PSYCHOLOGY
The Adaptive Mind

Third Canadian Edition

PSYCHOLOGY
The Adaptive Mind

Third Canadian Edition

D. Stephen Lindsay
University of Victoria

Delroy L. Paulhus
University of British Columbia

James S. Nairne
Purdue University

THOMSON

NELSON

Australia   Canada   Mexico   Singapore   Spain   United Kingdom   United States

THOMSON

NELSON

Psychology: The Adaptive Mind, Third Canadian Edition

by D. Stephen Lindsay, Delroy L. Paulhus, and James S. Nairne

Associate Vice President, Editorial Director:
Evelyn Veitch

Editor-in-Chief, Higher Education:
Anne Williams

Senior Marketing Manager:
Lenore Taylor-Atkins

Senior Developmental Editor:
Alwynn Pinard

Photo Researcher and Permissions Coordinator:
Sheila Hall

Senior Content Production Manager:
Tammy Scherer

Production Service:
Graphic World Inc.

Copy Editor:
Dawn Hunter

Proofreader:
Marcia Gallego

Indexer:
Mauri Baggiano

Production Coordinator:
Ferial Suleman

Design Director:
Ken Phipps

Interior Design:
Katherine Strain

Cover Design:
Studio Montage

Cover Image:
Inside Look by Alexej von Jawlensky. © Christie's Images/Corbis

Compositor:
Graphic World Inc.

Printer:
Courier Kendallville Inc.

Library and Archives Canada Cataloguing in Publication Data

Lindsay, D. Stephen
   Psychology : the adaptive mind / D. Stephen Lindsay, Delroy L. Paulhus, James S. Nairne. — 3rd Canadian ed.

Second Canadian ed. written by James S. Nairne ... [et al.].
Includes bibliographical references and index.

ISBN-13: 978-0-17-642408-4
ISBN-10: 0-17-642408-3

   1. Psychology—Textbooks.
I. Paulhus, Delroy L., 1950-
II. Nairne, James S., 1954- III. Title.

BF121.L55 2006   150
C2006-906048-7

Dedicated to Meg Lindsay, for inspiring me with a love of words as a child, and to Moira Cairns, for her loving support
—Steve Lindsay

To my parents, Laurie and Alice Paulhus
—Del Paulhus

To Virginia and Stephanie
—James Nairne

D. Stephen Lindsay

Steve Lindsay is a professor of psychology at the University of Victoria. He completed his undergraduate work at Reed College (B.A. 1981) and his graduate training at Princeton University (Ph.D. 1987). Steve specializes in the study of human memory, and much of his research has focused on memory source monitoring (e.g., studies of conditions under which people mistake memories of suggestions as memories of witnessed events). He has published numerous articles in scholarly journals, as well as chapters in edited professional books, and has co-edited two books on memory. Steve is a fellow of the Association for Psychological Science and was the editor of the *Journal of Experimental Psychology: General* from 2002 to 2007. He is on the editorial board of *Applied Cognitive Psychology* and has also served on the editorial boards of the *Journal of Experimental Psychology: Learning, Memory, and Cognition; Journal of Memory and Language;* and *Psychological Bulletin.*

Delroy L. Paulhus

Del Paulhus is a professor of psychology at the University of British Columbia. His undergraduate degree is from Carleton University (B.A. 1974), and his Ph.D. is from Columbia University (1981). He was also a visiting professor at the University of California (Berkeley) and the University of California at Davis. Del conducts research in a variety of areas of personality and social psychology. Topics include self-presentation (e.g., self-deception, faking, and impression management), aversive personalities (e.g., narcissism, Machiavellianism, subclinical psychopathy), and social judgment (e.g., perceptions of intelligence and personality). He has edited several books and published a number of psychological tests. Del was previously an associate editor for the *Personality and Social Psychology Bulletin* and is currently an associate editor for *Personality and Social Psychology Review.* He was also a member of the review committee for the Canadian federal granting agency, the Social Science and Humanities Research Council.

James S. Nairne

Jim Nairne received his Ph.D. in human memory and cognition from Yale University. He is a professor at Purdue University, where he specializes in cognition and human memory. He is a member of the American Psychological Association, American Psychological Society, and the Psychonomic Society. He was an associate editor of the *Journal of Memory and Language* from 1997 to 2001 and has served on the board of that journal since 1993. He was recently awarded the distinguished Outstanding Undergraduate Teaching Award, in memory of Charles B. Murphy, from Purdue University.

Brief Contents

Contents

Kevin Jordan/PhotoDisc Red/Getty Images

© Frank Conaway/Index Stock Imagery

Laurence Dutton/Getty Images

© Royalty-Free/Corbis

Eyewire/Getty Images

12 Personality 470

13 Social Psychology 512

14 Psychological Disorders 560

© Robert Gauthier

15 Therapy 600

Photos.com

To the Instructor

Our development of *Psychology: The Adaptive Mind*, Third Canadian Edition, focused on several goals:

- First and foremost was our goal of explaining the basic principles and discoveries of modern psychology in a way that both engages the reader and accurately communicates the scientific research that underlies our discipline.
- A second goal was to make the text particularly appealing and interesting for Canadian students. To this end, the text highlights the work of Canadian psychologists, many of whom have played significant roles in shaping modern psychology. The text also reviews how the profession of psychology is structured in Canada. More generally, throughout the text we have anchored the discussion of psychological topics to real-world examples that will be familiar and meaningful to Canadian students. In our experience, Canadian students have a strong preference for learning from texts that deal with issues, examples, and references relevant to their own experiences as Canadians, rather than from texts that might be topical in other countries.
- A third goal was to produce a text that affords some conceptual "hooks" for students—that is, core ideas that help students structure and organize the numerous theories and findings reviewed in the text. The adaptive problem-solving approach, originally developed by James Nairne and outlined below, provides a pedagogically effective means of understanding how the various aspects of modern psychology fit together.
- A fourth goal was to convey the dynamic nature of contemporary research in active and emerging areas, such as cognitive science and evolutionary psychology. We've added numerous new references to this third edition (many from 2004 and beyond).
- As a fifth goal, we strove to produce a volume that is aesthetically pleasing. The art, figures, and layout of this text all contribute to a lucid, enjoyable, and absorbing learning experience.
- Finally, we worked to develop a package of ancillaries that provides as much assistance as possible to instructors teaching this challenging course and to students learning about this diverse discipline.

The Adaptive Problem-Solving Approach

One of the first hurdles we face as instructors of introductory psychology is convincing students that psychology is more than just the study of abnormal behaviour. Introduce yourself as a psychologist and you're likely to get a response such as "Don't analyze me!" or "I'd better watch what I say around you!" It takes time for students to realize that psychology is a vast interdisciplinary field that includes all aspects of both normal and abnormal behaviour. Even after exposure to its breadth, students may still find the topics of psychology mysterious and forbidding. Take a look at a typical chapter on the psychology of learning, for example, and its contents seem to bear little resemblance to our everyday understanding of what it means to "learn." There are extended discussions of drooling dogs and key-pecking pigeons, but little about the connection between conditioning procedures and the learning problems we face on a daily basis.

In *Psychology: The Adaptive Mind*, Third Canadian Edition, we focus extensively on the function of psychological processes. Instead of leading with theories, methods, and findings specific to a topic, we introduce each topic as a "solution" to a "problem." For example, as one way of understanding how people and other animals learn about the signalling properties of events (problem), one can look to classical conditioning (solution). Notice the shift in emphasis: Instead of topic followed by function, it's function followed by topic. This is what we call the adaptive problem-solving approach, and it offers a number of advantages:

1. The student has a reason to follow the discussion; understanding the problem to be solved enables the student to appreciate the value of seeking a solution.
2. Because the discussion is about a problem, it naturally promotes critical thinking. The student sees the connection between the problem and the solution.
3. The adaptive problem-solving theme extends across chapters, enabling us to draw connections between what are typically treated as separate topics.

Thus, the adaptive problem-solving approach provides an effective learning framework.

Each chapter is organized around a set of problems that (1) focus the discussion on the functional relevance of the material and (2) demonstrate that people think and act for adaptive reasons. For example, electrochemical transmission in the nervous system is introduced as the solution to the adaptive problem of communicating internally, the experimental method is introduced as a solution to the conceptual problem of determining the causes of behaviour, and so on.

When behaviour is viewed as the product of adaptive systems, psychology begins to make more sense to students. They learn that behaviours (including the methods of psychologists!) are reactions to particular problems. Our emphasis on adaptation encourages students to step back from their egocentric view of the world and reflect on the significance of each behaviour for the greater good (i.e., the survival) of the organism. A greater appreciation of individuality and diversity will derive from understanding that human differences are natural consequences of adaptations to the environment.

Changes in the Third Canadian Edition

"Third time's a charm," people sometimes say. Whether there's general truth to this adage is an interesting (and unexplored) question, but the saying does hold true for this text. The first and second editions provided a strong foundation, and the detailed and extensive feedback we received from students and reviewers (including several who had taught from the prior editions) enabled us to build on that base to produce a text that communicates core concepts, theories, and findings of psychological science in a compelling and effective way. We have improved the clarity of the narrative throughout the text and made the prose style more engaging. We've also thoroughly updated the science content. Although we have kept primary and classic references in place where appropriate, we have included many new references to twenty-first century research—both Canadian and international. We've also improved the clarity and effectiveness of several of the figures, added some new ones drawn from recent media events, and cited normative data pertaining to psychological phenomena from recent Canadian surveys.

Following we list two examples of substantive changes made in each chapter; this is far from an exhaustive list, but it serves to illustrate the ways we've updated and improved the text.

Chapter 1: An Introduction to Psychology

- New section on Canadians in psychology
- Improved treatment of structuralism

Chapter 2: The Methods of Psychological Research

- Improved explanation of scientific method using a more student-relevant example
- Clarified treatment of the distinction between correlation and causation

Chapter 3: Biological Processes

- Clarified exposition of electrophysiological brain imaging and incorporation of new research in social neuroscience
- Enhanced discussions of neural plasticity and of individual and gender differences in brain function

Chapter 4: Sensation and Perception

- Improved treatments of audition and touch
- New material on the McGurk effect

Chapter 5: Consciousness

- New discussion of interactions between motivational states and the influence of subliminal stimuli
- Enhanced treatment of the topic of sleep, including tips on good sleep hygiene and recent science on melatonin as a sleep medication

Chapter 6: Learning: Conditioning and Observation

- New material explaining the relevance of classical and operant conditioning phenomena to students' real-world behaviour
- Improved exposition of the conditioning model of drug tolerance

Chapter 7: Memory

- Expanded discussion of false-memory phenomena such as schema- and suggestion-based false memories
- New material on the testing effect (i.e., that testing promotes long-term retention)

Chapter 8: Thought and Language

- New material on the relationship between language, thought, and problem solving
- New Practical Solutions feature on the benefits of taking a break from working on a difficult problem

Chapter 9: Intelligence

- New discussion of the Flynn effect (societal IQ gains over time)
- New treatment of the relationship between working memory and intelligence

Chapter 10: Human Development

- Added material on narrative approaches to identity development
- New approaches to moral development by Haidt and Krebs and Denton

Chapter 11: Motivation and Emotion

- Increased coverage of human sexuality, especially with regard to homosexuality and paraphilias
- Extensively updated material on eating disorders, including treatment of cultural influences

Chapter 12: Personality

- New critique and refinement of the Big Five personality trait theory
- Elaborated on and clarified research on the behavioural genetics of personality

Chapter 13: Social Psychology

- New Practical Solutions feature on combating prejudice
- Reworked the discussion of aggression to improve its clarity and integration with the rest of the chapter

Chapter 14: Psychological Disorders

- Updated the general approach to this topic to reflect the current state of the science (e.g., changed chapter title from "Abnormal Psychology," updated from *DSM-IV* to *DMS-IV-TR*)
- New sections on gender and cultural differences in psychological disorders and new coverage of biological influences on mental health

Chapter 15: Therapy

- New introduction that better situates therapy in the broader context of current psychological theory
- Clarified exposition of cognitive-behavioural therapy

Chapter 16: Stress and Health

- New material on physical effects of psychological stress and the relationship between socio-economic status and health
- Added discussion of recent research on links between depression and heart attacks

Appendix A: Statistics has also been thoroughly revised, cutting its length by about 15% and sharpening the focus on the most central ideas underlying statistical analyses.

Learning Aids

- Each major section within each chapter begins with Learning Goals and ends with a Test Yourself review to give students regular opportunities to check their understanding of the material.
- Concept Summaries are located throughout the chapter to help students review important themes, approaches, or subject areas.
- Comprehensive Chapter Summaries encourage students to review important points without taking extensive notes or wading through the entire text again. The summaries have been thoroughly revised to reflect the learning goals and content within each chapter.
- Annotated Recommended Readings and What's on the Web sections are located at the end of each chapter and offer brief descriptions of relevant books, articles, and websites to steer students toward further investigation. All of these have been checked for currentness, with many of them new to this edition.

- Suggested search terms and the URL for InfoTrac® College Edition are listed at the end of each chapter. Further suggestions for using InfoTrac® College Edition, including possible research projects, are found on both the student and instructor sections of the book site:
  http://www.adaptivemind3e.nelson.com
- References to Psyk.Trek 3.0 modules are listed at the end of each chapter to encourage further study of the concepts. Psyk.Trek's 65 interactive learning modules, simulations, and quizzes offer additional opportunities to interact with, reflect on, and retain the material.

Teaching and Learning Supplements

Psychology: The Adaptive Mind, Third Canadian Edition, is supported by a state-of-the-art teaching and learning package.

Study Guide (0-17-644269-3)
Revised for this edition by Susan Burns, this useful supplement is tied directly to the Learning Goals of each chapter and includes exercises for mastering the vocabulary, fill-in-the-blank exercises, and multiple-choice test items for each major concept. It also includes short-essay questions, matching exercises, and two additional sets of multiple-choice questions per chapter. Also included is a language enhancement guide that explains nontechnical terms and idioms that may be unfamiliar. Phonetic pronunciations of some of the more challenging words in each chapter are also included.

ThomsonNOW™ (0-17-644158-1)
ThomsonNOW is an online learning and homework assessment program created in concert with the text to present a seamless, integrated learning tool.

- With ThomsonNOW, instructors can dramatically affect student success. Assigning text-specific tutorials requires no instructor set-up. In addition, faculty can use the same system to create tailored homework assignments, quizzes, and tests that auto-grade and flow directly into the instructor's gradebook! This means instructors can actually assign marks to homework assignments, motivating students to study the material and come to class prepared.
- Students can improve their grades and save study time with ThomsonNOW. It isn't just reading—it provides a customized study plan that lets students master what they need to know without spending time on what they already know! The study plan provides a road map to interactive exercises, videos, ebooks, and other resources that help students master the subject. Pretests and posttests allow students to monitor their progress. Focused studying via ThomsonNOW will minimize student efforts and yet maximize results.

Instructor's Resource Manual (0-17-644083-6)
The Instructor's Resource Manual, revised by Jeff Pfeifer, includes detailed chapter outlines, learning goals, lecture elaborations, Focus on Research sections, demonstrations and activities, responses to Critical Thinking questions from the text and additional Critical Thinking questions, extensions for the Practical Solutions boxes, suggested readings, InfoTrac® College Edition key words, film and video suggestions, websites, and web activities. An electronic version of the Instructor's Resource Manual is also available through our instructor's website.

Test Bank (0-17-644261-8)
The Test Bank revision by Richard Madigan includes multiple-choice, sentence completion, and essay questions. The multiple-choice test items are organized into

different categories: text definition, applied definition, factual, text application, new application, and conceptual. Ten questions are drawn directly from the Study Guide and an additional ten questions are taken from the website.

Multimedia Manager/Instructor's Resource CD-ROM (0-17-644194-8)

This CD-ROM includes text-specific lecture outlines, a high-resolution digital version of each figure and illustration from the text, videos, animations, and Web content. These graphics can be combined with your own material to create powerful, personal, media-enhanced presentations. Also on the CD is an electronic version of the Test Bank, which is available for both Windows and Macintosh platforms. The ExamView software is a user-friendly program that allows instructors to insert their own questions and customize those provided.

Website: http://www.adaptivemind3e.nelson.com

This website is tied directly to the text. Chapter resources include practice quizzes, Web links from the text as well as additional links, crossword puzzles, glossary terms, InfoTrac® College Edition exercises, and animations and simulations (MediaWorks). The student site also includes study tips, information on degrees and careers in psychology, and further resources designed to enhance the learning experience. The password-protected, instructors-only area of the site includes downloadable ancillaries, suggestions for additional activities, and information to help instructors incorporate technology into their teaching.

CNN Today Videos: Introductory Psychology

Exclusive to Thomson Nelson, *CNN Today Videos* are course-specific to help instructors launch lectures and to encourage discussion. Organized by topics covered in a typical course, these 60-minute videos contain many exciting clips. Contact your publisher's representative for more information.

Psychology Digital Video Library 3.0 CD-ROM (0-495-09063-8)

A diversified selection of approximately 100 classic and contemporary clips, this CD-ROM offers a convenient way to access an appropriate clip for every lecture. Included is footage of prominent psychologists, as well as demonstrations and simulations of important experiments.

Psyk.Trek 3.0

Psyk.Trek 3.0 is a multimedia supplement that provides students with new opportunities for active learning. It consists of four components, including a set of 65 Interactive Learning Modules that present the core content of psychology in a dynamic new way. These tutorials feature thousands of graphics, hundreds of photos, hundreds of animations, approximately four hours of narration, 35 carefully selected videos, and about 160 uniquely visual concept checks and quizzes. Simulations allow students to explore complex psychological phenomena in depth through highly interactive, experiential demonstrations. Three new modules can be found on Psyk.Trek 3.0. A Multimedia Glossary allows students to look up over 800 psychological terms, access hundreds of pronunciations of obscure words, and pull up hundreds of related diagrams, photos, and videos. The Video Selector allows students to directly access 35 video segments.

InfoTrac® College Edition

A free subscription to this extensive online library is enclosed with every new copy of the book, giving students access to the latest news and research articles online. This easy-to-use database features thousands of reliable, full-length articles from hundreds of top academic journals and popular sources.

▶ Acknowledgments

We thank the superb team at Thomson Nelson—especially Evelyn Veitch, Alwynn Pinard, and Dawn Hunter. Producing a text like this is a team undertaking, and the Thomson Nelson professionals deserve a great deal of the credit for the final product. They've been unfailingly encouraging and friendly, prompt and effective, and highly skilled. Joanna Cotton, formerly of Thomson Nelson, was a stalwart and inspirational support through the first two editions and, along with Lesley Mann, the beginning stages of work toward the third edition.

Reviewers

Many instructors across Canada were involved in helping us develop this Third Canadian Edition. Their contributions can be seen throughout this edition and we thank them sincerely:

Glen Bodner, University of Calgary
Tara Burke, Ryerson University
Kimberly Clow, University of Ontario Institute of Technology
Ken Cramer, University of Windsor
Peter Graf, University of British Columbia
Ronald R. Martin, University of Regina
Karen Nicholson, Mount Allison University
Jeffrey Pfeifer, University of Regina
Maureen Reed, Ryerson University
Donald Sharpe, University of Regina
Sonya Symons, Acadia University

The following individuals played one or more important roles in the development of the First Canadian Edition of this book. Dr. Martin Smith of the University of Victoria was the driving force behind the First Canadian Edition, for which we extend our thanks; Ken Cramer, for his essential contribution to Chapter 12; Deborah Hunt Matheson, for assistance with Chapter 16; and Jennifer Lloyd and Laura-Lyn Stewart, for their friendly and efficient research assistance.

We would also like to thank P. Lynne Honey, Michael Picard, and Martin S. Smith for their feedback, which guided revisions for a reprinting of the Second Canadian Edition of this text.

First and Second Canadian Edition Reviewers and Contributors

Catherine Salmon, Simon Fraser University; Sally Walters, Simon Fraser University; Doug McCann, York University; Enrico DiTommaso, University of New Brunswick—Saint John; Bruce Bolster, University of Winnipeg; Robert Huxtable, Okanagan University College; Russell Powell, Grant MacEwan College; Michael MacNeill, Capilano College; Sonya Symons, Acadia University; Ken Cramer, University of Windsor; Jody Bain, University of Victoria; Bram Goldwater, University of Victoria; James Plant, University of Victoria; Glen Bodner, University of Calgary; Dianne Crisp, Kwantlen University College; Kathy Denton, Douglas College; Robert Moore, University of Regina; David Reagan, Camosun College.

▶ To the Student

Psychology is the scientific study of behaviour and mind. It can be a tough subject—partly because students often discover that they have mistaken ideas about the field. Nonetheless, we're confident that you'll find the journey of discovery rewarding and fascinating. Throughout this book we describe dozens of specific studies and hundreds of isolated facts, but our goal is for you to understand psychology in a way that will be useful throughout your life. Toward that end, we do our best to show you how particular behaviours, cognitive processes, and emotions help you solve important adaptive problems every day.

What Do We Mean by "The Adaptive Mind"?

We take the view that everything people do is influenced by their need to solve or adapt to problems in their environment. By "problems" we mean the threats people encounter and the various demands they need to meet as they navigate through everyday life. People are constantly digging into their psychological "tool kit" to solve one problem or another. For example, the sight of a charging enemy is a serious problem to be solved. To solve it, the body quickly creates extra energy in the form of general arousal that makes fighting or escaping more feasible. A more long-term example is the continual threat to an organism's survival created by an inability to communicate with others of its species. Survival is greatly enhanced by improved communication abilities. In this case, the solution—or adaptation—was the evolution of sophisticated language abilities in our species.

Each chapter in this book may be viewed as a set of scientific problems that need to be tackled by rigorous psychological research. Some have been solved, but we have only partial solutions for most of these scientific problems. We know, for example, that certain drugs can treat certain forms of mental illness, but we don't yet know how or why; nor do we yet understand why such medications are more effective for some individuals than for others.

We believe that viewing human behaviour and scientific research as short-term problem solving or long-term adaptions to recurring problems will facilitate your learning of psychology. Therefore, each chapter begins with three or four problems like the ones described above, and throughout the chapter we show you what psychologists have discovered about how these particular problems are solved by the human body and mind.

We hope that some of what you learn in this book will help you with situations in your daily life. The study of psychology is challenging, but it is most certainly relevant to everything you do.

How to Read This Book

Inexperienced students often read textbooks in a passive way. They start at the first assigned page, run their eyes along each sentence until the end of the assignment, and then close the book and go on to something else. Some students use a highlighter, diligently marking all of the bold and italic text (as if the fluorescent ink will somehow transmit the material to the brain). Still others study while listening to music or TV.

If you're used to listening to background music or TV when you study, you'll miss it at first. Music and TV are entertaining, and studying can be boring (especially if you're studying difficult and unfamiliar material in a passive way). But distracting background noises interfere with cognitive processing and hence are likely to make it more difficult for you to learn and retain what you're reading (see Chapter 6). Why make studying harder and less effective than it needs to be?

Studying will be more entertaining and valuable if you do it actively, striving to understand and think about the material rather than merely letting the words roll across your mind. You spontaneously read in an active manner if the text is something you care about and are interested in. For example, if you're a hockey fan reading an article about your favourite team, you don't just take in the words, but rather actively relate the new information to things you already know, form images of what the writer describes, question the author's claims, and so on. Reading in that way supports understanding and retention. It's easy when you are already an expert on and care about the topic, because you have a wealth of experience that facilitates this sort of intellectual engagement with the writing. It's harder with an introductory textbook, but with effort you can do it and it will pay off.

Our book includes numerous features designed to encourage you to work with the text in an actively engaged, thoughtful manner. We've included those features because we know that using them will benefit you (in the form of better understanding and retention of the material, not to mention better grades). This isn't just a matter of opinion, but rather something that has been amply demonstrated in rigorous scientific research. The features are there: Now it's up to you to use them.

We suggest that you begin each chapter by reading through the chapter outline. This will give you a general overview of the material to be covered. Also, ask yourself questions about the headings in the outline (e.g., "What's the difference between a clinical psychologist and an applied psychologist?" or "What does Darwin have to do with psychology?"). Generating these questions gets you actively engaged in thinking about the material and primes your mind to take in the parts of the text that address those questions.

As you read, strive to understand each sentence. If you don't understand it as you read it, you're not likely to remember it when tested. Also, understanding of many later points of the text requires understanding of earlier ones; if you don't make the effort to understand in the beginning, it will likely get harder as you go along.

When the text describes something concrete (such as a real-world example or the procedures of an experiment), form mental images of what the text is describing or think of similar examples from your own experience. Forming mental images and relating new knowledge to things you know will support understanding and subsequent recall. It will also help if you take notes as you read, especially if you write those notes in your own words; there is little value in simply copying material from the text, but paraphrasing key points in your own words can have substantial value.

Early in each chapter is a box previewing the key issues explored in the chapter, and toward the end of each chapter is another box reviewing those issues. It is important to read and think about these carefully. Doing so will help you grasp and retain the main points of the chapter.

The text includes a variety of materials in the margins: Almost every page has some sort of picture, drawing, definition, or exercise in the margin. There are also materials presented in boxes, such as Concept Summaries. Do not ignore any of these. They partly overlap with the text, but their purpose is to encourage you to think about central points in a slightly different way. Research has shown that thinking about material in multiple ways improves performance on subsequent memory tests.

Speaking of tests, each chapter includes several Test Yourself exercises, and you would be wise to do these as you go along, assessing your accuracy by checking your answers against Appendix B. It's easy to convince yourself that you know and understand the material, but if you want to do well in the course, then it's crucial to find out if you really do know it. Moreover, as we'll discuss in the chapter on memory, recent research has firmly established that taking a test on the ideas covered in a text has quite substantial benefits for memory of those ideas.

Each chapter also includes several Critical Thinking questions in the margins. As a student, your aim is not merely to memorize material, but also to develop intellectual skills that enable you to go beyond the information given. Don't just passively accept whatever the text says, but think critically about it; that is, question the text, think through the wider implications of its claims, note parallels between different issues raised in the text, and so on. The Critical Thinking items are designed to spark this sort of active, questioning approach to the text. Taking such an approach will simultaneously help you develop intellectual skills and encourage you to think about the ideas in the text in ways that support long-term memory.

When you finish reading a chapter, don't forget the end-of-chapter material. Go through the Chapter Summary and the list of Terms to Remember with care. Don't just look at the terms and decide whether or not they are familiar; rather, write down brief definitions of each term. If you encounter questions you cannot answer, review the relevant parts of the chapter until you can answer them. If questions remain after your best efforts, then seek help from your instructor, the course teaching assistant, or other resources available to you.

Comparing your understanding of a topic with that of other class members is useful, as is trying to communicate the material to friends and family. If they don't get what you're saying, then you may not understand the material as well as you think.

If you read the text in the ways we've suggested, you'll probably find that you don't need to do a lot of cramming the night before a test. Although cramming can be effective for improving performance on an immediate test, it isn't great for long-term memory. The best approach is to keep up with the reading in a deep and thoughtful way as the course goes along, and then spend time shortly before the test reviewing the material.

Of course, people are different in terms of which study techniques work best, but a general principle is that learning and retention are enhanced when readers engage with the material in an active, dynamic way (see Chapter 8). We hope that these comments will help you take advantage of the features of this book and that these features in turn will enable you to learn a great deal about psychology.

D. Stephen Lindsay
Delroy L. Paulhus
James S. Nairne

It was the best of times, it was the worst of times, it was the age of wisdom, it was the age of foolishness, it was the epoch of belief, it was the epoch of incredulity, it was the season of Light, it was the season of Darkness, it was the spring of hope, it was the winter of despair.

—Charles Dickens, *A Tale of Two Cities*

An Introduction to Psychology

I n the quotation with which we begin this book, Charles Dickens was speaking of pre-revolutionary France, but the contrasting extremes of his description capture the current moment as well. For example, here are some news items that are current as we write:

- Health researchers reported compelling evidence for a highly effective vaccine against cervical cancer.
- Two teenaged sisters in Mississauga, Ontario, were convicted of drowning their mother in a bathtub.
- A collector paid $135 million dollars for a painting by Gustav Klimt.
- Canadian Stephen Lewis, the UN secretary-general's special envoy for HIV/AIDS in Africa, expressed frustration with the developed world's response to that crisis.
- Some sources estimated the number of civilians killed by military intervention in Iraq at between 41 000 and 45 000.
- In the Darfur region of Sudan, the death toll from that genocidal ethnic conflict passed 200 000.
- Warren Buffett announced that he was donating most of his $50-billion fortune to the Bill and Melinda Gates Foundation.

By the time you read this, these "news" items will be a year or more out of date. Maybe democracy has blossomed in Bagdad, Canada has fulfilled its obligations to the international fight against HIV/AIDS, and Mr. Buffett's example has been followed by dozens of billionaires. Even so, these items serve to make two important points:

1. It's always both the best and the worst of times. At any given moment, some individuals are brimming with joy and others are drowning in sorrow.
2. To paraphrase Dickens, humans are the best of animals and the worst of animals. We are a species capable of discovering cures for diseases, unlocking the secrets of the atom, and raising graceful towers hundreds of metres into the air. Yet we are also capable of deliberately flying loaded passenger jets into skyscrapers, dropping atom bombs on cities, and enslaving our fellow humans. We create breathtaking works of art and stinking heaps of garbage. We soar at times, crash at others, and experience every gradation in between.

What makes us humans tick? Why and how do we do the things we do? Why are some people so different from others? What can be done to enhance the human potential to do good and to be happy and well, and to curtail the human potential to do harm and to suffer? Answers to such questions (and many others) can be sought through the study of **psychology,** the scientific study of behaviour and mind. This book is an introduction to that scientific discipline.

Many people have the idea that psychology is the study of mental illness. That is a misconception. The study and treatment of mental illness is certainly an important part of psychology, but the science of psychology focuses at least as much on normal behaviour as on abnormal or problem behaviour. In fact, most of the material in this book comes from studies of normal people (very often, university undergrads like you). Why focus on everyday, normal behaviour as well as abnormal behaviour? For one thing, to understand the abnormal, it's essential that we understand normal functioning first, just as medical doctors must understand the healthy body before they can understand sickness and disease. For another, the "normal" human animal is a marvellous scientific mystery, a great puzzle that is fascinating to study in its own right.

Psychology seeks to understand the essentials of behaviour and mind: how people act, think, and feel. You might think that these are simple matters of common sense, that everyone has intuitions about how and why people do and feel as they do. But one thing you'll learn by reading this book is that our everyday intuitions about how and why we do the things we do are often inaccurate. Rather than relying on intuition, psychologists have gradually built a knowledge base from systematic research, and they're continually using this knowledge to build a systematic science of behaviour and mind.

By studying psychology, you will receive several benefits:

- *You will see that psychologists have learned to predict behaviour in various situations.* Psychologists have developed theories of the causes of many different behaviours, both normal and abnormal. What you learn will help you to better understand your own actions, as well as those of the people around you.
- *You will learn about techniques that can help you modify your own behaviour.* Modern psychology has something to say about many issues, from the treatment of irrational fears (such as great fear of spiders) to the development of effective study skills and the design of technologies ranging from kitchen stoves to telephones to computers.
- *You will encounter a method of inquiry that will help you constructively analyze your own behaviour and that of other people.* You will learn how

psychology

The scientific study of behaviour and mind

psychological researchers ask questions about behaviour, how they draw conclusions about cause and effect, and how they develop theories that allow them to predict when particular behaviours will occur.

- *You will gain insight into why people differ in their actions, thoughts, and feelings.* Most psychologists believe that human actions are governed by general principles, but any given instance of behaviour—such as how you will act at dinner tomorrow night—is determined by multiple causes. Your actions are shaped by your current environment, the culture in which you were raised, and the genetic material passed along to you by your biological parents. Much of psychology is concerned with studying how people differ from one another in their thinking and behaviour.

From psychology, you may learn things about yourself that conflict with your familiar view of everyday experience. For example, you will discover that your personal memories are not always accurate; instead, what you remember is an elaborate—and fallible—reconstruction of the past created by adaptive memory mechanisms in your brain. You will learn that some beliefs you hold about yourself—how you act and treat others—are not rock solid and unchanging, as you might think; instead, they can be easily changed in the face of a demanding environment. You may even start to question the amount of control you have over your own behaviour. We'll consider the possibility (although with a critical eye) that your actions are controlled by unconscious forces, evolutionary dispositions, biological drives, and external stimuli that are not under direct willful control.

So be forewarned: The content of this textbook may make you feel uncomfortable at times. What you'll learn may change the way you view yourself, the world, and others around you. That may seem rather unlikely at the moment, but it's a possibility we hope you find intriguing as you begin your journey into the adaptive mind.

Suza Scalora/PhotoDisc/Getty Images

Most psychologists believe that human thoughts and emotions arise from complex interactions among the brain, other organs of the body, and the environment.

Introducing Psychology

Each chapter in this textbook is organized around a set of questions or problems. Most of these problems pertain to everyday life. The purpose of this organizational scheme is to show you how people use psychological processes to help them adapt to their environment.

For example, one of the most important things that you learn about in your environment is that certain events are reliable predictors, or signals, of other events. If you're walking along a wilderness path and hear a low growl, it's useful to surmise that a predator may be nearby. This may seem like a completely trivial problem, but imagine that you tried to build a machine that was capable of thinking "predator" and feeling fear when it heard a particular kind of noise. In Chapter 6, "Learning: Conditioning and Observation," you'll learn about a procedure that psychologists use to study how animals learn about signals in their environment. This procedure, called *classical conditioning*, is a solution to an important problem: how animals learn about events in the environment that signal things that can help or hurt

them. Similarly, in Chapter 3, "Biological Processes," you'll learn how we communicate information within our bodies through the vast communication network of the nervous system, and in Chapter 4 you'll learn about the psychoneurological mechanisms that underlie our perceptual experience. Internal communication and perception are crucial problems for your body to solve: If a cyclist suddenly weaves into the path of your car, the message needs to be communicated quickly and efficiently to the muscles controlling the foot-to-brake connection. The body uses its internal neural networks to solve this problem of internal communication.

At the beginning of each new topic in a chapter, it is useful to ask yourself the following question: How does the psychological process under discussion help me solve an adaptive problem in my life? Each of us is constantly adjusting our actions, often in a flexible and strategic way, to meet the demands of new conditions as they arise. We each carry around with us a psychological tool kit that has evolved over millions of years and been sharpened and refined by

our own personal learning experiences. Those tools enable us to initiate and control our behaviour in situation-appropriate ways. In the coming chapters, you'll see how these adaptive tools can be used to solve the obstacles and survival problems we face. (For a look ahead, you can find some of these tools listed in ▶ Table 1.1.)

In some instances, our focus will shift from adaptive problems that we each solve toward particular problems that psychologists seek to solve, either to advance basic knowledge or to help individuals in need. For instance, what are the best strategies to use to understand the cause of a behaviour (Chapter 2)? What are the best ways to conceptualize and then measure something as abstract as intelligence (Chapter 9)? Intelligence is not something that can be measured directly, like height or weight; it can only be inferred by measuring aspects of observable behaviour. How can abnormal behaviour be classified, and how can it be treated (Chapter 14)? These are practical problems that psychologists attempt to solve, and

▶ **Table 1.1** Examples of Adaptive, Scientific, and Practical Problems

Chapter	Problem to Be Solved	Example	Solution Tools
3 and 4	How to get information about the sounds in the environment	While walking through the woods, John hears a low growl.	Electrochemical coding of sound waves in the inner ear and transmission of those neural signals to the brain
6	Learning what events signal	John freezes in fear.	Associations between events acquired through classical conditioning
7	How to retain information about past events	John tries to remember what he read about what to do if a bear attacks.	Mentally generated retrieval cues that are similar to the to-be-remembered information
11	How to regulate eating	Stefanie has never been into eating breakfast—she's just not hungry in the morning.	A complex interplay between internal and external factors regulates hunger
13	Making inferences about others' behaviour	A grizzled man lurches from a doorway as you walk down the alley.	Knowledge-based schemas used to predict behaviour
15	How to treat mental illness	Omar is mired in the depths of depression.	Psychoactive drug therapy and psychotherapy

learning about the solutions and how they're reached is key to understanding how modern psychology works.

In this first chapter, you'll be exposed to three broad topics, which you can think of as conceptual problems that psychologists have attempted to solve. Each is designed to help acquaint you with the scientific study of behaviour and mind.

First, how do we define and describe psychology? That is, what are the topics with which this field is concerned, what methods are used to address those topics, and what are the goals of psychological study?

Second, how did current psychological perspectives develop? As you'll see, psychology as a scientific field has a short history, but the issues explored by psychologists have long captured the interest of scholars in other, older disciplines (especially philosophy and physiology). Understanding these historical roots will help you understand contemporary psychology.

Third, what is the dominant theoretical orientation of modern psychology? Over the course of more than 100 years since psychology first emerged as a distinct scientific field, various schools of thought have dominated psychological theory for periods of time. Such theoretical perspectives influence the questions psychologists ask, the methods they use, and the ways they apply their research. To anticipate, nowadays most psychologists combine multiple theoretical approaches, rather than adhering dogmatically to any single approach.

▶ Defining and Describing Psychology

LEARNING GOALS

1. Learn the modern definition of psychology.
2. Be able to discuss the different ways of studying the mind scientifically.
3. Learn about what psychologists do, distinguishing among clinical, applied, and research psychologists.
4. Learn about the schooling and qualifications required to become a psychologist.

As defined earlier, psychology is the scientific study of behaviour and mind. The word comes from the Greek *psyche*, which translates as "soul" or "breath," and *logos*, which means the study or investigation of something (as in biology or physiology). The word *psychology* was not in common use before the nineteenth century, and it did not become an independent subject matter of science until around the middle of the nineteenth century (Boring, 1950). Until then, "the study of the mind," as psychology was widely known, was conducted mainly by philosophers and physiologists. Sigmund Freud, for example, was not trained in psychology, despite his contributions to psychological theory and practice.

Notice that psychology is not simply the study of the mind; rather, it is the *scientific study of behaviour and mind*. The emphasis on science, and particularly the scientific method, helps to distinguish psychology from the related field of philosophy. An essential characteristic of the scientific method, as you'll see in Chapter 2, is *systematic observation*: Scientific knowledge is always based on some kind of direct or indirect observation, which is why psychologists emphasize behaviour; the only mind you can observe is your own—for all others you can only make inferences about mind from behaviour. Psychologists collect systematic observations, look for regularities, and then generate and test predictions based on what they've observed.

By **mind,** psychologists usually mean the contents and processes of subjective experience: sensations, thoughts, and emotions. Behaviour and mind are kept separate in the definition because only behaviour, not mind, can be directly measured by the scientific observer. Psychologists interpret the term

mind

The contents and processes of subjective experience: sensations, thoughts, and emotions

  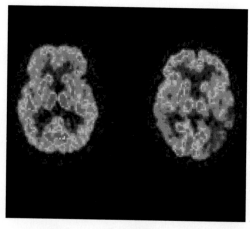

The term *behaviour* can mean many things to a psychologist: overt actions, verbal reports of thoughts and feelings, and even activities of brain cells as measured by recordings of physiological activity in the brain.

behaviour

Observable actions, such as moving, talking, gesturing, and so on; can also refer to the activities of cells, as measured through physiological recording devices, and to thoughts and feelings, as measured through oral and written expression

CRITICAL THINKING

Do you think it's possible to study behaviour independently of mind? Or does all behaviour result from the actions of a willful mind? Cockroaches, snails, and starfish all behave, but do they have minds?

behaviour in a quite general way. Besides referring to obvious actions, such as moving, talking, and gesturing, many psychologists consider the activities of cells within the brain (as measured through physiological recording devices) and the expressions of thoughts and feelings (as revealed through oral and written responses) to be types of "behaviour."

The Invisible and Dynamic Mind: How Can It Be Studied?

How can psychologists scientifically study the mind, given that it is invisible and intangible to all but the person whose mind it is? Asking people to report their own subjective impressions about how their minds work provides us with some interesting and potentially valuable data (Ericsson & Simon, 1993), but a science of the mind and behaviour cannot rest solely on such subjective self-reports. As will be further discussed later in this chapter, subjective self-reports may be inaccurate, and many mental processes are inaccessible to self-observation (Forgas, Williams, & Laham, 2005; Nisbett & Wilson, 1977; Schooler & Schreiber, 2004).

What about looking inside the brain as a way of studying the invisible mind? Many research psychologists do measure brain structures and activities as a way of exploring psychological questions, as you'll see in Chapter 3. However, a complete understanding of the human mind cannot be obtained solely by examining the physical structures and processes of the brain. Similarly, if you wanted to understand how your computer's spellchecker works, prying the cover off your computer and looking at the hardware wouldn't get you very far. Instead, measurements of the brain must be taken in the context of studies that also measure people's responses to carefully constructed questions and tasks. Therefore, research psychologists often study human behaviour in controlled settings, measuring such things as reaction times and response accuracy (e.g., on tests of memory) to make inferences about how the mind works. Some researchers include measurements of the brain or people's subjective self-reports in their studies, whereas others focus exclusively on people's behaviour responses while performing tasks. A complete science of mind and behaviour requires a combination of all three measures: subjects' self-reports of their subjective impressions, their behavioural responses, and their physiological (including neurological) processes.

▶ Figure 1.1 illustrates the above discussion by asking you to imagine the mind as a black box that you want to understand; it also illustrates the different ways you might attempt to understand how the box works. The black-box metaphor is useful because it is easy to understand; if the box emitted complex and sophisticated

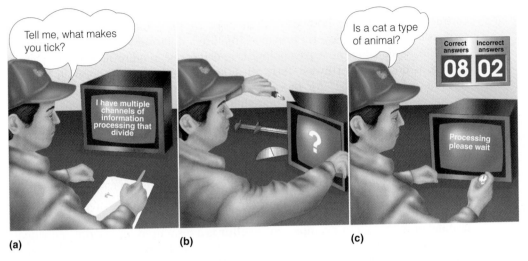

▶ Figure 1.1

Studying the Mind

It is difficult to study the mind because mental events are not directly observable. By using the analogy of a black box, these three panels depict some of the ways that we might attempt to study the mind: (a) ask the box itself for insight (*self-report measures*); (b) pry the box open to see what's inside (*physiological measures*); or (c) measure the box's behaviour and look for regularities (*behavioural measures*). If the box's "behaviour" was sophisticated and complex, you'd probably need to combine all three methods to figure out how it worked.

messages and you wanted to understand how it worked, you'd need to use a variety of converging methods to figure it out. (For a provocative discussion of whether or not a machine like our black box could be conscious, see Harnad, 2003.)

The black-box metaphor is limited, because the human brain and mind are not simple mechanical devices; rather, they are active, dynamic, living systems. Understanding and predicting human behaviour is arguably more akin to understanding and predicting atmospheric phenomena, such as rainstorms. Meteorologists have been studying the science of weather systems for a very long time and with massive levels of governmental funding, and they have developed sophisticated instruments and elegant theories. Yet it remains difficult to forecast the weather with precision and accuracy, because the systems that determine the weather are vast and dynamic and they interact in extraordinarily complex ways. So, too, are psychologists far from developing a complete understanding of the human mind and behaviour, but, as you'll see, we have made substantial progress toward revealing these intriguing mysteries.

What Psychologists Do

What do psychologists do on a daily basis? How do they earn a living? Where do they work? As shown in the Concept Summary on page 12, we can divide the job description into three main categories: clinical psychologist, applied psychologist, and research psychologist. These are not meant to be exclusive "either-or" categories—for example, clinical psychologists often work in applied settings and conduct research. The categorization scheme is designed merely to provide a useful way of subdividing the profession.

Clinical Psychologists   Most people believe that all psychologists work at treating psychological problems, such as depression, anxiety, phobias, or schizophrenia. Some psychologists, namely **clinical psychologists,** do indeed work in clinics or in private practice providing psychotherapy to individuals with psychological problems. Distinctions are often made between clinical and counselling psychologists, although the dividing line between the two is not clear and firm. **Counselling psychologists** generally deal with adjustment problems (e.g., marriage and family problems), whereas clinical psychologists tend to work with those kinds of problems as well as with more severe psychological disorders, such as schizophrenia. Together, clinical and counselling psychologists make up the majority of psychologists: More than half of all the professionals working in psychology are actively involved in the treatment of people with psychological problems.

clinical psychologists

Professional psychologists who specialize in the diagnosis and treatment of psychological problems

counselling psychologists

Professional psychologists who deal with milder problems, such as family and personal adjustment issues

In most provinces and territories, only clinical psychologists who have been certified by a regulatory body can call themselves "psychologists" to describe their professional services. Several provinces require a doctoral-level degree, such as a Ph.D., to be certified as a psychologist, and the rest require at least a master's degree, as does the Northwest Territories (see the subsequent section on "How to Become a Psychologist" for more information about such degrees). Almost all provinces and territories require that clinical and counselling psychologists complete internships or supervised practice periods of one to four years and achieve acceptable standards on professional psychology examinations. If you wish to check on the accreditation status of someone claiming to be a psychologist, you can contact your provincial or territorial Association of Professional Psychologists, or you can check his or her status with the Canadian Register of Health Service Providers in Psychology (**http://www.crhspp.ca**).

Not all individuals who help people with psychological problems have advanced training or degrees. For example, **counsellor** is a term used to describe individuals who provide some type of therapy or support-related service to clients. The term *counsellor* is not regulated by law in most provinces and territories, and there are generally no minimum educational requirements for people who describe themselves as "counsellors" or "therapists." Most counsellors do not have doctoral-level degrees in their specialties, and many have not completed an internship or period of supervised practice. Some such individuals are highly skilled, but others are not. Some provinces and territories are attempting to set minimum professional requirements for specific counsellor designations, such as "registered clinical counsellor."

Psychiatrists also specialize in the treatment of psychological problems, but psychiatrists are medical doctors. To become a psychiatrist you must graduate from medical school and complete further specialized training in psychiatry. Like clinical psychologists, psychiatrists treat mental disorders, but, unlike psychologists, they are licensed to prescribe medication.

Currently, debate is ongoing among mental health professionals about whether psychologists should be allowed to prescribe medication (Lavoie & Fleet, 2002; Welsh, 2003). Some states in the United States are considering legislation that will extend prescription privileges to licensed clinical psychologists; New Mexico recently passed a law giving properly trained psychologists the right to prescribe drugs, although the law has yet to be implemented. At present, psychologists and medical doctors typically work together. A clinical psychologist is likely to refer a client to a psychiatrist or a general practitioner if he or she suspects that a physical problem might be involved.

Applied Psychologists   Not all psychologists are concerned with understanding and treating abnormal behaviour or with helping people adjust. Many professional psychologists focus on "normal" people (we'll consider what it means to be normal or abnormal in Chapter 14). The goal of **applied psychologists** is to apply the principles of scientific psychology to practical, everyday problems in the real world. Applied psychologists work in various settings. For example, a *school psychologist* might work with students in primary and secondary schools to help them perform well academically and socially; an *industrial/organizational psychologist* might be employed in industry to help improve employee morale, train new recruits, or help managers establish effective lines of communication with their employees. *Forensic psychologists* apply psychological knowledge to the criminal justice and rehabilitation systems (see Schuller & Ogloff, 2001; Wells et al., 2000). *Human factors psychologists* play a key role in the design of new products: Why do you think telephone numbers were originally seven digits long, grouped in three, then four (e.g., 555-9378)? How about traffic lights—why red and green? Does it make a difference whether the word *delete, remove,* or *erase* is used in a word processing program? These are examples of practical problems that have been studied by human factors psychologists (Proctor & Van Zandt, 1994). See the Practical Solutions box for more information about human factors research in psychology.

counsellor

An individual who provides some sort of therapy or support to clients but who (typically) does not have advanced training in providing psychological treatment; some counsellors (or therapists) are skilled and effective, but others are not

psychiatrists

Medical doctors who specialize in the diagnosis and treatment of psychological problems; unlike psychologists, psychiatrists are licensed to prescribe drugs

applied psychologists

Psychologists who apply the principles of scientific psychology to practical, everyday problems in the world

PRACTICAL SOLUTIONS

THE PSYCHOLOGY OF STOVES AND DOORS

At the beginning of the chapter, we mentioned that psychologists have something to say about a variety of topics—even the design of the kitchen stove. You may not have thought too much about the role of psychology in stove design, but remember: Between every machine and its successful operation is a user, a human being. It's this human factor that often determines whether the product will be a success or a disaster. Let's see how a modern psychologist might analyze proper and improper stove design.

Does your stove look like the one depicted in the left panel of ▶ Figure 1.2? One of the authors of this textbook (DSL) has such a stove. Four burners are arranged in a rectangle, and four control knobs line up horizontally along the front (or sometimes the back). Your job as a user is to learn the relationship, or what psychologists call the *mapping,* between the control knobs and each burner. In this case you need to learn that the far left knob controls the back burner on the left. Or is it the front burner on the left? If you have a stove like this, which is psychologically incorrect, the odds are that you have trouble remembering which knob controls which burner. The reason is simple: The stove has been designed with an unnatural mapping between its controls and the burners. (By the way, the stove came with the house.)

"Mapping" is easier to understand when you look at a psychologically correct design, as depicted in the middle panel of Figure 1.2. Notice in this case that the arrangement of the burners

naturally aligns with the controls. The left-to-right display of the control knobs matches the left-to-right arrangement of the burners. There is no need to learn the mapping in this case: It's obvious at first sight which knob controls which burner. Alternatively, if you want to keep the rectangular arrangement of the stovetop, then simply arrange the control knobs in a rectangular manner that matches the burners, as shown in the far right panel. The point is that there are natural and unnatural ways to express the relationship between product control and product function. Taking advantage of the natural mapping requires that you consider the human factor—in this case, the fact that humans tend to rely on spatial similarity (left knob to left burner; right knob to right burner).

As we've stressed in this chapter, humans interact with the world with an adaptive tool kit—we tend to use certain strategies that have evolved over countless generations of interacting with objects in our natural environment. The stove example is a very simple one, yet it illustrates our natural tendency to map or link objects that share spatial nearness or similarity to one another. The more general point to be made is that it is crucial to take people's natural tendencies into account when designing devices for human use. As another example of that point, have you ever encountered a door like that shown in the top photo? The "push bar" clearly signals you to push, but you may have slammed your shoulder into such doors because they fail to

John Livzey

Examples of psychologically incorrect and correct door designs

signal which side opens. Likewise, the middle door has a large flat plate, which invites a natural response of pushing, not pulling. The fact that this door has a large "PULL" sign indicates how poorly it is designed. The bottom door, in contrast, is well designed: The large flat shape invites a natural pushing response, and the top plate on the left indicates which side should be pushed. The same issues arise in the design of more complex devices, such as cars, cell phones, and computers. Good design requires consideration of the human, psychological factor, and thus many manufacturers employ psychologists to assist in developing user-friendly designs for products and devices.

▶ Figure 1.2

The Human Factors of Stove Design

The stove on the left does not provide a natural "mapping" between the control knobs and the burners and is therefore difficult to use. The stoves in the middle and on the right provide psychologically correct designs that reduce user errors.

research psychologists

Psychologists who conduct experiments or collect observations designed to discover the basic principles of behaviour and mind

Research Psychologists   **Research psychologists** conduct experiments and collect systematic observations in an effort to discover the basic principles of behaviour and mind. Research psychologists specialize in a variety of areas. *Biopsychologists*, for instance, seek to understand how biological or genetic factors influence and determine behaviour. *Personality psychologists* focus on the internal factors that lead people to act consistently in different situations and that make people behave differently from one another. *Cognitive psychologists* research higher mental processes, such as memory, learning, and reasoning. *Developmental psychologists* study how people's behaviour and thinking change over a lifetime. *Social psychologists* are interested in how people think about, influence, and relate to one another. These are just a few of the specialties that research psychologists adopt. As you work your way through the chapters of this text, you will be exposed to a wide range of research interests.

How to Become a Psychologist

These days, most people who become psychologists majored in psychology as undergraduates, so if you are interested in a career in psychology then majoring in psychology is a sensible first step. Many students do not appreciate that the decisions they make during their first few years in university have long-term consequences. If you want to do well in the long run, it is important to learn the requirements of various potential majors. It is also important to earn good marks, even in your first-year courses, partly because admission to higher-level courses may be contingent on good marks in the earlier courses. Most, if not all, Canadian psychology departments have optional honours programs; earning an honours degree will give you a substantial advantage if you decide that you want to go on in

CONCEPT SUMMARY

TYPES OF PSYCHOLOGISTS

Type of Psychologist	Guiding Focus	Primary Workplace	Examples of What They Do
Counselling psychologists	Treatment of adjustment problems	Clinics, private practice, universities and colleges	Counsel clients who have adjustment problems
Clinical psychologists	Diagnosis and treatment of psychological problems	Clinics, private practice, universities and colleges	Counsel clients who have adjustment problems or more severe psychological problems; evaluate diagnostic techniques and therapy effectiveness
Applied psychologists	Applying psychological principles to practical problems in the world	Private industry, schools, universities and colleges	Help performance of students in school; improve employee morale and performance at work; design computers so that humans can use them efficiently
Research psychologists	Conducting research to discover the basic principles of behaviour and mind	Academic settings, private industry	Conduct experiments on the best study method for improving memory; assess the impact of daycare on children's attachment to their parents; observe the effects of others on a person's helping behaviour

psychology. Honours programs have quite stringent criteria; every year we encounter third-year students who would like to be in the honours program but are rejected because their grade-point averages are too low.

It also helps to get to know individual faculty members and advanced students. To go on for further education or get a skilled job after earning your undergraduate degree you will need letters of reference from at least two professors. Those letters will be much better if the professors who write them have had a chance to get to know you and can comment in detail about your skills and abilities. Ask questions in class. If your professors have office hours, go to them occasionally. If your department offers independent studies courses (sometimes called directed studies), consider taking such a course. Look for opportunities to work in professors' laboratories (or in community settings that are related to psychology) as a volunteer. Doing these things will make it easier to get good letters of reference and will enhance your résumé.

As Dr. Margaret Lloyd explains in her extraordinarily helpful website Careers in Psychology **(http://www.psywww.com/careers/index.htm),** students who earn a bachelor's degree in psychology typically develop good analytical thinking skills, people skills, and writing skills that prepare them for a wide variety of entry-level jobs. These include jobs related to counselling, social work, business, corrections, health, recreation, and education. It is possible to find work in these areas with a bachelor's degree, but those positions have certain limitations (e.g., you would likely work under supervision, with limited authority and pay).

To become a clinical psychologist, you would first need to earn a bachelor's degree. What you need beyond that depends on where in Canada you live, as different provinces and territories have different rules. In most provinces and territories, to qualify as a clinical psychologist you must have an advanced degree from a graduate program in clinical psychology. Canadian clinical psychology graduate programs have extremely stringent criteria for admission (as do programs in the United States); only students with very strong academic records are likely to be admitted (e.g., rejection rates are often around 80%). Completing a graduate degree in clinical psychology is a major undertaking: Students typically take two to three years to complete their master's degree, and then go on to spend another three or more years completing their doctoral degree, followed by an internship in which they further hone their clinical skills by working under supervision. Note that, as mentioned above, psychiatrists get their postgraduate training in medical school.

Qualifications for a career in research or applied psychology or related fields (e.g., education, social work) also begin with a bachelor's degree followed by some kind and amount of advanced training in graduate school. There is less competition for spaces in nonclinical psychology graduate programs, and therefore it is somewhat easier to gain admission (although only students with quite strong academic records are likely to be admitted). Here too, graduate school begins with two to three years of work toward a master's degree. Some graduate programs in nonclinical psychology are designed to terminate with the master's degree, and it is certainly possible to find a variety of good jobs with a master's degree in psychology. Most psychology graduate programs, however, are oriented toward a doctoral degree, which typically requires another two to three years of study and research beyond the master's. Almost all Canadian psychology professors, for example, have doctoral degrees.

You can see that it takes quite a commitment to earn the necessary qualifications for a career in psychology. We hope you'll also come to see, through reading this book, how incredibly rewarding and interesting such a career can be.

▶ Tracing the Evolution of Psychological Thought

LEARNING GOALS

1. Be able to explain what is meant by the mind-body problem.
2. Understand differing viewpoints on the origins of knowledge.
3. Be able to outline the development of the first scientific schools of psychology: structuralism, functionalism, and behaviourism.
4. Discuss the early clinical contributions of Freud and the humanistic psychologists.
5. Learn about some of the major contributions Canadian researchers made to early developments in the science of psychology.

The field of scientific psychology may have a relatively short past, but the study of psychological issues has a long and distinguished intellectual history. Indeed, the questions that interest psychologists (how and why people do and feel the things they do) have always interested people of all cultures, although here we focus on the roots of scientific psychology in Europe and North America. Thousands of years ago, the Greek philosopher Aristotle (384–322 B.C.E.) wrote extensively on such topics as memory, sleep, and sensation. Today, these topics form an important part of the subject matter of psychology. Aristotle argued that the mind of a baby could be seen as a kind of *tabula rasa*—a blank slate—on which experiences are written to form the basis of knowledge. The idea that knowledge arises directly from experience, a philosophical position known as **empiricism,** continues to be an important aspect of modern psychological thought (although no modern psychologists would agree with the idea that we are born with "blank" minds).

empiricism

The idea that knowledge comes directly from experience

Mind and Body: Are They the Same?

As mentioned earlier, the intellectual roots of modern psychology lie in the disciplines of *philosophy* and *physiology*. Psychology has always occupied a "middle ground" between these two areas (Bolles, 1993; Hunt, 1993). Ancient philosophers, such as Aristotle and Plato, helped to frame many of the fundamental questions that occupy the attention of psychologists today: Where does knowledge come from? What are the laws that govern sensory processes? How do we learn and remember?

Physiologists, however, focus on the workings of the human body. Years of research on the mechanics of physical movement and the anatomy of sensory systems produced volumes of data that were later used to develop a scientific understanding of behaviour and mind. In 1833, the German physiologist Johannes Müller

CRITICAL   THINKING

Psychology is the scientific study of behaviour and mind. Is it really surprising, then, that its intellectual roots lie in physiology and philosophy?

published the enormously influential *Handbook of Human Physiology* that proposed links between the nervous system and psychological effects. By the 1860s, clear connections had been established between brain damage and the loss of mental functions, such as language ability. Advances in brain research continue to influence psychological theory. We'll discuss some of these advances in Chapter 3 and later in this chapter.

Descartes's Solution   A fundamental problem in psychology involves the relationship between the physical *body*, as studied by the physiologists, and the *mind*, as studied by philosophers. Are the mind and body separate and distinct, or are they one and the same? Can we learn anything about one by studying the other? In the seventeenth century, the French philosopher René Descartes (1596–1650) argued that the mind and body are separate: The physical body, he claimed, cannot "think," nor is it possible to explain "thinking" by appealing to physical matter. This position is called *dualism*, because mind (or spirit) and body are considered to be two separate phenomena, each with distinct properties. Descartes did allow for the possibility, however, that mind can influence body and vice versa. The *mind*, he argued, controls the actions of a mechanical *body* through the pineal gland, a small structure at the base of the brain; Descartes did not, however, explain exactly how this works (see ▶ Figure 1.3).

Descartes stated the mind-body problem clearly, and his description of the human body in machine-like terms had an important influence on generations of physiologists. His specific ideas about the body turned out to be largely incorrect— the pineal gland, for example, plays a role in producing hormones, not muscle movements—but some of his ideas remain influential today. For instance, Descartes made pioneering observations and discussions of *reflexes*. Reflexes are automatic, involuntary reactions of the body to events in the environment. As you'll see in Chapter 3, reflexes play a very important role in our survival. But Descartes's solution to the mind-body problem did little to advance the scientific study of the mind. Talking about the mind as something separate from the physical world places a key aspect of the subject matter of psychology outside the boundaries of science.

Mind as a Product of Brain Activity   Most modern psychologists reject Descartes's separation of mind and body and assume no essential division exists between the two. The mind is considered to be a direct product of brain activity; put simply, the mind is what the brain does. Although we are still far from a complete understanding of how subjective mental states arise from physical processes in the brain and body, most psychologists believe that psychology is making progress toward solving this fascinating problem (Schall, 2004). As you'll read in this text, an extremely close link exists between the operation of the brain and behaviour. Many psychological problems appear to come directly from problems in the operation of the brain, and many of the symptoms can be treated effectively through biological means (usually the administration of drugs).

Nature and Nurture: Where Does Knowledge Come From?

Philosophers and psychologists have long sought to determine the origins of knowledge. Where does knowledge come from? As noted earlier, Aristotle adopted an empiricist position: He believed that knowledge comes entirely from our day-to-day experiences. Empiricism can be contrasted with a philosophical position called **nativism,** which holds that certain kinds of knowledge are inborn, or innate.

Nativists believe that babies arrive into the world knowing certain things, before any experience. For example, the German philosopher Immanuel Kant (1724–1804) believed that humans are born with a certain mental "structure" that determines how they perceive the world. He argued that people are born with a

▶ **Figure 1.3**

Wadsworth Photo

Descartes and Reflex

René Descartes introduced the concept of the reflex, which he described as an automatic, involuntary reaction of a mechanical body to an event in the world. He erroneously thought the mediating structure between body and mind was the pineal gland, shown here as a tear-shaped object in the back of the head.

nativism

The idea that certain kinds of knowledge and ideas are innate, or present at birth; innate ideas do not need to be learned

Charles Darwin believed that both physical and psychological characteristics were selected for their adaptive value.

natural tendency to see things in terms of cause and effect and to interpret the world in terms of space and time (Bolles, 1993; Wertheimer, 1987). Nativists do not believe that all knowledge is present at birth, but they reject the idea that all knowledge comes directly from experience.

Darwin's Theory of Evolution   Charles Darwin (1809–1882) provided some of the most important conceptual foundations of modern thinking about the human mind. Darwin proposed that all living things are products of an extended period of evolution, guided by the principles of natural selection. Cats have fur, seals have thick skin, and babies cry because these physical and behavioural traits have been selected for during the evolutionary history of the species. By *natural selection*, Darwin meant that some individuals survive and reproduce more than others because the successful individuals have heritable traits that make them better than others at overcoming obstacles and solving the problems present in their environment. For example, if an inborn tendency to cry helps to communicate feelings about hunger effectively, then crying increases the likelihood that a person will live long enough to pass this natural tendency on to offspring. Such tendencies are selected for naturally because they are *adaptive*—they improve the chances for meeting the needs demanded by the environment (Darwin, 1859, 1871).

Darwin believed that the principles of natural selection apply to characteristics that pass from parents to their offspring—not only physical traits but behavioural and psychological traits as well. By emphasizing the adaptive value of inherited characteristics, including psychological characteristics, Darwin's ideas greatly influenced psychological theorizing (Dennett, 1995). Psychologists now generally agree, for example, that humans have an inherited predisposition to acquire language, much as birds have an inherited predisposition to fly (Pinker, 1994).

Nature Plus Nurture   Today, it is widely recognized that most psychological phenomena—intelligence, emotion, personality—are influenced by innate genetic factors. At the same time, psychologists also agree that personal experience also plays a critically important role in thought, emotions, and behaviour. How a genetic message is expressed depends on the interaction between the genetic information and environmental influences during development. Recognition of this interaction has led virtually all psychologists to the following generalization: Human mind and behaviour are influenced by both nature (innate factors) and nurture (experience). So, the solution to the nature versus nurture debate isn't nature *or* nurture; it's nature *plus* nurture. A continuing challenge for psychologists is to discover the respective roles that innate and learned factors play in any given instance of behaviour. Psychologists often take on that challenge by studying psychological questions at multiple levels of analysis, ranging from the molecular and cellular (e.g., explorations of how the neurons in the brain function) to the phenomenological (e.g., studies of individuals' subjective experiences) to the social and cultural.

Certain physical characteristics, such as camouflage, are selected for in nature because they are adaptive; they improve the chances of an organism surviving and reproducing.

The First Schools: Psychology as Science

The first psychological laboratory was established in 1879 at the University of Leipzig by a German professor named

Wilhelm Wundt (1832–1920). Wundt was a medical doctor by training, and early in his career he worked with some of the great physiologists of the nineteenth century. Fittingly, Wundt was a professor of philosophy when he established his psychology laboratory. (Remember, the intellectual roots of scientific psychology lie at the union of philosophy and physiology.) Wundt is traditionally recognized as the founder of modern scientific psychology, and 1879 is seen as the year that psychology finally emerged as a unique field separate from philosophy and physiology. Before Wundt, there were no independent psychology departments or officially recognized psychologists (Bolles, 1993).

It is noteworthy that the birth of psychology is identified with the establishment of an experimental laboratory. Wundt's background in physiological research convinced him that the proper approach to the study of mental events was to conduct experiments. He believed that controlled observations should be collected about the phenomena of mind in the same way that one might observe twitching frog legs in an effort to understand the principles of nerve conduction. Wundt wasn't sure that all mental processes could be studied in this way, but he committed himself wholeheartedly to the use of scientific techniques.

Wilhelm Wundt, circa 1912, established the first psychological laboratory at the University of Leipzig in 1879.

Structuralism   Wundt (1896) believed that psychology should be the study of immediate conscious experience, by which he meant the things that people sense and perceive when they reflect inward on their own minds. Wundt analyzed conscious experience in terms of *elements*—sensations and feelings—and he suggested it was the job of the psychologist to identify these elements and discover how they combine to produce meaningful wholes. The idea was that any experience could be broken down into a number of constituent simple elements. This general approach was later named **structuralism** by one of Wundt's students, Edward Titchener (1867–1927). Structuralists believe that psychologists should seek to understand the *structure* of the mind by breaking it down into elementary parts, much like a molecular biologist might try to understand a compound (Titchener, 1899).

The structuralists' research method was *introspectionism:* They trained individuals to introspect, or look inward at the contents of their own minds, while performing various sorts of tasks. For example, the subject might be asked to introspect about what went on in his or her head when a particular musical chord was heard or a particular visual image was presented. By using this technique, the structuralists amassed volumes of data about subjects' reports of their elementary sensory experiences. Titchener's laboratory, for example, was one of the first to document that complex tastes could be broken down into combinations of four elementary tastes: salty, bitter, sour, and sweet (Webb, 1981; as you'll see in Chapter 4, researchers have recently confirmed the existence of a fifth elementary taste, called *umami*). Although introspectionism has fallen out of favour, psychologists studying perception still use some of the research techniques developed by the structuralists and still seek to identify basic elements of sensation. For a thoughtful (but unpublished) discussion of introspectionism, see **http://members. bainbridge.net/~bill.adams/introspection.htm.**

structuralism

An early school of psychology; structuralists attempted to understand the mind by breaking it down into its basic constituent parts, much as a molecular biologist might try to understand an organic compound

Functionalism   Once pioneer researchers, such as Wundt, helped establish psychology as an independent scientific discipline, psychology departments began to spring up rapidly throughout the world. This was particularly true in North America, where dozens of psychological laboratories were established between 1880 and 1900 (Hilgard, 1987). In Canada, James Mark Baldwin established a psychological laboratory at the University of Toronto in 1891; this event is generally considered to signify the beginning of an independent science of psychology in Canada (Hoff, 1992). By 1890, psychologists had established several journals for reporting research results and influential psychology textbooks had been published (e.g., James, 1890).

James Mark Baldwin opened the first Canadian psychology research laboratory in 1891 at the University of Toronto.

North American psychologists quickly departed from the strict structuralist approach advocated by many European psychologists. Whereas structuralists focused on the *content* of immediate experience, dissecting the mind into parts, North American psychologists worried more about the *function* of immediate experience. What is the *purpose* of the mental operations that underlie immediate experience? How are the components of mind used to achieve this end? Because the emphasis was on function rather than on content, this school of thought became known as **functionalism.** Functionalists believe that it's not the analysis of structure but the analysis of function and purpose that should occupy the attention of psychologists (Dewey, 1896; James, 1890).

Functionalists, such as William James (1842–1910), were convinced that it's not possible to understand a system like the mind by simply looking at its parts; that's like trying to understand a house by analyzing its bricks and mortar (James, 1884). It's necessary to first understand the goal—what the mental operation is designed to achieve—then you can try to decipher how the individual parts work together to achieve that goal. For example, to understand how memory works, you must first consider the purpose of memory: What specific problems do our memory systems help us solve in our everyday environments?

Darwin's ideas about evolution through natural selection were extremely influential in the development of functionalist thinking. If you want to analyze the colour markings on a butterfly's wings, a Darwinian theorist would argue, you must ask how those markings help the butterfly survive. Similarly, when analyzing the operations and processes of mind, a functionalist would argue, we need to focus first on the adaptive value of those operations—how they help people solve the problems they face.

Functionalism had a liberalizing effect on the development of psychology in North America. It greatly expanded the range of topics that scientific psychology could approach. For example, it became important to study how an organism interacts with its environment, which led to an early emphasis on learning (Thorndike, 1898) and to the study of individual differences (how people differ from one another). Later, some functionalists turned their attention to applied issues, such as how people solve practical problems in industry and in educational settings (e.g., Taylor, 1911). To a functionalist, just about any aspect of behaviour or mind was considered fair game for study, and psychology in Canada and the United States boomed.

Behaviourism Psychology changed even more radically from 1900 to 1920. Although functionalism and structuralism differed in their emphases, both perspectives considered that the fundamental aim of psychology was to understand immediate conscious experience. The great functionalist William James, in particular, is well known for his superb analysis of the content and purpose of consciousness, which he compared to a flowing and ever-changing stream (see Chapter 5). Around 1900, the technique of introspection—looking inward to observe your own mind—was the primary research method of the experimental psychologist. As previously mentioned, researchers using this technique would present certain stimuli and tasks to subjects and ask them to introspect and report about their perceptions, thoughts, and feelings while doing those tasks.

Yet not all psychologists were convinced that self-observation could produce valid scientific data. By definition, self-observations are private, and researchers have no way to be certain that people's reports accurately reflect their mental experiences. It was also recognized that introspection might change the mental operations being observed. If you're concentrating intently on introspecting about your perceptions of, say, a banana, you are probably experiencing "banana" in an atypical way—not as something to eat, but rather as a complex collection of sensations. Also, people lack introspective awareness of how their minds accomplish certain tasks (e.g., what are the mental processes that enable you to read these words?). Because of these

functionalism

An early school of psychology; functionalists believe that the proper way to understand mind and behaviour is to analyze their function and purpose; you can only truly understand a mental process, functionalists argue, by first knowing the purpose of that process

© Bettmann/Corbis/Magma

William James, shown here in 1868, was convinced that to understand a mental process, it's important to consider its function: How does the process help the individual solve problems in the environment?

© Underwood and Underwood/Corbis/Magma

John B. Watson rejected the study of the mind in favour of the study of observable behaviour.

problems, different laboratories often reported conflicting findings. The introspective method also limited the people and topics that could be studied; it's difficult to ask someone with a severe mental disorder, for example, to introspect and report systematically on his or her condition (Marx & Cronan-Hillix, 1987).

Starting around 1910, psychologists began to question the usefulness of studying immediate conscious experience. A shift began toward studying behaviour, rather than consciousness. The spokesperson of this new movement was a young professor at Johns Hopkins University named John B. Watson (1878–1958). Watson believed that psychology should discard all references to consciousness or mental events. Such events cannot be publicly observed, he argued, and therefore fall outside of the proper domain of science. Observable behaviour should be the proper subject matter of psychology, and the aim of the scientific researcher is to discover how changes in the environment can lead to changes in measurable behaviour. Because of its emphasis on behaviour, Watson called this new way of thinking **behaviourism** (Watson, 1913, 1919).

Behaviourism had an enormous impact on the development of psychology, particularly in North America. Remember, the psychology of Wundt and James was the psychology of mind and immediate experience. Yet by the 1920s, references to consciousness or immediate experience had largely vanished from the psychological vocabulary, as had the technique of systematic introspection. Researchers now concerned themselves with measuring behaviour, especially in animals, and studying how controlled laboratory conditions could change behaviour (Hull, 1943; Skinner, 1938). Influential psychologists, such as B. F. Skinner (1904–1990), provided repeated demonstrations of the practical value of the behaviourist approach. Skinner discovered principles of behaviour modification—how behaviour changes in response to reinforcement and nonreinforcement—that are now widely used in such settings as mental hospitals, schools, and the workplace (Skinner, 1969). We'll discuss these principles in some detail in Chapter 6.

The behaviourist approach dominated North American psychology for decades. However, as you'll see later in this chapter, its influence did not last. To help you put things in perspective, the Concept Summary on page 21 summarizes the three main schools of psychology's early days.

Freud and the Humanists: The Influence of the Clinic

At roughly the same time psychology in North America was undergoing its behaviourist reformation, a medical doctor practising in Vienna was mounting his own psychological revolution. Sigmund Freud (1856–1939) was trained as a neurologist (someone who studies the nervous system), but his psychological insights came not from the laboratory but from his experiences as a clinician. Freud regularly encountered patients whose physical problems appeared to him to be psychological in origin. Freud's efforts to treat these disorders led him to a comprehensive theory of mind that influenced legions of future psychologists and psychiatrists (Freud, 1900/1990, 1910, 1940).

Psychoanalysis   Freud called his theory of mind and system of therapy **psychoanalysis.** He believed that the mind and its contents—the *psyche*—must be *analyzed* extensively before effective treatments can begin. In his view, psychological problems need to be solved through *insight:* The patient needs to understand exactly how his or her mental processes lead to problem behaviours. For this reason, psychoanalysis is often referred to as a form of "insight" therapy.

Among Freud's major contributions were his ideas about unconscious determinants of behaviour. Freud believed each person has a hidden reservoir in the mind, filled with memories, urges, and conflicts that influence actions but that are not accessible to conscious awareness. Freud proposed that the conscious mind blocks people from consciously experiencing certain feelings and memories. If you

behaviourism

A school of psychology proposing that the proper subject matter of psychology is directly observable behaviour and the situations that lead to changes in behaviour, rather than immediate conscious experience

© Bettmann/Corbis/Magma

B. F. Skinner championed the behaviourist approach and was one of the most influential psychologists of the twentieth century.

psychoanalysis

A term used by Freud to describe his theory of mind and system of therapy, which involves analyzing the conscious mind to discover underlying unconscious influences

Sigmund Freud, developer of psychoanalysis, is shown here in the early 1920s.

CRITICAL THINKING

Although Freud was not technically a psychologist—he was a medical doctor—would you classify him as a clinical, an applied, or a research psychologist?

humanistic psychology

An approach to personality that focuses on people's unique capacity for choice, responsibility, and growth

accept Freud's reasoning, it follows that psychology should not be based solely on the study of immediate experience because thoughts and behaviours are influenced by unconscious forces.

Although Freud worked outside mainstream developments in scientific psychology, he too would have rejected systematic introspection as a viable technique for the analysis of mind—but for reasons different from the behaviourists'. Freud believed that recording immediate experience was of interest, but only as a way of discovering hidden conflicts and desires. Freud relied instead on the analysis of dreams—which he believed were largely symbolic—slips of the tongue, and free associations as his primary investigative data (although he also asked patients to report their conscious recollections of childhood). Freud spent hours listening to his patients relate their latest dreams or fantasies in the hope of discovering some symbolic key that would unlock the contents of his patients' unconscious minds. His complex analyses of the mind and its symbols led him to develop a theory of how the unconscious mind defends itself from those seeking to unlock its secrets. We'll consider this theory, as well as its applications for the treatment of psychological disorders, in more detail in Chapters 12 and 15.

In addition to emphasizing unconscious influences on behaviour, Freud believed that childhood experiences play an important role in shaping adult behaviour. He suggested that children go through stages of psychological development that involve a complex interplay between innate sexual urges and experience. He proposed, for example, that boys become erotically attached to their mothers during childhood and consequently experience anxiety about potential castration by their father. These urges and anxieties are unconscious, of course, so the adult male is unlikely consciously to remember these conflicts. Freud's theory was considered shocking when it was first introduced (during the highly moralistic Victorian era), and it continues to be criticized today. For example, Freud has been criticized for being biased against women (Lerman, 1986; Masson, 1984). However, there is no denying the impact of psychoanalytic thought. Psychodynamic theories of human personality—those that stress unconscious but emotionally charged forces in determining behaviour—continue to influence modern psychology.

The Humanistic Response   Freud's influence was substantial, especially among clinicians seeking to treat patients who had psychological disturbances. The familiar image of the client lying on a couch talking about his or her childhood, while the therapist silently jots down notes, is a fairly accurate description of the way early psychoanalysis was performed. However, not all psychologists were comfortable with this approach. Freudian psychology paints a pessimistic view of human nature. It presents human actions as the product of unconscious animalistic urges related to sex and aggression. Moreover, it dismisses any awareness that people might have about why they act the way they do as symbolic and misleading; instead, people's actions are thought to be motivated by deeply hidden conflicts of which they are unaware.

In the 1950s, negative reactions to Freud's view of therapy and mind led to the development of a new movement known as **humanistic psychology.** Humanistic psychologists, such as Carl Rogers (1905–1987) and Abraham Maslow (1908–1970), rejected the pessimistic views of Freud and focused instead on the unique human capacity for self-awareness, choice, responsibility, and growth. The humanists argued that people are not helpless unknowing animals, controlled by unconscious forces; they are ultimately in control of their own destinies and can rise above innate sexual or animalistic urges. Humans are built for personal growth, to seek their fullest potential, to become all they are capable of being (Maslow, 1954; Rogers, 1951).

The optimistic message of the humanists played a significant role in theories of personality development as well as in the treatment of psychological disorders. Carl Rogers, for example, promoted the idea of *client-centred therapy*, in which the therapist is seen not as an analyst or judge but rather as a supporter and friend. Humanistic psychologists believe that all individuals have untapped potential that can be nurtured by an empathic therapist. This idea remains influential among modern psychological approaches to therapy (see Chapters 12 and 15).

Scientific Psychology in Canada

It's likely that psychology is the most popular major at your university, as it is at most Canadian universities. That's partly because psychology is interesting, broadly applicable, and useful. But it doesn't hurt that Canada has long been at the cutting edge of psychological science. We already mentioned that James Mark Baldwin started Canada's first psychological research laboratory at the University of Toronto in 1892, making it one of the first such labs in the world. Today, more than 60 Canadian universities offer undergraduate majors in psychology (often including a selective honours degree appropriate for students who hope to go on to advanced studies in the field), and more than 40 offer graduate degrees in one or more areas of psychology (Adair, Paivio, & Ritchie, 1996). Visit your psychology department's website to learn about the various degrees offered and to find out about the research activities of the faculty members in your department.

In the remainder of this subsection, we highlight a few of the most prominent Canadians in the history of psychology up to the early 1960s. This is, necessarily, a very incomplete collection of brief snapshots. We'll have more to say about these (and other) great Canadian researchers in future chapters. For a much more detailed review of the history of psychology, see Benjafield (2004).

During his years at UofT, James Mark Baldwin took a trip to Massachusetts, where he participated in the creation of the American Psychological Association. He subsequently co-founded two of that association's most prestigious journals (*Psychological Review* and *Psychological Bulletin*, which remain among the top

Carl Rogers helped develop the humanistic perspective, which focuses on our unique capacity for self-awareness, responsibility, and growth.

CONCEPT SUMMARY

EARLY APPROACHES TO THE STUDY OF PSYCHOLOGY

General Focus	Specific Approach	Important Figures	Focuses of Approach
Research	Structuralism	Wundt, Titchener	Determine the structure of immediate conscious experience through the use of *systematic introspection,* in which a person attempts to describe the fundamental elements associated with simple thoughts and sensations.
	Functionalism	James, Dewey	Determine the *functions* of conscious experience through the use of introspection, naturalistic observation, and the measurement of individual differences. Influenced by Darwin, it greatly expanded the range of topics studied in psychology.
	Behaviourism	Watson, Skinner	Establish laws of observable *behaviour.* The approach rejects the study of immediate conscious experience and mental events, unless they are defined in terms of observable behaviour. It was the dominant approach to scientific psychology until the "cognitive revolution" of the 1950s.
Clinical	Psychoanalytic	Freud	Analyze personality and treat psychological disorders by focusing on *unconscious* determinants of behaviour. It contends that childhood experiences play an important role in shaping adult behaviour.
	Humanistic	Rogers, Maslow	Recognize that each person has a unique *self,* and a capacity for growth. Developing partly as a reaction against Freud, it emphasized that humans are basically good and have a unique capacity for self-awareness, choice, responsibility, and growth.

Pioneering neuropsychologist Brenda Milner

Montreal Neurological Institute, McGill University

Mary Salter Ainsworth, a pioneer Canadian psychologist and an important contributor to the study of child-parent attachment

Dan Grogan Photography

journals in psychology). Baldwin's research had to do with children's development, including such topics as how children learn their first language. His theorizing was influenced by Darwinian evolutionary theory. Baldwin left Toronto after a handful of years, returning to the United States. His career was cut short after his arrest in a brothel in 1908 led to a scandal that forced his resignation.

Another extraordinary figure in the history of psychology is Donald O. Hebb. As is further discussed in a subsequent section, Hebb's ideas about the neurological mechanisms underlying learning and memory continue to be influential. Hebb came to McGill at the invitation of another great Canadian brain scientist, Wilder Penfield. Penfield is best known for studies of individuals undergoing brain surgery; he used a tiny electrode to electrically stimulate their brains, thereby shedding light on the functions of various brain regions.

Brenda Milner of McGill University and the Montreal Neurological Institute is another extraordinary Canadian psychologist. Starting in the late 1950s, Milner published groundbreaking studies of a man known as H. M. who had severe amnesia. Milner's work continues to have tremendous impact, and she is justly considered one of the founders of neuropsychology.

McGill University was also home to yet another superstar of Canadian psychology: Ronald Melzack, who was born in Montreal in 1929. Melzack's research and theory led to a radical reconceptualization of the nature of physical pain. It showed that the brain plays a very large role in modulating the amount of pain a person experiences in response to a particular stimulus. This is why, for example, an athlete may experience little pain from an injury during an intense game, even though subsequently the pain may be quite intense.

One of the fundamental topics of psychology is how individuals influence one another. And one of the most influential theorists in that area is Albert Bandura. Bandura was born in Mundane, Alberta, in 1925, and earned his B.A. degree in psychology at the University of British Columbia in 1949. In the early 1960s he published works showing how children's behaviour is influenced not just by the rewards and punishments that they have received but also by their observations of other children's behaviour and the consequences that those children receive.

Mary J. Wright of the University of Western Ontario published a 2002 article with sketches of 10 pioneering Canadian psychologists specializing in child development. Wright herself is an important figure in the history of psychology, having been the first woman president of the Canadian Psychological Association (in 1969; the Americans were ahead of us in this regard; the American Psychological Association elected Mary Calkins as its president in 1905). Wright was a long-time friend of Mary Salter Ainsworth, another prominent Canadian psychologist. With British psychologist John Bowlby, Ainsworth made pioneering contributions to our understanding of the processes by which children become socially and emotionally attached to their parents (e.g., Ainsworth & Bowlby, 1954).

In the 50 or more years since the works referred to above were conducted, Canadian psychology has continued to thrive. According to a 2001 report by the Canadian Society for Brain, Behaviour and Cognitive Science (BBCS), Canadians make up only 3% of the world's psychologists in the BBCS areas, but publish more than 9% of the scholarly articles in those areas. Another way of measuring impact is citation counts—how often a paper is referred to or cited in subsequent papers. In terms of citation counts, Canada ranks third in the world (behind the United States and the United Kingdom, both of which have much bigger populations). Throughout this text we highlight first-rate Canadian psychological science when it is relevant. Sometimes we explicitly mention that a particular researcher or project is Canadian, but most of the time we simply talk about the content of the research itself.

Test your knowledge about how thinking in psychology developed by answering the following questions. (The answers are in Appendix B.)

Test Yourself 1.2

1. Most modern psychologists believe that the mind and the body are
   a. controlled by different sections of the pineal gland
   b. best considered as one and the same
   c. separate, but both can be studied with the scientific method
   d. best studied by philosophers and physiologists, respectively

2. Fill in the blanks in the following paragraph. Choose your answers from the following set of terms: behaviour, behaviourism, emotions, empiricists, functionalists, introspection, structuralists, thoughts.

   Functionalists and structuralists used the technique of _____ to understand immediate conscious experience. The _____ believed that it was best to break the mind down into basic parts, much as a chemist would seek to understand a chemical compound. The _____ were influenced by Darwin's views on natural selection and focused primarily on the purpose and adaptive value of mental events. _____, founded by John Watson, steered psychology away from the study of immediate conscious experience toward an emphasis on _____.

3. Freud's psychoanalysis differs from Rogers's humanistic approach in which of the following ways?
   a. Psychoanalysis is "client centred" rather than "therapist centred."
   b. Psychoanalysis is designed to promote self-awareness and personal growth.
   c. Psychoanalysis minimizes the influence of early childhood experiences.
   d. Psychoanalysis is designed to reveal hidden urges and memories related to sex and aggression.

4. Who was Mary Salter Ainsworth, and for what research was she particularly well known?

Understanding the Focus of Modern Psychology

LEARNING GOALS

1. Understand what it means to adopt an eclectic approach to psychology.
2. Be able to discuss the origins and central premises of the cognitive revolution.
3. Learn about recent developments in biology and neuroscience and how they have influenced modern psychology.
4. Understand how natural selection contributed to the evolution of the adaptive human mind.
5. Appreciate why psychologists believe that cultural factors are important determinants of behaviour and mind.
6. Grasp how psychologists strive to use their own adaptive minds to understand how and why people do and feel the things they do.

Psychology has changed substantially since Wundt established the first psychological laboratory in 1879 (see Robins, Gosling, & Craik, 1999, for an empirical analysis of trends in modern psychology). Psychologists have argued—often for decades—about the proper focus for psychology (mind or behaviour?), about how to conceive of human nature (e.g., do we have free will?), and about which research methods and forms of theorizing are appropriate for a science of psychology. Remember, the discipline is only a little more than a century old; psychology is still getting its theoretical feet wet.

Today, most psychologists have turned away from a strict allegiance to one theoretical orientation, such as behaviourism or psychoanalysis, and have adopted a more **eclectic approach.** This means that contemporary psychologists generally integrate from many different sources of ideas rather than relying entirely on one theoretical perspective. Eclecticism is common among both clinical psychologists helping people with psychological problems and research psychologists working primarily in the laboratory.

eclectic approach

The position adopted by many psychologists that it's useful to integrate information from several sources; we need not rely exclusively on any single theoretical perspective

In the case of the clinical psychologist, the best technique often depends on the preferences of the client and on the particular problem at hand. For instance, some kinds of phobias—irrational fears of things, like heights or spiders—can be treated effectively by focusing on the fearful behaviour itself and ignoring its ultimate origin. (We don't need to know why you're afraid of snakes; we can just try to deal with the fear itself.) Other psychological problems may require the therapist to determine how childhood factors influenced adult dysfunction. Modern clinical psychologists integrate perspectives in an effort to find the best solution for their clients' problems, and they increasingly rely on scientific evaluations of the efficacy of various treatment options rather than relying exclusively on their intuitions and casual observations.

Modern research psychologists also take an eclectic approach. For example, many psychological researchers now work in teams, pulling together the theoretical perspectives of psychologists with expertise in a variety of different sub-areas, such as biological psychology, social psychology, personality psychology, and cognitive psychology. Researchers recognize that it's possible to understand behaviour and mind from many different perspectives, at many different levels of analysis.

Four additional perspectives have become quite influential in recent years. Modern psychologists remain eclectic, but they generally refer to cognitive, biological, evolutionary, and cultural factors to explain behaviour. Because of the special emphasis these factors currently receive, we highlight them briefly in the following sections.

The Cognitive Revolution

By the 1950s, many psychologists had grown uncomfortable with the behaviourist idea that behaviour is the only proper subject matter for psychology. Researchers showed renewed interest in the study of consciousness and internal mental processes (Miller, Galanter, & Pribram, 1960; Neisser, 1967). A shift away from behaviourism began, and this movement, which is still going strong, is known as the **cognitive revolution.** The word *cognitive* refers to the process of knowing or perceiving; as you may remember from our earlier discussion, cognitive psychologists are research psychologists who study phenomena such as memory, learning, and reasoning.

Psychologists returned to studying internal mental phenomena for several reasons. One factor is the development of research techniques that enable investigators to infer cognitive processes from observable behaviour. Regularities in behaviour, such as reaction times or forgetting rates, can provide detailed information about internal mental processes, provided the experiments are conducted properly. You'll learn about specific tactics of psychological research in Chapter 2, and in subsequent chapters you'll see how those techniques have been used to study the mind as well as behaviour.

Another important factor that helped fuel the cognitive revolution was the development of the computer. Computers function through an interplay between *hardware*—the fixed structural features of the machine, such as the internal chips and disk drives—and *software*, the programs that tell the hardware what to do. Although the human mind cannot be compared directly to a computer, it's useful to conceive of behaviour as reflecting the interplay between biological (or genetic) factors—that is, the hardwired structures of the brain and nervous system—and the tactics and strategies (the software) we learn from interactions with the environment. Cognitive psychologists have developed explanations of human behaviour as reflecting the operation of *information processing systems*—internal structures in the brain that manipulate information from the environment in ways that solve problems (see Chapters 7 and 8). Such work has both inspired and drawn on parallel research on the development of artificial intelligence—that is, machines that are in some senses capable of intelligent action (Thagard, 2005).

cognitive revolution

The shift away from strict behaviourism, begun in the 1950s, characterized by renewed interest in the study of consciousness and internal mental processes

As you'll discover throughout this book, behaviour is often influenced by people's beliefs and mental strategies. Everything—from perceptions and memories to decisions about what foods to eat to our choice of friends—is critically influenced by prior knowledge and beliefs. Many psychologists believe that the key to understanding psychological disorders, such as depression, lies in the analysis of an individual's thought patterns. Depressed individuals tend to think rigidly and inflexibly, and some forms of therapy are directed specifically at challenging these entrenched thoughts and beliefs. You'll see many references to thoughts and cognitions as we investigate a range of psychological phenomena.

Developments in Biology

The focus of modern psychology has also been greatly shaped by the wealth of recent discoveries relating to the biological underpinnings of behaviour. As mentioned above, one of the most important researchers who attempted to understand the biological processes that underlie thought and action was the Canadian psychologist Donald O. Hebb. His 1949 book, *The Organization of Behavior: A Neuropsychological Theory*, is one of the most influential volumes in the history of psychology (Fentress, 1999; Klein, 1999) and has just been republished (thanks largely to the efforts of Professor Richard Brown of Dalhousie University's Neuroscience Institute). As a professor at McGill University, Hebb had a significant influence on fostering the cognitive revolution of the 1950s and 1960s (Wickelgren, 1999). He is the only psychologist to date to serve as president of both the Canadian Psychological Association and the American Psychological Association. Each year since 1998, the Canadian Society for Brain, Behaviour and Cognitive Science has celebrated Hebb's contributions by conferring the Hebb Award on a prominent Canadian researcher. Recent honourees include Doreen Kimura of Simon Fraser University and Shep Siegel of McMaster University (see **http://psych.mcmaster. ca/bbcs/hebb.html** for a complete list of Hebb Award winners).

Since Hebb, researchers have uncovered fascinating links between structures in the brain and the phenomena of behaviour and mind (see ❯ Figure 1.4). It is now possible to record the activity of brain cells directly, and it's been discovered that individual brain cells often respond to particular kinds of events in the environment. For example, cells in the "visual" part of the brain respond actively only when particular colours, or patterns of light and dark, are shown to the eye. Other cells respond to inadequate supplies of nutrients by "motivating" a person to seek food.

Canadian psychologist Donald O. Hebb of McGill University made important contributions to the cognitive revolution and to our understanding of the biological bases of behaviour.

Doreen Kimura has advanced our knowledge of differences between the brains of women and men.

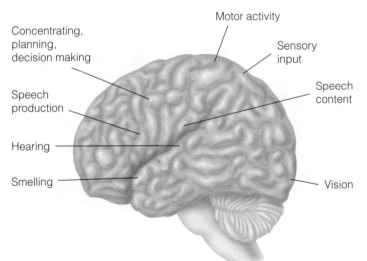

Concentrating, planning, decision making

Speech production

Hearing

Smelling

Motor activity

Sensory input

Speech content

Vision

❯ **Figure 1.4**

Specificity in the Brain

Researchers have discovered that bodily functions are largely controlled by specific areas of the brain. Developments in the biological sciences continue to have an enormous impact on the thinking of psychologists.

Moreover, technology is now allowing psychologists to take "snapshots" of mental life in action. As you'll see in Chapter 3, it is now possible to create images of how activities in the brain change as the mind processes different things. These images of the brain in action help researchers understand normal as well as abnormal brain activity. For example, it's possible to record brain activity during depression, during extreme anxiety, or even during auditory and visual hallucinations. This information is useful in determining where in the brain specific psychological disorders originate and in providing a "road map" for treatment.

Great strides have also been made in understanding brain chemistry, that is, how natural drugs inside the brain influence many behaviours. It turns out that certain psychological problems, such as depression and schizophrenia, may be related to imbalances among the chemical messengers in the brain. Cognitive neuroscientists have also learned a great deal about the functions of various parts of the brain and how those parts are interconnected. These developments, which we'll discuss in detail in Chapters 3, 14, and 15, are shaping the way psychological theories are constructed and how psychological problems are treated.

Evolutionary Bases of Thought and Behaviour

Another category of "biological" influence on modern psychological thinking involves researching the evolutionary origins of mind and behaviour. You will remember that Darwin's ideas influenced the early development of psychological thought, being particularly important in the development of functionalism. Darwinian ideas have recently re-emerged as a significant source of concepts and insights in understanding human psychology. This contemporary Darwinian perspective has been labelled **evolutionary psychology** (Barkow, Cosmides, & Tooby, 1992; Buss, 2004; Crawford & Krebs, 1998; Daly & Wilson, 1999b); it views human thought and behaviour as comprising somewhat independent "modules" that evolved to solve specific problems that repeatedly arose in the ecology of our evolutionary ancestors. In this perspective, the human mind evolved to include cognitive and social mechanisms to solve adaptive problems, such as how to find and reproduce with an appropriate mate (Buss, 1994), how to nurture and invest in offspring in a way that makes best use of limited resources (Daly & Wilson, 1998), and how to quickly make judgments and predictions about people's actions and motives (Krebs & Denton, 1997). The contemporary Darwinian perspective in psychology does not view evolutionary explanations as opposed to cognitive or cultural explanations of behaviour, but as complementary, providing a level of analysis of human behaviour that uses many of the same explanatory models used to understand the adaptive behaviour of nonhuman animals.

evolutionary psychology

The study of the human mind and behavioural processes as products of natural selection

Cultural groups can be based on numerous dimensions, such as ethnicity, geography, socioeconomic class, or political or religious allegiance.

The Importance of Culture

Modern psychological thinking also emphasizes the concept of culture and the role it plays in shaping people's thoughts and behaviours. By **culture,** psychologists mean the shared values, customs, and beliefs that characterize a group or community. Cultural groups can be based on obvious things, such as ethnicity, geography, or socioeconomic class, but also on political, religious, or other factors (e.g., those who share the same sexual orientation might be considered a cultural group). Culture is a broad construct, and its influences can be found in virtually all aspects of behaviour and mind.

Recognizing that culture exerts a strong influence on our thoughts and actions may seem obvious to you, but it was largely ignored in mainstream psychology for many years. In the introductory textbook used by one of this textbook's authors as an undergraduate student, group influences were not discussed except for a mere three paragraphs covering why individuals might differ in intelligence. Psychologists have always recognized that behaviour is influenced by the environment, which can mean culture, but it was the behaviour of individuals in isolation rather than the behaviour of individuals in groups that received the most attention. Researchers spent their time looking for universal principles of behaviour, those that cut across all people in all groups, rather than exploring how the shared values of a community might affect how people think and act. The search for universal principles continues today, but cross-cultural factors are now considered to be an integral part of the story of psychology, as shown in the *Handbook of Cross-Cultural Psychology*, compiled by Queen's University's cross-cultural psychologist John Berry, Ype Poortinga, and Janak Pandey (1997).

A few notable psychologists paid attention to culture early on, especially in attempting to explain cognitive and social development. More than half a century ago, the Russian psychologist Lev Vygotsky proposed that children's thoughts and actions originate from their social interactions, particularly with parents. Vygotsky believed that it's not possible to understand the mind of a child without carefully considering the child's social and cultural world. In an important sense, the properties of a child's mind are created by his or her social and cultural interactions. At first, these ideas were not very influential in psychology, partly because Vygotsky died young in the 1930s, but they've been rediscovered by psychologists in the last few decades and are now being actively pursued. (You'll read a bit more about Vygotsky in Chapter 10.)

Why have cultural factors become so important to psychologists? Most importantly, studies have demonstrated that culture matters, even when studying basic psychological principles, such as memory (DiMaggio, 1997; Mullen, 1994), perception (Davies & Corbett, 1997), self-presentation (Heine, Takata, & Lehman, 2000), and reasoning (Li, Sano, & Merwin, 1996). For example, in research conducted in New Zealand, MacDonald, Uesiliana, and Hayne (2000) asked adults from three different cultural backgrounds to report their earliest childhood memory: Maoris (the indigenous people of New Zealand), European New Zealanders, and Chinese people. The Maori culture places a strong emphasis on memory for the past, and Maori adults reported memories of significantly earlier childhood events than did individuals from the other cultures.

Most psychologists agree that a full understanding of behaviour and mind cannot be achieved without considering the individual in his or her social and cultural context. Although evolution has provided humans with a basic set of adaptive mental modules for solving problems that were important for the survival of our ancestors, cultural factors also play major roles in how we think, in how we interact with one another, and even in how we see the world.

culture

The shared values, customs, and beliefs that are characteristic of a group or community

CRITICAL   THINKING

Behaviour can be difficult to predict but can still be governed by understandable principles. Think about how difficult it is to predict the weather or even the movement of a ball rolling down an inclined plane. Would you claim that these activities are not controlled by principled "laws of nature"?

Solving Problems with the Adaptive Mind

We began this chapter by emphasizing the tremendous range of human behaviour, from acts of brutal violence to works of subtle genius. That range, from one person to another and from one moment to the next within individuals, is a telling characteristic of our species. It is telling because it illustrates the unusual (compared with other animals) extent to which our behavioural repertoire is determined by experiential and environmental factors as opposed to being genetically fixed and determined. As noted earlier (and elaborated in subsequent chapters), genes play important roles in the human experience, but our major evolutionary genetic endowment is of a mind/brain capable of an astounding flexibility and adaptiveness.

The ultimate aim of psychology is to develop a science of mind and behaviour, and an understanding of how and why people do, feel, and experience the things they do. Psychologists strive to use their own adaptive minds to unravel the mind's complex and mysterious nature. This science, and its practical application by clinical psychologists and applied psychologists, is still at an early stage of development. To put it another way, the science is still evolving, responding adaptively to new empirical evidence and new theoretical ideas. The 15 chapters that follow will introduce you to some of what we have discovered so far.

As we mentioned at the beginning of the chapter, each chapter in this textbook is organized around a set of adaptive or practical *problems*. The problem-solving approach is designed to promote the idea that we think and act for adaptive reasons; we use our psychological tool kit to help us solve problems every day. But this theme is also designed to provide you with a direct link between the topic discussions and the real world. For instance, in Chapter 13 you'll learn about a topic in social psychology called *attribution theory*. Why? Because attribution theory deals with a very important everyday problem: How do we assign a cause to someone's behaviour? You constantly need to interpret the behaviour of others, whether it's the sudden anger of a friend or the disapproving look of a professor. At first glance, attribution theory may seem like an abstract topic, but it's really quite relevant to your life.

The problem-solving approach is also intended to encourage you to think critically about the material. Rather than just memorizing the facts about a topic, you will learn more if you try to make the connection between the topic under discussion and solving the adaptive or practical problem. For example, how does a procedure like classical conditioning help psychologists understand how people learn about the signalling properties of events? (We'll discuss this in Chapter 6.)

Finally, the problem-solving approach is designed to provide some continuity across the different chapters. Human behaviour is easier to comprehend when it is viewed as the product of an adaptive mind. You are encouraged to understand that behaviours, as well as the methods of psychologists, are reactions to problems faced. Focusing on adaptiveness will sensitize you to the diversity of behaviour, both among people and across species. Although constrained by their shared evolutionary heritage, individuals respond to unique situations and use strategies that are influenced by culture and by transient biological states. The wide array of different behaviours and personal styles you encounter in daily life testifies to the diverse outcomes of our adaptive minds.

Test Yourself   1.3

Test your knowledge about the focus of modern psychology by answering the following questions. (The answers are in Appendix B.)

1. According to the eclectic approach, in choosing the best technique to use in therapy, you should consider the
   a. specific unconscious urges that are driving behaviour
   b. training and biases of the therapist or researcher
   c. preferences of the client and the particular problem under investigation
   d. availability of relevant monitoring equipment
2. Fill in the blanks in the following paragraph. Choose your answers from the following set of terms: biology, cognitive, computer, cultural, philosophy.

   Over the past several decades, psychologists have returned to the study of internal mental phenomena such as consciousness. This shift away from strict behaviourism has been labelled the _____ revolution. An important factor that helped fuel this revolution was the development of the _____ , which became a model of sorts for the human mind. Developments in _____ are also playing an important role in shaping modern psychology and in creating effective treatments for psychological problems.

3. Psychologists are increasingly appealing to cultural factors to help explain human behaviour. Which of the following statements about culture and psychology is *false*?
   a. Psychologists largely ignored cultural influences for many years.
   b. Culture influences social processes but not basic psychological processes, such as memory and reasoning.
   c. A few notable psychologists, such as Lev Vygotsky, studied cultural influences many decades ago.
   d. By culture, psychologists mean the shared values, customs, and beliefs that are characteristic of a group or community.

Introducing Psychology

R E V I E W

At the end of every chapter, you'll find a section that summarizes the main points of the chapter from the perspective of our "problems to be solved." This is a good point to stop and think about the facts and theories you've read about and to try to see how they relate to the particular problems we've discussed. This mental review will help consolidate your learning, making it easier for you to retain the material. In this chapter, our primary goal was to introduce you to the science of psychology. Our discussion involved three main issues.

First, how do we define and describe psychology? Psychology is the scientific study of behaviour and mind. Notice that this definition makes no specific reference to psychological problems or abnormal behaviour. Although many psychologists (especially clinical psychologists) work to promote mental health, applied psychologists and research psychologists work primarily to understand "normal" people. The goal of the scientific study of behaviour and mind is to discover general principles that can be applied widely to help people adapt more successfully—in the workplace, in school, or at home—and to unravel the great scientific mystery of how and why people do the things they do.

Second, how did current psychological perspectives develop? Psychology has existed as a separate subject matter of science for a little more than a century, but people have pondered the mysteries of behaviour and mind for thousands of years. Psychology has its roots in philosophy and physiology. Thinkers in these fields addressed several fundamental psychological issues, such as the relation between the mind and the body, and the origins of knowledge. Most modern psychologists solve the mind-body problem by assuming that the two are essentially one and the same—thoughts, ideas, and emotions arise out of the biological processes of the brain (although we are still far from a complete understanding of how this works). Most psychologists also assume that basic kinds of behaviours originate from natural evolved dispositions (nature) as well as from lifetime experiences (nurture).

Once the discipline of psychology was established by Wundt in 1879, vigorous arguments ensued over the proper way to characterize and study the mind. Structuralists like Wundt believed the world of immediate experience could be broken down into elements, much like how a chemist analyzes a chemical compound. In contrast, the functionalists argued that psychology should focus on the function and purpose of behaviour. The behaviourists rejected the world of immediate experience in favour of studying behaviour, without reference to consciousness. Sigmund Freud's psychoanalytic view outlined a quite different perspective on human psychology, with its emphasis on the unconscious mind. The pessimism of the Freudians was one factor that led to the reaction of the humanistic psychologists, who strongly advocate free will and the power of personal choice.

Third, what is the dominant theoretical orientation of modern psychology? Each of the earlier psychological perspectives has some continuing influence on psychological ideas today. But most modern psychologists adopt an eclectic approach: They choose from the perspectives based on the problem at hand. Many psychologists still focus on behaviour as a research strategy, but the world of inner experience is also a prime target for study, as evidenced by the cognitive revolution and by recent developments in the biological sciences. Recently, there has been a resurgence in efforts to use evolutionary ideas to help understand the functioning of the modules of the mind, and psychologists also increasingly include cultural factors in their explanations of behaviour and mind.

The problem-solving approach in this book is based on the concept of the adaptive mind: People, as well as other animals, use their mental machinery—forged in evolutionary history and rooted in the biological processes of the brain—to achieve certain fundamental ends. Individuals continually adjust their actions in an effort to solve the problems that arise from a complex and changing environment.

CHAPTER SUMMARY

▶ Defining and Describing Psychology

Psychology is the scientific study of *behaviour* and *mind* and of how people differ as a result of biological and environmental influences and cultural context. Psychological understanding lets us predict, control, and improve behaviour.

The Invisible and Dynamic Mind: How Can It Be Studied?

Psychologists use three types of measures to assess mental events. With *self-report* measures, people describe their own thoughts and feelings. With *biological* measures, scientists assess physiological processes, including brain activities. With *behavioural* measures, psychologists infer how the mind works from how the body behaves under particular conditions.

What Psychologists Do

Clinical psychologists diagnose and treat psychological problems, and they give advice. *Psychiatrists* also diagnose and treat psychological problems, but unlike clinical psychologists, they receive their training in medical school and are able to prescribe drugs. Some *counsellors* also provide services to people with psychological problems, but they vary widely in the kind and amount of training they have received. *Applied psychologists* help normal people in practical settings improve their performance. *Research psychologists* collect data on basic and applied issues through research and observation.

How to Become a Psychologist

The first step is to do well in your undergraduate years. A variety of psychology-related jobs can be held by an individual with a bachelor's degree in psychology, but to be classified as a psychologist per se, more advanced training is required. To provide therapy as a licensed psychologist, you need to complete a bachelor's degree (often, but not necessarily, in psychology) followed by a doctoral degree in clinical psychology (usually, a master's degree is earned en route to a doctoral degree). Most people working as applied psychologists have a master's degree or doctoral degree in psychology or both. Most research psychologists have a doctoral degree in psychology.

▶ Tracing the Evolution of Psychological Thought

The primary intellectual roots of psychology are in philosophy and physiology.

Mind and Body: Are They the Same?

Descartes believed that the mind is separate from the body, which it controls through the pineal gland. *Modern psychologists* believe that the mind and body are different aspects of the same thing, because the mind is a product of what the brain does.

Nature and Nurture: Where Does Knowledge Come From?

Empiricism holds that we learn everything through experience (Aristotle). *Nativism* holds that some knowledge is inborn (innate), including ideas regarding cause and effect, and space and time. *Darwin* proposed that natural selection guides evolution, and that some behavioural tendencies are inherited.

The First Schools: Psychology as Science

Structuralism was founded by *Wundt*, who established an experimental laboratory to study the components of immediate experience and how they sum to a meaningful whole. *Functionalism* was developed by North American psychologists who studied the adaptive purpose (*function*) of immediate experience. *Behaviourism*, led by *Watson*, was based on the premise that because immediate conscious experience cannot be observed, behaviour is the proper subject of psychology.

Freud and the Humanists: The Influence of the Clinic

Freud was a neurologist and clinician who used dreams and free association to analyze both the mind and the unconscious determinants of behaviour. According to Freud, much of human behaviour reflects unconscious drives to gratify sensual urges. Humanist psychologists, such as *Rogers* and *Maslow*, rejected Freud's pessimism and focused instead on positive traits. According to humanistic psychologists, people control their destinies and can attain their full potential through insight and personal growth.

Scientific Psychology in Canada

James Mark Baldwin established Canada's first laboratory of psychology at the University of Toronto. *Wilder Penfield* and *Donald O. Hebb* did groundbreaking work in neuropsychology. *Brenda Milner* of the Montreal Neurological Institute and McGill University is highly celebrated as one of the pioneers of neuropsychology, famed for her brilliant studies of patients with various kinds of brain damage. *Ronald Melzack*'s theorizing changed the way psychologists think about pain. *Albert Bandura* revolutionized thinking about children's learning with his work on how children are influenced by models. *Mary Wright* was the first female president of the Canadian Psychological Association. *Mary Salter Ainsworth* was a pioneer Canadian psychologist and an important contributor to our understanding of child-parent attachment.

▶ Understanding the Focus of Modern Psychology

An *eclectic approach* draws from diverse sources and theoretical perspectives and uses various methods to investigate psychological issues and to apply psychology in clinical and applied settings.

The Cognitive Revolution

The *cognitive revolution* was a shift away from strict behaviourism, characterized by a renewed interest in the study of consciousness and internal mental processes. The word *cognitive* refers to the process of knowing or perceiving that involves learning, memory, and reasoning, and underlies much human behaviour.

Developments in Biology

Biology has always played an important role in psychology, but that role has increased in recent years with the development of new knowledge concerning genetics and the anatomy and physiology of the brain, and new methods for studying the physiology of the brain in action. Psychological research informed by such knowledge and methods has led to new understandings of how human behaviour and experience are influenced by chemicals in the brain, and of how various components within the brain interact to give rise to mental phenomena.

Evolutionary Bases of Thought and Behaviour

Natural selection—the tendency for more successful organisms to survive to reproduce and hence pass their genes on to future generations—shaped specific modules of mind and behaviour to address problems faced by our evolutionary ancestors.

The Importance of Culture

Culture—the shared values, customs, and beliefs that characterize a group or community (Lehman, Chiu, & Schaller, 2004)—plays a major role in contributing to the diversity of human experience and behaviour. Differences between cultures affect not only relatively superficial things, such as clothing styles and language, but also more fundamental psychological processes, such as memory.

Solving Problems with the Adaptive Mind

Natural selection has endowed the human animal with a mind/brain capable of great flexibility and adaptiveness. Our behaviour and our understanding can shift dramatically with experience, and we are capable of solving (as well as creating!) a huge array of problems. Psychological scientists use their adaptive, problem-solving minds to explore fundamental questions of human behaviour and experience. By using your own *adaptive mind* in an actively engaged, problem-solving manner, you can enrich your understanding and retention of this (and other) texts.

Terms to Remember

psychology, 4

Defining and Describing Psychology
mind, 7
behaviour, 8
clinical psychologists, 9
counselling psychologists, 9
counsellor, 10
psychiatrists, 10
applied psychologists, 10
research psychologists, 12

Tracing the Evolution of Psychological Thought
empiricism, 14
nativism, 15
structuralism, 17

functionalism, 18
behaviourism, 19
psychoanalysis, 19
humanistic psychology, 20

Understanding the Focus of Modern Psychology
eclectic approach, 23
cognitive revolution, 24
evolutionary psychology, 26
culture, 27

Recommended Readings

Hunt, M. (1993). *The story of psychology*. New York: Anchor Books. This highly entertaining look at the history of psychology moves from the musings of the ancient Greek philosophers to modern theoretical approaches.

James, W. (1890/1983). *The principles of psychology*. Cambridge, MA: Harvard University Press. It's worth looking at James's classic work. The writing is poetic, the insights are many, and remember—this was once used as an introductory textbook in psychology!

Pinker, S. (1997). *How the mind works*. New York: W. W. Norton. This is a witty and lucid exploration of some of the basic concepts in contemporary cognitive and evolutionary psychology. It explains the "modules of mind" idea in some detail.

Wright, R. (1994). *The moral animal*. Toronto: Random House/New York: Pantheon. This book clearly explains the basic principles of modern evolutionary psychology, interweaves the story of Charles Darwin's life and ideas, and discusses which of Darwin's ideas have the most influence today.

For additional readings, explore InfoTrac® College Edition, your online library. Go to http://www.adaptivemind3e.nelson.com.

Hint: Enter these search terms: psychologist, psychoanalysis, behaviourism, history of psychology, cognitive psychology.

Media Resources

What's on the Web?

Please note that Web addresses are subject to change. Check out the accompanying website for updates: http://www.adaptivemind3e.nelson.com.

This site also presents practice quiz questions, hypercontent, information on degrees and careers in psychology, study tips, and more.

Instruments Used in Early Psychology Research

http://www.psych.utoronto.ca/museum/

This site provides images of and information about a variety of instruments (most made of brass and wood) used in Canada's first laboratory for experimental psychology.

Canadian Psychological Association

http://www.cpa.ca/

The national association for psychologists in Canada. The site includes information on careers for psychologists, provincial and territorial licensing requirements, educational opportunities, and links to Canadian psychology journals.

The Great Canadian Psychology Website

http://www.psych.ualberta.ca/GCPWS/

This site features videos and biographies on 11 of Canada's great psychologists. It also includes examples of the sorts of research done by each, including, for some, replications of classic studies that you can try out.

Bad Human Factors Designs

http://www.baddesigns.com/examples.html

Do you ever get frustrated with the stupid way that someone designed the things you work with every day? Do you have trouble telling the difference between the buttons on your stereo? Can't figure out which side of the door to push to get out? This site is full of stupid human factors designs, complete with pictures. Surf around and see if you can do some intelligent redesigning!

History of Psychology Website

http://elvers.stjoe.udayton.edu/history/welcome.htm

This is a comprehensive site, with a list of more than 100 clickable names that will give you a description of how that person contributed to psychology. The list ranges from Aristotle to St. Thomas Aquinas to B. F. Skinner. You can even sort the list of historical figures according to their birth date. See if any famous figures share your birthday!

ThomsonNOW™ ThomsonNOW

http://hed.nelson.com

Go to this site for the link to ThomsonNOW™, your one-stop study shop. Take a Pretest for this chapter and ThomsonNOW™ will generate a personalized Study Plan based on your test results. The Study Plan will identify the topics you need to review and direct you to online resources to help you master those topics. You can then take a Posttest to determine what concepts you have mastered and what you still need work on.

Psyk.trek 3.0

Check out Psyk.trek 3.0 for further study of the concepts in this chapter. Psyk.trek's 65 interactive learning modules, simulations, and quizzes offer additional opportunities for you to interact with, reflect on, and retain the material:

History and Methods: Psychology's Timeline

You can observe a lot by watching.

—Yogi Berra

The Methods of Psychological Research

Tara relaxed in the passenger seat as her friend Duncan wheeled his battered Toyota down the main street of town. Duncan's cell phone rang and he thumbed it open with characteristic aplomb and started chatting. Tara's dad always rants about how people shouldn't talk on the phone when driving, but Duncan argues that talking to a friend on the cell is no different from talking to a passenger. Anyway, Tara knows Duncan's a great driver, so she's not too worried about it.

Is cell phone use any more distracting to drivers than listening to the radio or conversing with a passenger? If so, why? If cell phones are especially distracting, what might be done to reduce the problem? Would it help if drivers used hands-free phones? Are some drivers more impaired by cell phone use than others are?

How would you go about answering such questions? Psychological scientists have worked toward such answers by using a variety of research techniques, including experiments with realistic driving simulators. That research is summarized in a Practical Solutions feature in Chapter 5; briefly, the evidence indicates that the use of a cell phone does indeed impair drivers' performance by reducing the extent to which they attend to visual stimuli. For now, our emphasis is on how psychologists go about gaining such knowledge.

As you know from Chapter 1, psychology is a scientific enterprise. Its methods combine basic principles of logic with systematic measurements of behaviour. Psychologists use the **scientific method** as their main tool for investigating

scientific method

A method for acquiring knowledge by combining (1) the principles of rational thought (that is, logic) with (2) information derived from systematic measurements of the object of study (that is, empirical research)

behaviour and mind. If you want to understand the effect of cell phones on driving, your first step is to employ the scientific method. Reduced to its barest essentials, the scientific method contains four important steps (see ▶ Figure 2.1):

1. *Generate a question.* An infinite number of questions can be explored scientifically, and the first step is to pick one to study. Psychological scientists get ideas about what to study from many sources, including casual observations of everyday life. Often, researchers are inspired to investigate a particular question by the work of other researchers who have explored that question.
2. *Gather information.* Next, the researcher looks for background information on the question of interest. What, if anything, have other scholars discovered about it? In addition to a search of the scientific literature, this stage may involve observing behaviour in settings related to the question (descriptive research).
3. *Formulate a hypothesis.* In step 3, the researcher forms a hypothesis, which is a testable prediction about the behaviour under study. Hypotheses can be expressed in the form of if-then statements: If some set of conditions is present, then a certain kind of behaviour is likely to occur. Often, hypotheses are guided by theories about the causes of the behaviours of interest.
4. *Test the hypothesis and interpret the results.* Finally, the prediction of the hypothesis is tested under controlled conditions. That is, the researcher sets up the conditions specified in the hypothesis and determines whether the predicted behaviour occurs. If the new data are consistent with the prediction of the hypothesis, the hypothesis is supported; if the data contradict the hypothesis, it is disconfirmed.

The hypothesis-testing step in the scientific method is, arguably, the defining characteristic of science. Scientists don't just make verbal arguments about why a hypothesis makes sense and should be accepted; rather, they put the hypothesis to the test in an actual situation.

Testing a hypothesis requires accurate measurements of the behaviour of interest. The information-gathering stage of the scientific method may also entail quantitative measures of behaviour in situations relevant to the research question. It is crucial for the scientific enterprise that such measures be accurate. To help ensure

▶ **Figure 2.1**

Steps in the Scientific Method

The scientific method has four major steps. In the first step, the researcher *generates a question*. For example, suppose a researcher casually observes (a) where students sit in a lecture hall and (b) how often they ask questions during a lecture, and wonders whether there might be a relationship between those two variables. In step 2, the researcher *gathers information* about this question by searching for prior research on the relationship between where students sit and how often they ask questions, and perhaps by observing these classroom behaviours more systematically. In step 3, the researcher *generates a hypothesis*: If the professor stands at the back of the lecture hall, more questions will come from the students at the back than from those at the front. In step 4, the researcher *tests the hypothesis*. Here the hypothesis has turned out to be wrong: Even when the teacher stands at the back of the room, it is still the students sitting in front who more often ask questions.

| Step 1 Generate a question | Step 2 Gather information | Step 3 Create a hypothesis | Step 4 Test the hypothesis |

the accuracy of their measurements, research psychologists use **operational definitions** to define the behaviours under investigation. An operational definition defines a to-be-measured variable in terms of the steps or procedures used to measure it (Levine & Parkinson, 1994; Stevens, 1939). For example, "intelligence" might be defined operationally as performance on a particular IQ test; "impatience" might be defined as the number of times the subject looks at his or her watch during a set period; "boredom" might be defined as how often a student yawns. One of the major challenges of psychological research is developing operational definitions that capture the underlying concepts of interest (e.g., creating IQ tests that measure what we have in mind when we think of "intelligence"). If your goal is to investigate the topic of attention in car drivers, for example, you must develop an operational definition of "attention." Can you think of one?

Our review of psychological research methods emphasizes the use of quantitative measurements to characterize aspects of human behaviour, thought, and feeling. We do this because quantitative approaches have long dominated psychological research and have yielded many insights into the human experience. But you should know that psychological research questions can also usefully be explored by using more qualitative methods. Qualitative methodology is complex and multifaceted and we cannot do it justice here, but the idea is for the researcher to attempt to apprehend (by close observation and painstaking analysis) the dynamic patterns of interactions among numerous variables in complex, naturalistic situations. For example, Prof. Kelli Stajduhar and her students at the University of Victoria use qualitative methods to explore the psychological and social dynamics that arise when family members care for a terminally ill loved one at home (e.g., Stajduhar & Davies, 2005). For an introduction to qualitative research methods in psychology, see Camic, Rhodes, and Yardley (2003), and for a discussion of qualitative research in Canadian psychology, see Rennie (2002).

operational definition

A definition that defines a concept in terms of the steps and procedures used to measure that concept

The Methods of Psychological Research

P
R
E
V
I
E
W

The primary goal of research psychologists is understanding. Psychologists want to know what causes behaviour; they want to understand how external events in the environment and internal processes in the individual conspire to produce the remarkable diversity of human thought, feeling, and action. However, understanding is neither easy to achieve nor the only acceptable goal of psychology. Sometimes it is enough merely to describe and predict behaviour. Consider TV sets, refrigerators, and computers. Most of us have little idea how these things work, but we know

how to use them. The same might be said of psychology; we may not always understand why people act the way they do, but if we can predict when people will act in a particular way then we gain a degree of control over our environment.

In this chapter you'll be introduced to the basic techniques of psychological research. The discussion focuses on four practical problems that researchers investigating behaviour and mind often attempt to solve. In each case, we'll discuss the technical solutions to these problems, and we'll pay particular attention to the pitfalls that can hinder the research process.

First, what are the best techniques for describing behaviour? One of the most important steps in any psychological research project is to develop ways of measuring the phenomena of interest. Measurement in research is more than just casual looking or listening; to yield reliable data, researchers must use rigorously systematic procedures. We discuss these issues below in the context of descriptive research.

Second, how can we predict behaviour? Descriptive research yields facts about behaviour, but psychologists are often interested not only in describing how people behaved at one time but also in predicting their future behaviour. Correlational research yields data on the extent to which particular measurements of persons' skills, abilities, and tendencies can be used to predict their future behaviour.

Third, how can psychologists determine the underlying causes of behaviour? Most psychologists want to understand *why* people act and feel as they do—that is, they want to understand the *causes* of particular behaviours and experiences. To determine causality it is necessary to use the *experimental method*. The key feature of experimental method is the controlled manipulation of one or more aspects of the environment independent of all other variables with the aim of determining the effect of that manipulation on behaviour. As discussed in the section on experimental research, experiments can provide powerful evidence regarding what causes behaviours to occur or change in particular situations.

Fourth, what procedures ensure that research participants are treated ethically? Psychologists seeking to describe, predict, and understand behaviour and experience must grapple with the important problem of how to pursue these goals while treating research participants ethically. The vast majority of psychological research with humans consists of straightforward, nonstressful procedures that do not put participants at risk, but even with such procedures, psychologists must take care to ensure that participants are aware of their rights. Some research procedures do expose participants to risks (e.g., stress or embarrassment). How can the value of such research be weighed against the potential costs to participants? Also, research with nonhuman animals raises many ethical issues.

▶ Descriptive Research: Describing Behaviour

LEARNING GOALS

1. Understand the goals, techniques, and challenges of descriptive research.
2. Learn how psychologists conduct naturalistic observations.
3. Appreciate the strengths and weaknesses of case studies.
4. Understand the advantages and limitations of surveys.
5. Learn the major purposes of psychological tests.

Because the observation and measurement of behaviour is so important to psychological research, we begin with a discussion of descriptive research. Descriptive research aims to measure what people do, say, feel, or believe. Returning to the issue of cell phone use while driving, researchers might undertake descriptive research to estimate how often Canadian men and women in various age groups use cell phones on the road. We note at the outset, however, that psychologists are usually not satisfied with purely descriptive research, because they want to know not only *what* people do but also *why* they do it. As will become clear, descriptive research by itself cannot provide compelling evidence of causal relationships (i.e., evidence about what causes people to do the things they do). Nonetheless, before we can attempt to understand *why* people do the things they do, we must know *what* they do; hence, descriptive research plays a vital role in psychological research by providing richly detailed and accurate information about behaviour.

Descriptive research consists of the methods used to measure and describe behaviour and experience. At face value, describing psychological phenomena seems simple enough; after all, people observe one another all the time. However, it's easy to be misled, even when the goal is simply to measure behaviour. Let's suppose, for example, that you want to characterize certain aspects of the behaviour of preschoolers in a local daycare centre. You arrive with cameras and recording devices in hand and begin systematic observations of the children at play. Right away, you notice that the children seem uneasy and hesitant to engage in the activities suggested by the teacher. Several children show outward signs of fear and eventually withdraw, crying, to a corner of the room. Later, in describing your results, you might conclude that children in daycare centres adjust badly and that some even show early signs of poor psychological health.

descriptive research

The methods used to measure and describe aspects of behaviour and experience

Michael Newman/PhotoEdit

Psychologists need to consider the problem of reactivity: Are the observed behaviours simply a reaction to the observation process? If the behaviour of these children is changed as a result of the observer's presence, then the observations may not generalize well to other situations.

It shouldn't take much thought to recognize that your research strategy may suffer from a basic problem. Whenever you observe the actions of someone else, the very act of observing can affect the behaviour of the people being observed. In the case of the daycare centre, it might be that your unexpected presence in the centre (with cameras and the like) made the children feel uncomfortable and led them to act in ways that were not representative of their normal behaviour. Psychologists refer to this phenomenon as reactivity. **Reactivity** occurs whenever an individual's behaviour is changed in some way by being observed. It's called "reactivity" because the subject's behaviour is altered in *reaction* to the observation (Orne, 1969; Webb, Campbell, Schwartz, Sechrist, & Grove, 1981). It may be that the children in the daycare centre are not normally hesitant and distracted; those behaviours may have been a reaction to you and your recording devices.

Reactivity can cause research to lack external validity. **External validity** refers to how well the results of a research study generalize to other situations or are representative of real life (Campbell & Stanley, 1966; Cook & Campbell, 1979). If the children's behaviour is largely a reaction to your presence as an observer, it's clearly not representative of their everyday behaviour. Moreover, even if these children are generally fearful, your observations may not be representative of children at other daycare centres. To improve external validity, you must minimize reactivity (as described below) and collect data at several daycare centres to see whether similar patterns of behaviour emerge.

reactivity

The extent to which an individual's behaviour changes as a result of being observed; the behaviour is altered in reaction to being observed

external validity

The extent to which the results of an observation generalize to other situations or are representative of real life

Dan McCoy/Rainbow

In naturalistic observation, the researcher records only naturally occurring behaviour, as opposed to behaviour produced in the laboratory, and a concerted effort is made not to interfere with the behaviour.

Naturalistic Observation: Focusing on Real Life

One way that researchers try to reduce the problem of reactivity and improve external validity is to observe behaviour in natural settings by using noninterfering measures (Martin & Bateson, 1993; Timberlake & Silva, 1994). In **naturalistic observation,** the researcher records naturally occurring behaviour in the everyday environment, as opposed to behaviour produced in the laboratory, and tries not to interfere with the behaviour in any way. If the recorded behaviour is natural and has not been affected by the researcher, then the recorded data are representative of real life (of course, it is also necessary to repeat the observations in different settings to be sure the results generalize). One way to avoid reactivity is to observe subjects without them knowing they are being observed: If the subjects are unaware of being observed, their behaviour cannot be a reaction to the observation process. Naturalistic observation has been used with great success by psychologists as well as by *ethologists*, biologists who study the behaviour of animals in the wild, such as Jane Goodall (e.g., 1990) and Konrad Lorenz (1958).

To observe natural behaviour while minimizing reactivity, researchers sometimes use a technique called *participant observation*, in which the observer becomes a part of the activities being studied. For example, in the 1950s a group of psychologists infiltrated a doomsday cult by passing themselves off as believers. This cult preached the impending end of the world on a specific date. Once they were on the inside, the psychologists recorded and studied the reactions of the cultists when the day of doom failed to materialize (Festinger, Riecken, & Schachter, 1956). In another classic project about which you'll read more in Chapter 14, a group of researchers had themselves committed to local mental hospitals—they complained of hearing voices—in an effort to obtain an honest record of patient life inside an institution (Rosenhan, 1973). As another example, a professor writing under the pseudonym Rebekah Nathan (2006) went undercover as a university student, living in a dorm room for a year and later publishing a book on her observations. Participant observation could also be used in our daycare centre example: You could simply introduce yourself as a new teacher, rather than as a researcher, and hide your cameras or other recording equipment.

Another useful technique is to measure behaviour indirectly, by looking at *indicators* of a behaviour rather than at the behaviour itself. For example, you might be able to learn something about the eating or shopping habits of kids at a local mall by measuring the amount and kinds of litter they leave behind. Administrators at museums have determined the popularity of various exhibits by noting how quickly floor tiles in front of each exhibit wear out (Webb et al., 1981) (see ◗ Figure 2.2). Neither of these examples requires direct observation of behaviour; it is the after effects—the products—of the behaviour that provide the insightful clues.

CRITICAL THINKING
Do you see any ethical problems with the technique of participant observation?

◗ **Figure 2.2**

Naturalistic Observation of Behavioural Results

In a study conducted at the Chicago Museum of Science and Industry, researchers gauged the popularity of exhibits by noting how quickly the vinyl floor tiles in front of each display needed to be replaced. The live chick-hatching exhibit proved to be extremely popular.

Naturalistic observation is an effective technique for measuring natural behaviour, and it can also be used to verify the generalizability of results of laboratory experiments (Miller, 1977; Timberlake & Silva, 1994). As we'll discuss later in the chapter, experiments are the best way to gain knowledge about *why* people do the things they do, but it's difficult to conduct experimental research in natural settings, so most experiments are conducted in the lab. Questions can be raised about the external validity of laboratory research. For instance, to what extent are the psychological principles gleaned from laboratory studies of human memory relevant to learning and remembering in natural settings? To answer this question, psychologists have conducted naturalistic observations of remembering and forgetting in real-world settings, such as eyewitness accounts of naturally occurring events, to determine whether the patterns resemble those collected in the lab (e.g., Bruce, 1985; Neisser & Hyman, 1999; Yuille, 1993). For reasons that will become clear later in this chapter, naturalistic observation, by itself, cannot be used to determine the causes of behaviour. It can, however, be used effectively to gather descriptive information about a phenomenon and to test the generality of psychological principles discovered in the lab.

Case Studies: Focusing on the Individual

Another descriptive research technique is the case study. In a **case study,** the researcher focuses on a single case and studies and describes that case in great detail and depth (Elmes, Kantowitz, & Roediger, 1995; Heiman, 1995). Usually the "case" is an individual person, although there are also case studies of groups (e.g., a case study of a company). Sometimes the case is an event or a response to an event (e.g., a case study of how emergency crews responded in the aftermath of hurricane Katrina). What makes a piece of research a case study is the very detailed description. Because a great deal of information is collected about the background and behaviour of one person (or group or event), case studies give the researcher a very important historical perspective that aids in forming hypotheses about the possible causes of a behaviour or psychological problem.

One of the most influential psychological theories of the twentieth century, the psychoanalytic theory of Sigmund Freud, was based primarily on descriptive data derived from case studies. Clinical psychologists continue to report and to be influenced by case studies. For example, case studies of individuals with brain damage have been tremendously influential in inspiring ideas about normal brain function (see Chapter 3). Some case studies have gained substantial popular interest as well. For example, in the 1960s the movie *The Three Faces of Eve* attracted lots of attention with its depiction of a woman who coped with emotional distress by apparently shifting among three wildly different personalities (Thigpen & Cleckley, 1957). Sybil, depicted in a television miniseries of the same name, was the subject of another famous case study of multiple personality disorder (now known as dissociative identity disorder).

Like naturalistic observation, the case study methodology suffers from some limitations (Yin, 1998). Because they explore only one or a few cases, questions are often raised about the external validity or generalizability of case studies: Are the experiences of the individual subject truly representative of others (Liebert & Liebert, 1995)? For example, Sybil's frightening descent into dissociative identity disorder may or may not be representative of how psychological disorders normally develop (see Rieber, 1999, for a skeptical discussion of the Sybil case; for critiques of the whole idea of dissociative identity disorder, see Piper, 1997, and Spanos, 1994). Another problem with case studies is that the claims of the individual under study are often difficult to verify. If the observations of the single subject are somehow tainted with inaccuracies—if the subject is lying, for example—the entire study must be viewed with suspicion (see Iverson, King, Scott, & Adams, 2001; Strauss et al., 2002; and Tombaugh, 1997, for techniques for catching people who

case study

A descriptive research technique in which the research effort is focused on one or a few individuals who are studied in great depth

pretend to have symptoms that they don't really have). Once again, as with naturalistic observation, case studies are excellent vehicles for generating ideas and hypotheses but cannot be used to determine cause-and-effect relationships.

Surveys: Describing Populations

survey

A descriptive research technique designed to gather limited amounts of information from many people, usually by administering a questionnaire

Whereas a case study focuses on one or a few individuals, psychologists use a **survey** to sample reported behaviour or opinions broadly by gathering responses from many people. Most surveys are administered in the form of a questionnaire: Individuals, or groups of individuals, are asked questions about some behaviour, psychological characteristic, or belief. You are probably familiar with opinion polls conducted by political campaigns or by the news media to capture the current attitudes of voters. Surveys are also used for research purposes, to gain valuable descriptive information about behaviour and mind. For example, researchers can use a survey to explore the personality characteristics and health problems of air traffic controllers (MacLennan & Peebles, 1996), to assess perfectionism and stress in school teachers (Flett, Hewitt, & Hallett, 1995), or to measure Canadians' emotional reactions to the terrorist bombings of September 11 (Asmundson, Carleton, & Wright, 2004).

▶ Figure 2.3 shows some of the results of a survey conducted to assess U.S. psychotherapists' beliefs and practices regarding therapeutic techniques that may help adult clients remember long-forgotten childhood sexual abuse. Poole, Lindsay, Memon, and Bull (1995) sent surveys to a randomly selected sample of psychotherapists and reported results from 145 respondents. What is most striking about the findings depicted in Figure 2.3 is the extent to which respondents disagreed with one another regarding the use of the techniques. For example, 29% reported that they used hypnosis to help clients remember childhood sexual abuse, but 27% indicated that hypnosis should not be used in this way. Similarly, 44% reported the use of dream interpretation as a way of helping clients remember childhood sexual abuse, but 26% judged that dream interpretation should not be used in this manner.

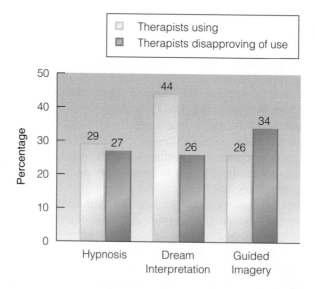

▶ **Figure 2.3**

Opinions about Memory Techniques in Psychotherapy

Selected results from the Poole et al. (1995) survey of psychotherapists show the percentage of respondents who reported the use of various techniques to help adult clients remember childhood sexual abuse and the percentage of respondents who indicated that those techniques should not be used to help clients remember childhood sexual abuse.

Surveys can be informative, if conducted properly, because they can provide researchers with valuable insights into individuals' opinions and beliefs. In this case, the Poole et al. (1995) data are worrisome because they reveal substantial disagreements among psychotherapists about the appropriateness of various therapeutic techniques. Such disagreements indicate a need for further research to develop widely accepted guidelines for which treatments are effective and appropriate and which are not. Moreover, a minority of the Poole respondents reported a constellation of beliefs and practices regarding ways of encouraging clients to remember childhood sexual abuse that many memory researchers view as suggestive (see Lindsay & Read, 1994, 2001; Loftus, 1993). As you'll see shortly, however, results of such surveys as this must be interpreted with caution because a variety of methodological problems can lead surveys to produce misleading results.

Sampling from a Population   The aim of a survey is to measure some of the characteristics of a large group (e.g., the memory-related beliefs of psychotherapists). Usually the group of interest is too large for researchers to measure everyone in it (e.g., all psychotherapists), so researchers attempt to select a representative subset of individuals to measure. The complete group that the researcher wants to learn about (e.g., psychotherapists) is called a *population*. The subset of individuals from the target population who are measured (e.g., the psychotherapists who completed and returned a questionnaire) is referred to as a *sample*.

A researcher needs to consider several technical details when sampling from a population. This is because it is easy to end up with an unrepresentative, or biased, sample unless the proper precautions are taken (Weisberg, Krosnick, & Bowen, 1989). Let's imagine that a researcher named Rosa wants to study Canadian university students' sexual behaviours. She places an ad with a toll-free telephone number in selected university newspapers. Her hope is that students will call the number and answer questions about their sex lives. However, not every university-aged student in the country will choose to participate, so Rosa will end up with only a subset, or sample, of the population of interest. Do you think the data collected from her subset will be truly representative of university students?

In this case, the answer is clearly "no" because the method of sampling depends on people volunteering to participate. Volunteers tend to produce biased samples, because people who volunteer usually have strong feelings or opinions about the study (Rosenthal & Rosnow, 1975). This tends to be especially problematic if the survey deals with an emotionally charged or sensitive topic. Think about it: Would you call in and tell a researcher about your sex life? Which of your friends would do so, and which would not?

Representative samples can be produced through **random sampling,** which means that everyone in the target population has an equal likelihood of being selected for the survey. In principle, for Rosa to achieve a truly unbiased sample she would need to sample randomly from the entire population of Canadian university students—everyone in the population must have an equal chance of being selected. Because this is difficult to achieve in practice, Rosa will probably need to limit herself to sampling randomly from the population of students going to a particular university. Even obtaining a truly random sample from a single university can be difficult. If you randomly selected survey recipients from a complete list of students, you might find that those who return the survey differ systematically from those who don't. The point is that survey researchers must strive to obtain representative samples; when representativeness is in doubt, survey researchers must be cautious in generalizing their results to the population of interest.

Now let's return to the Poole et al. (1995) survey of psychotherapists' reports regarding therapeutic techniques for helping adult clients remember childhood sexual abuse. The researchers sent their survey to a random sample from a large national list of qualified psychotherapists, so the sample of therapists who received the survey was very likely representative of the larger population of qualified

random sampling

A procedure for selecting a representative subset of a target population; the procedure guarantees that everyone in the population has an equal likelihood of being selected for the sample

psychotherapists. However, only 43% of the sample completed and returned the questionnaire. This raises the possibility that those who returned the survey had different views on the therapeutic techniques in question than those who did not; that is, it is possible that the sample was not representative of the population of qualified psychotherapists (although Poole et al. offered arguments against this concern).

Even if a proper representative sample of the population has been obtained, surveys can suffer from other problems (Taylor, 1997; Weisberg et al., 1989). A very general limitation of surveys is that they rely on respondents' verbal self-reports. This is a problem because people do not always respond truthfully and openly on questionnaires; they may exaggerate or disguise their views for any of a variety of reasons. For example, "social desirability bias" may lead people to respond in ways that they believe make them look good to the researcher. Furthermore, survey respondents may not even know the answers to some of the questions they are asked and may therefore guess or infer incorrect answers or leave questions blank. The results of a survey can depend on the particular wording of the questions and even on the order in which the questions are asked (Ellard & Rogers, 1993). Also, there is often room for debate about exactly what respondents mean when they give particular answers (see Lindsay & Poole, 1998, for discussion of disagreements about the interpretation of the Poole et al. survey, and see Gore-Felton et al., 2000, for a more recent survey on the same topic). Surveys can be written in ways that minimize these problems—for example, particular questions can be asked several times with slightly different wording to check on the consistency of each participant's responses—but inaccuracies and ambiguities in responses are difficult to eliminate entirely.

If conducted properly, surveys can be great vehicles for obtaining information about a target population. You can get a lot of information relatively quickly and easily with a survey. But, as with the other descriptive research methods that we've considered, surveys have limitations, as explained above. Most important, surveys are not appropriate for testing causal hypotheses. They are best used in conjunction with other techniques, such as case studies, naturalistic observation, and experimentation, in a broadly based research effort. As will be explained later in this chapter, when researchers want to understand what *causes* behaviours (e.g., what factors lead therapists to use or to disapprove of certain techniques), the best research approach is the experimental method.

Psychological Tests: Assessing Individual Differences

A major area of descriptive research in psychology is psychological testing. Psychological tests, which come in a variety of forms, are designed primarily to measure individual differences between people. For example, *achievement tests* measure a person's current level of knowledge or competence in a particular subject (such as mathematics or psychology) compared with others'; *aptitude tests* are designed to measure a person's potential for success in a given profession or area of study; *neuropsychological tests* (e.g., Strauss, Sherman, & Spreen, 2006) assess effects of various kinds of brain damage on cognitive performance. Researchers also use various kinds of intelligence and personality tests to classify ability or to characterize individuals' tendencies to act in particular ways. For example, Hewitt, Caelian, and Flett (2002) used personality tests in research exploring the relationship among perfectionism, anxiety, and depression.

Psychological tests have enormous practical value (Anastasi, 1985). For example, Anderson and Walsh (1998) reported evidence that IQ test performance of juvenile offenders is related to the likelihood of subsequent criminal behaviours; Ree and Earles (1992) showed that IQ is a good predictor of job performance; and Kuncel, Hezlett, and Ones (2001) summarized evidence that the Graduate Record Examination (GRE) predicts students' performance in

Psychologists use psychological tests to predict individuals' future behaviour as well as to help decipher the fundamental components of mind.

graduate school (for Canadian studies of the GRE, see Boudreau, 1983; Symons, 1999). Duckworth and Seligman (2005) found that a measure of individuals' self-discipline (that is, grit or determination) was an even better predictor of school performance than was a measure of intelligence. All these examples have obvious practical use (e.g., university admissions committees can use appropriate measures to predict who will do well in university).

Psychologists also analyze test performance to answer fundamental questions about the mind. For example, data collected from psychological tests have been used to tackle such questions as the following: Do people have a single and fixed amount of intelligence, present at birth, or do they have multiple kinds of intelligence that rise and fall with experience? Do people have consistent personality traits, such as honesty or pleasantness, that hold across situations, or do their behaviours change haphazardly across situations? You'll read more about these questions when we treat psychological tests in more detail in Chapters 9 and 12.

CONCEPT SUMMARY

DESCRIPTIVE RESEARCH METHODS

Specific Method	Description	Strengths and Weaknesses
Naturalistic observation	Record naturally occurring behaviour	+ Behaviour is natural; results are generalizable (high external validity) − Research lacks control; can't determine cause
Case studies	Gather a great deal of information on a single case	+ Richly detailed and give historical perspective − Difficulties in generalization based on one case; can't determine cause
Surveys	Gather responses from many participants	+ Can easily gather information from many people − Sampling bias; inaccurate self-reports; can't determine cause
Psychological tests	Measure individual differences between people	+ Practical predictions; insights into relationships among different psychological variables − Difficulties in test construction and validation; can't determine cause

To test your knowledge of descriptive research methods, fill in the blanks with one of the following words or terms: reactivity; external validity; measure; case study; random sampling; survey. (The answers are in Appendix B.)

1. To define a psychological variable operationally is to define it in terms of the steps or procedures that are used to _____ that variable.

2. The _____ technique, in which one or a few individuals are studied in depth, is open to criticism because its results may lack _____; that is, the results may not generalize to or be representative of the population as a whole.

3. When behaviour changes as a result of the observation process, the study may suffer from the problem of _____.

4. The descriptive research technique used to gather information from many people is called a _____.

▶ Correlational Research: Predicting Behaviour

LEARNING GOALS

1. Learn to define correlation and discuss how correlations can be used to predict behaviour.
2. Be able to explain why correlation does not necessarily imply causation.

When done well, descriptive research provides psychologists with facts about people's behaviour. Psychologists are rarely satisfied, however, with simply describing the facts of behaviour. At minimum, we would also like to be able to detect relationships among different variables that would enable us to predict behaviour. For example, the admissions officers at your university would like to be able to predict which high school graduates are likely to do well in university and which are not. Similarly, psychologists working with prison inmates want to be able to predict which prisoners will do well on parole and which will not. Or, to return to an earlier example, insurance agencies are interested in being able to predict whether individuals who use cell phones while driving are more likely than other drivers to have accidents.

Correlational Research

One step toward predicting behaviour is to determine whether a *relationship* exists between two measures, such as scores on an aptitude test and scores on a measure of job performance. Psychologists often use a statistical measure called a *correlation* to assess the relationship between a pair of measures applied to the same individuals. A correlation tells you whether two *variables*, or measures that can take on more than one value (such as test scores), tend to vary together systematically. Correlations are computed by gathering observations on both measures of interest from a sample of individuals and then computing a mathematical index called a **correlation coefficient.** A correlation coefficient indicates how accurately the value of one variable, such as job success, can be predicted based on the value of the other variable, such as an IQ test score.

When a correlation exists between two measures, those two variables tend to vary together in some way. For example, a correlation probably exists between exercise and body mass index: People who exercise a lot tend to have lower BMIs than people who rarely exercise. (BMI is a measure of weight status, weight in kilograms divided by the square of height in metres; scores below 18.5 are classified as underweight, those above 25, as overweight.) In this particular case, it is a *negative correlation*, which means that the two measures tend to vary in opposite directions: the more of one, the less of the other (e.g., people with high levels of

correlation coefficient

A statistic that indicates whether two variables are related or vary together in a systematic way; vary from +1.00 (perfect positive relationship) to 0.00 (no relationship) to −1.00 (perfect negative relationship)

Eyewire/Getty Images

Image Source/Jupiter Images

The building skills of the young girl on the left may or may not be predictive of a professional career in architecture.

exercise tend to have low BMIs). Conversely, a *positive correlation* exists when two measures tend to vary together in the same direction. For example, you would expect a positive correlation between hours of exercise per week and aerobic capacity, with people who frequently exercise tending to have high aerobic capacity compared with those who rarely exercise.

Calculating a correlation coefficient requires measurement of a relatively large number of observations. Moreover, you need to collect data on *both* measures. Correlation coefficients range between +1.00 and –1.00. The absolute value of the coefficient (the difference from 0, regardless of whether the value is positive or negative) indicates the *strength* of the correlation. A correlation coefficient of 0 indicates no relationship between the two variables. The closer the value is to 1.00 (either positive or negative), the stronger the relationship between the two measures and the more likely you are to be able to predict one variable correctly if you know the other. As a trivial example, the correlation between weight measured in kilograms and weight measured in pounds is +1.00; if you know a person's weight in kilograms you can perfectly predict it in pounds.

The sign of the coefficient indicates the direction of the correlation: A positive correlation indicates that people with high scores on one variable also tend to have high scores on the other variable, whereas a negative correlation indicates that people with high scores on one variable tend to have low scores on the other. For example, a correlation coefficient of 0.30 indicates that people with high scores on one variable also tend to have high scores on the other variable but that the strength of the relationship is quite weak (e.g., among a sample of university undergraduates, those who get high scores on a spelling test might also tend to get high scores on a math test, but there would be many exceptions to that general rule, resulting in a fairly weak positive correlation). Similarly, a correlation coefficient of –0.74 indicates that people with high scores on one variable tend to have low scores on the other variable and that this relationship is quite strong, such that knowing one enables you to fairly accurately predict the other (e.g., it might be that the more alcohol individuals had consumed, the worse they would do on a test of manual dexterity—the relationship would not be perfect, but depending on the characteristics of the sample and the specifics of the dexterity test, it might be quite a strong negative correlation).

▶ Figure 2.4 on page 48 shows how positive and negative correlations can be represented graphically, in the form of *scatter plots*. Each point in a scatter plot represents a person's scores on each of two measures. Part (a) depicts data from 40 individuals on the average number of hours of exercise per week and some measure of aerobic capacity. Part (b) shows, for the same 40 individuals, data showing for each person the average number of hours of exercise per week and the BMI score. Once the correlation has been computed, it can then be used to make predictions about a new subject's score on one variable based on his or her score on the other variable. So, if a correlation is present, you can predict (with some degree of

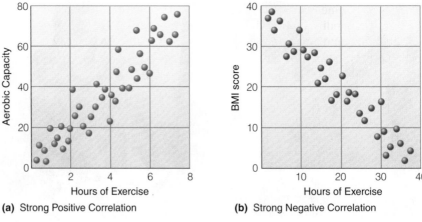

(a) Strong Positive Correlation

(b) Strong Negative Correlation

▶ **Figure 2.4**

Positive and Negative Correlations

Each point in the scatter plot shows an individual's scores on each of the two variables. (a) In a positive correlation, the values for the two variables move in the same direction; that is, as the average number of hours of exercise per week increases, so does the aerobic capacity. (b) In a strong negative correlation, the values for the two variables move in opposite directions; that is, as the average number of hours of exercise per week increases, the BMI score decreases. Note that the correlations depicted in these figures are much stronger than the real-world correlations between these variables.

confidence and accuracy) Danielle's BMI by knowing how many hours per week she exercises. Given that the correlation coefficient was calculated based on accurate measures of a large and representative sample, then the closer the correlation is to 1.00 (positive or negative), the more accurate your prediction is likely to be. This reasoning is used by most university admissions committees: They know a positive correlation exists between high school marks and university performance, so they predict how well people will do in university by looking at their marks in high school.

Many psychological variables are not correlated with one another, so knowing the value of one measure does not allow you to predict the value of the second measure with an accuracy greater than chance. Imagine, for example, trying to predict university grade point average by measuring how many times people wash their hands during the day. In this case, the correlation is almost certainly zero—you can't use hand-washing behaviour to predict GPA. Similarly, there's probably no correlation between shoe size and intelligence. As an interesting example, there's essentially zero correlation between wealth and happiness except when the poorest of the poor are included; once they cover the basic necessities of life, the amount of money people have is unrelated to how happy they are (Diener & Seligman, 2004).

It's worth emphasizing that even when no correlation exists between two variables, there are likely to be some cases with high scores on both variables (and some cases with high scores on one variable and low scores on the other, and others with low scores on both variables). Suppose, for example, that each day for two weeks you read your daily horoscope and scored its prediction for your day on a scale from 0 (a really bad day) to 10 (a really great day). Then, each night before bed, you scored your actual day on the same scale (see ▶ Figure 2.5). Suppose further that it turns out that no correlation exists between the horoscope predictions and the actual days. Does that mean that the horoscope's prediction would never agree with the actual day? No—indeed, there would have to be something magical about horoscopes if they always managed to be wrong! In this example, a zero correlation means that (1) sometimes the horoscope predicts that the day will be good and it turns out to be bad, (2) other times it predicts the day will be bad and it is good, (3) other times it predicts the day will be good and it is indeed good, and (4) yet other times it predicts that the day will be bad and it is indeed bad.

The point to remember is that if there is no correlation between two variables, then we cannot predict one variable on the basis of the other. People sometimes err in daily life by paying attention only to cases in which two variables appear to be related and ignoring the equally numerous cases in which the lack of relationship is obvious, leading them to perceive a correlation that isn't there (Chapman & Chapman, 1967).

Psychological measures rarely correlate perfectly; most correlations are only moderate. For example, Duckworth and Seligman (2005) found that the correlation between Grade 8 students' scores on an intelligence test and their grades at the end of the year was 0.32, which is greater than zero but not huge. These researchers found that a measure of self-discipline correlated with grades at 0.67 (so determination predicted grades about twice as well as intelligence did). But even 0.67 is far from a perfect 1.00, so when researchers make predictions about behaviour based on correlations, the accuracy of their predictions is usually limited. As another example, the correlation between adults' height and weight is only about 0.60; on average, taller people tend to weigh more than shorter people do, but obviously there are exceptions to this general rule. Correlation coefficients give researchers some important predictive ability, but they rarely enable exact predictions because correlations are rarely perfect.

Correlations and Causality

Determining whether a relationship (correlation) exists between two variables is important in everyday life because it helps people make predictions about their environment. It is useful to know, for example, whether someone who acts in a certain way at time 1 is likely to act in another certain way at time 2. Evidence of predictive relationships between variables can also have important real-world implications. Suppose, for example, that psychologists demonstrated a substantial positive correlation between the amount of violence children watch on television and how aggressively those children act later in life. Knowing about such a relationship would probably influence the behaviour of parents and might even lead to a social outcry demanding reductions in television violence (Bushman & Anderson, 2001).

We must, however, be cautious when interpreting correlational evidence. Correlations are useful devices for describing patterns of relationships between variables, but they are of limited value when it comes to understanding why behaviours occur and co-occur. The presence of a correlation between two behaviours may help psychologists predict one behaviour based on another, but correlations do not enable them to determine causality. For example, a correlation between watching violence on television and later aggression does not necessarily mean that television violence causes aggression, even if the correlation is very strong.

Third Variables   The main reason that it's not possible to determine causality from a correlation has to do with the presence of other factors in the situation. Two variables can appear to be connected—they might rise or fall together in a regular, predictable way—but the connection could be due to a common link with some third variable. Let's consider an example. On average, people who graduate from university end up with higher incomes than people who don't graduate from university. The 2001 Canadian census (Statistics Canada, 2004a) indicated that the average annual earnings of those whose highest degree was a high school diploma was $25 477, compared with $48 648 for those who had a university degree. Put in terms of a correlation, annual income is positively correlated with years of schooling. Does that mean that a university education *causes* better jobs and higher income? Perhaps, but not necessarily. Other variables could explain part or even all of the relationship.

Who goes to university? Do they represent a random sample of the population as a whole? Of course not. University students tend to do well on academic tasks, they tend to come from better high schools, they tend to be people who worked hard and succeeded in high school, and they tend to come from families in the

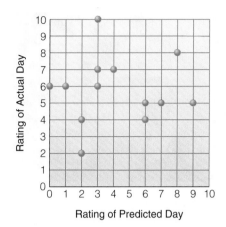

▶ **Figure 2.5**

Zero Correlation

This scatter plot shows a near-zero correlation between (a) daily horoscope predictions (rated on a scale of 0 for a very bad day to 10 for a really great day) and (b) ratings of actual days. Overall, it is not possible to predict the value of one variable by knowing the value of the other—the correlation is very near zero—even though the horoscope's predictions, on some days, will happen to agree perfectly with the actual day.

CRITICAL   THINKING

Pat doesn't make any decisions in her life without consulting a psychic. She's convinced that most of what the psychic tells her about her future comes true. Given what you know about correlations and causality, how might you convince her otherwise?

Do children model what they see on television? Many psychologists believe they do.

higher income brackets (partly because attending university is expensive). None of these factors is controlled for in the calculation of a correlation. You can predict with a correlation, but the mere presence of a correlation doesn't tell you what causes the relationship. University students might end up with higher incomes because they're richer, they work harder, or they are better educated. Any or all of these factors could contribute to the relationship between years of schooling and income that the correlation describes (Cook & Campbell, 1979).

Now let's return to the example of the relationship between TV violence and aggression. Can you think of a third variable that might explain the correlation? Try to answer that question before reading on. One possibility is that parents who allow their children to watch lots of violence on TV tend to be more aggressive than parents who do not let their children watch such shows. If so, the children who watch a lot of violent TV and later turn out to be aggressive might have grown up to be highly aggressive anyway, even if they had never seen a television show. That is, perhaps it's the parents' aggressiveness that causes the children's aggressiveness, and exposure to violent TV just happens to co-occur with having more aggressive parents. This is just one of many possible third variables that might underlie the TV–aggression correlation.

Even if a causal relationship exists between two variables, the direction of that relationship is not always obvious. For example, it might be that aggressive children simply like to watch violent programs on television. If so, then perhaps it's not that TV violence is causing the aggression, but rather that the children's aggressive tendencies are influencing their choice of programs. Once again, correlations describe relationships, but by themselves they cannot establish cause and effect. To determine causality, as you'll see shortly, researchers cannot simply describe and predict behaviour; they must manipulate it.

CONCEPT SUMMARY

CORRELATIONAL PATTERNS

Question to Be Addressed	Pattern of Correlation	Description
How does the number of hours of weekly exercise relate to aerobic capacity?	Positive	On average, the more exercise, the more aerobic capacity; the less exercise, the less aerobic capacity.
How does performance in high school relate to university GPA?	Positive	On average, the higher the high school GPA, the higher the university GPA; the lower the high school GPA, the lower the university GPA.
How does the number of hours of weekly exercise relate to BMI?	Negative	On average, the more exercise, the lower BMI; the less exercise, the higher BMI.
How does the amount of time spent partying relate to university GPA?	Negative	On average, the more time spent partying, the lower the GPA; the less time spent partying, the higher the GPA.
How does a person's shoe size relate to his or her score on an intelligence test?	No correlation	Knowing someone's shoe size tells you nothing about his or her IQ test score and vice versa.

Test Yourself 2.2

Test your understanding of correlations by identifying whether the following statements represent positive, negative, or zero correlations. (The answers are in Appendix B.)

1. The more Jeffrey studies his psychology notes, the fewer errors he makes on the chapter test: _____.

2. As Sadaf reduces her rate of exercising, her heart rate begins to slow:_____.

3. The longer Yolanda waits for her date to arrive, the higher her blood pressure rises: _____.

4. Eddie finds no relationship between his horoscope's predictions and what actually happens to him during the day: _____.

▶ Experimental Method: Explaining Behaviour

LEARNING GOALS

1. Grasp the differences between independent and dependent variables.
2. Be able to explain what is meant by experimental control and how it allows for the determination of causality.
3. Appreciate the problems created by expectancies and biases and be able to explain how these problems are avoided.
4. Understand the key issues regarding generalizing the results of an experiment.

As noted earlier, psychologists want to understand the *causes* of behaviour. To return to the cell phone example, correlational research might reveal that drivers who use cells while driving have more accidents than drivers who don't use cell phones while driving, but that wouldn't show that cell phone use caused the accidents (e.g., it might be that people who phone while driving tend to be less experienced and less careful drivers, and maybe those factors give rise to the correlation). As another example, psychologists studying teenagers' health-related behaviours are not satisfied by merely describing teens' patterns of drug use, unprotected sex, or risk taking; they want to know *why* some teens develop drug problems, contract sexually transmitted diseases, or take dangerous risks while others do not. Understanding why people do the things they do entails understanding causal relationships—that is, knowing the factors that influence people toward or away from performing particular behaviours or having certain thoughts and feelings. Given such an understanding, we can both predict behaviour (e.g., predict which high school graduates are likely to do well in university) and, more importantly, influence it (e.g., develop programs that effectively reduce teenage drug abuse).

If the ultimate goal of most psychologists is to establish the causes of behaviour, what research strategy will enable them to do so? Suppose you wanted to determine whether watching violent TV shows causes an increase in later aggression. What specific steps should you take? You must create a situation in which you can be confident that if aggressive behaviour increases after exposure to violent television, then it is indeed the television violence that is responsible for the change. Alternative possibilities need to be eliminated before you can confidently conclude that things are causally related. As you've just seen, the mere description of a relationship is not sufficient; correlation does not necessarily imply causation. Establishing causality requires *control*, one of the most important functions of an experiment.

Psychologists want to understand what causes people to do the things they do.

Scott Audette/CP Picture Archive

Karl Weatherly/PhotoDisc/Getty Images

experimental method

A technique in which the investigator actively manipulates or alters some aspect of the environment independently of other variables and observes the effect of the manipulation on behaviour

In research that uses the **experimental method,** the investigator actively manipulates or alters some aspect of the environment independently of other variables and observes the effect (if any) of that manipulation on behaviour. By the term *environment*, psychologists can mean just about anything. For instance, they might manipulate the external setting (room temperature, lighting, time of day), a person's internal state (hunger, mood, motivation to perform), or social factors (presence or absence of an authority figure or popular peer). The particular manipulation is determined by the researcher's hypothesis. As mentioned earlier, hypotheses in psychology can be expressed in the form of if-then statements about behaviour: If some set of conditions is present, then a certain kind of behaviour will be likely to occur. The purpose of the experiment is to set up the proposed conditions and see what happens.

To examine the role of television violence on aggressive behaviour, Wendy Josephson (1995) at the University of Winnipeg randomly assigned approximately half of a sample of 396 school-age boys to watch a violent TV program, while the remaining boys watched a nonviolent program. The boys watched the program in groups of six and, shortly afterward, were given an opportunity to play floor hockey. Aggressive behaviour during the floor-hockey play was greater among boys who had viewed the violent show than among those who had viewed the nonviolent show. This strategy of directly *manipulating* what TV show is watched, rather than simply observing what shows children happen to watch, is the essential feature of the experimental approach. Notice the difference from correlational research, in which the investigator simply records the viewing habits of a sample of children and then measures later aggressive acts. It is only through a direct manipulation by the experimenter that control over the environment can be exercised and causality determined. ▶ Figure 2.6 compares experimental research to the other two approaches we've discussed: descriptive and correlational research.

▶ **Figure 2.6**

Summary of Major Research Methods

The chart summarizes the purpose and research tactics for the three major research methods: descriptive research, correlational research, and experimental research.

Descriptive Method	Correlational Method	Experimental Method
Purpose Observing and describing behaviour	Predicting and selecting behaviour	Determining why behaviour occurs: Establishing cause and effect
Research Tactics Naturalistic observation Case studies Survey research Psychological tests	Statistical correlations based on two or more variables	Experiments manipulating the independent variable to note effects on the dependent variable

Independent and Dependent Variables

The aspect of the environment that is manipulated in an experiment is called the **independent variable.** Because it is a *variable* (i.e., something that can take on more than one value), any experimental manipulation must consist of at least two different conditions. In our example, the independent variable is the amount of television violence observed by the children, and the two conditions are (1) watching a violent program and (2) watching a nonviolent program. The aspect that is manipulated is called an *independent* variable because the experimenter produces the change, independently of the subjects' wants, desires, personality, or behaviour and independently of any other variables that might affect the subject.

The behaviour that is measured in an experiment is called the **dependent variable.** In our example, the dependent variable is the amount of aggressive behaviour that is seen following exposure to the violent or nonviolent program. The experimenter manipulates the independent variable (exposure to violent versus nonviolent TV shows) and observes whether the behaviour measured by the dependent variable (aggression) differs between the two conditions. Notice that the experimenter is interested in whether the dependent variable *depends* on the experimental manipulation (hence the name *dependent variable*).

independent variable

The aspect of the environment that is manipulated by the researcher in an experiment; manipulation must consist of at least two conditions

dependent variable

The behaviour that is measured in an experiment

Experimental Control

To conclude that changes in the dependent variable are *caused* by the independent variable, you need to be certain that the independent variable is the only thing changing systematically in the experiment (see ❭ Figure 2.7 on page 54). In the simplest sort of experiment, researchers compare subjects who get the special treatment, called the *experimental group*, with those who do not, called the *control group*.

In the TV-and-aggression experiment, the experimental group consisted of the subjects who watched the violent TV show, and the control group consisted of those who watched the nonviolent show. Given that subsequent levels of aggression differ between these two groups, and that the only systematic difference between them was the presence versus absence of violence in the TV show watched, then we can conclude that the violence of the TV show likely caused the difference in aggression.

Confounding Variables The determination of cause and effect hinges on the ability to be certain that the experimental and control groups are equivalent in all respects except for the critical independent variable manipulation. But how can you be certain that this is indeed the case? If some other factor differs between the groups, besides the independent variable, then interpretation of the results will be hopelessly compromised (Levine & Parkinson, 1994; Rosenthal & Rosnow, 1991). Uncontrolled variables that vary systematically with the independent variable are called **confounding variables** (the word *confound* means to throw into confusion). Suppose, for example, that researchers had not randomly assigned children to view the violent versus nonviolent show but instead had put all the children from Ms. Jones's class in the violent-show condition and all those from Mr. Phelp's class in the nonviolent-show condition. This would introduce a confounding variable because any differences in aggression between the groups could be due to differences between the classes rather than to the violence of the show. Similarly, if the children in one condition were tested before lunch and those in the other after lunch, you wouldn't know whether subsequent differences in the amount of aggression had to do with the TV shows watched or the time of day.

Researchers attempt to eliminate confounds by holding constant factors that might vary along with the experimental manipulation. In this case, Josephson (1995) took pains to ensure that the TV shows were virtually identical except that

confounding variable

An uncontrolled variable that changes along with the independent variable

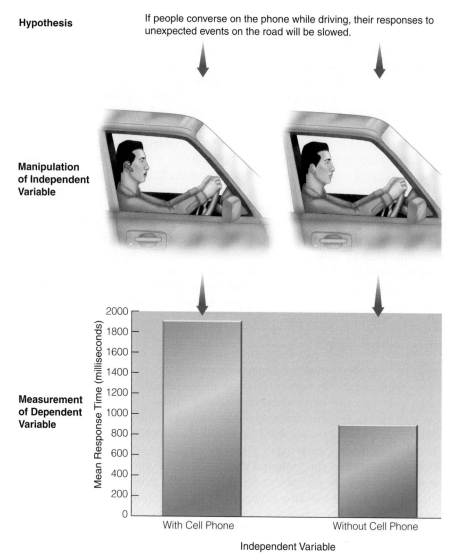

Hypothesis   If people converse on the phone while driving, their responses to unexpected events on the road will be slowed.

Manipulation of Independent Variable

Measurement of Dependent Variable

Mean Response Time (milliseconds)

With Cell Phone   Without Cell Phone

Independent Variable

▶ **Figure 2.7**

The Major Components of an Experiment

The hypothesis is tested by manipulating the independent variable and then assessing its effects on the dependent variable. If the only environmental thing changing systematically in the experiment is the independent variable, then the experimenter can assume that changes in the independent variable are likely *causing* any changes in the dependent variable.

one contained numerous violent scenes and the other didn't, and to test both groups under the same conditions (e.g., same time of day, same experimenter, same instructions). Factors that might affect the likelihood of aggression during the floor-hockey game, other than the independent variable manipulation, should be controlled—that is, held constant—across the different groups. When potential confounding variables are effectively controlled, allowing for the determination of cause and effect, the experiment is said to have high **internal validity.**

Random Assignment   Even in a perfectly controlled experiment, the problem of individual differences remains: How can experimenters be certain that the two groups of subjects are equivalent? People differ in many ways: aggressiveness, social skills, energy levels, and so on. Researchers cannot hold all these factors constant. Just think about the task of finding two or more groups of subjects with

internal validity

The extent to which an experimenter has effectively controlled for confounding variables; internally valid experiments allow for the determination of causality

exactly the same levels of aggression, the same moods, the same social skills, and so on. It would be impossible. This creates the problem that a difference between two experimental groups (e.g., the kids who were shown a violent TV program versus those shown a nonviolent one) could have to do with the particular people in each group, rather than with any effect of the independent variable. The solution to the problem of intrinsic individual differences lies in the concept of random assignment to conditions. In **random assignment,** the experimenter ensures that each participant has an equal chance of being assigned to any of the groups or conditions in the experiment. Each subject is assigned randomly to a group (e.g., by drawing names out of a hat). Neither the subject nor the experimenter chooses who gets assigned to which condition; the assignment is governed by random chance.

Random assignment does not eliminate differences between people: For example, some subjects will still be more naturally inclined to display aggression than others are. Random assignment increases the likelihood that these differences will be equally represented in each group (see ❱ Figure 2.8). Moreover, when participants are randomly assigned to conditions, only chance could lead to differences between the people in each condition. As will be discussed later, researchers use inferential statistical tests to estimate the likelihood that a particular difference between conditions would occur by chance.

> **random assignment**
>
> A technique that ensures that each participant in an experiment has an equal chance of being assigned to any of the conditions in the experiment

❱ **Figure 2.8**

Random Assignment

In random assignment, the experimenter ensures that each participant has an equal likelihood of being assigned to any of the groups or conditions in the experiment; that is, people are randomly assigned to the different levels of the independent variable. Random assignment increases the chances that subject characteristics will be represented equally in each condition.

Hypothesis   If people converse on the phone while driving, their responses to unexpected events on the road will be slowed.

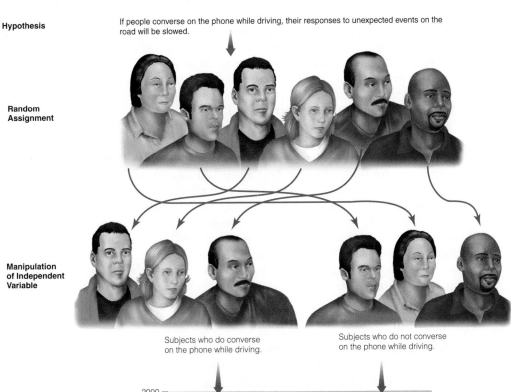

Random Assignment

Manipulation of Independent Variable

Subjects who do converse on the phone while driving.

Subjects who do not converse on the phone while driving.

Measurement of Dependent Variable

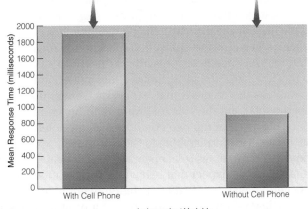

Mean Response Time (milliseconds)

With Cell Phone   Without Cell Phone

Independent Variable

Expectancies and Biases in Experimental Research

Research participants are not passive; they almost always have expectations about the purpose of the research and often try to act accordingly. These expectations can affect subjects' behaviour in ways that cloud interpretation of the results (Barber, 1976; Rosenthal, 2002; Rosenthal & Rosnow, 1969). Let's suppose, for example, that on the first day of class your teacher randomly selects half the students, including you, to participate in a special enrichment program. You receive instruction in a special room, with carefully controlled lighting and temperature, to see whether your learning will improve. The rest of the students, forming the control group, are left in the original classroom. The end of the semester arrives and, sure enough, the enrichment group performed better than the control group. What can you conclude from these results?

In some ways, this seems to be a well-designed experiment. It includes both an experimental and a control group, the subjects were randomly assigned to groups, and let's assume that many potentially confounding variables were carefully controlled. But there is still a problem. The subjects in the enrichment group *expected* to perform better, based on their knowledge of the experiment. After all, they knew they were in an enrichment group. Consequently, these students may have simply tried harder, or studied more, in an effort to live up to the perceived expectations of the researcher. At the same time, subjects in the control group were aware that they were failing to get special treatment; this knowledge may have lowered their motivation to perform, leading to poorer performance. The fact that the groups differed in performance doesn't necessarily mean that the enrichment program itself caused that difference.

One way to control *expectancy* effects is to be somewhat misleading in initially describing the study. This approach raises obvious ethical questions, but it is possible, under some conditions, to misrepresent some aspects of a study without severely violating ethical standards. (We'll return to the topic of research ethics later in the chapter.) In this example, the researchers could lead the control group to believe that they, too, are receiving a special experimental treatment. In that way, both groups have the same expectancy of doing well, so any difference between them at the end of the experiment must be due to something other than expectancy. This technique is often used in drug studies, in which participants in both the experimental and the control groups receive a pill or an injection, but the drug is actually present only in the substance given to the experimental group. The control subjects are given a **placebo**— an inactive, or inert, substance (e.g., a "sugar pill") that looks just like the drug (Shapiro, 1960; White, Tursky, & Schwartz, 1985). Even though placebos are used precisely because there is no reason that they should have an effect, people sometimes report effects of placebo treatments, presumably because they expect the treatment to work; for studies of the neurophysiological bases of such placebo effects, see de la Fuente-Fernandez and Stoessl (2002) and Mayberg et al. (2002).

Blind Controls   The kind of experimental procedure described above is an example of a **single-blind study;** that is, the subjects are kept "blind" about the condition in which they have been placed (e.g., they don't know whether they are getting the drug or the placebo). Single-blind studies effectively control for subject expectancies because the subjects don't know which condition they are in; any expectations that might be present are likely to be equivalent in both groups. Notice that the single-blind technique does not eliminate subject expectancies; it simply reduces the chances that expectancies will differ systematically between the experimental and the control groups and hence reduces the chances that any difference observed in the two conditions is due solely to differing expectations.

The individuals participating in the experiment as subjects aren't the only ones who expect certain things to happen; the experimenter does too (Rosenthal, 1966). Experimenters may expect that behaviour will be affected by the independent variable in a certain way, and that expectation might influence the results. Imagine, for example, that a researcher has developed a drug designed to cure influenza. The

---

CRITICAL THINKING

People sometimes experience effects of placebo treatments. If a placebo has an effect, how can it be used as a control condition?

---

placebo

An inactive, or inert, substance or treatment that resembles an experimental substance or treatment

---

single-blind study

An experimental design in which the participants do not know to which of the conditions they have been assigned (e.g., experimental versus control); used to control for subject expectancies

Subjects who participate in research studies usually have expectations about the research. They expect certain things to happen, and these expectations can influence the results.

researcher has worked hard to develop the drug and hopes for convincing scientific evidence that it is effective. So the researcher designs a single-blind experiment comprising two groups of influenza-suffering subjects. One group receives the drug and the other, a placebo. The researcher is pleased to find that people in the experimental group recovered more quickly than those in the control group did.

The experimenter's expectations might have influenced these results in two ways. First, unscrupulous investigators can deliberately fudge their data (e.g., by discarding data from subjects that didn't support the hypothesis or even falsifying the data). Sadly, cases of scientific fraud have been documented in most fields, including psychology (for discussion, see Barber, 1976; Broad & Wade, 1982; Martinson, Anderson, & de Vries, 2005). Second, researchers can unknowingly influence their results in subtle ways. Perhaps, for example, the researcher gave slightly more attention to the people in the experimental group and was more sympathetic and encouraging to them than to the people in the control group. Perhaps those subtle and unintended differences affected the subjects' health. Or perhaps the researcher measured recovery in a subjective way and was biased to score people who got the treatment as recovered even when they weren't (or vice versa). Such biases are not deliberate on the part of the researcher, but they can cloud interpretation of the results.

The solution to experimenter expectancy effects is similar to that for controlling subject expectancies: Keep the researcher blind to the assignment of subjects to conditions. If those administering the study do not know which subjects are receiving the experimental treatment, they are unlikely to treat members of each group differently. Obviously, someone needs to know the group assignments, but the information can be coded in such a way that the person doing the direct observation remains blind to the condition. To control for both experimenter and subject expectancies in the same context, a **double-blind study** is conducted, in which neither the subjects nor the observer is aware of who is in the experimental and the control conditions. Double-blind studies, often used in drug research, effectively eliminate bias effects.

Generalizing Experimental Conclusions

Properly designed experiments enable investigators to test hypotheses about the causes of behaviour in the context of the experiment. The determination of causality is possible if the experimenter has sufficient control over the situation to eliminate factors other than the experimental manipulation as contributors to a change in behaviour. But experimental control sometimes carries a cost. Sometimes, in the effort to control potentially confounding variables, the researcher creates an environment that is sterile or artificial and not very representative of

double-blind study

An experimental design in which neither the participants nor the research observers are aware of who has been assigned to the experimental and control groups; used to control for both subject and experimenter expectancies

everyday situations. The results of such an experiment may not generalize to real-world situations. As you learned previously, researchers use the term *external validity* to refer to how well results generalize across subjects and situations.

Consider again the issue of television violence and aggression: Does exposure to violent TV cause an increase in aggression? A number of experimental studies have explored this question (Bushman & Anderson, 2001; Friedrich-Cofer & Huston, 1986), but most have been conducted in the laboratory under controlled conditions. Subjects are randomly assigned to groups who watch violent programs or neutral programs, and their behaviour is then observed for aggressive tendencies, again under controlled conditions. In a study by Sanson and di-Muccio (1993), for example, preschool children were exposed to neutral or aggressive cartoons and then were given the opportunity to play with aggressive toys (such as guns); more aggressive acts were recorded for the children who watched the violent cartoon. These results clearly demonstrate that witnessed violence can increase the likelihood of aggressiveness. But this does not necessarily mean that these children would act similarly in their homes or that the effects of the brief exposure to violence were long lasting. In short, some experiments on TV and aggression may lack external validity. The Josephson study (1995) described above, in which the dependent measure was aggressive behaviours during a subsequent floor-hockey game, has higher external validity because the game was more comparable with children's everyday play behaviour. Huesmann, Moise-Titus, Podolski, and Eron (2003) provided even more compelling evidence of a long-term relationship between watching violent TV during childhood and aggressiveness.

Concerns about the generalizability of laboratory results should not be exaggerated—results of laboratory experiments very often *do* generalize to real-world environments (see, for example, Banaji & Crowder, 1989). But it's legitimate to question whether the findings of a particular laboratory experiment apply to the real world. The degree of skepticism regarding generalizing from laboratory research to everyday situations depends in part on the topic of the research. For example, if you studied basic sensory processes (say, the visual mechanisms involved in detecting a briefly presented, faint flash of light) in university undergraduates, your results would probably generalize to the wider population (because there probably are no qualitative differences in the basic sensory mechanisms of undergraduates versus other people). In contrast, if you explored hypotheses regarding social behaviours by testing undergraduates, you would want to be cautious about generalizing your results to others who differ in age, education, and other characteristics, because the principles that govern social behaviours on campus may well differ from those in force in other populations and other life situations. Ultimately, of course, the issue of generalizability must be addressed empirically (that is, by systematic observations and measurements) by conducting follow-up research with various samples and in various situations.

CRITICAL THINKING

Many psychology experiments use introductory psychology students as subjects, raising questions about the generalizability of the findings of such research to the broader population. Do you think problems with generalizing from studies of undergraduates to a broader population may be worse for some research questions than for others? Can you think of a research question for which it is probably reasonable to generalize from undergraduate subjects to the wider population?

CONCEPT SUMMARY

THE EXPERIMENTAL METHOD

Research Question (Variables in Bold)	Independent Variable (Experimenter Manipulates)	Dependent Variable (Experimenter Measures)
Does **watching television violence** increase **aggression**?	Experimenter *manipulates* the amount of exposure to TV violence	Experimenter *measures* the amount of aggression displayed
Does **exposure to subliminal messages** have an effect on **product sales**?	Experimenter *manipulates* whether or not subjects receive a hidden message	Experimenter *measures* product sales
Does **forming images of words** enhance **memory for those words**?	Experimenter *manipulates* whether subjects form images of words as they're being presented	Experimenter *measures* memory for the words

Test Yourself 2.3   *Answer the following questions to test your knowledge of experimental method. (The answers are in Appendix B.)*

1. Fill in the blanks with the term *independent* or *dependent*. In experimental research, the researcher actively manipulates the environment to observe its effect on behaviour. The aspect of the environment that is manipulated is called the _____ variable; the behaviour of interest is measured by the _____ variable. To draw conclusions about cause and effect, the experimenter must make certain that the _____ variable is the only thing changing systematically in the environment.

2. Jean-Paul wants to determine whether the presence of Brad Pitt in a movie increases the box office take. He randomly forms two groups of subjects. One group sees *Mr. and Mrs. Smith,* with Pitt as the male lead, and the other group sees *Barney's Big Adventure,* without Pitt. Sure enough, the Brad Pitt movie is rated as more enjoyable than the movie starring the purple dinosaur. Jean-Paul concludes that the presence of Brad Pitt in a film causes increased enjoyment. What's wrong with this experiment?

   a. The dependent variable—Brad versus Barney—is confounded with the content of the movie.

   b. The independent variable—Brad versus Barney—is not the only factor changing across the groups.

   c. Nothing has been manipulated; it's really a correlational study.

   d. Experiments of this type require independent variables with at least three levels.

3. Random assignment is an important research tool because it helps the researcher control for potential confounding variables. Which of the following statements about random assignment is true?

   a. Random assignment eliminates individual differences between people.

   b. Random assignment ensures that some participants will get the experimental treatment and others will not.

   c. Random assignment increases the likelihood that subject differences will be equally represented in each group.

   d. Random assignment controls for bias by ensuring that biased subjects will be placed in the control group.

▶ Statistics: Summarizing and Interpreting Data

LEARNING GOALS

1. Learn the basics of descriptive statistics, which are used to summarize data from research studies.
2. Know how to calculate three measures of central tendency (mean, median, and mode).
3. See that the scores in a data set can be characterized in terms of the extent to which those scores differ from one another.
4. Appreciate the purpose of inferential statistics, which help researchers make inferences about their data.

Descriptive Statistics: Summarizing Data

At the end of most research projects, regardless of the method used, the researcher is faced with lots of observations to analyze. Suppose, for example, that you studied the relationship between exercise and body mass index (BMI) in university undergraduates. You might measure each of a sample of undergraduates on how many hours of exercise they get in the typical week and on their BMI. These observations, or data, need to be organized and summarized in a form that allows for interpretation. It would be inappropriate to simply pick and choose from the results based on what looks interesting, because selective analyses of data can distort the interpretation (Barber, 1976; Rosenthal, 1994). Instead, the psychologist needs a principled way of describing and summarizing all the data. Descriptive statistics fill that need.

mean

The arithmetic average of a set of scores, obtained by dividing the sum of all scores by the number of scores

mode

The most frequently occurring score in a set of scores

median

The middle point in an ordered set of scores; half the scores fall below the median score and half fall above the median score

CRITICAL THINKING

Grade point average is typically calculated by using the mean. Suppose the mean were replaced with a grade point mode or a grade point median. What would be the advantages and disadvantages of calculating grade point in these ways?

Central Tendency If the recorded observations can be expressed in the form of numerical scores, the researcher can calculate statistics to summarize the results. For any set of numerical observations, such as hours of exercise per week, it is useful to begin with a measure of *central tendency,* or the value around which most of the scores tend to cluster. You are probably familiar with the **mean,** which is the arithmetic average of a set of scores. To calculate a mean, you add the numbers representing each observation and divide the total by the number of observations. So, if Jennifer works out 7 hours per week; Kim, 2; Jessica, 6; Hamead, 4; and Rowena, 6, the mean of these five scores would be 5 hours ($7 + 2 + 6 + 4 + 6 = 25$; $25 \div 5 = 5$). The mean summarizes the observations with a single representative number: On average, the students in your study worked out 5 hours per week. Notice that in this case none of the students worked out exactly 5 hours per week. The mean provides only an estimate of central tendency; it does not indicate anything about particular scores.

Another measure of central tendency is the **mode,** which is the most frequently occurring score (in the exercising example above, the mode is 6). The mode has the advantage that it always represents a real score—some students worked out 6 hours per week—and it is easy to calculate. Yet another measure of central tendency is the **median,** which is the middle score when scores are arranged in rank order. To calculate the median, order the scores from smallest to largest (2, 4, 6, 6, 7), then look for the middle score (6). If the number of scores is even, with no single middle score (e.g., 2, 3, 4, 6, 6, 7), the median is calculated as the mean of the two middle scores (e.g., $[4 + 6] \div 2 = 5$).

Researchers often compute more than one measure of central tendency for a set of scores. The mean is usually an excellent index of the average score, but it can sometimes be misleading. Imagine that you wait tables at a casual restaurant and that your total tips per day typically ranges between $20 and $70 (as shown in the upper-frequency histogram in ▶ Figure 2.9). Suppose that one day a big spender leaves a $100 tip, inflating your total for that day to $150 (as in the lower-frequency histogram of Figure 2.9). The arithmetic average, or mean, shifts rather dramatically—from $40 to $56—because of that one big tip, but neither the mode nor the median change at all. Because of the way they are calculated, means are very sensitive to extreme scores: The value shifts in the direction of the extreme score. The mode and the median are less affected by extreme scores. When an extreme value like this is included, the median or the mode may be a better sum-

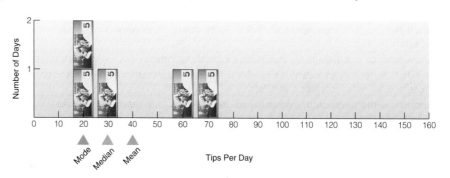

▶ **Figure 2.9**

Comparing the Mean, the Median, and the Mode

The top row shows the differences among the *mean* (arithmetic average), the *median* (middle point in a set of scores), and the *mode* (most frequently occurring score) for tips earned per day in a restaurant. The bottom row shows how the mean can be affected by an extreme score, in this case for the day you received $150 in tips. Notice that the extreme score has no effect on the median or mode.

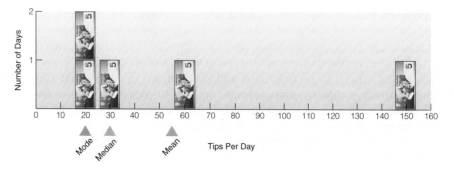

mary of the average than the mean. Thus researchers use the mean to index the central tendency of a set of data unless it includes a few very extreme scores that would distort the mean.

Variability In addition to measuring the central tendency of a set of data, researchers are also interested in summarizing **variability,** or how much the scores in the set differ from one another. The mean indicates the average, but it provides no information about how far apart the individual scores are from each other. A good way to get a sense of how much variability is in a set of data is to look at a frequency histogram of those data. A frequency histogram is a graph that displays the number (i.e., frequency) of cases that received various scores on the measurement scale used in a study. The horizontal axis of the chart represents different levels of the measurement scale, and the vertical axis represents the number of cases. For example, in the frequency histogram on the left side of ❱ Figure 2.10, about 30 students had a score of 75 and about 27 students had a score of 83. In the frequency histogram on the right side of Figure 2.10, in contrast, about 45 students had a score of 75, and only about 7 had a score of 83. There is much more variability in the scores depicted on the left of Figure 2.10 than in those depicted on the right of Figure 2.10.

To see why variability is important, think about your last exam score. Let's assume that you received an 83 and the average score was 75. What can you conclude about your performance? You might think that you did only slightly above average because your score was relatively close to the mean. But perhaps not. If the scores were all bunched toward the middle, your performance might have been spectacular; in fact, a grade of 83 could have been the highest in the class. Thus, researchers need to know more than the average of a set of scores; they also need to know something about variability.

Several measures of variability are available to researchers. A simple one is the **range,** which measures the difference between the largest and smallest scores in the distribution. If the highest score in the class was a 90 and the lowest score a 50, the range would be 90 − 50 = 40. In other words, the highest and lowest scores differed by 40 points. A more widely used index is the **standard deviation,** which provides an indication of the average extent to which individual scores vary from the mean score.

variability

A measure of how much the scores in a data set differ from one another

range

The difference between the largest and smallest scores in a distribution

standard deviation

An indication of how much individual scores differ or vary from the mean in a set of scores

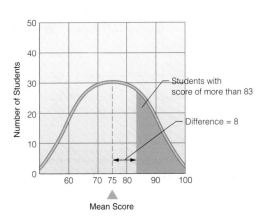
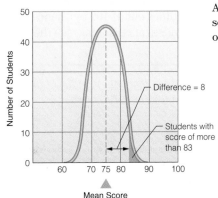

❱ **Figure 2.10**

Variability

Researchers are often interested in variability, or the extent to which scores in a set differ from one another. Each graph above shows the distribution of scores (i.e., how many students achieved each possible score; for example, in the left panel about 30 students received a score of 75). Each of these two distributions has the same average, or mean, but the distribution on the left has more variability. Notice that the raw difference between the mean (75) and a particular score, such as 83, is the same in both cases. But scoring 8 points above the mean is highly unusual in the distribution on the right and fairly common in the distribution on the left. If you received a score of 83, which class would you rather be in? How about if you received a score of 67?

If all the scores are very close to the mean score, then the average difference from the mean will be small, whereas if many scores differ dramatically from the mean then the average difference from the mean will be large (see Appendix A for more detail). The standard deviation is larger for the data set depicted in the frequency histogram on the left of Figure 2.10 than in that on the right. We'll return to the concept of standard deviation later in the text, particularly in Chapter 9, because psychologists often describe an individual's score on a psychological test, such as an IQ test, in terms of the extent to which that score deviates from the mean relative to other individuals' scores.

Inferential Statistics: Interpreting Data

descriptive statistics

Mathematical techniques that help researchers describe and summarize their data

inferential statistics

Mathematical techniques that help researchers estimate the likelihood that recorded behaviours are representative of a population or the likelihood that differences or relationships between observations are due to chance

Such statistics as the mean and the standard deviation form a part of what are called **descriptive statistics**—they help researchers describe their data. But it's also possible to use statistics to draw inferences from data—to help researchers interpret the results. Researchers use inferential statistics to decide (1) whether the behaviours recorded in a sample are likely to be representative of some larger population or (2) whether differences between groups are unlikely to have occurred by chance alone.

Inferential statistics are based on the laws of probability. Researchers always assume that the results of an observation, or a group of observations, might be due to chance. For example, suppose you find that the male servers in your restaurant average $38 a day in tips for the week whereas the female servers average $42 (a difference of $4). Is there really a gender difference in tip income? It could be that your recorded gender difference is accidental and unrepresentative of a true difference. Had you recorded tip income in a different week, you might have found that men produced more income. It is in your interest, then, to determine how representative your data are of true tipping behaviour.

Through inferential statistics, researchers estimate the likelihood, or probability, that results could have occurred by chance. The details of the procedures are beyond the scope of this text, but if you find that the chance probability is extremely low, then your findings can be treated as statistically significant. In most psychological studies, the probability that an outcome is due to chance must be lower than .05 (5%) for the outcome to be accepted as statistically significant. This means you can treat a female tipping advantage of $4 as significant only if that difference would occur less than 5 times out of 100 by chance factors alone. (To find out about our "intuitive" sense of statistical reasoning, see the Practical Solutions feature.)

Test Yourself 2.4   *You can test your learning of this brief introduction to statistics now. (The answers are in Appendix B.)*

1. The middle score in a rank-ordered set of scores is the
   _____.

2. The most common value in a set of scores is the
   _____.

3. The mean is calculated by dividing the
   _____ of all of the scores by the
   _____ of scores.

4. It's likely that in my intro psych class, the mean number of belly buttons per student is +1.00 and that the standard deviation is
   _____.

5. As explained in Appendix A, the three factors that inferential statistical tests use to estimate the likelihood that a difference between the scores observed in two groups would occur by chance alone are
   a. how motivated the subjects were, how big the difference is between the groups, and how much grant money the researcher has.
   b. how big the difference is between the groups, how much subjects within each group differed from one another, and how many subjects were tested.
   c. how many subjects were tested, how good the operational definitions were, and the practical significance of the research question.

PRACTICAL SOLUTIONS

INTUITIVE STATISTICS

Most people are intuitive statisticians, whether they recognize it or not. For example, when you meet someone new, you may try to determine which of his or her actions represent the "real" person and which are only momentary quirks. You may decide whether to stay in a course based on your impressions of the first few lectures. In all such cases you try to infer general truths from small samples of information. It's natural and reasonable to act in this way because everyday statistical intuitions help you describe and summarize your environment in ways that are often useful and efficient.

Unfortunately, evidence suggests that we're often not very good everyday statisticians. Let's consider an example taken from a study by Fong, Krantz, and Nisbett (1986) involving a statistical principle called the *law of large numbers*. Imagine that you recently went to a particular restaurant for the first time and that the meal was superb. You confidently recommend the place to your friends, and you all decide to visit there as a group. But this time the meal is mediocre, not terrible, but neither you nor your friends are impressed. What conclusion would you draw? If you're like most people, you will give a *deterministic* answer, which means that you come up with some simple, causal explanation for why the restaurant went from being great to being mediocre. You might speculate, for example, that the chef has changed.

Here's another example that demonstrates the same point. Suppose you are a hockey fan and were amazed by the brilliant play of the rookie backup goalie on your favourite NHL team the first time you saw him play. The guy did everything but stand on his head to make one spectacular save after another. The coach, too, must have been impressed, because the new goalie was put in for the next game, but this time he didn't play nearly as well. He wasn't terrible, but he didn't display anything like the skill he had on the previous outing. How would you explain the relatively poor performance in the second game?

Most people come up with simple, deterministic answers for why the goalie performed relatively poorly in the second game (e.g., the success of the preceding game put him under more psychological pressure than he could handle). Such explanations are not necessarily wrong, but the need for them is questionable from a statistical perspective. The problem arises from assuming that the original small sample of behaviour provided a reliable indication of true, stable characteristics. Dozens of variables affect how well a particular hockey player performs on a given night (e.g., which team is played, how well team mates perform, ice conditions, health). A player who has a spectacular night is likely to have had lots of luck in terms of such variables, and it's unlikely that chance will continue to be so kind night after night. You will be far above your own average some of the time but not consistently.

Behaviour varies dramatically as a consequence of a huge number of factors, whether you're talking about the behaviour of a restaurant kitchen or the behaviour of a person. Statistically, small samples of behaviour—such as one meal in a restaurant or one game in the NHL—cannot be expected to provide reliable indications of true quality or average ability. To achieve an accurate representation, you need lots of observations. This is the law of large numbers: The larger the random sample, the more likely the sample will accurately represent the population of interest (see ▶ Figure 2.11). Samples of one or two or three observations are particularly unreliable. Yet people tend to err by assuming that a small sample of behaviour is representative; consequently, they believe that any subsequent change in behaviour must be explained in terms of some simple cause.

Is there any way to avoid these kinds of errors? One answer is education: If you ask doctoral-level scientists with training in statistics to comment on the restaurant or rookie examples, they tend to give statistical rather than simple deterministic answers. They point to the concept of variability and say things like, "There are probably more instances of average restaurants that serve an occasional excellent meal than exceptional ones that serve only excellent meals" or "You may have hit it lucky at an average restaurant" (Fong & Nisbett, 1991). So there's hope for us all—as long as we take some stats courses!

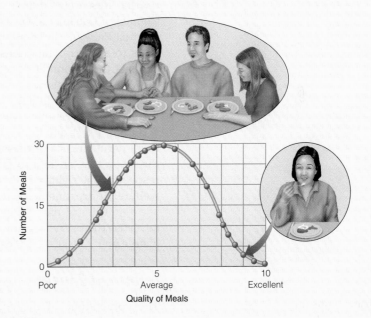

▶ **Figure 2.11**

The Law of Large Numbers

The larger the sample size, the more likely it is that the sample will accurately represent the true average of the population. Any single small sample may or may not reflect the average. If you have a great meal one time at a restaurant, that doesn't mean it represents the typical meal at that restaurant.

▶ Treating Research Participants Ethically: Human and Animal Guidelines

LEARNING GOALS

1. Grasp the principle of informed consent.
2. Be able to summarize the roles of debriefing and confidentiality in research.
3. Understand some of the key ethical issues involved in animal research.

Psychological research raises a host of ethical issues. Consider, for example, the methods researchers sometimes use to reduce the problem of reactivity. Is it ethical to observe people without their knowledge? Is it right to keep subjects blind to their condition in an experiment and to withhold treatment from some participants (through the use of placebos) in the interest of achieving experimental control? Would it be OK to randomly assign some drivers to talk on cell phones and others not to and then have them drive on busy streets during rush hour to see if those in the cell phone condition are more likely to have accidents? These are difficult questions—none of which can be answered with a simple yes or no. Rather, the costs and benefits of conducting research must be weighed carefully on a case-by-case basis.

To deal with such issues, professional organizations, such as the Canadian Psychological Association (CPA), have developed and published ethical guidelines and codes of conduct that members are expected to follow (Canadian Psychological Association, 1991). Canadian granting agencies that fund psychological research (e.g., the Canadian Institutes of Health Research, the Natural Sciences and Engineering Research Council, and the Social Sciences and Humanities Research Council) also require researchers to conform to strict ethical guidelines articulated in the *Tri-Council Policy Statement: Ethical Conduct for Research Involving Humans* (Canadian Institutes of Health Research, Natural Sciences and Engineering Research Council of Canada, Social Sciences and Humanities Research Council of Canada, 2005; see Adair, 2001, for a discussion of the impact of the Tri-Council Policy). Canadian universities also require researchers to submit applications to special committees before they conduct research with humans or with animals; these committees check to ensure that the proposed research conforms to the Tri-Council Policy.

All psychologists have a professional responsibility to respect the rights and dignity of other people. This responsibility is recognized around the world (Leach & Harbin, 1997), and it goes beyond research activities; the code of conduct applies to all psychologists' professional activities, from providing therapy to working in the laboratory or field to giving testimony in the courtroom. First and foremost, respecting the rights of others means showing concern for their health, safety, and welfare; no treatments or research procedures that are likely to harm people are allowed. Clinical psychologists are also expected to act responsibly in how they advertise their services, how they represent themselves in the media, and how they charge and collect their fees.

Informed Consent

informed consent
The principle that before consenting to participate in research, people must be fully informed of any significant factors that might affect their willingness to participate

The cornerstone of the code of ethical conduct is the principle of **informed consent.** Participants in any form of research or therapy must be informed, in easy-to-understand language, of any significant factors that might affect their willingness to participate (Mann, 1994; Meisel & Roth, 1983). Physical and emotional risks must be explained, along with the general nature of the research project or the therapeutic procedures that will be used, and only those who willingly give their consent in writing can be treated or tested (Charney, 2000). Clients or research subjects must also be informed that if they choose not to participate, for whatever reason, they will suffer no negative consequences.

But informed consent can raise problems for researchers. It can be argued that individuals cannot give truly informed consent unless they understand all the details of the project. Yet, as we've discussed previously, it is often desirable to keep subjects blind about group assignments and hypotheses so that their expectations won't affect their behaviour in the study. Most often, this can be done without deceiving subjects about what is involved in participating in the experiment. Suppose, for example, that you tested the hypothesis that Ginkgo biloba (an herbal extract sold in health food stores) enhances memorization by having some subjects take Ginkgo biloba and others take a placebo, then asking them to memorize a story, and finally testing their ability to recall the story. To avoid problems with reactivity, you would not tell subjects whether they were receiving the Ginkgo biloba or the placebo, but there would be no need to deceive them by telling them they were taking one substance when they were actually taking the other or to mislead them as to what they would be asked to do during the experiment. If, however, you were interested in assessing the effects of Ginkgo biloba on spontaneous or "incidental" memory (i.e., learning without intentional memorization), then you would not inform participants about the memory test until after they had taken the Ginkgo biloba or placebo and read the story. In a case like this, ethical problems can be reduced by using a two-stage consent procedure: You would first ask subjects to consent to participate in a study that involves taking Ginkgo biloba or a placebo and then reading a story, and then you would ask their consent to participate in the test phase. (See the Practical Solutions feature on page 89 of Chapter 3 for research on the effects of Ginkgo biloba on memory.)

Most psychological research topics can be studied rigorously without grossly deceiving subjects about what participating in the study will be like—they may not know all the details of the procedure, but they have an accurate understanding of what will be involved in participating. Some hypotheses, however, cannot be tested without deceiving subjects. Imagine, for example, that you were interested in studying why bystanders at an accident often fail to offer assistance to the victim. To gain experimental control, you might stage a mock accident in the laboratory, in front of waiting research subjects, to see how they react under various conditions (e.g., when the victim is a man versus a woman). To conduct this research in a meaningful way, you would have to mislead the subjects—you certainly could not fully inform them about the procedure by telling them that they will see a fake accident!

Most members of the psychological research community agree that it is sometimes justifiable to use deception in research procedures. Not all psychologists concur with this view (Baumrind, 1985; Ortmann & Hertwig, 1997), but it is the dominant opinion. According to the CPA code of ethics, deception in research is justified only if the prospective scientific, educational, or applied value of the study is clear and substantial and there is no way to answer the research questions adequately without deceiving the subjects. It is also agreed that deception must not be of a type that could cause subjects lasting physical or emotional harm, and that subjects should not be deceived into doing things they would not consent to do. Experimenters have a responsibility to respect the rights and dignity of research participants at all times. Most universities ensure that subjects' rights are protected by requiring investigators to submit detailed descriptions of their studies to committees before any human or animal subjects can be tested. If a study fails to protect subjects adequately, permission to conduct the study is denied.

Studying the behaviour of people in natural settings, such as the willingness of bystanders to help others in need, sometimes requires that the researcher mislead or withhold information from the people being observed.

debriefing

At the conclusion of an experimental session, informing the participants about the purpose of the experiment, including any deception that was involved

confidentiality

The principle that all personal information obtained from a participant in research or therapy should not be revealed without the individual's permission

CRITICAL THINKING

Can you think of any circumstances in which it might be ethical to conduct research with animals even though the results won't generalize to humans?

Debriefing and Confidentiality

Two other key ingredients of the psychologist's code of ethical conduct are the process of **debriefing** and the maintenance of confidentiality. Psychologists are expected to debrief subjects fully at the end of the experimental session, meaning that everyone involved is to be informed of the nature of the study. The primary aim of debriefing is to explain the purpose of the study so that individuals will appreciate why participating in the study was worthwhile (Gurman, 1994; Holmes, 1976). Good debriefing serves a valuable educational function, which is particularly important when students participate in research as part of a class. If deception was a part of the study, the full nature of the deception must be disclosed during the debriefing process. Debriefing gives the researcher an opportunity to counteract any anxieties that the subject might have developed as a result of the research. If the subject failed to help the victim of a staged accident, for example, the experimenter could explain that bystander passivity is a characteristic of most people (Darley & Latané, 1968). It is worth emphasizing that the vast majority of psychological research does not involve deception (that is, subjects are given an accurate idea of what participating will involve before the study begins). Research indicates that most people who participate in psychology experiments come away with positive views of the experience (e.g., Landrum & Chastain, 1995), although there is also evidence that debriefing procedures are not always as clear and effective as they should be (Brody, Gluck, & Aragon, 2000).

After participation is completed, the subject's right to privacy continues. Psychologists are obligated to respect the privacy of the individual by maintaining **confidentiality**—the researcher or therapist is not to discuss or report confidential information obtained in research or in therapy without the permission of the individual. Confidentiality makes sense for more than just ethical reasons. Research subjects, as well as people seeking help for psychological problems, are likely to feel more comfortable with the process, and to act more naturally, if they are convinced that their right to privacy will be respected.

The Ethics of Animal Research

The psychology departments of many universities in Canada and throughout the world include psychologists who study animals. Although some psychologists study animals by observing them in their natural environments, others do so in laboratory research. Animals are probably used in less than 10% of all current psychological research studies, but animal research has been and continues to be a very important source of psychological knowledge (Plous, 1996). As you'll see in later chapters, many of the most significant psychological principles were discovered through the study of animal behaviour (Domjan & Purdy, 1995).

Why use animal subjects? The most often cited reason is experimental control: Animal researchers can control the genetic background, diet, and experience of their subjects and thereby eliminate many of the extraneous variables that plague research with human subjects. Researchers can also study phenomena, such as life-span development, in ways that cannot be accomplished with human subjects. Studies of aging that would take 70 or 80 years with humans take only a few years with rats. Some research explores mechanisms of recovering from damage or stressors (e.g., testing treatments for brain injury): To develop effective interventions, researchers can cause and then treat damage in animals in ways they could not ethically do with human subjects. Yet another reason for studying animals is that they have relatively simple internal structures and systems. The basic biological mechanisms that underlie learning, for example, have been studied extensively with sea slugs; the number of neural connections in a sea slug is tiny compared with the billions of connections residing in a human brain. Research with

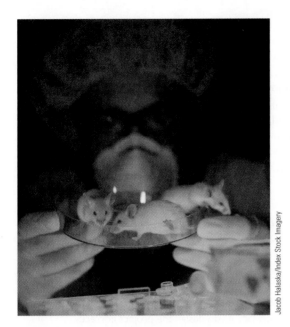

Many important insights in psychology have come from the study of animals, but the use of animals as laboratory subjects raises serious ethical questions.

nonhuman subjects often serves as a vehicle for developing hypotheses that are later elaborated and tested with humans. Such research has benefited many people and many animals.

But researchers cannot ask animals for informed consent, and if they could, the animals would likely decline. Can animal research be justified by its scientific value? For example, is it okay to destroy a part of a rat's brain to test the efficacy of treatments for brain damage? Obviously, the use of animals in research is a highly controversial subject. Many millions of dollars are spent every year by animal rights groups, some of which oppose all forms of animal research (see Hubbel, 1990). In one survey of animal rights activists, 85% advocated the complete elimination of all animal research (Plous, 1991). Other critics question the intrinsic value of animal studies, arguing that an understanding of animals reveals little about human functioning and may even mislead researchers into drawing inappropriate conclusions (see Ulrich, 1991).

While acknowledging these concerns, most psychologists believe that animal research has enormous value. They base their belief on the fact that animal studies have repeatedly led to significant breakthroughs in the understanding of behaviour and psychological disorders and in medical and biological research (see Johnson & Morris, 1987; Miller, 1985, 1991). To cite one instance, animal research has led to breakthroughs in our understanding of depression and to the development of drugs that lessen the symptoms of this disorder (see Chapters 14 and 15). In virtually every chapter in this textbook, you will be exposed to psychological principles that have been gained from research with nonhuman subjects.

Controversy regarding animal research has sometimes been inflamed by misinformation. For example, experiments that deliberately inflict pain and suffering on animals are extremely rare (see Coile & Miller, 1984). The CPA and agencies that fund psychological research (e.g., the Canadian Institutes of Health Research) enforce strict guidelines for the ethical treatment of nonhuman subjects. Those guidelines were developed by the Canadian Council on Animal Care (see http://www.ccac.ca). Psychologists who conduct research with animals are required to treat their subjects humanely. They are responsible for ensuring the animals have proper care and for minimizing their discomfort, pain, or illness. When surgical procedures are performed, the animals must be given the appropriate anesthesia, and proper medical procedures must be followed to eliminate infections and minimize pain. Failure to follow these standards can result in censure, loss of research funding, or termination of membership by the governing body of the association. Animal research raises legitimate and complex ethical issues about which reasonable people may disagree, but our opinion is that testing animal subjects is justifiable provided (1) the research has genuine potential to advance knowledge in important ways and (2) researchers minimize the distress experienced by their animal subjects.

Test Yourself 2.5

You can test what you've learned about ethics and research by answering the following questions. (The answers are in Appendix B.)

1. Fill in the blanks.
   All psychologists have a responsibility to respect the rights and dignity of other people. To ensure that research participants are treated ethically, psychologists use
   (a) _____, which means that all potential participants are fully informed about the potential risks of the project, (b) _____, which ensures that the subject's right to privacy will be maintained, and
   (c) _____, which is designed to provide participants with more information about the purpose and procedures of the research.

2. Sometimes it is necessary to deceive research participants in some way, such as keeping them blind to group assignments, so that expectations won't determine the outcome. Most psychologists believe that deception
   a. is always justified as long as it furthers scientific knowledge.
   b. is never justified unless the research involves clinical treatment.
   c. is justified but only under some circumstances.
   d. is never necessary if you design the project correctly.

3. The majority of psychologists believe that animal research has enormous value. But some question the ethics of using animals, primarily because
   a. no real scientific advancements have come from animal research.
   b. animals are typically treated cruelly.
   c. animals cannot give informed consent.
   d. animal research is too expensive.

The Methods of Psychological Research

R
E
V
I
E
W

The facts and theories that make up the discipline of psychology have arisen from the systematic application of a set of research tools. Consequently, to understand the field of psychology, you must learn about these methodological tools. In this chapter we divided our discussion of the methods of psychological research into four main problem areas.

First, what are the best techniques for describing behaviour? Psychologists use systematic techniques to describe behaviour. In *naturalistic observation*, the researcher observes behaviour in natural settings rather than in a laboratory environment. Naturalistic observation is a useful technique for generating research ideas and for verifying whether conclusions reached in the lab generalize to more realistic settings. In *case studies*, the focus is on one or a few individuals. This technique allows the researcher to obtain lots of background information on the individual being studied, but the results may not always generalize to wider populations. In *survey research*, behaviour is sampled broadly by gathering questionnaire or interview responses from many people. Finally, through *psychological tests*, differences between individuals can be quantified.

Once the descriptive data have been collected, they are summarized through the application of *descriptive statistics*. Such statistics include measures of the average or central tendency of a set of observations and measures of the extent to which individual scores in the set of observations vary. Researchers also use *inferential statistics*, based on the laws of probability, to test hypotheses. Inferential statistics help the researcher decide whether a difference between an experimental and a control group, for example, is unlikely to have occurred by chance.

Second, how can we predict behaviour? In *correlational research*, the researcher determines whether two measures of behaviour are systematically related to each other. For instance, do high school grades predict university performance? Correlation coefficients are statistics that provide an index of how well one measure predicts another: If two variables are highly correlated, then we can estimate a person's score on one variable on the basis of knowing that person's score on the other variable. Correlations are useful tools for predicting, but they do not allow the researcher to draw conclusions about what causes behaviour.

Third, how can psychologists determine the underlying causes of behaviour? If researchers want to know whether an activity, such as watching violence on television, *causes* a change in behaviour, they must conduct an *experiment*. In an experiment, the researcher manipulates the environment in a systematic way and then observes the effect of that manipulation on behaviour. The aspect of the environment that is manipulated is called the *independent variable;* the measured behaviour of interest is called the *dependent variable*. To determine that the independent variable is really responsible for the changes in behaviour, the researcher must exert experimental control—the only thing that can vary systematically between conditions is the experimenter's manipulation of the independent variable. Researchers conducting experiments encounter a variety of potential pitfalls, including potential confounding variables and subject and experimenter expectancies, that need to be controlled. Control strategies include the use of random assignment and blind research designs.

Fourth, what procedures ensure that research participants are treated ethically? Psychological research raises numerous ethical issues. As a result, it is important that all researchers follow a strict code of ethical conduct. An important safeguard is *informed consent*, which is designed to guarantee that participants are informed of any significant factors that could influence their willingness to participate. Other ethical standards govern proper *debriefing* and the maintenance of *confidentiality*. The same sorts of standards also apply to clinical psychologists when they provide psychological therapy. All psychologists have a professional responsibility to respect the rights and dignity of their research subjects and clients. This applies not only to human participants but also to animals used in research.

CHAPTER SUMMARY

Rather than relying solely on intuition or speculation, psychologists develop and test theories by using the *scientific method*: (1) Generate a research question, (2) gather background information related to that question, (3) formulate a testable research hypothesis, and (4) test that hypothesis and interpret the results of the test.

▶ Descriptive Research: Describing Behaviour

Descriptive research consists of tools and procedures for measuring behaviour systematically. One challenge of descriptive research is to minimize *reactivity* (i.e., the tendency for research participants to alter their behaviour when they know they are being observed).

Naturalistic Observation: Focusing on Real Life

Behaviour is observed in natural settings with noninterfering measures.

Case Studies: Focusing on the Individual

Intense focus on a single case yields richly detailed historical information that can be used to generate hypotheses. Unfortunately, however, it's often unclear whether the results of a case study can be generalized to other cases.

Surveys: Describing Populations

Responses can be gathered relatively easily from a large number of people, which helps establish generality. It is important to ensure that the sample of respondents to a survey is representative of the population to which the results are to be generalized. A major limitation of surveys is that they rely on verbal self-reports, which are not always accurate and are sometimes ambiguous.

Psychological Tests: Assessing Individual Differences

Psychological tests measure individual differences on variables, such as intelligence and various dimensions of personality.

Correlational Research: Predicting Behaviour

Correlational Research

Correlational research involves measuring a number of individuals on two variables and then determining whether the two variables are correlated (i.e., related) to each other. A positive correlation is observed if cases with high scores on one of the measures also tend to have high scores on the other (e.g., years of education and annual income). A negative correlation is observed if cases with low scores on one measure tend to have high scores on the other (e.g., test marks and hours spent watching TV the day before the exam). No correlation is observed if the two measures are unrelated to each other (e.g., shoe size and musical aptitude). Knowing that two variables are correlated means that an individual's score on one variable can be roughly predicted on the basis of his or her score on the other.

Correlations and Causality

A correlation between two measures of behaviour helps prediction but does not determine causality. For example, if IQ and income are correlated, that might be because having a higher IQ leads to better income or because greater income leads to better education or because some third variable (e.g., family background or motivation) has a causal influence on both IQ and income.

Experimental Method: Explaining Behaviour

Independent and Dependent Variables

The *independent variable* is the aspect of the environment that is manipulated in an experiment. The independent variable must consist of at least two conditions (e.g., experimental and control conditions). A *dependent variable* is the behaviour or response that is measured in an experiment.

Experimental Control

Experimental control is achieved by ensuring that the only systematic difference between conditions in an experiment is the independent variable. If, for example, the only systematic difference between two groups of subjects is whether they were given vitamin C or a placebo, then any difference in the dependent variable greater than what would likely occur by chance alone can be attributed to the effects of vitamin C.

Expectancies and Biases in Experimental Research

Researchers must control for expectations and biases that can affect subjects' and researchers' behaviour in ways that might distort an experiment's results. Blind experiments are often used to control for expectancies on the part of subjects (single-blind) and experimenters (double-blind).

Generalizing Experimental Conclusions

The effort to maximize experimental control can lead researchers to test hypotheses in artificial contexts, and this raises questions regarding the generalizability (or external validity) of the findings. Such questions are especially justified if the research explores an aspect of behaviour that is likely to differ across situations. Ultimately, conclusions from laboratory experiments must be confirmed by converging evidence obtained in naturalistic situations.

Statistics: Summarizing and Interpreting Data

Descriptive Statistics: Summarizing Data

Descriptive statistics summarize or "describe" the findings of research.

Inferential Statistics: Interpreting Data

Inferential statistics enable researchers to estimate the likelihood that the results of a study are representative of the larger population and the likelihood that observed differences (e.g., between groups of subjects) are due solely to chance.

Treating Research Participants Ethically: Human and Animal Guidelines

Informed Consent

Research participants must be informed of any factors that could affect their willingness to participate in psychological research or receive psychological treatment.

Debriefing and Confidentiality

Debriefing is the process of explaining to research participants the purpose of a study after their participation. *Confidentiality* protects the participant's privacy.

The Ethics of Animal Research

Although CPA guidelines require that animals be treated humanely, controversy remains over their use in psychological research. One fundamental issue is that animals cannot give informed consent (and would be unlikely to do so if they could). Balancing this issue is the fact that animal research has been tremendously valuable in advancing psychological knowledge, including in the development of treatments that have greatly enhanced the lives of humans and of animals.

Terms to Remember

scientific method, 35
operational definition, 37

Descriptive Research: Describing Behaviour
descriptive research, 38
reactivity, 39
external validity, 39
naturalistic observation, 40
case study, 41
survey, 42
random sampling, 43

Correlational Research: Predicting Behaviour
correlation coefficient, 46

Experimental Method: Explaining Behaviour
experimental method, 52
independent variable, 53
dependent variable, 53
confounding variable, 53
internal validity, 54

random assignment, 55
placebo, 56
single-blind study, 56
double-blind study, 57

Statistics: Summarizing and Interpreting Data
mean, 60
mode, 60
median, 60
variability, 61
range, 61
standard deviation, 61
descriptive statistics, 62
inferential statistics, 62

Treating Research Participants Ethically: Human and Animal Guidelines
informed consent, 64
debriefing, 66
confidentiality, 66

Recommended Readings

Pelham, B. W., & Blanton, H. (2003). *Conducting experiments in psychology: Measuring the weight of smoke* (2nd ed.). Pacific Grove, CA: Brooks/Cole. An interesting book that describes the essentials of research methods by using many real-life examples and hands-on activities.

Snodgrass, J. G., Levy-Berger, G., & Haydon, M. (1985). *Human experimental psychology.* New York: Oxford University Press. An excellent resource for designing experiments, setting up apparatus, testing subjects, analyzing and interpreting data, and writing up the results of research.

Stanovich, K. E. (2003). *How to think straight about psychology* (7th ed.). Reading, MA: Addison-Wesley. University of Toronto researcher Keith Stanovich provides an in-depth discussion of how to evaluate empirical evidence in psychology and avoid faulty conclusions.

 For additional readings, explore InfoTrac® College Edition, your online library. Go to
http://www.adaptivemind3e.nelson.com.

Hint: Enter these search terms: participant observation, survey research, psychological tests, experimental design, psychological research methods.

Media Resources

What's on the Web?

Please note that Web addresses are subject to change. Check the accompanying website for updates:

http://www.adaptivemind3e.nelson.com.

This site presents practice quiz questions, hypercontent, information on degrees and careers in psychology, study tips, and more.

The Natural Sciences and Engineering Research Council (NSERC)

http://www.nserc.ca/index.htm

NSERC is one of the largest Canadian federal agencies that provides grants for scientific research and is a major source of funding for research in scientific psychology. The NSERC website includes information about scholarships and grants for students and faculty in psychology as well as information about research ethics.

The Junk Science Homepage

http://www.junkscience.com

This page presents "all the junk that's fit to debunk." It's a very interesting site, chock full of phony claims and questionable science—a veritable feast for skeptical types—along with explanations of the flaws in the claims. Although many of the articles do not relate specifically to psychology, it's still a great site to visit to get a feel for the dogged skepticism of a scientist.

Psychology Research on the Net

http://psych.hanover.edu/Research/exponnet.html

This page is part of the American Psychological Society website and offers links to an array of research projects that will give you an idea of the range of phenomena that psychologists investigate. The projects linked to this site run the gamut of every area in psychology, from clinical to social to cognitive. Participate in projects on decision making, giving directions, anger, irrational food beliefs, and dozens of others.

CSICOP On-Line

http://www.csicop.org

This is the official home page of the Committee for Scientific Investigation of Claims of the Paranormal. CSICOP "encourages the critical investigation of paranormal and fringe-science claims from a responsible scientific point of view."

ThomsonNOW ThomsonNOW

http://hed.nelson.com

Go to this site for the link to ThomsonNOW™, your one-stop study shop. Take a Pretest for this chapter and ThomsonNOW™ will generate a personalized Study Plan based on your test results. The Study Plan will identify the topics you need to review and direct you to online resources to help you master those topics. You can then take a Posttest to determine what concepts you have mastered and what you still need work on.

Psyk.trek 3.0

Check out Psyk.trek 3.0 for further study of the concepts in this chapter. Psyk.trek's 65 interactive learning modules, simulations, and quizzes offer additional opportunities for you to interact with, reflect on, and retain the material:

History and Methods: Correlation
History and Methods: The Experimental Method

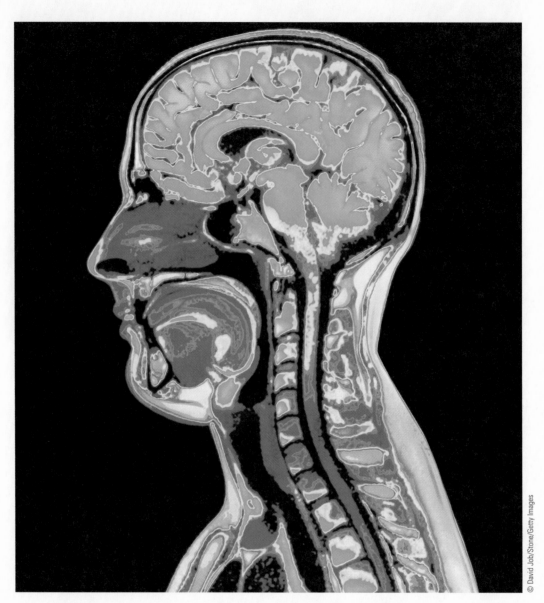

To discover that a particular feeling depends on activity in the [body] does not diminish the status of that feeling as a human phenomenon. Neither anguish nor the elation that love or art can bring about are devalued by understanding some of the myriad biological processes that make them what they are. Precisely the opposite should be true: Our sense of wonder should increase before the intricate mechanisms that make such magic possible.

—Antonio Damasio, *Descartes' Error: Emotion, Reason and the Human Brain*

What a piece of work is a man, how noble in reason, how infinite in faculties, in form and moving how express and admirable, in action how like an angel, in apprehension how like a god: the beauty of the world, the paragon of animals.

—William Shakespeare, *Hamlet*

Biological Processes

You, dear reader, are an amazing object. You are a specimen of the most complex thing in the known universe. One of the aims of this book is to help you appreciate that you (like the other 7 billion humans on Earth) are a marvel. Consider, for example, what you are doing now: As you'll learn in more detail in Chapter 4, light is bouncing off this page, sending a reflected pattern of shades and hues into the environment, with some of that reflected light entering your eyes and being transformed, through a remarkably complex cascade of processes, into thoughts, ideas, images, and feelings sparked by the black squiggles on this page. As another example, reach out and pick something up, such as a pen or a cup. Really—stop and do it. Now do it again, but this time notice the elegance of the trajectory of your reach (swiftly accelerating to a peak velocity, following a graceful arc, then smoothly braking as your hand nears the object, with your fingers oriented almost perfectly to grasp the object appropriately before your hand even reaches it).

The most remarkable thing about you, as a physical object, is your brain. This is an organ of bewildering complexity, with billions of intricately interconnected micro-components, and it plays the lead role in all your skills and abilities, from controlling the performance of physical acts (picking up a pencil, dancing, snowboarding) through constructing your experience of the world around you to giving rise to your innermost thoughts and feelings.

neuroscience

An interdisciplinary field of study directed at understanding the brain and its relation to experience and behaviour

central nervous system

The brain and the spinal cord

peripheral nervous system

The network of nerves that link the central nervous system with the rest of the body

This chapter introduces the field of **neuroscience,** which studies the connection among the brain, the mind, and behaviour. Although we'll focus primarily on the brain, your behaviour is controlled by a broader system that includes the spinal cord as well as neural connections to muscles, sensory organs, hormone-secreting glands, and other internal structures in the body. More specifically, the brain and spinal cord compose what is called the **central nervous system** (see ❱ Figure 3.1). An additional network of nerves, the **peripheral nervous system,** acts as the communication link between the central nervous system and the rest of the body. Later in this chapter, we'll expand on these basic divisions of the nervous system and outline their various functions in greater detail.

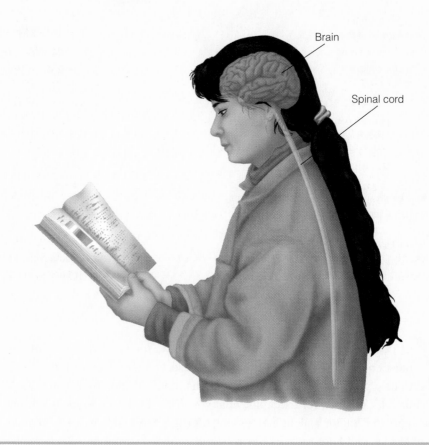

Brain

Spinal cord

❱ **Figure 3.1**

The Central Nervous System
The central nervous system consists of the brain and the spinal cord.

Biological Aspects of Psychology

P
R
E
V
I
E
W
I

We discuss biological processes that address four central problems of adaptation. Each problem can be viewed as a challenge to be solved by the systems of your body to help you survive and adapt to the environment. These biological solutions provide important insight into the workings of the adaptive mind.

First, how does your body communicate with the environment and internally? One reason behaviour is often adaptive is that people monitor their environment continuously and produce quick responses that fit the situations they face. If a child suddenly runs into the path of your car, you slam on the brakes and the child is saved. These rapid world-to-behaviour links are possible because of a complex communication network linking the outside world to the brain and linking the brain to the rest of the body.

Second, how does your brain generate your perception of the world around you and of your own internal states, and how does it initiate and coordinate behaviour? The brain consists of numerous regions specialized for performing particular kinds of tasks, with each region having vast numbers of densely interconnected neurons and being interconnected with other regions. Patterns of electrochemical activity across this extraordinarily

A vast communication network in the body helps us monitor the environment and produce quick adaptive responses when they're needed.

complex network give rise to and constitute perception, thought, and the control of action.

Third, how does the body regulate growth and other internal functions? Besides relying on the rapid transmission of information, the systems in your body also have widespread and long-term internal communication needs. To resolve these needs, structures in the body control the release of chemicals into the bloodstream that serve important regulatory functions, influencing growth and development, sexual behaviour, appetite, and emotions.

Fourth, how and why did evolution select the kind of brain structures and nervous system that humans have today, and how does the body store and transmit the genetic code? Natural selection has provided the human species with a unique set of physical, mental, and behavioural "solution tools" for solving the problems that our ancient ancestors encountered in their natural environments. The transmission of physical and behavioural characteristics from one generation to the next via genetics played a crucial role in our evolution, and your genetic inheri-

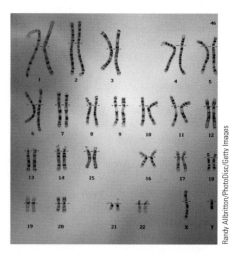

The genetic code is inherited from both biological parents and importantly shapes our physical and psychological characteristics.

tance continues to influence you today. The environments in which we live today are quite different from those of our evolutionary ancestors, yet our genetically coded "solution tools" have probably not changed very much, and this can cause problems.

Communicating Internally: Connecting World and Brain

LEARNING GOALS

1. Learn the basic structure of neurons and the three major kinds of neurons.
2. Understand how information is transmitted along a neuron and from one neuron to another.
3. Grasp how neurons work together in communication networks.

The Anatomy of Neurons

The main components of the nervous system are individual cells called **neurons,** which receive, transmit, and integrate information. Before it's possible to understand how the nervous system accomplishes communication between the external world and the body, you need to know the basic anatomical hardware of these cells. Neurons come in three major types—*sensory neurons, interneurons,* and *motor neurons*—that differ physically from one another and serve quite different functions.

1. **Sensory neurons** make the initial contact with the environment and are responsible for carrying the message inward toward the spinal cord and brain.

(**neurons**

The cells in the nervous system that receive, integrate, and transmit information by generating an electrochemical signal; the basic building blocks of the nervous system

sensory neurons

Neurons that make initial contact with the environment and carry the message inward toward the spinal cord and brain

interneurons

Neurons that make no direct contact with the external world but rather convey information from one neuron to another

motor neurons

Neurons that carry information away from the central nervous system to the muscles and glands that directly produce behavioural responses

glial cells

Cells in the nervous system that are not neurons and hence do not transmit or receive information but perform a variety of functions, such as removing waste, filling empty space, and helping neurons to communicate efficiently

myelin sheath

An insulating material that protects the axons of some neurons and helps to speed up neural transmission

2. **Interneurons,** the most plentiful type of neuron, make no direct contact with the world but rather convey information from one neuron to another.
3. **Motor neurons** carry information from the central nervous system to the muscles and glands that directly produce behavioural responses.

The nervous system also contains **glial cells,** which greatly outnumber neurons (by a factor of about 10 to 1) but do not directly communicate messages. Glial cells perform several functions in the nervous system, such as removing waste, filling empty space, and surrounding neurons with a physical environment that helps them to function efficiently (Kimelberg & Norenberg, 1989). Some types of glial cells wrap around the axons of neurons, creating a **myelin sheath** that insulates the neuron from interference from other neurons and that helps speed neural transmission (we'll have more to say about this shortly). Problems with glial cells play major roles in some kinds of brain dysfunction, including brain cancer and Alzheimer's disease (Saitoh, Kang, Mallory, DeTeresa, & Masliah, 1997).

As shown in ❱ Figure 3.2, neurons typically have four major structural components: *dendrites*, a *soma*, an *axon*, and *terminal buttons*. For any communication system to work properly, it must have a way to receive information, a way to process any received messages, and a means for transmitting information. The four structural components of the neuron play these distinct roles in the communication chain.

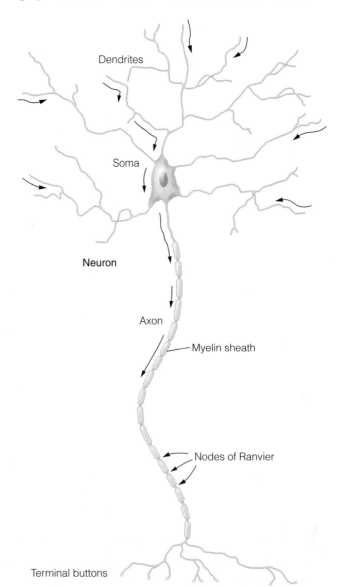

❱ **Figure 3.2**

The Components of a Neuron

The *dendrites* are the primary information receivers, the *soma* is the cell body, and the *axon* is the cell's transmitter device. The *myelin sheath* that surrounds the axon of some neurons helps speed up neural transmission, as do the *nodes of Ranvier*. At the end of the axon are the *terminal buttons,* which contain the chemical messengers used to transmit the message to the dentrites of other neurons.

The **dendrites,** which look like tree branches extending outward from the main body of the cell, are the primary information receivers. One neuron passes information to another neuron by chemically stimulating its dendrites. A particular neuron may have thousands of these dendritic branches, allowing the cell to receive input from many other neurons. Once received at the dendrites, the message is transmitted to the **soma,** the main body of the cell. The soma adds all the stimulation received by the dendrites within a brief period. If the soma receives sufficient stimulation, then it generates an electrical signal called an *action potential.*

The **axon** is the cell's transmitter device. When a neuron transmits a message, an action potential started in the soma is propagated along the length of the axon. In many neurons (like that depicted in Figure 3.2), the axon is covered with an insulating sheath of myelin, with small gaps in the myelin sheath called **nodes of Ranvier.** Axons vary dramatically in size and shape; in some cases, they can be more than a metre long (e.g., sensory and motor neurons between your feet and spinal cord). Near its end, the axon branches out in preparation to make contact with other cells. At the tip of each branch are tiny swellings called **terminal buttons.** Chemicals released by these buttons pass the message on to the next cell (e.g., the dendrites of another neuron, or muscle fibres).

Neurons don't actually touch one another. The **synapse** is a small gap between a terminal button of one neuron and a dendrite of another. When an action potential arrives at a terminal button, mechanisms in the terminal button release a chemical into the synaptic cleft. That chemical is taken up by the dendrites of the next neuron.

Neural Transmission: The Electrochemical Message

Neurons differ in size and shape, but the manner and direction of information flow are consistent across all neurons:

Dendrites → Soma → Axon → Terminal buttons

Information usually arrives at the dendrites from multiple sources—many thousands of synaptic connections might be made to the dendrites of a single neuron—and is passed along to the soma. Here, all the messages that have been received sum together; if sufficient energy is present, an action potential will be generated. The action potential travels down the axon toward the terminal buttons, where it causes the release of chemicals into the synapse. These chemicals move the message from the end of the axon to the dendrites of the next neuron, starting the process all over again. That's the general sequence of information flow: Messages travel electrically from one point to another within a neuron, but the message is transmitted chemically between neurons. Because the language that neurons use to communicate is part electrical and part chemical, it is referred to as electrochemical.

The Resting Potential   Neurons possess electrical properties even when they aren't receiving or transmitting messages. Specifically, a tiny electrical charge, called the **resting potential,** exists between the inside and outside of the cell. This resting potential is created by the presence of electrically charged atoms and molecules, called *ions,* that are distributed unevenly between the inside and outside of the cell. The main ions in neural transmission are positively charged *sodium* and *potassium* ions and negatively charged *chloride* ions.

Normally, ions will distribute themselves evenly in an environment, through a process called *diffusion.* However, they are unable to do so around a resting neuron because free movement is blocked by the neuron's cell wall, or *membrane.* The membrane of a neuron is selectively permeable, which means that it only allows certain ions to pass in and out through special ion "channels." As shown in

dendrites

The branchlike fibres that extend outward from a neuron and receive information from other neurons

soma

The cell body of a neuron

axon

The long tail-like part of a neuron that serves as the cell's transmitter device

nodes of Ranvier

Spaces separating the segments of the myelin covering of the neuron; they help speed the nerve impulse along the axon

terminal buttons

The tiny swellings at the end of a neuron's axon that contain chemicals that, when released into the synapse, are taken up by the dentrites of other neurons, thereby stimulating them

synapse

The junction, or small gap, between a terminal button of one neuron and a dendrite of another neuron

resting potential

The tiny electrical charge in place between the inside and outside of the resting neuron

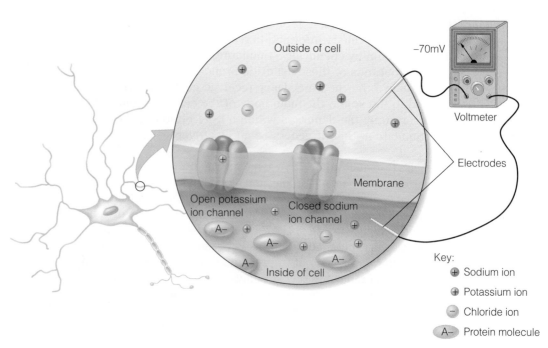

▌**Figure 3.3**

The Resting Potential

Neurons possess electrical properties even when they are neither receiving nor transmitting messages. The resting potential, a tiny negative electrical charge across the inside and outside of a resting cell, is created by an uneven distribution of ions across the cell membrane.

▌Figure 3.3, when the neuron is resting, there are different concentrations of various electrically charged particles inside versus outside the cell. Specifically, there are more negatively charged proteins and more positively charged potassium ions inside than outside the cell, whereas there are more negatively charged chloride ions and positively charged sodium ions outside than inside the cell. These unequal concentrations are maintained, in part, by a sodium-potassium pump that actively moves the ions into and out of the cell. If you used an electrode to measure the electrical potential of the neuron, you would find that the fluid inside the cell is *negative* with respect to the outside (between –60 and –70 millivolts). This negative charge defines the resting potential for the cell. Most of the negative charge comes from large protein molecules inside the cell, which are too big to pass through ion channels.

Why is it adaptive for neurons to have a resting potential? The resting potential helps the cell respond quickly when it's stimulated by other neurons. When one neuron communicates with another, it releases chemicals that change the nature of the stimulated neuron's membrane. Ions that are normally outside the cell can rush in quickly through newly opened channels. This changes the electrical potential inside the cell, which, as you'll see shortly, can lead to the production of an action potential.

action potential

The all-or-none electrical signal that travels down a neuron's axon

Generating Action Potentials   For a neuron to stop resting and generate an **action potential,** the electrical signal that travels down the axon, the electrical potential inside the cell must become less negative. This change occurs primarily as a result of contact from other neurons. Two types of messages can be passed from one neuron to the next: Excitatory messages and inhibitory messages. If the message is excitatory, the membrane of the contacted neuron changes and positively charged sodium ions begin to flow into the cell. This process, called *depolarization,* moves the electrical potential of the cell from negative toward zero and increases the chances of an action potential. When the message is inhibitory, the opposite happens: The cell membrane either pushes more positive ions out of the cell or pumps more negative ions in. The result is *hyperpolarization:* The electrical potential of the cell becomes more negative, and the chances of an action potential decrease.

It's important to remember that any given neuron in the nervous system is in contact with many other neurons. As a result, small changes in potential regularly occur in a neuron as messages are received (see ▌Figure 3.4). Near the point at

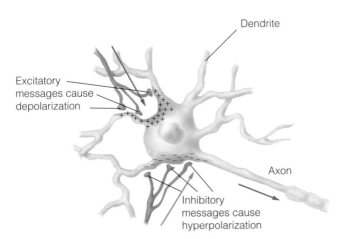

Dendrite

Excitatory
messages cause
depolarization

Axon

Inhibitory
messages cause
hyperpolarization

▶ **Figure 3.4**

Summing Excitatory and Inhibitory Messages

Each neuron is in contact with many other neurons. Some contacts initiate excitatory messages, or *depolarization*, and others initiate inhibitory messages, or *hyperpolarization*. A neuron generates its own action potential only if the summed messages produce sufficient depolarization (the negative potential moves close enough to zero).

which the axon leaves the cell body is a special trigger zone called the *axon hillock*. All the excitatory and inhibitory potentials in the soma combine at the axon hillock. If enough excitatory messages have been received—that is, if the electrical potential inside the cell has become sufficiently less negative—an action potential will be initiated. If not, the resting potential of the axon will be maintained.

Action potentials are the electrical signals that travel down a neuron's axon. They are generated in an *all-or-none* fashion; that is, the action potential will not begin until sufficient excitatory input has been received, but once the firing threshold is reached, they always travel completely down the length of the axon to its end. The process is somewhat analogous to the firing of a gun: Bullets don't travel farther or faster if you pull the trigger harder. Likewise, an action potential travels along the axon at the same rate regardless of the intensity of the messages that caused the firing. Also, the basic characteristics of action potentials are the same regardless of the type of information being transmitted: It doesn't matter whether the neuron is carrying a message about pleasure or pain, thought or reflex, the basic characteristics of action potentials are the same.

We have many different kinds of neurons, and although all action potentials are all-or-none, the speed of transmission does vary across different kinds of neurons. Transmission speed depends partly on the size and shape of the axon; in general, the thicker the axon, the faster the message will travel. Another feature that increases the speed of transmission in many neurons is the myelin sheath, which, as mentioned earlier, is made from a type of glial cell. Myelin provides an insulating wrap for the axon, like the plastic around the copper electrical wiring in a house, thereby protecting the neuron from interference from other nearby neurons. At regular points are the nodes of Ranvier—gaps in the insulation—which permit the action potential to jump down the axon from gap to gap rather than travelling more gradually along the whole length of the axon. This method of transmission from node to node is called *saltatory conduction* (from the Latin word *saltare*, which means "to jump"). Because of variations in size and in myelination, transmission speed varies across different sorts of neurons from about 3 km/h to 300 km/h (which is much slower than the speed of electricity through a copper wire).

Although action potentials are all or none, the nervous system can code the intensity of a stimulus through the frequency or rate at which neurons generate action potentials. The *firing rate* of a neuron is defined by the number of action potentials it generates per unit of time. The firing rate is subject to some natural limitations. For instance, a very brief **refractory period** follows the generation of an action potential, during which another action potential cannot be generated.

Many neurons have spontaneous firing rates; they generate a steady series of action potentials even without input from other neurons or the environment. A continuously active cell is adaptive for the nervous system because different information can be communicated by decreasing as well as by increasing the

CRITICAL   THINKING

The speed of neural transmission is quite slow, at least relative to the speed of processing in a computer chip. How do you think it's possible for people to make very quick decisions?

refractory period

The period of time following an action potential during which more action potentials cannot be generated

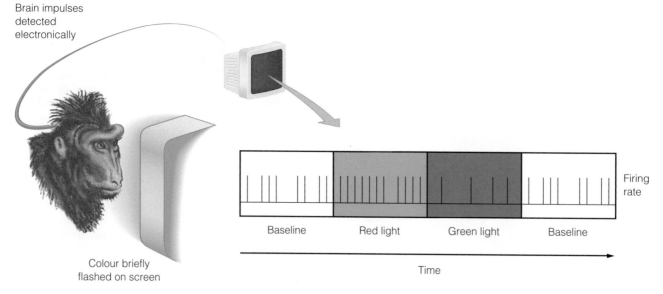

Brain impulses
detected
electronically

Colour briefly
flashed on screen

Baseline   Red light   Green light   Baseline

Firing
rate

Time

▶ **Figure 3.5**

Changes in Firing Rates

Information is communicated through changes in the firing rates of neurons. Here, certain neurons in the monkey's brain increase their firing rate (relative to baseline) when a red stimulus appears and decrease their firing rate (relative to baseline) when a green stimulus appears. Thus, the same neurons can code both red and green.

spontaneous firing rate. The colour red, for example, might be experienced when particular cells in the brain increase their frequency of firing, whereas green may be linked to a decrease in the rate of action potentials in the same cells (see ▶ Figure 3.5). In this way, the system can code more information. (You'll learn more about how colour is processed in the visual system in Chapter 4.) Patterns of changes in firing rate across large groups of interconnected neurons give rise to complex psychological phenomena.

Neurotransmitters: The Chemical Messengers   When the action potential reaches the end of the axon, it triggers the release of chemical messengers from small sacs, or vesicles, in the terminal buttons (see ▶ Figure 3.6). These chemical molecules, called **neurotransmitters,** spill out into the synapse and interact chemically with the cell membrane of the next neuron (called the *postsynaptic membrane*). Depending on the particular characteristics of the postsynaptic membrane, the neurotransmitter either will excite the recipient neuron toward generating an action potential or will inhibit it away from generating an action potential.

Each neurotransmitter molecule acts as a kind of key in search of the appropriate lock. The substance moves quickly across the synapse—it takes only about 1/10 000 of a second—and activates receptor molecules contained in the postsynaptic membrane. Depending on the particular type of receptor molecule that is present, the neurotransmitter will then either increase or decrease the electrical potential of the receiving cell. When the message is excitatory, the neurotransmitter causes channels in the postsynaptic membrane to open that allow positive sodium ions to flow into the receiving cell. When the message is inhibitory, negative chloride ions are allowed to enter the cell and positive potassium ions are allowed to leave. It's worth emphasizing that neurotransmitters, by themselves, are neither excitatory nor inhibitory. It's the nature of the receptor molecule that deter-

neurotransmitters

Chemical messengers that relay information from one neuron to the next; released from the terminal buttons into the synapse, where they interact chemically with the cell membrane of the next neuron; the result is either an excitatory or an inhibitory influence on the recipient neuron

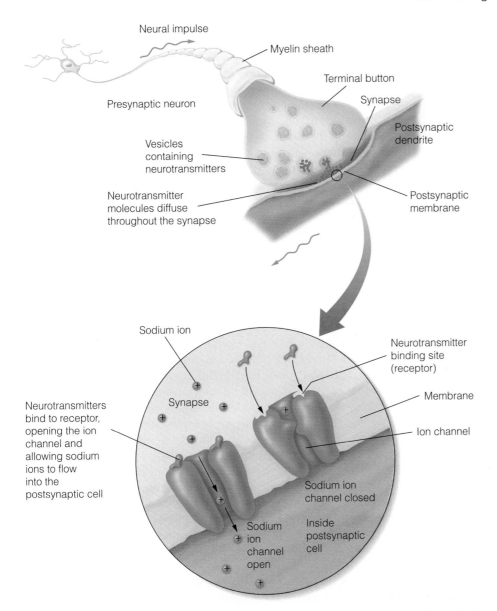

Neural impulse

Myelin sheath

Presynaptic neuron

Terminal button

Synapse

Vesicles
containing
neurotransmitters

Postsynaptic
dendrite

Neurotransmitter
molecules diffuse
throughout the synapse

Postsynaptic
membrane

Sodium ion

Neurotransmitter
binding site
(receptor)

Neurotransmitters
bind to receptor,
opening the ion
channel and
allowing sodium
ions to flow
into the
postsynaptic cell

Synapse

Membrane

Ion channel

Sodium ion
channel closed

Inside
postsynaptic
cell

Sodium
ion
channel
open

▶ Figure 3.6

Releasing the Chemical Messengers

When the action potential reaches the terminal buttons at the end of the axon, it causes the release of chemical messengers—neurotransmitters—into the synapse. The neurotransmitters interact with the postsynaptic membrane of the next neuron, opening or closing its ion channels. Here, the neurotransmitter is opening sodium channels, which will increase the chances of the receiving cell initiating its own action potential. In other synapses, neurotransmitters have inhibitory effects, decreasing the likelihood that the recipient neuron will generate an action potential.

mines whether a particular neurotransmitter produces an excitatory or inhibitory effect; the same neurotransmitter can produce quite different effects at different sites in the nervous system.

Dozens of neurotransmitters have been identified in the nervous system, along with their various functions. The neurotransmitter **acetylcholine** is a major messenger in both the central and the peripheral nervous systems; it acts, for example, as the primary transmitter between motor neurons and muscles in the body. When released into the synapse between motor neurons and muscle cells, acetylcholine tends to create excitatory messages that lead to muscle contraction. The neurotransmitter **dopamine** often produces inhibitory effects that help dampen and stabilize communications in the brain and elsewhere. Inhibitory effects help keep the brain on an even keel and allow us to do such things as produce smooth voluntary muscle movements, sleep without physically acting out our dreams, and maintain posture.

Dopamine is of particular interest to psychologists because it's thought to play a role in schizophrenia, a serious psychological disorder that disrupts thought processes and produces delusions and hallucinations. When schizophrenic patients take drugs that inhibit the action of dopamine, their hallucinations and delusions are

acetylcholine

A neurotransmitter that plays several roles in the central and peripheral nervous systems, including the excitation of muscle contractions

dopamine

A neurotransmitter that often leads to inhibitory effects; decreased levels have been linked to Parkinson's disease, and increased levels have been linked to schizophrenia; also plays an important role in the neurological mechanisms of reward

© Bettmann

For much of recorded history, psychological disorders were attributed to possession by evil spirits. Today, psychologists recognize that many disorders are the result of brain malfunctioning.

serotonin

A neurotransmitter that has been linked to sleep, dreaming, and general arousal and may also be involved in some psychological disorders, such as depression and schizophrenia

gamma-amino-butyric acid (GABA)

A neurotransmitter that may play a role in the regulation of anxiety; it generally produces inhibitory effects

often reduced or even eliminated. It has been speculated that perhaps an excess supply of dopamine is partly responsible for the disorder (O'Donnell & Grace, 1998; Sigmundson, 1994). Further evidence linking dopamine and schizophrenia has come from the study of Parkinson's disease. This movement disorder apparently results from the underproduction of dopamine. Parkinson's patients are often given the drug L-dopa, which increases the levels of dopamine in the brain, to reduce the tremors and other movement problems that result from the disease. For some patients, however, L-dopa causes thought disorders characteristic of schizophrenia (Braff & Huey, 1988). Dopamine also plays an important role in the "reward pathway" of the brain, which includes the parts of the brain that are most involved in transmitting feelings of pleasure (Holroyd & Coles, 2002; Nader, Bechara, & van der Kooy, 1997).

Neurotransmitters in the brain fundamentally affect people's thoughts and actions, but the particular mechanisms involved are not well understood. We know, for example, that people with Alzheimer's disease have damage to cells that play a role in producing acetylcholine (Quirion, 1993). Because memory loss is a common problem for Alzheimer patients, this suggests a connection between acetylcholine and certain kinds of memory functioning (Degroot & Parent, 2001; Hasselmo, Rolls, & Baylis, 1989; McDonald & Crawley, 1997; Pappas, Bayley, Bui, Hansen, & Thal, 2000). We also know that **serotonin,** another neurotransmitter that often acts in an inhibitory fashion, affects sleep, dreaming, and general arousal and may also be involved in such psychological disorders as depression, schizophrenia, and obsessive-compulsive disorder (Alda, 2001; McAllister-Williams, Ferrier, & Young, 1998; Potter & Manji, 1993; Thomsen, 1998). As you'll learn in Chapter 15, some medications used to treat depression, such as Prozac, act by modulating the effectiveness of serotonin. Similarly, many researchers believe that a neurotransmitter called **gamma-amino-butyric acid (GABA)** plays an important role in the regulation of anxiety (Adamec, 2000). Many oft-prescribed medications for anxiety (e.g., tranquillizers, such as Valium) regulate GABA in the brain (Stock, Werry, & McClellan, 2001).

In each of these cases, however, researchers still face the difficult task of determining the specific neural pathways and mechanisms involved. At this point, much of the evidence is correlational rather than experimental, so we cannot be certain about the causal roles of particular neurotransmitters (see Chapter 2). We know that as the levels of particular neurotransmitters vary in the body, so too do the symptoms of various disorders. This is useful information for treatment, but it doesn't establish a definitive cause-and-effect link between neurotransmitters and psychological characteristics (e.g., it could be that some unknown mechanism has parallel influences on both neurotransmitters and psychological characteristics).

Drugs and the Brain   Because the transmission of messages between neurons is chemical, chemicals that enter the body can affect the communication networks in the brain. Some drugs, called *agonists*, mimic the action of neurotransmitters. For example, the nicotine in cigarette smoke can act like the neurotransmitter acetylcholine. Nicotine has a general stimulating effect in the body (e.g., increases heart rate) because it produces excitatory messages in much the same way as acetylcholine does. (For arguments that agonists, such as nicotine, can change the physical structure of the brain, see Robinson & Kolb, 2004.)

Other drugs act as *antagonists*, which means that they oppose or block the action of neurotransmitters. The lethal drug curare, which some aboriginal peoples in South America use on the tips of hunting arrows and blow darts, is antagonistic to acetylcholine. Curare blocks the receptor systems involved in muscle movements, including the muscles that move the diaphragm during breathing. The result is paralysis and death from suffocation.

In the early 1970s, membrane receptor systems were discovered in the brain that react directly to *morphine*, a pain-killing and highly addictive drug derived from the opium plant (Pert & Snyder, 1973). It turns out that we have receptor systems that are sensitive to morphine because the brain produces its own morphine-like substances called **endorphins.** Endorphins serve as natural painkillers in the body. They are thought to act as *neuromodulators*, or chemicals that modulate (increase or decrease) the effectiveness of neurotransmitters. Apparently, the brain has evolved systems for releasing endorphins under conditions of stress or exertion to reduce pain and possibly to provide pleasurable reinforcement (Hoffmann, 1997; Schedlowski, Fluge, Richter, & Tewes, 1995). As shown by Christina Gianoulakis (2001) of McGill University, endorphins may also interact with ingested chemicals, such as alcohol. We'll return to the study of drugs, particularly their effects on conscious awareness, in Chapter 5.

endorphins

Morphine-like chemicals that act as the brain's natural painkillers

Many natural substances, such as coffee, curare, and the common groundcover St. John's wort, contain ingredients that affect the action of neurotransmitters.

CONCEPT SUMMARY

NEUROTRANSMITTERS AND THEIR EFFECTS

Neurotransmitter	Nature of Effect	Involved in
Dopamine	Generally inhibitory*	Dampening and stabilizing communication in the brain and elsewhere; helps ensure smooth motor function; plays a role in both schizophrenia and Parkinson's disease
Acetylcholine	Generally excitatory*	Communication between motor neurons and muscles in the body, leading to muscle contraction; may also play a role in Alzheimer's disease
Serotonin	Generally inhibitory*	Regulating sleep, dreaming, and general arousal; may also play a role in some psychological disorders, including depression
GABA	Generally inhibitory*	The regulation of anxiety; tranquillizing drugs act on GABA to decrease anxiety

Note: No neurotransmitter, on its own, is excitatory or inhibitory; the specific nature of a neurotransmitter's action depends on specific characteristics of the receiving cell's membrane.

The Communication Network

Up to this point, you've seen how information is transmitted electrically within a neuron, via the flow of charged ions that makes up an action potential, and how one neuron signals another through the release of chemical messengers. But the dynamics of activity within a neuron, and the way one neuron passes activation to another, are only small parts of the story. The nervous system consists of many millions of neurons, and billions upon billions of synaptic connections. No perception, thought, feeling, or action arises from the activation of a single neuron; rather, *patterns of activation* across large groups of interconnected neurons operating together underlie conscious experiences and complex behaviours. You may have heard claims to the effect that most people use only 10% of their brains, but this is a nonsensical myth: Everyone uses 100% of his or her brain (although some to greater effect than others!). It's the fine detail of how neurons are interconnected that, researchers believe, underlies what people can do with their brains. It is therefore necessary to pay attention to the specific ways in which neurons are interconnected.

Reflexes   As a first step toward understanding the role of neural interconnectivity, let's consider the mechanisms that give rise to the simplest form of neurally mediated behaviour, a **reflex.** If you inadvertently put your finger in a candle flame, you withdraw it very quickly, automatically. This action may not seem like much of an accomplishment, but it's obviously pretty important that organisms be able to do this sort of thing. Further, the problem is not as trivial as it may at first appear: Imagine trying to build a robot such that holding a match to any part of its body would cause it to very quickly jerk that part of its body away. What kinds of sensors and effectors would your robot need, and how, precisely, would you wire them all?

Here's how your body does it (see ❱ Figure 3.7). First, the flame stimulates sensory receptor neurons in your finger that are specialized to respond to pain, causing those cells to begin creating action potentials. Thus, a form of physical energy in the world (heat) is coded into the electrochemical language of the body. Those action potentials travel along the sensory cells' axons to specific sites in your spinal cord, where they synapse onto short interneurons in the spinal cord. The reflex is "wired" in such a way that when these interneurons receive activation they in turn pass activation directly to motor neurons with which they synapse. Moreover, the system is set up so that those motor neurons control muscles that effect movements of the body part from which the pain signals originated (i.e., the system "knows" the pain is in your right index finger rather than somewhere else

reflex

A largely automatic body movement, such as the knee jerk, that is controlled by a simple network of sensory neurons, interneurons in the spinal cord, and motor neurons

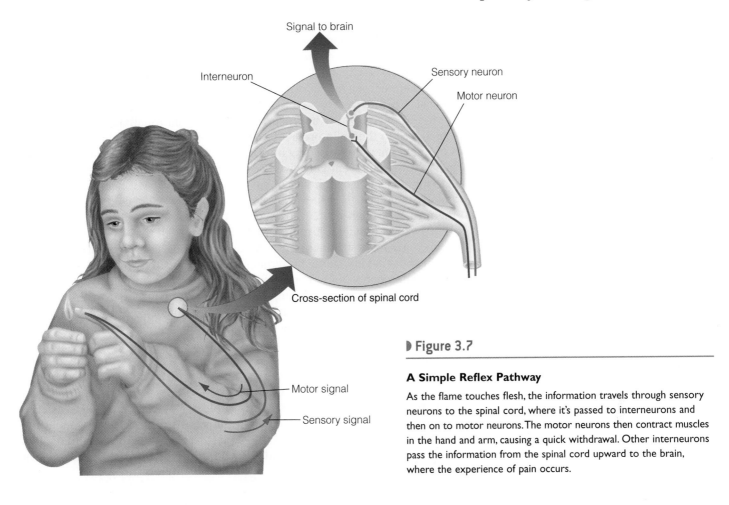

Signal to brain

Interneuron

Sensory neuron

Motor neuron

Cross-section of spinal cord

Motor signal

Sensory signal

▶ **Figure 3.7**

A Simple Reflex Pathway

As the flame touches flesh, the information travels through sensory neurons to the spinal cord, where it's passed to interneurons and then on to motor neurons. The motor neurons then contract muscles in the hand and arm, causing a quick withdrawal. Other interneurons pass the information from the spinal cord upward to the brain, where the experience of pain occurs.

in the body). The action potentials travel along the axon of the motor neurons from the spinal cord to the muscles of your hand and arm, causing those muscles to contract such that your hand quickly jerks away.

You may have noticed that the brain hasn't figured into our discussion of fingers and flames. This is because a reflex requires no input to or from the brain. The message normally *is* passed upward from the spinal cord to the brain via other interneurons, and it is in the brain that you consciously experience the heat of the flame, but the reflexive jerking away of your finger does not rely on the brain. If your spinal cord were cut near your neck, blocking communication between most of the body and brain, you wouldn't feel the pain or react with a facial grimace, but your hand would still twitch (although if you had been paralyzed for a long time the action would be greatly attenuated, partly because of muscle atrophy). Reflex pathways allow the body to respond very quickly to environmental events in a simple and direct way. We don't think or feel with our spinal cords, but reflex pathways are an important part of our ability to adapt successfully to the world.

Neural Plasticity   Of course, reflexes make up only a tiny fraction of human behaviour, and the sorts of psychological events that most people find especially interesting are driven primarily by the brain. Nonetheless, reflexes illustrate two key points. First, even the simplest behaviours (e.g., reflexes) require more than the operation of a single neuron; they require an interconnected system of neurons. More complex behaviours involve even more extensive collaborations of large numbers of neurons. Second, the effect of a given neuron depends largely on which other neurons and organs it synapses with. For example, what makes an interneuron an interneuron is that it receives activation from and sends activation

CRITICAL   THINKING

A reflex is a type of adaptive behaviour that does not arise directly from activity of the brain. If you were building a body from scratch, what types of reflexes would you build in and why?

to other neurons, rather than receiving activation from the external environment or sending it to muscles, glands, or other organs. More specifically, what makes a particular interneuron code information about, say, pain in the right index finger, is the fact that it synapses with pain-specialized receptor cells from the right index finger and with other neurons that control reactions to pain.

The same is true (but in a more indirect and complex way) when it comes to the brain. For example, the interneurons that carry information about pain from the spinal cord to the brain project to and synapse with other cells in specialized areas of the brain, thereby coding information about the location and intensity of the pain in ways that eventually give rise (through mechanisms that remain mysterious) to the subjective experience of being burned. This is why neuroscientists are particularly interested in discovering how neurons are connected to one another and the means through which those connections can be modified by experience (Hebb, 1949/2002; Kandel, 1991; Shaw & McEachern, 2001).

When you learn new things (e.g., right now, we hope!) the physical structure of your brain shifts in very subtle but crucial ways as the strength and even patterns of synaptic interconnections change to implement the new knowledge. If you have the misfortune to damage your brain, cellular processes will work toward repairing the damage; depending on the nature and extent of the damage, the recovery may not be complete, but recent evidence shows that the brain is better able to repair itself than once was thought. **Neural plasticity,** or the ability of neural systems to change and repair themselves, has been extensively studied by University of Lethbridge neuropsychologist Bryan Kolb and his co-workers. Kolb has conducted numerous studies of changes in the brains of rats as a consequence of experience or during recovery from brain damage (e.g., Kolb, 2004). Neural plasticity is at its greatest early in development—the brain of the fetus and newborn is wonderfully flexible and adaptable—but some degree of plasticity remains throughout life. For research on rehabilitation programs that foster recovery from brain damage, see Sohlberg and Mateer (2001) and Stuss, Winocur, and Robertson (1999).

CRITICAL   THINKING

Does it bother you when researchers generalize the results of studies of rats to humans? If so, does it also bother you that the basic principles of genetics were initially derived from studies of pea plants?

neural plasticity

Ability of neurons to alter synaptic connections during learning and during recovery from brain injury

---

Test Yourself 3.1

Test your knowledge about neurons and how they communicate. Select your answers from the following list of terms: dendrites, soma, axon, sensory, terminal buttons, spinal cord, action potential, interneurons, neurotransmitters, motor, refractory period. (The answers are in Appendix B.)

1. The main body of the cell, where excitatory and inhibitory messages combine: _____

2. The long tail-like part of a neuron that serves as the cell's main transmitter device: _____

3. The all-or-none electrical signal that travels to the end of the axon, causing the release of chemical messengers: _____

4. The branchlike fibres that extend outward from a neuron and receive information from other neurons: _____

5. Acetylcholine, serotonin, GABA, and dopamine are all examples of _____.

6. In a reflex response, _____ neurons carry information about a stimulus (such as intense heat) to the _____, where they synapse onto _____ neurons, which in turn synapse with _____ neurons that stimulate muscles to contract.

PRACTICAL SOLUTIONS

BETTER THINKING THROUGH CHEMISTRY?

Wouldn't it be great if you could take a pill that would make it easy for you to understand and remember the contents of this textbook? Because the brain operates electrochemically, it is plausible that there are drugs that can enhance its functioning, making users smarter, faster, and more retentive thinkers. And you've probably seen ads on TV and other media that make just such claims. Often, the attractiveness of the advertised substance is further enhanced by describing it as completely "natural." According to a 2005 Health Canada survey, 77% of Canadians believe that natural health products can be used to promote health. To take a case in point, an extract made from the leaves of the Ginkgo biloba tree has been touted as a natural and effective way to improve memory. Advertising has succeeded in making Ginkgo a big seller. Sales of Ginkgo were in the millions of dollars in 1999. Of course, it's a bargain at any price if the drug dramatically enhances memory.

As you may recall from Chapter 2, the best way to test the effectiveness of a drug or other experimental treatment is to conduct a double-blind, placebo-controlled experiment. In such an experiment, some subjects receive the drug and others receive an inert pill that looks and tastes identical to the drug, with neither the subjects nor the person administering the experiment knowing which subjects receive the drug and which receive the placebo. Several such experiments have assessed the effects of Ginkgo on human memory, but the results are mixed.

Wesnes, Ward, McGinty, and Petrini (2000) conducted what appears to be the first large double-blind, placebo-controlled study to yield clear evidence of the positive effects of Ginkgo (combined with ginseng) on memory-test performance. This study involved 256 healthy middle-aged volunteers who took the drug (or a placebo) daily

Some studies indicate that Ginkgo biloba may live up to its popular reputation as a memory enhancer. Unfortunately, other studies suggest it has no such effects.

Mitch Hrdlicka/PhotoDisc/Getty Images

for 12 weeks. Small but statistically significant effects were found on several measures of memory. Similarly, a study by Strough, Clarke, Lloyd, and Nathan (2001) involved 61 volunteers who took either Ginkgo or a placebo over a 30-day period. Statistically significant benefits of Ginkgo were found on tests of the speed and flexible control of mental processing.

The Wesnes and Strough findings are encouraging, and some other studies likewise reported beneficial effects of Ginkgo (e.g., Mix & Crews, 2002). Support seems to be particularly strong for beneficial effects among seniors who have age-related cognitive impairments (see Beaubrun & Gray, 2000, for a review). Unfortunately, however, a number of studies also reported null effects. For example, Moulton, Boyko, Fitzpatrick, and Petros (2001) tested 30 healthy young men who took Ginkgo or a placebo daily for five days and then completed a variety of standardized memory tests. They found no difference between the groups. An obvious criticism of this study is that five days may simply not be long enough for effects to be detected. The Moulton study also had a relatively small sample, and all subjects were young. However, a study by

Solomon, Adams, Silver, Zimmer, and DeVeaux (2002) tested 230 subjects, all over the age of 60, who took Ginkgo or a placebo for six weeks. Despite the large sample of people in an age group who might be expected particularly to benefit from a memory enhancer, no reliable benefits of Ginkgo were observed in this study. Similarly, van Dongen, van Rossum, Kessels, Sielhorst, and Knipschild (2000) tested 123 elderly individuals with dementia or age-associated memory impairments, with subjects randomly selected to receive either a placebo or Ginkgo daily over a 12-week period; the results did not support the efficacy of Ginkgo as a memory treatment. Likewise, neither Elsabagh, Hartley, Ali, Williamson, and File (2005) nor Nathan et al. (2004) found evidence that regularly taking Ginkgo enhances memory.

What are we to make of these results? On the one hand, it's possible that the experiments supporting the efficacy of Ginkgo biloba were flawed by undetected confounds or that the results were merely chance (see Chapter 2). On the other hand, it may be that Ginkgo has beneficial effects, but those effects are small, occur only in some people, or occur only under particular conditions. In any case, two things are sure. One is that Ginkgo does not have dramatic memory-enhancing effects for most people. The other is that further research is needed. Those same two conclusions also hold for other substances promoted and sold as sure-fire ways to increase intelligence or bolster memory. Many neuroscientists are optimistic that drugs eventually will be developed that improve mental functions, such as memory. Our recommendation, however, is to wait until solid scientific evidence supports the efficacy and safety of such substances before buying and trying them (and also to consult a physician before taking such supplements, as some can have dangerous side effects, especially when combined with other drugs).

The Nervous System: Processing Information and Controlling Behaviour

LEARNING GOALS

1. Know the basic organization of the nervous system.
2. Become familiar with some of the techniques that researchers use to study the brain.
3. Be able to describe the major structures of the brain and the functions associated with each structure.
4. Learn how the two hemispheres divide and coordinate brain functions.

The nervous system has many complex problems to solve through its communication network of neurons. In addition to generating physical behaviours and mental processes, such as thinking and feeling, the brain keeps constant track of more basic things, such as maintaining a beating heart, controlling breathing, and signalling the body that it's time to eat. If your body is deprived of food or water, or if its internal temperature changes, something must motivate you to seek sustenance or shelter. Moreover, even the most common everyday activities—speaking, walking, seeing—require a great deal of coordination between the muscles and sensory organs of the body. To accomplish such different functions, the nervous system divides its labour.

The Central and Peripheral Nervous Systems

As explained at the beginning of the chapter, the nervous system is divided into two major parts: the central nervous system and the peripheral nervous system. The central nervous system, consisting of the brain and spinal cord, acts as the central executive of the body. Decisions are made here, and messages are then communicated to the rest of the body through bundles of axons called **nerves.** The nerves outside the brain and spinal cord form the peripheral nervous system.

It is through the peripheral nervous system that muscles are moved, internal organs are regulated, and sensory input is moved toward the brain. As you can see in ❭ Figure 3.8, the peripheral nervous system is further subdivided into the *somatic* and *autonomic systems*. Information travels toward the brain and spinal cord through *afferent* (sensory) nerve pathways; *efferent* (motor) nerve pathways carry central nervous system messages outward to the muscles and glands. The **somatic system** consists of the nerves that transmit sensory information toward the brain as well as the nerves that connect to the skeletal muscles to initiate movement. Without the somatic system, information about the environment could not reach the brain, and we could not move voluntarily. The **autonomic system** controls the more automatic needs of the body, such as heart rate, digestion, blood pressure, and the activities of glands. These two systems work together to ensure that information about the world is communicated to the brain for interpretation, movements are carried out, and the life-sustaining internal activities of the body are performed.

One critical function of the autonomic system, besides performing the automatic "housekeeping" activities that keep the body alive, is to support the body's ability to handle and recover from emergency situations. The **sympathetic system** is a division of the autonomic system that helps the body respond to emergencies by triggering the release of chemicals that put it into a state of readiness to act quickly and vigorously (such as by increasing heart rate, blood pressure, and breathing rate). After the emergency has passed, the **parasympathetic system,** another division of the autonomic nervous system, calms the body down by slowing the heart rate and lowering the blood pressure. Parasympathetic activity also helps increase the body's supply of stored energy that may have been depleted as a result of dealing with an emergency situation.

nerves

Bundles of axons that make up neural "transmission cables"

somatic system

Nerves that transmit information from sensory organs to the brain, and from the brain to the skeletal muscles; part of the peripheral nervous system

autonomic system

Nerves that control the more automatic needs of the body, such as heart rate, digestion, blood pressure, and so on; part of the peripheral nervous system

sympathetic system

The division of the autonomic nervous system that helps the body respond to emergencies

parasympathetic system

The division of the autonomic nervous system that helps the body calm down

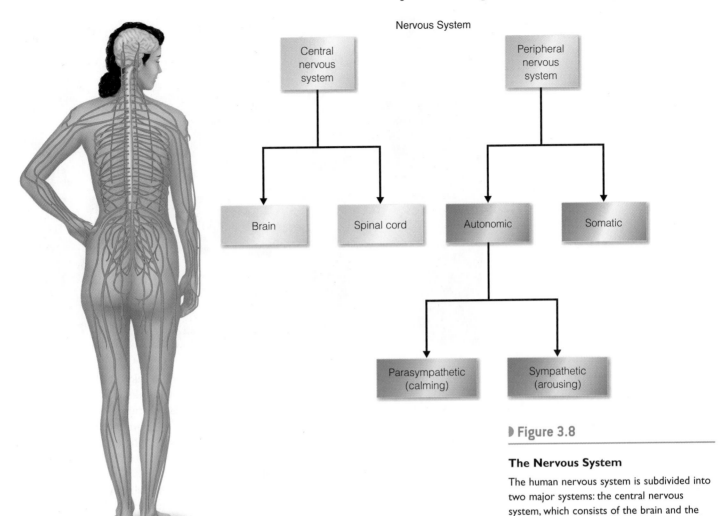

▶ **Figure 3.8**

The Nervous System

The human nervous system is subdivided into two major systems: the central nervous system, which consists of the brain and the spinal cord, and the peripheral nervous system, which includes the somatic system and the autonomic system. (Based on Kalat, 1996.)

Research Techniques for Exploring Brain Function

Before we embark on a detailed examination of the structure and function of the brain, let's consider some techniques that researchers use to explore what functions the different parts of the brain serve. The anatomical features of the nervous system as a whole—the various nerve tracts and so on—can be studied through dissection of the body. But the dissection of brain tissue, which contains billions of neurons, tells only a limited story. For one thing, when a brain is dissected, it no longer works, which makes it difficult to determine the relationship between particular structures and particular functions. To understand the brain, researchers need to draw on a broader set of tools. We'll briefly consider three general techniques: (1) the study of brain damage from injury or disease, (2) methods that allow the researcher to stimulate the living brain directly, and (3) methods that allow researchers to monitor the brain in action.

Brain Damage Studying individuals with brain damage is one of the oldest methods for investigating brain function. A patient with some specific localized region of damage—such as from a blow to the right side of the head—typically complains of a particular problem, such as trouble moving the left side of his or her body. This suggests a link between a brain area and a behaviour or function. By the middle of the nineteenth century, it was known that damage to specific areas on the left side of the brain creates distinct patterns of linguistic difficulties. Destruction

Researcher Cindy Bukach (left) demonstrates some of the tests used to detect brain damage in Professor Daniel Bub's laboratory at the University of Victoria.

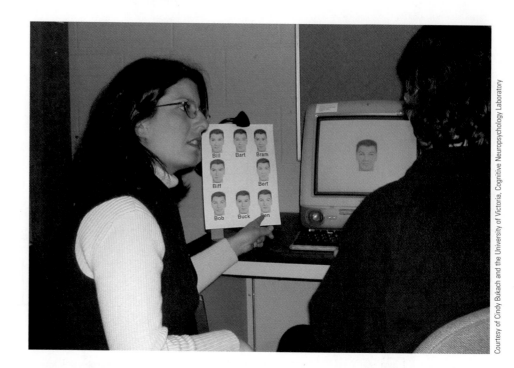

Courtesy of Cindy Bukach and the University of Victoria, Cognitive Neuropsychology Laboratory

of *Wernicke's area* results in a patient who speaks very quickly and incoherently and who cannot easily understand spoken language (Wernicke, 1874); damage to *Broca's area* results in a patient who can understand others' speech but whose own speech is very slow, halting, and effortful (Broca, 1861). Damage to other brain regions causes other problems (e.g., damage to the hippocampus can cause amnesia). Such cases suggest that particular psychological and behavioural functions are controlled by specific areas of the brain.

Unfortunately, relying on case studies of people who accidentally sustain brain damage has its limitations. For one thing, researchers must wait for the specific injury of interest to present itself for their inspection. Also, most instances of brain damage, either from an accident, a tumour, or a stroke, produce very general and widespread damage, making it difficult to know exactly which portion of the damaged brain is responsible for particular behavioural or psychological problems. Furthermore, it is difficult to determine the precise areas and extent of brain damage without performing an autopsy. Finally, as we saw in Chapter 2, case studies can be rich sources of information, but the researcher typically lacks important controls (e.g., an individual who sustains brain damage may have differed from most people even before the damage occurred).

To establish a structure-function relationship, it is necessary to observe in a controlled way the effects of systematic and localized removal of tissue. Researchers have used surgical techniques to explore brain function in lower animals, particularly rats. It's possible to destroy, or *lesion*, particular regions of an animal's brain by administering an electric current, injecting chemicals, or cutting tissue. Even here it is often difficult to pinpoint the damage exactly (because everything in the brain is interconnected), but lesioning techniques have become increasingly accurate in recent years. Some chemicals, for example, can selectively damage specific kinds of neurons in the brain without damaging neighbouring nerve pathways (Bergvall, Fahlke, & Hansen, 1996; Jarrad, 1993). The lesioning procedure is then followed by controlled examination of the animal's behaviour to see how it is affected. As discussed in Chapter 2, damaging animals' brains raises many ethical questions, but such research has provided much valuable information regarding brain functioning (e.g., Arvanitogiannis, Riscaldino, & Shizgal, 1999; Barnes, Floresco, Kornecook, & Pinel, 2000; Ellard, 2000; Mumby, Glenn, Nesbitt, & Kyriazis, 2002; Whishaw, Hines, & Wallace, 2001).

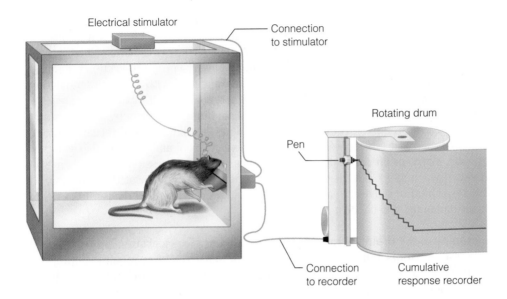

Electrical Stimulation

A rat presses a bar and a small pulse of electric current is delivered to the brain. Stimulation of certain brain areas appears quite rewarding to the rat, leading it to press the bar at a very rapid rate.

Talking to the Brain   It is also possible to "talk" to the brain directly by capitalizing on the electrochemical nature of the communication network. Essentially, neural activity can be induced artificially. One means of doing this is to inject chemicals that excite neurons in a particular area of the brain. Alternatively, researchers can insert tiny wire electrodes into brain tissue, allowing an area's cells to be stimulated electrically.

Electrical stimulation techniques have been used primarily with animals. It's possible to implant an electrode in ways that allow an animal to move freely about in its environment (see ▶ Figure 3.9). A small pulse of current can then be delivered to various brain regions whenever the researcher desires. Studies have shown that electrical brain stimulation can cause animals to suddenly start eating, drinking, engaging in sexual behaviour, or preparing for an attack, with the response depending primarily on what brain area is stimulated. In a classic study conducted at McGill University, researchers stimulated specific areas of rats' brains with electricity and found that certain areas in the brain act as pleasure centres, leading the rat to engage repeatedly in whatever behaviour led to the stimulation (Olds & Milner, 1954). For example, if rats are taught that pressing a metal bar leads to electrical stimulation of a reward area, they will press the bar thousands of times an hour.

The electrical stimulation technique is often used by researchers to link behaviour to patterns of activity in specific areas in the brain. For example, a behaviour that is produced by stimulation of brain region X but not by stimulation of brain region Y suggests that region X plays some role in the overall behaviour. Nonetheless, the precise mapping of behaviours to brain locations remains a difficult task. It is always possible to argue, for example, that a stimulated area is required to produce a particular behaviour but that it does not act alone—it might serve only as a communication link, or relay connection, to some other brain region that plays a bigger role in initiating and controlling the behaviour.

Famed neurosurgeon Wilder Penfield, working at the Montreal Neurological Institute at McGill University, developed what became known as the "Montreal procedure" for mapping the functions of specific areas of the human brain. During brain surgery (performed to treat a serious health problem, such as epileptic seizures), the patient was kept awake and the brain was stimulated with a tiny electrode. The primary purpose of the procedure was to determine the functions of particular brain areas before deciding whether or not to remove those areas to treat or correct the disorder. The procedure also revealed interesting things about the functions of the brain. Electrical stimulation under these conditions caused patients to produce involuntary movement, hear buzzing noises, and in some rare instances experience what they reported to be memories (Penfield & Perot, 1963).

Neurosurgeon Wilder Penfield established the Montreal Neurological Institute at McGill University and pioneered open brain stimulation techniques with human patients that helped establish the function of specific areas of the brain.

transcranial magnetic stimulation (TMS)

Powerful pulses of magnetic energy applied to the scalp stimulate action potentials in regions of the cortex; behavioural responses cast light on the function of the stimulated brain region

electroencephalograph (EEG)

A device used to monitor the electrical activity of the brain by measuring tiny changes in the electrical fields on the scalp

Direct electrical stimulation of brain tissue is a difficult and invasive procedure. An alternative method is known as **transcranial magnetic stimulation (TMS)**. In TMS, an electrical coil pressed to the scalp creates powerful magnetic pulses over the brain area of interest, causing the neurons in that area to propagate action potentials. Researchers can then observe the behaviours associated with action potentials in a particular brain area. For example, stimulating one area might cause the subject to move his or her right hand, whereas stimulating another area might lead the person to "see" a flash of red light. Although this technique is still quite new, research to date demonstrates that it has potential both as a research tool and perhaps also as a therapeutic intervention for, among other things, major depression (although a 2005 review by Jennifer Couturier, of the Department of Psychiatry at the University of Western Ontario, suggests that TMS is not as effective in treating depression as clinicians had initially believed it to be).

Listening to the Brain   Brain lesioning and direct electrical stimulation are effective research tools, but they are *invasive* in the sense that they require making contact with (or even destroying) actual brain tissue. Transcranial magnetic stimulation is less invasive than the other two techniques, and studies indicate that the procedure is safe, but some people might nonetheless be reluctant to undergo it. Fortunately, other techniques can eavesdrop on the brain without affecting brain functioning.

The **electroencephalograph (EEG)** is a device that monitors some of the electrical activity of the brain. Recording electrodes attached to the scalp measure global changes in the electrical potentials of many thousands of brain cells, representing those changes in the form of line tracings (brain waves). That is, the electrode picks up increases (or decreases) in the rate at which neurons near the electrode "fire" or have action potentials. The EEG is useful not only as a research tool (e.g., Bischof & Boulanger, 2003; Doucet & Stelmack, 1999) but also for diagnostic purposes (Barcelo & Gale, 1997; Connolly & D'Arcy, 2000). Brain disorders, including psychological dis-

Developmental neuropsychologist Sid Segalowitz of Brock University and a subject are shown here using an event-related potential (ERP) apparatus.

Courtesy of Professor Sid Segalowitz

orders and brain seizures, can sometimes be detected through abnormalities in brain waves (Lee, 1998; Sponheim, Clementz, Iacono, & Beiser, 1994). Most researchers who use EEG do so in the context of **event-related potentials (ERP)**: A computer is used to time-lock changes in the EEG to computer-presented stimuli (events), allowing researchers to produce graphs depicting the average increases and decreases in the amount of electrochemical activity in the cortex shortly after a stimulus is presented. For example, if the same stimulus (say, a picture of a cat) is presented over and over again, and then a different stimulus (e.g., a picture of a bottle) is presented, the amount of cortical neural activity in response to the repeated stimulus gradually declines across repetitions and sharply increases about 300 milliseconds after the appearance of the "oddball" stimulus (see Regan, 1981).

A detailed picture of the brain's anatomical structures, including abnormalities in brain tissue, can be obtained through a **computerized tomography scan (CT scan)**. CT scanners use computers to detect how highly focused beams of X-rays change as they pass through the body at various angles and orientations. CT scanners are most often used by physicians to detect tumours or injuries to the brain, but they can also be used to determine whether there is a physical basis for a chronic behavioural or psychological disorder.

Other imaging devices are designed to obtain a snapshot of the active brain at work. These techniques help the researcher determine how various tasks, such as reading, involve particular parts of the brain. In **positron emission tomography (PET)**, the patient ingests a harmless radioactive substance, which is absorbed into the cells of brain regions that are metabolically active. When the person performs a specific kind of task, such as speaking or reading, the active areas of the brain absorb more of the ingested radioactive material. The PET scanner reveals which brain regions are more versus less active during performance of a particular task. It is assumed that the parts of the brain with the most concentrated traces of radioactive material probably play significant roles in the task that the subject is performing. For example, Cabeza, Locantore, and Anderson (2003) used PET to measure which areas of the brain were particularly active as research participants performed various kinds of memory tasks.

Another technique that can be used to assess both structure and function in the brain is **magnetic resonance imaging (MRI)**. MRI is capable of producing extremely detailed, three-dimensional images of the brain. MRI technology capitalizes on the fact that atoms behave in systematic ways in the presence of magnetic fields and radio-wave pulses. Although expensive to build and use, MRIs have proven to be excellent diagnostic tools for spotting brain damage, tumour growth, and other abnormalities.

Perhaps the most sophisticated brain-imaging technique is *functional magnetic resonance imaging (fMRI)*. fMRI produces a very detailed map of the blood oxygen levels in the brain. More active areas use more oxygen, so this map is used to infer which areas of the brain are particularly important in performance of various tasks. fMRI has been used to identify brain regions associated with visual processing, visual imaging, language, attention, and memory (Gabrieli, 1998; Schacter, Norman, & Koutstaal, 1998). For example, Schacter (2001) reported fMRI evidence that brain activities differ when a person is experiencing a false memory (i.e., remembering something that hadn't really occurred) versus an accurate memory. As another example, there has recently been an explosion of interest in "social neuroscience," in which researchers use brain-imaging technologies, like fMRI, to explore issues in social psychology, such as prejudice, interpersonal attraction, or emotional evaluation (Cacioppo, Berntson, Sheridan, & McClintock, 2000; Cunningham, Raye, & Johnson, 2004).

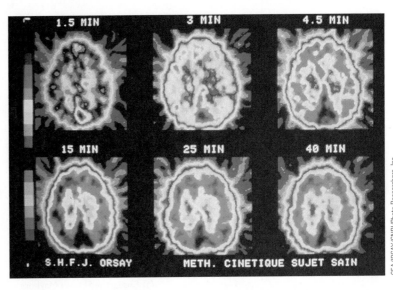

CEA/IRSAY/CNRI/Photo Researchers, Inc.

A series of eight PET scans demonstrates how a harmless radioactive substance is absorbed into the cells of active brain regions.

event-related potentials (ERP)

EEG patterns observed shortly after presentation of a stimulus

computerized tomography scan (CT scan)

The use of highly focused beams of X-rays to construct detailed anatomical maps of the living brain

positron emission tomography (PET)

A method for measuring how radioactive substances are absorbed in the brain; it can be used to detect how different tasks activate different areas of the living brain

magnetic resonance imaging (MRI)

A device that uses magnetic fields and radio-wave pulses to construct detailed, three-dimensional images of the brain

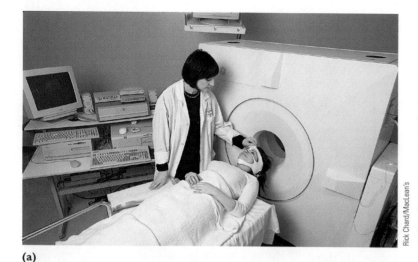

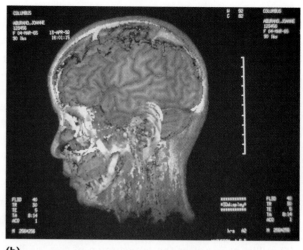

(a)   (b)

(a) Researcher Helen Mayberg of the Rotman Research Institute at the University of Toronto assists a patient undergoing an MRI procedure. The MRI is capable of providing information on both structure and function in the brain. (b) MRIs produce extremely detailed images of the brain and are therefore excellent diagnostic tools for spotting damage, tumour growth, and other physical abnormalities.

The interpretation of data from brain-imaging studies is not as straightforward as is sometimes implied (e.g., Bub, 2000). For example, when a particular brain area is more active during performance of one task than another task, there is room to debate what components of the tasks lead to the difference. Nonetheless, wide agreement exists that brain-imaging techniques are very useful tools and they are rapidly changing our understanding of the basic mechanisms of the brain and mind.

CONCEPT SUMMARY

BRAIN INVESTIGATION TECHNIQUES

Technique	Overview	What Can It Show?
Brain damage	Associates areas of brain damage with changes in behavioural function	Areas of the brain that may be partly responsible for different functions
Electrical brain stimulation	Uses direct electrical or chemical stimulation to excite brain areas	How activation of certain brain regions affects behaviour
Transcranial magnetic stimulation (TMS)	Uses a magnetic coil pressed to the scalp to excite brain areas	How activation of certain brain regions affects behaviour
Electroencephalograph (EEG)	Uses electrodes on the scalp to record gross electrical activity of the brain	How overall activity in the brain changes during certain activities, such as sleeping; may allow for detection of disorders
Event-related potentials (ERP)	Time-locks EEG records to computer-presented stimuli	How brain activity changes in response to particular kinds of stimuli (events)
Computerized tomography (CT) scan	Passes X-rays through the body at various angles and orientations	The location of tumours or injuries to the brain, as well as the structural bases for chronic behavioural or psychological disorders
Positron emission tomography (PET)	Uses an ingested radioactive substance, absorbed by active brain areas; uses a PET scanner to reveal distribution of the substance	How various tasks (such as reading) involve different parts of the brain
Magnetic resonance imaging (MRI)	Monitors systematic activity of atoms in the presence of magnetic fields and radio-wave impulses	A three-dimensional view of the brain, revealing which brain regions are involved in particular tasks and serving as a diagnostic tool for brain abnormalities, such as tumours

Brain Structures and Their Functions

Having discussed some of the research tools that scientists use to map brain structure and function, let's now turn our attention to the brain itself. Mental processes arise in the brain through the simultaneous activities of billions of densely interconnected individual neurons. Particular regions in the brain underlie unique aspects of an experience, collectively creating a psychological whole. Thus, your perception of a cat is not controlled by a single cell, or even by a single group of cells, but rather by different brain areas—each made of huge numbers of neurons—that detect the form, colour, texture, and movement of the beast, recognize a characteristic meow, and generate the expectation that the cat will saunter into the room because you just put down the food dish. As discussed earlier, knowledge about which brain areas perform particular mental functions comes, in part, from studies of patients with damage to specific parts of the brain. For instance, a patient might lose knowledge about living things but not about inanimate things (Dixon, Bub, & Arguin, 1997), or a person might lose the ability to see moving objects but not objects that are stationary (Goodale & Westwood, 2004).

Our discussion of the brain is divided into sections that correspond to the brain's three major anatomical regions: the *hindbrain*, the *midbrain*, and the *forebrain*. Please note that (unfortunately for students) different brain scientists use different terms for the various brain regions. Your professor (or professors in other classes) may prefer other terms. We've selected terms that we think are relatively easy to grasp and remember.

The Hindbrain: Basic Life Support   The **hindbrain,** which is the most primitive part of the brain, sits at the juncture where the spinal cord and brain merge (see ▶ Figure 3.10). "Primitive" is an appropriate term for two reasons. First, structures in the hindbrain control the basic life-support system for the body—no creative thoughts or complex emotions originate here. Second, from the standpoint of evolution, the hindbrain is the oldest part of the brain. Similar structures, with similar functions, can be found throughout the animal kingdom. You can think of the hindbrain as a kind of

hindbrain

A primitive part of the brain that sits at the juncture where the brain and spinal cord merge; structures in the hindbrain, including the medulla, pons, and reticular formation, control the basic life-support systems of the body

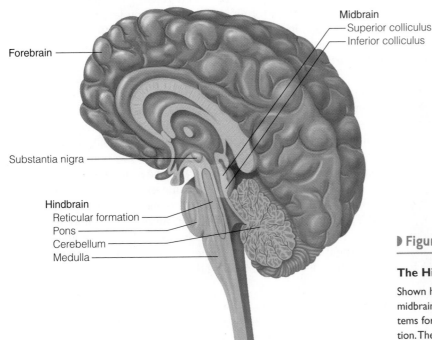

▶ **Figure 3.10**

The Hindbrain and Midbrain

Shown here are the various structures of the human hindbrain and midbrain. The hindbrain (blue) controls the basic life-support systems for the body, such as heart rate, blood pressure, and respiration. The midbrain (orange) relays some of the information from the spinal cord to higher brain regions.

base camp, with higher structures situated farther up into the brain controlling increasingly complex mental processes. Not surprisingly, damage to the hindbrain seriously compromises the ability of the organism to survive.

As you can see in Figure 3.10, the hindbrain contains several distinct anatomical substructures. The *medulla* and the *pons* are associated with the control of heart rate, breathing, blood pressure, and reflexes, such as vomiting, sneezing, and coughing. Both areas serve as pathways for neural impulses travelling to and from the spinal cord (the word *pons* means "bridge"). These areas are particularly sensitive to the ill effects of drugs, such as alcohol, barbiturates, and cocaine.

The hindbrain also contains the *reticular formation*, a network of nerves linked to the control of general arousal, sleep, and possibly certain movements of the head (Robbins, 1997). Damage to the reticular formation can lead to the loss of consciousness. Finally, at the base of the brain sits a structure that in general appearance resembles a smaller version of the brain. This is the **cerebellum** (which means "little brain"), a structure involved in the preparation, selection, and coordination of complex motor movements, such as hitting a golf ball, playing the piano, or writing (Yamaguchi, Tsuchiya, & Koboyashi, 1998). No one is certain about the exact role the cerebellum plays in movement—it may help guide movement through the integration of sensory information—but it clearly serves a vital function. The cerebellum may be involved in other functions as well; for instance, evidence suggests that the cerebellum becomes active during language, memory, and reasoning tasks (Schmahmann & Sherman, 1998), and Salman (2002) summarized evidence that the cerebellum may also be involved in timing neural processes.

The Midbrain: Neural Relay Stations

The **midbrain,** which lies deep within the brain atop the hindbrain, is enveloped by other structures that make up the forebrain. Perhaps because of its central position, the midbrain and its accompanying structures receive input from multiple sources, including the sense organs. The *tectum* and its component structures, the *superior colliculus* and *inferior colliculus*, serve as important relay stations for visual and auditory information and help coordinate reactions to sensory events in the environment (such as moving the head in response to a sudden sound).

The midbrain also contains a group of neurons, collectively called the *substantia nigra*, which release the neurotransmitter dopamine from their terminal buttons. As you learned earlier in the chapter, dopamine tends to produce inhibitory effects in the body, and it seems to be involved in a number of physical and psychological disorders (e.g., schizophrenia and Parkinson's disease). There is evidence that Parkinson's disease is caused by the death of neurons in the substantia nigra (Jenner, 1990; Keller & Rueda, 1998; Mendez, Baker, & Hong, 2000). Exactly why this portion of the midbrain degenerates in Parkinson's patients is not known, although environmental toxins may be contributors (Kuhn et al., 1998).

A number of important developments in the understanding and treatment of Parkinson's-like disorders have resulted from investigating the substantia nigra. A disturbing example comes from some recreational drug users who mistakenly ingested a substance called MPTP, which destroys the substantia nigra. Their minds remained active, but they lost the ability to speak and to move about freely. This tragic accident proved to be of great value to researchers of Parkinson's disease. By studying these individuals, researchers were

cerebellum

A hindbrain structure at the base of the brain that is involved in the coordination of complex motor skills (e.g., walking, throwing) and may contribute to the performance of other tasks as well

midbrain

The middle portion of the brain, containing such structures as the tectum, superior colliculus, and inferior colliculus; structures serve as neural relay stations and may help coordinate reactions to sensory events

Neuroscientist Sandra Witelson of McMaster University has conducted extensive research on the relationship between human brain anatomy and human behaviour. She is shown here with part of her collection of more than one hundred human brains.

able to confirm the link between the production of dopamine in the substantia nigra and the rigidity of movement that characterizes Parkinson's disease. It has even been possible to mimic Parkinson's disease in animals through the administration of MPTP (Schneider, Sun, & Roeltgen, 1994).

The Forebrain: Higher Mental Functioning   Moving up past the midbrain, we encounter the **forebrain** (see ❱ Figure 3.11). The most recognizable feature of the forebrain is the **cerebral cortex,** the greyish matter full of fissures, folds, and crevices that covers the outside of the brain (*cortex* is the Latin word for "bark"). The cortex is quite large in humans; it accounts for approximately 80% of the total volume of the human brain (Kolb & Whishaw, 2002). We'll look at the cerebral cortex in depth after a review of the other structures of the forebrain.

Beneath the cerebral cortex are subcortical structures, including the thalamus, the hypothalamus, and the limbic system. The **thalamus** is positioned close to the midbrain, and it's an important gathering area for input from the various senses. Indeed, the thalamus is thought to be the main processing centre for sensory input before that information is sent out to areas in the upper regions of the cortex. Besides acting as an efficient relay centre, information from the various senses is probably combined here.

The **hypothalamus,** which lies just below the thalamus, is important in the regulation of eating, drinking, body temperature, and sexual behaviour. In experiments on lower animals, administering an electric current to different regions of the hypothalamus initiates a variety of behaviours. For example, male and female rats show characteristic sexual responses when one portion of the hypothalamus is stimulated (Marson & McKenna, 1994), whereas damage to another region of the hypothalamus can seriously affect eating behaviour (Sclafani, 1994). (Chapter 11 has more information about the neural basis of hunger.) The hypothalamus also plays a key role in the release of hormones by the pituitary gland; you'll read about the actions of hormones when we discuss the endocrine system later in this chapter.

The **limbic system** comprises several interrelated brain structures, including the amygdala and the hippocampus. The *amygdala* is a small, almond-shaped piece of brain (*amygdala* means "almond") that has been linked to a variety of motivational and emotional behaviours, including fear, aggression, and defensive behaviours (Aggleton, 1993; Davis & Lee, 1998). Destruction of portions of the amygdala in lower animals, through brain lesioning, can produce an extremely passive animal—one that will do nothing in response to provocation.

The *hippocampus* (Greek for "seahorse," which it crudely resembles in shape) plays a central role in the formation of memories (Milner, 2005). People with severe damage to the hippocampus sometimes live in a kind of perpetual present—they are aware of the world around them, and they recognize people and things known to them before the damage occurred, but they recall almost nothing new. These patients act as if they

---

forebrain

The outer portion of the brain, including the cerebral cortex and the structures of the limbic system

cerebral cortex

The outer layer of the brain, considered to be the seat of higher mental processes

thalamus

A relay station in the forebrain thought to be an important gathering point for input from the senses

hypothalamus

A forebrain structure thought to play a role in the regulation of various motivational activities, including eating, drinking, and sexual behaviour

limbic system

A system of structures thought to be involved in motivational and emotional behaviours (the amygdala) and memory (the hippocampus)

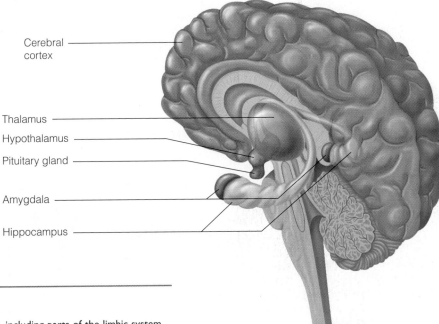

❱ **Figure 3.11**

The Forebrain

Shown here are the various structures of the forebrain, including parts of the limbic system and the cerebral cortex. Structures in the limbic system are thought to be involved in motivation, emotions, and memory. The cerebral cortex is the seat of higher mental processes.

Cerebral cortex
Thalamus
Hypothalamus
Pituitary gland
Amygdala
Hippocampus

are continually awakening from a dream; experiences slip away, and they recall nothing from only minutes before (Milner, Corkin, & Teuber, 1968). (We'll return to disturbances of this type, and memory loss in general, in Chapter 7.) It should also be noted that the limbic system is the site of most epileptic seizures (Wada, 1991).

The Cerebral Cortex   The cerebral cortex is considered the seat of the higher mental processes. Thoughts, the sense of self, reasoning—each arises primarily as a result of neurons firing in patterns in specialized regions of the cerebral cortex. The cortex of a young adult consists of about 20 billion neurons. It's been estimated that if all of your cortical neurons were laid end to end, they would stretch approximately 150 000 kilometres. But the number of neurons in the cortex is paltry compared with the number of synaptic connections, because each cortical neuron synapses with an average of around 7000 other neurons (Drachman, 2005). Patterns of electrochemical activity across these hundreds of trillions of synapses give rise to and constitute your experience of the world around you, and of your own internal states, and underlie your thinking, problem solving, and so on.

The cortex is divided into two *hemispheres*, left and right. The left hemisphere controls the sensory and motor functions for the right side of the body, and the right hemisphere controls these functions for the left side of the body. A structure called the *corpus callosum*, which we'll discuss later, serves as a communication bridge between the two hemispheres.

Each hemisphere can be further divided into four parts, or *lobes:* the *frontal, temporal, parietal,* and *occipital* lobes (see ❯ Figure 3.12). These lobes appear to control particular body functions, such as visual processing by the occipital lobe and language processing by the frontal and temporal lobes. However, although researchers have discovered that particular areas in the brain seem to control highly specialized functions, there is almost certainly considerable overlap of function in the brain. Most brain regions are designed to play multiple roles in helping us think, act, feel, and remember.

How can we possibly assign something like a "sense of self" to a specific area of the cerebral cortex? Once again, the evidence is primarily correlational—some portion of the cortex is damaged, or stimulated electrically, and behavioural changes are observed. We know, for example, that damage to the frontal lobe of the cerebral cortex can produce dramatic changes in personality. In 1850, a railroad foreman named Phineas Gage was packing explosive powder into a blasting hole when the powder accidentally discharged, driving a thick iron rod through the left side of his head (entering just below his left eye and exiting the left-top portion of

❯ **Figure 3.12**

The Cerebral Cortex

The cerebral cortex is divided into two hemispheres—left and right—and each hemisphere can be divided further into four parts, or lobes. The lobes are specialized to control particular functions, such as visual processing by the occipital lobe and language processing by the frontal and temporal lobes.

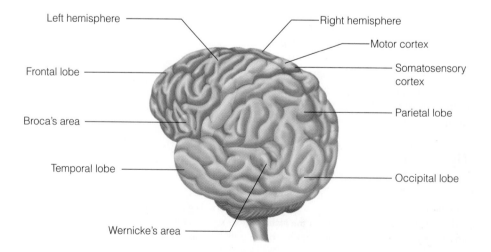

After a blasting accident substantially damaged the frontal lobe of Phineas Gage's brain, he was "no longer Gage" in the opinion of his friends and acquaintances.

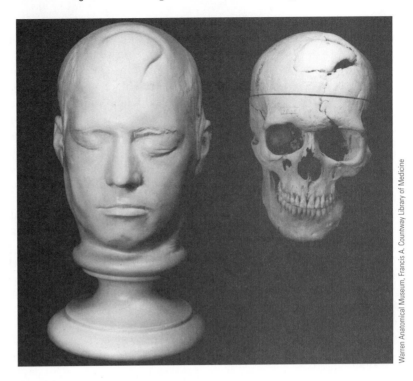

Warren Anatomical Museum, Francis A. Countway Library of Medicine

his skull). The result was a 7 cm hole in his skull and the complete shredding of a large portion of the left frontal lobe of his brain. Remarkably, Gage recovered, and with the exception of the loss of vision in his left eye and some slight facial paralysis, he was able to move about freely and perform a variety of tasks. But according to his friends and family he was "no longer Gage"; his personality had completely changed. Whereas before his injury he was known as "a shrewd businessman" with "a well-balanced mind," after the meeting of brain and iron he became "fitful, irreverent, indulging at times in the grossest profanity (which was not previously his custom)" (Bigelow, 1850).

The **frontal lobes** are the largest lobes in the cortex and are thought to be involved in a variety of functions, including planning and decision making, certain kinds of memory (particularly developing strategies for remembering), and personality (as our discussion of Phineas Gage indicated). The frontal lobes were once the site of a famous surgical operation, the prefrontal lobotomy, which was performed on people suffering from severe psychological disorders (before the development of modern psychopharmacological medications). The operation was performed to calm the patient and reduce symptoms, which it sometimes did, but the side effects were severe. Patients lost their ability to take initiative or make plans, and they often appeared to lose their social inhibitions (like Gage). For these reasons, the operation fell out of favour (see Valenstein, 1986, for a fascinating and accessible treatment of the history of lobotomy).

frontal lobes

One of four anatomical regions of each hemisphere of the cerebral cortex, located on the top front of the brain; contain the motor cortex and are involved in initiating higher-level thought processes

CONCEPT SUMMARY

BRAIN AREAS, STRUCTURES, AND FUNCTIONS

Brain Area	General Function	Structures and Specific Function
Hindbrain	Basic life support	**Medulla** and **pons**: associated with the control of heart rate, breathing, and certain reflexes **Reticular formation**: control of general arousal, sleep, and some movement of the head **Cerebellum**: involved in preparation, selection, and coordination of complex motor movement and likely other tasks as well
Midbrain	Neural relay stations	**Tectum** (components are **superior colliculus** and **inferior colliculus**): relay stations for visual and auditory information **Substantia nigra**: group of neurons that release the neurotransmitter dopamine and are involved in the control of movement
Forebrain	Higher mental functions	**Thalamus**: initial gathering point for sensory input; information combined and relayed here **Hypothalamus**: helps regulate eating, drinking, body temperature, and sexual behaviour **Amygdala** (part of **limbic system**): linked to fear, aggression, and defensive behaviours **Hippocampus** (part of **limbic system**): important to the formation of memories **Cerebral cortex**: the seat of higher mental processes, including sense of self and the ability to reason and solve problems

CRITICAL THINKING
Do you think it likely that personality is completely localized in a single region of the brain? What, exactly, would that brain region control?

parietal lobes

One of four anatomical regions of each hemisphere of the cerebral cortex, located roughly on the top middle portion of the brain; contain the somatosensory cortex, which controls the sense of touch

The frontal lobes also contain the *motor cortex*, which controls the initiation of voluntary muscle movements, as well as areas involved in language production and, possibly, higher-level thought processes (Baldo & Shimamura, 1998). Broca's area, which is involved in speech production, is located in a portion of the left frontal lobe in most people. The motor cortex sits at the rear of the frontal lobe in both hemispheres; axons from the motor cortex project down to motor neurons in the spinal cord and elsewhere. If neurons in this area of the brain are stimulated electrically, muscle contractions—the twitch of a finger or the jerking of a foot—can occur. Even more interesting, researchers have discovered an intriguing relation between body parts and regions of the motor cortex. It turns out that there is a mapping, or *topographic* organization, in which adjacent areas of the body, such as the hand and the wrist, are activated by neurons that sit next to each other in the motor cortex (Penfield & Boldrey, 1958).

This topographic organization is found in many regions of the cerebral cortex. For example, the **parietal lobes** contain the topographically organized somatosensory cortex, through which people experience the sensations of touch, temperature, and pain. Thus, the brush of a lover's kiss on the cheek excites neurons that lie close to neurons that would be excited by the same kiss to the lips. In addition, as ▶ Figure 3.13 demonstrates, a relationship exists

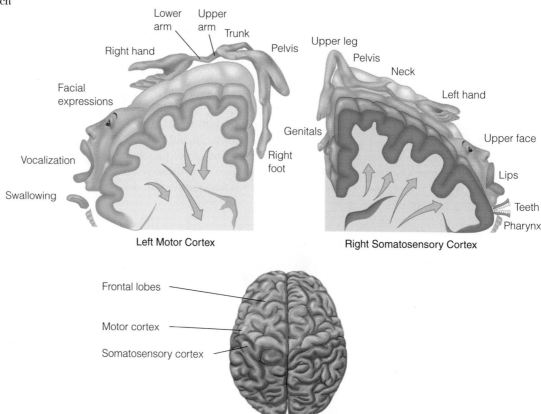

▶ **Figure 3.13**

Specialization in the Motor and Somatosensory Cortex

The motor cortex is located at the rear of the frontal lobes in each cerebral hemisphere. In a systematic body-to-brain relationship, adjacent parts of the body are activated by neurons in adjacent areas of the motor cortex. The somatosensory cortex, which controls the sense of touch, is located in the parietal lobes of each hemisphere; again, a systematic mapping arrangement exists. Notice that for each type of cortex, the size or amount of the representation relates to the degree of sensitivity or dexterity of the body part.

between sensitivity to touch (or the ability to control a movement) and the size of the representation in the cortex: Those areas of the body that show particular sensitivity to touch or are associated with fine motor control (such as the face, lips, and fingers) have relatively large areas of neural representation in the cortex.

The **temporal lobes,** which lie on both sides of the cortex, are involved in processing auditory information received from the ears. As you'll see in Chapter 4, a close relationship exists between the activities of particular neurons in the temporal lobe and the perception of sound. As noted earlier, one region of the temporal lobe, Wernicke's area, appears to play a large role in language comprehension (the ability to understand what someone is saying) as well as production. A person with damage to Wernicke's area might be able to repeat a spoken sentence aloud with perfect diction yet not understand a word of it. Converging evidence comes from brain-imaging studies revealing that Wernicke's area becomes active when people are asked to perform tasks that require meaningful verbal processing (Abdullaev & Posner, 1998). For most people, Wernicke's area is in the temporal lobe of the *left* cerebral hemisphere.

Finally, at the back of the brain sit the **occipital lobes,** where most visual processing occurs. We'll consider the organization of this part of the brain in more detail in Chapter 4; for now, recognize that it is here, in the far back of the brain, that the information received from receptor cells in the eyes is analyzed and turned into visual images. You have the perception of seeing these words on the page, but in a sense (so to speak!) the "seeing" is happening in the back of your brain. The brain represents the visual world through a remarkable division of labour—there appear to be separate processing stations in the occipital lobe designed to process colour, form, and motion independently (Shapley, 1990). Not surprisingly, damage to the occipital lobe tends to produce highly specific visual deficits—the person might lose the ability to recognize a face, a contour moving in a particular direction, or a colour (Goodale & Westwood, 2004).

The Divided Brain

Nowhere is the division of labour in the brain more evident than in the study of the two separate halves, or hemispheres, that make up the cerebral cortex. Although the brain is designed to operate as a functional whole, the hemispheres are *lateralized*, which means that each side has primary responsibility for performing different functions (Hellige, 1990). As you've seen, the right hemisphere of the brain controls the movements and sensations of the left side of the body, whereas the left hemisphere handles the body's right side: Stimulating a region of the motor cortex in the left cerebral hemisphere would cause a muscle on the right side of the body to twitch. Similarly, if cells in the occipital lobe of the right cerebral hemisphere are damaged or destroyed, a blind spot develops in the left portion of the visual world. **Lateralization** undoubtedly serves some adaptive functions. For example, it may allow the brain to divide its labour in ways that produce more efficient processing (Vallortigara & Rogers, 2005).

▶ Figure 3.14 on page 104 shows how information received through the eyes travels to each side of the brain. If you are looking straight ahead, an image originating from the left side of your body (the left visual field) falls on the inside half of the left eye and the outside half of the right eye; receptor cells in these locations transmit their images to the back of the *right* cerebral hemisphere. Both eyes project information directly to each hemisphere, as the figure shows, but information from the left visual field goes to the right hemisphere and vice versa. By capitalizing on the nature of these neural pathways, researchers can present information initially to just one side of the brain.

temporal lobes

One of four anatomical regions of each hemisphere of the cerebral cortex, located roughly on the sides of the brain; involved in certain aspects of speech and language perception

occipital lobes

One of four anatomical regions of each hemisphere of the cerebral cortex, located at the back of the brain; visual processing is controlled here

lateralization

Asymmetry in the functions of the right and left hemispheres of the cerebral cortex (e.g., in most individuals, most language skills are lateralized to the left hemisphere)

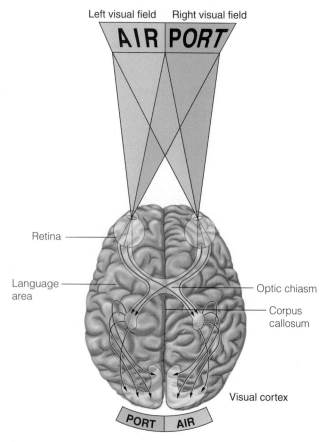

Left visual field   Right visual field

AIR PORT

Retina

Language area

Optic chiasm

Corpus callosum

Visual cortex

PORT   AIR

▶ **Figure 3.14**

Visual Processing in the Two Hemispheres

Images originating in the left visual field fall on the inside half of the left eye and the outside half of the right eye and are then projected to the right hemisphere. Information appearing in the right visual field, in contrast, projects to the left hemisphere. Because most language processing occurs in the left hemisphere, split-brain patients can vocally report only stimuli that are shown in the right visual field. In this case, the subject says only "port" because that is the word available for processing in the left hemisphere.

corpus callosum

The collection of nerve fibres that connect the two cerebral hemispheres and allow information to pass from one side to the other

Under normal circumstances, a visual object presented in only one visual field is eventually represented in both sides of the brain. This is because, as we noted earlier, a major communication bridge—the **corpus callosum**—connects the two hemispheres. Information arriving in the right hemisphere, for example, is transported to the left hemisphere through the corpus callosum in just a few thousandths of a second (Saron & Davidson, 1989). This transfer occurs automatically and requires no head movement or eye turning.

Splitting the Brain   If you think about it, you'll realize that it's important for both sides of the brain to receive information about objects in the environment. To see why, imagine what visual perception would be like for someone without a corpus callosum—someone with a "split brain." Suppose an object appears suddenly in the person's left visual field, and it is moving so quickly that the person has no time to move the head or eyes. Our patient would be incapable of a coordinated response, because the right side of the brain contains the machinery to control only the left side of the body. Moreover, the split-brain patient would be unable to name the menacing object, because the primary language comprehension and production centres are located, typically, on the left side of the brain.

Let's consider another experiment for our hypothetical patient. Suppose that we flash the word AIRPORT on a screen, very quickly, but arrange it so that the first part of the word, AIR, appears in the left visual field and the second part, PORT, appears in the right visual field (see Figure 3.14). What do you think the patient will report seeing? The answer is the word PORT, because that's the image received by the left hemisphere—the place where the language centres are located. The main language part of the brain wouldn't even know that AIR had been presented, because the image would remain locked in the visual centres of the right hemisphere.

Our hypothetical patient, as well as a version of the study we just described, is *real* (Gazzaniga, 1970). A number of individuals have split brains. Some were born without a corpus callosum (Lassonde & Jeeves, 1994; Sanders, 1989); others had their communication gateway severed on purpose by surgeons seeking to reduce the spread of severe epileptic seizures (Springer & Deutsch, 1989). Epilepsy is a kind of electrical firestorm in the brain that spreads across the cortex, producing convulsions and sometimes loss of consciousness. Severe epilepsy is a debilitating condition. Cutting the communication gateway from one hemisphere to another limits epileptic seizures to one half of the brain, thereby reducing their severity. Severing the corpus callosum is a rarely used procedure because modern antiepileptic drugs control seizures for most patients. However, it has proven effective in some instances for patients who fail to respond to medication.

The two hemispheres of split-brain patients are not broken or damaged by the operation; information simply cannot quickly pass from one side of the brain to the other. In fact, the behaviour of split-brain patients appears to be remarkably normal. It's extremely unlikely that you would be able to identify one of them in a crowd. Their behaviour appears normal because most input from the environment still reaches both sides of their brain. These patients can turn their heads and eyes freely as they interact with the environment, allowing information to fall on receptor regions that transmit to both hemispheres. The abnormal nature of their brains becomes apparent only under manufactured conditions, like those described above, and through the personal anecdotes that these patients sometimes report.

Much of the work on split-brain individuals was conducted by the late Nobel Prize–winning neuroscientist Roger Sperry and his colleagues. In one classic study by Gazzaniga, Bogen, and Sperry (1965), several images (pictures, words, or symbols) were presented visually to either the left or right visual fields of split-brain subjects. When an image was shown to the right visual field, it was easily named because it could be processed by the language centres of the left hemisphere. For left visual field presentations, the patients remained perplexed and silent. It was later learned, however, that their silence did not mean that the brain failed to process the image. If split-brain patients were asked to *point* to a picture of the object just shown, they could do so, but only with the *left* hand (e.g., Gazzaniga & LeDoux, 1978). The brain had received the input but could not respond verbally. Note that this result indicates that the right hemisphere has sufficient language to understand the instruction to point.

Studies of split-brain patients continue to the present day (for a brief review, see Gazzaniga, 2005). In one particularly intriguing recent study, Uddin, Rayman, and Zaidel (2005) showed that both right and left hemispheres of a female split-brain patient were able to recognize photographs of her, but only her right hemisphere could recognize photos of other people familiar to her.

Although split-brain patients behave relatively normally after surgery, they report some peculiarities. These reports are anecdotal, of course, and need to be viewed with some caution, but they are interesting nonetheless. For example, some patients report that sometimes their right and left hands act as if they have minds of their own, sometimes competing over things, such as what clothes to wear. One patient reported buttoning a blouse with one hand while, at the same time, unbuttoning the blouse with the other. Some patients have claimed that it is difficult to read a newspaper or a book, unless it is held by the right hand; the left hand, which maps to the nonverbal right hemisphere, apparently has no interest in reading as a leisure activity (Preilowski, 1975). Some researchers have even suggested that each side may have its own kind of separate consciousness (Victor, 1996; Wolford, Miller, & Gazzaniga, 2004).

Hemispheric Specialization   The available evidence strongly indicates that the two hemispheres of the cerebral cortex are specialized to perform certain kinds of tasks. The right hemisphere, for example, appears to play a more important role in spatial tasks, such as fitting together the pieces of a puzzle or navigating around in the environment. Patients with damage to the right hemisphere characteristically have trouble with spatial tasks, as do split-brain patients who must assemble a puzzle with their right hand (Kalat, 1992). The right hemisphere may also be involved in some important aspects of emotional processing (Spence, Shapiro, & Zaidel, 1996). The left hemisphere clearly contributes more to verbal tasks, such as producing and understanding speech, reading, and writing, than does the right hemisphere (Gernsbacher & Kaschak, 2003).

Still, you should understand that a great deal of cooperation and collaboration goes on between the hemispheres, and that the division of labour is not completely clear-cut. The right hemisphere does, for example, include regions that are involved in verbal tasks. The hemispheres interact continuously, and most mental processes, including language, depend on activity that arises in both sides of the brain. You think and behave with a whole brain, not a fragmented one. Moreover, if one side of the brain is damaged, regions in the other hemisphere can sometimes take over the lost functions (Gazzaniga et al., 1996). It's also worth noting that people vary in how specialized their right and left hemispheres are, and there is some indication that these variations in the degree of brain lateralization are related to individual differences on such dimensions as creativity (e.g., Weinstein & Graves, 2002). Handedness also appears to be related to hemispheric specialization: For example, about 20% of left-handers depart from the norm of left-hemisphere dominance for language, compared with only about 5% of right-handers (e.g., Szaflarski, Binder, & Possing, 2002).

It's adaptive for both sides of the brain to process information from the environment; otherwise, this child would probably have difficulty developing a coordinated response to this rapidly arriving ball.

CRITICAL THINKING
Besides as a treatment for epilepsy, can you think of any situations in which having a split brain might be beneficial?

The Brain Balancer!

Studies have shown that each side of the brain has different strengths. For instance—creativity lies in the right side of the brain. Further studies have shown that people are dominant in one side of their brain. It is also a known fact that only 10% of the brain is generally used. Think of all that brain power going to waste!

This needn't be you! With this kit, you will discover which side of your brain is dominant. Next, you will find out how to strengthen your less dominant half. Once your brain is equally balanced, there is no stopping!

Inner equilibrium brings outer equilibrium! With your brain's halves working together, you will increase your self-confidence, creativity, and ability to solve problems. **This will positively affect your life!**

With less of life's little annoyances to worry about, you can then concentrate on developing the 90% of the brain that is unused. It is believed that this is where motivation, intuition, and other such powers lie. The possibilities for personal, intellectual, and occupational growth are endless!

So, call and order your **BRAIN BALANCER** kit today! With a 30-day moneyback guarantee, you have nothing to lose and everything to gain! The kit includes the **BRAIN BALANCER** booklet, workbook, and tape.

Kalat, 1996

There is little, if any, scientific evidence to support claims of the type made in this advertisement.

Over the last two decades or so, there has been an explosion of interest—often promoted by individuals with limited training in neuroscience—in assigning a variety of psychological phenomena to the different sides of the brain. It has been suggested, for example, that the right side of the brain is holistic rather than analytic and accounts for such varied activities as fantasy, dance, and art and music appreciation. The left side of the brain is argued to be the rational mind, controlling not only language but also mathematical and scientific abilities. These ideas have some grains of truth, but some popular treatments of this topic grossly simplify hemispheric lateralization. One of the authors of this textbook once encountered a man who offered his left hand in greeting, explaining, "I'm trying to develop my right hemisphere." He apparently felt that shaking with his left hand would promote right-brain thinking. Some companies market packages designed to teach people to become more right-brained in their approach to the world or to develop ways to synchronize the two sides of the brain.

At present, little scientific evidence supports such claims. It's extremely unlikely that people can learn to develop a particular side of the brain or that individuals can be properly classified as "right brained" or "left brained." Far too often the striking and newsworthy claims are based on anecdotal reports or poorly designed studies. For example, students who listened to tapes designed to stimulate synchronization of the hemispheres were found to perform better on a variety of tasks than did students who weren't exposed to the tapes. But the students who participated were fully informed about the potential benefits of the tapes, so their task improvements could easily be attributed to a placebo effect (for further discussion, see Druckman & Swets, 1988).

Test Yourself 3.2

Test what you've learned about research into brain structures and their functions. Fill in each blank with one of the following terms: EEG, PET scan, hindbrain, midbrain, forebrain, cerebellum, hypothalamus, cortex, frontal lobes, limbic system, corpus callosum. (The answers are in Appendix B.)

1. A "primitive" part of the brain that controls basic life-support functions, such as heart rate and respiration: _____

2. A structure thought to be involved in a variety of motivational activities, including eating, drinking, and sexual behaviour: _____

3. The portion of the cortex believed to be involved in higher-order thought processes (such as planning) as well as the initiation of voluntary motor movements: _____

4. A structure near the base of the brain that is involved in coordination of complex activities, such as walking or playing the piano: _____

5. A device used to monitor the gross electrical activity of the brain: _____

▶ The Endocrine System: Regulating Growth and Internal Functions

LEARNING GOALS

1. Learn how the endocrine system controls long-term and widespread communication needs.
2. Be able to discuss the roles that hormones play in establishing sexual identity and how they may contribute to gender differences on psychological measures.

The nervous system starts and controls motor behaviours and gives rise to thoughts and to perceptions of the external world. But the body must also initiate and control growth and provide long-term regulation of numerous internal biological systems. A second internal system coordinates with the nervous system to serve these needs: a network of glands called the **endocrine system** (see ▶ Figure 3.15), which uses the bloodstream, rather than neurons, as its main information corridor. Chemicals called **hormones** are released into the blood by the various endocrine glands and serve to control a variety of internal functions.

endocrine system

A network of glands that uses the bloodstream to send chemical messages that regulate growth and other internal functions

hormones

Chemicals released into the blood by the various endocrine glands to help control a variety of internal regulatory functions

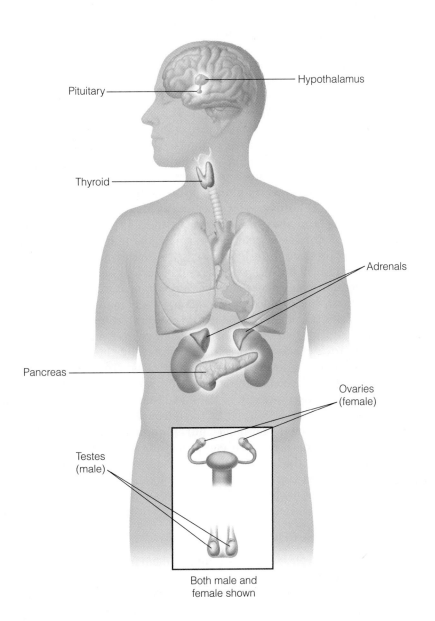

Pituitary — Hypothalamus

Thyroid

Adrenals

Pancreas

Ovaries (female)

Testes (male)

Both male and female shown

▶ **Figure 3.15**

The Endocrine System

The major glands of the human endocrine system. Collectively, they secrete more than 20 different hormones, or chemical messengers, into the bloodstream. Each hormone has specific effects on particular types of cells in the body, often at locations quite remote from the gland itself. (Used with permission © 2006 www.KidsHealth.org/ Nemours.)

The word *hormone* comes aptly from a Greek word meaning "to set into motion." Hormones play roles in many basic, life-sustaining activities in the body: Hunger, thirst, sexual behaviour, and the "fight-or-flight" response are all regulated in part by interplay between the nervous system and hormones released by the endocrine glands. The fact that the body has two internal communication systems rather than one makes sense from an adaptive standpoint. One system, communication among neurons, governs transmissions that are quick and detailed; the other, the endocrine system, initiates slower but more widespread and longer-lasting effects. In the following section, we'll consider the endocrine system in more detail and then consider how hormones influence some fundamental differences between men and women.

The Endocrine System

The chemical communication system of the endocrine glands differs in some important ways from the rapid-fire electrochemical activities of the nervous system. Communication in the nervous system tends to be *localized*, in that the activity of a neuron has a direct impact only on the neurons with which it synapses. Hormones, in contrast, travel throughout the body and affect numerous target sites. Also in contrast to neurotransmitters, hormones have long-lasting effects. Whereas neural communication operates in time scales bordering on the blink of an eye, the endocrine system can produce effects lasting minutes, hours, or even days. In some animals, for example, circulating hormones prepare the organism for seasonal migration or for hibernation. Thus, the endocrine system provides the body with a mechanism for widespread and long-term communication that cannot be produced by interactions among neurons.

The activities of the nervous and endocrine systems are closely coordinated (Anisman, Hayley, Staines, & Merali, 2001; P. E. Cooper, 1991). Structures in the brain (especially the hypothalamus) stimulate or inhibit the release of hormones by the glands; once released, these chemicals then feed back and affect the firing rates of neural impulses. The feedback loop balances and controls the regulatory activities of the body. The hypothalamus is of particular importance because it controls the *pituitary gland*. The **pituitary gland** can be thought of as a master gland that controls the secretion of hormones by other glands in response to signals from the hypothalamus; these hormones, in turn, regulate the activity of many of the other vital glands in the endocrine system. For example, the pituitary gland signals the testes in males to produce *testosterone* and the ovaries in females to produce *estrogen*—both of critical importance in sexual behaviour and reproduction.

Let's consider one example of the endocrine system at work. You leave a party late, convinced that you can walk the two kilometres home without incident. The streets, quiet without the noise of midday traffic, exert a calming influence as you walk along. But suddenly two shadowy figures emerge from an alleyway and move in your direction. You draw in your breath, your stomach tightens, and your rapidly beating heart seems ready to explode from your chest. These whole-body reactions, critical in preparing you to fight or take flight, are created by signals from the brain that lead to increased activity of the endocrine glands. The hypothalamus, acting through the pituitary gland, signals the **adrenal glands** (located above the kidneys) to begin secreting the hormones **norepinephrine** and **epinephrine** into the blood. These hormones produce energizing effects on the body, increasing heart rate, constricting the blood supply to the stomach and intestines, and increasing the amount of glucose (sugar) in the blood. The body is now prepared for action, enhancing the likelihood of survival (see ❱ Figure 3.16).

Gender, Hormones, and Psychology

Before birth, hormones released by the pituitary gland initiate developments in the fetus's reproductive anatomy, determining whether a child ends up with male or female sex organs. At puberty, an increase in sex hormones (testosterone and

pituitary gland

A kind of master gland that controls the release of hormones from other glands in response to signals from the hypothalamus

adrenal glands

Glands that secrete norepinephrine and epinephrine into the bloodstream

norepinephrine and epinephrine

Hormones that cause a surge of energy that increases the heart rate, directing blood to areas that require it (and away from the stomach and intestine) and making glucose available to the muscles

CRITICAL THINKING

Initiation of the fight-or-flight response clearly has adaptive value. But can you think of any circumstances in which this response might lower the chances of an adaptive response?

▶ Figure 3.16

The Fight-or-Flight Response

In potentially dangerous situations the endocrine system generates a fight-or-flight response. Hormones are released that produce energizing effects on the body, increasing our chances of survival.

Hypothalamus
Stimulates adrenal glands

Adrenal Glands
Secrete norepinephrine and epinephrine into bloodstream

Norepinephrine and Epinephrine
Cause energy to surge; heart rate to increase; cause blood to be shunted away from the stomach and intestine to areas that require it; make glucose available to the muscles

estrogen) leads males to develop facial hair and deep voices and females to develop breasts and to begin menstruation. It is now suspected that hormones released during development may affect basic patterns of neuronal connections within men's and women's brains. Evidence suggests that men and women may think differently as the result of gender-specific activities of the endocrine system.

Simon Fraser University psychologist Doreen Kimura and her colleague Elizabeth Hampson (1994), for example, reported that the performance of women and men on certain tasks changes significantly as the levels of sex hormones in the body increase or decrease. Women typically perform better than men do on some tests of verbal ability, and their performance on these tasks improves with their levels of estrogen. Similarly, men tend to show slightly better performance on some kinds of spatial tasks (such as mentally rotating visual images of three-dimensional objects), and their performance seems to be related somewhat to testosterone levels. Likewise, Bosco, Longoni, and Vecchi (2004) reported evidence that men and women tend to differ in the strategies they use to navigate through space. York University evolutionary psychologist Irwin Silverman and colleagues noted that, although men tend to do well on spatial tasks, such as mental rotation of objects and map reading, women tend to do better than males in remembering the contents and locations of arrays of objects (Silverman & Choi, 2005). These researchers suggest that such gender differences are linked to hormonal changes during puberty and may occur because human male brains were selected more by evolution to produce cognitive skills associated with hunting, whereas female brains evolved more for the cognitive skills associated with foraging for food. Most of the relevant evidence is correlational, rather than experimental, so we can't be sure that hormones cause such differences, but the data are suggestive of endocrine-based gender differences in cognitive task performance (Kimura, 2004).

Girls who have been exposed to an excess of male hormones during the initial stages of prenatal development, either because of a genetic disorder or from chemicals ingested by their mothers during pregnancy, tend to be particularly tomboyish during development (Resnick, Berenbaum, Gottesman, & Bouchard, 1986), preferring to engage in play activities that are more traditionally associated with boys. In one study reported by Kimura (1999), researchers compared the choice of toys by girls who either had been exposed to excess male hormones during early development with the choice of toys by girls who had not. The girls who had been exposed to the male hormones tended to prefer typical masculine activities—smashing trucks and cars together, for example—more than the control girls did. Of course, this does not

Although gender differences in brain anatomy and functioning may influence cognitive and behavioural differences between boys and girls, environmental factors also play a role.

mean that all girls who prefer masculine activities were exposed to excess male hormones; numerous factors interact to determine such preferences.

There is evidence that male and female brains differ somewhat anatomically, although such differences are often exaggerated (Shields, 1975). Animal studies have confirmed that male and female rat brains differ anatomically and that these differences in rat brains are due, in part, to the early influence of hormones (see Hines, 1982, for a review). For humans, the data are less clear and more controversial. It's been reported that the right cortex of males tends to be slightly thicker than the right cortex of females (Boone & Lu, 2000; Kimura, 1999), but whether this anatomical difference accounts, even in part, for the superiority that males show in performing certain spatial tasks is unclear. Other studies have reported that sections of the corpus callosum are more elaborate in women, suggesting that the two hemispheres communicate more effectively in females (de Lacoste-Utamsing & Holloway, 1982). However, McMaster University neuropsychologist Sandra Witelson (1992) failed to replicate this result.

Hormones released by the endocrine system produce permanent changes early in human development, and those changes may contribute to sex differences in certain kinds of cognitive performance. However, it should be noted that on many psychological and cognitive measures, men and women do not differ and that even on those tasks in which gender differences are observed, the differences are usually very small, with a great deal of overlap between the performance of men and women (Hyde & Lin, 1988). Some apparent differences between the sexes may have more to do with how abilities are tested than with real underlying differences; for example, a 2005 article by Spelke reviewed evidence that a widely used test of mathematical skill systematically overestimates boys' abilities. It's also very likely that cultural processes play major roles in fostering gender differences. Consistent with that idea, there is evidence that some cognitive gender differences can be eliminated with relatively brief training interventions (Kass, Ahlers, & Dugger, 1998).

To repeat a theme discussed in Chapter 1, it is difficult to separate the effects of biology (*nature*) from the ongoing influences of the environment (*nurture*) (see Karmiloff-Smith, Plunket, Johnson, Elman, & Bates, 1998). Men and women undoubtedly faced some differing problems of adaptation during our evolutionary history, and evolution likely selected for somewhat different "solution tools" in the brains of men and women. Furthermore, men and women are currently faced with different environmental pressures and cultural expectations during their lifetimes. These pressures also shape the actions they take, thereby influencing behavioural differences between the sexes. We will return to gender issues often in later chapters of this text.

Test Yourself 3.3

Test your knowledge about the differences between the endocrine system and the nervous system. For each statement, decide whether the endocrine or nervous system is the most appropriate term to apply. (The answers are in Appendix B.)

1. Communication effects tend to be localized, affecting only a small area: _____

2. Responsible for whole-body reactions, such as the fight-or-flight response: _____

3. The major determinant of sexual identity:
   _____

4. Communicates through the release of epinephrine and norepinephrine: _____

5. Operates quickly, with time scales bordering on the blink of an eye: _____

▶ Adapting and Transmitting the Genetic Code: Evolved Psychological Traits

LEARNING GOALS

1. Be able to explain what it means to say that a trait evolved through the process of natural selection.
2. Learn the basics of genetic transmission.
3. Become familiar with how psychologists study the role of genetics in psychological traits.
4. Understand how evolutionary mechanisms may have influenced human thinking, feelings, and behaviours, and appreciate the concept of the "environment of evolutionary adaptedness."

The human body, including the brain, developed over the course of thousands of millennia through the process of organic evolution (Forest & Gross, 2004). To understand humans and how and why they do and feel the things they do, it is important to understand the mechanisms of evolution that shaped their development. You are probably already familiar with the idea that plants and animals evolved via natural selection. In this section, we provide a brief introduction to evolutionary processes and discuss reasons for believing that our evolutionary heritage influences not only how our bodies look and operate, but also how we think, feel, and act.

Natural Selection

Darwin proposed the mechanism of **natural selection** to explain how species change, or evolve, over time. He recognized that having certain **traits,** or characteristic features of body or behaviour, can help an organism survive and reproduce in its environment. Further, he assumed that some such features are passed from one generation to the next. For example, if a sparrow is born with a special capacity to find nutritious seeds, then its chances of living long enough to mate and produce offspring increase relative to sparrows that are otherwise similar but lack the special feed-finding capacity. If that special capacity is heritable, then that sparrow's offspring will have a higher chance of sharing that evolutionary advantage than the offspring of other sparrows. Over many generations, the special seed-finding trait may become a stable characteristic of all sparrows (although there will still be variation from one sparrow to another in the strength of the trait). The seed-finding trait in this example is an **evolutionary adaptation,** a characteristic selected by nature because it increases the odds of survival. As illustrated in this example, natural selection refers to the differential reproduction and survival of offspring by members of a species who differ in some advantageous way from other members of that species (Crawford, 1998a).

For natural selection to produce evolutionary adaptations, there needs to be a mechanism for producing variation within a species. If all the members of a species were exactly the same, then obviously there could be no special trait for nature to select. In addition, there needs to be some mechanism by which an adaptive trait can pass from one generation to the next. During Darwin's time, the mechanism for creating variability and inheritance was unknown; Darwin made his case by documenting the abundance of variability and inherited characteristics that exist in nature. It was later learned that the mechanism that enables natural selection is the genetic code.

natural selection

The differential production and survival of offspring by species members with advantageous traits

trait

A distinguishable characteristic of an organism

evolutionary adaptation

A heritable trait that provided an organism with an advantage in surviving or reproducing during its evolutionary history

Genetic Principles

Let's briefly review some of the important principles of genetics. What are genes, what do they do, and what are the factors that produce genetic variability? The genetic message resides within chromosomes, which are thin, threadlike strips

The zebra's stripes presumably evolved because they benefit the zebra's survival and reproduction. Similarly, genetically coded tendencies toward loving offspring may constitute evolutionary adaptations that contributed to human survival and reproductive success in our evolutionary past.

Corel #3

Courtesy of Dr. Martin Smith

genes

Segments of chromosomes that contain chemically coded instructions for creating particular hereditary characteristics

dominant versus recessive genes

Many traits have two genes: one dominant and the other recessive; if the two such genes for a given trait differ, the dominant gene controls the observable characteristic

genotype

The genetic information inherited from parents

phenotype

A person's observable characteristics, such as hair colour; controlled partly by the genotype and partly by the environment

of DNA. Every cell in your body (except sperm cells or unfertilized egg cells) contains 46 chromosomes, arranged in 23 pairs. Half of each chromosome pair came from your mother through one of her eggs, and the other half from one of your father's sperm cells when it fertilized that egg. **Genes** are segments of chromosomes that contain chemically coded instructions telling cells how to manufacture various substances that, in turn, give rise to particular hereditary traits. Your genes, interacting with the environment, controlled the development of your body from a fertilized egg to whatever age you have attained, and they will continue to play roles in making you who you are throughout your life. For example, each person has genes that help determine height, other genes that help determine eye colour, and yet others that influence susceptibility to specific heritable diseases.

Most heritable characteristics, or traits, have two genes. People have two genes, for example, for hair colour, for blood type, and for facial dimples. If both genes are designed to produce the same trait (such as nearsightedness), there's little question the characteristic will develop (you'll definitely need glasses). But what if the two genes differ—for example, the father passes along the gene for nearsightedness, but the corresponding gene from the mother is for normal distance vision? Under these conditions, the trait is determined by the dominant gene; in the case of vision, the **dominant** "normal" **gene** will dominate the **recessive gene** for nearsightedness, such that the child will have normal vision. Thus, nearsighted individuals inherited a near-sightedness gene from each parent.

The fact that a dominant gene masks the effects of a recessive gene means that genetic material is not necessarily expressed in physical or psychological characteristics. A person may see perfectly but still carry the recessive gene for nearsightedness. This is why two parents with normal vision can produce a near-sighted child, or two brown-haired parents can produce a child with blond hair—it is the particular combination of genes that determines the inherited characteristics.

Thus it is important to distinguish between the **genotype,** which is the genetic code in an individual's chromosomes, and the **phenotype,** which is his or her observable characteristics. The phenotype, such as good vision, is influenced by the genotype, but it can also be influenced by the environment. A person's height and weight, for example, are strongly influenced by the genotype, but environmental factors, such as diet, also contribute significantly to these aspects of the phenotype. This is an important point to remember: Genes provide the materials from which characteristics develop, but the environment shapes the final product.

Across individuals, variations in the genetic message arise partly because the genetic information from each parent can be combined at fertilization in trillions of different ways. Each egg or sperm cell contains a random half of each parent's 23 chromosome pairs. According to the laws of probability, this means that there are more than 8 million (2^{23}) different combinations that a given individual could produce in his or her reproductive cells. The fertilization of a particular egg by a particular sperm is also a matter of chance, which means that the genetic material from your parents could be combined in 64 trillion ways. Thus, a very wide variety of traits (and combinations of traits) can emerge via reproduction, thereby contributing to variability across individuals. If a particular genetically coded trait produces a survival advantage, then individuals with that trait will be more likely to reproduce and their offspring will be more likely to have the trait. This is one way in which evolution proceeds.

Variation in the genetic code can also occur by chance via mutations. A **mutation** is a spontaneous change in the genetic material that occurs because of an error during the gene-replication process. Genetic mutations are essentially random errors in the biological mechanisms by which chromosomes are copied, and most mutations are harmful to the organism. Occasionally, however, by chance, a mutation leads to a new trait that confers a survival advantage to the organism. Mutations, along with the variations produced by unique combinations of genetic material, are key ingredients for natural selection because they introduce novelty into nature. Via natural selection, nature tends to discard novel organisms that are unfit and to favour those that are fit.

Genes and Behaviour

You probably find it pretty easy to accept the idea that your height and eye colour are influenced by your genes. But you may be less open to the idea that your genetic makeup affects your thoughts, feelings, and behaviours. However, as you'll see throughout this book, it is sometimes possible to predict (not perfectly, but above chance) things about the psychology of an individual by knowing something about his or her genes. Susceptibility to the psychological disorder schizophrenia is a case in point. Biological children of parents who have schizophrenia have a greater chance of developing the disorder themselves, when compared with children of parents without schizophrenia, even if the children were adopted by parents without schizophrenia at birth (Gottesman & Moldin, 1998). Thus, genes probably play some role in susceptibility to schizophrenia. (We will return to this issue in more detail in Chapter 14.)

One way that psychologists study the link between genes and behaviour is to investigate family histories in detail. In **family studies,** researchers look for similarities and differences between biological (blood) relatives versus unrelated individuals as a way of determining whether heredity has an influence. As you've just learned, the chances of schizophrenia increase with a family history, and many other psychological traits seem to run in families as well (e.g., intelligence and personality). The trouble with family studies, however, is that members of a family share more than just common genes; they are also exposed to similar environmental experiences, so it's difficult to separate the relative roles of nature and nurture in behaviour. Family studies can be useful sources of information—it helps to know, for instance, if someone has a greater than average risk of developing schizophrenia—but family studies can't be used to establish cause-and-effect links between genes and behaviour.

mutation

Error in the process by which chromosomes are copied that changes the genotype specified by those chromosomes

Genetic background plays an important role in determining physical appearance, and many researchers believe that it also helps shape certain psychological characteristics.

family studies

The study of similarities and differences between biological (blood) relatives to help discover the role heredity plays in physical or psychological traits; rarely provide conclusive evidence because genes and the environment are usually entangled

adoption studies

The traits of children adopted at an early age are compared with those of their biological parents and siblings, with whom they share genetic material but not rearing environment

twin studies

Identical twins, who share genetic material, are compared with fraternal twins in an effort to disentangle the roles of heredity and environment in giving rise to psychological traits

CRITICAL   THINKING

In what ways are the environmental experiences of identical twins more similar than those for fraternal twins? Why might this still be true if both sets of twins were raised apart starting at birth?

Adoption studies overcome some of the limitations of family studies. In adoption studies, researchers assess correlations between biological parents and children they gave up for adoption. Yet another approach is to conduct **twin studies,** in which researchers compare behavioural traits between *identical* twins, who share the same genetic material, and *fraternal* twins, who were born at the same time but whose genetic overlap is only roughly 50% (fraternal twins can even be of different sexes). In studies of intelligence, for example, identical twins tend to have much more similar intelligence scores than do fraternal twins, even when environmental factors are taken into account (Bouchard, 1997). Kerry Jang of the University of British Columbia and Phillip Vernon of the University of Western Ontario and their co-workers have collaborated on many such studies, emphasizing the interaction between genes and environment in, for example, susceptibility to alcoholism (Jang, Vernon, Livesley, Stein, & Wolf, 2001).

Identical twins make ideal research subjects because researchers can control, at least in principle, for nongenetic factors, such as home environment. Because identical twins have the same genetic makeup, any physical or psychological differences that emerge during development must be attributable to environmental factors. Similarly, if identical twins are raised in independent environments but still show similar traits, it's a strong indication that genetic factors are involved in expression of the trait. It's worth noting, though, that when identical twins are raised apart, they are often raised by close relatives (e.g., one twin with the mother and another with the mother's sister) and hence in somewhat similar environments, making it difficult to determine whether similarities between the twins are purely genetic (Kamin, 1974).

Evolutionary Adaptations and Human Behaviour

Having reviewed the basics of genetics, let's return to the issue of evolution. Evolutionary psychologists propose that humans evolved tendencies to think, feel, and behave in certain ways because humans (or prehuman hominids) who thought and behaved in those ways survived and reproduced better than those who thought and behaved differently. A potential example of this is the human tendency for fathers to love, nurture, and protect their children. From an evolutionary perspective, this tendency exists across the human species because, among ancient humans (and our prehuman ancestors), loving and protective fathering conferred a survival advantage. Note that we refer to a *tendency* here; although some human fathers do not demonstrate much loving behaviour toward their offspring, most do and as a species humans show much more fathering motivation and behaviour than males in closely related species, such as chimpanzees and orangutans (Smuts, Cheney, Seyfarth, Wrangham, & Struhsaker, 1987). This is what we mean when we say humans may have *evolved* a tendency for males in the species to love and protect their offspring. Males who had genes that built brains that disposed them toward fathering behaviours left more offspring who survived to reproduce than did males who did not have such genes, so over thousands of years genes for a degree of paternal love became "standard equipment" in the genetic complement of human males, just like genes coding for facial hair in males.

As is the case for facial hair, the claim that a trait evolved to be standard equipment across the human species does not mean that it shows no variability. Just as some men have a lot of facial hair and some have very little, some men show a great deal of fatherly love and some show very little. Although both traits are virtually universal across the human species (among adult males) and likely arose via natural selection, this does not mean that the expression of each trait will be similar in every man. Particularly in the case of psychological traits, what was likely selected was a *tendency* to respond in a certain way, not an invariant behavioural pattern. Such a tendency can be overridden by environmental or developmental circumstances (see Karmiloff-Smith et al., 1998).

A related point is that although human psychology may have been sculpted by evolution, those evolutionary adaptations are general and flexible, rather than specific and rigid. Humans have not, for example, evolved to understand a specific language, such as English or French. Instead, humans have evolved a tendency to learn the language or languages to which they are exposed in their environments, especially during childhood (Pinker, 1997b). We do not have genes for speaking English or French, but we do have genes that code for the construction of brain and mind mechanisms for learning whatever human languages are present around us during childhood. Evidently, natural selection favoured such genes in human evolution because language gave our ancestors an advantage in surviving and reproducing.

Evolutionary psychologists have suggested a number of aspects of human thought and behaviour that are likely evolutionary adaptations (Barkow et al., 1992; Bock & Cardew, 1997). These include the two examples discussed above: language mechanisms (Pinker, 1997b) and parenting motivations and behaviours (Wilson & Daly, 1997). Other examples include our tendency to find certain problems easier to solve if they are posed in a social and concrete context rather than in a nonsocial and abstract context (Cosmides & Tooby, 1997) and the tendency for people to feel jealous if they think a romantic partner is sexually attracted to someone else (Buss, 2000). Many of the "solution tools" to adaptive problems discussed in Chapter 1 are also likely evolutionary adaptations. For instance, the reason that our minds have the ability to form associations by using classical conditioning is that this ability helped some of our distant ancestors to survive and reproduce better than those who could not form associations.

How do we identify which human traits are evolved adaptations, as opposed to learned adaptations? This is a tricky and controversial topic among evolutionary biologists and psychologists, particularly with respect to mental processes. To be considered an evolutionary adaptation, a trait must be (1) *adaptive*, meaning it contributed to survival or reproduction in the ancestral environment of a species; (2) *heritable*, meaning that it can be passed from parents to offspring via genes; and (3) *universal*, meaning it occurs (if appropriate environmental conditions are present) in all genetically normal individuals of a species. It follows that not all human abilities evolved via natural selection. Consider, for example, your ability to read. This is a highly adaptive psychological ability, yet it could not have evolved through natural selection. Reading developed relatively recently in human history—too short a period for evolutionary change—and emerged long after the human brain had achieved its current size and form (Gould, 2000). We evolved eyes and a brain that is capable of learning to read (Dawkins, 1989), but reading itself did not evolve via natural selection.

A number of aspects of human behaviour probably reflect evolutionary adaptations but do not increase individuals' survival and reproduction in contemporary human environments. An example is humans' preferences for sweet foods. Although there is individual and cultural variability in fondness for sweets, some degree of fondness for sweet tastes is universal, and there is evidence of a genetic basis for sweet preference (e.g., Looy & Weingarten, 1992). This preference for sweet tastes probably evolved to encourage our ancestors to expend energy searching for foods that tasted sweet, which in our ancestral environments would usually have been fruits. Fruits are high in nutrients that our bodies cannot get from other sources, so it was advantageous for our ancestors to have a "sweet tooth" that encouraged them to search for fruits rather than more readily available but less nutritious foods. And in a natural environment, there was little danger of people "overdosing" on too many fruits.

The situation is quite different today. Modern humans learned to refine sugar and other highly concentrated sources of sweet tastes so that people can indulge their sweet tooth by consuming cookies, pies, candies, and thousands of other very sweet and non-nutritious concoctions. Our evolved fondness for sweetness, which was adaptive in our ancestral environments, was not designed to function in an environment where sweet tastes could be found in foods other than nutritious ones, such as fruits. So our evolved adaptation of a fondness for sweet tastes, which helped us survive in natural environments, backfires in contemporary environments and contributes to poor health, obesity, dental problems, and so on.

When considering the usefulness of a human trait, we must always consider how such adaptations would have contributed to human survival and reproduction in the human **environment of evolutionary adaptedness,** or **EEA** (Bowlby, 1969; Crawford, 1998b). The EEA refers to the environments in which our ancestors lived for millions of years before the rise of agriculture. Human evolutionary adaptations were selected to help people survive and reproduce in the human EEAs but not necessarily in other environments. The human EEAs that shaped most human adaptations probably included a hunting-gathering lifestyle, small groups of mostly related individuals living together, and considerable degrees of conflict between neighbouring groups. Evolutionary adaptations (especially in large, complex mammals, such as humans) take very long periods to evolve and change, so the human brain today comprises modules that evolved in and were adapted to our ancient environment of evolutionary adaptedness, rather than our modern environment of cities, cars, and computers. Incompatibilities between our evolved minds and the modern environment may contribute to the frequency of some psychological disorders, as we will see in Chapter 14.

environment of evolutionary adaptedness (EEA)

The environment, or environments, in which a species' evolutionary adaptations were selected

Test Yourself 3.4

Test your knowledge of the evolution of human psychological adaptations. Select your answers from the following list of terms: EEA, mutation, natural selection, heritable, trait, evolutionary adaptation, identical, recessive, universal, fraternal, adaptive. (The answers are in Appendix B.)

1. The differential reproduction of offspring by genetically different members of a population: _____
2. Any distinguishable aspect of a species: _____
3. Neither Eugene nor Kelly has red hair, but their daughter Colleen does. This suggests that the gene for red hair is _____.
4. An error in the process by which chromosomes are duplicated: _____

5. To the extent that a trait is inherited, _____ twins would be expected to be more similar to one another on that trait than would _____ twins.
6. To qualify as an evolutionary adaptation, a trait must be _____, _____, and _____.
7. Some human evolutionary adaptations may create problems for us because of differences between our modern environments and our _____.

Biological Aspects of Psychology

Psychologists believe that human thoughts, feelings, and actions are products of active biological systems. The human brain, along with the rest of the nervous system and all the other parts of our bodies, is a biological solution to problems produced by the natural environment. Out of these biological solutions arise the attributes that make up the human mind, including intellect, emotion, and artistic creativity. In this chapter we've considered four central problems of adaptation that were solved through the evolution of our biological systems.

First, how does your body communicate with the environment and internally? Networks of interconnected individual cells, called neurons, constitute the nervous system. To communicate internally, the nervous system has developed an electrochemical language. Messages travel electrically within a neuron, usually from dendrite to soma to axon to terminal button, and then chemically from one neuron to the next at a synapse. Combining electrical and chemical components creates a quick, efficient, and extremely versatile communication system. Neurotransmitters regulate the rate at which neurons fire, by producing excitatory or inhibitory messages, and the resulting global patterns of activation underlie behaviours, perceptions, feelings, and thoughts.

Second, how does your brain generate your perception of the world around you and of your own internal states, and how does it initiate and coordinate behaviour? To accomplish the remarkable variety of functions it controls, the nervous system divides its labour. Drawing on studies of animals and of people with brain damage, and using sophisticated brain-stimulating and brain-imaging technologies, researchers have begun to map out the localized regions of brain tissue that support particular psychological and life-sustaining functions. At the base of the brain, in the hindbrain region, structures control such basic processes as respiration, heart rate, and the coordination of muscle movements. Higher up are regions that control motivational processes, such as eating, drinking, and sexual behaviour. Finally, in the cerebral cortex more complex mental processes—such as thought, sensations, and language—arise. Some functions in the brain appear to be lateralized, which means that they are controlled primarily by one cerebral hemisphere or the other.

Third, how does the body regulate growth and other internal functions? To solve its widespread and long-term communication needs, the body uses the endocrine system to release chemicals called hormones into the bloodstream. These chemical messengers serve a variety of regulatory functions, influencing growth and development, hunger, thirst, and sexual behaviour, in addition to helping the body prepare for action. Hormones may underlie some of the behavioural differences between men and women.

Fourth, how and why did evolution select the kind of brain structures and nervous system that humans have today, and how does the body store and transmit the genetic code? Humans (and our prehuman ancestors) faced many threats to survival over the millions of years of our evolutionary history. Certain genetically coded brain structures provided solutions to the survival problems our ancestors faced, and these became part of the human makeup via natural selection. Physical and behavioural characteristics are passed on to offspring via portions of chromosomes called genes. The phenotypes an individual displays reflect interactions between his or her genotype and environment. Psychologists often try to disentangle the relative contributions of genes and the environment by conducting twin studies, comparing the behaviours and abilities of identical and fraternal twins who have been raised in similar or dissimilar environments. Discrepancies between our contemporary environments and those in which we evolved may cause problems for humans.

CHAPTER SUMMARY

Most scientists believe that behaviour arises from the activities of the brain. Every time you think, act, perceive, or feel, biological activity in your brain is playing a critical role. *Neuroscience* is the study of how the brain, mind, and behaviour are interconnected. Evolutionary processes shaped the human brain and nervous system, and the genetic code transmits information about how to construct the human body and mind to the next generation.

▶ Communicating Internally: Connecting World and Brain

Information is received, transmitted, and integrated by *neurons*, interconnected cells that communicate electrochemically.

The Anatomy of Neurons

Each neuron has *dendrites*, a *soma* or cell body, an *axon*, and *terminal buttons*. *Sensory neurons* carry information from sensory receptors to the spinal cord and brain. *Interneurons* convey information between internal processing sites. *Motor neurons* carry messages from the central nervous system to muscles and glands.

Neural Transmission: The Electrochemical Message

Messages travel electrically from one point to another within a neuron and chemically, through *neurotransmitters*, from the terminal buttons of one neuron to the dendrites of another at a *synapse*.

The Communication Network

The pattern of activation produced by vast numbers of densely interconnected neurons operating at the same time underlies both conscious experiences and complex behaviours.

▶ The Nervous System: Processing Information and Controlling Behaviour

The nervous system consists of several subparts that coordinate with one another (and with other systems in the body) to give rise to thinking, feeling, and behaving.

The Central and Peripheral Nervous Systems

The *central nervous system* consists of the brain and spinal cord, which communicate with the rest of the body through bundles of axons *(nerves)*. The *peripheral nervous system* is subdivided into the *somatic system* (which sends information from sensory receptors to

muscles) and the *autonomic system*, which controls the more automatic needs of the body, such as respiration and heartbeat.

Research Techniques for Exploring Brain Function

Studies of brain damage have revealed much about which areas of the brain perform particular functions. Researchers have also "talked" to the brain by way of *chemical injections*, *electrodes*, and *transcranial magnetic stimulation* (TMS). They can also "listen" to the brain with noninvasive techniques, such as *electroencephalography* (EEG and ERP) and *magnetic resonance imaging* (MRI and fMRI).

Brain Structures and Their Functions

The *hindbrain* provides basic life support through the *medulla, pons, reticular formation,* and *cerebellum.* The *midbrain* relays sensory messages. Higher mental functioning takes place in the *forebrain*, which uses the *cerebral cortex, thalamus, hypothalamus,* and *limbic system.*

The Divided Brain

The two *hemispheres* (halves) of the cerebral cortex are *lateralized*: Each side is responsible for somewhat different functions, but the two normally coordinate by communicating via the *corpus callosum*.

▶ The Endocrine System: Regulating Growth and Internal Functions

Long-term communication requirements are provided by the endocrine system, which uses the bloodstream as its communication corridor.

The Endocrine System

Endocrine glands release *hormones* into the blood that interact with the nervous system to regulate basic activities, such as the fight-or-flight response.

Gender, Hormones, and Psychology

Hormones released by the *pituitary gland* determine sexual identity before birth and direct sexual maturing at puberty. Endocrine activities may contribute to some differences in the way males and females think and behave.

▶ Adapting and Transmitting the Genetic Code: Evolved Psychological Traits

Humans evolved over millions of years, and our ancestral environments shaped our bodies and brains.

Natural Selection

If a physical or behavioural *trait* enhances an individual's chances of producing viable offspring, and if that trait is heritable, then by *natural selection* that trait may gradually become characteristic of the species.

Genetic Principles

Most cells of the human body contain 23 pairs of *chromosomes*. *Genes* are segments of chromosomes that contain chemical instructions that influence the development of hereditary traits. Genes can be *dominant* or *recessive*.

Genes and Behaviour

Family studies identify similarities and differences that may reveal the influence of heredity. In *twin studies*, researchers compare the traits of identical twins, who have the same genes, and fraternal twins, who have only about half their genes in common. Differences between identical twins can be attributed to the environment; similarities between identical twins are partly genetic but may also partly reflect similarities in twins' environments.

Evolutionary Adaptations and Human Behaviour

Gene-based physical and behavioural traits that increase the chances of producing viable offspring can, via natural selection, evolve as adaptations. Psychological traits are tendencies, with considerable flexibility and variability across individuals in how and the extent to which those tendencies are realized. Our bodies (including brains) evolved over millions of years, shaped by natural selection to the demands of a natural environment vastly different from that of most modern humans. Discrepancies between the environments in which we evolved and those in which we live may be a source of difficulty for humans.

Terms to Remember

Recommended Readings

Johnson, S. (2005). *Mind wide open: Your brain and the neuroscience of everyday life.* New York: Scribner. Steven Johnson is a writer who specializes in making science accessible to a wide audience. He became fascinated with recent brain-imaging technologies, and has written an engaging book about his explorations of them (which included undergoing some of the procedures you've read about in this chapter).

Kolb, B., & Whishaw, I. Q. (2001). *An introduction to brain and behavior.* New York: Worth. Written by two world-renowned neuroscientists at the University of Lethbridge, this introductory-level text explores the biological basis of behaviour, communicating the excitement of the tremendous advances in the field in recent years. Drawing on their teaching and research experiences, the authors organize this text around the key questions that intrigue brain researchers and students

(e.g., "Why do we have a brain?" "How is the brain organized?"). A strong focus on clinical issues and innovative art are incorporated.

Sacks, O. (1985). *The man who mistook his wife for a hat.* New York: Summit Books. A witty example of the case study approach applied to the neurosciences. Sacks presents examples and anecdotes from patients suffering from various forms of brain damage. All of Sacks's books are interesting, but this one is a classic.

 For additional readings, explore InfoTrac® College Edition, your online library. Go to http://www.adaptivemind3e.nelson.com.

Hint: Enter these search terms: neural transmission, sympathetic nervous system, cerebral cortex, brain imaging, behavioural genetics.

Media Resources

What's on the Web?

Please note that Web addresses are subject to change. Check out the accompanying website for updates: http://www.adaptivemind3e.nelson.com.

This site presents practice quiz questions, hypercontent, information on degrees and careers in psychology, study tips, and more.

Rotman Research Institute

http://www.rotman-baycrest.on.ca

Canada's renowned centre for the study of basic brain processes as well as associated functions of learning and memory. The website includes lists of publications and research projects and links to the home pages of the Rotman research scientists. If you have a QuickTime-equipped browser, you can even listen to audio clips of some of Canada's most distinguished neuroscientists explaining their research findings.

Neurosciences on the Internet

http://www.neuroguide.com

If you want to find information related to the brain or neurosciences, this is the place to do it! A very impressive site that serves as a sort of clearinghouse for information on the brain and nervous system. It provides up-to-date information on neurosurgery and brain disorders as well as psychiatry and psychology.

Neuroscience for Kids

http://faculty.washington.edu/chudler/neurok.html

Yes, the title says "for kids," but this site isn't just for children. It provides information on the brain and nervous system presented in a straightforward, engaging, and interesting fashion. Think of it as "Sesame Street Meets Chapter 3." Included are experiments, activities, and exercises to let you explore the nervous system, and links to other neuroscience resources. The site is part of a larger neuroscience site based at the University of Washington in Seattle.

Human Behavior and Evolution Society

http://www.hbes.com

This site includes essays introducing evolutionary psychological ideas, a list of recent books, publications, and conferences in this area, and RealAudio interviews with many of the leading researchers examining the evolved mechanisms underlying human social and cognitive behaviour.

ThomsonNOW™ ThomsonNOW

http://hed.nelson.com

Go to this site for the link to ThomsonNOW™, your one-stop study shop. Take a Pretest for this chapter and ThomsonNOW™ will generate a personalized Study Plan based on your test results. The Study Plan will identify the topics you need to review and direct you to online resources to help you master those topics. You can then take a Posttest to determine what concepts you have mastered and what you still need work on.

Psyk.trek 3.0

Check out Psyk.trek 3.0 for further study of the concepts in this chapter. Psyk.trek's 65 interactive learning modules, simulations, and quizzes offer additional opportunities for you to interact with, reflect on, and retain the material:

Biological Bases of Behavior: The Neuron and the Neural Impulse

When I enter most intimately into what I call myself, I always stumble on some particular perception or other, of heat or cold, light or shade, love or hatred, pain or pleasure. I never can catch myself at any time without a perception, and never can observe anything but the perception.

—David Hume, *A Treatise of Human Nature*

Sensation and Perception

4

At the end of this short paragraph, stop reading for a moment and pay attention to what you see and hear around you, the odours you smell, the tastes in your mouth, and what you can feel on your skin and inside your body. Really—take a moment and check it out.

Maybe you're reading this text in a frantically busy environment, such as a cafeteria at noon, with people moving all around you, the babble of many voices, and a complex mixture of powerful odours. Or maybe you're in the library, with its more muted sounds, the subtle dusty-gluey smell of books, and the slight discomfort of a too-hard chair. Or perhaps you're in your own room, flopped on your bed on top of a scratchy blanket with some music on. Wherever you are at the moment, you are being bombarded with stimulation from your environment. Even if you were reading this in the seclusion of an abandoned monastery, your sensory systems would be receiving many sorts of stimulation at every moment.

If asked to describe the input your sensory system is currently receiving, you would probably mention meaningful objects. You might say, "I smell the fish that someone is heating in the microwave," or "I see shelves full of books," or "I hear people talking and laughing on the television," or "I feel the band of my baseball cap on my forehead." These might be perfectly good descriptions of your

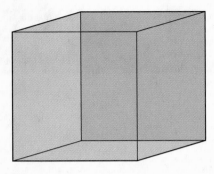

▶ Figure 4.1

The Necker Cube

perceptions, but notice that they are not really descriptions of the sensory stimulation itself. In the case of vision, for example, the sensory input is patterns of coloured light and dark: Light energy from some source—such as the sun or a light bulb—bounces in all directions off objects in the environment, and some of that reflected light enters your eyes and stimulates the visual system. Similarly, when you hear a voice or other sound, the sensory input to the auditory system consists of patterns of changes in air pressure.

Each sensory system transduces, or translates, the pattern of physical input it receives into electrochemical neuronal activities that code the characteristics of the sensory stimulation. This transduction and other brain processes involved in interpreting its products are the central topics of this chapter. We turn now to the important psychological processes of sensation and perception. It's through sensation and perception that we create our immediate experience of the world around us and of our own bodies.

To help understand the difference between the psychological terms *sensation* and *perception*, consider the image shown in ▶ Figure 4.1. It depicts a three-dimensional geometric figure—a cube—but it exists at another, more objective level of description as well. At that more objective level of description, the figure consists of two-dimensional lines, angles, patterns of light and dark, colours, and so on. These elementary features—the building blocks of the meaningful image—are processed by the visual system, through reasonably well-understood physiological systems, and the products of that processing are visual **sensations.** Psychologists have historically thought of sensations—such as a pattern of light and dark, a bitter taste, a change in temperature—as the fundamental, elementary components of experience. **Perception** is the collection of processes used to arrive at a meaningful interpretation of sensations. Through perception, the simple components are organized and interpreted by higher-order brain activities (which are less well understood) into a recognizable, meaningful form. In this case, you perceive a drawing of a three-dimensional *cube*.

Now, let's think about what *interpretation* really means in this context. Look closely at the cube in Figure 4.1. Stare at it for a while. The lines, the angles, and the colours remain fixed, but the cube may appear to shift its orientation periodically. For a while, the shaded surface of the figure is the front of the cube; then, in the next instant, it forms the back of the cube. First you see the cube from one perspective, and then from another. Why is this happening? Certainly the figure on the page remains fixed; the reflected light is not changing systematically with time. The answer lies in your *interpretation* of the sensory image. When you look at the Necker cube, the sensory input—the pattern of lines and colours that is stimulating your visual receptors—is ambiguous. Because the sensory input supports two quite different interpretations equally well, the brain engages in a perceptual dance, shifting from one interpretation to the other (Gaetz, Weinberg, Rzempoluck, & Jantzen, 1998). The extreme ambiguity of the Necker cube is not typical of real-world objects; usually, the pattern of light bouncing off an object and its surrounding environmental context provide the visual system with many cues as to the appropriate interpretation or perception of that object (Gibson, 1966). Nonetheless, the brain does a great deal of active work to interpret those cues to create our perceptions of the world around us.

Constructing Perceptual Experience

P R E V I E W

To appreciate how the brain creates its internal representation of the physical world, we'll discuss each sensory system from the perspective of three important adaptive problems. Each is a fundamental problem that our sensory systems need to solve, regardless of whether the system interprets light, sound, or some other kind of physical energy.

First, how is the external input from the environment translated into the language of the nervous system? As you learned in Chapter 3, communication in the nervous system is an electrochemical process. Input from the outside world takes a variety of forms, but none of it arrives in the electrochemical "language" of the nervous system. For example, you see by means of reflected light, which arrives in the form of electromagnetic energy; you hear by interpreting sound waves, which are rhythmic changes in air pressure. In a sense, it's like trying to listen to someone who speaks a language other than your own. The brain needs an interpreter, a process through which the incoming input is changed into an understandable form. The translation process is called **transduction,** and it's accomplished in a different way by each sensory system.

Second, how are the elementary components—the sensations—extracted from the input? Once environmental input has been successfully translated—represented now in the form of neural impulses—specific features of the input are extracted or pulled out of the complex sensory pattern. For example, any given part of the scene depicted in ❱ Figure 4.2 contains a great deal of overlapping information that must be decomposed into information about simple features of shape and colour

transduction

The process by which external inputs are translated into the internal language of the brain

(e.g., the curved triangular shape of the beak, the green of the feathers). To accomplish this feat, the newly formed neural code is transferred from the transduction sites (i.e., the sensory receptors) along a pathway of neural connections to areas deep within the brain. Each sensory system has a different pathway from the sensory receptors through particular brain regions. Along each pathway, specialized regions of the brain transform the initial neural coding of the input into elementary component sensations.

Third, how does the brain build and maintain a meaningful interpretation of these component sensations once they've been extracted? How, for example, does information about "green" and "curved" give rise to the perception of a leaf? You see objects, not patterns of coloured light and dark; you hear melodies or speech, not sequences of irregularly timed sounds. The biological and psychological mechanisms of perception—the processes that produce the interpretation that we experience as reality—are still under investigation, but we know a good deal about the principles of organization by which the brain interprets sensory input.

To get at these three major questions, this chapter first discusses each major sensory and perceptual system in turn, and then turns to broader issues that cut across the

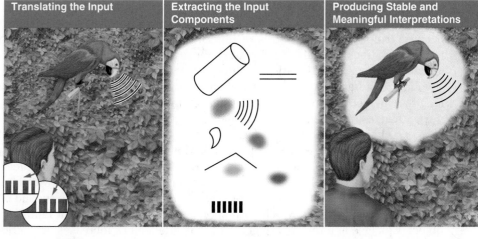

❱ **Figure 4.2**

Adaptive Problems of Sensation and Perception

To create its internal representation of the physical world, the brain needs to solve three fundamental adaptive problems for each sensory system: (1) translating the input from the environment into the language of the nervous system, here represented by the vertical black lines symbolizing bursts of action potentials in sensory neurons; (2) extracting the elementary components or features of the input, such as sounds of particular pitches, particular shapes and colours, and so on; and (3) creating a meaningful interpretation of those component sensations as objects of perception.

senses. As you read, it's important to keep in mind that our sensory and perceptual systems evolved to meet the needs of our ancestors. Also, although in most of the chapter we talk about each sensory and perceptual system separately, in the final section we emphasize that the systems are continually interacting with and affecting one another. Finally, an overarching theme of the chapter is that perception goes beyond the information given in the stimuli received by the sensory receptors; higher-level processes are involved in interpreting the sensory input in ways that resolve ambiguities, fill in missing information, and help us construct a meaningful and coherent perceptual experience.

▶ Vision: Creating a World of Meaningful Objects

LEARNING GOALS

1. Learn how light is translated into the electrochemical language of the brain.
2. Grasp how the essential features of the visual input, such as colour, are extracted by the brain.
3. Understand how a stable, meaningful interpretation of visual information is created and why the interpretation process sometimes leads to visual illusions.

Our discussion of sensation and perception begins with vision, the sense of sight. To understand vision, it's first necessary to know how the physical input—light— is translated into the language of the brain. Then, we'll trace some of the pathways in the brain that extract the basic components of the visual input. Finally, we'll tackle the topic of visual perception: How does the brain create a stable, meaningful interpretation of the pattern of light that stimulates the eyes?

Translating the Input: Visual Transduction

The physical input delivered to visual receptors, **light,** is a form of electromagnetic energy. Visible light is only a very small portion of an electromagnetic spectrum that includes other energy forms, such as X-rays, ultraviolet and infrared light, and even radio and television waves (see ▶ Figure 4.3). We've evolved to see visible light because it bounces off the sorts of things in our environment that matter to us (e.g., rocks, trees, animals); seeing X-rays or radio waves would have been of little advantage to our evolutionary ancestors.

Light can be classified by two main physical properties. The first is wavelength, which corresponds to the physical distance from one energy cycle to the next. Changes in the wavelength of light are generally experienced, psychologically, as changes in colour, or **hue.** Figure 4.3 shows that humans see wavelengths ranging from only about 400 nanometres to 700 nanometres (nm, billionths of a metre). Psychologically, these wavelengths are experienced as colours, ranging roughly from violet to red. Of course, light of other wavelengths also enters your eyes, but you cannot sense those wavelengths. The second physical property is intensity, which corresponds to the amount of light falling on an object. Changes in intensity are generally experienced as increases or decreases in **brightness.**

Light originates from a source, such as the sun or a light bulb, and usually enters the eye after bouncing off objects in its path. Most light is a mixture of many different wavelengths; after hitting an object, some of these wavelengths are absorbed by the object—which ones depends on the physical properties of the surface of the object—and the remaining wavelengths reflect outward. When you look at an object, some of the light bouncing off it enters your eyes through your pupils. It is here, in the eyes, that the important translation process occurs.

light

The small portion of the electromagnetic spectrum that is processed by the visual system; light is typically classified in terms of *wavelength* (the physical distance from one energy cycle to the next) and *intensity* (the amount of light falling on an object)

hue

The dimension of light that produces colour; hue is typically determined by the wavelength of light reflecting from an object

brightness

The aspect of the visual experience that changes with light intensity; in general, as the intensity of light increases, so does its perceived brightness

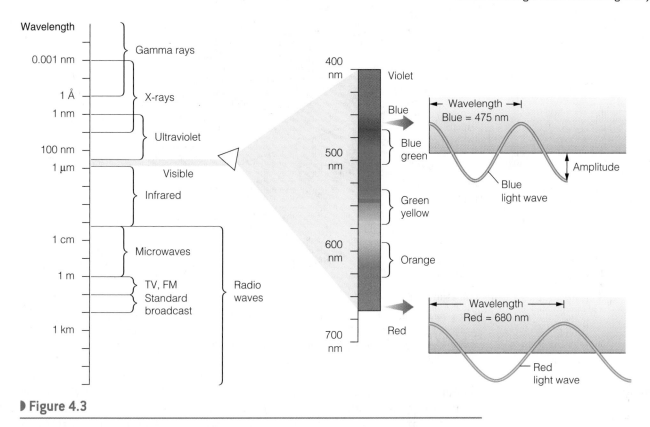

▶ **Figure 4.3**

Light and the Electromagnetic Spectrum

Visible light is only a small portion of the electromagnetic spectrum, which includes other forms of energy, such as X-rays, radio and TV waves, and light waves (such as ultraviolet and infrared), that are not sensed by the human eye. Changes in the wavelength of light from about 400 nm to 700 nm are experienced as changes in colour; short wavelengths are seen as violets and blues, medium wavelengths as yellows and greens, and long wavelengths as reds.

Entering the Eye   The first step in the translation process is to bring the incoming light energy to the light-sensitive receptor cells at the back of each eye. When light bounces off an object, the reflected wavelengths are scattered. They then need to be brought back together—focused—for a clear image to be processed. In the human eye, the focusing process is accomplished by the **cornea,** the protective outer layer of the eye, and by the **lens,** a clear, flexible piece of tissue that sits behind the pupil.

As shown in ▶ Figure 4.4 on page 128, light first passes through the cornea and the pupil before travelling through the lens. The **pupil,** which looks like a black spot, is actually a hole in a ring of coloured tissue called the **iris.** The iris gives the eye its distinctive colour (a person with brown eyes has brown irises), but the colour of the iris plays no role in vision. Relaxing or tightening muscles around the iris changes the size of the pupil, thereby regulating the amount of light that enters the eye. In dim light the pupil gets larger, which allows more light to get in; in bright light the pupil gets smaller, allowing less light to enter.

The lens focuses the light on the sensory receptors at the back of the eye, much as the lens in a camera focuses light on film or, in a digital camera, on a digital sensor array. In a camera, focusing typically involves changing the distance between the lens and the film, like moving a magnifying glass closer to or farther from an object; in the human eye, focusing is accomplished by changing the shape of the lens itself. The adjustment of the shape of the lens, known as

cornea

The transparent and protective outer covering of the eye

lens

The flexible, transparent disk of tissue that helps focus light toward the back of the eye

pupil

The hole in the centre of the iris through which light enters the eye; the size of the pupil changes with light intensity

iris

The ring of coloured tissue surrounding the pupil; if you have brown eyes, your irises are (mostly) brown

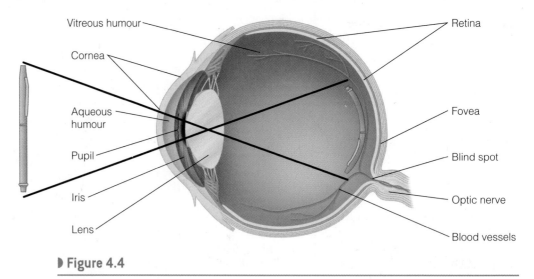

> ▶ **Figure 4.4**

The Human Eye

Light enters the eye through the cornea, pupil, and lens. As the lens changes shape in relation to the distance of the object, the reflected light is focused on the retina at the back of the eye. The light activates photoreceptors; thus, light is transduced into electrochemical neural activity.

---

accommodation

In vision, the process by which the lens changes shape temporarily to help focus light on the retina

---

retina

The thin layer of tissue that covers the back of the inside of the eye and contains the light-sensitive receptor cells for vision

---

CRITICAL   THINKING

It's been reported that pupil size increases with interest or level of emotional involvement (e.g., Tombs & Silverman, 2004). What might be the adaptive value of this phenomenon?

---

rods

Receptor cells in the retina, located mainly on the periphery of the retina, that transduce light energy into neural inputs; highly sensitive and are active in dim light

---

accommodation, depends on the distance between the lens and the object being viewed. When an object is far away, the lens is relatively long and thin; as the object moves closer, muscles attached to the lens contract and the lens becomes thicker and rounder. As people age, the lens loses some of this flexibility, making the accommodation process less efficient (Fukuda, Kanada, & Saito, 1990). This is one reason that people typically require reading glasses or bifocals when they reach middle age. The corrective lenses in the glasses partially substitute for the accommodation process, which the eyes can no longer successfully perform on their own.

Light completes its journey when it reaches a thin layer of tissue called the **retina,** which covers the back of the inside of the eye. Here the electromagnetic energy of light is translated into the electrochemical language of the brain. Embedded in the retina of each eye are about 126 million light-sensitive receptor cells that transduce, or change, the light energy into the electrochemical impulses of neural processing. The translation process is chemically based. Each receptor cell contains a substance, called a *photopigment*, that reacts to light. The light causes a chemical reaction in the cell that ultimately leads to a neural impulse, completing the transduction process. Thus, what begins as a pattern of electromagnetic information becomes a pattern of electrochemical signals, the language of the brain.

You may have noticed in Figure 4.4 that the image on the retina is upside down. The inverted image is created by the optical properties of the lens: The upper part of whatever we look at projects light to the lower part of the retina and vice versa. This process may seem strange, given that we don't see an upside-down world. It's important to remember that we don't see with our eyes. Our perceptual world is built in our brains. The main function of the eyes is to solve the problem of transduction and pass the information on to the brain. The brain later corrects the inversion problem and we see a sensible, right-side-up world.

Rods and Cones   We have two types of receptor cells in our retinas: **rods** and **cones.** Of the roughly 126 million receptor cells within each eye, about 120 million are rods and 6 million are cones. Each receptor type is named for its appearance: Rods are generally long and thin, whereas cones are short, thick, and tapered to a point. Rods are the more sensitive visual receptors; they can generate signals when very small amounts of light strike their surface. This makes rods useful at night and in any situation in which the overall level of illumination is low. Indeed, because of the sensitivity of the rods, people can detect a single photon of light. Rods tend to be concentrated along the periphery, or sides, of the retina. This is one reason that dim images can sometimes be seen more clearly out of the "corners" of your eyes.

Cones are concentrated mostly in the very centre of the retina, bunched in a small central pit called the **fovea.** Unlike rods, cones need relatively high levels of light to operate efficiently, as further discussed below. Cones perform a number of critical visual functions. For example, cones are used for processing fine detail, an ability called **visual acuity.** Cones also play an extremely important role in the early processing of colour, as we'll discuss later.

Dark Adaptation   When you move from a brightly lit environment to a dark one, at first you can see very little, but after a while your vision improves. It takes about 25 minutes for your eyes to adjust fully to very dim light, a process known as **dark adaptation.** As mentioned earlier, visual transduction occurs when light reacts chemically with photopigments in the receptor cells. Photopigments break down, or become "bleached," in the process of reacting to light, which makes them less able to generate a neural impulse. The receptor cells constantly regenerate photopigments, but in bright light the regeneration process cannot keep up with the rate at which photopigments are bleached.

As long as there is plenty of light around, your vision is fine because your eyes never completely run out of photopigment, but when the amount of light is suddenly reduced, your receptor cells don't have enough viable photopigments to detect the low levels of illumination. When there is little light, the rate at which photopigments are bleached is less than the rate at which the cells regenerate photopigments, so as time passes the receptor cells become increasingly sensitive and you can see more. Your eyes have adapted to the low light level.

The timing of the adaptation process is shown in ◗ Figure 4.5. This "dark adaptation curve" depicts the smallest amount of light that people can reliably see, plotted as a function of time spent in the dark. Over time, smaller and smaller amounts of light can be detected. Sensitivity increases because the visual receptor cells are recovering from earlier interactions with bright light, which broke down many of the visual pigments, by regenerating photopigments and hence becoming more sensitive.

Notice that a discontinuity occurs at about the eight-minute mark in the dark adaptation curve. This is because the rods and the cones adapt to the dark at different rates. Early in the dark adaptation function, the cones rapidly increase in

---

cones

Receptor cells in the central portion of the retina that transduce light energy into neural activity; operate best when light levels are fairly high, and they are primarily responsible for the ability to sense fine detail and colour

fovea

The "central pit" area in the centre portion of the retina where most of the cone receptors are located

visual acuity

The ability to see fine detail

dark adaptation

The process through which the eyes adjust to dim light

Each human retina contains two types of photoreceptor cells: rods and cones. As shown in this colour-enhanced photo, the rods are rod-shaped in appearance and the cones are cone-shaped.

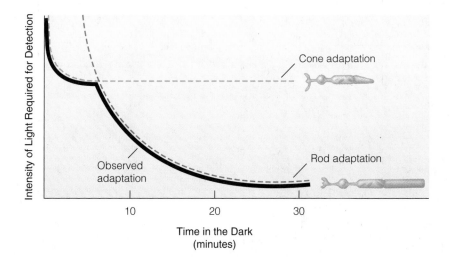

◗ **Figure 4.5**

The Dark Adaptation Curve

The photoreceptors in your eyes gradually adjust to the dark and become more sensitive; that is, you're able to detect light at increasingly low levels of intensity. The rods and cones adapt at different rates and reach different final levels of sensitivity. The dark adaptation curve represents the combined adaptation of the two receptor types. Notice that after about eight minutes a point of discontinuity occurs; this is where further increases in sensitivity are due to the enhanced functioning of the rods.

sensitivity, but they achieve their maximum responsiveness rather quickly. After about seven or eight minutes in the dark, the rods, which can detect quite low levels of illumination, begin to take over, gradually becoming more and more sensitive as they maximize the amount of viable photopigments they contain. Things look grey and lack fine detail in a very dim environment—only the rods are sufficiently sensitive to respond to very low levels of illumination, and rods do not detect colours, and the large receptive fields in the peripheral parts of the retina (where most of the rods are located) are not sensitive to fine details. We've talked about dark adaptation at some length because it is a phenomenon you've experienced many times and it dramatically illustrates that the entryway into vision is the stimulation of photoreceptive cells in the retina.

Early Processing in the Retina   Once an electrochemical signal is generated by a rod or a cone, it's passed along to other cells in the retina, particularly *bipolar cells* and *ganglion cells*, where further processing occurs (see ❯ Figure 4.6). Even at this early stage in visual processing, cells in the retina are beginning to interpret patterns in the incoming visual input. For example, the ganglion cells have what are called **receptive fields,** which means they receive input from a group of receptor cells and respond only to particular patterns of light shining on that group of receptors (Shapley, 1990). For example, the ganglion on the left side of Figure 4.6 might increase its firing rate only when one of the bipolar cells with which it synapses is firing and the other is not firing.

This concept of receptive fields is very important. The fact that a neuron, such as a ganglion cell, receives input from several receptor cells and responds only to a particular pattern across those receptor cells means that it can represent information about how light is spread out across the retina. One byproduct is that we can easily detect edges in visual scenes: Ganglion cells help the visual system tell where light stops and starts. As you'll discover shortly, the complexity of receptive fields increases at later stages of the visual-processing pathway in the brain.

The visual signals generated by the ganglion cells eventually leave the retina, en route to the higher processing stations of the brain, through a collection of nerve fibres called the *optic nerve*. The optic nerve consists of roughly 1 million axons that wrap together to form a sort of visual transmission cable. Where the optic nerve leaves each retina there is no room for visual receptor cells. This creates a biological **blind spot** because there are no receptor cells in this location to transduce the visual

receptive field

In vision, the portion of the retina that, when stimulated, causes the activity of a higher-level neuron (such as a ganglion cell or an even higher-level neuron in the visual cortex) to change

blind spot

The point where the optic nerve leaves the back of the eye; the blind spot has no rods or cones

❯ **Figure 4.6**

Rods, Cones, and Receptive Fields

Rods and cones send signals to other cells in the retina, such as bipolar cells and ganglion cells. Each ganglion cell has a receptive field. Ganglion cells in the fovea, which receive input from cones, tend to have smaller receptive fields than do ganglion cells in the periphery, which receive input from rods. The fovea provides better detail, and the periphery of the retina is more sensitive to low levels of light.

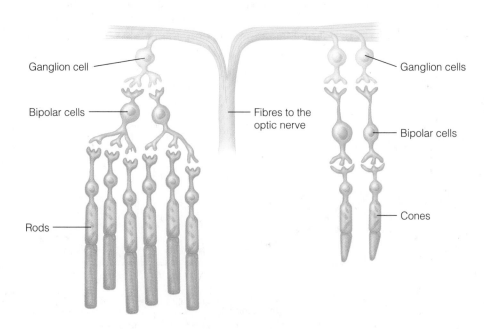

Ganglion cell — Ganglion cells
Bipolar cells — Fibres to the optic nerve
Bipolar cells
Rods — Cones

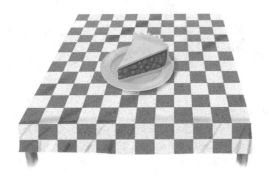

▶ **Figure 4.7**

The Blind Spot

To experience your blind spot, hold this book a few centimetres from your face; close your left eye and focus with your right eye on the boy's face. Then slowly move the book away until the pie mysteriously disappears. Notice that your brain fills in the spot—complete with the checkerboard pattern!

input. Interestingly, people normally experience no holes in their visual field; as part of its interpretation process, the visual system fills in the blind spots to create a continuous visual scene (Durgin, Tripathy, & Levi, 1995; Ramachandran, 1992; Sekuler, 1994). You can locate your blind spot with the exercise described in ▶ Figure 4.7.

Extracting the Input Components: Visual Pathways

After leaving the retina, the neural activity coding the input to each eye flows along each optic nerve until it reaches the *optic chiasm* (from the Greek word meaning "cross"), where the information splits into different tracts leading to the separate hemispheres of the brain (see ▶ Figure 4.8). Information that has been detected on the right half of each retina (from the left visual field) is sent to the right hemisphere, and information falling on the left half of each retina (from the right visual field) projects to the left hemisphere. The majority of the visual signals then move directly toward a major relay station in the thalamus called the *lateral geniculate nucleus*; other signals, perhaps 10% of the total, detour into a midbrain structure called the *superior colliculus*.

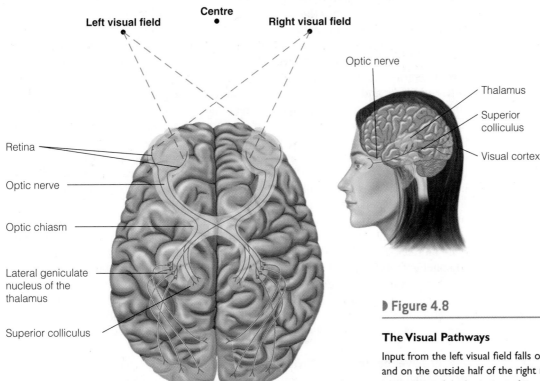

▶ **Figure 4.8**

The Visual Pathways

Input from the left visual field falls on the inside half of the left retina and on the outside half of the right retina and projects to the right hemisphere of the brain; input from the right visual field projects to the left hemisphere. Visual processing occurs at several places along the pathway, ending in the visual cortex, where highly specialized processing takes place.

CONCEPT SUMMARY

COMPARING RODS AND CONES

Characteristic	Rods	Cones
Number	Approximately 120 million per retina	Approximately 6 million per retina
Shape	Generally long and thin	Short, thick, tapered to a point
Location	Concentrated in the periphery of the retina	Concentrated in the centre of the retina, the *fovea*
Sensitivity		
–Light	Sensitive at low levels of illumination	Not very sensitive at low levels of illumination
–Detail	Not sensitive to visual detail	High level of sensitivity to detail; high *visual acuity*
–Colour	Not sensitive to differences in wavelength	Three types, each maximally sensitive to a different wavelength

Significant processing and interpretation of the visual input occur along these pathways. Neuroscientists believe that we have two primary visual pathways from the retina through the lateral geniculate nucleus. One pathway, called the P-channel, is specialized to process colour, texture, and possibly depth; the other, called the M-channel, seems to process movement (Livingstone & Hubel, 1988; Schiller, Logothetis, & Charles, 1990; Shapley, 1990). At the same time, processing in the superior colliculus, a somewhat more primitive structure, controls our ability to localize objects in space by moving our head and eyes (Sparks, 1988). Many of these activities are carried out simultaneously, through what is called **parallel processing:** Different brain regions work together, in parallel, to pull the essential features out of visual input.

parallel processing

Processing that occurs in many different brain regions at the same time, in parallel

Feature Detectors   From the lateral geniculate nucleus, the neural coding of the visual input moves toward the back of the brain, primarily to portions of the occipital lobe. Here, in the primary visual cortex, further elements of the transduced visual input are picked out and identified. For example, Hubel and Wiesel (1962, 1979) discovered **feature detectors** in the visual cortex of cats and monkeys. Feature detectors are cells that respond best to very specific visual events, such as a pattern of light and dark of a particular shape. One type of feature detector, which Hubel and Wiesel called a *simple cell*, responds actively only when a small bar of light shines onto a particular region of the retina. Cells of this type are orientation specific, which means that the visual bar needs to be presented at a particular angle for the cell to respond.

feature detectors

Cells in the visual cortex that respond to very specific visual events, such as bars of light at particular orientations

The properties of these cells were discovered by measuring neural impulses in individual cells by using implanted recording electrodes. An example of this type of experiment, and the equipment used, is shown in ▶ Figure 4.9. Remember: The brain has no pain receptors, which makes it possible for researchers to explore the reactions of brain cells without causing an animal great discomfort. The recorded cells increased, decreased, or showed no changes in their firing rates in response to specific visual stimuli placed in front of the eye. In Figure 4.9, experimenters were recording the reaction to the presentation of a small bar of light presented at a particular angle. Again, Hubel and Wiesel (1962, 1979) found that certain feature detectors in the monkey's brain reacted to this stimulus, and not to other stimuli, and only when the bar was shown at this particular angle.

CRITICAL   THINKING

Can you think of any reason why it might be adaptive for the brain to first break down the visual pattern into basic features—such as a pattern of light and dark—before recombining those features into a unified whole?

Higher-Level Detection   Obviously, the brain is sensitive to more complex visual inputs than just orientation-specific bars. Hubel and Wiesel (1962, 1979) also found cells that responded selectively to more complex patterns, such as corners, edges, bars that moved through the visual field, and bars of a certain length. Other researchers have found cells—once again in monkey brains—that respond most

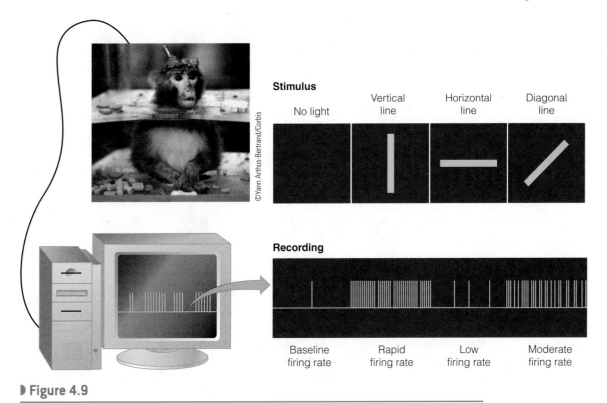

©Yann Arthus-Bertrand/Corbis

Stimulus

| No light | Vertical line | Horizontal line | Diagonal line |

Recording

| Baseline firing rate | Rapid firing rate | Low firing rate | Moderate firing rate |

▶ **Figure 4.9**

Feature Detectors in the Visual Cortex

Hubel and Wiesel discovered feature detectors in the brains of animals. A feature detector is a neuron that increases its firing rate in response to a particular pattern of visual input. Here a cell in a monkey's brain fires a lot when the monkey looks at a vertical line, very little when it looks at a horizontal line, and an intermediate amount in response to a diagonal line.

actively to realistic monkey faces; if the face is distorted or cartoonish, the cells do not respond as actively (Perrett & Mistlin, 1987). Evidence even suggests that some cells are "tuned" to respond selectively to certain facial expressions (Hasselmo et al., 1989). It is also clear that visual object-identification performance depends in part on experience: People with extensive expertise in a given domain (e.g., bird watchers) develop qualitatively different skills at identifying objects in that domain (Tanaka, Curran, & Sheinberg, 2005).

One way that researchers have collected evidence of how the brain parses the visual input is by studying people who have brain damage. Damaging certain parts of the brain leads to very selective, and sometimes bizarre, visual problems. For example, damage to a specific part of a brain area called the fusiform can produce a condition called *prosopagnosia*, in which a person loses the ability to recognize faces (Farah, 1994; Kanwisher, McDermott, & Chun, 1997). A person with prosopagnosia can fail to recognize acquaintances, family members, or even his or her own reflection in a mirror, but his or her ability to identify other sorts of objects seems fine. Patients with a related disorder, *visual agnosia*, have great difficulty recognizing everyday objects, such as fruits and vegetables (see ▶ Figure 4.10 on page 134). In some such cases the disorder is specific to particular categories; for example, the person might be unable to recognize fruits and vegetables but have little difficulty recognizing tools (Arguin, Bub, & Dudek, 1996). Some patients cannot identify the names of colours, even though their colour perceptions seem normal (e.g., Woodward, Dixon, Mullen, Christensen, & Bub, 1999). In another condition, called *akinetopsia*, patients possess normal vision only for objects at rest; if an object is placed in motion, it seems to vanish, only to reappear if it becomes

▶ **Figure 4.10**

Drawings by a Patient with Visual Agnosia

The right-hand side of each column shows the performance of a patient with brain damage who was asked to copy the particular letter, number, or shape. The patient had normal visual acuity and motor coordination but great difficulty perceiving even simple shapes.

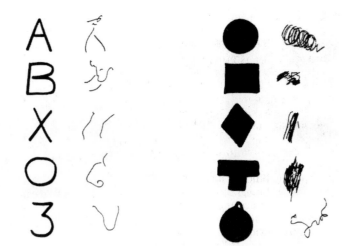

stationary once more. Conversely, patients with a lesion in another cortical location show the most sensitivity to objects that move rather than stay stationary (Zeki, 1992). That damage to specific areas of the brain leads to deficits in specific abilities suggests that the corresponding brain regions play key roles in those abilities.

Additional evidence for specialization in the human brain has come from studies that use PET (positron emission tomography) and fMRI brain-scanning procedures (described in the preceding chapter). While the person's brain is being scanned, a visual stimulus is presented, and the researcher measures which areas of the brain increase their activity. By using this technique, researchers have discovered that certain areas of the brain respond selectively to patterns of dots that move across the visual field (Dupont, Orban, De-Bruyn, & Verbruggen, 1994). Other areas respond selectively to particular tasks, such as matching faces or finding dots in an array (McIntosh, Grady, Ungerleider, & Haxby, 1994). Still other areas of the brain may be selectively involved in the processing of mental images (Kosslyn, Alpert, Thompson, & Maljkovic, 1993). Behrmann, Winocur, and Moscovitch (1992), of Toronto's Rotman Research Institute, described a patient with brain damage who had severe visual agnosia yet had preserved visual imagery (see Servos & Goodale, 1995, for a second such case). Mel Goodale and his colleagues at the University of Western Ontario have demonstrated that patients with brain damage who are grossly impaired in their ability to identify objects nonetheless reach for, grasp, and manipulate them in object-appropriate ways, suggesting that different visual systems underlie describing versus acting on visual stimuli (Goodale & Humphrey, 2000).

Such results as these suggest that the human brain, like the monkey brain, divides its labour. Certain regions of the cortex are specifically designed to process particular parts of the transduced visual input. In other words, there is specificity in the organization and function of the brain. The exact role that each of these parts plays in vision remains to be worked out, and it is likely that particular cells or regions of the brain perform more than one function, but the mysteries of how the brain solves the basic problems of vision are beginning to unravel.

Colour Vision: Trichromatic Theory   One of the most significant things the brain pulls out of the visual input is colour. It turns out that colour information is processed along the entire visual pathway: retina → lateral geniculate nucleus → visual cortex. In the retina, as you'll see shortly, colour information is extracted by comparing the relative activations of different types of cone receptors; higher up in the brain, neuronal representations of visual input encounter cells that are "tuned" to respond only to particular colours.

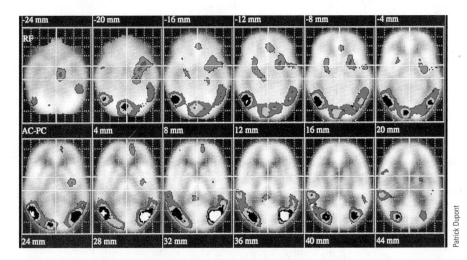

Patrick Dupont

Many areas in the human brain appear to respond selectively to visual motion. The highlighted regions, derived from PET scanning, show areas of the human brain that react more to a moving visual stimulus than to a stationary one.

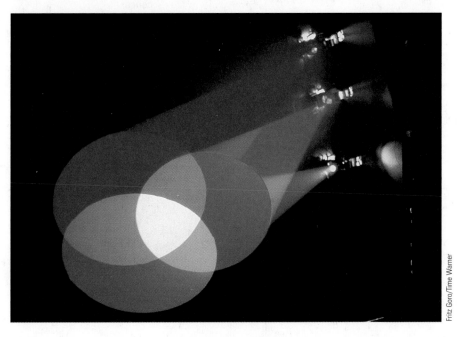

Fritz Goro/Time Warner

Mixing lights with different wavelengths can create a variety of perceived colours—even white.

Earlier you learned that colour is determined primarily by the wavelength of light reflected back into the eye. In general, short wavelengths (around 440 nm) produce blues, medium wavelengths (around 530 nm) produce greens, and long wavelengths (around 600 nm) produce reds. White light, which most people would classify as colourless, is actually a combination of all the wavelengths of the visible spectrum. The reason your neighbour's shirt looks red is that its fabric absorbs all but the long wavelengths of light; the long wavelengths are reflected back into the environment and you see the shirt as red. But in a sense the object itself, the shirt, has no colour; you perceive it as red only because it selectively "rejects," by reflecting outward, red light waves. In the dark, all objects are colourless.

When reflected wavelengths reach the retina, they stimulate photoreceptor cells. Stimulation of the cones plays a key role in colour perception. Physiological analysis of the human eye has revealed three types of cone receptors: One type generates neural impulses primarily to *short* wavelengths; another type responds most energetically to *medium* wavelengths; and a final type responds most to *long* wavelengths of light. The sensitivity of a particular cone type actually spreads across a relatively broad range of individual wavelengths and is determined by the photopigment that the receptor contains (Schnapf & Baylor, 1987). ▶ Figure 4.11 on page 136 shows the sensitivities for each of the types of cones, as well as for the rods.

▶ **Figure 4.11**

Receptor Sensitivity Curves

Blue-sensitive cones are most likely to respond to short wavelengths of light; green-sensitive cones respond best to medium wavelengths; red-sensitive cones respond best to long wavelengths. On the sensitivity curve for rods, notice that rods are not sensitive to long wavelengths of light. (Based on Jones & Childers, 1993.)

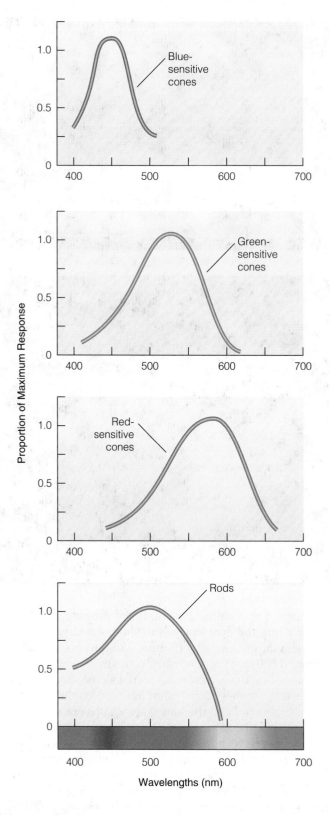

trichromatic theory

A theory of colour vision proposing that colour information is extracted by comparing the relative activations of three different types of cone receptors

The **trichromatic theory** of colour vision proposes that colour information is extracted through the activations of the three types of cones (*trichromatic* means "three-colour"). An early version of the trichromatic theory was proposed in the nineteenth century by Thomas Young and Hermann von Helmholtz, long before modern techniques had verified the existence of the different cone types.

As the basis for their theory, Young and Helmholtz used the fact that most colours can be made by mixing three basic, or *primary*, colours. They speculated that the brain must determine the colour of an object by comparing the relative activation levels of three primary receptors. When just one receptor type is strongly activated, you see one of the primary colours. For example, when a short-wavelength cone is strongly activated, you might see something in the violet to blue region of the spectrum; when a medium cone is active, you would see green. For long wavelengths, which activate the third type of cone, you sense the colour red. All other colours, such as a pumpkin orange, are sensed when more than one receptor type is activated. According to the trichromatic theory, most colours correspond to a mixture of wavelengths and are sensed by comparing the activations of the three receptors.

The trichromatic theory explains a number of interesting aspects of colour vision. For example, it explains certain kinds of colour blindness. At times, nature makes a mistake and fills a person's red cones with green photopigment or the green cones with red photopigment (Boynton, 1979). Under these rare conditions, which affect more males than females, individuals are left with two rather than three operational cone receptors. The trichromatic theory predicts that *dichromats*—people with two rather than three cone types—should lose their ability to discriminate between certain colours. Indeed, people who lack either the red or green cone type have a great deal of trouble distinguishing red from green. Other types of cone loss can produce trouble with blue–green discriminations. The particular type of colour deficiency depends on the particular type of lost receptor.

Colour Vision: Opponent Processes   The physiological evidence, combined with the colour mixing and colour-blindness patterns, provides strong support for the trichromatic theory. But the theory is not a complete account of colour vision. For one thing, the trichromatic theory has a problem with *yellow*. No cones are uniquely sensitive to yellow, but people perceive yellow as every bit as "pure" a colour as red, green, and blue; even four-month-old infants prefer dividing the colour spectrum into four colour categories rather than three (Bornstein, Kessen, & Weiskopf, 1976). In addition, people often report perceiving a yellowish-red or a bluish-green but rarely report seeing a yellowish-blue or a greenish-red. Why?

It turns out that certain colours are specially linked, such as blue and yellow, and red and green. You can discover this for yourself: If you stare at a patch of vivid colour (e.g., bright red) for a while and then switch your focus to a blank white space, you will see an **afterimage** of its *complementary* colour (e.g., green). Exposure to red produces an afterimage of green; exposure to blue results in an afterimage of yellow. The fact that people perceive yellow as a pure colour and that blue light can produce a yellow afterimage is quite difficult for the trichromatic theory to explain.

The McCollough effect (named after its discoverer, Celeste McCollough) is a particularly interesting kind of afterimage. The effect, which has been extensively studied by Lorraine Allan and Shep Siegel at McMaster University (Allan & Siegel, 1997) and by Keith Humphrey and his co-workers at the University of Western Ontario (Humphrey, James, Gati, Menon, & Goodale, 1999), is unusual in two ways. First, as you'll see if you try the demonstration in ▶ Figure 4.12 on page 138, the afterimage is specific to the orientation of the edges in the grid (once you have the afterimage, try rotating the book 45 degrees and notice how the illusory colours "move" to different grids). Second, the effect can last for hours (if you have a strong afterimage now, try it again when you finish reading the chapter). The mechanisms of the McCollough effect are as yet unknown—another of the many mysteries of perception—but it likely has to do with fairly high-level parts of the visual system rather than with the cells in the retina (partly because it involves the integration of information about colour and information about form).

afterimage

A sensation experienced after removal of a stimulus; for example, stare at a red maple leaf for several seconds; when you shift your focus to a blank part of the page, you will see a green afterimage

▶ **Figure 4.12**

The McCollough Effect

Look at the two coloured grids (alternating back and forth between them every few seconds) for at least two minutes. Then look at the black and white grid. You should see a greenish haze around the horizontal lines and a magenta haze around the vertical lines. If it doesn't work, try looking at the coloured grids for a longer period, and then return your gaze to the black and white grid.

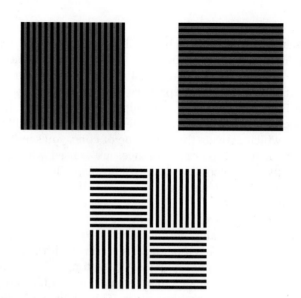

opponent process theory

A theory of colour vision proposing that certain cells in the visual pathway increase their activation levels to one colour and decrease their activation levels to another colour (e.g., increasing to red and decreasing to green)

CRITICAL   THINKING

Based on what you've learned about colour vision, why do you think traffic lights change between red and green?

The difficulties with the trichromatic view were recognized in the nineteenth century by the German physiologist Ewald Hering. Hering proposed an alternative view of colour vision: **opponent process theory.** He suggested that there must be cells in the visual system that respond positively to one colour (such as red) and negatively to another (such as green). Instead of three primary colours, Hering proposed six: *blue*, which is linked to *yellow* (therefore solving the problem with yellow); *green*, which is linked to *red*; and finally, *white*, which is linked to *black*. According to the opponent process theory, people have difficulty perceiving a yellowish-blue because activation of, say, the blue mechanism is accompanied by inhibition, or decreased activation, of the yellow mechanism. A yellowish-red does not present a problem in this scheme because yellow and red are not linked in an opponent fashion.

Like Young and Helmholtz, Hering was operating in a kind of physiological vacuum—he had no solid physiological evidence either for a three-receptor system or for specially linked opponent process cells. Such evidence now exists. For example, in addition to discovering different cone photopigments, researchers have found brain cells at various points in the visual pathway that code colour information in an opponent process fashion (DeValois & DeValois, 1980). The activity of these cells increases in response to one type of colour (e.g., red) and decreases to another (e.g., green).

So what underlies our ability to detect such a vast array of colours in the world? The visual system pulls colour information out of the visual input by relying on multiple processing stations. Colour information is extracted first at the retinal level through the activations of different cone types; farther up in the brain, opponent process neurons fine-tune and further process the visual information. Thus, a combination of the trichromatic and opponent process views best characterizes our current knowledge about colour extraction (but other types of neurons that also contribute to colour vision probably exist in the visual cortex; see Gegenfurtner, Xing, Scott, & Hawken, 2003).

Producing Stable and Meaningful Interpretations: Visual Perception

Let's return, for a moment, to the cube in Figure 4.1 (page 124). You've seen how the electromagnetic energy bouncing off the page is translated into an electro-chemical signal, and how specialized regions of the visual pathway break down the

CONCEPT SUMMARY

COMPARING TRICHROMATIC AND OPPONENT PROCESS THEORY

Theory	Stage of Processing	Processing Mechanism	Basic Description
Trichromatic	Early, in the retina	Three different cone types, maximally sensitive to short, medium, or long wavelengths of light, respectively	The brain compares the relative activity levels among the three cone types to determine the colour of a stimulus; helps to explain certain types of colour blindness (e.g., *dichromats*)
Opponent process	Later, in the visual pathway	Three types of mechanisms (e.g., cells) that respond positively and negatively to certain colour pairs (red-green; blue-yellow; black-white)	Mechanism responds positively to one member of a particular colour pair (e.g., blue) and negatively to the other (e.g., yellow); helps to explain complementary colour afterimages and prominence of yellow as a primary colour

visual information—the brain extracts lines, edges, colours, and even angles of orientation from the visual scene. But your perception is of seeing a cube—a particular object form—not a collection of elementary features.

To understand how the brain can generate perceptions of whole objects with visual machinery that seems designed to analyze parts, it helps to remember that perception is only partly determined by what comes in through the eyes. People also rely a great deal on their knowledge and expectations to construct what they see. Let's consider a simple example: Take a look at the two images depicted in ▶ Figure 4.13. You probably have no trouble seeing the image in part (a): It's the word SKY, written in white against a black background (although note that none of the letters is fully defined, and the figure could instead be seen as a series of irregular black shapes). Part (b) probably looks like a meaningless collection of black shapes (unless you read Chinese). Part (b) also shows the word SKY, but it's written in Chinese. People who can read English but not Chinese see part (a) as a meaningful image; those who can read Chinese but not English see part (b) as the meaningful image (Coren, Ward, & Enns, 1999). Thus, prior knowledge plays a critical role in how the brain interprets and organizes visual input.

People often use parts of a visual display to help interpret other parts. For example, take a look at each of the following lines of text:

A B C D E F G

10 11 12 13 14 15 16

The "B" in the first line is identical to the "13" in the second, but you "see" the letter B in the first line and the number 13 in the second because the other symbols in each line act as context that guides the perceptual interpretation of the ambiguous

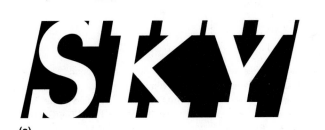

(a)

(b)

▶ **Figure 4.13**

Prior Knowledge and Perception

Whether you detect meaningful images in parts (a) and (b) depends on the prior knowledge you bring to your perceptual interpretation of these stimuli. (From Coren, Ward, & Enns, 2004.)

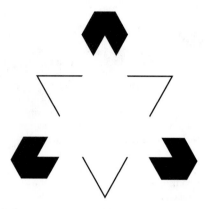

▶ **Figure 4.14**

Illusory Contours

Can you see the white upright triangle embedded in this figure? No physical stimulus corresponds to that triangular form. Nonetheless, people interpret the pattern as a triangle.

bottom-up processing

Processing that is driven by the physical input contacting the sensory receptors

top-down processing

Processing that is driven by beliefs and expectations about how the world is organized

stimuli. In some cases, how the elements are arranged in a visual display can even cause people to see things that aren't really there. Is a white triangle embedded in the middle of ▶ Figure 4.14? It sure looks like there is, but the perception is really an illusion—there is no physical stimulus, no reflected pattern of electromagnetic energy on the retina, that corresponds to the triangular form. Yet you interpret the pattern as a triangle.

There is more to perception than what meets the eye. Our perceptual world is constructed through a combination of two important kinds of mental activities. First, as we've been discussing throughout the chapter, the visual system analyzes the sensory input, the pattern of electromagnetic information on the retina. Psychologists refer to this as **bottom-up processing**—processing that starts with the raw physical input stimulating the sensory receptors and works its way up to higher brain areas. Second, we also use our knowledge, beliefs, and expectations about the world to interpret and organize information from lower-level sensory systems, something psychologists call **top-down processing**. Perception always reflects a combination of these two kinds of processes. What you see is determined by what's out there in the world and by what you *expect* to be out there.

Principles of Organization   You may recall that in Chapter 1 we briefly discussed the possibility that people are born with certain organizing principles of perception. This point of view was championed by a group of researchers known as *Gestalt psychologists* (the word *Gestalt* translates from the German as "configuration" or "pattern"). According to the Gestalt psychologists, people see objects as well-structured and organized wholes because people are born with tendencies to *group* the incoming visual input in sensible ways. For example, people have a natural, automatic tendency to divide any visual scene into a *figure* and a *ground*—we see the wine glass as separate from the table, the printed word as separate from the page. As you can see from ▶ Figure 4.15, the task of separating figure from ground is easy or difficult depending on whether strong or weak cues are available to guide the interpretation.

▶ **Figure 4.15**

Separating Figure from Ground

We have a natural tendency to divide any visual scene into a discernible "figure" and "ground." This task can be easy but ambiguous, as in the black and white image on the left (do you see a vase or a pair of profiles?), and it can be difficult, as in the painting on the right (how many faces can you find in the "ground" of the painting? We've found 10 so far!). (© Bev Doolittle, "The Forest Has Eyes," The Greenwich Workshop)

The Gestalt psychologists outlined a number of compelling and systematic regularities in human perception, known generally as the **Gestalt principles of organization,** that describe how people organize visual input to create the perception of whole objects:

1. *The law of proximity.* If the elements of a display are close to each other—that is, they lie in close spatial proximity—they tend to be grouped together as part of the same object. Here, for example, you see three groups of dots rather than a single collection.

Proximity

2. *The law of similarity.* Items that share physical properties—that physically resemble each other—tend to be perceived as belonging together. Thus, here you see rows of Xs and rows of Os rather than mixed-letter columns.

Similarity

3. *The law of closure.* If a figure has a gap, or a small amount of its border is missing, people nonetheless tend to perceive the object as complete. Below, for example, you likely perceive each figure as a circle, even though neither is a complete circle.

Closure

4. *The law of good continuation.* If lines cross or are interrupted, people tend to see continuously flowing lines. In the following figure you have no trouble perceiving the snake as a whole object, even though part of it is blocked from view.

Continuation

AMAZONIAN BOA

5. *The law of common fate.* If things appear to be moving in the same direction, people tend to group them together. Here the moving dots are classified together as a group, with some fate in common.

Common fate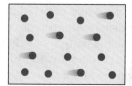

Gestalt principles of organization

The organizing principles of perception proposed by the Gestalt psychologists, which are the laws of proximity, similarity, closure, continuation, and common fate

Object Recognition   By imposing organization on a visual scene, the natural grouping tendencies described by the Gestalt principles simplify the problem of recognizing objects. Psychologist Irving Biederman (1987, 1990) suggested that the Gestalt principles of organization help the visual system break down complex visual inputs into components called *geons* (short for "geometric ions"). Geons are simple geometrical forms, such as blocks, cylinders, wedges, and cones. From a collection of only 36 geons, Biederman argues, more than 150 million possible distinct complex and meaningful objects can be created—far more than people would ever need to capture the richness of their perceptual world. Once the brain is familiar with the basic geons, it can recognize the basic components of any perceptual experience. Just as the 26 letters of the alphabet form the basis for a huge variety of words and an infinite variety of sentences, geons could form the alphabet for building any object a person might see.

One of the attractive features of Biederman's theory, which he calls **recognition by components,** is its ability to explain how people can successfully identify degraded or incomplete objects. In everyday life, parts of objects in the environment are often occluded by other objects. For example, when you are driving, the other vehicles you see are typically partially hidden behind other cars, and at the dinner table the cutlery may be obscured by your plate. Yet you have no trouble recognizing the car or the fork. According to Biederman (1987), only a few geons are needed for the rapid identification of most objects.

To illustrate, Biederman asked subjects to identify degraded drawings of objects, such as the ones shown in ▶ Figure 4.16. In some cases, the items were presented intact; in other conditions, the images were made more difficult to see by removing bits of information that either maintained (even-numbered items) or disrupted (odd-numbered items) the component geons. Not surprisingly, people had no problem recognizing the even-numbered objects but had considerably more trouble when the geons were obscured. In fact, Biederman found that identification of the geon-disrupted drawings was almost impossible—most people in this condition failed to identify any of the objects correctly.

It remains to be seen whether Biederman's theory will provide a complete account of object recognition. Not all researchers are convinced that a relatively small set of basic shapes is sufficient to allow us to identify and discriminate among all objects (Liu, 1996). Many objects share basic parts, yet we're able to quickly and efficiently tell them apart. Moreover, there may be certain kinds of objects, such as faces, that seem to be perceived and remembered immediately as wholes, without any breaking down or building up from parts. As you learned earlier, some cells in the brain respond selectively to faces; also certain kinds of brain damage make recognizing faces, but not other objects, difficult or impossible. We're capable of recognizing an enormous range of objects in our world without hesitation, and it may well be that our brains solve the problems of object recognition in a number of different ways (Hayward, 2003).

The Perception of Depth   The ability to perceive depth is one of the most amazing capabilities of the visual system. Think about it: The input to the visual system is a two-dimensional pattern of light falling on the surface of the retina. Yet, somehow, people extract a rich three-dimensional world from the "flat" image on the retina. As we will discuss in Chapter 10, the ability to perceive depth develops early in life (see also Tychsen, 2001): Infants as young as a few months can clearly tell the difference between the shallow and deep sides of a visual cliff (Gibson & Walk, 1960) and can even perceive depth in at least some kinds of two-dimensional displays (Schmuckler & Proffitt, 1994). How does the visual system create such a rich and vivid perceptual experience from the two-dimensional pattern of light falling on the retina?

Depth perception arises from a combination of bottom-up and top-down processing. People use their knowledge about objects, in combination with bottom-up processing of the visual input, to create the perception of a three-dimensional visual

---

recognition by components

The idea proposed by Biederman that people recognize objects perceptually through smaller components called *geons*

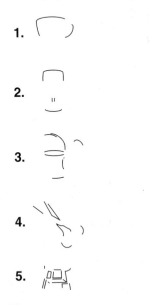

▶ **Figure 4.16**

Recognition by Components

Biederman proposed that we recognize visual forms in part by extracting simple geometric forms—geons—from the visual input. Above are degraded versions of drawings of common objects. Can you identify them? In drawings 1, 3, and 5, bits of lines that define geons have been removed, whereas in drawings 2 and 4 other bits of lines that do not define geons have been removed. You will likely find it easier to identify the objects in the even-numbered rows (intact geons) than those in the odd-numbered rows (disrupted geons). See page 148 for the answers. (From "Higher-Level Vision," by I. Biederman. In D. H. Osherson, S. M. Kosslyn, and J. M. Hollerback (eds.), *An Invitation to Cognitive Science: Visual Cognition and Action*, Vol. 2, p. 135. Copyright © 1990 MIT Press. Reprinted by permission.)

Donovan Reese/PhotoDisc/Getty Images

Edmond Van Hoorick/PhotoDisc/Getty Images

Kim Steele/PhotoDisc/Getty Images

Can you identify the types of cues present in these "flat" pictures that allow us to perceive depth?

world. For example, the brain knows and adjusts for the fact that distant objects produce smaller reflections on the retina. Thus, if you see two people whom you *know* to be of comparable height, but the retinal images they produce are of different sizes, your brain assumes that one person must be standing closer to you than the other is. Experience also makes it clear that closer objects tend to block the images of objects that are farther away: If your view of a TV screen is blocked by a human form, the visual system infers that the person is standing in *front* of the television and is therefore closer to you than is the television.

Another cue for distance, one that artists often use to depict depth in paintings, is *linear perspective*. As shown in the accompanying photos, parallel lines that recede into the distance converge toward a single point. Generally, the farther away two parallel lines are from the viewer, the closer together those lines will appear to be. The relative shading of objects in a scene can provide important cues as well: If one object casts a shadow on another, you can often tell which of the two is farther away. Objects that are far away also tend to look blurry and slightly bluish. If you look at a realistic painting of a mountain scene, you'll see that the distant hills lack fine detail and are painted with a tinge of blue. (See Loftus & Harley, 2005, for an interesting exploration of how and why distant faces appear blurrier, and hence harder to recognize, than closer faces.)

In everyday environments, the ground stretches away from the viewer to the visual boundaries of the environment (the walls of a room or the horizon line out of doors). The ground—whether it's a leaf-strewn lawn or a linoleum floor—has visual texture; that is, there are variations of light and dark and (usually) of colour across the surface of the ground. The texture of nearby ground appears relatively coarse or rough, and the texture of more distant ground looks progressively finer and smoother. For example, kneel on a carpet and look across its surface toward the far wall: The visual texture of the carpet close to your eyes appears coarse, whereas that far away appears fine. Gibson (1966) proposed that such **texture gradients** provide the visual system with a great deal of information about the distance between a viewer and objects on the ground.

Shaun Vecera and co-authors (Vecera, Vogel, & Woodman, 2002) documented another cue to figure-ground discrimination, which they call "**lower region**": All else being equal, the lower part of a scene tends to be perceived as "figure" and the upper part as "ground." ▶ Figure 4.17 on page 144 provides a simple example. In a natural setting, regions below the horizon line are usually closer to the observer than are regions above the horizon line, and the objects with which people typically

texture gradient

Gradual reduction, with increasing distance, of the apparent coarseness of a surface (such as the ground or floor); provides a powerful cue to the distances of objects located on that surface

lower region

Bias to perceive the lower part of a visual scene as the "figure" (meaningful object of perception) rather than "ground" (background)

▶ **Figure 4.17**

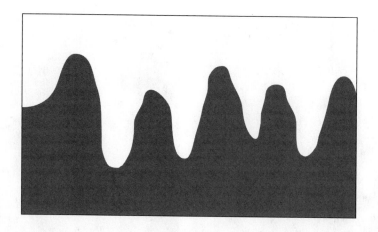

"Lower Region" Depth Cue

Most people see this drawing as consisting of black stalagmite-like figures rising up against a white background, but the drawing can also be perceived as white stalactite-like figures hanging down against a black background. Turn the page upside down: If you are like most people, you will still be biased to see the "lower region" (now coloured white) as the figure.

interact (rocks, plants, animals) are more often below than above the horizon line; presumably, the visual system has adaptively developed a bias to interpret stimuli in the lower region of a scene as figure rather than as ground. Lower region is a relatively weak bias—you can overcome it easily by changing the way you think about the stimulus—but nonetheless it biases us toward perceiving shapes in the lower region as ground.

The depth cues that we've been considering so far are called **monocular depth cues,** which means they can work even if there is input from only one eye. A person can close one eye and still see a world full of depth, based on the use of monocular cues, such as the ones we discussed above. But the brain also uses **binocular depth cues;** these are cues produced by two eyes, each with a slightly different view of the world. Hold your index finger up a few centimetres in front of your eyes. Now close and open each eye in alternation. You should see your finger jumping back and forth as you switch from one open eye to the other. The finger appears to move because each eye has a slightly different angle of view on the world (because the eyes are about 5 cm apart), producing different images in each retina. The difference between the images in the two eyes is called **retinal disparity.** The brain derives depth information, in part, by calculating the amount of disparity between the image in the left eye and the image in the right eye. Move your finger farther away and try looking at it with one eye shut and then the other; the amount of disparity is now much less than it was when your finger was close to your eyes. The brain also uses the degree that the two eyes turn inward to focus on an object, called **convergence,** to derive information about depth. The closer an object is to the face, the more the two eyes need to turn inward, or converge, for the object to be seen in focus.

We have described only some of the more important depth cues. Psychologists have identified many other kinds of information that the visual system also uses to infer the distance of objects and to create the compelling three-dimensional experience of seeing the world around us (see Coren et al., 2004). We hope that, in addition to learning about the cues to depth that we have discussed, you have developed an appreciation for the sophistication and complexity of visual perception. What to most people seems an effortless task—looking around and perceiving a three-dimensional world of people and objects—is in fact an enormous accomplishment. Interestingly, as described in the Practical Solutions box, the same mechanisms that enable us to perceive the three-dimensional depth of the world around us can also give rise to illusory perceptions of depth in two-dimensional images.

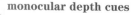

monocular depth cues

Cues for depth for which input from one eye is sufficient

binocular depth cues

Cues for depth that depend on comparisons between the two eyes

retinal disparity

A binocular cue for depth that is based on differences between the images in each eye

convergence

A binocular cue for depth that is based on the extent to which the two eyes move inward, or converge, when looking at an object

CREATING ILLUSIONS OF DEPTH

To survive in a three-dimensional environment, animals that move rapidly must perceive depth. Yet the pattern of light falling on the retina is only two-dimensional: It has height and width, but not depth. As you've read in this chapter, the visual system solves this problem by using multiple cues to depth (the dimension not directly represented on the retina).

The same processes that have evolved to enable us to perceive the depth of the real three-dimensional world can also give rise to illusions of depth in certain kinds of two-dimensional pictures. For example, three-dimensional movies are made by filming each scene twice, from slightly different angles, then projecting both versions simultaneously to viewers who are wearing special glasses with lenses that selectively deliver one image to the right eye and the other image to the left eye. If done just right, this arrangement simulates the *retinal disparity* (discussed in the section "The Perception of Depth") that would occur if the viewer were really looking at a three-dimensional object. Our two eyes are separated by several centimetres, and that means that when we look at a three-dimensional scene, each eye gets a slightly different view (e.g., looking at a cup on the desk, your left eye sees more of the cup's left side and less of its right side than does your right eye [and vice versa], and the amount of disparity is systematically related to the distance of the object). By using two cameras to record a scene, two projectors to present them, and a device (such as special glasses) to separate the projected images so that one image goes to each eye, three-dimensional movies mimic this natural retinal disparity, thereby giving rise to an illusion of depth from the two-dimensional stimulus of the movie. Some three-dimensional movies use red and green lenses to separate the signal to each eye, whereas others use polarized lenses, which selectively filter the light according to its angle.

The once-popular children's toy called a View-Master works on the same principle: When you look through the View-Master you are viewing two pictures of the same scene, taken from slightly different perspectives, and the device delivers one image to each eye, thereby producing the illusion of depth.

Neither three-dimensional movies nor the View-Master are currently in fashion, and you may never have seen either of them. But you probably *have* seen single-image random-dot stereograms like that shown in ▶ Figure 4.18. These enjoyed prolonged popularity throughout the 1990s, although the fad for them seems to be waning (perhaps partly because it is somewhat difficult to experience a three-dimensional effect with them). The best thing about stereograms is that you don't need special glasses or any other device to make them work—just a little patience. The pattern consists of two superimposed systematic patterns of dots (or blobs) that are slightly offset: One pattern taken from one perspective, another from a perspective about 7.5 cm (3 in.) to one side. One pattern corresponds to the pattern of stimulation your left eye would receive if it were looking at a three-dimensional object a few centimetres beyond the plane of the stereogram; the other pattern corresponds to what your right eye would receive. When you look at the images in the right way, as though you were focusing on an object a few centimetres beyond the plane of the stereogram, your brain fuses separate pairs of points in the image as though they were slightly different perspectives on the same point, thereby giving rise to a three-dimensional illusion.

Make sure you are in a brightly lit environment. Hold the book in front of your face, with Figure 4.18 several centimetres from your nose. Imagine that you are focusing on an object more than a metre in front of you. The stereogram will be blurry because it is very close but you are focused as though looking at something in the distance. Keep staring blankly forward as you gradually and smoothly move the book away from your eyes. What you are trying to do is set up a situation in which (1) the convergence of your eyeballs is appropriate for looking at a relatively distant object but (2) the image of the figure is in fairly good focus. If you achieve this, a three-dimensional image will arise. As in the other examples described above, this illusion arises from the adaptive mechanisms that enable us to perceive the depth of the real world around us. In turn, studies of stereograms have provided new insights into the nature and operation of those adaptive mechanisms (e.g., Grove, Gillam, & Ono, 2002).

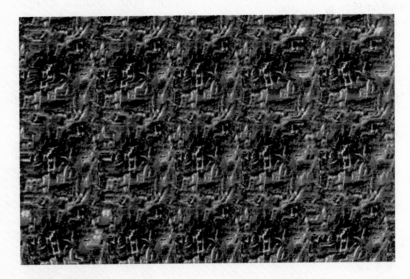

▶ **Figure 4.18**

Random-Dot Stereogram

An example of a single-picture random-dot stereogram

CONCEPT SUMMARY

DEPTH CUES

Type of Cue	Cue	Description
Monocular	Relative size	Comparably sized stimuli that produce different-sized retinal images are perceived as varying in distance from the observer.
	Occlusion	Closer objects tend to block the images of objects farther away.
	Linear perspective	Parallel lines that recede into the distance appear to converge on a single point.
	Shading	Shadows cast by objects on other objects assist in depth perception.
	Haze	Distant objects tend to look blurry and slightly bluish.
	Texture gradient	The texture of the ground on which an object is sitting appears relatively coarse if the object is near and relatively fine if the object is distant.
Binocular	Retinal disparity	The differences between the locations of the images in the two eyes; the amount of disparity changes with distance from a point of fixation.
	Convergence	The closer the stimulus, the more the eyes turn inward toward one another.

Perceptual Constancies   Yet another rather remarkable feature of the human visual system is its capacity to recognize that an object remains the same even when the image on the retina changes. As a case in point, consider how the size of an object's retinal image decreases with distance. As you walk away from a parked car, the size of its retinal image becomes smaller and smaller—so that it eventually resembles the image that might be reflected from a toy car held at arm's length. Do you ever wonder why your car has mysteriously been transformed into a toy? You don't, of course, because your visual system maintains a stable interpretation of the image—as a normal-sized car—despite the changes in retinal size.

When you perceive an object, or its properties, as remaining the same even though the physical input received by your eyes is changing, you are experiencing a **perceptual constancy.** In the car example, it is *size constancy*—the perceived size of the car remains constant even though the size of the reflected image is changing with distance. ▶ Figure 4.19 provides an example of *shape constancy*. Consider how many changes occur in the reflected image of a door as it moves from closed to open. Yet you still recognize it as a door, not as some bizarre shape that changes over time. Size and shape constancies are related. Both result, at least in part, from the visual system's use of cues to determine distance. Both are also extremely adaptive characteristics, because most of the time the size and shape of an object do, in fact, remain constant as the observer's distance or perspective changes—only its reflected image changes.

perceptual constancy

Perceiving the properties of an object as remaining the same even though the physical properties of the sensory input from that object are changing

▶ Figure 4.19

Shape Constancy

Think about all the changes in the image of a door as it moves from closed to open. Yet we perceive it as a constant rectangular shape.

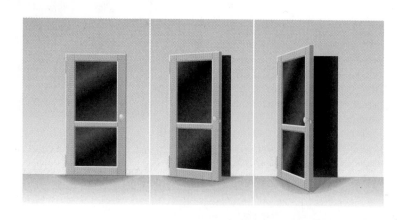

▶ **Figure 4.20**

Constancy Cues

We see these three planters, marked A, B, and C, as matching in size and shape partly because of depth cues in the environment: Each covers three tiles in its length and three in its width.

To see what kind of cues might be used to produce constancy, take a look at ▶ Figure 4.20. Take particular note of the rectangular shapes on the ground marked as A, B, and C. You see these planters as being the same size and shape, in part, because of the texture patterns covering the ground. Each open box covers three texture tiles in its length and an additional three in its width. The retinal image, however, differs markedly for each of the shapes (take a ruler and measure the physical size of each shape). You interpret and see them as the same because your experiences in the world have taught you that size and distance are related in systematic ways.

People experience perceptual constancies for a variety of object dimensions. In addition to size and shape constancy, the brightness and colour of an object typically appear to remain constant, even though the intensity and wavelength of the light change when ambient lighting conditions vary. Once again, these characteristics help us maintain a stable and orderly interpretation of a constantly changing sensory input. Think about how chaotic the world would appear if you saw a new and different object every time the physical properties of its reflected image changed. For example, instead of seeing a dancer gliding across the floor, you might see a series of dancers, each striking a unique pose.

Perceptual Illusions   The processes by which the brain interprets the ambiguous and incomplete information that reaches the retina can also give rise to **perceptual illusions,** or inaccurate interpretations of physical reality. For example, look at the two girls sitting in the room depicted in ▶ Figure 4.21 on page 148. The girl on the right appears to be much taller than the girl on the left. In reality, the two girls are approximately the same size. You're tricked because your brain uses cues in the environment—combined with the assumption that rooms are vertically and horizontally rectangular—to interpret the size of the occupants. Actually, as the rest of the figure shows, it is the room (known as the Ames room), not the sizes of the girls, that is unusual.

Based partly on your expectations about the shape of rooms and partly on the unique construction of the Ames room, as you look through the peephole you think you're looking at two people who are the same distance from your eyes. But the person on the left is actually farther away, so a smaller image is projected onto the retina (and onto the page). Because the brain assumes the two are the same distance away, it also assumes that the person on the right is larger (Dorward & Day, 1997). A related phenomenon is called the moon illusion: The full moon often looks huge as it

perceptual illusions

Inappropriate interpretations of physical reality; perceptual illusions often occur as a result of the brain's use of otherwise adaptive organizing principles

Answers to Figure 4.16

1.

2.

3.

4.

5.

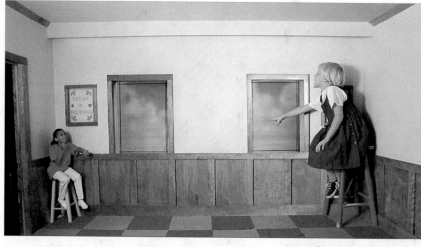

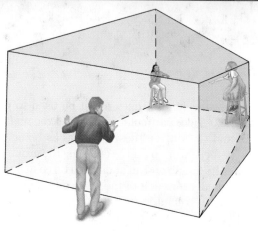

Richard Nowitz/Phototake

▶ **Figure 4.21**

The Ames Room

The girl on the right appears to be much taller than the girl on the left. But this is an illusion induced by the visual system's assumption that the room is rectangular. The sloping ceiling and floors and the angle of the back wall, along with systematic distortions of the shape and size of details in the room, provide misleading depth cues. For example, neither of the windows is really rectangular, and the window on the left is larger than that on the right. To the viewer looking through the peephole, the room appears perfectly normal. The misleading cues lead the visual system to perceive the two girls as being approximately the same distance away from the viewer; hence the girl on the right, who (because she is nearer) projects a larger image on the retina (and on the page), is perceived as larger. Here you see only a photo of an Ames room; the effect is even more compelling when you peep into an actual Ames room.

rises over the horizon, and appears to dwindle in size as it gradually mounts higher into the sky, but neither the size of the moon nor the size of its reflected image entering your eyes changes, as shown by photographs in which the moon's diameter does not change as a function of its position in the sky (see Coren, 1992).

The Ponzo illusion, shown in part (a) in ▶ Figure 4.22, operates in a similar way. You see two lines that are exactly the same size as quite different because the linear perspective cue—the converging parallel lines—tricks the brain into thinking that the horizontal line near the top of the display is farther away. Because it has the same-sized retinal image as the bottom line (remember, the two are physically the same size), the brain compensates for the "distance" by making the top line appear larger. Part (b) in Figure 4.22 shows a similar illusion: The monsters are really the same size (measure them with a ruler), but the one on the top appears to be much larger. This is yet another example of a key theme of this text: What you see is more than meets the eye!

CRITICAL THINKING

Our perceptual systems give rise to certain illusions (such as the Ponzo illusion illustrated in part (a) in Figure 4.22). How can this be squared with the idea that our brains have evolved adaptively?

(a)

(b)

▶ **Figure 4.22**

Illusion of Depth

These two figures, based on the Ponzo illusion, show that depth cues can lead to perceptual errors. In part (a) the horizontal lines are actually the same size, as are the monsters in part (b). (From *Mind Sights* by Roger N. Shepard. Copyright © 1990 by Roger N. Shepard. Reprinted by permission of Henry Holt and Company, LLC.)

Test Yourself 4.1

Check your knowledge about vision by answering the following questions. (The answers are in Appendix B.)

1. To test your understanding of how the visual input is translated into the language of the brain, choose the best answers from among the following terms: accommodation, cones, cornea, fovea, lens, opponent process, pupil, receptive field, retina, rods, trichromatic.
   a. The "central pit" area where the cone receptors tend to be located: _____
   b. Receptors that are responsible for visual acuity, or our ability to see fine detail: _____
   c. The process through which the lens changes its shape temporarily to help focus light: _____
   d. The "film" at the back of the eye that contains the light-sensitive receptor cells: _____
   e. The protective outer layer of the eye:

   _____

2. Decide whether each of the following statements about how your brain extracts components from visual input is true or false.
   a. Visual input tends to be analyzed primarily by structures in the superior colliculus, although structures in the lateral geniculate are important too. *True or False?*
   b. It's currently believed that information about colour and movement is probably processed in separate pathways in the brain. *True or False?*
   c. The opponent process theory of colour vision makes it easier to understand why most people think there are four, rather than three, primary colours (red, green, blue, yellow). *True or False?*

   d. Some feature detectors in the brain are "tuned" to respond only when certain patterns of light stimulate the retina. *True or False?*

3. Test your knowledge about visual perception by filling in the blanks. Choose your answers from the following terms: binocular depth cues, bottom-up processing, convergence, monocular depth cues, lower region, perceptual constancy, perceptual illusion, retinal disparity, recognition by components, top-down processing.
   a. The contribution of our beliefs and expectations about how the world is organized to our perceptual experience:

   _____
   b. Perceiving an object, or its properties, to remain the same even though the physical input received by the eyes is changing: _____
   c. The depth cue that is based on calculating the degree to which the two eyes have turned inward:

   _____
   d. The view that object perception is based on the analysis of simple building blocks called geons:

   _____
   e. People have a bias to perceive the

   _____ of a scene as the figure rather than as ground.

▶ Hearing: Identifying and Localizing Sounds

LEARNING GOALS

1. Understand how physical sound input is translated into the electrochemical language of the brain.
2. Learn how pitch information is pulled out of the auditory input.
3. Comprehend how the auditory input is interpreted to localize the source of a sound.

Imagine the world without sound. You wouldn't hear music, speech, or laughter. Hearing enriches our life and, like vision, it serves a variety of very adaptive functions. For example, sounds help us identify and locate objects, and it is through sound that we produce and comprehend the spoken word. Even our most private sense of self—the world inside our heads—often appears in the form of an inner voice, an ongoing speech-based monologue (see Chapter 7).

Translating the Input: Auditory Transduction

The physical input received by the auditory system, **sound,** is a form of energy that, like light, travels as a wave. However, sound—unlike light—is mechanical energy and requires a *medium* (such as air or water) through which to move. Sound cannot travel in a vacuum. Sound begins with a vibrating object, such as the movement of vocal cords, the plucking of a guitar string, or the pounding diaphragm of a woofer speaker. The vibration pushes air molecules out into space, where they collide with other air molecules, and a kind of travelling chain reaction begins.

The rate of vibration of the object that is the source of a sound determines the *frequency* of the sound, defined as the number of times the pressure wave moves from peak to peak per second (measured in units called *hertz*, where 1 Hz = 1 cycle per second). Psychologically, when the frequency of a sound varies, people hear changes in **pitch,** which corresponds to how high or low a tone sounds. For example, middle C on a piano has a frequency of 262 Hz, whereas the highest note on a piano corresponds to about 4000 Hz. Humans are sensitive to frequencies from roughly 20 Hz to 20 000 Hz, but we are most

sound

The physical input to the auditory system, a mechanical energy travelling in waves that requires a medium, such as air or water, through which to move

pitch

The psychological experience that results from the auditory processing of a particular *frequency* of sound

Dr. Mark A. Schmuckler, professor of psychology at the University of Toronto, examines a computer-generated spectrogram, which records the pattern of variation in the intensity and frequencies of sounds over time. For example, the spectrogram on the screen might depict the sounds of the word "relish" (with the *r* sound on the left and the *ish* sound on the right). If you have a PC, it may have a digital sound recorder that displays crude spectrograms (e.g., Windows Sound Recorder).

Courtesy of Dr. Mark A. Schmuckler

sensitive to frequencies in the 1000 Hz to 5000 Hz range (Gulick, Gescheider, & Frisina, 1989). Many important sounds fall into this range of maximum sensitivity, including the sounds that make up speech.

The other major dimension of sound is *amplitude*, the height a sound wave reaches. Psychologically, increases in amplitude are experienced as increases in **loudness.** The amplitude of a wave is measured in units called *decibels* (dB). The decibel scale is logarithmic: A 10 dB sound is 10 times more intense than the weakest sound a human can hear, a 20 dB sound is 10×10 (that is, 100) times more intense than the weakest audible sound, and so on. To give you some perspective, normal conversation is around 60 dB, whereas an incredibly loud rock band can produce sounds more than 120 dB in the front row.

It is not unusual for dance clubs to have ambient sound levels at or above 100 dB. Repeated and prolonged exposure to sounds 90 dB or higher can produce permanent hearing loss: The louder, longer, and more frequent the exposure, the more likely it will cause both short- and long-term hearing loss. As a rule of thumb, if the music is loud enough that you have to really raise your voice to be understood by someone less than a metre away, you are at risk. Many smart and cool people wear high-quality earplugs to clubs (stuffing tissue in your ears doesn't cut it).

Entering the Ear   Let's follow a sound as it enters the auditory pathway (see ❱ Figure 4.23). We saw that in the visual system, an optical pathway through the cornea, pupil, and lens focuses the light energy onto the visual receptors. In the auditory system, sound travels toward the auditory receptor cells through the ears. The external flap of tissue usually referred to as the "ear" is known technically as the **pinna;** it helps capture the sound, which then funnels down the auditory canal toward the *eardrum*, or **tympanic membrane.**

loudness

The psychological experience that results from the auditory processing of a particular *amplitude* of sound

pinna

The external flap of tissue commonly referred to as the "ear"; it helps direct sounds toward the tympanic membrane

tympanic membrane

The eardrum, which responds to incoming sound waves by vibrating

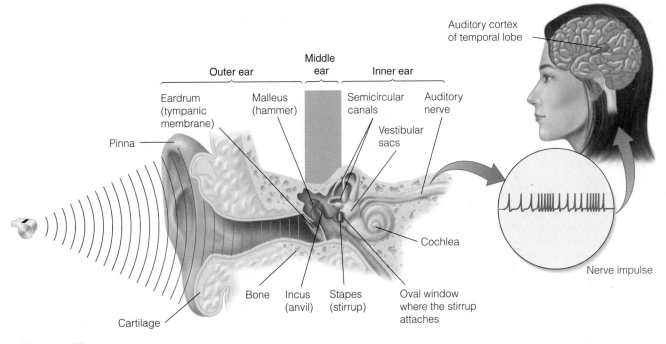

❱ **Figure 4.23**

The Structures of the Human Ear

Sound enters the auditory canal and causes the tympanic membrane to vibrate in a pattern that is then transmitted through three small bones in the middle ear to the oval window. The oval window vibrates, causing fluid inside the cochlea to be displaced, which moves the basilar membrane. The semicircular canals and vestibular sacs are not involved in audition; rather, they are part of the vestibular system, which senses the position and movement of the head.

middle ear

The portion of the ear between the eardrum and the cochlea containing three small bones (the malleus, incus, and stapes) that intensify and prepare the sound vibrations for passage into the inner ear

cochlea

The snail shell–shaped sound processor in the inner ear, where sounds are transduced into nerve impulses

basilar membrane

A flexible membrane running through the cochlea that, through its movement, displaces the auditory receptor cells (hair cells)

place theory

The idea that the *location* of auditory receptor cells activated by movement of the basilar membrane plays a role in the perception of pitch

▶ **Figure 4.24**

The Basilar Membrane

This figure shows an open slice of the cochlea. Sound vibrations cause fluid inside the cochlea to displace the basilar membrane that runs throughout the cochlear shell. Different frequencies trigger different patterns of movement along the membrane. Transduction takes place through bending hair cells. The hair cells nearest the point of maximum displacement will be stimulated the most, which helps the brain code information about pitch.

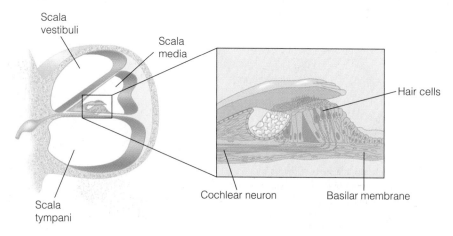

Scala vestibuli

Scala media

Hair cells

Cochlear neuron   Basilar membrane

Scala tympani

The tympanic membrane responds to the incoming sound wave by vibrating. The particular vibration pattern, which differs for different sound frequencies, is then transmitted through three small bones in the **middle ear:** the *malleus* (Latin for "hammer"), the *incus* (anvil), and the *stapes* (stirrup). These bones intensify the vibration pattern and prepare it for passage into the fluid-filled inner ear. Within the inner ear lies a snail-shell-shaped sound processor called the **cochlea;** here, the sound energy is transduced into the internal language of the nervous system— electrochemical activity in neurons.

Transduction in the Cochlea   The third bone in the middle ear, the stapes, is connected to an opening in the cochlea called the *oval window.* As the stapes vibrates, it causes fluid inside the cochlea to displace a flexible membrane, called the **basilar membrane,** that runs throughout the cochlear shell, somewhat like a long carpet. Transduction takes place through the activation of tiny auditory receptor cells, called *hair cells,* that lie along the basilar membrane. As the membrane starts to ripple—like a cat moving under a bed sheet—in response to the wave of pressure flowing through the fluid in the cochlea, tiny hairs called *cilia,* which extend outward from the hair cells, are displaced. The bending of these hairs causes the auditory receptor cells to fire, creating a neural impulse that travels up the auditory pathways to the brain (see ▶ Figure 4.24). It is these delicate cilia that can be permanently damaged by frequent prolonged exposure to loud noises.

Extracting the Input Components: Auditory Pathways

Less is known about the auditory pathways than about the visual route toward the cortex, but some general similarities are worth noting. The neural impulses generated by the hair cells leave the cochlea in each ear along the auditory nerve. Neural codings of sounds that have been received in the right ear travel mainly along pathways leading to the left hemisphere of the brain; left-ear sounds go primarily to the right hemisphere. As in the visual system, individual auditory nerve fibres also appear to be "tuned" to transmit a specific kind of input. In the visual system, the ganglion cells transmit information about regions of light and dark on the retina, with particular cells being particularly sensitive to certain shapes. In the auditory system, fibres in the auditory nerve pass on rough frequency information. Electrophysiological measurements of individual auditory nerve fibres show tuning curves—for example, a particular fibre might respond best to an input stimulus of around 2000 Hz and less well to others (Ribaupierre, 1997).

Extracting Pitch   Complex sounds, such as speech, consist of combinations of simple sound frequencies. The auditory system pulls out information about the simple frequencies, which correspond to different pitches, in several ways. Pitch is determined, in part, by the particular place on the basilar membrane that is most active. For example, stimulation of hair cells near the oval window leads to the perception of a high-pitched sound. This is called the **place theory** of pitch perception (Békésy, 1960): "Place" in this instance refers to the location of the activated hair cell along the basilar membrane. We hear a particular pitch partly because hair cells in a particular part of the basilar membrane are responding actively.

The physics of the cochlea underlie place theory. Different sound frequencies trigger different movement patterns along the basilar membrane. Higher frequencies of sound cause the membrane to be displaced the most near the oval window; low frequencies produce a travelling wave that reaches its peak deep inside the spiralling cochlea. If hair cells near the oval window are responding the most, the incoming sound is perceived as high in pitch. If many cells along the membrane are active, and the most active ones are far away from the oval window, the incoming sound is perceived as low in pitch.

Place theory helps to explain certain kinds of hearing loss. For example, as people grow older they typically have trouble hearing the higher frequencies of sound (such as those in whispered speech). Why might this be? Most sounds that enter the auditory system activate, to at least some extent, those hair cells nearest the oval window, which are most sensitive to high-frequency sounds. Cells in the interior portions of the cochlea respond actively only when low-frequency sounds are present. Thus, if receptor cells wear out from years of prolonged activity, those nearest the oval window should be among the first to go. Place theory thus explains, in part, why older people have difficulty hearing high-pitched sounds (especially if they went to lots of rock concerts when they were younger!).

Despite its successes, place theory does not offer a complete account of pitch perception. One problem with place theory is that hair cells do not act independently; often, many are activated in unison so that a broad range of "places" are activated simultaneously. As a result, it's thought that the brain also relies on the *rate* at which cells fire their neural impulses. According to **frequency theory,** pitch is determined partly by the frequency of neural impulses travelling up the auditory pathway: The higher the rate of firing, the higher the perceived pitch. This makes sense because high-pitched sounds are carried by high-frequency sound waves (i.e., ones in which peaks occur very frequently).

In summary, the brain uses two kinds of information to extract pitch. Remember that for colour vision the brain uses information from multiple cone receptors as well as from opponent process cells located in the upper regions of the brain. Similarly, to detect pitch the brain uses information about where on the basilar membrane activation is occurring (*place theory*) as well as the rate at which signals are generated (*frequency theory*). Neither place nor frequency information, by itself, is sufficient to explain our perception of pitch—both kinds of information are needed and used.

The Auditory Cortex   The neural activity caused by auditory input eventually reaches the auditory cortex, which is located mainly in the temporal lobes of the brain. Cells in the auditory cortex are frequency sensitive, which means that they respond best to particular frequencies of sound. They have a well-defined organizational scheme: Cells that respond to low-frequency sounds are clustered together in one area of the auditory cortex, whereas cells responsive to high-frequency sounds sit in another area (Scheich & Zuschratter, 1995).

Some cells in the auditory cortex appear to respond best to complex combinations of sounds. For example, a cell might respond only to a sequence of tones that move from one frequency to another in a rising series (Pickles, 1988). In animals, cortical cells have also been discovered that respond only to sounds that exist in the animal's natural vocabulary, such as a particular shriek, cackle, or trill (Godey, Atencio, Bonham, Schreiner, & Cheung, 2005). In people, PET scans have shown that specific

frequency theory

The idea that pitch perception is determined partly by the *frequency* of neural impulses travelling up the auditory pathway

Prolonged exposure to intense noise can cause permanent hearing loss.

©Marco Cristofori/Corbis

areas of the brain "light up" when complex auditory sequences are played, such as eight-note melodies (Zatorre, 2003). Much remains to be learned, though, about how complex sounds—such as patterns of speech—are represented in the cortex.

Producing Stable and Meaningful Interpretations: Auditory Perception

Say the phrase "kiss the sky" several times in rapid succession. Now do the same thing with the word "stress" or "life." Your perception of what you're saying may undergo some interesting changes. "Kiss the sky" may begin to sound like "kiss this guy"; "stress" may turn into "dress" and "life" into "fly." Even if the way you say the sounds doesn't change, your perception of it may. Indeed, the "kiss the sky/kiss this guy" example follows from a story about audiences' misperceptions of a lyric in the Jimi Hendrix song "Purple Haze." This is an auditory analogue to the Necker cube that we discussed at the beginning of the chapter. Input to the auditory system is ambiguous and must be interpreted by the brain.

Organizing the Auditory Input　As with the ever-changing Necker cube, the mapping between the physical and the psychological interpretation of a sound is not always straightforward. The brain is often faced with auditory ambiguity, which it usually resolves quickly and without your conscious awareness of any uncertainty. As with vision, the brain separates the incoming auditory stream into figure and ground. For example, at a party you focus on one voice (making it the figure) and other people's voices become part of the auditory background. The brain uses certain perceptual principles to accomplish figure-ground segregation: The auditory system tends to group sounds that are similar and that occur close together in time (Bregman, 1990; Hirsh & Watson, 1996). Sound frequency, for example, can be used as a grouping cue to distinguish between voices. Females generally speak at higher frequencies than males do, and as a result, it is usually easier to separate the signals of two people talking simultaneously if they are of different sexes (see Chapter 5).

The ability to identify and organize sounds increases with experience. People use their knowledge and expectations, through top-down processing, to interpret the incoming auditory sequence. Experienced car mechanics, for example, can often identify an engine problem simply by listening to the particular "knocking" that the engine makes; cardiologists, as a result of experience, can use the intricacies of the heartbeat to diagnose the health of a patient's cardiovascular system. Experience and expertise also play central roles in the perception of music (see Peretz & Zatorre, 2005, for a review of recent research on how the auditory system and brain process music).

Prior knowledge not only influences how we perceive sounds but also how we produce them. Read the following silently, then say it aloud while listening closely to the sounds:

Marzi doats n doze edoats n lidul lamzey divey.

Recognize anything familiar? The line is a lesson on the dietary habits of familiar barnyard animals; it's taken from a song of

When you listen to a band, you can separately pick out the sounds different musicians are creating, selectively attending to the guitar, vocals, or bass.

© Rune Hellestad/Corbis

the 1940s (Sekular & Blake, 1990). (Here's a hint: Mares eat oats and….) With a little knowledge and some expectations about the content of the input, you should eventually arrive at a meaningful interpretation of the lyric. Notice that once you've arrived at that interpretation, the same groupings of letters produce quite a different auditory experience when they are read aloud. In fact, Mattel now sells a board game called Mad Gab that works on this principle. The tag line for the game is "It's not what you say, it's what you hear!"

Sound Localization   Another adaptive characteristic of the auditory sense is the ability to identify the spatial location from which sounds emanate. For example, if you're driving down the street and hear a sudden screech of brakes, you very quickly identify the direction from which the sound came. How do you accomplish this feat? Just as comparisons between the retinal locations of images in the two eyes provide information about visual depth, comparisons between the auditory input to the right and left ears help people *localize* objects in space.

Let's assume that the braking car is approaching yours from the left side. Because your left ear is closer to the source of the sound, it receives the sound vibrations slightly sooner than your right ear. If an object is directly in front of or behind you, the input will arrive at both ears simultaneously. By comparing the arrival times between the left and right ears, the brain is able to localize the sound fairly accurately. What's amazing is that these arrival time differences are extremely small. For example, the maximum arrival time difference, which occurs when an object is directly opposite one ear, is only about 60 *milliseconds* (a millisecond is 1/1000 of a second).

Another important cue for sound localization is *intensity* differences between the ears. The sound that arrives first—to either the left or right ear—will be somewhat louder, or more intense, than the sound arriving second. Again, these intensity differences are not large, and they depend partly on the frequency of the arriving sound, but they are useful cues for sound localization. Thus, your brain calculates the difference in arrival times between the two ears, plus the difference in intensity, and uses this information to localize the source (Giguere & Abel, 1993). Just as infants demonstrate depth perception at an early age, they also demonstrate the ability to localize sounds (Morrongiello, Fenwick, Hillier, & Chance, 1994), although the precision of localization and the ability to integrate auditory and visual cues to localization improve during infancy (Fenwick & Morrongiello, 1998). Interestingly, individuals born blind are better at auditory localization than are other people (Gougoux et al., 2004).

CRITICAL THINKING

Can you think of any songs that you like now but didn't like when you first heard them? One possibility is that you've learned to organize the music in a way that makes it more appealing.

Test Yourself 4.2   *Check your knowledge about the auditory system by determining whether each of the following questions is true or false. (The answers are in Appendix B.)*

1. Sound is a form of mechanical energy that requires a medium, such as air or water, through which to move. *True or False?*

2. According to the frequency theory of pitch perception, the location of activity on the basilar membrane is the primary cue for determining pitch. *True or False?*

3. Sound pressure causes tiny hair cells, located in the pinna, to bend, thereby generating a neural impulse. *True or False?*

4. The separation of a sensory input into figure and ground occurs for vision but not for hearing. *True or False?*

5. We use multiple cues to help us localize a sound, including comparisons of arrival times and intensity differences between the two ears. *True or False?*

▶ The Skin and Body Senses: Experiencing Touch, Temperature, Pain, and Movement

LEARNING GOALS

1. Understand how touch information is translated and interpreted within the brain.
2. Learn how sensory receptors in the skin code information about temperature, and understand the basis of the subjective experience of temperature.
3. Know the basics of how we perceive and interpret pain.
4. Understand the sensory systems that give rise to (nonvisual) awareness of the position and movement of parts of your body (e.g., your arms).
5. Learn about the sensory systems that underlie the perception of the movement of your body through space.

Our perceptual experiences might appear to be driven primarily by what comes in through our eyes and ears. We often communicate through the spoken word; we usually identify objects through vision. But imagine a world without physical contact. Touch, such as a lingering kiss or the brush of a hand against a cheek, is obviously an important perceptual experience. Skin contact builds its own perceptual world: You can detect the location of a light switch in the dark, feel the warmth of a fire, or experience the pain of a collision in the mosh pit.

It's relatively easy to appreciate the adaptive significance of the skin and body senses. You need to be able to detect the presence of a spider crawling up your leg; if a blowing ember from the fireplace lands on your forearm, it's adaptive for you to respond quickly. It's also important to be able to detect the movement and position of our bodies: We need to know how our bodies are oriented in space and the current positions of our arms and legs, because that information is crucial for controlling our movements. Human sensory systems have evolved not only to detect the presence of objects in the environment but also to provide accurate information about the body itself.

In this section you'll learn about three skin senses—touch, temperature, and pain—as well as the body senses underlying the perception of movement and balance. In each case, as in our earlier discussions, the environmental input needs to be translated, transmitted to the brain, and interpreted in a meaningful fashion.

Touch

In the case of touch or pressure, the physical input delivered to the skin is mechanical. An object makes contact with the body and receptor cells embedded in the skin are disturbed. The mechanical pressure on the cell (it is literally deformed) produces a neural impulse, and the input is then transmitted to the spinal cord and up into the brain.

The skin has several different types of pressure-sensitive receptor cells. Some respond to constant pressure; others respond best to intermittent pressure, such as a tapping on the skin or a stimulus that vibrates at a particular frequency (Bolanowski, Gescheider, & Verrillo, 1994). As with vision and hearing, touch information is transmitted up the neural pathway through distinct channels to processing stations in the brain, where the inputs received from various points on the body are combined (Bolanowski, 1989). One kind of nerve fibre might carry information about touch location; other fibres might transmit information about whether the touch was brief or sustained.

At the level of the *somatosensory cortex*, located in the parietal lobe of the brain, a close connection is found between regions of the skin and representation in the cortex (Prud'homme, Cohen, & Kalaska, 1994). As you learned in Chapter 3, the somatosensory cortex contains multiple "body maps," in which adjacent cortical cells have areas of sensitivity that correspond to adjacent areas on the skin. Moreover, as in the visual cortex, some areas of the body are represented more elaborately in the somatosensory cortex than others are. For example, a relatively large amount of cortical tissue is devoted to the hands and lips, whereas the middle portion of the back, despite its size, receives little representation in the cortex. Maybe that's the reason that we kiss to display intense affection rather than pat our lovers on the back: A lot more cortex is devoted to the lips than to the back. Recent research suggests that different regions of the somatosensory cortex are involved in representing different kinds of touch-related information (e.g., one region represents information about the texture of an object, whereas another represents information about the firmness of that object) (Servos, Wilson, Gati, & Lederman, 2001).

People can recognize complex objects through touch. When blindfolded, people show near-perfect identification of common objects (such as toothbrushes and paper clips) after examining them by active touch (Lederman & Klatzky, 2004). Active skin contact with an object produces not only shape information but information about firmness, texture, and (if the object is held in the hand) weight. Andrea Kilgour and Susan Lederman (2002) of Queen's University showed that people can often identify another person by exploring his or her face with their fingertips. A follow-up study produced evidence that one brain area that is highly active when people look at faces is also activated by tactile exploration of the shape of a face (Kilgour, Kitada, Servos, James, & Lederman, 2005).

As with seeing and hearing, a person's interpretation of an object encountered via touch depends on a mixture of the physical stimuli the person receives and what he or she expects to feel. For instance, beliefs about objects' weights affect perceptions of weight (Ellis & Lederman, 1998). Similarly, if you expect to be touched by an object on a particular finger, you are more likely to identify the object correctly if it touches that finger than if it touches another (Craig, 1985). Changes in blood flow in the somatosensory cortex also occur when a person expects to be touched (Drevets, Burton, Videen, & Snyder, 1995). Thus, our knowledge, beliefs, and expectations alter our perceptions of tactile events.

Temperature

At present, researchers have only a limited understanding of how the body records and processes the temperature of an object. Electrophysiological research has detected the presence of **cold fibres** that respond to a cooling of the skin by increasing the production of neural impulses, as well as **warm fibres** that respond vigorously when the temperature of the skin increases. But the behaviour of these temperature-sensitive receptor systems is not yet well understood (Zotterman, 1959).

We do know, however, that the perception of warm and cold is only indirectly related to the temperature of the real-world environment or object. To demonstrate, try plunging one hand into a bowl of cold water and the other hand into a bowl of hot water. After 30 seconds, place both hands into a third bowl containing room-temperature water. The hand that was in the cold water will sense the water as warm; the other hand will register it as

cold fibres

Neurons that respond to a cooling of the skin by increasing the production of neural impulses

warm fibres

Neurons that respond vigorously when the temperature of the skin increases

Humans use the sense of touch to acquire information about shape, firmness, texture, and weight.

Skip Nall/PhotoDisc/Getty Images

cool. Same water, same temperature, but two different perceptual experiences. The secret behind this perceptual enigma lies in understanding that it is temperature *change* that determines your perception. When your cold hand touches warmer water, your skin begins to warm; it is the increase in skin temperature that you perceive as warmth.

These perceptual processes can lead to temperature "illusions." For instance, pick up a metal spoon and a wooden spoon. The two are exactly the same temperature, but if that temperature is below body temperature, the metal spoon will feel cooler. Why? Because metal is a better conductor of heat than wood, so it absorbs more warmth from the skin. Consequently, the brain perceives the more rapid loss of heat as a cooler physical temperature. Similarly, if both spoons were heated above body temperature, the metal spoon would feel hotter to the touch even if both were, for example, 50 degrees Celsius. You don't sense the temperature of the object per se, but rather the direction and amount of change in the temperature of your skin touching the object.

Pain

pain

An adaptive response by the body to any stimulus that is intense enough to cause tissue damage

gate-control theory

The idea that neural impulses generated by pain receptors can be blocked, or gated, in the spinal cord by signals produced in the brain

Pain is an adaptive reaction that the body generates in response to any stimulus that is intense enough to cause tissue damage. The stimulus can come from outside or inside the body; it does not need to be particularly intense (consider the effect of salt on an open wound). Animals lacking pain sensations rarely live for long.

Little is known about pain receptors in the skin, although cells have been discovered in some animals that react to painful stimuli (such as intense heat) by sending signals to the cortex (Dong, Chudler, Sugiyama, Roberts, & Hayashi, 1994). Pain is a complex psychological experience, and it often relies on much more than just a physical stimulus. For example, amputees often report experiencing feelings of itching or pain in the limb they no longer have. In this phenomenon, called "phantom limb," it is obvious that such sensations do not arise from receptors in the absent limb; rather, they arise in the central nervous system (Ramachandran & Hirstein, 1998). At the opposite extreme are well-documented examples of soldiers who report little or no pain after receiving serious injuries in battle; the same is true of many individuals entering an emergency room. In addition, some non-Western cultures use rituals that should, from a Western perspective, inflict great pain but apparently do not (Melzack, 1973). Perhaps related to this is evidence that hypnosis can significantly reduce pain (Patterson, 2004). For a recent book on psychological and social aspects of pain, see Hadjistavropoulos and Craig (2004).

The fact that these people can take a "polar bear swim" in the middle of winter demonstrates that the perception of temperature can be influenced by psychological factors.

Lon C. Diehl/PhotoEdit

Gate-Control Theory The interplay between the physical and the psychological in pain perception forms the basis for the **gate-control theory** of pain, developed by Ronald Melzack at McGill University (Melzack & Katz, 2004; Melzack & Wall, 1965). The basic idea is that the neural impulses generated by pain receptors can be blocked, or gated, in the spinal cord by signals produced in the brain. If you've just sliced your finger while cutting carrots, you would normally feel pain. But if a pan on the stove suddenly starts to smoke, the pain of that cut seems to evaporate while you try to prevent your house from burning down. According to the gate-control theory, the brain can "close the gate" and block pain signals from reaching higher neural centres when it is important to do so.

How is the gating action carried out? The details of the mechanisms are still under investigation, but two types of nerve fibres appear to be responsible for opening and closing the gate. So-called large fibres, when stimulated, produce nervous system activity that closes the gate; other small fibres, when stimulated, inhibit the effects of the large fibres and open the gate. Presumably, higher-level brain processes can stimulate the large fibres to gate out further processing of pain sensations. External stimulation—such as rubbing or placing ice on a wound—can also stimulate the large fibres, thereby reducing transmission of pain signals to the brain. The details of the neural circuitry remain to be worked out, but Melzack's idea of a pain gate that opens and closes is widely accepted.

In addition to gating pain signals, the brain can also control the experience of pain through the release of chemicals called *endorphins* (as we discussed in Chapter 3), which have pain-killing effects similar in some ways to morphine. The release of endorphins is thought to account, in part, for some instances in which pain should be experienced but is not. For example, sometimes swallowing a sugar pill can dramatically reduce pain even though there is no physical reason why sugar should be effective (a placebo effect) (see Wager & Nitschke, 2005). The locus of such effects, and other analgesic procedures, such as acupuncture, might lie in the brain's internal production of its own anti-pain medication.

The Kinesthetic Sense

The word **kinesthesia** literally means "movement"; when used in connection with sensation, the term refers to the ability to sense the position and movement of our own body parts. For example, as you reach toward a blossoming flower, feedback from your skin, tendons, muscles, and joints helps you maintain the correct line toward the target. That is, sensory receptors inside your limbs send signals to the central nervous system that communicate information about their movements and locations. The kinesthetic sense shares many properties with the sense of touch—a variety of receptor types in the muscles that surround the joints react to the physical forces produced by moving the limbs (Gandevia, McCloskey, & Burke, 1992; Verschueven, Cordo, & Swinnen, 1998).

The nerve impulses generated by the kinesthetic receptors travel, as in touch, to the somatosensory cortex. It is presumed that at the level of the cortex are increasingly complex cells that respond only when particular body parts, such as the right arm, are placed in certain positions (Gardner & Costanzo, 1981). But the psychological experience of movement is probably influenced by multiple factors, as with other kinds of perception (Jones, 1988). The visual system, for example, provides additional feedback about current body position, as does the sense of touch. We'll return to the issue of interactions among different sensory and perceptual systems later in this chapter.

The Vestibular Sense

Humans have yet another complex receptor system, attached to the cochlea of the inner ear, which responds not only to movement but also to acceleration and deceleration and changes in upright posture. Each ear contains three small fluid-filled **semicircular canals** that are lined with hair cells similar to those found in the cochlea. If you quickly turn your head toward some object, these hair cells are displaced and nerve impulses signalling acceleration are transmitted throughout the brain. Some of the nerve fibres project to the cortex; others direct inputs toward the eye muscles, so you can accurately adjust your eyes as your head is turning.

kinesthesia

In perception, the ability to sense the position and movement of one's body parts

semicircular canals

A receptor system attached to the inner ear that responds to movement, acceleration, and deceleration and to changes in upright posture

The vestibular sense helps people maintain balance by monitoring the position of the body in space.

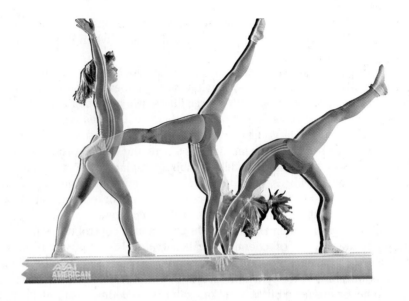

vestibular sacs

Small organs in the inner ear that contain receptors responsible for the sense of balance

The vestibular system is also responsible for the sense of balance. If you tilt your head, or hurtle through a 360-degree loop on a roller coaster, receptor cells located in other inner-ear organs, called **vestibular sacs,** quickly transmit the appropriate orientation information to the brain. Continual disturbance of the semicircular canals or the vestibular sacs can produce dizziness and nausea, as in motion sickness (Lackner & DiZio, 1991). When you were a kid, did you ever spin around and around to experience the rush of dizziness? Or have you ever spent several hours on a boat on the ocean, and later noticed the apparent heaving of the ground when you walked on land? Both of these examples are aftereffects of prolonged stimulation of the vestibular sense receptors.

The absence of gravity experienced by astronauts in a spaceship disables parts of the vestibular system, thereby impairing astronauts' perceptions of their own body movements. One effect is that most astronauts suffer "space sickness" (akin to motion sickness) for the first few days in space. Another consequence is that they experience a variety of interesting perceptual illusions when they first return to Earth and the previously disabled aspects of the vestibular system start working again (Young & Shelhamer, 1990).

Test Yourself   4.3

Check your knowledge about the skin and body senses by answering the following multiple-choice questions. [The answers are in Appendix B.]

1. Alicia holds her left hand in a bowl of cold water and her right hand in a bowl of hot water. She then transfers both hands to a bowl of room-temperature water. She finds that her left hand now feels warm and her right hand cool. Why?

  a. Cold and hot fibres rebound after continued activity.

  b. It's temperature change that determines perception.

  c. She expects a change; therefore, a change is experienced.

  d. Opponent process cells in the cortex are reacting.

2. According to the gate-control theory, psychological factors can influence the perception of pain by

  a. channelling pain signals to the occipital lobe

  b. reducing the supply of endorphins in the body

  c. blocking pain signals from reaching higher neural centres

  d. blocking pain receptors from relaying sensory information to the spinal cord

3. The vestibular sacs contain receptor cells that help us maintain our sense of balance. Where are they located?

  a. in the lateral geniculate nucleus

  b. in the superior colliculus

  c. in the joints and limbs of the body

  d. in the inner ear

▶ The Chemical Senses: Smell and Taste

LEARNING GOALS

1. Understand how chemical stimuli lead to neural activity that, in interaction with other perceptual processes, gives rise to the perception of odours.
2. Learn about the sensory and perceptual mechanisms that give rise to the perception of the taste or flavour of foods.

We end our review of the individual sensory systems with the chemical senses, smell and taste. We receive a vast array of stimulation from the environment, but few carry as much emotional impact as chemically based input. You can appreciate a loving caress or the visual beauty of a sunset, but consider your reaction to the smell of decaying meat or to the taste of milk left too long in the sun. Smells and tastes are enormously adaptive because they possess powerful signalling properties; like other animals, humans learn to avoid the off-odours or bitter tastes typical of noxious substances.

The perception of both smell and taste begins with the activity of receptor cells, called **chemoreceptors,** that react to molecules in the air or dissolved in liquids. These receptors solve the translation problem and project the newly formed neural impulses toward the brain. Psychologically, the two senses are related: Anyone who has ever had a cold knows that things "just don't taste right" with a plugged nose. You can demonstrate this for yourself by pinching your nostrils closed, closing your eyes, and trying to taste the difference between a piece of apple and a piece of raw potato. In fact, people can identify a taste far more efficiently if they are also allowed a brief sniff (Djordjevic, Zatorre, Petrides, & Jones-Gotman, 2004). Let's consider each of these chemical senses in more detail.

chemoreceptors

Receptor cells that react to molecules in the air or dissolved in liquids, leading to the senses of smell and taste

Smell

The technical name for the sense of smell is **olfaction,** which comes from the Latin word *olfacere*, meaning "to smell." Airborne molecules enter through the nose or the mouth and interact with receptor cells embedded in the upper region of the nasal cavity (Lancet, Gross-Isseroff, Margalit, & Seidemann, 1993). Like the receptor systems that are used to hear and detect motion, the olfactory receptor cells contain tiny hairs, or *cilia*. The airborne molecules bind with the cilia, causing the generation of a neural impulse. Receptor fibres then send the message forward to the *olfactory bulb*, located at the bottom front region of the brain. From here, the information is sent to several areas in the brain.

People have a thousand or more different kinds of olfactory receptor cells (Buck & Axel, 1991). It's not yet known whether each receptor type plays a special role in the perception of a particular odour, but there's almost certainly no simple one-to-one connection. For one thing, individual olfactory receptor cells are often activated by more than one kind of chemical stimulus. In addition, most odours are complex psychological experiences (Carrasco & Ridout, 1993). People have no problem recognizing the smell of frying bacon or the aroma of fresh coffee, but a chemical analysis of these stimuli fails to reveal the presence of any single defining molecule. Clearly, the ability to apply the label "frying bacon" to a set of airborne chemicals arises from complex perceptual processes. It's even possible to produce smell illusions—if you are led to expect that a particular odour is present, even though it is not, you are likely to report its presence (O'Mahony, 1978).

The neural pathway for smell is somewhat unusual, compared with the other sensory systems that we've discussed, because connections are made with forebrain structures, such as the amygdala, the hippocampus, and the hypothalamus (Buck, 1996). As you learned in Chapter 3, these areas have been linked with the regulation of feeding, drinking, sexual behaviour, and even memory. It's speculation, but part of the emotional power of olfactory cues might be related to the

olfaction

The sense of smell

A taster's ability to identify the smell, or "bouquet," of a fine wine depends on the constellation of airborne chemicals produced by the wine, as well as on the experiences of the taster.

Some smells and tastes are truly disgusting and lead to characteristic facial expressions and reactions. Can you think of any adaptive reasons why we might have such reactions?

gustation

The sense of taste

flavour

A psychological term used to describe the overall gustatory (eating) experience; flavour is influenced by taste, smell, the visual appearance of food, and expectations about the food's quality

involvement of this motivational pathway. Certainly in lower animals, whose behaviour is often dominated by odour cues (e.g., Brown, 1992), brain structures, such as the hypothalamus and the amygdala, seem to play a major role in the animal's reaction to odours in its environment.

Many animals release special chemicals, called *pheromones*, that cause highly specific reactions when detected by other members of the species. Often pheromones can provoke sexual behaviour or characteristic patterns of aggression, but a variety of reactions can be produced. Ants, for example, react to the smell of a dead member of the colony by carrying the decaying corpse outside the nest (Wilson, 1963). So far, much to the disappointment of the perfume industry, no solid support has been found for human pheromones: No scents have been discovered that reliably induce sexual interest in humans (Winman, 2004), although scents can certainly become associated with people who are perceived as arousing.

Taste

Gustation is the technical term for the perception of taste. Most textbooks tell students that we experience four basic tastes: sweet, bitter, salty, and sour. Recent research supports the existence of a fifth basic taste, called *umami* (Chaudhari, Landin, & Roper, 2000; Halpern, 2002). Umami was first proposed by Professor Kikunae Ikeda of Tokyo Imperial University in the early 1900s. Tastes are difficult to describe; the most common term used to describe umami is "savoury." Umami taste is often prominent in Japanese foods (dried seaweed and fish are particularly rich in umami), but cheese and tomatoes also have umami (think of a savoury tomato sauce).

When psychologists use the term *taste*, they are referring to the sensations produced by stimulation of the taste receptors, not to the overall richness of the experience of eating. The term **flavour** is used to describe the complete meal experience. Flavour is influenced by taste, smell, and the visual appearance of the food, as well as by expectations about the quality of the meal.

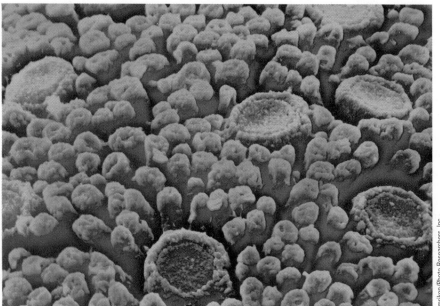

Taste buds, which contain the receptor cells for taste, are embedded within the folds of the papillae (shown here as the large, circular objects).

Taste receptors are distributed throughout the mouth, but most are on the upper surface of the tongue. If you coat your tongue with a sip of milk and look at it in a mirror, you'll see that your tongue is covered with tiny bumps called *papillae*. The **taste buds,** which contain the receptor cells, are embedded within the folds of the papillae. Many questions remain about how the transduction process for taste occurs. One possibility is that taste stimuli directly penetrate the membrane of the receptor cell, causing the cell to fire; another idea is that taste stimuli alter the chemical structure of the cell membrane without entering the cell itself (Shirley & Persaud, 1990). In any case, chemicals put in the mouth somehow stimulate the taste receptors, and the neural impulse is passed up toward the brain.

taste buds

The receptor cells on the tongue involved in taste

Compared with the neural pathway for olfaction, that for taste is more similar to the pathways for vision and audition: Information is passed toward the thalamus and then to the somatosensory area of the cortex (Rolls, 1995). Little work has been done on how cortical taste cells function, although taste-sensitive cells (analogous to visual feature detectors) have been discovered (Small et al., 1999). Stronger evidence for taste "tuning" has been found in analyses of the receptor neurons, but a given receptor cell seems to react to a broad range of gustatory stimuli. The neural code for taste is probably determined, to some extent, by the particular receptor cell that happens to react and by the relative patterns of activity across large groups of receptors. For an accessible article on the physiology of taste, see Smith and Margolskee (2001).

The brain can produce stable interpretations of taste stimuli, but the identification process is complex. For one thing, prior exposure to one kind of taste often changes the perception of another. If you've ever had a drink of orange juice shortly after brushing your teeth, you know tastes interact. To some extent, the interaction process depends on the similarity of successive tastes. For example, a taste of a sour pickle will reduce the sourness of lemon juice, but a taste of salty cracker will not. Some natural substances can completely change the normal perception of taste. A substance extracted from berries, called "miracle fruit," turns extremely sour tastes (such as from raw lemons) sweet. Another substance, taken from the leaves of a plant found in India and Africa, temporarily eliminates the sweet taste of sugar. It is also clear that expectations play a profound role in taste perceptions. Have you ever reached for one beverage and accidentally picked up and swallowed another? The discrepancy between expectation and the taste is experienced as distinctly unpleasant.

Test Yourself   4.4

Check your knowledge about smell and taste by filling in the blanks. Choose the best answer from among the following terms: chemoreceptors, flavour, gustation, hypothalamus, olfaction, olfactory bulb, pheromones, taste, taste buds. (The answers are in Appendix B.)

1. The general term for receptor cells that are activated by molecules in the air or dissolved in liquids:

   _____

2. One of the main brain destinations for odour stimuli:

   _____

3. A psychological term used to describe the entire gustatory experience: _____

4. The technical name for the sense of smell:

   _____

5. The technical name for the sense of taste:

   _____

▶ From the Physical to the Psychological

LEARNING GOALS

1. Learn the psychology of stimulus detection, including the technique of signal detection.
2. Learn about difference thresholds and understand Weber's law.
3. Comprehend the phenomenon of sensory adaptation and its adaptive value.
4. Understand that perceptual experiences involve the interaction of multiple sensory systems.

Throughout this chapter, you've learned that there is a transition from the physical to the psychological. Sensory stimuli originate in the physical world, but our conscious experiences of those inputs are influenced by expectations and beliefs about how the world is organized. We interpret the physical message, and this means that our conscious experience of the sensory input can be different from the one that is delivered by the environment.

In the field of **psychophysics,** researchers search for mathematical laws that describe the transition from the physical to the psychological. By quantifying the relationship between the physical properties of a stimulus and its subjective experience, psychophysicists hope to develop general laws that apply across all kinds of sensory input. Let's consider some examples of how such laws are established.

Stimulus Detection

Psychophysics is one of the oldest research areas in psychology; it dates back to the work of Wilhelm Wundt, Gustav Fechner, and others in the nineteenth century. One of the first questions these early researchers asked was: What is the minimum amount of stimulus energy needed to produce a sensation? Suppose we present you with a very faint pure tone—so faint that you cannot hear it—and gradually make it louder. At some point you will hear the tone. This point is known as the **absolute threshold** for the stimulus; it represents the level of intensity that lifts the stimulus over the threshold of conscious awareness. One of the early insights of pioneering psychophysicists, such as Fechner (1887/1987), was the realization that absolute thresholds are *not* absolute; that is, there is no single point in an intensity curve at which detection reliably begins. For a given intensity level, sometimes the person hears the tone, other times not (the same situation applies to detection in all the sensory modalities, not just auditory). For this reason, absolute threshold is redefined as the intensity level at which a person detects the presence of a stimulus 50% of the time (see ▶ Figure 4.25).

It might seem strange that a person's detection abilities change from moment to moment. Part of the reason is that trial-to-trial observations are "noisy," in that they are influenced by all sorts of essentially random factors. It is virtually impossible for a researcher to control all the things that can potentially affect someone's

psychophysics

A field of psychology in which researchers search for ways to describe the transition from the physical stimulus to the psychological experience of that stimulus

absolute threshold

The level of intensity that lifts a stimulus over the threshold of conscious awareness; it's defined as the intensity level at which a person detects the presence of the stimulus 50% of the time

▶ Figure 4.25

Absolute Threshold

The more intense the stimulus, the greater the likelihood that it will be detected. The absolute threshold of detection is defined as the intensity level at which the presence of the stimulus is detected 50% of the time.

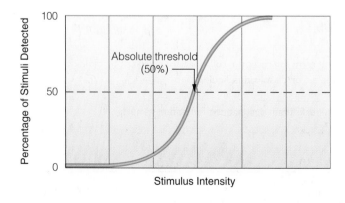

performance. For example, a subject might have a momentary lapse of attention that causes him or her to miss a presented stimulus on a given trial. Some random activity in the nervous system might create fluctuations in the sensitivity of the receptor systems. Subtle variations in the amount of ambient background noise may also affect performance. Experimenters overcome these problems by giving the subject many detection opportunities and averaging performance over trials to determine the threshold.

Psychologists have also developed sophisticated statistical techniques to pull the truth out of noisy data. Human observers often have biases that influence how they respond in a detection environment. For example, people will sometimes report the presence of a stimulus even though none has been presented. Why? Sometimes the observer is simply worried about missing a presented stimulus, so he or she says "Yes" on almost every trial. To control for these tendencies, which are called "response biases," researchers use a technique called **signal detection,** which mathematically compares *hits*—in which a stimulus is correctly detected— with *false alarms*—in which the observer claims a stimulus was presented when it was not.

Four types of outcome can occur in a signal-detection situation. Besides hits and false alarms, the subject can also fail to detect a stimulus when it was actually presented—called a *miss*—or correctly decide that a stimulus was not presented— called a *correct rejection*. These four outcomes are shown in ❯ Figure 4.26. Take a moment to think through why the names for the four outcomes make sense. Researchers compare the rates of hits and false alarms (over a large number of trials) to infer a subject's true detection ability.

To see why it's important to compare hits and false alarms, imagine that Katie is participating in a simple detection experiment and because she doesn't want to miss any of the signals her strategy is to say, "Yes, a stimulus occurred" on almost every trial (even when she is not sure that a stimulus was actually presented). If the researcher pays attention only to hits, it will appear as if Katie has almost perfect detection ability—she almost always correctly identifies a stimulus when it occurs. But saying "Yes" on every trial will also lead to lots of false alarms: She will often say "Yes" on trials when no stimulus was actually presented. By comparing hits and false alarms, the researcher is able to determine whether her high number of "hits" is really due to detection ability or to a strategic bias on her part. If Katie can truly detect the stimulus when it occurs, she should show lots of hits and very few false alarms (for an in-depth review of signal detection theory, see Macmillan & Creelman, 1991).

signal detection

A technique that can be used to determine an individual's ability to detect the presence of a stimulus and to measure the individual's response bias

CRITICAL THINKING

Can you think of any occupations requiring detection—such as air traffic controller—in which it might be advantageous to be biased toward saying yes, a stimulus has occurred?

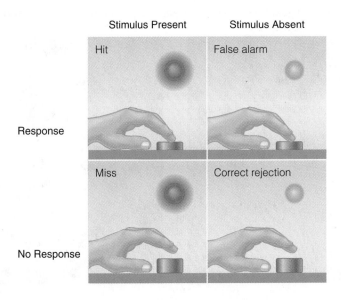

Stimulus Present   Stimulus Absent

Hit   False alarm

Response

Miss   Correct rejection

No Response

❯ **Figure 4.26**

Signal Detection Outcomes

Four outcomes are possible in each trial of a signal detection experiment. If the stimulus is present and correctly detected, it's called a *hit;* if the stimulus is absent but the observer claims it's present, it's a *false alarm.* A *miss* is when the stimulus is present but not detected, and a *correct rejection* is when the observer correctly decides that the stimulus was not presented.

Signal detection situations are ubiquitous in everyday life. Is that rustling in the bushes a tiger or just a breeze? Is that funny shape in a passenger's baggage a weapon or a hair dryer? Performance in these situations is jointly determined by sensitivity (i.e., the perceptual system's ability to differentiate between signal and nonsignal) and response bias (i.e., how willing or reluctant the person is to classify a stimulus as a signal). (For evidence that airport screeners likely do poorly when attempting to identify weapons in X-rayed luggage, see Smith, Redford, & Washburn, 2005.)

Difference Thresholds

Researchers in psychophysics have also been concerned with the measurement of **difference thresholds:** the smallest difference in the magnitude of two stimuli that an observer can detect. Suppose we present you with two tones in immediate succession, each equally loud. We then gradually increase the intensity of one tone until you notice it as being louder than the other (called the *standard*). How much of a change in magnitude do we need to make for you to detect the difference? As with absolute thresholds, the required amount changes slightly from one moment to the next, but an important general principle emerges.

It turns out that detection of a *just noticeable difference* (or *JND*) in magnitude depends on how intense the standard was in the first place. If you're at a rock concert and your friend Gillian wants to tell you something, she needs to yell; if you're in a library, a whisper will do. We can state this relationship more formally as follows: The JND for stimulus magnitude is a constant proportion of the magnitude of the standard stimulus. In other words, the louder the standard stimulus, the more volume will need to be added (or subtracted) before a difference in loudness will be detected. This general relationship, called **Weber's law,** works for more than just loudness; it applies across all the sensory systems. If the lights in your house go off, lighting a candle will make a big difference; if the lights are on, the addition of a candle will make little, if any, noticeable increase in brightness (even though the candle emits the same amount of light in both situations). Weber's law demonstrates once again that the relationship between the physical and the psychological is not always direct: Increases in the magnitude of a physical stimulus will not always lead to parallel increases in the psychological experience.

Sensory Adaptation

Another feature of all sensory systems also interested early researchers in psychophysics. Sensory systems are more sensitive to a particular kind of input when it first occurs than to its continued presence. Through **sensory adaptation,** the

---

difference threshold

The smallest difference in the magnitude of two stimuli that an observer can reliably detect

Weber's law

States that the ability to notice a difference in the magnitude of two stimuli is a constant proportion of the intensity of the standard stimulus; psychologically, the more intense a stimulus is to begin with, the more intense it will need to become for a person to notice a difference

sensory adaptation

The tendency of sensory systems to reduce sensitivity to a stimulus that remains constant

Burning candles in a brightly lit room would have little effect on perceived brightness; but lighting candles in a dimly lit room would noticeably increase brightness.

© Brownie Harris/Corbis/Magma

Jules Frazier/PhotoDisc

body quickly adapts, by reducing sensitivity, to input that remains constant—such as the feel of a shirtsleeve on your forearm or the hum of computers in the background. Think about what the world would be like without sensory adaptation. The water in the pool would never seem to warm up; the slightly musty smell of your friend's basement apartment would remain a pervasive force throughout your visit; you would be constantly reminded of the texture of your socks pressing on your ankles.

Adaptation is a feature of each sensory system. Images that remain stable on the retina vanish after a while; this doesn't normally occur because the eyes are constantly moving and refreshing the retinal image. Our sensitivity to many odours decreases by 70% over the course of a few minutes of exposure (one of the reasons your neighbour is probably unaware of his or her own BO!). If you are presented with a continuous tone, your perception of its loudness decreases over time (Evans, 1982). Sensory systems evolved to detect changes in the incoming input; sensitivity is reduced to those aspects of the input that remain the same, perhaps because they are not telling us anything new.

Interactions among Sensory Systems

In this chapter we've mostly considered the sensory systems one by one, in isolation, but in everyday life, they act together. Within a particular sensory system, the components of a stimulus (such as the shape and colour of a visual object) are picked out of the input and ultimately integrated (e.g., so that you see shape and colour as different aspects of the same visual object). Similarly, the internal representations of different sensory systems are also integrated, giving rise to a multifaceted but coherent perceptual experience. For example, you experience the smell, appearance, and texture of a pizza simultaneously as attributes of the same object.

It's not just that we see things at the same time as we are hearing, smelling, or feeling them, but also that the operations of different sensory systems influence one another. For example, we mentioned earlier that the flavour of food arises from a complex interaction of the taste, aroma, texture, and appearance of the food, together with higher-level psychological and social processes (such as expectations and mood). The same pizza that is delicious in one situation may be distasteful in another, partly because of interactions among different sensory systems.

Multiple sensory systems, such as audition and vision, often work together to help us localize and identify objects in the environment. For example, sounds and other sensations often capture our attention, leading us to direct our visual receptors toward some interesting object. As mentioned previously, even newborn infants look toward unexpected sounds. (Interestingly, studies at Queen's University by Symons, Hains, & Muir, 1998, found that 21-month-old babies are very sensitive to small shifts in adults' gazes, as though they realize that shifts of gaze reveal shifts of attention.) Even if no eye movements are required, sounds can be used to facilitate visual processing. For example, it is easier to detect a briefly presented visual stimulus if its onset is accompanied by a sound (McDonald & Ward, 2000; Woods, Alain, & Ogawa, 1998).

We benefit from interactions between sensory modalities, but they can also produce illusions. For example, objects that look heavy tend to be perceived as weighing more than they really do (Ellis & Lederman, 1999; Flanagan & Beltzner, 2000). Similarly, misleading visual cues can produce an astonishingly vivid illusion of motion; you may have had the experience of sitting in a stopped car when a car beside yours rolls backward a few metres, giving you the illusion that your car is moving forward (Telford & Frost, 1993). A related phenomenon can occur when people use "virtual reality" systems. In a driving simulator, for example, the visual, auditory, and kinesthetic sensory systems receive information that indicates that the driver is moving (accelerating, braking, turning) but the vestibular system is not receiving the stimulation that it would if the driver's body really were moving through space, and that incompatibility can make the person in the simulator feel nauseated (you may have experienced a weaker reaction of this sort from playing video games).

The McGurk effect is another example of the interaction among perceptual systems. This effect, named after psychologist Harry McGurk, arises when people watch a video of a person making one sound while listening to a synched recording of the person saying another sound. The subjective experience is of hearing a sound that blends the auditory and visual stimulus. You can try a demonstration of this effect at **http://www.faculty.ucr.edu/~rosenblu/VSMcGurk.html#**. In related work, Kevin Munhall and co-workers at Queens have shown that auditory perception of a speaker's utterances is better when the perceiver can see the speaker's natural head movements while speaking (Munhall, Jones, Callan, Kuratate, & Vatikiotis-Bateson, 2004).

A small proportion of people experience a phenomenon called synesthesia. Synesthesia occurs when a perceptual experience triggered by one kind of sensory processing is also accompanied by a perceptual experience associated with a different sensory system (e.g., sounds might be experienced as having colours as well as auditory properties). A synesthete known as C, for example, perceives digits as having colours (e.g., C reports that a black digit 9 looks orange, whereas 3 looks purple) (Dixon, Cudahy, Merikle, & Smilek, 2000).

Your everyday perceptual experiences of the world around you arise through interactions of the various sensory systems. Each sense is an exquisitely complex and sophisticated system that has evolved to create rich and vivid internal representations of reality, in ways that are consistent with prior experiences and beliefs. These systems sometimes err, but for the most part they serve us well.

Test Yourself 4.5

Check your understanding of psychophysics by deciding whether each of the following statements is true or false. (The answers are in Appendix B.)

1. The intensity level required to barely perceive a stimulus varies across individuals but remains constant for any given individual. *True or False?*

2. A "false alarm" occurs in signal detection when an observer claims a signal was present when, in fact, it was not. *True or False?*

3. According to Weber's law, the detection of a just noticeable difference (JND) in magnitude is constant across all intensity levels. *True or False?*

4. Sensory adaptation is a characteristic of all sensory systems. *True or False?*

5. Sensory systems interact with one another, such that the operation of one system can be altered by that of another. *True or False?*

Constructing Perceptual Experience

R
E
V
I
E
W

To interact successfully with the world, and to experience its richness, we rely on multiple sensory systems. The external world bombards the body with complex and ever-changing physical stimuli, but none arrives in the same form as the electrochemical neuronal language of the brain. Thus, the body faces three fundamental problems of adaptation: How can the external input be translated into the internal language of the nervous system? How are the elementary components extracted from the input? Finally, how does the brain build a stable and meaningful interpretation of the input components once they've been extracted?

First, how is the external input from the environment translated into the language of the nervous system? To solve the translation problem, the body relies on specialized receptor cells that transduce particular forms of physical energy input into neural impulses. In the visual system, receptor cells—rods and cones—react to light; in the auditory system, sound energy leads to movement of the basilar membrane, which in turn causes tiny hair cells to generate neural impulses. Other specialized receptors react to pressure on the skin, chemicals inhaled from the air or placed in the mouth, and the relative position or movement of the body. Each receptor system acts as a "translator," changing the input delivered by the external world into the electrochemical language of the nervous system.

Second, how are the elementary components—the sensations— extracted from the input? The initial neural coding of the sensory input receives further processing in the brain to extract the component sensations. A variety of neural pathways are specialized to process particular kinds of sensory information. For example, opponent process cells in the lateral geniculate region of the brain are specialized to process colour; they signal the presence of one kind of colour by increasing the rate at which they generate neural impulses, and they signal another kind of colour by decreasing their firing rate. Similarly, highly specialized cells in the visual cortex respond only to particular patterns of light and dark on the retina. One kind of cell might respond only to a bar of light presented at a particular orientation; another cell might respond only to a pattern of light that moves in a particular direction across the retina.

In the auditory cortex, the brain extracts information about the frequencies and amplitudes of sound in an auditory message. Psychologically, changes in frequency correspond to changes in perceived pitch, whereas changes in amplitude are experienced as variations in loudness. The brain detects frequency information by noting the place on the basilar membrane where hair cells are stimulated and by noting the rate at which neural impulses are generated over time.

The brain often relies on multiple kinds of processing to extract a particular component or aspect of a stimulus. The perception of colour, for instance, relies not only on opponent process cells but also on the relative activations of three different cone types that reside in the retina.

Third, how does the brain build and maintain a meaningful interpretation of these component sensations once they've been extracted? To create a coherent and meaningful interpretation of sensory input, people use a combination of bottom-up and top-down processing— beliefs and expectations work with the sensory input to create perceptions of the external world. The fact that people are able to maintain a stable perception of objects and actions is really quite a remarkable accomplishment. As we noted at the beginning of the chapter, the pattern of light reflected from a moving object changes continuously with time, yet you perceive it as the same object with the same properties. You can also recognize the voice of a friend in a crowded room, even though the auditory input reaching your ears also includes sound information from many different voices.

The brain solves the problems of perception, in part, by relying on organizational "rules." For example, we are born with built-in tendencies to group input components in particular ways. Figures are separated from ground, items that share physical properties are perceived as being grouped together, and so on. But we also rely on prior knowledge for help in the interpretation process. The perceptual systems use knowledge about how cues are related in the environment to arrive at sensible interpretations of ambiguous objects. For instance, if two parallel lines converge in the visual field, the brain assumes that the lines are stretching off into the distance. Such top-down processing is usually extremely adaptive—it helps us maintain a stable interpretation—although in some cases, these same top-down processes can lead to perceptual illusions.

CHAPTER SUMMARY

▶ Vision: Creating a World of Meaningful Objects

The first step toward understanding vision is understanding how the physical input—light—is translated into the language of the brain. Beyond that, you need to know what pathways in the brain are used to extract the basic components of the visual input. How does the brain create a stable, meaningful interpretation?

Translating the Input: Visual Transduction

Light is classified by two main physical properties: *wavelength* and *intensity*. Light reflected from an object passes through the *cornea*, and then through the *pupil* (the middle of the *iris*). The *lens* undergoes accommodation, focusing the incoming light onto a thin layer of tissue on the inside of the back of the eye, the *retina*. The visual receptors (rods and cones) are located here. Compared with the cones, the *rods* are more light sensitive but less able to detect fine details, are located primarily in the periphery of the retina, and are useful at low levels of illumination. The *cones* are concentrated in the centre of the retina (in the *fovea*), need more light to operate, and are responsible for processing fine detail and colour. *Bipolar* and *ganglion* cells process the activity of the receptor cells and send it to the brain through the *optic nerve*.

Extracting the Input Components: Visual Pathways

From the retina, patterns of activation flow to the *optic chiasm*, after which most of the incoming visual neurons project to a relay station in the thalamus, the *lateral geniculate nucleus*, and then on to the occipital lobes. Many processing activities are carried out simultaneously, through *parallel processing*. In the visual cortex (in the occipital lobes), *feature detectors* respond to particular aspects of a stimulus, such as orientation and patterns of light and dark. The *trichromatic theory* of colour vision proposes that colour information is extracted through the activation of three different types of cones. The *opponent process theory* proposes mechanisms in the visual system that respond positively to one colour type and negatively to others. Both theories account for certain aspects of colour vision.

Producing Stable and Meaningful Interpretations: Visual Perception

Perception involves both *bottom-up* processing (which starts with the physical input) and *top-down* processing (application of knowledge and expectation). People have a natural tendency to group incoming visual inputs according to *Gestalt principles of organization*, which include the laws of *proximity, similarity, closure, good continuation,* and *common fate*. Depth is perceived with the aid of *monocular depth cues* (such as *linear perspective, texture gradients,* and the bias to perceive the *lower region* of a scene as the figure rather than ground) and *binocular depth cues* (such as *convergence* and *retinal disparity*). Visual perception also demonstrates *perceptual constancy*; perceived properties (such as size) remain the same even when the physical input to the eye changes. *Perceptual illusions* are inappropriate interpretations of physical reality.

▶ Hearing: Identifying and Localizing Sounds

Hearing enriches our lives, and like vision, it serves a variety of adaptive functions. Sound helps us identify and locate objects in the environment. It allows us to produce and comprehend the spoken word. Even our private self often appears in the form of an inner voice.

Translating the Input: Auditory Transduction

The auditory system receives *sound*, which is waves of energy (moving through a medium, such as air) that vary in *frequency* and *amplitude*. Sound is funnelled by the *pinna* into the auditory canal and travels through the *tympanic membrane*, which it causes to vibrate. Vibration of the tympanic membrane causes patterns of movement to be transmitted through the three tiny bones in the *middle ear*, which in turn transmit the signal to the *cochlea* in the inner ear. Vibrations propagating through the fluid in the cochlea displace the *basilar membrane*, which causes auditory receptors (*cilia*, or *hair cells*) to be activated.

Extracting the Input Components: Auditory Pathways

According to the *place theory* of pitch perception, we hear a particular pitch because certain hair cells are responding actively. According to *frequency theory*, pitch is determined in part by the frequency of neural impulses travelling up the auditory pathway. Both theories explain aspects of pitch perception. Final processing of the input occurs in the *auditory cortex* in the temporal lobes of the brain.

Producing Stable and Meaningful Interpretations: Auditory Perception

Prior knowledge helps the brain organize and impose structure on incoming sound input. *Sound localization* involves comparisons between the auditory stimuli reaching the ears (arrival time and intensity).

▶ The Skin and Body Senses: Experiencing Touch, Temperature, Pain, and Movement

Although perceptual experiences seem to be driven primarily by seeing and hearing, sensory receptors in the skin and other parts of the body are also extremely important, allowing us to experience touch, temperature, pain, and movement.

Touch

The skin has several types of pressure-sensitive receptors. Touch information of different sorts is transmitted through distinct channels to processing stations in the brain. There, the somatosensory cortex (in the *parietal lobe*) further processes the input.

Temperature

Cold fibres respond to cooling of the skin by increasing the production of neural impulses; *warm fibres* respond vigorously when the temperature of the skin increases. Temperature change determines temperature perception.

Pain

Pain is an adaptive reaction that the body generates in response to any stimulus intense enough to cause tissue damage. According to the *gate-control theory* of pain, neural impulses generated by pain receptors are gated in the spinal cord by signals produced by the brain; the brain can block critical signals from reaching higher neural centres when appropriate. The brain also controls the experience of pain through the release of chemicals called *endorphins*, which produce morphine-like effects.

The Kinesthetic Sense

Kinesthesia refers to the ability to sense the position and movement of our own body parts. Nerve impulses generated by kinesthetic receptors travel to the somatosensory cortex in the parietal lobes.

The Vestibular Sense

The *vestibular sense* responds to movement, acceleration, and changes in posture. Each ear contains fluid-filled *semicircular canals* that help us detect the position of the head: When your head moves, fluid within these structures moves, triggering action potentials in receptor cells. The *vestibular sacs*, also in the inner ear, are primarily responsible for our sense of balance.

▶ The Chemical Senses: Smell and Taste

Smells and tastes are adaptive because they possess powerful signalling properties; like other animals, humans learn to avoid bad odours and very bitter tastes. The perception of smell and taste begins with *chemoreceptors*.

Smell

Olfaction occurs as airborne molecules enter the nose or mouth and interact with receptors in the nasal cavity. The input travels to the olfactory bulb in the brain. People have up to 1000 different types of olfactory receptor cells. Many animals release *pheromones*, chemicals that cause highly specific (often sexual) reactions when detected by other members of a species.

Taste

Gustation is smell's companion sense. We experience at least four basic tastes: sweet, salty, bitter, and sour; recent evidence supports the existence of a fifth basic taste, called *umami* (savoury). *Taste buds* containing the taste receptors are embedded within *papillae* (tiny bumps) on the tongue. Neural codes representing taste stimuli travel toward the thalamus and then to the somatosensory area of the cortex.

▶ From the Physical to the Psychological

Sensory stimuli originate in the physical world, but our conscious experience of them is also influenced by expectations and beliefs about how the world is organized. In the field of *psychophysics*, researchers try to describe the transition from the physical to the psychological in the form of mathematical laws.

Stimulus Detection

The *absolute threshold* for a stimulus is the level of intensity that lifts it over the threshold of conscious awareness. Absolute threshold is defined as the intensity level at which a person can detect the presence of a stimulus 50% of the time. To account for response biases, researchers developed a technique known as *signal detection* that mathematically compares *hits* with *false alarms*.

Difference Thresholds

A *difference threshold* is the smallest difference in the magnitude of two stimuli that an observer can detect. Detection of a *just noticeable difference (JND)* between two stimuli depends on the intensity of the standard stimulus. According to *Weber's law*, the JND for stimulus magnitude is a constant proportion of the intensity of the standard stimulus.

Sensory Adaptation

One important adaptive function of sensory systems is *sensory adaptation*, through which the body quickly adapts to a stimulus by reducing sensitivity to input that remains constant, such as the feel of a shirtsleeve on your arm.

Interactions among Sensory Systems

In everyday life, perceptual experience reflects the interactive operation of numerous sensory systems; messages processed by one system (e.g., vision) often influence the simultaneous operation of other systems (e.g., olfaction and gustation).

Terms to Remember

sensations, 124
perception, 124
transduction, 125

Vision: Creating a World of Meaningful Objects
light, 126
hue, 126
brightness, 126
cornea, 127
lens, 127
pupil, 127
iris, 127
accommodation, 128
retina, 128
rods, 128
cones, 128
fovea, 129
visual acuity, 129
dark adaptation, 129
receptive field, 130
blind spot, 130
parallel processing, 132
feature detectors, 132
trichromatic theory, 136
afterimage, 137
opponent process theory, 138
bottom-up processing, 140
top-down processing, 140
Gestalt principles of organization, 141
recognition by components, 142
texture gradient, 143
lower region, 143
monocular depth cues, 144
binocular depth cues, 144
retinal disparity, 144
convergence, 144
perceptual constancy, 146
perceptual illusions, 147

Hearing: Identifying and Localizing Sounds
sound, 150
pitch, 150
loudness, 151
pinna, 151
tympanic membrane, 151
middle ear, 152
cochlea, 152
basilar membrane, 152
place theory, 152
frequency theory, 153

The Skin and Body Senses: Experiencing Touch, Temperature, Pain, and Movement
cold fibres, 157
warm fibres, 157
pain, 158
gate-control theory, 158
kinesthesia, 159
semicircular canals, 159
vestibular sacs, 160

The Chemical Senses: Smell and Taste
chemoreceptors, 161
olfaction, 161
gustation, 162
flavour, 162
taste buds, 163

From the Physical to the Psychological
psychophysics, 164
absolute threshold, 164
signal detection, 165
difference threshold, 166
Weber's law, 166
sensory adaptation, 166

Recommended Readings

Coren, S., Ward, L. M., & Enns, J. T. (2004). *Sensation and perception* (6th ed.). New York: Wiley. This is an excellent undergraduate textbook by faculty at the University of British Columbia. It covers most of the material presented here in Chapter 4 but in much greater depth.

Ramachandran, V. S. (1992). Filling gaps in perception: I. *Current Directions in Psychological Science 1*, 199–205. This article, written for a general audience, describes fascinating research on how the visual system fills in information in the blind spot, along with numerous demonstrations of this filling-in phenomenon (and its limits).

Shepard, R. N. (1990). *Mind sights*. New York: W. H. Freeman. This provocative book is full of wonderfully original visual tricks and illusions. Accompanying the drawings are concise scientific explanations of the illusions. The two monsters shown in part (b) of Figure 4.22 came from this book.

For additional readings, explore InfoTrac® College Edition, your online library. Go to http://www.adaptivemind3e.nelson.com.

Hint: Enter these search terms: visual perception, pattern recognition, motion perception, optical illusions, speech perception, signal detection.

Media Resources

What's on the Web?

Please note that Web addresses are subject to change. Check out the accompanying website for updates: http://www.adaptivemind3e.nelson.com.

This site presents practice quiz questions, hypercontent, information on degrees and careers in psychology, study tips, and more.

Cow's Eye Dissection

http://www.exploratorium.edu/learning_studio/cow_eye

Yes, you read that right. This site, part of the wonderful Exploratorium site, provides you with the opportunity to dissect the eye of a cow online—it turns out there's a fair amount of similarity between our eyes and a cow's eyes. It's a fun way to find out more about the eye.

Illusionworks

http://psylux.psych.tu-dresden.de/il/kaw/diverses%20Material/www.illusionworks.com

Nothing's quite as fascinating as visual illusions. They're fun to look at and intriguing to learn about. This superb site, winner of numerous awards, presents a variety of visual illusions and interesting and informative explanations of the processes that are responsible.

Seeing, Hearing, and Smelling the World

http://www.hhmi.org/senses

Although many websites enable you to learn more about vision, relatively few are devoted to the other major senses. This site allows you to investigate these more "neglected" senses, with such articles as "A Secret Sense in the Human Nose?" and "Locating a Mouse by Its Sound."

H.E.A.R (Hearing Education and Awareness for Rockers)

http://www.hearnet.com

In addition to lots of information about the relationship between loud music and hearing damage (including inside information about musicians who wear earplugs and those

who wish they had because they're now partially deaf), this site includes a simple way to test the effect of a night in a club on your own hearing.

The Archive of Misheard Lyrics

http://www.kissthisguy.com

Mondegreens are misperceptions of song lyrics, as in the "kiss the sky/kiss this guy" example discussed on page 154. This fun site is an archive of hundreds of anecdotal accounts of these perceptual errors, such as the one from a woman who discovered at age 17 that Nirvana, in the song "Smells Like Teen Spirit," was not singing "Here we are now, in containers."

ThomsonNOW

http://hed.nelson.com

Go to this site for the link to ThomsonNOW™, your one-stop study shop. Take a Pretest for this chapter and ThomsonNOW™ will generate a personalized Study Plan based on your test results. The Study Plan will identify the topics you need to review and direct you to online resources to help you master those topics. You can then take a Posttest to determine what concepts you have mastered and what you still need work on.

Psyk.trek 3.0

Check out Psyk.trek 3.0 for further study of the concepts in this chapter. Psyk.trek's 65 interactive learning modules, simulations, and quizzes offer additional opportunities for you to interact with, reflect on, and retain the material:

Sensation and Perception: The Retina
Sensation and Perception: The Sense of Hearing

We learn the influence of our will from experience alone. And experience only teaches us, how one event constantly follows another; without instructing us in the secret connexion, which binds them together, and renders them inseparable.

—David Hume, *Enquiries Concerning the Human Understanding and Concerning the Principles of Morals*

Consciousness

Stop for a moment and take a look inside your own mind. Just let your thoughts go, and see where they take you. Pay attention to the movement from thought to thought to thought. Notice the transitions, the way that ideas and feelings and images spring forth, only to disappear a moment later, replaced by new thoughts. Does your "stream of consciousness" (James, 1890) flow smoothly and steadily along a single coherent line or thought, or does the content of your mental state shift sharply, such that you're thinking about psychology one moment, then focusing briefly on the discomfort of the chair in which you're sitting, then shifting to thoughts of food, then being grabbed by some interesting noise?

Consciousness can be defined in many ways; we focus here on consciousness defined as the subjective experience of internal and external events. Studying consciousness was one of the main jobs of psychologists in the nineteenth century. In fact, if you had taken a psychology course at the turn of the last century, the subject matter would likely have been defined as "the science which describes and explains the phenomena of consciousness" (Ladd, 1896, p. 1). At that time, the main research technique for studying psychology was introspection, in which research subjects were asked to report on their own internal thoughts. With the rise of behaviourism in the 1920s, however, psychologists shifted away from the study of internal experience toward an emphasis on behaviour. Such techniques as introspection fell strongly out of favour. Most psychologists became convinced

consciousness

The subjective awareness of internal and external events

that internal observations were difficult, if not impossible, to confirm objectively. Behaviourists argued forcefully that "psychology must discard all reference to consciousness" (Watson, 1913, p. 163) because it is impossible to measure conscious experience directly and objectively.

It's easy to understand why behaviourists were dissatisfied with the study of internal subjective experience. Turning inward and asking questions about the contents of consciousness is "like asking a flashlight in a dark room to search around for something that doesn't have any light shining upon it. The flashlight, since there is light in whatever direction it turns, would have to conclude that there is light everywhere" (Jaynes, 1976, p. 23). William James, one of the first psychological researchers, was also aware of the inherent difficulty of introspectively analyzing consciousness. In 1890 he wrote: "The attempt at introspective analysis . . . is . . . like seizing a spinning top to catch its motion, or trying to turn up the gas quickly enough to see how the darkness looks." It's tough to study the properties of something when your only tool of discovery is the object itself!

In recent decades, however, the study of consciousness has emerged from its intellectual Dark Age and has regained a measure of respectability (Cohen & Schooler, 1997; Milner & Rugg, 1992; Schooler & Schreiber, 2004). One major contributor to the renewed interest in the scientific study of consciousness was the development by cognitive psychologists in the 1950s and 1960s of clever experimental procedures for testing hypotheses about the nature of mental events (e.g., Broadbent, 1952; Brooks, 1968; Miller, 1956; Sperling, 1960). Examples of such procedures will be described later, but for now the point to appreciate is that these procedures provide an alternative to introspection: Rather than asking participants to report on their own mental events, cognitive psychologists make strong inferences about participants' mental processes by objectively measuring performance in such experiments (although cognitive psychologists sometimes also ask research participants to report on their subjective experiences).

Another contributing factor to the re-emergence of scientific studies of consciousness has been the development of technologies, such as the electroencephalograph (EEG) and positron emission tomography (PET) (see Chapter 3). These devices provide a window into the activities of the living brain, enabling researchers to measure how internal activity changes over time. Most neuroscientists are convinced that consciousness is linked directly to patterns of neural activity in the brain, although the biological basis of consciousness is not yet known (Miller, 2005; Revonsuo, 2001) and the interpretation of data from EEGs and PET scans is not as straightforward as is sometimes implied (for an elegant critique of brain imaging research, see Bub, 2000). Nonetheless, as our tools of discovery have broadened, psychologists' willingness to explore the workings of the inner world of the mind has increased.

Such technologies as event-related potentials (ERP), shown here, provide psychologists with a window through which the internal activities of the brain can be observed, but we do not yet know how electrochemical activity gives rise to consciousness.

Courtesy of Dr. Jim Tanaka

The Psychology of Consciousness

P
R
E
V
I
E
W

Consciousness can be defined as the subjective awareness of internal and external events. But what does it mean to be aware? Intuitively, everyone has a reasonably good idea of what the term means. To be aware is to experience the here and now, to re-experience the past in the form of memories, to think and feel internally and create a "view of the world" (Klatzky, 1984). Awareness has the additional property that it can be focused: You can choose to attend to that bug walking up the page of your text, to the beautiful sunset outside your window, or to the voice of a neighbour talking on the phone. You can also be consciously aware of developing strategies for future behaviour; you can think about what you want to say or do, and you can imagine the outcomes of those actions without actually performing them. You can also consciously imagine the content of others' minds—and hence predict the behaviour of other people and understand (or at least think you understand) their motivations (Nickerson, 1999; Weiskrantz, 1992).

Despite the importance of consciousness, many human actions are controlled by processes that operate without awareness. To take an extreme case, you're not aware of the processes controlling your heartbeat or (usually) your breathing rate, yet these functions carry on like clockwork in the body. You also lack awareness of many basic cognitive processes, such as the perceptual processes described in Chapter 4. For example, your brain is doing a phenomenal amount of sophisticated work to read the words on this page. You are probably aware that you are reading, but you lack awareness of the basic processes that are separating the black marks from the white background of the paper, identifying the letters and words, and so on. As you'll see later in this chapter, the brain can accomplish a lot without conscious awareness.

Your awareness also takes on different properties when you sleep, when you're hypnotized, if you take certain types of drugs, or when you are in different social settings or moods. As you'll see later in the

chapter, altering awareness can help people solve certain adaptive problems (see ▶ Figure 5.1).

First, how do people set priorities for mental functioning? Our performance of a task is typically better—faster and more accurate—when our efforts are focused on that task, rather than spread across several tasks. Have you ever tried to solve a difficult thought problem while someone is talking nearby? Obviously, it's critical for people to be selective about what they focus on. How do we set those priorities from moment to moment, and what mechanisms enable us to focus mental processing on some tasks or stimuli while largely ignoring others?

Second, what roles do sleep and dreaming play for the adaptive mind? Sleep clearly serves an adaptive function, as does dreaming. Some researchers believe that we sleep to give the brain a chance to rest and restore itself after the day's activities. Others believe that sleep protects us during periods when our sensory equipment is likely to function poorly (such as at night). Dreaming, with its sometimes

▶ **Figure 5.1**

Adaptive Problems of Consciousness

Here are the four adaptive problems that we consider in this chapter.

Nelson

Don Tremain/PhotoDisc/Getty Images

Nancy R. Cohen/PhotoDisc/Getty Images

Joaquin Palting/PhotoDisc/Getty Images

bizarre imagery, may help us work out hidden conflicts, or it may simply exercise the neural circuitry of the brain.

Third, how do certain chemicals, or drugs, produce profound alterations in awareness? You have probably heard about (if not experienced) the alterations of consciousness produced by psychoactive drugs, such as Ecstasy and marijuana. What you may not know is that the biological processes that produce those effects are natural and important ingredients of the adaptive mind. Psychoactive drugs can have long-lasting harmful consequences, but it's important to understand that artificial drugs operate, in part, by tapping natural adaptive systems.

Fourth, what happens under hypnosis and meditation, two other techniques that seem to alter awareness? Hypnosis is a social interaction that induces a heightened state of suggestibility in a willing subject. How can it serve an adaptive purpose? Well, for one thing, hypnosis can dramatically reduce the experience of pain (e.g., during dental treatments). Similarly, meditation may reduce stress and anxiety. Thus, you'll discover that both hypnosis and meditation can have adaptive benefits.

Setting Priorities for Mental Functioning: Attention

LEARNING GOALS

1. Learn how experiments on dichotic listening can be used to study attention.
2. Understand the concept of *automaticity*.
3. Learn about attention disorders, such as visual neglect and attention deficit/hyperactivity disorder.
4. Understand research on the influence of subliminal messages.

CRITICAL THINKING

Can you think of any circumstances in which your brain attends to things that you are not aware of?

attention

The internal processes people use to set and follow priorities for mental functioning

As you learned in Chapter 4, the world is a teeming smorgasbord of sensory information that offers an astonishing variety of sensory input. You don't consciously experience every stimulus at any given time; you sample selectively from the table, based partly on your current interests and needs. If you're searching desperately for a child lost in a shopping mall, you focus on the familiar sound of the child's voice or the colour of his or her shirt, and largely ignore other stimuli, such as the items displayed for sale. If you're trying to determine what's for dinner tonight, you sniff the air, selecting food aromas from the other scents stimulating your olfactory receptors. You tend to notice those things that are important to the task at hand, selecting them from the vast array of stimuli in the environment.

Psychologists use the term **attention** to refer to the internal processes people use to set and follow priorities for mental functioning. For adaptive reasons, the brain uses attention to focus selectively on certain parts of the environment while largely ignoring others. Obviously, the concepts of attention and consciousness are closely linked—you are consciously aware of only those things that receive some measure of attention. But why is attention selective? One reason is that any individual's mental resources are limited: Given the particular cognitive skills (both conscious and unconscious) that a person has developed, he or she will be limited in the number and kinds of cognitive tasks that he or she can perform simultaneously (Spelke, Hirst, & Neisser, 1976). Furthermore, some cognitive psychologists believe that certain kinds of cognitive operations can be performed only one at a time, which prevents us from performing those operations on different stimuli simultaneously (e.g., Pashler, 1992; Shapiro & Raymond, 1994; cf. Tombu & Jolicoeur, 2005). These limitations require us to make choices about which parts of the environment to process deeply and extensively (Broadbent, 1958; Kahneman, 1973).

In a mystery novel, certain events are relevant clues for solving the murder and others are red herrings, irrelevant points that lead the reader in the wrong direction and delay solving the crime. The trick is to be selective in deciding which components are worth selecting for focused attention. A first-rate detective knows not only what to look for but also what information to ignore. The same is true for even the simplest kind of action, such as walking across the room or reaching for a cup. The visual and motor systems must focus on the objects in the person's *path*, not every object in the room. If you tried to focus on and think about everything in the environment, you would suffer interference from irrelevant input. Prioritizing mental functioning is an important part of the coordination and control of human action (Allport, 1989).

Experiments on Attention: Dichotic Listening

Experiments on attention began in the 1950s with the development of the **dichotic listening** technique (Broadbent, 1952; Cherry, 1953). As shown in ▶ Figure 5.2, in a dichotic listening experiment subjects are exposed to two messages spoken simultaneously, each presented to one ear through headphones. To promote selective attention, the subject is asked to "shadow," or repeat aloud, one of the two messages as it goes along while essentially ignoring the other. This kind of listening is called *dichotic*, meaning "divided into two," because two messages are involved, delivered separately into each ear.

A dichotic listening experiment requires the subject to listen to two voices at the same time. Have you ever tried to listen to a lecture while someone next to you is filling you in on the details of his or her latest escapade? Not an easy task. In fact, you may have found yourself either ignoring one of the two or switching back and forth from one message to the other. This is essentially what happens in a dichotic listening experiment. Subjects are instructed to attend selectively to the to-be-shadowed message, based on both the spatial location and the sound qualities of that message (Mondor, Zatorre, & Terrio, 1998). Consequently, they process the other message poorly. For example, if at the end of the experiment subjects are given a surprise test for the nonshadowed message, they can usually remember very little about its content. They can usually report whether the speaker of the nonshadowed message was male or female, but they recall virtually nothing else about that message, even if it repeated the same statements over and over (Cherry, 1953; Moray, 1959).

People don't completely shut off the part of the world that is not bathed in the spotlight of attention. If they did, their actions wouldn't be very adaptive because the world is constantly changing. Some new, possibly critical, situation could suddenly arise, and we need to be able to switch our attention to such events quickly and flexibly when they occur. The brain must monitor many things at the same time, although the monitoring may be somewhat crude and accomplished without conscious awareness.

A case in point is something called the **cocktail party effect.** Imagine you're having a good time at a large and noisy party, engaged in conversation with a friend. In all

dichotic listening

A technique in which two different auditory messages are presented simultaneously, one to each ear; usually the subject's task is to shadow, or repeat aloud, one message while ignoring the other

cocktail party effect

The ability to focus on one auditory message, such as a friend's voice at a noisy party, and largely ignore others, yet notice when your own name is spoken among the auditory stimuli that you have been ignoring

▶ **Figure 5.2**

Dichotic Listening Technique

In dichotic listening, two different spoken messages are presented simultaneously, one to each ear; usually the subject is required to shadow—or repeat aloud—one of the messages while ignoring the other. The task taps the ability to *attend selectively*.

Shadowed channel
"Emily Carr was known for her eccentricity as well as for her art."

Nonshadowed channel
"When asked the question, 'what is consciousness?' we become conscious of consciousness."

"Emily Carr ... was known for her ... ah ... eccentricity as well as for her art."

The cocktail party effect: By using the processes of attention, it's possible to attend selectively to one of many conversations in a noisy environment. But if someone across the room speaks your name, you'll probably notice it.

likelihood, you won't be consciously aware of the content of the conversations around you; you'll be aware of hearing the babble of voices as background noise, but if asked to say what the people behind you had been discussing, you probably couldn't do it. You successfully select the sound of your friend's voice from all the other sounds stimulating your auditory receptors by using the processes of selective attention. Now suppose that someone behind you speaks your name. The odds are that you'll turn your head immediately. People in dichotic listening experiments have shown the same effect: They appear to ignore the contents of the nonshadowed message, but if their name is spoken in the non-shadowed channel, they notice and remember it later. This is the cocktail party effect, and it suggests that our brains are aware of more things than we think: You could not recognize the particular pattern of sounds that is your name unless your brain was analyzing *all* of the auditory input.

Another compelling example of how people monitor auditory input that they appear to be ignoring comes from a dichotic listening experiment by Anne Treisman (1960), one of the pioneers of cognitive psychology. People were presented with compound sentences, such as "Against the advice of his broker, the naive investor panicked" in one ear and "Released from his cage, the little lamb bounded into the field" in the other (see ▶ Figure 5.3). Subjects were to shadow the message in one ear. In the middle of some of the sentences, Treisman switched things around—the second half of each sentence moved to the opposite ear. Thus, in the to-be-shadowed ear the subject heard such a sentence as, "Against the advice of his broker, the little lamb bounded into the field," whereas in the other ear the message was "Released from his cage, the naive investor panicked." The interesting finding was that about 30% of the time subjects continued to repeat the meaningful sentence ("Against the advice of his broker, the naive investor panicked") smoothly and without hesitation, even though the message had switched midway from the to-be-shadowed ear to the to-be-ignored ear. Moreover, many of the subjects reported that they hadn't even realized that they had switched to shadowing the to-be-ignored ear.

The cocktail party effect and the findings of the ear-switching experiments suggest that the brain does not completely ignore stimuli that are not the focus of attention. Compare (1) what the brain does when we selectively attend to a source of stimuli to (2) what a TV does when tuned to a particular channel: For the TV, it

▶ **Figure 5.3**

Treisman's "Ear-Switching" Experiment

At one point in a dichotic listening experiment by Treisman, the to-be-shadowed message was abruptly switched to the to-be-ignored ear. Interestingly, subjects often continued to repeat the meaningful sentence without even noticing that they were now shadowing the message they were supposed to be ignoring.

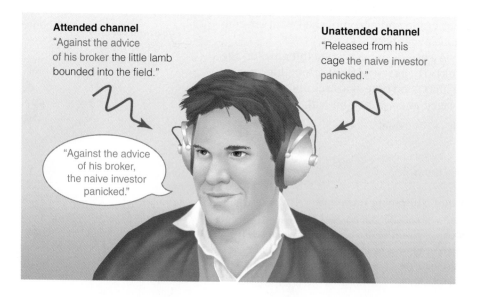

doesn't matter what happens on the other channels; as long as it is tuned to Much-Music, that's all you're going to see. In contrast, the brain focuses the spotlight of attention on the task at hand, but it carries on at least some unconscious monitoring of the rest of the environment as well. If something important happens in part of the environment that is outside of the focus of attention, the brain shifts the spotlight of attention and the new event becomes the focus of conscious awareness. In Treisman's experiment, the brain must have been following the meaning of the messages in both ears, even though the people who participated were only aware of monitoring one message. Exactly how all this works has been the subject of considerable debate over the last several decades (Cowan, 1995; Hirst, 1995; Pashler, 1998), but the process itself is clearly adaptive. Humans wouldn't survive for long if they processed only those things in the realm of immediate awareness.

Processing without Attention: Automaticity

The idea that the brain and body are doing things beyond current awareness may seem strange at first, but not if you think about it. After all, when's the last time you thought about breathing or keeping your heart beating or walking or even forming words from your repertoire of spoken sounds? You can drive a car and carry on a conversation at the same time; you don't need to focus an attentional spotlight on every turn of the wheel or press of the brake. You perform such tasks largely automatically (but see the Practical Solutions box for limits on the automaticity of driving).

Psychologists use the term **automaticity** to refer to fast and nearly effortless processing that requires little or no focused attention (Logan, 1991). When you practise a task, such as playing a piece by Mozart on the piano, overall speed steadily improves. You may even reach a point at which performing the task seems automatic—Mozart's music rolls off your fingertips with such ease that you're not even consciously aware of controlling your own finger movements. Automatic processes, once they develop, no longer seem to require much conscious control. The mind is free to consider other things, while the task itself is performed without a hitch. Many of the activities that people take for granted—such as reading, talking, and walking—are essentially automatic processes.

It's possible to measure how automaticity develops through what is called a *divided attention task* (Logan, 1988). In a typical experiment, people are asked to perform two tasks at the same time, such as playing a difficult piece on the piano while simultaneously trying to remember a short list of unrelated words. Automaticity is demonstrated when one task, the automatic one, doesn't interfere with performance on the other task (Hasher & Zacks, 1979; Shiffrin & Schneider, 1977). Clearly, if you are just learning to play the piece, you'll have enough trouble getting through it without error, let alone memorizing a list of words at the same time. But if you're an accomplished pianist—if your playing has become largely automatic—you can let your fingers do the playing and your mind can concentrate on remembering the word list.

The relationship between automaticity and awareness tells us something important about the function of consciousness. The better you are at performing a task—the more automatic the task has become—the less likely you are to be aware of the processes involved in performing the task. This is a very important characteristic of mental functioning: Performance of novel tasks seems to require conscious awareness of each step in performing the task, whereas highly practised tasks can be performed without conscious monitoring of all their component processes. Environmental conditions can change at any moment, so we need to be able to initiate new and adaptive behaviours when the unexpected occurs. It appears that people use consciousness for handling the new and demanding, while relying on the nearly effortless processes of automaticity to continue performing routine tasks.

automaticity

Fast and almost effortless processing that requires little or no focused attention

©Tim Hope/Shutterstock

If you practise a task, such as juggling, for extended periods, your performance may become largely automatic. Automatic processes, once acquired, no longer require much conscious control.

PRACTICAL SOLUTIONS

CELL PHONES AND DRIVING

You've seen that there are limitations on the brain's capacity to perform mental work. We attend selectively to current priorities, because we have limitations on how much information we can process at a given time. As we've discussed, with sufficient practice certain tasks (even quite complex ones) can become largely automatic, such that performing them has relatively little impact on our ability to perform another task simultaneously, and vice versa. Yet real-world tasks, such as driving, never become 100% automatic, partly because of unpredictable variations in the demands of driving. If something unexpected happens while you are driving (e.g., a cat darts into the path of your car), you cannot rely on well-practised routines but must respond very quickly in a way that fits the needs of that specific situation. Consequently, driving demands vigilance at all times. Yet studies suggest that a very substantial percentage of accidents involve lapses of drivers' attention.

According to a 2001 study, approximately half of Canadian adults use cellular phones occasionally, and about three-quarters of those who own cell phones report at least occasional use of them while driving (Leger Marketing, 2001). It seems likely that these numbers have increased in subsequent years. Studies have established a strong correlation between cell phone use and traffic accidents. In fact, it's been claimed that talking on a cell

phone increases the risk of accident to levels comparable with those of driving with a blood alcohol level above the legal limit (Redelmeier & Tibshirani, 1997). The presence of a correlation between cell phone use and accidents, however, is not sufficient to infer that cell phone use *causes* accidents. It could be that people who use cell phones while driving are just bad drivers. As you know, correlations do not imply causality (see Chapter 2).

To determine a causal link, you must have experimental control. A number of experiments have examined the effects of cell phone use on driving. Typically, these studies manipulate the type and extent of cell phone use during simulated driving—either in a driving simulator or by requiring people to perform a tracking task on a computer. In a recent study by Strayer and Johnston (2001), people were asked to use a joystick to move a cursor on a computer screen; the task was to keep the cursor aligned as closely as possible to a moving target (meant to correspond roughly to maintaining location on a road). At random intervals, either a red or a green light flashed on the computer screen. The subjects were instructed to react to the red light by pressing a "brake" button on the joystick.

Strayer and Johnston found that when people were engaged in a cell phone conversation while performing the simulated driving task, they missed twice as many red lights. Even when the red

light was detected and the brake applied, people talking on a cell phone were considerably slower to respond. Moreover, the impairments were found regardless of whether the cell phone was a hand-held or a hands-free model. Importantly, simply listening to the radio did not impair performance.

A study commissioned by Transport Canada and conducted by Harbluk, Noy, and Eizenman (2002) yielded similar findings. The Harbluk study used actual driving performance, with technology that enabled measurement of a large range of driving-related behaviours (braking, accelerating, eye movements). Even though the drivers in this study used hands-free phones, their performance was impaired when they were participating in a cognitively demanding phone conversation. For example, they spent more time looking centrally (and hence less time checking the sides of the road and their mirrors), and they more often braked hard.

The theoretical implications of these and other recent studies are clear: Cell phones are particularly distracting because (unlike other distractions, such as the radio or food or a companion in the car) they require the user to commit substantial cognitive resources to interacting with another person who is not in the vehicle. The practical implications are equally clear: Turn off the cell phone when you drive. If the call is important, then it's worth getting off the road.

Disorders of Attention

We've stressed the link between attention and consciousness because, in many respects, attention is the gateway to consciousness: We only become conscious of things that receive some measure of attention. It follows that if the brain systems that control attention are damaged, a corresponding loss in conscious awareness will occur. Brain researchers have used clinical cases of brain damage to examine this possibility, and they are in the process of mapping out what appear to be attention-related areas of the brain (Park, Moscovitch, & Robertson, 1999; Posner & Rothbart, 1992; Stuss, Rosenbaum, Malcolm, Christiana, & Keenan, 2005; Tulving, 2002). Other researchers are developing treatment strategies for people who have attention disorders as a consequence of brain injury (e.g., Mateer, 2005). Let's briefly consider two attention disorders that are related to brain dysfunction: *visual neglect* and *attention deficit/hyperactivity disorder*.

Visual Neglect   Damage to the right parietal lobe of the cerebral cortex can produce an odd and complex attention disorder called **visual neglect** (see ▶ Figure 5.4). People suffering from visual neglect tend to ignore things on the left side of the body (remember from Chapter 3 that the right side of the brain processes most information from the left side of the body). Visual neglect can cause people to read only the right side of pages and copy only the right side of pictures; patients with visual neglect may even dress, shave, or apply makeup to only the right side of the body (Arguin & Bub, 1993; Bisiach & Rusconi, 1990). It's as if an entire side of their visual field has vanished from awareness. Fortunately, the condition typically diminishes with time (Kerkhoff, Munssinger, & Meier, 1994).

Is the brain of patients with visual neglect really shutting off all visual information from one side of the body? Probably not. In one study, a patient suffering from visual neglect was shown drawings of two houses. One house was normal in appearance; the other was normal on the right side but had bright red flames and smoke billowing out from a window on its left side. The patient was asked to choose which of the two houses she would prefer to live in. "The houses look the same to me," she reported, presumably because she was attending only to the right side of each picture. Nevertheless, when forced to indicate which of the two she would prefer to live in, she consistently chose the house without the flames (Marshall & Halligan, 1988). This suggests that even though the brain mechanisms underlying conscious awareness had been damaged, her brain was still able to use information from the left visual field (Bisiach, 1992; Schweinberger & Stief, 2001).

A related disorder is called visual form agnosia. Patients with this disorder have great difficulty identifying common objects (e.g., a lemon, a pen) by looking at them. Such patients also have difficulty describing the shape, size, and orientation of visually presented objects. Yet when asked to pick up an object, patients with visual form agnosia tailor their grasp appropriately. Their studies of such patients, and of other patients who have impairments in visually guided movements but are able to describe their perceptions of objects, have led Goodale and co-workers at the University of Western Ontario to propose that there are two distinct but interacting visual systems: one for the conscious perception of objects and the other for acting on objects (Goodale & Westwood, 2004). According to this view, phenomena, such as visual agnosia, arise from damage to the former system.

Attention Deficit/Hyperactivity Disorder   The right hemisphere of the brain may also be involved in **attention deficit/hyperactivity disorder,** or ADHD, a psychological condition characterized by difficulties in concentrating and by high levels of fidgety physical activity. Individuals with ADHD have trouble sustaining attention for extended periods; they're easily distracted and have difficulty completing tasks. They also tend to squirm and fidget continuously and often act impulsively (e.g., blurt out answers to questions before the questions have even been completely asked) (Barkley, 1997). Attention deficits sometimes occur without hyperactivity (in which case the disorder is known simply as attention deficit disorder, or ADD) (Barlow & Durand, 2002). ADHD and ADD are among the most common psychological

visual neglect

A complex attention disorder characterized by a tendency to ignore things that appear on one side of the body, usually the left side

CRITICAL   THINKING

In what ways are the symptoms of visual neglect similar to the symptoms of the split-brain patients discussed in Chapter 3? How do they differ?

attention deficit/hyperactivity disorder

A psychological condition marked by difficulties in concentrating and sustaining attention and by high levels of fidgety physical activity; occurs most often in children

▶ **Figure 5.4**

Visual Neglect

Patients suffering from visual neglect might report that they see no differences between these two drawings of houses (because the flames in the lower one are on the left). But if pressed to choose, they would probably opt to live in the house without the flames.

problems in school-aged children. Only about 3% to 5% of all children meet criteria for either of these diagnoses (Cantwell, 1996), but these children make up a very sizeable portion of children identified as having behavioural problems. For example, a recent study of 324 schoolchildren in Quebec who were receiving special education found that three-quarters of them met criteria for ADHD or ADD (Déry, Toupin, Pauzé, & Verlaan, 2004).

Kerns and Price (2001) at the University of Victoria tested children's performance on a "prospective memory" task embedded in a computer game called CyberCruiser. The game involved controlling a car on a computer screen, and the player had to remember to check the gas level at appropriate times during the game. Compared with control children, children diagnosed with ADD or ADHD more often forgot to check the gas, suggesting that they had difficulty keeping that intention in mind while playing the game.

Some evidence exists that attention deficit disorder might be caused by mild damage to, or malfunctioning of, the right hemisphere of the brain (e.g., Manly, Cornish, Grant, Dobler, & Hollis, 2005). But the brain mechanisms involved in attention deficit disorder are still largely unknown, with different studies yielding differing results. PET scan studies, for instance, have indicated that various regions of the brain may be selectively involved (Zametkin et al., 1990). It's unlikely that any single brain location is responsible for ADHD, because the disorder is quite complex and can manifest itself in a variety of ways. As we might expect, experience and social influences play roles in the onset and maintenance of the disorder (DeGrandpre, 2000). Debate is ongoing even about the disorder's proper definition (Barkley, 2003). So, it may take some time before researchers arrive at a complete neurological understanding of the problem.

What about treatment? The news on this front is promising. It turns out that a majority of children who have attention problems can be helped with a combination of medication and training (Multimodal Treatment Study of Children with ADHD Cooperative Group, 1999). Children with attention problems need to learn coping strategies to help them perform well in school and in social settings. A complete training program typically includes teaching study skills, such as learning to write down important information (rather than relying on memory), and offering rewards for sitting still and not being disruptive in social interactions. Medications, such as Ritalin, seem to help concentration and they often reduce hyperactivity and disruptive behaviour. It's interesting to note that Ritalin, as well as many other drugs that are used to treat attention deficit disorder, comes from a class of drugs—called stimulants—that generally serve to increase nervous system activity. You'll read more about stimulants later in this chapter, but for present purposes the point to remember is that, in low doses, certain stimulants, such as Ritalin, appear to increase the ability to concentrate and focus attention in children with attention deficits. Finally, it's worth mentioning that some concern exists among psychologists that attention deficit disorder has been overdiagnosed in recent years and that drugs such as Ritalin have been overprescribed.

Subliminal Perception

Can people be influenced by stimuli of which they are entirely unaware? We briefly considered this topic in Chapter 2, when experimental methods were discussed, but we discuss it in greater detail here in the context of attention. You've seen how the brain uses attention to prioritize mental functioning; automatic processes can also develop that lead to fast and nearly effortless behaviours that require little or no conscious thought. So, from an adaptive perspective, it's reasonable to assume that people might be influenced by stimuli that bypass conscious awareness. But do subliminal messages really work?

Attention deficit/hyperactivity disorder involves distractibility, hyperactivity, and impulsive behaviour.

Dan McCoy/Rainbow

It's not known whether advertisers really try to influence people subliminally (the advertisers deny it) or, in fact, whether the subliminal tapes that some people buy to lose weight or gain confidence really do present the promised embedded messages (some evidence suggests that the messages are often not even present). It is possible, however, to conduct controlled experiments in which messages are purposely embedded in print advertisements or on audiotapes. Dozens of such studies have been conducted (Druckman & Bjork, 1991; Merikle, Smilek, & Eastwood, 2001; Rosen & Singh, 1992); the general consensus is that if subliminal messages have any effect at all it is a small and fleeting one.

It is sometimes claimed that subliminal messages lead to enhanced memory for the supraliminal material in which they are embedded. In a study conducted at the University of Lethbridge by Vokey and Read (1985), several instances of the word *SEX* were inserted into vacation slides; the words were placed into the pictures in such a way that they were not noticeable but could be detected if pointed out by the experimenters. Subjects viewed the slides (without being told about the hidden word) and then were tested on their ability to recognize them. Subjects did no better in recognizing the slides than control subjects who viewed the slides without the embedded words.

As another example, Rosen and Singh (1992) had people view one of three visually embedded subliminal messages: (1) the word *SEX*, (2) a picture of a naked woman and several phallic symbols, or (3) the word *DEATH* combined with pictures of skulls. The "embeds" were placed in print ads for liquor or cologne, and subjects viewed the ads as part of an experiment on advertising effectiveness. No mention was made of the embeds, which were present in some of the ads but not in others. This study is noteworthy because it used a variety of measures of advertising effectiveness to check for effects of the subliminal messages. None of these measures was affected by the hidden information.

Yet some studies do yield evidence of influences of subliminal stimuli on consumer behaviours. For example, Winkielman, Berridge, and Wilbarger (2005) exposed participants to subliminal presentations of photos of faces, then offered participants an opportunity to pour and drink a fruit-flavoured beverage. For some participants, the subliminally presented faces were smiling, for others they were frowning, and for the rest the faces had neutral expressions. Compared with subjects exposed to neutral faces, those exposed to smiling faces poured and drank more juice, and those exposed to angry faces poured and drank less. Interestingly, these results were observed only among participants who had previously reported that they were thirsty, suggesting that motivational states modulate the impact of subliminal stimuli.

With regard to self-help tapes with subliminal messages, no data support their efficacy. For example, Moore (1995) reported a study conducted at York University in which subjects listened to pairs of subliminal tapes and tried to discriminate between them; even after 400 trials, subjects scored no better than chance. Similarly, Greenwald, Spangenberg, Pratkanis, and Eskenazi (1991) at the University of Washington recruited subjects for a study of the effectiveness of subliminal tapes designed to improve either memory or self-esteem. Unknown to the subjects, the labels on the tapes had sometimes been switched, such that some subjects who thought they were listening to a self-esteem tape were actually given a memory tape, and vice versa. After regular listening, subjects improved on posttests of self-esteem or memory (depending on which tape they thought they had been listening to), but it didn't matter which tape they had actually been given.

Why the improvement? From a psychological perspective, it's important to remember that people who buy such tapes (and those who participate in studies of memory or self-esteem enhancement) are *motivated* to improve. Thus, we might expect to see some improvement over the course of a study, even if the tapes themselves have no effect at all. It is also possible that subliminal tapes act as a kind of *placebo*, leading to improvement because the listener believes in their magical powers. If subliminal self-help is placebo related, all that's necessary is that subjects *think* they are receiving something that will work. Consequently, we would expect the subject to improve regardless of whether or not the appropriate message was actually embedded in the background, just as occurred in the Greenwald study.

Such placebo effects are not always obtained, however. For example, in research conducted at the University of Waterloo by Merikle and Skanes (1992), subjects who had volunteered to participate in a study of the effects of subliminal messages on weight loss were randomly assigned to one of three conditions: Some listened to tapes with subliminal messages promoting weight loss, others listened to similar tapes but without any subliminal messages, and yet others did not listen to any tapes. Participants in all three conditions tended to lose weight over the course of the study, but the average amount lost was the same regardless of condition.

What about backward speech, such as that supposedly included in some rock music? Can the unconscious mind somehow reverse the backward speech, leading people to be influenced by it unawares? Vokey and Read (1985) reported several studies of backward speech: Their results indicate that people cannot tell the difference between innocent and sinister messages played backwards and, just as important, they showed that giving people suggestions about what they would hear in backward speech often led people to report hearing what was suggested. A 1993 study at McMaster University by Begg, Needham, and Bookbinder also found no effect of backward audio messages. In summary, we have no reason to believe that the unconscious mind can translate backward speech (a feat that would have had no adaptive value until the advent of audio recording devices). It's also worth noting here that no convincing evidence supports long-term memory for forward speech presented to people while they are asleep (Wood, Bootzin, Kihlstrom, & Schacter, 1992).

So what can we conclude about subliminal messages? Is it possible to alter behaviour without awareness? Perhaps. Most psychologists believe that a person's behaviour can be affected in small and transient ways without subjective conscious awareness of the source of the influence (Bodner & Masson, 2003; Cheesman & Merikle, 1986; Greenwald, Schuh, & Klinger, 1995; Kouider & Doupex, 2005). For example, Debner and Jacoby (1994) conducted a study at McMaster University in which subjects were asked to complete word fragments (e.g., "M O T _ _") presented on a computer screen. Immediately before each fragment appeared, a word was briefly flashed on the screen; on some trials, the briefly presented word could be used to complete the fragment (e.g., "MOTEL"). Subjects were warned about the briefly flashed words, told *not* to use them to complete the fragments, and instead asked to come up with different completions (e.g., "MOTOR"). If the briefly presented word was shown long enough for subjects to be consciously aware of it, they successfully avoided using it, but if its presentation was very brief they often did use it. The beauty of this design is that we can be sure that use of the briefly flashed word was mediated by unconscious influences, rather than by conscious perception of the word, because when subjects were aware of the word (i.e., when the word was flashed for a long enough time for subjects to see it), they avoided using it. This is strong evidence of an unconscious influence of the very briefly presented words.

Thus, we probably can be influenced by stimuli of which we are unaware, but there's not much evidence that such messages exist in advertisements—and even if they do, their influence is probably small and fleeting. Studying subliminal perception in a scientifically rigorous way is a difficult undertaking, partly because it requires a good operational definition of consciousness, so controversy about the topic is likely to continue for some time (Reingold, 2004).

CRITICAL   THINKING

Many people seem to want to believe in the ill effects of subliminal messages. Do you have any ideas about why this might be?

1. The cocktail party effect suggests that we cannot attend to more than one message at a time; we focus our attention on one thing and the rest of the environment is effectively blocked out. *True or False?*

2. In dichotic listening tasks, people are presented with two auditory messages, one in each ear, and the task is to repeat one of the messages aloud while essentially ignoring the other. *True or False?*

3. If a task—such as playing a piece on the piano—has become automatic, then you can perform a second task—such as

remembering a list of letters—with little or no interference with performance on the first task. *True or False?*

4. When visual neglect is caused by damage to the right side of the brain, people seem not to notice things that appear on the right side of the body. *True or False?*

5. Attention deficit/hyperactivity disorder is primarily a learned disorder that can easily be treated by special skills training. *True or False?*

6. Research has proven that there is no such thing as subliminal perception. *True or False?*

▶ Sleeping and Dreaming

LEARNING GOALS

1. Understand biological rhythms and how they are controlled.
2. Be able to describe the various stages and characteristics of sleep.
3. Learn about the function and adaptive significance of sleep.
4. Be able to summarize current theories of dreaming and its function.
5. Learn about the major sleep disorders.

Suppose you set out to design the perfect animal. What would such an animal look like? What characteristics would it have? You'd probably make it smart, strong, and perhaps swift. But would you design your animal so that it would sleep? If so, what purposes would that serve, and what mechanisms would regulate the timing and duration of sleep? What would go on inside the animal while it slept? Psychologists are not in the business of designing ideal animals, but we do strive to understand how and why animals—including humans—function as they do; hence we seek answers to these same sorts of questions. Why do we sleep? What mechanisms regulate when and for how long we sleep? What is going on inside us as we sleep?

Biological Rhythms

To understand sleep, you first need to appreciate that we live in a world of many rhythms and cycles, both in the environment (day to night, new moon to old, low tide to high, winter to spring, etc.) and within our bodies. The regular daily transition from waking awareness to sleep is an example of a cycle, or *biological rhythm*, in the body. Many body functions work in cycles, in humans and in other members of the animal kingdom. Sleep and waking vary daily, along with body temperature, hormone secretions, blood pressure, and other processes (for a review, see Hastings, Reddy, & Maywood, 2003). Activities that rise and fall along a 24-hour cycle are known as **circadian rhythms** (*circa* means "about," and *dias* means "day"). Other biological activities may follow other cycles that are either shorter or longer. The human female menstrual cycle operates on an approximately 28-day cycle, for example, whereas changes in appetite and the ability to perform certain tasks may change several times throughout the day.

circadian rhythms

Biological activities that rise and fall in a 24-hour cycle

What controls these internal rhythms? You don't consciously alert the endocrine system that it's time to secrete hormones or actively instruct some portion of your brain that your body temperature needs to rise. These functions are controlled automatically by structures in the brain, called **biological clocks,** that trigger the needed activities at just the right time. These clocks schedule the internal functions of the body and make sure that everything is performing as it should. Animal research has determined that a particular area of the hypothalamus, called the *suprachiasmatic nucleus*, plays a key role in regulating the clock that controls circadian rhythms (Antle & Silver, 2005; Mistlberger, 2005). Neurons in the suprachiasmatic nucleus contain what can be described as molecular clocks, triggering variations in the activity of those neurons in a cyclical manner.

The environment plays a critical role in helping our brains synchronize their internal biological clocks (Cermakian & Sassone-Corsi, 2002). Light is a particularly important controller, or *zeitgeber* (meaning "time giver"), of the pacing of internal clocks. If you were forced to live in a continuously dark or light environment without knowing the time of day, you would still sleep regularly (although your sleep might be disrupted somewhat). But the timing of the sleeping and waking cycles would likely drift and lose connection with night and day (see ❱ Figure 5.5). Rather than falling asleep at your usual 11:00 p.m. and waking at 7:00 a.m., after a while you might find yourself becoming sleepy at 2:00 a.m. and rising at 10:00 a.m. People use light during the day, as well as the absence of light at night, as a way of setting their internal sleep clock.

The fact that the environment is so important in maintaining internal body rhythms makes considerable adaptive sense. On average, the sun rises and sets approximately every 12 hours. Daily changes in air pressure and temperature

biological clocks

Brain structures that schedule rhythmic variations in bodily functions by triggering them at the appropriate times

❱ **Figure 5.5**

Pacing the Internal Clock

Light strongly influences our biological clocks. If you were forced to live without darkness and without knowing the time of day, you would still sleep a normal eight hours (shown by the length of the bar). But sleep onset times would probably drift. For example, if you usually fall asleep at 11:00 p.m. and wake at 7:00 a.m., after a while you might find yourself becoming sleepy at 2:00 a.m. and rising at 10:00 a.m.

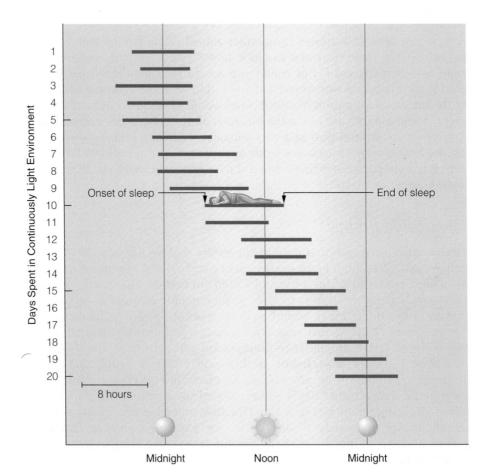

occur, caused, in part, by the continuous rotation of Earth on its axis. It's perfectly reasonable to assume that animals, including humans, have adapted to remain in harmony with these natural environmental cycles. As the cold of winter approaches, birds fly south for warmer temperatures and more plentiful food supplies; other animals stay put and prepare for hibernation. These changes in behaviour are sensible adaptations to cyclic changes in the environment that are not under the animal's control.

Jet lag is a good example of how the environment can play havoc with our internal clocks. When you travel to a new time zone, especially if you move east (which shortens your day), your usual signals for sleeping and waking become disrupted: It gets light and dark at unusual times for you. The net result is that you have trouble going to sleep, you get up at the "wrong" time, and you generally feel lousy. Your body needs to reset its clocks, in line with your new environment, and this process takes time. This is one reason that diplomats and business travellers often arrive at their destinations a few days before an important event or meeting; it gives them time to adjust their internal clocks and shrug off the jet lag.

Have you heard of melatonin? It is a hormone produced by the pineal gland. The production of melatonin is inhibited by light, so more of it is produced in the dark. Because of this, and because the suprachiasmatic nucleus includes receptors for melatonin, the hormone has been promoted as a cure for jet lag and as a way to improve sleep quality. A team of researchers at the University of Alberta published a major review of scientific studies of melatonin (Buscemi et al., 2006): Sadly, the bulk of the evidence suggests that it has little if any effect beyond placebos as a treatment for jet lag or other sleep problems.

CRITICAL   THINKING

Can you think of any workplace environments that might lead to symptoms similar to jet lag?

The Characteristics of Sleep

The transition from waking to sleep is sometimes described as a change in our state or level of consciousness. Rather than being "death's counterfeit" (as Shakespeare called it), sleep involves some awareness, although the focus of that awareness no longer connects as directly to events in the world as does our waking awareness. The problem facing researchers trying to understand the nature of consciousness during sleep is that they cannot collect reports of what sleep feels like to the sleeper (because the subject is unresponsive). Researchers can, however, measure what people say about a prior period of sleep after they awaken from it. Moreover, through *electroencephalograph* (EEG) recordings and other physiological measures, scientists can eavesdrop on the electrical activity of the brain during sleep and infer things about changes in the sleeper's state of consciousness by looking at how the patterns of brain activity change over time.

The activity levels of many animals are controlled by internal clocks that are set, in part, by the environment. Bears are active during the warm summer months and hibernate during the winter.

James Gritz/PhotoDisc

John Serrao/Photo Researchers, Inc.

As you may recall from Chapter 3, the EEG is a device that monitors the electrical activity of the brain. Electrodes are attached to the scalp, and changes in the electrical potentials of large numbers of brain cells are recorded in the form of line tracings, or brain waves. The EEG was first applied to the sleeping brain in the 1930s, and by the 1950s researchers had discovered some very intriguing and unexpected things about the sleep process. For example, EEG tracings revealed that sleep is characterized by cyclic changes in brain activity and that at certain points the electrical activity of the sleeping brain bears a striking similarity to the brain activity of a person who is wide awake (Aserinsky & Kleitman, 1955; Dement & Kleitman, 1957).

▶ Figure 5.6 presents typical EEG recordings made during waking and sleep states. The main things to notice are (1) the *height*, or amplitude, of the brain waves; (2) the *frequency*, or number of cycles per second (usually described in Hertz); and (3) the *regularity*, or smoothness, of the pattern. Regular high-amplitude waves of low frequency reflect neural synchrony, meaning that large

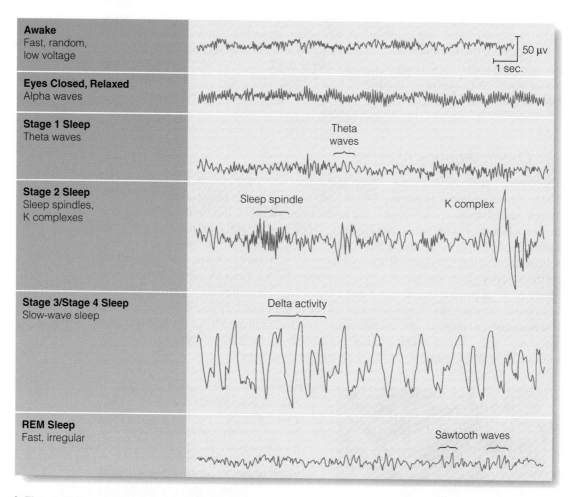

▶ **Figure 5.6**

EEG Patterns Associated with Sleeping and Wakefulness

As we move from a waking state into sleep, characteristic changes occur in the electrical activity of the brain. Generally, as we become drowsy and move through the first four stages of sleep, our brain waves become slower and more regular and show more amplitude. But during REM sleep, when we are presumed to be dreaming, the EEG shows a sawtooth pattern more closely resembling the waking state. (From *Current Concepts: The Sleep Disorders*, by P. Hauri, 1982, The Upjohn Company, Kalamazoo, Michigan. Reprinted by permission of the author.)

numbers of neurons are firing together. In the first row of tracings, measured when the subject was awake, you'll see no evidence of neural synchrony—the EEG pattern is fast and irregular, and the waves are of low amplitude. Presumably, when people are awake and focusing their attention on some task, the brain is busy dividing its labour; many cells are working on specialized individual tasks, so the combined brain activity looks irregular. In contrast, when the brain is in a relaxed state, it produces **alpha waves,** which have a higher amplitude and cycle in a slower, more regular manner.

Stages 1 to 4 of Sleep   As you settle down for the night and prepare for sleep, the fast and irregular wave patterns of the waking state are gradually replaced by slower, more synchronized alpha waves. You're not really asleep at this point, just relaxed and perhaps a little drowsy. The first stage of sleep—called *stage 1* sleep—is marked by a return to waves that are a bit lower in amplitude and slightly more irregular. The dominant wave patterns of stage 1 sleep are called **theta waves;** as you can see in Figure 5.6, they're different from the patterns found in the waking state. Scientists take the occurrence of theta waves, along with other physiological indicators, as evidence that stage 1 sleep truly is a stage of sleep, yet if people are awakened after entering stage 1 sleep they are likely to report that they had not really been asleep; instead, they usually claim that their thoughts were simply drifting.

The second stage of sleep, *stage 2* sleep, is defined by another change in the EEG pattern. Specifically, the theta activity that defines stage 1 sleep begins to be interrupted occasionally by short bursts of activity called *sleep spindles.* Sudden, sharp waveforms called *K complexes* occur from time to time. You're definitely asleep at this point, although your brain still shows some sensitivity to events in the external world. Loud noises, for example, tend to be reflected immediately in the EEG pattern by triggering a K complex (Bastien & Campbell, 1992; Cote, Etienne, & Campbell, 2001). Your brain reacts, as revealed by the K complex, but you're not really consciously aware of the environment. For instance, you'll do a very poor job of responding to prearranged signals delivered by an experimenter (such as instructions to raise your hand if you hear your name).

The next two stages of sleep, *stage 3* and *stage 4*, are progressively deeper states and show more synchronized slow-wave brain patterns called **delta activity;** for this reason, these stages are sometimes called delta or *slow-wave sleep.* Notice that the wave patterns for stage 3/stage 4 sleep in Figure 5.6 appear large (high in amplitude) and cycle slowly compared with the patterns of the earlier sleep stages. You're deeply asleep now and difficult to awaken. If someone shakes you awake during slow-wave sleep, you'll be confused and disoriented, and it'll take quite some time for you to reach a normal state of conscious awareness.

REM Sleep   It's fair to characterize the transition from stage 1 to stage 4 sleep as moving from a light to a deep sleep. Not surprisingly, measures of arousal, such as breathing rate, heart rate, and blood pressure, decline regularly as you progress through each of the stages. But about 70 to 90 minutes into the sleep cycle something very odd happens: Abrupt changes appear in the entire physiological pattern. Heart rate increases rapidly and becomes more irregular; twitching movements might begin in the hands, feet, and face; in males, the penis becomes erect, and in females vaginal lubrication begins; the eyes begin to move rapidly and irregularly, darting back and forth or up and down behind the closed eyelids. The EEG pattern

alpha waves

The pattern of brain activity observed in someone who is in a relaxed state, with his or her eyes closed

theta waves

The pattern of brain activity observed in stage 1 sleep

delta activity

The pattern of brain activity observed in stage 3 and stage 4 sleep; it's characterized by synchronized slow waves (also called *slow-wave* patterns)

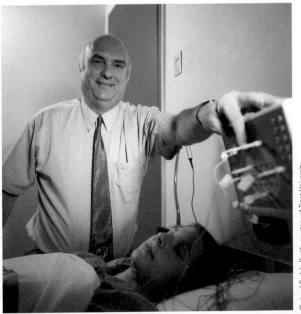

Professor Carlyle Smith of Trent University has published numerous articles reporting research on the relationship between sleep and memory.

Photo of Carlyle Smith, courtesy of Trent University

REM

A stage of sleep characterized by rapid eye movements and low-amplitude, irregular EEG patterns similar to those found in the waking brain; REM is typically associated with dreaming

CRITICAL   THINKING

Can you think of any adaptive reasons that sleep occurs in stages? What might be the advantage to starting off in a light sleep and moving to a deeper sleep?

loses its synchrony and takes on low-amplitude, irregular sawtooth patterns that resemble those of the waking state. But you're not awake—you've entered **REM** (rapid eye movement) sleep, sometimes called *paradoxical sleep*.

REM sleep is called "paradoxical" because the electrical activity of the brain during REM sleep resembles the "awake" pattern, yet the person is deeply asleep. The muscle tone is extremely relaxed, and the person is relatively difficult to awaken. But, as the EEG indicates, the brain is extremely active during this period; if the person is jostled awake from REM sleep, he or she will seem instantly alert. As noted above, this contrasts sharply with the reaction of people who are awakened from stages 3 and 4 of sleep, when they're likely to act confused. Perhaps most interesting, people who awaken from REM sleep are very likely to report an emotional and storylike dream. In fact, dreaming is reported more than 80% of the time among people awakened during REM sleep, even in people who previously denied that they dream (Goodenough, 1991).

Some debate continues among sleep researchers about the exact relationship between the REM state and dreaming. People usually report dreaming if they're awakened during REM, but dreaming also sometimes occurs during the earlier stages of sleep. Haven't you ever experienced a dream moments after going to sleep? Most people have, but it's unlikely that your brain was in the REM state. Systematic studies of dreaming and the sleep stages have revealed conflicting results. Some studies report low levels of dreaming during non-REM stages (Dement, 1978); other studies have found the percentages to be fairly high (over 50%; Foulkes, 1985).

The Sleep Cycle   In an average night, most adults cycle through the various stages of sleep, including REM sleep, about four or five times. Each sleep cycle takes about 90 minutes: You progress from stage 1 through stage 4, then back from stage 4 toward stage 1, ending in REM (see ▶ Figure 5.7). This sequence remains intact throughout much of the night, but the amount of time spent in each stage changes as morning approaches. During the first cycle of sleep, the majority of time is spent in stages 3 and 4 (slow-wave sleep), but REM sleep tends to dominate the later cycles. During a typical night, the amount of time spent in REM sleep, presumably dreaming, increases and the interval between successive REM states becomes shorter. In fact, by the end of the night, stage 4 seems to disappear and you end up spending almost all of your time in REM sleep (Webb, 1992). As you may have noticed, many dreams seem to occur toward the end of the sleep period, and these are the dreams you're most likely to remember.

▶ **Figure 5.7**

Sleep Cycles

During an average night, most adults pass through the various stages of sleep four or five times. A complete cycle usually takes about 90 minutes. As the figure shows, as morning approaches, we tend to spend more time in REM sleep, presumably dreaming. We also tend to spend brief intervals awake (indicated by the letter A in the figure) during the last hour or two of sleep. (Based on Kalat, 1996.)

Doug Menuez/PhotoDisc/Getty Images

Why do people sleep? It could be to restore or repair depleted resources, but research suggests that vigorous activity during the day has little effect on sleeping patterns.

The Function of Sleep

If you sleep eight hours a night and you live to the ripe old age of 75, you'll have spent a quarter century with your eyes closed, your limbs lying useless at your sides, and your outstretched body open to attack. Doesn't this seem a bit strange? Think about it. What could be the adaptive value of regularly entering a state in which the organism is unaware of resources and threats in the environment?

Repairing and Restoring At one level, it seems pretty obvious: People sleep because they get tired. The daily activities of waking life produce wear and tear on the body, and some mind and body downtime may be needed to put things back in order. During sleep, especially slow-wave sleep, the metabolic activity of the brain and the rest of the body is dramatically lowered (Sakai, Stirling Meyer, Karacan, Yamaguchi, & Yamamoto, 1979), and these decreased demands on use of the body may enable cellular processes to recover from fatigue. Consistent with that idea is the fact that if people are deprived of sleep for an extended period, their ability to perform complex tasks, especially those requiring problem solving, deteriorates (see below).

The trickier question is whether or not the brain actively performs special restorative processes during sleep. Many restorative activities do go on during sleep, but such activities also go on regularly throughout the waking day, and it is not clear if sleep is special in this regard. Despite people's intuitions, there isn't a strong relationship between the amount of activity in a day and the depth and length of the sleep period that follows (Horne & Minard, 1985). Rest and restoration are important consequences of a good night's sleep and, as discussed in a subsequent section, REM sleep may play special active roles in consolidating new learning, but sleep may have another important value as well.

Survival Value Sleep may be an adaptive response to environmental conditions, a behaviour that increases the likelihood of survival. Primates rely heavily on their visual systems; as a result, they aren't very efficient outside at night in low levels of

3 A.M.			4 A.M.				5 A.M.			6 A.M.		7 A.M.
2	3	2	REM	1	2	3 2 A 1	REM	A 1 A	2		REM	

illumination. Our ancestors could have moved about at night, groping around for food while trying to avoid being eaten by some lurking predator, but it was probably better for them to stay put in a tree or cave until dawn. Sleep at night thus may have been adaptive because it stopped our ancestors from venturing forth into a hostile environment.

We can find evidence supporting this idea by examining the sleeping patterns of animal species in the wild. If sleep is an adaptive reaction to light-dark cycles and susceptibility to predators, then we might expect animals that rely on senses other than vision to be active primarily at night, when vision-based predators would be at a hunting disadvantage. This is indeed the case for mice, rats, and other rodents. Second, large animals that must eat almost continuously and can't easily find places to hide should sleep very little. And, indeed, grazing animals, such as sheep, goats, horses, and cattle, which are vulnerable to surprise attack by predators, sleep only a few hours a day (see ▶ Figure 5.8). In one study, researchers found that body weight and susceptibility to attack could explain the majority of the differences among the sleeping patterns of different species (Allison & Cicchetti, 1976).

Sleep Deprivation   Earlier we mentioned that our ability to perform complex tasks is disrupted if we haven't received much sleep. This shouldn't come as too much of a surprise—you've probably pulled an all-nighter at some point and found yourself irritable and not good for much the next day. But how serious is prolonged sleep deprivation? Some individuals have tried to remain awake for very long periods—approaching two weeks—and the results have been generally negative: Some of the symptoms were slurred speech, sharp declines in mental ability, and symptoms of paranoia and hallucinations. Although severely sleep-deprived individuals can appear normal for brief periods, prolonged sleep deprivation generally wreaks havoc on virtually all aspects of normal functioning.

The harmfulness of extreme sleep deprivation has been dramatically demonstrated in animal studies. When rats and dogs are deprived of sleep for extended periods, their ability to regulate internal functions, such as temperature, is grossly

▶ **Figure 5.8**

Sleep Times for Various Species

Large grazing animals, such as cows and horses, eat frequently and are quite vulnerable to surprise attacks from predators. As the figure shows, such animals tend to sleep very little. Small, quick animals, such as cats and rodents, are less vulnerable to attack and sleep a great deal.

impaired, leading to considerable loss of weight (despite an increased intake of food). The immune system also starts to fail, along with various organs in the body. As time goes by, more and more extreme forms of stimulation are required to keep animals awake. After roughly three weeks of no sleep, the survival rate among these animals is virtually zero—most of them die, perhaps partly as a consequence of the methods used to try to keep them awake (Rechtschaffen, Bergmann, Everson, Kushida, & Gilliland, 2002). Sleep deprivation becomes torture.

Fortunately, people rarely if ever reach these levels of sleep deprivation, because we simply can't stay awake. Nonetheless, less extreme sleep deprivation contributes to thousands of deaths each year, mostly through traffic accidents and job-related mishaps. University of British Columbia professor Stanley Coren published a provocative and popular book on this subject (1996), arguing that most members of our culture are chronically sleep deprived. William Dement (whose pioneering research on the scientific study of sleep was mentioned above) made similar arguments in another engaging and accessible book with co-author Christopher Vaughan (1999). The bottom line is this: One of the easiest, simplest, and most effective things you can do to improve your daily life is to get an adequate amount of sleep each night (see also Horne, 2001).

The Function of REM and Dreaming

It's easy to see how sleep itself might have developed as an adaptive response, to repair, restore, and protect an organism struggling to survive. But why are there stages of sleep? Why, if people need to protect or rest the body, do they spend a significant amount of time in such an internally active state as REM sleep? Does dreaming serve some unique biological or psychological function? Unfortunately, we have no definitive answers to these questions.

It's not clear whether REM sleep is even a necessary component of normal functioning. It's possible to deprive people selectively of REM sleep by carefully monitoring the EEG and then waking the person whenever characteristic REM patterns appear in the recordings. Unlike the findings for sleep loss in general, losing significant amounts of REM sleep usually does not lead to dramatic effects. People may show a bit more irritability (compared with controls who are awakened during non-REM periods), and their performance on tasks requiring logical reasoning and problem solving is hurt, but the level of impairment is not large (Ellman, Spielman, Luck, Steiner, & Halperin, 1991). Some forms of severe depression even appear to be helped by REM sleep deprivation (Boivin, 2000), and some effective antidepressant drugs suppress REM sleep (Vogel, Buffenstein, Minter, & Hennessey, 1990).

However, an intriguing change does occur in sleep *patterns* after periods of REM deprivation. Sleep researchers have noticed that on the second or third night of REM deprivation it is necessary to awaken the subject with much greater frequency. When people lose REM sleep, their brains attempt to make up for the loss during the next sleep period by increasing the proportion of time spent in the REM stage. The more REM sleep lost, the more the brain tries to make it up the next night. This tendency, known as **REM rebound,** is one reason why many researchers remain convinced that REM sleep serves some unknown but extremely important function in the brain.

Memory Consolidation   One possibility is that REM sleep plays a role in strengthening or consolidating new memories. Several studies provide evidence for this idea. For example, Karni, Tanne, Rubenstein, Askenasy, and Sagi (1994) asked subjects to solve a perceptual task that required detecting a small target pattern in a complex visual array. Subjects practised the perceptual task shortly before going to sleep and were retested the next morning. The key finding was

REM rebound

The tendency to increase the proportion of sleeping time spent in REM sleep after a period of REM deprivation

that subjects who had a normal night's sleep, and those whose sleep was disturbed only when they were in stage 3 or 4 sleep, benefited from the practice session, but subjects who were deprived of REM sleep did not. Mednick and colleagues (2002) used the same perceptual task and showed that performance across blocks of trials was enhanced if subjects napped for 30 to 60 minutes during the breaks between blocks.

These results, and others reviewed by Stickgold, Hobson, Fosse, and Fosse (2001), suggest that activities during REM sleep are needed to consolidate some forms of learning overnight. But what are these activities? It's unclear at this point, but one possibility is that the neurotransmitter *acetylcholine* (ACh) may be involved. Studies with animals have shown that ACh increases in the brain during REM sleep. This important neurotransmitter is thought to play a role in storing memories. As we mentioned in Chapter 3, memory problems are common in patients who have Alzheimer's disease, and it's known that neurons in the brain that produce ACh often degenerate during the disease. Thus, ACh may be needed to consolidate the storage of experience, which may in turn explain why REM activity is important in the consolidation process. Unfortunately, at this point this account is purely speculative, and researchers even question the evidence that REM sleep is important for consolidating memories (e.g., Vertes & Eastman, 2000).

Wish Fulfillment   Historically, many psychologists viewed dreaming as an extremely important psychological phenomenon. Sigmund Freud (1900/1990) believed that dreams, once interpreted, could serve as a "royal road to the unconscious." Freud believed that dreaming was a psychological mechanism for *wish fulfillment,* a way to satisfy forbidden wishes and desires, especially sexual ones. He believed that dreams often look bizarre because the objects within our dreams are often symbolic. We hide our true feelings because our wishes and desires are too disturbing to be allowed to come to consciousness directly. To Freud, for example, a cigar or a gun (or any elongated object) in a dream might represent a penis, whereas a tunnel (or any entryway) could stand for a vagina. To establish the true meaning of the dream, Freud believed, it was necessary to distinguish between the dream's **manifest content**—the things seen and otherwise experienced by the dreamer—and its **latent content,** those hidden desires that are too disturbing to be confronted directly.

Compared with Freud, most modern psychologists are more reluctant to search for hidden meaning in dreams. Although certain kinds of dream events cut across people and cultures (e.g., people often dream of flying or falling or of having their teeth fall out), there is little evidence that particular dream contents (such as cigars) have any universal symbolic meaning. The interpretation of dreams is in the eye of the dreamer. Indeed, far from focusing on unconscious wishes, dreams often relate to the dreamer's waking concerns (Marquardt, Bonato, & Hoffmann, 1996; Nielsen & Powell, 1992). For example, students who care about their studies in their waking lives quite often report dreams with scholastic themes, such as trying to take an exam but not having anything to write with. In addition, no compelling evidence shows that dreams are a reliable source of accurate memories of childhood events (Brenneis, 1994). Even recurrent dreams don't necessarily have any hidden psychological significance. A troubling dream might lead you to wake up suddenly and think about the dream, so that it becomes firmly ingrained in memory and consequently is likely to occur again. It is also of interest to note that virtually all mammals experience REM, as do birds and some reptiles, such as turtles (Durie, 1981). Moreover, human infants spend a remarkable amount of time in REM sleep; even human fetuses show REM patterns in the womb. It seems very unlikely that the fetus or mouse in REM sleep is working out some hidden sexual desire or conflict. But if dreams are not about wish fulfillment, then what is the function of dreams?

manifest content

According to Freud, the objects and events experienced in a dream

latent content

According to Freud, the true psychological meaning of objects and events in dreams, which are said to represent hidden wishes and desires that are too disturbing to be confronted directly

Activation-Synthesis Hypothesis   An alternative to the notion that dreams are vehicles for imaginative wish fulfillment is the **activation-synthesis hypothesis** of Hobson and McCarley (1977; Hobson, Pace-Schott, & Stickgold, 2000). This view proposes that the initial seeds of dreams are random activity in the brain. During REM sleep, for reasons that are not particularly clear, cells in the hindbrain spontaneously activate the higher centres of the brain. This activity could arise simply to exercise the brain circuitry (Edelman, 1987), or it could be a consequence of random events in the room (e.g., the cat snoring or a mosquito buzzing around your face). Whatever the reason, the higher-brain centres have evolved to interpret lower-brain signals in meaningful ways. According to the activation-synthesis hypothesis, the brain creates a story in an effort to make some sense out of the signals that it's receiving. But in the activation-synthesis view, there's little of psychological significance in dreams: They are assumed to represent only a synthesis of random neurological activity (Weinstein, Schwartz, & Arkin, 1991).

The activation-synthesis hypothesis has received a lot of attention among sleep researchers because it takes into account how biological activity in the brain changes during sleep. It also provides another explanation for why dream content is often bizarre: Since the activated signals that produce dreams are random in nature, the higher centres of the brain have a tough time creating a storyline that is meaningful and consistent. Ironically, this view implies that reported dreams may have some psychological significance after all, but not for the reasons suggested by Freud. The biological mechanisms that generate the REM state may not be psychologically driven, but the brain's *interpretations* of those purely physiological activities may have psychological meaning. The story your brain creates probably tells us something about how you think when you're awake (Antrobus, 1991).

The activation-synthesis hypothesis is an intriguing alternative to the traditional Freudian view, but much remains to be worked out. The theory is a bit vague and consequently difficult to test. Also, in its present form the theory focuses primarily on brain activity that occurs during REM sleep but, as noted earlier, we also dream during non-REM states.

We've discussed two prominent views of dreaming—Freudian wish fulfillment and activation-synthesis—but there are others. For example, some psychologists have suggested that dreams serve a problem-solving function. We may dream to focus our attention on particularly troubling current problems in order to work toward possible solutions (Cartwright, 1991; Fiss, 1991). But the evidence for the problem-solving view is weak, relying mainly on anecdotes rather than on systematic research (Blagrove, 1996; Domhoff, 1996). Yet another recent view comes from evolutionary psychologists who have speculated that dreaming allows us to simulate threats from the environment and mentally practise the skills needed to avoid those threats (Revonsuo, 2000). People often do dream about aggressive events and threatening situations, but whether dreaming really evolved to help us handle real-world threats remains highly speculative (Flanagan, 2000). It's safe to assume that REM sleep and dreaming reflect some important property of the adaptive mind, but at the moment major questions remain unanswered.

Sleep Disorders

We end our review of sleep and dreaming with a brief discussion of sleep disorders. Psychologists and other mental health professionals divide sleep disorders into two main diagnostic categories: (1) *dyssomnias*, which are problems associated with the amount, timing, and quality of sleep, and (2) *parasomnias*, which are abnormal disturbances that occur during sleep. Let's consider some prominent examples of each type.

activation-synthesis hypothesis

The idea that dreams represent the brain's attempt to make sense out of random patterns of neural activity generated during sleep

CRITICAL THINKING

The activation-synthesis hypothesis proposes that dreams arise from the interpretation of random neural activity. Yet many people dream of flying, falling, or being unprepared for a test. How do you explain the fact that people have similar dreams if dreaming results from the interpretation of random neural activity?

CONCEPT SUMMARY

FUNCTIONS OF SLEEP AND DREAMING

Why Do We Sleep?

Theory	Description	Evaluation
Repair and restoration	Sleep restores and repairs the body and brain.	Not strongly supported by data; restorative activities of the body not limited to sleep; changes in physical activity do not lead to consistent changes in subsequent sleep patterns
Survival value	Sleep increases the chances of survival.	Receives some support from sleep patterns in different species of animals

Why Do We Dream?

Theory	Description	Evaluation
Wish fulfillment (Freud)	Dreaming is a psychological mechanism for fulfilling wishes, often sexual in nature. Dreams include both manifest and latent content.	Difficult to assess; most modern psychologists reluctant to ascribe hidden meaning to dreams; meaning of dreams is in the eye of the dreamer
Activation-synthesis	Dreaming is a consequence of random activity that occurs in the brain during REM sleep. The brain creates a story to make sense of these random signals.	Theory vague and difficult to test; dreaming not limited to REM sleep
Problem solving	Dreaming helps us focus on our current problems to find solutions.	Evidence weak and anecdotal
Threat simulation	Dreaming evolved to help us practise the skills needed to avoid threats.	Still speculation at this point

insomnia

A chronic condition marked by difficulties in initiating or maintaining sleep, lasting for a period of at least one month

Dyssomnias   The most common type of dyssomnia is **insomnia,** a condition marked by difficulties in initiating or maintaining sleep. Everyone has trouble getting to sleep from time to time, and most people have awakened in the middle of the night and been unable to get back to sleep. For the clinical diagnosis of insomnia, however, these difficulties must be chronic—lasting for at least a month. It's been estimated that perhaps 30% of the population suffers from some degree of insomnia, although the percentage of severe cases is thought to be closer to 15% (Bootzin, Manber, Perlis, Salvio, & Wyatt, 1993). Sutton, Mold-ofsky, and Badley (2001) reported on a survey of 11 924 Canadian adults, of whom 24% reported suffering from insomnia; the 2002 Canadian Community Health Survey produced an estimate of 13% (Statistics Canada, 2004b). Again, these differences across studies are probably primarily due to differences in how insomnia was defined. Even the lowest estimates indicate that millions of Canadians suffer insomnia.

Insomnia has many potential causes, including stress, emotional problems, alcohol and other drug use, as well as medical conditions. Some kinds of insomnia may even be learned; for example, children who regularly fall asleep in the presence of their parents often have trouble getting back to sleep if later they wake up alone (Adair, Bauchner, Phillip, Levenson, & Zuckerman, 1991). Presumably, these children have learned to associate going to sleep with the presence of a parent and consequently cannot return to sleep without the parent present.

Professor William Dement, one of the pioneers of the scientific study of sleep, offers a list of tips for "good sleep hygiene"—that is, practices that help people to get a good night's sleep—at his website, **http://www.stanford.edu/~dement/howto.html.**

His recommendations include (1) establishing a regular routine for going to bed and getting up, (2) avoiding caffeine, nicotine, and alcohol for several hours before going to bed, and (3) not using your bed for reading, eating, telephoning, and so on, so that bed is strongly associated in your mind with sleeping (and perhaps one other activity).

Whereas insomnia is characterized by an inability to sleep, in **hypersomnia** the problem is *too much* sleep. People who are diagnosed with hypersomnia show excessive sleepiness—they're often caught catnapping during the day, and they complain of being tired all the time. The cause of this condition is unknown, although genetic factors may be involved (Parkes & Block, 1989). Excessive sleepiness can also be caused by infectious diseases, such as mononucleosis.

Excessive sleepiness can also be a symptom of a sleep disorder called *sleep apnea.* Sleep apnea is a condition in which the sleeper repeatedly stops breathing, usually for short periods of 10 to 20 seconds. Most cases involve what is called obstructive apnea; the deep muscle relaxation of sleep causes the tissues around the upper parts of the airway to sag such that air cannot get through. The episodes typically end with the person briefly waking up, gasping for breath. Because these episodes occur frequently throughout the night (sometimes many times an hour), affected people feel tired during the day, but often they have no recollection of having awakened in the night. Until recently, it was thought that apnea was quite rare, but it turns out that many people with the disorder don't know they have it, which led to underestimates of its prevalence. Current estimates are that 1 in 25 middle-aged men, and 1 in 50 middle-aged women, experience clinically significant levels of obstructive sleep apnea. The disorder is less common among younger people and more common among older ones; obesity is also a risk factor for apnea.

Narcolepsy is a very rare sleep disorder, characterized by sudden extreme sleepiness. Sleep attacks can occur at any time during the day and can last from a few seconds to several minutes. What makes this disorder unusual is that the person seems to directly enter a kind of REM sleep state. He or she loses all muscle tone and can even fall to the ground in a sound sleep. Fortunately, not all instances of narcolepsy are this extreme, but it can be a disabling condition. Some evidence shows that the disorder has a genetic link (Barlow & Durand, 2002).

Parasomnias   The second category of sleep disorders, parasomnias, includes such abnormal sleep disturbances as nightmares, night terrors, and sleepwalking (Silber, 2001). **Nightmares** are frightening dreams that occur primarily during the REM stage of sleep. They inevitably cause the sleeper to awaken; if they recur frequently, they can lead to symptoms of insomnia. What causes nightmares? No one is certain at this point, although very frequent nightmares may indicate the presence of a psychological disorder.

Night terrors, which occur mainly in children, are terrifying experiences in which the sleeper awakens suddenly in an extreme state of panic. The child may sit in bed screaming and will show little responsiveness to others who are present. Night terrors are not considered to be serious indicators of psychological or medical problems, and they tend to go away with age.

Finally, **sleepwalking** occurs when the sleeper rises during sleep and wanders about. Sleepwalking happens mainly in childhood, tends to vanish as the child reaches adolescence, and is not thought to result from a serious psychological or medical problem. It's interesting to note that both night terrors and sleepwalking occur during periods of non-REM sleep, which suggests that neither is related to dreaming (although it remains possible that they are related to non-REM dreaming).

hypersomnia

A chronic condition marked by excessive sleepiness

nightmares

Frightening dreams that occur primarily during the REM stage of sleep

night terrors

A condition in which the sleeper, usually a child, awakens suddenly in an extreme state of panic

sleepwalking

A condition in which the sleeper rises during sleep and wanders about; not thought to be associated with dreaming

Test Yourself 5.2

To check your understanding of sleep and dreaming, answer the following questions. (The answers are in Appendix B.)

1. Choose the EEG pattern that best fits the following descriptions. Choose from the following: alpha waves, delta activity, K complex, sleep spindles, theta waves, sawtooth waves.
   a. The characteristic pattern found in stage 1 sleep:

   _____

   b. Often triggered by loud noises during stage 2 sleep:

   _____

   c. Another name for the slow-wave patterns that are found during stage 3 and stage 4 sleep:

   _____

   d. The characteristic pattern of paradoxical sleep:

   _____

2. Which of the following statements is most consistent with the view that we sleep because it keeps us away from hostile environments during times when we can't see well?
   a. Sleep deprivation leads to a breakdown in normal functioning.
   b. Fearful dreams make us wary of venturing outside.
   c. Cats sleep more than cows.
   d. People sleep less as they age.

3. Diagnose the following sleep disorders based on the information provided. Choose from the following: hypersomnia, insomnia, nightmare, night terror, sleep apnea, sleepwalking.
   a. Difficulty initiating and maintaining sleep:

   _____

   b. Sleeper awakens suddenly, screaming, but the EEG pattern indicates a period of non-REM sleep:

   _____

   c. Sleeper repeatedly stops breathing during the night, usually for short periods lasting less than one minute:

   _____

   d. A frightening dream that usually occurs during the REM stage of sleep: _____

▶ Altering Awareness: Psychoactive Drugs

LEARNING GOALS

1. Understand the relationship between neurotransmitters and psychoactive drugs.
2. Learn the different categories of psychoactive drugs, and provide examples of each.
3. Be able to discuss the psychological factors that influence the effects of psychoactive drugs.

The rhythmic cycles of sleep reveal how conscious awareness can shift in dramatic ways as the electrical activity of the brain changes. We haven't talked much about the biological factors that control these brain changes, but it shouldn't surprise you to learn that the brain's chemical messengers, the neurotransmitters, are primarily responsible. The start of REM sleep, for example, appears to be controlled by neurons in the hindbrain, particularly the *pons*, which release acetylcholine (Amzica & Steriade, 1996). In studies with animals, it's been found that levels of acetylcholine in the cortex are highest during REM and waking states and drop to lower levels during the stages of slow-wave sleep. Exactly when we fall asleep and how long we sleep may be affected by the actions of the neurotransmitter *GABA;* wakefulness and general arousal have been linked to *norepinephrine* and *dopamine.* Thus, the mind's own chemicals play important roles in controlling changes in consciousness through the sleep-wake cycle.

The brain is a kind of biochemical factory, altering moods and shifting awareness by moderating the release of its various neurotransmitters. For example, we've previously mentioned that the brain sometimes reacts to stress or injury by releasing brain chemicals called *endorphins*, which reduce pain and elevate mood. Altering awareness chemically in such a fashion is highly adaptive, because the delay of pain can enable an organism to escape from a life-threatening situation.

If an external chemical agent enters your body, it too can radically alter the delicate chemical balance that controls awareness and other mental processes. Obviously, drugs can have tremendously beneficial effects, especially in the treatment of psychological and medical disorders (see Chapter 15). But drugs can have negative effects as well, even if their short-term effects are pleasant. As you probably

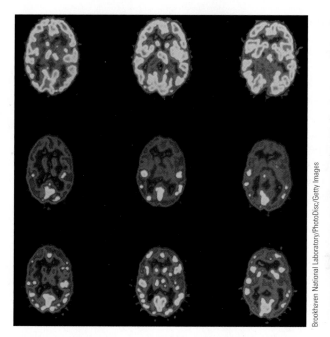

This series of PET scans shows how an opium-like drug affects general activity in the brain. The first PET scan in the top row shows a normal active brain; the last PET scan in the bottom row shows diminished activity after the drug has taken full effect.

know, drug abuse, particularly of alcohol and tobacco, is directly or indirectly responsible for tens of thousands of deaths annually in Canada (MacNeill & Webster, 1995; Single et al., 1996). Single and co-authors estimated that premature mortality because of drugs accounts for about one in five of the total number of deaths each year. In this section, we'll consider the actions of drugs labelled **psychoactive drugs,** those that alter conscious experience.

psychoactive drugs

Drugs that affect behaviour and mental processes, and produce alterations of conscious awareness

Drug Actions and Effects

Psychologists are interested in psychoactive drugs for three main reasons. First, some psychoactive drugs are effective in the treatment of psychological disorders, such as attention deficit/hyperactivity disorder, schizophrenia, and depression. Treating such disorders is a primary goal of many clinical psychologists and psychiatrists. Second, the abuse of some psychoactive drugs has tremendously destructive real-world consequences, harming users, their families, and the wider society. Many psychologists are interested in the development of scientifically validated approaches to discourage people from abusing psychoactive drugs and to treat and support those who have developed drug problems. Third, psychoactive drugs have powerful effects on behaviour and mental processes, and such effects are interesting in their own right and can help us understand the normal workings of the mind.

Psychoactive drugs, like the natural chemicals produced by the brain, exert their effects primarily by changing the normal communication channels of neurons. Neuron-to-neuron communication can be affected in a variety of ways. Some drugs, such as *nicotine*, duplicate the action of neurotransmitters by attaching themselves to neuronal receptor sites; this mimicking action allows the drug to produce the same effect as the brain's natural chemical messenger. Other drugs depress or block the action of neurotransmitters; some sleeping pills, for instance, decrease norepinephrine or dopamine stimulation. The psychoactive drug *fluoxetine* (known commercially as Prozac) is widely used to treat depression; it (as well as a wide variety of related drugs) slows the process through which the neurotransmitter serotonin is broken down and taken back up into the transmitting cell (Kramer, 1993; for a critique of Prozac, see Kirsch & Sapirstein, 1999).

Over time, repeated use of a drug can change the way the body reacts to that chemical. For example, a drug **tolerance** can develop, which means that increasing amounts of the drug are needed to produce the same physical and behavioural effects. Tolerance is a kind of adaptation that the brain makes to compensate for the effects of the drug. **Drug dependency** is manifested as either a physical or a psychological need for continued use (Woody & Cacciola, 1997). With physical dependency, the person experiences **withdrawal** symptoms when he or she stops taking the drug. These are clear, measurable physical reactions, such as sweating, vomiting, tremors, or changes in heart rate. Drug dependency is the primary cause of substance abuse, although the mechanisms that lead to dependency are still a matter of some debate. At this point, it's not certain whether dependency develops as a consequence of "urgings" produced by biological withdrawal or whether people essentially learn to become dependent on the drug with repeated use (Siegel, 2005; Tiffany, 1990).

Categories of Psychoactive Drugs

It's useful to classify psychoactive drugs into four categories—depressants, stimulants, opiates, and hallucinogens—based on their specific mind-altering characteristics. We'll briefly examine each type and then conclude with a discussion of some psychological factors involved in drug use.

Depressants   In general, drugs classified as **depressants** slow, or depress, the ongoing activity of the central nervous system. *Ethyl alcohol*, which is present in beer, wine, and distilled drinks, is a well-known example of a depressant. Biochemically, alcohol appears to lead to an increase in either the secretion or effectiveness of the neurotransmitters GABA and dopamine. Both usually act as inhibitory messengers in the brain, so neurons in a number of vital brain centres become inhibited (Suzdak et al., 1986). Drinkers feel "high" after a few drinks in part because the drug produces a calming effect on the body, which leads to a reduction in anxiety (Oscar-Berman, Shagrin, Evert, & Epstein, 1997). By the way, animals also find the effects of alcohol quite reinforcing; they will perform tasks that yield small amounts of alcohol as a reward (Wise & Bozarth, 1987).

As the consumption of alcohol increases, more complex psychological effects emerge because those brain centres that control judgment become sluggish from inhibition. As you're undoubtedly aware, after a few drinks some people start acting in ways that are contrary to their normal behavioural tendencies (Steele & Josephs, 1990). The normally demure may become loud and aggressive; the sexually inhibited may become flirtatious and provocative. Other individuals may simply become more extreme versions of their usual selves. These behavioural changes are produced, in part, because alcohol reduces self-awareness. Drinkers are less likely to monitor their behaviours and actions closely, and they tend to forget about their problems (Hull & Bond, 1986; MacDonald, Zanna, & Fong, 1996).

These carefree moments are stolen at a cost, of course, because the body eventually reacts to the drug in a more negative way. Nearly 1 in every 10 Canadian respondents to the General Social Survey of 1993 reported having problems with their drinking, and nearly a quarter reported exceeding the low-risk guidelines for alcohol consumption (one or two units a day) (Single, Brewster, MacNeil, Hatcher, & Trainor, 1995). A study by Statistics Canada in 2002 estimated that 641 000 Canadians have some degree of alcohol dependence (Tjepkema, 2002). Overconsumption of alcohol leads to impaired judgment, coordination, and reaction time while under the influence, and fatigue, nausea, and depression afterward. Every year, numerous Canadians die from alcohol overdose: If enough alcohol is consumed in

tolerance

An adaptation that the body makes to compensate for the continued use of a drug such that increasing amounts of the drug are needed to produce the same physical, psychological, and behavioural effects

drug dependency

A condition in which an individual experiences a physical or psychological need for continued use of a drug

withdrawal

Clear and measurable physical reactions, such as sweating, vomiting, tremors, or changes in heart rate, that occur when a person stops taking certain drugs after continued use

depressants

A class of drugs that slow or depress the ongoing activity of the central nervous system

CRITICAL   THINKING

Do you believe that all psychoactive drugs should be legalized for recreational use? If not, how can you justify the availability of alcohol, nicotine, and caffeine?

a short period of time, the result is death. Even consumption far short of a lethal overdose increases the likelihood of accidents. A disproportionate number of alcohol-related deaths are young people. Many such cases involve the combination of drinking and driving: Among Canadian drivers killed in automobile accidents in 1996, 35% had blood alcohol concentrations over the legal limit (Statistics Canada, 1997a). Finally, it is also clear that being drunk increases the likelihood that people will engage in a variety of risky behaviours, such as unprotected sex (e.g., MacDonald, Zanna, & Fong, 1998).

Barbiturates and *tranquillizers* are also classified as depressant drugs. Both are widely prescribed for the treatment of anxiety and insomnia, and they produce effects in the brain similar to those induced by alcohol (the neurotransmitter GABA is again involved; Gardner, 1997). Like alcohol, at low doses tranquillizing agents tend to produce pleasurable feelings of relaxation. But at higher doses the ability to concentrate is lost, memory is impaired, and speech becomes slurred. Barbiturate use also commonly leads to tolerance and dependency. With continued use, larger and larger doses of the drug are required to obtain the same effect, and the user becomes physically and psychologically dependent on the drug. Tranquillizers (such as the widely prescribed Valium and Xanax) are less habit forming than barbiturates.

Moderate drinking can be pleasurable, but consuming too much alcohol can have severe negative consequences on your health and well-being.

Stimulants   A **stimulant** is a drug that increases central nervous system activity. Examples of stimulants include *caffeine, amphetamines, cocaine, nicotine,* and *Ecstasy*. These agents generally increase alertness and can affect mood by inducing feelings of pleasure. The morning cup of coffee is an excellent example of how low doses of a stimulant—caffeine—can improve your mood and enhance concentration and attention. Other effects of stimulants include dilated pupils, increased heart and respiration rate, and decreased appetite. In large doses, stimulants can produce extreme anxiety and even convulsions and death.

Both amphetamines and cocaine produce their stimulating effects by increasing the effectiveness of the neurotransmitters norepinephrine and dopamine. Dopamine seems to be primarily responsible for the positive, reinforcing qualities of these drugs (Wise & Rompre, 1989). Research has shown that animals will work hard to administer themselves drugs that increase the activity of dopamine-based synapses. Cocaine, which is derived from the leaves of the coca plant, blocks the reabsorption of both norepinephrine and dopamine. When reabsorption is blocked, these transmitter substances are able to exert their effects for a longer period. Cocaine produces intense feelings of euphoria, although the effects of the drug wear off relatively quickly. A half hour or so after the drug enters the body, the user "crashes," in part because the drug has temporarily depleted the user's internal supply of norepinephrine and dopamine. Regular use of cocaine leads to dependence and tolerance and produces a number of very harmful side effects, including intense episodes of paranoia and delusions (Stein & Ellinwood, 1993), insomnia, impotence, and even death from heart attack, stroke, or seizure. Crack cocaine is a particularly powerful and dangerous form of this drug.

Nicotine, the psychoactive drug in tobacco, is also a stimulant. Approximately 100 000 Canadian teenagers take up smoking each year. Nicotine is highly addictive, and tobacco delivers a powerful mix of lethal substances to the user. It's estimated that smoking costs the Canadian economy $15 billion a year, and more than 30 000 Canadians die from tobacco each year (Single et al., 1996).

The psychoactive drug that has gained the most popularity in recent years is methylenedioxymethamphetamine (or MDMA), better known as Ecstasy (also called X, XTC, and a variety of other names). Canada Customs seized 120 kilograms of the drug (enough to make about 1.5 million pills, with an estimated street value of $52.5 million) in a single bust in October of 2002 (Walton, 2002). It is likely that

stimulants

A class of drugs that increase central nervous system activity, enhancing neural transmission

only a small fraction of the Ecstasy entering Canada is stopped by authorities, so numbers like these suggest that tremendous quantities of this drug are being used by Canadians. This drug combines characteristics of stimulants and hallucinogens (although hallucinations are likely to be experienced only when dangerously high doses are taken). Users report feelings of euphoria, interpersonal closeness with others, and boundless energy. That sounds great, but the drug also has some ill effects. According to Morton (2005, p. 79), "Chronic *ecstasy* use causes depletion of serotonin, which has subtle but important long-term effects on cognition and mood…. So little is known about the long-term effects of ecstasy on mood, emotional states and cognitive function that at present we cannot predict what impact their use of ecstasy will have on the middle-age of the average ecstasy user." Schifano (2004) provided a thoughtful review of the difficulty of interpreting cases in which people die while on Ecstasy; we know that such cases occur, but their cause is open to debate. One reason for this is that E tablets often contain a variety of drugs in addition to MDMA.

The most dangerous of currently popular street drugs is another amphetamine, called methamphetamine. More widely known as crystal meth, this is definitely a drug to avoid. It looks like little pieces of broken glass or shiny blue-white rocks. Most often it is smoked in a glass pipe, although some people inject it. Reportedly, the drug produces an immediate rush followed by a prolonged euphoria lasting about 12 hours. This drug has two huge problems: It is extremely addictive and it is extraordinarily neurotoxic. Whereas there is room to debate the prevalence and extremity of long-term ill effects of some recreational drugs, such as Ecstasy and marijuana, it is a simple matter of fact that crystal meth destroys dopaminergic neurons in the brain and has a barrage of other harmful effects (e.g., disrupted heart rhythms, overheating, dental problems ["meth mouth"]) (see Hanson, Rau, & Fleckenstein, 2004; Meredith, Jaffe, Ang-Lee, & Saxon, 2005). Regular use produces serious physiological and psychological problems, which may persist long after use of the drug is stopped.

opiates

A class of drugs that reduce anxiety, lower sensitivity to pain, and elevate mood; opiates often act to depress nervous system activity

Opiates   Drugs classified as **opiates** (also sometimes called *narcotics*) depress nervous system activity, thereby reducing anxiety, elevating mood (with small doses), and lowering sensitivity to pain. Well-known examples of opiates include opium, heroin, and morphine. As you learned previously, morphine, which is derived from the flowering opium plant, acts on existing neuronal receptor sites in the nervous system. Its pain-killing effects and pleasurable mood shifts (it's named after Morpheus, the Greek god of dreams) apparently arise from the fact that it mimics the brain's own chemicals, specifically *endorphins*, which are involved in reducing pain. Opiates, however, can quickly produce strong physical and psychological dependence. The brain is changed with continued use; once usage is stopped, the body rebels with intense and prolonged withdrawal symptoms.

People who are regular users of opiates, such as heroin or morphine, suffer in many ways, greatly overshadowing the fleeting pleasures that immediately follow drug use. Kicking an opiate habit is extremely tough because the physical withdrawal symptoms—which can include everything from excessive yawning to extreme nausea to severe chills—last for days. Users who opt for the typical method of administration—intravenous injection—run additional risks of contracting diseases, such as HIV and hepatitis C. Longitudinal studies of heroin addicts paint a grim picture: Addicts tend to die young (at an average age of about 40 years) from a variety of causes, including suicide, homicide, and overdose (Hser, Anglin, & Powers, 1993).

hallucinogens

A class of drugs that tend to disrupt normal mental and emotional functioning and produce distorted perceptions

Hallucinogens   For the final category of psychoactive drugs, **hallucinogens** (sometimes called *psychedelics*), the term "psychoactive" is particularly apt. *Hallucinogens* play havoc with your normal internal construction of reality. Perception itself is fractured, and the world may become awash in fantastic colours, sounds, and tactile sensations. Two of the best known examples of these drugs, *mescaline* and *psilocybin*, occur naturally in the environment. Mescaline comes from a certain kind of cactus, and psilocybin is a type of mushroom. Both of these

David Buffington/PhotoDisc/Getty Images

The flowering opium plant

drugs have been used for centuries, primarily in the context of religious rituals and ceremonies. Since the 1960s, they have served as potentially dangerous recreational drugs for those seeking alternative realities.

Lysergic acid diethylamide (LSD) is a synthetic psychedelic drug. LSD is thought to mimic the action of the neurotransmitter serotonin (Strassman, 1992); the drug acts on specific serotonin-based receptor sites in the brain, producing stimulation. For reasons that are not particularly clear, variations in sensation and perception are produced. A typical LSD experience, which can last for up to 16 hours, consists of profound changes in perception. Some users report a phenomenon called *synesthesia*, which (as previously mentioned in Chapter 4) is a blending of sensory experiences—colours may feel warm or cold, and rough textures may begin to sing. Also for unknown reasons, a user's experience can turn sharply wrong. Panic or depression can develop, increasing the likelihood of accidents and personal harm. Users also sometimes report the occurrence of "flashbacks," in which the sensations of the drug are re-experienced long after the drug has presumably left the body.

Marijuana, which comes from the naturally occurring hemp plant *Cannabis*, can also be classified as a hallucinogenic drug (although it doesn't usually lead to vivid hallucinations per se). Marijuana is probably the most widely used illicit drug. A 2002 study by Statistics Canada estimated that 41% of the population over age 14 reported that they had used marijuana at some time in their lives, and 12% reported that they had used the drug in the last year (Statistics Canada, 2004c). Marijuana can be smoked or swallowed, and its effects typically last around four hours. THC, the active ingredient in marijuana, inhibits release of a variety of neurotransmitters and may suppress inhibitory synaptic transmission involving the neurotransmitter GABA (Davies, Pertwee, & Riedel, 2002). Users often report a melting away of anxiety, a general sense of well-being, and an intensification of normal sensations. Changes in the perception of time and its passage are sometimes reported, along with increased appetite. As with other hallucinogenic drugs, marijuana does not always produce a pleasant experience. Indeed, reactions to marijuana vary dramatically, both across individuals and within an individual on different occasions. Some users report anxiety, extreme fearfulness, and even panic; others experience flat affect and doziness (Fackelmann, 1993). The effects of the drug are usually followed by feelings of mild fatigue.

A number of studies have shown that marijuana use impairs concentration, memory, motor coordination, and the ability to track things visually (Moskowitz, 1985; Sullivan, 2000); these side effects probably increase the likelihood of traffic accidents when driving under the influence. Less is known about the long-term effects of regular use (partly because it is not ethically possible to randomly assign people to long-term dope-smoking versus control conditions), but there's some evidence that marijuana

CONCEPT SUMMARY

PSYCHOACTIVE DRUGS

Category	Examples	General Effects
Depressants	ethyl alcohol barbiturates tranquillizers	Believed to enhance the effectiveness of GABA and dopamine, which often act as inhibitory messengers in the brain; produce pleasurable feelings of relaxation, but at high doses concentration and memory are impaired
Stimulants	caffeine amphetamines cocaine nicotine Ecstasy	Amphetamines and cocaine may work primarily by increasing the effectiveness of dopamine and norepinephrine; stimulants tend to increase alertness, elevate mood, and produce physical changes, such as increased heart and respiration rates
Opiates	opium morphine heroin	Depressing of nervous system activity, resulting in reduced anxiety, mood elevation, and lower sensitivity to pain; tend to produce strong physical and psychological dependence
Hallucinogens	LSD mescaline psilocybin marijuana	Produce variations in sensation and perception; LSD is believed to mimic the action of serotonin; some users report *synesthesia*, blending of sensory experiences; marijuana often leads to general sense of well-being and heightened awareness of normal sensations; negative side effects can include anxiety, fearfulness, and panic

may impair a variety of cognitive functions, including memory (Pope, Gruber, Hudson, Huestis, & Yurgelun-Todd, 2001; Solowij et al., 2002). A study by Croft, Mackay, Mills, and Gruzelier (2001) indicates that combined use of Ecstasy and marijuana has particularly deleterious effects on cognition. Evidence also shows that smoking marijuana can contribute to a variety of serious respiratory problems (Ashton, 2001). On the positive side, marijuana may help reduce some of the negative symptoms of chemotherapy (e.g., nausea), and in some cases it's proved helpful in treating eye disorders, such as glaucoma (Watson, Benson, & Joy, 2000).

Psychological Factors

Among the more interesting characteristics of psychoactive drugs, especially to psychologists, are the sharp differences that can be seen in the effects of any particular drug on different individuals. Two people can take the same drug, in exactly the same quantity, but experience completely different effects. A small amount of LSD consumed by Teo produces a euphoric "religious experience"; the same amount for Jane produces a frightening descent into a whirlpool of terror. Why? Shouldn't the pharmacological effects on the neurotransmitters in the brain produce similar psychological effects?

The answer is that the psychological effects are influenced by many factors. The environmental setting in which a drug is taken, for example, is known to affect the experience. Smoking marijuana for the first time in a car speeding at 120 km/h might limit the anxiety-reducing effects of the drug. Many users report that familiarity with the drug's effects is also important—users claim that you need to "learn" to smoke marijuana or take LSD before the innermost "secrets" of the drug are revealed. In fact, experienced users of marijuana have been found to experience a "high" after smoking a cigarette they only thought was marijuana; similar effects did not occur for novice users (Jones, 1971). Both familiarity and the environment affect the user's *mental set*, his or her expectations about the drug's harmful and beneficial consequences. Likely individual differences also exist in users' physiological metabolism and in their psychological reactions. For instance, some people develop resistance or tolerance to a drug faster than others do. The experience of a drug may even depend on such mundane things as whether the person has eaten recently or is well rested.

Test your knowledge about psychoactive drugs by picking the category of drug that best fits each of the following statements. Choose from among these terms: *caffeine, depressant, hallucinogen, opiate, stimulant.* (The answers are in Appendix B.)

1. Increases central nervous system activity: _____

2. Reduces pain by mimicking the brain's own natural pain-reducing chemicals: _____

3. Tends to produce inhibitory effects by increasing the effectiveness of the neurotransmitter GABA: _____

4. Distorts perception and may lead to flashbacks: _____

5. The active ingredient found in your morning cup of coffee: _____

▶ Altering Awareness: Induced States

LEARNING GOALS

1. Become familiar with the physiological and behavioural effects of hypnosis.
2. Learn the scientific status of hypnosis as a memory-retrieval technique.
3. Be able to describe the dissociation and role-playing accounts of hypnosis.
4. Understand the physical, behavioural, and psychological effects of meditation.

The setting is Paris, late in the year 1783. Dressed in a lilac silk robe, physician Franz Anton Mesmer works to restore the delicate balance of universal fluids within his patients. He attaches large magnets to each patient—the better to affect their animal magnetism—and then rhythmically passes an iron rod, in large wave-like motions, over their outstretched bodies. His patients fall into a trancelike state: They can still talk and move their limbs on command, but each appears to have lost all forms of voluntary control. On later awakening, many feel better, apparently cured of their various physical and psychological problems.

Although Mesmer eventually fell into disrepute, rejected by the scientific community of his time, the phenomenon of "mesmerizing" did not. Today, of course, we recognize that the unusual behaviours he induced in his patients had nothing to do with magnets or universal fluids. Modern psychologists would explain the bizarre behaviour of Mesmer's patients as an example of hypnosis. **Hypnosis** can be defined as a social interaction between a person perceived to be a hypnotist and a person who perceives himself or herself as a hypnotic subject; the interaction produces a *heightened state of suggestibility* in the subject. It is of interest to psychologists partly because, like the related topic of meditation, it's a technique that is specifically designed to alter conscious awareness. As you'll see shortly, hypnosis has some highly adaptive properties.

hypnosis

A social interaction between a person perceived to be a hypnotist and a person who perceives himself or herself to be a hypnotic subject; the interaction produces a heightened state of suggestibility in the subject

The Phenomena of Hypnosis

Despite some two centuries of work on the topic, our understanding of hypnosis remains incomplete. Researchers are not sure whether hypnosis is truly a unique state of awareness, qualitatively different from that of normal waking consciousness, or a kind of social role-playing in which the subject takes on the part of a hypnotized person. But we do know a few things about what hypnosis is *not*. For one thing, people who are hypnotized do not enter into anything resembling a deep sleep. The word *hypnosis* does come from the Greek *hypnos*, meaning "to sleep," but hypnosis bears little physiological relation to sleep. The EEG patterns of a hypnotized subject, along with other physiological indexes, more closely resemble

those of someone who is relaxed rather than asleep (Graffen, Ray, & Lundy, 1995; for a discussion of brain science as it relates to hypnosis, see Woody & McConkey, 2003). Moreover, certain reflexes that are commonly absent during sleep, such as the knee jerk, are still present under hypnosis (Pratt, Wood, & Alman, 1988).

Another myth is that only weak-willed people are susceptible to hypnotic induction. Everyone appears to be susceptible to a degree, in the sense that we all show heightened suggestibility under some circumstances. Individual differences exist among people—hypnotic suggestibility scales indicate that only about 20% of the population are highly hypnotizable (Hilgard, 1965)—but it's not clear what factors account for these differences. Personality studies have shown that people who are easy to hypnotize are not generally weak willed or highly conforming, although they may have more active imaginations than people who resist hypnosis (Nadon, Hoyt, Register, & Kihlstrom, 1991).

Yet another myth is that hypnosis can only be induced by going through a particular induction ritual. It is true that hypnotists do use such rituals, but a wide variety of methods can be used to induce hypnotic behaviour. The most popular induction technique is one in which the hypnotist, acting as an authority figure, suggests to the subject that he or she is growing increasingly more relaxed and sleepy: "Your eyes are getting heavier and heavier, you can barely keep your lids open," and so on. Often the to-be-hypnotized person is asked to fixate on something, perhaps a spot on the wall or a swinging pendulum. The logic here is that eye fixation leads to muscle fatigue, which helps convince clients that they are indeed becoming increasingly relaxed. Other approaches to induction rely on more subtle suggestions (Erickson, 1964), including ones that many people would not recognize as hypnotic induction procedures at all. No one method is necessarily better than any other. In the words of one researcher, "The art of hypnosis relies on not providing the client with grounds for resisting" the hypnotist's suggestions (Araoz, 1982, p. 106).

Once hypnotized, a person becomes highly suggestible, responding to instructions from the hypnotist in ways that seem involuntary. The hypnotist can then use his or her power of suggestion to achieve adaptive ends, such as helping the subject to reduce anxiety or increase self-esteem. Research indicates that hypnosis can be a significant adjunct to other forms of therapy in achieving such aims (Kirsch, Montgomery, & Sapirstein, 1995). Anesthetic effects are also possible at deep stages of hypnosis. Hypnotized patients report less pain during childbirth (Harmon, Hynan, & Tyre, 1990) and dental work (Houle, McGrath, Moran, & Garrett, 1988). It has even been possible to perform major surgeries (such as appendectomies) by using hypnosis as the primary anesthesia (Kihlstrom, 1985). Research is ongoing to determine the biological bases for these striking analgesic effects. It was once thought, for example, that the release of endorphins by the brain might be responsible, although this now seems unlikely (Moret, Forster, Laverriere, & Lambert, 1991).

If you ever see a stage hypnotist, you're likely to witness an astonishing variety of hypnotically induced behaviours. One impressive demonstration is **catalepsy:** One of the hypnotized person's limbs is placed in some unusual position (perhaps by raising a leg or an arm in the air), and the subject then retains this position rigidly for long periods without signs of tiring. In a related demonstration, the hypnotized person lies with his or her head on one chair and heels on another, remaining rigid in a way that seems miraculous. Apparent perceptual illusions are also common: The volunteer appears to see or hear things that are not really there or ignores loud noises that would normally cause someone to jump. Hypnotized individuals may also perform a variety of ridiculous behaviours, such as flapping their arms and quacking like a duck, in response to the hypnotist's suggestions. As you'll learn later in this chapter, these phenomena are less bizarre (and less specific to hypnosis) than they seem. First, however, we highlight a particularly important question regarding hypnosis: Does it enable people to recall things that they otherwise could not have remembered?

catalepsy

A hypnotically induced behaviour characterized by an ability to hold one or more limbs of the body in a rigid position for long periods without tiring

Hypnosis and Memory

It is popularly believed that hypnosis can dramatically improve recall performance through a phenomenon called **hypnotic hypermnesia.** Perhaps you've heard of crime investigations in which hypnosis apparently enabled witnesses to recall minute details of a horrific crime. In one famous kidnapping case from the 1970s, a bus driver was buried two metres underground along with 26 children inside a tractor trailer. Later, under hypnosis, he was able to recall the kidnapper's licence plate. A long-standing belief exists among some psychotherapists that hypnosis is an excellent tool for uncovering hidden memories of childhood abuse or other forms of psychological trauma (Poole et al., 1995; Pratt et al., 1988; Yapko, 1994). There have even been a number of well-publicized examples of *age regression* under hypnosis, in which the subject appeared to mentally travel backward to some earlier place (such as his or her grade 2 classroom, the experience of being born, or even a past life).

Unfortunately, little hard evidence supports the idea of hypnotic hypermnesia. A person's memory may indeed improve after a hypnotic session, but this fact does not allow us to conclude that hypnosis was responsible for the improvement (Spiegel, 1995). One possibility is that the hypnotic session simply provided the subject with another opportunity to recall the to-be-remembered material; everyone has had the experience of being unable to remember a particular piece of information at one time and then later recalling it. It is also possible that hypnotic procedures create effective and supportive environments in which to remember (Geiselman, Fisher, MacKinnon, & Holland, 1985). Another problem is that it's often difficult to judge whether memories recovered during hypnosis are, in fact, accurate representations of what actually occurred. You may "remember" a particularly unpleasant experience from your grade 2 classroom, but can you be sure that this traumatic episode indeed occurred as you remember it (Lindsay & Read, 1994; Loftus, 1993)?

As you'll see in a moment, evidence suggests that hypnotizable subjects adopt the role of being hypnotized. If the hypnotist suggests that the subject will be able to recall previously forgotten material, the subject will try to comply. What appear to be memories, then, may sometimes be fabrications—stories that the subject unintentionally makes up to please the hypnotist. To put this another way, the hypnotized individual may report as memories thoughts and images that are too vague or incomplete to normally be reported as memories; some of these may indeed be accurate, but many of them will be fabrications (Dywan & Bowers, 1983). If the hypnotist convincingly suggests that the subject will be able to remember a past life, highly hypnotizable subjects may comply with the suggestion and give a detailed report, but there is no reason to believe that the report corresponds to any real past event (Spanos, 1996). Controlled experiments in the laboratory have failed to find good evidence that hypnosis improves the ability to recall past experiences, but it sometimes increases false memories and sometimes inflates confidence in memory reports (Dinges, Whitehouse, Orne, & Powell, 1992; Lynn, Myers, & Malinoski, 1997; Steblay & Bothwell, 1994). For this reason, the use of hypnotic testimony in criminal court cases is rarely allowed. It's simply too difficult to tell whether the memory recovered after hypnosis is accurate or a product of suggestion by the hypnotist.

Explaining Hypnosis

Considerable debate ensues over how the phenomenon of hypnosis should be explained. As noted earlier, the EEG patterns of someone in a deep hypnotic trance resemble the patterns of someone in a relaxed waking state, and hypnosis does not appear to have any unique physiological indicators. So how do we explain the heightened suggestibility? Currently, two prominent interpretations of hypnosis are

hypnotic hypermnesia

The supposed enhancement of memory that is said to occur under hypnosis; little evidence supports the existence of this effect

CRITICAL   THINKING

Can you think of any situations in which memories accessed through hypnosis should be admitted in court? Why or why not?

favoured: (1) Hypnosis is a kind of dissociation, or true splitting of conscious awareness, and (2) hypnosis represents a kind of social role-playing. Let's consider each of these ideas in more detail.

Hypnotic Dissociations   Some researchers believe that hypnosis produces **hypnotic dissociations:** the hypnotized individual experiences a splitting of consciousness in which two forms of awareness coexist (Hilgard, 1992). One stream of consciousness follows the commands of the hypnotist, such as feeling no effects of painful stimulation, while another stream, called the "hidden observer," retains a more objective awareness of what is really going on (e.g., is painfully aware of the true stimulation) but does not reveal this awareness.

Hilgard (1992) supported his position with experiments in which subjects were hypnotized and asked to submerge one arm into a bucket of extremely cold ice water (a procedure to test for the analgesic effects of hypnosis). "You'll be aware of no pain," the subject was told, "but that other part of you, the hidden part that is aware of everything going on, can signal any true pain by pressing this key with your nonsubmerged hand." Subjects pressed the key repeatedly—reporting the pain—and the key presses became more frequent the longer the arm was kept submerged. During hypnosis, as well as afterward, the subjects claimed not to experience pain and to have no awareness of the nonsubmerged hand's behaviour. A hidden part of consciousness, Hilgard argued, maintains realistic contact with what's going on; it is the other hypnotized stream of awareness that feels no pain. For a recent defence of the concept of hypnotic dissociation, see Spiegel (1998).

This idea that conscious awareness is divided or split during hypnosis may seem mystical, strange, and worthy of skepticism. Yet you may have had everyday experiences that might reasonably be characterized as divided consciousness. At a movie theatre, for example, you can be deeply absorbed in the film yet be aware, at another level, of the theatre around you. As another example, you may have attended a party at which everyone, including you, seemed to be having a good time (animatedly laughing and chatting) but "deep down" you felt sad or troubled about something in your life. Some psychologists would characterize this as an example of split or divided consciousness; as you'll see below, others would describe it as an example of social role-playing.

Social Role-Playing   By definition, the behaviour of a hypnotized person is easily modified by the suggestions of the hypnotist. Such suggestions need not be blatant, and they do not need to be given while the person is hypnotized. Indeed, the

---

hypnotic dissociation

A hypothesized, hypnotically induced splitting of consciousness during which two streams of awareness are said to coexist: one that is fully under the sway of the hypnotist's suggestions and one that remains more aloof and objective

Hypnosis is often used for entertainment purposes. It can also have considerable clinical value.

suggestions do not even have to come from the hypnotist per se, but can be based on the subject's beliefs and expectations regarding hypnosis. For example, if people are told before being hypnotized that a rigid right arm is a prominent feature of the hypnotized state, then rigid right arms are likely to be demonstrated during hypnosis even when no such specific suggestion is made during the induction process (Orne, 1959). It often appears as if highly hypnotizable subjects are trying hard to "do whatever they can to achieve the suggested effects" (Kihlstrom & McConkey, 1990; Kirsch, 1999).

A number of researchers have suggested that hypnotic behaviour is a kind of social role-playing. Everyone has some idea of what hypnotized behaviour looks like: To be hypnotized, you must fall into a trance and slavishly obey the all-powerful hypnotist. So when people agree to be hypnotized, they implicitly agree to take on this role (Sarbin & Coe, 1972; Spanos, 1982). According to this view, people have not actually lost voluntary control over their behaviour; rather, they follow the lead of the hypnotist and obey his or her every command because they think, perhaps unconsciously, that involuntary compliance is an important part of what it means to be hypnotized (Lynn et al., 1997). The claim is not that people are merely "faking it"; rather, the idea is that hypnosis is a phenomenon of "creative role engagement, where people generate the sensations, subjective experiences, and mental representations scripted by the hypnotic context" (Lynn et al., 1997, p. 172).

Quite a bit of evidence supports this role-playing interpretation of hypnosis. One compelling finding is that essentially all hypnotic phenomena can be reproduced with *simulating subjects*—people who are not actually hypnotized but who are told to act as if they are hypnotized as part of an experiment. These issues were extensively explored by the late Nick Spanos of Carleton University (e.g., Spanos, 1996). For example, catalepsy looks very impressive, but it turns out that motivated nonhypnotized individuals can enact it just as well as hypnotized individuals. Moreover, many of the classic phenomena of hypnosis—such as posthypnotic suggestions—turn out to be controlled mainly by subject expectations. For example, if subjects are told to respond to some cue after the hypnotic session ends, such as tugging on their ear every time they hear the word *psychology*, they will often do so after hypnosis. However, posthypnotic suggestions of this kind are effective only if the subjects believe they are still participating in the experiment; if the hypnotist leaves the room or if the subjects believe the experiment is over, they stop responding appropriately to the cue (see Lynn et al., 1997, and Spanos, 1996, for reviews).

What can we conclude about hypnosis? Do hypnotic induction procedures produce a unique state of mind, qualitatively different from all other forms of awareness, in which the hypnotized part of consciousness slavishly follows the hypnotist's suggestions? Or do hypnotizable individuals merely take on a socially constructed role? Debate continues among psychologists, but we suggest that the two positions may not be very different from each other: If part of the role of hypnotized subjects is entering a peculiar state of mind, then individuals who truly get into that role will indeed experience a peculiar state of mind.

Meditation

Hypnosis and meditation have a number of parallels. For example, both are often said to produce an altered state of mind, both entail relaxation, and both typically involve some sort of induction ceremony. Most **meditation** techniques involve breathing in a special way while performing a mental exercise to focus the mind (e.g., silently repeating a string of words or sounds called a *mantra*) and cultivating a passive state of mind.

The variations in awareness achieved through meditation, as with hypnosis, are often described in mystical or spiritual ways. Meditators often report that they are able to obtain an expanded state of awareness, characterized by a pure and

meditation

A technique for self-induced manipulation of awareness, often used for relaxation and self-reflection

Daily meditation sessions can likely produce significant reductions in anxiety.

Ryan McVay/PhotoDisc/Getty Images

calm form of thought unburdened by self-awareness. Many forms of meditation and numerous induction procedures exist; most trace their roots back thousands of years to the practices of a variety of Eastern religions.

The general idea of meditation is to step back from the ongoing stream of mental activity and set the mind adrift in the oneness of the universe. Advocates of meditation claim it has many benefits, from improved health to spiritual insights. Meditation does lower heart and respiration rates, and regular meditation can reduce blood pressure. Also, EEG recordings reveal that alpha waves and theta waves significantly increase during meditation, and generally an overall frequency slowing of brain waves occurs. It's not clear, however, that the physiological effects of meditation differ from those of simple relaxation, nor do they necessarily signify a special state of consciousness. To quote from a review by Cahn and Polich (2006, p. 180), "EEG studies of meditative states have been conducted for almost 50 years, and no clear consensus about the underlying neurophysiological changes from meditation practice has emerged." At this point, researchers have even less to say about the subjective aspects of the meditative experience—whether, in fact, the meditator has indeed merged with the oneness of the universe—but most researchers agree that inducing a deeply relaxed state once or twice a day is likely to have genuinely beneficial effects.

Test Yourself   5.4

Check what you've learned about hypnosis and meditation by deciding whether each of the following statements is true or false. (The answers are in Appendix B.)

1. The EEG patterns of a hypnotized person resemble those of non-REM sleep. *True or False?*

2. Hypnosis improves memory under some circumstances because it reduces the tendency to fabricate, or make things up, to please the questioner. *True or False?*

3. The concept of hypnotic dissociation refers to a kind of splitting of consciousness, in which more than one kind of awareness is present at the same time. *True or False?*

4. Hilgard described his "hidden observer" experiments as providing support for the social role-playing explanation of hypnosis. *True or False?*

5. Meditation leads primarily to alpha wave rather than theta wave EEG activity. *True or False?*

The Psychology of Consciousness

R
E
V
I
E
W

Studying conscious awareness is not an easy task. Consciousness is by its very nature a subjective, personal experience. It is a difficult concept to define objectively, and the scribbling of an EEG pattern or a pretty picture from a PET scanning device may, in the minds of many, fail to capture the complexities of the topic adequately. Is consciousness some classifiable thing that can change its state, like water as it freezes or evaporates? For the moment, psychologists are working with a set of rather loose ideas about the topic, although conscious awareness is agreed to have many adaptive properties. We considered four adaptive characteristics of consciousness in this chapter; each revealed ways that the adaptive mind adjusts to solve problems faced in the environment.

First, how do people set priorities for mental functioning? The processes of attention allow the mind to prioritize its functioning. Faced with limited resources, the brain needs to be selective about the enormous amount of information it receives. Through attention, people can focus on certain aspects of the environment while largely ignoring others, adapting their thinking in ways that allow for selective and deliberate movement toward a problem solution. Attentional processes also enable the brain to divide its processing. People don't always need to be consciously aware of the tasks they perform; automatic processes allow us to perform multiple tasks—such as driving a car and following a conversation—at the same time. Certain disorders of attention, including visual neglect and attention deficit disorder, provide some insights into attention processes. In both of these conditions, which may be caused by malfunctioning in the brain, the person's ability to adapt to the environment is compromised.

Second, what roles do sleep and dreaming play for the adaptive mind? Sleep is part of a daily (circadian) rhythm, and sleep itself turns out to be composed of regularly changing cycles of brain activity. Studies that use the EEG reveal that people move through several distinct stages during sleep. Sleeping may allow the brain a chance to rest and restore itself from its daily workout, or it may simply be adaptive as a safe period of time out. Lying relatively motionless in the dark recesses of some shelter may have protected our ancestors at night when their sensory equipment was unlikely to function well. The function of dreaming, which occurs during the REM period of sleep (and sometimes during other stages of sleep), remains unclear. Some psychologists believe that dreaming may reveal conflicts that are hidden from conscious awareness or that dreaming may be one way to work out currently troubling problems. A third possibility is that dreaming is simply a manifestation of the brain's attempt to make sense of its own spontaneous neural activity.

Third, how do certain chemicals, or drugs, produce profound alterations in awareness? Psychoactive drugs alter behaviour and awareness by tapping into natural brain systems that have evolved for adaptive reasons. The brain, as a biochemical factory, can react to stress or injury by releasing chemicals (neurotransmitters) that help reduce pain or that shift mood in a positive direction. Many of the drugs that are abused in our society activate these natural systems. As a result, the study of psychoactive drugs has enabled researchers to learn more about communication systems in the brain.

There are four main categories of psychoactive drugs. *Depressants*, such as alcohol and barbiturates, lower the ongoing activity of the central nervous system. *Stimulants*, such as caffeine, nicotine, and cocaine, stimulate central nervous system activity by increasing the likelihood that neural transmissions will occur. *Opiates*, such as opium, morphine, and heroin, depress nervous system activity by mimicking the chemicals involved in the brain's own pain-control system. Finally, *hallucinogens*, such as LSD, play havoc with the user's normal internal construction of reality. Although the mechanisms involved are not known, it's believed that LSD mimics the actions of the neurotransmitter serotonin.

Fourth, what happens under hypnosis and meditation, two other techniques that seem to alter awareness? Two techniques have been designed specifically to alter conscious awareness: hypnosis and meditation. Hypnosis is a form of social interaction that induces a heightened state of suggestibility in the subject. Hypnotic techniques usually promote relaxation, but brain activity under hypnosis more closely resembles the waking than the sleeping state. In meditation, the participant manipulates awareness, often by mentally repeating a particular word or string of words, focusing on breathing in a particular way, and making efforts toward clear and calm thoughts. The biological mechanisms of both hypnosis and meditation are poorly understood at present, but each has some positive consequences. Pain and discomfort can be significantly reduced through hypnotic suggestion, and the regular practice of meditation has been linked to the reduction of stress and anxiety.

CHAPTER SUMMARY

▶ Setting Priorities for Mental Functioning: Attention

Attention refers to the internal processes we use to set and follow priorities for mental functioning. The brain uses attention to focus selectively on certain parts of the environment and not on others.

Experiments on Attention: Dichotic Listening

Different messages are presented simultaneously to each ear, and the subject tries to repeat (or "shadow")one message aloud while ignoring the other.

Processing without Attention: Automaticity

Automaticity refers to mental processing that, because of extensive skill development via practice, is fast and easy, requiring little or no focused attention.

Disorders of Attention

Visual neglect, caused by damage to one side of the parietal lobe, is a tendency to ignore everything on the other side of the body. *Attention deficit/hyperactivity disorder* is a psychological condition characterized by extreme distractibility, often with impulsivity or hyperactivity.

Subliminal Perception

Subliminal messages are stimuli that are presented so briefly, or in such a disguised fashion, that we cannot consciously perceive them. Contrary to popular beliefs, scientific research indicates that such messages can only affect behaviour in small and transient ways.

▶ Sleeping and Dreaming

Biological Rhythms

The internal cycles that regulate sleep, waking, and other physical processes are controlled by structures in the brain that trigger rhythmic variations at appropriate times.

The Characteristics of Sleep

During sleep, we experience repeated cycles of brain activity, each complete cycle being about 90 minutes long. *Stage 1:* "Drifting." *Stage 2:* Asleep but still dimly sensitive to the external world. *Stages 3 and 4:* Progressively deeper sleep. *REM sleep:* Abrupt physiological changes, brain waves look "awake," but motor movements are minimized; most dream activity occurs during this stage.

The Function of Sleep

Sleep helps to *repair* and *restore* the body and brain. It also helps us respond adaptively to environmental conditions for the sake of survival. Our ability to perform complex tasks is disrupted if we haven't received much sleep. Prolonged sleep deprivation generally wreaks havoc on virtually all aspects of normal functioning.

The Function of REM and Dreaming

REM sleep may serve an important function in the brain, such as strengthening certain kinds of memories. Dreams may be a form of *wish fulfillment* (Freud); the *activation-synthesis hypothesis* holds that dreaming is a product of random activity in the brain.

Sleep Disorders

Dyssomnias are problems associated with the amount, timing, and quality of sleep, such as *insomnia, hypersomnia,* and *narcolepsy. Parasomnias* are abnormal sleep disturbances, such as *nightmares, night terrors,* and *sleepwalking.*

▶ Altering Awareness: Psychoactive Drugs

Drug Actions and Effects

Like neurotransmitters, *psychoactive drugs* alter behaviour and mental processes by affecting the operation of neurons in the brain. Use of psychoactive drugs can produce lasting changes in the brain. These changes may include *tolerance,* a decreased susceptibility to the effects of the drug, and *dependence,* a physical or psychological need to use the drug. *Withdrawal* refers to physical and psychological symptoms when drug use stops. Many popular recreational drugs have been shown to impair mental functioning.

Categories of Psychoactive Drugs

Depressants, such as alcohol and barbiturates, slow the activity of the central nervous system. *Stimulants,* such as caffeine, amphetamines, cocaine, nicotine, and Ecstasy, increase central nervous system activity. *Opiates (narcotics),* such as opium, heroin, and morphine, depress nervous system activity and reduce anxiety and sensitivity to pain. *Hallucinogens (psychedelics),* such as LSD, mescaline, psilocybin, and marijuana, dramatically alter mood and perception.

Psychological Factors

Among the factors that can influence reactions to psychoactive drugs are *environmental setting, familiarity* with the effects of the substance, *physical state,* and *expectations and mental attitude.*

▶ Altering Awareness: Induced States

The Phenomena of Hypnosis

Hypnosis is a social interaction that produces a *heightened state of suggestibility* in a willing subject. It bears little physiological relation to sleep.

Hypnosis and Memory

People sometimes remember things under hypnosis that they previously failed to remember. Some such memories are accurate, but there is no convincing evidence that the hypnotic state gives people remarkable powers of memory.

Explaining Hypnosis

Some psychologists believe that hypnosis induces a true dividing of consciousness, with one stream of consciousness fully under the hypnotist's sway and the other more aloof and independent. Other psychologists describe hypnosis as a powerful form of *social role-playing* in which the subject enters into the role of being hypnotized.

Meditation

Meditation is characterized by self-induced altered awareness achieved by calming, relaxing, and concentrating on breathing or on a *mantra* (repetition of specific sounds). Daily meditation may reduce anxiety.

Terms to Remember

consciousness, 175

Setting Priorities for Mental Functioning: Attention
attention, 178
dichotic listening, 179
cocktail party effect, 179
automaticity, 181
visual neglect, 183
attention deficit/hyperactivity disorder, 183

Sleeping and Dreaming
circadian rhythms, 187
biological clocks, 188
alpha waves, 191
theta waves, 191
delta activity, 191
REM, 192
REM rebound, 195
manifest content, 196
latent content, 196
activation-synthesis hypothesis, 197
insomnia, 198

hypersomnia, 199
nightmares, 199
night terrors, 199
sleepwalking, 199

Altering Awareness: Psychoactive Drugs
psychoactive drugs, 201
tolerance, 202
drug dependency, 202
withdrawal, 202
depressants, 202
stimulants, 203
opiates, 204
hallucinogens, 204

Altering Awareness: Induced States
hypnosis, 207
catalepsy, 208
hypnotic hypermnesia, 209
hypnotic dissociation, 210
meditation, 211

Recommended Readings

Coren, S. (1996). *Sleep thieves*. New York: The Free Press. Written for the layperson by a top research psychologist at the University of British Columbia, this book presents a convincing case for the importance of a good night's sleep.

Dennett, D. C. (1991). *Consciousness explained*. Boston: Little, Brown and Company. Written by a philosopher, this book challenges the traditional commonsense view of consciousness. Generally easy to read—Dennett is a great writer—and it contains much food for thought.

Jaynes, J. (1976). *The origin of consciousness in the breakdown of the bicameral mind*. Boston: Houghton Mifflin. This is a fascinating and provocative book, full

of speculations about the origins of consciousness. Jaynes argued that conscious awareness developed relatively recently in human history and that ancient peoples from Mesopotamia to Peru were unable to think as we can today.

 For additional readings, explore InfoTrac® College Edition, your online library. Go to http://www.adaptivemind3e.nelson.com.

Hint: Enter these search terms: visual neglect, altered states of consciousness, stages of sleep, REM sleep, drugs and behaviour, hypnotic effects.

Media Resources

What's on the Web?

Please note that Web addresses are subject to change. Check out the accompanying website for updates: http://www.adaptivemind3e.nelson.com.

This site presents practice quiz questions, hypercontent, information on degrees and careers in psychology, study tips, and more.

The Need for Attention to See Change

http://www.psych.ubc.ca/~viscoglab/demos.htm

http://viscog.beckman.uiuc.edu/djs_lab/demos.html

In Chapter 4 you read about vision, and in this chapter you've read about attention. As you might expect, there are many interactions between attention and vision. A particularly interesting example is a phenomenon called "change blindness." The first of the two sites listed above, by Dr. Ronald A. Rensink (formerly of Nissan Technical Center, now at UBC), provides several demonstrations of the phenomenon and links to articles about it. The second site, by Professor Daniel J. Simons of the University of Illinois, provides a wide variety of demonstrations of the change-blindness phenomenon. The effect is quite amusing, as well as intriguing.

Canadian Centre on Substance Abuse

http://www.ccsa.ca

The Canadian Centre on Substance Abuse is a nonprofit organization working to minimize the harm associated with the use of alcohol, tobacco, and other drugs. The site is well designed and packed with authoritative and on-target information and useful resources.

Sleeping Better

http://www.healthyresources.com/sleep/apnea/index.html

http://www.stanford.edu/~dement

http://www.sleepnet.com

Some of the best sites on the Web for finding out more about sleep. Find out about snoring, dreams, insomnia, sleep aids, and much more.

Dream Sites

http://www.rider.edu/users/suler/dreams.html

http://psych.ucsc.edu/dreams/

Few topics pique the curiosity of the psychology student more than dreams. Why do we dream? What do dreams mean? These two sites will allow you to explore these questions in depth. They provide information about ongoing research on dreams as well as information for those who want to explore their own dreams.

ThomsonNOW™ ThomsonNOW

http://hed.nelson.com

Go to this site for the link to ThomsonNOW™, your one-stop study shop. Take a Pretest for this chapter and ThomsonNOW™ will generate a personalized Study Plan based on your test results. The Study Plan will identify the topics you need to review and direct you to online resources to help you master those topics. You can then take a Posttest to determine what concepts you have mastered and what you still need work on.

Psyk.trek 3.0

Check out Psyk.trek 3.0 for further study of the concepts in this chapter. Psyk.trek's 65 interactive learning modules, simulations, and quizzes offer additional opportunities for you to interact with, reflect on, and retain the material:

Consciousness: Biological Rhythms
Consciousness: Sleep
Consciousness: Drugs and Synaptic Transmission

And you may find yourself living in a shotgun shack
And you may find yourself in another part of the world
And you may find yourself behind the wheel of a large automobile
And you may find yourself in a beautiful house, with a beautiful wife . . .
And you may ask yourself—Well . . . How did I get here?
And you may ask yourself, How do I work this?

—Talking Heads, "Once in a Lifetime"

(From "Once in a Lifetime" by David Byrne, Brian Eno, Chris Frantz, Jerry Harrison, Tina (Martina) Weymouth. Copyright © 1980. Reprinted by permission of WB Music Corporation.)

Learning: Conditioning and Observation

Imagine that you suddenly traded places with someone from a different time and culture. You might, for example, awaken in a *yurt* on the steppes of Mongolia, home of a great horse-based, nomadic culture, perhaps in the time of Genghis Khan. If you're like most Canadian undergraduates, you won't know a word of the language, nor will you be an expert in the care of horses (let alone yaks and goats) and the handling of weapons. Indeed, even the most basic tasks of everyday living, such as finding water and food, will be challenging mysteries. Your counterpart, transported from the ancient Mongolian camp to your university, would probably be similarly discomfited. Yet, given experience, effort, and a bit of luck, each of you would learn to adapt to your new environment reasonably well. After all, each of you had learned to adapt to your initial cultures as children. You are genetically endowed with the ability to adapt to a very wide range of physical and cultural environments by learning from experience. The question explored in this chapter is how you do so.

Historically, much of scientific psychology's investigations of learning have focused on learning in relatively simple situations, often by using nonhuman species, such as rats, pigeons, or sea snails, as subjects. Indeed, much of what you'll read about in this chapter comes from animal research. The use of animals as models to understand human psychology makes sense when you consider that all species—even sea snails—need to learn to survive. Many psychologists believe that all organisms, including humans, share similar learning mechanisms (Roitblat & von Ferson, 1992). Different species differ in important ways, and humans are extraordinary in the extent to which they can adapt via learning from experience. Nonetheless, common principles, or laws, of learning appear to apply widely across species. We'll try to make clear, as we go along, the relevance of simple learning phenomena demonstrated in nonhuman animals for understanding why people do the things they do in everyday life.

Classical Conditioning, Instrumental Conditioning, and Observational Learning

What exactly is learning? Most people view learning as the process of acquiring knowledge and skill. In broad terms, psychologists would agree with this general description but, as you learned in Chapter 2, psychologists like to define concepts in terms of how those concepts are measured (i.e., operational definitions). "Knowledge" cannot be measured directly—if you looked inside someone's brain, you'd see neurons, glial cells, and so on, but not any accurate index of specific pieces of knowledge or skill. Instead, psychologists define **learning** in terms of behaviour—specifically, as a relatively permanent change in behaviour that

results from experience. (Keep in mind that speaking and writing are behaviours.) To determine that learning has occurred, we must observe a change in behaviour (Wasserman & Miller, 1997). Thus, psychologists make inferences about learning and the acquisition of knowledge and skill by observing behaviour and noting how behaviour changes with experience.

In this chapter our discussion revolves around four simple adaptive problems that are solved by our ability to learn. Later chapters will explore more conceptual or cognitive sorts of learning (in which language typically plays a major role). Here the focus is on four funda-

mental problems that all animals must solve:

First, how do we recognize consequential events when they occur and react to them appropriately? We need to recognize consequential events when they occur and react to them appropriately. We also need to learn to ignore events that occur repeatedly but have no consequences of interest to us. The cry of an infant, the screech of automobile brakes—these sounds demand our attention

learning

A relatively permanent change in behaviour, or potential to respond, that results from experience

The bright colours and screeching sirens of a fire engine are designed to draw our attention and to signal the need for us to get out of the way.

It's clearly adaptive to learn about the signalling properties of events. A distinctive rattle on a mountain trail signals the potential strike of the western diamondback rattlesnake.

This family dog has learned about the consequences of hanging around the dinner table. She's learned that her begging behaviour is instrumental in producing a tasty reward.

and cause us to react. Humans and animals note sudden changes in their environment; they notice things that are new and potentially of interest. Our reactions to these once-novel events change with repeated experience, and these changes are controlled by basic learning processes.

Second, how do we learn about the signalling properties of stimuli or events in the environment? When does one event predict that a second event is likely to follow? For instance, you know that lightning precedes thunder and that a dog's snarl may signal a bite. Often, you can't *do* anything about the co-occurrence of such events, but if you recognize the relationship, you can respond accordingly (you can take cover or move to avoid the dog).

Third, how do we learn about the consequences of our own behaviour? All species, sea snails as well as people, need to learn that when they act in a certain way in a particular situation, their behaviour is likely to have consequences. The child who flicks the tail of a cat once too often receives an unwelcome surprise. The family dog learns that if she hangs around the dinner table, a scrap of food might very well come her way. Behaviours often result in either rewards or punishments, and learning about such consequences plays a key role in adaptation via learning.

Fourth, how can we learn by observing others? People and many other kinds of animals often learn by observing the actions of others and the consequences those actions bring. Observational learning has considerable adaptive significance: A teenager learns about the consequences of drunk driving, we hope, not from direct experience but from observing others whose fate has already been sealed. A young monkey in the wild learns to be afraid of snakes not from a deadly personal encounter but from observing her mother's fear.

Allan Roberts

It's adaptive for all living things to notice sudden changes in the environment. In this case, the unexpected appearance of a red-tailed hawk elicits distinctive orienting reactions from an opossum family.

▶ Learning about Events: Noticing and Ignoring

LEARNING GOALS

1. Learn about the concept of the orienting response and be able to discuss its adaptive value.
2. Understand and be able to compare habituation and sensitization.

Let's begin with the first problem: How do we learn to notice consequential stimuli or events and to ignore inconsequential ones? We're constantly surrounded by sights, sounds, and sensations—from the sound of traffic outside the window to the colour of the paint on the wall to the feel of denim jeans against our legs. As discussed in Chapter 5, it's not possible to attend consciously to all these stimuli at once. Instead, you need to prioritize your mental functioning, directing your attention to some things while largely ignoring others. Some basic psychological processes help people and other animals determine which events deserve attention and which do not.

Orienting Responses, Habituation, and Sensitization

Humans are programmed from birth (and probably before) to notice novelty; when something new or different happens, we pay close attention. Suppose you hear a funny ticking noise in your car engine when you press the gas pedal. When you first

orienting response

An inborn tendency to shift our focus of attention toward a novel or surprising event

habituation

The decline in responsiveness to repeated stimulation; habituation has been used to investigate the perceptual capabilities of infants

sensitization

An increase in the tendency to respond to an event that has been repeated; sensitization is more likely when a repeated stimulus is intense

CRITICAL   THINKING

In Chapter 4 you learned about sensory adaptation, which refers to the tendency of sensory systems to stop or reduce responding to a stimulus source that remains constant. Do you suppose any connection exists between sensory adaptation and habituation?

notice the sound, it grabs your attention. You produce an **orienting response,** which is an automatic shift of attention toward the event. Perhaps you lean forward and listen; you may even repeatedly press the gas pedal to establish a link between acceleration and ticking. But suppose you keep driving, and the car performs as usual. After a while, your behaviour changes—the ticking becomes less bothersome, and you may even stop reacting to it altogether. Your behaviour in the presence of the event changes with repeated experience, which is the hallmark of learning. If you give an acquaintance a lift in your car, he or she might ask, "What's that ticking?" and you might reply, "What ticking? Oh yeah, *that* ticking! I've become so used to it I don't even hear it anymore."

When you respond less strongly to an event that has become familiar through repeated presentation, you are demonstrating **habituation.** (This process will be discussed in more detail in Chapter 10.) Most birds are startled and become agitated when the shadow of a hawk passes overhead, but their level of alarm rapidly declines if the shadow occurs repeatedly without a subsequent attack (Tinbergen, 1951). It makes sense for animals to produce a strong initial orienting response to a sudden change in their environment. If a bird fails to attend quickly to the shape of a potential predator, the bird is not likely to survive. Through the process of habituation, organisms learn to be selective about the things they orient toward. They attend initially to the new and unusual events but subsequently ignore events that occur repeatedly without significant consequence.

Sensitization is the opposite of habituation. It occurs when responsiveness to an event increases with repeated exposure to that event. Sensitization, like habituation, is a general learning phenomenon found throughout the animal kingdom. Both habituation and sensitization are natural responses to repeated events—they help us respond appropriately to the environment. Whether you become more or less responsive in any specific situation depends on the relative strengths of the habituation and sensitization processes (Groves & Thompson, 1970). Generally, increases in responsiveness—sensitization—are more likely when the repeated stimulus is intense. For example, if you are exposed to repetitions of a very loud noise, you may become "sensitized" to the noise—your reactions become more intense and prolonged with repeated exposure. If the noise is relatively modest in intensity, repeated exposure may lead to decreases in responsiveness (i.e., habituation). Habituation and sensitization also depend importantly on the timing of presentations—that is, whether the repetitions occur close together (which increases the likelihood of sensitization) or are widely separated in time (which is likely to lead to habituation) (Haerich, 1997; Staddon, 1998). Sensitization is adaptive because it prompts us to do something to escape potentially harmful stimuli (e.g., noises that could damage hearing).

Habituation and sensitization are both examples of learning because they produce changes in behaviour as a function of experience. The effects of sensitization generally tend to be short-lived (Domjan, 1998), whereas habituation can produce quite long-term effects. For example, when placed in a new environment cats are often skittish when they eat. The slightest sound or movement is likely to send them scurrying for cover. With experience the animal learns, and the adjustment is typically long lasting (see ▶ Figure 6.1).

Drug tolerance, which we discussed in more detail in Chapter 5, can be described in terms of long-term habituation. In humans, an initial dose of 100 mg to 200 mg of morphine produces profound sedation or even death, but morphine-tolerant subjects are capable of receiving more than 100 times that amount without negative effects (Baker & Tiffany, 1985). Similarly, regular Ecstasy users typically find they have to take more and more of the drug to experience the high (e.g., Parrott, 2005). The body's response to the drug changes after repeated use—that is, the body *habituates* to the drug. Most interestingly, drug tolerance depends, in part, on environmental context: A dose that would be tolerated when taken in the context in which the individual has often previously taken the drug may produce a lethal

Day 1   Day 2   Day 3   Day 4   Day 5

▶ Figure 6.1

Long-Term Habituation

Organisms notice sudden changes in the environment, but they learn to ignore them if they occur repeatedly without significant consequences. When a cat is eating, a novel sound leads initially to panic and escape, but if the sound is repeated over days, the cat gradually habituates and continues eating without the slightest reaction.

overdose if taken in a novel environment. As another example, Siegel, Baptista, Kim, McDonald, and Weise-Kelly (2000) found that university students were more affected by alcohol served in a novel blue beverage than by the same amount of alcohol served in beer. This suggests that these individuals had learned to produce physiological responses to cues associated with the drug (e.g., the look of the room in which a junky usually shoots up, or the appearance and aroma of a glass of beer) that attenuate the influence of the drug (Siegel, 2005). The exact nature of the learning that occurs as tolerance develops is still a matter of debate (Krank & O'Neill, 2002; Siegel, 2005), but tolerance shows clearly how responsiveness to an event can change as a consequence of repeated exposure.

Because it's a general kind of learning process that occurs throughout the animal world, habituation can be used as a psychological model for understanding how behaviours change with experience. Some learning theorists, for example, have used habituation as the basis for proposing theories about the structure of basic learning and memory systems (Staddon, 1998; Wagner, 1981). A number of neuroscientists have used habituation and sensitization as tools for mapping out the fundamental neural mechanisms of learning (Cleary, Lee, & Byrne, 1998; Rankin, 2002). Developmental psychologists have used habituation as an experimental technique for making inferences about infants' perceptions (Bornstein, 1992). For example, Easterbrook, Kisilevsky, Muir, and Laplante (1999) at Nipissing University repeatedly presented pictures of faces to one- to three-day-old infants. At first, the infants tended to look at each face quite a bit, but after a while they habituated to the faces and spent little time looking at them. The researchers then presented either yet another picture of a face or a picture that included facial features in scrambled positions (e.g., an eye below an ear, with a mouth to the side). The infants who were shown another normal face appeared uninterested, but those shown the scrambled face looked at it for quite a while, revealing that they perceived it as different from a nonscrambled face. Their habituation to photos of faces set the stage for the infants to reveal that they perceived the structure of faces.

As adaptive organisms, humans rely on simple learning processes, such as habituation, to adapt to the environment. The world is full of events to be noticed, far more than anyone can ever hope to monitor with conscious attention. Orienting responses help people notice the new and unusual, but through habituation we learn to ignore things that are repeated and are of little consequence. This helps solve a very important problem—how to be selective about the events that occur and recur in the world. However, there is more to learning than just noticing and ignoring events; it is also important to learn about relationships between events, as you'll see in the next section.

Test Yourself

Check your knowledge about noticing and ignoring by choosing the best answer for each of the following descriptions. Choose from the following terms: habituation, orienting response, sensitization. (The answers are in Appendix B.)

1. When Shawn practises his trumpet, he tries repeatedly to hit a high C note. The first time he tries, his roommate says nothing. By the third try, his roommate is banging on the door telling him to be quiet: _____

2. First-time driver Alonda reacts by screaming and slamming on the brakes when a passing car horn sounds: _____

3. Kesha loves clocks and has six different varieties in her apartment. Strangely, she rarely notices the ticking noises: _____

4. Your cat, Comet, used to jump about a metre in the air whenever you ground your gourmet coffee beans in the morning. Now he never seems to notice: _____

5. Drug users often develop tolerance, in that they need larger and larger doses of the drug to achieve the same effects. Tolerance may be considered an example of _____.

▶ Learning What Events Signal: Classical Conditioning

LEARNING GOALS

1. Be able to describe how the connection between a conditioned stimulus and an unconditioned stimulus is acquired.
2. Understand and discuss how and why conditioned responding develops.
3. Be able to explain the concept of second-order conditioning.
4. Understand and be able to differentiate between the concepts of stimulus generalization and stimulus discrimination.
5. Understand and explain the extinction of a conditioned response.
6. Learn about conditioned inhibition.

What happens shortly after a bolt of lightning flashes across a stormy sky? If you pour milk into your coffee and little white lumps float to the top, how's it going to taste? If you drink it anyway, how will your stomach react? In each of these cases, you've learned an association between two events; more specifically, you've learned that one event signals the likely subsequent occurrence of the other. This knowledge is adaptive because it allows you to prepare yourself for future events: You know to cover your ears or to avoid drinking the java. In this section, we'll consider how simple associations like these are learned and how they affect behaviour.

The scientific study of associations began in the early years of the twentieth century in the laboratory of a Russian physiologist named Ivan P. Pavlov (1849–1936). Pavlov developed a technique, now known as **classical conditioning,** to investigate how animals form associations between different environmental events. Pavlov didn't start with a plan to study learning. His main interest was in digestion, including salivation. Mammals (including humans) salivate when they eat, and saliva contains chemicals that help in the initial stages of digestion. Pavlov aimed to investigate the relation between various kinds of food and saliva production by putting particular kinds of food in dogs' mouths and measuring their salivary responses. Much to his annoyance, however, Pavlov found that his dogs often began to drool long before the food was placed in their mouths. Pavlov referred to these premature droolings as "psychic" secretions, and he began to study why they occurred, in part with the hope of learning how to eliminate this phenomenon in future studies of digestion.

classical conditioning

A set of procedures, initially developed by Pavlov, used to investigate how organisms learn about the signalling properties of events; leads to the learning of relations between events—conditioned and unconditioned stimuli—that occur outside of our control

CRITICAL THINKING

Can you think of any reason why it might be adaptive to begin the digestive processes before food actually gets into the mouth?

The Terminology of Classical Conditioning

Pavlov observed that psychic secretions developed as a result of experience. He assumed that, in contrast, drooling in response to food itself is not a learned response. That is, he proposed that certain kinds of stimuli, which he called **unconditioned stimuli (US)**, automatically lead to responses, which he called **unconditioned responses (URs)**. For example, food is an unconditioned stimulus that automatically produces salivation as an unconditioned response. Neither dogs nor humans need to be taught to drool when food is placed in their mouths; this response is a reflex similar to the jerking of your leg when tapped just below the knee. The occurrence of an unconditioned response (salivation) after presentation of an unconditioned stimulus (food in the mouth) is *unconditioned*—that is, no learning, or conditioning, is required.

The problem facing Pavlov was that his dogs began to drool merely at the *sight* of the food dish or at the sound of a food-bearing assistant entering the room. Food dishes and the footsteps of arriving assistants are not unconditioned stimuli that automatically cause a dog to salivate. Drooling in response to such stimuli is learned; it is *conditioned*, or acquired as a result of experience. For this reason, Pavlov referred to the psychic secretions as **conditioned responses (CRs)** and to the stimuli that produced them as **conditioned stimuli (CS)**.

Let's take footsteps as an example. The sound of an approaching feeder leads to the dog's drooling because the dog has learned that the sound *signals* the appearance of the food. Over time, footsteps and food come to bear a special relation to each other: When the footsteps are heard, the food is soon to arrive. To use Pavlov's terminology, the footsteps act as a conditioned stimulus that produces salivation, a conditioned response, in anticipation of food. This is what happens to you when your mouth begins to water as your waiter arrives with a delicious-looking meal. Conditioned stimuli typically lead to conditioned responses after the conditioned stimulus and the unconditioned stimulus have been paired together in time—the footsteps (the CS) reliably occur just before presentation of the food (the US). However, as you'll see shortly, simply pairing two events together does not always lead to the formation of this kind of association.

unconditioned stimulus (US)

A stimulus that automatically produces—or elicits—an observable response prior to any training

unconditioned response (UR)

The observable response that is produced automatically, before training, on presentation of an unconditioned stimulus

conditioned response (CR)

The acquired response that is produced to the conditioned stimulus in anticipation of the arrival of the unconditioned stimulus; often resembles the unconditioned response, although not always

conditioned stimulus (CS)

A neutral stimulus (one that does not produce the unconditioned response before training) that is paired with the unconditioned stimulus during classical conditioning and thereby comes to give rise to a conditioned response

In the summer of 1934, the Russian physiologist Ivan Pavlov watched one of his experiments on "psychic" secretions in dogs. Notice the dog's cheek, which is fitted with a device for measuring salivation.

Sovfoto

What Mechanisms Underlie Classical Conditioning?

Why should dogs drool in response to footsteps? At one time psychologists believed that the pairing of the conditioned stimulus and the unconditioned stimulus simply caused the unconditioned response to shift to the conditioned stimulus, in an automatic, mechanical manner. Pavlov, for example, was convinced that the conditioned stimulus came to act as a substitute for the unconditioned stimulus—organisms would respond to the conditioned stimulus as if it were the unconditioned stimulus. Over the last several decades, however, a number of experimental findings have shown that the traditional stimulus-substitution view of classical conditioning is incorrect.

One challenge to the traditional view of conditioning is that the response to the conditioned stimulus depends not only on the unconditioned stimulus, but also on the properties of the conditioned stimulus itself (Holland, 1977; Rescorla, 1988). For example, pigeons will quickly learn to peck (CR) a lighted disk (CS) that signals food (US) but will show little or no change in behaviour to a tone that predicts food (Nairne & Rescorla, 1981). The to-be-conditioned stimulus must be appropriate for the association to be learned, suggesting that conditioning cannot be explained in terms of a passive, mechanical process by which the CS becomes a substitute for the US as an automatic consequence of being paired with it.

Also, for an effective association to form, the conditioned stimulus needs to be presented *before* the unconditioned stimulus. If the two are presented at the same time (*simultaneous conditioning*), or if the conditioned stimulus is presented after the unconditioned stimulus (*backward conditioning*), little evidence of conditioning will be found. In both of these cases, the conditioned stimulus provides no information about when the unconditioned stimulus will appear, so conditioned responding does not develop (although this general rule has some exceptions: see, for example, Matzel, Held, & Miller, 1988; Rescorla, 1980).

It's also interesting that the unconditioned stimulus needs to follow the conditioned stimulus *closely in time*. Pavlov found that if there is a long delay between when the bell (CS) is struck and when the food (US) is delivered, dogs usually don't form a connection between the bell and the food (see ▶ Figure 6.2). As the gap between presentation of the conditioned stimulus and presentation of the unconditioned stimulus increases, one becomes a less efficient signal for the arrival of the other—that is, the conditioned stimulus provides less useful information about the appearance of the unconditioned stimulus. Once again, there are exceptions to the rule (DeCola & Fanselow, 1995; Gallistel & Gibbon, 2000; Williams, Frame, & LoLordo, 1991), but generally if the gap between the conditioned stimulus and the unconditioned stimulus is long, only a weak association forms.

One of the greatest challenges to the view that classically conditioned associations arise passively was a study that Leon Kamin conducted at McMaster University (1968). The conditioned stimulus needs to provide *new* information about the occurrence of the unconditioned stimulus. If the environment already has stimuli that signal the unconditioned stimulus, then presenting an additional stimulus before the unconditioned stimulus leads to little or no learning. For example, Kamin conditioned rats by preceding a mild electric shock with a tone. After the rats had acquired that association, they completed trials in which a shock was preceded by both a tone and a light. The rats never developed a CR to the light (even though a control condition showed that they were perfectly capable of doing so if they hadn't previously learned the tone-shock association). This result is called *blocking* because the tone appears to block acquisition of a CR to the light. The light is always presented just before the shock, but no conditioning occurs. Why? Because the light provides no new information about the occurrence of the shock—the tone already tells the rat that the shock is about to occur, so the rat learns nothing about the light.

CRITICAL THINKING

Why do you think it's adaptive to learn associations only when the conditioned stimulus provides new information about the unconditioned stimulus? Can you think of any situations in which it might be useful to learn that many stimuli predict the appearance of the unconditioned stimulus?

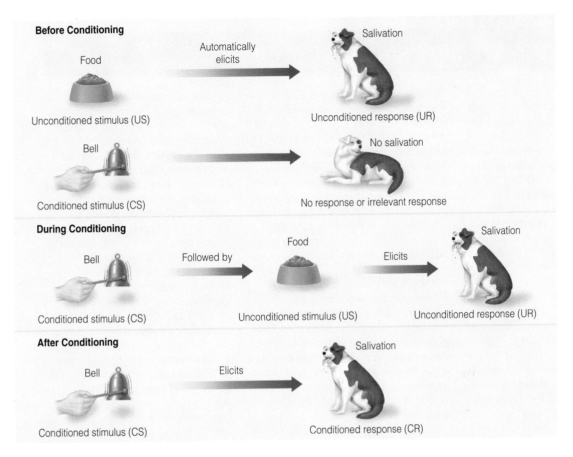

Before Conditioning

Food
Automatically elicits → Salivation

Unconditioned stimulus (US)   Unconditioned response (UR)

Bell
→ No salivation

Conditioned stimulus (CS)   No response or irrelevant response

During Conditioning

Bell
Followed by → Food
Elicits → Salivation

Conditioned stimulus (CS)   Unconditioned stimulus (US)   Unconditioned response (UR)

After Conditioning

Bell
Elicits → Salivation

Conditioned stimulus (CS)   Conditioned response (CR)

▶ **Figure 6.2**

Classical Conditioning

Through classical conditioning, organisms learn about the signalling properties of events. The presentation of an unconditioned stimulus (US) leads to an automatic unconditioned response (UR) before training. A neutral stimulus (one that does not produce a relevant response before conditioning) is paired closely in time with a US. Eventually, the animal learns that this conditioned stimulus (CS) predicts the occurrence of the US and begins to show an appropriate conditioned response (CR) on presentation of the CS.

Such findings as these have been taken as evidence for what is sometimes called the "cognitive" view of conditioning. Through classical conditioning animals learn that one event signals another event when the first event uniquely predicts, or provides information about, the second event. Rats and people don't acquire associations between conditioned stimuli and unconditioned stimuli in a *passive* way, through the simple pairing of the events in time. Rather, they actively process information in their environments—they seek to establish when events predict the occurrence of other events. Because the conditioned stimulus informs the animal that a significant event is about to occur, the animal responds in a way that is appropriate for the upcoming event. Learning such relations among events can be quite adaptive, as the Practical Solutions box discusses.

Second-Order Conditioning

In addition to discovering the basic phenomenon of classical conditioning, Pavlov found that a conditioned stimulus can be used to condition a second signal. In **second-order conditioning** an established conditioned stimulus,

second-order conditioning

A procedure in which an established conditioned stimulus is used to condition a second neutral stimulus

PRACTICAL SOLUTIONS

DEVELOPING TASTE AVERSIONS

On St. Thomas in the Virgin Islands, researchers Lowell Nicolaus and David Nellis encouraged captured mongooses to eat eggs laced with carbachol, a drug that produces temporary illness. The mongooses were hungry, but over a period of days they dramatically reduced their consumption of the tainted eggs (Nicolaus & Nellis, 1987). In research conducted in a different domain, children undergoing treatment for cancer ate ice cream flavoured with quinine (which has a very bitter taste) just before the onset of chemotherapy. Chemotherapy typically causes nausea and vomiting. Several weeks later, when offered the ice cream, only 21% of the children were willing to taste it again (Bernstein, 1978).

Both of these situations represent naturalistic applications of classical conditioning. Can you identify the critical features of each? How do these two examples involve the learning of a relation between two events, a conditioned stimulus and an unconditioned stimulus, that largely occurs outside the organism's control? First, let's look for the unconditioned stimulus—the stimulus that unconditionally produces a response before training. In both of these cases, the unconditioned stimulus is the illness-producing event, either the drug carbachol or the cancer-fighting chemotherapy. The response that is automatically produced, unfortunately for the participants, is stomach distress. Children don't need to learn to vomit from chemotherapy; a mongoose doesn't need to be taught to be sick after receiving carbachol. These are inevitable consequences that require no prior conditioning.

Now, what is the conditioned stimulus—the event that provides information about the occurrence of the unconditioned stimulus? In these examples, it is the taste of the food (the eggs or the ice cream) that signals the later onset of nausea. A conditioned response, feelings of queasiness, was produced whenever the opportunity to eat that food was presented. Taste aversions are easy to acquire and are sometimes learned after a single pairing

of a distinctive, novel food and illness. You may have conditioned taste aversions of your own.

Why would anyone want to do research studies like these? What possible value or relevance would such studies have? For one thing, it is extremely adaptive for people and mongooses to acquire taste aversions to potentially dangerous foods—it is in their interest to avoid those events that signal something potentially harmful—and discovering the principles and mechanisms that underlie such learning is a legitimate scientific aim. Moreover, in the two studies we've just considered, the researchers investigated the aversions for particular reasons. Mongooses often eat the eggs of endangered species (such as marine turtles). By baiting the nests of mongoose prey with tainted eggs and establishing a taste aversion, scientists reduced the overall rate of egg predation. Similar techniques have also been used to prevent sheep from eating dangerous plants in the pasture (Zahorik, Houpt, & Swartzman-Andert, 1990).

In the case of chemotherapy, Illene Bernstein was interested in developing methods for *avoiding* the establishment

of taste aversions: Cancer patients who are undergoing chemotherapy also need to eat, so it's critical to understand the conditions under which aversions are formed. Taste aversions often develop as a side effect of chemotherapy. Patients tend to avoid foods that they consumed just before treatment, potentially leading to weight loss, which impedes recovery. Researchers have found that associations are particularly likely to form between *unusual* tastes and nausea. Broberg and Bernstein (1987), for example, found that giving children an unusual flavour of candy just before treatment reduced the likelihood of their forming aversions to healthy parts of their normal diet. These children formed a taste aversion to the unusual candy rather than to their normal diet. Another helpful technique in preventing taste aversions from developing is to ask the patient to eat a very familiar, preferably bland, food before every treatment. Foods that do not have distinctive tastes and that people eat regularly (such as bread) are less likely to elicit taste aversions.

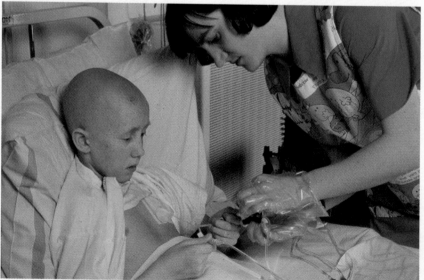

For children undergoing the rigours of chemotherapy, like this young boy who has leukemia, it's important to prevent taste aversions to healthy foods from developing as a negative side effect of the treatment. Broberg and Bernstein (1987) found that giving children an unusual flavour of candy just before treatment reduced the chances of a taste aversion forming to their normal diet.

CONCEPT SUMMARY

FACTORS AFFECTING CLASSICAL CONDITIONING

Factor	Relation to Conditioning Effectiveness
Appropriateness of CS	It is easier to condition a response to some conditioned stimuli than to others; prior experience may predispose animals to learn some associations more readily than they learn others.
Sequential relationship between conditioned stimulus and unconditioned stimulus	The conditioned stimulus should be presented *before* the unconditioned stimulus, not at the same time or after.
Temporal proximity of the CS and US	The unconditioned stimulus should follow the conditioned stimulus closely in time.
Informativeness of conditioned stimulus	The conditioned stimulus should provide new information about the occurrence of the unconditioned stimulus (to avoid blocking).

such as a tone that predicts food, is presented immediately *after* a new event, such as a light; the unconditioned stimulus itself is never actually presented. Several pairings of the tone with the light can be sufficient to produce conditioned responding to the light.

An example from Pavlov's laboratory helps to illustrate the procedure. One of Pavlov's associates, Dr. Frolov, first taught a dog that the sound of a ticking metronome signalled the application of meat powder in the mouth. The dog quickly started to drool in the presence of the ticking. A black square was then presented, followed closely by the ticking. After a number of these black square–metronome pairings, even though the ticking was never followed by food powder on these trials, the dog began to drool in the presence of the black square. The dog drooled in response to the square because it signalled the ticking, which the dog had previously learned signalled the food (see ◗ Figure 6.3).

◗ Figure 6.3

Second-Order Conditioning

In second-order conditioning, an established CS is used in place of a US to condition a second signal. In Dr. Frolov's experiment, a ticking metronome was first paired with food; after repeated pairings, the ticking elicited salivation as a CR. Next, a black square—which did not produce salivation initially—was paired with the ticking (no US was presented). After repeated pairings, the presentation of the black square produced salivation.

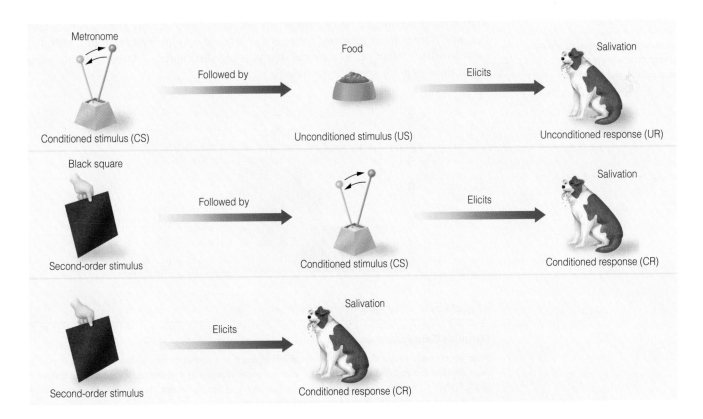

Metronome   Followed by   Food   Elicits   Salivation

Conditioned stimulus (CS)   Unconditioned stimulus (US)   Unconditioned response (UR)

Black square   Followed by   Elicits   Salivation

Second-order stimulus   Conditioned stimulus (CS)   Conditioned response (CR)

Second-order stimulus   Elicits   Salivation   Conditioned response (CR)

CRITICAL   THINKING

After reading about stimulus generalization, can you understand why some psychologists believe that certain psychological problems, such as specific fears called phobias, might result from learning experiences?

The fact that conditioned stimuli can be used to condition responses to other events is important because it greatly expands the number of situations in which classical conditioning applies. It is not necessary for an unconditioned stimulus to be physically present in a situation for you to learn something about the relationship between that situation and the likely occurrence of that US. Advertisers regularly use second-order conditioning to sell products. One example is the use of celebrities to endorse products. If the celebrity is an expert on the product being sold (e.g., Wayne Gretzky selling hockey equipment), then the endorsement makes sense on rational grounds. Often, however, the celebrity has no particular expertise related to the product being sold (e.g., Wayne Gretzky selling cars), and advertisers hope that prior associations between the celebrity and good feelings will, via second-order conditioning, create associations between their product and those good feelings.

Stimulus Generalization

Pavlov also discovered that a response conditioned to one stimulus tended to generalize to other, similar stimuli. If a bell with a particular pitch was conditioned as a signal for food, another bell that sounded similar also produced salivation—even though the dog had never before heard the second bell. When a new stimulus produces a response similar to the CR produced by the conditioned stimulus, **stimulus generalization** has occurred.

stimulus generalization

Responding to a new stimulus in a way similar to the response produced by an established conditioned stimulus

As a rule, stimulus generalization occurs when a new stimulus is similar to the conditioned stimulus (see ▶ Figure 6.4). If you get sick after eating clams, the chances are good that you'll later avoid eating oysters and mussels too; if you've had a bad experience in the dentist's chair, the sound of a neighbour's high-speed drill may make you uncomfortable. Generalization makes adaptive sense: Things that look, sound, or feel similar often share significant properties. It really doesn't matter whether it's a tiger, a lion, or a panther leaping at you—you should run.

Stimulus Discrimination

stimulus discrimination

Responding to a new stimulus in a way that is different from the response to an established conditioned stimulus

Stimulus discrimination occurs when you respond to a new stimulus in a way that is different from your response to the original conditioned stimulus. Through stimulus discrimination, you reveal that you can distinguish between stimuli, even when those stimuli are quite similar.

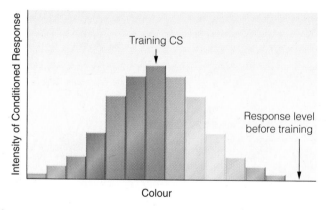

▶ **Figure 6.4**

Stimulus Generalization

After conditioned responding to a CS is established, another stimulus similar to the CS will often produce conditioned responding, too, through stimulus generalization. For example, if a red light is trained as a CS, then an orange light will also produce responding if tested. Notice that the less similar the new stimulus is to the trained CS, the less generalization occurs.

When stimuli do share properties—for example, two tones of a similar pitch—people often need experience to learn to discriminate. The natural tendency is to generalize—that is, to treat similar things in the same way. Because of this tendency to generalize, it typically takes many experiences to learn to discriminate between highly similar stimuli. For example, if one bell predicts food and a slightly different-sounding bell does not, at first the animal will respond as though both bells predict food; only after multiple trials does the animal demonstrate stimulus discrimination, responding only to the bell that predicts food. Also, the more similar the two bells are, the longer it takes for the animal to learn to discriminate between them. The same holds for humans. For example, one of the authors of this text was bitten, as a child, by a Pekinese dog; for a while afterward he was nervous about all dogs (generalization), but repeated positive experiences with other sorts of dogs led to discrimination; he never had much to do with Pekinese and still doesn't care for them.

Conditioning and Drug Tolerance   Earlier we discussed *drug tolerance* (i.e., decreasing effects of a drug as a function of repeated use) as an example of habituation. An alternative explanation, championed by Shepard Siegel and co-workers at McMaster University, describes tolerance in terms of classical conditioning (Siegel, 2005). Siegel's approach treats the immediate effects of a drug (say, physiological arousal caused by cocaine) as a US. He also assumes that certain USs give rise to automatic *compensatory responses*, which are URs that oppose the effects of a drug so as to return the body to baseline or homeostasis. So, for example, in response to a sudden increase in heart rate (US) your body releases chemicals that tend to reduce heart rate (UR). Over multiple administrations of a drug, the UR comes to be conditioned to environmental stimuli that co-occur with the drug, such as the sight of drug paraphernalia. Consequently, such environmental stimuli become CSs and the compensatory response is launched as a CR before the drug even enters the system, thereby reducing the drug effect.

One piece of evidence supporting this view is that habitual users of a drug are more likely to overdose if they take the drug in an unusual setting or in a novel way. The novelty of the setting or manner of taking the drug reduces its efficacy as a CS, such that a weaker CR occurs. If the CR is weak, it cannot prepare the body adequately for the full effect of the drug, and this lack of preparation can have fatal consequences. Debate continues as to how best to explain drug tolerance, and it may well be that multiple mechanisms contribute to it, but good evidence shows conditioning plays at least some role in its development (e.g., Ramsay & Woods, 1997).

Extinction: When Conditioned Stimuli No Longer Signal the Unconditioned Stimuli

Remember our general rule: A conditioned stimulus becomes a good signal when it provides *information* about the occurrence of the unconditioned stimulus. So what happens when the conditioned stimulus stops predicting the appearance of an unconditioned stimulus? In the procedure of **extinction,** after a conditioned response has been acquired the conditioned stimulus is presented repeatedly without being followed by presentation of the unconditioned stimulus. Under these conditions, the conditioned stimulus gradually loses its signalling properties because it stops predicting the appearance of the unconditioned stimulus. Not surprisingly, conditioned responding gradually diminishes as a result.

Notice the similarity between the procedure of extinction and the concept of habituation. Both involve the repeated presentation of an event accompanied by a gradual loss in responding. The difference between them is that extinction involves a loss in responding that has been acquired as a result of conditioning—you change

extinction

Presenting a conditioned stimulus repeatedly, after conditioning, without the unconditioned stimulus, resulting in a gradual loss of the conditioned response

your behaviour because the conditioned stimulus no longer signals the presence of another significant event. In habituation, no prior learning or conditioning is required to produce the changes that result from repeated exposure. You naturally orient toward sudden changes in your environment—no learning is required—but you'll learn to ignore those events that repeatedly occur without significant consequence.

Spontaneous Recovery   Sometimes conditioned responding that has disappeared as a result of extinction will recover spontaneously with the passage of time during which the CS is not presented. This phenomenon is known as **spontaneous recovery** (see ❭ Figure 6.5). For example, Pavlov's dogs stopped drooling if a bell that had previously signalled food was repeatedly presented alone, but when the bell was rung again the day after extinction, the conditioned response reappeared (although often not as strongly). Spontaneous recovery is another example of why it is important to distinguish between learning and performance. At the end of extinction, the conditioned stimulus seems to have lost its signalling properties, but when it is tested after a delay, we see that at least some of the learning remained (see also Bouton, 1991; Brooks, 2000).

Conditioned Inhibition: Signalling the Absence of an Unconditioned Stimulus

In the conditioning phenomena discussed so far, the organism learns that a previously neutral stimulus predicts the subsequent occurrence of an unconditioned stimulus (or, via extinction, gradually loses that association). Animals can also

spontaneous recovery

The recovery of an extinguished conditioned response after a period without exposure to the conditioned stimulus

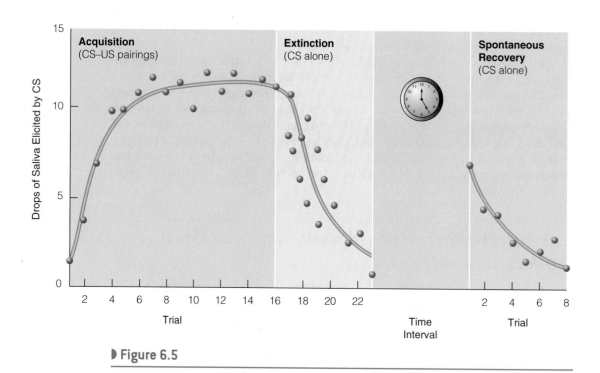

❭ **Figure 6.5**

Training, Extinction, and Spontaneous Recovery

During training, Pavlov found that the amount of salivation produced in response to the CS increased and then levelled off as a function of the number of CS–US pairings. During extinction, the CS is repeatedly presented without the US, and conditioned responding gradually diminishes. If no testing of the CS occurs for a rest interval following extinction, spontaneous recovery of the CR will often occur when the CS is presented again.

acquire **conditioned inhibition;** that is, they can learn to associate a previously neutral stimulus with the non-occurrence of an unconditioned stimulus. In the procedure illustrated in ❭ Figure 6.6, for example, a pigeon has been trained to associate the presence of a green light with the availability of food (a standard conditioned response) and so approaches the food hopper whenever it is hungry and the green light is on; the pigeon has also been trained, however, to associate a red light with the absence of food.

Typically, inhibitory conditioning produces a response that is opposite to the response that would be elicited by a CS that predicts the US. For example, after repeated pairings of a red light with the absence of food, a pigeon will actively move away from the food hopper when the red light is on (Hearst & Franklin, 1977; Jenkins, Barrera, Ireland, & Woodside, 1978). Note that it is just as adaptive to learn that a significant event will *not* occur under one set of conditions as it is to learn that it will occur under another. For example, the sight of troublemaker Randy might usually make Justin quake with fear and avoid the playground—but not if a teacher is around. The teacher signals the absence of a threat. In nature, inhibitory stimuli often act as "safety" signals, telling people or other animals when potential dangers are likely to be absent.

> **conditioned inhibition**
>
> Learning to associate a previously neutral stimulus with the absence of an unconditioned stimulus

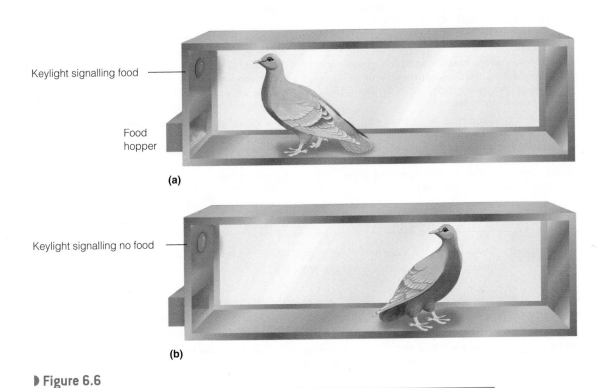

Keylight signalling food

Food hopper

(a)

Keylight signalling no food

(b)

❭ **Figure 6.6**

Conditioned Inhibition

The top panel illustrates a standard classical conditioned response: A green light has been repeatedly paired with the presence of food, and the pigeon has learned to associate the green light with availability of food and so approaches the hopper when the green light is on. The lower panel illustrates a conditioned inhibition response: A red light has repeatedly been paired with the absence of food, and the pigeon has learned to associate the red light with the lack of food and so moves away from the hopper when the red light is on.

CONCEPT SUMMARY

MAJOR PHENOMENA OF CLASSICAL CONDITIONING

Phenomenon	Description	Example: Pavlov's Dogs
Second-order conditioning	An established conditioned stimulus is presented immediately following a new event; after several pairings, the new event elicits the conditioned response.	After a dog has been conditioned to salivate in response to a conditioned stimulus (tone), the conditioned stimulus is presented immediately following a new signal (e.g., a light). After several pairings, the light then may come to elicit responding.
Stimulus generalization	A new stimulus that is similar to a conditioned stimulus produces a response similar to the one produced by the conditioned stimulus.	After a dog has been conditioned to salivate in response to a conditioned stimulus (e.g., a red light), the same response may be produced by a similar stimulus (e.g., an orange or purple light).
Stimulus discrimination	The response to a new stimulus is different from the response to the original conditioned stimulus.	After a dog has been conditioned to salivate in response to a conditioned stimulus (light), the response does not occur to a different stimulus, such as a ringing bell.
Extinction	Conditioned responding diminishes when the conditioned stimulus (after conditioning) is presented without being followed by the unconditioned stimulus.	After a dog has been conditioned to salivate in response to a conditioned stimulus (tone), the tone is presented repeatedly without the unconditioned stimulus (food). Responding to the conditioned stimulus lessens.
Spontaneous recovery	Conditioned responding that has disappeared in extinction recovers spontaneously with the passage of a period during which the conditioned stimulus is not presented.	After extinction, a dog no longer responds to the conditioned stimulus (tone). After a rest period, the dog once again will respond when presented with the conditioned stimulus (tone).
Conditioned inhibition	A stimulus that is repeatedly paired with the absence of an unconditioned stimulus leads to responding that is opposite in direction to that of the conditioned response that would be elicited by a conditioned stimulus that signals the presence of that unconditioned stimulus.	After repeated trials in which a red light signals the absence of meat powder, the dog produces even less saliva when a red light is turned on than it would normally do in the absence of any relevant stimuli.

Test Yourself 6.2

Check your knowledge about classical conditioning by answering the following questions. (The answers are in Appendix B.)

1. Growing up, your little sister, Leah, had the annoying habit of screaming, at the top of her lungs, every time she stepped into her bath water. Her screaming always made you wince and cover your ears. Now, years later, you still wince every time you hear running water. Identify the
   a. unconditioned stimulus: _____
   b. unconditioned response: _____
   c. conditioned stimulus: _____
   d. conditioned response: _____

2. Every two years when you visit the optometrist, you get a puff of air blown into your eye to test for glaucoma. It always makes you blink. Just before the puff is delivered, the doctor typically asks you if you're "ready." Now, whenever you hear that word, you feel an urge to blink. Identify the
   a. unconditioned stimulus: _____
   b. unconditioned response: _____
   c. conditioned stimulus: _____
   d. conditioned response: _____

3. A boy is repeatedly frightened by his neighbour's large dogs and soon begins to cry whenever he looks at the neighbour's yard, even if the dogs are not there. The neighbours (and their dogs) move away, and within a year the boy does not cry anymore when he looks at the yard. Which of the following probably best accounts for this development?
   a. Habituation
   b. Stimulus generalization
   c. Spontaneous recovery
   d. Extinction
   e. Inhibitory conditioning

4. You give your dog, Rascal, scraps from the table, except when your grandmother (who thinks this shows deplorable manners) is visiting. Normally, Rascal stays close to the table at dinnertime, but when Grandma visits, Rascal sprawls in the kitchen. Which of the following best fits this phenomenon?
   a. Habituation
   b. Stimulus generalization
   c. Spontaneous recovery
   d. Extinction
   e. Inhibitory conditioning

▶ Learning about the Consequences of Behaviour: Instrumental Conditioning

LEARNING GOALS

1. Be able to define instrumental conditioning, and discuss the law of effect.
2. Learn about B. F. Skinner's theoretical approach to psychology, which he called "radical behaviourism."
3. Be able to explain what is meant by the term "discriminative stimulus."
4. Understand the concept of reinforcement, and be able to distinguish between positive and negative reinforcement.
5. Be able to discuss different schedules of reinforcement, and compare their effects on behaviour.
6. Grasp how complex behaviours can be acquired through shaping.
7. Be able to describe the practical applications of instrumental conditioning and shaping.
8. Understand how biological factors may limit the responses that can be learned.
9. Be able to define punishment, and learn to distinguish between positive and negative punishment.
10. Be able to describe the practical applications of punishment.

Classical conditioning answers an important survival question: How do we learn that certain events signal the presence or the absence of other events? Through the processes tapped by classical conditioning, we learn to expect that certain events will or will not occur under certain conditions, and we react accordingly. Note that our actions under these conditions don't necessarily have any effect on the pairing of the signal and the unconditioned stimulus. Usually, occurrences of the conditioned stimulus and the unconditioned stimulus are outside our control. For example, you can't change the fact that thunder will follow lightning; all you can do is prepare for an event (thunder) when a prior event (lightning) tells you it's coming.

In another type of learning, studied through a procedure called **instrumental conditioning** (or **operant conditioning**), we learn that our own *actions*, rather than conditioned stimuli, lead to outcomes. If a child is given a treat as a reward for cleaning her room, she learns that her behaviour is *instrumental* in producing rewards; by *operating* on her environment, she produces a pleasing consequence. Instrumental (or operant) learning involves learning about the consequences of behaviour. Notice how classical conditioning differs from instrumental conditioning: In the former, you learn that events signal outcomes; in the latter, you learn that your own actions or behaviours produce outcomes (see ▶ Figure 6.7).

instrumental or operant conditioning

A procedure for studying how organisms learn about the consequences of their own voluntary actions: their behaviours are instrumental in producing rewards and punishments

▶ Figure 6.7

Classical versus Instrumental Conditioning

In classical conditioning, panel (a), food is delivered independently of the rat's behaviour. The light (CS) signals the automatic arrival of the food (US). In instrumental conditioning, panel (b), the rat must press the bar in the presence of the light to get the food (i.e., food is delivered to the hopper when the bar is pressed when the light is on). The light serves as a *discriminative stimulus* telling the rat that pressing the bar will now produce the food.

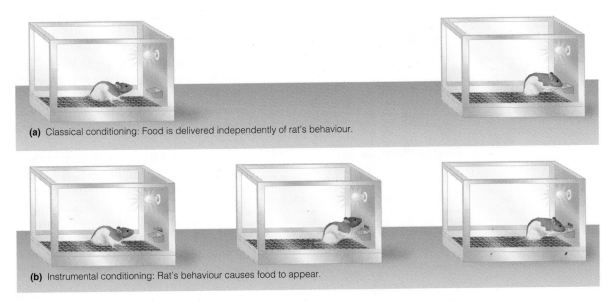

(a) Classical conditioning: Food is delivered independently of rat's behaviour.

(b) Instrumental conditioning: Rat's behaviour causes food to appear.

The Law of Effect

The study of instrumental conditioning predates Pavlov's historic work by several years. In 1895, Harvard graduate student Edward Lee Thorndike (1874–1949), working in the cellar of his mentor William James's home, began a series of experiments on "animal intelligence" by using cats from around the neighbourhood. He built a puzzle box, which resembled a tiny prison, and carefully recorded the time it took for the cats to escape. The boxes were designed so that escape was possible only through an unusual response, such as tilting a pole, pulling a string, or pressing a lever (see ▶ Figure 6.8). On release, the cats received a small amount of food as a reward.

Thorndike deliberately selected escape responses that were unlikely to occur when the animals were first placed in the box. In this way, he could observe how the cats learned to escape over time. Through trial and error, the cats eventually learned to make the appropriate response, but the learning process was gradual. Thorndike also found that the time it took for an animal to escape on any particular trial depended on the number of prior successful escapes. The more times the animal had successfully escaped in the past, the faster it could get out of the box on a new trial.

The relationship between escape time and the number of prior successful escapes led Thorndike to formulate the **law of effect:** If a behaviour in a particular situation is followed by a satisfying or pleasant consequence, the behaviour will be strengthened (i.e., the probability of the animal performing that behaviour in that situation will increase); if a response in a particular situation is followed by an unsatisfying or unpleasant consequence, the response will be weakened (i.e., its probability will decrease). According to the law of effect, all organisms learn to make certain responses in certain situations; the responses that regularly occur are those that have produced positive consequences in the past. If a response tends to occur initially (e.g., scratching at the walls of the cage) but is not followed by something good (such as freedom from the box), the chances of that response occurring again in the situation diminish.

B. F. Skinner and "Radical Behaviourism"

As you may recall from Chapter 1, from the late 1920s to the late 1950s psychological science was dominated by behaviourism. Behaviourists built on the work of such pioneers as Pavlov and Thorndike in an effort to develop a science of psychology based solely on observable environmental events and measurable behaviours. Behaviourists disdained attempts to explain psychological phenomena in terms of internal mental constructs, such as "consciousness" or "insight," preferring to conduct research (often with animal subjects) aimed at establishing lawful relationships between environmental stimuli and behavioural responses.

Probably the most influential behaviourist after Thorndike was B. F. Skinner (1904–1990). Skinner was responsible for major advances in our understanding of the details of animal and human learning. He developed a perspective regarding the explanation of behaviour that he called **radical behaviourism** (Skinner, 1974). Unlike earlier behaviourists, Skinner did

---

law of effect

If a response in a particular situation is followed by a satisfying or pleasant consequence, the response will be strengthened; if a response in a particular situation is followed by an unsatisfying or unpleasant consequence, the response will be weakened

▶ **Figure 6.8**

Instrumental Conditioning

In Thorndike's famous experiments on animal intelligence, cats learned that an unusual response—such as pressing a lever or tilting a pole—allowed them to escape from a puzzle box. The graph shows that the time required to escape gradually diminished over learning trials. Here the cat is learning that its behaviour is instrumental in producing escape. (From *Psychology: Themes and Variations,* Third Edition, by W. Weiten. Copyright © 1995. Reprinted with permission of Wadsworth, a division of Thomson Learning: http://www.thomsonrights.com. Fax 800 730-2215.)

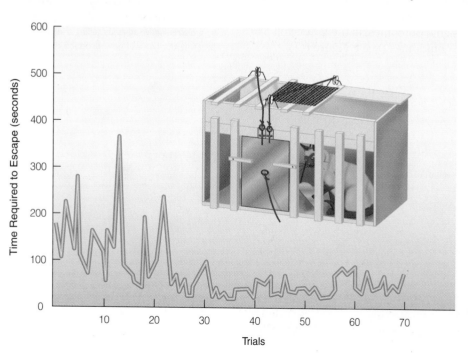

not completely rule out referring to private events like thoughts and feelings in explaining behaviour. Skinner argued that it is acceptable to speculate about events that take place "within the skin," as he put it, the things that only the person experiencing them can observe, as long as we treat them the same way we treat observable, public events—as physical in nature and subject to the same laws as external stimuli and behaviours.

As an example, Skinner talked about "conditioned seeing," as when a person listening to a particularly good recording of waves hitting a beach might "see," that is, imagine, the ocean waves crashing down on the shore. This "seeing" would be understood as involving some of the same brain activity as when we actually see waves when we're at the ocean. Skinner suggested that an event, such as a person "seeing" an ocean when there is no ocean there, should be treated just like any other behaviour. In this case, Skinner would claim that this covert "behaviour" is determined by exactly the same laws as the conditioned salivation in Pavlov's dogs, except that it's private rather than public.

Although Skinner allowed for a role of mental events in human behaviour, he was very cautious about making inferences about them. Instead, radical behaviourism emphasized the role of external, observable stimuli in influencing the behaviour of human and nonhuman animals. The idea was that an animal's behaviour can be understood as the product of that animal's history of reinforcement, as governed by the principles of classical and instrumental conditioning.

> **radical behaviourism**
>
> A perspective on the analysis of human and animal behaviour that emphasizes explaining behaviour in terms of environmental events and that minimizes the use of internal explanations, like thoughts, beliefs, and intentions

The Discriminative Stimulus: Knowing When to Respond

The law of effect tends to be situation specific. For example, if you are praised for raising your hand in class, your rate of raising your hand in class is likely to increase, but you're not likely to start raising your hand while walking down the street. What you've learned is something like the following: If some stimulus situation is present (the classroom) and you act in a certain way (raising your hand), then some reinforcing consequence (praise) is likely to follow.

Skinner (1938) referred to the situation as the **discriminative stimulus.** He suggested that a discriminative stimulus "sets the occasion" for a response to be rewarded. Being in class—the discriminative stimulus—sets the occasion for hand-raising to be rewarded. In some ways, the discriminative stimulus shares properties with the conditioned stimulus established in classical conditioning. For example, you often find *stimulus generalization* of a discriminative stimulus: If a pigeon is trained to peck a key in the presence of a red light, the bird will later peck the key more in the presence of a pink light than in the presence of a green light. If you're rewarded for asking questions in psychology class, you might naturally generalize your response to another course, such as economics, and raise your hand there. You might even find yourself raising your hand when you want to break into an animated conversation with friends outside the classroom. Conversely, *stimulus discrimination* also occurs, usually after experiencing reward in one situation but not in another. You may learn, for instance, that raising your hand in psychology class leads to positive consequences, but not in your economics class. In such a case, one setting (psychology) acts as an effective discriminative stimulus for a certain instrumental response, but another setting (economics) does not.

> **discriminative stimulus**
>
> The stimulus situation that sets the occasion for a response to be followed by reinforcement or punishment

Over the years, learning researchers have argued about exactly what is learned about the discriminative stimulus in instrumental conditioning, especially in studies with animal subjects. For example, if a rat is taught to press a lever to receive food, does the rat press the lever whenever it is there? Does the reward merely "stamp in" an association between a discriminative stimulus (the lever) and a response (pressing)? For many years, this was the traditional view in psychology: Instrumental conditioning leads to the formation of associations between stimuli and responses (Hull, 1943).

However, most psychologists now believe that more is learned in instrumental conditioning than simple connections between discriminative stimuli and responses. For example, it seems likely that the animal also learns something about the reward itself. Just as in classical conditioning, responding in the presence of the discriminative stimulus depends on how the animal feels about the reward—if a rat is taught to press a lever for a reward, and then the value of the reward is somehow changed, the rat will change its behaviour accordingly (Colwill & Rescorla, 1986). This suggests that the animal learns not only about the discriminative stimulus and the response but also about the specific reward that follows the response (Colwill, 1994).

Similarly, in recent years researchers have used instrumental conditioning procedures to explore other aspects of animals' "cognitive" processing of the learning experience. For instance, Marcia Spetch and Alinda Friedman at the University of Alberta (Spetch & Friedman, 2003) have used operant conditioning to explore differences and similarities in the ways humans versus pigeons perceive objects; and Santi, Weise, and Kuiper of Wilfrid Laurier University (1995) have used variations in the timing of the experimental procedures during conditioning trials to learn significant details about the memory systems of rats and pigeons. As another example, research conducted at Windsor University by Cohen, Simpson, Westlake, and Hamelin (2002) tested rats in sequences of operant conditioning trials, with reinforcement being provided on some trials but not on others (e.g., a rat might be reinforced for running a maze on trials 1 and 2 but not on trial 3 of a 3-trial sequence). After several such sequences, the rats run the maze more slowly on the nonreinforced trials, indicating that they have learned something about the temporal sequence of trials.

The Nature of Reinforcement

The law of effect states that responses will be strengthened if they are followed by a pleasant or satisfying consequence. By *strengthened*, Thorndike meant that a response was more likely to occur in the future in that particular situation. But what defines a pleasant or satisfying consequence? This is a tricky problem because the concept of a *pleasant* or *satisfying* event is highly personal—what's pleasant for me might not be pleasant for you. Moreover, something that's pleasing at one time might not be pleasing at another. Food, for example, is "positive at the beginning of Thanksgiving dinner, indifferent halfway through, and negative at the end of it" (Kimble, 1993). For these reasons, psychologists use a technical term—**reinforcement**—to describe consequences that increase the likelihood of responding. As you'll see, behavioural psychologists distinguish between two major types of reinforcement: *positive* and *negative*.

reinforcement

Response consequences that increase the likelihood of responding in a similar way again

Positive Reinforcement   Many behaviours have consequences. Some consequences increase the likelihood that the animal will repeat the behaviour; that is, some consequences reinforce performance of the behaviour that led to them. Such consequences are reinforcers. When the presentation of an event after a particular behaviour in a certain situation increases the likelihood of the behaviour being performed again in that situation, then that event was a **positive reinforcement.** Usually, positive reinforcers are *appetitive stimuli*—something the organism likes, needs, or has an "appetite" for. Food and water are obvious examples, but opportunities to perform behaviours can be reinforcing too (such as engaging in sexual activity or painting a picture). Such reinforcers are called "positive" because they are given to (rather than taken away from) the animal. Remember, though, it's not the subjective qualities of the consequence that matter from the behaviourist perspective—what matters in defining positive reinforcement is that it leads to an *increase* in the frequency of the behaviour that led to the reinforcement. As long as you're more likely to repeat a behaviour after receiving something as a consequence of performing that behaviour, then that consequence qualifies as positive reinforcement.

positive reinforcement

An event that, when *presented* after a response in a certain situation, increases the likelihood of that response occurring again in that situation

Negative Reinforcement   As we said above, a reinforcer is a consequence of a behaviour that increases the likelihood that the behaviour will be repeated. Positive reinforcement occurs when receiving something increases the likelihood of repeating the behaviour that led to that consequence. With **negative reinforcement,** in contrast, the *removal* of an event after a particular behaviour in a given situation increases the likelihood of that response occurring in that situation again. In most cases, negative reinforcement occurs when a response allows you to eliminate, avoid, or escape from an unpleasant situation. For instance, if you find that studying this text is unpleasantly difficult, then letting your mind drift while reading may be negatively reinforcing; mental drifting allows you to escape the unpleasant rigours of studying (see Schooler, Reichle, & Halpern, 2004, for research on "zoning out" while reading). To the extent you are negatively reinforced for zoning out, your rate of zoning out will tend to increase (which is why we do everything we can to make reading the text with comprehension as enjoyable as possible). The points here are that any reinforcer increases the rate of performing the behaviour that leads to that reinforcer and that a negative reinforcer is something whose removal increases performance of the behaviour that led to that removal.

Students are often confused by the term *negative reinforcement* because they think negative reinforcement is a bad thing. Whenever psychologists use the term *reinforcement*, both positive and negative, they are referring to outcomes that increase the probability of responding. The terms *positive* and *negative* simply refer to whether the response increases because of the presentation of something (positive) or because of the removal of something (negative). In both cases, the result is to reward or reinforce the contingent behaviour, and we can expect the response that produced the reinforcement to occur again in that situation.

Conditioned Reinforcers   Sometimes a stimulus can act as a reinforcer even though it seems to have no intrinsic value. For example, cash often serves as a powerful reinforcer, leading people to perform extravagantly arduous behaviours to get it (or to avoid losing it), even though it's only a well-made piece of paper marked with mildly interesting engravings. Money is useless in itself, but it predicts something of intrinsic value—you can buy things with it—and this is what gives it its reinforcing value. In the same way, if a stimulus predicts the removal of something negative, then its presentation is also likely to be reinforcing. Stimuli of this type are called **conditioned reinforcers** because their reinforcing properties are acquired through learning (they are also sometimes called "secondary" reinforcers to distinguish them from more "primary" reinforcers, such as food or water). These stimuli are reinforcing because they signal the presence or absence of other events that are themselves reinforcing.

negative reinforcement

An event that, when *removed* after a response in a situation, increases the likelihood of that response occurring in that situation again

CRITICAL   THINKING

Can you think of a case in which an unpleasant event increases the likelihood of the response that produces it?

CRITICAL   THINKING

When you study for an examination or try to do well in school, are you seeking positive reinforcement or negative reinforcement?

conditioned reinforcer

A stimulus that has acquired reinforcing properties through prior learning

CONCEPT SUMMARY

POSITIVE AND NEGATIVE REINFORCEMENT

Consequence	Description	Example
Positive reinforcement	The *presentation* of an event after a response increases the likelihood of the response occurring again.	Jean-Claude's parents reward him for cleaning his room by giving him $5. The presentation of $5 increases the likelihood that Jean-Claude will clean his room again.
Negative reinforcement	The *removal* of an event after a response increases the likelihood of the response occurring again.	Hannah's parents nag her continually about cleaning up her room. When she finally cleans her room, her parents stop nagging her. The removal of the nagging increases the probability that Hannah will clean her room again.

Schedules of Reinforcement

The law of effect implies that behaviours are more likely to be repeated if they are followed by positive or negative reinforcement. As in classical conditioning, however, the development of an instrumental response depends on how often, and when, the reinforcements are delivered. Instrumental learning is quickest if the situation makes it easy for the animal to link particular behaviours to particular consequences. If consequences occur in a haphazard way, learning can be slow or nonexistent (Dickinson & Charnock, 1985).

Many studies in the 1950s and 1960s explored the scheduling of reinforcements. A **schedule of reinforcement** is a rule used by the experimenter to determine when particular responses will be reinforced (Ferster & Skinner, 1957). If a response is followed rapidly by reinforcement every time it occurs, the reinforcement is said to be on a *continuous* schedule. If reinforcement is delivered only some of the time after the response has occurred, this is called a **partial reinforcement schedule.** There are four major types of partial reinforcement schedules: fixed ratio, variable ratio, fixed interval, and variable interval. Each produces a distinctive pattern of responding (see ▶ Figure 6.9).

schedule of reinforcement

A rule that an experimenter uses to determine when particular responses will be reinforced: in a continuous reinforcement schedule, a reward is delivered every time the target behaviour is performed; partial reinforcement schedules, in contrast, can be fixed or variable, and ratio or interval

partial reinforcement schedule

A schedule in which reinforcement is delivered only some of the time after the response has occurred

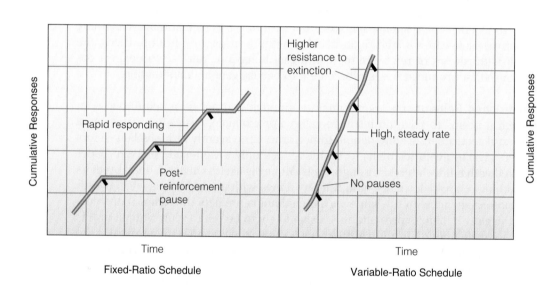

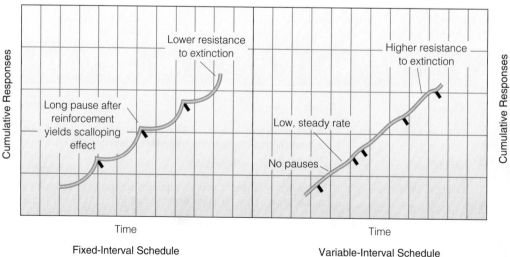

▶ **Figure 6.9**

Schedules of Reinforcement

Schedules of reinforcement are rules that the experimenter uses to determine when responses will be reinforced. Ratio schedules tend to produce rapid rates of responding because reinforcement depends on the number of responses. Interval schedules tend to produce lower rates of responding because reinforcement is delivered for only the first response after a specified time interval. In the cumulative response functions plotted here, the total number of responses is plotted over time. The short dark lines indicate delivery of reinforcement.

Fixed-Ratio Schedules   *Ratio* schedules of reinforcement require that you produce a certain *number* of responses before receiving reinforcement. In a **fixed-ratio schedule,** the number of required responses is fixed and doesn't change from one trial to the next. Suppose you are paid a dollar for every 100 envelopes you stuff for a local marketing firm. This schedule of reinforcement is referred to as an "FR 100" (fixed-ratio 100) because it requires 100 responses (envelopes stuffed) before the reinforcement is delivered (a dollar). You can stuff the envelopes as quickly as you like, but you must produce 100 responses before you get the reward.

Fixed-ratio schedules typically produce steady, consistent rates of responding because the relationship between the instrumental response and the reinforcement is clear and predictable. For this reason, assembly-line work in factories is often reinforced on a fixed-ratio schedule (e.g., workers may be paid a certain amount for every 100 widgets produced). Fixed-ratio schedules lead to an interesting behavioural quirk when the number of responses required for a reward is large. For example, if you have to pick 10 bushels of grapes for each monetary reward, you are likely to pause a bit in your responding (picking) immediately after the 10th bushel. This delay in responding after reinforcement is called the *postreinforcement pause.* Pausing after reinforcement is easy to understand in this situation—after all, you have to do a lot of work before you receive the next reward.

If you stop delivering the reinforcement after the fixed number of responses has occurred, the individual will change his or her behaviour accordingly: The rate of performing the behaviour will decrease and may even stop. Similar to what happens in classical conditioning, the introduction of nonreinforcement following a period of training is called *extinction.* How quickly subjects stop responding, or extinguish their behaviour, when reinforcements are no longer delivered is determined partly by the reinforcement schedule that had previously been in effect. Fixed-ratio schedules typically produce rapid rates of extinction because it quickly becomes clear to the animal being trained that the schedule has changed—the reinforcement no longer occurs after the required number of responses has been produced.

Variable-Ratio Schedules   A **variable-ratio schedule** also requires that a certain *number* of responses be made before a reward is given. However, with a variable-ratio schedule the number of responses required varies over trials. Reinforcement may be delivered after the first response on trial 1, after the seventh response on trial 2, after the third response on trial 3, and so on. It's called a variable-ratio (VR) schedule because the number of responses required to earn a reward *varies* (often in a random fashion).

Variable-ratio schedules differ from fixed-ratio schedules in that the animal being trained cannot predict which response will get the reward. These schedules typically produce high rates of responding, and the postreinforcement pause, seen in fixed-ratio schedules, is usually absent (after all, the very next response might get you the reward again). Gambling is an example of a variable-ratio schedule; because of chance factors, a gambler wins some bets and loses others, but the gambler never knows what to expect on a given bet.

The unpredictability of reward during a variable-ratio schedule makes it difficult to eliminate a response trained on this schedule when the response is no longer reinforced. Consider a compulsive slot machine player: Dollar after dollar goes into the machine; sometimes there's a payoff, more often not. Even if a machine was rigged so that rewards are never delivered (thus placing the responder on extinction), many established gamblers would continue playing long into the night. On a variable-ratio schedule, it's hard to see that extinction is in effect because you've never been able to predict when reinforcement will occur. (See Cox, Yu, Afifi, & Ladouceur, 2005, for a national survey of gambling problems in Canada.)

fixed-ratio schedule

A schedule in which the number of responses required for reinforcement is fixed and does not change from trial to trial

variable-ratio schedule

A schedule in which a certain number of responses is required for reinforcement, but the number of required responses typically changes from trial to trial

Fixed-Interval Schedules   In an *interval* schedule of reinforcement, the reward is delivered for the first response that occurs following a certain interval of time; if a **fixed-interval schedule** (FI) is in effect, the period remains constant from one trial to the next. Suppose we reward a pigeon with food when it pecks a lighted response key after two minutes have elapsed. In this case, we would be using an "FI 2 min." schedule. Note that the pigeon must still produce the response to receive the reward. (Otherwise, the learning procedure would not be instrumental conditioning.) Pecking just doesn't do any good until at least two minutes have elapsed.

You shouldn't be surprised to learn that fixed-interval schedules typically produce low rates of responding. Because no direct association exists between how much you respond and the delivery of reinforcement—you're rewarded only when you respond after the interval has passed—it doesn't make sense to respond all the time. Another characteristic of fixed-interval schedules is that responding slows down after reinforcement and gradually increases as the end of the interval approaches. If the total number of responses is plotted over time in a cumulative response record, the net effect is a *scalloping* pattern of the type shown in Figure 6.9 on page 240.

To appreciate scalloping, consider how people generally study in school. Because "reinforcement" occurs only on fixed test days, students often wait until the week (or night) before the test to start studying the material. Studying behaviour increases gradually throughout the test-to-test interval and peaks on the night before the exam. (Actually, studying is not usually reinforced on a true fixed-interval schedule because you must take the test on a specific day; in a true fixed-interval schedule, you can respond at any time after the fixed interval has elapsed and still get reinforcement.)

Variable-Interval Schedules   When a **variable-interval schedule** (VI) is in effect, the allotted time before a response will yield reinforcement changes from trial to trial. For example, we may deliver reinforcement for a response occurring after 2 minutes on trial 1, after 10 minutes on trial 2, after 30 seconds on trial 3, and so on. Variable-interval schedules are common in everyday life. Suppose you are trying to reach someone on the telephone, but every time you dial you hear a busy signal. To be rewarded, you know that you have to dial the number and that a certain amount of time has to elapse between now and when you are likely to get rewarded, but you're not sure exactly how long you need to wait.

Learning—that is, the increase in the rate at which the animal performs the target behaviour—tends to be slow in variable-interval schedules; the contingency between performing the behaviour and earning a reward is difficult to detect, because it is contingent on a randomly varying amount of time since the last rewarded response. Like variable-ratio schedules, however, variable-interval schedules help eliminate the pause in responding that usually occurs after reinforcement in fixed-reinforcement schedules. The rate of extinction also tends to be slower in a variable-interval schedule because of the uncertainty created about when the next reinforcement will be delivered. From the responder's point of view, the next response could very well produce the desired reward, so it makes sense to continue steady responding. For responding to cease, you need to recognize that the relationship between responding and reinforcement has changed.

There are many different types of reinforcement schedules. The four partial schedules we have considered here are representative and demonstrate that different reinforcement schedules produce strikingly different patterns of behaviour. Moreover, as Skinner (1956) argued, these principled behaviours are universal—the postreinforcement pause, for example, occurs regardless of the specific response, the nature of the reinforcement, or the species receiving the training. Reward, and the pattern with which it is delivered, exerts a powerful influence on everyday actions.

CRITICAL   THINKING

Do you think fishing is reinforced on a variable-interval schedule of reinforcement or a variable-ratio schedule? How might the answer depend on the skill of the person doing the fishing?

CONCEPT SUMMARY

SCHEDULES OF REINFORCEMENT

Type of Schedule	Description	Example	Effect on Behaviour
Continuous	Response is followed rapidly by reinforcement every time response occurs.	Every time Jean-Claude cleans his room, his parents give him $5.	It leads to fast acquisition of response, but response is easily extinguished.
Partial	Response is followed by reinforcement only some of the time.	Sometimes, Jean-Claude gets $5 after he cleans his room.	Acquisition is slower, but the learned response is more resistant to extinction.
—Fixed ratio	The number of responses required for reinforcement is fixed.	Jean-Claude gets $5 every third time he cleans his room.	Jean-Claude cleans his room consistently with a pause in cleaning after each $5; he stops quickly if reward stops.
—Variable ratio	The number of responses required for reinforcement varies.	Jean-Claude gets $5 after cleaning his room a certain number of times, but the exact number varies.	Jean-Claude cleans his room consistently with few pauses; he continues to clean his room even if the reward isn't delivered for a while.
—Fixed interval	Reinforcement is delivered for the first response after a fixed interval of time.	Every Tuesday, Jean-Claude's parents give him $5 if his room is clean.	Jean-Claude doesn't do much cleaning until Tuesday is approaching; he stops quickly if reward stops.
—Variable interval	Reinforcement is delivered for the first response after a variable interval of time.	On some random weekday, Jean-Claude gets $5 if his room is clean.	Jean-Claude cleans his room consistently and doesn't stop even if the reward isn't delivered for a while.

Acquisition: Shaping the Desired Behaviour

In principle, you should be able to gain control over any behaviour, such as getting your dog to sit, by reinforcing the appropriate response according to a specified schedule. For example, if you use a variable-ratio schedule to train your dog to sit and you use food as a reward, then your dog should continue to sit on command even when food is not available as a reward. In this case, the dog knows that sitting is reinforced only some of the time, so failure to receive a reward doesn't necessarily weaken the response.

In practice, however, it can be difficult to train a behaviour if that behaviour is unlikely to occur initially. How do you reward your dog for sitting if the dog never sits on command in the first place? Most people try to train a dog by saying "sit," pushing the dog's bottom down, and promptly giving the dog a food reward. This approach amounts to a kind of classical conditioning procedure—the dog is taught that having his bottom pushed downward is a *signal* for a pleasant unconditioned stimulus. If this was all you did, the dog would learn to salivate in response to the word "sit," but it would not learn that its own behaviour is instrumental in producing the outcome. What you want your dog to learn is that the word "sit" is a discriminative stimulus that signals that a behaviour (sitting) is instrumental in producing a reward.

To solve this problem, Skinner (1938) developed a procedure called **shaping,** in which reinforcement is delivered for successive *approximations* of the desired response. Instead of waiting for the complete response—here, sitting to the command "sit"—to occur, you reinforce some part of the response that is likely to occur initially. For instance, at an early stage of training you might give a dog a reward if it makes even a small movement toward sitting when you say "sit." As each part of the response is acquired, you become stricter in your criteria for what behaviour will be rewarded. A variety of animals (e.g., pigeons, rats, dogs, dolphins) can learn incredibly complex

shaping

A procedure in which reinforcement is delivered for successive approximations of the desired response

sequences of behaviours through the successive-approximation technique of shaping. For example, a chicken can be taught to peck out a simple melody on a toy piano, with the chicken playing one tune if a red light comes on and another if a blue light comes on. Other chickens have been taught to play a mean game of tick-tack-toe, rarely losing to their human competitors (see **http://www.reviewjournal.com/lvrj_home/ 2002/Jul-30-Tue-2002/living/19262071.html**).

Practical Applications   Shaping also works quite well as a technique for modifying behaviour in people. (In Chapter 15, you'll see how shaping can be applied in therapy to modify maladaptive thoughts, lessen fears, and help individuals handle stressful situations.) Children with developmental disabilities that grossly impair their language skills have been taught to speak by reinforcing verbal sequences with treats. Whereas the child might be reinforced initially for any kind of verbal utterance, gradually the reward is withheld until the child produces a more natural flow of sounds.

The same kind of training can be used with adult patients suffering from severe psychological disorders. Patients with serious mental problems sometimes lack normal living skills—for example, they might lose the ability to clean or bathe themselves properly or communicate effectively with others. Social skills can be trained, through shaping, leading to a significant improvement in the quality of the patient's life (e.g., Benton & Schroeder, 1990; Wong et al., 1993). For a more detailed review of how shaping and other behavioural interventions can help people control problematic behaviours and increase desirable ones, see Martin and Pear (1999).

Shaping also has enormous applications for teaching, both inside and outside the classroom. Most teachers, especially of the earlier grades, use principles of instrumental conditioning to encourage children to develop desired behaviours and avoid disruptive ones. Did you ever get a gold star, or get sent to the principal's office? B. F. Skinner and others advocated for the use of shaping as a technique for learning. Mastery of subject matter can be broken down into small steps accompanied by lots of positive reinforcement. Many computer programs used in schools and at home follow the shaping format—start small and gradually increase the requirements for reward. Shaping is also a great technique for sports activities. To teach someone an effective golf swing, it's best to begin by rewarding any contact between the club and the ball. Later, the teacher can fine-tune the person's swing by offering praise only when the mechanics of the swing are more technically correct.

So far, we've described shaping procedures in which a teacher or experimenter deliberately arranges contingencies, reinforcing some responses and not others and thereby gradually shaping a desired behaviour. But shaping can also be influenced by chance events that happen, by fluke, to coincide with reinforcement. As discussed in the Practical Solutions box, this can lead to the shaping of some quite odd behaviours.

Through shaping—in which reinforcements are delivered for successive approximations of a desired behaviour—it is possible to produce some unusual behaviours in animals. These rabbits are shown in the early stages of training for an advertisement that featured them popping out of top hats (circa 1952).

Courtesy of Drs. Robert and Marian Breland Bailey

PRACTICAL SOLUTIONS

SUPERSTITIOUS BEHAVIOUR

If you are a sports fan, you know that many professional athletes perform ritual actions in preparation for games or important shots. For example, basketball legend Michael Jordan wore his "lucky" North Carolina Tarheels trunks under his Bulls uniform. Similarly, baseball star Wade Boggs is said to believe that he hits better after eating chicken and, consequently, to have eaten chicken before every game for more than 20 years. Boggs also avoided stepping onto the foul line when running onto the field, and stepped onto it each time he left the field. Closer to home, after Canada won the 2002 gold medal in both women's and men's hockey, news got out that a Canadian coin had been buried at centre ice in the Salt Lake City rink in which the games had been played (the "lucky loonie" is now on display in the Hockey Hall of Fame).

Let's analyze these behaviours from the perspective of instrumental conditioning. According to the law of effect, these odd patterns of behaviour must have been reinforced—they occurred, perhaps by chance, and were followed by a reward (a hit or a successful free throw). But because the pairing of the behaviour with its consequence was really accidental, psychologists refer to this kind of reinforcement as *accidental* or *adventitious reinforcement*. In the player's mind, however, a cause-and-effect link has been formed, and he or she therefore repeats the rewarded behaviour when the next appropriate situation occurs. Maybe that trial and the next go unreinforced, but perhaps

on the fourth occasion once again the behaviour is followed by the reward. Once the player starts to perform the behaviour on a regular basis, it's likely that the behaviour will continue to be accidentally reinforced, although on a partial schedule of reinforcement. (Can you identify the particular schedule?) The result is called a superstitious behaviour, and because of the partial schedule (a variable-ratio one) it is difficult to eliminate.

In 1948, B. F. Skinner developed an experimental procedure to mimic and gain control over the development of superstitious acts. He placed hungry pigeons in a chamber and delivered bits of food every 15 seconds, irrespective of what the bird happened to be doing at the time. In his own words: "In six out of eight cases the resulting responses were so clearly defined that two observers could agree perfectly in counting instances. One bird was conditioned to turn counterclockwise about the cage, making two or three turns between reinforcements. Another repeatedly thrust its head into one of the upper corners of the cage. A third developed a 'tossing' response, as if placing its head beneath an invisible bar and lifting it repeatedly" (Skinner, 1948, p. 168).

Remember, from the experimenter's point of view, no cause-and-effect relationship existed between these quirky behaviours and the delivery of food. From the responder's point of view, illusory connections can form between behaviours and outcomes. By chance alone, a particular behaviour (typically,

Many athletes perform odd rituals on a regular basis. This baseball player feels the need to brush his teeth vigorously before every time up at the plate. A learning theorist might argue that the player's bizarre behaviour was somehow accidentally reinforced in the past, forming a superstitious cause-and-effect link between teeth brushing and successful performance.

one that the responder is likely to perform in the situation) happens to be followed closely by reward, and this leads the responder to perceive a systematic relationship where really only a fluky one exists. Once these connections have been made, if the animal comes to perform the behaviour frequently, then it is likely to continue to be accidentally reinforced every now and then (again, by chance alone) and this occurrence serves as the basis for a superstitious behaviour.

Biological Constraints on Learning

Is it really possible to train any behaviour, in any situation, provided that you have enough time and an effective reinforcer? No, because biological constraints limit the responses that can be taught. For one thing, animals of a given species are simply unable to make certain kinds of responses (e.g., you cannot condition a fish to fly).

More interestingly, even certain kinds of responses that an animal can make are very resistant to conditioning. For example, in his studies of cats in puzzle boxes, Thorndike found that he could not increase the probability of yawning in cats through the application of reinforcement. Similar observations were reported later by animal trainers Keller and Marion Breland (1961). The Brelands, who were former

CRITICAL THINKING

Do you perform any superstitious behaviours (in sports or school)? Why might a person who has read about superstitious behaviours, and accepts the explanation for them described in the Practical Solutions box, nonetheless decide to keep performing them?

students of Skinner, encountered some interesting difficulties while attempting to train a variety of species to make certain responses. In one case, they tried to train a pig to drop large wooden coins into a piggy bank (for a bank commercial). They followed a shaping procedure, with successive approximations of the desired sequence being reinforced, but they could not get the pig to complete the response. The animal would pick up the coin and begin to lumber toward the bank but would stop midway and begin "rooting" the coins along the ground; despite their best efforts, the Brelands failed to train the pigs to carry the coins all the way to the bank. They encountered similar problems trying to teach a raccoon to put coins in a bank:

> We started out by reinforcing him for picking up a single coin. Then the metal container was introduced, with the requirement that he drop the coin into the container. Here we ran into the first bit of difficulty: he seemed to have a great deal of trouble letting go of the coin. He would rub it against the inside of the container, pull it back out, and clutch it firmly for several seconds…. [With two coins] not only could he not let go of the coins, but he spent seconds, even minutes, rubbing them together (in a most miserly fashion) and dipping them into the container. He carried on this behavior to such an extent that the practical application that we had in mind—a display featuring a raccoon putting money into a piggy bank—simply was not feasible. The rubbing behavior became worse and worse as time went on, in spite of nonreinforcement. (Breland & Breland, 1961, p. 682)

In the cases of the pig and the raccoon, biological tendencies connected with feeding and food reinforcement interfered with the learning of certain response sequences. Pigs root in connection with feeding, and raccoons rub and dunk objects related to food (Domjan, 1998). These natural tendencies are adaptive responses for the animals—at least with respect to feeding—but they limit what the animals can be taught. Behaviour is a joint product of biology (nature) and experience (nurture), and both must be taken into account in a full description or account of learning.

Punishment: Lowering the Likelihood of a Response

Up to now, we have considered how the chances of a response increase, in the presence of a discriminative stimulus, when the response leads to reinforcement. If you perceive that performing a particular behaviour is instrumental in producing an appetitive event (positive reinforcement) or in removing something unpleasant (negative reinforcement), you're likely to behave in a similar fashion in similar situations in the future. But the law of effect has another side: Thorndike claimed that if a response is followed by an unsatisfying or unpleasant consequence, it will be weakened. The term **punishment** is used to refer to consequences that decrease the likelihood of responding in the presence of a discriminative stimulus. Like reinforcement, punishment comes in two forms: *positive* and *negative*.

Positive Punishment   When a response leads to the *presentation* of an event that lowers the likelihood of that response occurring again, this is **positive punishment.** Notice, as with reinforcement, the concept is defined in terms of its effect on behaviour—lowering the likelihood of responding—rather than on its subjective qualities. Usually, however, positive punishment occurs when a response leads to an *aversive* outcome. If you hassled the family cat with a new toy when you were a child, your parents might have scolded you. The scolding qualifies as positive punishment. If the aversive event—the scolding—is intense enough, the instrumental response that produced the punishment—hassling the cat—will tend to be *suppressed*.

Negative Punishment   When the removal of an event after responding lowers the likelihood of that response occurring again, **negative punishment** has occurred. For example, if a response leads to the removal of a positive outcome, you are unlikely to respond in that way again. Instead of scolding you for hassling the cat,

punishment

Consequences that decrease the likelihood of responding in a similar way again

positive punishment

An event that, when *presented* after a response, lowers the likelihood of that response occurring again

negative punishment

An event that, when *removed* after a response, lowers the likelihood of that response occurring again

your parents could simply take your toy away. They would be removing something you like when you engage in an inappropriate behaviour—this qualifies as negative punishment. Similarly, if they withheld your weekly allowance because your room was messy, they punished you by removing something good—money. As with positive punishment, negative punishment can rapidly suppress an undesirable response.

What accounts for the rapid suppression of the response that is punished? People simply learn the associative relationship between their behaviour and the particular outcome. You learn about the consequences of your actions—that a particular kind of behaviour will lead to an unpleasant consequence. In this sense, we don't really need two different explanations to account for the behaviour changes produced by reinforcement and punishment; the only major difference is that behaviour increases in one situation and declines in the other. In both cases, people simply use their knowledge about a behaviour and its consequences to maximize gain and minimize loss in a particular situation.

Practical Applications   In principle, punishment is an effective technique for suppressing an undesirable behaviour. However, difficulties often arise in everyday practice. For example, it can be hard to gauge the appropriate strength of the punishing event. When the punishment is aggressive or violent, such as the forceful spanking of a child, you run the risk of hurting the child either physically or emotionally. Another problem is that, if a child feels ignored, yelling at him or her can be reinforcing (rather than punishing) because of the attention it provides. Children who spend a lot of time in the principal's office may be causing trouble partly because of the attention that the punishment produces. In such cases as this, punishment leads to the exact opposite of the intended result. Another point is that for punishment to be effective it must be clear to the subject what particular behaviour is being punished. If your dog annoys you by barking, and you call the dog over to you and then deliver a punishment, the dog may learn not to come when you call, rather than not to bark.

CONCEPT SUMMARY

COMPARING PUNISHMENT AND REINFORCEMENT

Reinforcement: Consequences That Increase the Likelihood of Responding

Outcome	Description	Example
Positive reinforcement	Response leads to the removal of an event that increases the likelihood of that response occurring again.	Little five-year-old Skip helps his dad do the dishes. Dad takes him to the store and lets him pick out a candy bar. Giving Skip a candy bar increases the likelihood that he'll help with the dishes again.
Negative reinforcement	Response leads to the presentation of an event that increases the likelihood of that response occurring again.	Little Skip did such a nice job setting the table that his mum lets him leave his spinach on his plate. This increases the likelihood that Skip will set the table tomorrow.

Punishment: Consequences That Decrease the Likelihood of Responding

Outcome	Description	Example
Positive punishment	Response leads to the presentation of an event that decreases the likelihood of that response occurring again.	Little Skip nearly runs into the street; his mother pulls him back from the curb and scolds him. This decreases the likelihood that Skip will run into the street.
Negative punishment	Response leads to the removal of an event that decreases the likelihood of that response occurring again.	Little Skip teases his three-year-old sister at the dinner table. His parents send him to bed without his favourite dessert. Withholding the dessert decreases the likelihood that Skip will tease his sister at the dinner table.

You also need to recognize that punishment only suppresses an undesirable behaviour; it does not teach someone how to perform desirable behaviours. For instance, spanking a child for lying might reduce the lying behaviour, but it will not teach the child how to deal more effectively with the social situation that led to the initial lie. To teach the child about more appropriate forms of behaviour, you would need to reinforce some kind of alternative response. You must teach the child a positive strategy for dealing with situations that can lead to lying. That's the main advantage of reinforcement over punishment: Reinforcement teaches you what you should be doing—how you should act—whereas punishment only teaches you what you shouldn't be doing.

Punishment can also produce undesirable side effects, most notably anger, resentment, and aggression. Studies with animals in the laboratory have shown that aggressive behaviour is often a consequence of punishment procedures. Animals that are shocked together in the same experimental context will often attack one another (Domjan, 1998). Parents who punish their children regularly, without alternative reinforcement, invite future resentment and a loss in the quality of the relationship with their children. Few psychologists deny that punishment can be an effective means for stopping a behaviour, and it may even be appropriate in some circumstances (e.g., running into the street or sticking a fork into an electrical outlet). But punishment, by itself, is rarely a sufficient technique for teaching children—it needs to be supplemented with alternative strategies for behaving that provide the opportunity for a little tender loving care (positive reinforcement).

Test Yourself 6.3

Check your knowledge about instrumental conditioning by answering the following questions. (The answers are in Appendix B.)

1. For each of the following statements, decide which term best applies: negative punishment, positive punishment, negative reinforcement, positive reinforcement.

  a. Stephanie is grounded for arriving home well past her curfew: _____

  b. Greg receives a bonus of $500 for exceeding his sales goal for the year: _____

  c. Nikki gets a speeding ticket, at double the normal rate, for exceeding the posted limit in a school zone:

  _____

  d. Little Mowrer cries all the time when her mum is home because Mum always comforts her with a kiss and a story: _____

  e. With Dad, Mowrer is a perfect angel because crying tends to be followed by a stern lecture: _____

2. Identify the schedule of reinforcement that is at work in each of the following situations. Choose from the following: fixed interval, fixed ratio, variable interval, variable ratio.

  a. Rowena feels intense satisfaction after she calls the psychic hotline, but only when a psychic named Darlene reads her future: _____

  b. Prana likes to visit the Monster Truck rally because they always have good corn dogs: _____

  c. Sinéad constantly watches music television because her favourite show, *Puck Live,* comes on from time to time at odd hours: _____

  d. Mohamed has just joined a coffee club—he gets a free pound of gourmet coffee after the 10th pound that he buys: _____

  e. Charlie hangs around street corners for hours at a time. Occasionally, a pretty woman walks by and gives him a smile: _____

▶ Learning from Others: Observational Learning

LEARNING GOALS

1. Be able to describe observational learning and to specify the conditions that lead to effective modelling.
2. Be able to describe the practical applications of observational learning.

The world would be a very unpleasant place if you could only learn about the consequences of your behaviour through trial and error. You could learn to avoid poisonous foods through positive punishment, but only after eating them and getting sick. Through conditioning, children might learn not to play in the street, provided their initial injuries were not fatal. You could learn to avoid risky drugs, but only if you have a bad experience, such as an arrest or an overdose. Clearly, it's sometimes best not to undergo the experiences that lead to classical and instrumental conditioning.

In the wild, rhesus monkeys show an adaptive fear response in the presence of snakes. Because snakes are natural predators of monkeys, it makes sense for monkeys to avoid them whenever possible. But how do you suppose that fear is originally acquired? According to a strict interpretation of the law of effect, the animal must learn its fear through some kind of direct reinforcement or punishment—that is, through trial and error. This means that a monkey would probably need to approach a snake and be bitten (or nearly bitten) before it could learn to fear the snake; unfortunately, this single learning experience is likely to be fatal much of the time. This suggests that trial-and-error learning is not always adaptive, especially when you're learning about something dangerous or potentially harmful.

Fortunately, it turns out that it's possible to learn a great deal without trial and error—by simply observing the experiences of others. People and animals can learn by example, and this kind of learning, called **observational learning, social learning,** or **modelling,** has considerable adaptive value. For instance, McMaster University researcher Bennett Galef has demonstrated that in the wild, newly weaned rats acquire food habits by eating what the older rats eat (Galef, 1985). Similarly, red-winged blackbirds will refuse to eat a certain food if they have observed another bird getting sick after it has eaten the food (Mason & Reidinger, 1982), and chimpanzees in the wild learn how to use stone tools to crack open nuts by observing older chimpanzees eating (Inoue-Nakamura & Matsuzawa, 1997). Rhesus monkeys, it turns out, acquire their fear of snakes partly through social learning rather than through direct experience (Mineka, 1987). They watch other monkeys in their environment showing fear in the presence of a snake and thereby acquire the tendency to show fear themselves. It's also possible to learn by observing the mistakes of others—if one bird watches another bird consistently choosing the incorrect response in a discrimination task, the bird doing the observing is more likely not to make the same mistake (Templeton, 1998).

Modelling: Learning through Example

What conditions produce effective observational learning? One important factor is the presence of a significant role model. People naturally tend to imitate, or *model*, the behaviour of significant others, as do most members of the animal kingdom. You probably learned many things by watching your parents or your teachers—even though you may not have been aware of doing so. Research has shown that observational learning is particularly effective if the model is perceived as having positive characteristics, such as attractiveness, honesty, perceived competence, and some kind of social standing (Bandura, 1986; Brewer & Wann, 1998). It's also more likely if you observe the model being rewarded for a particular action, or if the model's behaviour is particularly successful.

CRITICAL THINKING

Do you think monkeys raised in captivity, such as in a zoo, will also show a strong fear of snakes?

observational learning, social learning, or modelling

Learning that occurs as a result of observing the experiences of others

The scientific study of learning from models was pioneered by Albert Bandura, who was born in Alberta and earned his B.A. degree at the University of British Columbia (we'll discuss his work further in Chapter 12). Bandura termed his approach "social learning theory." In one classic study, Bandura and his colleagues showed nursery school children a film that portrayed an adult striking, punching, and kicking a large, inflatable, upright "Bobo" doll. Afterward, when placed in a room with Bobo, many of these children imitated the adult and violently attacked the doll (Bandura, Ross, & Ross, 1963). In addition, the chances of the children kicking the doll increased if the adult was directly praised in the film for attacking Bobo ("You're the champion"). Bandura (1986) has claimed that the responses acquired through observational learning are strengthened through *vicarious reinforcement*, which occurs when the model is reinforced for an action, or weakened through *vicarious punishment*, in which the model is punished for an action. A clear parallel therefore exists between the law of effect and observational learning; the difference, of course, is that the behaviour of others is being reinforced or punished rather than our own.

Bandura believes that much of what we learn from an experience depends on our existing beliefs and expectations. You are unlikely to learn much from a model, for example, if you believe that you are incapable of ever performing the model's behaviour. You can watch a great pianist, singer, or athlete, but you're not likely to imitate his or her behaviour if you feel that you're incapable of performing the task. Our beliefs about our own abilities—which Bandura refers to as *self-efficacy*—significantly shape and constrain what we gain from observational learning.

Practical Applications   It's easy to see how the techniques of observational learning might be used to improve or change unwanted behaviours. Many studies have shown that observation of a model performing some desirable behaviour can lower unwanted or maladaptive behaviour. Children have been able to reduce their fear of dental visits (Craig, 1978) or impending surgery (Melamed & Siegel, 1975) by observing films of other children effectively handling their dental or surgical anxieties. Clinical psychologists use observational learning as a technique to deal with specific fears and as a method for promoting cooperative behaviour among preschoolers (Granvold, 1994).

We naturally tend to imitate, or model, the behaviour of significant others. Modelling is adaptive because it allows us to learn things without always directly experiencing consequences.

It's also important to recognize that observational or social learning can lead to undesirable effects. For example, it's been estimated that children now witness thousands of reinforced acts of violence just by watching Saturday morning cartoons. Although the causal connection between TV violence and personal aggression has not been firmly established (Freedman, 1988), the consensus among psychologists clearly supports a link (Bushman & Anderson, 2001; Hearold, 1986). In addition, it can be difficult for a society to overcome unproductive stereotypes if they are repeatedly portrayed through the behaviour of others. Many gender-related stereotypes, such as submissive or helpless behaviour in females, continue to be represented in TV programs and movies. By the age of six or seven, children have already begun to shy away from activities that are identified with members of the opposite sex. It's widely believed that television and other mass media play important roles in this trend (Blair & Sanford, 1999; Ruble, Balaban, & Cooper, 1981).

Even if people don't directly imitate or model a particular violent act, it's still likely that the observation itself influences the way they think. For instance, witnessing repeated examples of fictional violence distorts people's estimates of realistic violence—they are likely to believe, for example, that more people die a violent death than is actually the case. This can lead individuals to show irrational fear and to avoid situations that are in all likelihood safe. People who watch a lot of television tend to view the world in a fashion that is coloured by what they see on the screen. They tend to think, for example, that a large proportion of the population are professionals (such as doctors or lawyers) and that few people in society are seniors (Gerbner & Gross, 1976). It's not just the imitation of particular acts we need to worry about: Television and other vehicles of observational learning can literally change or determine our everyday view of the world (Bandura, 1986; Bushman & Anderson, 2001).

Conditioning, Observational Learning, and You

Many studies of classical conditioning, instrumental (operant) conditioning, and observational learning were conducted with animals as research subjects. This may make it difficult for you to appreciate the generalizability of these principles to your own life. Throughout this chapter we've drawn connections between research on conditioning, on the one hand, and everyday human life, on the other, but to drive the point home we reiterate some of those connections here.

Do you like the look of body piercings? If so, why? Perhaps there is something inherently aesthetically appealing about bits of metal protruding from the bridge of the nose. Maybe the individuals who sport such adornments would do so even if no one else did. But we doubt it. Rather, we suspect that principles of conditioning and observational learning play major roles in informing our fashion sensibilities. Fashion statements made by admired others, and looks that win us positive reinforcement from our peers, very quickly become good looks.

Are you a coffee connoisseur? Do you remember your first sip of coffee? Most novices find the beverage quite revolting at first, even if they are adults; it is, as they say, an acquired taste (as with alcoholic beverages, tobacco, etc.). Conditioning and observational learning are key to the acquisition of such tastes. Children observe their parents savouring coffee, which provides a motivation to imitate that behaviour. The nasty bitterness of the taste of coffee is at first aversive, but eventually the aroma and taste of coffee become pleasant via their association with pleasant consequences (e.g., social reinforcement and the alertness sparked by caffeine).

You may know songs that make you want to cry—if so, it's probably because they were associated with some sad experience in your past. Conditioning also plays roles in some psychological problems. For example, someone who was

Observational learning has powerful consequences that are not always what we intend. Children model the behaviour of significant role models, even when the model acts in a way that lacks adaptive value.

© Yuri Arcurs/Shutterstock

CRITICAL   THINKING

Given what you've learned about modelling, do you now favour the passage of laws that will control the amount of violence shown on television? Might you change your own viewing behaviours? Why or why not?

savagely bitten by a dog while on a walk might associate the attack with being outside (especially if he or she mentally relives the attack over and over) and so come to develop agoraphobia (fear of open spaces).

Thus, many of your likes and dislikes, your tastes and emotional responses, developed via basic principles of classical conditioning. Our examples in this section have emphasized classical conditioning, but instrumental conditioning (i.e., your history of being reinforced or punished in various ways—by parents, siblings, teachers, friends, and nature itself—for particular kinds of behaviours in particular situations) has undoubtedly also played important roles in making you the person you are. Likewise, your skills and proclivities have very likely been heavily influenced by observational learning. In summary, the basic principles of learning discussed in this chapter have played major roles in making you the person you are.

Test Yourself 6.4

Check your knowledge about observational learning by deciding whether each of the following statements is true or false. (The answers are in Appendix B.)

1. Observational learning, like classical conditioning, typically involves learning about events that occur outside your control. *True or False?*

2. People are more likely to imitate the behaviour of a role model if the model is observed being rewarded for his or her behaviour. Bandura refers to this reward process as vicarious reinforcement. *True or False?*

3. Observational learning is usually a passive process. Our beliefs and expectations about how well we can perform the model's behaviour play little or no role. *True or False?*

4. Most psychologists believe that television is a powerful vehicle for observational learning. *True or False?*

5. Clinical psychologists use observational learning to treat specific fears, such as phobias. *True or False?*

Classical Conditioning, Instrumental Conditioning, and Observational Learning

REVIEW

As organisms strive to survive and flourish in their environments, their capacity to learn—that is, to change their behaviour as a result of experience—represents one of their greatest adaptive tools. Psychologists have long recognized the need to understand how behaviour changes with experience; historically, research on learning predates research on all other topics except for basic sensory and perceptual processes.

In this chapter, we've concentrated on relatively basic learning processes. To meet the needs of changing environments, all organisms must solve certain types of learning problems, and the principles of behaviour that you've learned about apply generally across animal species. Although humans differ from other animals in that they are uniquely able to change their behaviour as a result of experience, many scientists believe that the same basic mechanisms of learning (habituation, sensitization, classical conditioning, operant conditioning, and modelling) play important roles in how all animals, including humans, learn to adapt to their physical (and for some animals, cultural) environments. Studying how individuals learn from experience can help us understand both similarities in the behaviour of individuals across cultures and differences between cultures.

First, how do we recognize consequential events when they occur and react to them appropriately? Everyone—people and animals—needs to *recognize* new events when they occur. Novel, or unusual, events lead to an orienting response, which helps ensure that we'll react quickly to sudden changes in our environment. The sound of screeching automobile brakes leads to an immediate reaction; you don't have to stop and think about it. You cannot attend to all the stimuli that surround you, so you must learn to ignore events that are of little adaptive significance. Through the process of habituation, characterized by the decline in the tendency to respond to an inconsequential event that has become familiar, you become selective about responding to events that occur repeatedly in your environment.

Second, how do we learn about the signalling properties of stimuli or events in the environment? We also need to learn about what events *signal*—it's helpful to know, for example, that when the cat's tail gets all bushy, it's likely to bite. Signals, or conditioned stimuli, can be established through classical conditioning. Events that provide information about the occurrence or absence of other significant events become conditioned stimuli. A conditioned stimulus elicits a conditioned response, which is a response appropriate for anticipating the event that will follow.

Third, how do we learn about the consequences of our own behaviour? It's also important to learn about the *consequences* of our own actions. People need to learn that when they act a certain way, their behaviours produce outcomes that are sometimes pleasing and sometimes not. In instrumental conditioning, the presentation and removal of events after responding can either increase or decrease the likelihood of responding in a similar way again. When a response is followed by reinforcement, either positive or negative, the tendency to respond in that way in that situation is strengthened. When a response is followed by punishment, either positive or negative, you are less likely to behave that way again. It's also important to consider the schedule of reinforcement (continuous or partial, ratio or interval, fixed or variable). Schedules affect not only how rapidly you will learn and respond but also the pattern of responding and how quickly you will change your behaviour if the reinforcement stops.

Fourth, how can we learn by observing others? Through observational, or social, learning we imitate and model the actions of others, thereby learning from example rather than from direct experience. We study how other people behave and how their behaviour is reinforced or punished, and we change our own behaviour accordingly. Observational learning can have both positive and negative effects on the individual and on society.

It is important to appreciate that we use all these mechanisms of learning. Classical conditioning is arguably more limited than is instrumental conditioning (because all the animal learns is to associate certain stimuli with certain automatic or reflexive responses), but organisms from sea slugs to humans learn via both types of conditioning. Observational learning is likely beyond sea slugs, but as mentioned earlier clear evidence shows that many species (including humans) learn from observing others. In later chapters we'll talk about more abstract, "cognitive" forms of learning that may be more uniquely human.

CHAPTER SUMMARY

Learning is a relatively permanent *change in behaviour*, or *in potential to respond*, that results from experience. Common principles of learning can be applied widely across situations and species; much of what we know about these basic principles of learning comes from animal research.

▶ Learning about Events: Noticing and Ignoring

Because the nervous system has limited resources, we cannot attend to every stimulus in the environment. Basic psychological processes help us prioritize our mental functioning.

Orienting Responses, Habituation, and Sensitization

When a novel event suddenly occurs in the immediate environment, animals exhibit an *orienting response*, an automatic turning of attention toward the unusual event.

Habituation occurs when one slows or stops responding to an event that has become familiar through repeated responding. *Sensitization* occurs when responsiveness to an event increases with repeated exposure. These general learning phenomena are found throughout the animal kingdom.

▶ Learning What Events Signal: Classical Conditioning

It's important to learn about the signalling properties of stimuli or events in the environment. We need to learn that one event predicts that a second event is likely to follow. It may not be possible to do anything about the co-occurrence of the events, but we can respond accordingly.

The Terminology of Classical Conditioning

Unconditioned stimuli (*US*) are stimuli that lead to automatic responses termed *unconditioned responses* (*UR*). After repeated pairings with an unconditioned stimulus, a *conditioned stimulus* (*CS*) can come to elicit a *conditioned response* (*CR*). An association between the conditioned stimulus and unconditioned stimulus has been acquired.

What Mechanisms Underlie Classical Conditioning?

For an effective association to be formed, the conditioned stimulus must be presented *before* the unconditioned stimulus, the unconditioned stimulus must follow the conditioned stimulus *closely in time*, and the conditioned stimulus needs to *uniquely predict* the unconditioned stimulus and provide *new information* about the unconditioned stimulus. Sometimes the conditioned stimulus and the unconditioned stimulus lead to different responses. The conditioned response depends on both the unconditioned stimulus and the conditioned stimulus.

Second-Order Conditioning

In *second-order conditioning*, an established conditioned stimulus (e.g., a tone that predicts food) is presented immediately following a new event, such as a light; the unconditioned stimulus itself is never presented. In this case, the pairing of the tone and the light can produce conditioned responding to the light.

Stimulus Generalization

Stimulus generalization occurs when a new stimulus produces a response similar to the one produced by the conditioned stimulus.

Stimulus Discrimination

Stimulus discrimination occurs when one responds to a new stimulus in a way that is different from the response to the original stimulus.

Extinction: When Conditioned Stimuli No Longer Signal the Unconditioned Stimuli

If the conditioned stimulus is presented repeatedly without being followed by the unconditioned stimulus, the conditioned stimulus loses its signalling properties and conditioned responding diminishes.

Conditioned Inhibition: Signalling the Absence of an Unconditioned Stimulus

Conditioned inhibition occurs when we learn that an event signals the absence of the unconditioned stimulus.

▶ Learning about the Consequences of Behaviour: Instrumental Conditioning

All species need to learn the consequences of particular behaviours. Behaviours play an important role in producing rewards and punishments; people and animals tend to adapt their behaviour to maximize rewards and minimize punishments.

The Law of Effect

Instrumental conditioning is a procedure for studying how organisms learn about the consequences of their own behaviour. Thorndike found that if a response is followed by a satisfying consequence, it will be strengthened; if a response is followed by an unsatisfying consequence, it will be weakened. This is the *law of effect*.

B. F. Skinner and "Radical Behaviourism"

B. F. Skinner discovered some of the basic principles of instrumental conditioning. He suggested that psychologists should refer mainly to environmental events and not to "internal" events in explaining behaviour, a view known as *radical behaviourism.*

The Discriminative Stimulus: Knowing When to Respond

The law of effect applies only to responses that are rewarded in *particular situations.* The situation is termed the *discriminative stimulus.*

The Nature of Reinforcement

When the presentation of an event after a response increases the likelihood of the response occurring again, *positive reinforcement* has occurred. When the removal of an event after a response increases the likelihood of the response occurring again, *negative reinforcement* has occurred. *Conditioned reinforcers* are stimuli that acquire reinforcing properties through learning (e.g., money).

Schedules of Reinforcement

A *schedule of reinforcement* is a rule used to determine when responses will be reinforced. In a *continuous schedule,* every response is followed by reinforcement; in a *partial schedule,* reinforcement is delivered only after some responses. Partial schedules include *fixed ratio, variable ratio, fixed interval,* and *variable interval.*

Acquisition: Shaping the Desired Behaviour

Training a behaviour can be accomplished through *shaping,* which refers to reinforcing *successive approximations* of the desired behaviour. Instrumental conditioning and shaping have proven to have numerous and important practical applications, from regulating the behaviour of wild animals to improving the performance of students and athletes. Instrumental conditioning and shaping can be used to promote the acquisition of desirable behaviours and skills and to discourage inappropriate or destructive behaviours.

Biological Constraints on Learning

Many psychologists believe that there are biological constraints, perhaps in the genetic code, that limit the responses that can be taught.

Punishment: Lowering the Likelihood of a Response

Punishment refers to consequences that decrease the likelihood of repeating a response in a situation. *Positive punishment* occurs when the presentation of an event decreases the response. *Negative punishment* occurs when the removal of an event decreases the response. Punishment has long been used to discourage undesirable behaviours in humans and other animals, in part because it is often quite effective.

▶ Learning from Others: Observational Learning

Often, our most important teachers are the actions of others; people, as well as most of the animal kingdom, learn by example. Learning through observation of others has considerable adaptive significance.

Modelling: Learning through Example

People naturally tend to model the behaviour of significant others. *Observational learning* is especially likely if the model has positive characteristics or is observed being rewarded. Observational learning (like punishment), can lead to undesirable effects, as in the case of children *modelling* the violence they see on TV.

Conditioning, Observational Learning, and You

Many studies of conditioning and learning are conducted with animals as research subjects, but they generalize to our lives as well. Principles of conditioning and observational learning probably play major roles in informing our fashion sensibilities, and they are key to the acquisition of such tastes as that for coffee. Conditioning also plays roles in some psychological problems, such as phobias. Instrumental conditioning undoubtedly plays important roles in shaping our behaviours too.

Terms to Remember

Recommended Readings

Domjan, M. (1998). *The principles of learning and behaviour* (4th ed.). Pacific Grove, CA: Brooks/Cole. This is a leading undergraduate textbook on learning. The material discussed in this chapter is covered in much more detail in Domjan's text.

Heyes, C. M., & Galef, B. G. (Eds.). (1996). *Social learning in animals: The roots of culture*. London: Academic Press. Co-edited by McMaster University social learning expert Bennett Galef, this volume examines such topics as how rats copy feeding behaviour, how other animals learn about mate choices through observation, and why yawning and laughing are contagious.

Martin, G., & Pear, J. (1999). *Behavior modification—What it is and how to do it* (6th ed.). New York: Prentice-Hall. Written by Garry Martin and Joseph Pear, experts on behavioural approaches to human performance at the University of Manitoba, this text covers theory, basic principles, and practical applications of learning theory as applied to everyday issues in child development, education, sports, and other areas.

Skinner, B. F. (1948). *Walden two*. New York: Macmillan. This is behaviourist B. F. Skinner's famous work of fiction describing how the principles of behaviour modification might be used to create a utopian society. Interesting and controversial.

 For additional readings, explore InfoTrac® College Edition, your online library. Go to
http://www.adaptivemind3e.nelson.com.

Hint: Enter these search terms: habituation, classical conditioning, schedule of reinforcement, consequences of punishment, observational learning.

Media Resources

What's on the Web?

Please note that Web addresses are subject to change. Check out the accompanying website for updates: http://www.adaptivemind3e.nelson.com.

This site presents practice quiz questions, hypercontent, information on degrees and careers in psychology, study tips, and more.

CBC Story on Ten Superstitious Athletes

http://www.cbc.ca/sports/columns/top10/superstition.html

We mentioned a couple of athletes who perform ritual behaviours that they believe are lucky. This site provides information about a number of such individuals, such as famed goal tender Patrick Roy.

Animal Training at Sea World

http://www.seaworld.org/infobooks/Training/home.html

After reading this chapter, you are no doubt aware that the basic principles of learning are instrumental (pun intended) in training animals to do the fantastic tricks they do at parks, such as Sea World. This website provides an overview of basic learning principles, presented within the context of the training done at Sea World. It's a very interesting explanation of basic learning principles in an applied context.

B. F. Skinner Foundation

http://www.bfskinner.org

This website is devoted to the legendary learning researcher. It provides a wealth of information about B. F. Skinner and his legacy, as well as a biography penned by Skinner's daughter, Julie S. Vargas.

Dr. P's Dog Training

http://www.uwsp.edu/psych/dog/dog.htm

Like the Sea World site described above, this site allows you to see the principles of learning applied to animal training. Learn how to teach an old dog new tricks with a visit to this site. It provides a wealth of information about dog training, including selections on assistance dogs, martial arts for dogs, and dog sledding.

ThomsonNOW™ ThomsonNOW™

http://hed.nelson.com

Go to this site for the link to ThomsonNOW™, your one-stop study shop. Take a Pretest for this chapter and ThomsonNOW™ will generate a personalized Study Plan based on your test results. The Study Plan will identify the topics you need to review and direct you to online resources to help you master those topics. You can then take a Posttest to determine what concepts you have mastered and what you still need work on.

Psyk.trek 3.0

Check out Psyk.trek 3.0 for further study of the concepts in this chapter. Psyk.trek's 65 interactive learning modules, simulations, and quizzes offer additional opportunities for you to interact with, reflect on, and retain the material:

Learning: Basic Processes in Classical Conditioning
Learning: Avoidance and Escape Learning

It's a poor sort of memory that only works backwards.

—Lewis Carroll

Memory

7

What if the flow of time suddenly fractured and you were forced to relive the same 10 minutes over and over again in an endless cycle? You might be driving your car or reading this book; it wouldn't matter—at the end of the interval you'd begin again, back at the same fork in the road or the same word on the page. Think about what this would be like. Would you notice that something was wrong? No; if your memories were truly erased before each new 10-minute interval, you'd be unaware of your hopeless plight; each repetition would seem new. It is through **memory,** broadly defined as the capacity to preserve and recover information, that such concepts as the past and the present gain meaning in our lives.

Certain brain injuries and neurological disorders greatly disrupt memory in various ways. Individuals suffering from *anterograde amnesia,* for example, appear normal at first sight. Their social skills and language abilities are largely intact, but they are forever locked in the present and distant past. In extreme cases, people with anterograde amnesia are unable to recognize people they have met since the onset of the disorder, even if they have interacted with those people many times. They can't remember what they ate for breakfast or the year in which they are living. Each morning begins like the previous one, devoid of any sense of recent personal history. They may read the same magazine

memory

The capacity to preserve and recover information

repeatedly, not remembering their prior readings; each time they are told of the death of a loved one, they mourn anew (Ogden & Corkin, 1991). If you've seen the movie *Memento*, you'll have a sense of what this might be like.

Even individuals with severe anterograde amnesia preserve many components of memory functioning. They retain the ability to communicate, which requires the use of memory for the meaning of words and the rules for stringing words together. They still have a basic understanding of the world and the objects in it, and their learned motor skills remain intact. They can even remember past personal experiences that happened before the brain dysfunction began. A world truly without memory would be devoid of thought and reason. You would never learn; you would not be able to produce spoken language or understand the words of others; your sense of personal history would be lost, and thereby much of your personal identity; even motor skills, such as walking, sitting in a chair, or feeding yourself, require memory for the complex set of muscle controls involved.

Memory

Like learning, memory is not something that can be directly observed. It is an inferred capacity, one that psychologists assume must be operating in situations in which people act on the basis of information that is no longer physically present. To understand how memory works, we need to consider how information is entered into memory (**encoding**), how information is maintained in memory (**storage**), and how the stored information is recovered and translated into performance (**retrieval**). We'll examine each of these psychological processes in more detail as we work through some adaptive problems that memory systems help solve.

First, how does the mind maintain information over the short term? Consider the interpretation of spoken language. Because speech unfolds over time, you must remember the early part of a sentence, after it has receded into the past, to comprehend the meaning of the sentence as a whole. Likewise, to perform mental tasks, such as solving math problems, certain bits of information must be retained during the ongoing solution process. By establishing short-term memories, we prolong the incoming information, giving us more time to interpret it properly.

Second, how do we retain accessible long-term memories of past experiences? To establish effective long-term memories, you must process, or think about, information in certain ways. For example, forming a visual image of to-be-remembered information enhances memory. It also helps to think about the meaning of the material and to relate it to other information you already know. We'll consider these techniques in some detail and provide some tips for improving your ability to remember.

Third, what initiates an act of remembering? What causes you to remember your appointment with the doctor this afternoon, what you had for breakfast this morning, or a fleeting encounter with a stranger yesterday? The retrieval of memories is triggered by an interaction among (1) events or cues encountered in the environment, (2) current "mindset" (i.e., what you are thinking about when the cues are encountered), and (3) information stored in memory.

Fourth, what mechanisms underlie forgetting? It can be frustrating to forget, but forgetting has considerable adaptive value: It keeps us current and prevents us from being overwhelmed by a flood of irrelevant memories when we encounter cues. Typically, it's today's study assignment that you need to remember to do, not the one from yesterday or the week before; it's your *current* address that you need to remember, not the one from a previous residence.

---

encoding

The processes that control the acquisition of information into memory

---

storage

The processes that determine how information is maintained over time

---

retrieval

The processes that control how information is recovered from memory and translated into performance

▶ Remembering over the Short Term

1. Understand the concept of visual sensory memory, be able to describe how it can be measured, and distinguish it from short-term memory.

2. Be able to define short-term memory and to describe the nature of the code used to represent verbalizable material in short-term memory.

3. Learn about the role of rehearsal in maintaining information in short-term memory, and how quickly information is lost from short-term memory without rehearsal.

4. Be able to explain what has been discovered about the limited capacity of short-term memory, and explain how chunking can increase memory span.

5. Become familiar with the working memory model and its three primary components: the articulatory loop, the visuospatial sketchpad, and the central executive.

The "classic" theory of memory is Atkinson and Shiffrin's (1968) multistore model of memory. According to the multistore model, people rely on two memory systems to help prolong incoming sensory information over relatively short terms. The first, called **sensory memory,** maintains the sensory stimuli in a relatively pure, unanalyzed form for a very brief period. Sensory memories are like fleeting snapshots of the world. The external message is represented in detail, as a kind of picture or echo that can last for a few moments (Crowder & Surprenant, 2000). The second system, **short-term memory,** is a limited-capacity "working memory" that we use to hold information after it has been analyzed into a meaningful form, usually for periods ranging from about a second to less than a minute. Short-term memories are usually rapidly forgotten, but they can be maintained for extended periods through rehearsal (internal repetition). The multistore model also allows for information in short-term memory being transferred into long-term memory, but we postpone discussion for now and focus on sensory and short-term memory. We'll take a look at each of these systems and consider some of their important properties.

Visual Sensory Memory: The Icon

Imagine that you are a commercial pilot, lazing along peacefully at 40 000 feet, your head in the clouds. Suddenly an alarm sounds, and you quickly look at the dozens of instruments and indicators in front of you. Quick action is a matter of life and death, and quick action depends on your ability to extract the critical information at a glance.

How much information can the human visual system extract in a single glance? This question gave rise to many studies in the 1950s. By using an apparatus called a *tachistoscope*, which presents visual displays for carefully controlled durations, researchers would briefly flash a matrix of letters (say, for 50 milliseconds, or 1/20 of a second) and ask subjects to report as many of the letters as they could. For example, a 12-letter matrix might look like this:

X L W F

J B O V

K C Z R

Typically, subjects reported only four or five letters from each matrix, suggesting a severe limitation on the amount of information taken in by the visual system in a single glance. Interestingly, however, subjects often said things like, "I *saw* all the letters in the matrix, but by the time I told you 4 or 5 of them I had forgotten the others." Of course, subjects might have made such claims to make themselves look good or because they had some sort of illusion of having seen more of the letters than they really did.

sensory memory

The capacity to preserve sensory information in a relatively pure, unanalyzed form for a very brief period

short-term memory

A limited-capacity "working memory" system that people use to hold information, after it has been perceptually analyzed, usually for less than a minute; the system used to temporarily store, think about, and reason with new information and with information retrieved from long-term memory

CRITICAL   THINKING

Do you consider the lingering afterimage left by a camera flashbulb to be a type of memory?

CRITICAL   THINKING

Can you think of a reason why it might be adaptive for icons to be lost so quickly?

iconic memory

The system that produces and stores visual sensory memories

Sperling's Partial Report Task   Did subjects really see all the letters in the matrix, thereafter forgetting them so quickly that by the time they had reported four or five they had forgotten the others? Or did they really see only the four or five letters that they reported? This is a question about what is going on inside people's minds, the very sort of question that behaviourists had argued cannot be studied scientifically.

More than 40 years ago, a psychology graduate student named George Sperling (1960) developed a clever procedure for answering this question. On each trial, a matrix of 12 letters was briefly presented and, *after* the matrix was removed, Sperling presented a tone. If the pitch of the tone was high, medium, or low, the subject was to report the top, middle, or bottom row of the display, respectively (see ▶ Figure 7.1). Sperling called this a *partial report* task because subjects were asked to report only a part of each display. Sperling found that subjects were usually able to report all of the letters in the to-be-reported row, even though they had no way of knowing which row they would be asked to report until *after* the matrix was removed. Because subjects never knew in advance which of the three rows they would be asked to report, the fact that they could usually report all the letters in the appropriate row supported the subjects' claims: They really did see all (or almost all) of the letters in the matrix. If they hadn't, they wouldn't be able to report whichever row of letters they were cued to report after the display was terminated.

Sperling's results suggested the existence of a visual sensory memory, which came to be known as **iconic memory.** Asking subjects to recall only a portion of the display, rather than the entire display, improved performance because subjects could report the relevant information before the iconic image had faded. In further experiments, Sperling measured the duration of visual sensory memory by varying the delay between removing the matrix and sounding the tone. He discovered that the fleeting image—iconic memory—faded in less than a second.

You are not usually aware of iconic memory, because its contents are replaced moment by moment by new incoming visual stimulation. In the Sperling task, the briefly flashed matrix was followed by a blank screen, so that the icon would not

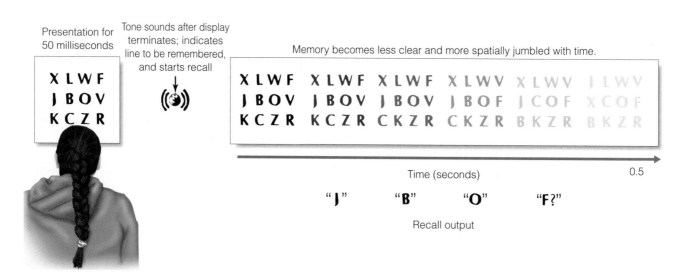

▶ **Figure 7.1**

Sperling's Partial Report Task

On each of many trials, a tone sounds *after* the visual display is removed, indicating which row of letters is to be reported on that trial. As soon as the display is turned off, the visual iconic memory of the letters begins to fade and memory for the spatial positions of individual letters becomes error-prone; the icon lasts only long enough for subjects to report about four or five letters before the image fades completely, but when only one line of letters is to be reported, this is usually enough time to report all the letters in that row.

Corbis Royalty Free/Magma

The trails of light created by a whirling sparkler are caused by visual sensory memories, which act as "still photographs" of the perceptual scene.

be overwritten by new input. You can get a related effect with a flashlight or sparkler on a dark night: Swing it in a quick circle and you will "see" the whole circle even though the light itself does not linger in the air. (For a critical discussion of the role of the icon in everyday perception, see Haber, 1985; for a more recent theoretical account of the nature and function of iconic memory, see DiLollo & Bischof, 1995.)

Sensory Memory in Other Modalities

Our discussion of sensory memory has focused on visual sensory memory or the icon, but other sensory systems have analogous forms of memory (Crowder & Surprenant, 2000). The second-most researched form of sensory memory is auditory sensory memory, known as the "echo" or echoic memory (Cowan, 1984). You've probably been aware of using your own echoic memory in everyday situations. For example, imagine you're watching TV when someone speaks to you (perhaps saying, "Do you want some pizza?"). You look up, knowing that someone has spoken to you but at first having no idea what he or she said. Yet a moment later you "hear" the statement in your echoic memory and then understand it (perhaps saying something like, "Huh? Oh, sure!"). Your echoic memory retained the information long enough for you to turn your attention to it and process the contents for meaning.

In addition to the icon and the echo, people have other forms of sensory memory, but these have not been studied as extensively. For example, Mahrer and Miles (2002) studied sensory memory for tactile stimuli (shapes momentarily pressed to the skin). Similarly, there is also evidence of a fleeting sensory memory for olfactory (odour) stimuli (e.g., Stopfer & Laurent, 1999). Some aspects of sensory memory differ from one sensory system to the next—for example, the icon lasts less than a second, whereas the echo lasts about two seconds—but the basic idea is the same across modalities: The system can briefly maintain a relatively unanalyzed representation of a recent stimulus, such that if attention is drawn to that sensory modality, the information can be more fully analyzed.

Short-term memory helps us maintain meaningful information, such as telephone numbers, over relatively brief intervals.

Short-Term Memory: The Mental Workspace

According to Atkinson and Shiffrin's (1968) multistore model of memory, attention selects some of the information available in the various sensory memory systems for further processing, transforming the selected information into meaningful representations in short-term memory. Short-term memory is the system we use to think about and consciously focus on information; whatever you are thinking about now is in short-term memory. The term *working memory* is sometimes used because this memory system often acts as a kind of mental workplace, allowing us to store the components of a problem as we work toward a solution (Baddeley, 2000; Nairne, 2002).

We address three important questions about short-term memory. First, what kinds of codes are used to maintain information over the short term? Second, how and why is information forgotten from short-term memory? Third, what is the capacity of short-term memory—that is, how much information can we maintain in short-term memory at any given moment? We'll consider each of these questions in the following sections.

The Short-Term Code   Sensory memory maintains a relatively exact representation of the physical stimuli received by the sensory receptors. But, as you know from Chapter 5, the conscious experience of perceiving things in the environment is the end result of perceptual analyses carried out on the contents of sensory memory. Consider the letters M O N E Y. Your iconic memory of that string of letters would represent only the shape, colour, and position of the various lines. But your internal experience when you perceive that string of letters is probably not about curved and straight lines, or even about letters. Your thoughts are likely to be about what the message stands for—in this case, a word that has particular meanings. If you do a little introspection, you'll also notice that you do much of your thinking in a kind of inner voice. Notice that you can repeat the word MONEY silently to yourself, either quickly or slowly; you can even insert internal pauses after each repetition. This repetition process has no visual aspect; you have recoded, or translated, the visual message into another form, a kind of inner voice.

The notion that people often use an inner voice to store verbalizable information over the short term is supported by the types of errors that people tend to make during short-term recall. When recalling from short-term memory, errors are usually acoustically based. That is, mistakes tend to *sound* like correct items even if the stimulus materials were not presented auditorily (Conrad, 1964; Hanson, 1990). For example, suppose you're given five letters to remember for a few seconds—B X R C L—but you make a mistake and misremember the fourth letter. Your error will probably be a letter that sounds like the correct one; you will probably incorrectly remember something like T or P. Notice that C and T and P all sound alike, but they *look* nothing alike. It is believed that errors in short-term recall tend to be acoustic because people recode the original visual input into an inner voice rather than an inner "eye" (see ❱ Figure 7.2).

Short-term memories of verbal material are typically stored acoustically, but you are capable of coding information in short-term memory in a variety of ways. For example, information is sometimes stored over the short term as visual images (Baddeley, 1992). To illustrate, stop for a moment, close your eyes, and mentally count the number of windows in your house or apartment. People usually perform this task by visualizing the rooms, one by one, and counting the number of windows they "see." Nevertheless, we often rely heavily on an inner voice when thinking about verbalizable information, partly because language is a handy way of representing ideas and partly because we're often called on to comprehend and produce spoken language. It makes sense to think in a way that is compatible with the way we communicate.

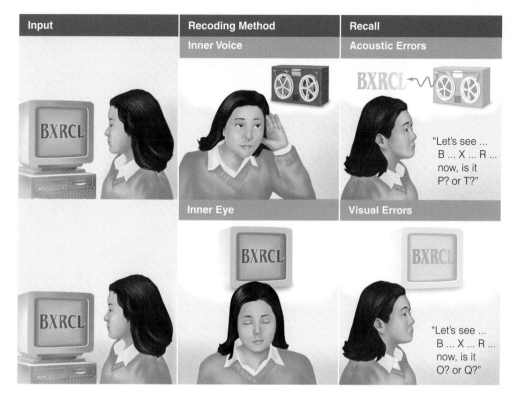

Input	Recoding Method	Recall
	Inner Voice	Acoustic Errors
	Inner Eye	Visual Errors

▶ Figure 7.2

Recoding and Memory Errors

Short-term memories are the results of cognitive processing and analyses. People recode, or translate, the sensory stimuli represented in sensory memory into meaningful representations. For verbalizable material, the recoding is usually from whatever form the stimuli were received into an inner voice. The top row presents a typical case, in which the subject recodes a visually presented message into an inner voice. Notice that recall errors are likely to sound like the letters that were presented. If to-be-remembered information was recoded into a visual form (an inner eye), as shown in the bottom row, recall errors would tend to be visually similar to the sensory input.

Short-Term Forgetting   What about forgetting from short-term memory? You've probably had the experience of looking up a phone number and then forgetting it before you get to the phone. Of course, it's possible to prolong short-term memories by engaging in **rehearsal,** which is a process of internal repetition, for as long as you continue the rehearsal process. (Think about the word *rehearsal* as re-*hear*-sal, as if listening to the inner voice.) Without rehearsal, as you'll see shortly, information is quickly lost from short-term memory.

Researchers at two different psychology labs (Brown, 1958; Peterson & Peterson, 1959) independently developed the same procedure to study forgetting from short-term memory. In the Brown/Peterson task, on each of a large number of trials the subject is asked to remember a triplet of letters (such as CLX) and then to report that triplet after a 3- to 18-second delay. The task sounds easy—remembering three letters for less than half a minute—but subjects were prevented from rehearsing, or thinking about the letters during the delay interval. To prevent rehearsal, the students were asked to count backward by 3s aloud from the time they were given the triplet until a recall signal appeared. You can try this experiment for yourself: Just ask someone to read you three letters, then immediately begin counting aloud backward by 3s from a three-digit number, and have your friend signal you to recall after about 10 to 20 seconds. Try several trials in a row, with a different triplet of letters and a different three-digit number each time. You'll

rehearsal

A strategic process that helps maintain short-term memories through the use of internal repetition

CRITICAL   THINKING

Do you believe that nonhuman animals think about things? If so, in what ways would their short-term memories differ from those of humans?

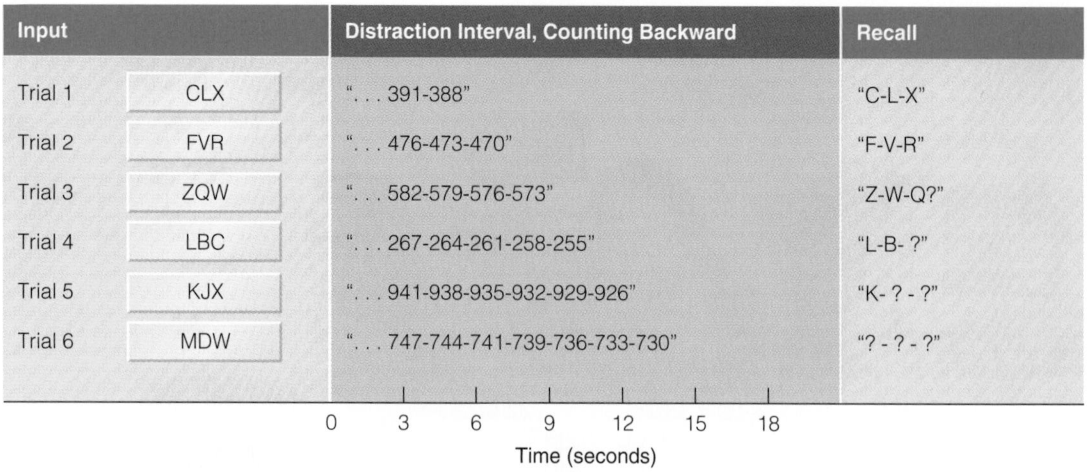

Input		Distraction Interval, Counting Backward	Recall
Trial 1	CLX	". . . 391-388"	"C-L-X"
Trial 2	FVR	". . . 476-473-470"	"F-V-R"
Trial 3	ZQW	". . . 582-579-576-573"	"Z-W-Q?"
Trial 4	LBC	". . . 267-264-261-258-255"	"L-B- ?"
Trial 5	KJX	". . . 941-938-935-932-929-926"	"K- ? - ?"
Trial 6	MDW	". . . 747-744-741-739-736-733-730"	"? - ? - ?"

```
       0    3    6    9    12   15   18
              Time (seconds)
```

▶ **Figure 7.3**

The Brown/Peterson Distractor Task

On each trial, subjects were asked to recall three letters in correct order, after counting backward aloud for from 3 to 18 seconds. The longer the subjects counted, the less likely they were to recall the letters correctly.

find that you often forget the letters, especially after the first few trials. In the Brown/Peterson experiments, subjects were reduced to guessing after about 10 to 15 seconds of counting backward (see ▶ Figure 7.3).

The Brown/Peterson task underestimates how quickly information is forgotten from short-term memory without rehearsal. When people are trying to remember material, as in the Brown/Peterson task, they sometimes "cheat" by turning their attention from the counting task to rehearsal for brief periods. If the task is redesigned so that subjects believe that the contents of short-term memory will not be tested but then a surprise test is given, results indicate that nonrehearsed information is lost from short-term memory after only a second or two (Marsh, Landau, & Hicks, 1997; Muter, 1980; Sebrechts, Marsh, & Seamon, 1989). Thus, short-term memory is an excellent system for maintaining information over the short term, but only while you're paying attention to it. In the absence of rehearsal, short-term memories are quickly lost.

Why is information lost from short-term memory so rapidly in the absence of rehearsal? Some researchers believe that short-term memories are lost spontaneously with the passage of time through a process called *decay*, unless those memories are kept active through rehearsal (Baddeley, 1992; Cowan, Saults, & Nugent, 1997). Other researchers believe that short-term forgetting is caused by *interference* from new information or because people confuse current memories with past memories (Crowder & Neath, 1991; Keppel & Underwood, 1962; Nairne, 1990, 2002). It is likely that both decay and interference operate together to produce information loss from short-term memory.

Short-Term Memory Capacity How much information can be stored over the short term—that is, what's the capacity of short-term memory? Research has shown that short-term **memory span**—the largest number of items a person can reliably recall in the exact order of presentation—is typically between five and nine pieces of information (as proposed in George Miller's classic 1956 article, titled "The magical number seven plus or minus two"). Most people find it easy to remember a list of four items but have great difficulty quickly mastering a list of 10 items.

memory span

The largest number of items that can reliably be recalled from short-term memory in their proper presentation order

Some psychologists believe that the capacity of short-term memory is limited because it takes time to execute the process of rehearsal. To illustrate, read the following list of letters aloud:

CA TFL YBU G

It probably took you about two to four seconds to read those letters aloud from C to G. Now look at the list again and then close your eyes and try cycling through the list with your inner voice, as if you were preparing for a short-term recall test. It turns out that the C to G cycling takes a similar amount of time when you are saying the words silently inside your head as it does when you are saying the letters aloud (Landauer, 1962). Items are lost from short-term memory in a second or two without rehearsal, so by the time you're finished with the last letter and ready to return to the beginning of the list, the early items may have already been lost from memory. You can think about this relationship between forgetting and rehearsal as roughly like juggling (see ▶ Figure 7.4). To juggle successfully, you need to win a constant battle against gravity. You throw the balls up, and gravity pushes them down. To prevent a ball from hitting the ground, it's necessary to catch it and toss it back up in the air before gravity pulls it down to the ground. Similarly, to prevent an item from being lost from short-term memory, you need to return to the rapidly fading short-term memory trace and reactivate it through rehearsal before the "force" of forgetting renders the memory unobtainable. It's a race between two opposing forces: rehearsal and forgetting.

This means that there should be a close link between the rate of rehearsal (or internal speech) and memory span. The sooner the rehearsal cycle is completed and begun again, the less chance that information will be lost through decay. This relationship is supported by a number of experimental findings. For example, over

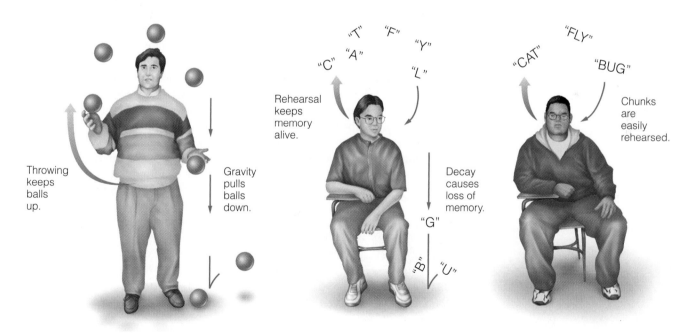

▶ **Figure 7.4**

The Capacity of Short-Term Memory

The amount of information that can be stored in short-term memory depends partly on the process of rehearsal, which you can think of as roughly analogous to juggling. You need to return to each rapidly fading short-term memory trace and reactivate it through rehearsal before it's forgotten. Forming "chunks" from the to-be-remembered material makes it easier and faster to rehearse and therefore increases the amount of information that can be retained.

CRITICAL   THINKING

Do you think it's an accident that local telephone numbers were originally seven digits long? Why do you suppose the telephone company encourages you to group the numbers into chunks, for example, 555-5854 or 905-555-2630?

chunking

A short-term memory strategy that involves mentally rearranging many pieces of information into a familiar and meaningful pattern; a single chunk can represent a wealth of information

the short term, it's more difficult to remember lists of long words (such as "rhinoceros") than it is to remember lists of short words (such as "bat"). It takes longer to cycle through a list of long words by using the inner voice, so more of these items are likely to be forgotten (Baddeley, Thomson, & Buchanan, 1975; Schweickert, Guentert, & Hersberger, 1990; Standing & Curtis, 1989). It also takes longer to count to 10 in Arabic than it does in English; consequently, people who speak English can remember longer lists of digits over the short term than those who speak Arabic (Naveh-Benjamin & Ayres, 1986). Finally, children's ability to remember information over the short term improves with language development; as they learn to speak more fluently, their rate of rehearsal improves, which contributes to an improved ability to recall information from short-term memory (Blake, Austin, Cannon, & Lisus, 1994; Hitch & Halliday, 1983).

As a general rule, memory span is roughly equal to the amount of material that can be internally rehearsed in about two seconds (which usually turns out to be about seven plus or minus two items). To improve your ability to remember over the short term, then, it's best to figure out a way to rehearse a lot of information in a short amount of time. One effective technique is **chunking,** which involves mentally rearranging the incoming information into meaningful or familiar patterns called *chunks*. A single chunk can represent a wealth of information. Remember that long list of letters presented earlier (CA TFL YBU G)? Perhaps you noticed that the spaces between the nine letters could be rearranged to form three words:

CAT FLY BUG

Forming the letters into words drastically reduces the time it takes to repeat the list internally (try saying CAT FLY BUG internally, compared with saying the list of letters internally). In addition, once you remember a chunk, it's easy to report the letters. In most cases, words are great storage devices for remembering sequences of letters. Of course, the trick lies in finding meaningful chunks in what can initially appear to be a meaningless jumble of information.

The ability to create meaningful chunks, thereby improving memory span, often depends on how much you know about the to-be-remembered material. Expert chess players can re-create most of the positions of a mid-game chessboard after only a brief glance (Chase & Simon, 1973). They recognize familiar attack or defence patterns in the game, which allows them to create easy-to-rehearse chunks of position information, each representing several pieces. Similar results are found when electronics experts are asked to remember complex circuit board diagrams (Egan & Schwartz, 1979). In both cases, if the materials are arranged randomly (e.g., the chess pieces are randomly scattered about the board), experts do no better than novices (see ▶ Figure 7.5).

Middle Game
Black

White

Random Middle Game
Black

White

▶ **Figure 7.5**

Expertise, Chunking, and Memory

Expert chess players recognize familiar configurations in a chess game and can re-create them easily from memory (left); however, when chess pieces are arranged randomly on a board (right), which precludes the chunking of familiar patterns, chess experts show memory similar to novices. (Chase & Simon, 1973.)

The Working Memory Model

Our discussion up to this point has focused on the characteristics of short-term memories, but we haven't discussed the psychological system that controls memory over the short term. Unfortunately, memory researchers still don't completely agree about the mechanisms that allow us to remember over the short term. Some psychologists believe that memory over the short term is controlled by the same machinery that underlies long-term memory (Melton, 1963; Nairne, 2002). Other psychologists assume we have special equipment for short-term memory. The most popular current account of the short-term memory system is the *working memory model* developed originally by Baddeley and Hitch (1974) and elaborated more recently by Baddeley (1992, 2000).

According to the working memory model, several distinct mechanisms are important for short-term retention. First, the temporary storage of acoustic and verbal information is controlled by the *phonological loop*. The phonological loop is the structure we use to store verbal information temporarily via repetitive rehearsal—it corresponds roughly to the inner voice and is believed to play a critical role in language (Baddeley, Gathercole, & Papagno, 1998). The short-term retention and processing of visual and spatial information relies on a different system—the *visuospatial sketchpad*. When you try to count the number of windows in your house by moving through its rooms in your mind's eye, you are using something like the visuospatial sketchpad. Finally, Baddeley and Hitch (1974) proposed that a *central executive* controls and allocates how processing is divided across the loop and the sketchpad. The central executive determines when the loop or sketchpad will be used with particular pieces of information and coordinates their actions.

One reason that the working memory model is popular among memory researchers is that it helps to explain the effects of certain types of brain damage. Some patients, for example, seem to lose very specific verbal skills, such as the ability to learn new words in an unfamiliar language. Other patients retain their language skills but have difficulties with memory for spatial or visual information (Baddeley, 2000). These results suggest that we have separate systems controlling verbal and visual storage, just as the working memory model proposes. Studies have also used neuroimaging techniques, such as PET scanning, which show that different areas of the brain are active when we remember verbal and visual information (Jonides, 2000; Wager & Smith, 2003).

Test Yourself   7.1

Check your knowledge about remembering over the short term by deciding whether each of the following statements best describes sensory memory or short-term memory. (The answers are in Appendix B.)

1. Information is stored as a relatively exact copy of the stimuli received by the sensory receptors: _____

2. Information can be stored indefinitely through the process of rehearsal: _____

3. System measured through Sperling's partial report procedure: _____

4. Recall errors tend to sound like the correct item even if the to-be-remembered items were presented visually: _____

5. Span is roughly equal to the amount of material that you can say to yourself in two seconds: _____

6. Capacity is improved through chunking: _____

7. The working memory model provides a theoretical account of its operation and use: _____

▶ Storing Information for the Long Term

LEARNING GOALS

1. Be able to differentiate among episodic, semantic, and procedural memories.
2. Be able to compare and contrast the effects of elaboration and distinctiveness on retrieval from long-term memory.
3. Appreciate how and why repetition influences later retrieval from long-term memory.
4. Understand how and why memory tends to be better for items near the beginning and end of a list than for mid-list items.
5. Learn how visual imagery can be used to improve retrieval from memory.
6. Learn about mnemonic devices.

Many of the processes used to store information in short-term memory also play key roles in the storage of information for the long term. At least some of the information in short-term memory also becomes encoded into **long-term memory.** (Remember, information in short-term memory lasts only for a few seconds without rehearsal, so any memories more than a few seconds post-rehearsal rely on long-term memory.) Most psychologists believe that long-term memory has no limit on the amount of material it can store. Whether, for how long, and under what circumstances information can later be *retrieved* from long-term memory depends partly on the processing activities performed during encoding, while the information was in short-term memory. To promote effective long-term retention, it's important to think about the information in certain ways during initial presentation. In this section, we'll consider the kinds of encoding activities that lead to effective long-term storage, but first we'll consider the general kinds of information that are stored.

What Is Stored in Long-Term Memory?

Stop for a moment and think about your first romantic kiss. Do you remember the person's name, the situation, the year? Memories of this type, in which you recall a particular moment of your own past experience, are called **episodic memories**— they are composed of particular events, or episodes, that happened to you personally. Most experimental research on remembering involves episodic memory; that is, subjects in most memory studies are asked to remember particular prior events, such as reading a word on a list or seeing a picture presented on a computer screen.

Now think of a capital city in Europe, located on the Seine, famous for its fashion, fine food, and wine. What is the square root of nine, and what is the capital city of Canada? Answering these questions certainly uses memory, in the sense that you must retrieve information from the past, but remembering these answers feels quite different from remembering your first kiss. When you use knowledge about language or the world but have no feeling of remembering a particular episode in your past, you are using **semantic memory** (*semantic* refers to "meaning"). Semantic memory represents knowledge and beliefs.

It's difficult to teach skills associated with procedural memory, such as golf, partly because it is difficult to verbalize such skills.

---

long-term memory

The system used to maintain information for extended periods, from several seconds to a lifetime

episodic memory

Remembering a particular past event or episode that happened to you personally, such as recalling having breakfast this morning or recollecting your high-school graduation ceremony

semantic memory

Knowledge about language and the world, retrieved as abstract facts or beliefs that make little or no reference to any particular episode in personal experience

CONCEPT SUMMARY

VARIETIES OF LONG-TERM MEMORY

Type of Memory	Description	Example
Episodic	Memories of moments of past experiences	Wanda, the mail carrier, remembers that yesterday 20 cm of snow fell, making the daily mail delivery very difficult.
Semantic	Knowledge about the world, with no specific reference to a particular past episode	Wanda knows that mailing a letter costs 51 cents.
Procedural	Knowledge about how to do something	Wanda drives along the streets of her mail route effortlessly, without really thinking about it.

Finally, recall how to tie your shoes, drive a car, or ride a bike. The memory for how to *do* things is called **procedural memory.** Most skills, including athletic prowess, rely on the use of procedural memories. Procedural memories differ from episodic memories in that they do not produce a conscious experience of "remembering," and they differ from semantic memory in that they are very difficult to verbalize. Most people have a difficult time reporting how to tie their shoes or ride a bike. For a summary of these three memory types—episodic, semantic, and procedural—see the Concept Summary table.

Elaboration: Connecting New Material with Existing Knowledge

If you want to remember something over the long term, you should relate the material to your existing knowledge. We all house an incredibly rich collection of information in long-term memory. This existing knowledge can be used to enrich, or elaborate, the new material you're trying to remember. Through **elaboration,** the process of relating new information to well-remembered previously acquired information, meaningful connections can be established that ease later retrieval of the stored material. This is one reason that experts in a given area (say, hockey fans) usually do very well at remembering new information in their domain of expertise (e.g., remembering the name of the captain of last year's Canucks).

Think about Meaning   In its simplest form, elaboration involves thinking about the meaning of information that you want to remember. In a famous experiment by Craik and Tulving (1975) of the University of Toronto, people were asked questions about a long list of words, such as MOUSE. In one condition, the task required judgments about the sound of the word (Does the word rhyme with HOUSE?). In another condition, people were required to think about the meaning of the word (Is a MOUSE a type of animal?). Substantially better memory-test performance was obtained in this second condition. Presumably, thinking about meaning, rather than sound, causes people to form more connections between presented events and other information in memory. The "deeper" and more elaborative the processing during study, the better memory performance on most tests of recall or recognition (Craik & Lockhart, 1972).

Notice Relationships   You can also use your existing knowledge to look for relationships between the items that you want to remember, to organize what you need to learn. Suppose you were asked to remember the following list of words:

NOTES PENCIL CHOCOLATE BOOK PAPER ERASER COFFEE

procedural memory

Memory for how to do things, such as ride a bike or swing a golf club

CRITICAL   THINKING

When you take a test in one of your university courses, is the test primarily tapping episodic, semantic, or procedural memory?

elaboration

An encoding process that involves the formation of connections between to-be-remembered input and other information in memory

If you think about what the words mean and look for properties that the words have in common—perhaps thinking of them as things that you might take to a late-night study session—you are engaging in what psychologists call *relational processing*. Relational processing is a kind of elaboration, and it turns out to be an extremely effective strategy for promoting long-term retention (Hunt & Einstein, 1981).

Relational processing works because you are embellishing, or adding to, the stimulus input. By thinking about how the word PENCIL relates to a study-session scenario, you create a rich, elaborate, and multifaceted memory record. Later, when you try to remember this particular word, several different kinds of cues may help you recall it. Thinking about notes, chocolate, drinking coffee, studying—any of these might lead to correct recall of PENCIL given that you encoded that word by thinking about it in relation to those varied but meaningfully interrelated concepts.

Notice Differences   Connections like those just described help memory, but it's also important to think about how the material you want to remember is different from other information in long-term memory. If you simply encode the fact that PENCIL is a writing implement, you might incorrectly recall such things as PEN, CHALK, or even CRAYON when later tested. You need to think about the to-be-remembered item in some detail—such as by thinking about a yellow number 2 pencil—so that the memory record becomes *distinctive*. Distinctive memory records are remembered better because they are easier to distinguish from other related material in memory that might otherwise interfere with retrieval of the appropriate information (Waddill & McDaniel, 1998).

Psychologists use the term **distinctiveness** to refer to how unique or different a memory record is, compared with other information in memory (Neath & Surprenant, 2003). One of the byproducts of elaboration is a distinctive, and therefore relatively easy-to-retrieve, memory record. By comparing the item that you're trying to remember with other information in memory, you'll notice both how the item is related to other information (elaboration) and how it is unique or different (Craik & Jacoby, 1979; Hunt & McDaniel, 1993). Generally, if you want to remember something, you should concentrate on encoding both its similarities to and its differences from other things you know.

distinctiveness

A term used to refer to how unique or different a memory record is, compared with other information in memory; distinctive memory records tend to be recalled well

Repetition of To-Be-Remembered Material: Diversify and Distribute

You probably already know that, compared with a single study opportunity, repeated studying improves memory for the studied material. You probably don't know, however, that repetition alone does little if anything to enhance memory. It's possible to encounter an item multiple times without substantially improving memory: If you think about the material in exactly the same shallow way every time it's presented, your memory won't improve very much with repetitions (Challis, 1993; Greene, 1992). This is why rote rehearsal (that is, simply repeating the to-be-remembered material over and over again) is a poor memorization technique. To benefit from multiple study occasions, you must use each opportunity to encode the material in a slightly different way. That is, you must diversify the way you think about the material. Doing so fosters the creation of multiple interrelated memory records, each of which is well elaborated and distinctive.

Many students put off serious studying until shortly before an exam, cramming almost all of their studying into the day or so leading up to the exam. This is known as **massed practice.** It is not a very effective way of learning, especially if you want to retain what you've learned after the exam is over. The better approach is to "distribute" your studying over wide periods, with other activities interspersed between study sessions. For example, rather than doing all of your psychology

massed practice

Clustering repetitions of to-be-remembered information close together in time

studying in one long session, it's better to study a little psychology, do something else, and then return to your psychology (Neath, 1998; Rea & Modigliani, 1988). This is called **distributed practice.**

Why does distributed practice lead to better long-term memory than massed practice does? The answer lies in how you process the material while studying it. If you engage in massed practice—where you simply reread the same material over and over again without a break—you're likely to think about the material in almost exactly the same way every time it is presented. If you insert a break between study sessions, when you see the material again, you have a better chance of noticing something new or different. Thus, compared with massed practice, distributed practice leads to memory records that are more diversified, elaborate, and distinctive. Also, distributed study sessions provide you with opportunities to practise retrieving memories of prior study episodes. Finally, distributing study sessions gives you a better sense of which things you have learned well and which things you haven't yet mastered (Metcalfe, 2002).

Effects of Temporal Order

Long-term memory also depends on the temporal order in which items are presented during study. For example, if you are given a long list of items to remember, such as 10 errands to complete, you will tend to remember the items from the beginning and the end of the list best. This pattern is shown in ▶ Figure 7.6, which plots how well items are recalled as a function of their temporal, or serial, position in a list (this graph is often called a *serial position curve*). The enhanced memory for items at the beginning of the list is called the **primacy effect;** the end-of-the-list advantage is called the **recency effect.** Memory researchers believe that primacy and recency effects arise partly because items that occur at the beginning and end of a sequence are more naturally distinctive in memory and are therefore easier to recall. Also, the first few items tend to be rehearsed more than later items, and if the memory test is immediate, then the last few items will still be available for report from short-term memory (Murdock, 1960, 1995; Neath, 1993).

Imagery: Remembering through Visualization

Another way to enhance memory is to form visual images of the to-be-remembered materials. **Visual imagery** is the process used to construct an internal vision-like image. Creating images during study can dramatically improve subsequent memory. If you're trying to remember the word COFFEE, for example, try forming a mental picture of a steaming hot, freshly brewed mug. As a more apt example, you might foster memory for a psychology experiment described in this text by forming an image of what the setting, equipment, and procedure of the experiment would look like.

Forming mental images is an effective memory strategy, partly because it naturally leads to elaborate, rich, distinctive encodings. That is, the process of forming an image of a to-be-remembered item leads you to think about various aspects of that item in novel ways that both connect it to things you already know well and make it distinctive and unique. Allan Paivio of the University of Western Ontario has argued that there is a second mechanism by which imagery enhances memory. According to Paivio's "dual code" hypothesis, when you form images as well as verbalize to-be-remembered material, you are creating two qualitatively different kinds of mental representations. When you later attempt to recall the item, either or both of those memory records could be retrieved, thereby increasing your chances of recall (Paivio, 1995).

distributed practice

Spacing the repetitions of to-be-remembered information over time

primacy effect

The better memory for items near the beginning of a studied list compared with mid-list items

recency effect

The better memory for items near the end of a studied list compared with mid-list items

visual imagery

The processes used to construct an internal visual image through the use of some of the same brain mechanisms as in perception

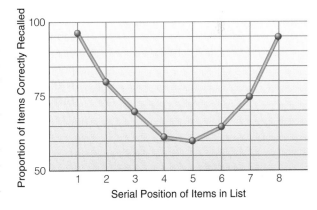

▶ Figure 7.6

The Serial Position Curve

When we are asked to recall a list of items, our performance often depends on the temporal, or serial, position of the items in the list. Items at the beginning of the list are remembered relatively well (the *primacy effect*) and so are items at the end of the list (the *recency effect*).

Good evidence shows that, consistent with Paivio's hypothesis, visual imagery involves cognitive codes and processes that are qualitatively different from those that support mental verbalization. For example, a classic study by Lee Brooks (1968) of McMaster University demonstrated that people have great difficulty holding a visual image in their mind's eye while performing a spatial pointing task, but have little difficulty holding an image in mind while performing a verbal task. This suggests that imaging and verbalizing involve separate mental machinery. That is, it is difficult to use the same piece of mental equipment to do two different tasks at the same time, but if each task involves a different piece of mental equipment, then it is relatively easy to perform them concurrently (also see Baddeley & Lieberman, 1980).

As evidence that mental imagery is perception-like, Kosslyn and colleagues showed that the time to answer questions that involve mentally "traversing" across imagined space is lawfully related to the distance "travelled" (Kosslyn, Ball, & Reiser, 1978). Similarly, Shepard and Cooper (1986) tested subjects on tasks that required them to mentally rotate an image of an object, and found that response times increased as a function of the number of degrees of mental rotation. These sorts of findings suggest that mental images represent spatial relations in ways that are directly analogous to perceptual spatial relations. Further supporting that claim, brain-imaging studies have shown that mental imagery involves some of the same brain areas as visual perception (Ganis, Thompson, & Kosslyn, 2004; Loverock & Modigliani, 1995; Raij, 1999). Also, some people with brain damage have parallel impairments in perceptual and imagery tasks (Levine, Warach, & Farah, 1985). For example, patients whose brain damage has caused them to lose their colour vision may also have difficulty forming a colourful visual image. Such results as these indicate that important links exist between the brain systems involved in visual perception and those involved in mental imagery (Ganis, Thompson, Mast, & Kosslyn, 2003).

Although mental imagery is similar to perception in some ways, imagery differs from perception in other ways. For example, try forming a very clear visual image of the "maple leaf" side of a penny. You've seen pennies thousands of times, so if you have good imagery skills this will probably seem easy. Now try to reproduce your image on paper—sketch the leaves, indicating the correct orientation, write in the words, and add the other details. Despite the apparent vividness of your mental image, you'll probably have difficulty with this task. Most people cannot reproduce the main features of the coin accurately, despite their belief that they can "see" an accurate representation in their mind's eye. Even more surprisingly, people have difficulty even recognizing the correct coin when it is presented along with incorrect versions, as shown in ❱ Figure 7.7 (Nickerson & Adams, 1979; for a British version of this study, see Jones & Martin, 1992).

❱ **Figure 7.7**

Can You Recognize a Penny?

Most people think that they can form an accurate mental image of a penny, but few can pick out a true penny from a group of alternatives. Can you find the real penny in this display? (Adapted from Nickerson & Adams, 1979.)

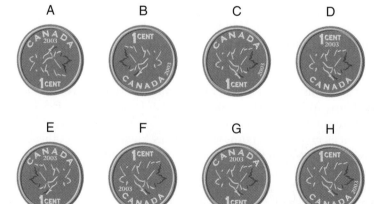

Another limitation of mental images is that people cannot change their interpretations of images as they can with visual perceptions. For example, if subjects are shown a Necker cube like that in Chapter 4 (see Figure 4.1 on page 124) and are then asked to form a visual image of it and examine their image, the imagined cube does not change perspective the way a visually present Necker cube does. Similarly, try imagining a line drawing of a Star of David (two superimposed upward- and downward-pointing equilateral triangles): Does the imagined line drawing have embedded within it any parallelograms (a four-sided figure with opposite lines parallel to one another but not meeting at right angles)? Most people are unable to "see" any embedded parallelograms in their images, but if they actually look at a Star of David, they easily spot four of them (try it!) (Reisberg & Chambers, 1991).

Such findings as those described in the preceding two paragraphs suggest that visual images are typically fairly vague or fuzzy, not entirely accurate, and different from perceptual images in some important ways. Even though images do differ from more word-like forms of mental representation, they can powerfully enhance memory, particularly when combined with other mental strategies, as described in the next section.

Mnemonic Devices

Mnemonic devices are special mental tricks that help people think about material in ways that lead to effective remembering of that material (*mnemonic* means "pertaining to memory"). Many of these devices were originally developed by the ancient Greeks (Yates, 1966). Mnemonic devices combine imagery and elaboration during study with a strategy or structure that guides retrieval when memory is tested.

One of the oldest mnemonic devices is the **method of loci** (*loci* is Latin for "places"). The method of loci (see ▶ Figure 7.8) has two primary components: visual imagery and a system for relating pieces of to-be-remembered information to well-remembered previously learned material that simultaneously encourages elaboration (and hence good encoding) and provides a strategy for searching memory. The technique begins with the choice of a familiar real-world pathway, such as a familiar route to work or school, and flawlessly memorizing a set of landmarks encountered along that pathway (e.g., the front hallway of your

mnemonic devices

Special mental tricks that help people think about material in ways that improve later memory; most use visual imagery and elaboration during encoding and a systematic strategy for searching memory during retrieval

method of loci

A mnemonic device in which you first memorize a series of locations along a familiar real-world pathway, such as the route from your residence to the university, and then form visual images of the to-be-remembered items sitting in the various locations along that pathway; to recall the items, you mentally traverse the pathway, checking each location as a retrieval cue

▶ **Figure 7.8**

The Method of Loci

To-be-remembered items are mentally imaged in various locations along a familiar path. These items will be easy to remember because the use of visual imagery promotes a distinctive and elaborate memory trace and because the pathway is well learned and hence provides a structure for searching memory. In this example, the locations are the kitchen counter, the TV, and the couch of the rememberer's apartment, and the to-be-memorized items are dry cleaning, dog food, and library books.

residence, the front steps, the bush close to the sidewalk, the mailbox down the street). The to-be-remembered material is then systematically placed, in your mind's eye, at the various landmarks along the path. So, if you wanted to remember to pay the gas bill, then feed the cat, then put a frozen pizza in the oven, and so on, you might form a mental picture of a large cheque made out to the gas company sitting in your front hallway, an image of your cat chowing down on your front steps, an image of your oven opening up to receive a pizza beside the bush close to the sidewalk, and so on. Then, when you want to remember this to-do list, you mentally traverse the pathway, checking each landmark. Ordinary people can remember very long lists with this technique (Bower, 1973; for a more general discussion of the relationship between imagery and memory, see Paivio, 1995).

Another mnemonic device, known as the **link-word system,** can be used to learn foreign language vocabulary (Gruneberg, Sykes, & Gillett, 1994). Suppose you wanted to remember the French word for rabbit (*lapin*). While studying, think of an English word that sounds like the French word; perhaps the word *lap* would do for *lapin*. Next, think about the meaning of the French word, and form a visual image of that meaning linked to the English term. For example, you could imagine a white rabbit sitting in someone's lap. When the word *lapin* later appears on a test, the English word should serve as an effective cue for bringing forth a remembered image of the rabbit. The use of this method can nearly double the rate of learning vocabulary words (Raugh & Atkinson, 1975).

The method of loci and the link-word technique are just two examples of mnemonic devices—there are many others (see Herrmann, Raybeck, & Gruneberg, 2002). The techniques are not necessarily easy, but diligent use of them can be extremely effective. How do they work? For one thing, most mnemonic techniques require the use of visual imagery. As noted earlier, the formation of a visual image often leads to an elaborate and distinctive memory record. Equally important, mnemonic techniques also require you to link to-be-remembered material to a set of easily available retrieval cues. By associating material to a well-learned sequence of landmarks, as in the method of loci, you establish retrieval cues that are easy to access at any time: All you need to do is mentally walk along that well-learned route, and the stored memory items are likely to come to mind. This illustrates a fundamental point, to be further explored in the next section: Memory performance is greatly influenced by the types of retrieval cues that are available when memory is tested.

Diligent use of mnemonics can enable ordinary people to perform seemingly impossible feats of memory. For example, Ericsson and Chase (1982) reported a study of a student volunteer who developed a mnemonic for memorizing random strings of digits. In the digit span task, digits are presented auditorily one at a time at a one-second rate, then the subject is asked to repeat back the string of numbers in order. At first, the student's digit span (i.e., the number of digits he could report back in order) was the standard 7, but over a period of weeks he got better and better, eventually being able to repeat back up to 80 digits. Similarly, Morris, Fritz, Jackson, Nichol, and Roberts (2005) showed that a simple strategy can dramatically increase undergraduates' ability to remember people's names. For other examples of feats of memory, see Kalakoski and Saariluoma, 2001; Neisser, 2000; and Parker, Cahill, and McGaugh, 2006.

link-word system

A mnemonic device for remembering foreign language vocabulary in which you (1) think of an English word that sounds similar to the to-be-learned foreign word and (2) form a visual image connecting the meaning of the to-be-remembered word with the similar-sounding English word

CRITICAL THINKING

Many people say, "I never forget a face, but I'm terrible at remembering names." Based on what you have learned in this chapter, generate several ideas about why people find it harder to remember names than faces.

1. For each of the following, decide whether the relevant memory is episodic, semantic, or procedural:
   a. The capital city of British Columbia is Victoria: _____
   b. I had a superb meal at Café Brio last night: _____
   c. My mother's maiden name is Hudlow: _____
   d. Executing a perfect golf swing: _____
   e. Tying your shoelaces: _____
2. Your little brother, Eddie, needs to learn a long list of vocabulary words for school tomorrow. Which of the following represents the best advice for improving his memory?
   a. Say the words aloud as many times as possible.
   b. Write down the words as many times as possible.
   c. Form a visual image of each word.
   d. Spend more time studying words at the beginning and end of the list than those near the middle of the list.

3. For each of the following, decide which term best applies. Choose from: distinctiveness, massed practice, distributed practice, elaboration, method of loci, link-word system.
   a. Visualize each of the items sitting in a location along a familiar pathway: _____
   b. Notice how each item is different from other information in memory: _____
   c. Form connections between the items that you want to remember and other things you already know: _____
   d. Form an image linking the meaning of a foreign word to the meaning of an English word that sounds similar to that foreign word: _____
   e. Study for a while, then do something else for a while, then do some more studying, and so on: _____
   f. Concentrate all of your studying in a single session: _____

▶ Recovering Information from Cues

LEARNING GOALS

1. Understand the ideas of cue-dependent forgetting, the encoding specificity principle, and the notion of transfer-appropriate processing.
2. Understand how reconstructive processes, such as schemas and source monitoring, can lead to inaccurate recollections of past events.
3. Learn about the differences between implicit and explicit memory.

Can you remember the memory list from a few pages back? You know, the one that included PENCIL? If you remembered the other items, such as BOOK, NOTES, and COFFEE, it's probably because you were able to use the common theme—things to take to a late-night study session—as a retrieval cue. Most psychologists believe that *retrieval*, which is the process of recovering previously stored memories, is guided by the presence of *retrieval cues*, which are either generated internally (thinking of the study session helps you remember PENCIL) or are physically present in the environment (as when the cue was presented here).

The Importance of Retrieval Cues

A classic study conducted by Tulving and Pearlstone (1966) at the University of Toronto illustrates the critical role that retrieval cues play in remembering. People were given lists to remember that contained words from a variety of meaningful categories (types of animals, birds, vegetables, and so on). Later, the participants were asked to remember the words either with or without the aid of retrieval cues. Half the subjects were asked to recall the words without cues (a condition known as **free recall**); the remaining subjects were given the category names to help them remember (an example of a kind of memory test known as **cued recall**). Subjects in the cued-recall condition recalled nearly twice as many words, even though the

free recall

A testing condition in which a person is asked to remember information without specific retrieval cues: subjects might simply be asked to "recall the words you studied a few minutes ago"

cued recall

A testing condition in which subjects are given specific retrieval cues to help them remember: subjects might be given hints or cues, such as "some of the words were fruits; others were vegetables"

Can you name all of your classmates from grade 2? Probably not, but your performance is likely to improve if you're given a retrieval cue in the form of a class photo.

cue-dependent forgetting

The idea that forgetting is caused by a failure to retrieve memories because of a lack of appropriate retrieval cues

encoding specificity principle

The idea that the effectiveness of retrieval cues depends on the extent to which they match the specifics of the to-be-remembered material; the more similar the cue and the testing situation to the to-be-remembered material and the studying situation, the more likely the memories will be accessed

two groups did not differ in how they had studied the words. Performance was better in the cued-recall condition because the category names helped subjects gain access to memories of the studied list.

Although these results may not seem surprising, they have important implications for how we think about remembering and forgetting. Consider performance in the free-recall condition. Because people performed poorly, it's tempting to conclude that they either never learned the material or simply forgot many of the items from the list. But the performance of the people who were cued shows that the poor memory in the free-recall condition resulted from a failure to access the relevant memory information. With the right retrieval cues, material that seems to have been lost, or never learned, can often be remembered with striking clarity. For this reason, many memory researchers believe that most, if not all, instances of forgetting are really **cue-dependent forgetting.** The information, once it's encoded in long-term memory, is available in the brain; you simply need the right kind of retrieval cues to recover it.

The Encoding–Retrieval Match   What conditions make retrieval cues effective? Psychologists believe that the effectiveness of a retrieval cue depends on how well and how uniquely the cue matches the memory that was encoded. If you thought about the meaning of the materials while studying them, then retrieval cues having to do with meaning will be most effective, but if you thought only about the sounds of the words while studying them, then sound-alike cues (such as rhymes) will be more effective. This idea is known as the **encoding specificity principle,** which holds that the effectiveness of a retrieval cue depends on the extent to which the cue and testing context match the to-be-remembered material (Tulving & Thomson, 1973).

Let's consider an example. Suppose you were asked to remember the two words BANK and WAGON. You know about the effectiveness of elaborative encoding and imagery, so you form a visual image of a WAGON perched on the BANK of a river (see ▶ Figure 7.9). Later, BANK is provided as a retrieval cue. Will it help you remember WAGON? Probably, but only if you interpret the retrieval cue

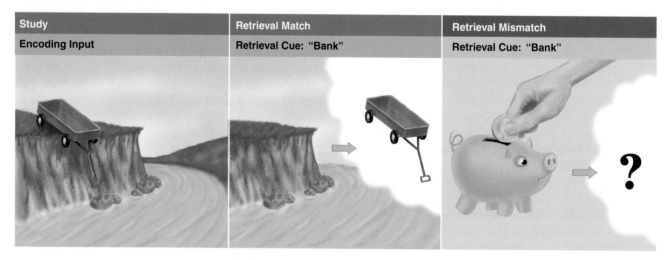

Study	Retrieval Match	Retrieval Mismatch
Encoding Input	Retrieval Cue: "Bank"	Retrieval Cue: "Bank"

▶ **Figure 7.9**

The Encoding–Retrieval Match

Memory performance depends partly on how well retrieval cues match the way information was originally studied or encoded. Suppose you're asked to remember the word pair BANK and WAGON. During study, you form a visual image of a wagon teetering on the edge of a riverbank. When later presented with the retrieval cue BANK, you're more likely to remember WAGON if you interpret that cue as land bordering a river than as a place to keep money.

BANK to mean "land bordering a river." If for some reason you think about BANK as a financial institution, you probably will not recover WAGON successfully. A retrieval cue will be effective only if you interpret it in a way that matches the original encoding.

The encoding specificity principle has a number of interesting implications for remembering. For example, it helps to explain context- and state-dependent remembering. Context-dependent remembering refers to the fact that memory tends to be better when study and test are performed in the same environmental context. That phenomenon was dramatically demonstrated in a study by Martin and Aggleton (1993), who had students in a diving school study information either on land or underwater, and then tested their memory either on land or underwater. Those who studied on land did better if tested on land, whereas those who studied underwater did better if tested underwater. Presumably, a better match between encoding and retrieval exists when information is learned and tested in the same environment. The concept of state-dependent remembering is similar, but here it is the match in internal state (e.g., mood) between study and test that matters (e.g., Eich & Schooler, 2000).

The encoding specificity principle may also explain the intriguing phenomenon of childhood amnesia. It is clear that very young children soak up new information at a prodigious rate, yet most adults remember few if any of their experiences before the age of three or four years (as though we were amnesic for early childhood). It's likely that we interpreted the world very differently when we were small. Childhood amnesia may result, then, from a poor match between the adult present and the early-childhood past. We see and interpret events differently now from how we did as children, so we have few effective retrieval cues available for remembering childhood events (Courage & Howe, 2004; Newcombe, Drummey, Fox, Lie, & Ottinger-Alberts, 2000).

Transfer-Appropriate Processing   The encoding specificity principle states that the more closely the content of cues matches the content of a memory, the more likely the cues will retrieve the memory. The concept of **transfer-appropriate processing** is a slightly different way of expressing the same basic idea. "Transfer" refers to effects of past performance on current performance. In the motor domain, for example, skill at one sport (e.g., tennis) may transfer to performance of another sport (e.g., squash); the more similar the processes involved in the two sports, the greater the transfer. Likewise, the more similar your current cognitive processes are to those you performed during a prior study session, the more likely that what you learned then will transfer to the present and hence be recollected (Jacoby & Dallas, 1981; Masson & MacLeod, 1997; Morris, Bransford, & Franks, 1977; Roediger, Weldon, & Challis, 1989). From this perspective, remembering is the transfer of aspects of your past experience to your current experience. This means that if you want to remember something at a certain future place and time, you should study the material by using the same kinds of mental processes that will be required during retrieval, as well as in a similar environmental context and emotional state.

To illustrate, you've learned at various points in this chapter that elaboration—relating to-be-remembered material to other information in memory—is an effective strategy for remembering. But the effectiveness of any encoding manipulation will depend on what kind of information is required by the memory test and what cues are available in the testing context. Let's assume

transfer-appropriate processing

The idea that the likelihood of correct retrieval increases as a function of the similarity between mental processes during encoding and those during test

Later, this couple may find it easier to remember their blissful reunion if they're happy rather than sad when they attempt recall. How does this conclusion follow from consideration of the encoding–retrieval match?

▶ **Figure 7.10**

Transfer-Appropriate Processing

Study by using the same type of mental processes that you'll use when tested. Suppose you form a visual image of a to-be-remembered word during study (panel 1). If the test requires you to recognize an image corresponding to this meaning of the studied word, you should do well (panel 2). But if the test asks how the word sounds (panel 3) or whether the word was studied in upper- or lower-case letters (panel 4), you're likely to perform poorly. It's best to study in a way that is appropriate for the test.

CRITICAL THINKING

We designed this text to encourage readers to process the material in ways that support excellent memory for the content. How many features of the text can you identify that are likely to have this effect?

that you're asked to remember the word TUG (see ▶ Figure 7.10). If you form a visual image of a tugboat during study and you are later specifically asked about a tugboat on the memory test, you will probably perform well. But suppose you are asked instead to remember whether the word TUG was printed in upper- or lower-case letters in the study materials. All the elaboration in the world isn't going to help you answer this question unless the elaboration had something to do with encoding the way the letters were shaped ("TUG," not "tug").

Another example of transfer-appropriate processing comes from a classic study by Morris et al. (1977). They had undergraduates study words with either a task that required them to think about the words or one that required them to think about the sound of the word. Later, subjects were either given a standard recognition test (which of these words did you study earlier?) or a rhyme recognition test (which of these words rhymes with a word you studied earlier?). On the standard recognition test, studying words in terms of meaning led to better performance than studying words in terms of sound, but on the rhyme recognition test the opposite was the case: Studying words in terms of their sounds led to better performance.

The practical implications of this idea of transfer-appropriate processing should be obvious. You should think about the characteristics of an exam *before* you study for it. Learn the material by reading the chapter and thinking about it in deeply elaborative ways, forming distinctive images, and relating the new knowledge to information you already know, all of which will help you both comprehend the material and encode it in ways that support recall. Importantly, though, when you go to prepare for an exam you should do so by doing the same kinds of things that will be required on that exam (Herrmann et al., 2002). Often, students prepare for exams by reading their notes and the text over and over again; this would make sense if the test was of reading speed or simple recognition, but exams rarely involve rereading passages of the text. An essay exam, for example, is a kind of *cued-recall* test: You are given a cue in the form of a test question, and you are to recall and write down the most appropriate answer. To study for such a test, it is best to practise cued recall: Make up questions that are relevant to the material, and practise recalling and writing down the appropriate answer. For a multiple-choice test, which is a kind of *recognition* test, it is necessary to discriminate a correct answer from a group of incorrect answers (called *distractors*). The best way to study for a multiple-choice test is to practise with multiple-choice questions; either make up your own or use questions from a study guide. For compelling evidence that practice tests dramatically promote learning and subsequent test performance, see Chan, McDermott, and Roediger (in press) and Roediger and Karpicke (2006). For more tips on studying for exams, see the Practical Solutions box.

PRACTICAL SOLUTIONS

STUDYING FOR AN EXAM

Motivation to learn does not, in itself, directly enhance memory. What matters is not how keenly you desire to remember the material, but rather how appropriately you process the material while studying. Here we synthesize the concepts discussed in this chapter in the context of their implications for studying. This may come across as "preachy," because in a sense we *are* preaching: We're teachers, our job is to promote, support, and facilitate your learning, and good evidence suggests that the practical solutions to the problem of studying for exams we offer here really work.

An essential starting point is to read the to-be-remembered material in an active, elaborative way. Simply running your eyes over the words will do little to support understanding and subsequent performance on a memory test. Even when a topic area is new to you, you can be creative in noting relationships, similarities, and differences between particular pieces of information and other things that you already know well. By pushing yourself to understand the material as you read it, you will process it in ways that create memory records that are distinctive and yet also relate to other knowledge. When the material describes something that has some concrete setting, forming visual images will both test your understanding and support later memory performance. A related point is that paying attention to the various pictures, graphs, quotations, and definitions provided in the margins of texts like this encourages you

to form distinctive memory records that are connected with your memories of the ideas in the main body of the text.

Many texts (including this one) include self-test items, summary review sections, and lists of terms to remember at the end of the chapter. Some students ignore these or look at them but don't use them. Answering the self-test questions (not just looking at them, but actually writing down answers to them and checking Appendix B to score your answers), reading the summaries thoughtfully, and testing yourself on the vocabulary after reading each chapter will have numerous benefits (Herrmann et al., 2002; Willoughby, Wood, McDermott, & McLaren, 2000). When you practise remembering by answering self-test questions, you practise what you want to do later. Now that you know about the notion of transfer-appropriate processing, it will be easy to see why integrating self-testing with your studying makes very good sense. Self-testing will also help you identify parts of the material that you did not initially understand or process effectively.

Long-term retention is better supported by distributed rather than massed practice. If you keep up with the reading as the school term goes along, and if you do the reading in an actively engaged, elaborative manner as described above, your need to "cram" at the last minute will be reduced (although additional studying will nonetheless be valuable) and the likeli-

hood that you will still remember the material months after the exam will increase.

To promote comprehension and retention of concepts presented in a lecture, it is a good idea to go over your lecture notes shortly after the lecture. Don't just look at them; think elaboratively about them, perhaps adding additional notes that amplify and clarify those you took in class and relate the material to other things you've learned.

When preparing for an exam, make your studying as similar to the test as you can (as per the notion of transfer-appropriate processing). Unless they'll be playing tunes or videos while you're taking the exam, don't study with such background distractions. Take steps to avoid distractions (e.g., turn off your cell and MSN). Include self-testing in your exam preparation, and tailor the self-tests to the nature of the real test. For example, if the test is multiple-choice, then your examination preparation should include answering multiple-choice questions, whereas if it will be short answers then you should practise writing short answers to those sorts of questions. Practice questions can be taken from a study guide if one is available for the text, or you can make up your own while looking at the text one day, and then test yourself on them the next. If you have a study partner preparing for the same exam, the two of you can make up practice questions for each other.

Reconstructive Remembering

Retrieval cues guide remembering in much the same way as physical stimuli guide perception. As you may recall from Chapter 4, what people "see" depends on both the incoming environmental stimuli and their expectations about what's "out there." In a similar way, remembering depends on more than just encoding processes and retrieval cues—beliefs and expectations can distort recollections of the past just as they can distort what people perceive in the present. Stop for a moment and try to remember what you had for breakfast exactly two weeks ago. It turns out that what you will "remember" in a case like this often corresponds more to habit than to actual fact. If you regularly eat a bowl of cereal in the morning, then you may "recall" eating cereal even if you broke your routine on that particular day and had a bagel.

Memory Schemas   To understand why memory acts in this way, you need to realize that we store more than just events and facts in long-term memory; we also store relationships between events and between facts. You know, for example, that houses contain rooms with walls, require insurance protection, and can catch fire. You know that two-year-old children drool, fall down, and put things into their mouths. You have a wealth of knowledge about everyday tasks and situations, such as shopping for groceries or doing your laundry. Psychologists refer to these large clusters of related knowledge as **schemas.**

Schemas can be about people, places, or activities, such as going to a restaurant, visiting the local drop-in medical clinic, or making breakfast. When you recollect a past experience, you use these organized knowledge clusters to help reconstruct what happened. So when someone asks you what you ate for breakfast two weeks ago, you may confidently answer "cereal" because you know that cereal is what you usually eat for breakfast. You don't have to remember the specific episode; you can rely on your general knowledge. More interestingly, thoughts and images that are based on schemas are sometimes erroneously experienced as if they were episodic memories; that is, you might feel that you are remembering a particular episode but really just be "filling in" from your schemas.

In a study of the influences of schemas on memories for crimes, Tuckey and Brewer (2003) showed undergraduate students a one-minute video of a simulated bank robbery. Some of the details in the video were consistent with the standard schema of a bank robbery (e.g., that the robber had a bag), whereas other details were schema-inconsistent (e.g., that the robber wore a business suit), and yet other details were unrelated to the bank-robbery schema (e.g., that the robber turned right after leaving). Participants in the study were then repeatedly interviewed about the video over a period of several days. Recall declined from the first to second interview, and that drop was greatest for schema-inconsistent details. Thus, participants' accounts became more schema-consistent from the first to the second telling. Also, participants sometimes recalled things that they hadn't really seen, and such false memories tended to be of details that, although not actually shown in the video, were consistent with the bank-robbery schema.

Schema-based remembering is usually reliable, because a schema corresponds to what most often happens. But schema-based remembering sometimes leads to inaccurate memories. You can remember something that is completely wrong—it didn't really happen—yet still be convinced your memory is accurate. In a well-known study conducted more than 60 years ago, Sir Frederick Bartlett asked English undergraduates to read an unfamiliar North American Indian folk tale about tribe members who battled with some warrior "ghosts" (the story's title was *The War of the Ghosts*). In recalling the story some time later, the students tended to distort facts, omit details, and fill in information that was not included in the original version. These errors were not random; rather, they often systematically changed the story in ways that made it more consistent with the English

schema

An organized knowledge structure in long-term memory

subjects' schemas. For example, familiar things were substituted for unfamiliar ones, such as the word "boat" being remembered rather than "canoe." Bartlett's subjects used their prior knowledge to reconstruct the story—even though they were often confident that they were remembering the material accurately (Bartlett, 1932).

You can demonstrate how easily schema-based remembering leads to false memories by reading the following list of words aloud to a group of friends:

BED REST AWAKE TIRED DREAM WAKE SNOOZE

BLANKET DOZE SLUMBER SNORE NAP YAWN DROWSY

After you've finished reading the list, ask your friends to write down all the words. The chances are good that someone will falsely remember the word SLEEP. In experiments that use lists of such related words as these, people recalled non-presented items, such as SLEEP, nearly 50% of the time (Deese, 1959; Read, 1996; Roediger & McDermott, 1995). The chances of false memory increase further when recognition memory is tested; that is, when subjects are given the word SLEEP and are asked if it was presented on the list (McDermott & Roediger, 1998). Subjects often indicate that they are highly confident that SLEEP was on the list and that they can recollect details of its presentation, such as the sound of the experimenter's voice when the word was read aloud.

What's behind this effect? Obviously, the word SLEEP is highly related to the words on the list. It seems likely that people recognize the relationships between the words and use this knowledge to help them remember, which in turn causes the word SLEEP to come to mind at test. This is a very effective strategy for remembering, but it can lead to false recollections. Other studies show that knowledge and beliefs can lead to false memories of significant life events. For example, research by Michael Ross and colleagues at the University of Waterloo has demonstrated that individuals' current beliefs about themselves can distort their recollections of their own pasts (Ross & Wilson, 2000).

CRITICAL THINKING
Do you think all remembering is reconstructive? What about sensory memory—isn't that a pure kind of remembering?

Eyewitness Testimony   The fact that memory tends to be reconstructive, sometimes leading to false memories, has important implications for eyewitness testimony. Loftus and Palmer (1974) conducted an experiment in which undergraduates were shown a short film depicting an automobile accident. When later questioned about the film, the students were asked to estimate the speed of the cars just before the accident. Some students were asked to estimate how fast the cars were going when they *smashed* into each other; others were asked how fast the cars were going when they *contacted* each other. Notice the difference between the words *smashed* and *contacted*. The schema for *smashed* implies that the cars were travelling at a high rate of speed, whereas *contacted* suggests that the cars were moving slowly. As shown in ◗ Figure 7.11 on page 284, subjects who heard the word *smashed* in the question estimated that the cars were travelling about 42 miles per hour (70 km/h); subjects in the *contacted* group gave an estimate about 10 miles per hour (16 km/h) slower.

Such results as these show that remembering is importantly influenced by general knowledge, beliefs, and social pressures. Everyone in the Loftus and Palmer (1974) experiment saw the same film, but what people remembered depended on whether the question implied that the cars were going fast or slow. In addition to giving estimates of speed, subjects were asked whether any broken glass was present in the accident scene. When *smashed* was used in the speed question, subjects were much more likely to remember seeing broken glass, even though there wasn't any in the original film. By asking the right kinds of questions during testing, it is possible to make a person think he or she experienced something that never really happened. As Loftus (1979, 1991) has emphasized, these findings suggest that caution must be exercised in interpreting the testimony of any eyewitness—

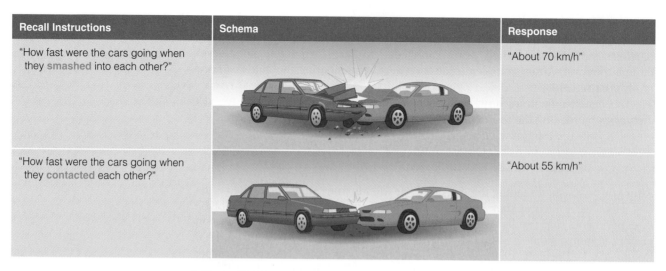

Recall Instructions	Schema	Response
"How fast were the cars going when they smashed into each other?"		"About 70 km/h"
"How fast were the cars going when they contacted each other?"		"About 55 km/h"

▶ **Figure 7.11**

Schema-Based Remembering

Loftus and Palmer (1974) found that subjects remembered that cars had been travelling at a faster speed when the test question used the word *smashed* as opposed to *contacted*. All subjects saw the same film, but their different schemas for the words *smashed* and *contacted* presumably caused them to reconstruct their memories differently.

reconstructive factors are always involved, and they can lead to memory errors (see also Lindsay, Brigham, & Brimacombe, 2002; Read, Connolly, & Turtle, 2001). Young children may be especially vulnerable to suggestive influences (e.g., Marche, 1999; Poole & Lindsay, 2002).

Suggestive influences do not always lead to false memories, and many variables interact together to determine the likelihood of false-memory development. In a study by Pezdek, Finger, and Hodge (1997), for example, undergraduates were exposed to a relatively weak suggestion to the effect that they had been given a rectal enema by their mothers when they were young children. Not one of Pezdek's subjects appeared to develop false memories of receiving the enema. As an example at the opposite end of the scale, Lindsay, Hagen, Read, Wade, and Garry (2004) used a variety of highly suggestive influences to foster false memories of having put Slime in the teacher's desk in elementary school, leading two-thirds of subjects to appear to develop false memories.

We have emphasized the errors that can be produced by reconstructive memory processes, partly because the errors are interesting and partly because they reveal the influence of reconstructive processes. Overall, though, schema-based reconstructive remembering has great adaptive value. By relying on pre-existing knowledge to "fill in the gaps" and to help interpret fuzzy recollections, people increase the chances that their responses will be appropriate; after all, our knowledge and beliefs are often accurate. People can also use their schematic knowledge to fill in minor details they may have missed during the original exposure. If you already have a pretty good idea of what goes on during a visit to a fast-food restaurant, your mind doesn't need to expend a great deal of effort attending to details when you enter a McDonald's. You can rely on your prior knowledge to capture the gist of the experience, even though, on the downside, you may later recollect a few things that didn't actually happen.

Source Monitoring   Have you ever had the experience of believing—if only for a few minutes—that something you had dreamed about had actually occurred? Have you ever remembered doing something (such as locking your door or turning off the oven) and later discovered that you had only *thought* about doing that action, not really performed it? Most people have experienced such memory confusions, and everyone has made similar memory errors, such as remembering hearing John say something that was actually uttered by Sean, believing they had seen a movie when really they had read the book, or thinking that a particular event had occurred yesterday when really it had happened two days before. These are examples of what Marcia Johnson and her co-authors refer to as *source-monitoring* errors (Johnson, Hashtroudi, & Lindsay, 1993).

Source-monitoring failures (being aware that you cannot identify the source of a memory) and source-monitoring confusions (mistakenly attributing a memory to a source other than its actual source) are among the most common of everyday memory problems. Indeed, all the reconstructive memory errors discussed above can be described as source-monitoring confusions. For example, information retrieved from a schema may mistakenly be attributed to memory for a particular episode. Source-monitoring difficulties can also contribute to certain kinds of illusory memories, such as *déjà vu*, in which you feel a sense of familiarity about a place you've never before visited. You probably encountered a similar place in the past, but you're unable to pinpoint the particular time and place and so you experience only a haunting sense of familiarity (Jacoby & Witherspoon, 1982; Whittlesea & Williams, 2000). Illusory feelings of remembering can also be produced by subtly manipulating the present. For example, if subjects are given "retrieval cues" that don't really correspond to any of the studied materials but that do cause nonstudied items to pop to mind, then they are likely to falsely report that they remember those items (Lindsay & Kelley, 1996; Whittlesea & Leboe, 2000). Here again, such memory illusions can be described as source-monitoring failures: The actual source of the item popping to mind is not apprehended by the subject, who instead erroneously attributes it to memory for the study list. Source-monitoring skills improve across childhood (e.g., Lindsay, 2002) but tend to decline in the senior years (e.g., McIntyre & Craik, 1987).

Flashbulb Memories Stop reading for a minute, and recall as much as you can about the moment you first learned of the terrorist attacks on September 11, 2001. Do you remember where you were, the approximate time of day, what you had been doing, and how you learned the news? Now recall as much as you can about where you were, what you were doing, and so on, at about the same time of day on September 10, 2001. We expect that most readers of this text will have very vivid recollections of hearing the news of the terrorist attacks, whereas their recollections of the day before are likely to be quite vague and schematic.

The term **flashbulb memories** refers to highly detailed and vivid recollections of the circumstances surrounding learning about an emotionally significant and surprising

flashbulb memory

Highly detailed and vivid recollections of the circumstances under which one first learned of an emotionally significant and surprising event

You may have a strong flashbulb memory for the events of September 11, 2001—but is the memory accurate?

AP/Wide World Photos

event (Brown & Kulick, 1977). Flashbulb memories have been reported for such events as the death of Princess Diana in 1997 and the assassinations of U.S. President John F. Kennedy and civil rights leader Martin Luther King, Jr. (see Conway, 1995, for numerous studies of flashbulb memories). Several researchers are currently studying flashbulb memories related to the events of September 11, 2001, and there may also be studies of memory for the tragic explosion of the space shuttle *Columbus* in 2003.

Flashbulb memories are interesting because of their great vividness and detail and the very strong confidence with which people hold them: People who experience flashbulb memories are convinced they can remember exactly what they were doing when they first heard the shocking news. Even more interesting, however, is that flashbulb memories are *not* necessarily accurate. This has been shown in studies in which people were asked about their memories on two occasions: shortly after the shocking news and months or years later. For example, the day after the space shuttle *Challenger* exploded in 1986 (live on TV, 73 seconds after take-off, killing all seven on board), Neisser and Harsch (1992) asked university students to describe how they learned of that accident, and then asked them the same question three years later. Most of the respondents were very confident about their recollections three years after the event, yet the original and delayed memories often differed in substantial ways. For example, one student initially reported being on the phone at work when the news was received, but later said that she first heard the news in class. The students were sure that they were remembering things accurately, but the data proved otherwise.

One reason flashbulb memories tend to be inaccurate is that we often combine memories of later experiences with memories of the initial event. When something shocking happens, we talk about it a lot, see footage of the event on TV, and hear other people analyze how and why it happened. The events of September 11 are a good example. When U.S. President George W. Bush was asked about his memory for the events some months later, he remembered having seen footage of the first plane hitting the tower before he learned about the crash of the second plane. At the time, of course, no footage was available on TV, so his memory of having seen the first plane attack was simply wrong. This led to some conspiracy theories on the Internet—"Bush films his own attack on the World Trade Center"—but a more reasonable explanation is that he simply mistakenly incorporated a later memory (viewing the footage) into his memory for the original event (Greenberg, 2004).

Why are flashbulb memories so vivid and detailed? Most memory researchers believe that the same basic processes we've discussed throughout this chapter account for the intensity of flashbulb memories: The events that give rise to flashbulb memories are highly distinctive and people tend to mentally elaborate on them extensively in the hours and days after the event, and to rehearse them frequently thereafter. The emotionality of the experiences that give rise to flashbulb memory reports also likely plays an important role. Intense emotion during an event contributes to distinctiveness and may encourage subsequent elaboration and rehearsal. Emotional experiences are characterized by large increases in neural activity in the amygdala of the brain, which facilitates attention to and encoding of relevant information (for an excellent review of the emotion-cognition link, see Phelps, 2006). Also, the fact that the recollections themselves have an emotionally charged quality may contribute to feelings of confidence in their accuracy. Despite that confidence, research indicates that the same sorts of reconstructive memory processes described in other parts of this chapter play roles in sculpting flashbulb memories, producing unusually vivid and detailed but nonetheless error-prone recollections. (For a discussion of the relationship between emotion and memory, including flashbulb memories, see Eich & Schooler, 2000.)

Remembering without Awareness: Implicit Memory

In the foregoing, we've concentrated on conscious acts of remembering; that is, we've emphasized situations in which someone is trying to remember something— such as what he or she ate for breakfast or the words from a memory list—and subsequently has the subjective experience of remembering. But people often use memory without meaning to and without being aware that they are doing so. You speak, walk to work, greet someone you know—all these activities require memory, but when you use memory in these ways you have no subjective experience of remembering the past. Most of the time, your awareness is focused on the present, but you are nonetheless constantly being influenced by your memories of the past.

Psychologists use the term **implicit memory** to refer to this kind of remembering, which occurs automatically and without a subjective feeling of remembering (Graf & Schacter, 1985; Roediger & McDermott, 1993). It turns out that implicit memory is in some ways similar to **explicit memory,** the name researchers use to describe deliberate uses of memory that are accompanied by a feeling of remembering. For example, both implicit and explicit memory are strongly influenced by retrieval cues in the environment. If you look at ▶ Figure 7.12, you'll see some examples of word and picture fragments. Your ability to complete fragments like these improves if you've recently read the solution word (e.g., the word fragment E_E_ _AN_ is easier to solve if the word ELEPHANT has been encountered in the prior 24 hours). But you don't need to consciously remember having seen the word to benefit from the fact that you had seen it. Your performance improves even if you don't consciously remember having recently seen the word, which makes the remembering *implicit* rather than *explicit.* The effect of prior exposure on fragment completion varies, depending on how closely the earlier encounter matches the fragment. If you need to solve a picture fragment, then you're helped more if the earlier encounter was in the form of a picture—such as seeing a picture of an elephant—rather than a word (McDermott & Roediger, 1994; Weldon & Roediger, 1987; Yonelinas & Jacoby, 1995). This is similar to what you learned earlier about explicit memory: Performance improves when the testing conditions match the study conditions; indeed, this is even more true of implicit memory than of explicit memory.

Implicit and explicit memory have similarities and differences. For example, study strategies that typically improve explicit remembering often have little or no effect on implicit memory (Roediger, Weldon, Stadler, & Riegler, 1992). If you elaborate material by thinking about its meaning, for example, your ability to remember that information will improve on most explicit tests of memory, such as recall or recognition. But the degree of elaborative processing has little or no effect if memory is tested indirectly by using an implicit test, such as solving word fragments (Graf, Mandler, & Haden, 1982; Jacoby & Dallas, 1981).

implicit memory

Use of memory that occurs automatically and without conscious awareness of remembering

explicit memory

Deliberate uses of memory with conscious awareness of remembering

▶ **Figure 7.12**

Implicit Memory Tests

Here are two examples of implicit memory tests. The subject's task in each case is to complete the picture or word fragment by identifying it as the object shown on the far right. Cues are presented one at a time, from most incomplete to complete. Recent prior exposure to the word "elephant" enables people to complete the fragments more easily than they otherwise would have.

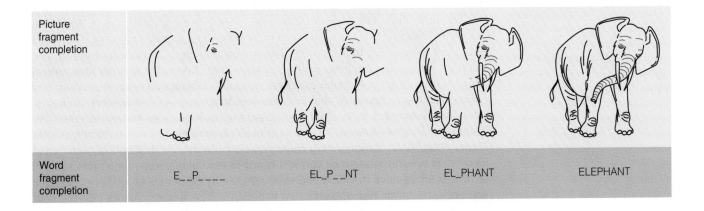

| Picture fragment completion | | | | |
| Word fragment completion | E_ _P_ _ _ _ | EL_P_ _NT | EL_PHANT | ELEPHANT |

One of the most fascinating things about implicit memory is that individuals who have grossly impaired explicit memory because of brain damage typically show normal or near-normal levels of implicit memory. We'll tell you more about this below, in a section on amnesia (unless we forget).

Illusions Produced by Implicit Memory

We previously discussed illusions of remembering; that is, cases in which people "remember" a past experience that never in fact occurred, such as hearing the word SLEEP on a list of words associated with the concept of sleep. Unconscious, or implicit, uses of memory can produce the opposite kind of illusion; that is, cases in which people's perceptions or judgments are distorted because they are using memory without realizing that they are doing so.

For example, Larry Jacoby and his colleagues at McMaster University (Jacoby, Woloshyn, & Kelley, 1989) led subjects to believe that made-up names were names of famous people. Subjects first read a list of made-up names (such as Sebastian Weisdorf). Half the subjects studied the list with their full attention, whereas others were required to perform a distracting task at the same time the list of made-up names was presented. Later, a test list was presented that contained three types of items: (1) slightly famous real names (such as Minnie Pearl), (2) made-up names that were presented on the study list, and (3) made-up names that were new to the experiment. The test task was to judge whether each name was famous. Before taking the test, subjects were accurately informed that none of the names on the study list was famous. The researchers found that subjects who had studied the list of made-up names with full attention were less likely to falsely call a made-up name famous if it had been on the study list than if it had not. This is because these subjects usually recognized the made-up names from the study list and so knew that those names were not famous. Subjects who had been distracted while studying the list of made-up names, in contrast, later often falsely judged those names to be famous. Distracting subjects during the first phase of the experiment, so that they were unable to process the made-up names elaboratively, decreased their ability to later consciously recognize the names as names presented on the study list, but it did not eliminate implicit memory for those names. Thus, the studied names seemed familiar and subjects erroneously attributed that familiarity to fame.

The false fame effect shows how prior experience can affect us in ways that escape awareness. Prior experience can make something seem familiar, but if you can't remember the specific time or place that you encountered the person or object, you can draw erroneous conclusions. Other studies have shown that unconscious uses of memory can distort perceptual experiences, make difficult problems seem easy, and create illusions of "knowing" that false answers to trivia questions are correct (Kelley, 1999; Whittlesea & Leboe, 2000). Unconscious uses of memory also account for instances of *cryptomnesia*, or unintentional plagiarism (Brown & Murphy, 1989; Marsh et al., 1997; Taylor, 1965). Have you ever discovered that one of your "great ideas" was actually something you had heard or read about some time previously? If so, this is an instance in which you were affected by memories of a prior experience without consciously remembering that experience. The stored memory affected your behaviour, but the memory was misidentified as a new idea (Johnson et al., 1993).

Memories of a prior experience can influence a person's behaviour, such as by producing a feeling of *déjà vu*, even though that prior experience is not consciously recollected.

Keith Brofsky/PhotoDisc/Getty Images

CRITICAL THINKING

Can you think of any ways that advertising agencies might use memory illusions to improve the image of a product?

Check your knowledge about how we use cues to help us remember by answering the following questions. Fill in the blanks with one of these terms: *cued recall, encoding specificity principle, explicit memory, free recall, implicit memory, schema, flashbulb memory, transfer-appropriate processing. (The answers are in Appendix B.)*

1. An organized structure of knowledge stored in long-term memory: _____

2. The use of memory automatically and without awareness of doing so: _____

3. Studying for a multiple-choice test by writing and answering your own multiple-choice questions: _____

4. Retrieval cues must match the information stored in the original memory record: _____

5. Detailed and vivid recollection of a surprising and consequential event: _____

6. Remembering material without the aid of any specific external retrieval cues: _____

▶ Updating Memory

LEARNING GOALS

1. Be able to describe the rate at which forgetting tends to occur, and explain why forgetting is adaptive.
2. Learn about the mechanisms that cause forgetting, including decay and retroactive and proactive interference.
3. Learn about motivated forgetting and the case for and against the concept of repression.
4. Be able to define retrograde and anterograde amnesia, and understand why it is unlikely that memories are stored in a single region of the brain.

Do you wish you never forgot anything? If you said yes, think again. If cues retained the same retrieval power indefinitely, then most cues would retrieve a flood of memories, challenging your ability to differentiate between memories from different sources. For example, if the cue "Where did you park your car?" was equally effective for retrieving all of your memories of episodes of parking, you'd have to sort through thousands of memories for the one of parking your car this morning. **Forgetting,** the loss in accessibility of previously stored information, is an important and adaptive property of your memory system (Bjork, 1989; Kraemer & Golding, 1997).

forgetting

The loss in accessibility of previously accessible memory information

How Quickly Do We Forget?

How quickly an item is forgotten depends on several factors: how the item was initially encoded, whether it was encountered again or mentally rehearsed at some later time, whether it is relatively unique versus very confusable with other memories, and the kinds of retrieval cues present when memory is tested. Such factors as elaboration, distinctiveness, rehearsal, and retrieval cues affect the absolute rate of forgetting, but the course of forgetting over time usually looks like the curve shown in ▶ Figure 7.13 on page 290. Most of the forgetting occurs early, with the rate of forgetting decreasing gradually for a long period following the initial exposure (Wixted & Ebbesen, 1991). Immediately after hearing a list of eight words, for example, you might be able to recall all eight of them; if recall was instead delayed for several minutes while you are engaged in some other task, you might recall only three or four of the words, yet even hours later you would probably still remember at least a couple of the words.

The forgetting curve shown in Figure 7.13 is taken from classic research by the German philosopher Hermann Ebbinghaus, who was one of the first people to investigate memory and forgetting scientifically (Ebbinghaus, 1885/1964).

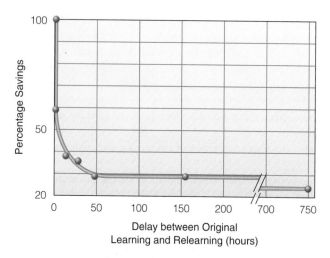

**Delay between Original
Learning and Relearning (hours)**

Hermann Ebbinghaus (1859–1909)

▶ **Figure 7.13**

The Ebbinghaus Forgetting Curve

The German philosopher Hermann Ebbinghaus learned lists of nonsense syllables and then measured how long it took to relearn the same material after various delays. Ebbinghaus termed the difference between times to learn the list on the two occasions "savings." Shown here are the percentage savings found after various delays. (A 50% savings means it took half as long to relearn the list as it did to learn the list originally; a 0% savings means that it took just as long to relearn the list as it did to learn the list originally.)

Ebbinghaus memorized lists of nonsense syllables (such as ZOK) and then measured how long it took to relearn the same material after various delays (his technique is called the *savings method*). As the graph shows, the longer the delay after original learning, the more time Ebbinghaus had to spend relearning the list. The form of the Ebbinghaus forgetting function—a rapid loss followed by a more gradual decline—is typical of forgetting in general. Similar forgetting functions are found for a variety of materials, and even for complex skills, such as typing (Baddeley & Longman, 1978) or performing cardiopulmonary resuscitation (McKenna & Glendon, 1985).

Memories of everyday experiences also tend to be forgotten over time, but some evidence suggests that material that has been retained in memory in accessible form without rehearsal for several years may be immune to further forgetting. Psychologist Harry Bahrick coined the term *permastore* to refer to this idea that information that has been retained for a number of years without rehearsal may be retained indefinitely. In one study, Bahrick (1984) looked at memory for a second language (Spanish) that had been studied in high school, with delay intervals ranging from about 1 to 50 years. In another study, Bahrick and Hall (1991) examined the retention of high school mathematics over 50 years. In both cases, the rate of forgetting was very rapid at first, followed by more gradual loss, but after three to six years the forgetting curve became almost flat (that is, forgetting seemed to stop). What's surprising about these studies is that a fair amount of the knowledge remained, even though the participants claimed to have not rehearsed or thought about the material in more than half a century. Bahrick's results suggest that if you can remember an early childhood experience now, you are likely to retain that memory for the rest of your life (see also Lindsay, Wade, Hunter, & Read, 2004). It's worth noting a caveat, though: Bahrick found that students who performed very poorly in the course very quickly forgot almost all of the little they had learned! It was only students who had mastered a fair amount of material who managed to retain some of that material for decades.

Why Do We Forget?

What causes forgetting? As we discussed earlier, most modern memory researchers believe that forgetting from long-term memory is *cue-dependent*—you fail to remember a prior event that had been stored in long-term memory because you don't have the right retrieval cues. Earlier psychologists believed that memories simply fade with the passage of time (through some spontaneous chemical process that happens over time, similar to rusting). But **decay**—the idea that memories fade just because time passes—cannot explain forgetting. For one thing, as you've seen, memories that appear to have been forgotten can sometimes be remembered later under the right retrieval conditions. In addition, people often remember trivial events (such as a joke) years later but forget more important things that once received a great deal of practice (such as knowledge about geography). If forgetting

decay

The proposal that memories are forgotten or lost spontaneously with the passage of time (or with some passive chemical processes that occur over time, akin to rusting) were merely a matter of passive decay, then we would expect that the extensively studied material would be retained longer. These observations suggest that other processes that occur over time must contribute to forgetting.

Retroactive Interference   What happens over time that could contribute to forgetting? Part of the answer is that we create new memories every moment and these new memories can compete, or interfere, with the retrieval of old memories. When you get a new apartment, you memorize your new address. After you succeed, it becomes more difficult to retrieve your old address. The retrieval cue "address" has now become associated with something new; as a result, its capacity to produce the old number is reduced. Psychologists use the term **retroactive interference** to refer to cases in which the formation of new memories hurts the retrieval of old memories.

In a classic study of retroactive interference, Jenkins and Dallenbach (1924) asked two students from Cornell University to learn lists of nonsense syllables either just before bed or early in the morning. The students were tested 1, 2, 4, or 8 hours after learning. The results, which are shown in ▌Figure 7.14, were clear: When the students slept during the delay interval, they remembered more than when they remained awake. Note that a constant amount of time passed in both conditions, so a decay theory would predict no differences between the conditions. The findings suggest that it was the activities that occurred during the students' waking hours that produced the information loss. When awake, the students formed many new memories, which interfered with retrieval of the studied material.

Proactive Interference   It is not only the learning of new information that produces forgetting. For one thing, previously learned information can also produce interference. **Proactive interference** occurs when old memories interfere with the retrieval of new memories. If you try to recall your new cell phone number (or computer password, street address, lock combination, etc.), memories of your old one may come to mind instead, interfering with your ability to recollect the new information. To consider another example, suppose that as part of an experiment you're asked to think of FORK as a weapon. You could think about the word in this way for the experiment, but as time passes you will almost certainly revert to thinking about FORK in the usual way. You would find it difficult to remember FORK as a weapon because the word has been used in a different way so many times before. Prior knowledge can interfere with the learning and retention of the new material.

Most memory researchers believe that forgetting from long-term memory is caused by various kinds of interference. Previously learned associations interfere with the acquisition of new ones, and as new memories are encoded, old retrieval

retroactive interference

A process in which the formation of new memories hurts the retrieval of old memories

proactive interference

A process in which old memories interfere with the establishment and retrieval of new memories

CRITICAL   THINKING

Can you think of any ways to lessen the influence of interference? Is there any way that you could study information so as to reduce interference?

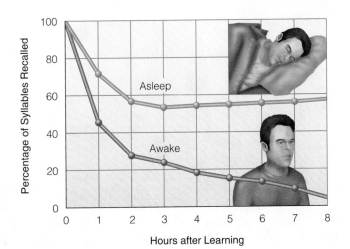

▌ Figure 7.14

Interference and Memory

The mental processes that occur after learning affect how well information is remembered. In this classic study by Jenkins and Dallenbach (1924), the students showed better memory if they slept during the retention interval than if they remained awake. Presumably, memories acquired during the waking activities interfered with retrieval of the studied material.

cues become less effective because those cues are now associated with new memories. If a particular cue is associated with many memories, that cue will not guide the rememberer uniquely to the relevant stored material. New experiences can also affect how people interpret retrieval cues, rendering those cues less effective (as in the idea of transfer-appropriate processing, discussed earlier). That is, as we learn and change, we are less likely to perceive or generate cues in ways that match memories created earlier in our lives (you may recall we made this point earlier, in the context of the phenomenon of childhood amnesia). Remembering depends on retrieval cues that are specific to the to-be-remembered material. Once again, you can see why elaboration is an effective strategy for remembering. If the original event is encoded in an elaborative and distinctive way, the memory record is less likely to be subject to competition from other remembered events because its mental representation will be less similar to those of such events.

Although most memory researchers attribute forgetting of material in long-term memory to interference, it is likely that decay—some passive neurochemical processes that occur spontaneously over time—contributes to forgetting over the very short term, that is, in sensory memory and short-term memory (Cowan, 1995; Cowan et al., 1997). Even in sensory memory and short-term memory, however, interference also plays important roles in forgetting. For example, in everyday situations the content of the sensory register is replaced or updated moment by moment by new sensory stimuli, and the content of short-term memory is replaced by new perceptions, thoughts, images, and feelings.

Motivated Forgetting

In our earlier comments about flashbulb memories, we suggested that highly unusual or emotional events tend to lead to distinctive, and therefore easy-to-remember, memory records. The adaptive value of a system that retains significant events is easy to understand—remembering these kinds of events could increase our ability to survive. But what about experiences it might be adaptive to forget, such as childhood abuse or witnessing a violent crime?

The idea that the mind can actively repress threatening memory records is an important ingredient of Freud's psychoanalytic theory, as you'll see when we discuss personality theories in Chapter 12. Freud described repression as a "defence mechanism" that people use, unknowingly, to push threatening thoughts, memories, and feelings out of conscious awareness. According to Freud, repressed memories retain the capacity to affect behaviour, but they cannot be consciously recollected.

Most people recall more pleasant than unpleasant experiences, perhaps partly because they think about and rehearse pleasant experiences more often.

Buccina Studios/PhotoDisc/Getty Images

The Evidence for Repression   Modern researchers are undecided about the scientific validity of repression. Evidence from laboratory studies shows that forming an intention to forget a subset of studied materials lowers subsequent memory performance on those materials (e.g., Allen & Vokey, 1998; MacLeod, 1999). Analogous effects have been demonstrated with instructions to forget autobiographical memories (e.g., Barnier, Conway, Mayoh, Speyer, & Avizmil, in press), and research with functional magnetic resonance imaging has shed light on the brain mechanisms of motivated forgetting (e.g., Anderson et al., 2004). Also, studies have found that people typically recall more pleasant than unpleasant events (Lindsay, Wade, et al., 2004; Linton, 1975; Wagenaar, 1986), and physically painful experiences, such as childbirth, are often not recollected well with the passage of time (Robinson, Rosen, Revill, David, & Rus, 1980). There are also many instances, reported mainly in clinical settings, in which people appear to have forgotten traumatic experiences.

In one study, for example, 475 adults who were undergoing psychotherapy and had reported experiencing childhood sexual abuse were asked about their memories. Each was asked the following question: "During the period of time when the first forced sexual encounter happened and your 18th birthday, was there ever a time when you could not remember the forced sexual experience?" (Briere & Conte, 1993). Fifty-nine percent responded "yes," which Briere and Conte took as evidence that the memories had been pushed out of consciousness for some time. In another study supporting the same conclusion, Williams (1994) interviewed 129 women who had been medically treated for sexual abuse as children approximately 17 years earlier. The women were not specifically asked about the recorded instance of abuse but rather questioned more generally about any childhood sexual experiences they may have had; 38% did not describe the particular instance of abuse recorded in the medical records, and 12% did not report *any* instance of childhood sexual abuse.

Do these data demonstrate repression? Not necessarily. The fact that painful childhood experiences are sometimes forgotten can be explained in many ways. Many childhood events are forgotten in adulthood, and so far we lack good data on whether or not forgetting of childhood sexual abuse differs from forgetting of other sorts of childhood experiences (Read & Lindsay, 2000). Even if future research shows that childhood abuse is much more likely to be forgotten than neutral or positive childhood experiences, such forgetting might be due to ordinary mechanisms of forgetting rather than to a special repression mechanism. For example, abuse may less often be mentally rehearsed than other sorts of events. Some psychologists (e.g., Brown, Scheflin, & Hammond, 1998) are convinced that a special forgetting mechanism is triggered by traumatic events, but the issue remains controversial. Of course, even if failures to recall childhood abuse are not due to a special repression mechanism, such "forgotten" events may nonetheless influence people in ways that bypass awareness (as per our discussion of implicit memory).

A lot of controversy arose throughout the 1990s about cases in which people reported that they had recovered memories of long-forgotten childhood sexual abuse (Lindsay & Read, 1994; Loftus, 1993; Pope, 1996). Debate focused on cases in which such reports emerged in the context of trauma-oriented psychotherapy. Critics argued that some therapists used highly suggestive therapeutic techniques (such as hypnosis) in well-intended but misguided efforts to help clients recover suspected repressed memories of abuse. Given what you have learned in this chapter about the reconstructive nature of remembering and about the effects of suggestive questions on memory, you can probably appreciate that such approaches to therapy might unintentionally lead some clients to develop false beliefs about abuse that never really happened. This does not mean that all or even most memories of abuse that emerge in therapy are illusory, but some of them may be (see Lindsay & Read, 2006).

CONCEPT SUMMARY

MECHANISMS OF FORGETTING

Mechanism	Description	Example
Cue dependence	Failure to remember is caused by a lack of appropriate cues.	Although Suni would recognize a definition of semantic memory on a multiple-choice test, she can't think of it for a fill-in-the-blank test.
Decay	Memories fade with the passage of time (or with some passive process that occurs spontaneously over time).	After the letters disappeared from the screen, Sarah's sensory memory of them rapidly faded.
Proactive interference	Old memories interfere with the retrieval of new memories.	Bruce acted in a high school production of *Hamlet*, and he now finds it difficult to memorize *Macbeth*.
Retroactive interference	New memories interfere with the retrieval of old memories.	Filling out a job application, Seth can only remember his most recent address, not the one before it.
Motivated forgetting	Traumatic experiences are forgotten to reduce anxiety.	Jackie remembers almost nothing about the day her parents were seriously injured in an accident.

The Neuroscience of Forgetting

To explain the instances of forgetting that we've encountered up to this point, we've appealed largely to the actions of normal, adaptive psychological processes. But forgetting can also be caused by physical problems in the brain from injury, aging, or illness. Psychologists use the term **organic amnesia** to refer to forgetting that is caused by physical damage to the brain. (Another type of amnesia is emotional in origin, but we'll delay our discussion of this kind of forgetting until Chapter 14.)

Types of Organic Amnesia   There are two major kinds of organic amnesia: *retrograde* and *anterograde*. **Retrograde amnesia** is memory loss for events that happened *prior* to the time of injury (*retro* means backward in time). People who receive a severe blow to the head often have trouble remembering the events immediately before the accident. The memory loss can apply to events that happened only moments before the accident, or the loss can be quite extensive; in some cases, patients lose their ability to recall personal experiences from the last several years leading up to the accident. In most cases, these memory losses are not permanent and recover slowly over time, although the moments immediately before the injury are usually not recovered (Cermak, 1982; Riccio, Millin, & Gisquet-Verrier, 2003).

Anterograde amnesia is memory loss for events that happen *after* the physical damage. People who suffer from anterograde amnesia, as we noted at the beginning of this chapter, seem to be forever locked in the present and distant past—they have great difficulty recollecting new experiences. The disorder develops as a result of brain damage, which can occur from the persistent use of alcohol coupled with poor nutrition (a condition called *Korsakoff's syndrome*), from brain infections (such as viral encephalitis), or, in some cases, as a byproduct of brain surgery. One of the most thoroughly studied amnesiac patients, known to researchers as H. M., developed the disorder after surgeons removed large portions of his temporal lobes. The operation was performed to reduce the severity of H. M.'s epileptic seizures; the surgery was successful—his seizures *were* dramatically reduced—but severe anterograde amnesia developed as an unexpected side effect.

What's Forgotten in Amnesia?   Over the past 25 years, considerable research has been conducted on anterograde amnesia. Led by the pioneering work of Brenda Milner at the Montreal Neurological Institute, such patients as H. M. have been

organic amnesia

Forgetting that is caused by physical problems in the brain, such as those induced by injury or disease

retrograde amnesia

Memory loss for events that happened before the brain injury

anterograde amnesia

Memory loss for events that happen after the physical injury

studied in great detail to determine exactly what kinds of memory processing are lost (Milner, 1966). It was originally believed that H. M. and other anterograde amnesiacs were incapable of forming new memories. It is now clear, however, that these patients can learn a great deal but must be tested in particular ways. If a patient like H. M. is tested indirectly, on a task that does not require *conscious* remembering, performance can approach or even match normal levels; that is, performance on tests of implicit memory is preserved in anterograde amnesia.

In one study, Jacoby and Witherspoon (1982) asked patients with Korsakoff's syndrome and anterograde amnesia to learn homophones for a later memory test. Homophones are words that sound alike but have different meanings and spellings, such as READ and REED. To "bias" a particular interpretation for each homophone, it was presented as part of a word pair, such as BOOK–READ or, for other subjects, SAXOPHONE–REED. (Because the words were presented aloud, the only way to distinguish between the homophones READ and REED was through the accompanying context word BOOK or SAXOPHONE.) Later, the subjects performed an explicit memory test in which they were shown some of the studied words mixed with nonstudied words and asked which words had been presented in the study list. The subjects performed very poorly on this test; they seemed not to have encoded the presented information. In a second test, however, other studied and nonstudied homophones were read aloud by the experimenter and the subjects' task was simply to spell them. The amnesiacs had a strong tendency to spell the words in a way that was consistent with their presentation during the study phase; for example, they were much more likely to spell "REED" if they had previously heard that word paired with SAXOPHONE than if they had heard it paired with BOOK.

These results demonstrate that the patients with amnesia had encoded and retained memories of the study phase of the experiment. Other experiments have revealed similar findings. For example, people with amnesia are more likely to complete a word fragment (such as E_E_ _AN_) correctly if they have recently seen the word, benefiting from the prior exposure just about as much as healthy people do, but if asked to recall the previously seen words, they cannot do so (Graf & Schacter, 1985). Patients who suffer from anterograde amnesia fail tests that ask them to recollect past experiences consciously; when memory is assessed indirectly, or implicitly, through a task that does not require conscious remembering, people with amnesia often perform at normal levels.

Our discussion of amnesia has focused on cases in which young to middle-aged adults sustained damage to parts of the brain that play critical roles in remembering. Similar phenomena are observed in a larger population of individuals with memory disorders—older adults suffering brain insults from diseases, such as Alzheimer's disease or strokes. Age-related changes in memory are discussed in Chapter 10.

CRITICAL   THINKING

What advice would you give to the family of someone suffering from anterograde amnesia?

What Parts of the Brain Underlie Memory, Forgetting, and Remembering?   The study of individuals with brain damage, such as the patients with Korsakoff's syndrome, has encouraged researchers to draw tentative conclusions about which parts of the brain underlie particular aspects of memory. We touched on this issue in Chapter 3, when we considered biological processes. At that point special attention was paid to a structure called the *hippocampus*, which most brain researchers believe is critically involved in the formation and storage of memories (Squire, 1992). Damage to the hippocampus, as well as to surrounding structures in the brain, leads to memory problems in a wide variety of species, including humans, monkeys, and rats. The hippocampus and surrounding areas also "light up" in PET scans when subjects are asked to recall past events (Raichle, 1994; Ranganath et al., 2004) (although it is worth emphasizing that other brain areas also light up in such studies). A related point is that certain memory disorders, such as those associated with Alzheimer's disease, have been linked to inadequate supplies of particular neurotransmitters (such as acetylcholine) (Albert & Moss, 1992).

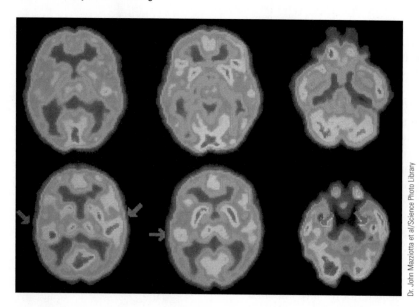

Dr. John Mazziotta et al/Science Photo Library

This PET scan shows regions of brain activity during auditory stimulation. The arrows are pointing to areas inside the temporal lobes that become active after words are heard; these areas are thought to be associated with some kinds of memory.

However, no single brain structure, or even group of structures, is responsible for all memory functions. The regions of the brain that are involved in memory depend on the type of processing involved. For example, episodic memory appears to involve different brain regions from those involved in procedural memory (i.e., learning and remembering skills) (Gabrieli, 1998; Wheeler, Stuss, & Tulving, 1997). There's also evidence that emotionally charged memories involve a structure in the brain called the *amygdala* (Herz, Eliassen, Beland, & Souza, 2004; Metcalfe & Jacobs, 2000), and different brain regions may contribute to true versus false memories (Okada & Stark, 2003; Schacter, 2001). More generally, different areas of the brain are richly interconnected with one another, and activities in one part of the brain often depend on activities in other parts. Similarly, damage to a part of the brain that produces a particular neurotransmitter, such as acetylcholine, probably has consequences for numerous other regions of the brain that depend on that neurotransmitter.

Thus, it is unlikely that any single "storehouse" for memory exists in the brain. Different kinds of memory tasks likely draw on different brain mechanisms. Even for a given type of memory, such as episodic recollections of mundane events, remembering draws on numerous regions of the brain. Most people think of remembering a past event as being akin to finding a book in a library, as though all the information about a particular moment in their past experience were stored in a single record, and as though remembering were merely a matter of locating that record and playing it back. As you've learned in this chapter, remembering is not this simple.

Test Yourself 7.4

Check your knowledge about forgetting and the updating of memory by deciding whether each of the following statements is true or false. [The answers are in Appendix B.]

1. Forgetting is usually slow at first and becomes more rapid as time passes. *True or False?*
2. Most psychologists agree that interference rather than decay is primarily responsible for long-term forgetting. *True or False?*
3. Proactive interference occurs when what you learn at time 2 interferes with what you learned previously at time 1. *True or False?*
4. Anterograde amnesia impairs memory for new information. *True or False?*
5. People tend to recall more pleasant than unpleasant events over time. *True or False?*
6. Psychologists believe that the hippocampus is involved in some, but not all, uses of memory. *True or False?*

Memory

Time flows continuously, so experiences quickly leave the present and recede backward into the past. To understand humans' capacity to preserve and recollect their own pasts, we considered some of the fundamental problems that memory systems help us solve.

First, how does the mind maintain information over the short term? To improve perception and aid ongoing comprehension, people have internal processes that help them maintain information over the short term. In the case of sensory memory, we retain a relatively pure copy of the physical stimuli picked up by our sensory receptors. Sensory memories represent the world as recorded by the sensory equipment, but they are very short lived, lasting between one and a few seconds at most. Short-term memory, in contrast, is the system used to store, think about, and reason with the products of perceptual analyses and with information retrieved from long-term memory. Verbalizable information is typically maintained in short-term memory in the form of an "inner voice," but short-term memory can also represent spatial information. Information in short-term memory is forgotten rapidly in the absence of rehearsal. The capacity, or size, of short-term memory is determined by a tradeoff between the factors that lead to forgetting over the short term (decay and interference) and the attention-demanding process of rehearsal.

Second, how do we retain accessible long-term memories of past experiences? To remember over the long term, it helps to produce elaborate and distinctive memory records. Focusing on the meaning of the input, relating it to things you already know, and forming visual images all lead to distinctive memory records that are relatively easily discriminated from other information in memory. Forming a visual image is particularly effective, and many memory aids, or mnemonic devices, are based on the use of imagery coupled with strategies for systematically searching memory. In the method of loci, for example, you form a visual image linking the to-be-remembered material to particular locations along a familiar pathway. Long-term memory also depends on the temporal order in which materials are presented: Items presented near the beginning and end of a sequence are remembered well compared to mid-sequence items. Repetition also improves memory, especially if the material is processed elaboratively and in slightly different ways across repetitions and is spaced or distributed across time rather than massed.

Third, what initiates an act of remembering? Most memory researchers believe that successful remembering depends largely on having the right kinds of retrieval cues. Most forgetting from long-term memory is cue-dependent, which means that stored information is not really "lost"; it's simply inaccessible because the appropriate retrieval cues are not present. According to the encoding specificity principle, effective retrieval cues are those that uniquely match the conditions that were present during original learning. Similarly, the notion of transfer-appropriate processing holds that memory depends on the extent to which the same sorts of mental processes are performed at study and at test. Remembering is not, however, simply a matter of retrieving episodic memory records. People use their general knowledge and beliefs to interpret and fill in gaps in information retrieved from memory. Such reconstructive remembering is adaptive because it is efficient and usually accurate, but it sometimes leads to inaccurate recollections.

Fourth, what mechanisms underlie forgetting? Forgetting is an adaptive process. If retrieval cues retained their efficacy indefinitely, most cues would prompt a flood of irrelevant memories, such as remembering where you parked your car last Wednesday when you try to remember where you parked it this morning. Although the psychological mechanisms of forgetting are still being investigated, it seems unlikely that long-term memories simply fade or decay passively over time. Rather, older memories can interfere with the retrieval of newer ones (proactive interference), and new memories can interfere with the retrieval of older ones (retroactive interference). Also, as we change and develop over time, our ability to cue ourselves in ways that match earlier memories declines. With the right kinds of cues, however—cues that uniquely match the memory records of a past event—previously forgotten material can often be retrieved.

CHAPTER SUMMARY

▶ Remembering over the Short Term

It's necessary to have some sort of internal machinery for remembering information over the short term. The performance of most mental tasks requires that certain bits of information be retained throughout the solution process.

Visual Sensory Memory: The Icon

The *icon* is a lingering visual sensory memory trace. These images allow visual sensations to be extended in time so the brain can more efficiently process the incoming physical stimuli. In a classic series of studies, Sperling compared *whole report* and *partial report* and found that the icon contains a large amount of information but lasts less than a second.

Sensory Memory in Other Modalities

Other sensory systems have analogous forms of memory to visual sensory memory, but have not been researched as extensively. Auditory sensory memory is known as the "echo" or echoic memory, and sensory memory for tactile stimuli and for olfactory (odour) stimuli also seem to exist. In all modalities, the system can briefly maintain a recent stimulus.

Short-Term Memory: The Mental Workspace

Short-term memory is the system we use to temporarily store, think about, and reason with information. Verbalizable information in short-term memory is typically recoded in the form of an "inner voice." Information is lost from short-term memory within a few seconds if not rehearsed, through *decay* and *interference* from other information. Short-term memory capacity is limited, as demonstrated by *memory span*, the number of items a person can reliably recall in their correct order from short-term memory. Memory span is equivalent to the number of items that can be rehearsed in about two seconds. It can be dramatically increased through *chunking*, mentally rearranging many individual pieces of information into a single familiar and meaningful pattern.

The Working Memory Model

According to the *working memory model*, the *central executive* controls which pieces of information are thought about and rehearsed at any given moment. The central executive relies on the *articulatory loop* to rehearse verbalizable information, and on the *visuospatial sketchpad* to rehearse visuospatial information.

▶ Storing Information for the Long Term

Once information is no longer being thought about in short-term memory, we need to store at least some of it internally so that it can later be recovered at the appropriate place and time. Certain types of thinking processes increase the likelihood that material will be remembered later.

What Is Stored in Long-Term Memory?

Episodic memories are those in which we recall a moment of our own past experience, *semantic memory* refers to knowledge and beliefs, and *procedural memory* refers to our tacit knowledge of how to do things.

Elaboration: Connecting New Material with Existing Knowledge

Elaboration (relating input to other knowledge) allows us to establish meaningful connections that ease later retrieval of the stored material. This can be accomplished by thinking about meaning and noticing relationships between different elements of the to-be-remembered material and between the to-be-remembered material and things that you already know. *Distinctiveness* refers to aspects of a to-be-remembered item or event that are unusual or unique. Attending to and noting distinctive aspects of an item or event facilitate later remembering by helping you differentiate between memories of that event versus memories of other events.

Repetition of To-Be-Remembered Material: Diversify and Distribute

Simply thinking about something you want to remember over and over in exactly the same way has little effect on memory, but if you think about the item in different ways, then memory improves with repeated rehearsal of to-be-remembered information. Benefits of repeated rehearsal for long-term memory tend to be greater if the repetitions are widely spaced in time, with other activities intervening between rehearsals (i.e., *distributed practice*), than if the repetitions are tightly clustered together in time (i.e., *massed practice*).

Effects of Temporal Order

Good memory for the first few items in a list is termed the *primacy effect*; good memory for the last few items in a list is termed the *recency effect*. *Repetition* also improves memory, particularly if the material is processed elaboratively each time and if the repetitions are *distributed* over time.

Imagery: Remembering through Visualization

Forming a *visual image* of presented material is a good way to produce an elaborative and distinctive memory trace, which in turn promotes long-term memory. According to Paivio's dual-code hypothesis, imagery also benefits memory because it leads to the creation of a second, qualitatively different kind of memory record than does thinking about the to-be-remembered material verbally. Research on visual imagery suggests that "mental pictures" are similar to visual perceptions in some ways but not in others. For example, some of the same brain areas are involved in perceiving and imaging visual objects, but visual images are less detailed than visual perceptions.

Mnemonic Devices

Mnemonic devices are special mental tricks that help people think about material in ways that lead to effective remembering and that provide strategies for searching memory. These techniques include the *method of loci* and the *link-word system*.

▶ Recovering Information from Cues

Our interactions with the world require us to retrieve information about both the immediate and the distant past. Retrieval is triggered directly or indirectly by other events, or cues, encountered in the environment.

The Importance of Retrieval Cues

Many researchers believe that most failures to remember are due to *cue-dependent forgetting*. Once encoded, the information is available in long-term memory, given the right type of cues. According to the *encoding specificity principle*, an effective retrieval cue is one that uniquely matches the encoded material. Similarly, according to the notion of *transfer-appropriate processing*, material should be studied by using the same kind of mental processes that will be used during retrieval.

Reconstructive Remembering

Remembering is influenced by beliefs and expectations. Remembering is aided by *schemas*, which are large clusters of related knowledge about people, places, and activities. Although schema-based reconstructive remembering has considerable adaptive value, it can lead to *false memories*, as shown in research on eyewitness testimony and *flashbulb memories*. *Source-monitoring* skills usually (but not always) enable us to differentiate between memories of a to-be-remembered event versus thoughts and images from other sources, such as schemas.

Remembering without Awareness: Implicit Memory

Explicit memory refers to conscious, willful remembering, whereas *implicit memory* refers to influences of memory that occur without awareness of remembering. Implicit and explicit memory are similarly affected by retrieval cues but sometimes behave differently; implicit memory is relatively unaffected by encoding strategies that help explicit remembering. Implicit memory can distort our perceptions, such as by leading us to think that we have just come up with a brilliant new idea when we have really merely remembered someone else's idea.

▶ Updating Memory

Forgetting refers to the loss in accessibility of previously stored material. Forgetting has considerable adaptive value: It reduces the likelihood that retrieval cues in the current environment will lead to retrieval of a flood of irrelevant, outdated information.

How Quickly Do We Forget?

Most forgetting occurs soon after initial exposure. Additional forgetting continues for a long period thereafter, with the rate of forgetting gradually decreasing. If material is retained in accessible form for a number of years without rehearsal, the rate of forgetting may approach zero (*permastore*).

Why Do We Forget?

The simple passage of time (*decay*) is not sufficient to explain forgetting from long-term memory. *Retroactive interference* (new material interfering with old) and *proactive interference* (old material interfering with new) play major roles in forgetting.

Motivated Forgetting

An important part of Freud's psychoanalytic theory is the assumption that the mind can actively *repress* certain memories. Modern researchers agree that seemingly memorable traumatic events are sometimes forgotten, but they remain undecided about the scientific validity of the concept of *repression*. Ordinary mechanisms may account for cases in which traumatic events are forgotten.

The Neuroscience of Forgetting

Organic amnesia refers to forgetting that is caused by some type of physical problem; *retrograde amnesia* is memory loss for events that happened before an injury; *anterograde amnesia* is memory loss for events that happen after the point of physical damage. Although the *hippocampus* is important for memory, no single brain structure is responsible for remembering.

Terms to Remember

Recommended Readings

Herrmann, D., Raybeck, D., & Gruneberg, M. (2002). *Improving memory and study skills: Advances in theory and practice.* Ashland, OH: Hogrefe & Huber Publishers. This book integrates scientific knowledge pertaining to study skills.

Neath, I., & Surprenant, A. (2003). *Human memory: An introduction to research, data, and theory* (2nd ed.). Pacific Grove, CA: Brooks/Cole. This is a leading undergraduate textbook on memory. The material discussed in this chapter is covered by Neath and Surprenant in much more detail.

Schacter, D. L. (2001). *The seven sins of memory: How the mind forgets and remembers.* Boston, MA: Houghton Mifflin. Schacter is a Harvard professor with a long-standing reputation for insightful empirical and theoretical work on human memory. This is a very readable and wide-ranging, yet scientifically grounded, survey of what researchers have learned about human memory.

Tulving, E. (1983). *Elements of episodic memory.* New York: Oxford University Press. This is a semi-autobiographical account of one of Canada's (and the world's) most renowned memory researcher's profound influence on modern memory theory. Although written as a professional book, it contains many personal observations and anecdotes that bring memory theory to life.

 For additional readings, explore InfoTrac® College Edition, your online library. Go to
http://www.adaptivemind3e.nelson.com.

Hint: Enter these search terms: short-term memory, long-term memory, autobiographical memory, visual imagery, implicit memory, explicit memory, amnesia.

Media Resources

What's on the Web?

Please note that Web addresses are subject to change. Check out the accompanying website for updates: http://www.adaptivemind3e.nelson.com.

This site presents practice quiz questions, hypercontent, information on degrees and careers in psychology, study tips, and more.

The Recovered Memories Controversy

http://web.lemoyne.edu/~hevern/nr-mem.html

Few topics in psychology have fuelled as much debate as the controversy about "recovered memories" of childhood sexual abuse. Throughout much of the 1990s, the debate was very polarized, with critics on one side claiming that most recovered memories were illusions produced by misguided therapy and countercritics dismissing such claims as anti-feminist, pro-abuser "backlash." More recently, various "middle-ground" perspectives have come to the fore, according to which some recovered memories are essentially false and others essentially accurate. This website offers an impressive array of links to sites presenting both sides (and the middle) of this complex issue.

Memory (at the Exploratorium)

http://www.exploratorium.edu/memory

This renowned science museum has an online memory exhibition, with some fun and informative memory demonstrations, facts, and figures. Read about a memory artist, learn more about memories for emotional events, play games with your memory, and explore "tricks" for improving your memory. This site is a bit dated, but the content is still quite interesting.

Gary Wells's Homepage

http://www.psychology.iastate.edu/FACULTY/gwells/homepage.htm

Faulty eyewitness identification decisions contribute to a large percentage of false convictions of innocent suspects. Gary Wells is widely regarded as the world's leading authority on the psychology of eyewitness suspect identifications. His work has had tremendous impact on the procedures used by police in Canada and in the United States (by the way, his first academic job was at the University of Alberta). His website is crammed with fascinating information about eyewitness identification evidence.

ThomsonNOW™ ThomsonNOW™

http://hed.nelson.com

Go to this site for the link to ThomsonNOW™, your one-stop study shop. Take a Pretest for this chapter and ThomsonNOW™ will generate a personalized Study Plan based on your test results. The Study Plan will identify the topics you need to review and direct you to online resources to help you master those topics. You can then take a Posttest to determine what concepts you have mastered and what you still need work on.

Psyk.trek 3.0

Check out Psyk.trek 3.0 for further study of the concepts in this chapter. Psyk.trek's 65 interactive learning modules, simulations, and quizzes offer additional opportunities for you to interact with, reflect on, and retain the material:

Memory: Memory Encoding

Common sense is the collection of prejudices acquired by age 18.

—Albert Einstein

Thought and Language

Wayne Inges, a devious soul, chuckles silently to himself as he completes the deal. "That's right," he says. "Centre court, floor level—$100 for the pair. Good deal, eh?" Having paid only $50 for the tickets himself, Wayne pockets a tidy little profit. But he knows there are more fools in the world, so he decides to buy the tickets back for $150. Just as game time approaches, he sells the pair for $200. Can you figure out Wayne's total profit for the evening?

Answering such a question requires a bit of thinking. **Thinking,** or cognition, can be broadly defined as the set of processes used to manipulate knowledge, images, and ideas. Through thought we can act on our knowledge in a directed and purposeful way to solve problems, to reason and make decisions, and to understand and communicate with others. Like most other internal psychological phenomena, it's not possible to measure thinking directly, but much can be learned by observing thinkers and listening to their rationales for actions or conclusions.

Let's see, Wayne made $50 on the first transaction but spent $150 to buy the tickets back, so he lost the original $50. He finally sold the pair for $200, so his total profit for the evening must be $50, right? Easy enough. We've used our knowledge about the world, and about mathematics in particular, to work

> **thinking**
>
> The processes that underlie the mental manipulation of knowledge, images, and ideas, often in an attempt to reach a goal, such as solving a problem

systematically toward a goal. It's easy to see the adaptive value of the process. Thinking increases your ability to survive because you can act on your knowledge in precise, systematic, and purposeful ways.

But, as you may have noticed, our reasoning in this case was completely wrong. We arrived at the wrong answer, as do many others who try this task. By using a slight variation of the same problem, Maier and Burke (1967) found that people come up with the correct answer less than 40% of the time. The correct answer is $100—Wayne paid out a total of $200 ($50 for the first transaction and $150 for the second) and received $300 back from the buyers. Simple subtraction yields the correct answer of $100.

What lies behind the error? The difficulty comes from thinking about Wayne's sales as one continuous event rather than as two separate transactions. This becomes clearer if you frame the problem slightly differently: Wayne bought tickets for Friday night's game for $50 and sold them for $100, then he bought tickets for Saturday's game for $150 and sold them for $200. When the problem is expressed this way, people rarely err. One of the challenges of the modern study of thinking, and of problem solving in particular, is to understand why human thought processes are sometimes led astray. How can illogical thought processes arise from an adaptive mind? In this chapter, we consider scientific evidence regarding the nature of human thinking. We begin with an examination of what may be the single greatest tool for thinking: language. We then turn to research on categorizing, solving problems, and making decisions. By the end of the chapter, you should have gained new insights into both strengths and weaknesses of human thinking.

Thought and Language

The topics of thought and language touch on a wide variety of psychological activities. Thinking relies on learning and involves conscious awareness. To manipulate the knowledge in your head, you need to remember things you learned in the past. When you solve problems or make decisions, you need to come up with criteria for what represents an acceptable solution. To express ideas symbolically in the form of language, you need rules for categorizing objects and guidelines for transforming ideas into the symbols of speech or writing.

For centuries, philosophers have struggled to understand the "higher mental processes" of thought and language. More recently, questions about thought and language have formed the focus of cognitive science, a diverse field that draws on a wide variety of disciplines, including psychology, linguistics, philosophy, biology, and even engineering and computer science. Once again, we'll discuss the insights of psychologists and cognitive scientists by considering a set of adaptive problems (see ▶ Figure 8.1).

First, how do we communicate with others? The ability to communicate through language may well be humanity's greatest success story. No other species approaches our ability to transmit knowledge through speech and writing. In fact, the use of language may be the "most pervasive and uniquely human characteristic of the species" (Wasow, 1989). Through language production we transmit thoughts, feelings, and needs to others; through language comprehension we understand and learn from others.

Second, how do we categorize objects in our world? To make sense of our environment, especially the objects in it, we carve the world into *categories.* Can you imagine a world where every encounter was new and unique—a world where no two things shared features in common, where each encounter with a cat, bird, or snake was a new and mysterious experience? The ability to see similarities between things, to classify objects as exemplars of meaningful categories (e.g., to perceive a round, orange-coloured object as a member of the category "orange," part of the larger category "fruit"), enables us to simplify our environment and make predictions.

Third, how do we solve problems, such as the ticket-scalping-profit problem posed at the beginning of

▶ **Figure 8.1**

The Adaptive Problems

Thought and language serve a variety of adaptive functions. Summarized here are the four adaptive problems that we'll be considering in this chapter.

the chapter? When you do problem solving, you want to reach a goal, such as answering a math problem or hooking up a new VCR, but you don't know exactly how to attain that goal. Think about the dozens of practical problems you face and solve every day. Did you have trouble finding your keys this morning or have a difficult time choosing what to wear or what to eat? The adaptive value of problem solving is obvious: If humans couldn't solve the problem of where to find food and water, *Homo sapiens* would quickly become extinct.

Fourth, how do we make decisions when confronted with a set of alternatives? Should I buy the tickets for $100, use the money to help pay this month's rent, or gamble it on the outcome of tonight's game? Should I keep working on my university education or go travelling? Note that an important ingredient of decision making is *risk*—choices have consequences, and an incorrect decision can lead to an unpleasant or even fatal outcome.

We discuss each of these issues in a different section, but you should know at the outset that communicating, categorizing, solving problems, and making decisions are all closely interrelated. For example, there is an obvious link between naming things with language (e.g., "chair" or "thief" or "envy") and categorizing; naming entails categorization, and the names we know may affect the ways we categorize things. As you'll see, problem solving and decision making are near cousins; indeed, solving problems invariably involves making decisions, and making a decision can itself be described as a sort of problem. And, of course, human problem solving and decision making very often rely on both language and categorization. Nonetheless, different researchers have focused on these subtopics, and it is therefore useful to present information about them separately.

▶ Communicating

LEARNING GOALS

1. Be able to evaluate the linguistic relativity hypothesis.
2. Learn about the structure of language and its basic units.
3. Appreciate the role of shared knowledge in language comprehension.
4. Be able to identify the major milestones of language development.
5. Evaluate whether or not nonhuman animals are capable of language.
6. Be able to summarize ideas about the evolution of language.

We begin our exploration of thinking with an extended discussion of language. It might seem odd to lump language and thought together, but the two are closely linked: Language importantly influences the way we think about and view our world. Remember from Chapter 7 how the use of the word *smashed* rather than *contacted* in a question changed witnesses' reports of a car accident?

linguistic relativity hypothesis

The proposal that language determines the characteristics and content of thought

CRITICAL THINKING

Do you think the study of colour perception is a fair way to test the linguistic relativity hypothesis?

Does Language Determine Thought?

How strong is the connection between language and thought? The **linguistic relativity hypothesis** proposes that language *determines* thought (Whorf, 1956). The idea is that the words and structures of a culture's language determine the perceptions and thoughts of members of that culture. For example, the Hopi language has no past tense for verbs, and Whorf argued that Hopi people consequently had difficulty thinking about the past.

To test the linguistic relativity hypothesis, researchers have turned to nature's laboratory to examine relationships between the idiosyncrasies of language and the way people think in different cultures. In the Philippines, for example, the Hanunoo people have 92 different names for rice (Anderson, 1990). According to the linguistic relativity hypothesis, language determines how people think about and perceive the world. Consequently, you might expect the Hanunoo people to perceive subtle distinctions in rice that members of other cultures, with a more limited "rice" vocabulary, do not.

The Cultural Evidence In some important cross-cultural research, Eleanor Rosch (publishing under her former name, Heider, in 1972) travelled to New Guinea to investigate the perceptual abilities of members of a tribe called the Dani. The Dani's language contains only two basic colour terms: *mola* for bright, warm hues, and *mili* for the darker, colder hues. If words completely shape thought, Rosch reasoned, the Dani should have trouble perceiving and remembering colours. By using a wide range of colour chips, Rosch discovered that volunteers from the tribe had no trouble remembering novel colours; moreover, the Dani did particularly well with focal colours (red, green, and blue) as opposed to nonfocal colours (such as teal), just as English speakers do.

Rosch interpreted her results as evidence that English speakers and speakers of the Dani language perceive colour in very similar ways. Colour perception appears to be universal, depending more on the physiology of the visual system than on the vocabulary of the perceiver (Heider, 1972). In research conducted after Rosch's pioneering study, the same general conclusion has been reached: Colour perception seems to be largely universal, regardless of language (Davies, 1998; Davies & Corbett, 1997; for a critique, see Saunders & van Brakel, 1997), although recent evidence also suggests that learning new colour categories can subtly influence colour perception (Ozgen, 2004; Ozgen & Davies, 2002).

The cross-cultural evidence has led most psychologists to conclude that linguistic differences across cultures do not cause dramatic differences in the operation of basic perceptual processes, such as colour perception. The evidence is less clear when it comes to the operation of higher-level perceptual and cognitive processes. One problem is that it is difficult to determine causation from cross-cultural comparisons. Suppose, for example, that research showed that Hanunoo people perceive rice differently from the way members of Western cultures do. Would that mean that the large Hanunoo rice vocabulary *causes* that difference? An alternative explanation is that different cultures place value on different sorts of things, and each culture develops vocabularies to communicate subtle distinctions in those things perceived as important. For example, most Canadians know hundreds of words for "automobile" (e.g., Cadillac, Camry, Camaro, car, and cab). Knowing these words may not, in itself, change the way we perceive automobiles but may merely go along with living in a culture in which people learn to talk about fine discriminations between automobiles.

Nonetheless, there is little question that language can influence thought. Both perception and memory depend on prior knowledge, and people often use words to summarize and represent prior knowledge. For example, verbal labels can strongly bias the perception of ambiguous pictures like those discussed in

The Quecha, who live in mountainous regions, have no word in their language for "flat." According to the linguistic relativity hypothesis, one might expect them to have a difficult time orienting themselves spatially in a flat environment.

Chapter 4. Language—in the form of an inner voice—also plays important roles in more abstract thinking. For example, a study conducted at Mount Allison University indicated that university students use internal speech as a cognitive tool in their studies (Duncan & Cheyne, 1999). Also, as you learned in Chapter 7, memory for an event depends significantly on how you thought about the event when it originally occurred. Furthermore, memory search is often mediated by language; for example, DODGE VIPER would be a powerful retrieval cue for memories of seeing a car for a person with expertise in automobiles, but it would be a poor cue for someone ignorant of the various makes and models.

Language is a tool of human thought, useful in many ways, but evidence also suggests that in some cases language can interfere with nonlinguistic processes. For example, Jonathan Schooler and his colleagues have shown that when people verbally describe hard-to-describe things (such as their memories of a person's face) their performance on subsequent judgment tasks involving those things (e.g., trying to recognize the person from a set of pictures) is sometimes impaired (Schooler, 2002). Language clearly affects thought in significant ways (Lucy, 1997).

The interplay between thought and language can be insidious: "The secretary hates his boss." Did you find yourself stumbling when you read this sentence? Many people do, which suggests that the "generic" male pronoun ("his") is not truly generic and that people tend to think of secretaries as women. Many words carry such gendered connotations. If used inappropriately, they become weapons, leading people to generate misleading expectations or draw inaccurate conclusions (Ehrlich, 1999; Henley, 1989; Mackay, 1983).

The Structure of Language

We now turn our attention to language itself. What is language? Birds communicate effectively through their songs. Some biologists believe that bees convey information about the exact location of nectar through a tail-wagging dance (von Frisch, 1967, but see also Wenner, 1998). Your neighbour's dog barks incessantly at outdoor noises. But to qualify as a true language, a communication system must have a generative **grammar** that enables the communicator to combine arbitrary symbols in an infinite number of ways to convey meaning.

Bees do a characteristic "waggle dance" that may communicate information about the location of nectar. But would you say bees have language?

grammar

The rules or procedures of language that allow the communicator to combine arbitrary symbols in an infinite number of ways to convey meaning; includes the rules of phonology, syntax, and semantics

phonology

The rules and procedures for combining sounds to make words in a language

syntax

The rules and procedures for combining words to form sentences

semantics

The rules and procedures for communicating meaning through words and combinations of words

phonemes

The smallest significant, difference-making sound units in speech

A generative grammar specifies which combinations of sounds are permissible in a particular language and which are not. Grammar has three aspects: (1) **phonology,** the rules for combining sounds to make words; (2) **syntax,** the rules for combining words to make sentences; and (3) **semantics,** the rules regarding the meanings of words and combinations of words. An English speaker would not normally say something like, "The cautious the at barked nasty man poodle." This particular combination of words violates a number of rules of syntax, such as the rule that articles (*the*) and adjectives (*nasty*) come before nouns (*man*). Most English speakers would also be unlikely to generate a sentence like "Colourless green ideas sleep furiously." Although this is a well-structured sentence with good syntax, it suffers from violations of semantics: It has no coherent meaning, even though the individual words are meaningful. We use our knowledge about semantics to pick the appropriate words to express thoughts (perhaps "people" can "sleep furiously," but "ideas" cannot) and to infer connections between words and other information in memory.

Phonemes and Morphemes   Language has a hierarchical structure: A fairly small set of simple sounds can be combined in various ways to make thousands of words, and words can be combined in innumerable ways to generate infinitely many sentences. At the base of the hierarchy are **phonemes,** which are the smallest significant, difference-making sound units in a language. Speech sounds are produced through a complex coordination of the vocal cords, lungs, lips, tongue, and teeth. ▶ Table 8.1 lists some examples of phonemes in the English language. Notice that there isn't a simple one-to-one mapping between a given letter of the alphabet and a phoneme. The letter *e*, for example, maps onto one phoneme in the word *head* and a different phoneme in the word *heat*.

English speakers use about 40 phonemes; some languages use considerably more, and others use fewer. Within a given language, a range of physically different sounds will be heard by speakers of that language as a single phoneme. For example, English speakers will hear a variety of physically different sounds as all being a "k" sound. Languages differ in where the boundaries between different sounds are drawn. Japanese, for example, does not differentiate between the sounds *r* and *l*; these are just different ways of saying a single phoneme. Similarly, English does not meaningfully distinguish between the initial consonant sounds in *keep* and *cool* (say these two words aloud, and notice how differently your mouth is shaped for each); here again, in English these two quite different sounds are perceived as a single phoneme. For example, if you force yourself to say the "k" sound from *keep* followed by the "ool" sound from *cool*, to an English speaker it will just sound like *cool*. That's what makes them the same phoneme in English, the fact that it doesn't matter which one you say. In Arabic, in contrast, those two "k" sounds correspond to two different phonemes, such that the meaning of a spoken word

▶ **Table 8.1** Some Examples of English Phonemes

Symbol	Examples	Symbol	Examples
b	**b**urger, ru**bb**le	ng	sti**ng**, ri**ng**er
ē	**e**asy, zomb**ie**	oy	c**oi**l, empl**oy**
ĕ	**e**nter, m**e**tric	r	**r**at, c**r**ust
f	**f**ungus, **ph**one	s	**s**todgy, be**s**t
ĭ	**i**cky, w**i**g	t	**t**ramp, mi**ss**ed
ī	**i**ce, sh**y**	th	**th**at, o**th**er
k	**k**itty, a**ch**e	ŭ	**u**gly, b**u**tter
n	**n**ewt, a**nn**oy		

changes depending on which one is used (just as, in English, the *r* and *l* sounds are treated as different). Part of the challenge of acquiring a foreign language is mastering the phonology of that language; it is difficult to learn to pronounce differences that you cannot hear.

At the next level in the hierarchy are **morphemes,** the smallest units of language that carry meaning. Most morphemes are single words, such as *cool* or *hip*, but prefixes and suffixes are also morphemes. For instance, the word *cool* contains a single morpheme, whereas *uncool* contains two: the root word *cool* and the prefix *un*. The grammar of a language dictates the acceptable order of morphemes within a word—*uncool* has a particular meaning in English; *coolun* does not. Similarly, the morpheme *s* when placed at the end of a word (*oar*) designates plural (two or more *oars*). But the phoneme *s* when placed at the beginning of that same word means something entirely different (*soar*). The average speaker of English knows and uses somewhere between 50 000 and 80 000 morphemes (see ▶ Figure 8.2).

Words to Sentences   At the higher levels of the language hierarchy are *words*, *phrases*, and *sentences*. Words combine to form phrases; phrases combine to form sentences. Sentences are not just collections of words, because the meaning of the sentence depends not only on what words it contains but also on how they are organized: "Beth shot John" has a meaning quite different from "John shot Beth."

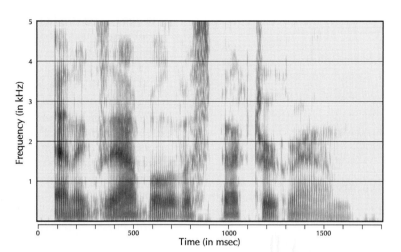

A spectrogram is a computer-generated visual image that represents sounds in terms of their frequencies (pitches, represented by the height of the lines) and amplitudes (loudness, represented by the darkness of the lines). Time is represented from left to right. The spectrogram above is a representation of the words "an example of a spectrogram." (Spectrogram provided by Professor R. Hagiwara of the University of Manitoba, see http://home.cc.umanitoba.ca/~robh/.)

▶ **Figure 8.2**

The Units of Language

Languages have a hierarchical structure, building from simple speech sounds to more complex levels of spoken conversation. Complex rules determine how fundamental speech sounds (phonemes) are combined to create the smallest units of meaning (morphemes) and words, and how words are combined into phrases and sentences. A small number of phonemes can be used to create many thousands of different words, and these can be combined to form an infinite number of different sentences.

morphemes

The smallest units in a language that carry meaning (words, prefixes, suffixes)

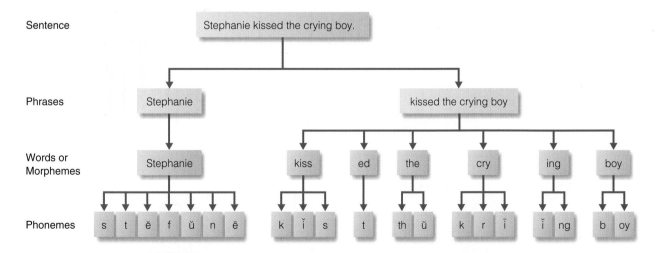

Language researchers have spent decades trying to decipher the rules of syntax that people use to combine words into phrases and phrases into sentences. It turns out that those rules are enormously complex.

Surface and Deep Structure   Noam Chomsky is widely heralded as the most important linguist of recent times. One of Chomsky's (1957) early contributions to the study of language was his distinction between the "surface" structure of a sentence and its more abstract "deep" structure. The **surface structure** of a sentence corresponds to its superficial appearance (the literal ordering of words), whereas **deep structure** refers to the underlying representation of meaning. Thus, a single surface structure can have two different deep structures. Chomsky used as an example the following sentence: "Visiting relatives can be a nuisance." Whether it is the relatives or visiting them that is a nuisance depends on the deep structure. Conversely, two different surface structures can represent essentially the same deep structure ("Beth shot John" and "John was shot by Beth").

According to Chomsky, language production requires the transformation of deep structure into an acceptable surface structure (see ❯ Figure 8.3), and comprehension involves transforming a surface structure into the appropriate deep structure. Most language researchers agree with Chomsky on this point, although there are disagreements over how the transformation process works (Treiman, Clifton, Meyer, & Wurm, 2003). Language is clearly more than sets of words or symbols organized in a fixed and rigid way. In the words of Canadian psychologist Steven Pinker (1997b), "hundreds of millions of trillions of thinkable thoughts" exist, and each can, in principle, be expressed through language in an understandable way. The challenge for language researchers is to discover how this flexibility arises.

Language Comprehension

How do you understand what a speaker is trying to communicate? This is not a trivial problem because language comprehension presents many difficulties: In normal speech, sounds are presented very quickly, without well-defined pauses between words; we don't always hear sounds clearly or correctly; word sounds often have many different meanings (e.g., consider the number of meanings that correspond to the sound of the word "rite"); and language is full of metaphors and other indirect speech acts that complicate the interpretation process (Glucksberg, 1998; Lakoff, 1987; Pinker, 1994).

Effective communication seems to rely a great deal on *common knowledge* among speakers (Clark, 1992; Keysar, Barr, Balin, & Paekm, 1998). When you're having a conversation with someone about a mutual friend, you can say "That's typ-

---

surface structure

The literal ordering of words in a sentence

deep structure

The underlying representation of meaning in a sentence

CRITICAL THINKING

Based on what you've learned about Chomsky's work, why might it be difficult to program a computer to understand speech?

❯ **Figure 8.3**

Surface Structure and Deep Structure

The surface structure of a sentence is its "surface" appearance, the literal ordering of words. Deep structure is the underlying meaning of the sentence. The left and right panels of this figure show how the same surface structure—"Visiting relatives can be a nuisance"—can reflect two different deep structures. Similarly, the panel on the far right shows how a single deep structure can be transformed into two or more acceptable surface structures.

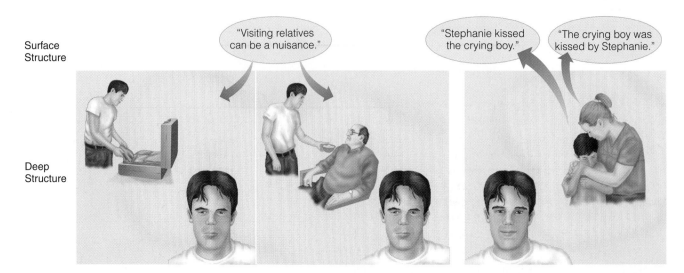

ical of her" and be understood. You both know that "her" refers to your friend, and you can both list examples of your friend's "typical" behaviour. You go beyond the information given in the spoken message by using shared knowledge. Similarly, everyday language is rife with ambiguity, yet we usually resolve the ambiguity without even being aware that it is there. Someone says to you, "They're shooting stars," and in one context you immediately comprehend that this refers to meteorites, in another to expert sharpshooters, in yet another to victimized movie actors or a scene from *Star Wars*. Like other forms of perception, language comprehension involves a combination of top-down and bottom-up processing (McClelland & Elman, 1986). Sometimes the system breaks down and we become aware of ambiguity or even misunderstand one another, just as we sometimes misperceive objects, but most of the time language comprehension is very fluent.

Pragmatic Rules   Language researchers use the term **pragmatics** to describe how practical knowledge is used to comprehend the intentions of speakers and to produce appropriate responses. Consider your response to an *indirect* request, such as, "Could you close the window?" If you process the request directly—that is, if you take its literal interpretation—you might respond, "Yes, I'm capable of putting enough steady pressure on the window to produce closure." You have answered the question, but clearly you have violated an important pragmatic rule. The speaker was making a request, not asking you about your ability to perform the task. In fact, if you answered the question in this way, the speaker would probably infer that you were using *irony* or *sarcasm* (Katz, Blasko, & Kazmerski, 2004; Kreuz, 2000; Pexman & Olineck, 2002).

The pragmatics of language add to its complexity. How you interpret someone's words depends on the shared context of the conversation as well as on the expectations and beliefs that you bring to the exchange. To facilitate effective communication, good speakers follow certain pragmatic guidelines, or conversational maxims (Grice, 1975):

- Be informative.
- Tell the truth.
- Be relevant.
- Be clear.

If you choose to answer an indirect request literally ("Yes, I can close the window"), then you're not being relevant; you're violating an accepted guideline for communication. If you don't tell the truth or are purposely vague in answering a request, then you'll soon have trouble finding people who want to talk with you. By following the simple rules listed above, and by assuming the same of your conversational partner, you can enhance the ease and flow of the conversational process.

Language Development

How does language develop? Are humans born with a genetic blueprint that directs and shapes their communication skills? Or do we acquire language exclusively as a product of experience? There are thousands of different languages, so experience must certainly play an important role. But most language researchers are convinced that babies are genetically prepared to learn language, much as they are genetically prepared to learn to walk. There is a regularity to language development, as there is to the development of motor skills, that is difficult to explain by appealing solely to the environment (Chomsky, 1986; Pinker, 1994; see also Gopnik, 1999). Moreover, the complexity of language is so great that some scholars have argued that it would be impossible to learn any language from scratch without innately specified linguistic mechanisms that constrain and guide language development.

pragmatics

The practical knowledge used to comprehend the intentions of a speaker and to produce an appropriate response

Infants and small children develop rather sophisticated ways to communicate meaningfully (cooing, kicking, looking, pointing, crying, and so on), even though their language skills are limited.

The universality of language is apparent even at birth. Most babies cry in similar ways, and they move quickly through vocalization milestones that precede formal language development. By three to five weeks of age, *cooing*—repeating vowel sounds like "ooh" and "aah"—has been added to the baby's vocalization patterns. *Babbling*—repeating consonant/vowel combinations, such as "kaka" or "baba"—begins in virtually all babies between the ages of four and six months. It doesn't matter where you look in the world, this same sequence—crying then cooing then babbling—is found. Babbling also progresses through a regular series of stages, beginning with simple sound sequences and culminating with complex and speech-like (but meaningless) vocalizations known as "expressive jargon."

Between the ages of 6 and 18 months, experience begins to play a noticeable role, shaping and fine-tuning the baby's babblings into language-specific sounds. Babies begin to restrict their vocalizations to the phonemes of the language(s) they hear every day; they even acquire a kind of language-specific "accent" by around eight months of age (de Boysson-Bardies, Sagat, & Durand, 1984; Locke, 1994). Six-month-old babies perceive subtle phonemic differences from other languages that their parents cannot detect, but by one year children no longer hear those differences (Werker & Tees, 1999; for a more general overview of infants' perceptions of speech sounds, see Werker & Desjardins, 2001). Simple words appear by the end of the first year, and by 24 months most babies have developed a vocabulary of nearly 200 words (Nelson, 1973).

Language comprehension also develops rapidly during this period; in fact, infants develop the ability to understand language faster than they learn to produce it. At first thought, you might assume that learning to understand words would be relatively simple, but deeper consideration shows that here too children's ability to learn is amazing. For example, suppose I point at a dog and say "flug." Is flug the word for dog? Or is it the word for that particular breed of dog (a collie, perhaps) or the name of that specific dog (Flug)? Or maybe it means "bark" or "bite" or refers to some specific part of the dog (collar, nose, whatever), or perhaps it refers to the rug the dog is standing on. Young children use a variety of sophisticated inferential strategies to solve problems like this and hone in on the meanings of new words (Nelson & Shaw, 2002; Welder & Graham, 2001).

Child Speak   As every parent knows, infants and young children develop rather sophisticated ways to communicate meaningfully, even though their language skills are limited. An 18-month-old child can point to the jar on the counter and say "ookie," and Mom or Dad immediately knows what the child has in mind. An enormous amount of information can be packed into a single word, even if that word is spoken incorrectly, especially if its utterance is combined with a gesture or occurs in the right context.

As the child approaches the end of his or her second year of life, a phase of *telegraphic speech* begins. Telegraphic speech involves combining two words into simple sentences, such as "Daddy bad" or "Give cookie." It's called telegraphic speech because, as in a telegram, the child characteristically omits articles (*the, a*) and prepositions (*at, in*). But a two-year-old's first sentences reflect a rudimentary knowledge of the syntax of his or her language: Words are almost always spoken in the proper *order*. For example, a child will say, "Want cookie," not "Cookie want," and "Me push!" will mean something quite different from "Push me!" During the rest of the child's preschool years, up to around age five or six, sentences become increasingly complex, such that the average child of Kindergarten age can produce and comprehend sentences that reveal most of the important features of adult syntax.

CONCEPT SUMMARY

HIGHLIGHTS IN LANGUAGE DEVELOPMENT

Age	Linguistic Highlight(s)	Interpretation
3–5 weeks	Cooing, or the repetition of vowel sounds, such as "ooh" and "aah"	Both cooing and babbling are vocalization milestones that occur before formal language development, and their occurrence is similar across cultures, highlighting the universality of language.
4–6 months	Babbling, or the repetition of vowel–consonant combinations, such as "kaka" and "baba"	As above.
6–18 months	Vocalizations specific to the native language; first word spoken by the end of the first year	Experience plays a role in vocalization as a baby's babblings are shaped into language-specific sounds. Language comprehension develops rapidly.
24 months	Vocabulary of nearly 200 words; child shows telegraphic speech, grammatical two-word combinations	Speech reflects knowledge of syntax, as words are almost always combined in the proper order.
Preschool years	Ability to produce and comprehend sentences; vocabulary growing at an astounding rate	The child is now showing most of the important features of adult syntax.

The linguistic rules children learn during their preschool years are revealed by the errors that they make. For example, preschoolers acquire the rule "Add *ed* to the ends of verbs to make them past tense." Interestingly, children tend to *overgeneralize* this rule—they say such things as "goed" and "falled," which are incorrect in English but represent an application of the rule. Notice that children are not rewarded for saying *goed*, nor do they hear the word being used by their parents. Rather, children appear to be naturally "tuned" to pick up linguistic rules and apply them generally, even if a rule sometimes leads to an incorrect utterance. This natural tendency to learn and apply rules is then further refined and shaped by experience as the child learns the exceptions to the rules.

Language development continues throughout the school years, as children fine-tune their articulation skills and knowledge about grammar. Vocabulary expands at an astounding rate, as does the child's ability to communicate abstract concepts. Ultimately, the sophistication of any child's language ability will depend, at least in part, on his or her level of cognitive development. Children think differently as they mature, and their increasingly sophisticated cognitive abilities are reflected in the conversations they generate. You should keep this fact in mind when we turn our attention to language abilities in nonhuman species.

Acquiring our first language has been described as "the greatest intellectual feat any of us is ever required to perform" (Bloomfield, 1933). How do children develop such sophisticated language skills so quickly? Few parents sit down with their preschoolers and teach them the rules of grammar (such as the differences between present and past tense). Moreover, as we will discuss further in Chapter 10, children at this age lack the ability to understand most abstract concepts, so they couldn't consciously understand grammatical rules even if parents tried to explain them. Children pick up their language skills implicitly, not through explicit instruction. It's also clear that children do not simply imitate the speech they hear around them. For example, children's first words are *not* the words they most often hear (articles, such as *the* and *a*, or perhaps their own names), but rather names for things that move and that they find interesting. Similarly, children's early telegraphic grammar is not something they hear others use. Also, deaf children raised without exposure to sign language often develop their own gestural languages (Pinker, 1994). It's worth mentioning that manual languages, such as

CRITICAL   THINKING

If imitation played the major role in the development of language, what words would babies first use?

American Sign Language, are just as complex, sophisticated, and generative as spoken languages. Research conducted at McGill University by Petitto (2000) showed that the acquisition of sign language by young children follows a developmental trajectory that parallels that of the acquisition of spoken language, and some of the same brain areas are involved in spoken and signed language use.

Most psychologists are convinced that humans have an innate "language acquisition device" that enables them to develop linguistic skills astonishingly quickly. This inherent tendency toward language development must be sufficiently flexible to allow for the acquisition of any of the many thousands of languages used by humans (including sign language). All languages use comparable building blocks (nouns and verbs, subjects and objects, interrogatives and negations, etc.), and although considerable variation exists in surface structure across languages, those variations all fit within certain common constraints. Thus, all human languages can be described as dialects or variants of an innate universal grammar.

Language in Nonhuman Species

Anyone who has ever been bossed around by a cat knows that nonhuman animals can communicate. The question is whether such forms of communication should be called *language*. There's no doubt that an animal's actions can convey meaning. But to qualify as having a true language, the animal would need to possess at least a rudimentary grammar, that is, a set of procedures for generatively combining arbitrary symbols to convey innumerable possible messages.

Several teams of researchers have explored nonhuman animals' linguistic skills by attempting to teach them a language. For example, chimps were raised in human homes in an effort to provide the ideal environment for language development. In one case, a chimp named Gua was raised along with the researchers' son, Donald (Kellogg & Kellogg, 1933). Donald and Gua were exposed to the same experiences, and careful attention was paid to rewarding the appropriate vocalizations. But in the end the Kelloggs had merely produced a fine-speaking son and an effectively mute chimp (legend has it that Donald also developed into an excellent tree climber). Later efforts to teach chimps to speak yielded the same discouraging results (Hayes & Hayes, 1951).

Signs and Symbol Communication   Attempts to teach chimps to speak were doomed because chimps' vocal apparatus cannot produce most of the sounds required for human speech (Hayes, 1952). It's like a bird trying to teach a human to fly by raising a child in a nest—without wings, that baby just isn't going to fly. For this reason, subsequent researchers turned to visual communication mediums. Allen and Beatrice Gardner tried to teach a simplified form of American Sign Language to a chimp named Washoe (Gardner & Gardner, 1969; Gardner, Gardner, & Van Cantfort, 1989). By four years of age, Washoe was capable of producing about 160 appropriate signs, and apparently she understood a great deal more. Even more impressive was her ability to produce various word combinations, such as "more fruit" or "gimme tickle."

Koko, a gorilla trained by Francine Patterson (1978), also demonstrated impressive use of sign language. Similarly, David Premack taught a chimp named Sarah to manipulate plastic shapes that symbolized words (e.g., a plastic triangle stood for the word *banana*). Sarah eventually learned to respond to simple symbol-based sentences that were arranged on a magnetic board (such as "Sarah insert banana into pail"; Premack, 1976). In a lab in Georgia, pigmy chimpanzees were taught to communicate by pressing keys that represented objects, such as food or toys (Rumbaugh, 1977; Savage-Rumbaugh, McDonald, Sevcik, Hopkins, & Rupert, 1986). Again, not only did these chimps learn to associate particular symbols with words or actions, but they also showed the capacity to generate combinations of words by pressing the symbols in sequence.

Susan Kuklin/Photo Researchers, Inc.

Chimpanzees lack the vocal equipment needed to produce most of the sounds of human speech. But chimps can be taught to communicate in relatively sophisticated ways by using American Sign Language or by pressing keys that symbolically represent objects, such as food or toys.

Work in Savage-Rumbaugh's Georgia laboratory has also shown that pygmy chimpanzees can understand some spoken English. A chimp named Kanzi can press the appropriate symbol key when a word is spoken (e.g., banana). He can also respond appropriately to a variety of spoken commands. When asked, "Can you pour the ice water in the potty?" Kanzi picked up the bowl of ice water, headed to the potty, and carefully poured it in (Savage-Rumbaugh et al., 1993). When asked to "Hide the toy gorilla," Kanzi picked up the toy gorilla and attempted to push it under a fence.

Is It Really Language?   These are very impressive demonstrations and are quite convincing when you see them on video. But have chimps, such as Kanzi, really acquired *language*? The jury is still out on this issue. Some psychologists believe that the chimps' behaviour simply reflects reinforced learning—like a pigeon who has been taught to peck a key for food—rather than true language (Terrace, 1986). But this view is challenged by reports that chimps, such as Washoe and Kanzi, can generate new combinations of words and respond to requests that they have never heard before. Washoe, for example, could apparently respond to environmental events by producing novel signs. On seeing a duck for the first time, she reportedly signed "water bird." Moreover, it's been shown that chimps can acquire these language skills through observing other chimps, without being trained directly (Savage-Rumbaugh et al., 1986).

This debate is nowhere near a firm resolution. Most psychologists who work with chimps are firmly convinced that the language abilities are real. Kanzi, for example, doesn't seem to follow rigid scripts; he can respond appropriately to a request that is worded in various ways, which is far beyond what you would expect from a pigeon trained to peck a key. Yet Seidenberg and Petitto (1987) offered strong arguments that Kanzi's behaviours were like the nonlinguistic gestural communication of very young children, not comparable with the generative grammar of language users. Moreover, much of the critical evidence (such as Washoe's "water bird") has come from trainer anecdotes, so there is room for multiple interpretations. For example, some of the novel combinations generated by the chimps may merely be imitations of their trainers or flukes of chance; it is also possible that trainers' beliefs and expectations have sometimes distorted their perceptions (as discussed in Chapter 4). We just don't know at this point. It is clear, however, that even if chimps or other nonhuman animals are capable of acquiring language, their abilities in this regard are qualitatively different from humans. For one thing, untutored three-year-old humans have linguistic skills far beyond those of the most intensively trained nonhuman animals. For another, it seems likely that nonhuman animals have relatively little to say; as emphasized in a preceding section, language is intimately related to thought, and to date we have little evidence that our nonhuman cousins are capable of the sophisticated sorts of cognitions entailed by all but the most primitive of conversations. We can't say for sure—according to one of Kurt Vonnegut's short stories, Thomas Edison's dog broke a fundamental canine rule against talking in front of humans when he told Edison to use tungsten as the filament in a light bulb—but to date there's no compelling evidence for truly human-like language in nonhumans.

The Evolution of Language

Given that human linguistic competence differs qualitatively from the communicative skills of nonhuman animals, how did our species acquire that competence? It's easy to say that language "evolved," but by itself that isn't much of an explanation. Darwinian evolution works through random genetic errors; mutations that turn out to be advantageous tend to be preserved because animals with advantageous mutations are more likely to survive and propagate and their progeny are likely to share the mutation. It is easy to see that language has survival value. The major difficulty is that any given random genetic mutation is likely to produce a subtle variation on its predecessors, not a large and qualitative difference, so evolution occurs gradually. Thus, "there must have been a series of steps leading from no language at all to language as we now find it, each step small enough to have been produced by a random mutation ... and each intermediate grammar useful to its possessor" (Pinker & Bloom, 1992). Where is the evidence of all of these small steps?

Most linguists agree that all known human languages are comparable in terms of complexity and sophistication (as noted earlier, each language appears to be a variant of an underlying "universal grammar" shared by all humans) (Cartwright, 2000). Presumably, then, language evolved gradually in early forms of human life (e.g., *Australopithecus afarensis*) (Pinker & Bloom, 1992). If early forms of human life had survived rather than becoming extinct, then perhaps we would share the planet with creatures with protogrammars of varying degrees of complexity. Perhaps, for example, some of our prehuman relatives would use a gestural language (see Merlin, 1999, for a discussion of what such prehuman protogrammars might have been like).

As you think about this topic for yourself, try to avoid adopting an anthropocentric view of the world. It's important to keep in mind that chimpanzees did not evolve to understand or produce human language. Chimps evolved to solve their own problems, problems that arise from their own unique environments. The human mind has evolved to solve human problems, and those problems may or may not overlap with the challenges faced by other members of the animal kingdom. You would probably have difficulty performing the honeybee's waggle dance effectively, and your climbing skills are likely but a faint echo of those of the chimpanzee.

Check your knowledge about language by answering the following questions. (The answers are in Appendix B.)

1. Choose the term that best fits the following descriptions. Choose your answers from the following: deep structure, linguistic relativity, morphemes, pragmatics, phonemes, phonology, semantics, surface structure, syntax.
   a. The smallest significant, difference-making sound units in speech: _____
   b. The practical knowledge used to understand the intentions of a speaker and to produce an appropriate response: _____
   c. The idea that language determines the characteristics and contents of thought: _____
   d. The rules governing how words are combined to form sentences: _____
   e. The smallest units in language that carry meaning: _____

2. Decide whether each of the following statements about language is true or false.
   a. Across the world babies cry, coo, and begin to babble in similar ways. *True or False?*
   b. Children learn the rules of language primarily by copying the words and phrases of their parents. *True or False?*
   c. Telegraphic speech begins toward the end of the child's second year of life. *True or False?*
   d. Chimpanzees lack the vocal equipment needed to produce human speech. *True or False?*
   e. Chimpanzee Kanzi learned to associate symbols with a variety of words but cannot follow spoken instructions from his trainers. *True or False?*
   f. Early (now extinct) forms of human life likely possessed a more primitive grammar than *Homo sapiens. True or False?*

▶ Categorizing

LEARNING GOALS

1. Understand why psychologists have rejected the idea that natural categories have defining features, in favour of the idea that category members share a "family resemblance."
2. Be able to compare the prototype and exemplar views of categorization.
3. Learn about the hierarchical organization of categories.

As discussed above, one use of language is as a tool to think and talk about things. By "things" we mean both concrete things (objects and animals) and more abstract ones (concepts, ideas, feelings). Thus, language includes a large number of symbols that are used to refer to various sorts of things (e.g., "tree" or "lust"). Some of these verbal labels refer to a particular single instance (e.g., "Brad Pitt"), but most refer to categories of things (e.g., "hammer" or "doctor" or "fruit"). In this section we turn our attention to the cognitive processes that underlie our knowledge of categories.

Categorizing is an essential cognitive skill. By carving the environment into meaningful categories, people create a world that is manageable, predictable, and sensible. Imagine what it would be like if each time you encountered a new ballpoint pen you did not perceive it as a member of the category "pen" but rather as a novel object (after all, you've never encountered that particular pen before). Without categorization, every new object and event would be a one-of-a-kind mystery, and you would have to explore each one to discover its nonapparent properties.

A **category** is a collection of objects (people, places, or things) or events that people in a given culture agree belong together (Smith, 1989). "Vegetables" is a category that contains such things as peas, carrots, and Brussels sprouts; "psychologists" is a category that includes researchers, clinicians, and other professionals working within particular areas of expertise. Categories allow people to *infer* invisible properties of objects. For example, by perceiving a particular object as an orange you immediately access information about what the inside of that object

category

A collection of objects (people, places, or things) or events that most people in a given culture agree belong together

People automatically classify objects, and even other people, into categories. How would you categorize this individual, and what "invisible" properties would you infer about him? Can you predict how he might act in a social situation?

defining features

A set of features that define membership in a category, such that all members of that category (and no nonmembers of that category) have all those features; for example, the defining features of the category *triangle* might be (1) a two-dimensional figure that is (2) composed of three straight lines with (3) each end of each line joined to an end of one of the other lines

looks, tastes, and feels like, what can be done with it, and so on. Once you have successfully categorized something, you can also make *predictions* about the future. You know, for example, that if you throw an orange against a wall with sufficient force it is likely to splatter, and that if you plant its seeds and tend the soil properly, they will sprout.

We'll divide our discussion of categorizing into three main topics. First, what properties of an object make it a member of a particular category? Second, do we form and store an abstract representation of the most typical member (or "prototype") of each category, or are category judgments based on memory for individual encounters with category members? Finally, we'll end the section by considering the structure of categories: When people categorize an object, do they usually do so in a very general or a highly specific manner?

Defining Category Membership

Researchers have spent a lot of time studying how people categorize objects and events in everyday experience. How do we know that a trout is a member of the category "fish"? How is it that we quickly and effortlessly classify a sparrow as a bird? These questions probably sound pretty silly to you at this point, but as you read on you will (we hope) come to appreciate that the question of how people categorize things is quite interesting.

The intuitively obvious answer is that people classify a sparrow as a "bird" because it has features that all members of the bird category share. We'll refer to this as the **defining-features** account of categorization: If the object in question has all the defining features of a category, it must be a member of that category; if the object lacks one or more of these characteristics, it must be something else (Medin, 1989). For example, to be a member of the category "bird" an object might have to be a living thing that flies, sings, lays eggs, and nests in trees. From this standpoint, categorizing an object is simply a matter of learning and applying the right set of defining features (see ▶ Figure 8.4).

▶ **Figure 8.4**

Natural Categories Do Not Have Defining Features

According to the defining-features account, all members of a category (and no nonmembers) share a set of defining features. This account works well for certain artificial categories (e.g., geometric forms) but fails for most everyday categories, such as birds, furniture, or games. The problem is that members of most categories don't share any unique set of defining features. All of the objects shown here are birds, for example, but they don't all share the same set of "defining" features. (Based on Smith, 1989.)

Properties	Robin	Sandpiper	Vulture	Chicken	Penguin
Flies regularly	+	+	+	−	−
Sings	+	+	−	−	−
Lays eggs	+	+	+	+	+
Is small	+	+	−	−	−
Nests in trees	+	−	+	−	−

Corel 3 British Columbia

Does this monorail train fit into your category for "vehicle"? If so, what "defining features" does it share with other members of the category?

As is often the case, the intuitively obvious answer is inadequate. The defining-features account of categorization works fine for mathematical categories, such as "triangle," but it breaks down for natural objects. Take the category "vehicle," for example. What are the defining features of a vehicle? Something that moves along the ground, has wheels, and can transport people? That applies well to cars and trucks, but what about monorail trains and snowmobiles, which many would describe as vehicles but don't run on wheels? What about inline skates, which have all of those "defining" features but most people would not describe as a vehicle? Research on natural categories, such as birds, vehicles, furniture, and games, demonstrates that people cannot agree on just what constitutes the defining features of a natural category (Malt & Smith, 1984; Rosch & Mervis, 1975).

Most natural categories have *fuzzy boundaries*. For example, in ▶ Figure 8.5 you can see a series of objects within the fuzzy boundaries of the category "cup." In an experiment by Labov (1973), people were presented with a set of these objects, such as objects 1 through 4 in the figure, and were required to name each object as it was presented. As the ratio of width to depth increased (as the object appeared wider), subjects were increasingly likely to reject the "cup" label and categorize the object as a "bowl." But the crossover point was gradual rather than fixed. Subjects who began at the "cup" end of the series (object 1) usually called the object labelled 3 a cup, and a significant number of them also confidently

1   2   3   4

▶ **Figure 8.5**

Fuzzy Category Boundaries

Are all these objects members of the category "cup"? Labov (1973) discovered that as the width of the object increased, people were more likely to label it as a "bowl." But the cup category boundary was fuzzy rather than fixed: When the objects were presented from 1 to 4, a significant number of people confidently judged that the fourth object was a cup. (From *Introduction to Psychology*, First Edition, by Goldstein. Copyright © 1994. Reprinted with permission of the author.)

categorized object 4 as a cup. Other subjects, who started at the "bowl" end of the series, almost always called the object labelled 4 a bowl and usually called object 3 a bowl as well. One implication of these results is that category members have typical features that are characteristic of the category rather than fixed defining features.

Family Resemblance   Another way to think about the idea of typical features is in terms of what Rosch and Mervis (1975), following the great Russian thinker Ludgwig Wittgenstein, called **family resemblance.** Members of the same category usually share some of a set of characteristic features, but it isn't necessary for each member to have them all. Within an extended human family there may be a characteristic drooping nose, close-set beady eyes, receding hairlines, and a prominent cleft chin. Cousin Theodore may lack the cleft chin or the beady eyes, but he could still possess a family resemblance in his drooping nose and balding pate that would enable outsiders to identify him as a member of that family. For the category "vehicle," people know that a monorail train doesn't have wheels, and it's not shaped like a car, but in other senses it fits the category so most people agree that a monorail is a vehicle (albeit a somewhat atypical one).

The degree of family resemblance is determined by how many of the characteristic features of the category an object possesses. Again, members of a category share some of a set of characteristic features, but it's unlikely that any single member will have them all. If a given object has most of the family features, it will be seen as a good member of the category; if an object has only a few, it will be seen as a poor member of the category. For North Americans, a car has most of the basic features of the category "vehicle"; an elevator does not. A robin has most of the features of "bird"; an ostrich or a flamingo has just a few. Through the notion of family resemblance, we can begin to see how natural categories achieve their fuzzy status. There is no absolute set of criteria for what constitutes a vehicle or a bird; there are only good and poor examples of a class of objects that share at least some of a set of features (Rosch, Mervis, Gray, Johnson, & Bayes-Braem, 1976).

family resemblance

The idea that categories are defined by a set of characteristic features, which category members share in varying degrees; each member of the category will have some but not necessarily all of these features

CRITICAL THINKING

Although categories are usually adaptive, can you think of any instance in which categorizing an object or a person might not be adaptive?

Members of the same family often share physical features, creating a family resemblance, but it's unlikely that any single member of the family will have them all.

Do People Store Category Prototypes?

The concept of family resemblance, combined with the idea that there are good and poor members of a category, leads naturally to the concept of a *prototype*. In this context, a **prototype** is the best or most representative member of a category. For most Canadians, a robin is close to the prototype for the category "bird"; an apple resembles the prototype for "fruit." Some psychologists believe that we store abstract representations of category prototypes in long-term memory and use them to help decide category membership. If an object, say a small fuzzy creature with a beak, is similar to the prototype for the category "bird," then we assume that the object must be a member of the prototype's category (Goldstone & Kersten, 2003).

Reference to stored prototypes is not the only way people can classify things into categories. We can also store memories of all of the category examples (or **category exemplars**) that we encounter. To decide whether a new object is a member of a specific category, we might compare the object with all of these stored examples (or with a sample of them from memory) rather than with a single prototype. If the object is similar to many examples in a particular category, then we would categorize the object as a member of that category (see ◗ Figure 8.6). You should note the main difference between prototype and exemplar views of categorization: In prototype theory, you compare the object with one thing—the stored prototype; in the exemplar view, there is no single stored prototype and the object is compared with many things—the category exemplars.

Whether prototypes or exemplars are used in categorization is currently unknown, although many cognitive psychologists favour the exemplar view (Hintzman, 1986; Jacoby & Brooks, 1984; Medin & Shaffer, 1978; Nosofsky, 1992). One reason for preferring the exemplar view is that people know a lot about the individual members of a category. For example, people know about what features tend to go together—such as the fact that small birds are more likely to sing than

prototype

The best or most representative member of a category (such as robin for the category "bird")

category exemplars

Specific examples of category members that are stored in long-term memory

◗ **Figure 8.6**

Prototypes versus Exemplars

How do we decide whether an object is a member of a particular category? According to prototype theory, we compare the object with a stored representation of the abstract "best" example of the category (a generic bird). If the new object is similar to the prototype, it is assigned to the prototype's category. Exemplar theories of categorization propose instead that we compare the new object with the individual examples of the category that have been stored in memory. Category membership is based on the summed similarity between the new object and the exemplars.

large birds—and this kind of knowledge is more easily explained by theories proposing that we store exemplars (because a single prototype could not represent, say, the relationship between size and singing in birds). Another reason for favouring the exemplar account is that the number of categories is boundless because we can make up a category (and judge how well particular items fit that category) on the spot (e.g., "things to save if your house catches fire"; "foods that are good barbecued") (Barsalou, 1983). It's difficult to imagine that we have abstracted and stored an ideal prototype for every possible category. Also, prototypes are supposed to be quite stable, changing only gradually as a result of experience, but studies have shown that categorization judgments are greatly affected by recent exposure to exemplars. For example, research at McMaster University has shown that physicians are more likely to diagnose an ambiguous set of symptoms as a particular disease if they have recently encountered (or read about) a case of that disease (Hatala, Norman, & Brooks, 1999).

Given the flexibility of the human mind, it seems likely that people can perform categorization in more than one way. Sometimes we may form prototypes; other times we may rely on rules for deciding category membership; and in many situations we may appeal only to category exemplars (e.g., Erickson & Kruschke, 1998; Smith, Patalano, & Jonides, 1998; Vokey & Brooks, 1992; Whittlesea, Brooks, & Westcott, 1994).

The Hierarchical Structure of Categories

Virtually any object or event can be described at numerous levels of abstraction, ranging from very broad and general categorizations to very narrow and specific categorizations. Consider the class of "living things." Under the umbrella of "living things," there are categories, such as "animals" and "plants"; under "animals" there are "cats" (and other animals); under "cats" there are "Siamese cats," and so on. These levels of description are hierarchical, in that they differ from one another in terms of their degree of inclusion. The more general the level, the more inclusive it is—the category "living things" is more inclusive (i.e., includes more members) than the category "animals," which is in turn more inclusive than the category "cats" (Murphy & Lassaline, 1997).

Not all levels in the hierarchy of categories are psychologically equivalent. When people refer to an object during an everyday conversation, they tend to use what is called its **basic-level category** name (see ▶Figure 8.7). When a furry

basic-level categories

The level in a category hierarchy that most efficiently provides a lot of useful and predictive information; the basic level is usually an intermediate level in a category hierarchy

CONCEPT SUMMARY

DEFINING CATEGORY MEMBERSHIP

View of Categorization	Basis for Categorization	Example
Defining features	The presence of certain features defines membership in the category.	Amiko knows that a particular shape is a triangle because it has all the features that define a triangle, such as three straight lines joined at their ends.
Family resemblance	This is the degree to which category members share certain core features. A prototype is the most representative member of a category.	James knows that a robin is a bird because it has several features that are characteristic of birds. In North America, "robin" might be considered the prototype for the category "bird."
Exemplars	All category examples (category exemplars) that we encountered in the past are used for categorization.	Sehar knows that a robin is a bird because it matches fairly closely so many of the examples of birds stored in her memory.

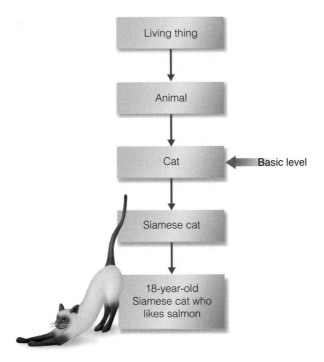

▶ Figure 8.7

Category Hierarchies

Most things can be described at a variety of levels of abstraction, ranging from very broad and general category terms (such as "living thing") to very narrow and specific terms (such as "Siamese seal-point cat"). When people refer to something during normal conversation, they often use its intermediate, or *basic-level*, category label. In most everyday contexts, we would refer to an animal like the one depicted in the figure as a "cat" rather than as a "living thing" or an "18-year-old Siamese cat who likes salmon."

feline saunters by, you typically call it a cat (a basic-level category term), not a thing or an animal (a more general, or *superordinate*, category) or a Siamese seal point (a more specific, or *subordinate*, category). Basic-level category terms tend to be short words, yet they communicate a lot of useful and predictive information (Markman & Wisniewski, 1997; Rosch et al., 1976). For example, in most situations the term "cat" provides just the right amount of relevant information: People know you're talking about a medium-sized, four-legged pet that likely has certain characteristic features and behaviours (much more information than would be provided if you used the nondescriptive "animal"), but you haven't burdened the conversation with a needless amount of detail. Typically, people use subordinate terms only when doing so provides additional information that is important in the conversational context (e.g., if there is something important about the cat being a Siamese).

Rosch and her colleagues found that when people were asked to list the distinguishing features of superordinate categories (such as "living things"), they generated only a few features. (Try it yourself: List the properties that characterize "living things.") At the basic level, many more properties were generated, and the generated properties tended to be ones that most subordinate members of the category share (i.e., many of the characteristics of cats are shared by most varieties of cats) (Rosch et al., 1976). It's of interest to note that basic-level categories are also the category names that children first learn to use. It is through basic-level categorization that the adaptive mind most efficiently cuts the world into useful and informative slices.

Check your knowledge about how people form categories by answering the following questions. [The answers are in Appendix B.]

1. For each of the following statements, decide on the category term that seems most appropriate. Choose from the following: category exemplars, defining features, family resemblance, prototype.
   a. It must be a bird because all birds (and no nonbirds) have wings, feathers, and a beak. _____
   b. It must be a bird because it looks like most of the other birds that I've seen. _____
   c. It must be a bird because it has several features that are typical of birds. _____
   d. It must be a bird because it looks a lot like a robin. _____

2. When people refer to an object during normal conversation, they tend to use what kind of category descriptor?
   a. superordinate ("Look, it's an object on the planet Earth.")
   b. basic level ("Look, it's a cat.")
   c. subordinate ("Look, it's a seal-point Siamese.")
   d. functional ("Look, it's something to cuddle.")

▶ Solving Problems

LEARNING GOALS

1. Be able to list the steps in the IDEAL problem-solving technique.
2. Describe factors that influence how a problem is identified and defined.
3. Understand the distinction between algorithms and heuristics as problem-solving strategies, and learn about several commonly used problem-solving heuristics.
4. Appreciate the importance of looking back and assessing how well a problem was solved for improving future problem solving.

We're rarely aware, in daily life, of the cognitive processes involved in categorizing things; most of the time, we categorize things quickly, effortlessly, and without reflection. We're much more aware of active cognitive processes when it comes to solving problems. In this section we'll consider some of the thought processes people use when they solve problems.

Obviously, problem solving is an extremely adaptive skill. When you're faced with a problem, such as how to get your car started in the morning, there is a goal, a running motor, and some uncertainty about how to reach that goal. To study the solution process, psychologists often use problems like the following:

> It's early morning, still dark, and you're trying to get dressed. Your 2-month-old baby, snuggled in her crib at the foot of the bed, sleeps peacefully after a night of sustained wailing. You can't turn on the light—she'll wake up for sure—but your five pairs of black socks and four pairs of blue socks are unpaired and mixed up in the drawer. You don't care what colour you wear today, but you want them to match. How many single socks do you need to take out of the drawer to guarantee a pair of matching colours?

Notice there is a goal (selecting a pair of matching socks), and it's not immediately obvious how to attain that goal. Psychologists call this a **well-defined problem** (even though you may have no idea how to solve it) because there is a well-defined starting point and a well-defined goal (i.e., with regard to the problem, you know exactly where you are starting out and you know exactly what goal you want to achieve). Other kinds of problems do not have a clearly defined starting point or a clearly defined goal, and these are called **ill-defined problems.** Maybe, for example, you'd like to become a better person. This can be described as a problem, with a starting point and a goal, but it would probably be difficult to provide an exact specification of either so the problem is ill defined.

well-defined problem

A problem with a clear starting point and a fully specified goal

ill-defined problem

A problem, such as "becoming a better person," for which the starting point and goal cannot be clearly specified

Certain kinds of problems are well defined, such as trying to find the correct route on a map. Other problems are ill defined and may not even have a solution. Can you decipher the true meaning of the artwork on the left?

Most of the research done on problem solving has examined performance on well-defined problems, such as our sock problem. We'll focus on well-defined problems in this section, but ill-defined problems can be tackled with some of the same strategies. It's believed that ill-defined problems may sometimes require unique cognitive processes (Jausovec, 1997), but generally the same psychological processes are assumed to operate in the vast majority of problem-solving settings.

The IDEAL Problem Solver

Let's start by considering a set of guidelines that highlight the psychological processes relevant to problem solving. These guidelines were developed by psychologists John Bransford and Barry Stein and are recommended in their book *The Ideal Problem Solver* (1993). Bransford and Stein use the letters of the acronym IDEAL to stand for the five major steps that underlie effective problem solving. These steps are briefly described here and are summarized in the Concept Summary table.

1. *Identify* the problem. Before you can solve a problem, you need to recognize that there is, in fact, a problem that needs solving. Strange knocking sounds, little spots of oil, and uneven acceleration are signs of car problems, but they need to be recognized as symptoms before the appropriate diagnosis and repairs can begin.
2. *Define*, or represent, the problem information in the clearest and most efficient way. Not only is it important to define the goal—What exactly are you trying to achieve?—it's also important to conceptualize the problem information in ways that will make it easier for you to generate effective problem-solving strategies. The ticket-scalping problem discussed at the beginning of the chapter is difficult because most people don't describe it to themselves as a situation in which Wayne made two separate ticket transactions. They tend to think about just one pair of tickets, so the cost of the second transaction is applied incorrectly to the first.
3. *Explore* a variety of problem strategies. Once you have identified the problem, defined the goal, and developed an appropriate representation of the information you have to work with, it's time to try to move forward toward a possible solution. To do this, you must decide on a strategy. Most solution strategies amount to "rules of thumb." They don't guarantee a solution, but they usually move you closer to your goal.

4. *Act* on the problem strategy that you chose in step 3. Work through the solution strategy, and as part of the process, try to anticipate any dead ends or obstacles that might prevent you from reaching the goal.

5. *Look back* and evaluate the effectiveness of your selected strategy. Have you in fact solved the problem? It's important to identify and correct any errors that have occurred before moving on and trying something new.

If you follow these five problem-solving guidelines, you will approximate the IDEAL problem solver (Bransford & Stein, 1993). Now let's consider some of the processes involved in greater detail.

Identifying and Defining: Problem Representation

To identify and define a problem correctly, it's essential to represent the problem information in an appropriate way. *Problem representation* refers to your understanding of the starting point, the goal, the difference between them, and the kinds of actions that are appropriate for moving from the starting point to the goal.

Take the sock problem, for example. The correct answer is three. There are only two colours, so with three samples you will get two that match. If you're like most people, you let the math get in your way. Did you start worrying about the four-to-five ratio of blue-to-black? Did you consider calculating some sort of probability? To solve this problem, you must pay attention to the right problem components—you need to see the problem in the right way. Most people fail to detect which information is relevant and which is not. They get hung up with ratios and probabilities and the like. Let's consider another example.

> Dr. Adams is interrupted from his daily rounds by the arrival of a new patient, a child, who has been seriously injured in a fall. "My God!" Adams cries. "It's my son!" Moments later, Dr. Henderson arrives, sees the injured child, and sobs, "My son, my dear son!" Is it a tragic mix-up?

You probably solved this one almost immediately, but it demonstrates the point. The two doctors are the mother and the father of the injured child. The gender connotations of the word "doctor," along with the fact that the two doctors have different last names, lead some people to represent this problem inappropriately, thereby making it difficult. (It is likely that this problem stumped people more often a few decades ago, when the gender connotation of "doctor" was stronger than it is today.) The point to appreciate is that we often make problems difficult for ourselves by making inaccurate assumptions.

CRITICAL THINKING

Think back to the linguistic relativity hypothesis we discussed earlier. Do you think the "doctor" problem supports the hypothesis?

CONCEPT SUMMARY

THE IDEAL PROBLEM SOLVER

State of Problem Solving	Description	Example
Identify	Recognize that a problem exists.	In the basement, Greg notices a small amount of water underneath the washing machine.
Define	Represent the problem information in the most efficient way.	Greg notices that there is water dripping from the ceiling, just under where the bathroom is. He tests and confirms the hypothesis that the shower upstairs is leaking.
Explore	Consider possible solutions.	Greg considers showering at the gym for the rest of the semester; then he considers calling a plumber; then he considers caulking the base of the shower stall.
Act	Employ the chosen strategy.	Greg caulks the base of the shower stall.
Look back	Evaluate the effectiveness of the chosen strategy.	Greg notices that the pool of water is gone and that the ceiling has stopped leaking.

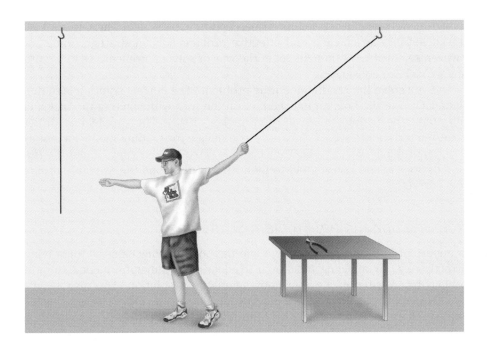

The Maier Two-String Problem

Can you figure out a way to tie these two strings together? Notice there's a pair of pliers on the table.

Functional Fixedness   The two-doctor problem illustrates a common obstacle to correct problem representation. People often allow their preconceptions and prejudices to lock them into an incorrect view of the problem information (Bassok, Wu, & Olseth, 1995; Dixon & Moore, 1997). Consider another example, illustrated in ▶ Figure 8.8, called the Maier two-string problem (after Maier, 1931). Imagine you are standing in a room with two strings hanging from the ceiling. The strings are hung such a distance apart that, when holding one of the strings, you cannot reach the other. By using only a pair of pliers, which happen to be sitting on a table in the room, can you tie the strings together?

This is a difficult problem because most people have a certain set, or fixed, way of viewing the function of pliers. The solution is to tie the pliers to one string and swing it, like a pendulum, while you hold on to the other string. Solving the problem requires you to change the way that you normally think about pliers. Pliers are designed for gripping, but they can also serve as pendulum weights.

Psychologists use the term **functional fixedness** to refer to this tendency to see objects, and their functions, in certain fixed and typical ways. Doctors are men, pliers are for gripping, and so on. Functional fixedness is an obstacle to problem solving because it prevents you from recognizing the problem-solving tools that are present in the situation. Now try solving the problem illustrated in ▶ Figure 8.9. You enter a room in which a candle, a box of tacks, some matches, and a hammer lie on a table. You are told to mount the candle on the wall so that it will burn properly, by using only the objects on the table. Work on the problem for a while; we'll return to its solution shortly.

Let's stop for a moment and think about the adaptive significance of functional fixedness. How can such a tendency possibly be adaptive? Wouldn't it be better to consider all possible object uses? Well, how many possible uses does each object have? If you think about this for a moment, you can see that it would be very inefficient if we went around thinking about every possible use for every object. Most of the time, if you view objects in fixed ways or use fixed strategies that have worked well in the past, you're likely to be successful. After all, pliers usually do solve problems having to do with holding and gripping. Generally,

functional fixedness

The tendency to see objects, and their functions, in certain fixed and typical ways, and thereby to fail to see alternative uses of objects that would enable us to solve a problem

The Duncker Candle Problem

By using only the materials shown, figure out a way to mount the candle on the wall so it will burn properly.

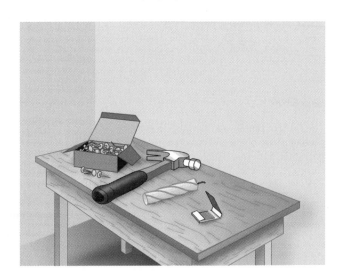

mental sets

Well-established habits of perception and thought used to solve problems; typically efficient and effective, but sometimes make problem solving more difficult

relying on well-established habits of perception and thought (sometimes called **mental sets**) is an efficient and effective problem-solving strategy. Sometimes, however, such habits of thought get in the way of solving problems, as in the problems we've been considering.

Did you solve the candle-mounting problem? The correct solution is to dump the tacks out of the box, mount the box on the wall with some of the tacks, and then stand the candle in the box (Duncker, 1945). The problem is difficult because most people see the box only as a device for holding the tacks, not as a potential problem-solving tool. They become *fixed* in their views about the *functions* of objects and thereby fail to identify and define all the available problem tools correctly.

Exploring and Acting: Problem Strategies

It's important to represent a problem and the potential mechanisms for solving it correctly (e.g., by avoiding functional fixedness and unhelpful mental sets), but problem representation alone cannot guarantee a solution. You also need an arsenal of problem *strategies*, techniques that allow you to move toward a problem solution. There are two large classes of problem-solving strategies: *algorithms* and *heuristics*.

algorithms

Step-by-step rules or procedures that, if applied correctly, guarantee a problem solution eventually

Algorithms   For some well-defined problems you can use **algorithms,** which are step-by-step rules or procedures that guarantee a solution. You can use algorithms to solve simple math problems, for example, because there are fixed rules for addition, subtraction, and so on. As long as you use the rules properly, you will always arrive at the correct solution. Solving word jumbles, such as MBLOPRE, is another case in point. There are seven letters in the word, which means there are 5040 possible combinations of the letters. If you systematically work out each of the possible sequences, you will eventually solve the PROBLEM. But it could take a long time.

Computers are often programmed to use algorithms because computers can perform lots of simple transformations very quickly. But algorithms are not always practical strategies for problem solution, even for computers. Consider chess, for example. In principle, it would be possible to use algorithms to play chess—the computer would simply need to consider all the possible consequences of a particular move. But practically, even the most advanced computers cannot examine all the possible outcomes in a chess game; they can examine only some of them. Some 10^{40} possible game sequences exist, so even if a computer could calculate a game in under one-millionth of one-thousandth of a second, it would still require 10^{21} centuries to examine all the game possibilities (Best, 1989). Another problem with algorithms is that they work only for certain kinds of well-defined problems. There is no algorithm, for example, for figuring out how to be happy, choose an appropriate career, or create a great website.

heuristics

The rules of thumb we often use to solve problems; are quick and easy but do not guarantee a correct solution

Heuristics   In cases in which it's not feasible to use an algorithm, it's possible to use **heuristics,** which are problem-solving "rules of thumb." To solve a word jumble, especially one with many letters, it's not expedient to use an algorithmic approach (e.g., the 5040 possible letter sequences for a seven-letter word jumble). Instead, you use heuristics. For example, you know that English words don't usually begin with MB, or end with BL, so you don't even check out those possibilities. In other words, you can use your knowledge about English words to make guesses about elements of the most likely solutions. Heuristics are extremely adaptive problem-solving tools because they often open the door to a quick and accurate solution. In natural environments, quick solutions can mean the difference between life and death. An organism cannot spend its time wrapped in thought, systematically working through a long list of solution possibilities. Instead, it's

People use heuristics—"general rules of thumb"—when they play chess because the human mind cannot examine all the possible moves and their consequences during a game. Even chess masters do not consider a huge number of potential moves; instead, they usually consider only two or three moves. What makes them masters is that the few moves they consider are among the best possible moves in the given situation.

Duncan Smith/PhotoDisc/Getty Images

adaptive for the organism to make informed guesses, as long as those guesses are usually at least close to correct. Below we describe some commonly used problem-solving heuristics.

One common heuristic that people use to solve problems is **means-ends analysis,** which attacks problems by devising *means*, or actions, that are designed to reduce the gap between the current starting point and the desired goal, or *end* (Newell & Simon, 1972). Usually, this strategy requires breaking down the problem into a series of simpler subgoals, in which the appropriate means to an end are more immediately visible. Let's assume that Peter, an underachieving undergraduate, wants to start a relationship with Jill, the brightest student in his psychology class. Obviously, asking Jill out immediately is unlikely to succeed, so Peter breaks the problem down into more manageable components.

First, he reasons, he'll impress her by making insightful comments during lectures. He now has a new goal, acting intelligently in class, for which he has relatively straightforward means—he needs to study so he can master the material. If he is successful (everyone now thinks he is an amazingly bright guy), he devises a new subgoal: making some kind of sustained contact with Jill. Forming a small study group would be a good means to that end, he surmises, so he approaches the recently impressed Jill with the idea. Notice the key ingredients of the problem-solving strategy: Establish where you are, figure out where you want to be, and then devise a means for effectively getting from here to there. Often, as in Peter's case, means-ends analysis is made more effective by working systematically through a series of subgoals.

Another effective heuristic is **working backward**—starting mentally at the goal and moving back toward the starting point. Suppose someone asked you to generate an anagram or word jumble. How would you proceed? Would you create a random set of letters and then see if they can be rearranged to form a word? Of course not. You would start with the solution, the word, and work backward by mixing up the known sequence.

Let's consider another example. You're working on a biology project tracking the growth of bacteria in a Petri dish. You know that this particular strain of bacteria doubles every 2 hours. You discover that the Petri dish is exactly full after 12 hours. After how many hours was the Petri dish exactly half full? To solve this one, it's better to work backward. If the dish is full after 12 hours, and it takes 2 hours for the bacteria to double, what did the dish look like 2 hours ago? This turns out to be the answer, which is attained fairly easily by working backward.

Another useful heuristic for problem solving is **searching for analogies.** If you can see a resemblance between the current problem and some problem that you solved in the past, you can often quickly obtain a solution. Let's test your analogy-searching skills. Imagine that a woman buys a horse for $60 and sells it for $70. Later, she buys the same horse back for $80 and sells it again for $90. How much money did she make in the horse-trading business? The attentive reader will not miss this one. It's a different version of the ticket-scalping problem that opened this chapter. If you see the relationship between the two problems, you're unlikely to suffer the same problem-solving pitfalls you encountered before.

means-ends analysis

A problem-solving heuristic that involves devising actions, or means, that reduce the distance between the current starting point and the desired end (the goal)

working backward

A problem-solving heuristic that involves mentally starting at the goal and mentally moving backward toward the starting point to see how the goal can be reached

searching for analogies

A problem-solving heuristic that involves trying to find a connection between the current problem and some previous problem you have solved successfully

PRACTICAL SOLUTIONS

HAVING DIFFICULTY? TAKE A BREAK!

Have you ever been frustrated with a problem, given up, only to find that the solution suddenly and mysteriously comes to mind at a later time? Psychologists refer to this as an *incubation effect*—sometimes we do better at solving a problem when we stop working on it for a while. What accounts for this effect? Why should putting a problem aside increase the chances of reaching a solution?

One possibility is that our brain continues to work on the problem, even though our conscious awareness is directed elsewhere. The problem is placed in the background where, over time, our unconscious mind churns out a solution. The trouble with this explanation is that we don't really have any solid scientific evidence for this kind of unconscious processing. Psychologists remain undecided about the nature of unconscious mental processes, with few believing that they are capable of sophisticated problem solving.

A more likely explanation is that the break stops you from thinking about the problem in the wrong way. When people have trouble solving a problem, they often continue with the same ineffective strategy, coming up with the same wrong answer again and again. You can get locked into a particular way of viewing the problem components and can't break free. As you know, successful problem solving often requires thinking about the

Sometimes we do better at solving a problem when we stop working on it for a while.

problem components in a novel and creative way. When you take a break and stop thinking about the problem, you're able to approach it later in a fresh and new way.

Another possibility is that during the break, while you're doing something else, you will come across information that ultimately helps solve the problem. The additional activity may provide clues or hints that lead to a problem breakthrough. Suppose you're having a difficult time solving a word jumble, such as THREAGUD. You stop working on it and turn on a television program that shows a happy mom with her children, a boy and a girl, playing nearby. That's it, you shout—the solution to the word jumble is DAUGHTER! The new activity, watching television, provided the necessary clue to solve the problem. Regardless of the interpretation, it's a good idea to take a break periodically when you're trying to solve a tough problem. A fresh mind can do wonders for seeing a problem in a new way or simply for renewing your enthusiasm for finding a solution.

Interestingly, people often fail to detect the relationship between a new problem and analogous past problems. The same Duncker who came up with the candle problem described earlier also came up with the following problem: A person has a brain tumour that cannot be operated on. There is an X-ray that could destroy the tumour if fired with sufficient strength, but unfortunately at that strength it would also destroy the healthy brain tissue on the path to the tumour. What can be done? Most people find this a difficult problem; take a few minutes and see if a solution comes to mind. Now consider another problem: A general wants to attack a fortress that is surrounded by a large moat, with various bridges leading across the moat. The general wants as many soldiers to reach the fort at the same time as possible, but if he masses them all on any one bridge the bridge will collapse. What can be done? Most people find this an easier problem: Break the army up into smaller groups, send each of them across a bridge timed to converge on the fort together. There are two points to be made here: The first is that a closely analogous solution also works for the tumour problem (i.e., aim multiple weak rays to converge on the tumour) and the second is that giving people the solution to the fort problem has little if any effect on their ability to solve the tumour problem. That is, they often fail to see the analogy (Gick & McGarry, 1992). It is important, when working on a problem, to look for analogies with other problems you have solved in the past, yet people often fail to do so.

Looking Back and Learning

The IDEAL problem solver identifies and defines the problem, seeks the best problem representation, and explores and acts on problem strategies. But the process is incomplete unless you also *look back* and *learn* from your experience (Bransford & Stein, 1993). The IDEAL problem solver "debugs" performance in an effort to maximize the information gained.

By analyzing your performance in detail and noting your mistakes as well as your successes, you can determine whether your strategy helped solve one kind of problem but not another. Through an after-the-fact analysis, you can also gain insight into *why* a particular heuristic failed or succeeded. Look and learn from your experience so that the next time you can do better still.

Test Yourself 8.3   *Check your knowledge about problem solving by answering the following questions. (The answers are in Appendix B.)*

1. Decide whether each of the following problems is well defined or ill defined. Justify your answer.
   a. Finding your way to a new restaurant in town:
   _____
   b. Receiving an A in your psychology course:
   _____
   c. Making your lab partner in chemistry fall madly in love with you: _____
   d. Baking a delicious cherry cheesecake:
   _____

2. Try to identify the problem-solving strategy at work in each of the following examples. Choose from the following terms: algorithm, means-ends analysis, working backward, searching for analogies.

   a. On the final exam Myka looks for connections between the physics problem on the test and the ones he solved while studying. _____
   b. Rachel needs a three-letter word that begins with R to complete the crossword puzzle. She mindlessly considers all possible two-letter combinations, placing them after R until she arrives at an acceptable word. _____
   c. Hector really needs an A in his philosophy class, but he has no idea what it takes. He decides to start by doing the assigned readings before each class. _____
   d. Courtney needs to generate a set of anagrams for a school project. To generate each anagram, she starts with a word and then scrambles the letters to make a new word.
   _____

▶ Making Decisions

LEARNING GOALS

1. Learn about framing effects and their influence on decision making.
2. Understand the human tendency toward confirmation bias and how this bias can contribute to illusory correlations.
3. Learn about two common decision-making heuristics: representativeness and availability.
4. Be able to discuss the pros and cons of the use of heuristics.

We turn our attention now to the topic of **decision making,** which deals with the thought processes involved in evaluating and choosing from among a set of alternatives. Decision making can be considered a subset of problem solving; making a decision could be described as solving the problem of which of several options to select. Choosing almost always entails risk, because the wrong choice can have

decision making

The thought processes involved in evaluating and choosing from among a set of alternatives; it usually involves some degree of risk

long-lasting unpleasant consequences, so it's in your interest to evaluate and select from among the alternatives wisely. Consider a doctor deciding whether or not to prescribe a risky drug that may save a patient but that may also have harmful side effects, or a student whose decisions about which courses to take may have life-long career implications. We make decisions virtually every moment of our waking lives, and some of them have substantial consequences.

Like problem solving, decision making is influenced by how you represent the alternatives in your mind and by the decision-making strategies you use. Let's examine how each of these processes affects the choices we make.

The Framing of Decision Alternatives

framing

The way the alternatives in a decision-making situation are structured and described

The way the alternatives are structured and described, called **framing,** can dramatically influence decision making. In a study by Tversky and Kahneman (1987), for example, subjects were asked to choose between two programs designed to combat a deadly disease: If program A is adopted, 200 people will be saved, whereas if program B is adopted, there is a one-in-three probability that 600 people will be saved and a two-in-three probability that no people will be saved. Which program would you choose? There is no right answer to this question—there are good arguments for and against each alternative—but about three-quarters of the subjects preferred the less risky (but potentially less rewarding) program A. Other subjects were asked to choose between the same two programs, but the programs were framed negatively (in terms of who will die). They were told that under program A 400 people will die, whereas under program B there is a one-in-three probability that nobody will die and a two-in-three probability that 600 people will die. This pair of alternatives is mathematically identical to the first pair, but when the question was framed in this way, three-quarters of the subjects preferred the more risky (but potentially more rewarding) program B.

In general, when people are confronted with decisions in ways that emphasize potential gains, they tend to avoid taking risks—they choose certainty or the best approximation to it. But if the choice is framed negatively, in terms of potential losses, people are much more likely to take a gamble to limit or avoid the loss. More generally, the way alternatives are structured and described often affects decisions. Framing effects are commonplace and are used by marketers and public relations firms. For example, people prefer beef that is labelled "75% lean" to beef that is labelled "25% fat" (Levin & Gaeth, 1988), and condoms are perceived as more effective if they are described as having a 95% success rate than if they are said to have a 5% failure rate (Linville, Fischer, & Fischhoff, 1993). A study by McNeil, Pauker, Cox, and Tversky (1982) revealed analogous effects on decisions made by medical doctors. Thus, human decision making is not always rational, partly because our minds weigh information differently depending on how alternatives are framed (Kahneman, Slovic, & Tversky, 1982).

CRITICAL   THINKING
Do you think problem solving is a part of decision making, or is decision making a part of problem solving?

Confirmation Bias and Illusory Correlations

confirmation bias

The tendency to emphasize hypothesis-confirming evidence when making decisions

Suppose you were offered $100 if you could find out, just by asking a yes-or-no question, whether Jane is socially outgoing. What question would you ask? Think about it for a moment. Now, what if the task was to ask a yes/no question to find out if Jack is introverted? What question would you pose? If you are like most people, you'd ask Jane a question, such as "Do you enjoy being the centre of attention?" and you'd ask Jack a question like "Do you like to spend a lot of time quietly by yourself?" That is, in each case you'd seek evidence that would confirm your hypothesis, as opposed to evidence that would disconfirm it. This is an example of **confirmation bias,** the tendency to emphasize hypothesis-confirming evidence when making decisions.

As another example of confirmation bias, Reisberg (2001) noted that roosters might believe that their crowing causes the sun to rise each morning (assuming roosters only crow at dawn, they would have lots and lots of evidence that every time they crow, up comes the sun, and when they don't crow, it doesn't rise). To do a better job of testing that hypothesis, the rooster must try *not* crowing some mornings and crowing in the middle of the night, thereby seeking evidence that something else is responsible for the sunrise (and hence disconfirming his hypothesis). This example is amusing, but it illustrates a serious point: Our human tendency to focus on confirming evidence can lead us to make very poor judgments. For example, there is evidence that medical doctors show a confirmation bias when making diagnoses (e.g., Travis, Phillippi, & Tonn, 1989), thereby increasing the likelihood that they will falsely diagnose a condition as being what they initially hypothesized it was rather than as what it really is.

Confirmation bias often leads to **illusory correlations,** perceptions of relationships between variables that do not really exist. In a classic study, Chapman and Chapman (1967) showed psychology students drawings done by psychiatric patients. Each drawing had a psychiatric diagnosis (e.g., schizophrenia, depression, paranoia) attached to it. The students were asked to examine the drawings and determine whether there were any relationships between features or characteristics of drawings and patients' diagnoses. Sure enough, the students detected such relationships. For example, many of them noted that patients diagnosed with paranoia tended to draw faces with exaggerated or otherwise peculiar-looking eyes. What makes this interesting is that, unknown to the students, the researchers had paired the diagnostic labels and drawings randomly; that is, there was no relationship at all between the drawings and the diagnostic labels. Students perceived such relationships, however, because they tended to focus their attention on and remember cases in which, by chance alone, a drawing happened to confirm their hunches about the kinds of drawings patients with particular disorders would make.

Confirmation bias and illusory correlations are powerful influences on human thought. It is very likely that they play important roles in supporting superstitions and beliefs in various paranormal phenomena, such as telepathy and astrology. Consider, for example, the pseudoscience of graphology, according to which a person's handwriting reveals important information about his or her personality. Scientific tests of graphology have failed to produce any compelling evidence in support of it, but many people persist in believing in it. In research at the

illusory correlation

Perception of a relationship between variables (e.g., handwriting and personality) that does not really exist

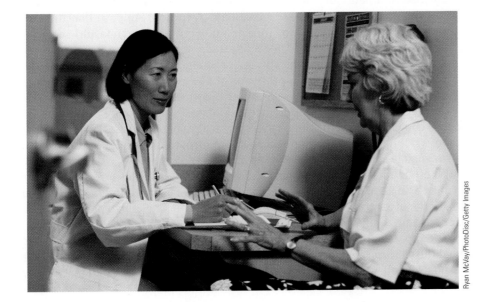

How doctors interpret treatment options, as well as how the information relevant to those treatments is framed, can critically influence the decision-making process.

CRITICAL **THINKING**

We've mentioned that confirmation bias may undermine the accuracy of physicians' judgements. Can you think of any other individuals who might be similarly affected by this bias?

representativeness heuristic

The tendency to base judgments on similarity to an abstract ideal, expectation, or stereotype; for example, when deciding whether a sequence of coin-toss outcomes is random, people who use the representativeness heuristic focus on how irregular the sequence looks, because they think short random sequences should look irregular

University of Waterloo, King and Koehler (2000) provide evidence that confirmation bias and illusory correlations underlie this persistent belief. As another example, DiBattista and Shepherd (1993) proposed that confirmation bias and illusory correlations support exaggerated beliefs regarding the effects of sugar on children's activity levels.

Decision-Making Heuristics

People usually rely on heuristics, or rules of thumb, when making decisions, just as they do when solving problems. Heuristics simplify the decision-making process and often lead to correct judgments, but they sometimes lead to errors.

Representativeness   When people are asked to estimate the likelihood that an object or event belongs to a particular class, they often rely on a rule of thumb called the **representativeness heuristic.** They arrive at their decision by comparing the object or event in question with their idea of the average, or prototypical, member of the class. The representativeness heuristic is similar to the idea, discussed earlier in this chapter, that people categorize perceptual objects by comparing them with prototypes, except that the representativeness heuristic is used when people make explicit judgments of probability. An example of the representativeness heuristic at play is "the gambler's fallacy." On each spin of a fair roulette wheel, the odds that the ball will land on red rather than black are 50%. Suppose we spin the wheel ten times and on every one of the first nine times the ball lands on red; R R R R R R R R R. What now are the odds that the ball will land on red on the tenth and final spin? If you are susceptible to the gambler's fallacy you'll think those odds are low—after all, the pattern so far doesn't resemble (is not representative of) the sort of random pattern you'd expect, so it may seem like a correction in that direction is long overdue (Ayton & Fischer, 2004; Roney & Trick, 2003). But assuming the wheel is fair, the odds of red are exactly 50% on the 10th spin regardless of the outcome of the prior spins. The device has no memory, so it doesn't "know" that red has come up on the last nine spins.

People frequently use the representativeness heuristic to make decisions in real-world settings. For example, clerks in stores use the type of products that a shopper buys as a way of judging age. If someone loads his or her shopping cart with products normally thought to be representative of an older consumer, the clerk's estimate of the shopper's age increases (McCall, 1994).

The use of a heuristic, such as representativeness, is adaptive and beneficial most of the time, but it can lead to irrational decisions. Suppose that the public relations office at the University of Toronto randomly selected a faculty member to be interviewed for a newsletter. The faculty member selected is a man who is fairly short, slight, quiet, and somewhat shy, and who enjoys nature. Which do you think is more likely, that the man is a professor of Chinese studies or that he is a professor of psychology? Most people asked this question chose Chinese studies, because the man fits their stereotype of a Chinese studies scholar. But this is an illogical choice, because in Canada professors of psychology vastly outnumber professors of Chinese studies. The University of Toronto, for example, currently has approximately 100 professors in the Department of Psychology, but no Department of Chinese Studies (and the Department of East Asian Studies has only 17 faculty members). In choosing Chinese studies, people have failed to think about the *base rate*, or the proportion of times that an object or event is likely to occur in the population being sampled.

The representativeness heuristic also dupes people into committing what is called the *conjunction error.* Consider the following: Linda is 31 years old, single, outspoken, and very bright. She majored in philosophy. As a student she was deeply concerned with issues of discrimination and social justice and participated in demonstrations against logging. Which of the following alternatives is more likely?

1. Linda is a bank teller.
2. Linda is a bank teller and active in the feminist movement.

In a study conducted by Tversky and Kahneman (1983), 85% of the participants judged alternative 2 to be the more likely. Why? Because Linda's description is more representative of someone active in the feminist movement than it is of a bank teller. But think about it—how can the odds of two things happening together be higher than the odds of either of those events happening alone? Notice that the second alternative is a subset of the first alternative and therefore cannot be more likely. Consequently, it is illogical to choose option 2, but most people do so, presumably because it better fits (i.e., it is more representative of) their impression of Linda.

Availability   When asked to estimate the odds of some event occurring in the future, or the frequency with which it has occurred in the past, people usually rely on the **availability heuristic.** Imagine you're asked to estimate the likelihood that you will forget to turn off your alarm clock on Friday night. If you can easily remember lots of Saturday mornings on which your sleep was interrupted by a blasting alarm, your estimate is likely to be high. You have relied on the availability of memories of relevant prior events as a basis for judging probability of a future event.

The availability heuristic is usually reliable: Compared with rare events, common events are more likely to come to mind and more likely to occur in the future, so availability is often a good basis for judging past frequency and for predicting future probability. But, as with the representativeness heuristic, in some situations this decision-making heuristic leads us astray. Which do you think is more common, English words that begin with the letter K or English words with K as their third letter? By now you're probably justly skeptical about your intuitive choice, but most naive subjects judge that English words that begin with K are more likely (Tversky & Kahneman, 1973). In fact, English words that have K in the third position are about three times more common. Which do you think is more likely, someone dying from any kind of accident or someone dying from a stroke? Accidents, right? Nope. It's not even close. More than twice as many people die from stroke than from all kinds of accidents (Slovic, Fischoff, & Lichtenstein, 1982). People make the error because examples of the incorrect alternative are more likely to come to mind. It's easier to search your memory for words by first letter, and accidental deaths get much more publicity than deaths from stroke and so are more memorable.

The Value of Heuristics

We've briefly reviewed evidence of the way reliance on the representativeness and availability heuristics sometimes leads human decision makers astray. Representativeness and availability are not the only heuristics people use when making decisions. Cognitive psychologists have identified several other "mental shortcuts" that decision makers often use and that sometimes lead to erroneous judgments (for some interesting examples, see Buehler, Griffin, & Ross, 1994; Kunda, 1999; Sharpe & Adair, 1993). What are we to make of such an imperfect decision maker? Well, imperfect as heuristics are, there are several points worth making in their favour. First,

availability heuristic

The tendency to base estimates of frequency or probability on the ease with which examples come to mind; for example, if you've just heard about a plane crash, your estimate of the likelihood of plane crashes may increase because the recent plane crash easily comes to mind

People are much more likely to worry about terrorism if a recently publicized disaster (such as the attack on the Pentagon) is fresh and available in their minds.

Steve Helber/CP Picture Archive

CRITICAL   THINKING

Try to come up with some examples in your own life in which you used the availability heuristic when judging the frequency or likelihood of some thing or event.

the use of heuristics leads to errors under some circumstances but, as Tversky and Kahneman (1974) argued, they are usually quite effective. Second, heuristics are economical. Optimal, or rational, decision making can be a complex, time-consuming activity; indeed, in many situations it is not feasible to make a perfectly rational decision (e.g., the needed data may not be on hand, so we are forced to rely on availability, or the number of potential steps may be too large to allow for a systematic consideration of all of them). Think back to our discussion of perceptual illusions in Chapter 4. Just because your visual system can be tricked by an illusion doesn't mean it's a bad system. Indeed, it is precisely the strengths of the visual system (such as its use of top-down processing) that leads it to create illusions under some conditions. Similarly, when you make decisions, you rely on adaptive systems that serve you very well in the majority of situations, even though they sometimes lead you to make errors (Gigerenzer, 1997).

Moreover, the fact that people often make errors in certain situations (as when they judge that Linda is more likely to be a feminist bank teller than she is to be a bank teller) does not mean that people are unable to think rationally. Rather, it appears that people often fail to think about problems or decisions in ways that would lead them to access and use the appropriate rational decision-making rules. In the "Linda is a bank teller" example, for instance, people know that there are more bank tellers in the world than feminist bank tellers. The mistake is made because people focus their thoughts on a single case, Linda, and base their decision solely on representativeness, rather than thinking about probabilities in general (Fiedler, 1988; Gigerenzer, 1996). Under conditions that encourage people to pay attention to considerations, such as probabilities and base rates, they often do so. Note, too, that people differ widely from one another in the extent to which they rely on heuristics in situations in which doing so leads to errors (Stanovich, 1999). Also, formal training in statistics and rational decision making can lessen inappropriate reliance on heuristics (Gebotys & Claxton, 1989; Kosonen & Winne, 1995; Nisbett, 1993).

It is also worth noting that apparent errors in reasoning may sometimes be caused by reliance on linguistic conventions rather than by irrationality. Earlier in this chapter, we mentioned that good language users follow certain conversational conventions or maxims, such as "be informative." In view of such maxims, some subjects may reinterpret some decision-making questions. For example, the choice "Linda is a bank teller" versus "Linda is a bank teller and an active feminist" may be understood as a choice between "Linda is a bank teller who is *not* a feminist" and "Linda is a bank teller who *is* a feminist." If so, then there is nothing irrational about selecting the latter alternative (Slugoski & Wilson, 1998). It is clear, however, that such linguistic conventions don't account for all of the reasoning and decision-making errors described in this chapter (Stolarz-Fantino, Fantino, & Kulik, 1996).

CONCEPT SUMMARY

DECISION-MAKING HEURISTICS

Heuristic	Description	Example
Representativeness	We arrive at a decision by comparing the object or event in question with our image of the average member of potential categories.	Juan meets his new college roommate, Bryce, who is 208 cm tall and very athletic looking. Juan assumes that Bryce is a basketball player, probably on scholarship.
Availability	We estimate the odds of some event occurring based on the ease with which examples come to mind.	Stella reads so much in the newspaper about car accidents that she believes her chances of dying in a car accident are greater than her chances of dying from a stroke.

Test Yourself 8.4

Check your knowledge about decision making by picking the term that best fits the following statements. Choose your answer from the following: framing, representativeness heuristic, availability heuristic, confirmation bias, illusory correlations. (The answers are in Appendix B.)

1. Matt used to fly to visit his parents during the holiday break, but after seeing nonstop coverage of a gory plane accident, he now chooses to drive. _____

2. Chantelle is a firm believer in the herb Echinacea; whenever she has a cold she takes lots of Echinacea and she always gets over the cold within a few days. _____

3. Larry, a broker, used to tell people that his mutual fund lost money only three times in the last ten years. Now he tells them that the fund has made money in seven of the last ten years. He's noticed a marked improvement in sales of the fund.
_____

4. Jing has a theory that extroverted people tend to be less bright than introverted people, which she supports with numerous examples of boisterous dullards and reserved scholars.
_____

5. Kelley sleeps until noon, parties at night, and carries around a big backpack the rest of the time. Her neighbour Eileen assumes that Kelley must be a university student.
_____

Thought and Language

REVIEW

In this chapter, we've discussed how people use their higher mental processes to communicate, categorize, solve problems, and make decisions. Each of these abilities illustrates how the mind draws on its adaptive tool kit to thrive in the human environment.

First, how do we communicate with others? One of the defining characteristics of the human species is that we have a complex, generative linguistic grammar—a system of rules and procedures for combining arbitrary symbols in meaningful ways to express thoughts, feelings, and needs to others. A grammar consists of rules and procedures for combining sounds (phonology), for expressing particular meanings in words (semantics), and for constructing sentences from words to express complex messages (syntax). To understand how language works, it is important to distinguish between the surface structure of a sentence—the literal ordering of words—and its deep structure, which taps the underlying representation of meaning. Human communication also relies on mutual knowledge, or pragmatics, to interpret statements or requests that would otherwise be ambiguous or anomalous (such as, "Can you pass the salt?").

Are we born with a natural blueprint for language, or does language develop exclusively as a product of experience? The sequence of language development is quite universal—it doesn't matter where you look in the world, babies show similar milestones in language development. This and other findings have led most researchers to conclude that people are born ready to learn language in the same way they are born ready to learn to walk.

Second, how do we categorize objects in our world? When people categorize, or put objects or events into meaningful groups, they create a world that is more sensible and predictable. Categorization skills enable us to infer invisible properties about objects—if X is a member of category Y, then X will have at least some of the characteristics of category Y members. As a result, we can make accurate predictions about the things we encounter. How do people identify category membership? Research suggests that the mind uses "family resemblance" to identify the category to which an object or event belongs. Members of the same category tend to share at least some of a set of basic or core features of that category. Categories are remarkably flexible; their boundaries are fuzzy, which enables us to classify things adaptively even when those objects don't share all the typical features of the category members. Any given object or event can be categorized at numerous levels of abstraction, ranging from very broad and general categories (such as "living things") to very narrow and specific ones ("adult female Siamese seal-point cat"). People have a bias toward the use of basic-level category terms (such as "cat"), which tend to be at intermediate levels of the hierarchy and communicate a great deal of information very efficiently.

Third, how do we solve problems, such as the ticket-scalping-profit problem posed at the beginning of the chapter? When people are faced with a problem, there is a starting point and a goal, and there is some uncertainty over how to move from the former to the latter. Some problems are well defined, others ill defined. What thought processes are involved in finding an appropriate solution? According to the model of the IDEAL problem solver, good problem solving involves five main steps: (1) Identify the problem. (2) Define, or represent, the problem. (3) Explore strategies for a solution. (4) Act on those problem strategies. (5) Look back and learn from the experience. To identify and define a problem correctly, it's important to see the problem in an appropriate way. One of the common pitfalls with problem solving is that people allow their preconceptions to influence how they represent problem information. For example, most people fall prey to functional fixedness, or the tendency to see objects and their functions in certain fixed ways.

People use a variety of problem-solving strategies. Algorithms are procedures that guarantee a solution, but they're often time consuming and cannot always be applied. Heuristics are problem-solving rules of thumb that can be applied quickly but do not always lead to the correct solution. Examples of problem-solving heuristics include means-ends analysis, working backward, and solving through analogies.

Fourth, how do we make decisions when confronted with a set of alternatives? Decision making involves evaluating and choosing from among a set of alternatives. Choice in decision making is usually accompanied by risk, so it's adaptive to evaluate and select from among

the alternatives with care. As with problem solving, decision making is influenced by how the alternatives are viewed or represented. For example, the framing or structuring of the alternatives can affect the decision that is made. We reviewed two common decision-making heuristics, representativeness and availability. These strategies sometimes lead us to make errors, but they are quick and easy and often lead to good decisions. Humans have a tendency to focus on evidence that supports their hypotheses, and this confirmation bias can contribute to illusory correlations (i.e., unfounded beliefs about relationships between variables).

CHAPTER SUMMARY

▶ Communicating

The ability to communicate with others through the use of spoken and written language is one of humanity's greatest success stories. Through language production, we transmit thoughts, feelings, and needs to others; through language comprehension, we learn from and understand one another.

Does Language Determine Thought?

The *linguistic relativity hypothesis* proposes that language determines thought; if you lack words to describe an experience, the experience is literally "out of mind." Cross-cultural evidence suggests that a literal interpretation of this hypothesis cannot be true. But there is little doubt that language influences thought in many ways.

The Structure of Language

To qualify as true language, a communication system must have rules, collectively termed *grammar*. A grammar specifies how arbitrary symbols can be combined to generate and comprehend any of an infinitely large number of ideas. Grammar has three aspects: *phonology*, the rules for combining sounds to make words; *syntax*, the rules for combining words to make sentences; and *semantics*, the rules used to communicate meaning. Language has a hierarchical structure, ranging from *phonemes* (the smallest significant

sound units in speech) to *morphemes* (the smallest units of language that carry meaning) to words, phrases, and sentences. Language is generative, in that the fairly small set of phonemes can be combined to express an infinite number of different sentences. According to Chomsky, sentences have a *surface structure* (superficial appearance) and a *deep structure* (underlying representation of meaning). Language production involves the transformation of deep structure into an acceptable surface structure, and comprehension involves translating a surface structure into the appropriate deep structure.

Language Comprehension

Effective communication relies heavily on *shared knowledge* among speakers and involves a combination of bottom-up and top-down processing. The term *pragmatics* is used to describe how practical knowledge is used to comprehend the intentions of speakers and to produce appropriate responses.

Language Development

Researchers believe that human infants are innately prepared to learn language. Crying, cooing, and babbling are important vocalization milestones that are attained in similar ways across cultures. Between 6 and 18 months, experience begins to play a larger role. Simple words are usually uttered by the end of the first year. Two-year-olds develop a *telegraphic grammar* that omits articles and prepositions but reflects a rudimentary version of adult syntax. As children learn grammatical rules, they pass through a stage during which they *overgeneralize* those rules (e.g., saying such things as "goed").

Language in Nonhuman Species

Early attempts to teach chimps to speak were unsuccessful, partly because chimps lack the necessary vocal equipment for speech. Subsequent researchers have taught chimps to communicate with visual mediums, such as American Sign Language. Chimps can associate particular symbols with words and actions, and understand some spoken English, but not all researchers are convinced that the chimps' achievements constitute true language. In any case, it's clear that the linguistic abilities of nonhumans are vastly and qualitatively different from those of *Homo sapiens*.

The Evolution of Language

If all humans share a "universal grammar" (with the thousands of languages being variants on that underlying shared grammar), how did they acquire it? Presumably, universal grammar evolved gradually by way of natural selection. It is easy to appreciate that possessing language confers great selective advantage. What is amazing is that the gap between humans' and nonhumans' linguistic abilities appears to be so great. Because evolution occurs gradually in small steps, it is likely our prehuman ancestors possessed protogrammars of varying degrees of complexity.

▶ Categorizing

To make sense of our environment and the objects in it, we carve the world into meaningful chunks called categories. A *category* is a class of objects (people, places, or things) or events that most people agree belong together. The ability to see similarities between different things, to classify objects and events into meaningful categories, allows us to simplify our environment, apprehend nonapparent properties of objects, and make predictions.

Defining Category Membership

What criteria do people use to determine *category membership*? According to the *defining-features* account, things are classified as members of a category if they have certain features that all members of that category share. This works fine for mathematical categories (e.g., triangle) but breaks down for natural categories (e.g., weapon), which tend to have *fuzzy boundaries*. The *family resemblance* view is that members of a category share at least some of a set of core features that are characteristic of that category, but it isn't necessary for each member to have them all. By this view, some members of a category are more typical, or better exemplars, of that category than others.

Do People Store Category Prototypes?

The notion that categories are defined by family resemblance leads to the concept of a *prototype:* the best or most representative member of a category. Objects may be categorized by comparing them to stored representations of the prototypes of various categories. Alternatively, we may store memories of all of the category examples (*category exemplars*) that we encounter and use these remembered examples to determine category membership.

The Hierarchical Structure of Categories

Any object or event can be categorized at numerous levels of abstraction within a hierarchy, ranging from very general to highly specific. *Basic-level category* terms are mid-level in the hierarchy and communicate a wealth of useful and predictive information in an efficient manner. Higher-level (*superordinate*) category terms are less informative, and lower-level (*subordinate*) category terms tend to be longer and deliver only a small amount of additional information over basic-level terms.

▶ Solving Problems

Problem solving refers to situations in which someone wants to reach a goal, but the way to do so is not immediately obvious. The ability to solve problems is important for everyday survival. *Well-defined* problems have a clearly defined starting point and a well-specified goal. *Ill-defined* problems do not have clear starting points or well-specified goals.

The IDEAL Problem Solver

The five major steps in problem solving are (1) identifying the problem, (2) defining (representing) it in the most efficient way, (3) exploring problem strategies, (4) acting on the problem strategy chosen, and (5) looking back to evaluate the effectiveness of the selected strategy.

Identifying and Defining: Problem Representation

To identify and define a problem, you must understand exactly what information is given and how that information can potentially be used. One obstacle in representation is *functional fixedness*, the tendency to see objects and their functions in certain fixed and typical ways. People typically rely on well-established patterns of perception and thought (*mental sets*); most of the time this is an effective strategy, but it sometimes leads us astray.

Exploring and Acting: Problem Strategies

For some well-defined problems, you can use *algorithms*, step-by-step procedures that guarantee a solution. Algorithms can be used only for certain well-defined problems, and even for such problems they are not always practical. When algorithms are not feasible, we use *heuristics*, or problem-solving "rules of thumb." Three common problem-solving heuristics are *means-ends analysis*, *working backward*, and *searching for analogies*.

Looking Back and Learning

The problem-solving process is incomplete unless we look back and learn from the experience. By analyzing performance in detail, we can learn whether the strategy worked for some aspects of the problem but not for others and gain insight into why a particular heuristic failed or succeeded.

▶ Making Decisions

Decision making involves choosing from among a set of alternatives. Choosing entails risk because an incorrect decision can have unpleasant consequences.

The Framing of Decision Alternatives

The way alternatives are structured (*framing*) can dramatically influence decision making. When choices are framed in ways that highlight potential gains, people tend to avoid taking risks. If decisions are framed in ways that emphasize potential losses, people are more likely to take a risk that may limit or avoid the loss.

Confirmation Bias and Illusory Correlations

People have a bias to seek, remember, and emphasize evidence that confirms their hunches, often failing to look for evidence that could potentially disconfirm them. This *confirmation bias* can lead people to have faith in unfounded ideas. Confirmation bias can also contribute to *illusory correlations*, beliefs that two variables are correlated when in truth they are not, because people tend to assess relationships between variables by trying to remember cases in which variables they think should go together (e.g., a patient's diagnosis and unusual characteristics of that patient's drawings) did happen to go together.

Decision-Making Heuristics

When asked to judge the likelihood that something belongs to class A or B, people often rely on a rule of thumb termed the *representativeness heuristic*, which involves comparing the thing in question with beliefs regarding the average member of each class. When asked to estimate the odds of some event occurring, we often rely on the *availability heuristic*, basing estimates on the ease with which examples of the event come to mind. Both heuristics are beneficial most of the time, but they can lead to irrational decisions.

The Value of Heuristics

Although heuristics are imperfect, they are usually effective. Also, heuristics are economical, because they lead to quick decisions with little cost. In any case, we often must rely on heuristics because many of the problems and decisions that people confront have no feasible algorithms.

Terms to Remember

Recommended Readings

Bransford, J. D., & Stein, B. S. (1993). *The ideal problem solver* (2nd ed.). New York: Freeman. This fun book, written by a pair of famous cognitive psychologists, is full of great advice on how to solve problems effectively.

Christiansen, M. H., & Kirby, S. (2003). (Eds.). *Language evolution.* New York: Oxford University Press. This edited volume pulls together chapters by a dozen of the world's leading experts on language, each considering the problem of understanding how our linguistic competence evolved.

Pinker, S. (1994). *The language instinct.* New York: Morrow. In this very readable and insightful book, Canadian-born (but Harvard-based) psychologist Pinker addresses language, how it evolved, and whether it truly represents a unique human ability.

For additional readings, explore InfoTrac® College Edition, your online library. Go to http://www.adaptivemind3e.nelson.com.

Hint: Enter these search terms: language development, animal communication, problem solving, decision-making heuristics.

Media Resources

What's on the Web?

Please note that Web addresses are subject to change. Check out the accompanying Website for updates: http://www.adaptivemind3e.nelson.com.

This site presents practice quiz questions, hypercontent, information on degrees and careers in psychology, study tips, and more.

Koko and Penny

http://www.pbs.org/wnet/nature/koko/index.html

This site from the Public Broadcasting Service includes a brief video clip of Koko the gorilla and trainer Penny Patterson, along with numerous photographs and text about Koko's communicative skills. Patterson and Koko have worked together for some 30 years.

Mind/Brain Resources

http://plato.stanford.edu/entries/cognitive-science/

You've read a bit about the field of cognitive psychology. Now find out about the exciting interdisciplinary field of cognitive science (mentioned in the chapter introduction), a group of disciplines all working together to explain the mysteries of the mind. Cognitive science includes such diverse areas as philosophy, computer science, psychology, linguistics, and neuroscience. Explore the common threads that these disciplines share.

The Jane Goodall Institute

http://www.janegoodall.org

This site is relevant to this chapter in at least two ways. First, the institute was started by pioneering primatologist Jane Goodall, who changed our understanding of chimpanzees and of humans with her discoveries of chimps' impressive abilities (e.g., they modify sticks for use as termite-catching tools, challenging the uniqueness of "humans the toolmakers"). Second, one focus of this chapter was problem solving, and the JGI is dedicated to solving the pressing problems facing our natural environment.

ThomsonNOW™ ThomsonNOW™

http://hed.nelson.com

Go to this site for the link to ThomsonNOW™, your one-stop study shop. Take a Pretest for this chapter and ThomsonNOW™ will generate a personalized Study Plan based on your test results. The Study Plan will identify the topics you need to review and direct you to online resources to help you master those topics. You can then take a Posttest to determine what concepts you have mastered and what you still need work on.

Psyk.trek 3.0

Check out Psyk.trek 3.0 for further study of the concepts in this chapter. Psyk.trek's 65 interactive learning modules, simulations, and quizzes offer additional opportunities for you to interact with, reflect on, and retain the material:

Cognition and Intelligence: *Problem Solving*

The Gods do not give all men gifts of grace—nor good looks, nor intelligence.

—Homer

It's not that I'm so smart, it's just that I stay with problems longer.

—Albert Einstein

Intelligence

Late at night, students in the dormitory are arguing about who is the epitome of intelligence. Jennifer, a physics major, argues: "Obviously it's the person who figured out how the universe works—Albert Einstein." Dan, a business major, retorts: "If Einstein was so smart, how come he wasn't rich? I've got to pick Bill Gates because he's the richest person in the world." Carlo, a psychology major, says: "It's got to be the person who can charm, control, and entertain anyone she wants: That's Oprah Winfrey." Who's right? Or is it totally a matter of opinion? Given how different the three nominations were, could it be that the students' own majors influenced their choices?

After getting back their marks on the history exam, Larry Knoway argues with his friend: "Sure, we both got the same mark—but I didn't study. That makes me more intelligent." His friend disagrees: "No way, Larry—working hard is part of intelligence." Who's right? Is a person's personality part of their intelligence?

Jane interviews candidates for jobs in a computer software company. She has trouble with the immigrant applicants because they don't seem to catch on to her explanations very well. Her job is important and she doesn't want to hire incompetent applicants. But she wonders whether they are really incompetent or whether their language skills are giving her the wrong impression about their intelligence. Can a person's accent and appearance affect our judgments of their intelligence?

Albert Einstein's name is almost synonymous with intelligence. Is it partly because few people really understand his complex physics and mathematics?

Bill Gates created a business empire based on personal computers. Many others tried to take advantage of the computer revolution, but Gates's technical and business savvy proved incomparable.

Oprah Winfrey also became rich but primarily on the basis of her social skills. Can a person decide to be popular, or is it an inborn talent?

intelligence

An internal capacity hypothesized to explain people's ability to solve problems, learn new material, and adapt to new situations; its strength appears to differ across individuals

subjective definition

A definition based on personal opinion; each person's definition seems designed to suit his or her personal needs and worldviews

objective test

A test that is scored in a standardized fashion so that anyone calculating the result gets the same answer

These three anecdotes illustrate that the concept of **intelligence** is an especially elusive one. It seems evident to all of us that some people we meet are smarter than others are. Yet, as with all psychological concepts, we can't directly see intelligence. Nonetheless, we constantly judge people's intelligence (or lack of it) on the basis of such behaviour as their school grades or the salary they make or the way they talk. The concept is also especially sensitive, so the act of labelling arouses people's emotions.

Surveys show that the trait of intelligence is rated as both highly important and highly desirable. This high value may explain why polls asking people to rate themselves as either "above average" or "below average" in intelligence find an odd result: Virtually everyone reports being above average! Although this result upsets statisticians, it is quite understandable to psychologists. Research by David Dunning and colleagues explains how this can happen (e.g., Beauregard & Dunning, 1998). Because the concept of intelligence is so vague, people can define it the way they want. So they simply define "intelligence" subjectively in such a way that they personally rate highly on it. As a result, we can all be geniuses in our own minds!

Rather than accept a completely **subjective definition** of intelligence, psychologists have expended considerable energy on developing an **objective test.** Subjective definitions have no fixed meaning and depend on who is doing the judging; objective definitions (i.e., scores on a test) yield the same concrete score no matter who calculates it. More than one hundred years of research has been devoted to developing objective tests that are able to predict important consequences, such as school performance and job success.

Intelligence

P
R
E
V
I
E
W

Intelligence is commonly viewed as the ultimate human adaptation. More than any other trait, intelligence distinguishes us from other species. Nonetheless, the relatively small differences within our species are given huge significance within human societies. We judge ourselves and others—often on the basis of very little information.

As psychologists began to measure these differences, a variety of scientific and practical, and even ethical, problems arose. This chapter deals with the four most important problems.

First, how should intelligence be conceptualized? Although we cannot see intelligence directly we all believe it exists in varying degrees in our fellow human beings.

We also sense that it is not a single thing but may have several forms. As you will see, verifying our belief in these assumptions has proved to be a serious scientific and practical problem for psychologists.

Second, how can we measure intelligence in an objective fashion? Regardless of how we may choose to conceptualize intelligence, we are still faced with the practical problem of measuring it. Doing it right is extremely difficult. Near the beginning of this chapter, we'll explain how psychological measurement works in general. You will find that understanding qualities of tests, such as reliability and validity, is worth the effort. It will prove valuable for other chapters of this book.

Third, what are the origins of intelligence? Does intelligent behaviour come primarily from your genetic background or from life experiences? This traditional nature versus nurture question should sound familiar by now. Today, the importance of this question is more scientific than practical. We do not—or at least, should not—care about the source of abilities when we hire someone or select them for medical school. Nonetheless, the origins of intelligence continue to occupy the research careers of many academic psychologists.

Fourth, how accurate are we in judging intelligence? It would be adaptive if we could judge intelligence in others; however, we might also be better off if others could not judge us accurately.

▶ Conceptualizing Intelligence

LEARNING GOALS

1. Comprehend the psychometric approach to conceptualizing intelligence, including Spearman's *g*-factor theory.
2. Understand cognitive approaches to conceptualizing intelligence.
3. Learn the differences among the various expanded theories.

From the perspective of the adaptive mind, intelligence is simply the degree to which a person is successful in adapting. You are considered intelligent if you can solve the particular problems that you confront in your environment (Matthews, 1997; Sternberg, 1997). This adaptive interpretation of intelligence presents many advantages. For one thing, focusing on adaptation deters us from assuming that *human* thoughts and actions are the only proper measuring tools for intelligent behaviour. The fact that the nutcracker bird can efficiently hide and relocate thousands of seeds is certainly intelligent from the standpoint of adapting to the harshness of winter (Kamil & Balda, 1990). From this perspective, University of British Columbia psychologist Stanley Coren (1995) argues that all flourishing species are intelligent because they are all well adapted to their unique environments. This notion that different species (and cultures) have different survival problems previews the fact that we may need to establish a wide range of criteria for what constitutes intelligence.

However, conceptualizing intelligence simply in terms of adaptability does not tell us much about what produces *individual differences* within a species, such as our own. Human beings differ substantially in their ability to fit successfully into their environments—even when the problems they face are very similar. We need

CRITICAL THINKING
Should scientists stick with concrete observations and avoid abstract ideas, such as intelligence (and anxiety and gravity)?

psychometrics

The use of psychological tests to measure the mind, especially individual differences

to understand the factors that account for such individual differences. In this section of the chapter, we'll consider three general ways to accomplish this end: (1) the *psychometric* approach, (2) the *cognitive* approach, and (3) *expanded conceptions of intelligence*. Each approach is designed to provide a general framework for conceptualizing intelligence, with the express goal of explaining how people differ in mental ability.

The Psychometric Approach: Measuring the Mind

The psychometric approach assumes that intelligence is a mental capacity that can be understood by analyzing performance on cognitive ability tests. The word **psychometric** literally means "measuring the mind." A person's intelligence is evaluated by scores on tests that measure his or her specific mental skills, such as vocabulary, memory, or spatial ability. The results are then analyzed statistically and conclusions are drawn about underlying mental abilities.

Englishman Sir Francis Galton (1822–1911) was one of the first researchers to examine intelligence in a systematic fashion. Galton was a half-cousin of Charles Darwin, and, like his famous relative, was deeply committed to the idea of "survival of the fittest." He believed that individual differences in intelligence had their basis in heredity and could be measured through a series of tests of sensory discrimination and reaction time. For a small fee, visitors to Galton's laboratory were given a variety of psychological and physical tests, measuring such things as visual acuity, grip strength, and reaction time to sounds. At the end of the test session, they were handed a card with a detailed record of their scores (Hilgard, 1987; Johnson et al., 1985).

As it turned out, Galton's laboratory investigations into the measurement of intelligence were too crude and his tests were shown to be poor predictors of actual intellectual performance, for example, academic success (Wissler, 1901). But his general approach captured the attention of other researchers, who went on to develop the psychometric approach in a more rigorous way. Among the more influential of those who carried on the Galton tradition was a mathematically inclined psychologist named Charles Spearman.

Sir Francis Galton (1822–1911) and his "anthropometric" laboratory, which he used to measure intellectual ability.

Spearman and Factor *g* One problem with Galton's approach was that he didn't know how to combine his multitude of measurements. British intelligence researcher Charles Spearman (1904) provided a solution by applying a mathematical technique he called **factor analysis** to the testing of mental ability. Results showed a single common factor in the analysis, which he called *g* for **general intelligence.** The implication was that intelligence could be estimated by combining scores on a variety of ability tests.

Although *g* helped to explain performance on a wide variety of mental tests, it did not explain the unique part of each test. The correlations among the test scores were highly positive but not perfect. Spearman argued, therefore, that each test includes a **specific residual, *s*,** which is the leftover part unique to each individual test (see ▶ Figure 9.1). For example, the leftover part of a test of verbal comprehension represents an extra aptitude or life experience not captured by *g*. Note that special talents, like musical and mechanical ability, did not show any connection with *g*: The tests for such talents were all *s* and no *g*.

Hierarchical Models of Intelligence Over the years, some researchers have challenged Spearman's conclusions, especially the overarching concept of *g*. Psychologist Leon Thurstone, for example, applied a somewhat different version of factor analysis, as well as a more extensive battery of tests, and discovered evidence for seven **primary mental abilities:** verbal comprehension, verbal fluency, numerical ability, spatial ability, memory, perceptual speed, and problem solving (Thurstone, 1938). He rejected Spearman's notion of a single general intelligence, *g*, because Thurstone's analysis indicated that these seven primary abilities are sometimes discrepant. Just because someone is good at verbal reasoning, for example, doesn't guarantee that he or she will be good at memory or perceptual speed. Although the correlations among the primary abilities tended to be positive, Thurstone argued that it was informative to score the seven abilities separately.

Modern intelligence tests include a variety of subtests similar to Thurstone's, although an overall score is usually provided. Rather than the term *mental abilities*, current psychologists favour use of the term *cognitive abilities*.

Psychologists continue to debate (1) the proper way to apply factor analysis, (2) the particular kinds of ability tests that should be used, and (3) whether single or multiple factors are needed to explain the data (Jensen & Weng, 1994). The

CRITICAL THINKING

How well does the notion of general intelligence describe you and your friends? If you're good at one subject, does that predict how well you will do in others?

factor analysis

A statistical procedure developed by Charles Spearman that determines how many subsets of highly correlated items are in a larger test; each subset is called a common factor, useful for summarizing the subset under a single name

***g* (general intelligence) factor**

The large underlying factor that contributes to performance on a variety of ability tests

***s* (specific) residual**

The remainder part of a specific ability test that is unique and not explained by *g*

primary mental abilities

The seven distinct forms of intelligence Thurstone uncovered with modern forms of factor analysis

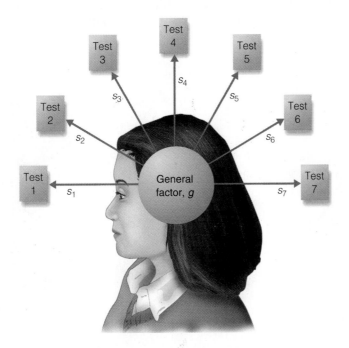

▶ **Figure 9.1**

Spearman's *g*-Factor and Specific Residuals

To explain performance on a variety of cognitive ability tests, Spearman distinguished (1) a common factor, called *g* for general intelligence, that contributes to performance on all the tests from (2) specific residuals—labelled here as *s*1 through *s*7—which are the remainder skills specific to the particular tests.

Some people seem to be all-round athletes. Deion Sanders performed at the highest levels in both professional football and professional baseball. Do his skills support the existence of a *g*-factor of athletic ability?

Mark Lyons/Getty Images

Ezra Shaw/Getty Images

statistical debates will not be considered here. But the evidence for a central *g* is hard to dismiss completely, especially when intelligence is defined by performance on tests of scholastic ability. For this reason, most modern psychometric theories of intelligence retain the concept of general intelligence but propose more of a hierarchical structure, such as that shown in ▶ Figure 9.2. General intelligence, *g*, occupies a position at the top of the hierarchy, and various sub-factors sit at a lower level. This compromise between Thurstone's view—that there is more than one primary mental ability—and Spearman's concept of *g* is well supported by the data.

Fluid and Crystallized Intelligence   Other psychologists believe strongly in the notion of general intelligence, but they contend that it should be broken down into two separate dimensions: *fluid* intelligence and *crystallized* intelligence (Cattell, 1963, 1998; Horn & Cattell, 1966). **Fluid intelligence** is the basic ability to solve problems, reason, and remember in ways that are relatively uninfluenced by expe-

fluid intelligence

The natural ability to solve problems, reason, and remember; thought to be relatively uninfluenced by experience

▶ **Figure 9.2**

Hierarchical Models

Many psychologists now argue for hierarchical models of intelligence, which include elements found in the theories of both Spearman and Thurstone. Like Thurstone did, hierarchical models propose separate factors that contribute independently to certain types of tests (e.g., factor 1 contributes to tests 1 to 3 but not to tests 4 to 9). But, as Spearman did, these models also assume that all factors are influenced by an overall *g*.

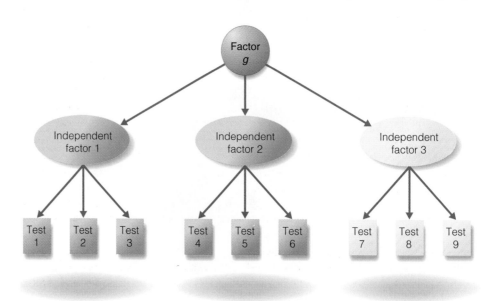

rience. Fluid intelligence is probably determined primarily by biological or genetic factors. **Crystallized intelligence,** however, refers to knowledge and ability acquired from experience. You might learn things about the world, such as tricks to deal with arithmetic problems, and learn words used only at higher levels of schooling and in certain cultural groups.

The distinction between fluid and crystallized intelligence is important because it helps to explain how mental abilities differ with age and across different cultures (Horn & Noll, 1997; Parkin & Java, 2001). As you'll see later in the chapter, there are reasons to expect fluid and crystallized intelligence to change in different ways as we age. It's also common to find striking differences in people's ability to perform on psychometric tests of mental ability. Performance differences between different cultures and socioeconomic classes are also difficult to explain from the perspective of general intelligence, unless we assume that an important part of general intelligence is acquired from experience. Distinguishing between fluid and crystallized intelligence can help explain how two people born with the same amount of natural (fluid) intelligence can end up performing quite differently on tests of mental ability.

The Cognitive Approach

The cognitive approach assumes that intelligence is best understood by clarifying the sequence of internal mental processes. We must analyze how people differ on the complex mental tasks detailed in Chapter 8. The required analysis typically comes in one of two forms: (1) measurement of the speed of mental processing and (2) an analysis of the specific mental operations that produce intelligent thought.

Mental Speed   Some cognitive psychologists have suggested that intelligence reflects, in part, the speed of transmission among the neural pathways of the brain (see Deary, 2001; Hunt, 1985; Jensen, 1993; Vernon, 1983). The faster the brain communicates internally, the higher an individual's intelligence. The reason that communication speed might be important is that the brain has limited resources and must quickly allocate, or divide, its processing to perform efficiently (see Chapter 4). In support of this position, Jensen and his colleagues typically find a significant correlation between measures of neural communication speed and performance on mental tests of intelligence (Reed & Jensen, 1992). Similarly, Linda Miller, Philip Vernon, and their colleagues at the University of Western Ontario have found a positive relationship among speed of information processing, working memory, and intelligence; they have also found that this relationship holds true for children as well as adults (Miller & Vernon, 1996, 1997). Other researchers have linked the speed difference to genetic factors (Rijsdijk, Vernon, & Boomsma, 1998).

Working Memory   Cognitive theorists also attempt to identify the specific mental components that contribute to superior test performance. One such component— working memory—is receiving increasing attention from researchers (e.g., Conway, Kane, & Engle, 2003; Gray & Thompson, 2004). Like the working memory in a computer, it is the most direct and active part of memory: It holds information ready for use in problem solving, reasoning, and comprehension.

Scores on simple memory tasks (e.g., "repeat the words you heard in the same order") do not show the same connection with intelligence as do multiple memory tasks (e.g., "repeat back the words you heard while keeping track of numbers on the screen"). In other words, intelligent individuals can avoid being distracted while keeping several ideas in their mind. Individuals with better working memories are then likely to score higher on intelligence tests as well as perform better on a variety of life's challenges.

crystallized intelligence

The knowledge and abilities acquired as a result of experience (as from schooling and cultural influences)

CRITICAL   THINKING

Which do you think contributes the most to performance on an essay exam: fluid or crystallized intelligence?

Like the psychometric theorists, cognitive theorists hope that once they identify the fundamental components and processes of intelligence, those elements can be used to predict and explain individual differences in task performance. If we can get a measure of your ability to analyze analogies, for instance, we might be able to predict how well you will perform on a wide variety of tests of mental ability. One special approach called **artificial intelligence** involves developing computer programs that mimic human intelligence, or at least expert thinking in more narrow domains. We already know, for example, that the famous IBM computer program called Deep Blue can defeat the best human chess player, Garry Kasparov. Another program called Liza can actually do psychotherapy at a bargain price (free). Other programs under development can diagnose medical conditions and solve physics or engineering problems (Simon, 1969, 1992). By conceptualizing intelligence in terms of underlying mental processes and then modelling those processes by using computer programs, cognitive theorists hope to go beyond just measuring intelligent behaviour to understanding and explaining its causes.

Expanded Conceptions of Intelligence

In recent years, several psychologists have argued that the traditional unitary conception of intelligence needs to be expanded to include a wider variety of abilities and talents. They reject the idea that intelligence can be adequately conceptualized through the analysis of test performance or artificial laboratory tasks (as used by the psychometric and cognitive approaches). Criticizing the narrow definition implied by a single underlying g, they argue that we should acknowledge a wider variety of human talents and abilities.

Gardner's Multiple Intelligences   Howard Gardner (1983, 1993) has been the most powerful voice calling for the expansion of current conceptions of intelligence with his theory of **multiple intelligences.** An *intelligence* (rather than "the" intelligence) is defined as "an ability or set of abilities that permits an individual to solve problems or fashion products that are of consequence in a particular cultural setting" (Walters & Gardner, 1986). Although Gardner believes that each of these separate intelligences may be rooted in the biology of the brain, the way that each is manifested may depend on a person's culture.

Rather than studying intelligent behaviour in the laboratory, Gardner has used a case study approach. He analyzed detailed reports of particular individuals with special abilities or talents, such as superior musicians, poets, scientists, and savants. For example, he closely studied biographies on Einstein. Gardner has also looked extensively at the effects of damage to the brain. He has noted, for example, instances in which brain damage can affect one kind of ability, such as reasoning and problem solving, yet leave intact other abilities, such as musical skill. Based on his research, Gardner has identified what he believes to be nine kinds of intelligence:

1. *Musical intelligence* is the type of ability displayed by gifted musicians or child prodigies.
2. *Bodily-kinesthetic intelligence* is the type of ability shown by gifted athletes, dancers, or surgeons who have great control over body movements.
3. *Logical-mathematical intelligence* is the type of ability displayed by superior scientists and logical problem solvers.
4. *Linguistic intelligence* is the type of ability shown by great writers or poets who can express themselves verbally.
5. *Spatial intelligence* is the type of ability shown by those with superior navigation skills or an ability to visualize spatial scenes.
6. *Interpersonal intelligence* is the type of ability shown by those who can easily infer other people's moods, temperaments, or intentions and motivations.

artificial intelligence

The attempt to understand the meaning of intelligence by building intelligent machines; such machines—usually computer programs—can simulate or surpass many human capabilities

multiple intelligences

The notion proposed by Howard Gardner that people possess a set of separate and independent "intelligences" ranging from musical to linguistic to interpersonal abilities

CRITICAL   THINKING

Do you think the average person on the street thinks that athletic ability or dancing ability qualifies as a type of intelligence? What other intelligences could be added to Gardner's list?

7. *Intrapersonal intelligence* is the ability shown by someone who has great insight into his or her own feelings and emotions.

8. *Naturalist intelligence* is the ability to observe and interact with diverse species in nature and is the type of ability shown by a biologist or environmentalist.

9. *Spiritual intelligence* is the ability to sense spiritual aspects of human experience and use them to adapt to the environment.

Notice that some forms of intelligence, as described by Gardner, are covered well by conventional tests of cognitive ability. The psychometric and cognitive approaches focus extensively on logical-mathematical intelligence and to some extent on linguistic and spatial intelligence. Certainly, some psychometric researchers argued for the need to distinguish between subtypes of intelligence, but they rarely, if ever, included special intelligences, such as mechanical ability, musical ability, or athletic skill. As a result, the multiple intelligences approach is a direct challenge to traditional unitary conceptions of intelligence.

Clearly, Gardner's multiple intelligences approach has an adaptive flavour and fits snugly into this textbook's general conception of the adaptive mind. The idea is that everyone has a life niche where he or she displays intelligence. Gardner's framework has been applied successfully in educational settings (Krechevsky & Seidel, 1998). Many grade school and high school teachers like the idea of multiple intelligences because it can help increase the lower self-esteem of some students. Some critics say that Gardner is really talking about multiple talents rather than intelligences, and his theory remains primarily descriptive without much hard scientific evidence. But many psychologists (and real people too!) are coming to agree with Gardner that intelligence should be broadly conceived—it's not simply performance on a battery of primarily verbal-linguistic or sensory tests.

Exemplars of Intelligence   Instead of relying on Gardner's case studies, Paulhus and his colleagues (2002) asked ordinary people to suggest famous individuals whom they consider to be intelligent. These researchers from the University of British Columbia had collected data from thousands of people over many years—1982 to 1997. When the voting was compiled, Albert Einstein topped the list in every year. In the 1997 survey, the rest of the top 10 were (in order): Bill Gates, Bill Clinton, Stephen Hawking, Isaac Newton, Leonardo da Vinci, William Shakespeare, Sigmund Freud, Charles Darwin, and Ludwig van Beethoven.

The Canadian who received by far the most nominations over the years was Pierre Trudeau. In fact, in Canadian surveys, Trudeau was the only nominee to ever come close to "beating" Einstein (in 1982). Although more than 60% of the participants in this study were female, they nominated only three women to be among the top 15 over the years: Margaret Thatcher, Madonna, and Oprah Winfrey. Paulhus and his colleagues concluded that there is remarkable consistency in the "exemplars" nominated, that powerful individuals are often seen as intelligent, and that people seem to differentiate several different subtypes of intelligence: scientific, communicative, entrepreneurial, moral, and artistic intelligences (Paulhus, Wehr, Harms, & Strasser, 2002). These popular subtypes show some overlap with the multiple intelligences arising from Gardner's case study approach.

Sternberg's Three Facets of Intelligence   Robert Sternberg has also challenged the unitary notion of intelligence suggested by psychometric researchers. He agrees that it's important to understand the analytic mental operations that are involved in the planning and execution of specialized tasks, but he also believes that any complete account of intelligence must address behaviour outside the laboratory. For example, what is the form of intelligence that enables people to apply their mental processes creatively to problems that arise in the external environment? Furthermore, how does intelligence relate to the practical experience of the

People possess unique abilities that Gardner views as types of intelligence. For example, the performers from Cirque du Soleil (left) possess high levels of bodily-kinesthetic intelligence; Jim Carrey (right) rates highly in interpersonal and bodily-kinesthetic intelligence.

Paul Chiasson/CP Picture Archive

CP Picture Archive (Chris Pizzello/AP)

> **Sternberg's three facets of intelligence**
>
> Robert Sternberg's theory of intelligence that includes three types of intelligence: analytic, creative, and practical

individual? In short, like Gardner, Sternberg sees the need for more than one intelligence. Instead of Gardner's nine types, **Sternberg's three facets of intelligence** include *analytic, creative,* and *practical* types (Sternberg, 1985, 1988b).

Sternberg believes that any complete theory of intelligence must refer in some way to basic analytic skills. Some people are simply better than others are at processing information—they're good at representing (or seeing) problems in the right way and can generate effective strategies for solutions. People with high degrees of *analytical intelligence* tend to perform well on conventional tests that tap reasoning and logical-mathematical ability—such as the Scholastic Aptitude Test (SAT). Because most psychometric tests of intelligence require these kinds of abilities, people who are high in analytic intelligence tend to be assigned a high *g*. If you know someone who performs well in school or who claims to be highly intelligent based on a standardized test, he or she is likely to score highly on analytic intelligence.

Sternberg proposes that *creative intelligence* expresses how well people are able to cope with new or novel tasks. Being analytic and processing information well does not guarantee that you will be creative or be able to apply the skills you've mastered in a new context. The world is full of people who are good at school or who perform well on assigned tasks but have nothing to contribute when the situation changes. They lack creativity and seem to have trouble applying what they've learned. A child who is motivated to read widely after acquiring the rudiments of language, for example, is said to be high in creative intelligence (Sternberg, 1985).

Finally, people differ in *practical intelligence*, which taps how well they fit into their environments. People with lots of practical intelligence solve the problems that are uniquely posed by their cultural surroundings. They mould themselves well into existing settings and move to new environments, if required, that provide a better fit or niche for their talents. In a nutshell, these individuals have "street smarts"; they size up situations well and act accordingly. You probably know someone who seems to lack analytic skills—who fails school or drops out—but still manages to succeed in life. Such success involves adapting to the environment and doing what it takes to succeed.

Sternberg's theory fits the current trend toward a broadening of the concept of intelligence. Like Gardner's approach, Sternberg's theory deals with behaviours and skills that are not normally covered by the psychometric and purely cognitive approaches. Also like Gardner's theory, Sternberg's distinctions can be applied successfully in classroom settings, where multiple types of intelligence can be nurtured and developed (Sternberg, 1998; Sternberg, Torff, & Grigorenko, 1998). Nonetheless, breadth is gained with some cost: Such concepts as practical and creative intelligence are not defined with precision and, consequently, can be somewhat difficult to measure and test (Sternberg, Castejon, Prieto, Hautamaeki, & Grigorenko, 2001). Moreover, even if it is desirable to broaden our conception of intelligence, that doesn't mean that the cognitive or psychometric approaches to intelligence have no value. As you'll see in the next section, psychometric tests are often quite useful in predicting performance, even though they may be measuring only narrow dimensions of intelligence.

CONCEPT SUMMARY

VIEWS OF INTELLIGENCE

Approach	Example(s)	Intelligence is
Psychometric	Spearman's g-factor	A general mental capacity evaluated by performance on cognitive ability tests
	Seven primary abilities	A set of correlated cognitive abilities
Cognitive	Cognitive strategies	Strategies and components of specific mental operations
	Mental speed	Overall speed of mental operations
Gardner's multiple intelligences	Musical intelligence Spatial intelligence	A variety of abilities that permit an individual to succeed in a particular achievement setting
Sternberg's three facets of intelligence	Analytic intelligence	The ability to process information analytically
	Creative intelligence	The ability to cope with novel tasks
	Practical intelligence	The ability to solve problems uniquely posed by cultural surroundings

Test Yourself 9.1

For each of the following statements, pick the term that best describes the approach to conceptualizing intelligence from the following: psychometric, cognitive, Gardner's intelligences, Sternberg's intelligences. (The answers are in Appendix B.)

1. Mitsuko has street smarts—she can mould herself successfully into any situation. _____

2. Celia wants to measure her intelligence so she volunteers to participate in a reaction time experiment in the psychology department. _____

3. Jeremy flunks most of his classes, but he's a brilliant pianist so he considers himself to be highly intelligent. _____

4. Lucy has just finished an exhaustive battery of mental tests; she's waiting to find out if she has a high g. _____

5. Natalie wants to understand the concept of intelligence so she has signed up for a class on factor analysis. _____

6. Verne shows great insight into the feelings of others, which makes him score highly on tests of interpersonal intelligence. _____

7. Sheila scored a perfect 4.0 GPA in high school but has trouble applying what she's learned to new situations. She's beginning to feel like she might not be so intelligent after all. _____

▶ Measuring Individual Differences

LEARNING GOALS

1. Recognize the components of a good test: reliability, validity, and standardization.
2. Understand the intelligence quotient (IQ) and how it is interpreted.
3. Learn how mental retardation, giftedness, and savant are defined.
4. Understand the validity of IQ tests.
5. Be able to explain creativity and emotional intelligence.

We have now discussed several ways to conceptualize the idea of intelligence. We have yet to discuss how individual differences are actually measured and scored. Although the different conceptions take different approaches, they all acknowledge the need to perform objective measurement. As noted earlier, objective tests give the same number no matter who calculates the score. A scientific analysis of intelligence cannot proceed without collecting objective scores that we can use to compare people.

Of course, there is no guarantee that a test score is useful just because it is objective. We might all agree on how many freckles you have, but this agreement is hardly a good reason for using your freckle score as an indicator of your intelligence. This section of the chapter deals with various ways of distinguishing a good test from a bad one.

First, we have to decide on exactly what we want to measure. It is easy to confuse similar concepts, such as intelligence with aptitude, achievement, or achievement motivation. They all have different implications for a person's future. **Achievement motivation tests** evaluate a person's ambition or desire to be successful. Some people devote all their energies toward future achievements and others choose to pass their time entertaining themselves or helping others. **Achievement tests** measure someone's actual level of knowledge or competence in a particular subject (such as math or reading). Researchers and teachers can use the results of an achievement test to assess the effectiveness of a learning procedure or a school curriculum. Achievement tests are also used to make predictions about the future, such as how well you can be expected to perform in your chosen profession or whether you are likely to succeed at university. **Aptitude tests** measure your ability to learn in a particular area and to acquire new knowledge needed for success in a given domain. Aptitude test results can be used to help choose a career path and to avoid those in which your specific lack of ability may hold you back. (You probably don't want to waste 10 years learning a career that you don't have a knack for.) **Intelligence tests** are similar to aptitude tests but they are assumed to measure a more generalized form of aptitude. Intelligence should reveal itself in successful performance in many domains.

The Characteristics of a Good Test

We'll begin by discussing the qualities or characteristics of a "good" test (i.e., a dependable test that can be expected to provide a meaningful measure of individual differences). Given that we recognize the need to measure these differences, it's crucial that our measurement device yield information that is scientifically useful. Researchers generally agree on three characteristics that are needed for a good test: reliability, validity, and standardization.

Reliability   The first good test characteristic, **reliability,** refers to the consistency of the test results. Reliable tests produce similar scores when the test is administered more than once. Suppose we want to measure creativity and we design a test that produces a score from 0 to 100. On their first try, Al gets a score of 53 and Cynthia scores much higher at 86. It seems that Cynthia is much more

---

achievement motivation tests

Psychological tests that measure your desire to perform challenging tasks and reach difficult goals

achievement tests

Psychological tests that measure your current level of knowledge or competence in a particular subject

aptitude tests

Psychological tests that measure your ability to learn and solve problems in a particular subject area

intelligence tests

Tests that evaluate your overall cognitive ability to learn and solve problems

reliability

A measure of the consistency of test results; reliable tests give people similar scores across time and across parts of the test

creative than Al is. To be sure about the results, we administer the test again. This time Al scores 77 and Cynthia 43. Unfortunately, our new creativity test lacks reliability: That is, it does not produce consistent scores from one administration to the next. Cynthia may very well be more creative than Al is, but this particular test is not helpful in drawing that conclusion. Either the new test is unreliable or we have to give up on the idea that some people are consistently more creative than others are.

It's important for a test to be reliable. Otherwise, we cannot draw firm conclusions from people's scores. One way to measure a test's reliability is to give it to the same group of individuals again after an interval of time, say a month. **Test-retest reliability** is then calculated by comparing the scores across the repeated administrations. Often, a correlation coefficient is computed to put a number on how well

Throughout the school years, children regularly take standardized tests that are designed to measure aptitude or achievement.

scores on the second test can be predicted from scores on the first. The closer the test-retest correlation comes to a perfect $+1.00$, the better the test is. Another kind of reliability is calculated by correlating people's scores on the first half of the test with their scores on the second half. A high value of this **split-half reliability** is even more important than a high test-retest reliability, because test scores cannot be trusted if they change from the first half of the test to the second half.

Validity   The second good test characteristic, **validity,** refers to how well a test measures what it is supposed to measure. In other words, is the label of the test (intelligence, height, sociability) truly justified? A test can yield reliable numbers (i.e., consistent results across repeated administrations), yet not truly measure the psychological characteristic of interest. If a test of creativity just uses your shoe size, then the data are likely to be quite reliable but not very valid. Shoe size isn't going to change much from one measurement to the next, but it has little to do with creativity.

Validity has several different forms. Content validity measures the degree to which the content of a test samples the entire domain of interest. If you're trying to get a general measure of creativity, your test should not be limited to one kind of creativity, such as artistic creativity. For the test to have a high degree of content validity, it should probably measure artistic, verbal, mechanical, mathematical, and other kinds of creativity.

Sometimes psychologists are interested in designing a test that predicts a particular outcome, such as job performance or success in school. For a test to have predictive validity, it needs to predict this outcome adequately. An example of predictive validity is provided by researcher Douglas Symons (1999) of Acadia University, in a study of the predictive validity of the Graduate Record Exam (GRE). The GRE is designed to measure the likelihood of success in graduate school, and most graduate schools require applicants to submit scores on the GRE as part of the application process. To examine the predictive validity of the GRE in a master's program in clinical psychology, Symons examined the correlations between GRE scores and success on several goals, including whether students graduated on time, whether they received external grants and scholarships, and whether they published their master's theses. Symons concluded that the GRE did correlate highly with these variables and, therefore, that the GRE did have high predictive validity for students in the program that was studied.

test-retest reliability

The ability of a test to give consistent scores across time

split-half reliability

The ability of a test to give the same scores in the first and second halves of the test

validity

An evaluation of how well a test measures what the label of the test says it is measuring: *Content validity* assesses the degree to which the content of a test samples broadly across the domain of interest; *predictive validity* assesses how well the test predicts an important criterion; *construct validity* assesses how well the test captures all the details of the theoretical construct

CRITICAL THINKING

Do you think the class tests that you've taken so far have been valid? What specific kind of validity are you using as a basis for your answer?

standardization

Keeping the testing, scoring, and interpretation procedures similar across all administrations of a test

A more general kind of validity, construct validity, measures how well a test captures all the details of the theoretical concept or construct. Suppose we have a theory of creativity that is developed well enough to generate a wide variety of predictions—how creative people act, the kinds of books that creative people are interested in, the susceptibility of creative people to mental disorders, and so on. To have high construct validity, our test must show the predicted connections with each of these variables, rather than with just one. So if the theory predicts that creative people are more likely to suffer from depression, then people who score high on the creativity test should have a greater likelihood of being depressed. Finally, the test should also avoid measuring other constructs, such as achievement motivation or g, if your theory of creativity says that these are different.

Standardization   The third characteristic of a good test of individual differences is **standardization.** When you take a test, such as the SAT or any widely used aptitude or achievement test, you quickly learn that the testing procedures are extremely rigid to ensure fairness. You can break the test seal only at a certain time, a serious administrator reads the instructions in monotone, and you must put down your yellow number 2 pencil immediately when the time elapses. Clearly, these tests are *standardized*, which means that the testing, scoring, and interpretation procedures are kept similar across all administrations of the test. Rigid adherence to standardization is important because it ensures that all test takers will be treated the same.

In fact, the proper interpretation of a test score absolutely demands standardization. Remember: We're concerned with individual differences. It doesn't make much sense to compare two people's scores if different amounts of time or scoring procedures were used in the two test sessions. A person's score on a test of individual differences can be understood only with respect to a reference group, often called a *norm group*, and everyone within the group must receive the same test and administration procedures. We'll return to this notion of a norm reference group momentarily, as we consider the concept of the IQ.

CONCEPT SUMMARY

COMPONENTS OF A GOOD TEST

Component	Description	Example
Reliability	Consistency of test results	Taking a test twice should yield similar scores both times.
Validity	The test measures what its label says it measures.	
Content	The degree to which the content of a test samples broadly across the domain of interest	The items on a test of creativity should cover different types of creativity, such as artistic, mathematical, and verbal.
Predictive	The degree to which a test predicts a particular outcome	Performance on the Scholastic Achievement Test (SAT) should correlate with later performance in university classes.
Construct	The total evidence that a test actually measures the intended concept	Performance on a test of creativity should correlate with other characteristics or indexes thought to be associated with creativity.
Standardization	Testing, scoring, and interpretation procedures are kept similar across all administrations of the test.	Everyone who takes the SAT receives the same instructions, uses a yellow number 2 pencil and standard answer sheet, and completes the test within the same specified time.

IQ: The Intelligence Quotient

A critical step in developing an intelligence measure is deciding how to operationalize the concept; that is, how should assessors assign numbers to people to represent their intelligence? They could use each individual's salary, or school grades, or shoe size. Instead of those questionable operationalizations, psychologists typically administer a test containing questions of varying difficulty. Most people get the easy questions but very few get the difficult ones. Much research is required to choose the appropriate questions, to demonstrate that the test has reliability and validity, and to provide large samples of comparison data to standardize the test. Whatever questions are on the test, it has become traditional to convert overall scores to a single number labelled **IQ,** which stands for **intelligence quotient.** You will see in the rest of this section that the calculation of this number can be complicated.

The historical roots of the intelligence quotient trace back about a hundred years to the work of the French psychologist Alfred Binet and his associate, Théopile Simon. Binet and Simon were commissioned by the French government in 1904 to develop a test that would identify children who were considered "dull"—specifically, children who would have a difficult time grasping concepts in school. It was the French government's intention to help these children, once they were identified, through some kind of special education. Thus, the mission of the test was primarily practical, not theoretical; the goal was to develop a test that would accurately assess individual differences in future academic performance.

Mental Age Not surprisingly, Binet and Simon designed their test to measure the kinds of skills that are needed in school—such as memory, reasoning, and verbal comprehension. To form a meaningful scale, they came up with the notion of **mental age,** defined as the chronological age that best describes the child's current level of intellectual performance. Thus, it is actually a performance measure in disguise. Mental age is calculated by comparing a child's test score with the average scores for different age groups. For example, let's suppose that 8-year-old Jenny is able to answer the questions that an average 12-year-old can answer. Then Jenny would be assigned a mental age of 12. Her actual (chronological) age is irrelevant.

Thus, individuals can have a mental age that is higher or lower than their chronological age. When averaged over the whole group, they will be the same: By definition, an average 8-year-old solves problems at the average 8-year-old level. By using mental age, Binet and Simon (1916/1973) were able to diagnose the slow and quick learners and recommend appropriate curriculum adjustments.

However, mental age does not allow an easy comparison of the ability of children of different ages. Intuitively, we recognize that an 8-year-old child who has a mental age of 10 is smarter than a 10-year-old with the same mental age.

Ratio Formula for IQ German psychologist William Stern solved the problem of comparisons across age. He suggested the use of a formula called IQ that compares a child's mental age and chronological age, that is, their true physical age:

Intelligence quotient (IQ) = Mental age ÷ Chronological age × 100

The IQ is a useful scoring system because it establishes an easy-to-understand baseline for "average" intelligence: People of average intelligence will have an IQ of 100 because their mental age will always be equal to their chronological age. People with IQs greater than 100 will be above average in intelligence; those below 100 will be below average in intelligence.

IQ (intelligence quotient)

A single number calculated to represent a person's intelligence; originally, mental age divided by chronological age and then multiplied by 100; more recently, defined in terms of deviation from the average score on an IQ test

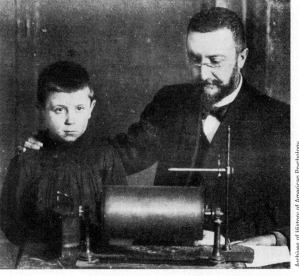

Alfred Binet, shown here with an unidentified child, was commissioned by the French government to develop a test that would help teachers identify students who might need special education.

Archives of History of American Psychology

mental age

The chronological age that best fits a child's level of performance on a test of mental ability; typically calculated by comparing a child's test score with the average scores for different age groups

Binet's intelligence test was revised several times and was ultimately translated into English for use in North America. The most popular American version was developed by psychologist Lewis Terman at Stanford University. Thus, it became known as the *Stanford-Binet* test of intelligence. It was also Terman who refined the standardization and conducted large-scale studies of intelligence. With him the term "IQ test" became a short form for intelligence test and it still is today.

Deviation Formula for IQ   Defining IQ simply in terms of the ratio of mental age to chronological age has some problems. The main problem is that performance on mental tests seems to level off around age 16. For example, the number of items a person can hold in mind or remember does not increase after that age. Chronological age, however, keeps getting larger. It doesn't seem fair to continue dividing by a bigger and bigger number when the mental age is not growing along with the chronological age. The ratio formula makes it look as if people are getting less and less intelligent with age. One solution has been to divide by 16 for all people aged 16 and older.

Another way to overcome this problem is to define IQ in terms of a *deviation*, or difference, rather than as a ratio. A **deviation IQ** still uses 100 as the average, but people are compared only against others of the same age. A particular person's IQ is then calculated by determining where his or her test score lies relative to the average score, in the overall distribution of scores. ▶ Figure 9.3 shows the typical **bell curve** of scores that would result from administering an IQ test, such as the Stanford-Binet, to a large group of people aged 25. The average score of the distribution is converted to 100 and everyone else's score is converted accordingly. Therefore, half the test takers will be given scores above 100 and the other half below 100. The standard deviation is 15.

One of the characteristics of modern intelligence tests is that they tend to produce very regular and predictable distributions of scores (see Figure 9.3). This regularity allows us to know the percentages of people scoring in each range of scores. For example, 68% of the people will receive an IQ score between 85 and 115, and 95% between 70 and 130. We can also easily calculate the percentage of the population likely to score at or below a particular IQ score. For example, 50% of scores fall below 100 (by definition), and about 98% of the people will receive a score at or below 130. Notice once again that IQ in this case is defined in terms of the relative location of a person's score in a frequency distribution of scores gathered from people in the same chronological age group.

deviation IQ

An intelligence score that is derived from determining where your performance sits in an age-based distribution of test scores

bell curve

The plot of frequencies obtained for many psychological tests; most people's scores are in the middle range, and the decline in frequencies is similar whether scores get higher or lower than the mean

▶ **Figure 9.3**

The Distribution of IQ Scores

IQ scores for a given age group will typically be distributed in a bell-shaped, or normal, curve. The average and most frequently occurring IQ score is defined as 100. Roughly 68% of the test takers in this age group received IQ scores between 85 and 115, which includes everyone scoring between one *standard deviation* above and below the mean. People labelled as "being gifted" (an IQ of 130 and above) or "having mental retardation" (an IQ of 70 or below) occur infrequently in the population—about 2% each.

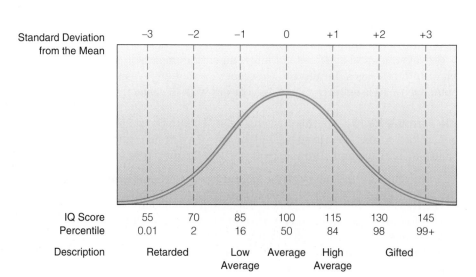

Standard Deviation from the Mean	−3	−2	−1	0	+1	+2	+3
IQ Score	55	70	85	100	115	130	145
Percentile	0.01	2	16	50	84	98	99+
Description		Retarded	Low Average	Average	High Average	Gifted	

Extremes of Intelligence

Tests, such as the Stanford-Binet or the related Wechsler Adult Intelligence Scale, have been given to many thousands of people. Consequently, we know a great deal about how IQ scores tend to be distributed in the population. All but 5% of people score between 70 and 130. Individuals who fall above or below this range represent extremes in intelligence.

Mental Retardation   A score of 70 or below on a standard IQ test qualifies an individual for a diagnosis of **mental retardation.** It is rare, however, that a single test score leads to a final diagnosis of mental retardation; other factors (such as daily living skills) contribute to the diagnosis (Fredericks & Williams, 1998). A four-level classification scheme, as shown in ▶ Table 9.1, has been developed by the American Association on Mental Deficiency. The table shows how each category level for retardation is defined in terms of IQ. It also lists some of the adaptation skills that can be expected, on average, for individuals who meet the diagnostic criteria.

What causes mental retardation? There are many possible sources, some genetic and some environmental. Down syndrome, for example, is typically associated with low IQ scores and is caused by a genetic abnormality—usually an extra chromosome. Environmental factors during development, such as birth trauma, inadequate nutrition, and maternal illness, have also been linked to mental retardation.

Giftedness   At the other end of the IQ scale are people considered **gifted,** with IQs at or above approximately 130. The highest score ever assigned—to Johann Goethe—was estimated posthumously at 210 (Cox, 1926). The estimate was based on records confirming that Goethe performed at the level of university students when he was only five years old. Of course, we don't have his score on a standard IQ test. Nor do we have the scores of most acknowledged geniuses, such as Einstein or Shakespeare.

But several studies have tracked the intellectual and social accomplishments of gifted children. One of the most famous studies was started in the 1920s by Lewis Terman (1925; Terman & Ogden, 1947). Terman was interested in whether children identified as gifted early in life would achieve success throughout their lives. Generally, this turned out to be the case: Terman's gifted subjects earned more college degrees than average, made more money, wrote more books, generated more successful patents, and so on.

CRITICAL THINKING

Do you see any similarities between the way that deviation IQ is interpreted and the way that you interpret your test scores in a class?

mental retardation

A label commonly assigned to someone who scores below 70 on a standard IQ test; other factors, such as the ability to adapt to the environment, are also considered before putting someone in this category

gifted

A label commonly assigned to someone who scores above 130 on a standard IQ test

▶ **Table 9.1** Types of Mental Retardation

Type	IQ Range (approximate)	Adaptation Potential
Mild	50 to 70	May develop academic skills comparable to a grade 6 educational level; with assistance, may develop significant social and vocational skills and be self-supporting
Moderate	35 to 50	Unlikely to achieve academic skills past a grade 2 level; may become semi-independent
Severe	20 to 35	Speech skills will be limited, but communication is possible; may learn to perform simple tasks in highly structured environments
Profound	Below 20	Little or no speech is possible; requires constant care and supervision

Ten-year-old Eddie Bonafe was born with severe physical and mental disabilities. But he could reproduce on the piano every hymn he heard sung in church before he had learned to walk. Individuals with Eddie's intellectual pattern are called savants.

Interestingly, these kids also turned out to be both emotionally stable and generally socially adept, which is surprising given the bookworm stereotype that people have of highly intelligent people. Most had successful marriages, and the divorce rate was lower for them than for the general population (Terman, 1954). A more recent study examining gifted children who skipped high school and moved directly to college also found evidence for better-than-average social adjustment (Nobel, Robinson, & Gunderson, 1993). Conversely, if we look at profoundly gifted children—those with IQs above 180—some different patterns emerge. Ellen Winner (1997) found that profoundly gifted children typically showed only average adult achievement and were more likely to have emotional problems and become socially isolated.

savant

An individual with a special talent despite generally low intelligence

Savants   Even more fascinating are the cases of **savants** (formerly known as "idiot savants" because they display both retardation and giftedness). They are generally deficient in most standard mental abilities but have some special mental talent, such as musical ability, memory for dates, or skill at calculating numbers. The existence of such individuals adds further support to the idea that intelligence is not a unitary ability. The neurology of the brain must involve some separation of mental abilities.

The Validity of Popular Intelligence Tests

In the section on characteristics of a good test, we discussed the central importance of validity. Now we can ask the critical question: Are standard tests of intelligence valid? Do IQ scores truly tap some hidden mental power (i.e., cognitive ability) that accounts for individual differences? Do intelligence tests adequately measure the ability to adapt and solve the problems of survival? Remember, the term *validity* has a technical meaning to the psychologist: How well does the test measure the thing that it is supposed to measure? To assess the validity of IQ tests, then, we need to ask: How well do IQ scores predict the appropriate criteria? Let's consider several of the popular tests.

The most widely applied intelligence tests today are the Stanford-Binet, the Wechsler Adult Intelligence Scale (WAIS), and the Wechsler Intelligence Scale for Children, third edition (WISC-III). These are not the only tests, of course. In fact, if we combine intelligence tests with measures of scholastic aptitude, then we can identify at least 120 different tests currently in use (Jensen, 1992). Usually these tests are given for the same reasons that originally motivated Binet and Simon—to predict some kind of academic performance, usually grades in high school or university. From this perspective, IQ passes the validity test with flying colours: IQ, as measured by Stanford-Binet or the Wechsler tests, typically correlates about 0.50 or higher with school grades (Ceci, 1991; Kline, 1991). Notice that the correlation is not perfect, but it is high in comparison with other attempts to predict real-world behaviour from a psychological test. Consider all the other factors that can affect grades in school (motivation, home environment, participation in extracurricular activities, teacher bias, and so on). IQ is also a reasonable predictor of real-world job performance, although its success in this domain is more modest (see the Practical Solutions box on page 361).

Critics of IQ tests often argue that the tests fail to provide a broad enough index of intelligence. In part, this is a complaint about content validity. People can fit successfully into their environments in many ways—and it's certain that not all

PRACTICAL SOLUTIONS

DOES INTELLIGENCE PREDICT SUCCESS IN THE WORKPLACE?

Theories and measures of intelligence have traditionally focused on school performance. But a much larger part of people's lives is spent at work. How well does the concept apply there? It is essential to employers to have some ability to predict who will function well in the job being filled. Interviews, although widely used, are poor predictors. The research is clear that general cognitive ability (g) is the best predictor of overall job performance (Jensen, 1993; Ree & Earles, 1992; Schmidt & Hunter, 1998). Nonetheless, this predictive power is far from perfect and it seems intuitively obvious that other factors, such as personality and motivation, play a role in people's performance on the job (Hogan, Hogan, & Roberts, 1996).

Even the concept of intelligence has been expanded to deal with workplace performance. Standard intelligence tests contain questions that have right and wrong answers. There is usually only one path or method for solving the problem. But success on a job typically requires knowledge that is not so cut-and-dried. Often a workplace has unspoken rules and strategies that are not taught formally. They help people to think quickly and efficiently in workplace situations. This kind of unspoken practical "know-how" is called **tacit knowledge,** and some psychologists believe that it will

turn out to be an even better predictor of job performance than g is (Wagner & Sternberg, 1985).

Such knowledge is rarely written in books and is not usually taught directly. Instead, it comes primarily from experience—from watching and analyzing the behaviour of others. But some workers pick up tacit knowledge more quickly than others do. Some managers learn the rules for maximizing the performance of their subordinates better than others do. Tacit knowledge tests contain "inside knowledge" questions provided by experts.

Here's a multiple-choice question on the tacit knowledge about becoming a famous academic:

What is the best strategy early in one's career?
a. Publish as many articles as possible in as many places as possible.
b. Publish your articles in prestigious journals.
c. Gain good teacher ratings at your school.
d. Acquire contacts at the higher levels of school administration.

The answer, as judged by successful academics, is (b).

Although the evidence is sparse so far, Sternberg and Wagner (1993) found that tacit knowledge correlates positively with such indicators as salary,

performance ratings, and the prestige of the business or institution where the person is employed. They also showed that tacit knowledge improves with work experience, which is what you would expect.

A telling example was provided by a study at the racetrack (Ceci & Liker, 1986). A sample of people were asked to spend a day betting on horses. Some were experts on horseracing and some were not. Standard tests were administered to ensure that the experts and nonexperts had the same IQ scores. When the accounts were examined at the end of the day, the experts had won an average of $92 as opposed to the $30 lost by the nonexperts. So IQ is not everything. As with most jobs, racetrack professionals draw on their experience to succeed in their chosen profession.

Let's now take a moment to critique the concept of tacit knowledge. The idea that it's useful to develop and use multiple strategies to perform successfully is almost certain to be true. The adaptive mind soaks up knowledge where it can and, as we've seen in earlier chapters, modelling is an important vehicle for guiding behaviour. But critics of Wagner and Sternberg's research have questioned whether tacit knowledge is really anything new. It sounds much like job experience or specific knowledge (Schmidt & Hunter, 1993). It may not be some human ability, like g, that can be tapped by the appropriate test; instead, measures of tacit knowledge may simply be indexes of what has been learned on the job. Other critics have questioned the claim that tacit knowledge scores really help predict job performance over and above g (Jensen, 1993). At this point, the jury is still out on whether tacit knowledge is a separate component of intelligence.

Successful managers understand the unspoken rules and strategies—called "tacit knowledge"—that are rarely, if ever, taught directly.

tacit knowledge

The special knowledge in a particular area that allows one to think quickly and efficiently

Wechsler Adult Intelligence Scale (WAIS)		
Test	**Description**	**Example**
Verbal scale		
Information	Taps general range of information.	On what continent is France?
Comprehension	Tests understanding of social conventions and ability to evaluate past experience.	Why are children required to go to school?
Arithmetic	Tests arithmetic reasoning through verbal problems.	How many hours will it take to drive 150 miles at 50 miles per hour?
Performance scale		
Block design	Tests ability to perceive and analyze patterns by presenting designs that must be copied with blocks.	Assemble blocks to match this design:
Picture arrangement	Tests understanding of social situations through a series of pictures that must be arranged in the right sequence to tell a story.	Put the pictures in the right order: 1 2 3
Object assembly	Tests ability to deal with part-to-whole relationships by presenting puzzle pieces that must be assembled to form a complete object.	Assemble the pieces into a complete object:

▶ **Figure 9.4**

Examples from the WAIS

The Wechsler Adult Intelligence Scale (WAIS) was designed to measure both verbal and performance aspects of intellectual ability. Included here are samples of the various question types. (From *Psychology: Themes and Variations,* Third Edition, by Weiten. Copyright © 1995. Reprinted with permission of Wadsworth, a division of Thomson Learning: www.thomsonrights.com. Fax 800 730-2215.)

CRITICAL   THINKING

Do you think it makes sense for elementary schools to use "streaming" systems, that is, to divide children early on into different academic streams based on early performance on standardized tests?

forms of multiple intelligence are tapped by traditional IQ tests. This criticism has been recognized for years by the community of intelligence test researchers, and efforts have been made to develop tests that tap a variety of abilities. The influential tests of David Wechsler, for example, were developed in part to measure nonverbal aspects of intellectual ability. The Wechsler tests include not only verbal-mathematical questions of the type traditionally found on the Stanford-Binet test but also performance questions requiring physical movement, like the completion or rearrangement of pictures (see ▶ Figure 9.4). Scores are then broken down into a verbal IQ and a performance IQ.

Again, most intelligence tests were designed to measure *g* and, therefore, are successful in predicting future academic performance; they were not designed to provide an all-encompassing index of multiple intelligences. So if you develop a test to predict university performance, it probably isn't reasonable to expect it to predict creativity, originality, or the ability for moral insight. For their purpose, then, standard IQ tests have good predictive validity. Whether they have construct validity is a more complex issue: The psychologist's answer will depend on whether IQ tests match that psychologist's concept of intelligence.

As we'll discuss later, this also means that intelligence tests can suffer from cultural limitations—a test designed to measure the abilities of high school students in suburbia may not be valid for students in the inner city or from a different region of the world. This doesn't mean that intelligence tests aren't useful—you just need to be aware of what the tests were designed to measure.

The developer of the WISC test has recently conducted research that compared the performance of American and Canadian children, and the results indicated that Canadian children tend to score slightly higher than American children do on certain test items (Beal, Dumont, Cruse, & Branche, 1996; Wechsler, 1996). As a result, new tables for interpreting the results of the test have been provided to Canadian psychologists who use the WISC-III, so that a valid assessment of each child in comparison to the Canadian norm is possible.

Other Individual Differences Related to Intelligence

To end our discussion of the measurement of individual differences, we'll briefly consider two psychological characteristics that are often aligned with the topic of intelligence: *creativity* and *emotional intelligence*. Neither creativity nor emotional intelligence is necessarily related to general intelligence, but both represent quite adaptive characteristics that can potentially increase our ability to survive.

Creativity   The term **creativity** refers to the ability to generate ideas that are original and novel. Creative thinkers think in unusual ways, which means that they can look at the usual and express it in an unusual way. Creative thinkers tend to see the "big picture" and are able to find connections between things that others might not see. Importantly, however, it's not just the generation of new and different ideas that makes a person creative; those ideas must also be useful and relevant—they must potentially have adaptive value.

> **creativity**
>
> The ability to generate ideas that are original, novel, and useful

How is creativity measured? Psychologists have devised a number of ways to measure individual differences in creative ability (Cooper, 1991; Cropley, 1996). One popular technique is to give someone a group of unrelated words, or unrelated objects in a picture, and then ask him or her to generate as many connections among the items as possible (Mednick, 1962; Torrance, 1981). Try it yourself: Take the words FOOD, CATCHER, and HOT and try to think of a fourth word (or words) that relates to all three. It turns out that measures like these reveal individual differences among people—some find this task to be quite easy; others find it extremely difficult. Moreover, performance on these creativity tests can then be correlated with other abilities, such as IQ or job success, to see if there is a connection.

What's the relation between creativity and intelligence? When intelligence is conceptualized in a broad way, then creativity fits in nicely as a part of general intellectual ability. You'll remember, for instance, that Sternberg's three facets of intelligence include the concept of creative intelligence. However, we noted that IQ tests aimed at g show relatively little overlap with measures of creativity. Correlations between creativity and IQ are always positive but modest (Horn, 1976; MacKinnon, 1962). What this means, however, is not clear—traditional IQ tests don't really measure creative thinking, so perhaps it's not surprising that the correlations are not very high. Perhaps being intelligent is a necessary but not sufficient condition for being creative. Furthermore, this issue still suffers from disagreement about which is the best test of creativity.

Emotional Intelligence   The second psychological characteristic, emotional intelligence, has recently gained some popularity among psychologists and is worthy of discussion here.

Emotional intelligence is essentially the ability to perceive, understand, and express emotion (Bar-On & Parker, 2000; Parker, 2000; Salovey & Mayer, 1990). The concept applies to perceiving and understanding the emotions of others, as well as to understanding and controlling our own emotions. Emotions, as you'll see in Chapter 11, can play a large role in behaviour, so it's clearly adaptive to manage and express them appropriately.

> **emotional intelligence**
>
> The ability to perceive, understand, and express emotion in ways that are useful and adaptive

People who score highly on emotional intelligence can read others' emotions well and tend to be empathetic as a result. They're good at managing conflict, both their own and the conflicts of others. Not surprisingly, emotional intelligence is believed to be an excellent predictor of success in career and social settings. In fact, some have argued that emotional intelligence may be a more important predictor of success in life than are more traditional conceptions of intelligence (Goleman, 1995). Critics have argued that emotional intelligence is not really a form of intelligence at all but an aspect of personality (e.g., Block, 2002). Research on emotional intelligence is in its infancy, so we'll need to wait before concluding anything about its ultimate usefulness (Pfeiffer, 2001).

Check what you know about the measurement of individual differences by answering the following questions. (The answers are in Appendix B.)

1. For each of the following statements, pick the test characteristic that is most appropriate. Choose from the following: reliability, standardization, and validity.
   a. Donna performs poorly on the SAT, so she takes it again and finds herself performing poorly again: _____
   b. Larry has devised a new test of intelligence, but he finds that it predicts nothing about school performance or success on the job: _____
   c. Chei-Wui wants to see how consistent the scores are on his new intelligence test, so he correlates answers across repeated administrations of the test: _____
   d. Robert's new job is to administer the Graduate Record Exam. He is very careful to keep the testing and scoring procedures the same for everybody who takes the test: _____

2. Decide whether each of the following statements is true or false.
   a. Lucinda has a mental age of 8 and an IQ of 160—this means that she must be five years old chronologically. *True or False?*
   b. Average IQ, based on the deviation IQ method, varies with chronological age. *True or False?*
   c. Lewis has just scored below 70 on his IQ test, which means that he will soon be labelled as having mental retardation. *True or False?*
   d. Creativity increases with intellectual ability, as measured by IQ. *True or False?*

▶ Discovering the Sources of Intelligence: The Nature-Nurture Issue

LEARNING GOALS

1. Understand the stability of IQ, and discuss why IQ might change across the life span.
2. Learn how twin studies are used to evaluate genetic contributions to intelligence.
3. Recognize environmental influences on intelligence.
4. Understand how genetic and environmental factors interact to determine intelligence.

We've seen that people differ, and we've considered some of the ways to measure these individual differences. We've also discussed methods for conceptualizing these differences theoretically—people may differ in *g*, they may differ in the speed of their brain cells, or they may lack some of the mental operations needed for intelligent performance. But what accounts for these differences in the first place? Why is one person's *g* higher or lower than another person's *g*? Is there anything that can be done about these differences, or are they fixed?

How differences in intelligence might arise can essentially be explained in two ways. First, you can appeal to heredity, particularly the internal *genetic code*—those strands of DNA that determine eye colour, thickness of hair, and possibly *g*. According to this view, intellectual potential is established at conception through some particularly fortunate (or unfortunate) combinations of genes. The second way is to appeal to an external cause, specifically, the *environment*. Variations in *g* might be attributable to past history: A high scorer might have been reinforced for intellectual pursuits or might have gone to an excellent school. Perhaps a low score might be traced to exposure to toxins as a child (such as lead paint). In this section, we'll frame this classic *nature versus nurture* debate and consider the evidence relevant to each position. But first, we have a practical issue to consider: How stable is the IQ measure itself?

CRITICAL THINKING

Seniors are often said to possess wisdom. In what ways do you think the label "wise" differs from the label "intelligent"?

The Stability of IQ

One way to answer questions about the origins of intelligence is to ask whether IQ changes significantly over a lifetime. If intelligence is caused by something like a "fast brain," then we might expect intellectual ability to change very little over time until the brain deteriorates along with the rest of the body. Conversely, if intelligence is determined mainly by the environment, we would probably expect to find variation over time: IQ might rise and fall depending on recent experience or current environmental setting. Neither of these arguments is airtight, however. For instance, your environment might remain constant over time, or the genetic code might express itself differently at different ages. It might also be the case that IQ is determined by early experience and remains fixed after a certain point in development. Still, examination of the stability of the IQ measure is a reasonable place to start the search.

Pictured is intelligence researcher J. P. Das, working with a child at his clinic at the University of Alberta. Although tests are available to measure intelligence in small children, it's difficult to obtain reliable estimates of intelligence before age four (see Das, 2002).

When intelligence is measured in the standard way, through performance on a battery of tests, the stability of the measure depends on when the measuring process begins. Before the age of about three or four, it's difficult to get an accurate assessment of intellectual ability. Infants can't talk or show sustained attention, so conventional testing procedures can't be used. Investigators resort to indirect measures, such as recording whether babies choose to look at old or new pictures presented on a screen. Some evidence shows that babies who quickly "habituate," or lose interest, in response to repeated presentations of the same picture, and who prefer to look at novel pictures when they're shown, score higher on intelligence tests later in childhood (Bornstein, 1989; McCall & Carriger, 1993). But in general, it's widely believed that you can't get reliable assessments of IQ until somewhere between ages four and seven; from that point onward, IQ scores tend to predict performance on later IQ tests reasonably well (Honzik, Macfarlane, & Allen, 1948; Sameroff, Seifer, Baldwin, & Baldwin, 1993).

Longitudinal Studies   One of the best ways to measure the stability of IQ is through a longitudinal study, which involves testing the same people repeatedly as they age. The most widely known investigation of the stability of adult intelligence is the Seattle Longitudinal Study, which has examined mental test performance for approximately 5000 adults ranging in age from 25 to 88 (Schaie, 1983, 1989, 1993). The subjects have been tested in seven-year cycles, dating back to 1956, by using a battery of tests to assess such things as verbal fluency, inductive reasoning, and spatial ability. Schaie and his colleagues have found great stability in intellectual ability throughout adulthood. From age 21 to about age 60, there appears to be no serious decline in general intellectual ability, as measured through the test battery (see ▶ Figure 9.5 on page 366). After age 60, abilities begin to decline a bit, although the losses are not great. Large individual differences also exist—some people retain their performance well into their 80s, whereas others do not (Schaie, 1998).

It's difficult to interpret changes in IQ with age because many factors change concurrently with age. Older people are more likely to have physical problems, for example, that can affect performance. Declines in intelligence with age also depend on the type of intellectual ability measured. Earlier, we discussed the distinction between fluid intelligence, which taps basic processing skills, and crystallized intelligence, which taps acquired knowledge. The current thinking is that fluid

▶ **Figure 9.5**

The Stability of Intellectual Ability

Data from the Seattle Longitudinal Study show how performance changes on a variety of mental tasks between the ages of 25 and 88. Notice that average performance is remarkably stable up to about age 60, at which point some declines are seen. (Data from Schaie, 1983.)

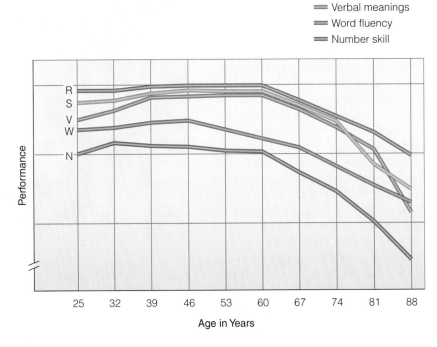

▬ Inductive reasoning
▬ Spatial orientation
▬ Verbal meanings
▬ Word fluency
▬ Number skill

CRITICAL   THINKING

Do you think it's possible to separate the relative contributions of nature and nurture to intelligence by studying animals in the laboratory?

intelligence declines with age—perhaps because the biology of the brain changes—whereas crystallized intelligence remains constant, or perhaps even increases, until late in adulthood (Horn, 1982; Kaufman & Horn, 1996; Schretlen et al., 2000). The brain may become a bit slower with age, but people continue to add knowledge and experiences that are invaluable in their efforts to solve the problems of everyday life.

Nature: The Genetic Argument

A number of pioneers in intelligence testing, including Galton, strongly believed that individual differences in mental ability are inherited. After all, Galton argued, it's easy to demonstrate that intellectual skill runs through family lines. (Remember: His cousin was Charles Darwin; in addition, his grandfather was another famous evolutionist, Erasmus Darwin.) But family-tree arguments do not lead to firm conclusions. Environmental factors, such as social and educational opportunities, can explain why members of the same family might show similar skills. Growing up in a family that places value on intellectual pursuits determines to some extent what sort of behaviours will be rewarded in a child, or the particular type of role models that will be available. To capture this debate, Galton coined the phrase "nature versus nurture" (Galton, 1869, 1883).

To establish a genetic basis for a psychological or physical characteristic, it's necessary to control for the effects of the environment. In principle, if two people are raised in exactly the same environment and receive exactly the same experiences, we can attribute any reliable differences in IQ to inherited characteristics (i.e., *nature*). Because any nurturing effects of the environment are held constant, then any differences must be due to genetics. Alternatively, if two people are born with exactly the same genes but end up with quite different intelligence scores, it must be the environment, not genes, that is responsible (*nurture*). We can't do a true experiment to confirm these arguments, for obvious reasons, but we can look for natural comparisons that are relevant. As we discussed in Chapter 3, psychologists often study identical twins, who share nearly complete genetic overlap, to tease apart the nature and nurture components of mind and behaviour.

Twin Studies   In twin studies, researchers search for identical twins who have been raised together in the same household or who have been separated at birth through adoption (Bouchard & McGue, 1981; Bouchard, Lykken, McGue, Segal, & Tellegean, 1990). The effects of the environment are assumed to be similar for the twins raised together but quite different, at least on average, for twins raised apart. If intelligence comes primarily from genetic factors, we would expect identical twins to have very similar intelligence scores, regardless of the environments in which they have been raised. One way to measure similarity is by correlation. More specifically, we can attempt to predict the IQ of one twin when given knowledge about the IQ of the other.

If genes are entirely responsible for intelligence, we would expect to get a strong positive correlation between IQ scores for identical twins. We wouldn't necessarily expect it to be exactly +1.00 because of measurement error or other uncontrolled factors. In reviewing the research literature on this issue, Bouchard and McGue (1981) found strong evidence for the genetic position: The IQ scores of identical twins are indeed quite similar, irrespective of the environment in which the twins have been reared. As shown in ❱ Figure 9.6, the IQ scores for twins reared together showed an average correlation of 0.86; even when reared apart, the average correlation remained strongly positive at 0.72 (Bouchard & McGue, 1981).

Researchers who conduct twin studies are actually interested in many different comparisons. For instance, it's useful to compare intelligence scores for fraternal twins (who are genetically no more similar than normal siblings are) and among unrelated people who have been reared together or apart. In general, the impressive finding is that the closer the overlap in genes, the more similar the resulting IQs. Notice, for example, that the average correlation for adopted siblings who have been reared together (0.30) is much lower than the average correlation for identical twins reared apart (0.72). Thus, similarity in environmental history is not as strong a predictor of intelligence as similarity in genetic background.

Some kinds of abilities tend to run in families, such as musical ability in the Rankin family. It's difficult, though, to separate the influences of nature and nurture.

❱ **Figure 9.6**

Nature versus Nurture

The horizontal bars show the mean correlation coefficients for pairs of people with differing amounts of genetic overlap who have been reared in similar or different environments. For example, the top bar shows the average correlation for identical twins who have been reared together in the same environment. The bottom bar shows the correlation coefficient for adopted siblings reared together. Higher correlations mean that the measured IQ scores are more similar. (Data from Bouchard & McGue, 1981.)

Type of Relationship

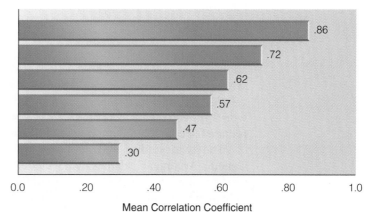

*One or both of the siblings were adopted.

Adoption Studies   Adopted children have two sets of parents: The biological parents have a genetic impact on the child's IQ and the adopting parents have an environmental effect. Whom will the child most resemble? Studies show that the child's IQ is correlated with the IQs of both sets of parents; however, the correlation with the biological parents is higher and it increases with time (Plomin, Fulker, Corley, & DeFries, 1997). Together, the twin data and the adoption data suggest that genetic background plays an important role in intelligence, at least when intelligence is measured through conventional IQ testing.

Heritability   Intelligence researchers often use a concept called heritability to describe the influence of genetic factors on intelligence. **Heritability** is a mathematical formula that indicates the extent to which IQ differences within a population can be accounted for by genetic factors. For any group with differences in IQ scores, heritability measures the role that genetic factors play in producing these differences. Its value is expressed as a percentage, so if the heritability of intelligence were 100%, that would mean that all differences in measured IQ could be explained by genetics. Most estimates of the heritability of intelligence, derived from twin studies, hover at around 50%, which means that approximately half the differences in IQ have a genetic basis (Sternberg & Kaufman, 1998). Other researchers propose values that are higher, perhaps closer to 70% (Bouchard, Lykken, et al., 1990). There is some debate over the fact that heritability estimates are somewhat higher in twin studies than in adoption studies.

It's important to understand that estimates of heritability apply only to groups, not to individuals. A heritability estimate of 70% does not mean that 70% of someone's intelligence is due to his or her genetic blueprint. To see why, imagine two groups of people with the same genetic histories. Group A maintains rigid control of the environment—everyone is treated exactly the same. Group B allows the environment to vary. If IQ scores are influenced by the environment in any way, we would expect the heritability values to be quite different for the two groups, even though the groups' genetic backgrounds are identical. Because the environment is held constant in group A, all the variability in measured IQ will be due to genes. In group B, the heritability index will be lower because some of the differences in IQ will be due to environmental effects. Heritability tells us only that for a given group, a certain percentage of the differences in intelligence can be explained by genetic factors.

Nurture: The Environmental Argument

You may have noticed in Figure 9.6 that identical twins and siblings reared together have IQs that are more similar than do twins or siblings reared apart. This means that individual differences in intelligence cannot be explained completely through genetic background. The environment also plays an important role.

Most psychologists acknowledge that different learning experiences result in different performance on intellectual tasks. Zajonc (1983), for example, details how intellectual stimulation of a child accumulates over childhood to determine adult scores on IQ tests. Chapter 10 provides much more detail on this topic. There are significant economic differences between individuals even within ethnic groups. And these differences correspond well to differences in IQ scores. In other words, poverty may contribute to low scores: The most obvious reason is the reduced access to education among the poor.

The twin studies and adoption studies noted in the section "Nature: The Genetic Argument" also provide evidence for environmental influences on IQ scores. Although it may be lower than the genetic contribution, the environmental influence is significant and well established.

---

heritability

A mathematical index that represents the extent to which IQ differences in a particular population can be accounted for by genetic factors

Group Differences   Most intelligence researchers agree that different ethnic and socioeconomic groups score, on average, somewhat differently on intelligence tests, and these differences are relatively stable. At the same time, it's very important to understand that group differences are averages. The bell curves always overlap. So the average differences don't tell us anything about single individuals.

Still, the group differences are real and should be explained. How can we account for these differences? Some researchers have suggested that evolutionary and genetic factors are the most important factors in such IQ differences between ethnic and racial groups (e.g., Eysenck, 1991; Jensen, 1992; Rushton, 2000).

A consistent pattern of sex differences remains even in modern samples. Men tend to score higher on spatial ability and women higher on verbal ability (Benbow, Lubinski, Shea, & Eftekhari-Sanjani, 2000). The origin of such differences, however, remains controversial. For example, the difference in spatial ability might be traceable to sex differences in the brain or to the fact that boys more often play sports (Halpern, 2000; Kimura, 1999). In sum, the research literature is more certain about the existence of group differences than about their origins in nature or nurture.

Finally, generational differences in IQ scores are now becoming apparent. Average IQ scores have increased slightly every decade since the 1930s. This trend, known as the Flynn effect, has been documented world-wide but remains largely unexplained. Most psychologists are doubtful that biological changes are responsible given that the gene pool is unlikely to have changed uniformly in the positive direction across so many countries in so little time. Environmental explanations include better nutrition, better schooling, and increased availability of daycare and preschooling. Exposure to new technologies (e.g., radio, television, computers) may have promoted thinking processes to new levels every generation.

Whatever the reason, it has been necessary to renorm IQ tests to adjust for the fact that scores are rising. The average of each generation has to be reset to 100. Otherwise, current students would have to perform better than previous students to get the same IQ score. And more individuals would be classified as having mental retardation.

Jonathan Hayward/CP Picture Archive

Many psychologists suggest that cultural background plays an important role in the measurement of intelligence. The cultural background of this Innu family should be taken into account when assessing intelligence.

Economic Differences   Significant economic differences exist between racial and ethnic groups that make interpretation of intergroup IQ differences difficult. For example, Black and Aboriginal Canadians are more likely to live at or below the poverty level than are White Canadians. Poverty, of course, may lead to nutrition problems and difficulties in gaining proper health care, and may hurt a person's chances of entering adequate schools. Black and Aboriginal Canadians are also more likely to experience racial discrimination than are Whites. The impact of these factors on intelligence testing is not completely understood, although they may play an important role. Black, Aboriginal, and White Canadians also tend to live in somewhat different social worlds; consequently, it is difficult to disentangle the effects of the environment from any genetic differences that might contribute to group differences in intelligence.

Test Bias   Some indication exists that test biases might contribute to group differences in IQ scores (Bernal, 1984). Racial or ethnic group differences depend, to a certain extent, on the type of intelligence test that is administered (Brody,

CRITICAL THINKING

Do you think it's possible to eliminate cultural influences completely from a psychological test?

1992). Most traditional IQ tests of the type that we've discussed in this chapter are written, administered, and scored by White, middle-class psychologists, which raises the very real possibility that cultural biases might be contaminating some of the test questions. For example, if you are asked a question, such as "Who wrote *Faust*?" (which once appeared on a Wechsler test), your ability to answer correctly will depend partly on whether your culture places value on exposure to such information. In general, it is most likely that White students of European descent would have been exposed to the information necessary to answer such a question. Therefore, failure to answer it might not be a sign of lower intelligence, but rather of a culture that places a higher value on other types of information. Some observers have even argued that because of such problems, conventional intelligence tests have little validity with some populations, such as many Aboriginal groups, and should not be used (Darou, 1992; Kleinfeld & Nelson, 1991).

Psychologists have worked hard to remove bias from standard intelligence and achievement tests (Raven, Court, & Raven, 1985); in some cases, the development of **culture-fair tests** has reduced racial differences in measured ability. However, significant group differences usually remain even after culture-bound questions have been altered or removed. In sum, bias is recognized as a contributor to measured intelligence, although it's unlikely to be the sole determinant of group differences in IQ (Cole, 1981; Kaplan, 1985).

Adoption Studies   A more direct test of environmental explanations of racial or ethnic differences comes from studies looking at the IQs of Black children who have been reared in White homes. If the average Black childhood experience puts children at a disadvantage (for whatever reason) on tests of intelligence, then Black children raised in White, middle-class homes should be expected to produce higher IQ scores. In general, this assumption is supported by the data. Scarr and Weinberg (1976) investigated interracial adoptions in Minnesota and found that the average IQ for Black children reared in economically advantaged White households was significantly higher than the national Black mean score. This finding was confirmed again in later follow-up studies (Waldman, Weinberg, & Scarr, 1994; Weinberg, Scarr, & Waldman, 1992). You should not conclude from this finding that White, middle-class households are better in every way. The results simply imply that certain cultural experiences give an advantage on the IQ tests currently being used to assess intelligence.

The Interaction of Nature and Nurture

So what are we to conclude about the relative contributions of genetics and the environment to intelligence? Nature-nurture issues are notoriously difficult to resolve, and this is especially true in the politically sensitive area of intelligence. It's extremely difficult to control for the effects of either the environment or genetics. Consider the twin studies—how reasonable is it to assume that twins who have been reared apart have had unrelated environmental experiences? Are children who are adopted really representative of the racial or ethnic populations from which they have been drawn? It's difficult to answer questions like these, because neither the environment nor genetic structure can be manipulated directly in the laboratory (at least for humans).

The most reasonable position to take today is that your intelligence, like many other psychological attributes, is determined by a mixture of genes and environment. The genes that you inherit from your parents place upper and lower bounds on intellectual ability (sometimes called a reaction range). Genes may importantly determine how your brain is wired and, possibly, the speed of neural transmission, but the expression of your genetic material is strongly influenced by the environment.

---

culture-fair test

Tests that avoid the use of language (e.g., by using only pictures or symbols) so that the test is fair to all cultures

CRITICAL   THINKING

Genetic and environmental theories are both scientific in origin. Then why is it that different people—even scientists—tend to have an emotional preference for one approach or the other?

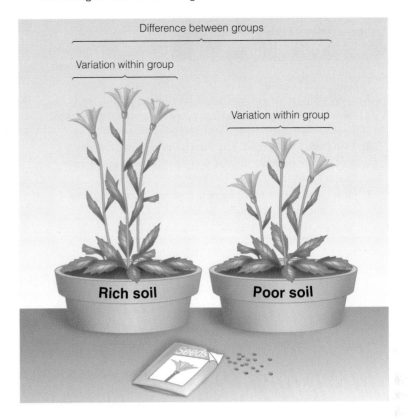

▶ **Figure 9.7**

Between- and within-Group Variation

In the plant analogy, all the variation in plant height within a pot is due to genetics, but the overall height difference between the two pots is attributable to the environment (rich soil versus poor soil).

Recall from Chapter 3 that geneticists use the term *genotype* to refer to the genetic message itself and *phenotype* to refer to the observable characteristics that actually result from genetic expression. An analogy that is sometimes used by intelligence researchers compares the development of intelligence to the nurturing of flowering plants (Lewontin, 1976). Imagine that we have a packet of virtually identical seeds and we toss half into a pot containing fertile soil and half into a pot of barren soil (see ▶ Figure 9.7). The seeds tossed into the poor soil will undoubtedly grow, but their growth will be stunted relative to that of the group planted in the rich soil. Because these are virtually identical groups of seeds, containing similar distributions of genetic information, any differences in growth between the pots are due entirely to the environment (the soil). So, too, with intelligence—two people can be born with similar genetic potential, but the degree to which their intellectual potential "blossoms" depends critically on the environment.

Consider as well that within each handful of seeds there will be variations in genetic information. Some plants will grow larger than others will, regardless of the soil into which they have been thrown. A similar kind of result would be expected for intelligence—variations in the genetic message will produce individual differences in IQ that cannot be adequately explained by environmental variables. In fact, after analyzing the differences within a pot, we might conclude that all the differences are due to inherited factors. But even if the differences within a group are due to genes, the differences between groups would still be due to the environment (fertile or barren soil). This kind of insight might help account, in part, for the racial or ethnic differences in IQ that we discussed earlier. Even though genes may exert a strong influence within a population, between-population differences could still be determined primarily by the environment (Eysenck & Kamin, 1981; Lewontin, 1976).

One other feature of the interaction between nature and nurture is worth noting. Environmental experiences do not occur independently of inherited factors. It's a two-way street. The environment will partly determine how genetic information is expressed, but so too will genetic information determine experience. If you're born with "smart" genes, then early on you're likely to be exposed to opportunities that will help you realize your full intellectual potential; conversely, if you're born "slow," the environment is likely to shape you away from intellectually nurturing experiences (see ▶ Figure 9.8). Even in the domain of intelligence, the rich tend to get richer.

▶ **Figure 9.8**

Reaction Range

Each person may have genes that set limits for intellectual potential, sometimes called a reaction range. In this case, Tom inherited a capacity for obtaining an IQ anywhere between 80 and about 112. The IQ that Tom actually obtains (shown as the dark bar) is determined by the kind of environment in which he is reared. Notice that Miguel inherited a greater IQ potential than Tom, but if Tom is raised in an enriched environment, his IQ may actually turn out to be higher than Miguel's.

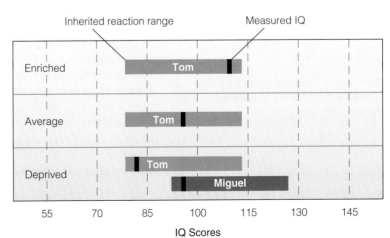

Quality of Environment for Realizing Intellectual Potential

Test Yourself 9.3

1. Longitudinal studies of intelligence reveal that fluid, but not crystallized, intelligence remains largely constant across the life span. *True or False?*

2. Twin studies have shown that fraternal twins raised together tend to have more similar IQs than identical twins raised apart. *True or False?*

3. Most psychologists now believe that genetic factors definitely play a role in intelligence. *True or False?*

4. A heritability estimate of 70% means that 70% of someone's intelligence is due to his or her genetic blueprint. *True or False?*

5. Test bias is recognized as a contributor to measured intelligence, but it's unlikely to be the sole determinant of group differences in IQ. *True or False?*

▶ Perceptions of Intelligence

LEARNING GOALS

1. Understand the common tendency to judge people's intelligence.
2. Recognize the potential abuses in applying the concept.

At the beginning of the chapter, we noted that the concept of intelligence looms large in people's lives. Its high value in society leads people to have strong opinions about who deserves the label and who does not. Of course, we all believe that we deserve the label: Everyone believes that they are above average in intelligence (Beauregard & Dunning, 1998). However, we do not extend that generosity to other people. Indeed, "stupid" and "idiot" are common terms in some people's daily descriptions of others. Here we discuss our natural human tendency to judge other people's intelligence.

Judging Intelligence

Several times in an average day, we find ourselves commenting on people's intelligence: "Man, he's smart" or "What an idiot!" Typical situations include when a classmate makes a comment in class or when a politician makes a controversial remark. We tend to attribute high intelligence to those who talk fast (Amabile, 1983), those with a confident voice (Reynolds & Gifford, 2001), those who criticize others, and those who wear glasses (Beech & Whittaker, 2001; Kellerman & Laird, 1982). But these cues have little validity. We also make complex judgments based on people's accents. In Canada, for example, we tend to make biased judgments against those with "Newfie" accents (Edwards, 1999). Conversely, when we use cues, such as confident voice and careful speech, we are accurate (Borkenau & Liebler, 1995). According to Sternberg (1988b), our overall judgment of a person will correspond to the proportion of apparent matches between an individual's characteristics and our **intelligence prototype,** that is, our list of the characteristics of (what we think constitutes) a perfectly intelligent person. Personal prototypes differ from person to person and from situation to situation (we use different prototypes at school versus in the business world).

But how accurate are people in judging intelligence? When IQ scores are used as the criterion, the correlation with rated intelligence is roughly 0.30 (Paulhus, Lysy, & Yik, 1998). Does it matter who does the rating? Research shows that your friends are more accurate than strangers and just as accurate as you are in judging your intelligence. But those with lower ability are also blissfully unaware of their competence (Dunning, 2005). Despite this rather mediocre success in judging intelligence, we indulge in such attributions several times a day without ever being proven wrong. Unfortunately such decisions

intelligence prototype

The characteristics each person believes are present in the perfectly intelligent person influence our lives and those of others without recourse (Kunda & Thagard, 1996). For each time that we are evaluated by a standard test, our intelligence is evaluated a thousand times by those who meet us.

Ordinary people also differ in their general style of judging people's intelligence. Carol Dweck and her colleagues at Columbia University make the distinction between people who see intelligence as fixed (**entity theorists**) and people who see intelligence as malleable (**incremental theorists**). Entity theorists believe that intelligence is a permanent quality that people are born with. Incremental theorists believe that people gradually acquire intelligence through hard work. According to Dweck, it is more adaptive to be an incremental theorist, especially when judging oneself (Dweck, 1999; Dweck, Chiu, & Hong, 1995). Recent evidence suggests that Asian students tend to be incremental whereas European-heritage students tend to be entity theorists (Tweed & Lehman, 2003).

entity theorists

People who see intelligence as fixed, a permanent quality that people are born with

incremental theorists

People who see intelligence as malleable and something that people gradually acquire through hard work

The Potential for Abuse

Because of our strong tendency to judge others—accurately or not—intelligence testing has the potential for abuse. As noted earlier in the chapter, the high value placed on having intelligence and the correspondingly strong emotional reaction to being labelled as unintelligent pose a number of dangers. As with any form of psychological assessment, wrong conclusions might be drawn but the consequences of those conclusions can be more serious with intelligence testing. The pronouncements of an authority figure, such as a teacher or psychologist, are taken much more seriously than a schoolyard insult.

Consider the potentially serious problem of labelling. Once a child takes an IQ test, his or her performance becomes part of a continuing academic record. A label tends to be applied—you're smart, you're below average, and so on. As a result, your expectations of yourself are altered accordingly. Expectations are also altered in those who have access to your score. Some studies have suggested that intelligence-related labels influence how teachers interact with their students in the classroom. The kids with the "smart" label are exposed to more educational opportunities and are treated with more respect (Oakes, 1985; Rosenthal & Jacobson, 1968). More recent research suggests that such effects are detectable but rather weak (Jussim, 1989). Overall, the effects may be weak because not all teachers react the same way: The most diligent and nurturant teachers might actually increase their assistance once a student is labelled as less able.

Labelling effects were serious in the early decades of the twentieth century, when intelligence tests were in their formative stages of development. Tests were widely administered to newly arriving immigrants and all army recruits well before the impact of cultural and educational factors on test performance was widely understood by test administrators. As noted earlier, people can perform poorly on an intelligence test because the test has certain built-in biases with respect to language and cultural lifestyle.

The result was that certain population groups, such as immigrants from southern and eastern Europe, generally performed poorly on these tests. Some psychologists even went so far as to label these immigrant groups as "feeble minded" or "defective" based on their test performance. One result was that immigration laws enacted in the 1920s in the United States discriminated against poorly performing groups. For many years, several Canadian provinces permitted forced sterilization of individuals who performed very poorly on intelligence tests. In modern times, psychologists are more aware of test bias, but its impact on test performance remains controversial to this day.

To be fair, any critique of intelligence tests should answer the question "compared with what?" It is unlikely that society will stop evaluating people—the only question is how they will make the evaluations. Aptitude and intelligence tests were designed to counter the biases inherent in previous methods of evaluating people (e.g., interviews and letters of recommendation). Compared with the alternatives, intelligence tests seem rather unbiased. Of course, the optimal assessment approach would take advantage of a variety of information sources to minimize the effects of any one bias. Whether we use standard IQ tests, people's intelligence will continue to be evaluated in both job situations and everyday interactions.

Test Yourself 9.4

Check your knowledge about perceptions of intelligence by deciding whether each of the following statements is true or false. (You will find the answers in Appendix B.)

1. People show a general tendency to believe that others are above average in intelligence. *True or False?*
2. Our perceptions about others' intelligence are totally inaccurate. *True or False?*
3. Entity theorists believe that intelligence is malleable. *True or False?*

4. Labelling people as intelligent or unintelligent can affect how we treat them. *True or False?*
5. IQ test scores have been used unfairly to mistreat whole groups of people. *True or False?*

Intelligence

R E V I E W

Our analysis of the concept of intelligence has confirmed its adaptive significance in the life of human beings. True, the nutcracker bird, in its successful search for a cache of seeds, fits the adaptive view of intelligence just as well as the humans who build cities. But the ecological niche of the human species is so sweeping and powerful that our mental abilities allow us to control (or destroy) our ecosystem in ways that other species cannot.

Within our species, we seem to automatically judge and then exaggerate relatively small differences—despite the looseness in people's definitions. The intense human need to evaluate each other's intelligence has motivated a vast scientific literature. The concept seems necessary to explain individual differences in life success, especially scholastic achievement. Everyone seems to agree that people differ in intelligence and that objective tests are more useful—both scientifically and practically—than are subjective judgments. Yet the long-standing attempts to create objective

intelligence tests continue to raise scientific and practical problems that both challenge and excite researchers interested in intelligence. This chapter was organized around four of these problems.

First, how should intelligence be conceptualized? The attempts of researchers and everyday people to conceptualize intelligence have yielded a long list of methods. Proponents of the psychometric approach try to understand the concept by analyzing performance on a battery of mental tests. They traditionally debate distinctions between a general factor of intelligence, *g*, which applies broadly, and distinct sets of abilities. Cognitive approaches to intelligence seek to discover the internal processes that account for intelligent behaviour. Some evidence suggests that performance on traditional tests of mental ability might be traced to an individual's cognitive processing speed and a good working memory.

Recently, a strong resistance to psychometric and behavioural

definitions of intelligence has developed. Like the nutcracker bird, isn't everyone intelligent in their own way? Multiple intelligence approaches, such as Howard Gardner's and Robert Sternberg's, have recommended ways in which the concept of intelligence should be dramatically expanded. Fortunately, with nine types of intelligence, we all stand a much better chance of scoring high. As a practical device, however, the scientific evidence does not (yet) support this subdivision of mental abilities.

Second, how can we measure intelligence in an objective fashion? To diagnose individuals and be able to conduct research on intelligence, we needed a numerical index of mental performance. This need has been met—for more than 100 years now—by IQ test scores.

Popular measures, such as the Stanford-Binet and the SAT, are reliable tests that can predict important life outcomes. Nonetheless, debates continue about the construct validity of intelligence itself.

Third, what are the origins of intelligence? The variation that we see in measured intelligence can be explained in two primary ways: genetics and the environment. Twin and adoption studies provide convincing evidence that at least some proportion of mental ability is inherited and some is environmental in origin. Therefore, part of the scientific problem has been solved. The details of what genes and what experiences interact with one another is far from solved.

Fourth, how accurate are we in judging intelligence? We learned that, with regard to our own intelligence, we are interested in looking good as well as in being accurate. Perhaps that bias is adaptive because it keeps up our spirits and encourages us to continue our efforts. So the accuracy of our self-judgments is a tradeoff between two adaptive tendencies: being realistic and staying confident.

Judgments of others' intelligence are not hampered by that bias, but they are hampered by the fact that we have less information about others than about ourselves. Therefore, overall, judgments of ourselves and others are comparable in validity. Nonetheless, the fact that we automatically judge others and are overconfident about it can cause harm to society.

CHAPTER SUMMARY

▶ Conceptualizing Intelligence

The Psychometric Approach: Measuring the Mind

The *psychometric approach* proposes that intelligence is a mental capacity that can be understood by analyzing performance on mental tests. Galton and Spearman are two pioneers of this approach. Spearman used *factor analysis* to analyze the relationships among subtest scores and isolate the "factors" that account for test performance. Spearman proposed that intelligence tests measure *g*, or general intelligence, plus a residual, *s*, for each subtest included. Later models have emphasized more than one kind of ability, as in *hierarchical models*. Cattell proposed that general intelligence comprises two abilities: *fluid intelligence* (ability to solve problems and reason) and *crystallized intelligence* (acquired knowledge).

The Cognitive Approach

The cognitive approach argues that intelligence can be understood by analyzing internal mental processes. Such analyses include measuring the speed of mental processing and the specific mental components that produce intelligent thought. Research supports the notion that intelligence reflects faster neural processing and a larger working memory.

Expanded Conceptions of Intelligence

Gardner has proposed that traditional views of intelligence should be broadened to include special abilities or talents and that *multiple intelligences* exist. By using a case study approach, Gardner has identified nine kinds of intelligence: *musical, bodily-kinesthetic, logical-mathematical, linguistic, spatial, interpersonal, intrapersonal, naturalist,* and *spiritual*. The psychometric and cognitive approaches focus on logical-mathematical, linguistic, and spatial intelligence. Many of Gardner's intelligences match those found by Paulhus and his colleagues when they collected ordinary people's nominations of *intelligent exemplars*.

In contrast, Sternberg's conceptualization of intelligence includes three facets: *Analytic intelligence* refers to a person's basic ability to process information; *creative intelligence* expresses how well people are able to cope with new or novel tasks; *practical intelligence* taps how well people fit into their environments.

▶ Measuring Individual Differences

Regardless of how psychologists conceptualize intelligence, an important practical consideration is how to measure intelligence. Accurate measurement of abilities through the use of psychological tests allows for the tailoring of people's activities to fit their skills. *Achievement tests* measure someone's current level of knowledge in a particular topic; *aptitude tests* measure the ability to learn in a particular area.

The Characteristics of a Good Test

Three characteristics are needed for a good test. *Reliability* is a measure of the consistency of a test. *Test-retest reliability* is calculated by comparing test scores across repeated administrations. *Validity* tells us whether a test measures what it is supposed to measure. *Content validity* measures the degree to which the content of the test samples broadly across the domain of interest. *Predictive validity* measures the degree to which the test predicts a particular outcome. *Construct validity* measures how well a test captures the whole theme or construct. *Standardization* means that the testing, scoring, and interpretation procedures are similar across all administrations of the test.

IQ: The Intelligence Quotient

The *IQ*, or *intelligence quotient*, dates back to Binet and Simon, who were commissioned to develop a test to identify children who might have trouble in school. Their goal was to determine a child's *mental age*, which is typically calculated by comparing a child's test score with the average score for different age groups. The IQ was originally calculated by the *ratio method*—dividing mental age by chronological age and multiplying by 100. Now it is specified in terms of a *deviation IQ*, in which a person's IQ is calculated by determining where his or her test score sits relative to the average score.

Extremes of Intelligence

A score of 70 or below on a standard IQ test (along with some other factors) is likely to lead to a diagnosis of *mental retardation*. Numerous factors, both genetic and environmental, may cause mental retardation. *Giftedness* is seen in individuals with IQs at or above 130. Terman's longitudinal study of gifted children showed that these kids were likely to achieve later success and were stable emotionally and socially adept, contrary to the bookworm stereotype. *Savants* exhibit characteristics of both giftedness and retardation.

The Validity of Popular Intelligence Tests

Scores on traditional IQ tests correlate well with school grades. Critics of IQ tests argue that they fail to provide a broad index of intelligence. Also, a particular IQ "label" influences how teachers interact with students. These labelling effects were particularly serious in the early twentieth century, when many immigrants were given intelligence tests and labelled as feeble-minded or defective.

Other Individual Differences Related to Intelligence

Creativity refers to the ability to generate ideas that are original and novel and is an important component of broad conceptualizations of intelligence. *Emotional intelligence* is the ability to perceive, understand, and express emotion. According to some, it is also an important component of intelligence.

▶ Discovering the Sources of Intelligence: The Nature-Nurture Issue

Does intelligent behaviour come primarily from genetic background or from life experience? The study of intelligence serves as an investigation into the plasticity of the mind.

The Stability of IQ

The Seattle Longitudinal Study of Adult Intelligence found great stability in intellectual ability throughout adulthood. Current thinking is that *fluid intelligence* (which taps basic reasoning skills) may decline with age, whereas *crystallized intelligence* (which taps acquired knowledge) remains constant and perhaps even increases.

Nature: The Genetic Argument

Twin studies are one method for addressing the role of heredity in intelligence. The IQ scores of identical twins are quite similar, irrespective of environment. Similarity of genetic background is a stronger predictor of intelligence than is similarity of environment. *Heritability* is a mathematical index that tells a researcher the extent to which IQ differences within a population can be accounted for by genetic factors; estimates of heritability apply to groups, not individuals. Estimates of the heritability of intelligence range from 0.50 to 0.70.

Nurture: The Environmental Argument

Individual differences in intelligence cannot be explained completely through genetic background. Most intelligence researchers agree that stable differences exist in IQ across racial, ethnic, and socioeconomic groups. These differences, however, reflect average *group* differences. Possible sources of these differences could be economic factors and test bias. Adoption studies have supported the role of the environment in explaining group differences.

The Interaction of Nature and Nurture

Intelligence is determined by a mixture of genes and environment. Genes place lower and upper bounds on intellectual ability, but the expression of genetic material is strongly influenced by the environment. The *genotype* is the genetic message itself, and the *phenotype* is the observable characteristic that results from the genetic expression. Genetic expression depends critically on the environment, and genetic background affects how a person interacts with the environment.

▶ Perceptions of Intelligence

The importance of the dimension of intelligence guarantees that people frequently judge each other. People have strong reactions to such judgments likely because the consequences can be substantial.

Judging Intelligence

On a daily basis, we tend to judge other people's intelligence by using a variety of cues—some valid and some invalid. Our accuracy is modest at best, but that doesn't stop us. Our judgments may be automatic. People also differ in their tendency to perceive intelligence as fixed or malleable.

The Potential for Abuse

Because we judge other people so readily on this important dimension, the consequences of an official declaration of mental incompetence can be devastating. Being labelled as unintelligent can have continuing negative effects on self-esteem and motivation. Low scores obtained by minority group members are sometimes used to justify mistreatment.

Terms to Remember

intelligence, 344
subjective definition, 344
objective test, 344

Conceptualizing Intelligence
psychometrics, 346
factor analysis, 347
g (general) factor, 347
s (specific) residual, 347
primary mental abilities, 347
fluid intelligence, 348
crystallized intelligence, 349
artificial intelligence, 350
multiple intelligences, 350
Sternberg's three facets of intelligence, 352

Measuring Individual Differences
achievement motivation tests, 354
achievement tests, 354
aptitude tests, 354
intelligence tests, 354
reliability, 354
test-retest reliability, 355

split-half reliability, 355
validity, 355
standardization, 356
IQ (intelligence quotient), 357
mental age, 357
deviation IQ, 358
bell curve, 358
mental retardation, 359
gifted, 359
savant, 360
tacit knowledge, 361
creativity, 363
emotional intelligence, 363

Discovering the Sources of Intelligence: The Nature-Nurture Issue
heritability, 368
culture-fair test, 370

Perceptions of Intelligence
intelligence prototype, 372
entity theorists, 373
incremental theorists, 373

Recommended Readings

Bar-On, R., & Parker, J. D. A. (Eds.). (2000). *The handbook of emotional intelligence.* New York: John Wiley/Jossey-Bass. If the idea of emotional intelligence intrigues you, this volume will provide you with a comprehensive review of contemporary research and applications. The book was edited by the scholar who coined the term "EQ" (emotional quotient), Reuven Bar-On, and James Parker, who conducts research on emotions and emotional intelligence at Trent University.

Gardner, H. (2004). *Frames of mind: The theory of multiple intelligences* (20th anniversary ed.). New York: Basic Books. A very readable introduction to Gardner's theory of multiple intelligences.

Sternberg, R. J. (1999). *Thinking styles.* New York: Cambridge University Press. A very readable book, written by a leading intelligence researcher, that explains how aptitude tests, school grades, and classroom performance often fail to identify real ability because of differences in thinking styles.

 For additional readings, explore InfoTrac® College Edition, your online library. Go to http://www.adaptivemind3e.nelson.com.

Hint: Enter these search terms: intelligence tests; general intelligence; mental retardation; giftedness; psychometrics; nature, nurture, and intelligence.

Media Resources

🌐 What's on the Web?

Please note that Web addresses are subject to change. Check out the accompanying website for updates: http://www.adaptivemind3e.nelson.com.

This site presents practice quiz questions, hypercontent, information on degrees and careers in psychology, study tips, and more.

Mensa Canada

http://www.canada.mensa.org

Mensa is an organization for people who score in the top 2% on standardized intelligence tests (on the WAIS, that would be over 130). This page explains what the organization is about and how to apply to join, and has links to puzzles and tests.

J. P. Das Developmental Disabilities Centre

http://www.ualberta.ca/~jpdasddc/INDEX.html

Located at the University of Alberta, this centre acts as a research, training, informational, and clinical service for people with disabilities, including intellectual impairments. Includes links to resources for people with disabilities and related problems.

Great Thinkers and Visionaries

http://www.lucifer.com/~sasha/thinkers.html

This website reviews the concept of genius and looks at examples of extremely high intelligence. Detailed histories of geniuses, such as Einstein, Goethe, and Marie Curie, are reviewed in detail.

Online IQ Tests

http://www.geocities.com/CapitolHill/1641/iq.html

http://www.iqtest.com

People have a fascination with intelligence testing. As you were reading the material in the chapter, you may have been thinking, "I wonder what my IQ is." These sites purport to help you find out. (But beware! Consider the standardization, reliability, and validity of these tests.) You'll even find tests of your emotional IQ, "political IQ," and "jewellery IQ."

Upstream: **Issues: Psychology: Intelligence and IQ**

http://www.psych.utoronto.ca/~reingold/courses/intelligence/cache/index.html

The book *The Bell Curve* helped to re-ignite the controversies that surround intelligence testing, such as the validity of scores, group differences, and the sources of intelligence. This site provides a wealth of links to the writings of prominent figures in the debate, such as Arthur Jensen and Stephen Jay Gould. The Upstream site also has general information on the controversial book as well as reviews and analyses.

ThomsonNOW™ ThomsonNOW

http://hed.nelson.com

Go to this site for the link to ThomsonNOW™, your one-stop study shop. Take a Pretest for this chapter and ThomsonNOW™ will generate a personalized Study Plan based on your test results. The Study Plan will identify the topics you need to review and direct you to online resources to help you master those topics. You can then take a Posttest to determine what concepts you have mastered and what you still need work on.

Psyk.trek 3.0

Check out Psyk.trek 3.0 for further study of the concepts in this chapter. Psyk.trek's 65 interactive learning modules, simulations, and quizzes offer additional opportunities for you to interact with, reflect on, and retain the material:

Cognition and Intelligence: Understanding IQ Scores
Cognition and Intelligence: Key Concepts in Testing
Cognition and Intelligence: Heredity, Environment, and Intelligence

What creature walks in the morning on four feet, at noon upon two, and in the evening upon three?

—Sophocles, *The Riddle of the Sphinx*

Human Development

T he famous saying "The apple doesn't fall far from the tree" is a literary way of pointing out that children tend to resemble their parents. As detailed in Chapters 9 and 12, the reasons for adult differences in intelligence and personality are often debated by using the phrase "nature versus nurture." By now, you should recognize that the origins of behaviour and knowledge rarely lie exclusively in either nature or nurture but most often in the interaction between them.

Here in Chapter 10, we track the path to adulthood in detail. You will read about the process of how nature interacts with nurture to determine physical, intellectual, and social characteristics.

Let us define human **development** as the age-related physical, intellectual, and social changes that occur throughout an individual's lifetime. The incredible change from the newborn through the adolescent, adult, and elderly human being is one of nature's most wondrous spectacles. How does it happen? Theories of modern *developmental psychologists*—those who study the developmental process—inevitably allude to the concept of *interaction*. This interactive notion first became prominent with Freud's theories but is now key to most developmental approaches. Different theories suggest different ways in which social, cultural, and biological forces affect one another during development.

> **development**
>
> The age-related physical, intellectual, social, and personal changes that occur throughout an individual's lifetime

As you saw in Chapter 3, messages emerge automatically from the infant's genetic makeup to direct the body to change over time, but the environment modifies how those messages are realized. Thus, the idea of interaction goes beyond realizing that both heredity and the environment contribute to development: It means that you can't understand one without the other. Instead, development is better seen as a series of adjustments that occur throughout the life span: From conception to death, the developmental process continues.

We might pose the blunter question "why do humans develop?" One straightforward reason is that a mother's womb has no room for a full-sized adult—nature is forced to start small. At the same time, however, extending the process of human development over time enables us to fine-tune our physical, intellectual, and social capabilities to better adapt to the demands of varied environments.

Human Development

P R E V I E W

Nature has built a considerable degree of flexibility or plasticity into the developmental process. This flexibility permits exceptional adaptation to environmental circumstances (Kolb, 1999). This chapter focuses on three main problems that face the developing human child (see ▶ Figure 10.1).

First, how do we go from fertilized eggs to fully functioning adults, capable of producing our own offspring? Although the environment helps shape the process of growth, most physical changes in our species are regular and predictable. In general, the timing of development is a product of evolutionary history and reflects the problems of survival that the human species has been required to solve.

Second, how do we develop the intellectual tools needed to solve survival problems? The developmental changes that occur in how people think—what is called cognitive development—have been studied extensively by psychologists. Intellectually, the newborn is not simply a miniature adult or simply an adult with less world knowledge. You'll discover that infants see and think about the world quite differently from adults.

Third, how do we form the social relationships and sense of personal identity needed for personal protection, nourishment, and continuation of the species? Humans are social animals. They are continually interacting with each other, and these relationships help people adapt successfully to their environments. In this section, we'll consider the milestones of social development, beginning with the formation of attachments to parents and caregivers and ending with a discussion of how relationships change in middle and late adulthood.

▶ Figure 10.1

Adaptive Problems of Development

Humans face three main developmental problems: developing physically, intellectually, and socially.

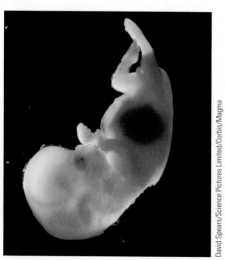

David Spears/Science Pictures Limited/Corbis/Magma

Corbis Royalty Free/Magma

Corbis Royalty Free

▶ Developing Physically

LEARNING GOALS

1. Understand the physical changes that occur during prenatal development.
2. Learn about growth from infancy through adolescence.
3. Be able to explain adulthood and the aging body and brain.

To a child, it seems to take forever to grow up. In fact, humans do take a relatively long time to reach full physical maturity, compared with other species. At birth, for example, the brain of a chimpanzee is at about 60% of its final weight, whereas the brain of a human newborn is only at about 25% of its ultimate weight (Corballis, 1991; Lenneberg, 1967). Humans do a lot of developing outside the womb. Still, the main components of the body—the nervous system, the networks of glands, and so on—develop at an astonishingly rapid rate after conception.

Guided by the genetic code and influenced by the release of hormones by the endocrine system, individuals in the early years change physically at rates that will never again be matched in their lifetimes. To place the growth rate in some perspective, it's been estimated that if children continued to develop at the rate they show in the first two years of life, adults would end up being more than three metres tall and weighing several thousand kilograms! Fortunately, things slow down considerably after the first few years of life; but they never completely stop—we continue to change physically until the very moment of death.

The Stages of Prenatal Development

The human developmental process begins with the union of egg and sperm at conception. Within the fertilized egg, or **zygote,** the 23 chromosomes from the father and the 23 chromosomes from the mother pair up to form the master genetic blueprint. Over the next 266 days or so (approximately nine months), the organism undergoes a steady and quite remarkable transformation. It begins as a single cell and ends as an approximately three-kilogram newborn composed of literally billions of cells. The period of development that occurs *before* birth is called prenatal development and is divided into three main stages: *germinal, embryonic,* and *fetal.*

The **germinal period** lasts approximately two weeks, from conception to the time when the zygote migrates from the mother's fallopian tubes to implant itself on the wall of the uterus (often called the womb). The **embryonic period** lasts for about six weeks: from implantation to the eighth week after fertilization. In this period, arms, legs, fingers, toes, and a distinctly beating heart appear, and the embryo starts to develop the sexual characteristics of either a male or a female (see ▶ Figure 10.2).

At the ninth week of prenatal development, the **fetal period** begins and continues until birth. Early in this period, the bones and muscles of what is now called the *fetus* start

zygote

The fertilized human egg, containing 23 chromosomes from the father and 23 chromosomes from the mother, which pair up to form the master genetic blueprint

germinal period

The period in prenatal development from conception to implantation of the fertilized egg in the wall of the uterus

embryonic period

The period of prenatal development lasting from implantation to the end of the eighth week; during this period, the human develops from an unrecognizable mass of cells to a somewhat familiar creature

fetal period

The period of prenatal development lasting from the ninth week until birth, during which the fetus develops functioning organ systems, and increases are seen in body size and in the size and complexity of brain tissue

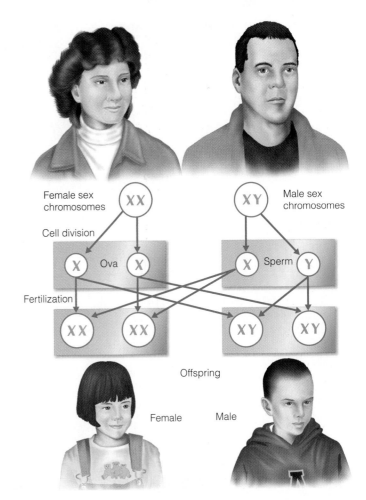

Female sex chromosomes · Male sex chromosomes
Cell division
Ova · Sperm
Fertilization
Offspring
Female · Male

▶ Figure 10.2

Genetic Determinants of Gender

If the father contributes an X chromosome, the child will be a girl; if he contributes a Y chromosome, the child will be a boy.

teratogens

Environmental agents—such as disease, organisms, or drugs—that can potentially damage the developing embryo or fetus

▶ **Figure 10.3**

Critical Periods of Susceptibility during Prenatal Development

Specific organs and body parts are at greatest risk from teratogens during certain critical periods of prenatal development. The light part of each bar signifies the period of greatest susceptibility. (Adapted from *Life-Span Human Development,* Second Edition, by Sigelman/Shaffer. Copyright © 1995. Reprinted with permission of Wadsworth, a division of Thomson Learning: http://www. thomsonrights.com. Fax: 800 730-2215.)

to develop. By the end of the third month, the skeletal and muscular systems allow for extensive movement—even somersaults—although the fetus at this point is still only about seven centimetres (Apgar & Beck, 1974). The final three months of prenatal development are marked by extremely rapid growth, both in body size and in the size and complexity of brain tissue.

Environmental Hazards   Although the developing child is snugly tucked away within the mother's womb, it is by no means completely isolated from the effects of the environment. The mother's physical health, as well as exposure to toxins, can seriously affect the developing child. Mother and child are linked physically, so if the mother gets sick, smokes, drinks, or takes drugs, the effects can transfer to the fetus or embryo. Some psychologists believe that the mother's psychological state, such as her level of anxiety during pregnancy, can exert an effect and may even influence the personality of the child (Dawson, Ashman, & Carver, 2000; Oldani, 1997).

Environmental agents that can potentially damage the developing child are called **teratogens.** The developing fetus or embryo is generally most susceptible to teratogens during its initial formation. For example, if the mother contracts German measles (rubella) during the first six weeks of pregnancy, the child is at risk for developing heart defects because it is during this period that the structures of the heart are formed. ▶ Figure 10.3 shows the periods of greatest susceptibility— called critical periods—for various structures in the body. The embryonic period is the point of greatest susceptibility, although the central nervous system can be affected throughout prenatal development.

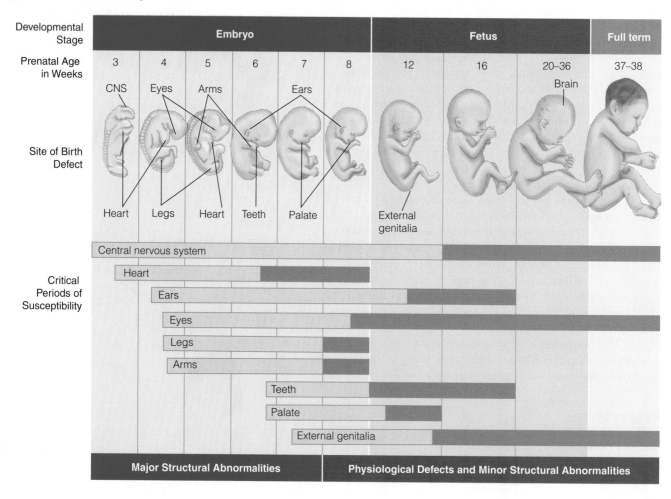

Evolutionary biologist Margie Profet has suggested that the morning sickness often experienced in the first three months of pregnancy may be an adaptive defence against the influence of teratogens (Profet, 1992). Because this is a critical period of embryonic growth, women have to be especially careful about the food they ingest. Thus, the food aversions and nausea associated with morning sickness are thought to protect the development of the embryo by influencing the mother toward eating bland foods; they are less likely than stronger-tasting foods to contain toxins that could damage or even terminate embryonic development. Women who experience morning sickness are less likely to suffer miscarriages than those who do not (Flaxman & Sherman, 2000). Finally, the fact that morning sickness occurs in every culture strengthens the view that it is an evolutionary adaptation.

Growth during Infancy

We've stressed the negative impact of the environment, such as how teratogens can prevent expression of the normal genetic plan. However, the fetal environment usually has a nurturing effect on the developing organism. The internal conditions of the mother's uterus are perfectly tuned for physical development. The temperature is right; the fetus floats cushioned in a protective fluid; and regular nourishment is provided through the umbilical cord and placenta. Life is rarely as perfect again. More often than not, the result is a healthy baby, with normal physical systems, who is ready to take on the world.

The average newborn weighs in at about 3 kg and is roughly 51 cm long. Over the next two years, as the child grows from baby to toddler, this weight will quadruple and the child will reach about half of his or her final adult height. Along with the rest of the body, the brain continues its dramatic growth spurt during this period. As mentioned earlier, a newborn enters the world with a brain that is only 25% of its final weight; but by the second birthday, the percentage has increased to 75%. Remarkably, this increase in brain size is not due to the formation of new neurons, since most of the cells that make up the cerebral cortex are in place well before birth (Nowakowski, 1987; Rakic, 1991). Instead, the cells grow in size and complexity, and a number of supporting glial cells are added. Each of us has essentially all the neurons we're ever going to possess at the moment we're born.

CRITICAL THINKING

Given that the environment plays such an important role in shaping brain development, what advice would you give new parents to enrich the development of their baby's intellectual capabilities?

Experience Matters   The fact that most neurons are intact at birth does not mean that the brain of the newborn infant is mature—far from it. The brain still needs to refine its vast internal communication network, and it needs experience to accomplish this task. During the final stages of prenatal development, and especially during the first year or two after birth, tremendous changes occur in the neural

The child on the left is one of thousands born each year with fetal alcohol syndrome. The age of the mother is also a risk factor in pregnancy, but most women over the age of 35, such as the woman on the right, deliver normal, healthy babies.

David H. Wells/Corbis/Magma

Jose Luis Pelaez Inc/Getty Images

circuitry. More branches (dendrites) sprout off from the existing cells, to receive information from other cells, and the number of connections, or synapses, greatly increases. Even a kind of neural pruning process occurs in which neurons that are not used simply atrophy or die (Dawson & Fischer, 1994).

The key principle at work is *plasticity*. The genetic code does not rigidly fix the internal circuitry of the brain; instead, a kind of rough wiring pattern is established during prenatal development that is filled in during the important first few years of life. Studies with animals have shown that the quality of early experience may be extremely important during this period. For example, rats raised in enriched environments (with lots of social contact and environmental stimulation) show significantly more complex and better functioning brain tissue than do rats raised in sterile, barren environments. There is also better recovery of function after brain injury if rats spend their recovery time in an enriched environment (van Rijzingen, Gispen, & Spruijt, 1997).

From Crawling to Walking

Most children learn to crawl, stand alone, and walk at predictable ages. ▶ Figure 10.4 shows the major stages of an infant's motor development. The sequence of development, from lifting the head to walking alone, is stable, orderly, and predictable. The baby sits before it stands and crawls before it walks partly because of the way that the nervous system develops. The figure also shows the typical range of ages for each stage. Roughly 90% of all babies can roll over at 5 months of age, sit without support at 8 months, and then walk alone by 15 months.

However, psychologists hesitate to tie developmental milestones directly to age. One baby might stand alone consistently at 9 months, while another perfectly normal baby might not accomplish the same feat until nearly 14 months of age.

▶ **Figure 10.4**

Major Stages of Motor Development

Approximate time periods are given for the major points in motor development. Within the ranges indicated, psychologists are reluctant to evaluate developmental progress in terms of age.

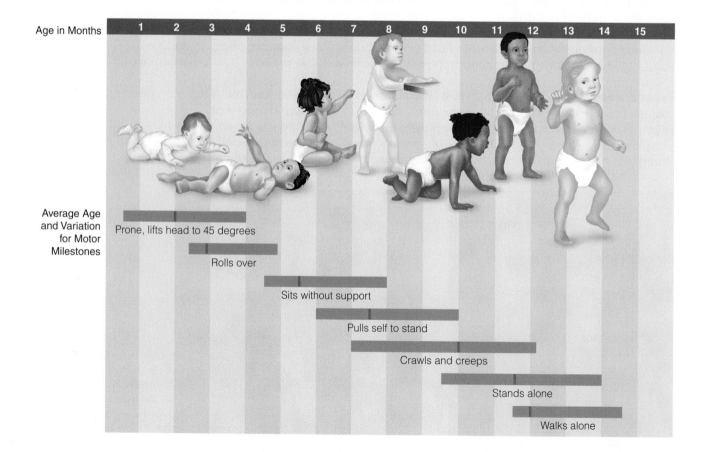

Age in Months | 1 | 2 | 3 | 4 | 5 | 6 | 7 | 8 | 9 | 10 | 11 | 12 | 13 | 14 | 15

Average Age and Variation for Motor Milestones

Prone, lifts head to 45 degrees

Rolls over

Sits without support

Pulls self to stand

Crawls and creeps

Stands alone

Walks alone

Individual Differences   What accounts for individual differences in early motor development? Each infant has a genetic recipe that determines when he or she will develop physically; environmental and cultural influences play only a minor role. For example, Hopi babies are traditionally swaddled and bound to cradleboards for much of the first year of life, yet these babies begin walking at roughly the same time as babies who are not bound in this manner (Dennis & Dennis, 1940; Shaffer, 2002). To learn to walk at a reasonable age, the infant simply needs to be given the opportunity to move around at some point—to "test the waters" and explore things on his or her own (Bertenthal, Campos, & Kermoian, 1994). Such evidence suggests that individual differences in early motor development are more attributable to genetic and other constitutional factors than to environmental differences.

From Toddlerhood to Adolescence

A notable change occurs in hand-to-eye coordination as the child matures. Three-year-olds lack the grace and coordination in movements that are so obvious in a six-year-old. The brain also continues to mature, although far more slowly than during prenatal development or during the first two years of life. General processing speed—how quickly people think and react to sudden changes in their environment—also increases consistently throughout childhood (Kail & Salthouse, 1994).

Between the end of childhood and the beginning of young adulthood lies an important physical and psychological transition period called *adolescence*. Physically, the two most dramatic changes that occur during this time are the adolescent *growth spurt* and the onset of **puberty,** or sexual maturity (the word *puberty* is from the Latin for "to grow hairy"). As with crawling and walking, it's not possible to pinpoint the timing of these changes exactly, particularly for a specific individual, but changes usually start occurring for girls at around age 11 and for boys at about 13. Hormones released by the endocrine system trigger a rapid increase in height and weight accompanied by the maturation of internal and external sexual organs.

Maturing Sexually   Puberty is the developmental period during which individuals mature sexually and acquire the ability to reproduce. For the adolescent female, high levels of estrogen in the body lead to external changes, such as breast development and broadening hips, and eventually to the beginning of *menarche* (the first menstrual flow) at around age 12 or 13. For boys, hormones called *androgens* are released, leading to the appearance of facial hair, a lower voice, and the ability to ejaculate (release semen) at around age 13 or 14. Yet these indicators do not guarantee that the adolescent is ready to reproduce—ovulation and sperm production may not occur until months later. But psychologically these "firsts" tend to be highly memorable and emotional events (Golub, 1992).

The onset of puberty is another classic instance of how the master genetic plan interacts with the nurturing effects of the environment. The average onset age for menarche has dropped from about 16 in the 1880s to the current 12 to 13. Physically, people are maturing earlier than in past generations, and it's almost certainly not due to genetics. Instead, better nutrition, better living conditions, and improved medical care are responsible for the trend. Even today, in parts of the world where living conditions are difficult, the average age of menarche is later than in industrialized countries, such as Canada (Chumlea, 1982). Although the environment does not cause sexual maturation—that's controlled by the genetic code—the environment modulates the expression of the code, either accelerating or delaying the point when changes start to occur (Graber, Brooks-Gunn, & Warren, 1995).

Research by Mount Allison University developmental psychologist Michelle Surbey indicates an intriguing factor that may influence the age of menarche in girls. Surbey has reported that girls who grow up with high levels of stress and in father-absent homes tend to go through menarche earlier than girls who grow up in less stressful environments with their fathers present (Surbey, 1990, 1998). Surbey

Grace and coordination in motor movements take time to develop. This two-year-old will probably have little trouble throwing and catching a baseball successfully by the time he enters elementary school.

puberty

The period during which a person reaches sexual maturity and is potentially capable of producing offspring

Not all children reach the adolescent growth spurt at the same age. Boys can lag behind girls by two years during this stage.

suggests that this pattern may reflect evolved psychobiological mechanisms that allow females to unconsciously adjust their rate of pubertal development in ways that would have been adaptive in the evolutionary history of human ancestors. Although this finding needs to be confirmed by further research, it illustrates the range of possible factors that may contribute to the timing of puberty.

Reaching Adulthood

The adolescent years are marked by dramatic changes in appearance and strength. Motor skills, including hand-to-eye coordination, improve to adult levels during the teenage years. As you're undoubtedly aware, some world-class swimmers and tennis players are barely into their teens. The brain reaches adult weight by about age 16, although the myelination of the neurons—so critical in early motor development—continues throughout the adolescent years (Benes, Turtle, Khan, & Farol, 1994). The continued maturation of the brain can also be seen in the gradual quickening of reaction times that occurs throughout adolescence (Kail & Salthouse, 1994).

When do individuals actually cross the threshold to adulthood? That's a difficult question to answer because becoming an adult is, in some sense, a state of mind. There are differences in how the transition from adolescent to adult is defined across the world. Some cultures have specific rites of passage and others do not. And, as you know, not all adolescents are willing to accept the socially defined responsibilities of adulthood at the appropriate time. But by the time people reach their 20s, they are physically mature and at the height of their physical prowess.

menopause

The time during which a woman's menstrual cycle slows down and finally stops

A strenuous daily exercise program may delay the onset of puberty.

The Aging Body   It's barely noticeable at the time, but most people begin slowly and steadily to decline physically, at least with respect to their peak levels of strength and agility, after their 20s. This loss applies to virtually all physical functions, from strength to respiration rate to the heart's pumping capacity (Whitbourne, 1985). Individual differences occur in the rate of decline, of course, depending on such factors as exercise, illness, and heredity. We're sure you can think of a 40-year-old who is in better physical shape than a 25-year-old. But wrinkles, age spots, sagging flesh, and loss of muscle tone are all reliable and expected parts of the aging process.

By about age 50, the average woman begins **menopause,** the time during which the menstrual cycle slows down and finally stops. Ovulation also stops, so women at this point lose the ability to bear children. These events are caused by hormonal changes, in particular by a decline in the level of female hormones in the body. Despite what you might have heard, menopause is not disruptive for all women, either physically or psychologically (McKinlay, Brambilla, & Posner, 1992). The main physical symptoms, such as hot flashes, can be controlled with medication and only a minority of women undergo any sustained mood disruption (Matthews, 1992). Men experience a more gradual loss of androgen production, which can diminish overall life energy, including sexual motivation and performance. Sometimes called *andropause* or *male climacteric*, this phenomenon does not occur in all men.

The Aging Brain   Throughout a person's lifetime, the connections between neurons in the brain are continually changing. New pathways are formed and others are abandoned in response to environmental experiences. Synapses are constantly in flux. This *neuroplasticity*—the ability to change and adjust its connections—is extremely adaptive, especially during the early years of development. Because the master genetic plan has no way to predict the environments that a person will encounter after birth, the intrinsic capacity for change is built in.

Some new but controversial research has even challenged the notion of a fixed number of brain cells. The phenomenon of *neurogenesis* suggests that, under some conditions, some cells can be added to the brain. So far, this notion has been confirmed only in animal research.

Nonetheless, many individuals eventually suffer brain degeneration, that is, a significant loss of brain cells. This loss may appear as gradual senility or even the disabling condition called Alzheimer's disease. But the good news is that the majority of older people never experience these problems; fewer than 1% of people at age 65 are afflicted with **dementia,** the technical name for physically based loss in mental functioning. Although that percentage may rise to as much as 20% for individuals over age 80 (Cavanaugh & Blanchard Fields, 2002), significant losses in mental functioning or mental health are still the exception rather than the rule. The bad news is that everyone loses brain cells with age—the extent of the loss depends on the particular site in the brain (Kemper, 1994; Selkoe, 1992). The associated declines occur in certain kinds of memory, sensory abilities, and reaction time, as shown in ❱ Figure 10.5 (Cavanaugh, 1993; Salthouse, 1994). Later in this chapter, we'll take a closer look at how memory changes with age.

Interestingly, physical deterioration in the aging brain may not necessarily affect performance. Neurons are lost, and the loss is apparently permanent, but the remaining neurons may in some instances increase in complexity. In a famous autopsy study by Buell and Coleman (1979), it was found that dendrites were significantly longer and more complex in samples of normal brain tissue taken from elderly adults when compared with those of middle-aged adults (see ❱ Figure 10.6). It appears that the brain may compensate for the losses it experiences by making

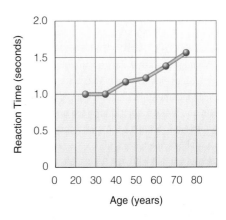

❱ **Figure 10.5**

Age and Reaction Time

This figure shows how average reaction time changes between age 20 and age 80 for a cognitive task requiring subjects to match numbers with symbols on a computer screen. Although there is a gradual quickening of reaction time from childhood through adolescence, after age 20 reaction time gradually slows. (Based on Salthouse, 1994.)

(**dementia**

Physically based losses in mental functioning

❱ **Figure 10.6**

Aging Neurons

Samples of hippocampal neurons taken from people in their 50s, 70s, and 90s and from adults afflicted with Alzheimer's disease. Notice that the dendrites of the samples actually increase in length and complexity from the 50s to the 70s, declining only in late old age or with Alzheimer's disease. (Photos courtesy Dr. Dorothy G. Flood/University of Rochester Medical Center.)

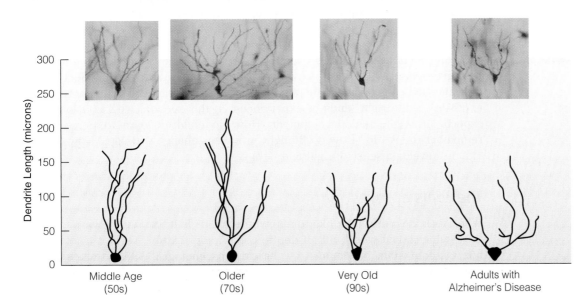

How might you test the idea that mental activity or exercise helps to counteract the decline in mental skills that occurs with age? Can you make predictions based on choice of profession? Should people who choose intellectually challenging professions show less mental decline with age?

better use of the structures that remain intact. Some researchers have even argued that sustained mental activity in later years may help promote neural growth, thereby counteracting some of the normal decline in mental skills (Mirmiran, van Soneren, & Swaab, 1996).

Test Yourself 10.1

Check your knowledge about the physical changes that occur during development by deciding whether the following statements are true or false. (The answers are in Appendix B.)

1. The period in prenatal development lasting from implantation of the fertilized egg to the end of the eighth week is called the germinal period. *True or False?*

2. The initial development of arms, legs, fingers, and toes occurs during the embryonic period of prenatal development. *True or False?*

3. The large increases in brain size that occur in the first two years of life are due primarily to increases in the number of neurons in the brain. *True or False?*

4. The timing of motor development—when a baby begins to crawl, walk, and so on—is affected to a small extent by nature (biology) and to a large extent by nurture (the environment). *True or False?*

5. Everyone loses brain cells with age, and roughly half of all people over 70 can expect to develop dementia. *True or False?*

▶ Developing Intellectually

LEARNING GOALS

1. Understand the research tools used to study infant perception and memory.
2. Be able to explain the perceptual capabilities of an infant.
3. Comprehend the characteristics of memory loss in the elderly.
4. Understand and evaluate Piaget's theory of cognitive development.
5. Understand and evaluate Kolhberg's theory of moral development.

As the brain changes physically in response to the environment, so do the corresponding mental capabilities. Cognitive processes—how individuals think and perceive—change over time. As with learning to walk, growth in intellectual performance depends on adequate physical maturation within the brain as well as on exposure to the right kinds of experiences. In this section, we'll consider three aspects of intellectual development: How do children learn to perceive and remember the world? How do thought processes change with age? How do individuals develop a sense of right and wrong?

The Tools of Investigation

What does the world look like to a newborn child? Is it like our view—a complex three-dimensional world, full of depth, colour, and texture? Or is it a "blooming, buzzing confusion," as claimed by the early psychologist William James (1890)? Answering such questions is not a simple matter. Babies can't tell us what they see or hear.

Researchers who study the developmental process typically use either a *longitudinal* or a *cross-sectional research design*. In a **longitudinal design,** the same individuals are tested repeatedly over time. If you wanted to study the stability of intelligence, you might give an IQ test to the same set of participants at ages 10, 20, 30, and 50. In a **cross-sectional design,** participants of those different ages are studied at one point in time. Each research strategy has advantages and disadvantages.

If the research is on infants or small children, then other methodological problems arise. Because infants don't communicate as adults do, it is necessary to devise creative methods to infer intellectual development.

Fortunately, babies already possess several capabilities that can be exploited to understand their level of mental development: (1) They show *preferences*, which means they prefer some stimuli to others; (2) they notice *novelty*, which means they notice new or different things in their environment; and (3) they can *learn* to repeat activities that result in a reward.

The Preference Technique   In the "preference technique" developed by Robert Fantz (1961), an infant is presented with two visual displays simultaneously, and the investigator simply records how long the infant looks at each (see ▶ Figure 10.7). Suppose that one of the displays shows a male face and the other a female face; and suppose we find that the baby looks at the female face for a significantly longer period of time. By "choosing" to look longer at the female face, the infant has shown a preference. By itself, this preference indicates very little. Perhaps the baby tends to turn its head to the left; or perhaps it prefers to look at smaller faces. To draw clear inferences, it's necessary to repeat the test a number of times with different male and female faces, and switching the male–female relative positions from trial to trial. If the baby continues to look longer at the female face—even when it's larger and on the right—we can infer that the baby has the visual capability to tell the difference between the two displays. The infant "tells" us that he or she can detect differences by exclusively tracking the female face. Notice that we didn't need to ask the baby anything; we simply inferred things about his or her visual system by measuring overt behaviour.

Habituation Techniques   One preference babies consistently show is for novelty—they like to look at new things. But they tend to ignore events that occur repeatedly in their environment without consequence. For instance, if you show newborns a blue-coloured card and track how their eyes move (or how their heart rate changes), you'll find that they spend a lot of time looking at the card when it first appears—it's something new. But if you present the same card over and over again, their interest wanes, and they'll begin to look at something else. This decline in responsiveness to repeated stimulation, called **habituation,** provides an effective tool for researchers seeking to map out the infant's perceptual world (Colombo, Frick, & Gorman, 1997). By acting bored, which is defined operationally by how long they look at the card, babies reveal that they remember the stimulus from its previous presentation and recognize that it hasn't changed. It's as if the baby is saying, "Oh, it's that blue card again."

longitudinal design

A research design in which the same people are studied or tested repeatedly over time

cross-sectional design

A research design in which people of different ages are compared at the same time

habituation

The decline in responsiveness to repeated stimulation; habituation has been used to investigate the perceptual capabilities of infants

▶ **Figure 10.7**

The Preference Technique

Babies prefer some visual stimuli to others. In this case, a preverbal infant is demonstrating a preference for a female face by tracking its location across trials. The preference can be determined by simply recording how long the baby looks at each face.

CRITICAL THINKING
Why do you think nature built in a tendency to habituate?

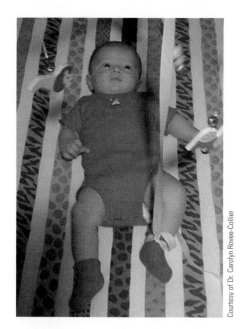

Courtesy of Dr. Carolyn Rovee-Collier

In research by Carolyn Rovee-Collier, infants learn that leg kicking can produce movement of a mobile hanging overhead.

Habituation can be used to discover specific information about how babies perceive and remember their worlds (DeSaint, Smith, Hull, & Loboschefski, 1997; Granrud, 1993). For example, suppose we wanted to discover whether newborns have the capacity to perceive colour. We could show the blue card for a while, and then suddenly switch to a green card that matches on all other visual dimensions (such as size and brightness). If the infant shows renewed interest in the card—treating the stimulus as if it were novel—we can infer that the baby can discriminate, or tell the difference, between blue and green. However, if the baby continues to ignore the new green card, it suggests that the baby lacks colour vision at this stage in development. We can also study memory by varying the time that elapses between presentations of the card. If the baby continues to act bored by the blue card even though we insert long pauses between successive presentations, we know that he or she is remembering the card over those particular intervals.

The Use of Rewards   A researcher can also gain insight into what a baby sees, knows, and remembers by *rewarding* a simple motor movement, such as kicking a leg or sucking on an artificial nipple, in the presence of particular kinds of events (Siqueland & DeLucia, 1969). For example, in research by Carolyn Rovee-Collier (1993), two- and three-month-old infants were taught that kicking their legs could produce movement of a crib mobile hanging overhead. A moving mobile is quite rewarding to babies at this age, and they'll double or triple their rate of leg kicking in a matter of minutes if it leads to movement. We can then study cognitive abilities—such as memory—by taking the mobile away, waiting for some period of time, and then replacing the mobile. If the baby begins leg kicking again at rates comparable to those produced at the end of training, we can infer that the baby has remembered what he or she has learned. We can also change the characteristics of the mobile after training and learn things about a baby's perceptual abilities. For example, if we train an infant with a blue mobile and then switch to a green one, differences in leg kicking help us infer whether the baby can discriminate between green and blue.

The Growing Perceptual World

Based on such techniques, researchers have discovered that babies greet the world with sensory systems that function reasonably well. Although not yet operating at peak efficiency, babies already see a world of colour and shape (Banks & Shannon, 1993). They even arrive with built-in preferences for some colours and shapes. One-day-old babies, for example, respond more to patterned stimuli than to unpatterned ones. As shown in ❱ Figure 10.8, they even prefer to look at correctly drawn faces rather than scrambled faces with features placed in incorrect positions (Johnson, Dziurawiec, Ellis, & Morton, 1991; see also Walton & Bower, 1993). Such research indicates that reasonably sophisticated perceptual processing can occur rapidly after birth.

Newborns also hear reasonably well, and they seem to recognize their mother's voice within a day or two after birth (DeCasper & Fifer, 1980). Remarkably, evidence suggests that newborns can even hear and remember things that happen before birth. By week 28, fetuses will close their eyes in response to loud noises presented near the mother's abdomen (Parmelee & Sigman, 1983). Infants will also choose to suck on an artificial nipple that produces a recording of a story that was read aloud to them repeatedly before birth (DeCasper & Spence, 1986). This is an adaptive quality for the newborn to possess, since the newborn needs nourishment and is dependent on others for survival. Consequently, babies born with a visual system that detects shapes and forms and an auditory system tuned to the human voice have an increased likelihood of survival.

In addition to sights and sounds, babies are quite sensitive to touch, smell, pain, and taste. Place a drop of lemon juice in the mouth of a newborn and you'll see a distinctive grimace. Place a small amount of sugar in the baby's mouth, and

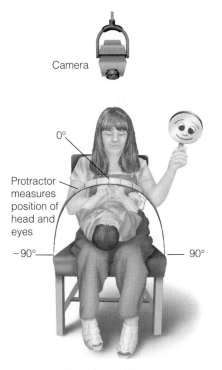

Camera

0°

Protractor measures position of head and eyes

−90°

90°

Experimental Setup

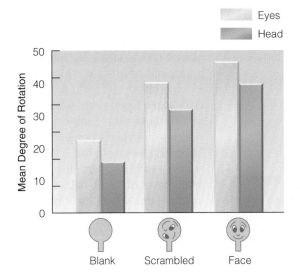

Eyes

Head

Mean Degree of Rotation

50

40

30

20

10

0

Blank

Scrambled

Face

▶ **Figure 10.8**

Infant Preferences

In the experiment, babies were shown either a blank stimulus, a stimulus with scrambled facial features, or a stimulus with a face. Each stimulus was positioned over the baby's head and then moved from side to side. The dependent variable was the extent to which the baby tracked each stimulus by rotating his or her head and eyes. As the results show, the babies tracked the face stimulus more than the other stimuli. (Graph adapted from M. H. Johnson, S. Dziurawiec, H. Ellis, & J. Morton (1991). Newborns' preferential tracking of face-like stimuli and its subsequent decline, in *Cognition, 40,* 1–19. Copyright © 1991. With permission from Elsevier.)

This baby is a few months old, but even newborn infants show distinctive reactions to a variety of tastes (lemon, sugar, and salt are shown here).

© John Livzey

© John Livzey

© John Livzey

the baby will smack its lips. These distinctive reactions are present at birth and are found even before the infant has had a single taste of food (Steiner, 1977). A baby's sense of smell is developed well enough that the newborn quickly learns to recognize the odour of its mother's breast (Porter, Makin, Davis, & Christensen, 1992). As for pain and touch, babies will reject a milk bottle that is too hot, and, as every parent knows, the right kind of pat on the baby's back is pleasurable enough to soothe the newborn into sleep.

Babies even seem to recognize that the world is three-dimensional. When placed on a visual cliff, such as the one shown in the accompanying photo, six-month-old babies are reluctant to cross over the apparent dropoff, or cliff, even to reach a reward (Gibson & Walk, 1960). Even babies as young as two months show heart rate changes when they're placed on the glass portion covering the deep side of the visual cliff (Campos, Langer, & Krowitz, 1970).

But the infant's perceptual world is not the same as the one viewed by an adult. In general, newborn babies cannot see as well as adults. For example, newborns are not very good at discriminating fine detail in visual patterns: Compared with the ideal acuity level of 20/20, babies see a blurry world that is more on the order of 20/600, meaning that what newborns see at 20 feet (6 metres) is like what adults with ideal vision see at 600 feet (180 metres) (Banks & Salapatek, 1983). In addition, newborns apparently do not perceive shapes and forms in the same way as adults do (Johnson, 1997). Nor can they hear as well as adults. For example, infants seem to have some trouble listening selectively for certain kinds of sounds, and infants need sounds to be louder than adults do before they can detect the noises (Bargones & Werner, 1994).

Infants' perceptual systems improve markedly during the first few months, partly because of continued physical development but also because experience plays a role in the fine-tuning of sensory abilities. Research with nonhuman subjects, such as cats or chimpanzees, has shown that if animals are deprived of visual stimulation during the early weeks or months of life, permanent visual impairments can result (Gandelman, 1992). Thus, perceptual development relies on experience as well as on physically mature sensory equipment.

By the time we leave infancy, our perceptual systems are reasonably intact. Most of the changes that occur during childhood and adolescence deal with the ability to use the equipment we have. For example, as children grow older, their attention span improves, and they are better able to attend selectively to pertinent information. Memory improves throughout childhood, partly because kids learn strategies for organizing and maintaining information in memory. Moreover, as you saw in Chapters 4 and 7, the way individuals perceive and remember the world depends on what they know about the way the world works. We use our general knowledge about people and events to help us interpret ambiguous stimuli and to remember things that happen in our lives. Perception and memory are influenced by the knowledge gained from experience, which is one of the reasons that perceptual development is really a lifelong process.

In the visual cliff apparatus, a plate of glass covers the dropoff or "cliff." Beginning at roughly six months of age, babies are reluctant to cross over to reach a beckoning parent.

Enrico Ferrorelli

Do We Lose Memory with Age?

What happens to memory as we age? Is there an inevitable decline in the ability to remember? It's quite common for the elderly to report memory problems. We know from recent research that there are declines in both prospective memory and retrospective memory (Craik, 1994; Uttl, Graf, Miller, McIsaac, & Tuokko, 2001) and both the speed of and the capacity for information processing (Graf & Uttl, 1995). Beyond that, the relationship between aging and memory is rather complex. Some kinds of memory falter badly with age, but other kinds do not. For example, age-related deficits appear to be restricted to tasks that require conscious memory. If memory is tested in ways that do not require conscious awareness (such as testing to see whether your ability to solve a puzzle increases when you've seen the puzzle before), age-related differences disappear (Balota, Dolan, & Duchek, 2000).

A cross-sectional design was used in a famous study conducted at the University of Toronto by Craik and McDowd (1987). They compared both recall and recognition memory in 20-year-olds and 70-year-olds. All were asked to learn memory lists that consisted of short phrases (e.g., "a body of water") presented together with associated target words (e.g., "pond"). The lists were followed by either an immediate recall test, in which the short phrase was given and the subject needed to recall the target word, or a delayed recognition test, which required the subjects to decide whether a word had or had not been presented in one of the earlier lists.

In such experiments, researchers try to match the participants on as many variables as possible—such as educational level and verbal ability—so that the only difference between the groups is *age*. Any performance differences can then be attributed uniquely to the independent variable (age) and not to some other confounding factor (see Chapter 2). The results of the Craik and McDowd (1987) study are shown in ▶ Figure 10.9. As you can see, the young subjects outperformed the old subjects on the test of recall, but the advantage vanished on the recognition test. Conclusions about memory loss in older people therefore depend on how memory is actually tested. Other studies have shown that performance also depends on the types of materials tested. When older subjects are asked to remember materials that fit naturally into their rich knowledge base (e.g., vocabulary), they may even perform better than their younger counterparts (Zacks & Hasher, 1994).

Although many people past age 60 or 70 are able to perform well on certain kinds of memory tests, it is still the case that seniors generally perform quite poorly on tests that require recalling lists of newly presented information (Hultsch,

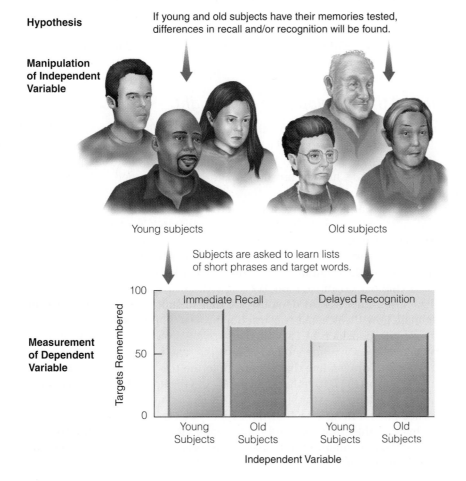

Hypothesis   If young and old subjects have their memories tested, differences in recall and/or recognition will be found.

Manipulation of Independent Variable

Young subjects   Old subjects

Subjects are asked to learn lists of short phrases and target words.

Measurement of Dependent Variable

Immediate Recall   Delayed Recognition

Targets Remembered

100

50

0

Young Subjects   Old Subjects   Young Subjects   Old Subjects

Independent Variable

▶ **Figure 10.9**

Memory and Aging

In the study by Craik and McDowd (1987), two groups, one with an average age of 20.7 years and one with an average age of 72.8 years, were asked to learn and then recall or recognize target words. Although the younger subjects recalled more targets than the older group did, the advantage disappeared for recognition.

Jean Piaget

Hertzog, Small, & Dixon, 1999). UBC researchers are actively trying to determine why these memory deficits occur (Graf & Uttl, 2001). One possibility is that older adults lose the ability to suppress irrelevant thoughts or to ignore irrelevant stimuli (Hasher, Stolzfus, Zacks, & Rypma, 1991). Because they are unable to focus selectively on the task at hand, they fail to process the information to be remembered in ways that are conducive to later recall (Craik, 1994).

Can anything be done to prevent these age-related memory decrements? This question has been addressed by University of Victoria life-span developmental psychologists David Hultsch, Roger Dixon, and their colleagues (Hultsch et al., 1999). These researchers examined data from the Victoria Longitudinal Study, a major Canadian study of age-related changes in people's cognitive functioning, particularly their memory processes. The researchers tested the hypothesis that people who continue to engage in intellectually demanding activities throughout their life span, including old age, may not experience the same decline in memory processes experienced by other older people. This idea has come to be known as the "use it or lose it" hypothesis. The results generally supported this idea, with cognitive activities that involved processing novel information, such as playing bridge or learning a language, apparently being particularly related to "buffering" older people against the usual decreases in memory processes in old age. However, the researchers caution that it is difficult to ascertain cause and effect in this kind of study. As abilities deteriorate, a person is likely to lose interest in challenging intellectual tasks. So "losing it" may actually precede "using it."

One fascinating argument from evolutionary theory is that the deterioration of short-term memory in older people is adaptive for our species. The elders must retain the accumulated cultural information that helps prevent hasty decisions being made by young people. If older folks learned everything new that came along during their lives, it would interfere with their function as society's storehouse of wisdom (Pinker, 1997a). The adaptive value of such wisdom is often expressed in the phrase "Those who do not remember history are doomed to repeat it."

Piaget and the Development of Thought

Much of what we know about how thought processes develop during childhood comes from the collective works of a Swiss scholar named Jean Piaget (1929, 1952, 1970). It was Piaget who first convinced psychologists that children think quite differently from adults. Children are not little adults, he argued, who simply lack knowledge and experience; instead, they view the world in unique and idiosyncratic ways. Piaget argued that we are all born with a natural tendency to organize the world meaningfully. People construct mental models of the world—called **schemas**—and use them to guide and interpret their experiences. But these schemas are not very adult-like early in development—in fact, they tend not to reflect the true world accurately—so much of early intellectual development is spent modifying our cognitive models of how the world operates. One of Piaget's primary contributions was to demonstrate that mistakes in children's reasoning can illuminate how the schema-construction process is proceeding.

For example, consider the two tilted cups shown on the left. When young children are asked to draw a line indicating how the water level in a tilted cup might look, they tend to draw a line that is parallel to the top and bottom of the cup, as shown in the cup on the left, rather than parallel to the ground, as shown in the cup on the right. This kind of error is important, Piaget argued, because children can't have learned such a thing directly from experience (water never tilts that way in real life). Instead, the error reflects a fundamental misconception of how the world is structured. Young children simply have an internal schema of that aspect of the world that is inaccurate.

schemas

Mental models of the world that people use to guide and interpret their experiences

CONCEPT SUMMARY

RESEARCH DESIGNS FOR STUDYING DEVELOPMENT

Type of Design	Overview	Advantages and Disadvantages
Cross-sectional	Researchers compare performance of different people of different ages	A: Faster, more practical than longitudinal D: Other variables may be confounded with age
Longitudinal	Researchers test the same individuals repeatedly over time	A: Can examine changes in individuals D: Cost intensive; subject loss over time

Assimilation and Accommodation   As their brains and bodies mature, children build more accurate mental models of the world, based in part on their experiences. Piaget suggested that this process of cognitive development is guided by two adaptive psychological processes: **assimilation** and **accommodation.** Assimilation is the process through which people fit—or assimilate—new experiences into their existing schemas. For example, suppose a small child who has been raised in a household full of cats mistakenly concludes that the neighbour's new rabbit is simply a kind of kitty. The new experience—the rabbit—has been assimilated into the child's existing view of the world: Small furry things are *cats*. The second function, accommodation, is the process through which people change or modify existing schemas to accommodate new experiences when they occur. When the child learns that the new "kitty" hops rather than walks and seems reluctant to purr, he or she will need to modify and revise the existing concept of small furry things; the child is forced to change the existing schema to accommodate the new information. Notice that the child plays an active role in constructing schemas by interacting directly with the world (Piaget, 1929).

Piaget believed that children develop an adult worldview by proceeding systematically through a series of four stages or developmental periods: *sensorimotor*, *preoperational*, *concrete operational*, and *formal operational*. Each period is tied roughly to a particular age range—for example, the preoperational period usually lasts from age two to about age seven—but individual differences may occur in how quickly children progress from one period to the next. Although the timing may vary from child to child, Piaget believed that the order in which individuals progress through the stages is invariant—it remains the same for everyone. Let's consider these cognitive developmental periods in more detail.

> **assimilation**
>
> The process through which people fit—or assimilate—new experiences into existing schemas

> **accommodation**
>
> The process through which people change or modify existing schemas to accommodate new experiences when they occur

> **sensorimotor period**
>
> Piaget's first stage of cognitive development, lasting from birth to about two years of age; schemas revolve around sensory and motor abilities

The rooting reflex is adaptive because it helps the newborn receive needed sustenance.

The Sensorimotor Period: Birth to Two Years

From birth to about age two, schemas about the world revolve primarily around the infant's sensory and motor abilities (hence the name **sensorimotor period**). Babies initially interact with the world through a variety of evolved reflexes. For example, they'll start sucking when an object is placed in their mouth (called the *sucking reflex*), and they'll automatically turn their head in the direction of a touch or brush on the cheek (called the *rooting reflex*). This means that when an object comes into a newborn's view, that object is interpreted in terms of how it can be sucked. Of course, this behaviour is far different from an adult's, but it's *adaptive* for a newborn. These reflexes increase the likelihood that adequate nourishment will follow, and attaining adequate nourishment is a significant problem the newborn needs to solve.

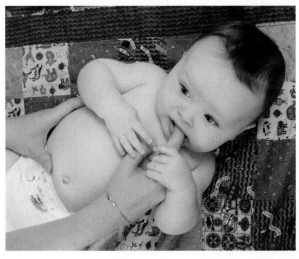

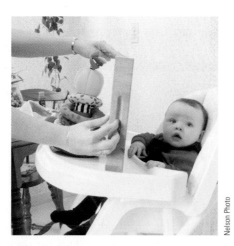

According to Piaget, until object permanence develops, babies fail to understand that objects still exist when they're no longer in view. Notice how this boy loses interest when he can no longer see his favourite toy.

object permanence

The ability to recognize that objects still exist when they're no longer in sight

Object Permanence   As infants develop intellectually over the first year, they begin to use their maturing motor skills to help them understand how they can voluntarily interact with the world. Babies start to vocalize to gain attention; they learn that they can kick their legs to make sounds; they acquire the ability to reach with their arms to touch or grasp objects. The initial stirrings of symbolic thought also begin during the sensorimotor period. The infant gradually develops the ability to represent things internally as mental images or symbols. Early in the first year, for example, babies lack **object permanence,** which means that they fail to recognize that objects exist when they're no longer in sight. The photos above illustrate how psychologists have measured object permanence. Notice that the baby loses interest when the toy is covered, suggesting that the baby is only capable of thinking about objects that are directly in view. Babies at this point are unable to represent objects symbolically—out of sight equals out of mind. But by the end of the first year, Piaget argued, the child has a different reaction to the disappearance of a favoured toy; as object permanence develops, the child will begin to search actively for the lost toy.

The Preoperational Period: Two to Seven Years

preoperational period

Piaget's second stage of cognitive development, lasting from age two to about age seven; children begin to think symbolically but often lack the ability to perform mental operations, like conservation

From about ages two through seven, the child's schemas continue to grow in sophistication. Children in the **preoperational period** no longer have difficulty thinking about absent objects, and they can use one sort of object to stand for another. A four-year-old, for example, can easily use a stick to represent a soaring airplane or a cardboard box for a stove. The child realizes that these are not the real objects, but he or she can imagine them to be real for the purposes of play. However, as Piaget demonstrated in a number of clever ways, the child still thinks about the world quite differently from an adult. The preoperational child lacks the ability to perform certain basic mental *operations*—hence Piaget's use of the term *preoperational* to describe a child's mental abilities during this period.

conservation

The ability to recognize that the physical properties of an object remain the same despite superficial changes in the object's appearance

Conservation   Something that children at the preoperational stage often fail to understand is the principle of conservation. To understand **conservation,** children need to be able to recognize that the physical properties of an object can remain the same despite superficial changes in its appearance (see ❱ Figure 10.10). If four- or five-year-old children are shown two modelling clay balls of exactly the same size and we ask them which object contains more clay, most of the children will say that the two balls contain the same amount. But if one ball is then rolled into a long, sausage-like shape, the children are likely to think that the two quantities of clay are

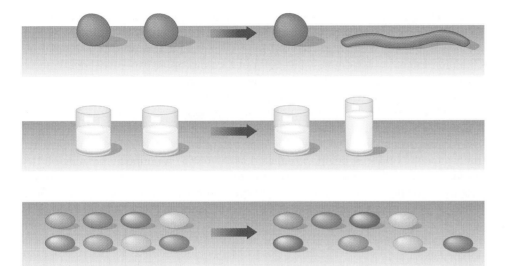

▶ Figure 10.10

Examples of Conservation Problems

Understanding conservation means recognizing that the physical properties of objects remain the same even though the objects may superficially change in appearance. Preoperational children often fail conservation problems—they fail to detect, for example, that the objects to the right of the arrows still retain the same volume or number as those on the left.

no longer the same, saying that either the sausage or the ball has more modelling clay. Children at this age simply do not understand that a basic property of an object, in this case its mass, doesn't change as the object changes shape.

Typically, preoperational children will fail to conserve a basic quantity even if they directly observe the change in appearance taking place. Suppose that we ask five-year-old Sam to pour a cup of water into each of two identical glasses. Sam performs the task and accepts that the two glasses now contain the same amount of water. We then instruct him to pour the water from one of the glasses into another glass that is tall and thin. Do the glasses now contain the same amount of water? "No," Sam explains. "Now the tall one has more water." Sam is not showing any evidence of conservation; he does not yet recognize that how the water looks in the glass has no effect on its volume.

Piaget argued that the reason children in the preoperational period make these kinds of errors is that they still lack the capacity to think in truly adult-like ways. For example, the thinking of preoperational children demonstrates *centration*, the tendency to focus attention on one particular aspect of a situation and to ignore other aspects. Sam believes that the tall glass has more water because he cannot simultaneously consider both the height and the width of the glass; he focuses only on the height and is therefore convinced that the taller glass must contain more water. In addition, children at this age have difficulty understanding *reversibility*—they don't understand that one kind of operation can produce change and that another kind of operation can undo that change. For example, Sam is unlikely to consider what will happen if the water from the tall glass is poured back into the original glass. The capacity to understand that operations are reversible doesn't develop until the next stage.

Egocentrism   Piaget also discovered that children in the preoperational period tend to see the world, and the objects in it, from primarily one perspective: their own. Children at this stage have a tough time imagining themselves in another person's position. If you ask a child in the preoperational period to describe what another person will see or think, the child will usually describe what he or she personally sees or thinks. Piaget called this characteristic **egocentrism**—the tendency to view the world from your own unique perspective only.

Children's Theory of Mind   An important aspect of children's cognitive development that occurs during the preoperational stage is the child's development of a "theory of mind." This refers to how children view the process of acquiring

CRITICAL   THINKING

Do you think Piaget's insights about cognitive development have any implications for education? For example, should teachers be giving students in Grade 1 and Grade 2 abstract math problems to solve?

egocentrism

The tendency to see the world from your own unique perspective only; a characteristic of thinking in the preoperational period of development

knowledge. Developmental researchers Christopher Lalonde of the University of Victoria, Michael Chandler of the University of British Columbia, and Kang Lee of Queen's University have examined this issue (Chandler & Lalonde, 1996; Lalonde & Chandler, 1995; Lee & Homer, 1999). Although infants appear to have mental mechanisms that contribute to a primitive theory of mind (Baron-Cohen, 1994; Muir, Hains, & Symons, 1994), Lalonde and Chandler suggest that a fundamental shift in children's theory of mind takes place around the age of six or seven. Before this, three- to five-year-olds think of the mind very much as a tape recorder: a passive tool for making copies of whatever is in the environment. At six or seven, however, things change: Children begin to realize that the mind can impose meaning on the world and that knowledge is often a matter of interpretation. By realizing that other people can be mistaken, children are (unfortunately) better able to deceive others (Chandler, Lalonde, & Sokol, 2000). This is a considerably more sophisticated view of people's thinking processes than that held by preschoolers, and it is another example of the relatively rapid changes in cognitive development in the preoperational stage.

The Concrete Operational Period: Seven to Eleven Years

concrete operational period

Piaget's third stage of cognitive development, lasting from age 7 to age 11; children acquire the capacity to perform a number of mental operations but still lack the ability for abstract reasoning

Between the ages of 7 and about 11, children enter the **concrete operational period** and gain the capacity for true mental *operations*. By mental operations Piaget meant the ability to perform mental actions on objects—to verbalize, visualize, and mentally manipulate objects. A child of eight can consider the consequences of rolling a long strip of modelling clay into a ball before the action is actually performed. The result is that children in the concrete operational period have fewer difficulties with conservation problems because they are capable of reversing operations on objects; they can mentally consider the effects of both doing and undoing an action.

Children at the concrete operational stage also show the initial stirrings of logical thought, which means they can now mentally order and compare objects and perform more sophisticated classifications. These children can do simple math problems and solve problems that require elementary reasoning. Consider such a problem as the following: Stan is faster than Kenny; Kenny is faster than Eric. Is Stan faster or slower than Eric? Children of 9 or 10 have little trouble with this problem because they can keep track of ordered relations in their heads. Younger preoperational children will probably insist on actually seeing Stan and Eric race— they cannot easily solve the problem in their heads.

Although concrete operational children possess a growing array of mental operations, Piaget believed that they are still limited intellectually in an important way. The mental operations they can perform remain concrete, or tied directly to actual objects in the real world. Children at this age have great difficulty with problems that do not flow directly from everyday experience. Ask an eight-year-old to solve a problem involving four-armed people and barking cats and you're likely to see a blank look on his or her face. Basically, if something can't be seen, heard, touched, tasted, or smelled, it's not going to be something that concrete operational children can easily consider in their heads (although these children can imagine non-real-world objects they have encountered, as in cartoons or fairy tales). The ability to think truly abstractly doesn't develop until the final stage of cognitive development.

The Formal Operational Period: Eleven to Adulthood

Piaget repeatedly stressed the idea that children tend to think differently from adults. Children's schemas, or mental models of the world, are limited because they lack the proper amounts of biological maturation and experience. These limitations in turn lead to errors in reasoning or judgment, although the child's view of the world can be adaptive for solving the particular problems that children face (as when a baby's viewing of an object as something to be sucked increases the likelihood of obtaining nourishment). But by the time children reach their teenage years, many of them will be in the formal operational period, during which their thought processes become increasingly more like those of an adult. Neither teenagers nor adults have problems thinking about imaginary or artificial concepts; they can consider hypothetical outcomes and make logical deductions about places they've never visited or that might not even exist. Teenagers and adults can develop systematic strategies for solving problems—such as the use of trial and error—that are beyond the capability of most preteens.

The **formal operational period** is the stage in which individuals start to gain mastery over abstract thinking. Ask a concrete operational child about the meaning of education, and you'll likely hear about teachers and grades. The formal operational adolescent is able to answer the question in a general and abstract way, perhaps describing education as a system organized by parents and the government to foster the acquisition of useful knowledge. Piaget believed that the transition from concrete operational thinking to formal operational thinking probably occurs gradually, over several years, and is not achieved by everyone (Piaget, 1970). Once it is reached, the adolescent is no longer tied to concrete real-world constructs and can invent and experiment with the possible rather than with the here and now alone.

formal operational period

Piaget's last stage of cognitive development; thought processes become adult-like, and people gain mastery over abstract thinking

Challenges to Piaget's Theory

Most psychologists agree that Piaget's contributions to the understanding of cognitive development have been substantial. He successfully convinced the psychological community that children have unique internal schemas, and he provided convincing demonstrations that those schemas, once formed, tend to change systematically over time. However, not all Piaget's ideas have withstood experimental scrutiny. It's now common for researchers to challenge the specifics of his theory, primarily his assumptions about what children really know and when they know it (Feldman, 2003).

It now seems clear that Piaget was simply wrong in some of his conclusions about the young child's mental capabilities. Children and young infants are considerably more sophisticated in their models of the world than Piaget believed (Flavell, Miller, & Miller, 1993; Kuhn, 1992). For example, Piaget stated that object permanence doesn't develop until late in the child's first year. Although it's true that children will not search for a hidden toy in the first few months of life, more sensitive tests have revealed that even one- to four-month-old infants are capable of recognizing that vanished objects still exist (Baillargeon, 2004).

In a classic study by T. G. R. Bower (1982), very young infants watched as a screen was moved in front of a toy, blocking it from view (see ▶ Figure 10.11 on page 402). Moments later, when the screen was removed, the infants acted surprised if the toy was absent (it could be secretly removed by the experimenter). If objects no longer exist when removed from view, then infants shouldn't be surprised by a sudden absence (see also Hofstadter & Reznick, 1996). Other researchers have demonstrated that small infants can show symbolic thought—they understand, for instance, that objects move along continuous paths and do not jump around—and they gain this understanding at points in development far earlier than Piaget imagined (see Mandler, 1992; Spelke, Breinlinger, Macomber, & Jacobson, 1992).

Problems with the Stage View   Piaget has also been criticized for sticking to the notion of distinct stages, or periods of development (Flavell et al., 1993). This criticism may not be fair because, in fact, he did not insist on such sharp

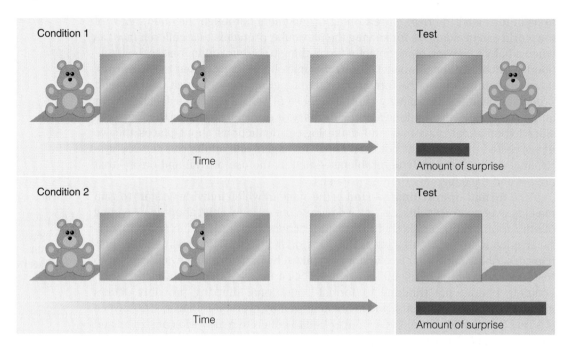

Condition 1   Test

Time

Amount of surprise

Condition 2   Test

Time

Amount of surprise

▶ **Figure 10.11**

Re-evaluating Object Permanence

In this experiment by T. G. R. Bower, young infants watched as a screen was moved in front of a toy, blocking it from view. Moments later, the screen was removed and the baby's level of surprise was measured. In the condition where the toy had vanished, the infants seemed to be surprised. Piaget would not have predicted such surprise because children that age are not supposed to have object permanence.

transitions (Chapman, 1988). Most modern developmental psychologists believe that cognitive development is better viewed as a process of continual change and adaptation (Siegler, 1996). If we adopted a strict stage view, we should expect that once the child undergoes a stage transition—say, from the preoperational stage to the concrete operational stage—the child should relatively quickly show the capacity to perform a variety of new tasks. But this is not usually the case.

Rather than rapid change, children's thought processes tend to show slow and inconsistent change over long periods (Flavell, 1971). For example, it is not uncommon to find a five-year-old who understands conservation of number but has no idea about conservation of mass or volume. Such a child seems to contradict the notion of an overall schema shift with age. Instead, children gradually adapt to the world and to tasks and problems that might occur only in particular situations. So it's not surprising that they act in ways that are difficult to fit into any specific cognitive stage or that the transitions from one developmental point to the next are not rapid and well defined (Munakata, McClelland, Johnson, & Siegler, 1997).

The Role of Culture   Piaget was also rather fuzzy about the mechanisms that produce cognitive change. His demonstrations that infants, toddlers, and school-aged children think in fundamentally different ways were brilliant, but he never clearly accounted for the psychological processes that produce those changes. Although he did not totally ignore social factors (Carpendale, 1997), he emphasized them less than did other theorists. Cross-cultural research has shown that children across the world develop cognitively in similar ways, but significant cultural differences occur in the rate of development (Matsumoto, 1994). For example, children raised in nomadic societies, which move frequently from place to place, seem to acquire spatial skills (the ability to orient themselves in their environment) earlier and better than do children raised in single, fixed locales. Schooling may also be a factor: Ample cross-cultural evidence indicates that people who never attend school may have a difficult time reaching the formal operational stage of thinking, at least as measured through the use of traditional Piagetian tasks (Cole, 1992; Segall, Dasen, Berry, & Poortinga, 1990).

CONCEPT SUMMARY

PIAGET'S STAGES OF COGNITIVE DEVELOPMENT

Stage	Basic Characteristics	Accomplishments	Limitations
Sensorimotor period (birth to two years)	Schemas about the world revolve primarily around sensory and motor abilities.	Children develop object permanence; they learn how to vocalize and they learn their first words.	Schemas are limited primarily to simple sensory and motor function; problems occur in thinking about absent objects (early).
Preoperational period (two to seven years)	Schemas grow in sophistication. Children can think about absent objects and can use one object to stand for another.	Children readily symbolize objects, and imaginary play is common; they make great strides in language development.	Children are prelogical; they fail to understand conservation, because of centration and a failure to understand reversibility; children show egocentrism in thinking.
Concrete operational period (7 to 11 years)	Children gain the capacity for true mental operations (i.e., verbalizing, visualizing, mental manipulation).	Children understand reversibility and other simple logical operations, like categorizing and ordering.	Mental operations remain concrete, tied to actual objects in the real world; children have difficulty with problems that do not flow from everyday experience.
Formal operational period (11 years to adulthood)	Mastery is gained over abstract thinking.	Adolescents can think and answer questions in general and abstract ways.	No limitations: development of reasoning is complete; however, not all people reach this stage.

The idea that we cannot fully understand the development of mental processes without considering social and cultural influences was promoted by a Russian psychologist, Lev Vygotsky, around the same time that Piaget was developing his theoretical ideas. Vygotsky died in 1934, after only a decade of work in psychology, but his ideas continue to exert a powerful influence on modern developmental psychologists (Duncan, 1995; Wertsch & Tulviste, 1992). Vygotsky argued that cognitive abilities emerge directly out of our social interactions with others. He proposed, for example, that inner speech, which people use to think and plan activities, is simply a natural extension of the outer speech that people use to communicate with others. In general, children see social situations as challenges that can be mastered in part by asking for and getting assistance from others. In sum, development cannot be understood by considering the individual in isolation; we must always consider the child in his or her social context (Vygotsky, 1978).

This Vygotskyian perspective on inner speech has recently been examined by developmental psychologist Robert Duncan of Mount Allison University and his colleagues from the University of Waterloo (Duncan & Cheyne, 1999; Duncan & Pratt, 1997). Duncan and his colleagues found support for Vygotsky's suggestions that inner speech is an important cognitive "tool," although it is internalized during childhood and hence it is not readily apparent in adults.

Corel 3 Indonesia

Children in nomadic societies move frequently from place to place and may be able to orient themselves in an environment faster and more efficiently than can children raised in fixed locales.

Beyond Formal Operational Thought   Another active area of controversy surrounding Piaget's theory concerns the issue of adult cognitive development. Does intellectual development really end with the acquisition of formal operational thinking at some point during adolescence, as claimed by Piaget? A number of researchers believe that mastery over abstract thought, which is the hallmark of the formal operational period, is only one part of a much more extensive process of adult cognitive development (Cavanaugh, 1993; Riegel, 1976). Fundamental differences probably exist between adolescent and adult thought processes that cannot be explained without the introduction of new, *postformal* stages of cognitive development.

According to Vygotsky, cognitive abilities arise directly out of the social and verbal interactions that children have with other people, including their friends and relatives.

Jack Hollingsworth/PhotoDisc/Getty Images

Currently, no general consensus exists over exactly what these postformal thoughts represent. One popular idea is that postformal cognitive development is characterized by *relativistic thinking*. Adults tend to think about "truth" in a much more relative way than teenagers do; adults recognize, for instance, that the correct answer to a moral dilemma might vary from one situation to the next. Adults are also more tolerant of ambiguity in their thinking than teenagers are (although too much ambiguity in thought is obviously a problem). Adolescent thinking is typically rigid and absolute in the sense that teenagers tend to rely on fixed rules of right and wrong and show little intellectual flexibility (Labouvie-Vief, Hakim-Larson, & Hobart, 1987; Perry, 1970).

Other researchers have argued that adolescents are also less capable of thinking about *systems* of ideas. Teenagers who have reached the formal operational stage might be able to deal with abstract ideas, but they will have trouble dealing with higher-order systems of ideas of the type found in a scientific theory (Richards & Commons, 1990). Systematic comparisons among ideas, as in the analysis of the similarities and differences among theories, require postformal thought processes. Ironically, many modern developmental psychologists argue that Piaget himself must have been operating at a level of cognitive development beyond the formal operational stage when he developed his own theory.

Moral Development: Learning Right from Wrong

Developing intellectually means more than just learning to think logically and form correct internal models of the world. As children mature intellectually, they also acquire a sense of morality, which provides them with a way to distinguish between appropriate and inappropriate thoughts and actions. Piaget had strong opinions on this topic, arguing that the sense of **morality** is closely tied to the stage of cognitive development and to social experiences with peers. For example, from Piaget's perspective children in the concrete operational stage would not be expected to show sophisticated moral reasoning skills, because morality is basically an abstract concept—something that cannot be handled until the formal operational stage of development. Partly for this reason, researchers have largely focused on the moral development of adolescents and adults, rather than of children.

morality

The ability to distinguish between appropriate and inappropriate actions; a child's sense of morality may be tied to his or her level of cognitive development

Kohlberg's Stage Theory   The most influential theory of moral development is the stage theory proposed by Lawrence Kohlberg. Strongly influenced by the writings of Piaget, Kohlberg framed his theory around the idea that individuals progress through an orderly series of stages of moral development (Kohlberg, 1963, 1986). His investigative technique was to give people of various ages a hypothetical moral dilemma and use their solutions to identify their current state of moral development. Let's consider in detail an example, based on Kohlberg (1969).

A woman is stricken with a rare and deadly form of cancer. There is a drug that can save her, a form of radium recently discovered by a druggist in town. But the druggist is charging an impossible amount for the medicine, in fact, 10 times what the drug cost him to make. The sick woman's husband, Heinz, tries desperately to raise the money but can raise only half the needed amount. He pleads with the druggist to sell him the drug at a reduced cost, or at least to allow him to pay for the drug over time, but the druggist refuses. "No," the druggist says. "I discovered the drug and I'm going to make money from it." Frantic to save his wife, Heinz considers breaking into the druggist's office to steal the drug.

What do you think? Should the husband steal the drug? Why or why not? You probably have an answer to this dilemma. Whether you answer "yes" or "no" doesn't matter to Kohlberg. Instead, it is the reasoning behind your answer, the kind of intellectual justification that you give, that is important. Kohlberg argued that an adult's moral development can be evaluated by matching it against the three levels through which children progress. Few children progress through them all, leaving all adults fixed at one of the three levels: the *preconventional*, the *conventional*, or the *postconventional* level (see the Concept Summary table on page 407).

At the lowest level of moral development—the **preconventional level**—decisions about right and wrong are based primarily on external consequences. Young children will typically interpret the morality of a behaviour in terms of its immediate individual consequences—that is, whether the act will lead directly to a reward or to a punishment: "Heinz shouldn't steal the drug because he might get caught and punished" or "Heinz should steal the drug because people will get mad at him if his wife dies." Notice the rationale is based on the immediate external consequences of the action rather than on some abstract moral principle.

At the **conventional level** of moral reasoning, people start to justify their actions on the basis of internalized rules. Now an action is right or wrong because it maintains or disrupts the *social order*. Someone at this level might argue that Heinz shouldn't steal

preconventional level

In Kohlberg's theory, the lowest level of moral development, in which decisions about right and wrong are made primarily in terms of external consequences

conventional level

In Kohlberg's theory of moral development, the stage in which actions are judged to be right or wrong based on whether they maintain or disrupt the social order

Children need to develop a sense of morality, which helps them tell the difference between appropriate and inappropriate actions.

James Frank/Index Stock Imagery/Jupiter Images

the drug because stealing is illegal, whether or not he gets caught. Or Heinz should steal the drug because husbands have a traditional obligation to protect their wives. Notice here that the moral reasoning has moved away from immediate individual consequences to societal consequences: What if everyone did that? Moral behaviour is conduct that conforms to the rules and conventions of society. In general, individuals at the conventional level of moral reasoning tend to consider the appropriateness of their actions from the perspective of cultural traditions and current authority figures.

At the final level of moral development, the **postconventional level,** morality is based on abstract principles that may even conflict with accepted laws and standards. The individual adopts a moral standard—not to seek approval from others or an authority figure, but to follow some universal ethical principle. "An individual human life is more important than society's dictum against stealing," someone at this level might argue. In this case, moral actions are driven by general and abstract personal codes of ethics that may not agree with societal norms.

Evaluating Kohlberg's Theory   The idea that we progress through periods of moral development, from an early focus on immediate individual consequences toward a final principled code of ethics, remains popular among many developmental psychologists (see Damon & Hart, 1992). A number of observational studies have confirmed aspects of Kohlberg's views. For example, research by University of British Columbia developmental psychologist Lawrence Walker suggests that people do seem to move through the various types of moral reasoning in the sequence suggested by Kohlberg (Walker, 1989). Furthermore, the link that both Piaget and Kohlberg made between moral reasoning and level of cognitive development has clear merit. But Kohlberg's theory has attracted criticism and amendment suggestions from many subsequent researchers—not unlike any major theory in psychology.

A strong competitor to Kohlberg's theory of moral development comes from psychologists who view morality from an evolutionary perspective. Social and developmental psychologist Dennis Krebs of Simon Fraser University reviewed some of the likely factors leading to the evolutionary selection of moral behaviours in humans (Krebs, 1998). This analysis of moral development leads to two main differences from Kohlberg's view. The evolutionary perspective suggests that people's cognitive mechanisms for thinking about morality are probably not as unified as Kohlberg suggested. Indeed, people's minds probably contain relatively unconnected "modules" or submechanisms for thinking about different aspects of morality, such as obeying authority and treating people fairly. Therefore, all modules are there from the beginning and they may sometimes come into conflict in ways not anticipated by Kohlberg.

An evolutionary analysis leads to the second difference from Kohlberg's view: Kohlberg (1984) suggested that people first think about moral dilemmas, then come up with a judgment on a moral way to proceed, and then behave in a way suggested by their moral judgment. Evolutionary psychology suggests that the system evolved the other way around: Certain social tendencies were selected because they proved to be adaptive. For example, it was adaptive to help other humans in distress because the whole group benefited. People often help first and think later. These socialized behaviours become so common and accepted that people get upset with their own and others' deviations from the norm. The bad feeling (e.g., anxiety, disgust) associated with deviations from the norm then tells us that something is immoral (Krebs & Denton, 2005).

Other critics of Kohlberg's theory argue that he tied the concept of morality too closely to an abstract code of *justice*—that is, to the idea that moral acts are those that ensure fairness to the individual (Damon & Hart, 1992). For example, suppose

CONCEPT SUMMARY

KOHLBERG'S STAGE THEORY OF MORAL DEVELOPMENT

Stage	Basis for Moral Judgment	Possible Response to "Was Heinz Right?"
Preconventional	External consequences	Yes: "He won't be able to look after the house and family without his wife." No: "He may go to jail and his life will be ruined."
Conventional	Social order	Yes: "Spouses must protect each other to maintain the family unit." No: "Stealing is against the laws that maintain social order."
Postconventional	Abstract ethical principles	Yes: "Individual lives are more important than society's laws." No: "Stealing is inherently wrong."

that your sense of morality is not based on fairness but rather on concern for the welfare of others. You might believe that the appropriate action is always one that doesn't hurt anyone and takes into account the happiness of the affected individual. This moral code is appropriate for women, according to Harvard psychologist Carol Gilligan (1982). She has argued that women in our culture are conditioned to adopt such a view (a moral code based on caring), whereas men are taught to make moral decisions on the basis of an abstract sense of justice. Given the way Kohlberg's scale is scored, however, this socialization difference means that women will tend to be classified at a lower level of moral development than men are. Gilligan sees this result as an unfair and unjustified gender bias.

The Role of Culture   It now appears that Gilligan may have overstated the evidence for sex differences in moral reasoning. Modern samples of educated men and women (e.g., college students) show minimal differences on the types of moral dilemmas studied by Kohlberg (Walker, 1989). At the same time, other evidence indicates that important cross-cultural differences occur due to social environment. For example, studies of moral decision making in India reveal striking differences from those typically found in Western cultures (Miller, 1994). Shweder, Mahapatra, and Miller (1990) found that traditional Hindu children and adults are likely to find it morally acceptable for a husband to beat a disobedient wife; in fact, keeping disobedient family members in line is considered to be the moral obligation of the head of the family. In Canada, such actions would be widely condemned. In some cultures, allowing women to show their hair in public is considered to be an outrageous sexual display. To most Canadians, this view seems silly: Here a woman covering her head is probably having a "bad-hair day." However, Canadians appear to be more troubled than are Europeans with women exposing their breasts in public.

In sum, evidence supports the cross-cultural consistency in the developmental ordering of moral thinking. Nonetheless, the development of morality is a complex process that involves influences from the larger culture, the community in which the child resides, the relationship between the child and the parent, and the child's own personality and disposition (Grusec & Kuczynski, 1997).

The Role of Emotion   Kohlberg's approach has long been criticized for leaving emotion out of the theory. A newer theory (Haidt, 2001) argues for the primacy of emotion. We automatically react with disgust or elation to certain behaviours we observe. Moral reasoning comes later when we have to explain our reactions to what we intuitively feel.

Test Yourself 10.2   *Check your knowledge of intellectual development by answering these questions. (The answers are in Appendix B.)*

1. Pick the appropriate research technique from among the following terms: cross-sectional, habituation, longitudinal, preference, reward.
   a. Baby learns to kick her leg when a blue, but not a red, card appears. _____
   b. Baby grows bored and stops looking at repeated presentations of the same event. _____
   c. Comparisons are made among three groups of children; each group contains children of a different age.

   _____
   d. The development of memory is studied by testing the same individual repeatedly throughout his or her lifetime. _____
2. According to Piaget, children develop mental models of the world, called schemas, that change as the child grows. During the preoperational period of development, children often fail to recognize that the physical properties of an object can stay the same despite superficial changes in its appearance (e.g., rolling a ball of clay into a sausage shape doesn't change its mass). Piaget referred to this ability as
   a. conservation
   b. object permanence
   c. accommodation
   d. relativistic thinking
3. Pick the appropriate level of moral development, as described by Kohlberg. Possible answers include conventional, preconventional, and postconventional.
   a. Actions are justified on the basis of whether or not they disrupt social order. _____
   b. Actions are justified on the basis of abstract moral principles. _____
   c. Actions are justified on the basis of their immediate consequences. _____

▶ Developing Socially

LEARNING GOALS

1. Be able to explain the notion of temperament.
2. Understand the short-term characteristics and long-term consequences of early attachments.
3. Comprehend Erik Erikson's stage theory of personal identity development.
4. Understand gender-role development and the role of the family in adult development.
5. Recognize the social and psychological factors that older people face.
6. Appreciate the psychological issues connected with death and dying.

Human beings do not develop in isolation. The unfolding of their biological makeup occurs in a social context. Their social and emotional relationships critically affect how they act and view themselves. For infants, relationships with caregivers go beyond the basics of adequate nourishment and a safe and secure environment. For children, the social task is to become part of a social group and thereby learn what it means to get along with peers and follow the rules and norms of society. For adults, whose social bonds become increasingly intimate, the task is to learn to accept responsibility for the care and support of others. As with most aspects of development, social and personal development is a continuous process that is shaped by innate biological forces as well as by learned experiences.

Temperament

temperament

Behavioural tendencies that have biological origins

The child's social and personal development begins with a biologically based set of behavioural predispositions called **temperament.** Included are such factors as sociability, moodiness, inhibition, and energy level. Although mostly genetic in origin, part of temperament is due to congenital factors—that is, biological forces that alter the fetus during pregnancy. For example, environmental stress on the mother can cause fluctuations in hormones that, in turn, alter fetal development. Whatever their source, these temperament factors continue to interact with the environment to produce the more complex adult personality (see Chapter 12).

Early work on temperament proposed that infants can be categorized into types. As you might guess, some babies are *easy*: They are basically happy, readily establish daily routines, and tend not to get upset very easily. Other babies are *difficult*: They resist new experiences, resist the establishment of routines, and often get upset. Fortunately, only about 10% of babies fall into the difficult group, with about 40% classified as easy (Thomas & Chess, 1977). The remaining 50% are more difficult to categorize. For example, some babies are *slow to warm up*, which means they show a more complex mixture of different temperaments.

Modern research on temperament has moved to a more complex dimensional approach. Instead of a few categories, infants can now be scored on as many as 15 different dimensions (Rothbart, Ahadi, Hershey, & Fisher, 2001; Soudino, Plomin, & DeFries, 1996). One dimension now attracting attention seems to be the antecedent of adult shyness. Jerome Kagan developed novel techniques to demonstrate how infants differ in terms of being *inhibited* (i.e., fearful of unfamiliar people or new events) versus *uninhibited* (i.e., calm in the face of the unfamiliar or novel). In several longitudinal studies, he showed that the same babies who acted fearful when a complex mobile was activated in front of them (about 20%) later developed into shy adolescents (Kagan, 1997; Kagan & Snidman, 1991).

Research on other dimensions of temperament has also demonstrated stability across childhood (Caspi & Silva, 1995; Eaton & Saudino, 1992; Schwartz, Snidman, & Kagan, 1996). For example, infants who seem very energetic show that same energy later in life. Most important is the evidence that identical twins, who share the same genetic material, show more similarities in temperament than do fraternal twins or regular siblings raised in the same home (Braungart, Plomin, DeFries, & Fulker, 1992; Jang, Livesley, & Vernon, 1996b). One implication of the power of temperament is that children may be affecting their parents' behaviour rather than the reverse. A tense, angry, hyper-reactive mother may actually be the creation of her difficult child (Johnston, 1988; Johnston & Freeman, 1997).

The attachment process involves an interaction between child temperament and parental reactions.

Forming Bonds with Others

To gain the nourishment needed to live, as well as protection from danger, the newborn relies on interactions with others—especially the mother. The newborn forms what psychologists call **attachment,** a strong emotional tie to one or more close others. The need for early attachment is so critical that many researchers believe that innate, biologically driven behavioural systems may be involved in their formation (Bowlby, 1969, 1988; Maestripieri, 2001).

According to child psychiatrist John Bowlby, both caregiver and infant are preprogrammed from birth to respond to certain environmental signals with attachment behaviour. The newborn typically cries, coos, and smiles, and these behaviours lead naturally to attention and support from the caregiver. It's no accident that adults like to hear babies coo or watch them smile—humans probably evolved to derive pleasure from observing happy babies (Bowlby, 1969; Sigelman & Shaffer, 1995). Parents also seem to derive a great deal of pleasure from singing to their infants (Trehub, Hill, & Lamenetsky, 1997).

Similarly, newborns are biologically predisposed to respond to nurturance from a caregiver. For example, newborns imitate the facial expressions of their parents (Maratos, 1998), which presumably enhances their social interactions with mom and dad (Bjorklund, 1997). Queen's University infant researchers Lawrence Symons, Sylvia Hains, and Darwin Muir (1998) have demonstrated that even five-month-old infants are quite sensitive to the direction of another person's gaze, and their apparent interest in a social interaction decreases substantially when a person looks away from them even a little bit. Both the infant and the caregiver are active participants in a reciprocal relationship—the attachment is formed because both parties are prepared to respond to the right kind of environmental

attachments

Strong emotional ties formed to one or more intimate companions

events by bonding. The bond usually is formed initially between baby and mother because it is the mother who provides most of the early care (Lamb, Ketterlinus, & Fracasso, 1992).

The Origins of Attachment

The idea that humans are evolutionarily predisposed to form strong emotional attachments makes sense from an adaptive standpoint—it helps to ensure survival. But what determines the strength and quality of the attachment? Differences clearly exist in the quality of the bond that forms between infant and caregiver—some infants are securely attached to their caregivers; others are not. Research with animal subjects suggests that one very important factor is the amount of actual contact comfort—the degree of warm physical contact—provided by the caregiver.

Contact Comfort   In his classic research on early attachment, psychologist Harry Harlow noticed that newborn rhesus monkeys, when separated from their mothers at birth, tended to become attached to soft, cuddly things left in their cages, such as baby blankets. If one of these blankets was removed for cleaning, Harlow noticed, the monkeys would become extremely upset and cling to it frantically when it was returned. Intrigued, Harlow began a series of experiments in which he isolated newborn monkeys and raised them in cages with a variety of surrogate, or artificial, "mothers" (Harlow & Zimmerman, 1959). In one experiment, baby monkeys were exposed to two surrogate mothers: One consisted simply of wire mesh fitted with an artificial nipple that delivered food. The other was a nipple-less mother made of soft cloth and a padding of foam rubber.

Which of the two surrogate mothers should the infant monkeys prefer? If early attachments are based primarily on who provides nourishment, we would expect the monkeys to prefer the wire mother: That is, infants should love the one who feeds them. But in the vast majority of cases, the monkeys actually preferred the cloth mother. If startled in some way, perhaps by the introduction of a foreign object into the cage, the monkeys ran immediately to the cloth mother, hung on

If forced to choose between two surrogate mothers, baby monkeys prefer a soft and cuddly cloth "mother" to a wire one, even when the wire mother provides the food.

Children orphaned by the 1989 war in Romania were housed in a hospital under conditions that led to its being dubbed "the children's Auschwitz."

tight, and showed no interest in the wire mother that provided the food. Harlow and his colleagues concluded that contact comfort—the warmth and softness provided by the terry cloth—was the primary motivator of attachment (Harlow, Harlow, & Meyer, 1971).

For obvious reasons, similar experiments have never been conducted with human babies. However, it is clear that human infants are like rhesus infants in their desire and need for contact comfort. Many studies have looked at how children fare in institutional settings that provide relatively low levels of *contact comfort* (e.g., Hodges & Tizard, 1989). Children reared in orphanages with poor infant-to-caregiver ratios (e.g., 1 caregiver for every 10 to 20 infants), on average, show many more developmental problems than do children reared in less deprived environments (Shaffer, 1993). Recent research has looked at orphaned children in Romania who, for some time, were literally "warehoused with minimal food, clothing, heat, or caregivers" (Kaler & Freeman, 1994). When the social and intellectual functioning of these orphans is compared with children reared in their own homes, the orphans show significant and sometimes severe deficits.

Interaction with Time and Temperament   In many mammals, the influence of environment must occur during what is called a *critical period*—an ideal time in infancy when certain events must occur to have their maximum effect (Lorenz, 1970). This notion appears to apply to human attachment processes (Ainsworth, Blehar, Waters, & Wall, 1978; Cox, Owen, Henderson, & Margand, 1992). Mother–child contact must occur during early infancy to maximize its impact on both mother and child.

In addition, the child's own temperament can influence whether the infant will receive the contact he or she needs. Difficult or fussy babies tend to elicit fewer comforting and responsive reactions, and the quality of the attachment between parent and child suffers as a result (Thomas & Chess, 1977). Temperament determines parental reactions, which then determine contact comfort, which then influences the child's attachment tendencies.

How children react when they are in a strange situation provides insight into the type of attachment they've formed with their parent or caregiver.

Nelson Photo

Types of Attachment

strange situation test

Gradually subjecting a child to a stressful situation and observing his or her behaviour toward the parent or caregiver; this test is used to classify children according to type of attachment: secure, resistant, or avoidant

For such reasons, systematic differences exist in the types of bonds that are formed. To investigate these differences, psychologists have used a technique called the **strange situation test.** This test, which was developed by Mary Ainsworth and her colleagues, can be used to classify 10- to 24-month-old children into three main attachment groups (e.g., Ainsworth & Wittig, 1969; Ainsworth et al., 1978). This experimental situation gradually subjects the child to a stressful situation and notes how his or her behaviour toward the parent changes. After arrival in the lab, the parent and child are ushered into a waiting room filled with toys; the child is encouraged to play with the toys. Various levels of infant stress are then introduced. A stranger enters the room; the parent steps out for a few moments, leaving the child alone. The researchers measure several dependent measures of stress or discomfort: Initially, how willing is the child to move away from the parent and play with the toys? How much crying or distress does the child show when the parent leaves the room? How does the child react to the parent when the parent comes back into the room—does the child greet and cling to the parent, or does he or she move away?

Most infants—approximately 70%—react to the strange situation test with what Ainsworth called *secure attachment.* With the parent present, even if the situation is new and strange, these children play happily and are likely to explore the room looking for interesting toys or magazines to shred. But as the level of stress increases, they become increasingly uneasy and clingy. If the mother leaves the room, the child will probably start to cry but will calm down rapidly if the mother returns.

About 10% of children show a pattern called *resistant attachment.* These children react to stress in an ambiguous way, which may indicate a lack of trust for the parent. Resistant children are wary in a strange situation, refusing to leave their mother's side and explore the room, and they do not deal well with the sudden appearance of strangers. If the mother leaves the room, they cry, yet they are unlikely to greet the mother with affection on her return. Instead, these children act ambivalent, scorning their mother by temporarily resisting her affection.

The final group of children—about 20%—show a pattern of *avoidant attachment.* These children demonstrate no strong attachment to the mother in any aspect of the strange situation test. They are not particularly bothered by the appearance of strangers in the room, nor do they show much concern when the mother leaves the room or much interest when she returns. Ainsworth discovered that the parents of these children tend, on average, to be unresponsive and impatient when it comes to the child's needs and may even actively reject the child on a regular basis (Ainsworth, 1979). Why? It's difficult to tell because the parent–child relationship depends on several factors: the particular personality characteristics of the parent, the temperament of the child, and the child-rearing practices of the culture.

PRACTICAL SOLUTIONS

DO PARENTS REALLY MATTER?

Can any idea in child development be more accepted than the assumption that parents have an influence on the way their children turn out? Indeed, much of the field has been built on debates and subsequent recommendations about how best to raise children. Nonetheless, several psychologists have recently been bold enough to challenge this almost sacred claim. In her review of the literature, Judith Harris (1995, 1998) concluded that the research literature points to factors other than the parents' child-rearing behaviour as the real causes behind the differences seen in the personal and social behaviour of children and adults. A consequence of the traditional view, she complained, was that parents—especially mothers—were blamed for everything their children did. As we did in our discussion of temperament, Harris noted that parents are often just reacting to their child's behaviour rather than causing it.

Harris accepts that parents do matter in the limited sense that they pass on their genetic predispositions to their children. In fact, she cites the accumulating evidence for the behavioural genetics of personality. Roughly half the variation observed in children's personality can be attributed to the genes inherited from their parents (e.g., Jang, Livesley, & Vernon, 1996a, 1996b). Of course, that leaves a substantial amount for the environment to explain.

But the evidence about environmental effects is even more surprising. It appears that these effects are primarily within the family (Plomin et al., 1997; Plomin, Corley, Caspi, Fulker, & DeFries, 1998). That means that children of the same parents are experiencing different environments. The most obvious difference among siblings is their birth order. The effects of birth order—once thought to be disproved (Ernst & Angst, 1983)—have been rehabilitated by the work of

Who affects you more—your parents or your friends?

Frank Sulloway (1997). The research now indicates that first-born children are more domineering, dutiful, and conservative in their political beliefs, while later-born children are more rebellious and open to new ideas. These differences in personality are created not by parents treating the birth orders differently, but by the siblings treating each other differently. First-borns are always older and, therefore, have physical and status superiority over the later-borns. During childhood, first-borns are constantly trying to reassert their higher status in the sibling community. Later-borns are always trying to break down the hierarchy. So, their adult personalities become structured around these issues of status and dominance. Sulloway's results have been replicated in large samples of students and adults (Paulhus, Trapnell, & Chen, 1999).

Rather than birth order, Judith Harris (1998) argues that children in the same family end up with different personalities primarily because they have different friends. She provides evidence that siblings who share friends do end up with personalities that are more similar than siblings who do not share friends. Other environmental factors that could make

siblings different are different teachers and various chance experiences. For example, one child might have the good fortune to be taught by an inspiring teacher while the other child was turned off school by a bullying incident. Note again that these are differences among children with the same parents. The differences between families appear to be explicable by genetics, so that the differences we see in parents' child-rearing styles may not actually be having the effect that psychologists have always assumed.

As you might expect, many developmental psychologists have reacted negatively to Harris's ideas (Borkowski, Ramey, & Bristol-Power, 2001; Maccoby, 2000). The counterarguments have included that (1) the behaviour genetics studies are flawed, (2) there is evidence that children in different cultures have different personalities, and (3) extreme parental treatment (e.g., child abuse) is known to have long-term effects. Such controversies as these often take years to clarify, but the challenge to re-think such a basic issue always has positive scientific benefits. Stay tuned—there is bound to be more debate about this issue.

CRITICAL **THINKING**

Do you think the findings of the strange situation test would change if the test were conducted in the child's home? Why or why not?

Do Early Attachments Matter Later in Life?

Given that infants can already be divided into these attachment groups by age one, it's reasonable to wonder about the long-term consequences. For instance, are the avoidant children doomed to a life of insecurity and failed relationships? Evidence suggests that children with an early secure attachment do indeed have some social and intellectual advantages. For instance, Acadia University developmental psychologists Douglas Symons and Sharon Clark have reported that five-year-old children with more secure attachments to their mothers do better at cognitive tasks, such as locating objects (Symons & Clark, 2000). In other research, teachers rate securely attached children as more curious and self-directed in school (Waters, Wippman, & Sroufe, 1979). By age 10 or 11, securely attached children also tend to have closer and more mature relationships with their peers than do children who were classified as insecurely attached (Elicker, Englund, & Sroufe, 1992). Other researchers have found that early attachment relationships do predict patterns of social interactions and other important behaviours in adulthood (Bartholomew, Henderson, & Dutton, 2000; Mikulincer & Shaver, 2005).

However, early patterns of attachment are not perfect predictors of later behaviour. One problem is stability: Sometimes a child who appears to be insecurely attached at 12 months can act quite differently in the strange situation test a few months later (Lamb et al., 1992). In addition, a child who has a particular kind of attachment to one parent may show quite a different attachment pattern to the other. It's also important to remember that when psychologists talk about predicting later behaviour based on early attachment patterns, they are referring mainly to correlational studies. As you learned in Chapter 2, it's not possible to draw firm conclusions about causality from simple correlational analyses. The fact that later behaviour can be predicted from early attachment patterns does not guarantee that early bonding caused the later behaviour patterns; other factors might be responsible. For instance, children who form secure attachments in infancy typically have caregivers who remain warm and responsive throughout childhood, adolescence, and adulthood. So it could be that securely attached infants tend to have successful and meaningful relationships later in life because they live most of their lives in supportive environments.

Evolutionary Bases of Family Interactions

It is understandable that humans, like other mammals, have evolved attachment mechanisms that serve to maintain contact between pairs of intimate individuals. Whether it is child to parent, parent to child, or spouse to spouse, these mechanisms are of great benefit.

A number of Canadian psychologists have studied the complexities of these family interactions. McMaster University psychologists Martin Daly and Margo Wilson (1998, 1999a) have suggested that human parenting behaviour should be considered as a form of "reproductive strategy" that human parents evolved to "invest resources," including food, protection, and nurturance, in ways that will promote the optimal number of offspring for an individual parent. Daly and Wilson offer an example in the fact that rates of child abuse and neglect are considerably higher in families with stepparents as compared with those with two biological parents present. They suggest that people may have evolved so that they tend to be more nurturant and protective of children who are biologically related to them, and that stepparenting situations involve a decrease in the "buffering" effect that biological relatedness provides against the frustrations and stresses of parenting; thus, stepparents display higher rates of child abuse and neglect than biological parents do. Daly and Wilson are quick to point out that many stepparents are excellent parents and that most do not abuse their children. However, they suggest that an evolutionary perspective on this phenomenon provides important insights into the traumatic problem of child abuse and may suggest some targets for programs aimed at preventing such abuse.

In other research, Daly and colleague Catherine Salmon of Simon Fraser University (1998) suggest that evolutionary theory predicts that parents should invest more in first-born children and last-born children, and invest the least in middle-born children. First-born children were expected to be favoured partly because they have a higher "reproductive value," which means, all things being equal, favouring older children would have resulted in more descendants for human ancestors. Last-born children are expected to be favoured, to some degree, as well, but for different evolutionary reasons. On average, parents of last-borns are older than parents of first- or middle-borns. Older parents are generally expected to invest more in children, since there is no point in "holding back" resources for future children (unlike the case for parents of first- and middle-borns). But middle-born children have neither the reproductive value advantage of first-borns nor the older-parent advantage of younger children. Salmon and Daly found these predictions indirectly confirmed in a sample of Canadian undergraduate students (1998). When asked what person in the world they felt closest to, 64% of first-borns named a parent, compared with 39% of last-borns and only 10% of middle-borns. Similarly, when asked who they would go to for emotional support after a trauma, 42% of first-borns named a parent, as did 44% of last-borns, compared with only 21% of middle-borns. Instead, middle-borns were five times as likely as first-borns or last-borns to say they would go to a sibling for emotional support, rather than to their parents.

Although these patterns do not directly indicate that parents invested in the ways predicted by Salmon and Daly, they can be interpreted as quite possibly resulting from the predicted patterns of differential parental investment.

An evolutionary view of family relationships does not deny that culture and environment play important roles in influencing parental and other family behaviours (Surbey, 1998). However, it does suggest that people have evolved psychological dispositions that provide a foundation for parenting and other family behaviours and that cultural and other environmental forces interact with these basic evolved dispositions to produce the range of behaviours that we see in contemporary families (Janicki & Krebs, 1998).

It should be noted that infant survival was definitely a prime factor in shaping the evolved psychological adaptations that underlie cultural variations in parenting behaviour (Crawford, 1998b; Daly & Wilson, 1987). Many recent researchers who have examined these issues suggest that variability between cultures in behavioural patterns, such as childcare, are best thought of as deriving from complex interactions between such evolved psychological adaptations and influences from environmental and cultural sources (Barkow et al., 1992; Janicki & Krebs, 1998). This "co-evolutionary" perspective emphasizes the usefulness of considering both biological adaptations and cultural or environmental pressures in understanding differences between cultures in important behaviours, such as child-rearing patterns.

Friendships   There's no question that early attachments are important. But the relationships formed after infancy, especially during later childhood and adolescence, also significantly affect our social behaviour. Under the right circumstances, there are good reasons to believe that individuals can counteract negative experiences that occur during infancy or childhood (Lamb et al., 1992). The significance of friendship is a case in point. Psychologists now recognize that a child's social network—the number and quality of his or her friends—has a tremendous impact on social development and well-being (Berndt, 1988; Harris, 1998; Hartup & Stevens, 1997).

Children with friends interact more confidently in social situations, they are more cooperative, and they report higher levels of self-esteem (Newcomb & Bagwell, 1995). Children with friends, compared with those without friends, are also less likely to seek help for psychological problems, and they're more likely to be seen as well adjusted by teachers and adult caretakers. Such trends are true for young children and adolescents and continue into adulthood (Berndt & Keefe, 1995). When you read Chapter 16, which deals with stress and health, you'll find that social support—particularly our network of friends—predicts how well we're able to cope and deal with stressful situations and how well we're able to recover from injury or disease. This is just as true for children as it is for adults (Hartup & Stevens, 1997).

Obviously, general conclusions like these need to be qualified a bit. For example, the quality (or closeness) of the friendship matters, as does the identity of the friends. If you have very close friends who recommend drug use or a life of crime, then the developmental consequences will be less than ideal. It's also unclear at this point what aspects of friendship matter most. For instance, people often share similarities with their friends (such as common attitudes and values). Does this mean that friends merely play the role of reinforcing our values and making us more secure in our attitudes? In-depth research on friendships is ongoing, in part, because psychologists recognize the value of friendship across the life span. When asked to rank what is most important in their lives, children, adolescents, and adults often pick "friends" as the answer (Klinger, 1977).

At adolescence, peer culture becomes increasingly important, and a conflict between family-oriented behaviours and peer-oriented behaviours has often been perceived. Developmental researcher Sherry Beaumont, of the University of Northern British Columbia, examined this issue by focusing on differences between the conversational styles that Canadian adolescent girls adopted with their mothers as compared with their friends. Beaumont found that, with their friends, adolescent girls used a fast-paced conversational style that included many interruptions and considerable mutual talking at the same time, and this pattern increased from preadolescence to mid-adolescence. In contrast, mothers tended to speak more slowly than their daughters, and this resulted in the mothers being interrupted much more by their daughters than the reverse (Beaumont, 1995, 1996). Adolescents also rated their conversations with friends as friendlier and as more involved than conversations with their mothers. Beaumont suggests that differences in conversational styles may be one of the reasons that adolescents rate their parents as less understanding, less interesting, and more controlling than their friends (Beaumont & Cheyne, 1998).

Unfortunately, children's peer relationships have a dark side, namely, bullying. Developmental psychologists Debra Pepler, of York University and The LaMarsh Centre for Research on Violence and Conflict Resolution, Wendy Craig, of Queen's University, and their colleagues have extensively studied the development and remediation of bullying in children and adolescents (e.g., Craig, Pepler, & Atlas,

The quality of a child's social network—the number and quality of friends—can have a tremendous influence on his or her social development and well-being.

2000; Pepler, Craig, & O'Connell, 1999). Their research has led to "systemic recommendations for anti-bullying interventions," some of which are the following (Connolly, Pepler, Craig, & Taradash, 2000):

1. Change must occur in the entire system, that is, with the bully, victim, peers, school staff, parents, and community.
2. Parents of both bullies and victims must intervene.
3. Both bullies and victims must receive counselling.
4. Implementing an anti-bullying program is a complex and prolonged process but can be successful.

Pepler and Craig's research on bullying is a good reminder of the fact that research in developmental psychology is not just of theoretical interest; it can often be applied to important real-world problems.

Forming a Personal Identity: Erikson's Crises of Development

One of the most important parts of social development is the formation of **personal identity**—a sense of self, of who you are as an individual and how well you measure up against peers. We recognize ourselves—that is, that we represent a unique person different from others—quite early in our development. Children as young as six months of age will reach out and touch an image of themselves in a mirror; by a year and a half, if they look into a mirror and notice a smudge mark on their nose, they'll reach up and touch their own face (Butterworth, 1992; Lewis & Brooks-Gunn, 1979).

As noted earlier in the chapter, many psychologists are convinced that people use social interactions—primarily the ones with parents during childhood and with peers later in life—to help them come to grips with who they are as individuals. One of the most influential theories of how this process of identity formation proceeds is the stage theory of Erik Erikson. Erikson (1963, 1968, 1982) believed that personal identity is shaped by a series of psychosocial crises that each person must confront at a characteristic stage in development (see the Concept Summary table on page 418).

Infancy and Childhood   As you know, human infants are largely at the mercy of others for their survival. According to Erikson, this overwhelming dependency leads infants to their first true psychosocial crisis, usually in the first year of life: *trust versus mistrust.* Psychologically and practically, babies face an important problem: Are there people out there in the world who will meet my survival needs? Resolution of this crisis leads to the formation of an initial sense of either trust or mistrust, and the infant begins to develop some basic knowledge about how people differ. Some people can be trusted and some cannot. It is through social interactions, learning whom to trust and whom not to trust, that the newborn ultimately resolves the crisis and learns how to deal more effectively with his or her environment.

As the child progresses through toddlerhood and on into childhood, other fundamental conflicts appear and need to be resolved. During the "terrible twos," the child struggles with breaking his or her dependence on parents. The crisis at this point, according to Erikson, is *autonomy versus shame or doubt:* Am I capable of independent self-control of my actions, or am I generally inadequate? Between the ages of three and six, the crisis becomes one of *initiative versus guilt:* Can I plan things on my own, with my own initiative, or should I feel guilty for trying to carry out my own bold plans for action? In late childhood, beginning around age 6 and ending around age 12, the struggle is for a basic sense of *industry versus inferiority:* Can I learn and master new skills? Can I be industrious and complete required tasks? Or do I lack fundamental competence?

personal identity

A sense of who we are as individuals and how well we stack up against peers; Erik Erikson's theory postulates that personal identity is shaped by a series of personal crises that each person confronts at characteristic stages of development

Part of the process of developing socially is the development of personal identity. This child may be experiencing self-awareness as she examines her reflection in the mirror.

CONCEPT SUMMARY

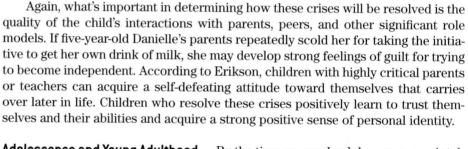

ERIKSON'S STAGES OF PERSONAL IDENTITY DEVELOPMENT

Life Period	Stage	Conflicts Revolve Around
Infancy and childhood	Trust versus mistrust (first year of life)	Developing a sense of trust in others: Are there others present who will fulfill my needs?
	Autonomy versus shame or doubt ("terrible twos")	Developing a sense of self-control: Can I control my own actions?
	Initiative versus guilt (ages three to six)	Developing a sense of drive and initiative: Can I carry out plans? Should I feel guilty for trying to carry out my own plans?
	Industry versus inferiority (ages 6 to 12)	Developing a sense of personal ability and competence: Can I learn and develop new skills?
Adolescence and young adulthood	Identity versus role confusion (adolescence)	Developing a single, unified concept of self, a sense of personal identity: Who am I?
	Intimacy versus isolation (young adulthood)	Questioning the meaning of our relationships with others: Can I form a committed relationship with another person, or will my personal insecurities lead to isolation?
Adulthood and older adulthood	Generativity versus stagnation	Concern over whether we have contributed to the success of children and future generations. Older adulthood: Have I contributed to the community at large?
	Integrity versus despair	Acceptance of life—successes and failures: Am I content, looking back on my life?

Again, what's important in determining how these crises will be resolved is the quality of the child's interactions with parents, peers, and other significant role models. If five-year-old Danielle's parents repeatedly scold her for taking the initiative to get her own drink of milk, she may develop strong feelings of guilt for trying to become independent. According to Erikson, children with highly critical parents or teachers can acquire a self-defeating attitude toward themselves that carries over later in life. Children who resolve these crises positively learn to trust themselves and their abilities and acquire a strong positive sense of personal identity.

Adolescence and Young Adulthood   By the time we reach adolescence, our intellectual development has proceeded to the point where we naturally begin to consider personal qualities that are both general and abstract. In particular, Erikson argued, adolescents have to deal with the fundamental crisis of *identity versus role confusion*. They become concerned with testing roles and finding their true identity: Who am I? What kind of person do I really represent? In a very real sense, the teenager acts as a kind of personality theorist, attempting to integrate various self-perceptions about abilities and limitations into a single unified concept of self. Erikson (1968) coined the term *identity crisis* to describe this transition period, which he believed is often filled with turmoil.

Observational studies of how adolescents actually come to grips with the identity crisis reveal many individual differences (Offer & Schonert-Reichl, 1992; Peterson, 1988). Not all teenagers become paralyzed with identity angst and anxiety—most, in fact, show no more anxiety during this transition period than at other points in their lives. Simon Fraser University psychologist James Marcia found that individual differences also occur in how young people commit to a particular view of themselves (e.g., Marcia, 1966). Some adolescents choose an identity by modelling others: "I'm honest, open, and cooperative because that's the way I was brought up by my parents." Others develop a personal identity through a soul-searching evaluation of their feelings and abilities. Some adolescents even reject the crisis altogether, choosing instead not to commit to any particular view of themselves. The specific course or

Erik Erikson would probably argue that this young man is concerned with testing roles and finding his true identity.

Nick Koudis/PhotoDisc/Getty Images

path an individual takes depends on many factors, including his or her level of cognitive development, the quality of the parent–child relationship, and outside experiences (Compas, Hinden, & Gerhardt, 1995). The ethnic and sociocultural groups that the adolescent is part of and identifies with can also play an important role in identity formation (e.g., Leadbeater & Way, 1996).

Entrance into young adulthood is marked by the crisis of *intimacy versus isolation*. Resolution of the identity crisis causes us to question the meaning of our relationships with others: Am I willing or able to form an intimate, committed relationship with another person? Or will my insecurities and fears about losing independence lead to a lifetime of isolation and loneliness? People who lack an integrated conception of themselves, Erikson argued, cannot commit themselves to a shared identity with someone else. Some have argued that this particular conclusion may be more applicable to men than women (Gilligan, 1982). Historically, women have been forced by societal pressures to deal with intimate commitments—raising a family and running a home—either at the same time as, or before, the process of searching for a stable personal identity. This trend may well be changing, however, because more women are establishing professional careers before marriage.

Adulthood, Middle Age, and Beyond   With the establishment of career and family arrives the crisis of *generativity versus stagnation*. The focus at this point shifts from resolving intimacy to concern about children and future generations: Am I contributing successfully to the community at large? Am I doing enough to ensure the survival and productivity of future generations? Failure to resolve this crisis can lead to a sense of meaninglessness in middle life and beyond—a condition Erikson calls *stagnation*.

For some people, especially men in their 40s, this point in psychosocial development is marked by soul-searching questions about personal identity reminiscent of those faced in adolescence (Gould, 1978; Levinson, Darow, Klein, Levinson, & McKee, 1978). According to such psychologists as Gould and Levinson, the so-called midlife crisis arises as people begin to confront their own mortality—the inevitability of death—and as they come to grips with the fact that they may never achieve their lifelong dreams and goals. There is no doubt that this can be an emotionally turbulent period, but recent evidence suggests that the midlife crisis is a relatively rare phenomenon. It gets a lot of attention in the media, and it's certainly consuming for those affected, but probably fewer than 5% of people in middle age undergo anything resembling a turbulent midlife crisis (McCrae & Costa, 1990).

The final stage in the process of psychosocial development, which occurs from late adulthood to the point of death, is the crisis of *integrity versus despair*. It is at this stage in people's lives, Erikson argued, that they strive to accept themselves and their pasts—both failures and successes. Older people undergo a kind of life review in an effort to resolve conflicts in the past and to find meaning in what they've accomplished. If successful in this objective search for meaning, they acquire wisdom; if unsuccessful, they wallow in despair and bitterness (Reker, 1995, 1997). An important part of the process is the preparation for death and dying, which we'll discuss in more detail near the end of the chapter.

Evaluating Erikson's Theory   Erikson's stage theory of psychosocial crises has been enormously influential in shaping how psychologists view personal identity development (Steinberg & Morris, 2001). Among its most important contributions is the recognition that personal development is a lifelong process. Individuals don't simply establish a rigid personal identity around the time they reach Piaget's formal operational stage; the way that people view themselves and their relationships changes continually throughout their lives. Erikson's theory is also noteworthy for its emphasis on the role of social and cultural interactions in shaping human psychology (Douvan, 1997).

Erik Erikson

CRITICAL · · · THINKING

How well do Erikson's ideas describe your own personal identity development? Are you going through any fundamental crisis at the moment, or are you aware of having solved one in the past?

The influence of Erikson's ideas can be seen in the growing field of narrative research (e.g., McAdams, 2001). According to this approach, people's identity is best assessed by asking them to tell stories about their lives. Research by Kate McLean (2005) at the University of Toronto emphasizes the fact that people rely heavily on critical incidents to define their identities: "Mrs. Reid, my Grade 3 teacher, taught me why good people are honest with themselves as well as with others." Whether the incidents actually happened the way that people recount them is not as important as how the story helps organize the person's life.

Nevertheless, Erikson's theory suffers from the same problems as any stage theory. Although people may confront psychosocial crises in an orderly sequence, overlap occurs across the stages (Whitbourne, Zuschlag, Elliot, & Waterman, 1992). As noted earlier, the search for identity is not confined to one turbulent period in adolescence—it is likely to continue throughout a lifetime. Furthermore, like Piaget, Erikson never clearly articulated how a person actually moves from one crisis stage to the next: What are the psychological mechanisms that allow for conflict resolution, and what determines when and how they will operate (Achenbach, 1992)? Finally, Erikson's theory of identity development, although useful as a general organizing framework, lacks sufficient scientific rigour. His concepts are vague enough to make scientific testing difficult.

Additional Issues in Adolescent Development

Developmental researchers have examined many aspects of psychological development during adolescence besides moral development and the development of personal identity. Adolescence has often been considered a period of life when people take greater risks than at other stages of development. To examine the development of risk-taking behaviour in adolescents and young adults, Nancy Galambos and Lauree Tilton-Weaver (1998) studied the following four risk-taking behaviours among a sample of almost 2000 young Canadians aged 15 to 24: smoking, binge drinking, sex with multiple partners, and sex without a condom. Binge drinking was the most common of these risk behaviours among the 15- to 19-year-olds, with 52% of males and 35% of females reporting consuming five or more alcoholic beverages during a single occasion at least once in the previous year. Approximately 5% of both males and females in the sample reported engaging in all four risk behaviours, although far more reported engaging in none of the four risk behaviours: 39% of the females and 32% of the males. The researchers found that multiple-risk behaviour was higher among young people who were not students, as well as among those who did not live with their parents and those who felt distressed. Adolescents who regularly attended religious services, however, did not report engaging in risk-taking behaviours as much as other teens did.

Adolescents display gender differences in many other behaviours besides risk taking. For example, female teenagers tend to show far more "internalizing" psychological problems than males do, such as depression, anxiety, suicidal feelings, and eating disorders. Males, on the other hand, have more "externalizing" problems: oppositional behaviour, delinquency, and school problems (e.g., Leadbeater, Blatt, & Quinlan, 1995). Developmental psychologist Bonnie Leadbeater and her colleagues suggest that one factor leading to more internalizing problems in girls is a greater sense of interpersonal vulnerability in teenage girls—a tendency to see themselves as helpless, together with a fear of being abandoned. Leadbeater suggests that even normal pressures during adolescence moving girls toward greater autonomy could result in "interpersonally vulnerable" girls becoming depressed or anxious. Leadbeater also suggests that teenage boys at risk for externalizing problems seem to suffer more from the effects of self-criticism than girls. Such boys tend to view themselves and others negatively, and this leads to difficulties in interpersonal relationships that may be steppingstones to acting out and delinquency. Leadbeater suggests that one avenue for preventing such externalizing problems may be programs that promote interpersonal involvement during adolescence and that give all teenagers opportunities for leadership, valued community service, and caring for others (Leadbeater, Kuperminc, Blatt, & Hertzog, 1999).

Gender-Role Development

By the time children are in elementary school, gender is seen as a permanent condition—"I'm a boy (or a girl) and always will be." At this point, children tend to act in accordance with reasonably well established **gender roles**—specific patterns of behaviour consistent with how society dictates males and females should act. Children at this age have strong opinions about how boys and girls should behave, what occupations they should have when they grow up, and how they should look. Can you imagine the reaction that a seven-year-old boy might receive if he walked into his Grade 2 class wearing a dress or with his fingernails polished a bright shade of pink? Indeed, there is much evidence that boys are punished more than girls for deviating from their standard sex role. It is more acceptable for a girl to be a "tomboy" than for a boy to be a "sissy" (Ruble & Martin, 1998).

Nature or Nurture?   How do these firm ideas about gender roles develop? Are they the inevitable byproduct of biological differences between male and female brains, or do they grow out of experience? We encountered this issue in Chapter 3, where we considered the evidence supporting gender-based differences in brain anatomy and functioning. Behavioural sex differences, such as activity level, can be detected even in the womb (Campbell & Eaton, 1999). Hormones released by the endocrine system early in development likely account for some gender differences in behaviour and thought (Kimura, 1999), and it is likely that natural selection has shaped males and females to have evolved psychological adaptations that differ in some respects (Buss, 1999; Miller, 1998). However, many psychologists have focused on environmental factors in gender-role development because they are more subject to modification.

The development of **gender schemas** may play an important role in maintaining gender roles in children and adults (Bem, 1981). A gender schema is an organized set of beliefs and perceptions held about men and women. Once established, these schemas guide and direct how individuals view others, as well as how they view their own behaviour. For example, men's gender schemas might direct them to judge their own behaviour, as well as the behaviour of other men, in terms of strength, aggression, and masculinity. We encountered the concept of schemas earlier in the chapter when we talked about Piaget, and we'll have more to say in later chapters about schemas and the role they play in directing behaviour. For the

CRITICAL THINKING

Do you think that society should work hard to eliminate specific gender roles? Do you believe that men and women can ever be taught to think and act similarly?

gender roles

Specific patterns of behaviour that are consistent with how society dictates males and females should act

gender schemas

The organized sets of beliefs and perceptions held about men and women

Many negative stereotypes about seniors are exaggerated. The majority of older people are not sick and most don't have disabilities; they lead active lives.

Steve Mason/PhotoDisc/Getty Images

Scott T. Baxter/PhotoDisc/Getty Images

Corbis Royalty Free/Magma

moment, you can think of schemas as knowledge organizers that people carry around inside their heads. Gender schemas are acquired through learning, they set guidelines for people's behaviour, and they underlie the expectations that people hold about the appropriateness of actions. As you can probably guess, gender schemas are mostly adaptive—they help us interpret the behaviour of others—but they can lead to inaccurate perceptions of specific individuals and even to discrimination.

Growing Old in Society

With the passage of time, and the inevitable physical declines that accompany the aging process, come constant new challenges for the developing individual. Of course, not all the changes that greet us in our older years are negative—far from it. In fact, some kinds of intelligence seem to increase with age (see Chapter 9), marital satisfaction often grows (Carstensen, 1995), and many seniors remain actively involved in the community and report high levels of contentment. One recent survey found that people in their 70s, on average, report more confidence in their ability to perform tasks than do people in their 50s (Wallhagen, Strawbridge, & Shema, 1997).

At the same time, older people have definite hurdles in their pathways, many related to health care. Seniors need more physical care, require more doctor visits, and can be at an economic disadvantage because of retirement; they also have an elevated rate of depression (Reker, 1997). Although most older adults do not live in nursing homes, many need continuing care. Whatever form this care takes, it is likely to be expensive. The scope of the problem should not be underestimated, especially as the "greying of Canada" continues. Over the next 50 years, there is expected to be a large increase (perhaps as much as sixfold) in the number of people over age 85.

Death and Dying

Death and the dying process have many psychological aspects, including how people come to grips with their own mortality and how they grieve and accept the loss of others. One of the most influential approaches to the dying process is the stage theory of Elisabeth Kübler-Ross (1969, 1974).

Kübler-Ross proposed that people progress through five distinct psychological stages as they face death. She based her theory on a set of extensive interviews conducted with hundreds of patients with terminal illnesses. Her fundamental insight was that people appear to react to their own impending death in a characteristic sequence: (1) *denial:* "There must be some terrible mistake"; (2) *anger:* "Why is this happening to me?"; (3) *bargaining:* "What can we do to stop this terrible thing?"; (4) *depression:* "Blot out the sun because all is lost"; and (5) *acceptance:* "I am ready to die." As a stage theorist, Kübler-Ross essentially implied that people move through each of these five stages, from denial to acceptance, as a normal part of their emotional acceptance of death.

Kübler-Ross's views on the dying process have been highly influential, in both psychological and medical circles, primarily because she was one of the first people to treat the topic of dying thoroughly and systematically. She sensitized legions of physicians to the idea that denial, anger, and depression are normal reactions to dying and that they should be treated with respect rather than dismissed. However, most psychologists today are not convinced that people progress through a fixed set of orderly stages in the way Kübler-Ross described; too many individual differences exist to support the theory. Not all dying people move through distinct emotional stages, and, even if they do, the stages do not seem to follow any particular set order. Stages might be skipped, might be experienced out of order, or might alternate, with the person being angry one day and accepting the next. In sum, no firm evidence supports a stage approach to the process of dying.

Many psychologists find it more appropriate to talk about *dying trajectories*. A dying trajectory is simply the psychological path people travel as they face their impending death. Different people show different trajectories, and the shape of the path depends on the particular illness as well as on the personality of the patient (Bortz, 1990; Glaser & Strauss, 1968). Trajectories are preferred to stages because stages imply that all people react to impending death in fixed and characteristic ways. But there is no right or wrong way to deal with dying—some people may react with anger and denial, others with calm acceptance. The best that witnesses to the dying process can do is offer support and allow the individual to follow his or her own unique path.

End-of-Life Decisions   One current topic of particular interest to psychologists is the decision-making processes that surround the end of life. Should people have the right to control how and when they die, especially if they're faced with a poor quality of life (e.g., constant pain, immobility, or dependency)? Is suicide, assisted suicide, or "pulling the plug" justified under any circumstance (Brigham & Pfeifer, 1996)? In some sense, these are legal and ethical questions rather than psychological ones, but questions about controlling the end of life occupy the attention of many people, especially seniors.

Very little research has been conducted on the psychological factors that influence end-of-life decisions. It seems likely that religious convictions, value systems, life satisfaction, and even fear of death play a role in how people feel about the various end-of-life options. A recent study by Cicirelli (1997) confirms these expectations. Older adults, ranging in age from 60 to 100, were asked their views of various end-of-life options. Each person was given sample decision situations, such as the following:

> Mrs. Lee is an elderly widow who has terminal bone cancer. She has had chemotherapy to try to cure the cancer but it has not helped her, and the side effects from the chemotherapy itself have been difficult to deal with. She is slowly getting worse, and the pain is unbearable. Drugs for pain help some but leave her in a stupor.

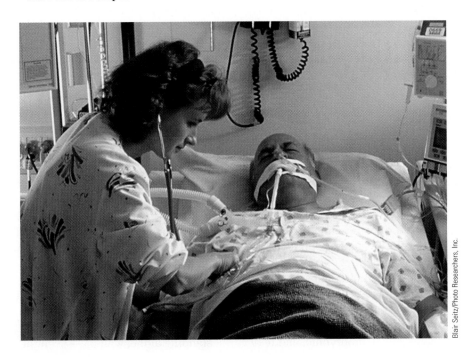

Blair Seitz/Photo Researchers, Inc.

The shape and form of the final dying trajectory depends on the particular illness, the conditions of care, and the personality of the individual.

The participants were then asked to make judgments about various end-of-life options, such as the following: strive to maintain life, refuse medical treatment or request that it be removed, commit suicide, or allow someone else to the make the decision about terminating life. Cicirelli (1997) found that people were often willing to endorse more than one option, but the majority opinion was to strive to continue life (51% of the participants endorsed this view). Psychosocial factors, such as religious convictions and fear of death, played a significant role in the decision-making process. For example, a significant minority favoured the ending of life under these circumstances, but these individuals tended, on average, to be less religious and to value the quality of life more.

Test Yourself 10.3

Test your knowledge about social and personal development by answering the following questions. (The answers are in Appendix B.)

1. The strange situation test is often used to study attachment. Identify the type of attachment that best characterizes the following reactions: avoidant, resistant, secure.
   a. When Mom leaves the room, the child begins to cry but calms down rapidly when she returns. _____
   b. When Mom leaves the room, the child couldn't care less. There is little reaction or interest when she returns.

   _____
   c. When Mom leaves the room, the child cries but shows little or no affection on her return. _____
   d. When Mom is in the room, the child refuses to leave her side and does not react well to the sudden appearance of strangers. _____

2. According to Erik Erikson, adolescents face a psychosocial crisis called *identity versus role confusion*. Current research suggests that
   a. This is a time of rebellion for all adolescents.
   b. Erikson made a mistake—no such crisis occurs.

   c. The identity crisis has mostly a genetic basis.
   d. Not all teenagers suffer anxiety during this period.

3. Gender identity doesn't develop until a child enters elementary school—it's only at that point that gender-role curricula begin to exert an effect. *True or False?*

4. Which of the following statements about seniors and growing old in society are true and which are false?
   a. Most elderly people are sick and have disabilities. *True or False?*
   b. Stereotypes about seniors are always harmful. *True or False?*
   c. Most older people have little, if any, confidence in their abilities. *True or False?*
   d. Seniors, on average, would rather die than suffer the consequences of a painful and terminal disease. *True or False?*

Human Development

R E V I E W

As people grow from infancy through childhood and on to adulthood, they experience fundamental changes in physical, intellectual, and social functioning. For the most part, these developmental changes can be viewed as adaptive reactions to environmental change as individuals grow and learn from experience. As with other species, the changes in developing humans seem to show regularities that can be seen as stages of development. At the same time, the exact psychological effects of the stages can vary dramatically according to the environment in which they occur.

First, how do we go from fertilized eggs to fully functioning adults, capable of producing our own offspring? Individuals begin life as a fertilized egg, or zygote, which contains genetic material packed into chromosomes received from the mother and father. Prenatal development—which is divided into the germinal, embryonic, and fetal stages—takes place between conception and birth. The body develops rapidly during this time and is especially susceptible to both positive and negative influences from the environment. Infancy and childhood are marked by rapid growth in height and weight and by a further maturing of the nervous system. One of the byproducts of nerve cell maturation is motor development. The major milestones in motor development—crawling, standing alone, walking—occur at similar times for most individuals, in part because of the systematic manner in which the nervous system develops.

As people move through adolescence and into early adulthood, their physical systems continue to change. Puberty is the developmental period in which individuals mature sexually, and it's marked by dramatic changes in physical appearance driven primarily by the release of gender-specific hormones. Once people reach their 20s, their bodies become physically mature, and most begin a gradual across-the-board decline in physical ability. Some declines occur in mental ability over time, especially in old age, although significant losses in mental functioning or mental health are still the exception rather than the rule. Evidence suggests that losses in the number of brain neurons may be counteracted by increases in the complexity of the remaining nerve cells. In general, individual differences exist in how the aging process proceeds; both the positive and the negative consequences of aging are affected by a person's genetic blueprint and lifestyle choices (for instance, how much a person exercises).

Second, how do we develop the intellectual tools needed to solve survival problems? Psychologists use the term *cognitive development* to refer to the changes in intellectual functioning that accompany physical maturation. Several innovative techniques have been used to map out the internal perceptual world of infants. Newborns have remarkably well-developed tools for investigating the world around them: They can see, hear, smell, feel, and taste, although not at the same level as

they will later in childhood. Individuals leave infancy with well-developed perceptual systems and use the experiences of childhood to help fine-tune and use their sensory equipment.

Much of what we know about how thought processes develop during infancy and childhood comes from the work of Jean Piaget. Piaget's theory of cognitive development proposes that children use mental models of the world—called schemas—to guide and interpret ongoing experience. Central to the theory is the idea that as children grow physically and acquire new experiences, their mental models of the world change systematically. Piaget argued that children pass through a series of cognitive stages (sensorimotor, preoperational, concrete operational, and formal operational) characterized by unique ways of thinking. Piaget's theory has been criticized for a number of reasons, but the idea that children do not function as "little adults" continues to be widely accepted among developmental psychologists. Piaget's theory is complemented by Lawrence Kohlberg's theory of moral development. Like Piaget, Kohlberg proposed a stage theory, suggesting that individuals pass through qualitatively different levels of moral development, which differ in the extent to which moral actions are seen as driven by immediate external consequences or by general abstract principles.

Third, how do we form the social relationships and sense of personal identity needed for personal protection, nourishment, and continuation of the species? Humans use relationships with others to help them solve the problems that arise

throughout development. Infants, burdened with limited motor skills and immature perceptual systems, form attachments with others to gain the sustenance they need for survival. Both the infant and the caregiver are active participants in the attachment process and are prepared to respond, given the right kinds of environmental events, with mutual bonding. Ainsworth identified three main categories of attachment—secure, resistant, and avoidant—that may have long-term consequences. These attachment styles have a significant influence on the relationships formed later in life.

Another aspect of social development is the formation of personal identity—a sense of who one is as an individual. Erik Erikson argued that personal identity is shaped by a series of "psychosocial" crises that individuals confront over the life span. During infancy and childhood, individuals address questions about their basic abilities and independence and learn to trust or mistrust others. During adolescence and adulthood, individuals deal with the identity crisis and come to grips with their roles as participants in intimate relationships. In the later years, individuals struggle with questions of accomplishment, concern for future generations, and meaning. Other important aspects of social development include the learning of gender roles—how each person learns to think and act as a member of a gender group—and the critical influences of the family structure. The chapter ended with a discussion of the social and psychological factors that confront the elderly and some of the important stages and decisions that accompany death and dying.

CHAPTER SUMMARY

▶ Developing Physically

The environment helps shape the physical process of growth and can determine its ultimate outcome, but most physical changes are surprisingly consistent and predictable.

The Stages of Prenatal Development

The fertilized egg is referred to as the *zygote*. Prenatal development is divided into three main stages. The *germinal period* is the period from conception to implantation. The *embryonic period* occurs over the next six weeks. The *fetal period* goes from the ninth week to birth and includes the development of skeletal and muscular systems.

Growth during Infancy

The average newborn weighs about 3 kg and is approximately 51 cm long. Over the next two years, there is tremendous physical development and increasing complexity of brain networks. The newborn's brain shows *plasticity;* changes are constantly occurring in neural circuitry. Generally, the nervous system develops from the head down and from the centre out.

From Crawling to Walking

The sequence of development, from lifting the head to walking alone, is stable and predictable. Both nature and nurture contribute to individual differences.

From Toddlerhood to Adolescence

After toddlerhood, general processing speed and coordination improve rapidly. *Adolescence* is an important physical and psychological transition period that features the *growth spurt* and the onset of *puberty*.

Reaching Adulthood

By their 20s, people are physically mature and at the height of their physical prowess. A small decline begins to occur in the 20s. Some individuals suffer brain degeneration with age, but fewer than 1% of people at age 65 have *dementia* or physically based loss in mental functioning.

▶ Developing Intellectually

The developmental changes that occur in how people think (cognitive development) are of major importance to psychologists. There are good reasons to believe that infants see and think about the world differently from adults.

The Tools of Investigation

In the *preference technique*, an infant is presented with two visual displays simultaneously, and the researcher notes how long the infant looks at each. Researchers also use *habituation*, the decline in responsiveness to repeated stimulation, by *rewarding* simple motor movements to investigate infants' preferences and abilities.

The Growing Perceptual World

Babies greet the world with sensory systems that function reasonably well. They show preferences for some colours and shapes; they recognize their mothers' voices within a day or two after birth; they are sensitive to smell, taste, and touch; and they seem to perceive a three-dimensional world.

Do We Lose Memory with Age?

Many memory functions decline but some do not. Least affected are those involving recognition rather than recall and nonconscious rather than conscious testing. Older individuals who maintain an active intellectual life are less subject to decline.

Piaget and the Development of Thought

Piaget believed that everyone is born with a natural tendency to organize the world meaningfully and do so through the use of *schemas*. Cognitive development is guided by *assimilation* (people fit new experiences into existing schemas) and *accommodation* (people modify existing schemas to accommodate new experiences). Piaget proposed four stages of cognitive development: *sensorimotor*, *preoperational*, *operational*, and *formal operational*.

The Sensorimotor Period: Birth to Two Years

From birth to about age two, schemas about the world revolve primarily around sensory and motor abilities. Children develop *object permanence*; they learn how to vocalize and they learn their first words.

The Preoperational Period: Two to Seven Years

From about ages two through seven, schemas grow in sophistication. Children can think about absent objects and can use one object to stand for another. Children readily symbolize objects, and imaginary play is common; they make great strides in language development. Children show *egocentrism* in thinking.

The Concrete Operational Period: Seven to Eleven Years

Between the ages of 7 and about 11, children gain the capacity for true mental operations (i.e., verbalizing, visualizing, mental manipulation). Children understand reversibility and other simple logical operations, like categorizing and ordering. Mental operations remain concrete, tied to actual objects in the real world; children have difficulty with problems that do not flow from everyday experience.

The Formal Operational Period: Eleven to Adulthood

From the age of about 11 to adulthood, mastery is gained over abstract thinking. Adolescents can think and answer questions in general and abstract ways. No limitations: development of reasoning is complete; however, not all people reach this stage.

Challenges to Piaget's Theory

Not all Piaget's ideas have withstood experimental scrutiny. Children and infants are more sophisticated in their models of the world than he believed. Cognitive development is better viewed as a process of continual change and adaptation than as a series of stages. Vygotsky argued that cognitive abilities emerge directly out of our social interactions with others. Some researchers contend that intellectual development doesn't end with the acquisition of formal operational thinking.

Moral Development: Learning Right from Wrong

Kohlberg proposed three major levels of development. At the *preconventional level*, decisions about right and wrong are based primarily on external consequences. At the *conventional level*, people start to justify their actions on the basis of internalized rules and whether an action maintains or disrupts the social order. *Postconventional* morality is based on abstract principles that may even conflict with accepted standards. Kohlberg's critics argue that his views lack generality.

▶ Developing Socially

Social relationships help people adapt successfully to their environments.

Temperament

In-born behavioural tendencies are called *temperament*. Although originally thought of as categories (e.g., easy or difficult), they are now considered dimensions, including activity level and degree of inhibition.

Forming Bonds with Others

Newborns form *attachments*, strong emotional ties to one or more intimate companions.

The Origins of Attachment

Some believe that both caregiver and infant are preprogrammed from the baby's birth to respond to environmental signals with attachment behaviour.

Types of Attachment

Systematic differences exist in the types of bonds that are formed, which psychologists have investigated by using a technique called the *strange situation test*. Children respond with secure attachment, resistant attachment, or avoidant attachment.

Do Early Attachments Matter Later in Life?

Children with an early secure attachment seem to have some social and intellectual advantages later in life. However, early patterns of attachment are not perfect predictors of later behaviour.

Evolutionary Bases of Family Interactions

People have evolved psychological dispositions that provide a foundation for parenting and other family behaviours. Cultural and other environmental forces interact with these dispositions to produce the range of behaviours in contemporary families. Ensuring infant survival helped shape the evolved psychological adaptations that underlie cultural variations in parenting behaviour. Children's social networks have a tremendous impact on social development and well-being. At adolescence, peer culture becomes increasingly important.

Forming a Personal Identity: Erikson's Crises of Development

Erikson believed that *personal identity* is shaped by a series of psychosocial crises. During infancy and childhood, the crises experienced include *trust versus mistrust, autonomy versus shame or doubt, initiative versus guilt, and industry versus inferiority*. During adolescence and young adulthood, we experience *identity versus role confusion*. Entrance into young adulthood features the crisis of *intimacy versus isolation*. As career and family are established, the conflict is *generativity versus stagnation*, and in later adulthood we face the conflict of *integrity versus despair*.

Additional Issues in Adolescent Development

In adolescence people take greater risks than at other stages of development. Adolescents display gender differences in many behaviours.

Gender-Role Development

The foundations of gender identity are in place by age two or three, and by the time children are in elementary school, they tend to act in accordance with *gender roles. Gender schemas* guide and direct our perceptions and behaviours.

Growing Old in Society

Seniors face challenges presented by physical decline and society. Some of the more common myths claim that older people are sick, in mental decline, or depressed.

Death and Dying

Kübler-Ross proposed that people progress through five stages as they face death: denial, anger, bargaining, depression, and acceptance. Many psychologists find it more appropriate to speak in terms of *dying trajectories*, the paths people travel as they face their impending death.

Terms to Remember

development, 381

Developing Physically
zygote, 383
germinal period, 383
embryonic period, 383
fetal period, 383
teratogens, 384
puberty, 387
menopause, 388
dementia, 389

Developing Intellectually
longitudinal design, 391
cross-sectional design, 391
habituation, 391
schemas, 396
assimilation, 397
accommodation, 397
sensorimotor period, 397

object permanence, 398
preoperational period, 398
conservation, 398
egocentrism, 399
concrete operational period, 400
formal operational period, 401
morality, 404
preconventional level, 405
conventional level, 405
postconventional level, 406

Developing Socially
temperament, 408
attachments, 409
strange situation test, 412
personal identity, 417
gender roles, 421
gender schemas, 421

Recommended Readings

Gopnick, A., Meltzoff, A. N., & Kuhl, P. K. (1999). *The scientist in the crib: Minds, brains and how children learn.* New York: William Morrow. A cognitive science perspective on how babies recognize people, interpret the world around them, and develop language and theories about the world, and how these activities help build their brains.

Hultsch, D. F., Hertzog, C., Dixon, R. A., & Small, B. J. (1998). *Memory change in the aged.* New York: Cambridge University Press. By University of Victoria lifespan development researchers, this book reports on data from the Victoria Longitudinal Project, a major Canadian longitudinal study of memory and personality changes in older people.

Pinker, S. (2002). *The blank slate.* New York: Viking. Originally from McGill University, MIT psychologist Steven Pinker writes in a persuasive style to decry the tendency of social scientists to assume that most human behaviour is learned.

 For additional readings, explore InfoTrac® College Edition, your online library. Go to http://www.adaptivemind3.nelson.com.

Hint: Enter these search terms: motor development, cognitive development, moral development, psychosocial development, death and dying.

Media Resources

⬡ What's on the Web?

Please note that Web addresses are subject to change. Check out the accompanying website for updates: http://www.adaptivemind3e.nelson.com.

This site presents practice quiz questions, hypercontent, information on degrees and careers in psychology, study tips, and more.

Canadian Psychological Association's Developmental Psychology Section

http://www.cpa.ca/aboutcpa/cpasections/developmental/

Provides information on membership, their newsletter, and contacts for Canada's national association of researchers in developmental psychology.

Descriptions of the Developmental/Life-Span Programs at Several Canadian Centres of Developmental Research

University of Waterloo

http://www.psychology.uwaterloo.ca/gradprog/programs/phd/developmental/

University of Toronto

http://www.psych.utoronto.ca/grad/develop.htm

University of Victoria

http://web.uvic.ca/psyc/lifespan

University of British Columbia

http://www.psych.ubc.ca/research.psy?lab=Developmental

University of Toronto Institute for Life Course and Aging

http://www.aging.utoronto.ca/

The site of one of Canada's centres for research in adulthood and aging, it includes extensive links to Canadian and international sources on aging and human development.

University of Victoria Centre on Aging

http://www.coag.uvic.ca

This site includes links to many aging-related sites, including research centres, such as the University of Manitoba Centre on Aging, the Gerontology Research Centre at Simon Fraser University, the Nova Scotia Centre on Aging, and the McGill University Centre for Studies in Aging.

Child Development Institute

http://www.cdipage.com

This award-winning site provides information to parents on such topics as caring for young infants, improving learning skills, and dealing with learning disabilities.

Adolescence: Change and Continuity

http://www.oberlin.edu/faculty/ndarling/adolesce.htm

This site can help you gain some insight into the turbulent years of adolescence. You can choose to explore basic domains, such as social transitions that occur in adolescence; you can explore the important contexts of adolescence, such as schools, family, and peer groups; and you can explore how certain issues, such as achievement, sexuality, and delinquency, interact with this developmental stage.

ThomsonNOW™ ThomsonNOW

http://hed.nelson.com

Go to this site for the link to ThomsonNOW™, your one-stop study shop. Take a Pretest for this chapter and ThomsonNOW™ will generate a personalized Study Plan based on your test results. The Study Plan will identify the topics you need to review and direct you to online resources to help you master those topics. You can then take a Posttest to determine what concepts you have mastered and what you still need work on.

Psyk.trek 3.0

Check out Psyk.trek 3.0 for further study of the concepts in this chapter. Psyk.trek's 65 interactive learning modules, simulations, and quizzes offer additional opportunities for you to interact with, reflect on, and retain the material:

Human Development: Prenatal Development
Human Development: Piaget's Theory of Cognitive Development

The emotion creates the idea, which is then more direct and more powerful.

—Alfred North Whitehead

Motivation and Emotion

Taking the short cut through the park at night was a bad mistake. A sudden rustle and a rapid movement. A glint to your right and the feel of cold metal on your cheek. You gasp as a bony arm wraps itself around your neck. "Don't move or I'll cut you bad," barks a desperate voice. "All your money—right now! Cell phone too." Inside, your sympathetic nervous system jumps into action, flooding your body with adrenalin. Your mind is paralyzed with confusion. Run? Fight? Money is not worth a knife in the face. Can't think. But you're in a meltdown—you see a flash of wild eyes and needle tracks dotting the arm around your neck. Suddenly, he's gone. Only then do you notice the uncontrollable shaking in your knees. And the drenching sweat.

An ugly interaction but so very human. Two individuals brought by circumstance into a high-stress encounter. For psychology, the interaction raises a variety of basic questions about the tight interplay of two broad constructs, namely, *motivation* and *emotion*. What factors initiated and energized the attacker's behaviour? Was it the pull of money or just excitement? Was it the loss of inhibition driven by the need for a fix? And what about the emotions that rock the victim—surprise, desperation, fear? How can such an emotion as fear, with its often-paralyzing consequences, possibly be considered adaptive? These are some of the topics we'll consider in this chapter.

The set of factors that initiate and direct behaviour, usually toward some goal

A psychological event involving (1) a physiological reaction, usually arousal, (2) some kind of expressive reaction, such as a distinctive facial expression, and (3) some kind of subjective experience, such as the conscious feeling of being happy or sad

Motivation can be defined as the set of factors that *initiate* and *direct* behaviour, usually toward some goal. If you're motivated, your behaviour becomes activated and goal directed. Hunger is a classic example of an internal condition or *state* that stimulates an organism to pursue food. The desire for a fix motivates the drug user to search for the drug for relief. As you saw in Chapter 6, people are also likely to become motivated if they've recently been rewarded for behaving in a particular way—they're likely to act in a similar way again to get the reward. An **emotion** is a complex psychological event often associated with the initiation and direction of behaviour. It can involve (1) a *physiological* reaction, usually arousal, (2) some kind of *expressive* reaction, such as a distinctive facial expression, and (3) some kind of *subjective experience*, such as the conscious feeling of being happy or sad.

Most psychologists agree that the concepts of motivation and emotion are closely linked. Both terms, in fact, derive from the Latin *movere*, meaning "to move." Many conditions that are motivating also give rise to the experience of emotion. Consider the sequence that begins with you noticing your thirst. Your thirst motivates you to put money into a drink machine. You feel excited about the imminent quenching of your thirst. If the money gets stuck, stalling the pursuit of your goal, frustration and anger are likely. Moreover, once aroused, the emotional experience affects your ability to direct your behaviour successfully. If you start to curse aloud and kick the machine, you may never get that soft drink that keeps looking more and more delicious. The point is that a whole series of emotions can get intertwined with a simple motivational state. That's why it's difficult to discuss the topic of motivation without also considering emotion.

Motivation and Emotion

**P
R
E
V
I
E
W**

To study motivation, we need to ask questions about the fundamental causes of behaviour, so the topic is relevant to much of psychology. The preceding chapters each connect in one way or another to motivational issues, but we'll focus our discussion in this chapter on a set of specific adaptive problems that relate to motivation.

First, what activates goal-directed behaviour? Any organism seeking to survive in a changing environment must react quickly to its needs. It must anticipate future outcomes and act accordingly, *now*, with vigour and persistence. Much of the time our actions are controlled by *internal* factors that push us in the direction of a goal. For example, if your body is deprived of food or water, a delicate internal balance is

disrupted inside your body. A specific need is signalled, which you seek to satisfy in order to restore the internal balance. At other times we're motivated by *external* events, things in our environment that exert powerful pulling effects. The sight of an attractive person or a slice of chocolate cake can be sufficient to initiate and direct your behaviour.

Second, what factors create hunger and control eating? Obviously, we all need to eat—it's a requirement of living. Consequently, the body and mind must have mechanisms that make us hungry and interested in eating at regular intervals. To understand how our bodies maintain the proper levels of internal energy, we'll consider the relevant *internal* and *external* cues that activate and control eating. For

example, we'll discuss how the body monitors internal physiological states and uses brain mechanisms to check on levels of energy reserves (e.g., the amount of sugar in the blood). We'll also discuss how external cues in the environment compel us to eat and how these cues can influence the food selection process. Whether you like broccoli, reject mushrooms, or happily consume squid depends on a variety of factors, including what you've learned about these foods.

Third, what factors promote sexual behaviour? Although you may know someone who is "consumed" by sex, sexual activity is not necessary for individual survival. In principle, people can live perfectly productive lives without ever once engaging in sexual behaviour or exploring their sexuality. But sexual behaviour is needed for survival of the *species*. It's reasonable to assume, then, that internal cues, based in our genetic code and found in active biological systems, help motivate an interest in sex. We'll discuss some of the biological and psychological mechanisms that motivate sexual behaviour as well as some of the physiological characteristics of the human sexual response.

Fourth, how are emotions expressed and experienced, and what functions do they serve? All psychologists agree that emotions have considerable adaptive significance. Consider an emotion like *anger*. Anger typically arises in response to an environmental event, usually the perceived misdeed of another, and the body enters a highly aroused state. The arousal activates behaviour and leads to reactions that may substantially

increase (or decrease) the likelihood of survival. Once the emotion gains hold, overt physical expressions arise, particularly in the form of easy-to-identify facial expressions. From an adaptive perspective, the sight or sound of an angry person carries important signalling properties—others know to back away and avoid interaction. As you'll see, emotions are easy to identify but difficult to define.

▶ Activating Behaviour

LEARNING GOALS

1. Comprehend the role of instincts and drive in activating behaviour.
2. Be able to explain incentive motivation and discuss how it activates behaviour.
3. Understand achievement motivation.
4. Understand intrinsic motivation.
5. Learn about Maslow's hierarchy of needs, and discuss how each need influences behaviour.

Let's turn our attention to the first question: What factors activate and control goal-directed behaviour? At first, psychologists considered the possibility that there might be a single source of motivation, grounded either in the internal workings of the body or in the external environment. It's possible, for example, that people are born with biological machinery that compels them to act in certain ways, irrespective of what they learn from experience. But this idea is largely rejected by psychologists today, who believe instead that no single explanation of goal-directed behaviour, based on either biological or environmental factors, is likely to be found. The reason is simple: Virtually all forms of behaviour are determined by multiple causes. Factors both inside and outside the body—internal and external factors—contribute to motivation. In the following sections, we'll consider some examples of these influences.

instincts

Unlearned characteristic patterns of responding that are controlled by specific triggering stimuli in the world; not thought to be an important factor in explaining goal-directed behaviour in humans

The factors that are initiating and directing this bobcat's behaviour include both internal factors, such as depleted energy resources, and external factors, such as the sight of an attractive meal. As you'll see, internal and external factors often interact to produce motivated behaviour.

© PhotoDisc Collection/Getty Images

Internal Factors: Instincts and Drive

Birds don't need to be taught to build nests in the springtime or to fly south in the winter; cats don't need to be taught to show interest in small, rapidly moving creatures. These are unlearned, characteristic patterns of responding—called **instincts**—that are controlled by specific triggering stimuli in the world. Instincts share properties with *reflexes*, which we discussed in Chapter 3, but instincts typically involve more complex patterns of behaviour than those covered by the simple reflexes.

Human Instincts   It is widely accepted that instincts play a role in the behaviour of nonhuman species. But do instincts play any role in controlling human behaviour? A number of early psychologists followed the lead of Charles Darwin in suggesting that

The behaviour of many animals is motivated, at least in part, by instincts—unlearned, characteristic patterns of responding that are controlled by specific triggering stimuli in the environment.

instincts are a central factor in human motivation. Humans don't need to be taught to take care of their young, William James (1890) argued, or to cry as infants, to clean themselves when dirty, or even to play, love, imitate, or be curious. These are ingrained biological "musts" that are as natural to the human as nest building is to the bird.

However, just because a behaviour occurs on a regular basis doesn't guarantee that it's instinctive—that is, unlearned and inflexible in its display. We have no way to open up the body and directly measure an instinct, so it's easy to fall into a trap of circular reasoning: People demonstrate some regular behaviour, such as showing sympathy for a child in need, and the temptation is to propose a corresponding sympathy instinct (Holt, 1931). Over the years, psychologists argued about which behaviours qualify as instinctive. For example, William James (1890) suggested some 20 physical and 17 mental instincts in his writings. William McDougall (1908), however, was convinced of only 12 (he later changed his mind and upped the number to 17). For these and other reasons, instincts eventually fell out of favour as a widely applied explanation for goal-directed human behaviour. There was simply no agreement about how to confirm or categorize human behaviours as instinctive.

Although psychologists avoid the term, the notion of instinct has been reintroduced by evolutionary psychologists. They argue that our species is born not only with neural "hardware" but also with mental "software" that directs and controls at least part of our behaviour. For example, it's possible that we're born with natural reactions to certain types of facial features, or to be on the lookout for people who cheat or engage in deception (Cartwright, 2000; Tooby & Cosmides, 1995). But these "innate" tendencies are not as fixed as traditional instincts, nor are they necessarily automatically triggered by particular stimuli in the environment. Inborn mental software establishes a goal and may bias us toward a particular kind of strategy, but it allows for multiple ways to achieve that goal.

primary drive

A psychological state that arises in response to an internal physiological need, such as hunger or thirst

homeostasis

The process through which the body maintains a steady state, such as a constant internal temperature or an adequate amount of fluids

secondary drive

A drive learned by association with a primary drive (e.g., the need for money)

Drive   To replace instinct, psychologists turned to the concept of *drive*. A **primary drive** is a psychological state that arises in response to an internal physiological *need*, such as hunger or thirst. It's clear that the human body is designed to seek fairly stable and constant internal conditions. For example, it's important for the body to maintain an adequate internal supply of fluids or a constant internal temperature. Psychologists use the term **homeostasis** to refer to the process through which the body maintains its steady state, much like the thermostat in a house maintains a constant internal temperature by turning the heat on or off (Cannon, 1929). Once a specific need is detected, drive serves a general activating function: Drive energizes the organism, causing it to seek immediate reduction of the need (Berridge, 2004). So if your water supply is used up, you are driven to drink and restore the appropriate balance. Similar processes are assumed to operate for other biological drives, such as hunger and for the maintenance of internal body temperature (see ▶ Figure 11.1).

Additional drives are learned by association with primary drives. These **secondary drives** (e.g., the need for money) can eventually act like primary drives. A loss of money, for example, motivates action to relieve the need.

Drive is a considerably more flexible concept than instinct. An organism seeks to reduce drive—to restore homeostatic balance—but it doesn't really matter how balance is restored. People can use what they've learned from experience to help them satisfy the need; they're not stuck with one fixed pattern of behaviour that is

▶ **Figure 11.1**

Homeostasis

It's adaptive for the body to maintain stable and constant internal conditions. If your internal temperature rises above or falls below an optimal level, you are driven to perform actions that will restore the "steady state."

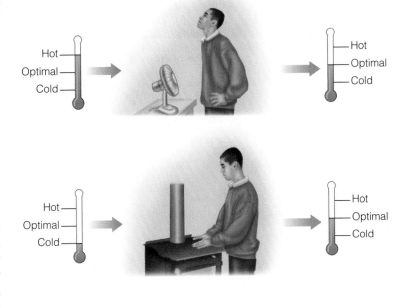

triggered only by a restricted set of stimuli. You can think about drive as somewhat analogous to the engine of a car. A properly running engine is necessary for the car to move, as drive is necessary to initiate goal-directed behaviour, but it's not sufficient to get across town. Other factors, such as knowledge about the layout of the town, must be used in conjunction with the operating engine to move about. As you'll see shortly, it's also the case that the vigour or intensity with which someone acts depends critically on the value, or incentive, of the goal. You are much more likely to be motivated to eat if you like the food, even though a wide variety of food options may satisfy the internal need. You sometimes eat even in the absence of an internal need, as in the case in which you have that second brownie just because it looks good.

Ultimate and Proximate Factors in Motivation   Evolutionary psychology requires a distinction between *ultimate* and *proximate* levels of explanation. Why do we feel like eating a banana at one time and not at another? An explanation that focuses on changes in our internal body physiology, such as blood glucose level (see the "Internal Factors Controlling Hunger" section later in the chapter), can be referred to as a **proximate** explanation of our eating motivation, that is, an explanation that involves causal factors in the immediate internal or external environment of the person. However, another question we can ask about our motivation for eating bananas is: Why do we eat them in the first place? Why, when we are hungry, are we motivated to eat bananas and not dirt? Answering this question requires attention to the **ultimate factors** that led to the type of motivational systems humans have today. At some point in our evolution, liking the taste of bananas paid off with enhanced likelihood of survival; liking the taste of dirt has never paid off.

Although most psychological explanations of human motivation focus on proximate factors influencing our eating, sexual, and aggressive motivations, human motivational systems are most fully understood when we also consider the ultimate evolutionary factors that led to the construction of our present-day motivational systems (Daly & Wilson, 1995).

proximate factors

Causes of behaviour that derive from an organism's immediate internal or external environment

ultimate factors

Causes of behaviour that refer to the evolutionarily adaptive significance and reproductive consequences for the organism

External Factors: Incentive Motivation

By itself, the concept of drive is insufficient to explain motivated behaviour. Goal-directed behaviour requires connecting the drive reduction with what people learn from experience. External cues tell us when and where to exert our efforts. Generally, whether you will be motivated to perform an action depends on the total value—positive or negative—of the incentive. For this reason psychologists often use the term **incentive motivation** to explain specific goal-directed behaviour. For example, Whitney is motivated to jog for an extra five minutes so that she can eat that extra brownie; conversely, Charlie is motivated to avoid the kitchen because of the extra calories (and guilt) that he knows the brownie consumption

incentive motivation

External factors in the environment—such as money, an attractive person, or tasty food—that exert pulling effects on people's actions

CONCEPT SUMMARY

GENERAL APPROACHES TO MOTIVATION

Approach	Source of Motivation	Summary and Evaluation
Instinct	Internal	Unlearned, inflexible patterns of responding that are controlled by specific triggering mechanisms in the environment. The traditional notion has been rejected as too fixed, but evolutionary psychology has reintroduced a more complex and compelling version.
Drive	Internal	A psychological state that arises in response to a physiological need, such as hunger or thirst. People are motivated to reduce that drive state and feel pleasure when that happens. Drive is a more flexible concept than instinct, but it does not explain behaviour in the absence of need.
Incentive motivation	External	Helps to explain goal-directed behaviour. People are driven by external rewards that exert powerful pulling and guiding effects on their actions.

will produce. Note that the emphasis here is quite different from drive: Drive is an internal push that compels a person to action; incentives are external pulls that tempt or deter people with the prospects of rewards or punishments.

Of course, internal factors interact with external factors in a number of ways. Whether a person is thirsty, for example, clearly affects the incentive value of water; water tastes better and is more rewarding when you've been deprived of it for a while (Blundell & Rogers, 1991; Bolles, 1972). Motivating students with an end-of-chapter test, a good incentive for them to study, has more of an effect when a student is a high procrastinator, that is, someone who finds it difficult to motivate himself or herself to study (Tuckman, 1998). Internal states of deprivation can also act as cues for responding. A person might learn to perform a certain type of action when he or she is thirsty or hungry (Hull, 1943); alternatively, a person might learn that hunger or thirst means that food or water will be especially rewarding (Davidson, 1993, 1998). It's important to remember that motivated behaviour is virtually always jointly determined by internal and external factors. Neither factor alone is sufficient to explain the complexities of human motivation.

achievement motive

A need that varies in strength across individuals; its strength on any given task depends on (1) expectations about success and (2) how much value a person places on succeeding at the task

Achievement Motivation

One example of motivated behaviour that clearly depends on both internal and external factors is striving for achievement (Elliot & Thrash, 2001). A number of psychologists have argued that each of us, to varying degrees, has an internally driven need for achievement (Atkinson, 1957; McClelland, Atkinson, Clark, & Lowell, 1953; Murray, 1938). The **achievement motive** pushes us to seek challenging tasks and significant accomplishment in life. People high in achievement motivation tend to work harder and more persistently on tasks, and they tend to achieve more than those who rate low in achievement motivation (Atkinson & Raynor, 1974; Cooper, 1983).

Charles Gupton/Stone/Getty Images

Every society in the world sets standards for achievement—what skills are important and unimportant—and these standards influence what members of the society seek to achieve.

How can the achievement motive be measured? Questionnaire tests simply ask people various questions about their achievement tendencies. But the evidence suggests that measurement is more valid if conducted with projective tests. They examine people's fantasies, wishes, and dreams. This method is covered in detail in Chapter 12.

Achievement motivation on any particular task depends on (1) your expectations about whether your efforts will be successful and (2) how much you value succeeding at the task (Atkinson, 1957; Molden & Dweck, 2000). This dual requirement means that even people with a high internal need for achievement may not persist at a task either because they do not value success on the task or because they lack confidence in their ability to succeed. For example, young children who experience failure on mathematics problems early in life can develop a negative attitude that prevents them from persisting and succeeding on valued mathematical tasks later in life (Smiley & Dweck, 1994; Wigfield, 1994). Conversely, you may place high value on becoming a professional basketball star but have low expectations because of your height. In both the math and the basketball cases, the individual's achievement motivation will be low with respect to that specific task.

Parents and teachers play an important part in determining achievement motivation. If parents value a task, it's likely that their child will value it as well and will appear more motivated to succeed (Eccles et al., 1983). What children are told about their performance on a task is also important. For example, if children are praised for their effort, they tend to work harder, report more enjoyment, and show more interest. Conversely, if they're told that performance is tied to ability, such as natural intelligence, children show less achievement motivation, especially if they fail or perform poorly on the task (Mueller & Dweck, 1998; Ziegert, Kistner, Castro, & Robertson, 2001).

All these ideas assume that boosting achievement motivation will boost actual achievement. However true, we must acknowledge that the causation also runs in the opposite direction. If we show a natural talent in school or sports or music, then our achievement motivation will naturally be focused in the domain of our best ability. So educational programs designed to boost achievement must consider individual differences in talent (Gardner, 1993).

Cultural Factors   Every society in the world establishes standards for achievement—what skills and tasks are deemed important and unimportant—and these standards influence what the members of the society seek to achieve and perhaps the level of productivity of the society as a whole (McClelland, 1961). For example, whether a society values individual success or places more emphasis on the collective success of the society seems to affect individual levels of achievement motivation (Sagie, Elizur, & Yamauchi, 1996). Middle-school athletes in the United States report more self-confidence than comparable students in Korea do, and they are more easily motivated, presumably because a greater emphasis is placed on individual success in the United States (Kim, Williams, & Gill, 2003).

Intrinsic Motivation

Sometimes we choose to engage in actions that have no obvious internal or external motivational source. A child spends hours carefully colouring a picture or playing with a doll; you might become transfixed by a crossword puzzle or by a long walk on the beach. Certainly, no biological *need* drives colouring or walking. There's also no clear-cut external incentive: Nobody pays the child for colouring or you for finishing the crossword puzzle. Psychologists use the term **intrinsic motivation** to

Children who experience failure on mathematical problems early in life can develop a negative attitude that prevents them from persisting and succeeding in mathematics later in life.

intrinsic motivation

Goal-directed behaviour that seems to be entirely self-motivated

describe situations in which behaviour appears to be entirely self-motivated (Sansone & Harackiewicz, 2000). We engage in the action for its own sake, not because someone offers us a reward or because the action restores some internal homeostatic balance.

What convinced many researchers that intrinsic motivation deserves special status was a counterintuitive finding: It's possible to lower someone's interest in performing a task by giving an external reward. In a classic study by Lepper, Greene, and Nisbett (1973), preschool children who were naturally interested in drawing were asked to draw either for its own sake or to win a "Good Player" certificate. Psychologically, we would expect the external reward to encourage drawing behaviour even more than normal—after all, drawing is now associated with a concrete positive consequence. Instead, the children in the reward condition showed *less* interest in drawing a week later. The reward apparently undermined the children's motivation, making it less rewarding or interesting than it otherwise would have been.

This study has been repeated with other rewards and with activities other than drawing (see Deci & Ryan, 1985). The story is much the same: Externally supplied rewards can lower a person's desire to perform a task. Once someone receives a reward for performing a task, he or she seems less likely to enjoy that task for its own sake in the future. Think about professional athletes. Many sports fans complain that the external reward of money has ruined professional sports. Even players sometimes complain that the game was more fun when they were amateurs—before millions of dollars complicated the motivational chain.

Control and Overjustification

How can a reward lead to a negative effect? One possibility is that people see external rewards as an indirect way of controlling behaviour. Drawing loses its value because it's now something you do to please the person giving you the reward—you're no longer drawing simply because it pleases *you* (Rummel & Feinberg, 1988). Thus, the so-called reward is not really a reward at all. When coupled with the loss of control, the consequence loses its reinforcing value and becomes negative.

Another possibility is that external rewards lead to what has been called *overjustification:* When a second motivation is added, it eats away at your intrinsic motivation. Eventually, you conclude that it's the external reward that motivates you to perform the task (Bem, 1972; Deci & Ryan, 1985). Rewarding someone for performing a task in a sense degrades the value of that task (e.g., the baseball player begins to believe that it's the money that makes him play, rather than love of the game). Some researchers have even suggested that things like creativity should never be rewarded, lest the positive internal value of engaging in a creative act be destroyed (Amabile, 1983; Schwartz, 1990).

But not all psychologists are comfortable with these conclusions (Covington & Mueller, 2001; Pittenger, 1996). External reward can enhance creativity under some circumstances, and the negative effects of reward on task motivation may occur only in restricted circumstances (see Dickinson, 1989; Eisenberger, 1992). For example, in the Lepper et al. study (1973), children did indeed choose to draw less frequently when they were rewarded for drawing, but this effect occurred only when the children expected the reward. When children were given an unexpected reward for drawing, they later spent more time drawing than did a group who had not received a reward. Therefore, the negative effect of reward on intrinsic motivation may be related to the expectation or *promise* of reward rather than to the reward itself (Cameron & Pierce, 1994). In sum, the way we think about rewards strongly influences the way they motivate us.

Do you think these two volunteers at a local food bank would feel better about their work if they were also paid for their activities?

Maslow's Hierarchy of Needs

Most general theories of motivation rest on a foundation of biological need. The body seeks to maintain a delicate internal balance (homeostasis), and if that balance is disrupted, we're motivated to restore it. But as you've just seen, not all needs are biological in origin—such as the need for achievement (Murray, 1938). For this reason, some psychologists have tried to classify needs and to determine whether some are more important than others.

Among the more influential of these classification systems is the **need hierarchy** introduced by the humanistic theorist Abraham Maslow (see Chapter 12). The essential component of Maslow's theory is the *prioritizing* of needs. Some needs, he argued, have special priority and must be satisfied before others can be addressed. Obviously, if people don't eat or drink water on a regular basis, they'll die. Maslow's theory is usually represented in the form of a pyramid, to emphasize the fact that human motivation rests on a foundation of biological and security "musts" (see ▶ Figure 11.2). It is only after satisfying the survival needs—such as hunger and thirst—that we can consider personal security and more social or spiritual needs, such as the need for love or self-esteem. At the top of the structure sits the need for self-actualization, which Maslow believed represented people's desire to reach their full potential as human beings.

The pyramid is an appropriate symbol for Maslow's system because it captures the upward thrust of human motivation. As a humanistic psychologist, Maslow believed that all people have a compelling need to grow, to better themselves as functioning individuals. In his own words: "A musician must make music, an artist must paint, a poet must write if he is ultimately to be at peace with himself" (Maslow, 1954). Maslow was strongly influenced by people who, he felt, had reached their fullest potential, such as Albert Einstein and Mother Teresa. He used their personality characteristics as a way of defining what it means to sit at the top of the pyramid—to be self-actualized. These characteristics included spontaneity, openness to experience, and a high degree of ethical sensitivity (Mook, 1995; Ryckman, 2004). (We'll return to humanistic views on personality in Chapter 12.)

It is easy to dispute the specific order of needs that Maslow proposed. Many daily examples confirm that people sometimes sacrifice a lower need to gain a higher one. For example, we hear of people going on a hunger strike to gain higher esteem from others. We also hear of people risking their lives for their love needs.

Nonetheless, we must acknowledge Maslow's point that how we act is often influenced by unfilled needs. If you have to worry about putting food on the table and consequently steal from others on a regular basis, you might appear to lack moral or ethical values. But this isn't necessarily a permanent aspect of your personality: Under different circumstances and with a full stomach, you might be a model citizen in the promotion of ethical values.

need hierarchy

The idea popularized by Maslow that human needs are prioritized in a hierarchy; some needs, especially physiological ones, must be satisfied before others, such as the need for achievement or self-actualization, can be pursued

CRITICAL **THINKING**
Can you think of other examples in which Maslow's ordering of needs doesn't hold up?

▶ **Figure 11.2**

A Hierarchy of Needs

Maslow organized his need hierarchy in a pyramid to highlight the fact that the higher needs are built on a foundation of lower, more basic needs.

Test Yourself 11.1

Check your knowledge about activating behaviour by answering the following questions. (The answers are in Appendix B.)

1. Which of the following statements best captures the difference between an instinct and a drive?
   a. A drive is a reflex; an instinct is not.
   b. Instincts are learned; drives are not.
   c. Instincts lead to fixed response patterns; drives do not.
   d. Instincts restore appropriate internal balance; drives do not.

2. Which type of motivation best describes each of the following behaviours: achievement, incentive, or intrinsic?
   a. Whitney never misses her daily jogging session—she loves the brownie she gives herself at the end: _____
   b. Celine spends hours practising the piano—she just seems to love playing: _____

   c. Candice studies at least six hours a day—she is obsessed with the idea of finishing first in her class: _____
   d. Jerome rarely paints for fun anymore, not since he started teaching art classes at the local college: _____

3. According to Maslow's hierarchy of needs, we can reach our true potential as human beings only after
   a. restoring a proper level of homeostatic balance.
   b. satisfying basic survival and social needs.
   c. satisfying our need for achievement.
   d. eliminating the need for rewards.

▶ Meeting Biological Needs: Hunger and Eating

LEARNING GOALS

1. Understand the internal factors that influence when and why we eat.
2. Understand the external factors that influence when and why we eat.
3. Be able to explain how body weight is regulated, including the concept of a set point.
4. Learn about the eating disorders anorexia nervosa and bulimia nervosa.

We now turn our attention to an important motivational problem that must be dealt with every day: initiating and controlling eating behaviour. Eating is a constant in everybody's life, but we eat for reasons that are more complex than you might think. If asked why we eat, children will explain that we eat "because we're hungry" or "because my tummy hurts." An adult's response will appear more sophisticated, but it usually amounts to much the same thing: "We eat because our bodies need food, internal energy." This is true; eating is a biologically driven behaviour. But eating is a psychologically driven behaviour as well. We sometimes feel hungry when there is no physical need and, as any dieter knows, a strong will can stop consumption even when the physical need is present.

Internal Factors Controlling Hunger

Researchers have spent decades trying to understand the internal mechanisms that influence when and why we eat. We now know, for example, that the body monitors itself, particularly its internal supply of resources, in a number of ways. For example, a connection exists between the volume and content of food in the stomach and the amount that neurons will fire in certain areas of the brain (Sharma, Anand, Due, & Singh, 1961). Psychologically, people report little, if any, hunger or interest in food when their stomach is full, and hunger increases in a relatively direct way as the stomach empties (Sepple & Read, 1989).

Chemical Signals   It's not only the contents of the stomach that are monitored. The body has several important suppliers of internal energy that it checks regularly. One critical substance is **glucose,** a kind of sugar that cells require for energy production. Receptors in the liver are thought to react to changes in the amount of glucose in the blood or perhaps to how this sugar is being used by the cells, and

glucose

A kind of sugar that cells require for energy production

appropriate signals are communicated upward to the brain (Mayer, 1953; Russek, 1971). When the amount of usable glucose falls below an optimal level, which occurs when you haven't eaten for a while, you start to feel hungry and seek out food (Campfield, Smith, Rosenbaum, & Hirsch, 1996). If blood glucose levels are high, which occurs after a meal, you lose interest in food. This link between blood sugar levels and hunger is not simply correlational: In the laboratory it is possible to increase or decrease how much an animal will eat by artificially manipulating the amount of glucose in its blood (Smith & Campfield, 1993).

Another key element the body monitors is **insulin,** a hormone released by the pancreas. The body needs insulin to help pump the nutrients present in the blood into the cells, where they can be stored as fat or metabolized into needed energy. At the start of a meal, the brain sends signals to the pancreas to begin the production and release of insulin in preparation for the rise in blood sugar produced by the food. As insulin does its job, the levels of blood sugar go down and you eventually feel hungry once again. It's probably a glucose-insulin interaction that is actually monitored internally because both substances play pivotal roles in the metabolic, or energy-producing, process. If laboratory animals are given continuous injections of insulin, they tend to balloon in weight and grossly overeat—the insulin keeps the blood sugar level low, which tells the animal to start looking for something to eat. Researchers are also actively studying a hormone called **leptin** that may regulate the amount of energy stored in fat cells; high levels of leptin are often found in obese individuals, and leptin levels typically drop when individuals go on a diet (Woods, Schwartz, Baskin, & Seeley, 2000). Leptin is undoubtedly only one of many important signals in the body, along with insulin and glucose, that tell us when it's time to start or stop eating (Berthoud, 2004).

Both glucose and insulin are believed to play key roles in motivating eating behaviour, but it's unlikely that any one single chemical (or even two) completely controls whether you will feel hungry. Other internal stimuli, such as the overall level of body fat (Keesey & Powley, 1975), also play important roles. Of course, ultimately the experience of hunger originates in the brain. It is the activation of brain structures that initiates and directs the search for food. You learned in Chapter 3 that structures in the limbic system are involved in controlling a number of motivational and emotional behaviours. As you'll see momentarily, structures associated with the *hypothalamus* have long been thought to be of central importance in eating.

Brain Regions   A number of years ago it was discovered that if a particular portion of the **ventromedial hypothalamus** is lesioned in laboratory animals, a curious transformation occurs. Lesioned animals appear to be hungry all the time and show a striking tendency to overeat. In fact, each animal becomes an eating machine—if allowed, it balloons up to several times its normal weight (Hetherington & Ranson, 1942). If this same area is stimulated electrically, rather than destroyed, the opposite pattern emerges. Electrical stimulation causes the animal to lose all interest in food, even if it has a real need for nutrients in its body. These results suggested to many researchers that the ventromedial hypothalamus functions as a kind of "stop," or *satiety*, centre in the brain. Activation of the region, which presumably occurs whenever we've eaten enough to fulfill the body's energy needs, turns off hunger and eating. This process would be adaptive because it prevents us from accumulating too many nutrients in the blood—more than our bodies can handle.

If activation of the ventromedial hypothalamus stops eating, then what starts the eating process? One logical candidate was the **lateral hypothalamus** because it acts as a kind of mirror image of the ventromedial hypothalamus. In the laboratory, damage to the lateral hypothalamus creates an animal that typically starves itself, even to the point of death. Electrical stimulation of the same area causes the animal to immediately start eating. This suggested that the lateral hypothalamus

insulin

A hormone released by the pancreas that helps pump nutrients in the blood into the cells, where they can be stored as fat or metabolized into needed energy

leptin

A hormone that may regulate the amount of energy stored in fat cells

ventromedial hypothalamus

A portion of the hypothalamus that, when lesioned, causes an animal to typically overeat and gain a large amount of weight; once thought to be a kind of "stop eating," or satiety, centre in the brain; its role in eating behaviour is currently unknown

lateral hypothalamus

A portion of the hypothalamus that, when lesioned, causes an animal to be reluctant to eat; probably plays some role in eating behaviour, but the precise role is unknown

Richard Howard

If a particular portion of the ventromedial hypothalamus is destroyed, rats become eating machines and can balloon up to several times their normal weight.

CRITICAL   THINKING
Can you think of any factors, besides behaviour modelling, that might help to determine eating habits? What about the availability of food? When was the last time you saw sheep's eyes on a menu?

may act as a kind of eating "start-up" centre to counteract the stop centre located in the ventromedial hypothalamus. This division of labour in the brain paints a cohesive picture—two regions of the hypothalamus working together to initiate and control eating behaviour.

Unfortunately, this simple story turns out to be wrong. Researchers remain convinced that both regions of the hypothalamus help to control eating, but they're uncertain about the precise roles. Part of the problem is that destruction of either area tends to affect the nervous system in a number of ways, so it's difficult to determine the exact causes of the eating changes. Lesions to the ventromedial hypothalamus, for example, may affect the secretion of insulin (Weingarten, Chang, & McDonald, 1985) or damage the effectiveness of other important pathways in the brain (Kirchgessner & Sclafani, 1988). Moreover, a closer examination of animals with lesions to the ventromedial hypothalamus revealed that they're somewhat picky and won't eat certain foods (Ferguson & Keesey, 1975). They don't eat everything, as the start-stop hypothesis seems to predict.

Just as the brain monitors the levels of several internal chemicals to determine the need for food, several important locations in the brain besides the hypothalamus help to control eating behaviour (Woods, Seeley, Porte, & Schwartz, 1998). Evidence shows that portions of the brainstem are critical in the initiation of eating (Grill & Kaplan, 1990), and the hippocampus may be involved as well. You may remember from Chapter 7 that we discussed an amnesiac called H. M. who was doomed to live in a kind of perpetual present—he could remember nothing of what happened to him moments before. H. M., who has damage to his temporal lobes and hippocampus, also has trouble monitoring his need for food. He is sometimes convinced that he's hungry immediately after finishing a meal. He may have simply forgotten that he's eaten; but, as Davidson (1993) points out, H. M. clearly is also unable to use internal signals from his body as cues for hunger or satiety. These data suggest an important role for the hippocampus in feeding behaviour (see also Davidson & Jarrard, 1993).

External Factors Controlling Eating

From an adaptive standpoint, it's obviously critical that you eat. You can't let your internal energy sources fall too low; otherwise, you won't have an adaptive mind to consider. But it would be a mistake to think about eating as simply a means of satisfying a variety of internal energy needs. We often eat for reasons that are unrelated to restoring internal homeostatic balance (Capaldi, 1996; Epel, Lapidus, McEwen, & Brownell, 2001). Have you ever eaten to reduce stress or simply to make yourself feel good? Have you ever eaten to promote social interaction, as in going out to dinner with friends? We all have. People even eat at times to make artistic, aesthetic, or moral judgments. For example, some people are vegetarians because they believe it's wrong to eat other animals.

Eating Habits   Most people have established eating habits, which develop through personal experience and by modelling the behaviour of others. These learned habits control much of our decision making about food. For example, you're probably used to eating at certain times and in certain places. If you're offered a tasty snack, how much you eat is determined partly by the time of day— if the offer comes shortly before dinner, you take less than if the offer comes in the middle of the afternoon (Schachter & Gross, 1968). You also know from past experience how much food you can eat and still feel well. You know, for instance, that if you eat a whole pizza you will probably feel sick afterward, even though the pizza probably tasted great at the time.

Your cultural and ethnic background is another powerful influence on when and what you choose to eat (Rozin, 1990). Most people who grow up in Canada will not willingly choose to eat dogs or sheep's eyes, but these are considered delicacies in some parts of the world. Are you hesitant about eating pork or beef? You probably are if you're an Orthodox Jew or a Muslim (in the case of pork) or a Hindu (in the case of beef). And it's not just the appearance of food or where it comes from. People around the world often discriminate about whom it is appropriate to eat with. For example, members of some social classes would never consider eating with those that they consider to be social inferiors.

Food Cues   The decision to eat is also strongly influenced by the presence or absence of food cues. Animals know that certain kinds of food signal positive consequences, and the sight of these foods is often enough to make them start eating. Researcher Harvey Weingarten at the University of Calgary has shown that if hungry rats are taught that a flashing light signals food, later on they'll start eating in the presence of the light even if they've been fully fed moments before (Weingarten, 1983). Waiters at fine restaurants push the dessert tray under your nose after a filling meal because they know that the sight (or presentation) of the sugar-filled array will be more likely to break down your reserve than just hearing about what's for dessert will. Again, your choice of the cheesecake is not driven by internal need. Your blood contains plenty of appropriate nutrients— the sight of the food, and its associations with past pleasures, acts as an external pull, motivating your choice to consume.

Cultural and ethnic background exert a powerful effect on food selection. Would you be willing to consume the insect delicacies shown in the picture above? How about the more traditional desserts shown in the top picture?

Regulating Body Weight

What determines your everyday body weight? Why are some people thin and others obese? Not surprisingly, internal and external factors combine to regulate body weight. It turns out that some factors, such as genetic predisposition, play a particularly important role (Kowalski, 2004). This has been demonstrated in animals. For example, Linda Wilson and her colleagues at the University of Manitoba used

CONCEPT SUMMARY

FACTORS INVOLVED IN HUNGER

Type of Factor	Factor	Its Role in Hunger
Internal	Chemical signals	Receptors in the liver respond to changes in the amount of *glucose* in the blood. The body also monitors *insulin,* a hormone released by the pancreas. The glucose-insulin interaction is monitored internally. Insulin lowers blood glucose levels, leading to hunger.
	Brain	The lateral and ventromedial regions of the hypothalamus help to control eating, but the precise role of each is unclear. Portions of the brainstem also seem important in the initiation of eating.
External	Eating habits	Learned habits develop through personal experience and modelling the behaviour of others. Cultural and ethnic background also plays a critical role in when and what you eat.
	Food cues	Factors, such as the attractiveness of food and its association with past pleasures, can serve as an external pull, motivating eating behaviour.

strains of genetically obese and genetically lean mice to try to tease apart genetic, environmental, and physiological factors involved in obesity (Currie & Wilson, 1993; Wilson, Stewart, & McAnanama, 1989).

In humans, we know that when identical twins—those sharing the same genetic material—are fed identical diets, they tend to gain virtually the same amount of weight. But if two unrelated people are given matched diets, the differences in weight gain can be substantial (Bouchard, Tremblay, et al., 1990). No doubt you know people who appear to eat continuously and never gain weight; others balloon considerably after only a small daily increase in caloric intake. In short, the amount of food that you eat only partly determines what you normally weigh.

set point

A natural body weight, perhaps produced by genetic factors, that the body seeks to maintain; when body weight falls below the set point, people are motivated to eat; when weight exceeds the set point, people feel less motivated to eat

Set Point   Some earlier researchers suggested that we have a natural body weight, or **set point,** that more or less controls our tendency to gain or lose weight (Keesey & Powley, 1975). Most people show little variation in weight from year to year, presumably because their bodies manipulate the motivation to eat, as needed, to maintain the appropriate set point weight. When people go on a diet and dip below their natural weight, more than 90% of them eventually gain that weight back (Martin, White, & Hulsey, 1991). Here again, the idea is that the body adjusts how much it eats, rebounding after a diet, to produce stability in body weight.

Assuming that people do indeed have such set points, what might determine them? Set point theorists have suggested that genetic factors might be responsible: Different people are born with different numbers of fat cells, and this number may constrain just how much weight someone can hope to gain or lose (Faust, 1984). Your metabolic rate—how quickly you burn off calories—could be another important internal factor; again, it's determined in part by your genetic makeup. Recent research in rats indicates that nicotine may lower metabolic set point; if so, although speculative, this may help explain why people sometimes gain weight after they stop smoking (Frankham & Cabanac, 2003).

Evolutionary Theories of Hunger and Eating   It should be noted that recently researchers, notably John Pinel and his colleagues from the University of British Columbia and Harvey Weingarten from McMaster University, have criticized set point theory on several grounds (Assanand, Pinel, & Lehman, 1998; Pinel, 1997; Weingarten, 1985). Instead, they propose an evolutionary theory of hunger and eating that suggests that the "mammalian feeding system evolved to anticipate and prevent energy deficits, rather than to merely react to them" (Assanand et al., 1998, p. 1003). These researchers suggest that among most people with adequate access to food, the main cause of hunger is not a decline of energy below fixed set points. According to this view, human food supplies were unpredictable in the human environments of evolutionary adaptedness that forged our eating mechanisms. We could not afford to pass by the opportunity to store significant quantities of sweet, salty, and fatty foods when they were available, so we evolved mechanisms to normatively eat more quantities of such foods if they are available than set point theory would suggest. Although this would be an adaptive mechanism in natural environments, the result in modern societies is what appears to be overeating when compared with our actual ongoing nutritional requirements.

obesity

A weight problem characterized by excessive body fat

Obesity   What causes **obesity,** the condition characterized by excessive body fat? Obesity rates are on the rise, startlingly so over the last decade or so (Corsica & Perri, 2003). Think about how easy it is to get tasty fast food or packaged meals or to stuff yourself at an all-you-can-eat buffet. At one time it was thought that obese people simply lacked sufficient willpower to resist overeating, especially when appealing food was in view (Schachter, 1971). At the University of Toronto, researchers Peter Herman and Janet Polivy conducted studies showing that obese people (but not people who are not obese) are more likely to order a specific dish

 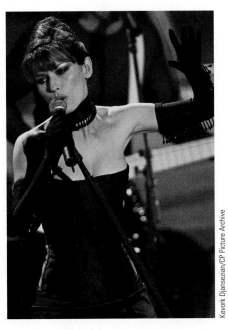

Social standards concerning weight "ideals" have changed considerably over the years.

in a restaurant after being given a tasty description (Herman & Polivy, 1988). Obese people are also more likely than people who are not obese to report that food still tastes good after a filling meal.

However, to explain obesity by appealing to willpower or to any one psychological factor is simplistic and misleading. It's increasingly apparent that genetic factors predispose people to become overweight (Corsica & Perri, 2003). The causes of obesity lie in a complex combination of biology and psychology: Metabolic rate, number of fat cells, learned eating habits, cultural role models, and level of stress all contribute in one way or another to weight control (Hill & Peters, 1998; Rodin, 1981).

Eating Disorders

Unfortunately concerns with obesity can be taken too far. The pursuit of unrealistic weight goals, ones that you can never hope to reach because of your genetic background, can lead to significant psychological and physical problems. Unhappiness and depression are the all-too-often byproducts of the failure to reach the ideal (Rodin, Schank, & Striegal-Moore, 1989).

Interestingly, people's assessments of their own weight, and its relation to these standards, are typically inaccurate. In addition, most people are simply wrong about what members of the opposite sex consider to be an ideal body weight (Fallon & Rozin, 1985). On average, women tend to think men prefer thinner women than men actually do; when men are asked about their own ideal weight, it tends to be heavier than what the average woman rates as most attractive. Not surprisingly, these mistaken beliefs help promote a negative body image. One of the consequences of a negative body image is increased susceptibility to eating disorders, such as *anorexia nervosa* and *bulimia nervosa* (Polivy & Herman, 2002).

Anorexia Nervosa   A recent survey of students in grades 8 and 10 revealed that more than 60% of the females and 28% of the males were dieting (Hunnicutt & Newman, 1993). The concern—some would say obsession—with weight and dieting starts early in Western cultures, and for an unfortunate few the consequences can be life threatening. In the condition called **anorexia nervosa,** an otherwise healthy person refuses to maintain a normal weight level, typically

anorexia nervosa

An eating disorder diagnosed when an otherwise healthy person refuses to maintain a normal weight level because of an intense fear of being overweight

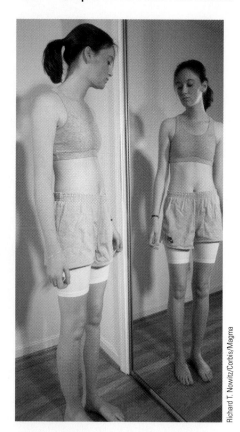

Richard T. Nowitz/Corbis/Magma

This young woman has anorexia nervosa, a condition characterized by an intense fear of being overweight.

bulimia nervosa

An eating disorder in which the principal symptom is binge eating (consuming large quantities of food), followed by purging in which the person voluntarily vomits or uses laxatives to prevent weight gain

because she or he has an irrational fear of being overweight. In such cases, a person can literally be starving to death and still see an overweight person in the mirror. The condition affects mainly young women between the ages of 12 and 18 (perhaps as many as 1% of female adolescents), and it's been estimated that as many as 20% of those with the disorder will eventually die as a result, either from medical problems or from suicide (Herzog, Greenwood, Dorer, Flores, & Ekeblad, 2000).

The causes of this disorder are complex and may involve genetic as well as psychological factors (Allison & Faith, 1997; Gorwood, Bouvard, Mouren-Simeoni, Kipman, & Ades, 1998). Psychological factors that may contribute include a perfectionistic personality and an exaggerated adherence to some social demand: Such demands could arise from current fashion, athletic competition, or competitive dancing. Some evidence of abnormally low levels of certain neurotransmitters also exists. Our lack of understanding makes the disorder very difficult to treat (Grice, Halmi, & Fitcher, 2002).

The existence of anorexia is a challenge to evolutionary psychology. Michele Surbey of Mount Allison University and Charles Crawford and Judith Anderson of Simon Fraser University have suggested that a disposition toward anorexia may have evolved because it would be adaptive for young women to be able to "automatically" avoid reproduction when they are feeling extreme stress. One of the features of anorexia in women is that menstruation ceases, thus decreasing or eliminating the ability of the woman or girl to conceive. Although the behaviour may have had adaptive roots, it is obviously unnecessary and, indeed, harmful in modern environments where birth control is available (Anderson & Crawford, 1992; Crawford, 1989; Surbey, 1987). Besides interfering with reproductive functions, the condition is associated with low blood pressure, loss of bone density, and gastrointestinal problems, and it can lead to death. Anorexia nervosa is a very serious and chronic condition that needs immediate and prolonged treatment.

Bulimia Nervosa   In the eating disorder known as **bulimia nervosa,** the principal symptom is *binge eating*. A binge is an episode in which a person consumes large quantities of food, often junk food, in a short time. You might find a person who has bulimia locked in a room, surrounded by his or her favourite snacks, eating thousands of calories in a single sitting. The condition is marked by a lack of control—the person feels unable to stop the eating or control the content of the food being consumed. A binging episode is often followed by *purging*, in which the person induces vomiting or uses laxatives in an effort to stop potential weight gain. Like anorexia, bulimia primarily affects women and is characterized by an obsessive desire to be thin.

Although associated with a variety of medical problems, bulimia nervosa is not usually life threatening. People with bulimia can appear normal without excessive weight loss but repeated vomiting can damage the intestines, cause nutritional problems, and even promote tooth decay.

Until recently, social scientists assumed that eating disorders, such as bulimia and anorexia, were caused primarily by cultural factors, specifically, the fixation in Western cultures on staying thin. However, recent work indicates that anorexia nervosa may be neither recent nor culture-bound. Cases can be traced back to medieval times and the disorder occurs today in all parts of the world. Bulimia nervosa, however, may follow a different pattern. A large increase occurred in the latter half of the twentieth century and little evidence for the condition currently exists outside cultures with Western influence. This suggests a strong cultural influence although genetics is undoubtedly involved as well (Keel & Klump, 2003).

Check your knowledge about hunger and eating by deciding whether each of the following statements is true or false. (The answers are in Appendix B.)

1. A high level of glucose, or blood sugar, is associated with an increased desire for food. *True or False?*
2. The principal symptoms of anorexia nervosa are binging and purging. *True or False?*
3. The lateral hypothalamus serves as the brain's stop centre for eating. *True or False?*

4. Obesity is primarily caused by poor dietary habits. *True or False?*
5. Destruction of the ventromedial hypothalamus causes a rat to refuse food and dramatically lose weight. *True or False?*

Meeting Biological Needs: Sexual Behaviour

LEARNING GOALS

1. Be able to explain the role that hormones play in human and animal sexual behaviour.
2. Understand external influences on sexual behaviour.
3. Recognize the factors that influence mate selection.
4. Learn the possible origins of sexual orientation.

Does your world revolve around sex? Perhaps not, but there's no denying that sex is a powerful motivator of people around the world. Recent findings by Sandra Byers and Christine Purdon of the University of Waterloo and David Clark of the University of New Brunswick illustrate the powerfully compelling nature of sexual motivation (Byers, Purdon, & Clark, 1998). These researchers found that 89% of Canadian university students reported regularly having sexual fantasies. Perhaps the rest were too embarrassed to admit it.

To regulate and restrict this powerful motivation, every culture has legal and moral rules related to courtship, marriage, and sexual acts. Why should sex be so important to humans? What adaptive problem is solved by so much focus on the pursuit and completion of intercourse? People won't die if their goal-directed sexual pursuits fail, as they would from an unsuccessful search for nutrients. But eventually, the species would disappear. Thus, the ultimate value of sexual motivation is to encourage people to engage in behaviour that leads to the replication of their genes. Evolution has selected us to be reactive to sexual cues and enjoy sexual activity, because, from an evolutionary point of view, reproduction is even more important than our own survival (Dawkins, 1989).

Of course, sexual motivation has adaptive benefits apart from replicating genes. Besides the pleasurable aspects of sex, sexual desire is often a motivation for people to pursue a mate, thereby opening the door for companionship, protection, and love. We'll first look at the internal and external factors that motivate sexual behaviour, and then conclude with a look at issues involved in mate selection and sexual orientation.

Beginning with Kinsey's groundbreaking work, research on human sexuality has met with unique impediments. Psychologists remain cautious about accepting the validity of self-reports on such intimate matters. But the alternative—observing human sexuality in natural situations—has ethical problems. Moreover, much of society still believes that such research is unacceptable—no matter what the purpose.

CRITICAL THINKING

Is there a connection between the importance of sex for the replication of our genes and the emphasis that some theorists place on sex in their theories of behaviour and mind (e.g., Freud)?

Internal Factors

Hormones and Human Sexuality   We have learned much about human sexuality by studying animals experimentally and then testing humans with less intrusive measurements (Pfaus, Kippin, & Coria-Avila, 2003). For example, humans show regular cyclic variations in the hormones relevant to sex and reproduction. These sets of hormones—*estrogens* in women and *androgens* in men—play a critical role in physical development, affecting everything from the development of the sex organs to the wiring structure of the brain (see Chapter 3). But the initiation and control of adult sexual behaviour does not appear to be simply a matter of mixing and matching the right internal chemicals. We retain a large degree of control over our sexual behaviour, with learned social and cultural factors having an important influence. Instead of instinctive mounting and fixed courtship rituals, people in most human cultures largely choose when and where they engage in sex and the particular manner in which the sexual act is consummated.

Therefore, the role that hormones play in human behaviour is still not well understood. Some evidence suggests that a woman's peak of sexual desire occurs in the middle of her menstrual cycle, near the time of ovulation (Pillsworth, Haselton, & Buss, 2004). Evidence also suggests that testosterone affects both male and female sexual desire. For example, when testosterone levels are reduced sharply—as occurs, for instance, following removal of the testes (medical castration) in men—people often experience a loss of interest in sex. In fact, sex offenders are sometimes treated by administering drugs that block the action of testosterone (Roesler & Witztum, 1998).

But humans are not rigidly controlled by these hormones. Some castrated men continue to enjoy and seek out sexual encounters, even without hormone replacement therapy. Similarly, women continue to seek out and enjoy sexual relations after menopause, when the levels of female sex hormones decline (Matlin, 2003). Interestingly, new research at Simon Fraser University indicates that testosterone is higher in unmarried individuals (van Anders & Watson, 2006). It is not clear which is the cause and which is the effect of that link.

External Factors

Animals often show rigid courtship and mating rituals that are largely under the control of internal hormones.

Rather than appealing to the flow of hormones, an alternative way to explain sexual desire is to appeal to the value, or incentive, of sex. Clearly, something about the internal wiring of the brain makes sexual stimuli immensely rewarding for most people. We are regular recipients of an ongoing array of sexual signals in our environments, and these signals often stimulate sexual desire. Most men and women are sexually aroused by explicit visual stimuli, although women, if questioned, are less likely to report the arousal (Kelley, 1985; Murnen & Stockton, 1997). If excitement is measured through physiological recording devices attached to sensitive genital regions, men and women show very similar arousal responses to erotic pictures and movies (Meston, 2000; Rubinsky, Eckerman, Rubinsky, & Hoover, 1987). The argument for external factors suggests that the amount people think about and actually engage in sex is determined by the degree of external stimulation.

© Michael Melford Inc./The Image Bank/Getty Images

Touch and Smell   Touch is a particularly important external source of sexual arousal. Careful stimulation of certain regions of the body (commonly known as *erogenous zones*) is highly arousing for most people and may be one of the few completely natural, or unlearned, arousal sources. We frequently communicate through touch; in fact, it is an important source of information in every society (McDaniel & Anderson, 1998).

In contrast, for many animals it is odour or smell that initiates sexual interest. In Chapter 4, we discussed chemicals called pheromones that are released by the females of many species during periods of receptivity. Pheromones are odour-producing chemicals, and they drive dogs, pigs, and many other creatures into a sexual frenzy. At this point, no solid evidence shows that human pheromones affect sexual desire, although one recent study reported increased sexual activity for men wearing synthetic human pheromones compared with a placebo control (Cutler, Friedmann, & McCoy, 1998). How a person smells matters—both men and women report that odour is an important factor in selecting a lover (Herz & Cahill, 1997). In all likelihood, however, experience, rather than biological wiring, is responsible for these reports of sexual triggers.

Mate Selection

The initiation of sexual activity is guided by one very important factor—a person's selection of and acceptance by an appropriate mate. Not surprisingly, what people consider attractive is strongly influenced by sociocultural factors. In our own society, the ideal female body is much thinner than the ideal at the turn of the last century. Societies have unique cultural definitions of attractiveness, their own rules for attracting a mate, and different views on what kinds of sexual behaviour are considered appropriate. In some societies, for example, sexual activity is encouraged at very young ages—even five- and six-year-olds are allowed to engage in casual fondling of a willing partner's genitals. In other societies, sexual expression in childhood is strictly prohibited.

Sexual Scripts   The sequence of sexual activity between partners tends to unfold according to **sexual scripts:** learned programs that instruct people on how, why, and what to do in their interactions with sexual partners (Gagnon & Simon, 1973). These scripts may differ from one culture to the next, and they contribute to many of the differences seen in male and female sexual behaviour. Among other things, sexual scripts affect the attitudes we hold toward the sexual act. Boys typically learn, for example, to associate sexual desire with genital fondling; girls are more likely to identify sexuality with romantic love. These scripts affect expectations and sometimes are responsible for miscommunication between the sexes. For instance, more than 50% of teenage girls who engage in premarital sex expect to marry their partners, but this expectation is true for only 18% of the male partners (Coles & Stokes, 1985). York University researcher Michaela Hynie and her colleagues have conducted research exploring how women's sexual scripts relate to their use of condoms (Hynie, Lydon, Cote, & Weiner, 1998). They surveyed the sexual scripts of undergraduate students at McGill University and concluded that the women in their sample did indeed hold sexual scripts that were more "relational" in nature than those of men, and that condom use was not an integral part of women's relational sexual scripts. In other words, women generally tended to see sexuality as ideally part of a committed relationship, and condom use did not figure prominently in their scripts for such relationships. Sexual scripts may also account, in part, for why men sometimes employ aggression or strategies based on force to help them achieve their sexual interests (Ryan, 2004).

Evolutionary Influences   Despite cultural differences in sexual scripts, some fundamental similarities among peoples reflect the evolutionary history of the species. For example, in nearly every culture men are more likely than women to pursue

sexual scripts

Learned cognitive programs that instruct us on how, why, and what to do in our interactions with sexual partners; their nature differs across gender and may vary across cultures

Besides reproduction, finding an appropriate mate opens the door for companionship, protection, and love.

what David Buss and David Schmitt call short-term sexual strategies—brief affairs or one-night stands. In interviews with college students, Buss and Schmitt (1993) confirmed that most men had few qualms about the idea of having sexual intercourse with a woman they'd met only an hour before. For most women, however, the idea of such casual sex was a "virtual impossibility." Across all parts of the world, men seem to value attractiveness in a long-term mating partner and universally tend to prefer to mate with women who are on average younger than they are (Schmitt, 2003). Women, conversely, place greater value on a mating partner's financial prospects—a pattern that is consistent with their preference for older partners (see ❱ Figure 11.3).

The fact that these differences are present in virtually every society strongly suggests that these sex differences in mating behaviours might constitute evolutionary adaptations (see Chapter 3). The argument begins with the biological imperative: Only women bear children. Therefore, the ideal strategy for ensuring the perpetuation of genes necessarily differs between the sexes. Men should have evolved stronger and less discriminating desire for sexual partners in an effort to increase the likelihood of successful reproduction. A recent review of the literature seems to support the belief that men have a stronger sex drive than women do (Baumeister, Catanese, & Vohs, 2001).

But why would men have a preference for young and physically attractive women? During human evolutionary history, relative youth (ages 18–30) and physical attractiveness were the best cues as to whether a woman was fertile and healthy enough to bear children. Unattractiveness was associated with disease and parasites. Therefore, men who preferred youth and beauty were more likely to successfully reproduce (Buss, 1999).

In contrast, the responsibility of carrying and nurturing a child typically falls on the woman's shoulders. Natural selection should therefore have shaped a preference for males who would be able to contribute resources that would aid in the survival of offspring. The best cues are age, power, and evidence of commitment. From an evolutionary perspective, then, the differing sexual strategies we observe in men and women are not at all surprising (Buss & Schmitt, 1993). Throughout evolutionary history, men and women have faced different reproductive problems; their mating attitudes and behaviours undoubtedly have developed, in part, to solve these different adaptive problems (Buss, 2000, 2004).

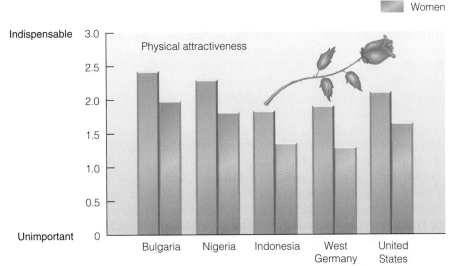

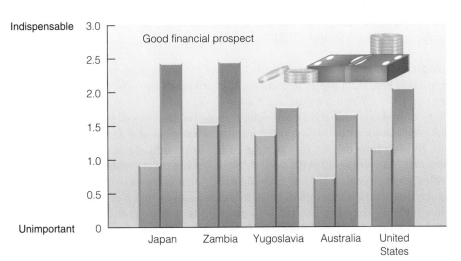

▶ Figure 11.3

Cross-Cultural Mating Strategies

Men and women in different parts of the world were asked to rate the importance of physical attractiveness and financial prospects in a long-term partner. On average, men rated physical attractiveness as more important than women did, whereas women were more likely than men to consider a partner's financial prospects important. (From "Cross-Cultural Mating Tendencies" from *Psychological Review 100*, by Buss & Schmitt, pp. 204–232. Copyright © 1993 by the American Psychological Association. Reprinted with permission.)

As noted before, human sexual behaviour shows considerable flexibility—evolutionary adaptations influence but need not determine our final behaviour. Moreover, it's worth reiterating a point from Chapter 2: Behavioural tendencies that developed during our species' evolutionary history may no longer be adaptive or socially constructive.

Sexual Orientation

The term **sexual orientation** refers to whether a person is sexually attracted to members of the same sex or the other sex. The label *homosexual* is applied to those with same-sex attraction and *heterosexual* to (the more common) other-sex attraction. Estimates of the number of people in North America who fit the description of homosexual vary, ranging from 2% to 10% (Rogers & Turner, 1991). Exact numbers are difficult to determine, partly because people are often reluctant to disclose such personal information.

Moreover, some types of sexual orientation (e.g., bisexuality, pedophilia, paraphilia) do not seem to fit into fixed boundaries. Many heterosexuals—women more than men—have had sexual experiences with members of the same sex. Indeed, women more than men seem to have an *erotic plasticity*—an ability to shift from

sexual orientation

The direction of a person's sexual and emotional attraction: homosexuality, heterosexuality, and bisexuality are all sexual orientations

one sexual orientation to another and back (Baumeister, 2004). Consider the famous case of actor Anne Heche: Originally heterosexual, she had a long-term relationship with comedian Ellen Degeneres but then eventually married a cameraman and had a child. Such plasticity is extremely rare in men: For social reasons, male homosexuals sometimes seek out heterosexual relationships. But true bisexuality may be rare: Men tend to be strictly heterosexual or homosexual (Lippa, 2006). Yet, as we'll see in Chapter 14, it is largely males who engage in paraphilias (e.g., pedophilia, sadomasochism, foot fetishes). This sexual stimulation from unusual sources occurs in only 1% of males and an even smaller percentage of women.

Despite its existence in every human society, the existence of homosexuality is difficult to explain with evolutionary theory. If the ultimate evolutionary function of sexual desire is procreation, how can homosexuality be considered adaptive? For many years psychologists were convinced that homosexuality developed as the result of experience, particularly the experiences children have with their parents. Homosexuality was considered to be an abnormal condition that arose from dysfunctional home environments, usually as a consequence of having a domineering mother and a passive father. But this view is no longer widely accepted, primarily because a close examination of family histories revealed that the home environments of heterosexuals and homosexuals are actually quite similar (Bell, Weinberg, & Hammersmith, 1981).

Biological and Environmental Factors The evidence is accumulating that sexual orientation is at least partly determined by biological factors (Crooks & Baur, 2002; Gladue, 1994). When researcher Simon LeVay (1991) compared the autopsied brains of homosexual and heterosexual men, he discovered that a cluster of neurons associated with the hypothalamus was consistently larger in heterosexual men. Exactly how or why this portion of the brain influences sexual orientation is unknown. But it does fit with new evidence of a genetic basis. For example, twin studies have revealed that if one identical twin is homosexual, there is a 50% chance that the other twin will be homosexual—even when reared apart. This rate is much higher than the 11% rate of homosexuality for fraternal twins or non-twin siblings of homosexuals (Bailey & Pillard, 1991; Bailey, Pillard, Neale, & Agyei, 1993). In fact, a systematic analysis of the chromosomes of homosexual brothers suggests evidence for what the researchers believe might be a "gay gene" (Hamer, Hu, Magnuson, Hu, & Pattatucci, 1993).

Other researchers have provided evidence thought to be consistent with biological influences on the development of homosexuality. J. Hall of the University of Western Ontario and Doreen Kimura of Simon Fraser University have reported that fingerprint "asymmetries" are more pronounced in gay men as compared with heterosexual men (Hall & Kimura, 1994). Martin Lalumière and colleagues at the University of Toronto reviewed 20 studies that compared rates of handedness (primarily left-handedness versus right-handedness) and found that gay men and women had a 39% greater chance of being non-right-handed than heterosexuals did, and the researchers suggested that prenatal exposure to sex hormones and maternal immune system reactions may be among the factors that influence developing fetuses toward a homosexual developmental path (Lalumière, Blanchard, & Zucker, 2000). Ray Blanchard and his colleagues at the University of Toronto found that the more boys a mother produces, the greater the chance that the next son will be gay (Blanchard, 1997; Bogaert, 2005). The researchers suggest that this pattern may result from a maternal immune response that strengthens after each boy baby. All these effects are consistent with the notion that homosexuality results from prenatal events that alter the fetal environment. This notion is backed up by controlled experiments on animals.

If there are purely environmental effects, such as attachment and learning, they must operate very early in development. Kenneth Zucker and his colleagues have determined that homosexual adults displayed a heightened level of cross-gender characteristics even as young children (Bailey & Zucker, 1995; Zucker, 1987).

Research is accelerating in this field and it's simply too early to be sure what the current data truly mean. They do suggest that biological factors (largely genetic and prenatal) play a significant role in the determination of sexual orientation. The biological findings are largely correlational—that is, we know that sexual orientation may be associated with certain brain structures or genetic markers. But these correlational studies do not guarantee that the cause of sexual orientation is biological. Some are susceptible to the alternative explanation that homosexual behaviour somehow alters the biology of the individual (Bailey & Pillard, 1995). Moreover, it seems unlikely that biological factors alone determine sexual orientation in all cases (after all, 50% of identical twins of homosexuals are straight). The environment likely plays a role, but the nature of that role has yet to be determined.

Test Yourself 11.3

Check your knowledge about the internal and external factors that control sexual behaviour by deciding whether each of the following statements is true or false. (The answers are in Appendix B.)

1. It is possible to affect sexual desire in men by altering the natural levels of the hormone testosterone in the body. *True or False?*

2. Condom use plays a role in the sexual scripts of women when they are thinking about committed relationships but not when they are thinking about more casual sexual encounters. *True or False?*

3. Across the world, men value attractiveness in a long-term mating partner and universally prefer to mate with women who are, on average, younger than they are. *True or False?*

4. Twin studies have revealed that if one identical twin is homosexual, there is an approximately 50% chance that the other twin will share the same sexual orientation. *True or False?*

▶ Expressing and Experiencing Emotion

LEARNING GOALS

1. Be able to identify the basic components of emotions and discuss their adaptive value.
2. Appreciate the evidence for and against basic emotions.
3. Learn about the role that arousal plays in the emotional experience.
4. Understand the subjective experiences of anger and happiness.
5. Recognize the differences among the James-Lange, Cannon-Bard, and Schachter theories of emotion.

As we discussed at the beginning of this chapter, an emotion is a complex psychological event that involves a mixture of reactions: (1) a *physiological response* (usually arousal), (2) an *expressive reaction* (distinctive facial expression, body posture, or vocalization), and (3) some kind of *subjective experience* (internal thoughts and feelings). Each of these components, which are shown in ▶ Figure 11.4 on page 454, can be measured, although some, especially the subjective-cognitive reaction, are difficult to measure reliably.

What is the function of emotions in the first place? The general belief among psychologists is that emotions help us adapt to rapidly changing environmental conditions. Emotions are powerful motivators of behaviour—they help us

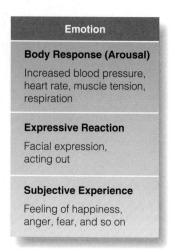

> **Figure 11.4**

The Components of Emotion

Emotions are complex experiences involving
(1) a *physiological response*, (2) an *expressive reaction*, and (3) some kind of *subjective experience*.

prioritize our thoughts, and they force us to focus on finding solutions to problems. Physiological arousal, for instance, prepares the body for "fight or flight" and helps us direct and sustain our reactions in the face of danger. Through expressive behaviours, such as the characteristic facial grimace of anger, it's possible to communicate our mental state instantly to others. Emotions can even regulate social behaviours. People perform better and are more likely to help others when they feel happiness (Hoffman, 1986); people are also more likely to volunteer aid after doing something for which they feel guilt (Carlsmith & Gross, 1969).

Are There Basic Emotions?

Most languages contain hundreds of words that relate in one way or another to emotions. Does that mean that there are hundreds of emotions, or are some more basic? This seems like a simple question, but it's one that has perplexed researchers for decades (Russell, 2003). Most emotion researchers agree on about six basic emotions. These lists usually include anger, fear, happiness, and sadness, for example (Ortony & Turner, 1990). Researchers who believe that such emotions are basic, or universal, argue convincingly that certain emotions, such as anger, increase the chances of survival. People also have no trouble recognizing expressions of anger, fear, sadness, and happiness in other people. For example, Paul Ekman and his colleagues asked volunteers to match photographs of grimacing, smiling, or otherwise provocative facial displays to a number of basic emotion labels. Volunteers showed wide agreement on six fundamental emotions: happiness, surprise, fear, sadness, anger, and disgust combined with contempt (Ekman, 1992; Ekman & Friesen, 1986).

Research by Maxine Wintre at York University supports the notion of a common understanding of emotions. She found that children as young as eight already understood emotional situations in the same way as adults do (Wintre, Polivy, & Murray, 1990).

Facial Expressions and Culture   Regardless of where you look in the world, people recognize that facial expressions are associated with certain emotional states. For example, a furrowed brow and a square mouth with pursed lips signify anger worldwide (Boucher & Carlson, 1980; Ekman & Friesen, 1975). In one case, Ekman and Friesen (1975) even tested members of a rural, isolated culture in New Guinea. These people had no experience with Western culture, yet they correctly identified the emotions expressed in photographs of Caucasian faces. Similarly, when North American college students were later shown photos of the New Guinea people acting out various emotions, they too were able to identify the emotions with a high degree of accuracy. Although it's not clear that emotion labels necessarily mean the same thing across cultures (Russell, 1994), most researchers are convinced there's some universal recognition of emotion from facial expressions (Russell, Bachorowski, & Fernandez-Dols, 2003).

Although most researchers are convinced that universal recognition of emotion from facial expressions exist (Ekman, 1994; Izard, 1994), there are some variations on this basic finding. For instance, Manas Mandal of Banara Hindu University and Philip Bryden and Barbara Bulman-Fleming of the University of Waterloo collaborated on a study that compared Canadian and Indian university students in their ability to distinguish Ekman's six basic facial expressions (Mandal, Bryden, & Bulman-Fleming, 1996). One of their findings was that Indians found fearful and angry expressions to be more unpleasant than did Canadians. Another finding was that happy, sad, and disgusted emotions were judged the most consistently in both cultures and may be the most basic of the basic emotional expressions. Although the ratings of the emotions surprise, anger, and fear were less consistent, the researchers suggest that this does not necessarily mean they are not universal, but that culturally specific "display rules" may influence these basic expressions to some degree.

Different emotions are often associated with particular facial expressions. Can you identify the emotion expressed in each of these photos?

In another cross-cultural study, Michelle Yik of Hong Kong University and James Russell of the University of British Columbia showed Canadian, Chinese, and Japanese respondents the expressions of basic emotions. They found that in addition to showing a considerable degree of agreement regarding the basic emotion expressed, the respondents also tended to agree on other information conveyed in the expressions, such as social messages (Russell & Yik, 1996; Yik & Russell, 1999).

Several researchers have suggested that the expression of emotion may have an evolutionary origin. Babies show a wide range of emotional expressions (Izard, 1994), and even babies who are born blind or born with hearing impairments and blind show virtually the same facial expressions as sighted babies (Eibl-Eibesfeldt, 1973). It appears, then, that people may purse their lips and furrow their brow when they're mad because these tendencies are built directly into the human genetic code rather than having been learned. The idea that there are universal facial expressions certainly makes adaptive sense; as noted before, facial expressions are excellent signals to others about our current internal state (Ekman & Keltner, 1997).

The Facial-Feedback Hypothesis　Some researchers have argued that feedback from the muscles in the face may even determine the internal emotional experience. According to the **facial-feedback hypothesis,** muscles in the face deliver signals to the brain that are then interpreted, depending on the pattern, as subjective emotional states (Tomkins, 1962). Other researchers point out that direct connections may exist between expressions and physical changes in the brain; for example, smiling can alter the volume of air that is inhaled through the nose. These changes, in turn, can affect the temperature of the brain which, in turn, might affect mood (McIntosh, Zajonc, Vig, & Emerick, 1997; Zajonc, Murphy, & McIntosh, 1993).

facial-feedback hypothesis

The proposal that muscles in the face deliver signals to the brain that are then interpreted, depending on the pattern, as a subjective emotional state

Patrick Clark/PhotoDisc/Getty Images

Babies show a wide range of emotional expressions.

CRITICAL   THINKING

Have you ever heard actors talk about how they "become the role" when they're playing emotional parts? What might a psychologist tell an actor to help him or her understand why this happens?

The facial-feedback hypothesis makes the unique prediction that if people are asked to copy a particular facial expression, they should experience a corresponding change in emotionality. Indeed, forced smiling, frowning, or grimacing does appear to modulate emotional reports, although the effects may be small (Matsumoto, 1987). You can try this yourself: Try forcing yourself to smile or grimace in an exaggerated way. Do you feel any different? Some therapists recommend that clients literally force themselves to smile when they are feeling depressed.

How Convincing Is the Evidence?   The link among facial expressions, biology, and emotion seems to support the idea that certain emotions are universal. But does the fact that people have similar facial expressions for fear, anger, or happiness really allow us to conclude that these emotions are somehow more primary or basic than others? Some psychologists think not. Remember: Many psychologists disagree about which emotions belong on the basic list.

For example, evidence is accumulating that a number of other emotions need to be added to the basic list. Research by University of British Columbia psychologist Jessica Tracy points to pride as a basic emotion (Tracy & Robins, 2004). It is signalled by a small smile, head tilted slightly back, and an open posture. You should easily be able to pick it out from the photos on page 455.

What about interest, wonder, or guilt? How about shame, contempt, or elation? Each of these terms has been identified as basic by at least one prominent emotion researcher. The problem is that humans are capable of an enormous range of emotional experiences. Consider the differences among fear, terror, panic, distress, rage, and anxiety. It is clearly appropriate to use any of these terms in some circumstances and not in others. How can we explain a complex emotion, such as terror? If it's not a basic emotion, is it somehow manufactured in the brain by combining or blending more fundamental emotions, like fear, surprise, and possibly anger?

Psychologists Andrew Ortony and Terence Turner (1990; Turner & Ortony, 1992) believe that it's not possible to explain the diversity and complexity of human emotional experiences by manipulating and combining a set of basic emotions. Rather than basic emotions, they argue, it's better to think of basic response components that are shared by a wide variety of emotional experiences. For example, the furrowed brow commonly seen in anger also occurs when people are frustrated, puzzled, or even just working hard on a task. The furrowed brow may occur in any situation in which a person is somehow blocked from reaching a goal. Hence its appearance, by itself, is not sufficient to infer that the person is angry.

It may help to think about the analogy of human language. Hundreds of different languages are spoken across the world, and each follows certain universal rules (relating to sound and word combinations). But it doesn't make any sense to argue that some of these languages are more basic than others. Human languages are built from basic components and share many features in common. But the components—the rules of sound and meaning—are not themselves languages (Ortony & Turner, 1990). Similarly, when people are in the grip of an emotion, they may experience many basic and universal conditions (such as a tendency to smile or frown, approach or avoid), but these are merely the components of emotion, not the emotions themselves (Russell, 2003; Turner & Ortony, 1992). Sticking out your tongue, for example, may be a playful sign of resentment in North America; in some regions of China, it indicates surprise.

The Emotional Experience: Arousal

Psychologists may disagree about whether people experience a special set of basic emotions, but everyone agrees about certain aspects of the emotional *experience*. Virtually all emotions, for instance, lead to *physiological arousal*. Muscles tense, heart rate speeds up, and blood pressure and respiration rates skyrocket. These emotional symptoms arise from activity of the autonomic nervous system as it prepares the body's muscles and organs for a fight-or-flight response. We usually experience emotions in situations that are significant for one reason or another—for

PRACTICAL SOLUTIONS

DOES THE POLYGRAPH WORK?

The link between emotions and arousal naturally led to the assumption that arousal could be used as a reliable index of emotional experience. If you're experiencing an emotion, your body ought to show the characteristic patterns of physiological arousal. This assumption lies behind the device commonly called a "lie detector." The technical term is the *polygraph*, a multi-measure of arousal. It is not a mysterious and magical device that measures truth—there's no secret location in the brain, chest, or fingertips that sends up a red flag when you're lying (Lykken, 1998). The polygraph test simply measures mundane things like heart rate, blood pressure, breathing rate, and perspiration. The assumption is that lying leads to greater emotionality, which can then be picked up through measurements of general physiological arousal.

This man is undergoing a polygraph test, which is based on the idea that lying leads to greater emotionality, which can then be picked up through measurements of general physiological arousal.

In a polygraph test, the critical comparisons are made between the arousal levels produced by what are called *relevant* and *control* questions. Testers understand that people might become aroused just from taking the test, whether they're lying or not. Therefore, the critical comparison is how arousal levels of the same person change across different question types. During the test, you're typically asked a series of neutral questions (e.g., "What's your name?") to establish a kind of baseline arousal level. Relevant questions are then asked about a specific event (e.g., "Did you change the bank records?"), and the examiner compares the amount of recorded arousal with the various baseline controls.

In the words of Lykken (1998), however, "polygraph pens do no special dance when we are lying." There-

fore, this approach has serious problems. First, the person being accused—guilty or not—will naturally react more emotionally to critical questions. Moreover, people can learn to beat the test. If you can control your arousal responses, it's possible to pass the test even if you're lying. Clever criminals can mask lying by increasing their level of arousal on control questions—perhaps by pinching themselves or biting their lip. If arousal levels on the control questions are high, the critical difference between the readings on relevant and control questions will be reduced. If arousal levels are similar across the different question types, the criminal is likely to pass the test. Many hardened criminals may pass the test because they feel little, if any, guilt about their crimes, so their reactions will be minimal anyway.

For these reasons, the polygraph test leads to frequent false positives: That is, innocent people are judged to be lying when, in fact, they are telling the truth. This is a significant problem. Consider that even if testers falsely accused people of lying only 5% of the time, that would still mean 50 out of 1000 people might be falsely accused of a crime. For these reasons, most courtrooms do not allow the results of polygraph tests to be used as evidence for guilt or innocence.

The modern technique that avoids some of these problems is the "guilty knowledge" approach. The polygraph tester can ask about crime scene details that can only be known to someone who was there. A stronger reaction to such details compared with control questions is, therefore, revealing.

instance, the car of a drunken driver swerves sharply into our path, or the sound of breaking glass from the basement window startles us awake. It's adaptive for the body to react quickly in such cases, and the rapid onset of physiological arousal serves that function well. Psychologists have developed instruments for objective measurement of arousal. A device that combines several of these measurements is called the **polygraph.** The Practical Solutions box on page 457 describes the pros and cons of using this device for lie detection.

Arousal and Performance   The relationship between arousal and performance is not simple and direct—emotional arousal can have a negative side as well. Too much arousal can lead to a breakdown in behavioural, biological, or psychological functioning. ❱ Figure 11.5 shows the relationship that exists between level of arousal and task performance. Notice that the pattern looks like an arch or an inverted U. For a given task, as arousal levels increase from low to moderate, performance generally rises. You may perform better on a test if the test is important. But too much pressure, which leads to too much arousal, leads to a sharp dropoff or breakdown in task functioning. You might have more trouble thinking if your entire grade depended on one test. Note that we can also explain individual differences with this idea: Some people perform better under pressure than others because the peak of their arch is closer to the high arousal side of Figure 11.5.

Understanding the relationship between arousal and performance has helped psychologists interpret behaviour in a variety of situations. For example, you may remember from Chapter 7 that people who witness crimes are sometimes inaccurate in their later recollections. One factor that contributes to these inaccuracies is the high level of arousal generated when someone witnesses a crime. If someone is holding a gun to your head, your arousal levels are so high that you may be incapable of normal cognitive processing. You are simply too aroused to process the details of the crime scene in a manner that will lead to effective recall. Moreover, as you'll see in Chapter 13, the relationship between arousal and performance also helps us to understand how our behaviour changes in the presence of other people—our performance is either facilitated or impaired when other people are around, perhaps because the presence of others changes our overall level of arousal.

The Emotional Experience: Subjective Reactions

Experiencing an emotion involves much more than just a facial expression or a flood of physiological arousal. Your thoughts, your perceptions, the things you notice in the environment—these all change when you experience an emotion. But as we discussed before, it's difficult to measure the internal experience accurately and reliably. After all, the emotional experience is by definition personal and subjective. We can ask someone to report what it feels like to be angry, happy, or scared, but the natural constraints of language restrict the answers we receive. Some cultures don't even have a word in their language to describe the concept of an emotion. For example, the Ifaluks of Micronesia have only the word *niferash*, which roughly translates as "our insides" (Lutz, 1982; Matsumoto, 1994).

Anger   What causes *anger*? Not surprisingly, the causes are many (Berkowitz & Harmon-Jones, 2004). Generally, people tend to get angry when their expectations are frustrated. If you're counting on someone to act a certain way or counting on a place or thing to deliver certain rewards, and these expectations are violated, you will probably get angry. This is one of the reasons we are often angry with the ones we love. We tend to expect more from the people we love, which, in turn, increases the chances that our expectations will be violated.

Is it better to express your anger or hold it in? Psychologists remain undecided about the benefits of "venting" anger, or blowing off steam. On the one hand, expressing your feelings may have a cathartic effect: The expression of anger can

---

polygraph

A device that measures various indexes of physiological arousal in an effort to determine whether someone is telling a lie; the logic behind the test is that lying leads to greater emotionality, which can be picked up through such measures of arousal as heart rate, blood pressure, breathing rate, and perspiration

CRITICAL   THINKING
Do you think people make distinctive facial expressions when they lie?

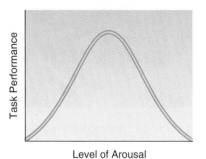

❱ **Figure 11.5**

Arousal and Task Performance

For a given task, performance tends to be best at intermediate levels of arousal. Too little or too much arousal often leads to a decrease in performance.

lead to an emotional release that is ultimately calming. On the other hand, getting physically angry could well increase the chances that you'll get angry again (Mauss, Evers, Wilhelm, & Gross, 2006). When you express anger and feel the calming effect that follows, you reinforce or reward the anger response. Hence, encouraging people to express their feelings of anger or hostility leads to more expressions of anger in the future. The expression of anger can also lead to increased risk taking and other kinds of self-defeating behaviour (Leith & Baumeister, 1996). (We'll return to the effects of anger, specifically on stress and health, in Chapter 16.)

Disgust   As you go to brush your teeth, you notice an unwelcome visitor among the bristles—a cockroach. The mirror captures your reaction: You wrinkle your nose and your mouth drops open in a characteristic gape. Internally, arousal coupled with nausea rise up as your mind plots the exact form of its soon-to-be expressive behaviour. What you are experiencing, of course, is a highly adaptive, usually food-related emotion known as disgust.

If there is a core group of basic emotions, *disgust*, a marked aversion toward something distasteful (literally meaning "bad taste"), is a likely candidate for inclusion. It's easy to appreciate why this emotion is an important tool for the adaptive mind, especially as a mechanism to ensure that we select and reject the appropriate foods. The facial expression that typically accompanies disgust is itself an adaptive reaction to a potentially harmful substance: Wrinkling the nose closes off the air passages, cutting off any offending odour; the gaping expression "causes the contents of the mouth to dribble out" (Rozin & Fallon, 1987).

But in recent years, researchers have come to recognize that the psychology behind the emotion of disgust extends beyond its role in food rejection. To illustrate, consider this question: What are the odds that you're going to use that toothbrush again? Suppose you were to drop it into boiling water for a period to ensure sterilization. Would you use it now? Probably not by choice. In a study by Paul Rozin and his colleagues, a dead but sterilized cockroach was dropped into a glass of juice and offered to thirsty subjects. Not surprisingly, few people showed any interest in drinking the juice, even though they knew the roach had been sterilized (Rozin, Hammer, Oster, Horowitz, & Marmara, 1986). Most people are also reluctant to consume their favourite soup if they witness the bowl being stirred by a never-used comb or fly swatter (Rozin & Fallon, 1987).

What accounts for these effects? According to some researchers, we are likely to succumb to what has been called *sympathetic magic* (Frazer, 1890/1959; Mauss, 1902/1972; Rozin & Fallon, 1987). People tend to believe that when two objects come in contact, they acquire like properties. The juice acquires some of the disgusting properties of the cockroach, perhaps through a process akin to contagion. The soup becomes associated with flies, even though you know that the fly swatter has never come into contact with a fly. Objects apparently need only to be associated with other disgusting objects to cause an emotional reaction. These are not conscious rational processes at work here, although they may be thought processes that are fundamental and common to all people (Rozin & Fallon, 1987). (It may also be that classical conditioning is involved—some kind of higher-order association may be formed between the juice, for example, and an object that elicits disgust; see Chapter 6.)

The experience of disgust seems to be universal—appearing cross-culturally—but the emotion takes a while to develop in all of its various forms. For example, if children under age four are presented with what adults would consider to be a disgusting odour (feces or synthetic sweat), they tend not to be bothered, or they may even react positively (Stein, Ottenberg, & Roulet, 1958). Children under age two, as any parent knows, are happy to put just about anything into their mouths, even "disgusting" objects. In one study, it was found that 62% of tested children under age two would put imitation dog feces in their mouths; 31% would mouth a whole,

Would you brush your teeth with this toothbrush?

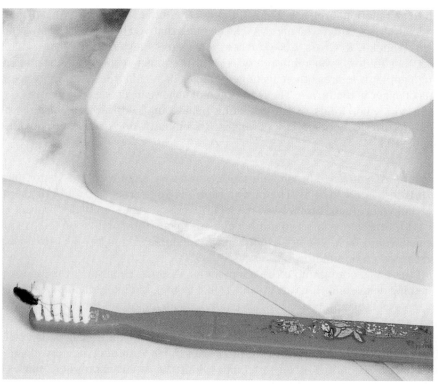

Nelson Photo

sterilized grasshopper (Rozin et al., 1986). Children simply have no conception that these objects are potentially harmful—they must learn what not to put in their mouths.

It also apparently takes a while for the idea of object contamination to become ingrained in people's minds. You won't brush your teeth with a toothbrush that once housed a cockroach, but a seven-year-old might. Children of this age typically report that a drink has been returned to normal after a disgusting object has been removed (Fallon, Rozin, & Pliner, 1984). In several studies, children under the age of seven were quite willing to drink a beverage after the experimenter simply removed an object like a fly—they were even willing to drink if a tiny bit of the disgusting object remained in the bottom of the glass (see Rozin, 1990, for a review). Notions about contagion and contamination clearly develop with experience and may even require the child to reach a certain developmental stage.

Happiness   Overall, little, if any, relationship exists between observable characteristics, such as age, sex, race, or income, and the experience of happiness (Myers & Diener, 1995). Instead, people seem to gain or lose happiness as a result of the comparisons they make—either with others (a well-known tendency called *social comparison*) or with things or experiences from their past. People set standards for satisfaction, and they're happy to the extent that these standards are maintained or surpassed. The trouble is that our standards are constantly changing—Homer and Marge may be able to keep up with the Flanders next door, but there's always the Fockers down the street who just bought that new boat. Once people obtain one level of satisfaction, they set higher goals and thereby immerse themselves in a spiral that never quite leads to utopian bliss.

Actually, many psychological judgments, not just emotions, arise from comparisons with some standard, or *adaptation level*. You may recall from Chapter 4 that whether people will hear one tone as louder than another depends on how loud the standard tone is to begin with. Human judgments are relative—there is no sense in judging whether a tone is loud, a light is bright, or a person is happy or sad without answering the question "Relative to what?" The fact that the subjective experience of happiness is relative helps explain some seemingly inexplicable phenomena. Why is that couple who just won the multimillion-dollar lottery now bickering? How can that homeless man, with only scraps to eat and tattered clothes, wake up every morning with a smile on his face? Happiness is not an absolute Nirvana that can be pursued and grasped: Instead, it's an elusive and fickle condition that depends on constantly changing standards and comparisons.

Note that happiness is the only positive emotion in our list. Indeed it seems that psychologists tend to focus on the dark side of human behaviour, including emotions. For every published article on happiness, joy, or well-being, there are 17 articles on depression, anxiety, and anger. This complaint has led to the recent rise of *positive psychology*, a movement toward studying the good side of human beings (Seligman, 2002). This movement may have good practical applications. We know, for example, that good moods lead to good behaviour. Making people happy induces them to help others (Lyubomirsky, King, & Diener, 2005).

Theories of Emotion: Body to Mind

We've seen that emotions are complex events. People subjectively experience happiness or sadness, but they also experience important changes in their body and on their face. Questions about how these various components interact have perplexed emotion researchers for decades. For example, what exactly causes the bodily reaction? Is the arousal caused by the internal subjective experience, or is someone happy or sad because his or her body has been induced to react in a particular way?

Several explanations are possible (for an overview, see ▶ Figure 11.6 on page 462). The most commonsense argument is that the subjective experience drives the physiological reaction. People tremble, gasp, and increase their heart rate because some event has caused them to become afraid. They detect the grasp of an arm around their neck, they feel fear, and their body reacts with physiological arousal. Surprisingly, this straightforward view of emotion has been essentially rejected by emotion researchers for more than a century. William James (1890) saw the commonsense view as backward. In his own words: "The more rational statement is that we feel sorry because we cry, angry because we strike, afraid because we tremble, and not that we cry, strike, or tremble because we are sorry, angry, or fearful" (p. 1066). Although James did not deny that our interpretation of the situation is also important (Ellsworth, 1994; James, 1894), he believed that the body reaction occurs before the subjective experience of emotion, rather than the other way around.

The James-Lange Theory   The idea that the body reaction drives the subjective experience of emotion became known as the **James-Lange theory** of emotion. Lange is coupled with James because Danish physiologist Carl Lange proposed a similar idea at roughly the same time as James. Why reject the commonsense approach in favour of such a counterintuitive view? Actually, neither James nor Lange presented much evidence in support of this account (other than personal impressions). However, some significant predictions can be derived from the view. For instance, imagine that we could somehow reduce or eliminate significant body reactions. The James-Lange theory predicts that we should lose the corresponding experience of emotion. To test this idea, a number of interviews have been conducted with people who have spinal cord injuries. Because of nerve damage, these people have either lost feeling in major portions of their bodies or at least have reduced sensory feedback. In

Despite what you might think, winning millions of dollars in the lottery does not guarantee future happiness.

James-Lange theory

A theory of emotion that argues that body reactions precede and drive the subjective experience of emotions

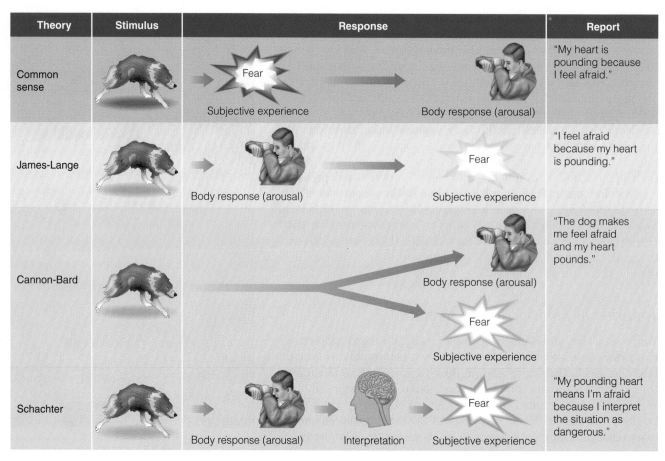

Theory	Stimulus	Response			Report

Figure 11.6

Four Views of Emotion

The *commonsense view*, largely rejected by psychologists, assumes that an environmental stimulus creates a subjective experience (fear), which in turn leads to a physiological reaction (arousal). The *James-Lange theory* proposes instead that the physical reaction drives the subjective experience. In the *Cannon-Bard theory*, the physical reaction and the subjective experience are assumed to be largely independent processes. In the *Schachter theory*, it is the cognitive interpretation and labelling of the physical response that drives the subjective experience.

support of the James-Lange view, some paraplegics report a corresponding dropoff in the intensity of their emotional experience (e.g., anger loses its "heat") (Hohmann, 1966). But at least some strong emotional feelings remain intact despite the loss of body feedback (Lowe & Carroll, 1985).

The James-Lange theory also predicts that unique physical changes should accompany each different emotional experience. That is, a particular body response must produce anger, happiness, fear, and so on. But as we noted before, the dominant physiological response during an emotion is *arousal*, and heart rate changes, sweaty palms, and increased breathing rate seem to be characteristic of virtually all emotions rather than just a select few. Think about how your body feels just before an important exam. Do you notice any similarities with the feelings that you get before an important and long-awaited date? Would you describe the emotions as similar?

Recently, however, sophisticated measuring devices have enabled researchers to record small, previously undetectable changes in body reactions. These new data may eventually help us distinguish the body reaction for one emotional state from the body reaction of another (Lang, 1994; Levenson, 1992). It turns out that anger, fear, and sadness, for example, may lead to greater heart rate acceleration than such an emotion as disgust; also, a greater increase in finger temperature apparently occurs during fear than during anger (Levenson, 1992). Neuroimaging studies also reveal differences in patterns of brain activity when people experience different emotions (e.g., Sato, Kochiyama, Yoshikawa, Naito, & Matsumura, 2004). Establishing definitive links between emotional states and physiological responses is an important step for emotion researchers, although perhaps not an unexpected one. After all, anger and happiness certainly are experienced differently and therefore must ultimately reflect differences in brain activity.

The Cannon-Bard Theory   Historically, it didn't take too long for critics of the James-Lange theory of emotion to emerge. Physiologist Walter Cannon mounted an influential attack in the 1920s. Cannon (1927) recognized that the body reacts in essentially the same way to most emotional experiences. He also argued that the conscious experience of emotion has a rapid onset—people feel fear immediately after seeing an attacking dog—but the physiological reactions that arise from activity of the autonomic nervous system have a relatively slow onset time (glands need to be activated, hormones need to be released into the bloodstream, and so on). Cannon felt that the subjective experience of emotion and the associated body reactions are independent processes. Emotions and arousal may occur together, but one doesn't cause the other. Cannon's view was later modified somewhat by Philip Bard, so this approach is now generally known as the **Cannon-Bard theory** of emotion.

The Schachter Theory   You've now been exposed to three different theories of emotion: (1) people experience emotions subjectively, which then leads to body reactions, such as arousal (the commonsense view), (2) the body generates a characteristic internal reaction, which then produces the appropriate emotional experience (James-Lange), and (3) body reactions and subjective experiences occur together but independently (Cannon-Bard). None of these views remains popular among modern emotion researchers.

The major problem with this trio of emotion theories is that they fail to take into account the cognitive side of emotion. To understand exactly what this means, you need to consider a rather complex study that was conducted in 1962 by psychologists Stanley Schachter and Jerome Singer (see ▶ Figure 11.7).

Cannon-Bard theory

A theory of emotion that argues that body reactions and subjective experiences occur together but independently

▶ **Figure 11.7**

The Schachter and Singer Experiment

Volunteer subjects were injected with a drug that produced physiological arousal symptoms. Half the subjects were informed about the drug's effects; the other half were not. When placed in a room with either a euphoric or an angry accomplice, only the uninformed subjects adopted the mood of the accomplice. Presumably, the informed subjects interpreted their arousal symptoms as due to the drug, whereas the uninformed subjects interpreted the arousal symptoms as an emotional experience.

College students were recruited to participate in an experiment that they thought was designed to test the effects of vitamin injections on vision. What the subjects didn't know, however, was that the vitamin cover story was a ploy: Rather than vitamins, they were actually injected with either a dose of epinephrine (which produces physiological arousal symptoms) or a dose of saline (which produces no effects). A second manipulated variable was subject expectation: Half the subjects in each of the injection groups were told to expect arousal symptoms ("It's a side effect of the vitamins, you see") and the other half were told to expect no reaction of any kind.

Now let's consider what effect these conditions might be expected to have on emotional reactions. Suppose you're sitting in a room, waiting for further instructions from the experimenter, when suddenly your heart begins to race and your palms begin to sweat. According to James-Lange, this arousal should translate into some kind of emotional experience; you might, for example, expect to become scared or irritated. But what Schachter and Singer (1962) found was that the experience of emotion was determined entirely by expectation. Those subjects who were told to anticipate arousal from the injection showed little emotional reaction to the arousal when it occurred. Only when the arousal was unexpected did people begin to report experiences of emotion. Importantly, participants who were injected with saline experienced no emotion *whether or not* they were told to anticipate arousal.

Even more interesting, Schachter and Singer were able to influence *which* emotion occurred. Joining the subject in the waiting room was an experimental accomplice, introduced as another participant in the experiment. Unknown to the real subject, the accomplice was instructed to act in a fashion that was either playful and euphoric or angry and disagreeable. In later assessments of mood, Schachter and Singer found that aroused but uninformed subjects tended to adopt the mood of the accomplice. If the accomplice was playful, the subjects reported feeling happy; if the accomplice was angry, the subjects reported feeling irritation.

The results of the Schachter and Singer experiment led to the proposal of the **Schachter theory** of emotion, sometimes called the *two-factor theory*. In this theory, autonomic arousal is still a critical determinant of the emotional experience (factor 1). But equally important is the *cognitive appraisal* or *interpretation* of that arousal when it occurs (factor 2). An intense body reaction may be necessary for the full experience of an emotion, but it's not sufficient. It's how you *interpret* the arousal that ultimately determines your subjective emotion. Thus, you're scared when you face an out-of-control bakery truck not only because your body is aroused but also because your mind understands that the source of the reaction is dangerous. You *label* the arousal and thereby determine the emotion that is experienced.

Like the other theories of emotion we've discussed, the Schachter theory has generated its share of criticism. For example, some researchers remain convinced that emotions like anger and fear can arise directly without higher-level interpretation or appraisal (Russell, 2003; Winkielman & Berridge, 2004). However, it's possible to draw several tentative conclusions. First, it's reasonably clear that arousal contributes to the experience of emotion. Second, the situation in which the arousal occurs and our expectations about the source of the arousal contribute to the emotional experience. Third, rather than saying that the body reaction creates the emotion or vice versa, it's better to conclude that emotions arise from interactions among several sources: the stimulus event that leads to the reaction, autonomic changes in arousal, and the expectation-based cognitive labels applied to everything involved.

Schachter theory

A theory of emotion that argues that the cognitive interpretation, or appraisal, of a body reaction creates the subjective experience of emotion

CRITICAL   THINKING

If expectations play an important role in determining whether an emotion will be experienced, would you expect to find cultural differences in the expression of emotion?

Test Yourself 11.4   *Check your knowledge about expressing and experiencing emotion by answering the following questions. (The answers are in Appendix B.)*

1. For each of the following, pick the component of emotion that best fits the situation: body response, expressive reaction, or subjective experience.

   a. Suzette likes to dance when she's happy: _____

   b. Yolanda grimaces and wrinkles her nose when she sees spaghetti with clam sauce: _____

   c. Mei feels her heart start racing whenever she sees her boyfriend approach: _____

   d. Robert would rather use the words *delighted, glad, pleased,* and *excited* to describe how he feels, instead of the word *happy*: _____

2. Which of the following situations is most likely to produce happiness?

   a. Receiving a B on a test when you were expecting a C

   b. Receiving an A on a test when you were expecting an A

   c. Receiving a C on a test when you were expecting to flunk

   d. Stimulation of the ventromedial hypothalamus

3. For each of the following, pick the theory of emotion that best fits the situation: James-Lange, Cannon-Bard, or Schachter.

   a. I love it when my heart starts racing because it makes me feel happy: _____

   b. I must be in love because she just gave me a wink and my heart is racing: _____

   c. I really feel happy right now and, by the way, my heart is also racing: _____

   d. You're not really in love; you just drank too much coffee this morning: _____

Motivation and Emotion

R
E
V
I
E
W

Your adaptive mind is designed to initiate, direct, and control behaviour. Motivation and its intimate companion, emotion, are vehicles that enable you to accomplish these things—to react to sudden changes in the environment, to maintain your internal energy needs, and even to prolong the species. We all have certain things we simply must do—consume food, drink liquids, maintain a constant internal temperature—and psychologists have struggled for decades to discover appropriate ways to describe the mechanisms that ensure our accomplishment of them.

First, what activates goal-directed behaviour? As you've seen, motivation depends on interplay between internal and external factors. Much of the time behaviour is controlled by internal factors that compel us in the direction of a goal. Our bodies are constantly monitoring internal energy levels, and once a disruption in the homeostatic balance is detected, we feel hungry or thirsty and seek to restore the appropriate balance. In these cases, it's likely that motivated behaviour arises directly as a consequence of biological factors and requires no direct experiences with the environment.

But even something as biologically significant as eating or drinking cannot be explained by appealing just to innate internal factors. All forms of motivated behaviour are influenced by external factors as well. External rewards, or incentives, exert powerful pulling and guiding effects on our actions. Understanding motivation then becomes a matter of specifying how these *external* factors interact with *internal* factors to activate and control behaviour. One way in which internal and external factors interact is described by Maslow's notion of a need hierarchy. The essential component of Maslow's theory is the prioritizing of need: Some needs, especially those critical to survival, must be satisfied before others, such as the need for self-actualization, can be pursued.

Second, what factors create hunger and control eating? What are the internal and external sources that initiate and control eating? Internally, the body monitors everything from the amount and content of food in the stomach to the level of glucose in the blood to determine its energy needs. If the level of glucose falls below a certain point, for example, you start to feel hungry and seek out food. Although researchers are uncertain about its precise role in controlling eating, the hypothalamus is believed to play an important role in initiating and controlling eating. But we also eat for reasons that appear unrelated to restoring homeostatic balance. People likely evolved to anticipate and prevent energy deficits, rather than to merely react to them. Food, and eating in particular, is clearly reinforcing. People are much more likely to motivate themselves to eat if they like the food—the vigour or intensity with which they respond depends critically on the value, or incentive, of the food. A number of factors, both genetic and environmental, play a role in regulating body weight. Eating disorders, such as anorexia nervosa and bulimia nervosa, tend to have psychological origins related to body image and to the need for (or lack of) control, and they may also reflect evolutionary adaptations that helped young women delay reproduction when they were feeling extreme stress.

Third, what factors promote sexual behaviour? Why do individuals in sexually reproducing species have such a strong motivation to pursue sexual activity? Sexual activity is necessary for individuals to replicate copies of their genes in the next generation. Humans therefore evolved to find sex to be very reinforcing, and sexual desire compels us to pursue a mate, thereby opening the door for companionship, protection, and love. Hormones apparently influence sexual desire in humans much less than in other animals. Different cultures have different views of attractiveness and different codes of conduct for sexual activity. Many psychologists believe that people acquire sexual scripts that instruct them on how, why, and what to do in their interactions with potential sexual partners. Mate selection and sexual orientation, however, are influenced by biological as well as environmental factors.

Fourth, how are emotions expressed and experienced, and what functions do they serve? Emotions typically involve a mixture of reactions, including a physiological response (arousal), a characteristic expressive reaction (such as a distinctive facial expression), and some kind of subjective experience (such as the feeling of happiness or sadness). The physical expression of an emotion allows us to communicate our feelings to others. The internal components— arousal, for example—prepare us for action. Thoughts become prioritized, and muscles are ready to respond. Emotions are powerful adaptive tools: They not only increase the likelihood of survival, but also, for many, make life itself worth living.

The internal subjective experience of emotion is often relative— whether we feel happy, for example, seems to depend on the comparisons we make with others and with our past experiences. Although a number of theories have tried to explain the relation between arousal and the experience of emotion, most psychologists believe that the experience of emotion depends partly on the presence of a body response— general arousal—and partly on the cognitive appraisals one makes about the origin of arousal when it occurs.

CHAPTER SUMMARY

▶ Activating Behaviour

Any organism that seeks to survive in an ever-changing environment needs motivational mechanisms to be able to react quickly to its needs and to anticipate future outcomes.

Internal Factors: Instincts and Drive

Instincts are unlearned, characteristic patterns of responding that are controlled by specific triggering stimuli in the world. Instincts do not adequately explain human behaviour. A *primary drive* is a psychological state that arises in response to a physiological need. *Secondary drives* are learned by association with primary drives. The body is designed to seek stable and constant internal conditions through a process termed *homeostasis*. It is useful to consider both *proximate* and *ultimate* factors in explaining motivational systems.

External Factors: Incentive Motivation

External rewards exert powerful "pulling" effects on behaviour. Psychologists use the term *incentive motivation* to explain goal-directed behaviour. Whereas drives serve as an internal "push," incentives serve as an external "pull" toward specific goals. Motivation is determined jointly by both internal and external factors.

Achievement Motivation

The *achievement motive* pushes you to seek success and significant accomplishment in your life. People who rate high in achievement motivation tend to work harder and more persistently on tasks. How hard you work on a task depends on your expectations about whether you will be successful and how much you value success on the task. Cultural factors play a role in achievement motivation and gender-related differences.

Intrinsic Motivation

Psychologists use the term *intrinsic motivation* to describe situations in which behaviour seems to be entirely self-motivated. This form is often contrasted with incentive motivation from externally provided rewards: They can lower a person's intrinsic motivation for a task. One explanation for this is that a reward may be perceived as controlling behaviour. Another account is that external rewards lead to overjustification; you conclude that you're engaging in the behaviour because of the reward, rather than because you enjoy doing it.

Maslow's Hierarchy of Needs

Maslow's *need hierarchy* provides a prioritizing of needs. Usually represented as a pyramid, the theory proposes that certain fundamental needs (biological "musts") take priority; once fulfilled, we seek to fulfill more personal security, spiritual, and relationship needs. At the top of the hierarchy is the need for self-actualization (reaching our potential).

▶ Meeting Biological Needs: Hunger and Eating

Eating is a critical part of living. Both internal and external cues help activate and control eating.

Internal Factors Controlling Hunger

A number of internal signals influence when and why we eat. The contents of the stomach is one such signal. Also, levels of *glucose* and *insulin* are monitored. It's likely that a glucose-insulin interaction is monitored because both substances play a role in metabolic processes. Brain regions also play a role in signalling hunger. Early research isolating the *ventromedial hypothalamus* and *lateral hypothalamus* as "stop-eating" and "start-eating" centres was overly simplified. Later research indicates that the brainstem and hippocampus are also involved.

External Factors Controlling Eating

We often eat for reasons not related to restoring internal homeostatic balance. Our eating behaviour is partially determined by our eating habits and food cues, such as the sight of food and its association with past pleasures.

Regulating Body Weight

Some researchers suggest that we have a *set point* (a natural body weight) that controls our tendency to gain or lose weight. However, more recent researchers have criticized set point theory and suggest that people eat to prevent energy deficits, not in reaction to them. The causes of *obesity* are varied and complex; a combination of biological and psychological factors, including genetics, metabolic rate, and learned eating habits, is likely involved.

Eating Disorders

People's assessments of their own weight and its relation to societal standards are typically inaccurate and help promote a negative body image. This increases susceptibility to the eating disorders *anorexia nervosa* (in which a person refuses to maintain a healthy body weight because of a fear of being overweight) and *bulimia nervosa* (binge eating coupled with purging to control body weight). The reproductive suppression model suggests that anorexia may constitute part of an evolved disposition for young women to suppress reproduction when under perceived extreme stress.

▶ Meeting Biological Needs: Sexual Behaviour

Although sexual activity is not necessary for individual survival, it is necessary to ensure that our genes are represented in the next generation. Internal and external cues help motivate an interest in sex.

Internal Factors

For much of the animal kingdom, sexual behaviour is controlled by internal (hormonal) mechanisms. Humans also show cyclic variation in hormones related to sex and reproduction (*estrogens* in females, *androgens* in males). But human sexual behaviour is subject to strong societal regulation as well as self-regulation.

External Factors

Sexual desire can also be explained by appealing to the incentive value, that is, stimulation by environmental cues. Visual and informational cues are both important. Touch is one important external source of sexual arousal; stimulation of *erogenous zones* is highly arousing for most people under the right circumstances. Also, *pheromones* (chemicals released by the females of many species during periods of receptivity) play a role in producing sexual arousal but not necessarily in humans.

Mate Selection

What people consider attractive in a mate is strongly influenced by both cultural and evolutionary factors. Our culture provides men and women with different *sexual scripts* that instruct us on how, why, and what to do in our sexual encounters. Evolutionary factors are implicated by sex differences observed in nearly every culture. Men are more likely than women to pursue short-term sexual strategies and focus on youth and attractiveness. These patterns reflect evolutionary adaptations that were responses to the differing reproductive problems faced by males and females in ancestral environments.

Sexual Orientation

Sexual orientation refers to whether a person is sexually and emotionally attracted to members of the same sex or the opposite sex. Research suggests that sexual orientation is at least partly determined by biological factors. It is possible that the environment plays a role as well.

▶ Expressing and Experiencing Emotion

Most psychologists believe that emotions help us adapt to rapidly changing environmental conditions and act as powerful motivators of behaviour.

Are There Basic Emotions?

Appreciate the evidence for and against basic emotions. Most people agree on about six basic emotions, typically including anger, fear, happiness, and sadness. Recognition of certain basic facial expressions of emotions seems to be universal, suggesting that expression of emotion may have a biological or genetic origin. Some researchers have argued that the feedback from muscles in the face may determine the internal emotional experience (the *facial-feedback hypothesis*). Some psychologists remain unconvinced that one set of emotions are "basic" and "universal." One alternative is that a set of basic response components appear in different combinations in different emotions.

The Emotional Experience: Arousal

Emotions are associated with *physiological arousal*. The relationship between arousal and performance is complex. The general relationship is an inverted U function; extremely high or low levels of arousal are likely to disrupt performance. The measurement of arousal serves as the basis for the *polygraph test*. The purpose of a polygraph test is to determine whether someone is being truthful or lying. However, polygraphs are fairly easy to beat and do produce a fair number of false positives.

The Emotional Experience: Subjective Reactions

The emotional experience is personal and subjective. Anger is typically associated with the violations of our expectations. The value of venting anger is a controversial issue. Some psychologists have found that encouraging people to express anger or hostility leads to experiencing more anger in the future, along with increased risk-taking and self-defeating behaviours. *Happiness* seems to rely on the comparisons we make—with others or with things or experiences from our past. Many psychological judgments (like emotions) arise from comparisons with some *adaptation level*.

Theories of Emotion: Body to Mind

The most natural way to relate emotion to body and mind is to assume that the subjective experience drives the physical reaction. The *James-Lange theory* assumes the opposite, that the body reaction drives the subjective experience of emotion. This theory predicts that unique physical changes should accompany different emotions, and this is typically not the case. The *Cannon-Bard theory* proposes that the subjective experience of emotion and associated body reactions are independent processes that occur together. The *Schachter theory*, formerly known as the *two-factor theory*, assumes that emotion is a product of autonomic arousal and cognitive appraisal of that arousal. Recent data seem to support some version of this theory.

Terms to Remember

Recommended Readings

Capaldi, E. D. (Ed.). (1996). *Why we eat what we eat: The psychology of eating.* Washington, DC: American Psychological Association. This is a broad collection of chapters, written by leading researchers, covering all aspects of eating and food selection.

Peterson, C., & Seligman, M. E. P. (2005). *Character strengths and virtues.* New York: Oxford. This book has its origins in the positive psychology movement. It breaks with the tradition of books listing human problems and what to do about them. Instead, it focuses on what we know about positive human traits and how to measure them. Among those traits covered are forgiveness, bravery, humour, and spirituality.

Taylor, G. J., Bagby, R. M., & Parker, J. D. A. (1997). *Disorders of affect regulation: Alexithymia in medical and psychiatric illness.* Cambridge: Cambridge University

Press. What happens when people are unable to regulate their emotions in an adaptive way? These people can be said to be suffering from alexithymia, and this volume, by University of Toronto researchers Graeme Taylor and Michael Bagby and Trent University researcher James Parker, explores the possible causes and consequences of this puzzling disorder.

 For additional readings, explore InfoTrac® College Edition, your online library. Go to http://www.adaptivemind3e.nelson.com.

Hint: Enter these search terms: achievement motivation, intrinsic motivation, eating disorders, sexual drive, sexual orientation, happiness, anger.

Media Resources

 What's on the Web?

Please note that Web addresses are subject to change. Check out the accompanying website for updates: http://www.adaptivemind3e.nelson.com.

This site presents practice quiz questions, hypercontent, information on degrees and careers in psychology, study tips, and more.

National Eating Disorder Information Centre

http://www.nedic.ca

This informative Canadian site provides a great deal of helpful information about eating disorders as well as other health-related issues. Find out the answers to such questions as these: How does body image distortion relate to eating disorders? What is the history of eating disorders? What is the relationship between exercise and eating disorders?

American Polygraph Association

http://www.polygraph.org

This association describes itself as "dedicated to providing a valid and reliable means to verify the truth and establish the highest standards of moral, ethical, and professional conduct in the polygraph field." This is a great site to visit if you're curious about the practice of lie detection with polygraphs. Find answers to the following questions: Who uses polygraph examinations? What factors lead to errors in polygraph results? Is voice stress analysis a valid indicator of lying?

The Kinsey Institute

http://www.indiana.edu/~kinsey

This is the official website (housed at Indiana University) of the famous institute, founded by one of the pioneers of human sexuality research. As documented in the recent film *Kinsey*, the institute "supports and coordinates a range of research on human sexuality." The site includes a wealth of information about and links to other sites dealing with sexology.

ThomsonNOW™ ThomsonNOW™

http://hed.nelson.com

Go to this site for the link to ThomsonNOW™, your one-stop study shop. Take a Pretest for this chapter and ThomsonNOW™ will generate a personalized Study Plan based on your test results. The Study Plan will identify the topics you need to review and direct you to online resources to help you master those topics. You can then take a Posttest to determine what concepts you have mastered and what you still need work on.

Psyk.trek 3.0

Check out Psyk.trek 3.0 for further study of the concepts in this chapter. Psyk.trek's 65 interactive learning modules, simulations, and quizzes offer additional opportunities for you to interact with, reflect on, and retain the material:

Motivations and Emotion: Elements of Emotion

Character is like a tree and reputation like its shadow. The shadow is what we think of it; the tree is the real thing.

—Abraham Lincoln

Personality 12

I n the most popular books, plays, and films throughout history, it is made clear who are the good characters and who are the bad. Indeed, the appeal of such stories would be lost without both good and evil represented in the cast of characters. Most appealing to psychologically minded people are stories in which good and evil reside within the same person. A classic example is R. L. Stevenson's 1886 novel, *The Strange Case of Dr. Jekyll and Mr. Hyde,* which explored the dual nature of human personality through the characters of Jekyll and Hyde. The good Dr. Jekyll could transform himself into the ghastly Mr. Hyde—the personification of evil—simply by drinking a special potion.

As you'll see in this chapter, psychologists, such as Sigmund Freud, have argued that human nature has multiple sides and that these sides fight a continual internal battle within the mind of ordinary people. Although not as dramatic as psychoanalysis, several other theories of personality accept the idea that people's behaviour can be inconsistent across situations.

Nonetheless, it is the consistency in social behaviour that is the focus in the study of personality. Note that your sadness after a funeral, grouchiness after bumping your knee, or elation after your team wins the big game do not justify labelling your personality as sad, grouchy, or elated. Such temporary departures from your character are best described with such terms as *mood* or *state* or *feeling.* Certainly, the idea of personality consistency seems to be a necessary assumption of living a normal life. How could we pick friends, get married, or select employees unless we assumed that they will have the same character tomorrow as they do today?

The fact that some people are shyer than others is indisputable, but is it a fixed characteristic? Is it even consistent across situations?

personality

The entire organization of psychological characteristics—thinking, feeling, and behaving—that differentiates one person from another

trait

A stable predisposition to act or behave in a consistent fashion

Personality can be defined as the overall organization of psychological characteristics—thinking, feeling, and behaving—that differentiate us from others and lead us to act consistently across time and situations. As with intelligence, the emphasis is on individual differences (Cronbach, 1957). People seem to differ in lasting ways: Sarah is warm, creative, and energetic; Karla has a cold social style and is generally untrustworthy. These central elements of personality are called **traits,** that is, predispositions to respond consistently across time and situations. Of course, the full richness of a person's personality cannot be captured by just listing his or her traits. Good personality theories must explain how the traits are integrated. They must be able to explain how good and bad qualities, as well as stability and change, can be present in every human being.

Personality

P R E V I E W

An individual's personality may be viewed as his or her typical way of adapting to life's challenges. Everyone runs into problems but, to be successful, we must cope with such difficult situations. Different people respond to these problems in different ways. Some people tackle their problems aggressively; others manipulate to get around the problem; others simply fret and hope it goes away. Not surprisingly, then, some personality styles are more adaptive; that is, some people overcome the challenges to lead more successful and happier lives than others do. These adaptive styles may be learned through trial and error but are constrained by temperament.

In one respect, the whole topic of personality represents a challenge to evolutionary theory, which is not designed to explain *differences* within a species (except for sex differences). The theory can certainly explain why the human species is characterized by traits, such as cooperativeness, conscientiousness, and even self-deception, because those traits increase the likelihood of survival (Buss, 1988; Kenrick, 1994; Krebs & Denton, 1997). The idea of individual differences, however, requires a more complex version of the theory. Why don't human beings all have the same traits— those that are ideal for our niche within the ecosystem? One argument is that two different levels of

the same personality trait (e.g., anxious and calm) both stay in the gene pool because each is adaptive in an important life situation (Buss & Shackelford, 1997). Calm people often have an advantage. But if everyone were calm, who would warn us of possible dangers? Another possible explanation for variation in personality is that random mutations of genes are necessary for new evolutionary development.

As with other chapters, we will show how psychologists have attempted to resolve the scientific and practical problems that are central to the study of personality. As you read this chapter, think back to the issues we considered in

Chapter 9. Many similarities exist between the study of intelligence and the study of personality.

First, what is the proper way to enumerate and measure the traits that make us both consistent and unique? To understand anyone's personality, it is necessary to summarize and integrate a wide range of his or her behaviours. People can't be judged based on their actions in a restricted situation or even in several situations. We need to capture the enduring aspects of behaviour—those *traits* that distinguish one person from another consistently across time. Of the many traits listed in the dictionary, we don't want to measure too many or too few. Describing people by using only a couple of traits may oversimplify personality. We need to go beyond saying Sarah is sweet and Karla is nasty. However, it would be impractical to use hundreds

of traits. The first part of this chapter outlines various research programs attempting to get the number of important traits just right.

Second, how do personality traits develop? What are the deeper processes that lead to stable and consistent behaviours? Does the surface stability hide a deeper turbulence? Different views on these questions will be clarified by turning to the grand theories of personality, such as the psychodynamic, learning, and humanistic perspectives. We covered some of the historical issues of these theories in Chapter 1 and some of the developmental issues in Chapter 10. But this chapter discusses the most thorough integration theories of psychology—the ones that try to paint the big picture of the human condition. We'll do this in the second part of the chapter.

Third, how do personality theories deal with variation and change in the same person's behaviour? Some critics have gone so far as to say that situational inconsistencies prove that traits don't even exist (e.g., Mischel, 1968). Most psychologists now dismiss that extreme view. Nonetheless, most psychologists also believe that human personality is more complex than trait theories seem to imply. Both traits and situations must be considered in any serious theory. The data from behavioural genetics confirms the importance of both genetics and environment. In the third section of the chapter, we'll discuss the controversies and lay out the most recent evidence.

▶ Enumerating and Measuring Personality Traits

LEARNING GOALS

1. Appreciate how factor analysis is used to identify basic personality traits.
2. Understand Allport's distinction among cardinal, central, and secondary traits.
3. Be able to explain the advantages and disadvantages of self-report questionnaires, projective tests, and indirect methods.

We must introduce personality measurement before we go on to detailed theories, such as psychoanalysis. After all, we need some systematic way of enumerating and measuring the various traits before we can deal with their organization and dynamics. **Trait taxonomies** are systems for counting and organizing the important dimensions on which people differ. As a general rule, trait approaches seek to identify stable individual differences by analyzing the responses of large groups of people. The assessment devices are then evaluated with psychometrics, that is, statistical indexes of measurement quality.

Three modes of measurement are common in this psychometric approach. The first is self-report: People describe themselves in interviews or questionnaires. The second is observer-report: Here the person is rated by others who have relevant information (e.g., friends, family, or trained observers, such as therapists or job interviewers). The third is actual behaviour, a concrete indicator that can be measured objectively (e.g., speed of initiating conversation, heart rate, number of parties attended in a month).

Whatever the mode of measurement, we have to decide what traits to measure. It has been estimated that comprehensive English dictionaries contain approximately 4500 trait terms (Allport & Odbert, 1936). Understandably, most research participants would not appreciate filling out questionnaires that long. Nor can we

trait taxonomies

Systems for distinguishing the most important individual differences in personality; these trait taxonomies are usually associated with an inventory of psychometric tests designed to measure these traits

communicate personality with such an overdose of facts. We need a trait taxonomy that reduces these thousands of descriptive terms into a smaller set of more basic terms that summarize groups of related terms. For example, when you describe someone with words like *kind*, *trusting*, and *warm*, you are actually citing related facets of a more fundamental trait, namely, agreeableness (Goldberg, 1993; Graziano & Tobin, 2002). But how can we identify the basic traits from among the thousands of personality descriptors in the language?

The Factor Analytic Approach

One way to approach the problem is to use *factor analysis*. Recall from Chapter 9 that factor analysis is a mathematical procedure used to analyze the correlations among a large number of variables—in this case trait words. The goal is simplification; that is, to reduce a large set of trait word variables to a small number of factors by clustering similar traits into subsets. Traits are considered similar if they are highly correlated (e.g., greater than 0.50). But, in a typical personality study of 100 traits, the resulting correlation table is huge (100 × 100). To say the least, this large dataset of 10 000 numbers is not easily analyzed by eye—even the trained eye of the personality researcher.

Factor analysis provides a dramatic simplification. It examines all the correlations to find subsets of trait words that are highly correlated. For example, people who rate themselves as *kind* also tend to rate themselves as *warm* and *trusting*. Together, they measure some broader personality characteristic. The final step is to name each factor in a way that captures the meaning of the whole cluster. Agreeableness or pleasantness seems like an appropriate summary label for the cluster of kind, warm, and trusting. If we end up with only 10 factors instead of the original 100 trait words, we can proceed in a much more efficient way to ask questions about the consistency and validity of personality. This is the logic behind factor analysis: determine the common denominators for personality by uncovering all the subclusters of traits.

Cattell's Source Traits   Raymond Cattell was the first to conduct a factor analysis of all the traits in the English dictionary. This feat became practical around 1960, when university computers became available for this purpose (Cattell, 1963). His analyses yielded 16 basic personality factors from a set of traits that originally numbered in the thousands. Thus, an individual's personality could now be summarized by their scores on 16 summary factors: *outgoing, calm, dominant, cheerful, conscientious, venturesome, tough-minded, trusting, imaginative, shrewd, self-assured, conservative, self-sufficient, controlled, relaxed,* and *intelligent.* The 16 factors were measured by a questionnaire—still popular today—that was appropriately labelled the **16 Personality Factors** inventory **(16PF)** (Cattell, Eber, & Tatsuoka, 1970). To Cattell, all 16 factors were *source traits*, meaning that they represent the underlying causes of behaviour. In contrast, he used the term *surface traits* for the many consistent behavioural tendencies (e.g., interrupts others) typically observed in people. The latter number far more than 16 and do not necessarily map onto the same source for different individuals. For example, the tendency to interrupt might be due to impulsivity for one person, callousness for another, and creativity for a third.

Eysenck's Three Dimensions   The major complaint about Cattell's factors was that they overlapped with each other; that is, even the factors were intercorrelated. To solve this problem, Eysenck used a type of factor analysis that produced nonoverlapping factors; they should show zero correlations with each other. The three resulting dimensions were quite clear: (1) the dimension of *extroversion*, which refers roughly to how outgoing and sociable you are; (2) the dimension of *neuroticism*, which captures your degree of anxiety, worry, or moodiness; and (3) the dimension of *psychoticism*, which represents your tendencies to be irresponsible and nasty toward others (Eysenck, 1991).

---

16 Personality Factor (16PF)

A self-report inventory developed by Cattell and colleagues to measure 16 primary personality factors

Eysenck's Three Primary Dimensions of Personality

Hans Eysenck measured three dimensions of personality: extroversion, neuroticism, and psychoticism. Included in each circle are sample questions of the type used to measure a person's standing on that dimension. (Questions from Eysenck & Eysenck, 1975.)

With only three primary dimensions (see ▶ Figure 12.1), Eysenck's theory is certainly simpler and, therefore, more practical for use in research and testing. Eysenck also theorized about the underlying biological systems required to explain the emergence of these three dimensions (Eysenck, 1970). Many have complained about his choice of labels: *neuroticism* and *psychoticism* are extreme terms that other psychologists reserve for clinical disturbances, not normal traits.

The Big Five   Who was right—Cattell or Eysenck? A simple answer is that Eysenck and Cattell were operating at different levels of analysis: Eysenck, with his three primary dimensions, was interested in mapping out the more distinct and general aspects of human personality, whereas Cattell's analytic techniques paint a more fine-grained set of overlapping traits (see Feist, 1994). More recently, researchers seem to be settling on an intermediate solution to the factoring problem: the "Big Five"—that is, the five basic personality dimensions (Goldberg, 1993; McCrae & Costa, 1985; Wiggins & Pincus, 1992).

The so-called **Big Five** personality dimensions include *extroversion, agreeableness, conscientiousness, neuroticism,* and *openness to experience.* Each is listed in ▶ Figure 12.2 on page 476 along with some of the descriptors that identify each trait. So, for example, people who score highly on the extroversion dimension tend to see themselves as talkative, sociable, fun-loving, and affectionate. Notice that extroversion and neuroticism are two of the three primary dimensions suggested by Eysenck, and psychoticism neatly translates into a combination of conscientiousness and disagreeableness.

Why 5 factors in the Big Five model instead of 2 or 3 or even 16? Part of the reason is technical, having to do with what current researchers believe is the most appropriate way to apply the factor analytic technique (see Digman, 1990; Goldberg, 1993). But there are other reasons. For example, a number of studies have analyzed trait ratings collected from people around the world. Regardless of the language used—and different languages can have quite different personality descriptors—five basic dimensions still appear to best explain the ratings (Digman,

Big Five

The five dimensions of personality—extroversion, agreeableness, conscientiousness, neuroticism, and openness—that have been isolated through the application of factor analysis; it is widely believed that virtually all personality terms in language can be accounted for by appealing to one or more of these basic dimensions

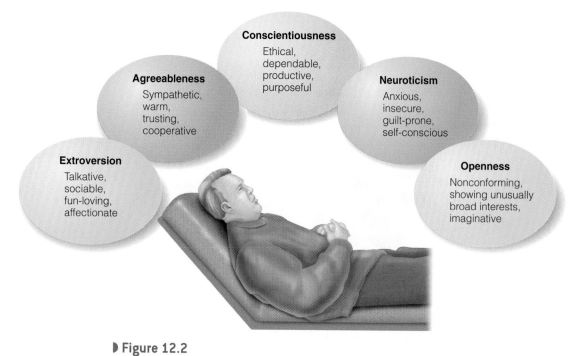

▶ Figure 12.2

The Big Five Dimensions

There is a growing consensus that personality traits can be summarized in terms of five fundamental personality dimensions: extroversion, agreeableness, conscientiousness, neuroticism, and openness.

1990; McCrae & Costa, 1997). Such data suggest that the basic structure of personality may be universal rather than dependent on cultural background (McCrae, Costa, & Yik, 1996). At the same time, the fact that five factors can be used to categorize people doesn't tell us anything about the internal processes that determine a personality profile. To truly understand personality, some critics argue, you need to understand the ability of people to *change* as well as their consistency across situations (Mischel & Shoda, 1998; Srivastava, John, Gosling, & Potter, 2003). We'll discuss how the environment affects the consistency of behaviour later in the chapter.

The Interpersonal Circle   What if we are interested only in dimensions that relate directly to interpersonal behaviour? In that case, personality can be reduced to two primary dimensions of interpersonal behaviour, namely, *agency* and *communion*. Canadian researchers have been especially important in developing this model. The importance of these two dimensions was first pointed out by York University's David Bakan (1966) and later explored in detail by other Canadian researchers, including Ross Broughton and Paul Trapnell of the University of Winnipeg, Jerry Wiggins and Del Paulhus of the University of British Columbia, Debbie Moskowitz of McGill University, and Krista Trobst of York University (Moskowitz, 1994; Trapnell & Wiggins, 1990; Trobst, 2000; Wiggins, 1979; Wiggins & Broughton, 1991).

The key idea is that the interpersonal traits form a statistical and conceptual circle, as in ▶ Figure 12.3. The closer two traits are on the circle, the more highly correlated they are. Moreover, any interpersonal trait can be summarized by how much it reflects each of the two basic social values—agency and communion. The concept of agency refers to "getting ahead," that is, achieving more than others do. The concept of communion refers to "getting along," that is, fitting in with and supporting others. Of central importance is the idea that they are not mutually exclusive: You can be agentic and communal, too. Successful leaders, for example,

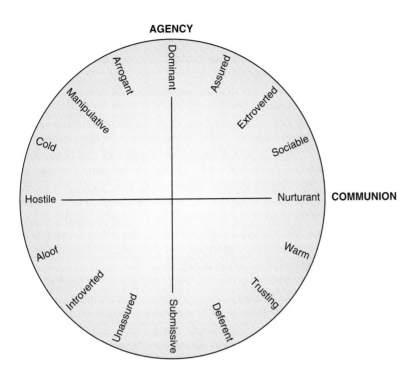

AGENCY

Arrogant
Dominant
Assured
Manipulative
Extroverted
Cold
Sociable
Hostile — Nurturant   **COMMUNION**
Aloof
Warm
Introverted
Trusting
Unassured
Submissive
Deferent

▶ **Figure 12.3**

Wiggins's Interpersonal Circle of Personality Traits

Personality researcher Jerry Wiggins of the University of British Columbia suggested that this two-dimensional figure provides a useful summary of important personality traits relating to the interpersonal domain. Traits that are close on the circle are those that are most highly correlated.

require both. Note that four out of the Big Five dimensions can be mapped onto the interpersonal circle (Paulhus & John, 1998; Wiggins & Trapnell, 1997). Extroversion and openness to experience are associated with agency, whereas agreeableness and conscientiousness are associated with communion.

Recent Alternatives to the Big Five   Several Canadian psychologists have addressed the limitations of the Big Five factor model. The University of Western Ontario's Sampo Paunonen (1998) wondered how specific lower-order traits (e.g., talkativeness and sociability) would compare with broader Big Five dimensions (e.g., extroversion) in predicting observable behaviour. Ninety-six undergraduates completed a general inventory of 22 lower-order traits, a measure of the Big Five, and a set of 14 behavioural criteria: These included number of dates per month, whether the student was a smoker, choice of major, religiosity, and fraternity or sorority membership. When compared with the Big Five, the lower-order traits produced significantly better prediction. In short, specific behaviours are better predicted by narrower, more focused traits. The bigger lesson is that we should use a measurement instrument that is at the same level as the outcome we want to predict.

Another challenge to the Big Five is the recommendation to subdivide the conscientiousness dimension of the Big Five into two parts: dutifulness and ambition (Jackson, Paunonen, Fraboni, & Goffin, 1996). Another is the radical proposal by Michael Ashton of Brock University and Sibeom Lee of the University of Calgary. They have suggested adding a sixth dimension to the Big Five. In a series of factor analyses, they provided evidence for a dimension they called honesty-humility, that is, the tendency to be honest and forthright in social relations (Ashton, Lee, & Son, 2000). Low scorers on this factor include the so-called dark triad of personality: Machiavellianism, narcissism, and psychopathy (Paulhus & Williams, 2002).

Allport's Trait Theory

Like the factor analysts, psychologist Gordon Allport (1897–1967) was convinced that all people possess underlying personality traits, or "predispositions to respond." But he was less convinced that the search for a common set of

CRITICAL   THINKING

When comparing Allport's approach with the factor analytic approach, think back to our discussions in Chapter 2. What are the advantages and disadvantages of using case studies, which examine single individuals, versus surveys, which rely on responses from large groups?

underlying dimensions was the way to go. Instead, Allport believed that personality should focus on the uniqueness of the individual. His approach, which he called *idiographic* (which means "revealing the individual"), was to study particular persons in great detail. An advantage of this kind of case study approach is that consistencies in behaviour can be recorded across an entire lifetime of experiences in a variety of settings (Barenbaum, 1997).

One of Allport's main contributions was his general classification scheme for identifying personality traits (Allport, 1937). Allport believed that some people display what he called *cardinal personality traits*. **Cardinal traits** are the ruling passions that dominate an individual's life. If you spend your life huddled in a mountain monastery, rejecting all worldly possessions, your passion "to serve God" would likely satisfy Allport's description of a cardinal trait. Perhaps you know someone whose every thought or action seems to revolve around the pursuit of wealth, fame, or power. We can't really capture something like a cardinal trait by applying a technique, such as factor analysis, because cardinal traits are uniquely defined by the individual rather than the group.

Allport believed that cardinal traits are rare. Most people have personalities that are controlled by several lasting characteristics, which Allport labelled as *central traits*. **Central traits** are the 5 to 10 descriptive terms that you would use to describe someone you know. Consider Sarah. She's warm and friendly, very trustworthy, sentimental at times, and honest to the core. In addition to central traits, Allport suggested that everyone has **secondary traits,** which are less obvious because they may not always appear in an individual's behaviour. For example, Sarah might also have a secondary trait of *grouchiness* that always shows up in morning meetings. Personality characteristics, therefore, can be appropriately described in terms of levels ranging from dominant (cardinal) to representative (central) to occasional (secondary).

Assessment Methods

We have now covered the best-known systems for organizing traits, the basic dimensions of human personality. Confirmation of these traits is a major advance in our search to find distinguishing patterns of psychological characteristics. But there are also practical reasons why it's important to measure personality traits—they provide an efficient screening process for job selection and clinical diagnosis.

---

cardinal traits

Allport's term to describe personality traits that dominate an individual's life, such as a passion to serve others or to accumulate wealth

central traits

Allport's term to describe the 5 to 10 descriptive traits that you would use to describe someone you know—friendly, trustworthy, and so on

secondary traits

The less obvious characteristics of an individual's personality that do not always appear in his or her behaviour, such as grouchiness at morning meetings

Cardinal traits are the ruling passions that dominate a person's life, such as a compelling need to help the needy at the expense of personal comfort.

© Bettmann/Corbis/Magma

Suppose you're the personnel director at a large nuclear power plant. You need to hire responsible people to run the plant—people who have the right stuff to handle potentially dangerous materials in an emergency. You wouldn't want to hire someone like Karla, with her tendency toward dishonesty, or the forgetful Homer Simpson.

But what is the best way of assessing an individual's traits? The three modes of measurement mentioned earlier (self-report, observer-rating, behaviour) have led to a wide variety of assessment devices. The trait taxonomies detailed above (e.g., the Big Five factors) were developed primarily from questionnaires. Observer versions of these measures often consist of the same questions as the self-report, except you are asked to answer the questions about someone else. Behaviours often have the advantage of being scored objectively (e.g., counted or measured). But they are time-consuming and generally difficult to collect.

Of these three modes of measurement, we will discuss only *self-report questionnaires* in detail. We will also discuss two methods that go beyond the three standard modes, namely *projective tests* and *indirect methods*.

Self-Report Questionnaires   Sometimes the best way to learn what someone is like is to ask the person directly. The questions could be posed by an interviewer or a computer, but they are usually presented in a standardized questionnaire. Responses are scored objectively, and the results are then compared with test averages that have been compiled from the performances of thousands of other test takers. The major advantage of **self-report questionnaires** is their ease of administration: Responses can be collected from thousands of people in a short time. Self-report questionnaires paint a reliable picture of how someone differs from the average. Karla's answers, for instance, would probably raise red flags on a number of measures; her answers are likely to show some disdain for others (compared with the average) and a marked tendency toward impulsiveness. If you were the personnel director, you could easily make your hiring decision (presumably "no hire") based on the test results.

Many kinds of self-report questionnaires are employed by professionals. Some tests are based on popular trait theories. For example, to assess normal personality traits you can administer the 16 Personality Factor (16PF), which is the 187-item questionnaire designed to measure the 16 primary personality factors identified by Cattell, discussed earlier in the chapter (Cattell et al., 1970). Alternatively, the **NEO-PI-R** was designed by Costa and McCrae (1989) to measure the Big Five personality traits identified in Figure 12.2. For clinical purposes, the most widely used self-report inventory is the **Minnesota Multiphasic Personality Inventory (MMPI).** The MMPI requires test takers to answer hundreds of true-false questions about themselves (e.g., "I never get angry"). Although originating almost 60 years ago, the instrument has recently been revised (see Butcher, 1995). An individual's answers are expressed in a personality profile that describes his or her scores on various subscales (see ▶ Figure 12.4 on page 480). Note that all the self-report questionnaires listed above have been validated by showing significant correlations with alternative measures, such as peer-reports and behavioural measurement.

The main advantage of self-report questionnaires is their efficiency. Large numbers of individuals can be scored quickly with objective scoring keys—they're standardized, everyone takes the same test, and they can easily be scored by a computer. This efficiency of questionnaires facilitates research so that hundreds of studies have been conducted on the reliability and validity of the major instruments, especially the MMPI (Butcher & Rouse, 1996; Helmes & Reddon, 1993). At the same time, self-report questionnaires depend on the accuracy of the information provided by the test taker. If people choose to be deceptive on the test or try to make themselves look good in some way, the results can be of limited usefulness (Nichols & Greene, 1997).

self-report questionnaires

Personality tests that ask the person of interest a set of questions about how he or she thinks, acts, or feels

NEO-PI-R

A self-report inventory developed to measure the Big Five personality dimensions

Minnesota Multiphasic Personality Inventory (MMPI)

A widely used self-report inventory for assessing personality traits and for diagnosing psychological problems

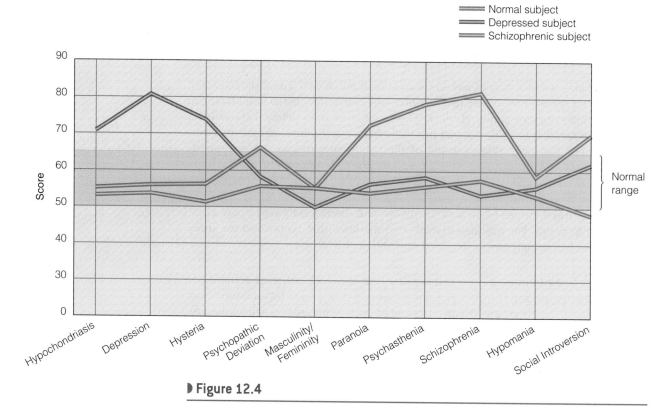

Normal subject
Depressed subject
Schizophrenic subject

Normal range

Score

Hypochondriasis
Depression
Hysteria
Psychopathic Deviation
Masculinity/ Femininity
Paranoia
Psychasthenia
Schizophrenia
Hypomania
Social Introversion

▶ **Figure 12.4**

MMPI Profiles

The MMPI is often used to help psychologists diagnose psychological disorders. A client's scores on the various clinical scales can be compared with average scores from people who do not have psychological problems as well as average scores from people who have been diagnosed with specific problems (such as depression or schizophrenia). (Adapted from Weiten, 1995.)

Assumptions behind Self-Reports A number of Canadian researchers have either developed or evaluated scales to assess many important personality constructs. These include Ron Norton's work at the University of Winnipeg on social anxiety or shyness (Norton, Cox, Hewitt, & McLeod, 1997), Ken Cramer's work at the University of Windsor on loneliness and self-concealment (Cramer & Barry, 1999a, 1999b), Gordon Flett's work at York University on perfectionism (Flett, Hewitt, Blankstein, & Gray, 1998; Flett, Hewitt, Blankstein, & Pickering, 1998), Gerald Wilde's work at Queen's University on risk taking (Wilde, 1994), and Donald Saklofske and Peter Greenspoon's work at the University of Saskatchewan on student life satisfaction (Greenspoon & Saklofske, 1998; Saklofske & Greenspoon, 2000). In fact, personality scale construction and evaluation may become easier following an important finding from University of Calgary researchers Karen Pasveer and John Ellard (1998). They found that scale data can be collected on the World Wide Web with the same reliability as when collected traditionally in a classroom or in person. Moreover, Internet samples have the advantage of larger and more diverse sample sizes (Vazire & Gosling, 2004).

Of course, a researcher who uses self-report questionnaires typically makes a series of assumptions about the validity of such data. Suppose you asked two friends to fill out a loneliness scale. You hope not only that their answers are honest but also that they have enough insight to accurately evaluate their own loneliness. Your own knowledge of your friends might make you doubt the accuracy of their questionnaire answers. Given that psychologists often study very sensitive personality variables, such as loneliness, depression, authoritarianism, and sexual tendencies, they have devoted considerable energy to evaluating such distortions. For example, questionnaire responses are usually screened for **socially desirable responding,** that is, the tendency of some people to describe themselves as having positive, or at least normal, traits. Therefore, personality inventories often include extra items that are desirable but very unlikely to be true (e.g., "I have never stolen anything" or "I have no prejudices"). Initial research in this area began decades ago with work by the University of Waterloo's Douglas Crowne (Crowne & Marlowe, 1964) and Western University's Douglas Jackson (Jackson & Messick, 1961). More recently, the University of British Columbia's Paulhus and Reid (1991) made the distinction between two forms of desirable responding: One is conscious and based on purposeful distortion (known as *impression management*) and the other is based on an unconscious bias (known as *self-deception*).

In one application, University of Saskatchewan researchers Ken Cramer and Kim Neyedley (1998) investigated whether males' and females' reports of their loneliness were influenced by the negative social stigma associated with our perceptions of the lonely individual. Over 250 respondents completed one scale that measured how lonely they felt and another that measured how masculine they felt. The researchers originally found no sex differences in loneliness but after adjusting the data for the fact that males scored higher on masculinity, the results suggested that males were significantly lonelier than females. It seemed that males were not honest about their feelings of loneliness: Their masculinity forced them to deny that they were lonely. Note that this form of "dishonesty" is more a matter of self-deception than impression management. To avoid such problems, most modern personality scales are evaluated for possible contamination with either form of desirable responding.

Projective Tests   Based on the theories of Sigmund Freud (whom we'll discuss shortly), psychologists sometimes use what are called projective personality tests. In a **projective test,** you're asked to interpret an unstructured or ambiguous stimulus. The underlying assumption is that you will "project" your thoughts and true feelings during your interpretation, thereby revealing elements of your personality. For example, take a look at the inkblot shown in ▶ Figure 12.5, which is similar to the kind of unstructured stimulus used on the **Rorschach test.** Different interpretations of such a stimulus are unlikely to be pure coincidence. If Karla sees snakes and dragons in such images whereas Sarah sees butterflies and flowers, it's not too difficult to infer that they have quite different personalities.

> **socially desirable responding**
>
> The tendency to describe ourselves as having positive, or at least normal, traits

> **projective test**
>
> A type of personality test in which individuals are asked to interpret ambiguous stimuli; the idea is that subjects will project their true thoughts and feelings into the interpretation, thereby revealing elements of their personality

> **Rorschach test**
>
> A projective test that requires people to interpret ambiguous inkblots

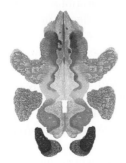

▶ **Figure 12.5**

Projective Tests

In projective tests, we are asked to interpret unstructured or ambiguous stimuli. Our answers are presumed to provide insight into our personalities. What do you see hidden in this inkblot? Is it an angel longing to return to the Garden of Eden—or just a flattened frog? (From Kalat, 1996.)

This image, taken from the Thematic Apperception Test, can be interpreted in many ways. What do you think the character in the picture is thinking and feeling? Your answers may reveal something about your personality.

From *Abnormal Psychology* by Barlow, Durand, and Stuart. © 2006 Nelson, a division of Thomson Canada Limited.

Thematic Apperception Test (TAT)

A projective personality test that requires people to make up stories about the characters in ambiguous pictures

Another popular projective test is the **Thematic Apperception Test (TAT)**. Instead of an inkblot, you are shown an ambiguous picture, such as the one above. You are asked to make up a story that explains what is happening in the picture. Again, the idea is that you will reveal aspects of yourself in the themes of your stories. Many clinical psychologists prefer to use tests like the TAT or the Rorschach rather than other approaches because projective tests are revealing without being directly confrontational. After all, you are just making up stories about pictures!

But how do we know what your responses really mean? Reliable standards have been developed for interpreting responses on projective tests. Both the TAT and the Rorschach, for example, use a standardized set of stimuli so that your responses can be compared with those of thousands of other people. Of course, many clinicians tend to look for traditional psychodynamic themes in interpretation (such as a tendency to see sex, death, or aggressiveness) or for such qualities as originality (Edberg, 1990; Hurt, Reznikoff, & Clarkin, 1995). They may also look for such things as the degree of realism in the interpretation: Does the response really match the perceptual structure of the stimulus? If you claim to see a dragon in an inkblot like the one in Figure 12.5, your general view of the world may slant toward fantasy rather than reality. The degree to which you seek help in your interpretation may also be instructive. For example, individuals who constantly seek guidance from the clinician before giving an answer are likely to be classified as dependent.

Despite the improvements, projective tests continue to come under fire. The scoring procedures still tend to be somewhat unreliable. The same person's answers change from session to session and different administrators may arrive at quite different interpretations of the same subject's responses (see Beutler & Berren, 1995). Questions about the validity of the interpretations have also been raised (Lilienfeld, Wood, & Garb, 2000).

CRITICAL **THINKING**

Do you think there is any connection between the interpretation of projective tests and the interpretation of dreams? Do you think we could use dream interpretation as a way of discovering someone's true personality?

▶ **Figure 12.6**

Nonverbal Personality Assessment

In nonverbal personality assessments, respondents are shown line drawings and asked to rate the likelihood that they would act similarly themselves. Panel (a) is meant to portray aggressive behaviour, and (b) portrays thrill-seeking behaviour. (Figure taken from Paunonen et al., "The structured nonverbal assessment," from *Journal of Personality, 58,* 1990, pp. 481–501. Reprinted by permission of Blackwell Publishers.)

Despite these criticisms, projective tests remain extremely popular with therapists (Butcher & Rouse, 1996). As well, some major researchers continue to hold that projective tests are the only valid way to capture such tendencies as power motivation (Winter, John, Stewart, Klohnen, & Duncan, 1998) and uncertainty motivation (Sorrentino & Roney, 2000).

Indirect Methods   To avoid the problems of projective testing and self-report inventories, a number of other indirect methods have been developed. Sampo Paunonen and colleagues at the University of Western Ontario have devised a unique form of nonverbal personality assessment (Paunonen, Jackson, & Keinonen, 1990; Paunonen, Zeidner, Engvik, Oosterveld, & Maliphant, 2000). In this nonverbal assessment method, the items are drawings of a figure performing trait-relevant behaviours in specific situations, like getting angry over a missed tennis volley or returning a lost hat to a stranger (see ▶ Figure 12.6). Respondents rate the likelihood that they themselves would engage in similar behaviours. These researchers found that the nonverbal personality scales have compared favourably in reliability and validity with the standard verbal scales, even when administered to diverse samples of university undergraduates from Canada, England, the Netherlands, Finland, Norway, and Israel. In fact, the factor structure of the nonverbal scales is very similar to the familiar Big Five factor model found in more conventional personality assessments. This approach has some advantages in cross-cultural applications and in the assessment of illiterate populations, non-native language groups, dyslexic individuals, young children, and some psychiatric patients with attention problems.

A variety of other indirect methods have recently been developed, including those based on posture, facial photographs, and even websites. One novel approach—room analysis—is detailed in the Practical Solutions box on page 484.

PRACTICAL SOLUTIONS

DOES YOUR ROOM GIVE AWAY YOUR PERSONALITY?

Does your room give away your personality? Sam Gosling and colleagues investigated this possibility with both college residence rooms and workplace offices (Gosling, Ko, Mannareli, & Morris, 2002). They hypothesized that the environments people create around themselves are rich with information about the occupants' personalities. It seems likely, for example, that the pictures a student selects to hang on the wall and the books on the shelf both reflect aspects of his or her personality. An office may be equally revealing. The way that office furniture is arranged and the items on the worker's desk are likely to reveal some aspect of the occupant's personality.

To conduct a systematic investigation, Gosling arranged for a team of raters to examine the residence rooms of 83 college students and judge their personalities. The raters had no direct contact with the occupants and had to base their judgments solely on the qualities of the room. As a criterion for accuracy, Gosling collected personality ratings of the 83 students from their close friends.

Of course, to get the most accurate information on a student's room, it would have been better to sneak into the rooms without warning. Such a practice would be unethical, however, so the researchers obtained the consent of the students to examine their rooms while they were away. Their roommates reported that the students in the study tidied up a little more than usual for a few days but eventually went back to their typical room habits.

Results showed that the raters were quite confident of all their personality judgments and they agreed with one another. But accuracy was restricted to two of the Big Five personality dimensions. They were accurate on judging the occupant's conscientiousness and openness to experience. A valuable cue for the former was the general state of neatness and organization evident in the room. A valuable cue for the latter was the type of books on the shelf. If the books were creative, intellectual, or politically radical, then the individual was judged accurately as higher in openness. Take a look at room photos A and B. Which one is higher in conscientiousness? Which one is higher in openness to experience? (After you guess, see the answer below.)

Residence Room A

Courtesy of Dr. Del Paulhus

Residence Room B

Courtesy of Dr. Del Paulhus

For a more detailed look, go to **http://www.psych.ubc.ca/~dpaulhus/textbook/photos.**

A parallel investigation of 94 offices and their residents yielded a similar pattern of results, although somewhat weaker. Students' personal living spaces may have provided unusual insight into the minds of their occupants for several reasons. First, college is a time when individuals are negotiating identity issues, so students may be particularly prone to self-expression. Second, people generally have the freedom to decorate their personal living spaces as they please, but office decor is often restricted by company guidelines. Third, individuals in offices, both voluntarily and because of extrinsic pressure and norms, are typically concerned about the positive and professional image they project. As a result, they may be pressured to arrange and decorate their offices in ways that are contrary to their actual preferences and personalities. Fourth, the observers in both studies were students themselves and perhaps were relatively well versed in the cultural meaning of the possessions and icons found in student living spaces but less so in the meanings of cues in office spaces. Fifth, the rooms in the study of residences were often multipurpose spaces where the occupants spent a great deal of their time and used them for a variety of activities, such as working, sleeping, relaxing, and entertaining. Thus, the personal living spaces in the study of residence rooms may have been informationally richer environments than the office spaces were.

Gosling's room research is only part of a growing **personality profiling** approach based on the notion that people can be judged by their behavioural residue. People can be judged by the music they listen to (Rentfrow & Gosling, 2003), the pets they choose (Coren, 2000; Roy & Christenfeld, 2004), the food they eat (Goldberg & Stycker, 2002), their tattoos and piercings (Nathanson, Paulhus, & Williams, 2006), and even their websites (Vazire & Gosling, 2003). The most important application to date is criminal profiling: Details about the perpetrator of a crime are assembled to create a character sketch (Kocsis, Irwin, Hayes, & Nunn, 2002). The hypothesized character is then used to make predictions about the perpetrator's habits, which could then be used to make an arrest.

(The answer to the room question above is high conscientiousness and low openness for Room A and vice versa for Room B.)

personality profiling

Estimating the personality makeup of an individual based on indirect evidence, such as his or her eating habits, room arrangement, and so on

Test Yourself 12.1

Check your knowledge about conceptualizing and measuring personality by answering the following questions. (The answers are in Appendix B.)

1. For each of the following, identify the personality dimension of the Big Five that the statement best describes. Choose from the following terms: extroversion, agreeableness, conscientiousness, neuroticism, openness.

   a. Joey is known as a risk taker; he just loves to bungee jump: _____

   b. It's difficult to get Rachel to stop talking: _____

   c. Phoebe is very cooperative; she's virtually always sympathetic to my needs: _____

   d. Chandler is very insecure; he always seems to feel guilty about something: _____

   e. Monica is very productive and has very high ethical standards: _____

2. For each of the following, pick the personality test that the statement best describes. Choose from the following: MMPI, NEO-PI-R, 16 Personality Factor, Rorschach, TAT.

   a. An ambiguous picture is shown and the client is asked to make up a story about its contents: _____

   b. An objective self-report inventory that is often used in clinical settings: _____

   c. A test used primarily to measure someone's standing on the Big Five: _____

   d. A projective personality test that uses standardized inkblots as stimuli: _____

   e. Designed to create a trait profile representing Cattell's source traits: _____

▶ Determining How Personality Develops

LEARNING GOALS

1. Be able to explain Freud's psychodynamic theory of personality and mind.
2. Understand and evaluate humanistic approaches to personality, including the specific proposals of Carl Rogers and Abraham Maslow.
3. Assess cognitive-behavioural theories of personality, and understand how cognitions and the environment interact to produce behaviour.

As you've just seen, we can describe the personality traits of people like Karla or Sarah—perhaps by their standing on the Big Five—and there is a good chance that our measurements will be reasonably accurate and reliable. But description is not the same thing as explanation. We may know that Sarah has a bright and sunny disposition, but trait theories provide little insight into the origin of those characteristics. Why do Karla and Sarah differ? What mechanisms in the mind produce and maintain those differences?

In this section we'll consider three quite different approaches to understanding personality development: the psychodynamic theory of Sigmund Freud, the humanistic theories, and the cognitive-behavioural theories. Each claims that individual uniqueness comes from the operation of general psychological principles. We're not unique or consistent in our behaviour by accident or chance; rather, processes are at work inside our heads, or in the external environment, that shape and mould our predispositions. In each case, personality is a product of general adaptive processes that help initiate and control behaviour in widely different situations.

The Psychodynamic Approach of Freud

Consider the following scenario. You're a practising clinician and your latest patient, 18-year-old Katarina, complains of persistent physical problems. "I'm often overcome with a frightful choking feeling," she insists. "I have trouble catching my breath, my head begins to spin, and I truly think I must be about to die." Extensive examinations reveal no physical cause and the attacks appear without warning.

A young Sigmund Freud is shown here in 1891, at a time when he was becoming increasingly convinced that certain physical problems may have psychological origins.

Archive/PhotoResearchers, Inc.

Katarina herself provides no insight: "There's nothing in my head when the attacks begin; my mind is a blank." The only additional information you have about Katarina is that she makes a face when the idea of sex is mentioned and she has a persistent dream in which a young child is pursued from room to room by a shadowy figure.

Long before the advent of modern psychology, this sort of clinical case intrigued Sigmund Freud (1856–1939). As you learned in Chapter 1, Freud began as a medical doctor in Vienna, where he dealt with a wide variety of patients. But he was particularly intrigued by patients like Katarina, who reported serious physical symptoms without any discernable physical cause. Explaining such cases seemed to require an entirely new way of thinking. The idea that traumatic life events might manifest in physical symptoms was the basis for Freud's **psychodynamic theory** of personality, as well as for his method of treatment known as *psychoanalysis*. The theory gradually grew into an extremely complex set of ideas that tried to explain every aspect of humanity. The great creative accomplishments of culture as well as the everyday slip of the tongue all derive from the deep recesses of the human mind. Two prominent themes—sex and aggression—were said to play a leading role in all human emotions, thoughts, and behaviour.

The Structure of Mind   Freud believed that the human mind was divided into three levels of awareness: the *conscious*, the *preconscious*, and the *unconscious*. The **conscious mind** consists of the contents of current awareness—those things that occupy the focus of your attention at the moment. As you read the words on this page and think about Freud's theory, you are using the processes of the conscious mind. The **preconscious mind** contains inactive but accessible thoughts and memories—those things that you could easily recall, if desired, but are simply not thinking about at the moment. If asked what you had for breakfast, you can summon the information from your preconscious into your conscious mind. Finally, the **unconscious mind** houses all the memories, urges, and conflicts that are beyond awareness.

To Freud, the important contents of the mind are not politics, sports scores, or the Dow-Jones average, but deep conflicts related to sex and violence. These topics are at once the most alluring and the most disturbing aspects of life. Important psychological events involve the transfer of information among the different levels of awareness. For instance, try to picture your mother and father having sexual intercourse. Because you exist, your parents must have had sex, but the mental image is still disturbing to most of us. The aversiveness of this idea (and others far worse than copulating parents) explains why we might be motivated to push some images out of consciousness. The actual experience of seeing this event as a child—the inexplicable noises and apparent suffering—creates a conflict that the child is motivated to forget.

Even from the depths of the unconscious mind, however, such conflicts continue to exert powerful and enduring influences on behaviour. Indeed, to Freud and subsequent psychoanalysts, the phenomenon of repressed conflicts is thought to be the primary reason for mental illness.

Given these assumptions, as Katarina's psychoanalyst, you would try to trace her panic attacks back to memories of sex or aggression recorded in her unconscious. Consider her repetitive dream of being chased through her house by a shadowy figure. She can remember the details of the dream—her appearance as a young child, perhaps the colour and shapes of the rooms—but her conscious memory of the dream is likely to be superficial and misleading. The parts of the dream that she remembers, its *manifest content*, are merely symbolic of the dream's true unconscious meaning, or *latent content*. As we discussed in Chapter 5, according to Freud, dreams represent a mental mechanism for wish fulfillment; dreams are simply one way that the mind attempts to gratify desires or deal with forbidden conflicts that are normally stored in the unconscious. In

---

psychodynamic theory

An approach to personality development, based largely on the ideas of Sigmund Freud, which holds that much of behaviour is governed by unconscious forces

conscious mind

The contents of awareness—those things that occupy the focus of your current attention

preconscious mind

The part of the mind that contains all the inactive but potentially accessible thoughts and memories

unconscious mind

The part of the mind that Freud believed housed all the memories, urges, and conflicts that are truly beyond awareness

Katarina's case, the pursuing shadowy figure may well have arisen from a traumatic childhood experience—perhaps sexual abuse by a relative—or even from her own unconscious desire for a forbidden sexual experience. In his early years, Freud relied heavily on such dream interpretation as a technique for mapping out the contents of the unconscious mind. Dreams, Freud argued, represent a "Royal Road" to the unconscious (Freud, 1900/1990).

The Structure of Personality   The two powerful instinctual drives—sex and aggression—are said to motivate and control much of our behaviour. Rather than revealing themselves in fixed traits, however, these two motives are played out in conflicts among the mind's three dynamic elements: the *id, ego,* and *superego* (see ◗ Figure 12.7). Freud used the term **id** to represent the portion of personality that seeks immediate satisfaction of innate urges, without concern for the morals and customs of society. It pursues immediate satisfaction of animalistic urges. A central aspect—the *life instinct*—is the desire to explore and enjoy life's pleasures, especially sex. It is this optimistic side of personality that promotes survival of our genes by motivating a desire for sexual contact. A darker side of the id, the *death instinct*, is required to explain suicide and other self-destructive human behaviour. All human societies throughout history have documented such negativistic behaviour. Another aspect of every human society—aggression toward others—was explained by Freud as an indirect display of the death instinct: Self-aggression turned outward. In short, psychoanalysis specifically acknowledges the dark side of personality.

At the same time, Freud understood that human behaviour involves more than just sexual and aggressive instincts. The forces of the id are appropriately balanced by a moral arm of personality called the superego. The **superego** is the component of our personality that deters us from breaking the moral customs we learned from our parents and other conveyors of culture. The superego is acquired primarily from punishing experiences. But the details of these experiences are mostly forgotten and the superego exerts its influence as a conscience—a self-inflicted punishment mechanism that makes us feel ashamed and guilty when our behaviour strays from accepted standards. Like the id, the superego is essentially irrational—its only goal is to avoid sin. Left to its own devices, the superego would undercut or block satisfaction of the more basic urges, even though those urges benefit fundamental survival needs. In short, the superego follows a *moralistic principle:* Always act in a proper and decent fashion as defined by parents and culture.

 **CRITICAL THINKING**

How do the modern memory concepts of short-term and long-term memory relate to Freud's three-part theory of the mind?

id

In Freud's theory, the portion of personality that is governed by inborn instinctual drives, particularly those related to sex and aggression

superego

In Freud's theory, the portion of personality that motivates people to act in a proper fashion, that is, in accordance with the moral customs defined by parents and culture

 **CRITICAL THINKING**

What are the adaptive qualities of the superego? What would happen to the human species if the superego always controlled behaviour?

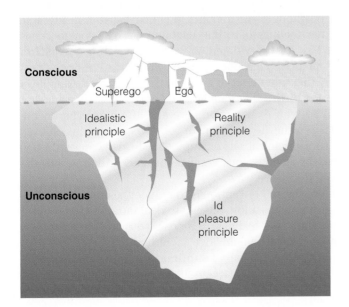

◗ **Figure 12.7**

Freud's View of Personality

Freud believed that our personalities are influenced by three forces. The *id* is the unconscious and unrepentant seeker of pleasure; the *superego* is the moral critic of unacceptable behaviour; and the *ego* is the executive that acts in accordance with reality. Just as most of an iceberg lies beneath the water, much of personality operates at an unconscious level. (From *Psychology: The Science of Behaviour,* Second Canadian Edition, by Carlson, Buskist, Enzie and Heth (p. 466), Toronto: Allyn-Bacon (Pearson Education). Copyright © 2002. Reprinted with permission by Pearson Education Canada Inc.)

ego

In Freud's theory, the portion of personality that induces people to act with reason and deliberation and helps them conform to the requirements of the external world

defence mechanisms

According to Freud, unconscious processes used by the ego to ward off the anxiety that comes from conflicts between the superego and the id

denial

A defence mechanism involving the refusal to accept an external reality that creates anxiety

repression

A defence mechanism used to bury anxiety-producing thoughts and feelings in the unconscious

projection

A defence mechanism in which unacceptable feelings or desires are dealt with by attributing them to others

reaction formation

A defence mechanism used to transform an anxiety-producing desire into a kind of opposite—people behave in a way counter to the way they truly feel

sublimation

A defence mechanism used to channel unacceptable impulses into socially acceptable activities

Sitting between the forces of the id and superego, and acting as a mediator, is the third component of personality—the **ego.** This component serves a managerial role in Freud's conception of personality and resembles later theories about a "self." The ego encourages you to act with reason and deliberation and helps you conform to the requirements of the external world. Freud suggested that the ego obeys a *reality principle* in that it monitors the real world, looking for appropriate outlets for the id's needs. But, to avoid punishments, such as guilt, the ego also considers the moralistic preaching of the superego. Its goal is compromise among three demanding masters: the external world, the id, and the superego.

Defence Mechanisms   As just noted, Freud argued that we're unaware of most of the conflicts that occur among the id, ego, and superego. We consciously experience only the side effects of these battles. For example, Freud believed that the experience of *anxiety* (an unpleasant feeling of dread) often comes from confrontations between the id and superego. To regain control, the ego must often resort to its most powerful weapon—the ability to alter reality. This task is accomplished with a variety of **defence mechanisms,** which are unconscious processes designed to ward off anxiety.

Most crude of the defences is **denial,** the refusal to accept an external fact because it causes anxiety. It is usually the first reaction when people receive devastating news: "No, that's not true. I can't have cancer." An even more powerful weapon in the arsenal of defences is **repression,** a process that actively keeps anxiety-producing thoughts and feelings buried in the unconscious. When a primitive urge from the id conflicts with the superego, the ego actively represses the thought or feeling. The urge is blocked out, jammed down into the dark recesses of the unconscious. Because they are the most common sources of conflict, we are particularly likely to repress sexual or aggressive thoughts or experiences. Unrestricted sexual activity is typically shamed by parents and society, and eventually by our own superego. So sexual thoughts and feelings need to be actively blocked by the reality-driven ego. The type of aggression most likely to cause id-ego conflict is hostility toward parents. In contrast, we would probably have few repressed thoughts or memories about eating or drinking, although both are instinctual urges, because these behaviours tend to violate few, if any, societal norms.

Repression is a kind of self-deception: The mind deals with the anxiety-producing impulse by acting as if it isn't there. Different kinds of self-deception occur with the other defence mechanisms that Freud proposed (Sackeim, 1983). For example, through a process called **projection,** you deal with unacceptable feelings or desires by attributing them to others. A person harbouring strong sexual feelings toward a married neighbour—an impulse likely to cause considerable guilt—might project his or her feelings onto the neighbour: "That woman keeps trying to turn me on—just like all the women at work!" **Reaction formation** occurs when you transform an anxiety-producing desire into a kind of opposite—you actually behave in a way that counters the way you truly feel. For example, a mother who secretly resents the birth of her daughter and unconsciously wants her to die might smother the child with exaggerated care and affection. The unconscious anti-Semite, who desires the degradation of all Jews, might become an active and tireless volunteer for organizations championing Jewish causes. Notice that, in each of these cases, the unconscious conflict receives attention, but the attention is disguised in a self-deceptive way.

Note again that the point of the self-deception is to reduce the conscious experience of anxiety. Defence mechanisms allow the ego to deal indirectly with unacceptable psychological thoughts and feelings. Suppose you are an extremely aggressive person who unconsciously would love to hurt others. According to Freud, you might use the defence mechanism of **sublimation,** in which unacceptable impulses are channelled into socially acceptable activity, to deal with the potential anxiety. Perhaps you would pursue a career in professional hockey or

Freud believed that people sometimes deal with unacceptable feelings by attributing them to others through a process called *projection*. Freud might argue that the woman on the left is projecting her anger from some deeper conflict onto the man on the right. Through *sublimation*, unacceptable impulses, such as a desire to hurt others, are channelled into socially acceptable activities.

even the local police force. Here, the aggressive impulse would be satisfied but in an indirect and socially acceptable manner. Similarly, a strong sex drive could be channelled into sensual creative activities, such as sculpting figures or even composing symphonies. To Freud, the great artistic accomplishments of human culture are actually a side effect of sublimation.

The idea of defence mechanisms has strongly influenced subsequent psychological research, although new labels are often used. Consider the current debate over the consequences of positive illusions. Some researchers have argued that positive illusions about ourselves can be beneficial to mental health (Taylor & Brown, 1988). The tendency to err on the positive side when evaluating ourselves could explain why some people are more optimistic about life and seem to bounce back from failure when others seem paralyzed. Two questionnaires have been developed to measure the tendency of individuals to have positive illusions about themselves. One is a measure of self-deception (Paulhus & Reid, 1991); the other is a measure of narcissism (John & Robins, 1994; Morf & Rhodewalt, 2001). Although they sound different, they both seem to measure people's tendency to exaggerate their positive qualities (Paulhus, 1998).

The research with these new questionnaires has shown that positive illusions are, at best, a mixed blessing. In one study at the University of Manitoba, Edward Johnson, Norah Vincent, and Leah Ross (1997) investigated whether self-deception helps or hurts task performance after failure. Results showed that self-deceivers felt good about themselves but performed poorly on a task that was preceded by a failure experience. It would appear that individuals who have to self-deceive to feel good about themselves after a failure experience are also too distracted to perform well on the next task. A different sort of tradeoff was demonstrated in studies conducted at the University of British Columbia. Delroy Paulhus (1998) arranged for members of discussion groups to rate one another's behaviour over seven meetings. Group members enjoyed the self-deceivers at the first meeting but, after seven weeks, hated them. The results of both these studies are consistent with Freud's idea that defence mechanisms have advantages and disadvantages.

oral stage

The first stage in Freud's conception of psychosexual development, occurring in the first year of life; in this stage, pleasure is derived primarily from sucking and placing things in the mouth

anal stage

Freud's second stage of psychosexual development, occurring in the second year of life; pleasure is derived from the process of defecation

phallic stage

Freud's third stage of psychosexual development, lasting from about age three to age five; pleasure is gained from self-stimulation of the sexual organs

Freud believed that people can become "fixated" at a particular psychosexual stage if activities associated with that stage, such as toilet training during the anal stage, are particularly traumatic or frustrating.

Psychosexual Development   To Freud, the unconscious mind is a bubbling cauldron of hidden conflicts, repressed memories, and biological urges. In the case of the biological urges, their origin is relatively clear—people are born with instinctual drives for self-preservation and sex. But where do the other conflicts come from? Freud argued that conflicts are almost inevitable as children pass through a series of stages of psychosexual development (Freud, 1905/1962). How children deal with their emerging sexuality importantly affects the way they feel about their family and their other relationships when they reach adulthood.

Each developmental stage is associated with a particular region of pleasure, which Freud called an *erogenous zone*. In the first year or so of life—during the **oral stage**—pleasure is derived primarily from sucking and from placing things in the mouth (such as the mother's breast). The adaptive significance of this first stage is clear—gaining pleasure through sucking or crying for milk or warmth increases the probability that you will get the nourishment and care you need for survival. In the second year of life, the focus of pleasure shifts to the anus. During this **anal stage,** pleasure arises from the process of defecation—both the withholding and the expelling of feces. The stage also marks greater self-control and more autonomous activity of the ego. From ages three through five, in the **phallic stage,** the genital regions of the body receive the focus of attention. The child notices the pleasure obtained from stimulation of the sexual organs. A sense of relationships is also developing, and the emerging sexuality is naturally associated with the currently most prominent individuals—the parents, of course.

Freud argued that we move through these stages for primarily biological reasons. All organisms, including humans, need to learn how to gain nourishment, control the elimination of waste, and satisfy the sexual drive. Unfortunately, it's possible to become stalled, or fixated, at a particular stage, which, in turn, can have important and long-lasting effects on personality. By *fixation*, Freud meant that a person will continue to act in ways that are appropriate for a particular stage, seeking pleasure in stage-dependent ways, even long after he or she has physically matured. Fixations result from traumatic events, often excessive parental punishment, during a particular stage.

Notice that the oral and anal stages are associated with the potentially traumatic experiences of weaning and toilet training. Freud emphasized these experiences because a child can become easily frustrated during either event. People who are fixated in the oral stage, Freud believed, continue to derive excessive pleasure from oral activities in adulthood. They become smokers or constant eaters, or bite their nails or chew on pencils. (By the way, are you doing any of these at the moment?) Fixation at the anal stage can lead to either excessive neatness or excessive messiness. The pleasure-seeking activities in these instances are symbolic, of course: Compulsive room cleaning might be a symbolic attempt at the gratification derived earlier from the retention of feces. Phallic fixations involve overvaluing the male organ, which translates into narcissism in men and aggressiveness in women. This sampling of Freud's ideas makes it clear how adult personality can be viewed as the symbolic acting out of events that occurred during the first few years of childhood.

Freud's interpretation of the events that surround the phallic stage of psychosexual development remains particularly controversial. He was convinced that small children have intense sexual urges that focus on the parents during this stage. Boys, for example, become erotically attracted to their mother while sensing the threat from a major competitor, their father. Freud called this psychological drama the *Oedipus complex* (after the Greek tragedy of Oedipus, who unknowingly killed his father and married his mother). Girls play out a different drama by blaming their mothers for their lack of a penis in what has been called the *Electra complex* (after the mythical Greek Electra, who hated and conspired to murder her mother). In both case, a desire for the opposite-sex parent creates enormous unconscious conflicts in the developing child. Freud believed that many adult sexual or relationship problems can be traced back to a failure to resolve these conflicts adequately. Needless to say, the idea of childhood sexuality was considered outrageous in his time, and still remains offensive to many people.

One prediction from Freudian theory is that parent-child conflict should be greater between same-sex combinations (i.e., father-son, mother-daughter) than opposite-sex combinations. This prediction was evaluated by McMaster University researchers Martin Daly and Margo Wilson (1990) in a study looking at same-sex and opposite-sex family homicides. No difference in homicide rates was found. This pattern is consistent with evolutionary theory (see Chapter 10) but fails to support Freudian theory. This one study may not convince those of you who are currently having trouble with your same-sex parent.

After the age of five or six, boys and girls enter a kind of psychosexual lull—called the **latency period**—during which their sexual feelings are largely suppressed. During this period children direct their attention to social concerns, such as developing solid friendships. Finally, with the onset of puberty, they enter the **genital stage.** Here, their sexuality reawakens, but in a more mature and appropriate fashion. Erotic tendencies now tend to be directed toward members of the opposite sex outside the family.

The Neo-Freudians: Adler, Jung, and Horney

A number of Freud's early disciples became famous in their own right because they extended Freud's theory while disagreeing with part of it. One of the first to split from Freud's inner circle was Alfred Adler (1870–1937). Adler strongly disagreed with Freud about the role of early psychosexual experience. Rather than sexual gratification, he believed that it is our natural drive for superiority that explains human motivation (Adler, 1927). But because we grow up with older people, we struggle to compensate for our relative inadequacy; some never do and their later personalities are centred on an *inferiority complex*. Adler also hypothesized another source of motivation, social interest. This is the desire to help society rather than just ourselves. He was also the first to speculate about the role of birth order in personality development (see Chapter 10).

Adler was not the only dissenting voice. One of the biggest personal blows to Freud was the alienation of his disciple Carl Jung (1875–1961), whom Freud had originally picked as his intellectual heir. Jung, like Adler, was dissatisfied with Freud's narrow reliance on sexuality as the dominant source of human motivation. Jung believed instead in the idea of a "general life force," which he adopted from his extensive study of Eastern religions and mythology. This general life force was sexual in part but included other basic sources of motivation as well, such as the need for creativity (Jung, 1923).

Among Jung's more influential ideas was his concept of the **collective unconscious.** He argued that people have a shared unconscious, in addition to the personal unconscious described by Freud. This shared portion is filled with mystical symbols and universal images that have accumulated over the lifetime of the human species. These symbols are inherited, that is, passed genetically from one generation to the next. They include enduring concepts (or *archetypes*), such as God, evil, mother, hero, wise old man, earth, and water. Actually, the idea

Karsh/Woodfin Camp

Carl Jung believed that all people share a collective unconscious filled with mystical symbols and universal images.

latency period

Freud's period of psychosexual development, from age five to puberty, during which the child's sexual feelings are largely suppressed

genital stage

Freud's final stage of psychosexual development, during which a person develops mature sexual relationships with members of the opposite sex

CRITICAL   THINKING

Most people deny that they've ever had sexual feelings toward their parents. If you were Freud, how would you explain these denials?

collective unconscious

The notion proposed by Carl Jung that certain kinds of universal symbols and ideas are present in the unconscious of all people

Karen Horney rebelled against what she felt was Freud's male-dominated view of sexuality.

that all humans share certain concepts (like fear of the dark) can also be found in the writings of Freud, but Jung expanded on the idea and assigned it a central importance.

Jung was a charismatic figure whose ideas continue to attract followers. His version of psychodynamic psychology was a predecessor to humanistic psychology (which we'll discuss shortly) and continues to have an almost cultlike following. In fact, most major Western cities still have a Jungian society for advocates to meet regularly.

Another historic blow to Freud was the dissenting voice of Karen Horney (pronounced HORN-eye). She was one of the first women to learn and practise psychodynamic theory. Horney (1885–1952) agreed with Freud's basic approach, but she rebelled against what she felt was Freud's male-dominated view of sexuality. Freud had argued in his writings that women are fundamentally dissatisfied with their gender—they suffer from what he called *penis envy*—a view that Horney found unsatisfactory in many ways. She boldly confronted Freud, both personally and in her writings, and offered revised forms of psychodynamic theory that treated women in a more balanced way (Horney, 1967). One of her more lasting theoretical contributions was her insistence that a link exists between the irrational beliefs people hold about themselves and their psychological problems (Horney, 1945). As you'll see in Chapters 14 and 15, this idea continues to be influential in the conceptualization and treatment of psychological disorders.

Evaluating Psychodynamic Theory   No psychological theory has been as influential as Freud's. Many of the terms and concepts he introduced—particularly his ideas about the unconscious and defence mechanisms—have become part of modern culture and have now been accepted by all psychologists. You were probably familiar with such Freudian terms as *repression, ego,* and *denial* before you opened this psychology text. Moreover, the suggestion that personality is determined in part by how we learn to satisfy basic biological drives, as well as coping with traumatic childhood events, is now undisputed (Buss, 1991; Revelle, 1995; Westen, 1998). But psychodynamic theory, as envisioned by Freud, has been steadily losing its influence on scientific psychology over the past several decades.

Part of the problem is that many of the ideas that Freud proposed lack scientific rigour. He never articulated such concepts as the id, superego, and ego with precision. Moreover, he changed his mind on many issues over his 40 years of writing about psychology. As a result, it's been difficult, if not impossible, to subject his ideas to proper scientific testing. Consider the concept of repression, which Freud believed to be the bedrock of psychodynamic theory. If repressed memories are hidden behind the veil of the unconscious, expressing themselves only in masked and largely symbolic ways, can we ever be certain that we have correctly identified and interpreted the source and content of these unconscious influences? Patients of psychoanalysts can feel frustrated when their therapist scolds them: "Well of course, you deny that you're acting defensively. It's all unconscious."

Debates about psychoanalysis often centre on the contradiction between clinical evidence and experimental evidence. Many practising therapists are certain that they regularly see defences like repression operating in their patients. But these are uncontrolled case studies of individuals who are not representative of the general population. In the laboratory, experimental psychologists have been unable to create repression (i.e., the forgetting of threatening events). The consistent finding in lab studies is that threatening events are actually remembered *better* than nonthreatening events (Loftus, 1993). Therapists reply that, of course you can't simulate real repression in the lab: After all, it would be unethical to create the severe level of trauma required to send someone into a repression episode.

Besides the problems of testability and lack of scientific rigour, Freud's theory is often criticized for its biases against women. There is no question that Freud viewed women as the weaker sex psychologically. As mentioned earlier, he painted women as unsatisfied with their gender and more subject to neurosis. Women were even said to be morally inferior, partly because they don't have to overcome as many temptations as men do. Freud also argued that memories of sexual abuse were sometimes false. Instead, they could be a child's confused recollections of sexual feelings toward his or her parents. Even some modern psychologists consider these ideas to be offensive (Masson, 1984; Vitz, 1988).

But, to give Freud his due, no theory other than psychoanalysis ever postulated that children could forget traumatic events (such as sexual abuse) and yet suffer their negative consequences for the rest of their lives. And what other theory could begin to explain why teenage girls who repeatedly cut themselves almost invariably suffered sexual abuse in their childhood? Although many of Freud's speculations may have been off the mark, it is important to recognize that many modern views of childhood, unconscious processes, dreams, and even the sexual revolution stem in part from his pioneering work.

Humanistic Approaches to Personality

Many psychologists have another reason why they simply don't like Freud's psychodynamic approach: They see it as a dark and dismal view of human nature. In particular, they don't like the idea that the mind's primary concerns are the animalistic urges related to sex and aggression. Nor do they like the idea that the unconscious is in charge of the bulk of our behaviour.

Humanistic psychology provides a more optimistic alternative to Freud's pessimistic view of the human spirit. Humanistic psychologists don't talk about battlefields and conflict; instead, they talk about growth and potential. It is not animalistic urges that are stressed in explaining personality; it is the human being's unparalleled capacity for self-awareness, choice, responsibility, and growth. Humanistic psychologists believe that each of us can control our own behavioural destiny—we can consciously rise above whatever animalistic urges might be coded in our genes. We're built and designed for personal growth, to seek our fullest potential, to self-actualize—to become all we are capable of becoming.

To a humanistic psychologist, every human being is considered naturally *unique*. People are more than the sum of a set of predictable parts—everyone is a unique and individual *whole*. However, the environment influences the natural growth process. Like plants, people will grow best in fertile and supportive environments; barren environments can't stop the growth process, but they can prevent us from realizing our own true potential (Rogers, 1963).

A central theme in humanistic psychology is the validity of subjective experience. How we act is determined by our unique view of the world—our interpretation of reality. Moreover, our personal view of ourselves and of the environment is as genuine and valid as anyone else's view. Nonetheless, some people's subjective experience of reality is not very adaptive. Notice the emphasis is on conscious mental processes. We're assumed to be responsible for our own actions, and accepting this responsibility is key to good adjustment. The ideas of two humanistic psychologists, Carl Rogers and Abraham Maslow, have been especially influential.

Carl Rogers and the Self   To Carl Rogers (1951, 1961, 1963), the essence of personality lies in the concept of the self. He defined the **self-concept** as an organized set of perceptions about our own abilities and characteristics: It amounts to that keen sense of the self, what it means to be "I" or "me." The self-concept comes primarily from social interactions, particularly the interactions we have with our parents, friends, and other significant role models throughout our lifetimes. The people around us mould and shape our self-image through their ongoing evaluations of our actions.

humanistic psychology

An approach to personality that focuses on people's unique capacity for choice, responsibility, and growth

self-concept

An organized set of perceptions that we hold about our abilities and characteristics

positive regard

The idea that we value what others think of us and constantly seek others' approval, love, and companionship

conditions of worth

The expectations or standards that we believe others place on us

incongruence

A discrepancy between the image we hold of ourselves—our self-concept—and the sum of all our experiences

Rogers argued that we have a basic need for **positive regard.** We value what others think of us and constantly seek others' approval, love, and companionship. Unfortunately, in real life, **conditions of worth** tend to be attached to the level of approval we get from others. For instance, suppose that you come from a family that values education and intellectual pursuits. You, however, couldn't care less about such things—your interests are in popular music and athletics. To gain acceptance from your parents, you may well deny your true feelings and modify your self-concept to bring it more in line with what your parents believe: "I'm not someone who cares about a trivial activity like sports; I'm someone who cares intensely about the pursuit of knowledge."

Rogers called this condition **incongruence,** which he defined as a discrepancy between the image you hold of yourself—your self-concept—and the sum of all your experiences. Incongruence leads to the experience of anxiety and ultimately forms the basis for a variety of psychological problems. True psychological health, Rogers suggested, comes when the self-concept is *congruent* (agrees) with your true feelings and experiences, that is, when your opinions and beliefs about yourself accurately reflect your everyday experiences. The larger the discrepancy is, the greater your anxiety and the lower your self-esteem will be.

Undoubtedly, the greatest influence of Carl Rogers has been to turn psychologists' attention to the study of the self. This topic is now a major focus in both personality and social psychology and, in fact, now bridges the two fields (Baumeister, 1997). The self has enduring features, to be sure, but it can also be affected by contextual features (Sorrentino & Higgins, 1996).

Modern laboratory techniques are now being used to tease apart the complexities of the self. In a series of studies at the University of Waterloo, Ziva Kunda and colleagues have shown how the self-concept can be manipulated by altering the value of different attributes. For example, if extroversion is made to sound valuable, participants reported higher levels of that trait (Kunda & Sanitioso, 1989). Even more dramatic was McGill University researcher Mark Baldwin's demonstration of how others' perceived approval affects the experience of the self (Baldwin, Carrell, & Lopez, 1990). Baldwin's research participants were graduate students who wrote down recent research ideas they had been working on. Participants were presented with subliminal images of either (1) an approving, smiling face or (2) a disapproving, scowling face (both faces were unfamiliar). The participants then evaluated the research ideas they had indicated earlier. Their ratings of their own research ideas tended to be higher immediately following a presentation of the approving face than following the disapproving face. This experiment demonstrated that self-evaluations can be influenced by minimal exposures to positive and negative evaluative stimuli, which is in line with the humanistic belief that unconditional positive regard can foster self-esteem development.

With respect to personality and its development, Rogers believed that regularities in behaviour come largely from the structure of the self-concept. We tend to act consistently, Rogers argued, simply because our actions consistently mirror the self-concept we have established. We act in ways that support rather than contradict our beliefs about ourselves. More often than not, we will actively seek to protect our self-image. Given a choice, you might purposely choose to read philosophy rather than watch television because it's consistent with your vision of yourself. If you consistently choose television, at some point, you'll need to reconsider who you really are—exactly the sort of confrontation that people tend to avoid.

Carl Rogers proposed that people have an ingrained need for positive regard—we value what others think of us and constantly seek their approval and companionship.

Photos.com

The Self in Flux   Although Rogers felt that there was only one "true self," the sense of self can be changed just by putting people in a different context. This effect was shown in simple studies where people were asked to fill out a "Who Am I" questionnaire in different situations. This measure simply asks people to report the most important aspects of who they are. When responding to the questionnaire in a room full of men, women are more likely to mention their gender than when they respond in a room with only 50% men. Similar effects are found for race (McGuire & McGuire, 1988).

A more dramatic claim is that each of us may have multiple internal selves (Kihlstrom & Cantor, 1984). No one would disagree that we act differently in different contexts. When we go home to visit our parents, we show a different set of behavioural reactions from those we show with our friends. Even our self-image changes. But these different selves seem to be triggered so quickly and effortlessly that they become automatic. These different senses of self have been labelled "self-schemas" (Markus, 1977). They are organized packages of information about ourselves. They help us interpret the present, reconstruct the past, and guide our actions.

Not surprisingly then, the self-concept can change after immigration to another country. Canadian researchers have been at the forefront of addressing acculturation effects on the self-concept. Clarry Lay from York University investigated ethnic self-definition in a study comparing the level of self-esteem between Canadian-born and foreign-born Chinese adolescents (Lay & Verkuyten, 1999). Because of their greater breadth of experiences in Canada, Canadian-born Chinese adolescents may feel more accepted and less like members of a minority group compared with their foreign-born counterparts. Therefore, Canadian-born Chinese adolescents should attend less to their ethnic origins. As predicted, results showed that foreign-born Chinese adolescents were more likely to label themselves "Chinese" (rather than "Chinese Canadian") and were more likely to make reference to their ethnicity in the "Who Am I" questionnaire.

Recognized as a major figure in cross-cultural psychology, John Berry at Queen's University developed a two-factor system for categorizing various strategies for acculturating to a new country (Berry, 1999). Immigrants can acquire the new culture to varying degrees, and they can lose the old culture to varying degrees. Most important, one change does not necessarily affect the other. Berry hypothesized that the best strategy for bolstering self-esteem was to acquire the new culture without losing the old. When tested on Asian immigrants at the University of British Columbia, Andrew Ryder and colleagues found only partial support for Berry's hypothesis. Acquiring the new culture did boost self-esteem, but retaining the old culture did not matter (Ryder, Alden, & Paulhus, 2000).

People commonly adopt different roles, and employ unique "self-schemas," in the various situations of life.

The take-home message from all this work is that despite its central importance to people's sense of well-being, the self seems quite sensitive to external influences. The notion of personality that follows from this view is obviously much more variable and flexible than trait psychology implies.

Abraham Maslow and Self-Actualization   Consistent with the humanistic approach, Abraham Maslow took a very positive perspective on psychology. At our core, he argued, we are all creative individuals yearning to fulfill our personal potential. This idea that everyone has a basic need for **self-actualization**—the need to move forward toward the realization of potential—has already been discussed in Chapter 11, under the topic of motivation. Recall Maslow's explanation that human motivation is grounded in the satisfaction of *need*. And higher-level needs can be addressed only when the lower-level needs have already been satisfied.

Your personality characteristics will reflect where you are positioned in the *hierarchy of needs*. Maslow was convinced that all people are inherently good; a person may consistently act in an unkind, defensive, or aggressive manner, but these personality traits reflect a failure to satisfy basic needs—they will never be fundamental to the human spirit. To support this claim, Maslow pointed to the behaviour of individuals whom he felt had progressed through the entire hierarchy. The characteristics of human personality, he argued, are highly consistent across individuals at the highest levels of the hierarchy. People who are self-actualizing show none of the darker personality traits exhibited by those locked in at lower levels; self-actualized people tend to be positive, creative, accepting individuals (Leclerc, Lefrancois, Dube, Hebert, & Gaulin, 1998).

Maslow's conclusions were based largely on the study of particular individuals, people whom he knew and admired. He also noted the personality traits of individuals who had reached the pinnacle of success, such as Albert Einstein, Abraham Lincoln, and Mother Teresa. All self-actualizing people, he argued, share certain personality traits. They tend to be accepting of themselves and others, to be self-motivated and problem-oriented, and to have a strong ethical sense and hold democratic values. Self-actualizing people also often undergo what Maslow called *peak experiences*—emotional, often religious, experiences in which their place in a unified universe becomes clear and meaningful. Notice that these are all quite positive traits; self-actualizing people tend to be at peace with themselves and with the world that surrounds them.

Evaluating Humanistic Theories   The humanistic approach, with its optimistic emphasis on positive growth, has had considerable influence in psychology. Such concepts as the *self* are now receiving a great deal of attention among researchers and, as you'll see in Chapter 15, humanistic approaches to psychotherapy are popular and widely applied. The humanistic approach provides a welcome balance to the pessimism of Freud. Rather than ignoring the conscious influences on behaviour, humanists champion personal choice and responsibility. Take a trip to your local bookstore and check the shelves devoted to psychology—you'll find that many of the books emphasize the control *you* can exert over your own behaviour. This is one indication of the humanists' widespread impact, especially in tapping the general population's interest in psychology.

As contributors to scientific psychology, however, humanistic psychologists are often criticized (Funder, 2001). Many of the fundamental concepts we've discussed, such as the potential for growth and self-actualizing tendencies, are vague and difficult to pin down. It's also not clear where these tendencies come from and under which conditions they will fully express themselves. Remember too that the humanists place important emphasis on personal, subjective experience. This means that researchers must often rely on self-reports by individuals to generate data, and we cannot always be sure that these reports are reliable and accurate representations of internal psychological processes (Leclerc et al., 1998). So in addition to problems of conceptual vagueness, the approach lacks adequate testability.

self-actualization

The ingrained desire to reach our true potential as human beings

The highlighting of the self in human motivation and cognition is reason enough to recognize the importance of the humanistic approach. Although it may be the most abstract of mental concepts, the self has become a key part of developmental psychology, social cognition (see Chapter 13), and other branches. Research on the self has become much more rigorous as the latest laboratory technology is applied to it. Given the central themes of humanistic psychology, these developments would not necessarily meet with Carl Rogers's approval.

The humanistic approach to personality is also criticized for adopting too optimistic a view of human nature. In part, the arguments of humanists, like Rogers and Maslow, are reactions against the pessimism of Freud and the mechanical depiction of humans outlined by Skinner. Humanistic theorists may have gone too far in the other direction to adopt an extremely optimistic view of human nature: People are basically good, unless constrained in some way by social conditions of worth, and are driven to pursue lofty goals. And self-actualized people seem to be almost God-like in their perfection. Thus, we have the dark view described by Freud (people are all driven by unconscious animalistic urges) countered by the extremely optimistic views of the humanists.

Some humanistic psychologists believe that it's probably better to adopt a more balanced approach: People are neither inherently good nor evil; they sometimes act in self-interested ways that may appear animalistic, but these actions are often adaptive and increase the likelihood of survival. At the same time, the message of humanistic psychology is that we can exercise considerable conscious control over both good and bad behaviour.

Cognitive-Behavioural Approaches to Personality

One particularly important characteristic of both the psychodynamic and humanistic approaches to personality is their emphasis on built-in determinants of behaviour. People are born with animalistic urges that must be satisfied, or they greet the world naturally good with a compelling need for personal growth.

But in Chapter 6, you learned about the power of conditioning. People may simply *learn* to act in consistent ways that differentiate them from others. Isn't it possible that Karla's nasty tendency to lie and Sarah's outgoing and sunny disposition come entirely from experience? Maybe Karla stole candy when she was four and was rewarded by not being caught; maybe Sarah learned at an early age that smiles are often met with smiles and that a good deed will be returned in kind. According to **cognitive-behavioural theories** of personality, human experience, not human nature, is the primary cause of personality growth and development. The *behavioural* side of the approach emphasizes the actual experiences delivered by the environment; the *cognitive* side emphasizes how interpretations and expectations about the events we experience play a significant role in determining what we learn.

Rewards and Punishments   An exclusively behavioural approach to personality development would propose that it is the outside world alone that influences our actions. As we discussed in Chapter 1, behaviourists believe that psychologists should look to observable behaviour for answers to psychological questions; the research goal of most behaviourists is to understand how *observable* behaviour changes when rewards and punishments are applied. Personality, then, might really be nothing more than the collective actions we've learned to produce in various situations. As with all other animals, if our behaviour is rewarded in a particular situation, we will be more likely to perform that behaviour again the next time we encounter the same situation.

People acquire situation-specific response tendencies in three main ways (see Chapter 6). First, through *classical conditioning*, we learn that certain kinds of events signal other events. Imagine that as a small child little Ravi is frightened in

CRITICAL   THINKING

Think about how good it makes you feel to talk to a really close friend. From the perspective of humanistic theory, why should this be the case?

cognitive-behavioural theories

An approach to personality that suggests it is reward-punishment experiences, and interpretations of those experiences, that determine personality growth and development

the presence of a white furry rat; he develops a specific fear, or phobia, of small furry animals that continues on into adulthood. His behaviour is consistent and regular over time—he panics at the sight of anything small and furry—in large part because of this early childhood experience. Second, through *instrumental conditioning*, we learn about the consequences of our behaviour. If we're rewarded in some context for acting aggressively, we will tend to act aggressively in the future. If we are repeatedly put down at parties for acting outgoing, we will learn to be withdrawn and to avoid social situations. Here it is the environment alone—the past history of rewards and punishments—that is shaping behaviour.

The third way that regularities in behaviour can develop is through observational learning, or *modelling*. We observe the behaviour of others around us—especially role models—and imitate the models' behaviour. As we discussed in Chapter 6, it's adaptive for organisms to mimic the behaviour of others because in this way, they can learn appropriate behaviour without directly experiencing the consequences of an inappropriate action. Rhesus monkeys, for example, learn to show fear in the presence of snakes through modelling their parents' behaviour, not from directly experiencing the negative consequences of a bite (Mineka, 1987). According to **social learning theory,** many important personality traits come from copying the behaviour of others, especially when the behaviour of the model regularly leads to positive, reinforcing outcomes (Bandura, 1986; Mischel, 1968).

Expectations and Cognitions Very few psychologists actually believe that the environment *alone* determines personality growth. The reason is that the psychological effect of most experiences—positive or negative—depends crucially on the expectations and beliefs you hold about the experience. For example, suppose we ask two groups of people to perform a relatively difficult task, such as predicting sequences of numbers. We tell one group that performance on the task is based on skill; the other group is told that success or failure is due entirely to chance. (Unknown to the participants, we actually rig the procedure so that people in both groups will succeed and fail the same number of times.) What you'll find in such a situation is that task effort, as well as the amount that is learned, depends on how much control a person thinks he or she has over the outcome. That is, people who believe that their performance is skill based work harder and learn more from the task (Rotter, Liverant, & Crowne, 1961).

social learning theory

The idea that most important personality traits come from modelling, or copying, the behaviour of others

The way we act and feel often depends on how much control we think we have over the environment. Externals, who perceive little connection between their own actions and the occurrence of rewards, tend to see themselves as powerless and possess low levels of self-esteem.

David Ximeno Tejada/Stone/Getty Images

The important point here is that the groups perform differently even though everyone receives exactly the same number of rewards and punishments. So it is not only the literal distribution of rewards and punishments that matters; your *beliefs* about the origins of those consequences are equally important. Some psychologists have suggested that people acquire enduring personality traits based on their perceived **locus of control**—how much control they feel they can actually exert over their environment (Rotter, 1966). People who are oriented externally, known as *externals*, perceive little connection between their own actions and the occurrence of rewards; such people tend to see themselves as powerless and generally have low levels of self-esteem (Lefcourt, 1982). Internally oriented individuals (*internals*) view the world as fundamentally responsive to their actions; they feel confident that they can control the occurrence of rewards and punishment. Internally oriented people display high levels of self-confidence and tend to score higher than externally oriented individuals on a variety of academic and social indexes (see Ryckman, 2004).

locus of control

The amount of control that a person feels he or she has over the environment

Researcher Ross Broughton of the University of Winnipeg has investigated one aspect of cognitive personality psychology—*prototypes*, which are defined as the clearest case or best example of a category. Although prototypes do not occur in nature, the prototype approach to personality suggests that scales and factors can be represented by unique words (e.g., demanding, interrupting, bold, pushy). Researchers have recently investigated prototype theory with respect to occupational preferences. For example, after thinking about the prototypical dominant person, what sort of job would best suit that person? Broughton, Trapnell, and Boyes (1991) took this approach a step further and considered whether unique occupational clusters exist for specific interpersonal personality types.

Subjects in their study rated occupations according to the extent to which the ideal person in that role had any of the following eight personality traits from Wiggins's Interpersonal Circle: dominant, quarrelsome, submissive, agreeable, arrogant, introverted, unassuming, and gregarious.

Results showed the following features by trait: dominant (business executive, hotel manager); quarrelsome (credit investigator, cost estimator); submissive (bank teller, astronomer); agreeable (playground director, missionary); arrogant (broker, bank examiner); introverted (poet, author); unassuming (concert singer; wildlife specialist); and gregarious (master of ceremonies; drama coach). The results supported the idea that people do show considerable agreement regarding the types of personalities they attribute to people in different professions and that simply by knowing a person's occupational preference, you can predict interpersonal aspects of his or her personality with some degree of accuracy.

The concept of locus of control is related to another psychological concept called **self-efficacy** (Bandura, 1986, 1993). Whereas locus of control refers to your beliefs about how much control you can exert over the environment, self-efficacy is defined as the beliefs you hold about your own ability. For example, Raymond might be convinced that people can control their environments but feels that he personally lacks the skill. In this case, he would be rated as low in self-efficacy, with an internal locus of control. Conversely, John might be extremely confident in his basic abilities (high self-efficacy) but believes that he can do little to control the things around him (external locus of control). Often a person's degree of self-efficacy is related to particular situations or tasks. You might believe strongly in your ability to excel academically but lack any measure of confidence in your social skills.

self-efficacy

The beliefs that we hold about our own ability to perform a task or accomplish a goal

Such concepts as locus of control and self-efficacy are important because they indicate that what we learn from the environment depends on more than just the delivery of rewards and punishments. Expectations and beliefs about the world and your abilities influence the types of tasks you will choose to engage in, as well as the effectiveness of rewards and punishments. If you're convinced you have little or no ability in social settings—your self-efficacy is low—you will either tend to avoid going to parties or be nervous and uncomfortable if you do go. If you feel you have no chance of succeeding in your psychology course because the teaching assistant doesn't like you—that is, you've adopted an external locus of control— your motivation to work hard is likely to be low. Note that in these cases your internal beliefs end up affecting your overt behaviour (avoidance of parties or class), which, in turn, affects the likelihood that you will be rewarded. Psychologist Albert Bandura (1986) has referred to this relationship between beliefs, overt behaviour, and the environment as one of **reciprocal determinism:** beliefs, behaviour, and the environment interact to shape what is learned from experience (see ▶ Figure 12.8).

The Pure Cognitive Approach   The cognitive-behavioural theories just discussed have kept their roots in learned behaviour. The most recent ones have emphasized the cognitive aspect to the exclusion of behaviour. Here the central ingredients are mechanisms, such as the particular tasks or problems that the person is trying to solve. Such psychologists as Nancy Cantor and Brian Little suggest thinking about personality as being something that a person *does* rather than something that a person *has* (Cantor, 1990; Little, 2000). Each person approaches life with a unique set of goals or personal projects. Individuals differ in what is important to them and in their own personal agenda for accomplishment. Karla may be concerned with accumulating wealth and fame; Sarah may be seeking to master her interpersonal skills. To solve these problems or life tasks, we use strategies or characteristic ways of responding that help us meet the challenges that arise (Cantor & Harlow, 1994). The strategies we adopt may cause us to act consistently, but only to the extent that the goal is met or the problem resolved.

The important point to remember is that you cannot understand a person's personality without considering these strategies for solving life tasks. Cantor and her colleagues have found that students in academic settings often adopt quite different

reciprocal determinism

The idea that beliefs, behaviour, and the environment interact to shape what is learned from experience

CRITICAL THINKING

Mariko receives an A in her psychology class but attributes it to the fact that her professor is undemanding. Does she have an internal or external locus of control, and how confident do you think she is of her own abilities?

▶ **Figure 12.8**

Reciprocal Determinism

Bandura proposed that personality is shaped by complex interactions among expectations, beliefs, behaviour, and the rewards and punishments delivered by the environment. In this case, the expectation of failure in class (personal/cognitive factors) affects studying (behaviour), which in turn affects the likelihood of success on the test (environment). Note that the arrows point both ways, suggesting that these factors can all interact.

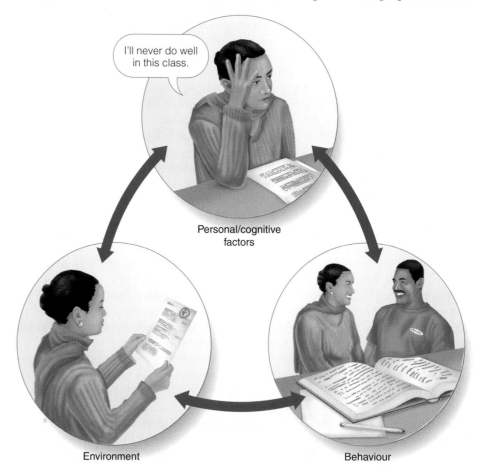

strategies to cope with the same task, such as performing well in school. Some students adopt pessimistic strategies, in which they ignore past accomplishments and consistently report low expectations for success on assignments and exams; pessimists spend lots of time thinking and worrying about their academic performance. Other students are optimists, which means they set high expectations for themselves and try not to worry or dwell on negative thoughts. But surprisingly, Cantor has found that these two types of students often perform equally well on exams. They simply have different strategies for meeting the same end. The pessimists are able to confront their anxieties effectively by dwelling on the possibility of failure, whereas the optimists prepare better by accentuating the positive. The pessimists and the optimists seem to have different personalities, but those special characteristics may have arisen simply as a result of the strategies they've adopted to solve a particular life task.

How students cope with the problem of performing well in school depends on the type of "life task" strategy that they adopt.

Now let's consider two final points. First, this view of personality predicts that if someone's personal life tasks change, he or she may well adopt new strategies that will affect how he or she behaves. Thus, an individual's personal actions could appear to change, or be inconsistent, across situations, but only because he or she is trying to solve a different kind of problem. Second, this problem-solving description of personality also predicts that individuals from different cultures or social groups may appear to possess unique personality traits. As the problems of a culture change, so too should the strategies that its people adopt. (We'll have more to say about the relationship between culture and the individual in Chapter 13.)

CONCEPT SUMMARY

VIEWS OF PERSONALITY DEVELOPMENT

Approach	Description	Example
Psychodynamic	Personality is influenced by forces originating in the unconscious and is made up of three components: the *id* (instinctive urges), *ego* (conscious decision making), and *superego* (conscience).	Laurie is strongly attracted to men, but her parents are very strict about dating, so her sexual feelings are repressed. As a result, she tends to avoid men and is uncomfortable when she is around them.
Humanistic	We all control our own behavioural destiny. Personality reflects our uniqueness and our self-concept as well as our environment and our personal view of the world.	Because of criticism from her parents during childhood, Laurie has developed a poor self-concept. She has not experienced unconditional positive regard. As a result, she feels uncomfortable with who she is.
Cognitive-behavioural	Personality results from an interaction between the experiences delivered by the environment and our interpretations of and expectations about those experiences.	Laurie had bad experiences with men in sexual situations although not in other situations. As a result, she's a bit uncomfortable in sexual situations.

Evaluating Cognitive-Behavioural Theories All psychologists recognize that behaviour is importantly influenced by what we learn from the environment. Thus, the idea that at least some personality traits might be learned is not considered controversial. Furthermore, the idea that cognitive factors are involved in learning, in the form of expectations and beliefs, has also gained relatively wide acceptance. Critics of the cognitive-behavioural approach simply argue that it is insufficient as a general account of personality development (Feist, 1994; Ryckman, 2004). Cognitive-behavioural theory, for example, tends to neglect the individual as a *whole*, choosing instead to concentrate on how people have learned to respond in particular situations. The pure cognitive theories do move substantially in that direction, however.

The approach has also been criticized for failing to adequately emphasize the role of biological and genetic factors in development. Perhaps ingrained drives and urges are not the main determinants of personality, but biological ancestry cannot be ignored completely. By choosing to focus primarily on the environment, the cognitive-behaviourists sometimes ignore potentially important motivational factors that are controlled largely by biological processes.

Test Yourself 12.2

Check your knowledge of how personality develops by deciding whether each of the following statements is most likely to have been made by a psychodynamic, humanistic, or cognitive-behavioural personality theorist. (The answers are in Appendix B.)

1. Estelle talks a lot, but that's only because she's trying to cover up her true feelings of inadequacy: _____

2. Teresa is very demanding, but that's because her boyfriend always gets her what she wants: _____

3. Sally can't help herself—her basic needs are preventing her from realizing her true potential: _____

4. Sharma seems to be a tireless volunteer, but in truth she secretly resents people in need: _____

5. Kevin isn't really an intellectual—he just acts that way because both of his parents are famous academics and he desperately wants to please them: _____

6. Henri is shy because he lacks confidence in his abilities and he's convinced that he cannot really influence or control the people who are around him: _____

7. Ralph sleeps around a lot, but that's because he doesn't have enough moral virtue to control his animalistic nature: _____

▶ Resolving the Person-Situation Debate

LEARNING GOALS

1. Understand both sides of the person-situation debate.
2. Learn the role genetic factors play in personality.
3. Appreciate how the different approaches to personality may not be contradictory.

According to cognitive-behavioural theories, behaviour is primarily the product of the environment. As a result, you might be expected to act somewhat inconsistently from one situation to the next. If you are rewarded for acting bold and aggressive when negotiating a deal (such as buying a car), you will almost certainly act bold and aggressive in such situations in the future. But if similar actions lead to rejection in the classroom or in social situations, you might very well turn meek and mild in class or when you go to a party. If you think about it, you probably know people whose behaviour does vary dramatically across situations.

However, this possibility really strikes at the core of personality. Remember, personality is defined in terms of lasting qualities—distinguishing patterns of characteristics that differentiate us from others and lead us to act consistently from one situation to the next. Throughout this chapter, we've assumed that such traits exist and that they can be measured and interpreted through the application of psychological principles. But the assumption of cross-situational *consistency* in behaviour has been challenged by some prominent psychologists, notably Walter Mischel, and the issue has come to be known as the **person-situation debate.**

The Person-Situation Debate

The argument is really a simple one. If people possess unique and enduring personality traits, we should be able to predict their behaviour from one situation to the next. If you believe Karla to be dishonest—perhaps because you witnessed her peering over Sarah's shoulder during a history test—then you also expect her to be dishonest in the future. You predict that she will take a fallen wallet or jewellery that someone left lying on the counter. In statistical terms, we expect that trait behaviours should *correlate* across situations; that is, given that you know a person's tendency to be extroverted in situation A, you should be able to predict his or her tendency to be extroverted in situation B.

Unfortunately, as Walter Mischel (1968) pointed out almost four decades ago, the cross-situational consistency seems weak. If you look carefully at studies reporting correlations between measures of behaviour that tap a particular kind of personality trait (such as honesty), the correlations are virtually always low. Although a correlation of 1.00 implies perfect behavioural consistency across situations, Mischel found that actual correlations rarely exceeded 0.30. To say the least, Mischel's conclusions were quite controversial; in fact, they rocked the foundation of personality theory. Without consistency in behaviour, the psychological construct of personality has little meaning.

Situational Consistency   Despite those pessimistic data, very few psychologists (including Mischel) reject personality altogether as a viable psychological construct. People may not always act consistently *across* situations, but they do tend to act consistently *within* a situation. For example, in a famous study by Hartshorne and May (1928), the honesty of schoolchildren was tested by placing them in situations in which they could act dishonestly without much likelihood of being caught (money was left on a table, cheating on a test was possible, and so on). Little evidence of cross-situational consistency was found, but the children did tend to act the same way in a similar situation. For instance, kids who cheated on a test were not necessarily more likely to steal money, but they were more likely to cheat on a test again if given the chance. In short, people do act consistently from one situation to the next, as long as the situations are similar (Mischel & Peake, 1982; Mischel & Shoda, 1995). This is exactly the type of finding you would expect if people are simply learning specific kinds of actions in particular circumstances. So the evidence for greater within-situational consistency is often used to support cognitive-behavioural approaches to personality development.

Other psychologists have pointed out that low cross-situational correlations, by themselves, are misleading. Data of the type reported by Hartshorne and May (1928) and others (see Mischel, 1968) are based primarily on the observation of single behaviours (did the child steal the money on the table?) rather than on collections of behaviours. But, as we noted earlier, single observations tend to be unreliable indicators of any concept. To get an accurate estimate of a true personality trait, you have to collect many observations, not just one (Epstein, 1979). When calculated properly, cross-situational consistency is clear on established traits, such as the Big Five (Kenrick & Funder, 1988).

Self-Monitoring   Some psychologists have argued that the tendency to act consistently or haphazardly across different situations may itself be a kind of personality trait. People differ in the extent to which they engage in chameleon-like

person-situation debate

A controversial debate centring on whether people really do behave consistently across situations

Tom Hanson/CP Picture Archive

self-monitoring

The degree to which a person monitors a situation closely and changes his or her behaviour accordingly; people who are high self-monitors may not behave consistently across situations

CRITICAL THINKING

Decide whether each of your friends is a high or a low self-monitor. Whom do you prefer to be around—the high self-monitors or the low self-monitors?

Successful politicians are often high self-monitors, which means they attend closely to the situation and change their behaviour accordingly.

self-monitoring, which can be defined as the tendency to alter your behaviour to fit the situation at hand (Snyder, 1974, 1987). People who are high self-monitors attend closely to their present situation and change their behaviour to best fit their needs. They are likely to alter their behaviour, and even their stated opinions and beliefs, simply to please someone with whom they are currently interacting. People who are low self-monitors are less likely to change their actions or beliefs and therefore are more likely to show consistency in their behaviour across situations (Gangestad & Snyder, 1985).

Scales have been developed to measure self-monitoring tendencies. Typically, you're asked to respond to such statements as the following: "I'm not always the person that I appear to be" or "I might deceive people by acting friendly when I really dislike them." People who score highly on self-monitoring, not surprisingly, are likely to conform to social norms. They also tend to be aware of how their behaviour is affecting others. High self-monitors even seem to remember the actions of others better than low self-monitors, especially when those actions are unexpected or unusual (Beers, Lassiter, & Flannery, 1997). Thus, self-monitoring can be quite adaptive: It is usually in our interest to monitor the environment and change our behaviour accordingly (Graziano & Bryant, 1998; Mischel & Shoda, 1998).

The Current Resolution   Currently, the majority of psychologists resolve the person-situation debate simply by assuming that it is necessary to take both the person and the situation into account. It is unlikely that either alone, the person or the situation, is going to explain behaviour or allow us to predict consistency.

People *interact* with situations, and the expression of lasting qualities or traits will depend partly on what's required by current needs. Personality traits will tend to reveal themselves primarily in situations in which they are relevant (Kenrick, McCreath, Govern, King, & Bordin, 1990) and may not otherwise. Similarly, given the right situational demands, each of us can act in ways that seem to violate our basic nature. (We'll return to this issue, and provide some compelling illustrations of the power of the situation, when we take up the general topic of social psychology in Chapter 13.)

Genetic Factors in Personality

As noted in Chapters 9 and 10, the evidence has accumulated that individual differences must be at least partly genetic in origin. People appear to be born with certain genetic predispositions that induce them—but not compel them—to act in an idiosyncratic and regular fashion throughout their lifetime. It is not unusual for family members to show similar personality traits, but normally we cannot rule out the role of experience in producing these similarities. At the same time, as we all know, siblings can show strikingly different personality traits: These differences often appear early in life and can be strong, even for siblings raised under apparently similar environmental conditions. Observations like these indicate that more may be at work in determining personality than the environment.

Special methods, such as twin analysis and adoption studies, are required to separate the genetic and environmental effects. This approach is called "behavioural genetics." Note that this method does not tell us the details about the biological differences. Likely suspects are different brain structures, different chemical balances, and different speeds of neural transmission. Research on the nature of these genetic differences is one of the most active and exciting topics in psychology. The genome project is currently revealing exciting results, but we are only beginning to point to specific genes that can explain personality differences.

Twin Data   As in the study of intelligence, most of the evidence for genetic factors in personality comes from twin studies. Identical twins are compared with fraternal twins under conditions in which the twins have been reared together or apart. Perhaps you've seen reports in the popular media of identical twins who were separated at birth but ended up sharing many of the same personality traits. One example is the case of identical twins Oscar and Frank—one raised as a Nazi in Czechoslovakia and the other as a Jew in Trinidad. When they were reunited in 1979, it was discovered that they shared numerous odd but regular behaviours. For example, they both had a habit of sneezing deliberately in elevators to surprise people, and they both liked to flush toilets before and after use.

However, isolated reports like these do not make a convincing scientific case. Coincidences are possible, and some of the more famous reunited twins may have had ulterior motives for manufacturing shared traits (e.g., Oscar and his brother eventually sold the rights to their story in Hollywood). More compelling evidence comes from large-scale studies in which the personality characteristics of different types of twins are analyzed. In one such study (Tellegen et al., 1988), 217 pairs of identical twins who had been reared together and 44 pairs of twins who had been reared apart were compared with 114 pairs of fraternal twins reared together and 27 pairs reared apart. Each participant was administered the MMPI, which, as you remember from our earlier discussion, is a widely used questionnaire for measuring personality traits.

Loehlin's (1992) review of recent Big Five studies is summarized in ▶ Figure 12.9. The bars in this graph indicate the degree of similarity between members of a twin pair, expressed in terms of correlation coefficients. As the figure indicates, identical twins tend to show higher correlations than fraternal twins, regardless of the Big Five factor. Twins who share the same genes but have been reared in different households tend to have more similar personality traits than

CRITICAL   THINKING

Do you think identical twins who are reared apart live in totally different environments? How might their environments still be similar?

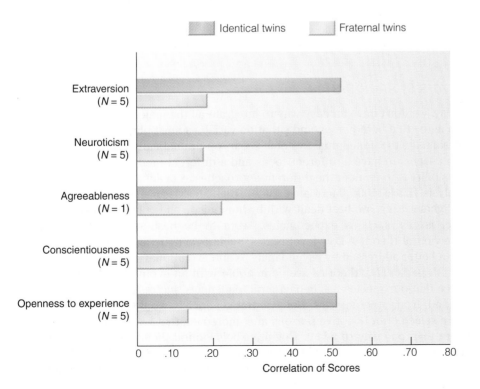

▶ **Figure 12.9**

The Genetics of Personality

Are identical twins more likely to share basic personality traits than fraternal twins? These average correlations from Loehlin (1992) provide solid support. The results suggest that genetics play a role in all of the Big Five personality factors. (Adapted from Loehlin, 1992.)

fraternal twins who have been reared together. Other evidence suggests that this same difference is observed whether or not the studies were conducted on twins raised together or twins raised apart (Tellegen et al., 1988).

Such evidence has convinced psychologists that at least some enduring psychological traits have their origins in genetic predispositions. Of course, as we discussed in Chapter 9, the expression of genetic tendencies depends on the nurturing conditions (the environment): Nature interacts with nurture in determining a person's final physical and psychological makeup. Therefore, although genes may play a critical role in determining how personality develops, environmental factors are also extremely important (Beer, Arnold, & Loehlin, 1998; Plomin et al., 1998).

Among the world leaders in the behavioural genetics of personality are the University of Western Ontario's Philip Vernon and the University of British Columbia's Kerry Jang and John Livesley. In one recent study, these researchers considered the role of culture in the heritability of personality across culture (Jang, McCrae, Angleitner, Riemann, & Livesley, 1998). They reasoned that although culture may affect the expression of a trait, it does not instill those traits in the individual. As a result, basic traits should be heritable in all cultures, and we should expect heritability scores to be similar in Canadian and German twins. These studies examined identical and fraternal Canadian twins from the Vancouver area and German twins sampled from across Germany. Respondents completed the NEO-PI-R, and correlations were calculated to predict one twin's personality score based on the other twin's score. All of the Big Five dimensions showed similar heritabilities— around 0.50. Moreover, both the genetic and the environmental effects on personality traits were essentially the same in form and magnitude in Germany and Canada, offering strong support for the idea that the genetic roots of personality are very similar in different cultures. These data are consistent with earlier findings of Jang et al. (1996a) that the correlation among identical twins was significantly and noticeably higher compared with the correlation among fraternal twins.

By using a cross-sectional twin design, Jang et al. (1996b) considered whether the heritability of personality dimensions was consistent across the life span, which would help explain the stability of adult personality. They found that whereas correlations were higher for identical compared with fraternal twins, this was especially true in the older sample. This suggests that genetic influence on personality increases over time, a finding that contradicts the widely held belief that personality should somehow be *more* heavily influenced by genes early in life, with a greater influence from the environment later in life.

Levels of Analysis

Today, we don't have an easy way to integrate all the major theories. Although we can agree that both person and situation variables must play a role in determining personality, the conceptual systems seem too dramatically different to integrate. Each seems to have a different focus and a different method of assessment. One possibility is to think of the different approaches as dealing with different levels of analysis (Little, 1996; McAdams, 2000). High-level issues, such as consciousness and goal setting, are best dealt with by humanistic and cognitive theories. Middle-level issues, such as expectancies, seem to be best addressed by cognitive-behavioural theories. Low-level issues, such as genetic and unconscious factors, seem better addressed by psychoanalysis and evolutionary approaches.

All personality theories are compatible with an evolutionary analysis. We all agree that our species has behavioural tendencies that differ in degree, and likely in kind, from other species. Behavioural geneticists would say that human traits were selected for adaptive reasons and, moreover, that we differ because there is more than one way to adapt. Cognitive-behavioural theorists would say that our main adaptive advantage is that we have a superior ability to learn from experience. Humanistic theorists might say that consciousness is our distinctive trait.

Psychoanalysis argues that we are gifted with a complex structural system that engages in a symbolic fashion with the environment. In short, all personality theories can be viewed as an answer to the general adaptive question: What allows human beings to adapt so well to their environments?

Finally, the person-situation debate can be resolved by the levels of analysis distinction. People are born with genetically endowed traits that, without counter forces, produce consistent tendencies in behaviour. The higher levels of analysis deal with the varieties of ways in which these traits are channelled by environmental forces or overridden by conditioning. And at the highest level, humans are able to recognize their own tendencies, reflect on them, and, when necessary, regulate their maladaptive tendencies (Baumeister & Vohs, 2004).

Test Yourself 12.3

Check your knowledge about the person-situation debate by deciding whether each of the following statements is true or false. (The answers are in Appendix B.)

1. In the Hartshorne and May (1928) study, kids who cheated on a test were not more likely to steal money, but they were more likely to cheat on a test again if given the chance. *True or False?*
2. People do tend to act consistently from one situation to the next, as long as the situations are similar. *True or False?*
3. People who are low self-monitors tend to change their behaviours to fit the situation at hand. *True or False?*
4. Identical twin studies show little evidence for genetic contributions to personality characteristics, as measured by the MMPI. *True or False?*
5. Most psychologists believe that personality traits are revealed in all situations, regardless of the relevance of the trait. *True or False?*

Personality

R E V I E W

There is little question in most people's minds about the existence of personality—anyone will tell you that people differ in enduring ways. We all have behavioural quirks that differentiate us from others, and most of us at least give the impression of acting consistently across situations. If asked, people also have little trouble making judgments about the personality of others. Without hesitation, we identify Sarah as agreeable and open and Karla as disagreeable and unbalanced. These differences in personality can be viewed as different adaptive styles. Thus, personality is clearly an important aspect of the adaptive mind.

To psychologists, however, the study of personality has proven to be a source of controversy. As we've seen, questions have even been raised about the validity of the concept itself—how useful is such a concept as personality in describing individual differences in behaviour? (Remember, similar issues were raised about the study of intelligence.) Still, the vast majority of psychologists agree that the concept of personality is needed to describe the full range of human psychological functioning. Personality is indeed something to be studied, and understanding it is both a conceptual and practical problem to be solved by the psychological community.

First, what is the proper way to enumerate and measure the traits that make us both consistent and unique? Trait taxonomies are formal systems for measuring and identifying personality characteristics, such as emotional stability or extroversion. Currently, the trait theorists seem to agree that there are five basic personality dimensions—the so-called Big Five (extroversion, agreeableness, conscientiousness,

neuroticism, and openness)—that accurately and reliably describe a person's unique and consistent attributes. Psychometric techniques, such as factor analysis, along with the development of personality tests, such as the NEO-PI-R and the MMPI, have proven useful in advancing theory and in applying what we've learned about personality to practical settings. For example, the NEO-PI-R has proven itself in business settings as part of the decision-making process for hiring new employees.

Second, how do personality traits develop? Identifying stable personality traits, however, leaves unanswered the general question of how those traits originate. Noted psychologists have developed several grand theories of personality development, including the psychodynamic approach of Freud, the humanistic perspective of Rogers and Maslow, and the cognitive-behavioural approach of Bandura, Mischel, and others. These theoretical frameworks propose very different mechanisms for personality development and offer quite different conceptions of basic human nature. The pessimism of Freud, with his emphasis on battling unconscious biological urges, is counterbalanced by the optimism of the humanists. To the cognitive-behaviourists, the

environment and beliefs about controlling that environment underlie the consistent actions that define personality. Each of these perspectives has been enormously influential in the past and remains so today.

Third, how do personality theories deal with variation and change in the same person's behaviour? The concept of personality demands at least some consistency in behaviour across situations. Early worries

about low cross-situational consistency have been clarified by aggregation across large numbers of behaviours. The current consensus is that a proper analysis of behaviour requires consideration of the *interaction* between the person and the situation. The growing evidence from behavioural genetics rules out any approach to personality that is focused entirely on situational effects.

CHAPTER SUMMARY

▶ Enumerating and Measuring Personality Traits

What is the proper way to conceptualize and measure the *traits* that make us both consistent and unique? Psychologists have suggested several ways to organize traits within a manageable system that permits communication of the stable aspects of character.

The Factor Analytic Approach

Factor analysis is used to reduce the huge number of traits to a smaller number of factors. By using this method, Cattell identified 16 *source traits* to cover the full range of personality. Eysenck reduced this number to three independent factors (extroversion, neuroticism, and psychoticism). Current thinking is that five dimensions—the *Big Five* (extroversion, agreeableness, openness, neuroticism, and conscientiousness) provide the best compromise between simplicity and a full coverage of personality.

Allport's Trait Theory

Allport proposed a classification scheme for identifying personality traits. *Cardinal traits* are ruling passions that dominate an individual's life. *Central traits* are the 5 to 10 descriptive terms you would use to describe someone you know. *Secondary traits* are less obvious traits that do not always appear in an individual's behaviour.

Assessment Methods

The most common method—*self-report questionnaire*—uses a paper-and-pencil format to identify personality characteristics. Examples are the *16 Personality Factor*, the *NEO-PI-R*, and the *Minnesota Multiphasic Personality Inventory* (*MMPI*). Self-report questionnaires are objective

and standardized. *Projective tests*, such as the *Rorschach* and the *Thematic Apperception Test* (*TAT*), require the test taker to interpret an unstructured or ambiguous stimulus, thereby revealing elements of personality. *Indirect methods* have been developed for use in populations with language difficulties and have been found to provide personality assessments similar to standard verbal scales.

▶ Determining How Personality Develops

What underlying factors account for differences in personality? How are the components organized into an overall personality? Is personality more dynamic than it appears on the surface?

The Psychodynamic Approach of Freud

Freud argued the mind could be partitioned into the *conscious*, the *preconscious*, and the *unconscious*. The unconscious mind was said to exert powerful effects on behaviour. Dreams are one window into the unconscious and include a *manifest content* and *latent content* (the hidden meaning). Personality has three components: the *id* (governed by inborn drives and the pleasure principle), the *superego* (the conscience, following the moralistic principle), and the *ego* (the executive of personality, following the reality principle). Conflict among the forces of personality results in anxiety. To cope with the anxiety, we employ *defence mechanisms*, such as *denial, repression, projection, reaction formation*, or *sublimation*. Children progress through a series of *psychosexual stages* of development (*oral, anal, phallic, latency*, and *genital*) that help determine later personality. Neo-Freudians, such as Jung, Adler, and Horney, de-emphasized the role of sexuality in personality, emphasizing other factors as central to the development of personality.

Humanistic Approaches to Personality

Humanistic psychology developed partly as a reaction against Freud's pessimistic view of the human spirit. This approach emphasizes self-awareness, choice, responsibility, and growth as important factors in personality. According to Carl Rogers, the essence of personality is tied to the *self-concept*. We have a basic need for *positive regard*, and problems arise when our acceptance by others is tied to *conditions of worth*. Problems may also arise from *incongruence*, a discrepancy between your self-concept and the sum of your experiences. Maslow stressed the drive toward *self-actualization* as important in determining personality. He proposed a need hierarchy, which explains the priority with which needs must be fulfilled. Personality reflects where you are within the hierarchy of needs.

Cognitive-Behavioural Approaches to Personality

The *cognitive-behavioural* approach emphasizes the role of learning in personality. Human experience, not human nature, is the primary cause of personality growth and development. People acquire situation-specific response tendencies through classical conditioning, instrumental conditioning, and modelling. According to *social learning theory*, many personality traits come from copying the behaviour of others. Our interpretation of our experiences also plays a critical role in personality. Perceived *locus of control* (how much control people feel they have over their environment) and *self-efficacy* (the beliefs you have about your own ability) determine how experience is interpreted and how it affects personality.

▶ Resolving the Person-Situation Debate

Is behaviour across situations as consistent as many people, including trait psychologists, assume? How can situational variation be integrated into personality theories?

The Person-Situation Debate

Do people show cross-situational consistency in their behaviour? This question is at the heart of the *person-situation debate*. According to Mischel, the evidence for consistency looks weak across situations although reasonable within situations. However, proper aggregation of behaviours indicates a fair degree of consistency in both. Some psychologists have suggested that the tendency to act consistently or inconsistently across different situations may itself be a personality trait. This tendency is termed *self-monitoring*. High self-monitors attend closely to their behaviour and change it to best fit their needs, whereas low self-monitors are less likely to change their actions and beliefs. Current thinking is that both the person and the situation need to be taken into account to explain personality.

Genetic Factors in Personality

Evidence from twin and adoption studies indicates that genetic factors play a substantial role in determining individual differences. Correlational studies of personality traits as measured by the MMPI and NEO-PI-R reveal that identical twins show higher correlations than fraternal twins, regardless of being raised in the same or different environments. Such genetic evidence helps explain why all of the Big Five factors show substantial persistence across the life span. Nonetheless, we know little about the actual biological mechanisms.

Levels of Analysis

The best perspective to date is to consider that different theories are not in conflict but consider people's personalities at different levels of analysis.

Terms to Remember

personality, 472
trait, 472

Enumerating and Measuring Personality Traits
trait taxonomies, 473
16 Personality Factor (16PF), 474
Big Five, 475
cardinal traits, 478
central traits, 478
secondary traits, 478
self-report questionnaires, 479
NEO-PI-R, 479
Minnesota Multiphasic Personality Inventory (MMPI), 479
socially desirable responding, 481

projective test, 481
Rorschach test, 481
Thematic Apperception Test (TAT), 482
personality profiling, 484

Determining How Personality Develops
psychodynamic theory, 486
conscious mind, 486
preconscious mind, 486
unconscious mind, 486
id, 487
superego, 487
ego, 488
defence mechanisms, 488
denial, 488

Recommended Readings

Coren, S. (2000). *Why we love the dogs we do: How to find the dog that matches your personality.* New York: Fireside. Noted research psychologist and popular psychology author Stanley Coren of the University of British Columbia has researched both the personalities of dogs and the personalities of dog owners. In this book, he uses that research to suggest the matches between breeds of dog and owner personality that are likely to lead to the best outcome.

Dutton, D. G. (1998). *The abusive personality: Violence and control in close relationships.* New York: Guilford. Donald Dutton of the University of British Columbia has studied people with abusive personalities for many years, and this volume addresses such issues as the structure and origins of the abusive personality.

Hoyle, R. H., Kernis, M. H., Leary, M. R., & Baldwin, M. W. (Eds.). (1999). *Selfhood: Identity, esteem, regulation.* New York: Westview. Co-edited by Mark Baldwin of McGill University, this collection summarizes research and findings pertaining to people's perceptions of themselves and how their self-esteem influences their self-perceptions.

Wiggins, J. S. (Ed.). (1996). *The five-factor model of personality: Theoretical perspectives.* New York: Guilford. Jerry Wiggins of the University of British Columbia is one of Canada's foremost personality researchers, and this collection of articles examines a variety of issues pertaining to the Big Five factors.

 For additional readings, explore InfoTrac® College Edition, your online library. Go to http://www.adaptivemind3e.nelson.com.

Hint: Enter these search terms: personality traits, personality tests, Sigmund Freud, defence mechanisms, humanistic psychology, locus of control.

Media Resources

 ## What's on the Web?

Please note that Web addresses are subject to change. Check out the accompanying website for updates: http://www.adaptivemind3e.nelson.com.

This site presents practice quiz questions, hypercontent, information on degrees and careers in psychology, study tips, and more.

Freud Museum

http://www.freud.org.uk

This site provides some very interesting information about the founder of psychoanalysis. You can also look at some fascinating pictures from the museum, including Freud's original couch and tub chair that he used in his psychoanalytic sessions.

The Personality Project

http://personality-project.org/personality.html

This fascinating site serves as a sort of clearinghouse for information related to personality measurement and personality theory. The pages are "meant to guide those interested in personality theory and research to the current personality literature." The site provides pages that allow you to find out more about psychoanalytic theory, behavioural genetics, and evolutionary psychology.

ThomsonNOW™ ThomsonNOW™

http://hed.nelson.com

Go to this site for the link to ThomsonNOW™, your one-stop study shop. Take a Pretest for this chapter and ThomsonNOW™ will generate a personalized Study Plan based on your test results. The Study Plan will identify the topics you need to review and direct you to online resources to help you master those topics. You can then take a Posttest to determine what concepts you have mastered and what you still need work on.

Psyk.trek 3.0

Check out Psyk.trek 3.0 for further study of the concepts in this chapter. Psyk.trek's 65 interactive learning modules, simulations, and quizzes offer additional opportunities for you to interact with, reflect on, and retain the material:

Personality Theory: Freudian Theory
Personality Theory: Behavioral Theory

Whatever you may be sure of, be sure of this—that you are dreadfully like other people.

—James Russell Lowell

Social Psychology

It's the annual Christmas party for the Jersey Sanitation Company. Chris M. has been a loyal member of the unit for three years now, and he's hoping for a promotion. Chris and several other co-workers are chatting when the boss, Tony Alto, comes over. The boss's incompetence is recognized by everyone in the group—except him.

The boss complains about the results of his recent takeover plan, which was a disaster. "My brilliant plan—ruined," he spouts arrogantly. "Not a single one of my managers could do it right. It's amazing how they all screwed it up."

"They're all just stupid," agrees Paulie. "They wouldn't know a good plan if they saw one."

"Absolutely," adds Silvio. "Your plan was brilliant."

The little voice inside Chris's head whispers, *I'm working with spineless yesmen. None of them will tell the boss the truth—that his plan was inept.*

"And what about you, Chris?" the boss says, looking directly at him. "What do you think?"

"Excellent plan, sir," Chris says, hesitating only slightly. "The work of a genius!"

Let's analyze Chris M.'s behaviour. From this brief exchange, can you draw any conclusions about what kind of person he is? He clearly violated his own beliefs and publicly conformed to social pressure. But so did all the employees. He thought they were wimps, but will he now draw the same conclusion about himself? Do you suppose they all would have acted differently if the boss wasn't there? How might you have acted in this situation—would you have conformed to the opinions of others? Would you, like Chris, have left the conversation thinking your co-workers—but not you—have a pathetic personality? All these questions are studied by social psychologists.

Throughout this text we've stressed that behaviours, as well as thoughts and feelings, are influenced by the immediate context. Not only do you behave differently in different situations, but you also think differently. Nor do we judge ourselves by the same standards that we use to judge others. Chris M.'s example is relatively harmless, but other situations can have more far-reaching and disturbing consequences. Suppose, for example, that Tony was not simply a company head but a commanding officer in the military, and the situation was a Middle-Eastern battlefield. Suppose the issue under consideration was not a company expansion campaign, but rather the leader's decision to execute all the inhabitants, including women and children, of a just-captured village. How would you react then? Would you still conform to the opinions of your superior? Clearly, the answers to such questions have powerful implications for society.

Undoubtedly, it's adaptive for us to monitor the environment closely and to change our behaviour accordingly. But the social environment has an especially complex effect on us. The mere presence of other people, as well as their behaviours, can be among the most powerful and pervasive of environmental influences. Thinking about other people is also different from thinking about objects. After we get to know others, our relationships with them can be the source of joy or cause of aggression. These uniquely social aspects of psychology are the focus of this chapter.

Social Psychology

P
R
E
V
I
E
W

Social psychology studies how people think about, influence, and relate to other people. Research topics include obedience, interpersonal attraction, attitude formation and change, and the behaviour of groups. Understanding people's social behaviour involves three important adaptive problems (see ▶ Figure 13.1).

social psychology

The study of how people think about, influence, and relate to other people

Thinking about the social world

Behaving in the presence of others

Establishing relations with others

▶ **Figure 13.1**

Summarizing the Adaptive Problems

In this chapter we address three main adaptive problems studied by social psychologists.

First, how do we think about the social world? As social animals, we must constantly think about other people. But what features do we use to form impressions of friends, teachers, and workplace colleagues? How do we infer the causes of their behaviour and form attitudes about them? Do we show any consistent biases in our interpretation of social events?

Second, how does our behaviour adapt to the presence of others? Exactly how is our behaviour influenced by the social context? For example, do we think differently, make different decisions, and perform better when others are present or when we are alone? What about when authority figures are present? What implications do these answers have for the structure of society?

Third, how do we establish relationships and when are they adaptive? We have to be able to develop positive relations with others to make society function. Exactly how and with whom do these relationships develop? How is it that all societies continue to report substantial aggression? How can that be adaptive?

▶ Thinking about the Social World: Social Cognition

LEARNING GOALS

1. Understand how physical attractiveness, stereotypes, and social schemas influence our impressions of others.
2. Learn how we attribute causality to the behaviour of others and the biases and errors that we show when making attributions.
3. Appreciate the complexity of attitudes and how they are formed and changed.

We begin our treatment of social psychology with a discussion of how people think about other people—how impressions of others are formed, how people attribute causes to behaviour, and what mental mechanisms construct our attitudes about people and things. Together, these topics are labelled **social cognition,** which can be defined as the study of how people use cognitive processes—such as perception, memory, and thought—to help make sense of other people as well as of themselves. First is the topic of person perception, which deals specifically with how we form impressions of others.

social cognition

The study of how people use cognitive processes—such as perception, memory, thought, and emotion—to make sense of other people as well as themselves

Person Perception: How Do We Form Impressions of Others?

When we first discussed the topic of perception in Chapter 4, we focused on the processes used to interpret elementary sensations as meaningful wholes. In that chapter you learned that perception is driven by a combination of *bottom-up processing*—building the whole from details received by the sensory equipment—and *top-down processing*, which begins with global expectations and beliefs about the world. Either way, we do not simply see what's out there in the physical world; our perceptions of objects are also influenced by our *expectations* of what's out there.

A similar process applies when we perceive people. When you encounter a person for the first time, your expectancies tend to be dominated by obvious physical factors—gender, physical attractiveness, skin colour, clothing. If you see a raggedly dressed, unshaven man staggering toward you on the street, you would likely form a negative first impression, because past experience has taught you to avoid people who fit this description. You could be wrong about this individual, of course; it could be one of your professors! But it's adaptive to use your background knowledge to anticipate the possible consequences of an interaction.

Physical Appearance   Of the possible cues for judging people, physical appearance produces the strongest expectancies. A person's age, gender, race, and physical attractiveness are the most powerful cues. We tend to assume that attractive people are more intelligent, better adjusted, and healthier than those with only average looks (Chia, Allred, Grossnickle, & Lee, 1998; Eagly, Ashmore, Makhijani, & Longo, 1991; Feingold, 1992; Kalick, Zebrowitz, Langlois, & Johnson, 1998). These expectancies translate into behavioural reactions: Attractive students are less likely to be carded in bars and are less likely to be convicted of crimes (McCall, 1997). Moreover, these tendencies don't diminish as we age: Even seniors attribute positive personality characteristics to attractive people (Larose & Standing, 1998).

Why do we rely on physical appearance to form a first impression? After all, it seems like a rather shallow way to judge a person. The reason is simple: When you form a *first* impression, you use the most *salient* information, that is, the cues that are most dramatic and available. You can't avoid noticing race, gender, and attractiveness, and facial expressions and posture. These raw materials are combined with your background knowledge to generate an expectation of what an encounter with that person might be like. Your cultural background may influence your final judgment to a certain extent—some cultures do not rely on attractiveness as much as others do (Wheeler & Kim, 1997)—but all people, across cultures, rely on physical appearance as an important part of impression formation.

Obviously, judging a book by its cover is not always an effective long-term strategy for impression formation (Feingold, 1992). Collecting objective facts about a person will generally create more valid judgments (Paulhus & Reynolds, 1995). But because of their speed, appearance-based judgments can be adaptive as a short-term strategy. If the person approaching you on the street appears clean and well dressed, at least you know that he or she follows some of the accepted standards and norms of the culture (Damhorst, 1990). Think about it. If you were in trouble and needed help, whom would you approach—someone with poor personal hygiene and tattered clothes or someone neat, clean, and well dressed?

Social Schemas   Our expectancies about such a huge amount of our background knowledge require substantial organization. The subsets of those expectancies that organize specific topics are called *schemas* (Bartlett, 1932). They are general knowledge structures about a particular topic in memory, such as knowledge about how houses are constructed or about what to expect at a restaurant or the doctor's office. We use schemas to help reconstruct the past and to organize and interpret our experiences. A schema can be formed about just about anything—a person, a place, or a thing. When schemas are about social experiences or people, they are commonly called **social schemas** (Fiske, 1993).

social schema

A general knowledge structure, stored in long-term memory, that relates to social experiences or people

The physical appearances of these individuals are likely to activate "social schemas" that will direct and guide your behaviour. Social schemas are generally adaptive, but they can lead to inappropriate conclusions or actions under some circumstances.

Returning to the dirty, ragged man on the street, your initial impression is likely to be negative because his tattered appearance activates one of your social schemas about people. A ragged appearance is associated with negative social characteristics—such as an offensive smell or even criminal behaviour—and his weaving gait signals possible drunkenness. All these things lead you to categorize the man as "trouble" and make it less likely that you will either ask him for help or respond to his requests (Benson et al., 1980). Both the man's physical appearance and his behaviour feed into your existing social schema about seedy characters, and, once he has been categorized, the schema quickly directs you to alter your behaviour accordingly.

Stereotypes   When social schemas concern traits and behaviours of groups and their members, they are called **stereotypes.** We form stereotypes about many kinds of social groups, from car salespeople to university professors, but three of the most common are based on gender, race, and age (Fiske, 1993). Most people carry around a collection of impressions about men and women, for example, that can importantly influence behaviour: Men are typically seen as strong, dominant, and aggressive; women are typically seen as sensitive, warm, and dependent (Deaux & Lewis, 1984). The central problem with stereotypes is that they lead us to judge individuals on the basis of our expectancies about the group they belong to.

> **stereotypes**
>
> The collection of beliefs and impressions held about a group and its members; common stereotypes include those based on gender, race, and age

Stereotypes share many of the properties of categories covered in Chapter 8. For example, *prototype theories* of stereotypes assume that we store abstract representations of the typical features of a group; we then judge particular individuals based on their similarity to the prototype (Cantor & Mischel, 1978; Sternberg, 1988a). *Exemplar theories* assume instead that we store memories of particular individuals, or exemplars, and these individual memories form the basis for stereotypes (Paulhus et al., 2002; Smith & Zárate, 1992). So, for example, the stereotypic belief that Black people are athletic would be based on information about particular individuals (e.g., Perdita Felician or Tiger Woods) rather than on some abstract representation (Hilton & von Hippel, 1996). Either way, these categories speed up our thinking but can lead to misjudgments about individuals.

Research by Kerry Kawakami at York University has confirmed that stereotypes are activated automatically (Kawakami, Young, & Dovidio, 2002). They are especially likely to be activated if we have recently been exposed to stereotypic beliefs and actions. For example, men are more likely to behave sexually toward a woman if they've recently seen a television commercial in which women were presented as sexual objects (Rudman & Borgida, 1995). In addition, witnessing a Black man engaging in a negative stereotypic behaviour influences how a White male evaluates other Black men (Henderson-King & Nisbett, 1996). Recent exposure to a behaviour relevant to a stereotype apparently activates, or "primes," the stereotype, which in turn affects behaviour (Smith, Stewart, & Buttram, 1992; Stewart, Doan, Gingrich, & Smith, 1998). Finally, a stereotype that is easily communicable (e.g., simple and salient) will be more frequently activated and therefore will persist longer within a culture (Schaller, Conway, & Tanchuk, 2002).

It is important to note that stereotypes are not always wrong: For example, the stereotype that older people are not as accurate as younger people in eyewitness testimony has some justification (Brimacombe, Jung, Garrioch, & Allison, 2003).

The Self-Fulfilling Prophecy Effect   Once stereotypes are activated, we expect certain kinds of behaviour from members of groups. These expectations can produce the **self-fulfilling prophecy effect,** which is the power of expectations about a person's actions to cause that person to behave in the expected way (Merton, 1948). If you expect someone to be unreliable, and you act in accordance with your expectations (such as snubbing or avoiding the person), the chance that their future behaviour is unreliable may actually increase.

> **self-fulfilling prophecy effect**
>
> When our expectations about the actions of another person actually lead that person to behave in the expected way

CRITICAL **THINKING**

Do you think the social schemas that were activated in the telephone study were different for the men and the women? If so, in what way?

Let's consider an experiment demonstrating the self-fulfilling prophecy effect. In a study by Snyder, Tanke, and Berscheid (1977), undergraduate men were asked to talk to undergraduate women, whom they had never met, on the telephone. Before the conversation, the men were shown a photograph of their prospective telephone partner. The partner appeared as either physically attractive or unattractive. In reality, the photos were not really those of the women participating in the study. The intention of the experimenters was simply to lead the men to *believe* they were talking to a woman who was attractive or unattractive. As for the women, they were not given a photo of their partner, nor were they told that the man was looking at a misleading photo. All the telephone calls were taped, and the quality of the men's and women's conversational styles was then rated by independent judges who were unaware of the misleading photos.

Not surprisingly, if the men thought they were talking to an attractive female, their conversational styles tended to be rated as friendly and positive, more so than if their partner had been depicted as unattractive. But the important finding of the study focused on the women. It turned out that the women's conversational styles also differed, depending on whether the man they were talking to thought they were attractive. The women who were presumed by their partners to be attractive were rated by the judges as more friendly, open, and poised and generally more pleasant than the women depicted as unattractive. Remember, these women had no idea that their male partners had formed opinions about their attractiveness. Apparently, the friendly, positive conversational styles of the men were able to elicit similar qualities from the women. This is the self-fulfilling prophecy effect: The expectations that we have of others, along with our actions, can actually influence them to act in the expected way (see ▸ Figure 13.2). Self-fulfilling prophecies can have either positive or negative effects on people. As you've just seen, if someone expects you to be unattractive, or intellectually challenged, those expectations can bring out the worst in you. One recent study found that parents' beliefs about whether their adolescent child would engage in illegal drinking predicted the

Perceiver's impression of the other person

Perceiver's behaviour based on that impression

Corresponding behaviour elicited from the other person

Leads to

Produces

She looks nice and she's very attractive!

"You sound like a very nice person."

"Thank you. It's going to be fun talking to you."

Confirms . . .

▸ **Figure 13.2**

The Self-Fulfilling Prophecy Effect

Our impressions of another person can affect how that person behaves, leading him or her to act in the expected way. In the study by Snyder and his colleagues (1977), if a male participant thought he was talking to an attractive female, his conversational style was rated as more friendly and positive—but so too was the conversational style of his female telephone partner.

child's subsequent drinking behaviour—if both parents expected their child to drink illegally, there was a greater chance their child would, in fact, drink illegally. But if a parent thought illegal drinking was unlikely, then this, too, predicted subsequent drinking behaviour (Madon, Guyll, Spoth, & Willard, 2004). The fact that expectations can importantly shape behaviour has many implications for society, especially when it comes to the expectations generated about groups and cultures.

Prejudice: The Canadian Context   As you've seen, stereotypes can lead to rigid interpretations of people. Stereotypes can cause us to overgeneralize and focus on the differences *between* groups (for instance, between men and women), rather than acknowledging the differences that exist *within* groups. Not all women are dependent, nor are all men strong. Furthermore, when the beliefs we hold about a group are negative, stereotypes increase the likelihood of **prejudice** (unfair negative feelings) and actual **discrimination** (unfair behaviour). Someone can be excluded from a job, or even criminally assaulted, because of negative beliefs activated by his or her skin colour or sexual orientation.

However, stereotypes are not the only cause of prejudice. University of Waterloo social psychologist Mark Zanna has suggested that we can distinguish at least three other components of prejudice in addition to stereotypic beliefs: (1) symbolic beliefs about the **out-group** (the group to which you do not belong), (2) emotional responses to the out-group, and (3) past experiences with the out-group (Esses, Haddock, & Zanna, 1993; Zanna, 1994). Zanna and his colleagues define symbolic beliefs about the out-group as beliefs that the out-group violates essential traditions or values. To examine this more complex view about the structure of prejudice, Zanna and his colleagues asked undergraduate participants at the University of Waterloo about their attitudes toward five groups in Canadian society: one **in-group** (the group to which the person does belong, in this case English Canadians) and four out-groups (French Canadians, Native Canadians, Pakistanis, and homosexuals). The responses did indicate some degree of prejudice, on average, toward the four out-groups. On a scale from 0 to 100, where 100 was "extremely favourable" and 0 was "extremely unfavourable," the participants rated English Canadians as approximately 81, but rated French Canadians as 69, Native Canadians as 66, Pakistanis as 59, and homosexuals as 44. The researchers also found that, although the stereotyped beliefs of the participants were an important aspect of their prejudice, the participants' emotional reactions to the groups, independent of their cognitive stereotypes of the groups, were also a very important aspect of their prejudiced attitudes. Similarly, it was found that

prejudice

An unrealistic negative evaluation of a group and its members

discrimination

Behaving in an unfair way toward members of another group

out-group

A group of individuals that you do not belong to or identify with

in-group

A group that you belong to or identify with

CONCEPT SUMMARY

FACTORS IN PERSON PERCEPTION

Factor	Role in Person Perception	Example
Physical appearance	We tend to assume that physically attractive individuals are more intelligent, well adjusted, and more socially aware.	Tyrone encounters Michelle at a party. He finds Michelle quite attractive. In addition, he perceives her as very personable, good humoured, and intelligent.
Social schemas	We use schemas (e.g., stereotypes) to organize and interpret experiences.	Tyrone believes most women are very sensitive, warm, and dependent. He finds that Michelle's behaviour fits this pattern.
Self-fulfilling prophecies	The activation of stereotypes leads to expectations of certain behaviours. These expectations can cause the person to behave in the expected way.	Tyrone is very attentive toward Michelle at the party, bringing her refreshments and introducing her to all his friends. Michelle relaxes; she begins to open up and make witty comments.

the more an individual believed that a group blocked or spurned a cherished value (such as "family values" or "respect for law and order"), the greater the degree of prejudice toward that group, and this "symbolic belief" component was somewhat independent of the "stereotyped belief" and the "emotional" components of prejudice. In other words, a person who held strong negative emotions about an out-group did not always express equally strong negative stereotypes about the group. Zanna and his colleagues suggest these data support their contention that prejudice consists of far more than simple negative stereotypes about out-groups.

Of course, some people are more prejudiced than others. The tendency is higher in those who are rigidly conservative or authoritarian (Adorno, Frenkel-Brunswik, Levinson, & Sanford, 1950). This tendency is commonly measured with the right-wing authoritarianism (RWA) scale developed by social psychologist Bob Altemeyer of the University of Manitoba (Altemeyer, 1988, 1994, 1996). People high in RWA tend to agree with items on the RWA scale, such as "Obedience and respect for authority are the most important virtues children should learn" (Adorno et al., 1950). Right-wing authoritarians tend to have especially strong tendencies to favour the in-group over out-groups. Zanna and his colleagues also found that the prejudiced attitudes of people high in RWA tend to be more related to their concern that out-groups are disregarding or even interfering with essential values and traditions ("symbolic beliefs") than to stereotyped beliefs about the out-groups.

How early in life do people begin to display prejudicial attitudes toward out-groups, and what can we do to try to promote tolerance rather than prejudice among children? These are among the questions addressed in a research program by Frances Aboud of McGill University and Anna Beth Doyle of Concordia University (Aboud, 1988, 1993; Aboud & Doyle, 1996; Doyle & Aboud, 1995). In one study (Aboud & Doyle, 1996), prejudice among 8- to 11-year-old White children in Montreal was measured by using the Multi-response Racial Attitude measure: It assessed whether a child tended to evaluate White, Black, and Chinese children positively or negatively. Children who scored high in prejudice as measured by this scale were then paired with a friend who had scored low in prejudice, and they were asked to discuss two items that they had disagreed on. In general, high-prejudice children displayed less prejudice following these discussions, particularly when their low-prejudice partner made more statements relating to similarity among groups (e.g., "Everyone can be mean sometimes"). Happily, the low-prejudice children did not become more prejudiced as a result of the discussions.

Aboud and Doyle suggest that these results indicate one strategy for decreasing prejudice among children is to systematically arrange for high-prejudice children to engage in such discussions with low-prejudice peers. They also suggest that, although parents and teachers might be hesitant to engage children in any discussions of racial differences and similarities, such discussions might have a positive effect if they are structured to promote tolerance and respect for diversity among children. The Practical Solutions box discusses ways to combat prejudice among adults as well.

At Queen's University, John Berry and Rudolf Kalin have studied Canadians' attitudes toward multiculturalism and ethnic groups within Canada. Much of the research on the psychology of prejudice in the United States has focused on how a majority group (usually Americans of European origin) views minority groups (often Black people). Berry and Kalin suggest that in Canada's multicultural environment, a wider perspective is more appropriate, one that involves examining the attitudes of multiple ethnic groups toward each other, not just the attitudes of the majority group toward minority groups (Berry, 1999; Berry & Kalin, 1995; Kalin & Berry, 1996). In one such study, the researchers analyzed a 1991 survey of more than 3000 Canadians from across the country. Respondents were asked to rate how comfortable they were being around people from 14 different ethnic groups: British, French, Ukrainians, Sikhs, Indo-Pakistanis, Germans, Chinese, West Indian

PRACTICAL SOLUTIONS

COMBATING PREJUDICE

It's generally adaptive for us to form stereotypes—they help us categorize our social world and make quick and efficient decisions about how to act. But when stereotypes lead to prejudice or discrimination, it's in our interest to reduce their influence. Combating stereotyping can occur in many ways. Learning more about other groups makes us less prone to negative beliefs and actions. It's also possible to actively suppress stereotypic beliefs. For example, if undergraduates are asked to write essays about well-defined groups, such as seniors or Aboriginal peoples, the essays will show less stereotypic content if the students are first instructed to actively avoid preconceptions about the target group.

Unfortunately, when people are directly told to suppress thoughts and beliefs, some evidence shows rebound effects. When no longer attempting to suppress them, those very thoughts seem to become more accessible and influential (Macrae & Bodenhausen, 2000; Wegner, 1994). For example, after suppression of a stereotype, people are more likely to recall words consistent with the stereotype. Therefore, thought suppression may not be the best solution to reducing prejudice and discrimination.

Recent research suggests a more promising alternative may be to practise taking the perspective of others. Galinsky and Moskowitz (2000) asked undergraduates to write a narrative essay about a day in the life of an older man. One group was told to adopt the perspective of the man: "to imagine a day in the life of this individual as if you were this individual, looking at the world through his eyes and walking through the world in his shoes" (p. 711). Compared with control conditions, those who adopted the man's perspective produced fewer stereotypic words in their essays and, in fact, tended to write about the subject in a more positive way. Moreover, they showed no rebound effects. Similar results were found when American students were asked to take the perspective of a Black person. Among other things, perspective-taking increased the subjects' awareness of the continued discrimination that is directed against Black people.

Negative stereotypes, which form the basis for prejudice and discrimination, are widespread and hard to avoid. As our familiarity with group members increases, however, the likelihood of prejudice and discrimination decreases. One reason may be that familiarity enables us to better see the world through another's eyes. Such techniques have already proved successful in overcoming the intrusion of stereotypes into job hiring decisions (Kawakami, Dovidio, & van Kamp, 2005).

Blacks, Jews, Arabs, Italians, Portuguese, Aboriginal Canadians, and Muslims. The good news is that people reported being relatively comfortable with all the groups, which could be taken as validation of Canadians' self-schema of being tolerant.

On average, however, these subgroups of Canadians evaluated their own group more positively than other groups, a tendency referred to as *ethnocentrism*. In addition, if one group ranked another group highly, the second group tended to rank the first group highly as well ("reciprocity"). For instance, the British tended to rate Ukrainians highly, and Ukrainians also rated the British highly. Berry and Kalin's multiethnic comparison approach to studying ethnic attitudes provides some clear advantages over the older, more simplistic assessments of majority views of minorities, and it provides psychologists and social planners with a detailed analysis of the psychological complexity of the Canadian multicultural experience.

In an additional study, Kalin (1996) reported that people tend to have more positive attitudes toward ethnic groups that they often see around them, compared with groups who are not present in their environment. Kalin suggests that this pattern may be partly a result of the "mere exposure" effect (Zajonc, 1968), discussed later in this chapter. People feel more comfortable with a given ethnic group simply because they have seen members of the group around them more often. Another factor that is possibly at work here is the "contact" effect (Allport, 1954; Hewstone & Brown, 1986), which states that under certain circumstances, repeated interactions between members of ethnic groups are likely to lead to more positive attitudes.

Discrimination: The Personal/Group Discrepancy   Social psychologists have discovered an interesting anomaly regarding how the targets of discrimination perceive their situation. It appears that members of groups that are discriminated against, such as gay people and visible minorities, tend to report that although they believe discrimination against their group is quite significant, they themselves have experienced relatively little discrimination (e.g., Taylor, Wright, Moghaddam, & Lalonde, 1990). Although such a situation might be possible for a few fortunate members of out-groups, it is logically impossible for discrimination to be high against a group as a whole, yet minimal toward most members of the group. Nonetheless, that is what is reported by members of disadvantaged groups in numerous studies. This anomaly has been labelled the **personal/group discrimination discrepancy,** and it has been examined by several Canadian social psychologists trained at McGill University. Their research indicates that two somewhat-independent psychological processes may be operating to create this discrepancy. One is a tendency for members of discriminated-against groups to minimize discrimination as a possible explanation for failures in their lives. Taylor, Ruggiero, and Louis (1996) suggest that, contrary to previous suggestions, this reluctance to invoke an explanation involving discrimination, even when good evidence exists for such discrimination, may be adaptive for individuals, allowing them to distance themselves from a potentially unpleasant explanation and permitting them to maintain an adaptive belief that evaluations of their performance are largely under their control and not the result of the vagaries of unfair prejudices.

Why, then, are members of disadvantaged groups willing to believe that their group as a whole suffers from such discrimination, if they generally minimize such discrimination when it happens to them? Taylor and colleagues (1996) suggest that when asked about discrimination against their group, disadvantaged group members are influenced by an **auto-stereotype** regarding societal discrimination against their group—that is, a belief system about discrimination that is widely shared by group members. And where does this auto-stereotype come from, if it is not a product of perceived instances of discrimination against individuals? The researchers suggest that it is possible that the auto-stereotype is largely created by media portrayals of discrimination against the group that become part of the belief system of the group members, to be automatically invoked when they think about discrimination against their group as a whole. This argument is supported by the fact that Inuit, a geography-isolated minority, perceive little discrimination from mainstream Canadians (Poore et al., 2002).

Another aspect of ethnically based stereotypes that has been recently researched involves assessing the stereotypes that individuals feel other groups hold about them. Jacquie Vorauer and her colleagues at the University of Manitoba refer to these as **meta-stereotypes.** They found, for instance, that White Canadians believe that Aboriginal Canadians hold a negative stereotype of White Canadians (Vorauer, Hunter, Main, & Roy, 2000; Vorauer, Main, & O'Connell, 1998). Furthermore, the researchers have also reported the somewhat paradoxical finding that White Canadians who are less prejudiced against Aboriginal Canadians rate Aboriginal Canadians as holding a more negative view of White Canadians than do more prejudiced White Canadians. This research indicates the complex nature of ethnic stereotyping and confirms the need to consider multiple causal factors and processes when attempting to understand and explain prejudice and discrimination.

Attribution Theory: Attributing Causes to Behaviours

It's natural to interpret the behaviour of others. A wife tries to understand why her husband forgot about their anniversary dinner; a student tries to understand why the teacher refuses his plaintive appeal for a grade change. Television viewers try to understand why the bachelor picked that woman. When people assign causes to

---

personal/group discrimination discrepancy

The tendency for members of groups experiencing discrimination to minimize discrimination directed toward themselves as individuals, but to agree with other group members that discrimination against the group as a whole is significant

auto-stereotyping

A belief system about discrimination that is widely shared by group members

meta-stereotyping

A person's beliefs regarding the stereotype that out-group members hold about his or her own group

behaviours, psychologists refer to these inferences as **attributions.** Attribution theories are concerned with the psychological processes that underlie these inferences of cause and effect (Heider, 1944; Jones & Davis, 1965).

Let's consider an example of the attribution process at work. Suppose you notice that your friend Larry's mood improves noticeably on Monday, Wednesday, and Friday afternoons, after he returns from lunch. He smiles a lot, exchanges pleasantries, and offers advice freely. These behaviours contrast sharply with his normal gruff manner and generally sour disposition. You wonder what accounts for the behaviour change. According to the *covariation model of attribution* (Kelley, 1967), the first thing you'll look for is some factor that happens at the same time as, or *covaries* with, the behaviour change. You will try to identify an event or some other factor that is present when the behaviour change occurs and is absent when the behaviour change does not occur. In this particular example, it turns out that Larry goes to his aerobic exercise class between 12:00 and 1:00 on those three days.

But covariation by itself is not an infallible criterion for attributing causality, for much the same reason that we cannot infer causality from the presence of a correlation (see Chapter 2). Just because Larry's mood improves after he leaves his exercise class does not guarantee that exercise is the cause of the change; other factors could be involved. Perhaps he meets a certain someone at the exercise class. According to the covariation model, we rely on three additional pieces of information to help us make the appropriate inference: *consistency, distinctiveness,* and *consensus.* When assessing *consistency,* we try to determine whether the change occurs regularly when the causal event is present—does Larry's mood consistently improve after exercise class? *Distinctiveness* provides an indication of whether the change occurs uniquely in the presence of the event—does Larry's mood improve after lunch only if he's been exercising? Finally, we look for *consensus,* which tells us whether other people show similar reactions when they are exposed to the same causal event—is elevation of mood a common reaction to exercising?

Internal versus External Attributions   These three factors—consistency, distinctiveness, and consensus—work in combination to help us form an attribution. In the particular example we've been considering, it's likely that we'll assume it's the external event—the exercise class—that is the cause of Larry's mood change. People tend to make an **external attribution,** which appeals to external causes, when the behaviour in question is high in consistency, distinctiveness, and consensus. In the case of Larry's pleasant demeanour, it's highly consistent (it happens every Monday, Wednesday, and Friday afternoon); its occurrence is distinctive (it occurs only after exercise class); and there is a high level of consensus (exercise tends to make other people happy too).

But what if no single event or situation in the environment can be used to explain someone's behaviour? For example, suppose Larry consistently smiles and acts pleasant in the afternoon, but he also smiles during the mornings and on days he has skipped the exercise class. Under these conditions it's doubtful that you will appeal to the environment to explain his behaviour; instead, you'll likely make an **internal attribution,** which means you'll attribute his pleasant behaviour to some *internal* personality trait or disposition: "Larry just has a great personality; he's a friendly, pleasant guy." Internal attributions are common when the consistency of a behaviour is high but its distinctiveness and consensus are low. If Larry is pleasant all the time, his post-lunch behaviour lacks distinctiveness, and you'll be unlikely to appeal to some lunch activity to explain his behaviour. Similarly, if the consensus is low—suppose exercise rarely improves mood for most people—you'll again resist attributing his good mood to this particular event (see ▶ Figure 13.3 on page 524).

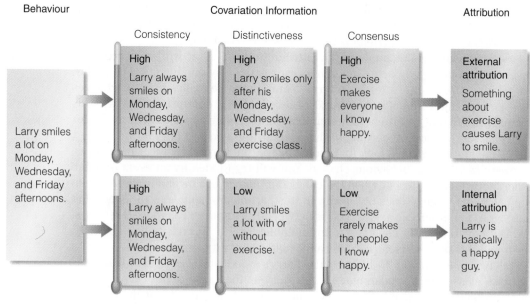

Behaviour | Covariation Information | Attribution

> ▶ **Figure 13.3**

The Covariation Model of Attribution

When people make internal attributions, they attribute behaviour to internal personality characteristics; in external attributions, they attribute behaviour to factors in the environment. In Kelley's (1967) attribution model, whether an internal or external attribution will be made about a particular behaviour depends on *consistency, distinctiveness,* and *consensus*. Generally, consistent behaviours that are highly distinctive and show consensus are attributed to the environment, whereas consistent behaviours that are not distinctive and show little consensus are attributed to internal characteristics.

The Fundamental Attribution Error So far, it seems as if the attribution process is quite logical and rational, but this characterization is a bit misleading. Social psychologists have discovered that it's common for us to take shortcuts in the attribution process, probably because we're often required to make attribution judgments quickly, and it's effortful and time consuming to consider all potential factors logically (Gilbert, 1989). What happens, however, is that these shortcuts produce consistent biases in the judgment process. One of the most pervasive of these is the **fundamental attribution error:** When we interpret someone's behaviour, we overestimate the influence of internal personal factors and underestimate the role of external situational factors (Jones, 1990; Ross, 1977).

In a classic demonstration of this bias, Jones and Harris (1967) had college students read essays expressing either positive or negative opinions about Fidel Castro's communist regime in Cuba. Before reading the essays, one group of students was told that the person writing the essay had been allowed to write freely and choose the position adopted in the text. A second group was told that the writer had no choice and had been forced to adopt a particular pro or con position. Afterward, the students in both groups were asked to speculate about the writer's true opinion on the topic. Thinking logically, you might assume that if the writer had been given a choice, then the essay position probably reflected his or her true opinion on Castro. Alternatively, if the writer were simply following directions, it would be difficult to tell. To the surprise of the experimenters, however, the students tended to believe that the essay always reflected the writer's true opinion, even when the students knew that the essay writer had been forced to adopt a particular position. This example represents the fundamental attribution error at work: People tend to attribute an individual's activities to internal personal factors,

fundamental attribution error

The fact that causal attributions tend to overestimate the influence of internal personal factors and underestimate the role of situational factors

CRITICAL THINKING

Suppose you were forced to make an attribution quickly, without much time for thought. Do you think quickly formed attributions are more likely to be internal or external? Why?

Getty Images

People often think that popular game show hosts, such as Alex Trebek, are extremely knowledgeable individuals. What attribution processes might underlie such an inference?

even when something in the situation (in this case, being compelled to take a certain position) provides a more likely explanation for their behaviour (Jones, 1990; Ross, 1977).

Now consider a more everyday example: You're driving down the road at a perfectly respectable speed, when you glance in your rear-view mirror and see a pickup truck bearing down on your bumper. You speed up a bit, only to find the truck copying your every move. Being tailgated like this is a relatively common experience. But what kind of attribution do you typically make about the driver? Do you attribute the behaviour to the person or the situation? If you're like most people, your first response is likely to be an internal attribution—you assume that the driver behind you has some severe personality flaw. Put simply, the driver is an aggressive jerk. You overlook the possibility that situational factors might be compelling the driver to appear aggressive. Perhaps he's desperately late for work or is taking a sick child to the hospital emergency room. These kinds of attributions, which focus on the situation, don't usually enter our minds because our visual focus is on the individual. The fundamental attribution error is one of the most powerful aspects of our social thinking and clarifies a range of social phenomena, from prejudice to helping.

Self-Attributions   Most of these biases also apply when we make attributions about our own behaviour. But there are some differences. Suppose, in the above example, you're the one doing the tailgating. It's unlikely that under these conditions you'll blame your behaviour on the fact that you're a long-term jerk; instead, your attribution will be situation-based. You're tailgating, you explain, because you're late for an appointment, or because the driver in front of you is simply driving too slowly. This difference is called the **actor-observer effect:** We tend to attribute our own behaviour to external sources but the behaviours of others to internal sources. The explanation may simply be our direction of vision. Because we are looking outward, we see others in action and draw conclusions about them; but we seldom view ourselves in action, just the ever-changing events around us.

One exception to the rule about external self-attributions is called the **self-serving bias:** We do make internal attributions when our actions produce positive outcomes. But of course we blame external forces when the action produces negative outcomes (Miller & Ross, 1975). When they receive an A grade on a psychology exam, students attribute the success to their own intelligence. When they fail, however, they tend to say that the exam was too difficult or the teacher was unfair. They seldom say that the exam was "too easy" if they achieve a high mark. This same bias shows up even when people are explaining the causes privately and anonymously. So it's not just a public excuse to other people. This self-serving bias is adaptive because it allows us to bolster and maintain our self-esteem and project a sense of self-importance and confidence to the world (Greenwald, 1980).

Attribution biases can have important implications for society. The tailgating attributions just discussed may sustain the high rate of car accidents because we all tend to believe that we are in the right. When we compare the

actor-observer effect

The tendency to attribute others' behaviour to internal forces and our own behaviour to external forces

self-serving bias

The tendency to make internal attributions about our own behaviour when the outcome is positive and to blame the situation when our behaviour leads to something negative

behaviour of other countries with that of Canada, we will always assume that Canada has the correct perspective. Even broader social values and worldviews can be affected; think about discussions of welfare policy or homelessness. Because of attribution biases, you might naturally attribute someone's receiving welfare or losing a job to laziness, incompetence, or some other negative internal trait. You may not consider that, in many cases, an individual is on welfare or out of work because of situational factors, perhaps a catastrophic life event. Attribution biases may have considerable adaptive value—first because they allow us to make quick decisions about the causes of behaviour, and second because they make us feel more comfortable about ourselves and the world as a whole. As usual, however, they do have a downside: They can sometimes lead to incorrect conclusions.

Evolutionary and Cultural Sources of Biases   We noted in Chapter 8 the adaptive value of cognitive biases. The same arguments can be made for the presence of consistent biases and errors in social judgments—including assessments of our own abilities and accomplishments. Social and developmental psychologists Dennis Krebs of Simon Fraser University and Kathy Denton of Kwantlen College suggest that natural selection may have shaped human minds to process social information in a systematically inaccurate fashion (Krebs & Denton, 1997). Not only do we have biases but our brains are also structured to deceive us about them. According to Krebs and Denton, the advantages of our biases have outweighed the disadvantages to such a degree that they contributed to the reproductive success of our ancestors. People who overvalued their abilities and overlooked their baser motives were more successful because of their confidence and optimism. Evolutionary pressure to favour those who exploit other people (e.g., psychopaths) may exist. However, the growth of this group will be limited because a society cannot sustain a large proportion of exploiters (Mealey, 1995). Eventually they would end up trying to exploit other exploiters.

Research by Joan Lockard and University of Victoria's Catherine Mateer suggests that the brain is capable of storing information in such a way that self-deception is possible: Information in one part of the brain can be isolated from other parts of the mind/brain system (Lockard & Mateer, 1988). Such findings suggest a possible neuropsychological basis for adaptive mechanisms of self-deception and social biases (Lockard & Paulhus, 1988). As with mechanisms selected by evolution, there is no guarantee that they are adaptive in all modern situations. For example, Edward Johnson of the University of Manitoba showed, in laboratory studies, that self-deception can boost people's self-esteem but interfere with their task performance after failure (Johnson, 1995; Johnson et al., 1997). Research by Shane and Peterson (2004) at the University of Toronto has shown that self-deceivers fail to learn from their mistakes.

The human tendency to classify people into in-groups and out-groups is also likely to have some evolutionary basis (Pinker, 2002). Our ancestors often needed to make critical but immediate life decisions: For example, "Is this stranger likely to harm me or help me?" Thus evolutionary selection would shape our minds with structures that quickly classify people into "friend or foe" categories—even if mistakes are sometimes tragic. Recent laboratory work on stereotypes has supported such speculations: Differences in brain activation have been detected when individuals are making judgments about a disliked out-group compared with judgments about an in-group (Phelps et al., 2000).

If the tendency to classify people into in-groups or out-groups does have an evolutionary origin, this does not mean it can never be overcome. Research has shown that society can at least modify people's ethnic and other prejudices. However, knowledge of the origins of the basic cognitive processes that underlie group categorization will be useful in attempting to eliminate ethnic and other prejudice.

Although all cultures show the fundamental attribution error under some circumstances, the effect is easier to find among Westerners (Masuda & Kitayama, 2004). Moreover, the claims for universality of cognitive biases have been challenged by recent work at the University of British Columbia. Steve Heine and Darrin Lehman have demonstrated that the Japanese show little in the way of self-serving biases or any sort of self-enhancement (e.g., Heine & Lehman, 1999). Moreover, Ara Norenzayan and his colleagues have shown that people in Eastern cultures are generally more situationist and, therefore, less susceptible to the fundamental attribution error (Norenzayan, Choi, & Nisbett, 2002). When members of such cultures do think of dispositions, they consider them to be more malleable than do Westerners (Norenzayan & Nisbett, 2000). The field awaits a theory that can integrate the evolutionary and cultural positions.

Attitudes and How They Change

The final topic we'll consider in our discussion of social cognition is the study of attitudes and attitude change. An **attitude** is simply a positive or negative evaluation or belief held about something, which in turn may affect behaviour. Like the other forms of social cognition we've discussed, attitudes are beneficial for a number of reasons. When they guide behaviour, attitudes help us remain consistent in our actions and help us use our knowledge about individuals or situations. Attitudes also play an important role in our perception and interpretation of the world. They help us focus our attention on information relevant to our beliefs, particularly information that can help confirm an existing belief. As a result, attitudes may serve as a kind of defensive function, protecting people's basic beliefs about themselves and others (Fazio, 1986).

The Components of an Attitude   Typically, social psychologists divide attitudes into three main components: a *cognitive* component, an *affective* component, and a *behavioural* component (Olson & Maio, 2003). The cognitive component represents what people know or believe about the object of their attitude; the affective component is made up of the feelings that the object engenders; and the behavioural component is a predisposition to act toward the object in a particular way.

To see how these three components work together, let's suppose that you've formed an unfavourable attitude toward your landlord. Your attitude rests on a collection of facts and beliefs about behaviour. You know, for instance, that the landlord has raised your rent three times in the last year, that he enters your apartment without first asking permission, and that he won't let you keep your pet cat, Mr. Wigglesworth, without paying a huge deposit in advance. These facts and beliefs form the cognitive component of your attitude. Accompanying these facts are your emotional reactions, which make up the affective component: When you see or think about your landlord, you get angry and feel slightly sick to your stomach. Finally, the behavioural component of your attitude predisposes you to act in certain ways. You may continually scan the classified ads looking for a new apartment; you may constantly complain about your landlord to anyone who'll listen. These three factors in combination—cognitive, affective, and behavioural— reinforce one another to create an attitude (see ▶ Figure 13.4).

Notice that the behavioural component of the attitude is described as a *predisposition to act*. This label is important to remember because attitudes do not always culminate in a behaviour. As you know, people sometimes act in ways that are inconsistent with their attitudes (Ajzen, 2001; Ajzen & Fishbein, 1977). When talking to your landlord, for instance, you may be all smiles even though underneath you're steaming. Attitudes do not always lead to behaviour because the latter is determined by multiple factors, especially external factors, such as the situation. In some situations, it is simply unwise to express true feelings, such as when dealing with your boss or the landlord. In other situations, people act quickly and

attitude

A positive or negative evaluation or belief held about something, which in turn may affect behaviour; are typically broken down into cognitive, affective, and behavioural components

▶ Figure 13.4

The Three Components of Attitudes

Social psychologists typically divide attitudes into three main components: cognitive, affective, and behavioural.

mindlessly without considering the true meaning or ramifications of their behaviour (Langer, 1989). For example, people often sign petitions for activities they may not completely believe in or buy products that they don't really want, simply because they're in a hurry and don't want to be bothered further. For an attitude to guide behaviour, it needs to come to mind—that is, it needs to be accessible—and it should be appropriate or relevant to the situation (Kraus, 1995; Pratkanis & Greenwald, 1989).

How Are Attitudes Formed? Where do attitudes come from, and how are they acquired? Attitude formation has many routes. We use our everyday experiences as the basis for many of our beliefs. How we interpret those experiences depends partly on our inborn intellectual and personality traits (Tesser, 1993). But even something as simple as *mere exposure* can be sufficient to change your feelings about an object. In a classic study by Robert Zajonc (1968), participants were shown photographs of undergraduate men taken from a school yearbook. Some of the photos were shown only once or twice; others were shown up to 25 times. Following exposure, participants were asked to give an estimate of how much they liked each man. The results revealed that the more often a photo had been presented, the more the participants claimed to "like" the person shown. It shows how easily some attitudes, particularly new ones or those that are not strongly held, can be modified (Zajonc, 2001).

Direct positive or negative experience with an attitude target is generally agreed to be the single most important factor affecting attitude formation. A great deal of evidence suggests that attitudes can be conditioned, through experiences of the type discussed in Chapter 6. Events that occur outside of our control can acquire signalling properties, through classical conditioning, and then serve as an initial foundation for an attitude (Baldwin, Granzberg, Pippus, & Pritchard, 2003; Petty, DeSteno, & Rucker, 2001). Advertisers commonly try to manipulate how people feel toward consumer products by pairing the product with something pleasurable, such as an attractive model or a successful athlete. Through instrumental conditioning, attitudes are influenced by the rewards and punishments people receive for their actions. Certainly if you express a tentative opinion on a subject—"We've got too much big government in this country"—and this opinion is reinforced by people whom you respect, you're likely to express this same attitude again.

CRITICAL THINKING

Do you think it's likely that all people have an innate attitude, or preference, for pleasurable things over painful things? What other kinds of attitudes might be influenced by genetic factors?

How closely do your attitudes mirror the positions and beliefs of your peer group?

Scott Bohaker

Finally, much of what we learn, including attitudes, is the result of *observational learning.* We model significant others—our parents, peers, teachers, and so on—when it comes to both attitudes and behaviour. The political convictions of most people, for example, mirror quite closely the political attitudes of their parents (McGuire, 1985). People also use their peers as a reference group for judging the acceptability of their behaviours and beliefs. Simply observe teenagers in the local mall to see how important modelling behaviour can be. Everything from language to musical taste to hairstyle to shoe type is replicated from one teen to the next. Ask yourself: How differently do you think and act from the people in your immediate circle of friends? Modelling is not the only reason why people act and think like their peers, but it is a large part of the reason.

Central and Peripheral Routes to Persuasion

For decades, social psychologists have been interested not only in how attitudes are formed initially but also in how attitudes can be changed (Petty, Wheeler, & Tormala, 2003). Although we are bombarded daily by dozens of persuasion attempts from sources in business, politics, religion, and arts, only a limited number are actually successful in changing our attitudes. One popular theory of attitude change, the *elaboration likelihood model,* suggests that two primary routes to persuasion exist: one that is central and one that is peripheral (Petty & Cacioppo, 1986).

We are particularly likely to change our attitudes when we're motivated and inclined to process an incoming persuasive communication with care and attention, that is, when we listen carefully to the arguments and then judge them according to their merits. Imagine you've recently changed your views on the topic of abortion after listening to a persuasive speaker at your school. If you carefully weighed the quality and strength of the arguments and then changed your attitude accordingly, your attitude change is likely to be stable and long lasting (Olson & Zanna, 1993). This is referred to as the *central route* to persuading someone to change his or her attitude. However, another way that advertisers in particular attempt to change our attitudes is called the *peripheral route* to attitude change. This approach works on the affective component of the attitude and usually involves simply exposing people to the attitude or product to be adopted, without any deep processing of rational arguments. For instance, an advertiser that suggests you buy a Zippo car because it gets good gas mileage is using the central route to persuade you to buy the car; an advertisement that simply shows you attractive actors enjoying themselves in a Zippo car is using the peripheral route.

The Festinger and Carlsmith Study

We can also be persuaded to change our attitudes because of our own actions. In an influential study of attitude change conducted by Festinger and Carlsmith (1959), college students were asked to perform an incredibly boring task for a full-hour session. At the end of the hour, some of the participants (the two experimental groups) were asked to tell the next participant that the experiment was actually fun and interesting. To provide an incentive, the experimenter offered participants in one experimental group a monetary reward of $1 and those in the other experimental group a reward of $20.

The point of the offer was to get the members of the two experimental groups to act in a way that contradicted their true feelings, or attitudes, about the experiment. The task was clearly boring, so they were essentially asked to lie for either a small or a large reward. Festinger and Carlsmith were interested in what effect this behaviour would have on participants' attitudes about the experiment. After students accepted the offer and tried to convince the next participant, their attitudes about the boring tasks were assessed through an interview. The researchers found that attitudes about the tasks did indeed change: They became more positive relative to the attitudes of the members of the control group, who had not been asked to lie. Moreover, the positive shift was larger for participants

CRITICAL THINKING
Next time you watch television, notice which commercials rely on logical arguments and which use humour or celebrity endorsers. Do you see any connection between the type of product and the style of persuasion? What kinds of products are more likely to induce us to use central rather than peripheral processing?

In situations in which a person's level of involvement or commitment to a message is low, advertisers tend to capitalize on the peripheral route to persuasion by using celebrity endorsers or humour in the persuasive message.

CP Picture Archive (Brendon Dlouhy)

receiving $1 as opposed to $20. The more participants were paid to act inconsistently with their true feelings, the less likely their attitudes were to change (see ▶ Figure 13.5).

Cognitive Dissonance   Festinger and Carlsmith's (1959) results may seem perplexing. You would probably have predicted that the students receiving $20 would show the greatest attitude change; after all, wouldn't a large reward have a greater reinforcing effect? The answer, according to Festinger's (1957) theory of **cognitive dissonance,** is that the inconsistent behaviour produces psychological distress, or what he called *dissonance*. Think about it. Which action is going to lead to greater internal turmoil and distress: lying to receive $1 or lying to receive $20? Most people can easily justify a simple white lie when offered a reasonable amount of money, especially when asked by an authority figure (remember that $20 was worth a lot more in the 1950s than it is now). But to lie for a mere $1 is tough to justify—unless, of course, you weren't really lying. Maybe it wasn't so bad after all.

cognitive dissonance

The tension produced when people act in a way that is inconsistent with their attitudes; attitude change may occur as a result of attempting to reduce cognitive dissonance

▶ **Figure 13.5**

Cognitive Dissonance

Festinger proposed that attitudes change when a discrepancy exists between what we believe and how we act. People who lied about the boring experimental task for a mere $1 later claimed to enjoy the task more than did people who lied for $20 or who were not asked to lie. (Data from Festinger & Carlsmith, 1959.)

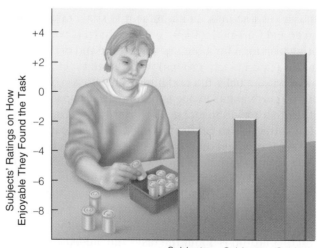

According to cognitive dissonance theory, if the discrepancy between what you believe and how you act is great, you will tend to change your beliefs to match the behaviour.

Since cognitive dissonance theory was first introduced in the 1950s, hundreds of follow-up studies have been conducted (Aronson, 1992). Most have confirmed Festinger and Carlsmith's basic finding: When people are induced to act in ways that are inconsistent with their attitudes, those attitudes tend to change as a consequence. For instance, suppose you are asked to eat fried grasshoppers either by an experimenter who behaves in a rude and disrespectful way toward you or by a nice experimenter. If you do eat the grasshoppers offered by the rude experimenter, you are more likely to report later that you actually liked them; otherwise, it is difficult to explain to yourself and others why you would do something you dislike for someone who treated you rudely. It is much easier to explain why you did something you dislike for someone who treated you well.

But not all psychologists are convinced that internal tension, or dissonance, results from acting inconsistently with your beliefs. You might, for example, feel personally responsible for creating an unwanted or negative situation (Blanton, Cooper, Skurnik, & Aronson, 1997; Cooper, 1992). Some psychologists are also uncomfortable with the concept of cognitive dissonance because it seems rather vague and is not easy to measure directly. It's also difficult to predict when dissonance will occur and, if it's present, how people will choose to reduce it (Joule, 1986). However, the idea continues to be influential among social psychologists, especially when the motivational and cognitive components of dissonance are taken into account (Aronson, 1997; Petty, Wegener, & Fabrigar, 1997; Wood, 2000).

Self-Perception Theory   One of the best-known alternatives to dissonance theory is psychologist Daryl Bem's (1967, 1972) **self-perception theory**. The idea behind self-perception theory is that we are active interpreters of our own behaviour. We learn from our behaviour and use our actions as a basis for inferring internal beliefs. For example, if I sit down and practise the piano for two hours a day, I must like music and think I have at least a bit of musical talent. If I regularly stop for hamburgers and fries for lunch, I must like fast food. The basis for the attitude is self-perception—behaviour is observed, and attitudes follow from the behaviour (see ▶ Figure 13.6). Note that this theory makes no reference to distress or any kind of emotion.

self-perception theory

The idea that people use observations of their own behaviour as a basis for inferring their internal beliefs

▶ **Figure 13.6**

Self-Perception Theory

Some psychologists believe that we form attitudes at least in part by observing our own behaviour. If I regularly eat hamburgers, then my attitude about hamburgers must be positive.

Many experimental findings support these basic ideas. For example, the Festinger and Carlsmith study can be interpreted from this perspective. You observe yourself telling someone that a boring task is interesting, for a mere $1, and conclude that since you engaged in this behaviour your attitude toward the task must not have been that negative. Another phenomenon that may be explained this way is the persuasion method known as the *foot-in-the-door technique*. Jonathan Freedman and Scott Fraser (1966) convinced a group of California house-holders to sign a petition expressing support for safe driving. Several weeks later, the researchers returned with a request that the householders now place a large and quite ugly "Drive Safely" billboard in their yards. The petition signers were three times more likely to comply with this new request than a control group of people who were never asked to sign a petition. What's the interpretation? The memory of signing the original petition triggered *self-perception*, which then helped shape the attitude: If I signed the petition, then I must be a strong advocate for safe driving (see also Burger & Caldwell, 2003). Another more troublesome outcome of self-perception processes involves the development of prejudiced attitudes. A person who finds himself or herself avoiding a minority group in public places, for instance, may reflect on this pattern and conclude: "I tend to move away from people of that minority group; I suppose this means I must believe they are undesirable."

Of course, these effects have boundary conditions—we do not always simply match our attitudes to our behaviours—but monitoring our own behaviour is clearly an important ingredient of attitude formation and change. It may be that we are particularly likely to use our own actions as a guide when we're unsure of or undecided about our attitude. Or we may use our own behaviour to see if our

CRITICAL   THINKING

How might you use cognitive dissonance theory to explain the foot-in-the-door technique*?*

CONCEPT SUMMARY

ROOTS OF ATTITUDES AND ATTITUDE CHANGE

Mechanism	Description	Example ("Whom should I vote for?")
Central route	When motivated to process an incoming message, we listen carefully to the arguments given and judge them on their merits.	Jason is not sure whom to vote for in the upcoming federal election. He obtains detailed information on the candidates' views on the major issues, and after considering each, decides on the Liberal candidate.
Peripheral route	When we are unable or unwilling to process a message carefully, our attitudes are more affected by superficial cues or mere exposure.	Yvette hasn't really kept up with the election coverage, but she has seen some commercials during her nightly TV viewing. She gets a kick out of the New Democratic Party candidate's humorous ad, so decides to vote for her.
Cognitive dissonance	Behaviour that is inconsistent with attitudes produces psychological tension (i.e., *dissonance*). If this discrepancy is large enough, attitudes or behaviour will change.	Jeremy has always considered himself a Conservative and backs the Conservative candidate for member of Parliament. Lately he's been dating a woman involved with the Christian Coalition Party. At first, Jeremy feels distressed, but gradually he becomes more favourable toward the Christian Coalition Party.
Self-perception	We learn from our behaviour and use our actions as a basis for inferring beliefs. Behaviour is observed, and attitudes follow from the behaviour.	Felicia gets a phone call from the Green Party campaign headquarters pleading for help. The Green Party can't compete with the other campaigns unless it raises more money for its candidate. Felicia agrees to donate $20 to the cause. Looking back on it, she decides she must really favour the Green Party candidate.

attitudes or opinions have recently changed: "Do I still like playing video games? Well, let's see. I haven't played a game for a while, so I must not be crazy about them any more." It's adaptive for us to use multiple sources of information for establishing our beliefs, including our own actions.

Test Yourself 13.1

Check your knowledge about how we form impressions of others by answering the following questions. (The answers are in Appendix B.)

1. Decide whether each of the following statements about person perception is true or false.
   a. On average, attractive people are assumed to be more intelligent, better adjusted, and more socially aware than people with average looks. *True or False?*
   b. Prototype theories assume that we represent stereotypes with particular individuals, or exemplars. *True or False?*
   c. The prejudiced attitudes of people who also express authoritarian attitudes appear to be more related to their stereotyped beliefs about out-groups than to their concern that such groups disrespect traditional values. *True or False?*
   d. The degree of discrimination that people believe is directed toward their group is usually closely correlated with the discrimination that individuals in the group report experiencing personally. *True or False?*

2. For each of the following, decide whether you are most likely to make an internal or an external attribution for the behaviour described.
   a. You get a perfect score on your psychology exam:
      _____

   b. Josie always smiles after her psychology lecture, but everyone else in the class leaves angry: _____
   c. You get a failing score on your psychology exam:
      _____

   d. Eagerly anticipating your food, you notice your waiter seems to spend a lot of time talking to the hostess:
      _____

3. Decide whether each of the following statements about attitudes and attitude change is true or false.
   a. For an attitude to guide behaviour, it should be appropriate or relevant to the situation. *True or False?*
   b. The peripheral route to persuasion operates when our level of involvement in or commitment to a message is high. *True or False?*
   c. According to cognitive dissonance theory, it is inconsistencies between internal beliefs and our actions that lead to attitude change. *True or False?*
   d. Mere exposure can lead to attitude change, but only if we're processing an incoming communication with care and attention. *True or False?*

▶ Behaving in the Presence of Others: Social Influence

LEARNING GOALS

1. Understand social facilitation and interference, including the relationship among task difficulty, arousal, and performance.
2. Be able to explain the bystander effect and the concept of diffusion of responsibility.
3. Learn how behaviour changes in a group setting.
4. Understand some aspects of group decision making.
5. Be able to describe the Milgram experiment and discuss its implications for the power of authority.

We now turn our attention to the topic of **social influence:** How is our behaviour affected by the presence of others? The evidence shows that the presence of other people can cause us to act in new or different ways or to change our attitudes and beliefs. Think back to the ambitious underling, Chris M., whom we met at the beginning of the chapter. His behaviour certainly changed in the presence of others: He violated his beliefs and conformed to the opinions of his colleagues and his arrogant boss.

> **social influence**
>
> The study of how the behaviours and thoughts of individuals are affected by the presence of others

Social Facilitation and Interference

social facilitation

The enhancement in performance that is sometimes found when an individual performs in the presence of others

CRITICAL THINKING

Under what conditions do you think the presence of an audience might actually lower someone's arousal? What implications does this possibility have for social facilitation?

social interference

The impairment in performance that is sometimes found when an individual performs in the presence of others

Demonstrating the phenomenon of social facilitation, people tend to eat more when they're in the presence of others.

One of the simplest and most widely documented examples of social influence is the phenomenon of social facilitation. **Social facilitation** is the *enhancement* in performance that is sometimes found when we perform in the presence of others. To demonstrate social facilitation, we need to compare someone's task performance in two conditions: when performing alone and when performing in the presence of other people. The "other people" could be either co-actors (often people performing the same task or a related one), or they could be audience members (for instance, friends and family watching a piano recital). If performance improves when other people are around, you've demonstrated social facilitation. In the very first social psychology study, Norman Triplett (1898) discovered that people would wind in a fishing reel faster when working in pairs than when working alone. Task performance improved in the presence of others, which is the defining characteristic of social facilitation.

Social facilitation is a widespread effect, occurring in many kinds of social environments and for many kinds of tasks (Aiello & Douthitt, 2001). Motorists drive through intersections faster when another car is travelling in the lane beside them (Towler, 1986); people run faster when others are present (Worringham & Messick, 1983); people even eat more when dining out with friends than when eating alone (Clendenen, Herman, & Polivy, 1994). In fact, the effect is not restricted to humans: Ants will excavate dirt more quickly to build their nests when other ants are present (Chen, 1937); hungry chickens will peck food more when other chickens observe passively through a clear plastic wall (Tolman, 1968); cockroaches will even run faster down an alleyway when a "spectator" roach watches from a small plastic enclosure (Zajonc, Heingartner, & Herman, 1969).

But there is another side to the coin. It's easy to think of examples of how we've "risen to the occasion" and excelled when an audience was present, but the opposite can be the case as well. Sometimes performing in a crowd impairs performance—we choke, a tendency referred to as **social interference.** Talented Angela, who finally performs Bach's Invention No. 1 perfectly in her last practice session, finds her fingers fumbling helplessly during the piano recital. Confident Marco, who thought he had memorized every fact in his psychology textbook, finds that his mind goes blank in a large auditorium full of other students. Social interference is the opposite of social facilitation, but both represent cases in which our ability to perform a task is influenced by the presence of others.

Task Difficulty and Arousal So what determines whether the presence of others will help or hinder performance? Psychologists have determined that *task difficulty* is one important factor: If the task is relatively easy, the presence of others will spur the person on, and you'll see social facilitation; if the task is new or difficult, the presence of others can have an inhibitory effect, and you'll find social interference.

According to psychologist Robert Zajonc (1965), it's possible to explain the relationship between task difficulty and performance by appealing to how an audience's presence influences *arousal*. When others are watching, Zajonc argued, it's reasonable to assume that our general level of arousal increases. Arousal, in turn, naturally biases us toward engaging in well-learned responses. If the task is a relatively easy one, such as running or solving simple multiplications, then such well-learned responses are likely to be useful and help performance. But when tasks are difficult, we're likely to need new or unusual responses that are less well learned. For difficult tasks, then, performance is likely to be impaired because the high arousal levels will bias us toward responses that are not very useful. For instance, think about trying to perform a complicated jump for the first time in front of your gym class. The high arousal level involved in attempting this difficult task in front of other people would probably decrease your performance compared with trying

Ryan McVay/PhotoDisc/Getty Images

When a task is difficult, performing in the presence of others can lead to social interference. What seemed easy in private becomes a nightmare in public.

Associated Press/Harr Cabluck

it by yourself. Evidence shows that home teams tend to lose important hockey games played in their home stadium. Apparently, teams feel more pressure when their own fans are watching (Wright, Voyer, Wright, & Roney, 1995). Thus, the influence that others have on performance is explained by the relationship between general arousal and its effects on task performance.

Social Influences on Helping: The Bystander Effect

In addition to task performance, the presence of other people can dramatically influence whether we help others in need. Think about the last time that you were driving on the highway and noticed some poor person standing alongside a disabled car by the side of the road. Did you stop and help? Did you at least get off at the nearest exit and telephone the police or highway patrol? If you're like most people, you probably did nothing. In all likelihood, you failed to accept responsibility for helping; you left that job for someone else.

The problem is more serious than you might think. In March 1964, while walking home from work at 3:30 in the morning, Catherine "Kitty" Genovese was stalked and then brutally attacked by a knife-wielding assailant outside her apartment building in New York City. "Oh my God, he stabbed me!" Kitty screamed. "I'm dying! I'm dying!" Inside the apartment building, awakened by the screams, some 38 of her neighbours sat silently listening as the attacker finished the job. Kitty was stabbed repeatedly before she eventually died; in fact, the attacker actually left and came back to assault her again and then kill her. No one in the apartment building came to her aid or called the police until approximately 30 minutes after the first attack. Only in New York, you say? A similar incident happened in Vancouver in December 2002. Fifteen people heard a girl scream as she was murdered, but none responded in a helpful way. Were bystanders simply afraid to get involved in these situations, or was some other more general psychological process at work?

The reluctance to come to someone's aid when other people are present is known generally as the **bystander effect** (Darley & Latané, 1968). Although it's relatively easy to document examples in the news, it's also possible to study the

bystander effect

The reluctance to come to the aid of a person in need when other people are present

bystander effect in the laboratory. Consider the following scenario. You've volunteered to participate in a psychology experiment that involves groups of students discussing the problems of university life. To minimize embarrassment, you're allowed to sit in a small cubicle where you can communicate with the others by using an intercom system. Before the experiment begins, you're told that one, two, or five other people will be participating. The session begins and suddenly one of the group members, who had previously mentioned being prone to epileptic seizures, begins to have a seizure. Over the intercom, his voice begins to garble—"Somebody-er-er-help-er-uh-uh-uh"—followed by silence. What do you do? Do you get up and help or sit where you are?

In the experiment, of course, no one actually had a seizure; the incident was manufactured by the experimenters to observe the bystander effect. The experiment had only one real participant; the "others" were simply voices recorded on tape. The researchers found that the likelihood that the real participant would offer some kind of help to the imaginary seizure victim depended on how many other people the participant believed to be present. When the participant was convinced that only one other person was participating in the group, he or she almost immediately rose to intervene. But when it was presumed that four others (in addition to the seizure victim) were present, only 62% of the participants offered aid (Darley & Latané, 1968).

Diffusion of Responsibility   Most social psychologists believe that the behaviour of the people in these situations, including the actions of the New York apartment dwellers, is not unusual, nor does it simply reflect widespread societal apathy. Instead, the reluctance to help the needy in the presence of others can be explained by a specific kind of social influence. We avoid helping, or getting involved, because the presence of others leads to **diffusion of responsibility**—we believe that others have already done something to help or will soon get involved. If we know that others are present in the situation, and certainly many occupants of the apartment building heard the terrible screams, we allow our sense of responsibility to *diffuse*, or spread out widely, among the other people presumed to be present.

The bystander effect is a disturbing but powerful example of social influence. The more witnesses present, the less likely it will be that any one will step forward to offer aid. The effect has been replicated many times in numerous social settings that extend beyond the laboratory. It extends to other social situations where several people have the opportunity to contribute to a worthwhile goal (Latané & Nida, 1981). Although you may not have witnessed a murder, you surely have witnessed a messy kitchen. Everyday experience, as well as research, confirms that the more people involved in messing up a communal room, the less likely any one of them will clean it up.

Of course, helping behaviour has many other social determinants. For instance, people are more likely to help if they have recently observed others being helpful. It is the counterintuitive nature of the bystander effect—that there is danger in numbers rather than safety in numbers—that makes it a fascinating social phenomenon. In trying to explain the bystander effect, it is tempting (and much more comfortable) to suggest that it was the weak character of the reluctant nonhelpers rather than a complex social effect, such as diffusion of responsibility. For instance, in the Kitty Genovese incident, many commentators suggested that this phenomenon is peculiar to New Yorkers, who have a reputation for being collectively callous and indifferent. Such a suggestion can be interpreted as being an example of the fundamental attribution error (discussed earlier in the chapter): The reason for the failure to intervene in the Genovese case was New Yorkers' callousness (an internal explanation) rather than diffusion of responsibility dynamics (a more external attribution). Although local norms regarding helpfulness undoubtedly play a role in interventions and intervention failures, people seem particularly quick to blame such failures on the lack of character in people ("That couldn't

diffusion of responsibility

The idea that when people know, or think, that others are present in a situation, they allow their sense of responsibility for action to diffuse, or spread out widely, among those who are present

happen here in Canada" or "I would never behave that way"), rather than considering the more complex external explanations. Of course, people do not have easy access to the driving forces of social situations. Given our inability to pinpoint the true causes of our own social dynamics, it is understandable that we resort to explanations that make us feel more comfortable.

The Power of the Group

The social context is particularly powerful in well-defined groups. Our behaviour is shaped not only by the characteristics of the group—its size and the unanimity of its members—but also by the mere fact that we're *in* the group. Among the most impressive demonstrations of the power of the group involves its ability to get group members to conform to the behaviour of other people in the group. Also powerful are the tendencies of individuals in groups to shirk responsibility for their own actions. We discuss these group pressures toward conformity in the following section.

Social Loafing   During our discussion of social facilitation you learned that a person's performance often changes when others are present. Whether performance improves or declines depends on factors, such as the difficulty of the task or the general level of arousal. But when participating as a member of a group, most people show a strong tendency to engage in **social loafing,** which means they put out less effort than when the task is theirs alone (Latané, Williams, & Harkins, 1979). Social loafing is easy to demonstrate in the laboratory. In one study, volunteer subjects were instructed to clap and cheer as loudly as possible while blindfolded and listening to noise over headphones. Just before they began the task, the participants were told they would be clapping either with a group of other subjects or by themselves. When the volunteers believed they were part of a clapping group, their individual output dropped considerably.

Like many of the phenomena we've discussed in this chapter, social loafing is complex. Whether it occurs in a particular situation will depend on many factors, including the importance of the task, the cohesiveness of the group, and the personalities of the group members (Karau & Hart, 1998; Smith, Kerr, Markus, & Stasson, 2001). The effect occurs widely across cultures, although it may be especially common in cultures that stress individuality (Karau & Williams, 1993). Some social psychologists make a connection between social loafing and the bystander effect. Bibb Latané (1981), in particular, has argued that both effects result from diffusion of responsibility. In the bystander effect, people suspect that others either will or have become involved; in social loafing, we assume that others will carry the load. In both cases, the fact that we are simply one of many makes us feel less accountable for our behaviour. We fail to step up and take full responsibility, or to work to our fullest capabilities, because the responsibility can be diffused or spread to the other members of the group.

Deindividuation   The idea that we feel less accountable for our behaviour when we're in a group setting can lead to a phenomenon called **deindividuation.** Imagine yourself at a particularly lively party: The people around you are acting crazy—they're drinking too much, damaging the furniture, and some are even beginning to shed their clothes. Are you likely to start doing the same? Some psychologists believe that when people are in large groups, they lose their sense of individuality. We can enter a depersonalized state of mind, called deindividuation, that increases the chances of engaging in destructive, aggressive, or deviant behaviour. Under most circumstances, it's highly unlikely that you would trash the furniture in a friend's home. But when you're part of a large rowdy group, deindividuation can lead you to do things that you might not otherwise do.

---

social loafing

The tendency to put out less effort when several people are supposed to be working on a task than when only one is working

CRITICAL   THINKING

What situations are subject to social loafing as opposed to social facilitation?

deindividuation

The loss of individuality, or depersonalization, that comes from being in a group

CP Picture Archive (Stephan Savoia)

People can feel less accountable for their behaviour in a group setting, a phenomenon known as deindividuation.

conformity

The tendency to go along with the wishes of the group; when people conform, their opinions, feelings, and behaviours generally start to move toward the group norm

Once again, diffusion of responsibility is likely to play a role in such situations. When you're in a large group, you're less likely to feel accountable for your actions. You feel anonymous, which lowers your normal restraints on destructive actions. You also feel less self-conscious—you go along with the group, as a whim, because you're not thinking about your normal standards, values, and morals. Whether you truly enter a depersonalized state of mind is debatable, but your actions do differ from your normal tendencies. Some psychologists have argued that deindividuation is simply an example of situation-specific behaviour; your behaviour is being controlled by an unusual situation and your actions probably don't provide much information about how you typically behave (Postmes & Spears, 1998).

Conformity   One of the most important behavioural consequences of group membership is **conformity,** the tendency of a member's opinions, feelings, and behaviours to move toward the group norm. Its effects are powerful even when that person has not been explicitly asked to behave in the same way as others do. Normally conformity is an adaptive function for group success and a cohesive society. We agree to drive on the right side of the road. We go to Aunt Sarah's for the holidays because that's what the family tradition is. If your friends all want to see *Titanic* for the fifth time, why cause a fuss? The downside, of course, is that your group may not always do the right thing. Smoking, racism, shoplifting, violence, and promiscuous sex can often result from pressure to feel part of a group. Studies investigating issues of conformity to group norms are among the oldest and best known of all social psychology experiments.

In one classic study of conformity, psychologist Solomon Asch (1951, 1955) rigged the following experimental setup. Participants were asked to take part in a simple perception experiment that required them to make judgments about line length. Two cards were shown: one displaying a standard line of a particular length and the other showing three comparison lines of differing lengths. The participant was required to state aloud which of the three comparison lines was the same length as the standard line (see ▶ Figure 13.7). The task was really quite simple—there was no question as to what the correct answer should be. The catch was that the participant was part of a group and the other members of the group were really *confederates* of the experimenter—they were there to put social pressure on the true participant.

The confederate participants were instructed to lie on some of the trials. They were told to give a response, aloud, that was clearly wrong (such as picking comparison line 1 as the correct answer). Asch was mainly concerned about how often these incorrect answers would affect the answers of the real participant. Imagine yourself in this situation: You know the answer is line 2, but four of your fellow participants have already given line 1 as a response. Do you conform to the opinions of your peers, even though doing so conflicts with what you know to be true? Asch found that in approximately 75% of the sessions, participants conformed on at least one of the trials, and the overall rate of conformity was around 37%. Although peer

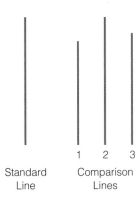

Standard
Line

Comparison
Lines

William Vandivert/Scientific American

▶ **Figure 13.7**

The Asch Study of Conformity

Do you think you would have any trouble choosing the correct comparison line in this task? Asch found that people often conformed to the group opinion—even when it was clearly wrong. The photo shown here is taken from one of his actual experiments.

pressure wasn't always effective in altering the behaviour of the participants—in fact, only 5% of the participants conformed on every trial—its power was surprising.

As you might imagine, the Asch experiments had quite an impact on the psychological community. It was disturbing to many that intelligent college students could be pressured by a group of strangers to agree with a clear falsehood. Similar experiments have been conducted on dozens of occasions in many countries around the world. Generally, Asch's results have held up well, although a number of variables affect the likelihood that conformity will occur. Asch himself found, for example, that the rate of conformity dropped dramatically when one of the confederates dissented from the majority and gave the correct answer. It was also discovered that the size of the group is not as important as you might think. Conformity increases as the size of the pressure group gets larger, but it levels off relatively quickly. The pressure to conform does not increase directly with group size; after a certain point, usually when the majority group contains three to five members, adding even more pressure has a minimal effect (Tanford & Penrod, 1984). Finally, attitudes about the group as a whole also matter; if people have little respect for the group, they're less likely to conform. Conformity is particularly likely when pressure comes from an in-group—that is, a group of individuals with whom you share features in common or with whom you identify (see Cialdini & Goldstein, 2004).

Group Decision Making

As you've just seen, members of an in-group can exert considerable pressure on one another to conform to the standards or norms of the group. One of the consequences of these internal pressures is that groups tend to take on behavioural characteristics of their own, especially when group decisions need to be made. Obviously, the psychology of group decision making is critically important—it affects everything from how verdicts are reached by juries, to how families decide where to go on vacation, to decisions made by government Cabinet members. Psychologists have identified two important characteristics of group decision making: group polarization and groupthink.

CRITICAL THINKING

Notice that when people conform they often act in ways that are inconsistent with their attitudes. What implications should this have for attitude change?

group polarization

The tendency for a group's dominant point of view to become stronger and more extreme with time

Group Polarization   When members of an in-group arrive at a consensus of opinion, there is a tendency for the group's opinion to polarize. **Group polarization** means that the group's dominant point of view—which is usually determined by the initial views of the majority—becomes stronger and even more extreme with time. If you join a local action group dedicated to exposing corporate corruption and the group tends to believe initially that corporate corruption is a significant and rising problem, it's likely that over time you and the rest of the members of the group will become even more convinced of that position (Myers, 1982; Nowak, Vallacher, & Miller, 2003).

What accounts for group polarization? Not surprisingly, some of the same factors that promote conformity promote polarization. For example, group discussions tend to provide information that consolidates initial opinions. Those who enter the group with strong opinions make strong cases for their viewpoint and dissenting viewpoints are less likely to be heard (Stewart & Stasser, 1995). At the same time, the social aspects of the discussion play an important role. People want to be liked by the other members of the group, so they shift their attitude toward the group consensus. You're more likely to be accepted by the group if you forcefully argue in favour of the group's dominant viewpoint.

groupthink

The tendency for members of a group to become so interested in seeking a consensus of opinion that they start to ignore and even suppress dissenting views

Groupthink   The trend toward consensus and polarization of opinion may also be influenced by what psychologist Irving Janis has labelled **groupthink:** Members of a group become so interested in seeking a consensus of opinion that they start to ignore and even suppress dissenting views. Janis (1982, 1989) found evidence for groupthink when he looked at how well-established in-groups arrived at decisions, particularly policy decisions by members of the government. He and others analyzed a number of watershed events in U.S. policymaking, including the decision to escalate the war in Vietnam, the decision by President John F. Kennedy to invade Cuba in 1961, and even the decision by NASA to launch the ill-fated *Challenger* space shuttle. Not all psychologists are satisfied with the interpretations that Janis provided for groupthink (e.g., Kramer, 1998), but there is still wide agreement that the phenomenon exists (Esser, 1998).

In an alarming number of cases, Janis discovered that group members systematically sought consensus at the expense of critical analysis. Group members often acted as if they were trying to convince themselves of the correctness of their position. When alternative views were expressed, those views were either suppressed or dismissed. The management at NASA had clear evidence that freezing launch temperatures might pose a problem for the *Challenger* space shuttle, but the managers chose to ignore that evidence in the interest of going forward with the mission. The result of groupthink is general closed-mindedness and an overestimation of the uniformity of opinion.

Polarization occurs when a group's majority opinion becomes stronger and more extreme with time. What's the likelihood that people in this group will adopt more tolerant views in the future?

Can groupthink be avoided? According to Janis (1982), it is possible to counteract groupthink by following certain guidelines. For instance, it helps to have a leader who acts impartially, one who does not quickly endorse a particular position. One or more members of the group can also be assigned a kind of "devil's

CONCEPT SUMMARY

VARIETIES OF SOCIAL INFLUENCE

Phenomenon	Description
Social facilitation	An improvement in performance is sometimes found when we perform in the presence of others. It is especially likely with easy or well-practised tasks.
Social interference	A decline in performance is sometimes found when we are in the presence of others. It is especially likely with tasks that are unique or not well learned.
Bystander effect	This is the reluctance people show to come to someone's aid when other people are present. It is characterized by diffusion of responsibility, the tendency to believe that others will help.
Social loafing	Most people show a strong tendency to put in less effort when they are working in a group compared with when they work alone.
Deindividuation	When in large groups, we can lose our sense of individuality and be more likely to engage in destructive, aggressive, or deviant behaviour.
Conformity	A person's opinions, feelings, and behaviours start to move toward the group norm.

Group–Decision-Making Effects

Phenomenon	Description
Group polarization	A group's dominant point of view become stronger and even more extreme with time.
Groupthink	Members of a group become so interested in seeking a consensus of opinion that they ignore and suppress dissenting views.

advocate" role in which they are expected and encouraged to represent a dissenting position. Perhaps most important, however, is making the group members aware that social influences, such as groupthink, are real phenomena that can lead to bad decisions, irrespective of group members' intelligence or commitment to the truth. Groupthink can be avoided, although it requires reconsidering how group decision making is normally conducted.

The Power of Authority: Obedience

Up to this point in our discussion of social influence, we've concentrated on how our behaviour is affected by the presence of others of comparable status to us. But what if those other individuals have higher status than us? Think back once again to our story about Chris M., who opened the chapter. Do you think he would have agreed so readily with his co-workers if the boss had not been standing there, drink in hand, listening intently to his opinions? To what degree was Chris's behaviour influenced because it was someone in a position of authority who had asked him his opinion? The question of how behaviour changes in the presence of authority has produced some of the most intriguing and controversial studies in the history of psychology.

Psychologists use the term **obedience** to refer to the form of compliance that occurs when people respond to the orders of an authority figure. You're of course aware of the fact that during World War II, millions of Jewish men, women, and children were systematically executed by German soldiers working under orders from Nazi officials. In a rural area of Guyana, South America, in 1978, hundreds of converts to the religious teachings of Reverend Jim Jones chose, under his direct orders, to commit mass suicide. Most people find it extremely difficult to understand such events and consider them to be social aberrations committed by people far different from themselves. Admittedly, you might toe the line in front of your boss and do and say things that you don't really believe, but murder innocent people? Would you follow orders to take a poisoned drink and give the same lethal

obedience

The form of compliance that occurs when people respond to the orders of an authority figure

Obedience to authority reached shocking levels in 1978 when followers of Reverend Jim Jones chose, under his direct orders, to commit mass suicide by willingly taking a poisoned drink.

© Bettmann/Corbis

concoction to your children (as parents did at Jonestown)? Most people would say, "Not a chance." However, the certainty with which most people answer these questions might partly be another reflection of the fundamental attribution error, which, as you remember, involves a basic unwillingness to fully acknowledge the extraordinary power that situational forces can have on us.

The Milgram Experiment   In the most famous social psychology experiment ever conducted, psychologist Stanley Milgram (1963) set out to determine how far an average person would go in complying with the directions of an authority figure. He placed a newspaper ad recruiting men for what was described as a study looking at the effects of punishment on learning. The participants were told that they would be paid a small fee to play one of two roles in an experiment: either a *learner*, which required memorizing and then recalling lists of word pairs, or a *teacher*, whose task it would be to administer an electric shock to the learner whenever he made any recall errors. Each session required two participants—one teacher and one learner—and the assignment of roles was decided by drawing slips of paper out of a hat.

But things were not exactly what they appeared to be. In fact, in every case the true volunteer, the one who had actually responded to the ad, was picked to be the teacher. The learner was a confederate of the experimenter, someone who pretended to be another participant. Although it was rigged to look as though he was receiving shocks throughout the session, he never actually did. The idea was to see how willing the teacher would be to give the learner electric shocks when the authority figure—the experimenter—told him to do so.

To begin the setup, the two men were introduced and the teacher watched as the learner was led away to an adjacent room and hooked up to a shock-administering apparatus. Back in the original room, the teacher was then placed in front of an imposing-looking electrical shock generator, which contained some 30 different switches. It was explained that each switch was able to generate a particular level of shock intensity, ranging from 15 V (slight shock), through 150 V (strong shock), and finally up to 450 V (labelled simply XXX). With the experimenter standing by his side, the teacher was instructed to begin reading and then testing the learner's memory for the words, over an intercom, and to administer a shock whenever the learner failed to call out the correct answer. Moreover, to see how far the teacher would go, he was instructed to increase the voltage level of the shock (by clicking up the switch) after each new mistake.

Remember: No one was actually shocked in this experiment; the learner was in on the experiment, and he was told to make mistakes consistently throughout the session and the apparent "mistakes" were preprogrammed. A tape recording made it seem as if the learner was responding. At first, when the shock levels were low, there wasn't much response. But as the prearranged mistakes continued—which, of course, necessitated the teacher to continue increasing the voltage of the shock—loud protests began to come over the intercom. By the time the mistake-prone learner was receiving 150-V shocks, he was demanding to be released from the experiment. By around 300 V, he was screaming in pain in response to each delivered shock and pounding on the wall; after the 330-V level, the shocks yielded no response at all—simply silence.

Listening to these disturbing pleas for help did not, of course, make most "teachers" very comfortable. Most expressed concern about the shocks and wanted to discontinue the experiment. But the teacher's concerns were met with resistance from the authoritative experimenter, who demanded that the shocks go on. "Please continue," the experimenter responded. "The experiment must go on." What would you do in this situation? You're participating in an experiment, which is being conducted in the name of science, but the task requires you to inflict pain and suffering on someone else. Do you continue, delivering shocks in compliance with the requests of the authority figure, or do you quit and give the experimenter a piece of your mind? This was exactly the question of interest to Milgram: How obedient would people be to unreasonable requests by an authority figure?

Before the experiment began, Milgram asked several people, including psychological professionals, to predict how much shock participants would be willing to deliver in his task. Most predicted that obedience would be low; the estimates were that only a few people in a thousand would deliver shocks up to 450 V and that most participants would defy the experimenter after discomfort was expressed by the learner. In reality, the results were far different. Milgram found that 65% of the 40 participants who participated were willing to deliver shocks up to 450 V, and no participant quit before the pounding on the wall started (see ▶ Figure 13.8 on page 544). This means that 26 of the 40 participants went all the way to the final switch—the one with the ominous XXX label—despite the agonizing pleas from the learner. (Subsequent research found approximately the same rate of compliance in women participants as in men.) Milgram's remarkable finding rocked the psychological community and initiated a great deal of subsequent research as well as a firestorm of controversy.

Controversies and Ethical Concerns   Milgram's (1963) experiment was controversial for two main reasons. First, the manner in which it was conducted raises serious ethical questions. The participants in his study were misled from the beginning and became severely distressed during their participation. Milgram observed many indications of distress during the experiment: The "teachers" sometimes groaned, bit their lips, trembled, stuttered, and even broke into a sweat. Some critics feel that this kind of psychological manipulation—even though it was conducted to advance knowledge—cannot be justified (Baumrind, 1964; Schlenker & Forsyth, 1977). In response, Milgram (1974) argued that his participants were thoroughly debriefed at the end of the experiment—they were told in detail about the true nature of the experiment—and generally said they were glad they had participated. Follow-up questionnaires sent to the participants months later revealed that only a few felt negative about the experiment.

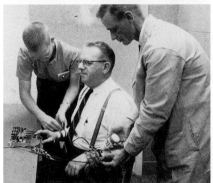
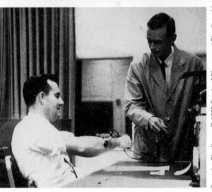

From the Obedience © 1965 Stanley Milgram and Distributed by Penn State Media Sales. Permission granted by Alexandra Milgram.

These photos were taken during one of Milgram's early experiments on obedience to authority. The first photo shows the shock generator used during the experiment; the second photo shows the "learner," who was actually a confederate of the experimenter, being hooked up to the shocking apparatus; the third photo shows the "teacher" with the demanding experimenter (in the lab coat) standing over him.

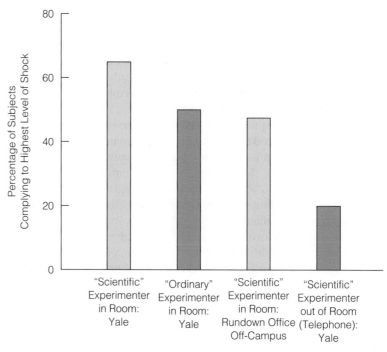

▶ **Figure 13.8**

Milgram's Study of Obedience

Milgram was astonished to discover that 65% of the people he tested gave (what they thought was) a life-threatening electric shock to another person simply because a Yale University experimenter told them to. You can see from the lower bars on the graph that obedience was reduced if the experimenter was out of the room or looked nonscientific, or if the location was off-campus in a run-down building.

CRITICAL　THINKING

Why might it be adaptive for us to respond so readily to the demands of an authority figure?

Other criticisms concerned the validity of conclusions about obedience. Some critics argued that the participants had seen through the cover story and were simply trying to please the experimenter. They said that participants would assume that the procedure was OK; otherwise, how could such an experiment be allowed? Milgram again pointed out the extreme distress that his participants exhibited: That suggests that they had *not* figured out the hoax. Other critics argued that the results, although interesting, had no general applicability beyond the laboratory. That argument does not seem very comforting when we consider that many important life situations involve the same psychological elements. Think about the plight of soldiers ordered to behave in a barbaric fashion. Think about orders from employers who want you to ignore potential environmental damage caused by the company's new policies.

In the four decades since Milgram's original experiment was conducted, his general procedure has been repeated a number of times, in many countries around the world (see Blass, 2000; Meeus & Raaijmakers, 1987). Few psychologists today question the validity of the basic findings, although it's clear that the degree of compliance that people will show to authority depends on many factors. For example, the Milgram experiment was conducted at a prestigious university (Yale); when the same study was conducted in a less prestigious setting—a run-down office building—compliance dropped (although it remained alarmingly high). People were also less likely to comply if the authority figure left the room after explaining the experiment or if the person giving the orders looked ordinary rather than official or scientific (Milgram, 1974). Thus, obedience to authority is not absolute; it depends on the characteristics of the situation as well as on the characteristics of the person giving the orders.

Test Yourself 13.2 *Check your knowledge about social influence by answering the following questions. (The answers are in Appendix B.)*

1. Pick the psychological term that best fits each of the statements below. Choose from the following: social facilitation, social interference, bystander effect, social loafing, deindividuation, conformity, group polarization, groupthink, obedience.
   a. Jerry is convinced that his study group is dead wrong about their interpretation of the Milgram experiment, but he chooses to nod in agreement with the others in the group: _____
   b. Kramer never calls 911 when he sees a broken-down car by the side of the road; he assumes everyone has a cell phone: _____
   c. Elaine notices that she always talks more when she's at a large party: _____

   d. George is normally shy and polite, but at the rock concert last night he was loud and shouted obscenities at the police: _____
   e. Landlord Newman notices that the grievances coming from his tenant group have become increasingly more rigid and demanding over time: _____
   f. Jane writes extremely well, but she contributes little to group discussions during class: _____

2. Which of the following situations should lead to the greatest reduction in obedience to authority?
   a. The authority figure wears a uniform in front of the teacher.
   b. The authority figure stands close to the teacher.
   c. The experiment is conducted in a federal building.
   d. The experiment is conducted in the teacher's home.

▶ Relationships with Others: Positive and Negative

LEARNING GOALS

1. Understand the factors that influence our perception of facial attractiveness.
2. Distinguish how proximity, similarity, ingratiation, and reciprocity influence liking and loving.
3. Be able to define the components of romantic love and discuss the triangular theory of love.
4. Understand the psychology of aggression and how it can be reduced.

Human beings have a fundamental need to belong (Baumeister & Leary, 1995). But how do we establish and maintain relationships with others? What differentiates the pleasant relationships from the unpleasant ones? For most of us, our personal relationships are the best part of life. We depend on our interactions with colleagues, friends, lovers, and family for protection and inspiration. At the same time, personal hostility and aggression are major disruptions. Both positive and negative relationships give meaning to our lives. Each type of relationship (e.g., parent-child, siblings, friends, lovers, colleagues, competitors, enemies) may invoke quite different schemas to guide our behaviour. In evolutionary terms, these different "mind modules" were selected for dealing with the normal relationships necessary for the continuation of our species (Daly, Salmon, & Wilson, 1997; Daly & Wilson, 1998; Krebs & Denton, 1997).

We've actually encountered the topic of social relationships several times in earlier chapters. In Chapter 10, when we discussed social development, we dealt in detail with the topic of attachment. But in that case we were concerned with the function of social bonds for solving the problems that arise during development. Infants are born with limited motor skills and somewhat immature perceptual systems; consequently, they need to establish strong bonds with their caregivers to survive. In Chapter 11, when we discussed motivation and emotion, we saw how people use facial expressions to communicate their emotions to others and how people are motivated to secure sexual partners. Again, in that discussion we emphasized the adaptive value of the relationship rather than the role that the social context plays in the process. In this section we'll first consider interpersonal

Our relationships with others protect us, nurture us, and give meaning to our lives.

attraction, which usually precedes relationship development, and then we'll discuss how psychologists have tackled the mysterious phenomenon of love. We'll also address the darker side of relationships—aggression—and whether it can be reduced.

What Makes a Face Attractive?

We often resent it. We even deny it. Like it or not, beauty is a powerful motivator of human behaviour. Psychologists have confirmed that people's physical attractiveness often shapes how their behaviour is interpreted and how they are treated by others. As you learned earlier in the chapter, the mind utilizes social schemas to form impressions, and physical attractiveness is used as a cue to generate expectations about others (Eagly et al., 1991). The nineteenth-century German poet Johann Schiller captured the tendency of humans to equate beauty with worthiness when he wrote, "Physical beauty is the sign of an interior beauty, a spiritual and moral beauty." Schiller's contention pervades modern advertisements, but research has shown that physical attractiveness is not actually correlated with people's character or mental health (Hatfield, 1988).

An Evolutionary Perspective   What exactly is it that makes a face physically beautiful? What are the qualities that determine whether someone's looks are considered desirable? One way to think about this problem is from the perspective of evolutionary theory. Like other animals, humans likely evolved to prefer mating with someone with a high reproductive capacity or someone who is able to provide protection for offspring and compete successfully for needed resources. This reasoning predicts that people should be attracted to opposite-sex members who are youthful, vigorous, and healthy looking because these qualities used to be correlated with the likelihood of successful reproduction and child rearing (Alley & Cunningham, 1991; Buss, 2004; Johnston, 2000).

Another prediction of evolutionary theory is that features of attractiveness should transcend cultural boundaries. If attractiveness is grounded somewhere deep in our evolutionary heritage, then it shouldn't matter much where you are raised and what experiences you have; in general, worldwide agreement should exist about what constitutes attractiveness. This conclusion contrasts sharply with the generally accepted idea that "beauty is in the eye of the beholder," but it's supported by empirical research. People from quite different cultures rate the same basic structural facial features as attractive (Bernstein, Lin, & McClelland, 1982; McArthur & Berry, 1987). It's also been discovered that babies, within hours of birth, prefer to look at pictures of attractive faces compared with those that have been rated as unattractive by adults (Langlois et al., 1987; Slater et al., 1998). Culturally based standards of beauty cannot account for this very early human preference.

Attractive Faces May Be Average   Psychologists Judith Langlois and Lori Roggman (1990; Langlois, Roggman, & Musselman, 1994) suggest that the universality of attractiveness may be partly due to the fact that people are programmed to prefer faces that are *average* representations of faces in the population. By average, Langlois and Roggman do not necessarily mean common, typical, or frequently occurring faces. Instead, they mean prototypical faces—that is, faces that are good representations of the category "faces." In Chapter 8, we defined category prototypes as the best or most representative members of a category—a robin, for example, is probably close to the prototype for the category "bird." According to Langlois and Roggman, attractive faces are those that are particularly *facelike*, or representative of the category of faces.

They based their conclusions on research in which people were asked to rate the attractiveness of average faces that were generated electronically on a computer. To create these faces, hundreds of individual black and white photographs of either male or female Caucasians, Asians, and Hispanics were scanned into a computer and then digitized into matrices of individual grey values. Each of these grey values corresponded to a shade of grey sitting at a particular small location on the scanned face. A whole face was represented by many thousands of these grey values, as they are in a typical newspaper photo or video display. As you probably know, any image you see in a newspaper or on a video monitor is actually a configuration of many rows and columns of individual-intensity dots or pixels. When viewed as a whole, the dots blend together to form a familiar image on the page or screen.

The unique feature of the Langlois and Roggman research was that people were sometimes shown faces that were generated by averaging the grey values across a large collection of individual faces. An individual dot in one of these composite faces was set by averaging the values of all the dots at the same relative location in the face pool. The result was a kind of blended face that did not look exactly like any one of the individual faces but rather represented a kind of prototype face in the population. Volunteer participants were asked to rate these faces for attractiveness, along with the individual faces that had been used to form the composite. The surprising result was that people generally rated the composite faces as more attractive than the individual faces (see also Rhodes & Tremewan, 1996).

Why would people prefer faces that are prototypical? Langlois and Roggman (1990) offer several speculative reasons. One possibility is that prototypical faces are easy to identify and classify as human faces. Classifying something as a face may not seem like much of a task for adults, but it could well be for the newborn infant. It is critical that infants be able to recognize a looming visual configuration as a face because they are dependent on their social interactions with people for survival. Yet the visual acuity of the newborn is limited, so faces that are particularly facelike may make this critical classification process easier. Another possibility is that people are programmed biologically to prefer prototypical faces because individuals with average features may be less likely to harbour potentially harmful genetic mutations. Generally, it is the average or normal characteristics that tend to be preferred over extreme ones in a population.

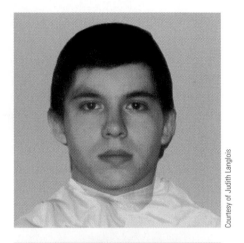

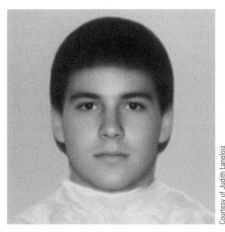

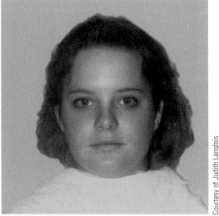

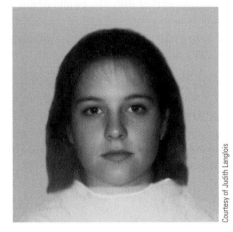

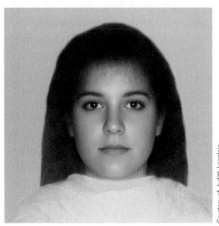

The faces shown in each row are composites created by averaging either 2 individual faces (far left), 8 faces (middle photos in each row), or 32 faces (far right). The stimuli were created by using the averaging process employed by Langlois and Roggman (1990).

There are subjective components to the perception of beauty that are culturally dependent.

The Socialized Components   Despite the evidence for universality in how people conceive of attractiveness, most psychologists recognize that there is a strong socialized component to the perception of beauty as well. As we discussed in Chapter 11, standards of beauty have changed over time in most cultures of the world. In Western societies, for instance, our icon of beauty, the fashion model, has ranged from a "curvaceous bustiness" at one point to slender tomboyishness at the next (Silverstein, Perdue, Peterson, & Kelly, 1986). It's also the case that features considered attractive in one culture—pierced noses, liposuctioned thighs, elongated earlobes—may be considered unattractive in another. Nevertheless, people can generally identify which people from other quite different cultures are considered beautiful by others within that culture.

Perceptions of attractiveness and beauty also clearly change with experience. We generally rate people we like as more attractive than people we don't like. Moreover, if you've just been shown a picture of a strikingly attractive person, your ratings of average-looking people go down (Kenrick, Gutierres, & Goldberg, 1989). Beauty is not entirely in the eye of the beholder, as the research of Langlois and Roggman (1990) indicates, but it indeed has a measurable subjective component that cannot be ignored.

Determinants of Liking and Loving

Do we form friendships, or choose marriage partners, based on some relationship equation that sums desirable and undesirable attributes in a logical and rational way? One of the most important lessons of this textbook, and certainly of this chapter, is that our behaviour is strongly influenced by external forces in the environment. People act the way they do partly because of conscious, internally driven processes, and partly because the environment shapes and constrains behaviour in an unconscious fashion. In the case of interpersonal attraction, the environment usually plays a major role in determining both whom you choose to spend time with and whom you consider to be an appropriate mate. As you learned earlier in the chapter, even mere exposure to something can be sufficient to increase its likeability (Zajonc, 1968). People like things that are familiar, even when that familiarity has been created by simple repetition.

Proximity   In a classic study conducted 50 years ago, psychologists Leon Festinger, Stanley Schachter, and Kurt Back (1950) analyzed the friendships that formed among students living in an apartment complex near the Massachusetts Institute of Technology. Festinger and his colleagues found that they could predict the likelihood of a friendship forming by simply noting the *proximity*—defined in terms of the closeness of living quarters—between two people in the building. When the students were asked to list their three closest friends, two-thirds of the time they named students who lived in their same apartment complex. Moreover, when a fellow apartment dweller was listed as a friend, two-thirds of the time he or she lived on the same floor as the respondent. Clearly, the choice of friends is strongly influenced by where you live. People tend to end up with friends who live nearby.

Of course, it isn't really proximity by itself that leads to liking and loving. When somebody lives close by, you see him or her a lot, and it may be the increased exposure that promotes the attraction. We've already seen that increased exposure leads to an increase in rated likeability, but it also provides the opportunity for interaction. When you consistently interact with someone, mutual feelings of connectedness and belonging tend to follow (Cantor & Malley, 1991). You tend to see each other as members of the same in-group. In fact, you don't even have to interact physically with someone for increased liking to occur. Psychologists John Darley and Ellen Berscheid (1967) found that even the anticipation of an interaction with someone you don't already know can cause you to rate that person as more attractive.

Similarity   It's also the case that we tend to like and form relationships with people who are *similar* to us (Byrne, 1971). Friends and intimate partners typically resemble each other in age, social status, education level, race, religious beliefs, political attitudes, intelligence, and even physical attractiveness; we even pick dogs that, at least on some dimensions, seem to resemble us physically (Roy &

CRITICAL   THINKING

Think about your own relationship experiences. Have you ever felt peer or parental pressure to find a partner who meets a well-defined set of standards? How important were these factors in your decisions?

Birds of a feather do tend to flock together; more often than not, we form lasting relationships with people who are similar to ourselves.

Christenfeld, 2004). People may report preferring physically attractive mates, but most end up marrying someone who is comparable to them in degree of physical attractiveness (Feingold, 1988, 1990). The only case where "opposites attract" is on the vertical dimension of the interpersonal circle (see Chapter 12). Specifically, a couple that differs on the dimension of dominance versus submission is more stable than a couple that does not differ on that dimension (Wiggins, 1979).

Although few psychologists question the finding that similarities attract, they disagree about how best to interpret this finding. The fact that similarities are found between the appearance and attitudes of friends and lovers doesn't explain why these similarities exist. As we discussed in Chapter 2, correlations do not imply causality. One possibility is that we like others who share our beliefs and attitudes because they *validate* those beliefs, which further helps convince us that our beliefs are the right ones (Byrne, 1971; Laprelle, Hoyle, Insko, & Bernthal, 1990). Another possibility is that we spend time with others like ourselves because we *dislike* people who hold different views (Rosenbaum, 1986). It's not so much that we want to spend time with those who resemble us; it's that we don't want to spend time with those we despise.

Reciprocity There is also a role in the dynamics of interpersonal attraction for **reciprocity,** or our tendency to return in kind the feelings that are shown toward us. If someone doesn't like you and displays hostility at every turn, you usually have similar negative feelings toward him or her. If someone likes you, or even if you simply *think* the person likes you, then you tend to like that person back (Kelley, 1983). In a study by Curtis and Miller (1986), participants were asked to have a conversation with someone whom they believed had been told either positive or negative information about them (actually, the conversation partner hadn't been told anything). If the participants believed they were talking to someone who perceived them in a positive light, they tended to be friendlier and more open in their conversation; they acted as if they liked their partner more.

Reciprocity helps lead to interpersonal attraction because it is self-fulfilling and because people who like you tend to be reinforcing and accepting of your actions. But it doesn't always work. If you feel that the positive actions of another are motivated for some selfish reason—as part of a con job or to get something, such as a promotion—then your reaction will typically be negative (Jones, 1964). **Ingratiation,** in which a person consciously tries to win the affections of another for some ulterior motive, is likely to backfire as a strategy if it is discovered.

reciprocity

The tendency for people to return in kind the feelings that are shown toward them

ingratiation

The attempt to get someone to like you for some ulterior motive

Meeting someone in an exciting place can mislead you into feeling more attracted than you really are.

Courtesy of Dr. Del Paulhus

General Level of Arousal   We learned in Chapter 11 that our bodies can experience a global feeling of arousal without our understanding what is going on. An example relevant to this chapter is that people can misattribute arousal from one source (e.g., exercise or fear) as sexual attraction to someone nearby. Psychologists at the University of British Columbia showed how men's fear of an unsteady suspension bridge could transfer into feelings of attraction for a female interviewer (Dutton & Aron, 1974). As young men finished walking across two kinds of bridges in a Vancouver mountain park, they were interviewed by an attractive young woman. The men were more likely to ask the interviewer for a date if they had just walked across the fear-arousing suspension bridge than if they had just walked across a small nonthreatening bridge. This same effect was recently shown by measuring attraction to a female interviewer just after men had experienced a scary ride at the fair (Meston & Frolich, 2003). Think about how similar misinterpretations of your feelings could occur if you met someone in an exciting location; for example, a loud, crowded bar with flashing lights.

CRITICAL THINKING

Does it really matter how relationships begin (e.g., based on arousal misattribution versus similarity of interests)?

The Psychology of Romantic Love

When psychologists study a topic, such as *interpersonal attraction*, it's likely to be seen as an interesting and important research endeavour by most casual observers. But when psychologists turn to the study of love, as you might imagine, the reactions are often more skeptical. How, you ask, can someone understand, define, or attempt to measure something like love? Love is a topic to be tackled by the poet or the artist, not the questionnaire-bearing social psychologist. Perhaps. But that hasn't stopped psychologists from trying.

Defining Love   Psychologists recognize that love is a complex emotion that can be expressed in many ways. There is the love that exists between parent and child, between lovers, between husband and wife, even between friends. In each case, when it's measured through a questionnaire, the relationship is typically characterized by the giving and receiving of support, mutual understanding, and intense personal satisfaction, according to University of Winnipeg social psychologist Beverley Fehr and her colleagues (Fehr & Russell, 1991; Sternberg & Grajek, 1984). Although fundamental similarities may exist in how love is experienced, the amount of love that is reported depends on the type of relationship studied. Women, for example, often report loving their lover more than a best friend, but liking their best friend more; men, on the other hand, report liking and loving their lover more than they report these feelings for their friends (Sternberg, 1986).

When the relationship between two individuals is romantic, it is possible to distinguish further between passionate love and companionate love. **Passionate love** is an intense emotional state in which the individual is enveloped by a powerful longing to be with the other person (Hatfield, 1988). For many people, passionate love resembles a ride on a kind of emotional roller coaster—they experience intense joy if the feelings are reciprocated and intense pain and despair if their feelings are unrequited. **Companionate love** is less emotional and intense, but its feelings of trust and warmth can be more enduring. Whereas passionate love leads to intense arousal, companionate love leads to self-disclosure—we are willing to reveal our innermost secrets because the relationship sits on a bedrock of trust. It is, of course, possible for both passionate love and companionate love to be present in the same relationship, but this is not always the case.

The Triangular View of Love   Psychologist Robert Sternberg (1986, 1988a) has argued for what he calls a triangular view of love. He sees love as triangular because it comprises three major dimensions—*intimacy*, *passion*, and *commitment*—that vary in relation to one another (see ▸ Figure 13.9 on page 552). Intimacy is the

passionate love

An intense emotional state characterized by a powerful longing to be with a specific person; marked by a combination of intimacy and passion, but commitment may be lacking

companionate love

A kind of emotional attachment characterized by feelings of trust and companionship; marked by a combination of intimacy and commitment, but passion may be lacking

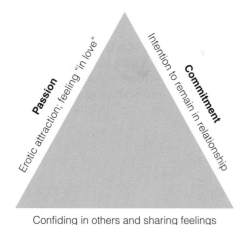

Confiding in others and sharing feelings

Intimacy

Passion	Intimacy	Commitment	Type of Love That Results
+	−	−	Infatuated love
−	+	−	Liking (friendship)
−	−	+	Empty love
+	+	−	Romantic love
−	+	+	Companionate love
+	−	+	Fatuous love

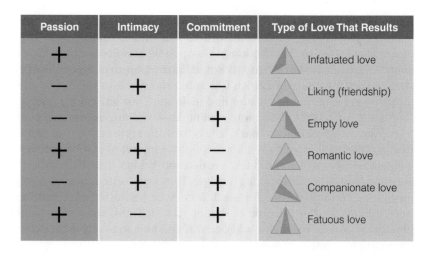

▶ **Figure 13.9**

The Triangular View of Love

Robert Sternberg has proposed that many kinds of love exist, each defined by the degree of *passion, intimacy,* and *commitment* present in the relationship. For example, infatuation is a kind of love with lots of passion but little intimacy or commitment, whereas empty love has commitment but little passion or intimacy. (Based on Sternberg, 1986.)

CRITICAL THINKING

If you had to write a recipe for a successful marriage, what priority would you give to the three dimensions of Sternberg's triangle?

emotional component that brings closeness, connectedness, and warmth to a relationship. Passion is the motivational component that underlies arousal, physical attraction, and sexual behaviour. Commitment is the decision-making arm of love: How willing are the partners to stick with the relationship in times of trouble? All forms of love can be seen as some combination of these three components. For example, according to Sternberg (1986), *romantic love* is marked by a combination of intimacy and passion (but it may lack the commitment); *companionate love* is high in intimacy and commitment (but without passion); and *empty love* occurs when there is commitment but little or no passion or intimacy. Sternberg has suggested the term *consummate love* for the love relationship in which passion, intimacy, and commitment are all present. Although many people might find this the "ideal" kind of love, we should note that people do differ in their preferences for ideal love arrangements and that forms of love relationships other than consummate love are quite satisfying for many people.

In addition to using his triangle as a vehicle for defining love, Sternberg has followed other researchers in attempting to map out how the components of love change over time (see Berscheid, 1985; Hatfield & Rapson, 1993). What patterns have been found? Do couples gain intimacy? Lose passion? Become increasingly willing to commit? It is impossible to predict for any particular relationship, but the theory proposes some general trends. On average, for example, the passion component of love builds early and rapidly in a relationship—it can even be experienced almost immediately on meeting another—but it's difficult to sustain for long periods. Commitment, conversely, is slow to develop but can be quite long lasting. Intimacy, too, is unlikely to be found early in a relationship (there is too much uncertainty), but it grows and maintains itself in most successful relationships. Therefore, the components of love are conceived as fluid, changing over time in ways that reflect the developmental trajectory of the couple and their changing circumstances.

Predicting the Longevity of Love Relationships Predicting whether a specific love relationship will last or not is a topic of interest to most people, particularly those embarking on such a relationship. Researchers Tara MacDonald of Queen's University and Michael Ross of the University of Waterloo examined this question in a study that focused on first-year undergraduates at the University of Waterloo who were in dating relationships that had lasted at least one month but less than a year at the time of the study (MacDonald & Ross, 1999). The students, their roommates, and their friends were all asked questions about these relationships, including questions assessing relationship quality (e.g., How satisfied are they with the relationship? How serious is it?) and predictions about the relationship (e.g., What is the likelihood that the relationship will last beyond six months? two years? five years? What is the likelihood that the couple will marry? How likely is it that the relationship will last a lifetime?).

MacDonald and Ross (1999) found, surprisingly, that the roommates were better at predicting the longevity of the relationship at six months and one year after the original predictions than the lovers themselves. Intriguingly, the students' original *ratings of the quality of the relationship* correlated more highly with the outcome of the relationship than did the students' *predictions* about the relationship. That is, relationships that were rated by the participants as higher quality (e.g., more satisfying, more serious) tended to last compared with those rated as less serious, less satisfying. But evidently, the lovers did not attend very much to those factors in making their predictions about the relationships. MacDonald and Ross suggest that the students' predictions may have reflected their hopes for the relationships to continue, rather than an objective evaluation of that likelihood, and that people in the early stages of love relationships may engage in "tunnel vision" and ignore evidence of current relationship problems when asked to predict the future of the relationship. The researchers conclude by suggesting that to get a more realistic view of what the future holds, lovers should focus more on the quality of the current relationship, rather than being overly sentimental about the prospect of relationship problems improving in the future. And they should pay attention to what their roommates and parents predict; these observers are evidently not as swayed by the "longing in their hearts" that lovers feel and can therefore be a little more accurate in predicting the course of true love.

Aggression

Social psychologists also study the dark side of human behaviour. Of all the negative events documented in daily newspapers, most disturbing are the widespread examples of humans purposefully harming others. We will use the term **aggression** for behaviour meant to harm someone. Its manifestation in wars between democratic countries has shown some decline over the last century. But aggression within such modern societies as Canada, Britain, and the United States has not shown any clear reduction. High levels of violent aggression are documented in crime statistics, but aggression is also prominent in sports and driving styles; nonphysical aggression is encouraged in business, science, and even everyday interpersonal interactions.

aggression

Behaviour meant to harm someone

News events highlight the fact that aggression appears in all societies—sometimes when we least expect it. One of the most well-known examples is the case of the shootings at Columbine High School in Littleton, Colorado, in 1999. Two intelligent White children of middle-class parents massacred 13 of their schoolmates and then committed suicide, bringing the death toll to 15. But such outbursts are restricted to the violence-prone American society. Right?

Hardly. Similar incidents have since taken place in Canada, Australia, Germany, and Scotland. One particularly disturbing example took place near Victoria, British Columbia, in 1997. A group of mostly White, middle-class teenagers—all female except one—swarmed and murdered another teenage girl. They burned her with cigarettes and set her hair on fire, apparently over a boyfriend jealousy issue. So much for the claim that poverty and disadvantaged ethnicity are necessary conditions for violence. In the continuing case of the missing Eastside Vancouver women, close to 50 women were murdered without the benefit of firearms. So much for the argument that guns are necessary for the perpetration of serial murder. Although often rated as the best country in the world to live in, Canada nonetheless has a serious violence problem. There have even been a number of serious street riots over sporting events, once when a team won the Stanley Cup (Montreal) and once when they lost it (Vancouver).

Can it be that humans are not the civilized species that we claim to be? In fact, our species shows the highest rate of within-species murder (Lorenz, 1966). Even harder to explain is why human beings often enjoy seeing others get hurt. People seem to be highly entertained by watching violent sports, films, television, video games, and car crashes.

The possible psychological explanations of aggression map onto the various theories of personality outlined in Chapter 12. To Freud, aggression is a natural component of human nature tied to the death instinct. In strict learning theories, aggression is learned by receiving repeated rewards for aggressive behaviour (Skinner, 1938). In cognitive-behavioural theories, aggression is learned by observing others behaving aggressively (e.g., Bandura, Ross, & Ross, 1963). Evolutionary theories explain that aggression was an adaptive behaviour—especially for males—that was selected into our gene pool because it led to successful reproduction (Daly & Wilson, 1983). In contrast, humanistic psychologists argue that aggression results from society's perversion of the naturally good selves that we are born with. These traditional theories have guided a variety of attempts to reduce aggression but none has been entirely successful at changing human nature.

What factors seem to promote aggression? Aggression has clear links with sociological variables, that is, the ways in which contemporary society is organized. These include such demographic factors as being poor, being male, and being between 16 and 30 years of age. In conjunction with testosterone, a biological factor, high status in a group has also been linked to aggression (Sellers, Mehl, & Josephs, in press). But violence often occurs without any of these factors.

Neither can these variables explain the psychological processes involved in aggression. In this chapter, we have already dealt with two examples, namely, the aggression encouraged by authority figures and deindividuation, the reduction in individuality and personal responsibility that occurs when people are in groups, especially mobs. More generally, aggression occurs when people are frustrated or otherwise provoked by insults, hot temperatures, or spousal abuse. As noted in Chapter 6, the evidence is becoming clearer that violence in films and on television provides modelling that promotes aggression (Anderson et al., 2003).

Gender Differences   Research has firmly established sex differences in aggression but they are more complex than we might expect. Physical aggression is certainly higher in males but, in some studies, verbal aggression is higher in females (e.g., Eagly & Steffen, 1986). By verbal aggression, these studies are usually referring to such behaviours as purposely spreading false rumours about someone you dislike. Of course, physical aggression is a greater concern—especially the male tendency toward murder (Buss, 2005). Greater physical aggression in males is consistent with research on sex differences in testosterone: Its effects seem to alter the brain structure as well as physical appearance of the developing fetus (Dabbs, 2000; Halpern, 1989; Mazur & Booth, 1998).

According to Taylor and her colleagues, it is not adaptive for females to react to potential harm by attacking or fleeing (Taylor et al., 2000). They often lack the necessary physical power to ward off threats through aggression but cannot retreat because they have to care for the young. Their tendency to protect and calm offspring will increase the chances of offspring survival. They may have to cooperate with the adversary or, at least, attempt to maintain peace. These reactions are also reflected in longer-term strategies: Females appear more likely to develop and maintain social networks that potentially can aid in protecting themselves and their offspring (Haselton & Buss, 2000).

The proposal that males and females differ fundamentally in their behavioural reactions to threat is new and likely to be controversial—especially the idea that gender-specific reactions may be adaptations arising from evolutionary pressures. However, the evidence supporting gender differences appears across the animal kingdom and seems to have some basis in the biology of male and female brains (Kimura, 1999). As with other analyses of sex differences, it is difficult to provide definitive evidence for either nature or nurture (Taylor et al., 2000).

Test Yourself 13.3

Check your knowledge about how we establish relationships with other people by deciding whether each of the following statements is true or false. (The answers are in Appendix B.)

1. Babies, within hours of birth, show a preference for attractive over unattractive faces. *True or False?*
2. Blending studies of facial attractiveness indicate that faces that are unusual or distinct tend to receive higher ratings of attractiveness than averaged faces. *True or False?*
3. Studies have found that if you've just been shown a picture of a strikingly attractive person, your ratings of an average-looking person go up. *True or False?*
4. Friends and intimate partners typically resemble one another in age, social status, education level, race, religious beliefs, political attitudes, intelligence, and even physical attractiveness. *True or False?*
5. According to the triangular theory of love, infatuated love represents passion without intimacy or commitment. *True or False?*
6. Passionate love typically leads to more feelings of warmth and trust than does companionate love. *True or False?*
7. "Tend and befriend" is a notion more associated with females than males. *True or False?*

Social Psychology

R E V I E W

The human tendency to affiliate with others and live in larger and larger groups has raised a variety of problems for our species. Our actions, thoughts, and feelings arise out of the necessity to deal with ever-changing and more demanding social environments. In this chapter we tackled the topic areas of social psychology from the perspective of three major adaptive problems.

First, how do we think about the social world? As we move through the social world, we try to make sense of the people around us. We form initial impressions of others and must make decisions on that basis. In fact, we have to make important decisions about an impossibly complex world, sometimes in a split second. Such a feat can only be accomplished by economic cognitive shortcuts called schemas. In general, they serve us well, but schemas can also have maladaptive consequences, such as stereotypes, prejudice, and discrimination.

We must also go beyond superficial facts about people to form mini-theories called attributions. These inferences about the causes of behaviour allow us to understand other people. For example, the use of a single behaviour to make a trait attribution about person X is a theory predicting that X will act similarly in the future. Such attributions are often quite rational, based on an overall assessment of how certain factors—consistency, distinctiveness, and consensus—covary with the behaviour: The attributions we draw then permit us to make logical decisions. However, we also show basic attribution biases—such as the fundamental attribution error. Although they appear irrational, overall, attributions are more beneficial than harmful.

It is useful for us to have summary evaluations of certain people, situations, and other entities in our social world. These attitudes include cognitive, affective, and behavioural components. Each one is helpful in guiding our tendency to approach some people and avoid others. At the same time, we are gifted with the ability to change our attitudes when important new information is collected.

In short, our thought processes are adaptive in allowing us to organize our social world in a way that allows us to make decisions and predict the future. Although these processes can lead to errors, they are generally adaptive in allowing us to make quick decisions that are largely rational.

Second, how does our behaviour adapt to the presence of others? We are affected by the presence of other people in our environment— sometimes for the better, as in social facilitation, and sometimes for the worse, as in social interference. The presence of other people can have an arousing effect, which magnifies our tendency to give our dominant response. Given that arousal is an indicator of stress or threat, it is adaptive to revert to our usual simple response rather than a more complex and, therefore, slower response. The presence of other people also seems to reduce our willingness to help people in need. This bystander effect seems to harm victims but it may simply be a logical deduction that, when others are around, our help is not as urgently needed. Instead, we should act out of self-interest and carry on with our own lives.

Our behaviour is also guided in certain directions by the powerful social pressures of groups and authority figures. In general, we tend to conform to what others around us do and obey our authorities, whether they be parents, teachers, police, doctors, or religious leaders. These tendencies to conform and obey are adaptive in maintaining solidarity of the groups to which we belong as well as stabilizing the larger culture. The tendency for group decisions to polarize also helps to maximize consensus in group decisions. The downside of obedience to authority, as in Milgram's famous experiment, is the surprising power of such pressure. Because our groups and authorities do not always make ideal decisions, it is fortunate that their pressures can be overcome by some of the people some of the time.

Third, how do we establish relationships and when are they adaptive? The human tendency to develop relations with specific others is essential to human adaptation. We have to get along in pairs as well as in larger groups. Obviously, the processes that guide attraction and romantic love are essential to initiating reproduction. But so is commitment to romantic partners and friends and co-workers who populate our larger social world. These processes are adaptive from a cultural perspective and from an evolutionary perspective.

The dark side of relationships, namely aggression, may have had adaptive value to our ancestors. Although it has little adaptive value today, it remains in all human societies. Such mismatches between our ancestral environment and our contemporary environment may explain some of our most difficult social problems.

The adaptive significance of social psychological processes can be viewed either in evolutionary or cultural terms. The fact that some social behaviour is observed across cultures may suggest a genetic commonality of our species or simply a norm that evolved in all cultures because it works.

CHAPTER SUMMARY

▶ Thinking about the Social World: Social Cognition

As social animals, we're constantly trying to interpret the behaviour of other people. We form impressions of people we encounter, devise theories about why they behave the way they do, and maintain attitudes about them. The interpretation processes we use to make these judgments have systematic biases.

Person Perception: How Do We Form Impressions of Others?

Our perception of people is guided by *bottom-up processing* (actual physical sensations) and *top-down processing* (our expectations and beliefs). Physical appearance is a powerful determinant of a first impression. Physically attractive individuals are perceived as superior on a variety of dimensions. *Social schemas*, our schemas about social experiences and people (e.g., *stereotypes*), exert a strong influence on our perception of others. An example is the *self-fulfilling prophecy effect*, in which we expect certain kinds of behaviour from members of groups, and these expectations can cause the person to behave in the expected fashion. Stereotypes can also increase the likelihood of *prejudice* and discriminatory behaviour. People tend to show preferences for their *in-group* and are more likely to display prejudice against *out-groups*. Prejudice can be reduced through repeated exposure to individuals in the stereotyped group. People in groups that are discriminated against tend to deny experiencing discrimination themselves but agree that the group as a whole is discriminated against. *Auto-stereotyping* refers to a belief system about discrimination that is widely shared by group members, while *meta-stereotyping* refers to a person's beliefs regarding the stereotype that out-group members hold about his or her own group.

Attribution Theory: Attributing Causes to Behaviours

The *covariation model* assumes that we look for some factor that covaries with the behaviour we're judging. In addition, we rely on *consistency*, *distinctiveness*, and *consensus* to make the appropriate inference. We tend to make *external attributions* (appealing to external causes) when a behaviour is high on these three dimensions; we tend to make *internal attributions* (appealing to internal personality traits) when a behaviour is high in consistency but low in consensus and distinctiveness. The *fundamental attribution error* refers to our tendency to overestimate the role of internal factors and underestimate the role of external factors. The *actor-observer effect* is the tendency to make internal attributions for others' behaviour and external attributions for our own. The *self-serving bias* refers to our tendency to take internal credit for actions that produce positive outcomes and to blame the situation when behaviours lead to failure. Evolutionary researchers have suggested that natural selection may have shaped human minds to systematically misrepresent and oversimplify social phenomena because such distortions may have been adaptive for humans during our evolutionary history.

Attitudes and How They Change

Attitudes are positive or negative beliefs we hold about something and include a *cognitive*, *affective*, and *behavioural* component. The behavioural component is a predisposition to act; attitudes do not always directly affect behaviour. Attitudes are formed primarily through experience, through the mechanisms of classical conditioning, instrumental conditioning, and observational learning. Attitudes can be changed in several ways. The *elaboration likelihood model* suggests that two primary routes to persuasion exist: the central route and the peripheral route. According to *cognitive dissonance theory*, inconsistency between behaviour and attitudes results in tension that may be relieved through attitude change. *Self-perception theory* states that we use our own actions as the basis for beliefs about ourselves. The *foot-in-the-door technique* provides support.

▶ Behaving in the Presence of Others: Social Influence

Everyone's behaviour is strongly influenced by the social context. The ability to perform a task might improve or fall apart in the presence of others. How we act is also profoundly influenced by the presence of authority figures and by the opinions of fellow members in a group.

Social Facilitation and Interference

Social facilitation is an enhancement in performance sometimes found when we perform in the presence of others. *Social interference* occurs when performing in front of a crowd impairs performance. Task difficulty helps determine when the presence of others will help or hinder performance. When a task is easy, social facilitation is likely; when it's difficult, social interference is likely.

Social Influences on Helping: The Bystander Effect

The presence of others can affect *helping*, whether we will act in a way that shows unselfish concern for others. The reluctance to come to someone's aid when others are present is termed the *bystander effect*. The presence of others leads to a *diffusion of responsibility*; we believe that others have already done something to help.

The Power of the Group

People have a tendency toward *social loafing*, putting out less effort when working with a group than when working alone. *Deindividuation* occurs when we feel less accountable in the presence of others than when we're on our own. *Conformity* occurs when a person's opinions, feelings, or behaviours move toward the group norm and is especially likely when the pressure is coming from an *in-group*.

Group Decision Making

When the dominant point of view within a group becomes stronger and more extreme with time, *group polarization* has occurred. When group members become so interested in achieving consensus that they ignore and even suppress dissenting views, *groupthink* has taken over.

The Power of Authority: Obedience

Obedience refers to following the orders of an authority figure. The Milgram experiment found that a surprisingly high proportion (65%) of research participants were willing to follow an experimenter's orders to deliver shocks, despite pleas from the participant. Milgram's study has been criticized on ethical grounds as well as for the general procedures used.

▶ Relationships with Others: Positive and Negative

Among our most important social actions are the relationships that we share with others. It's unlikely that the human species would survive without attraction and romantic love. In addition, we rely on our relationships within the family as well as on the social structures in society to help protect and nurture us. At the same time, the worst of human behaviour can be seen in aggression and hostility toward others.

What Makes a Face Attractive?

An evolutionary perspective on physical attractiveness predicts that we will be attracted to opposite-sex members who are youthful, vigorous, and healthy looking. Also, features of attractiveness should cut across cultural boundaries. The evolutionary view has some research support. The universality of attractiveness may be due to the fact that we seem programmed to prefer faces that are average representations of faces in a population. Our perception of beauty also has a strong socialized component.

Determinants of Liking and Loving

The environment plays a major role in determining interpersonal attraction. Attraction to others is determined by others' *familiarity*, *similarity*, *proximity*, *ingratiation*, and *reciprocity*, our tendency to return in kind the feelings that are shown toward us. We can also misinterpret arousal from other sources as evidence for attraction to someone.

The Psychology of Romantic Love

Love is a complex emotion that can be expressed in a variety of forms. *Passionate love* is an intense emotional state in which the individual is enveloped by a powerful longing to be with the other person. *Companionate love* tends to be less intense and is characterized by trust and warmth. According to the *triangular theory*, love comprises three major dimensions: *intimacy, passion,* and *commitment.* These components are fluid, changing over time.

Aggression

Aggression (behaviour meant to harm someone) remains at high levels in crime statistics, but it is also widespread in business, sports, driving styles, and even interpersonal interactions. In modern societies, links exist between rates of aggression and sociological factors, but there remains much that we don't understand about the psychology of aggression. Although aggression now seems to be uniformly harmful to society, its roots in evolutionary psychology suggest that the capability to be aggressive has been adaptive and the greater physical aggression among males is predictable.

Terms to Remember

Recommended Readings

Altemeyer, B. (1996). *The authoritarian specter.* Cambridge, MA: Harvard University Press. Based on years of research into the authoritarian personality by University of Manitoba psychologist Bob Altemeyer, this book explores the origins and development of authoritarian attitudes and the social problems related to these attitudes.

Gladwell, M. (2005). *Blink.* New York: Little-Brown. Although not a trained psychologist, Malcolm Gladwell presents psychological research in a delightfully clear and entertaining fashion.

Simpson, J. A., & Kenrick, D. T. (1997). *Evolutionary social psychology.* Mahwah, NJ: Erlbaum. The evolutionary bases of social phenomena, such as social perception, attraction, and mating; includes articles on social illusions and self-deception by Simon Fraser University psychologists Dennis Krebs and Kathy Denton, and on kinship by McMaster University evolutionary psychologists Martin Daly, Catherine Salmon, and Margo Wilson.

 For additional readings, explore InfoTrac® College Edition, your online library. Go to http://www.adaptivemind3e.nelson.com.

Hint: Enter these search terms: social cognition, stereotypes, persuasion and attitude change, conformity, interpersonal attraction, romantic love.

Media Resources

 What's on the Web?

Please note that Web addresses are subject to change. Check out the accompanying website for updates: http://www.adaptivemind3e.nelson.com.

This site presents practice quiz questions, hypercontent, information on degrees and careers in psychology, study tips, and more.

Descriptions of the Nine Largest Canadian University Social Psychology Programs

University of British Columbia
http://www.psych.ubc.ca/research.psy?lab=Social%20Personality

University of Calgary
http://www.psych.ucalgary.ca/Social/StrategicMission.html

University of Manitoba
http://umanitoba.ca/faculties/arts/psychology/grad/programs/social.php

McGill University
http://www.psych.mcgill.ca/grad/resar.htm#s

University of Waterloo
http://www.psychology.uwaterloo.ca/gradprog/programs/phd/social/index.html

Simon Fraser University
http://www.psyc.sfu.ca/index.php?topic=social

University of Saskatchewan
http://www.usask.ca/psychology/programs/applied_social/index.htm

University of Toronto
http://www.psych.utoronto.ca/grad/social.htm

York University
http://www.psych.yorku.ca/sp

Social Psychology Network

http://www.socialpsychology.org

This is *the* website for social psychology. It's a clearing-house with a tremendous amount of information about social psychology, including areas of study within social psychology, Ph.D. programs in social psychology, and even online experiments that allow you to take part in actual online research. The links to research include student projects on interpersonal relations, social perception, and judgment and decision making.

The Influence at Work Website

http://www.influenceatwork.com

This website is devoted to the psychology of persuasion and contains a wealth of information about the dynamics of social influence and how it is implemented in everyday settings. There's even a test to measure your "influence quotient." Cruise to this site to find out how influence relates to courtrooms, cults, Aristotle, and George W. Bush.

ThomsonNOW™ ThomsonNOW™

http://hed.nelson.com

Go to this site for the link to ThomsonNOW™, your one-stop study shop. Take a Pretest for this chapter and ThomsonNOW™ will generate a personalized Study Plan based on your test results. The Study Plan will identify the topics you need to review and direct you to online resources to help you master those topics. You can then take a Posttest to determine what concepts you have mastered and what you still need work on.

Psyk.trek 3.0

Check out Psyk.trek 3.0 for further study of the concepts in this chapter. Psyk.trek's 65 interactive learning modules, simulations, and quizzes offer additional opportunities for you to interact with, reflect on, and retain the material:

Social Psychology: Attribution Processes
Social Psychology: Attitude Change
Social Psychology: Theories of Love
Social Psychology: Conformity and Obedience

Though this be madness, yet there be method in it.

—William Shakespeare, *Hamlet*

Psychological Disorders

O ver the next two chapters, we turn our attention to the classification and treatment of psychological disorders. They are thought to be the underlying mental problems responsible for abnormal behaviour. But defining abnormality turns out to be more difficult than you might think. Let's suppose you arrive home tonight and find your roommate slumped in a corner with his cap pulled down over his eyes. You ask him to explain, but he tells you to "mind your own business." Later that night, you hear sobbing and crying coming from behind his locked bedroom door. He has never acted this way before and it continues for days. He refuses to respond to questions, he stops going to class, and he refuses to eat or clean himself. He's been hit with some psychological illness, right? Perhaps, but what if we tell you that his father and mother were just killed in an automobile accident? What would your reaction be now? You might well change your mind and conclude that he's showing an intense but totally normal grief reaction.

Psychological Disorders

In the psychological literature, various terms, such as insanity, abnormal behaviour, mental illness, and psychopathology, all seem to be used more or less equivalently. In this chapter, we will try to be more specific and, therefore, more clear. Here's a quick guide. *Abnormal behaviour* refers to an observed problem behaviour, whereas the term *psychological disorder* refers to the underlying psychological problem. The more general terms *mental illness* and *psychopathology* often refer to both the abnormal behaviours and the disorders. Finally, the term *insanity* is reserved for criminal situations, and officially only in the United States; therefore, it will be covered very briefly. The terms *abnormal behaviour* and *psychological disorder* are key to both this chapter and the next.

Throughout this book, our theme has been that the mind generally operates in an adaptive fashion. In this chapter, however, our concern is with the most maladaptive of human states and traits. We will consider the possibility that these states and traits are simply good features taken to a maladaptive extreme. As it turns out, very few disorders have any possible adaptive explanation.

So, instead of focusing on adaptive interpretations, we organize this chapter as a scientific problem to be solved. How can we best define and organize this field of psychology? To answer this question, we break it down into three more basic questions: What is the proper way to conceptualize abnormal behaviour? How can the underlying disorders best be organized to reveal their similarities and differences? Finally, what are the environmental and biological origins of disorders?

First, how should we conceptualize abnormal behaviour? As you will see, defining the term **abnormal behaviour** has proved to be more difficult than you might expect. Despite a long history of attempts, even psychologists have had difficulty with this term. Among the approaches to be covered are statistical deviance, cultural deviance, dysfunction, and emotional distress. In contrast, the term **psychological disorder** refers to the underlying psychological problem that is assumed to be responsible for the abnormal behaviour.

Second, how do we classify psychological disorders? We will cover a wide variety of psychological disorders (e.g., depression, schizophrenia, psychopathy), many of which overlap in terms of their symptoms. Therefore, it is essential that health professionals, including psychologists and psychiatrists, have a recognized set of terms and diagnoses. We will cover this "bible" of disorders—the *Diagnostic and Statistical Manual of Mental Disorders*—in detail. It provides the most up-to-date labels and criteria for diagnosing disorders on the basis of specific symptoms.

Third, what are the root causes of disorders? What causes depression, schizophrenia, or a snake phobia? Is the cause biological or environmental? When someone has a prolonged depression, for example, is it because of a problem with brain chemistry? Or has the person learned to act in depressed ways either through modelling the behaviour of others or because acting depressed has received some reinforcement?

The answers to such questions are important in advancing our basic understanding of psychological disorders. We will consider the standard theoretical approaches that you have become familiar with (e.g., psychoanalysis, learning, trait theory). Each has something to say about the origins of disorders and possible therapies. Not surprisingly, the answer to many psychological problems lies in an interaction among biological, cognitive, and environmental factors.

---

abnormal behaviour

An observed behaviour that is unusual, maladaptive, socially deviant, or accompanied by continuing distress

---

psychological disorder

A specific psychological problem that causes abnormal behaviour to occur

---

▶ Conceptualizing Abnormal Behaviour

LEARNING GOALS

1. Understand and evaluate the various criteria that have been proposed to define abnormality.
2. Understand how the medical and sociological models view disorders.

If you meet someone in the street who babbles about voices in his head that are warning about a Klingon invasion, you would likely categorize this behaviour as abnormal. Clearly, this person is in trouble and in need of some professional help.

But as you've seen, sharp dividing lines don't always exist between normal and abnormal behaviour. Sometimes behaviour that appears abnormal can turn out to have a reasonable explanation, for example, the roommate's reaction to the death of his parents. And the Klingon example above is a standard plot in science fiction stories: Someone babbling a nonsensical story turns out to be telling the truth but no one will listen. To paraphrase comedian Woody Allen, even paranoids are sometimes right. And a depressed person might well say, "If you knew what was going on in the world today, you'd be depressed too!"

It's certainly true that a behaviour that seems abnormal in one culture can appear to be perfectly normal in another (Castillo, 1997; Marsella & Yamada, 2000). Entering a trance state and experiencing visual hallucinations are considered abnormal in Western cultures, but in other cultures they may not be (Bentall, 1990). Even within a culture, conceptions of abnormality can change over time. For many years homosexuality was considered deviant and abnormal by the psychological community. This view is rejected by most psychologists today. Fifty years ago, a strong dependence on tobacco would not have raised many eyebrows, but today if you're hooked on tobacco you're likely to be classified as having a substance-related disorder by many professionals (see Chapter 16). As times change, so do conceptions of what are appropriate and inappropriate actions. For these reasons, psychologists are justifiably cautious when it comes to applying the label of abnormality. Many professionals try to stick to clear behavioural criteria so that the diagnosis can be reliably communicated to other professionals (Widiger & Sankis, 2000).

The extreme version of this critique goes so far as to argue that the term *abnormality* is purely in the mind of the beholder and that mental illness does not really exist outside of our arbitrary societal biases (e.g., Szasz, 1961, 1990). Indeed, evidence suggests that once an authority labels someone as abnormal, people interpret any behaviour as being more evidence for that abnormality (Rosenhan, 1973). Of course, it would be irresponsible for us to ignore such unusual behaviours as those exhibited in the above examples of your roommate and Mr. Klingon: If such individuals do indeed have a psychological disorder, they can be dangerous to themselves and others.

Psychological distress is a normal reaction to a negative event. But how long and severe must the distress be for it to be called abnormal?

Criteria for Defining Abnormal Behaviour

We could just give up on the idea of defining abnormal behaviour. Instead, let's consider a number of attempts that have to be taken seriously. In each of the four approaches, as you'll see, the proposed criteria capture some but not all of the important features of what is agreed to be abnormal behaviour.

Statistical Deviance One way to define abnormal behaviour is in terms of **statistical deviance,** or infrequency. Any given behaviour, such as talking to yourself out loud, has a small probability of occurring in society at large. Most people have talked to themselves at one time or another, but few have actually had excited conversation with a cabbage. According to the concept of statistical deviance, a behaviour is abnormal if it occurs infrequently among the members of a population. As you've learned elsewhere in this text, it's not unusual for psychologists to classify behaviour on the basis of statistical frequency. For example, such terms as *gifted* and *mentally retarded* are defined with respect to statistical frequencies. So it should come as no surprise that statistical frequencies have been used to define abnormality.

But statistical deviance cannot be used as the sole criterion for labelling a behaviour as abnormal. It's easy to come up with a list of behaviours or abilities that are statistically infrequent but are not abnormal in a psychological sense. For example, Tiger Woods and Sidney Crosby have athletic skills that are extreme, and thereby statistically deviant, but being a great athlete does not make someone

statistical deviance criterion

A criterion for abnormality based on a low frequency of occurrence among the members of a population

Entering a trance state is likely to be classified as "abnormal behaviour" in Western cultures, but in other cultures it may not be.

abnormal. Similarly, only a handful of individuals have reached the intellectual heights of Albert Einstein or Isaac Newton, but superior intelligence is not abnormal in the usual psychological sense of the word. Even restricting the definition to extremely bad or poor performance seems to include far too many people. You might claim to be the world's worst singer or hockey player, but that won't convince your instructor to give you more exam time because you are "abnormal." An additional problem is the establishment of a cut-off point: Just how infrequent or unusual does a behaviour need to be, to be characterized as abnormal? 1 percent of the population? 10 percent? The statistical deviance approach cannot provide a satisfactory answer to such questions.

cultural deviance criterion

Behaviour is abnormal if it violates the rules or accepted standards of society

Cultural Deviance   Another criterion is **cultural deviance,** which compares behaviour with existing cultural norms. In this case, a behaviour would be considered abnormal if it violates the accepted standards of society. In most cultures, for example, it is not considered normal or acceptable to go to church naked or to defecate in a classroom. These behaviours break the established rules of our culture, and if you engage in either, it's likely that people will think you have a serious problem.

But once again, cultural deviance by itself fails as a sufficient criterion. Some people—especially university students—purposely engage in behaviour that is countercultural and anti-authority. But it seems clear that their motivation is to express their values and identity as free thinkers: Rarely is such behaviour indicative of a psychological disorder. And many criminals violate the established norms of society—stealing cars or embezzling money, for example. Such behaviour might be abnormal by both statistical and cultural standards, but that doesn't mean all criminals have psychological disorders. As noted above, behaviours that are abnormal in one culture may be considered normal in another. In some cultures public nakedness is totally acceptable, and in others women have to cover everything but their eyes. Views of deviance also change over time in the same society. Twenty years ago, the idea of body piercings (other than earrings) was considered repulsive; today, it is common. Finally, there are exceptions of the opposite sort: Many people who have psychological problems—those with depression, for example—rarely violate laws or act in culturally deviant ways.

John Felstead/CP Picture Archive

© Nancy Kaszerman/ZUMA/Corbis

The late Kenneth Thomson (Canada's richest person until his death in June 2006, with an estimated worth of $19.6 billion) and actor Pamela Anderson are statistically deviant in some respects, but does that mean they would necessarily be categorized as abnormal in a psychological sense?

Emotional Distress   A third criterion for labelling someone's behaviour as abnormal is the presence of **emotional distress.** People who have psychological disorders often experience great despair and unhappiness. They feel hopeless, lost, out of control, and alienated from others. In fact, it is the emotional distress that usually leads them to seek professional help for their problems. But not all disorders make people unhappy. There are people, for example, who have little contact with reality but seem perfectly content in their fantasy world. Others, as you will see, show no distress because they have a dangerous lack of any emotions. Conversely, there are many distressed people in the world—for example, those who have recently lost a loved one or a job—who would not be classified as abnormal by the psychological community.

emotional distress criterion

Behaviour is abnormal if it regularly leads to personal distress or emotional upset

Dysfunction   A final criterion for abnormality considers the general adaptiveness of the individual's behaviour. Is there a breakdown in normal functioning— a **dysfunction**—that prevents the person from functioning successfully in typical daily activities? They may not be able to eat properly, clean themselves, buy groceries, or hold a job. They may have such an impairment in thinking and judgment that it affects their ability to adapt successfully to minor changes in their environment. As you'll see later, the assessment of global functioning—defined as the ability to adapt in social, personal, and occupational environments—plays a large role in the diagnosis and treatment of psychological disorders.

dysfunction criterion

Behaviour is abnormal if it interferes with the ability to pursue daily activities, such as work and relationships

Summarizing the Criteria   You've seen that abnormal behaviour can be defined in terms of statistical or cultural deviance, personal or emotional distress, or dysfunction. Normal behaviour, then, could be any behaviour that is relatively common, is socially acceptable, does not cause personal distress, or generally leads to adaptive consequences.

None of these four criteria seems to be foolproof by itself. Psychologists will usually refuse to label any behaviour as normal or abnormal unless it satisfies several of these criteria rather than just one. Among those four elements, psychologists would place the most emphasis on how distressed the patient is and how well they can function on their own.

As in our introductory story, crying hysterically for hours at a time may be a normal grief reaction, or it may signal a serious disorder. Even a behaviour that seems to be clearly abnormal—such as a paranoid delusion that people are out to get you—might be adaptive in some environments.

CRITICAL THINKING

Suppose a 70-year-old entered university and started acting exactly the same way as an 18-year-old first-year student. Would you consider his or her behaviour to be abnormal?

CONCEPT SUMMARY

CRITERIA FOR DEFINING ABNORMALITY

Criterion	Description	Example
Statistical deviance	Behaviour that occurs infrequently among the members of a population	Jon goes back to make sure his front door is locked exactly 12 times each morning. As he walks to the door, he mutters over and over, "Lock the door." No one else in the neighbourhood does this.
Cultural deviance	Behaviour that violates the accepted standards of society	Jon notices that each time he comes back to his front door, talking to himself, his neighbours look at him rather nervously and tend to avoid him at other times.
Emotional distress	Experiencing great despair and unhappiness	Jon is very distressed by his compulsive behaviour.
Dysfunction	A breakdown in normal everyday functioning	Jon's routine of checking his front door 12 times every morning has made him late for work a number of times, and his job is in jeopardy.

Even when the criteria are clear, psychologists warn against our natural tendencies to categorize people as "abnormal" and "normal." Each of us can relate in one way or another to the criteria of abnormality we've just discussed. We all know people who have occasionally acted unusually, experienced emotional distress, or failed to follow an adaptive strategy. Many psychological disorders are characterized by behaviours or feelings that are merely exaggerations of normal ones, such as anxiety, feelings of sadness, or concerns about health. Consequently, it's better to think about normal and abnormal behaviour as endpoints on a *continuum* rather than as non-overlapping categories (see ❱ Figure 14.1). (For a discussion of the legal concept of insanity, which differs from the concept of a psychological disorder, see the Practical Solutions box.)

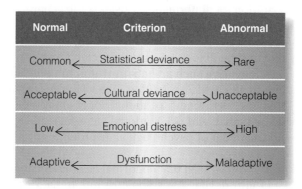

❱ **Figure 14.1**

The Normal-to-Abnormal Continuum

In this view, "abnormal" and "normal" are not fixed and rigid categories. They are better seen as endpoints on a continuum. To a certain degree, everyone has acted unusually, behaved unacceptably, experienced emotional distress, or failed to follow an adaptive strategy. Abnormality is a matter of degree, not a matter of kind.

PRACTICAL SOLUTIONS

THE INSANITY DEFENCE

As we've just discussed, it's a challenge to find a perfect scientific definition for abnormal behaviour. Nonetheless, regardless of where you travel in the world, some kinds of behaviour are always recognized as abnormal. Consider, for example, the behaviour of Chicago serial killer Jeffrey Dahmer, who admitted to butchering and having sex with the dead bodies of more than a dozen young men and boys. Then, he went on to eat selected body parts. But you may be surprised to hear that Jeffrey Dahmer was judged by a jury to be sane! In a 2002 case, Andrea Yates (see photo) drowned her five young children while trying, she believed, to follow instructions from God. She was judged to be sane in her first trial.

How is this possible? The answer lies in the fact that *insanity* is a *legal* concept rather than a *psychological* one. Legally, in

© Reuters/Corbis

From a legal standpoint, Andrea Yates was considered sane because she was judged capable of understanding the wrongfulness of her actions.

the United States, an insane person cannot be guilty. So, Yates's and Dahmer's lawyers tried to have them declared mentally unfit and, therefore, not responsible for the crimes. In both cases, however, the prosecution lawyers were successful in having them declared legally sane and, therefore, guilty.

Although the legal definition varies somewhat across U.S. jurisdictions, **insanity** is usually defined in terms of the defendant's thought processes at the time of the crime. The definition used in the American legal system is the inability to know right from wrong. Instead of the term *insanity*, Canadian law uses the phrase "not criminally responsible on account of a mental disorder."

Often this defence can be refuted by showing that the individual was acting in a rational and manipulative fashion in other respects—such as evading the police and carefully hiding the bodies. It is clear that cases of horrendous crimes put judges and juries in a difficult dilemma: The worse the crime, the more they want to hold the offender responsible, *but* the more likely the offender is actually insane. Jeffrey Dahmer was judged capable of understanding the wrongfulness of his actions; that is, the jury determined that he was fully aware of the fact that his actions were wrong. As a result, he failed the insanity test, even though he was clearly experiencing serious psychological problems.

The concept of legal insanity has generated considerable controversy over the years. But the controversy has not usually come from cases like the above in which someone with a disorder has been declared legally sane. Instead, the brunt of the concern has been over instances of acquittal—in which someone who obviously committed a crime has been judged not guilty by reason of insanity. The classic case was the landmark trial of Daniel M'Naghten back in 1843. Driven by

"voices from God," M'Naghten set out to kill the British prime minister, Sir Robert Peel, but ended up killing Peel's secretary instead. The court acquitted M'Naghten for reasons of insanity. This particular ruling was strongly criticized by the public, even though M'Naghten spent the rest of his life in a mental hospital. But it remains important because the so-called M'Naghten rule for insanity—which focuses on what the criminal understands at the time of the crime—is still the foundation for most current standards of insanity (De Jesus-Zayas, Baker, Banes, & Lozano-Blanco, 2001).

The insanity defence is not a widely used legal loophole, despite the impressions of the general public. Note that being declared insane does not mean that you can go right home and carry on with your life: You will likely be sent to a mental institution until there is clear evidence that the mental illness has subsided. In many cases, this amounts to a life sentence. Nonetheless, the form of supervision you receive in an institution is likely to be more sensitive to the specific psychological disorder. Most mental health professionals concur with this abnormality-insanity distinction and agree that people with serious psychological disorders are sometimes incapable of judging the appropriateness of their actions. As this chapter will illustrate, psychological disorders can lead to distorted views of the world—affected individuals not only act in ways that are abnormal, but their very thoughts, beliefs, and perceptions of the world can be wildly distorted as well.

insanity

A legal term in the United States usually defined as the inability to understand that certain actions are wrong, in a legal or moral sense, at the time of a crime

The Medical Model versus the Sociological Model

When abnormality is present, is it better to think of the person as having a physical problem—that is, something that is broken or not working properly in the body—or is the person simply psychologically unsuited to the environment? We'll discuss the possible causes of psychological disorders in detail later in the chapter, but to understand how disorders are actually classified, you need to understand what is called the *medical model* of diagnosis. According to the **medical model,** abnormal behaviour is caused by an underlying *disease*—a kind of mental *illness*—that can be cured with the appropriate therapy.

This conception of abnormality has been quite influential. As you already know, good reasons support the view that behaviour is strongly influenced by biological factors, such as an oversupply or undersupply of neurotransmitters in the brain. In addition, biomedical therapies, such as the administration of psychoactive drugs, are often effective in treating a variety of psychological problems. As you'll see shortly, it's also the case that most psychological disorders can be classified in terms of *symptoms*. Depression, for example, typically leads to one or more of the following: sad mood, diminished interest in pleasure, difficulty sleeping, and feelings of worthlessness. The medical influence is deeply ingrained in the very language that psychologists use—they talk about mental health, mental illness, or psychopathology in much the same way as a physician describes a medical condition.

But is the medical model the only way to view abnormality? Both strep throat and depression lead to a set of reliable symptoms. Strep throat is caused by a physical problem, namely, specific bacteria. Application of the medical model to depression may be less appropriate because social and cultural factors have more of an influence on its meaning to the person with depression and on other people's reaction to it.

The **sociological model** argues that the interpretation of psychological symptoms as abnormal is arbitrary and depends on the particular social or cultural context. We pointed out earlier that some kinds of behaviour thought to be abnormal in one culture could be considered normal in another. In the case of extreme shyness, for example, it might be cured (based on any of the four criteria discussed above) by moving to an East Asian country, where shyness is more common and modesty is highly valued (Chen, Rubin, & Sun, 1992).

We will see in Chapter 15 that some psychotherapies are as simple as changing our perspective on life. Such flexibility is consistent with the sociological model. Moving to the country or avoiding those irritating relatives may solve your problem. If such simple strategies can actually make the distress go away, they seem more like effective lifestyle changes than like medical cures. A true disease would not go away so easily. In short, the arbitrariness and flexibility of a disorder will help us determine the degree to which the disorder fits the sociological model better than it fits the medical model.

Extreme versions of the sociological model argue that psychological disorders don't even exist—except in a totally subjective sense. Society decides that certain behaviours and people are "sick" and psychologists go along with it (Rosenhan, 1973; Szasz, 1961). From this perspective, psychological disorders are nothing more than labels for behaviours that society considers to be deviant or nonconformist. As we will see below, such an extreme view is challenged by our increasing understanding of the chemical and biological basis of many psychological disorders. Moreover, this extreme view seems to minimize the suffering of people with disorders.

The sociological model does remind us that scientific theories are all tentative and cannot be taken as absolutes. And scientific theories of psychology, in particular, are influenced by current social views.

---

medical model

The view that abnormal behaviour is symptomatic of an underlying "disease" that can be "cured" with the appropriate therapy

sociological model

The view that abnormality is a label that each society assigns to behaviours that it finds unacceptable, even if the behaviours are not criminal in nature

Test Yourself 14.1   *Check your knowledge about how abnormality is conceptualized by deciding whether each of the following statements is true or false. (The answers are in Appendix B.)*

1. When a behaviour occurs infrequently among members of a population, it meets the criterion of cultural deviance. *True or False?*

2. To be diagnosed with a psychological disorder, a person must be experiencing a certain amount of emotional distress. *True or False?*

3. In many cases, abnormal behaviours are simply exaggerated versions of normal behaviours. *True or False?*

4. According to the medical model, psychological disorders can and should be classified in terms of measurable symptoms. *True or False?*

▶ Classifying Psychological Disorders: The *DSM-IV*

LEARNING GOALS

1. Understand the *DSM-IV*, and discuss the pros and cons of this multiaxial system.
2. Identify and describe the common anxiety disorders.
3. Identify and describe the somatoform disorders.
4. Identify and describe the common dissociative disorders.
5. Identify and describe the common mood disorders.
6. Identify and describe the characteristics of schizophrenia.
7. Identify and describe the common personality disorders.
8. Understand the debate over cult membership and Internet addiction.

As mentioned earlier, specific psychological disorders are often diagnosed in terms of a set of defining criteria or symptoms. This is the approach taken by the *Diagnostic and Statistical Manual of Mental Disorders (DSM)*. The *DSM* was developed over many years by a diverse committee of health professionals from Canada and the United States. It is now used as the standard diagnostic reference by clinicians (both psychologists and psychiatrists) in North America. (Europe has a somewhat different, less integrated system.) Because it is in its fourth edition, the manual is currently referred to as the **DSM-IV.** (The manual is continually being revised, and the latest version is labelled *DSM-IV-TR.*) The *DSM-IV* provides clinicians with a well-defined classification system based on objective and measurable criteria, so that reliable diagnoses of psychological disorders can be produced across the continent (Maser, Kaelber, & Weise, 1991; Spitzer, Gibbon, Skodol, Williams, & First, 1994). In a way, the *DSM-IV* is like a dictionary that allows a psychologist in Alberta to communicate with a psychiatrist in Alabama about the nature of a particular individual's psychological disorders. The *DSM-IV* is intended only for diagnosis and classification; it does not suggest therapies or methods of treatment for its various listed disorders.

How does the classification system work? The *DSM-IV* is composed of five major rating dimensions, or *axes* (see ▶ Figure 14.2 on page 570). We'll focus our attention mainly on the first axis, which lists the major clinical disorders (such as depression and schizophrenia), although all five are important to the complete diagnostic process. The clinician uses the criteria outlined in Axis I (Clinical Disorders) and Axis II (Personality Disorders) to classify and label any abnormal behaviour that may be present. Axis III allows the clinician to record any *medical* conditions that the individual has. It's important for the clinician to know a person's medical history because some medical conditions (such as Alzheimer's disease) can contribute to abnormal behaviour. Axis IV indicates

DSM-IV

The *Diagnostic and Statistical Manual of Mental Disorders* (4th ed.), which is used for the diagnosis and classification of psychological disorders; comprises five major rating dimensions, called *axes*

Axis I	Axis II	Axis III	Axis IV
Clinical Disorders	Personality Disorders and Mental Retardation	General Medical Conditions	Psychosocial and Environmental Problems
Examples	**Examples**	**Examples**	**Examples**
Substance-related disorders Schizophrenia and other psychotic disorders Mood disorders Anxiety disorders Somatoform disorders Dissociative disorders Sexual and gender identity disorders Eating disorders Sleep disorders	Paranoid personality disorder Schizotypal personality disorder Antisocial personality disorder Borderline personality disorder Narcissistic personality disorder Dependent personality disorder	Infectious and parasitic diseases Endocrine, nutritional, and metabolic diseases and immunity disorders Diseases of the nervous system and sense organs Diseases of the circulatory system Diseases of the respiratory system Diseases of the digestive system Diseases of the genitourinary system Congenital anomalies	Problems with primary support group Problems related to the social environment Educational problems Occupational problems Housing problems Economic problems

Axis V

Global Assessment of Functioning (GAF) Scale

Code	Examples of symptoms
100	Superior functioning in a wide range of activities
90	Absent or minimal symptoms, good functioning in all areas
80	Symptoms transient and expectable reactions to psychosocial stressors
70	Mild symptoms or impairment in social, occupational, or school functioning, but general functioning is pretty good
60	Moderate symptoms or impairment in social, occupational, or school functioning
50	Serious symptoms or impairment in social, occupational, or school functioning
40	Major impairment in work or school, family relations, judgment, thinking, mood; some communication impairment
30	Influenced by delusions or hallucinations, serious impairment in communication or judgment
20	Some danger of severely hurting self or others, gross impairment in communication, sporadic personal hygiene
10	Persistent danger of severely hurting self or others

▶ **Figure 14.2**

The Five Axes of the *DSM-IV* Diagnostic System

The *DSM-IV* is composed of five major rating dimensions or axes. Information collected from each axis is integrated into final diagnosis and treatment decisions. (Reprinted with permission from the *Diagnostic and Statistical Manual of Mental Disorders,* Fourth Edition. Copyright © 1994 American Psychiatric Association.)

any environmental or psychosocial problems that may be present. For example, is the client going through a difficult divorce, or has he or she recently been fired? Finally, on Axis V, the clinician codes the individual's current level of adaptive or global functioning. Is the client able to function adequately in social, personal, and occupational settings?

The clinician uses this multiaxial classification system to get the widest possible assessment of the individual's current psychological status. It matters to the clinician how someone is functioning in daily life, for example, because it often

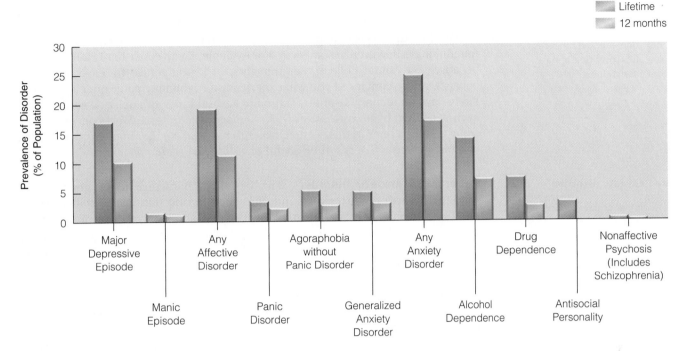

Lifetime

12 months

▶ **Figure 14.3**

Prevalence Rates for Various Psychological Disorders

Each bar shows the percentage of individuals in a large sample (more than 8000 participants) who reported experiencing the listed psychological disorder during the past 12 months or at some point in their lifetime. Note: A given individual might have reported experiencing more than one of these disorders concurrently. (Data from Kessler et al., 1994.)

determines the most effective kind of treatment program. If the person is so severely impaired that he or she cannot hold a job, go to school, or even keep clean, it may be necessary to initiate a period of hospitalization. Our discussion will focus primarily on the diagnostic criteria that are used to classify the most common psychological disorders, as depicted on Axis I. We'll consider the major clinical syndromes and then end the section with a brief discussion of Axis II–based personality disorders. But remember, categorizing the disorder is only part of the diagnostic process; the remaining axes also play an important role in the diagnosis. ▶ Figure 14.3 summarizes some of the disorders we'll be discussing and presents data showing how likely each disorder is to occur in the population at large.

Anxiety Disorders: Beyond Rational Fear

We all understand rational fear, that is, the normal sense of aroused distress we experience when confronting real danger. Anxiety is a similar distressed feeling when the threat is less clear and nonphysical. We may become anxious when meeting strangers, when awaiting an important exam, or on suddenly remembering that we forgot to pay our taxes for the past five years. Even though the physical and psychological changes that accompany anxiety can seem unpleasant, anxiety is ultimately an *adaptive* human response. The physical changes prepare the body to take action—to fight or flee—and thereby increase the chances of survival. The psychological changes cause us to become attentive—we monitor our environment more closely so we're more apt to notice a potentially dangerous event when it occurs.

anxiety disorders

A class of disorders marked by excessive apprehension and worry that in turn impairs normal functioning

generalized anxiety disorder

Excessive worrying, or free-floating anxiety, that lasts for at least six months and cannot be attributed to any single identifiable source

panic disorder

A condition marked by recurrent discrete episodes or attacks of extremely intense fear or dread

agoraphobia

An anxiety disorder that causes an individual to restrict his or her normal activities; someone who has agoraphobia tends to avoid public places out of fear that a panic attack will occur

In panic disorder, a person has recurrent episodes, or attacks, of intense fear or dread.

But anxiety has a maladaptive extreme. When it becomes too persistent and intense, it interferes with your everyday activities. **Anxiety disorders** are diagnosed when the levels of apprehension and worry become so extreme that normal functioning is impaired in some way. For example, if you consistently fail on exams because you cannot collect your thoughts, or if you refuse to leave the house because you're convinced you will experience a frightening panic attack, then you likely have an anxiety disorder. There are several kinds of anxiety disorders, and each is defined by its own set of *DSM-IV* diagnostic criteria. We'll concentrate on some common ones in this section: *generalized anxiety disorder*, *panic disorder*, *obsessive-compulsive disorder*, *social phobia*, and *specific phobias*.

Generalized Anxiety Disorder   The defining characteristic of **generalized anxiety disorder** is excessive and chronic worrying that lasts for at least six months. The anxiety is "free floating," as Freud described it, and cannot be attributed to any single identifiable source. People who have this problem tend to worry about very minor things (Brown, O'Leary, & Barlow, 2001) as well as life *in general* (Sanderson & Barlow, 1990). To qualify as a disorder, the worrying must be unrealistic; that is, it's not rationally related to the chances that the feared event will actually occur (Brown, Barlow, & Liebowitz, 1994).

Because anxiety is associated with activity of the autonomic nervous system, generalized anxiety disorder tends to be accompanied by a range of physical symptoms, including high pulse and respiration rates, chronic diarrhea, a need to urinate frequently, and chronic digestive problems. Someone burdened with generalized anxiety disorder is likely to have trouble sleeping and becomes easily irritated; he or she is also likely to spend a lot of time worrying about the future—more so than someone who has the other anxiety disorders we'll consider (Dugas et al., 1998). These kinds of symptoms are an understandable result of living in a world of perpetual fear.

Panic Disorder   In **panic disorder,** people experience recurrent episodes, or attacks, of extremely intense fear or dread (Craske & Barlow, 1993). A *panic attack* is a sudden and unexpected event, and it can make a person feel as if he or she is about to die (or, sometimes, go crazy). Panic attacks are brief, but they produce high levels of anxiety and, as a result, are accompanied by a collection of physical symptoms: a pounding heart, shortness of breath, sweating, nausea, chest pains, and so on. These symptoms can be devastating experiences, and they often lead to persistent concern about the possibility of having additional attacks (Barlow, 1988). It's worth noting that a single isolated panic attack is not sufficient for diagnosis of a panic disorder; the attacks need to occur repeatedly and unexpectedly.

Remarkably, panic attacks can even occur while you're asleep, a condition referred to as *nocturnal panic* (Craske & Rowe, 1997). Nocturnal panic attacks usually occur in the middle of the night—between 1:30 a.m. and 3:30 a.m.—and they're associated with slow-wave sleep rather than REM sleep (Barlow & Durand, 1999). This fact suggests that the attacks are not a consequence of bad dreams or nightmares, which tend to be associated with REM sleep (see Chapter 5). Nocturnal panic attacks are poorly understood at the moment, although they may be related to night terrors, which commonly occur in children, or to a sleep-related breathing problem called *sleep apnea*. Not surprisingly, people who experience nocturnal panic attacks are terrified after an attack and, in some cases, are very reluctant to go to sleep at night.

Panic disorder is sometimes associated with an additional complication, called *agoraphobia*, that arises from the worry that further panic attacks might occur. **Agoraphobia**—which translates from the Greek as "fear of the marketplace"—causes a person to restrict his or her normal activities in an extreme way (Mennin, Heimberg, & Holt, 2000). People who have agoraphobia typically stay away from crowded or public places, such as shopping malls or restaurants, because they're afraid they'll experience a panic attack and be rendered helpless. In severe cases, people with agoraphobia might simply refuse to leave their house. Home, they decide, is the only really safe place in the world. For obvious reasons, panic disorder with accompanying agoraphobia can significantly reduce a person's ability to function successfully in the world.

Obsessive-Compulsive Disorder   In **obsessive-compulsive disorder,** anxiety manifests itself through persistent, uncontrollable thoughts, called *obsessions,* or by the presence of a compelling need to perform one or more actions repeatedly, which is called a *compulsion* (Foa & Franklin, 2001; Swinson, Antony, Rachman, & Richter, 1998). Compulsions are related to obsessions in the sense that the repetitive action is usually performed in response to some kind of obsessive thought (Riggs & Foa, 1993). Have you ever had part of a song or jingle in your head—one that keeps repeating despite your best efforts to stop it? This phenomenon is somewhat like an obsession, although in obsessive-compulsive disorder the obsessions tend to focus on fears (such as being contaminated by germs), doubts (such as forgetting to turn off the stove), and impulses (such as hurting oneself or others) (Jenike, Baer, & Minichiello, 1986; Salkovskis, 1985).

Compulsions consist of such actions as cleaning or checking or actions that prevent some inappropriate impulse from occurring. For example, someone might repeat the alphabet aloud over and over in an effort to divert his or her thinking away from a frightening or an inappropriate aggressive or sexual impulse. In extreme cases, the compulsions are so repetitive and ritualistic that they essentially prevent the person from leading anything resembling a normal life. Some people become housebound, relentlessly cleaning rooms; others feel irresistibly compelled to leave work 10 to 15 times a day to check and make sure the stove wasn't left on. Interestingly, in the majority of such cases the individuals understand that their actions are irrational and of little adaptive value (Stern & Cobb, 1978). The disorder simply compels the action.

Social Phobia   The most commonly reported fear is **social phobia,** an incapacitating fear of social interactions (Alden, 2001). This fear is maximized with larger audiences, authority figures, and strangers. The very idea of speaking in front of a group is terrifying to many students. They would rather quit school than face such a horror. Its milder form, social anxiety or shyness, appears to be a combination of two normal personality dimensions, namely, introversion and neuroticism (Coplan, Rubin, Fox, Calkins, & Stewart, 1994; Paulhus & Trapnell, 1998). In its extreme form, this tendency to avoid (even important) interactions is considered by some psychologists to be a personality disorder (Widiger, 1998).

obsessive-compulsive disorder

An anxiety disorder that manifests itself through persistent and uncontrollable thoughts, called *obsessions,* or by the compelling need to perform repetitive acts, called *compulsions*

social phobia

An incapacitating fear of social interactions

People who have agoraphobia are often reluctant to leave the house; they're afraid that once outside they will experience a panic attack and be rendered helpless.

A person who has obsessive-compulsive disorder may feel the need to engage in a repetitive activity, such as compulsively lining up candies, to reduce anxiety or to avoid thinking inappropriate thoughts.

specific phobic disorder

A highly focused fear of a specific object or situation

CRITICAL   THINKING

Can you think of reasons why it might be adaptive for people to show specific reactions for each of the four classes of phobic stimuli described in the text?

Specific Phobic Disorder   The defining feature of a **specific phobic disorder** is a highly focused fear of a specific object or situation (other than social situations). These include bugs, snakes, heights, animals, closed places, storms, or flying. Like the other anxiety disorders we've discussed, specific phobias are irrational, which means that the level of anxiety the object or situation produces is in no way justified by reality. True, elevators do fall, snakes can bite, and planes do crash, but these events are rare and do not justify daily worry. Many people show mild forms of phobic reactions, but in specific phobic disorder the fear and distress can be severely disabling. To avoid the anxiety-producing object or situation, individuals with a specific phobic disorder might significantly disrupt their normal routines; they might avoid going to work or school or travelling to anywhere different if there is even a slight chance that they will encounter the object of their fear.

Specific phobias typically revolve around one of four classes of fear-inducing objects or situations: (1) animals (insects, snakes, dogs, etc.), (2) natural environments (storms, heights, water, etc.), (3) blood-injection-injury (the sight of blood or even the thought of an injection), and (4) specific situations (fears associated with public transportation or closed-in places). These four categories capture the majority of phobic reactions, although there are others—such as fear of choking or fear of costumed characters—that do not fit easily into these established categories. Most people who have specific phobias tend to have more than one and often more than one type (Hofmann, Lehman, & Barlow, 1997). For a look at how likely the various specific phobias are to occur among the general population, see ▶ Figure 14.4.

Somatoform Disorders: Body and Mind

A common phenomenon, called the *medical student syndrome*, often plagues medical students as they first learn about the various diseases of the body. The students find that the symptoms described in class, or in the text, become increasingly familiar and personal. A pain that appears suddenly in the night is interpreted as a signal for a heart attack; that darkening blemish on the forehead becomes the rare

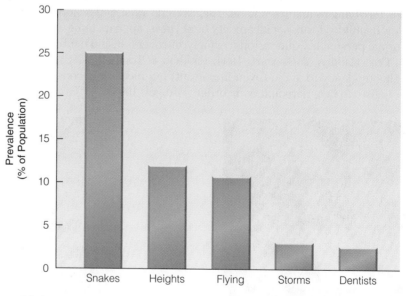

▶ **Figure 14.4**

Prevalence Rates for Various Specific Phobias

Each bar shows the percentage of people in a large sample who reported having a particular kind of phobia. (Data from Agras, Sylvester, & Oliveau, 1969.)

CONCEPT SUMMARY

ANXIETY DISORDERS

Disorder	Description
Generalized anxiety disorder	Excessive and chronic worrying that lasts for a period of at least six months; accompanied by excessive autonomic activity (e.g., increased respiration, heart rate)
Panic disorder	Recurrent episodes or "attacks" of extremely intense fear or dread; sometimes accompanied by agoraphobia, the fear of being in public due to anticipation of another panic attack
Obsessive-compulsive disorder	Anxiety is manifested through *obsessions* (persistent uncontrollable thoughts) or *compulsions* (a compelling need to perform one or more actions repeatedly) or both
Social phobia	Extreme fear of social interactions that interferes with everyday work and relationship requirements
Specific phobic disorder	A highly focused fear of a specific object or situation; most revolve around animals, natural environments, blood-injection-injury, or specific situations

form of skin cancer that often accompanies AIDS. In almost every case these students are perfectly healthy, but their mind has started over-interpreting normal physical feedback as some kind of serious physical problem. We all do the same from time to time after seeing a television show or reading an article about some new illness: "Uh-oh, I've got that one, too!"

It can be adaptive for us to pay attention to physical symptoms, but when the preoccupation with bodily functions or symptoms is excessive and not grounded in any physical reality, a true psychological disorder may be indicated (Iezzi, Duckworth, & Adams, 2001). Mental health professionals classify psychological problems that focus on the physical body as **somatoform disorders** (*soma* means "body"). The *DSM-IV* lists a number of basic somatoform disorders; we'll focus briefly on three: *hypochondriasis, somatization disorder,* and *conversion disorder.*

somatoform disorders

Psychological disorders that focus on the physical body

Hypochondriasis   The main symptom of **hypochondriasis** is the persistent preoccupation with the idea that you've developed a serious disease, based on what turns out to be a misinterpretation of normal bodily reactions. The pain in the side, the slight case of indigestion, the occasional irregular heartbeat—these are interpreted as symptomatic of a serious medical condition. Moreover, unlike the situation for the normal medical student, these preoccupations persist for months and often cause significant distress and impaired functioning. Hypochondriasis is typically associated with excessive anxiety and, in fact, may be strongly related to the types of anxiety disorders we discussed earlier (Otto, Demopulos, McLean, Pollack, & Fava, 1998).

hypochondriasis

A long-lasting preoccupation with the idea that one has developed a serious disease, based on what turns out to be a misinterpretation of normal body reactions

Somatization Disorder   **Somatization disorder** is related to hypochondriasis; in fact, mental health professionals sometimes have a difficult time distinguishing between the two. Both involve the persistent complaint of symptoms with no identifiable physical cause, but in somatization disorder it is the *symptoms* that receive the focus of attention rather than an underlying disease. In both cases, the person searches endlessly for doctors who will confirm his or her symptoms, but usually with little success (because no real physical problem exists). The major difference between hypochondriasis and somatization disorder seems to be that in hypochondriasis the anxiety arises because of a presumed underlying disease, whereas in somatization disorder the presence of the symptoms themselves causes the anxiety. People with somatization disorder are not typically afraid of dying from a serious disease; rather, they are looking for someone to understand and sympathize with their countless physical problems.

somatization disorder

A long-lasting preoccupation with body symptoms that have no identifiable physical cause

Corbis Royalty Free

A person who has hypochondriasis is prone to misinterpreting normal bodily reactions as symptomatic of a serious disease.

Conversion Disorder　In **conversion disorder,** unlike the other two somatoform disorders we've considered, there appears to be real physical or neurological impairment. Someone who has a conversion disorder might report being blind, paralyzed, or unable to speak. The affected person might even experience seizures resembling those found in epilepsy or other neurological disorders (Bowman, 1998). These are not feigned symptoms; that is, these problems are not intentionally invented by the individual to gain sympathy or attention. These are real problems, although no physical cause can be discovered.

Obviously, in such cases it is always possible that a true neurological or other physical problem does exist. Indeed, physical problems are sometimes misdiagnosed as conversion disorders (Fishbain & Goldberg, 1991; Slater & Glithero, 1965). But when the reported problems disappear after effective therapy, a psychological origin is usually indicated. You may remember from our discussion of personality in Chapter 12 that Sigmund Freud often used his psychoanalytic techniques to treat patients with conversion disorders (although the problem was known as *hysteria* in his day). In fact, the term *conversion*, as used here, originates from psychodynamic theory and the proposal that unconscious conflicts have been converted into a physical form.

Dissociative Disorders: Disruptions of Identity or Awareness

Some of the more colourful types of psychological disorders, at least as seen by Hollywood or the popular press, come from a class of problems called **dissociative disorders.** Dissociative disorders are defined by the separation, or *dissociation*, of conscious awareness from previous thoughts or memories. If you're affected by one of these disorders, you lose memory for some specific aspect of your life, or even for your entire sense of identity. The theme of the confused amnesiac, searching for his or her lost identity, has been explored repeatedly in books and films throughout the years. Another fascinating example is the so-called multiple personality. As usual, the actual clinical versions are more complex than those depicted in popular movies. We'll focus our attention on three types of dissociative disorder: *dissociative amnesia*, *dissociative fugue*, and *dissociative identity disorder*.

Dissociative Amnesia　In Chapter 7, when we tackled remembering and forgetting, we discussed various kinds of *amnesia*, or the inability to remember or retain personal experiences. It was noted that amnesia could result from either physical factors (such as brain damage) or psychological factors (such as traumatic stress). In **dissociative amnesia,** which is assumed to be psychological in origin, the person is unable to remember important personal information. The amnesia can be quite general, as in the failure to remember personal identity or family history, or it can be localized, such as the failure to remember a specific traumatic life experience (Loewenstein, 1996). In dissociative amnesia, the forgetting can last for hours or for years. It often disappears as mysteriously as it arises.

Dissociative Fugue　In **dissociative fugue,** there is also a loss of personal identity—people forget who they are—but it's accompanied by an escape or a flight from the home environment (*fugue* literally means "flight"). Imagine leaving for work or school as usual only to "awaken" some time later in a different city. One example is Canadian actor Margot Kidder, famous for her film roles as Superman's girlfriend in the 1970s and 1980s. She disappeared for a week and was found dishevelled, dirty, carrying a knife, and ranting about phantom pursuers. Sometimes the fugue state can last months or even years, and some individuals experiencing this disorder have even adopted different identities in their new locale. Recovery can be sudden and often complete, but affected individuals typically report that they have no knowledge of their activities during the blackout period.

---

conversion disorder

The presence of real physical problems, such as blindness or paralysis, that seem to have no identifiable physical cause

---

dissociative disorders

A class of disorders characterized by the separation, or dissociation, of conscious awareness from previous thoughts or memories

---

dissociative amnesia

A psychological disorder characterized by an inability to remember important personal information

---

dissociative fugue

A loss of personal identity that is often accompanied by a flight from home

Dissociative Identity Disorder In what is perhaps the most baffling of all dissociative disorders, **dissociative identity disorder,** a person alternates between what appear to be two or more distinct identities or personality states (hence the previous label for this condition, *multiple personality disorder*). Some cases of this disorder have been widely publicized. The classic 1950s case was Sybil Dorsett, who was diagnosed with 16 personalities (Schreiber, 1973); she was portrayed by Sally Field in the television movie *Sybil*. Another well-known case is Eve, who alternated among three personality types (Thigpen & Cleckley, 1957); she was portrayed by Joanne Woodward in the film *The Three Faces of Eve*.

In dissociative identity disorder, the unique personalities or identities appear to take control of the affected person's thoughts and actions, one personality at a time. More important, the personality in control will profess to have only limited awareness of the other personality inhabitants. Commonly, there is interpersonality amnesia, which means that events experienced while the person is inhabited by personality A cannot be remembered when he or she is occupied by personality B (Eich, Macaulay, Loewenstein, & Dihle, 1997). It is for this reason that the disorder is classified as *dissociative*—a separation occurs between current conscious awareness and prior thoughts and memories. Dozens of different identities may be involved, including both males and females, and a given identity will tend to have unique physical attributes, such as a distinct tone of voice, facial expression, handwriting style, or behavioural habit (Putnam, Guroff, Silberman, Barban, & Post, 1986).

Dissociative identity disorder is recognized as a legitimate disorder in the *DSM-IV*, but not all mental health professionals are comfortable with this designation (Fahy, 1988). Controversy often surrounds the diagnosis, for a number of reasons. First, this disorder often co-occurs with other psychological problems (such as depression and somatization disorder), so it's quite difficult to pinpoint the ultimate cause of any particular symptom (Ross et al., 1990). Second, although each of the observed personalities may be distinguished on the basis of personality tests or physiological measures, we still cannot be completely sure about the true origins of these differences—other factors, such as mood or arousal differences, may partly account for the distinct performance patterns (Fahy, 1988; Lilienfeld, 1994).

The third reason for skepticism is that researchers, such as Nicholas Spanos of Carleton University, have shown that it's relatively easy to fake or simulate multiple personalities (Spanos, 1994; Spanos, Weeks, & Bertrand, 1985). This research raises the possibility that people with dissociative identity disorder may actually be role-playing in some fashion, perhaps in a way comparable to those who have been hypnotized. As you might recall from Chapter 5, many psychologists question whether hypnosis really represents some kind of dissociated state; instead, hypnotized people often seem eager to please the hypnotist by acting in accordance with a hypnotized role. This is not necessarily a conscious choice made by those who have been hypnotized; instead, it may represent a kind of unconscious or involuntary compliance (Lynn, Rhue, & Weekes, 1990). Some researchers are convinced that dissociative identity disorder is best interpreted as a kind of self-hypnosis that arises partly to please the therapist. An unusually rapid rise in the number of cases of dissociative identity disorder has occurred since the disorder has been publicized in the media, which lends support to the role-playing hypothesis.

Despite the controversy, dissociative identity disorder was retained as a diagnostic disorder in the *DSM-IV*, which was published in 1994. It does seem clear that not all aspects of the disorder can be consciously faked (Kluft, 1991). Highly specific physiological differences have been reported across personalities—such as differences in visual acuity or eye muscle balance (Miller, 1989)—and it seems unlikely that such things could be easily faked (see ▶ Figure 14.5 on page 578). After all, these differences are not part of the stereotype. Certain similarities in the past histories of affected individuals have convinced many of the validity of the diagnosis. For example, in a recent study of 97 cases, 95% of the individuals were found

dissociative identity disorder

A condition in which an individual alternates between what appear to be two or more distinct identities or personalities (also known as *multiple personality disorder*)

Kenneth Bianchi, known as the Hillside Strangler, claimed that he could not be held responsible for the rape and murder of a number of California women because he had dissociative identity disorder. The evidence presented at trial suggested that Bianchi was "faking" the disorder, and he was later convicted and sentenced to life imprisonment.

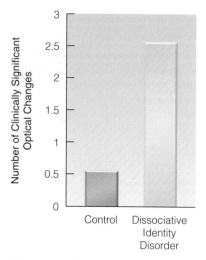

▶ **Figure 14.5**

Optical Changes across Personalities

In a study by Miller (1989), individuals diagnosed with dissociative identity disorder were asked to undergo ophthalmological (eye) exams while "inhabited" by each of three different personalities. Significant differences were found in optical functioning across personalities, whereas no differences were seen when normal control subjects were asked to fake different personalities. (Data from Miller, 1989.)

mood disorders

Prolonged and disabling disruptions in emotional state

CRITICAL THINKING

Can you think of any reason that a client who is seeking help for a psychological problem might want desperately to please the therapist?

major depressive episode

A type of mood disorder characterized by depressed mood and other symptoms

to have endured some form of abuse, usually sexual or physical, most often during childhood (Ross et al., 1990). The diagnosis of dissociative identity disorder remains controversial, but it is considered to be a legitimate disorder by the psychological community at large (Gleaves, May, & Cardena, 2001).

Mood Disorders: Depression and Mania

From time to time everyone experiences depression, that overwhelming feeling that things are completely hopeless and sad. For most, thankfully, the experience is brief; moreover, most of us can usually account for our depressed mood by pointing to a particular experience or event in our lives: We failed a test; our beloved pet died; our once-trusted romantic partner now prefers the affections of another. But when an extreme mood swing is prolonged and accompanied by other symptoms, such as a loss of appetite and a negative self-concept, a mood disorder may be present. **Mood disorders**—which are defined as prolonged and disabling disruptions in emotional state—come in two main varieties: (1) *depressive disorders*, in which the person experiences primarily depression, and (2) *bipolar disorders*, which are characterized by *mood swings* between extreme highs, called manic states, and the lows of depression. We'll consider each of these types of disorders separately.

Depressive Disorders   The *DSM-IV* lists specific criteria for the diagnosis of depressive disorders, which are among the most common of all psychological disorders. For something to qualify as a **major depressive episode,** for instance, you must show five or more of the following types of symptoms for a period of at least two weeks:

- Depressed mood for most of the day
- Loss of interest in normal daily activities
- A significant change in weight (either a loss or a gain)
- Difficulty sleeping or a desire to sleep all the time
- A change in activity level (either extreme restlessness or lethargy)
- Daily fatigue or loss of energy
- A negative self-concept, including feelings of worthlessness or excessive guilt
- Trouble concentrating or making decisions
- Suicidal thoughts

In a major depressive episode, the world is seen through a kind of dark filter. You feel extremely sad and full of self-doubt, and the environment seems overwhelming, imposing, and full of obstacles that cannot be overcome (Young, Beck, & Weinberger, 1993). This worldview of a depressed person is a particularly grim aspect of the disorder—if you're depressed, the future seems hopeless, with little or no possibility of a reprieve. Moreover, depressed people are absolutely convinced about the truth of their hopelessness, which tragically leads some to consider suicide as their only outlet.

It is important to understand that major depression is more than just feeling sad. You literally view and interpret the world differently when you're depressed, which tends to feed and confirm your negative self-concept. Normal activities are interpreted as indicating some dire consequence (e.g., if a friend fails to call, it must mean the friend no longer likes you). As you'll see in the next chapter, one goal of therapy in treating depression is to change depressed individuals' thought patterns—to make them see the world in a more realistic way.

Mental health professionals distinguish among several types of depressive disorders, based partly on the length and severity of the depressive episode. For example, a major depressive episode can be classified as *recurrent*, which means that it has occurred more than once in an individual's lifetime (but separated by a period of at least two months). There is also a condition called *dysthymic disorder*, in which the depressive symptoms tend to be milder and less disruptive but more chronic. Most major depressive episodes end after a period of weeks or months and the person returns to normal, but people affected by dysthymic disorder show a relatively continuous depressed mood for a period of at least two years (Akiskal & Cassano, 1997). A major depressive episode can even occur at the same time as dysthymic disorder, in which case the condition is referred to as *double depression* (Hellerstein & Little, 2000; Keller & Shapiro, 1982).

McMaster University researcher David Offord and colleagues have reported that approximately twice as many women as men experienced a major depressive episode (Offord et al., 1996). However, Simon Fraser University researchers Marlene Moretti, Amy Rein, and Vanessa Wiebe point out that this gender difference is not typically found in university-aged people (Moretti, Rein, & Wiebe, 1998). These researchers also point out a factor that might be involved in explaining some aspects of gender differences in depression. They found that although both men and women experienced considerable unhappiness when their perceived self-image was far from their ideal self-image, only the women in their sample tended to be unhappy when they perceived themselves as not meeting other people's ideal standards for them. Moretti and colleagues suggest that this potential double source of unhappiness relating to women's self-images may be involved in the higher rates of depression found among women in general.

David Zuroff of McGill University has proposed, together with his colleagues, that people who are highly self-critical or dependent on others will tend to be more depressed than people low on those traits (Blatt & Zuroff, 1992; McBride, Zuroff, Bacchiochi, & Bagby, 2006). Following this suggestion, researchers Jennifer Aubé and Valerie Whiffen of the University of Ottawa found that self-critical people tended to have worse social acuity than other people, and they suggest that a deficit in social acuity (i.e., judging the reactions and feelings of others) may be a factor contributing to the development or continuation of depressive states in self-critical individuals (Aubé & Whiffen, 1996).

Bipolar Disorders   Major depression can be described as unipolar because the disorder is defined by a mood shift in only one direction—toward the negative. In a **bipolar disorder,** you experience mood shifts in two directions: travelling from the depths of depression (a major depressive episode) to a hyperactive, euphoric condition called a **manic state** (Miklowitz, 2001). When you're in a manic state, you act as if you're on top of the world—you're hyperactive, talkative, and seem to have little need for sleep. These symptoms may seem positive and desirable, but they get exaggerated toward grandiosity, distractibility, and risk taking. In a manic state, a person might attempt a remarkable feat—such as climbing a dangerous cliff—or perhaps will go on a sudden spending spree, cashing in all his or her savings. People who are in a manic state report feeling great, even euphoric—but their thinking is far from normal or rational. Their speech can appear disrupted because they shift rapidly from one fleeting thought to another.

To be classified as a manic episode in the *DSM-IV*, this abnormally elevated mood state must last for at least a week, although it can last for months. Like a depressive episode, the manic state typically goes away, even without treatment, and the person either returns to normal or roller-coasters into another depressive episode. People who have bipolar disorders live lives of extreme highs and lows: As a result, their ability to function normally in society is often severely impaired. Moreover, tragically, it's been estimated that as many as 19% of individuals who are affected with bipolar disorders end up committing suicide, usually during one of their episodes of depression (Jamison, 1986). (For a discussion of the possible connection between bipolar disorders and creativity, see the following Practical Solutions box.)

bipolar disorder

A type of mood disorder in which the person experiences disordered mood shifts in two directions—from depression to a manic state

manic state

A disordered state in which the person becomes hyperactive, talkative, and has a decreased need for sleep; a person in a manic state may engage in activities that are self-destructive or dangerous

PRACTICAL SOLUTIONS

ARE CREATIVE PEOPLE MAD?

It is commonly believed that inside the hearts and minds of truly creative people lies an element of madness. If you take a journey through history and consider the psychological health of prominent individuals, it's not difficult to find examples of psychological problems. In the twentieth century alone, at least five Pulitzer Prize–winning poets (including Sylvia Plath) have committed suicide in the midst of depression. So, too, have a number of fiction writers (e.g., Ernest Hemingway) and song writers (e.g., Kurt Cobain). It is now recognized that Abraham Lincoln, Cole Porter, and Winston Churchill all probably had bipolar disorder, marked by swings between manic states and depression, and Canadian Prime Minister Mackenzie King may well have had recurrent delusions.

Such examples are intriguing, but they don't constitute solid scientific evidence. More systematic data have come from studies in which pools of highly creative and "average" people are matched on a number of dimensions and the rate of psychological problems is then compared. In one such study, Nancy Andreasen (1987) compared the psychiatric diagnoses of 30 creative writing faculty at the University of Iowa Writers' Workshop (a highly regarded creative writing program) with those of 30 control individuals who were matched to the writers on age, sex, and educational status. Andreasen discovered that the writers had a substantially higher rate of psychological disorders than the controls—in fact, 43% of the writers were found to have experienced the symptoms of a bipolar disorder at some point in their lives. This was the case for only 10% of the controls. Andreasen also found a higher likelihood of mental problems among the writers' first-degree relatives (parents and siblings). According to University of British Columbia psychologist Mark Schaller, the disorder becomes even worse when writers become famous. His argument is that fame increases their self-consciousness to a degree that pushes their already frenetic minds over the edge (Schaller, 1997).

Kay Redfield Jamison (1989) looked to see whether similarities might exist between creative states and the characteristics of manic states. She interviewed 47 famous British writers and artists—all had won at least one prestigious literary or artistic prize—and asked them to describe their moods, thoughts, and actions during spurts of creative activity. She found striking similarities between their answers and the symptoms found in manic states: Virtually all the subjects reported experiencing creative states characterized by a decreased need for sleep; increases in energy, enthusiasm, self-confidence, and speed and fluency of thoughts; as well as an elevated mood and sense of well-being. Moreover, when Jamison asked the subjects how important these extremes in mood and thoughts were to the creation of their work, 90% of the participants stated that the moods and feelings were integral, necessary, or very important (Jamison, 1989).

But this kind of evidence does not indicate that the psychological disorder is *causing* the creative activity. Other factors might be involved. For example, one possibility is that when creative individuals are in a manic state, they simply do more work because of their high energy levels. This can make it look like the mania is enhancing creativity, even though it is the *quantity* rather than the *quality* of the work that is really changing. Suppose that you're capable of writing one really good poem for every 10 attempts you make. If you normally make 10 attempts in a month, you will end up with one excellent result. Now suppose you enter a manic state, which increases your output to 30 poems in a month. Even if the mania doesn't affect the quality of your work one bit, it will still look as if you have tripled the number of "great" works that you have produced. Madness and creativity may co-occur, but one is not directly causing the other.

To examine the possibility that it may be the quantity rather than the quality of output that is affected by a mood disorder, Robert Weisberg (1994) conducted a detailed case study of the composer Robert Schumann (1810–1856). Schumann is believed to have had bipolar disorder; throughout his life, he repeatedly entered either manic or depressive states, and he eventually starved himself to death in an institution at age 46. Schumann is an excellent case to study because there are medical records, as well as other data, that pinpoint on a year-by-year basis which kind of mood state he was in. Weisberg found a clear relationship between Schumann's mood state and his productivity as a composer: For the years that he was primarily in a state of depression, he completed, on average, fewer than three compositions per year. Conversely, his output during manic years was a little more than 12 compositions per year.

But were the compositions from his manic years of high quality? To find out, Weisberg (1994) determined the number of times Schumann's compositions had been recorded professionally over the years. If a composition is recorded often by professionals, Weisberg argued, it's reasonable to conclude that the piece is of high quality. Weisberg found that when the quality of Schumann's compositions—defined as the average number of recordings available for each composition in a particular year—was compared across manic and depressive years, no significant differences emerged. Although Schumann composed more during his manic periods, he was not more likely to produce works of extremely high quality. In this particular case, then, madness affected the quantity of creative output but not the quality.

Determining whether a causal relationship really exists between certain kinds of psychological problems and genius or creativity is a difficult thing to do. Obviously, psychologists cannot conduct a well-controlled experiment (creating madness in one randomly sampled group of creative people and not in another), so they are typically forced to rely on correlational studies or anecdotes as the basis for their opinions. Weisberg's research, with its careful and objective separation of quality from quantity, suggests that the anecdotal evidence may be wrong or misleading, at least for people who have bipolar disorders. The link between madness and creativity may turn out to be quite weak, despite centuries of belief to the contrary.

Suicide is the third leading cause of death among adolescents.

Suicide As just noted, suicide can be one fatal consequence of having a mood disorder, such as bipolar disorder. It's worth pausing for a moment and considering suicide because it's quite a significant problem worldwide; suicide rates have been on the rise for decades, especially among adolescents. It's now the third leading cause of death among adolescents and the eighth leading cause of death overall. Men are four to five times more likely to commit suicide than women. Women are slightly more likely to attempt suicide, but they often use nonlethal methods (Statistics Canada, 1997b). It's been estimated that more than 90% of people who kill themselves have some kind of psychological disorder (Garland & Zigler, 1993).

What are the risk factors associated with suicide? Besides the presence of a psychological disorder, many different factors can be involved. Alcohol use and abuse is particularly likely in adolescent suicides, existing in perhaps 50% of suicides (Kelly, Lynch, Donovan, & Clark, 2001; Woods et al., 1997). In Canada, Aboriginal people and people living in remote northern communities have a higher suicide rate than other groups (Statistics Canada, 2000). Another important factor is the sudden occurrence of a very stressful event—something, such as the death of a loved one, the failure of or rejection in a personal relationship, or even a natural disaster. Convincing evidence suggests that suicide rates increase after natural disasters, such as floods, hurricanes, or earthquakes (Krug et al., 1998). Suicide may also be contagious: Suicide rates increase following widely publicized suicides, especially among adolescents, suggesting that imitation or modelling is an important factor (Gould, 1990; Gould & Kramer, 2001).

Among the most significant predictors of suicide, however, are prior suicide attempts and suicidal thoughts. Among adolescents there is a ratio of 3:1 to 6:1 between serious suicidal thoughts and an actual suicide attempt. Not everyone who thinks about suicide makes an attempt—and the ratio of attempted suicides to successful suicides is perhaps 50:1 (Garland & Ziegler, 1993)—but suicidal thinking is a serious warning sign. We'll discuss treatment options for the psychological conditions that are associated with suicide in Chapter 15, but a variety of intervention programs are currently being used to tackle the suicide problem nationally. One suggestion is that teams of mental health professionals be sent to schools, for counselling and screening, whenever a student or visible member of the community commits suicide. Moreover, most cities and towns now have 24-hour suicide hotline services that allow people in need to voice their concerns and learn about alternative ways of dealing with their crises. Most psychologists are optimistic that as the risk factors associated with suicide are identified, and treatment options become more accessible, suicide rates can be slowed or reversed (Holden, Kerr, Mendonca, & Velamoor, 1998; Kosky, Eshkevari, Goldney, & Hassan, 1998).

Shown here are areas of the brain that appear to be selectively activated during auditory and visual hallucinations. The highlighted areas were captured through the use of a PET scanning procedure, during which a young man who has schizophrenia was asked to press a button, initiating the scan, every time he experienced a hallucination.

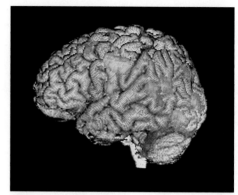

Wellcome Dept of Cognitive Neurology/SPL/ PhotoResearchers, Inc.

Schizophrenia: Severe Thought Disturbance

schizophrenia

A class of disorders characterized by fundamental disturbances in thought processes, emotion, or behaviour

Schizophrenia is actually a group or class of disorders. Different subtypes of schizophrenia exist, defined by different *DSM-IV* criteria, but each case is identified with some kind of fundamental disturbance in thought processes, emotion, or behaviour. Schizophrenia is a bit unusual compared with the other disorders we've considered because it doesn't always reveal itself in the same way: Whereas everyone who has an anxiety disorder feels apprehensive, or in depression feels sad, each symptom of schizophrenia need not be shared by all affected individuals. Schizophrenia is a complex disorder that is expressed in a variety of complex ways—no single symptom must be present for the diagnosis to be applied (Walker, Kestler, Bollini, & Hochman, 2004).

It is important to understand that schizophrenia is not the same thing as a dissociative identity disorder, despite the misleading translation of schizophrenia as "split mind." Schizophrenia leads to faulty thought processes and inappropriate emotions—not to dissociations among distinct personality types. In fact, when the Swiss psychiatrist Eugen Bleuler (1908) originally introduced the term *schizophrenia*, he was referring primarily to the fact that affected individuals have trouble holding on to a logical line of thought. Their thinking is disorganized; their thought lines and associations seem to split apart and move forward in inconsistent ways. Both schizophrenia and dissociative identity disorder are serious psychological problems, but they fall into completely different categories in the *DSM-IV*.

Diagnostic Symptoms   Psychologists distinguish *positive symptoms* and *negative symptoms* of schizophrenia. These terms do not refer to good versus bad but to the appearance of abnormal behaviours versus the absence of normal behaviours. Positive symptoms usually include delusions or hallucinations. Negative symptoms consist of reduced interest in life and diminished ability to express emotion. The *DSM-IV* requires that two or more characteristic symptoms be present for the diagnosis of schizophrenia, but a particular person may have only positive symptoms or a combination of both positive and negative symptoms. As with the other disorders we've considered, these symptoms need to last for a significant time, they must cause social or job distress, and they cannot be due to the effects of a general medical condition or to the use of a drug or medication.

Let's consider some of the major positive symptoms of schizophrenia in more detail. As noted earlier, one of the main problems in schizophrenia is distorted or disorganized thinking. People with schizophrenia often experience delusions, which are thoughts with inappropriate content. If someone sitting next to you in class leaned over and claimed to be Elvis in disguise or Jesus Christ or Adolf Hitler, the content of his or her thoughts would clearly be inappropriate or deviant—this individual would be experiencing a delusion. People who have schizophrenia sometimes hold a *delusion of grandeur*, which is a belief that they are more famous or important than they actually are, or a *delusion of persecution*, which is a belief that others are conspiring or plotting against them in some way.

It is also not unusual for people with schizophrenia to report distorted perceptions of the world. For them, objects can seem to change their shape or size; distances can be perceived in ways that are different from reality. Frequently, these *hallucinations*—which are perceptions that have no basis in external stimulation—are auditory. People with schizophrenia claim to hear disembodied voices in their heads, giving them commands or commenting on the quality of their activities ("You're an idiot," "You should stay away from that person," and so on). Some researchers believe that these voices may originate from the same areas of the brain that control language production. It may be the case that people with schizophrenia are actually "listening" to their inner voice (see Chapter 7) but fail to recognize the voice as their own. Instead, they falsely attribute the source of the voice to something external (Cleghorn et al., 1992; Evans, McGuire, & David, 2000; McGuire, Shah, & Murray, 1993).

Two other positive symptoms of schizophrenia that may be present are *disorganized speech* and *catatonia*. Sometimes the speech patterns of a person with *schizophrenia* appear quite jumbled and incoherent; the affected individual jumps repeatedly from one disconnected topic to another. ("I went to the beach today where the moon pulls the rabbit out of the hat. I'm the world's greatest cook, but that's because volcanic magma heats the glaciers and makes the water and the sand.") It's as if the mind has lost its internal editor—ideas or thoughts no longer flow in a connected way. In addition to displaying speech problems, someone with schizophrenia can behave in ways that are quite disorganized and bizarre. The person might engage in repetitive activities, such as swirling his or her arms repeatedly, or will appear to laugh or cry at inappropriate times. When *catatonia* is present, people will sometimes adopt a peculiar stance or position and remain immobile for hours; or they may wildly and suddenly change position for no apparent reason.

Negative symptoms of schizophrenia are expressed by the elimination or reduction of normal behaviour. For example, it's quite common for people with schizophrenia to display *flat affect*, which means that they show little or no emotional reaction to events. Show someone with flat affect an extremely funny movie or a tragic, heart-rending photo, and the person is unlikely to crack a smile or shed a tear. People with schizophrenia also often refuse to engage in the most basic and important of everyday activities. They may refuse to wash or clean themselves, eat, or dress themselves. Activities that are pleasurable to most people become unpleasurable or uninteresting to some individuals with schizophrenia.

For obvious reasons, people with schizophrenia are often unable to cope successfully at school or at work. In many cases, their behaviour becomes so maladaptive that

Grunnitus/Monkmeyer Press

When catatonia is present as a positive symptom of schizophrenia, the affected person might adopt a peculiar stance or position and remain immobile for hours.

hospitalization is required. As you'll see later in the chapter, there are reasons to believe that people with schizophrenia may be experiencing a kind of "broken" brain—fundamental neurological problems may underlie the bizarre thinking and behaviours that plague people affected with the disorder.

Personality Disorders

personality disorders

Chronic or enduring patterns of behaviour that lead to significant impairments in social functioning

paranoid personality disorder

A personality disorder characterized by pervasive distrust of others

dependent personality disorder

A personality disorder characterized by an excessive and persistent need to be taken care of by others

antisocial personality disorder

A personality disorder characterized by repeated criminal behaviour and a failure to learn from punishment

psychopathy

An alternative construct to the antisocial personality disorder; as well as criminal tendencies, it focuses on the underlying personality traits of manipulation, callousness, and impulsive thrill-seeking

All the psychological disorders we've considered up to now are described on Axis I of the *DSM-IV* (Clinical Disorders). Axis II describes **personality disorders,** which are essentially chronic or enduring patterns of behaviour that lead to significant impairments in social functioning (Livesley, 2001). People with personality disorders have a tendency to act repeatedly in an inflexible and maladaptive way. They may show an exaggerated distrust of others, as in **paranoid personality disorder,** or they may show an excessive and persistent need to be taken care of by others, as in **dependent personality disorder.** One of the best-known examples of a personality disorder, occurring mainly in males, is the **antisocial personality disorder.** People with this type of disorder pay no attention to society's rules and laws. They freely engage in any activity—from lying to murder—to get their way. Although often punished for their misconduct, they fail to learn and end up in prison. Even among other prison inmates, they stand out because of their long criminal records and the wide variation in the type of crimes they commit (Cunningham & Reidy, 1998).

As with other *DSM* diagnoses, the emphasis in defining antisocial personality disorder is on observable behaviour—in this case criminal behaviour. The closely related concept of **psychopathy** is more psychological and emphasizes the underlying personality traits (Hare, 1996, 2003). Therefore, it includes malevolent individuals who have not (yet) been arrested. This movement has been led by University of British Columbia psychologist Robert Hare and his colleagues (those in Canada include Stephen Hart, Adelle Forth, Jim Hemphill, Hughes Herve, Steve Wong, and Del Paulhus). Hare's most recent outline of the syndrome includes four facets: interpersonal manipulation, impulsive thrill seeking, callous affect (lack of guilt), and social deviance (criminal history). Hare developed the standard instrument for assessing psychopathy entitled the Psychopathy Checklist Revised (PCL-R): It requires that a trained assessor complete a 20-item rating scale, based on a semi-structured interview and detailed information from files or other corroborating sources (Hare, 2003).

Other researchers have also used the PCL-R to advance our knowledge of psychopaths and other violent offenders. Among these are Marnie Rice and Grant Harris of Mental Health Centre, Penetanguishene; Vernon Quinsey of Queen's University; and Martin Lalumière of the Clarke Institute of Psychiatry. One of the surprising findings of these researchers was that group therapy programs designed to rehabilitate violent psychopathic offenders actually increased their rate of reoffending. Perhaps the program raised their self-confidence and, therefore, their subsequent aggression, or it provided them with practice in appearing empathic, which they later used to manipulate other people more effectively (Harris, Rice, & Cormier, 1994; Rice, 1997). Nonetheless, use of the PCL-R and other data has permitted prediction of the likelihood of violent offenders reoffending with far more accuracy than has ever been possible (Hare, 2003; Harris, Rice, & Quinsey, 1993; Quinsey, Harris, Rice, & Cormier, 1998).

Whether we refer to antisocial personality disorder or psychopathy, the constructs are unique in the classification of psychological disorders. For one thing, these individuals show no personal distress or desire to change—unlike those afflicted with other disorders. And it would seem outrageous to find psychopaths not guilty of all their crimes just because they have a psychological disorder.

Some experts suggest that psychopathy better fits the notion of a "cheater-warrior strategy" that evolved during our evolutionary history and is passed along genetically to a small percentage of the human population today (Harris et al., 1994;

Paul Bernardo and his wife, Karla Homolka, abused and murdered several young women in the Hamilton, Ontario, area. The nature of their crimes, including the callousness, the manipulation, and the thrill-seeking, led psychologists to diagnose them as psychopathic.

Lalumière & Quinsey, 1999; Book & Quinsey, 2003). Other researchers suggest that it may be common even among non-offenders, including university students (Williams, Paulhus, & Hare, in press). Although these perspectives do not overlook the seriousness of the criminal activity, they do shift the emphasis of psychopathy from a rare disorder found in prisoners to a more common personality trait.

The **perfectionistic personality disorder** has been elaborated primarily by Canadian researchers Paul Hewitt, of the University of British Columbia, and Gordon Flett, of York University. Perfectionists have an exaggerated need to make things of the highest quality, organization, or precision. Instead of handing in a less-than-perfect assignment, they will continue to work on it until they have no time for other necessary tasks. As a result, their lives are full of stress, anxiety, and depression—with no particular successes to show for it (Flett & Hewittt, 2003). The disorder has not yet been given a distinct location in the *DSM*. Given its overlap with eating disorders, obsessive-compulsive disorder, and narcissism, some experts have argued that it is a combination of symptoms of other known disorders.

What is it about personality disorders that requires them to be placed on their own classification axis? Do personality disorders have characteristics that fundamentally distinguish them from the major clinical syndromes described on Axis I? Most mental health professionals believe that personality disorders are unique primarily because they tend to be more *ingrained* and *inflexible* than the major clinical syndromes outlined on Axis I (Barlow & Durand, 2002). These are not problems that typically appear and disappear over time, which is the case with many psychological disorders. They may not be accompanied by a sense of distress. Instead, these disorders arise from someone's basic personality and, as a result, tend to continue throughout adulthood and are quite resistant to therapy. Personality disorders are placed on a separate axis in the *DSM-IV* in part to force clinicians to consider the possibility that it is a personality characteristic, rather than a major clinical syndrome, that underlies the problem behaviour.

Because personality disorders are linked to an individual's personality, some mental health professionals have argued that it's wrong to think of them as *disorders* in the same sense as something like a specific phobia or depression (Gunderson, 1992; Trull & McCrae, 1994). In Chapter 12, we discussed the idea that personality can be defined by the Big Five personality dimensions (McCrae & Costa, 1985). Some researchers have argued that it is better to think about people with personality disorders as simply extreme or deviant on one or more of the five dimensions: extraversion, agreeableness, conscientiousness, neuroticism, and openness (Clarke & Livesley, 1994; Wiggins & Pincus, 1992). For example, the dimension of *agreeableness* measures how kind, warm, and trusting an individual is. It's possible that people classified with a paranoid personality disorder may simply lie at the extreme low end on the agreeableness scale—they trust almost no

perfectionistic personality disorder

A personality disorder characterized by an excessive and rigid need to achieve the highest level of quality in achievements

CRITICAL THINKING

Think back to our earlier discussion of how to conceptualize abnormality. Do you think personality disorders should be labelled as "abnormal" behaviours?

one. Similarly, perfectionism may be an exaggerated combination of conscientiousness and neuroticism (Alden, Ryder, & Mellings, 2002). At present, questions are still being raised about the proper way to think about personality disorders and whether the Big Five will be sufficient to account for the complexities of the disorders is still an unresolved question (Trull & Widiger, 2003).

Cult Membership and Internet Addiction: Psychological Disorders?

Psychologists are constantly debating whether other maladaptive tendencies should be added to the *DSM*. Some candidates have insufficient evidence to conclude that the condition is a psychological disorder rather than simply a social or personal problem. Some conditions are linked to new technologies, substances, or social conditions. Cult membership and Internet addiction are considered to be indications of psychological disorders to some observers, but they have not yet received official *DSM* status.

Cult Membership   James Ogloff of Simon Fraser University and Jeffrey Pfeifer of the University of Saskatchewan conducted a survey and examination of Canadian and American university students' attitudes toward cults (Ogloff & Pfeifer, 1992). Only about 2% of the respondents reported ever having been a member of a cult. Students generally reported feeling negative toward cults (including satanic cults) and alternative religious movements, but they expressed the most negative attitudes toward satanic cults and the least toward alternative religious movements. However, the fact that most university students hold negative attitudes toward cult membership does not mean that cult members are necessarily psychologically disordered. Other researchers have examined whether cult membership is generally psychologically harmful (Aronoff, Lynn, & Malinoski, 2000), and they conclude that, perhaps surprisingly to many, cult members generally seem to be well adjusted psychologically and show few obvious signs of greater-than-average levels of psychological disorders. The authors caution, however, that the usual cult environment of extreme conformity may mask some underlying psychological problems. They also note that former cult members who have recently left cults may experience some significant psychological problems (referred to as adjustment difficulties). Therefore, although cult membership can be problematic and severely stressful, particularly for the family and friends of cult members, current evidence does not indicate that cult membership by itself constitutes a psychological disorder or is highly correlated with such disorders.

Internet Addiction   Many substance-related addictions, such as those to alcohol, nicotine, and cannabis, are considered to be psychological disorders and are described in the *DSM-IV*. What about addiction to the Internet? Can obsessive interest in and time spent online constitute a "real" addiction? Some psychologists think so, particularly Kimberly Young. She has suggested (1998, 1999) that pathological Internet use can be considered very similar to pathological gambling (which is a disorder listed in the *DSM-IV*) insofar as it also involves a failure of impulse control without involving an intoxicant. Young has listed several criteria of "pathological Internet use." To be considered Internet addicted, she suggests people would meet four or more of the following criteria:

- Being preoccupied with the Internet (thinking about it while offline)
- Having an inability to control Internet use
- Using the Internet to escape from problems
- Showing signs of withdrawal when offline
- Staying online longer than originally intended

(See "What's on the Web?" for online information. But don't spend too much time there!)

CRITICAL   THINKING

What characteristics of the Internet make it likely to facilitate a variety of addictions?

Although it may appear on the next *DSM*, maladaptive Internet use was too recent a phenomenon to be included in the current version. In the meantime, people with such problems should seek help from psychologists, counsellors, or self-help groups (Cooper, Scherer, Boies, & Gordon, 1999). Other repetitive behaviours that are being considered for addition to the *DSM* include pornography addiction and video-game addiction.

Test Yourself 14.2

Check your knowledge about classifications of psychological disorders by picking the diagnostic category that best describes each of the following behaviour patterns. Pick from among the following terms: anxiety disorder, somatoform disorder, dissociative disorder, mood disorder, schizophrenia, personality disorder. (The answers are in Appendix B.)

1. Lynette is convinced that the ringing in her ears means she has a brain tumour, even though a variety of doctors can find nothing wrong: _____

2. Gabrielle is a checker—she often drives home five or six times a day to make sure that she hasn't left the oven on: _____

3. Orson hasn't left his house for six years—it's the only place he really feels safe: _____

4. Morty hates himself. He's convinced that he's worthless, stupid, and unlovable. No one can convince him otherwise: _____

5. Mike is found wandering aimlessly in the park. When questioned, he can't remember who he is or how he got to the park: _____

6. Bree is a habitual con artist with little regard for the truth. She steals regularly and feels no guilt or remorse about her actions: _____

7. Karen is convinced that her psychology professor is beaming his thoughts directly into her brain; she feels empowered and ready to complete her takeover of the world: _____

8. Carlos shows little or no emotional reaction to events in his world; in fact, he usually stands in the corner for hours at a time with his right arm resting on his head: _____

▶ Understanding Psychological Disorders: Biological, Cognitive, or Environmental?

LEARNING GOALS

1. Understand how biological and genetic factors can contribute to psychological disorders.
2. Learn how maladaptive thoughts can contribute to psychological disorders.
3. Be able to explain how environmental factors can contribute to psychological disorders.

The *DSM-IV* classification system is designed to provide a reliable way for mental health professionals to diagnose psychological problems. The word *reliable* in this case refers to whether professional clinicians will tend to arrive at the same or similar diagnoses for people with a given set of symptoms. In general, the *DSM* system is considered to be quite reliable, although agreement is higher for some diagnostic categories than for others (Nathan & Langenbucher, 2003). But it's important to remember that the *DSM-IV* is only a classification system—it does not indicate anything about the origin, or *etiology*, of the underlying disorder. What factors, alone or in combination, conspire to produce a major clinical syndrome, such as depression, anxiety, or schizophrenia? The answer, in a nutshell, is that we don't know for sure. But most current explanations, as well as most approaches to therapy, appeal to *biological*, *cognitive*, or *environmental* factors.

The recognition that psychological disorders are influenced by biological, cognitive, and environmental factors is sometimes called the **bio-psycho-social perspective.** Biological factors (*bio*) include physiological problems with the

bio-psycho-social perspective

The idea that psychological disorders are influenced, or caused, by a combination of biological, psychological (cognitive), and social (environmental) factors

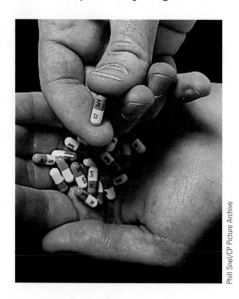

Some psychological disorders, such as depression, can be effectively treated by administering drugs that correct neurotransmitter imbalances in the brain.

Phill Snel/CP Picture Archive

body, particularly the brain, and genetic influences that are present at birth. Cognitive factors (*psycho*) include our beliefs, styles of thought, and any other psychological mechanisms that potentially influence behaviour. Finally, environmental factors (*social*) include what we learn from the environment, cultural influences, and how other people treat us in our daily lives. We'll consider each of these three major factors in greater detail in the following sections.

Biological Factors: Genes, Brain, and Hormones

Over the past several decades, significant advances have been made in our understanding of the brain and its functions. Most psychologists are now convinced that at least some kinds of abnormal behaviour result directly from brain dysfunction. The disordered thoughts of someone with schizophrenia, for example, may be partly due to a broken or at least malfunctioning brain. What is the evidence? Biological accounts are typically supported by two kinds of findings. First, it's been discovered that abnormal brain chemistry or abnormal brain structures accompany some kinds of mental disorders. Second, through the close study of family histories, it has been determined that a number of psychological disorders may have a powerful genetic component—psychological disorders tend to run in families in ways that cannot be easily explained by environmental histories. We discussed some of these findings in Chapter 3; we'll review and expand on that discussion here.

Neurotransmitter Imbalances   As you may recall from Chapter 3, schizophrenia has been linked to an excess supply of the neurotransmitter *dopamine* (Seeman, Lee, Chau Wong, & Wong, 1976; Snyder, 1976), or possibly to an interaction between dopamine and the neurotransmitter *serotonin* (Carlsson et al., 2001; Caspi et al., 2003). Support for the link has come primarily from studying how different drugs affect the disorder. Among the most effective treatments for schizophrenia are medications that act as dopamine *antagonists*, which means they reduce or block dopamine use in the brain (Gershon & Reider, 1992). It's also the case that drugs that increase the level of dopamine in the brain can sometimes produce side effects that resemble the symptoms found in schizophrenia (Braff & Huey, 1988; Davidson et al., 1987). Abnormal dopamine levels may not be the only cause of schizophrenia—for example, not all people with schizophrenia are helped by dopamine-reducing medications—but problems in brain neurochemistry are widely believed to be at least partly responsible for the disorder (Csernansky & Bardgett, 1998). Currently, the neurotransmitters glutamate, GABA, and serotonin are also being considered as factors in the development and maintenance of schizophrenia (Walker et al., 2004).

Neurotransmitter imbalances may also contribute to mood disorders, such as manic states and depression. Once again, most of the effective medications for these problems act by altering the actions of neurotransmitters in the brain. Fluoxetine (more commonly known by its brand name, Prozac) is one of the most commonly prescribed treatments for depression; it acts by slowing the reuptake of serotonin, thereby prolonging the neurotransmitter's effectiveness. More generally, depression and mania have been linked to a group of neurotransmitters called *monoamines*, which include serotonin, norepinephrine, and dopamine. Researchers currently believe that these neurotransmitters are involved in the regulation of mood, although the specifics have yet to be worked out (Hammen, 2003). It's unlikely that mood disorders are caused by a single neurotransmitter deficit. Instead, a decrease in one may have multiple effects on the others. A decrease in serotonin, for instance, may permit the levels of other neurotransmitters in the brain to vary more widely; these more complex interactions probably work together in some way to alter mood abnormally (Goodwin & Jamison, 1990). Recent research suggests that stress hormones, such as cortisol, may play an important role as well in mood disorders like depression (Sher, 2004).

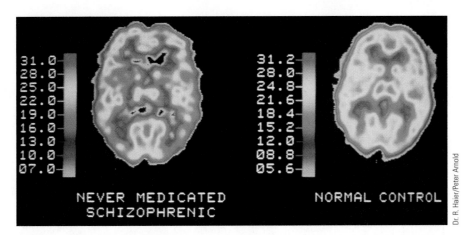

NEVER MEDICATED SCHIZOPHRENIC   NORMAL CONTROL

Dr. R. Haier/Peter Arnold

People who have such disorders as schizophrenia may possess malfunctioning brains. These two PET scans, taken from a person diagnosed with schizophrenia (left) and one without the disorder (right), show dramatic differences in brain activity levels. The blue and purple colours in the scans show areas of relatively low brain activity.

Structural Problems   In addition to neurochemical problems, such as imbalances in neurotransmitters, people who have serious psychological problems may also have structural problems in their brains. In the case of schizophrenia, anatomical and brain-imaging studies have revealed that people with schizophrenia tend to have larger *ventricles*, which are the liquid-filled cavities in the brain. (For reasons that are not yet clear, increased ventricle size tends to be more likely in men who have schizophrenia.) Larger ventricles are associated with the loss, or shrinkage, of brain tissue, and this factor may help explain some instances of schizophrenia (Pahl, Swayze, & Andreasen, 1990). Evidence also suggests that activity in the frontal areas of the brain may be abnormally low in patients with schizophrenia (Berman & Weinberger, 1990). Although it's not clear why these activity levels are low, decreased brain activity in certain prefrontal regions may directly or indirectly alter the neural pathways associated with the neurotransmitter dopamine (Davis, Kahn, Ko, & Davidson, 1991). Postmortem studies have also found abnormalities in how neurons are interconnected in certain regions of the brain, suggesting that schizophrenia may involve faulty wiring in the neural circuits (Walker et al., 2004).

These data are convincing, but it's important to remember that not all people with schizophrenia show these kinds of neurological problems. Not all people with schizophrenia have larger ventricles or show lower frontal lobe activity. Moreover, not all people who have been diagnosed with depression respond to drug therapies that alter the levels or actions of monoamines. So we're left with a somewhat cloudy picture. There's little doubt that psychological disorders are sometimes associated with observable abnormalities in brain chemistry or function. But whether these factors are the true cause of such disorders as schizophrenia or depression, or simply one cause, or even occur as a consequence of having the disorder, is not currently known. For example, larger ventricle size is observed more often in people who have had schizophrenia for a long time, so it's conceivable that the structural abnormality is partly a consequence of the disorder or even of its treatment (DeLisi et al., 1997).

Genetic Contributions   Increasingly, researchers are concluding that people may inherit predispositions toward abnormality. For example, the odds that any particular individual in the population will develop schizophrenia are roughly 1 in 100. But if you have a brother, sister, or parent with the disorder, the odds increase dramatically, perhaps to 1 in 10. If you have an identical twin—someone who has essentially the same genetic information as you do—and your twin has been diagnosed with schizophrenia, the odds that you will develop the disorder during your lifetime jump to about 1 in 2 (Gottesman, 1991) (see ▶ Figure 14.6 on page 590). Notice that the disorder cannot be explained entirely by appealing to genetic factors—otherwise, identical twins would always share the disorder—but these data suggest that genetic background plays a significant role.

CRITICAL   THINKING
Why don't all people who are diagnosed with schizophrenia show the same neurological problems?

▶ **Figure 14.6**

Schizophrenia Concordance Rates

Each bar shows the risk of developing schizophrenia under various conditions. For example, if one identical twin has schizophrenia, there is a roughly 50% risk that the other will also develop the disorder. In general, the closer the individual is related genetically to the person with schizophrenia, the more likely he or she is to develop the disorder. (From *Schizophrenia Genesis: The Origins of Madness* by Irving Gottesman. Copyright © 1990 by Irving Gottesman. Reprinted by permission of Henry Holt and Company, LLC.)

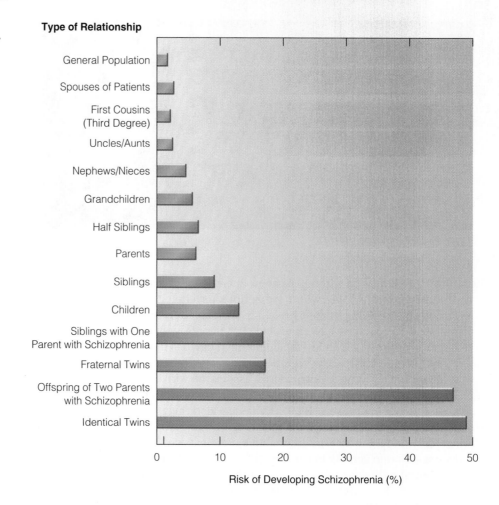

A similar pattern emerges with mood disorders. Depression and bipolar disorder tend to run in families, and the *concordance rate*, which measures the likelihood of sharing a disorder, is quite high between identical twins. A number of studies have shown that if one twin is diagnosed with depression, there is a 50% or greater chance that the other twin will also be diagnosed with depression; the concordance rate may be even higher for bipolar disorders (Gershon, 1990). It is also the case that adoptees with biological parents who have a mood disorder are themselves more likely to have a mood disorder. It is the biological history rather than the environmental history that, on average, predicts the chances of becoming affected by the disorder (Wender et al., 1986).

Genetic factors help predict the likelihood that someone will experience certain psychological disorders, but genetic factors are not necessarily sufficient to explain abnormal behaviour. Anxiety disorders, for example, are more likely to occur in people born with sensitive temperaments, but experience will influence whether a full-blown disorder actually develops.

Cognitive Factors: Thinking Maladaptive Thoughts

If you look closely into the mind of someone who has a psychological disorder, you will often find fixed and disordered styles of thinking. People with anxiety disorders, somatoform disorders, or just about any of the other disorders we've discussed typically believe things about themselves or the world that have little or no basis in reality. Robert, who is depressed, is convinced that he lacks ability and drive, even though he is a successful banker. Jill, who has agoraphobia, refuses to leave her house because she's convinced that something terrible will happen outside, even though she can think of no real reason for this belief.

Many psychologists feel that such faulty beliefs may be more than just symptoms of an underlying disorder—they may contribute to, or even cause, the disorder itself. To see how this might work, suppose we are able to convince you, by feeding you false but convincing reports, that your city was soon going to be bombed. Your anxiety level would certainly shoot up, and there's little question that your behaviour would change. You might not leave your house, and you might, in fact, end up spending a lot of time crying and huddled under a table in your basement. This behaviour is not irrational if the belief about the attack is true. Similarly, many people with psychological disorders act the way they do because they have incorrect beliefs. If you're absolutely convinced that you're no good and can never succeed at anything, it's not surprising that you withdraw from social situations and fail to secure steady employment.

Maladaptive Attributions Psychologists use the term *attribution* to refer to the processes involved in assigning causality to a behaviour (see Chapter 13). When you fail at something, such as a test or a new job, you attribute the failure to a cause, such as your own incompetence or the lousy teacher. It turns out that people who have psychological disorders, particularly depression, have relatively distinctive and predictable attributional or explanatory styles. Unfortunately, the attributions that these people make are often maladaptive, which means that they lead to behaviours that are abnormal or unproductive (McFarland & Miller, 1994).

As ▶ Figure 14.7 shows, when something bad happens to a person prone to depression, he or she is likely to explain it in terms of *internal* ("I'm to blame rather than the situation"), *stable* (long-lasting), and *global* (widespread) attributions (Abramson, Metalsky, & Alloy, 1989; Foersterling, Buehner, & Gall, 1998). Let's suppose you fail a test at school. If you're depressed, you will probably attribute that failure to some personal inadequacy (internal) that is likely to be long lasting (stable) and that will apply in lots of situations other than school (global). People who are not prone to depression tend to have more flexible explanatory styles. They might attribute the failure to some *external* source ("I've got a rotten

CRITICAL   THINKING
Try to identify your own attributional style. Do you tend to attribute outcomes to global, stable, and internal causes?

Stable
"I was born stupid."

Internal
"It's totally my fault."

Global
"I'll probably fail all my courses."

▶ **Figure 14.7**

Maladaptive Thoughts in Depression
Depressed individuals tend to attribute failure to internal, stable, and global conditions.

teacher") and consider the failure to be *unstable* ("I had a bad day"), and they will probably make a *specific* rather than global attribution. Nondepressed people have less of a tendency to overgeneralize from a situation at school to other areas of life. They are also less likely to process every event as having implications for their self-evaluation (Moretti, Segal, McCann, & Shaw, 1996).

Learned Helplessness   What produces these different explanatory styles? It's difficult to know whether people who make maladaptive attributions do so because they are depressed or whether it is the unfortunate explanatory style that creates the depression. Some researchers have argued that prolonged experience with failure may be one contributing factor. According to the **learned helplessness** theory of depression (Seligman, 1975), if you repeatedly fail while attempting to control your environment, you acquire a general sense of helplessness. You give up and become passive, which, the theory proposes, leads to depression. Still, it's unlikely that we can account for all forms of depression by appealing simply to repeated failure. Experience with failure may be a necessary condition for acquiring depression, but it is not a sufficient condition. Many people fail repeatedly yet show no tendencies toward depression.

Moreover, it isn't really the failure that leads to depression but rather your attributions about the failure. Instead of learning to be helpless, it is really the sense of *hopelessness*—the belief that things cannot become better because of internal, stable, and global factors—that is more likely to produce depression (Alloy & Clements, 1998; Joiner et al., 2001). Whether this sense of hopelessness can be explained by appealing to experience alone or to some interaction between experience and biological or genetic predispositions remains to be seen (Alloy et al., 2001). In a recent study, researcher Kenneth Cramer of the University of Windsor and his colleagues demonstrated two important determinants of feeling helpless: believing that you were going to fail in a task and feeling that you have no control over outcomes that are important to you (Cramer, Nickels, & Gural, 1997). They also found that an uncertain outcome did not seem to have the same effect in creating a feeling of helplessness; people seem to be able to cope with uncertainty better than with lack of confidence or lack of control.

learned helplessness

A general sense of helplessness that is acquired when people repeatedly fail in their attempts to control their environment; learned helplessness may play a role in depression

Prolonged exposure to stressful situations may play a role in the onset of psychological disorders.

Peter Turnley/Corbis

Environmental Factors: Do People Learn to Act Abnormally?

All theories of psychological disorders ultimately appeal either directly or indirectly to environmental factors. Even if a researcher believes that a disorder, such as schizophrenia, is primarily caused by a genetically induced brain dysfunction, it is still necessary to explain why identical twins don't always share the disorder. Experience clearly plays a pivotal role. Similarly, the irrational beliefs and explanatory styles that characterize depression must be learned somewhere, although two people with the same experiences may not always end up with the same set of beliefs. Once again, experience is the bedrock on which the psychological interpretation is built.

Culture's Role   Cultural factors also play an obvious and important role (Harper, 2001). Although the symptoms of most serious psychological disorders—such as schizophrenia and depression—are generally similar across the world (Draguns, 1997), culture-based differences emerge. For example, the types of delusions found in schizophrenia depend to a certain extent on cultural background (Tateyama, Asai, Hashimoto, Bartels, & Kasper, 1998). Different cultural groups may also be more or less likely to show symptoms of disorders because of cultural "rules" for expressing emotion and action (Manson, 1995). If you live in a culture, for instance, that discourages the expression of emotion, then depression will be somewhat more difficult to detect and treat.

Your cultural background may also determine the likelihood that you will be exposed to environmental events that could trigger the onset of psychological disorders. Obviously, if you live somewhere in the world where war or extreme poverty is a way of life, you are likely to encounter more stressful events that, in combination with a genetic predisposition, could lead to psychological problems (Bonanno, Field, Kovacevic, & Kaltman, 2002). Cultural goals or ideals can also influence your psychological health. For example, living in a society that places enormous emphasis on weight ideals can increase the chances that you'll develop an eating disorder, such as bulimia or anorexia nervosa (see Chapter 11). (You'll learn more about how cultural ideals and stressors in everyday life can affect your physical and psychological health in Chapter 16.)

Conditioning Disorders   Mental health professionals who follow a social learning model feel that psychological disorders may be essentially *learned*. People can learn to act and think abnormally in perhaps the same way they might learn how to bake a cake, make friends, or avoid talking in class. Experts with this view of abnormality propose that learning principles of the type we discussed in Chapter 6 help explain why psychological disorders develop and how they can be best treated. A specific phobia, for example, could be acquired through *classical conditioning;* you might learn to associate a particular stimulus or event with another event that makes you afraid. Alternatively, you might learn to act abnormally, through *instrumental conditioning*, because you've been reinforced for those actions. Acting in a strange way thus becomes more likely than it was before.

Learning theorists believe that modelling, or observational learning, might play a particularly important role in the development of some psychological disorders. As we discussed in Chapter 6, evidence suggests that specific phobias are sometimes acquired through modelling (Bouton, Mineka, & Barlow, 2001). Parents who react in terror to the sight of snakes might easily transfer this reaction to their children in this fashion. Some of the best evidence has come from animal studies, in which it is possible to control how the fear reaction is initially acquired. Rhesus monkeys raised in the wild show an extremely strong fear response to snakes; monkeys reared in the laboratory will show a similar reaction, but only if

CRITICAL   THINKING

Do you have any kind of specific phobia? Can you trace the fear to any particular experience in your life? Does anyone else in your family share the same fear**?**

they've witnessed other monkeys reacting fearfully when snakes are introduced into the cage. This research has made it clear that it is not necessary for the animal to directly experience something negative, such as getting attacked and bitten by the snake; the animal can acquire its fear simply by watching other monkeys act afraid (Cook & Mineka, 1989). Modelling in this case makes adaptive sense because appropriate actions can be learned without directly experiencing negative consequences.

The monkey data are important because they show how modelling can lead to the acquisition of a strong fear response. Obviously, for monkeys in the wild it's quite adaptive to be afraid of snakes. For humans, we know that modelling is also a powerful way to learn, but the evidence that modelling underlies specific phobias—which, after all, are essentially irrational fears—is still largely indirect at this point. Stanley Rachman and Sheila Woody of the University of British Columbia have pointed out that many people with specific phobias cannot remember having a traumatic experience with the object of their fear (Rachman, 1990). It's also the case that specific phobias tend to run in families—if your father was afraid of heights, for instance, there's an increased chance that you too will be afraid of heights (Fyer et al., 1990). This kind of evidence is consistent with a modelling account of specific phobias but it does not preclude alternative accounts (Woody & McLean, 2001). From our adaptive perspective, it's interesting to note that modelling, which is essentially an adaptive process, might under certain conditions lead people to acquire behaviours that are not very adaptive.

As with the biological, genetic, and cognitive factors we've considered, it's unlikely that learning principles alone will be able to account for why people develop psychological disorders. People probably can't learn to be schizophrenic, for example, although stressful events in the environment may play an important role in this disorder (Walker et al., 2004). Even with phobias, which may be largely learning based, it is probably necessary to be predisposed to anxiety for a full-blown phobia to develop (Barlow, 1988). Experience plays a significant role in the development of most psychological disorders, but it does not act alone. Behaviour, both normal and abnormal, is virtually always produced by multiple causes.

CONCEPT SUMMARY

CAUSES OF PSYCHOLOGICAL DISORDERS

Factor	Description	Example
Biological	Physiological problems, particularly in the brain; could include neurotransmitter imbalances, structural problems, and genetic influences	Jennifer feels extremely depressed. She goes to a psychologist, who asks her whether anyone else in her family has experienced depression. Jennifer reports that her mother and grandmother did have bouts of severe depression.
Cognitive	Our beliefs and styles of thought, such as maladaptive attributions and a sense of hopelessness	Jennifer is struggling with her studies. She receives a D on a big exam. She is disgusted with herself and keeps thinking, "How could I be so stupid? I am such a loser!"
Environmental	The influence of experience and culture; cultural background, events, and learning all have an impact on psychological disorders	Jennifer's family has always struggled financially, and now her parents are going through a nasty divorce. Jennifer acts disruptively because it's one of the few ways she can get any attention from them.

Test Yourself 14.3

Check your knowledge about how psychologists have attempted to understand psychological disorders by answering the following questions. (The answers are in Appendix B.)

1. Which of the following biological conditions is most likely to be a contributing factor in schizophrenia?
   a. slowed reuptake of the neurotransmitter serotonin
   b. excessive amounts of the neurotransmitter dopamine
   c. smaller than normal ventricles in the brain
   d. increased random activity in the frontal lobes

2. Studies examining the genetics of schizophrenia have discovered that
   a. Schizophrenia is a learned rather than an inherited disorder.
   b. Living with two parents with schizophrenia increases your risk of developing schizophrenia by about 65%.
   c. Identical twins are more likely to develop schizophrenia than are fraternal twins.
   d. If your identical twin has schizophrenia, you have about a 50% chance of developing the disorder yourself.

3. Psychologists studying depression have found that depressed people tend to make the following kinds of personal attributions:
   a. external, stable, and global
   b. internal, unstable, and global
   c. internal, stable, and specific
   d. internal, stable, and global

4. Studies examining how monkeys develop a strong fear response to snakes have been used to support which of the following accounts of specific phobias?
   a. instrumental conditioning
   b. observational learning
   c. learned helplessness
   d. classical conditioning

Psychological Disorders

R
E
V
I
E
W

This chapter has focused on the most maladaptive states and traits endured by the human mind, namely, psychological disorders. They are the underlying mental problems assumed to explain various kinds of abnormal behaviour. Could they actually be adaptive processes in disguise? For example, some have argued that depression is a mechanism for disengaging from a current lifestyle, a message from nature to back off. Others have suggested that amnesias are adaptive in preventing recall of traumatic events. Such claims are reminiscent of Shakespeare in that there may indeed be some method (i.e., a function) in our madness.

Or psychological disorders may simply be adaptive processes gone wrong. Anxiety, for example, is an adaptive bodily response that prepares us for action and keeps us vigilant for danger. Only when prolonged does it impair normal functioning. Personality disorders include perfectionism and narcissism: They may simply be exaggerated, and therefore, maladaptive versions of two adaptive traits, conscientiousness and self-esteem.

However, these notions can take us only so far. Most psychological disorders seem to have no adaptive value. Instead, we have structured this chapter more in terms of the scientific problems confronted by psychologists. How do we define abnormal behaviour and organize psychological disorders? The practical side of these issues will be dealt with in the next chapter on therapies.

First, how should we conceptualize abnormal behaviour? This task has turned out to be more difficult than expected. A number of criteria have been proposed, including the notions of statistical and cultural deviance, emotional distress, and dysfunction. None of these criteria alone seemed sufficient to capture it all. Instead, the presence of abnormality is usually defined by observing some combination of these factors.

Many mental health professionals conceive of abnormal behaviour in terms of a medical model. According to this view, psychological disorders are best described as illnesses that explain an individual's abnormal behaviour. They can be "cured" through appropriate treatment. Note that a given abnormal behaviour, like a physical symptom, could have more than one possible cause. So mental illness is better classified in terms of psychological disorders than by the specific abnormal behaviour.

In contrast, the sociological model assumes that labelling an individual's behaviour as abnormal is more of a declaration that the individual's social environment disapproves of the behaviour. This model provides a useful warning that a patient might be fine in a different setting. But it should not be taken too literally. No change of setting will help someone with schizophrenia or other serious conditions. And society is unlikely to change to suit the patient's behaviour. So psychologists must do their best to alleviate the patient's distress.

Second, how do we classify psychological disorders? Because much similarity and overlap occurs between psychological disorders, a standardized manual called the *DSM* has proved to be invaluable. Most mental health professionals in North America rely on the *DSM-IV*, which lists objective criteria for the diagnosis of each psychological disorder. The latest revision—called the *DSM-IV-TR*—is a temporary transition to the upcoming *DSM-V*. All these versions include five major rating dimensions, or axes, which are used to record the presence of

clinical or personality disorders, existing medical conditions, environmental problems, and the ability of the individual to function globally. In this chapter we focused our attention primarily on Axis I, which lists the major clinical syndromes.

The huge majority of psychologists feel that the DSM classification system is a great benefit to the field. Nonetheless, debate continues about what alterations to make for the next version. Many experts feel that the concept of psychopathy should replace antisocial personality disorder. Others want to add disorders regarding Internet addiction and cult membership. In short, the DSM should always be considered to be a work in progress.

Third, what are the root causes of disorders? Mental health professionals currently believe that the root cause, or etiology, of most disorders lies in a combination of biological, cognitive, and environmental factors. Evidence supports the idea that some psychological problems result from neurotransmitter problems in the brain or perhaps from structural problems in brain anatomy. Many psychological disorders also appear to have a genetic basis—individuals may inherit a predisposition for a particular kind of problem. Nonetheless, other approaches, including learning theories and cognitive science, continue to advance our understanding of disorders.

CHAPTER SUMMARY

▶ Conceptualizing Abnormal Behaviour

The term *abnormal* is often used as roughly equivalent to the term *psychological disorder*. But psychologists have had an ongoing struggle with how to best define the concept of abnormality. No single criterion is sufficient to capture the concept.

Criteria for Defining Abnormal Behaviour

A number of criteria have been proposed to define abnormality. *Statistical deviance* refers to infrequency. *Cultural deviance* compares behaviour with existing cultural norms. Behaviour is considered abnormal if it violates the accepted standards of society. A third criterion for defining abnormality is *emotional distress*. A final criterion is *dysfunction*, a breakdown in the ability to perform daily tasks. *Abnormal* and *normal* are best seen as ends of a continuum rather than as distinct categories.

The Medical Model versus the Sociological Model

According to the *medical model*, abnormal behaviour is seen as an underlying disease that can be cured. This conception of abnormality has been quite influential; drugs are effective in treating a variety of disorders, and most disorders can be classified in terms of symptoms. The *sociolog-*

ical model argues that mental illness does not lie directly in the patient but in the context and perceptions of the individual and society as a whole.

▶ Classifying Psychological Disorders: The *DSM-IV*

Even if we successfully define abnormality, we still need a means for naming and classifying the underlying disorders that lead to abnormal behaviour. The purpose of the *Diagnostic and Statistical Manual of Mental Disorders* (*DSM-IV*), now in its fourth edition, is to provide clinicians with a well-defined classification system for psychological disorders. Based on objective and measurable criteria, the *DSM-IV* consists of five major ratings dimensions, or *axes*, that assess clinical and personality disorders, health status, environmental stressors, and the client's ability to cope.

Anxiety Disorders: Beyond Rational Fear

Anxiety disorders are diagnosed when levels of worry and apprehension become so extreme that behaviour is impaired in some way. *Generalized anxiety disorder* is characterized by excessive and chronic worrying. *Panic disorder* is characterized by sudden "attacks" of extremely intense fear or dread and is sometimes associated with the complication *agoraphobia* (a fear of being in public places). In *obsessive-compulsive disorder*, anxiety manifests itself through persistent uncontrollable thoughts (*obsessions*) or by the compelling need to perform one or more actions repeatedly (*compulsions*). *Social phobia* is an extreme fear of social interactions. The defining feature of *specific phobic disorder* is a highly focused fear of a specific object or situation.

Somatoform Disorders: Body and Mind

Somatoform disorders are psychological problems that focus on the physical body. *Hypochondriasis* involves a preoccupation with the idea that one has developed a serious disease based on a misinterpretation of normal bodily reactions. A related problem, *somatization disorder*, involves a focus on physical symptoms rather than an underlying disease. In *conversion disorder*, real physical impairment exists in the absence of an apparent physical cause.

Dissociative Disorders: Disruptions of Identity or Awareness

Dissociative disorders are defined by the dissociation of conscious awareness from previous thoughts or memories. In *dissociative amnesia*, a person is unable to remember certain events after experiencing traumatic stress. *Dissociative fugue* involves a loss of personal identity, accompanied by flight from the home environment. In *dissociative identity disorder*, a person alternates between distinct identities or personality states. Controversy surrounds the diagnosis of dissociative identity disorder for a number of reasons.

Mood Disorders: Depression and Mania

Mood disorders (prolonged and disabling disruptions in emotional state) come in two varieties: *depressive disorders* and *bipolar disorders*. A *major depressive episode* is characterized by a number of symptoms, including loss of interest in daily activities, daily fatigue or loss of energy, trouble concentrating, and suicidal thoughts. In *dysthymic disorder*, depression tends to be milder but more chronic. In a *bipolar disorder*, a person alternates between depression and *mania*, a hyperactive, euphoric condition. *Suicide* is one fatal consequence that can result from a mood disorder. Risk factors for suicide include substance abuse, the sudden occurrence of a very stressful event, and the occurrence of other suicides.

Schizophrenia: Severe Thought Disturbance

People with *schizophrenia* live in an internal world marked by delusions, hallucinations, and generally disordered thinking. Schizophrenia can be expressed in a variety of complex ways. Two major types of symptoms in schizophrenia are *positive symptoms* and *negative symptoms*. Positive symptoms are observable expressions of abnormal behaviour, such as *delusions* (thoughts with inappropriate content), *hallucinations* (perceptions that have no basis in external stimulation), *disorganized speech*, and *catatonia*. Negative symptoms involve the reduction of normal behaviour, as in *flat affect*.

Personality Disorders

Personality disorders are chronic or enduring patterns of behaviour that lead to significant impairments in social functioning. They include *paranoid personality disorder* (an exaggerated distrust of others), *dependent personality disorder* (an excessive need to be taken care of by others), *perfectionistic personality disorder* (an excessive need to accomplish tasks that are error-free), and *antisocial personality disorder* (a repeated tendency toward criminal activity). *Psychopathy* resembles antisocial personality disorder but emphasizes the underlying personality traits. Some researchers argue that all personality disorders are simply extreme or deviant on one or more of the Big Five personality dimensions.

Cult Membership and Internet Addiction: Psychological Disorders?

Although most university students have negative attitudes toward cults, little evidence suggests that cult members have more psychological disorders than noncult members. However, they may experience some significant adjustment problems on leaving the cult. Some psychologists have suggested that Internet addiction constitutes a psychological disorder much like pathological gambling. However, the phenomenon is too recent to have been included in the *DSM-IV*, and it is too soon to tell whether the problem of excessive Internet use will eventually be found to meet all the criteria to be considered a psychological disorder.

▶ Understanding Psychological Disorders: Biological, Cognitive, or Environmental?

What are the causes of psychological disorders? The answer to many psychological problems lies in an interaction among biological, cognitive, and environmental factors. This view is sometimes called the *bio-psycho-social perspective*.

Biological Factors: Genes, Brain, and Hormones

Abnormal brain chemistry accompanies some psychological disorders. Schizophrenia has been linked to an excess supply of dopamine or to an interaction between dopamine and serotonin. Neurotransmitter imbalances may also contribute to mood disorders. Structural problems in the brain are also sometimes associated with some psychological disorders. Also, research indicates that genetic factors probably play a role in psychological disorders. People may inherit predispositions toward certain disorders. The *concordance rate* (likelihood of sharing a disorder) is quite high between identical twins.

Cognitive Factors: Thinking Maladaptive Thoughts

People with psychological disorders, particularly depression, have distinctive and predictable attributional or explanatory styles. When something bad happens to someone prone to depression, he or she is likely to make internal, stable, and global attributions. According to the *learned helplessness* theory of depression, people who repeatedly fail to control their environment give up, leading to depression.

Environmental Factors: Do People Learn to Act Abnormally?

Experience plays a pivotal role in psychological disorders. Culture, for example, can affect how disorders are expressed and the likelihood that you will be exposed to events that could trigger the onset of psychological disorders. Some professionals feel that disorders can be learned through classical or instrumental conditioning, or through modelling.

Terms to Remember

abnormal behaviour, 562
psychological disorder, 562

Conceptualizing Abnormal Behaviour
statistical deviance criterion, 563
cultural deviance criterion, 564
emotional distress criterion, 565
dysfunction criterion, 565
insanity, 567
medical model, 568
sociological model, 568

Classifying Psychological Disorders: The DSM-IV
DSM-IV, 569
anxiety disorders, 572
generalized anxiety disorder, 572
panic disorder, 572
agoraphobia, 572
obsessive-compulsive disorder, 573
social phobia, 573
specific phobic disorder, 574
somatoform disorders, 575
hypochondriasis, 575

somatization disorder, 575
conversion disorder, 576
dissociative disorders, 576
dissociative amnesia, 576
dissociative fugue, 576
dissociative identity disorder, 577
mood disorders, 578
major depressive episode, 578
bipolar disorder, 579
manic state, 579
schizophrenia, 582
personality disorders, 584
paranoid personality disorder, 584
dependent personality disorder, 584
antisocial personality disorder, 584
psychopathy, 584
perfectionistic personality disorder, 585

Understanding Psychological Disorders: Biological, Cognitive, or Environmental?
bio-psycho-social perspective, 587
learned helplessness, 592

Recommended Readings

De Silva, W. P., & Rachman, S. J. (1996). *Panic disorder: The facts.* New York: Oxford University Press. These succinct summaries of research and treatment of several of the anxiety disorders were co-written by Stanley Rachman of the University of British Columbia.

Flett, G. L., & Hewitt, P. L. (2003). *Perfectionism: Theory, research and treatment.* Washington, DC: American Psychological Association. Co-written by researchers from York University and the University of British Columbia, this volume provides up-to-date summaries of several perspectives on perfectionism.

Hare, R. D. (1993). *Without conscience: The disturbing world of the psychopaths among us.* New York: Pocket Books. University of British Columbia psychologist Robert Hare has been studying psychopaths, both criminal and noncriminal, for more than 30 years and is one of the world's foremost experts on the subject. This

volume summarizes his research in a popular format. The detailed sketches include those of Ted Bundy and Clifford Olson.

Woody, S., & McLean, P. D. (2001). *Anxiety disorders in adults: An evidence-based approach to psychological treatment.* New York: Oxford University Press. Co-authored by University of British Columbia researchers, this volume makes clear recommendations about treating various anxiety disorders.

 For additional readings, explore InfoTrac® College Edition, your online library. Go to http://www.adaptivemind3e.nelson.com.

Hint: Enter these search terms: diagnosis of mental illness, anxiety disorder, dissociative identity disorder, bipolar disorder, schizophrenia, causes of mental illness.

Media Resources

🖧 What's on the Web?

Please note that Web addresses are subject to change. Check out the accompanying website for updates: http://www.adaptivemind3e.nelson.com.

This site presents practice quiz questions, hypercontent, information on degrees and careers in psychology, study tips, and more.

Centre for Addiction and Mental Health

http://www.camh.net

The CAMH is now Canada's most comprehensive organization for all issues relating to psychological disorders. It recently incorporated a number of other institutions, including the Clarke Institute of Psychiatry.

Canadian Mental Health Association

http://www.cmha.ca

CMHA combats mental health problems and emotional disorders through research and information services, sponsored research projects, workshops, seminars, pamphlets, newsletters, and resource centres. The site includes such items as stress tests and "10 Tips for Mental Health."

Mental Health, Law, and Policy Institute

http://www.sfu.ca/mhlpi/

Located at Simon Fraser University, this institute promotes collaboration among research practitioners and policy-makers working in the area of mental health law and policy. Includes a useful set of links to sites, such as the Canadian Supreme Court and Statistics Canada.

Center for Internet Addiction Recovery

http://www.netaddiction.com

Are you addicted to the Web? Try the "Internet Addiction Test" link and see.

The Phobia List

http://www.phobialist.com

Who thinks these things up? According to the author of this site, "all of the phobia names on this list have been found in some reference book." So find out for yourself what you would call a fear of being forgotten (athazagoraphobia). You probably didn't know that there was such a thing as a fear of gravity (barophobia). Hundreds of phobias are listed at this site.

Dr. Ivan's Depression Central

http://www.psycom.net/depression.central.html

This site, according to its author (Dr. Ivan), "is the Internet's central clearinghouse for information on all types of depressive disorders and on the most effective treatments" for individuals who have various mood disorders. Topics you can find at this site include famous people with mood disorders, seasonal affective disorder, and postpartum depression.

Internet Mental Health

http://www.mentalhealth.com

This website includes an alphabetical list of links for dozens of psychological disorders. Click on "Disorders" in the menu on the left. Click on each link, and you'll be able to read detailed information about the disorder. The site even has a tool for diagnosis of disorders (although it goes without saying that you should view such a tool with more than a little caution!).

ThomsonNOW™ ThomsonNOW™

http://hed.nelson.com

Go to this site for the link to ThomsonNOW™, your one-stop study shop. Take a Pretest for this chapter and ThomsonNOW™ will generate a personalized Study Plan based on your test results. The Study Plan will identify the topics you need to review and direct you to online resources to help you master those topics. You can then take a Posttest to determine what concepts you have mastered and what you still need work on.

Psyk.trek 3.0

Check out Psyk.trek 3.0 for further study of the concepts in this chapter. Psyk.trek's 65 interactive learning modules, simulations, and quizzes offer additional opportunities for you to interact with, reflect on, and retain the material:

Abnormal Behavior and Therapy: Anxiety Disorders
Abnormal Behavior and Therapy: Mood Disorders
Abnormal Behavior and Therapy: Schizophrenia Disorders

© Anne Dowie/Index Stock Imagery

You cannot teach people anything. You can only help them discover it within themselves.

—Galileo

The art of medicine consists in amusing the patient while nature cures the disease.

—Voltaire

Therapy

I f you weep eight hours a day, hear voices shouting in your head, or have to check everything you do exactly 333 times, you'll have trouble leading a normal life. It helps to know—as you learned in the last chapter—that these are well-known symptoms of mood disorders, schizophrenia, and obsessive-compulsive disorder, respectively. But what can be done about them? This chapter takes us beyond putting labels on disorders to details about how to treat them.

To take the step from Chapter 14 to Chapter 15, we begin with the distinction between two categories of mental health professionals: researchers and psychotherapists (therapists, for short). Researchers help advance our understanding of disorders, but therapists are the hands-on specialists who deal with patients. Therapists have a variety of techniques—summarized by the term **psychotherapy**—to help people regain their ability to function.

The particular technique used by the therapist will depend on a number of factors, including the specific type of psychological disorder being treated and the personality of the person seeking treatment. A treatment can be administered in several ways. Some people respond well to one-on-one sessions with a therapist, whereas others thrive best in group settings. As we discussed in Chapter 1, good therapists are often *eclectic*, meaning they draw on a variety

psychotherapy

Treatment designed to help people deal with mental, emotional, or behavioural problems

of therapeutic techniques to meet the needs of the particular client. This commitment to eclecticism doesn't mean that therapists must abandon all theoretical orientations (Lazarus & Messer, 1991), but it does require flexibility. Good therapists recognize that a method that proves effective for one patient may not work for another.

Therapy

P R E V I E W

As you saw in Chapter 14, psychological disorders can be caused by physical problems, biological problems, maladaptive thinking, or maladaptive conditioning. As a result, most kinds of psychotherapy are usually designed to treat either the body, the mind, or the environment (see ❱ Figure 15.1). Current therapists can draw on any one of these approaches or even combine them. In this chapter, we'll consider the problems—both scientific and practical—associated with each approach to psychotherapy.

First, what are the most effective biologically based treatments?
From Chapter 14, you know that abnormal brain functioning is thought to contribute to a number of psychological disorders. Schizophrenia, for example, appears to be traceable in part to imbalances in neurotransmitters. Depression and mania have also been linked to the activities of neurotransmitters. To address these kinds

of problems, it makes sense to consider treating the body itself through biomedical therapies.

Second, how can maladaptive thinking be changed?
Chapter 14 also discussed those disorders associated with irrational beliefs and faulty attributions. Here, the appropriate path to improvement lies in insight, that is, better awareness of our own thought processes. Several prominent therapies (e.g., psychoanalysis, cognitive, humanistic) take this approach. Sometimes labelled as "the talking cure," the idea that therapist and patient must interact closely and talk out the problem remains prominent in current psychotherapy.

Third, how can the environment be altered to reduce maladaptive behaviour?
In Chapter 14 we discussed the idea that some psychological disorders are learned responses to specific situations. People can learn to think and act in abnormal ways in

much the same way that they acquire other thoughts and actions, that is, via instrumental conditioning, classical conditioning, or modelling the actions of others. If so, maladaptive learning might best be undone by applying similar principles to psychotherapy.

Fourth, how can we evaluate the effectiveness of psychotherapy?
Do all forms of therapy work, or are some more effective than others? Given how costly and time-consuming therapy can be, it's important to evaluate the advantages and disadvantages of the intervention. At the same time, it may not be easy to do studies that have sufficient controls to draw firm conclusions. After all, they cannot be done in the laboratory with average university students. As you'll see, most studies demonstrate the effectiveness of psychotherapy, but some of the findings may surprise you. We'll also look at factors to consider when choosing a therapist.

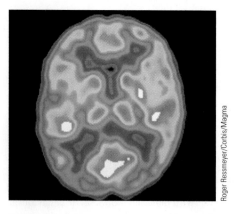

Treating the body

Treating the mind

Treating the environment

❱ **Figure 15.1**

Treatment Options

Psychologists face three main scientific and practical problems as they seek to administer and evaluate therapy.

▶ Treating the Body: Biomedical Therapies

LEARNING GOALS

1. Learn how drug therapies can be used to treat psychological disorders.
2. Understand and evaluate electroconvulsive therapy.

Psychological disorders have affected people since the beginning of history. And for almost as long, people have speculated about what causes abnormal behaviour and have offered remedies for its treatment. At one time, people who exhibited bizarre or deviant behaviour were believed to be possessed by evil spirits or demons. Early "therapies" included chaining, drowning, or torturing the sufferer in an effort to drive out the evil inhabitants.

Less barbaric methods have also been around for some time. In fact, more than 2000 years ago, Hippocrates (469–377 B.C.E.) and his followers suggested that psychological disorders should be treated as manifestations of the body. Hippocrates believed that people get depressed or exhibit manic states for much the same reason we fall victim to the common cold—the body and, hence, the mind are affected by some kind of "disease." Hippocrates even went so far as to recommend changes in diet and exercise as a way of treating depression, a course of action that many modern therapists consider appropriate today.

The medical approach to understanding disorders was placed on firmer scientific ground in the nineteenth and early twentieth centuries as scientists began to establish links between known physical problems and psychological disorders. For example, by the end of the nineteenth century it was recognized that the venereal disease syphilis is responsible not only for a steady deterioration in physical health (and eventually death) but also for the appearance of paranoia and hallucinations. Establishing a link between syphilis and mental problems was an important step in the eventual development of biologically based therapies.

In this section of the chapter, we'll consider several modern biological approaches to the treatment of psychological disorders. **Biomedical therapies** use physiological interventions in an effort to reduce or eliminate the symptoms of psychological disorders. By far the most popular approach is treatment with drugs, but other biomedical therapies are also available, including electroconvulsive therapy and psychosurgery. We will say very little about psychosurgery (operating on the brain in an attempt to cure or alleviate psychological disorders) because it is now rarely used and then only for quite specific conditions.

> **biomedical therapies**
>
> Biologically based treatments, including drug therapies, shock treatments, and, very rarely, psychosurgery

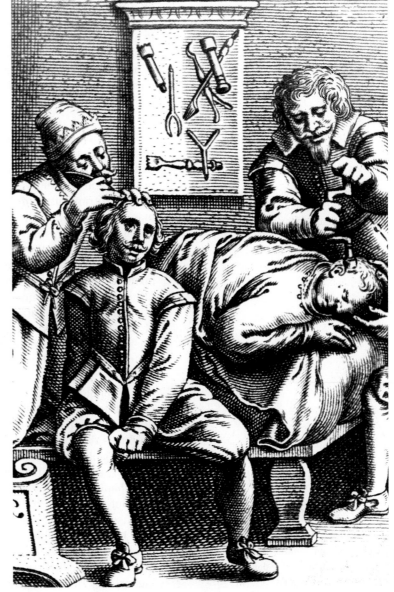

This engraving from 1598 demonstrates an early form of "therapy" for psychological disorders—drilling holes in the head to promote the release of evil spirits. Believe it or not, this method, called trephination, is still recommended today by certain cult groups.

© Bettmann

Drug Therapies

In the early 1950s two French psychiatrists, Jean Delay and Pierre Deniker, reported success in treating the positive symptoms of schizophrenia with a drug called *chlorpromazine* (now sold under the brand name Thorazine). Patients who had severe delusions and hallucinations showed considerable improvement after prolonged use of the drug. Since that time, dozens of other drugs have proven successful in treating a wide variety of psychological disorders. In fact, specific medications are now available to treat most of the disorders that we considered in Chapter 14—everything from obsessive-compulsive disorder to depression. Unfortunately, these drugs do not work for all patients, and some drugs have disturbing side effects. Nonetheless, the drugs have helped thousands of people, and in many ways they have revolutionized the mental health profession.

The use of medications, such as chlorpromazine, has greatly reduced the number of patients who require extended stays in mental hospitals or institutions. Before the 1950s, hundreds of thousands of people were institutionalized in North America because their symptoms were too severe for them to cope in everyday settings. Partly through the administration of drugs, it is now possible to control the severity of these symptoms, allowing individuals to be treated outside a hospital or an institution. The results have been dramatic: By the 1980s, the number of people institutionalized for psychological problems had dropped to less than 25% of what it had been in the 1950s. Effective medications are not the only reason for the decline in the number of hospitalized patients. Other factors include improvements in alternative forms of therapy (including behavioural and cognitive), cutbacks in government funding needed to maintain adequate institutional care, and stricter laws governing commitment.

Antipsychotic Drugs   Medications that treat the positive symptoms of schizophrenia—delusions, hallucinations, disorganized speech—are commonly called **antipsychotic drugs.** Chlorpromazine is an example of such a drug, but others are also effective. Most of these antipsychotic drugs are believed to act on the neurotransmitter *dopamine* in the brain. As we discussed in Chapter 14, many researchers believe that schizophrenia is caused by excess supplies of dopamine. Chlorpromazine acts as a dopamine *antagonist*, meaning that it blocks or slows down the use of dopamine in the brain (Gershon & Reider, 1992) (see ▶ Figure 15.2). The fact that dopamine antagonists work so well in treating positive symptoms is strong support for the dopamine hypothesis of schizophrenia (Barlow & Durand, 2002; Walker et al., 2004).

But dopamine antagonists do not work for all sufferers of schizophrenia. Moreover, these drugs tend to work almost exclusively on positive symptoms. The negative symptoms of schizophrenia, such as the sharp decline in the normal expression of emotions, are not affected very much by the administration of antipsychotic medications. Antipsychotic drugs can also produce unwanted and persistent side effects in some patients, including drowsiness, difficulties in concentrating, blurry vision, and movement disorders (Windgassen, 1992). One particularly serious side effect is a condition called *tardive dyskinesia*, which produces disabling involuntary movements of the mouth and face (Kane et al., 1986). These side effects can be permanent and they act as a two-edged sword: Not only are they extremely uncomfortable for the patient, but they also increase the chances that the patient will stop taking the medication (Tugrul, 1998). Without the medication, of course, it's very likely that the positive symptoms of the disorder will reappear.

Over the past decade or so, a number of new medications, including *clozapine* and *risperidone*, have been introduced that work well for patients who don't respond to the more traditional dopamine antagonists (Chakos, Lieberman, Hoffman, Bradford, & Sheitman, 2001). These medications do not

antipsychotic drugs

Medications that reduce the positive symptoms of schizophrenia; the majority act on the neurotransmitter dopamine

CRITICAL   THINKING

Just because dopamine antagonists reduce the positive symptoms of schizophrenia does not necessarily mean that dopamine causes schizophrenia. Why not?

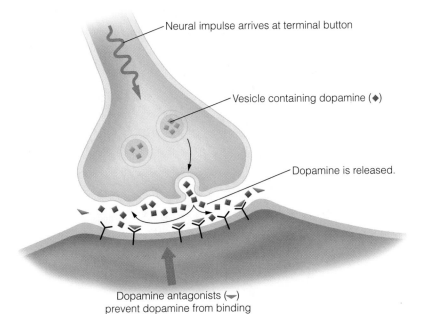

Neural impulse arrives at terminal button

Vesicle containing dopamine (◆)

Dopamine is released.

Dopamine antagonists (◖) prevent dopamine from binding to the membrane receptors (Y).

Dopamine Antagonists

Some antipsychotic medications act as antagonists, which means they block or slow down the action of neurotransmitters in the brain. Here, a dopamine antagonist is binding with the receptor membrane, blocking the neurotransmitter.

produce movement side effects, such as tardive dyskinesia, although medical complications can still be a concern in some cases (Hector, 1998). From a research standpoint, the effectiveness of the newer "second-generation" medications is noteworthy because they don't work simply by regulating the amount of dopamine in the brain. It's believed that they affect a number of neurotransmitters, including dopamine, serotonin, and others (Carlsson et al., 2001). Thus, dopamine alone, as we noted in Chapter 14, cannot account entirely for schizophrenic disorders.

Antidepressant Drugs   Medications for treating manic states and depression were also introduced in the 1950s. Mood disorders have been linked to several neurotransmitters, including norepinephrine and serotonin. **Antidepressant drugs,** like the antipsychotic drugs, act by modulating the availability or effectiveness of these kinds of neurotransmitters. The group of antidepressants called *tricyclics*, for example, alters mood by acting primarily on norepinephrine: They apparently allow norepinephrine to linger in synapses longer than normal, which eventually modulates its effectiveness. A different class of antidepressants called SSRIs (selective serotonin reuptake inhibitors) includes fluoxetine, sold commercially as Prozac, as well as Zoloft and Paxil. These drugs act primarily on serotonin, again by blocking its "reuptake" into the neuron, thereby allowing it to linger in the synapse (see ▶ Figure 15.3 on page 606).

At present, researchers do not know exactly how these medications affect mood, outside of the fact that they alter the effectiveness of neurotransmitters. Fortunately, it's clear that they do work well for many individuals affected with depression. It's been estimated that sustained use of antidepressants successfully controls depression in more than 50% of all depressed patients (Hammen, 2003). On the downside, it typically takes several weeks for these medications to begin working (the time may differ across the different types of antidepressants), and potential side effects must be monitored. Prozac, for example, can produce agitation or restlessness, difficulty sleeping, as well as diminished sexual desire and performance. A few early reports claimed that Prozac might also induce violent or suicidal tendencies, but these claims have not been substantiated in follow-up research (Khan, Khan, Kolts, & Brown, 2003).

antidepressant drugs

Medications that modulate the availability or effectiveness of the neurotransmitters implicated in mood disorders; Prozac, for example, increases the action of the neurotransmitter serotonin

▶ **Figure 15.3**

Reuptake Blockers

Some antidepressant medications block the reabsorption of neurotransmitters, which then linger longer in the synapse and continue to activate receptor neurons. Prozac is in the class of antidepressants that block the reabsorption of serotonin.

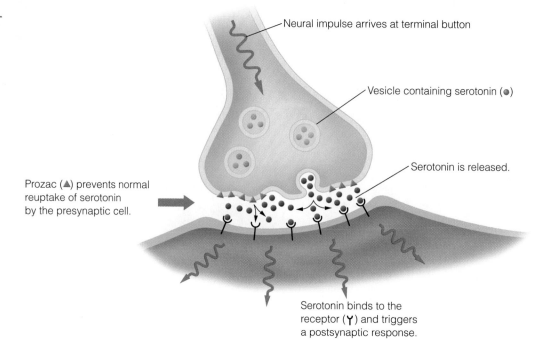

Neural impulse arrives at terminal button

Vesicle containing serotonin (●)

Serotonin is released.

Prozac (▲) prevents normal reuptake of serotonin by the presynaptic cell.

Serotonin binds to the receptor (Υ) and triggers a postsynaptic response.

Effective medications are also available for treating bipolar disorders, which are characterized by mood swings between depression and hyperactive manic states. Bipolar disorders are usually treated by administering a common salt called *lithium carbonate*. Lithium is more effective for bipolar disorder than the antidepressants because it works well on the manic state; it puts affected individuals on a more even keel and helps to prevent the reoccurrence of future manic episodes. But it too needs to be monitored closely because lithium use can lead to a variety of medical complications (Holtzheimer & Neumaier, 2003).

Antianxiety Drugs   To treat anxiety-related disorders, mental health professionals typically use **antianxiety drugs,** known more generally as *tranquillizers*. Tranquillizers include a class of chemicals called *benzodiazepines*—Valium and Xanax are popular trade names—and they are quite effective for reducing tension and anxiety. In the mid-1970s it was estimated that 10% to 20% of adults in the Western world were taking tranquillizers (Greenblatt & Shader, 1978), which gives you some idea of their widespread use. In recent years tranquillizer use has been on the decline, primarily because mental health professionals recognize a downside to their continued use.

Most benzodiazepines appear to work on a neurotransmitter in the brain called gamma-amino-butyric acid (GABA), which tends to produce primarily inhibitory effects. The effectiveness of GABA increases after taking the drug, which leads to a lowering of excitation in affected neurons (Lickey & Gordon, 1991). Potential side effects include drowsiness, impaired motor coordination, and possible psychological dependence (Rickels, Schweizer, Case, & Greenblatt, 1990). Tranquillizers can act as a psychological crutch after lengthy use, so most therapists now recommend that they be used primarily as a short-term remedy for anxiety rather than as a long-term cure. Some newer antianxiety drugs on the market, such as *buspirone*, may not produce the same degree of dependency, but whether they will turn out to be as useful as traditional medications remains to be seen (Carrazana, Rivas-Vazquez, & Rey, 2001). Increasingly, therapists are finding that antidepressants, particularly SSRIs, are effective in treating anxiety disorders, and they're now being widely prescribed (Golden, 2004).

antianxiety drugs

Medications that reduce tension and anxiety; many work on the inhibitory neurotransmitter GABA

CONCEPT SUMMARY

DRUG THERAPIES

Type of Drug	Used in the Treatment of	Examples and Effects
Antipsychotic	Positive symptoms of schizophrenia, including delusions, hallucinations, and disorganized speech	*Chlorpromazine* acts by impeding the flow of dopamine in the brain. *Clozapine* has also proven effective in alleviating some symptoms of schizophrenia.
Antidepressants	Mood disorders	*Tricyclics* alter mood by acting primarily on norepinephrine, allowing it to linger in synapses longer. *Fluoxetine* (e.g., Prozac) works primarily on serotonin, blocking its reuptake into the neuron. *Lithium carbonate* is used to treat bipolar disorder.
Antianxiety	Psychological problems associated with anxiety	Commonly known as *tranquillizers*. Tranquillizers come from a class of chemicals called *benzodiazepines;* they inhibit excitation in affected neurons, reducing tension and anxiety.

Electroconvulsive Therapy

When traditional medications for depression fail, therapists turn to a different form of biomedical therapy: "shock" treatment. At face value, few psychological therapies seem as radical as the idea of strapping someone down on a table and passing 100 V or so of electricity into his or her brain. During this procedure, a brief brain seizure occurs that produces convulsions and loss of consciousness. When **electroconvulsive therapy (ECT)** was first introduced in the 1930s, it was a terrifying and hazardous procedure; patients suffered serious side effects that included the occasional broken bone from the convulsions. Thankfully, modern applications of ECT are much less physically traumatic; the patient is given a light anesthetic and medications that relax the muscles so that injuries will not occur (Sackeim et al., 2000).

electroconvulsive therapy (ECT)

A treatment used primarily for depression in which a brief electric current is delivered to the brain

Most mental health professionals believe that ECT, as currently administered, is a safe and effective treatment for patients who have severe depression. Some experts believe it may benefit other psychological problems as well (Fink, 2001; Krystal & Coffey, 1997). Nonetheless, most professionals consider it to be a treatment of last resort. It is used in cases in which people have shown little or no response to conventional antidepressant drugs or talk therapies. Controlled studies have found that ECT is successful some 50% to 70% of the time in lessening the symptoms of depression in patients who have not responded to any other treatment (Prudic, Sackeim, & Devanand, 1990; UK ECT Review Group, 2003).

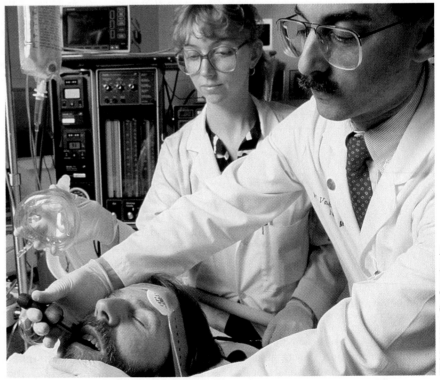

ECT, as currently administered, is a reasonably safe and effective form of treatment for patients who have severe depression, but its use is still debated by some mental health professionals and advocates.

Will & Deni McIntyre/PhotoResearchers, Inc.

Controversies   Despite the demonstrated effectiveness of ECT as a treatment for severe depression, the procedure remains controversial for several reasons. First, no one is certain exactly why the treatment works. It's possible that shocking the brain affects the release of neurotransmitters or changes some structural feature of the brain (Mann, 1998), but at present there is no definitive answer to why the procedure changes mood (Kapur & Mann, 1993). Second, ECT produces side effects, particularly confusion and a loss of memory for events surrounding the treatment (Breggin, 1991). These side effects are usually temporary, and they're not serious for most patients, but some observers remain concerned that ECT might cause long-term brain damage. Finally, the third reason for controversy is the emotional revulsion many people feel about putting an electric current through a patient's brain—a treatment not unlike that used to execute convicted murderers.

Is ECT worth the risks? The medical consensus has become more optimistic over the last two decades (Sackeim, 1999). Certainly, for the deeply depressed individual who has tried but received no relief from other treatment options, ECT might literally be a lifesaver. Psychologist Norman Endler of York University definitely would agree. Endler suffered from severe depression himself and found that the only treatment that was effective in alleviating it was ECT, as recounted in his book *Holiday of Darkness* (1990). Many clinicians believe that if it comes down to a desperate choice between ending your life and suffering some confusion and memory loss, trying ECT is certainly worth the risk. Newer treatment options on the horizon may eventually prove more effective and have fewer side effects. For example, transcranial magnetic stimulation (TMS) works by placing a magnetic coil around your head, which, in turn, sets up a magnetic field that alters electrical activity in the brain. Early results have been promising in treating major depressive disorders (Paus & Barrett, 2004).

Test Yourself 15.1

Check your knowledge about biomedical therapies by answering the following questions. (The answers are in Appendix B.)

1. Pick the psychological disorder that is best treated by each of the following therapies or medications. Choose your answers from among the following: depression, manic state, generalized anxiety disorder, schizophrenia, hypochondriasis.
   a. clozapine: _____
   b. Prozac: _____
   c. ECT: _____
   d. benzodiazepine: _____

2. Which of the following statements about ECT is false?
   a. ECT is an effective treatment for depression.
   b. Researchers are uncertain why ECT works.
   c. ECT can produce confusion and some memory loss.
   d. ECT is used regularly to treat schizophrenia.

▶ Treating the Mind: Insight Therapies

LEARNING GOALS

1. Understand and evaluate psychoanalysis as a form of insight therapy.
2. Understand and evaluate cognitive therapies.
3. Understand and evaluate humanistic therapies.
4. Learn about group and family therapy.

insight therapies

Treatments designed to give clients self-knowledge, or insight, into their psychological problems, usually through one-on-one interactions with a therapist

People who have psychological disorders often carry around faulty or irrational beliefs about the world and about themselves. Many therapists believe that their role is to challenge these irrational thoughts and beliefs directly through what are called insight therapies. **Insight therapies** are designed to give clients self-knowledge, or *insight*, into their psychological problems, usually through extensive one-on-one verbal interactions with the therapist. The hope is that, with insight, the person will adopt a more realistic, adaptive view of the world, and behaviour will change accordingly.

Many forms of insight therapy are available for use by mental health professionals. We'll consider three in this section: *psychoanalysis*, *cognitive therapies*, and *humanistic approaches*. Most of the other insight therapies are related in one form or another to these three main approaches. The common thread that ties them all together is the belief that cognitive or mental insight can produce significant changes in a person's psychological condition. The therapies differ in the kinds of beliefs or memories that are considered of vital importance and in how the client's insight can best be obtained. Finally, we'll end the chapter by briefly discussing the value of group and family therapy.

Psychoanalysis: Resolving Unconscious Conflicts

The best-known insight therapy is **psychoanalysis,** an elaborate set of ideas and techniques emanating from the psychodynamic theory of Sigmund Freud and his disciples. As discussed in Chapter 12, Freud emphasized the impact of the *unconscious mind.* We can't directly think about the urges and memories stored in the unconscious mind, but they affect our behaviour nonetheless. Freud argued that through psychoanalysis, these hidden impulses and memories could be brought to the surface of awareness, thereby freeing us from the insidious harm they wreak on our thoughts and behaviours.

Freud based his ideas on two sources: (1) self-analysis and (2) case studies of individuals he encountered in his private practice. He routinely treated patients who had troubling psychological problems, and he discovered that he could often help these people by getting them to recall and relive traumatic experiences that they had apparently forgotten, or repressed. Freud was particularly interested in the emotionally significant experiences of childhood because he believed that during childhood we progress through a number of psychologically "fragile" stages of psychosexual development (see Chapter 12). Traumatic experiences are, by definition, anxiety provoking and therefore difficult for the young mind to deal with. If sufficiently traumatizing, the ideas are buried in the unconscious. Although no longer consciously available, these experiences continue to influence feelings and behaviour in ways that are beyond the person's awareness.

The Tools of Psychoanalysis   The goal of psychoanalysis is to help the patient uncover, and thereby relive, these unconscious conflicts. Obviously, because the patient is unaware of the conflicts, the therapist needs certain tools to gain access to the contents of the unconscious mind. Freud liked to compare psychoanalysis to excavating a buried city; but instead of picks and shovels, his tools were the uncensored expressions and feelings of his patients. In the beginning, Freud tried hypnosis and other new techniques of his era. Later he developed a technique called **free association,** in which patients were asked to relax on a couch and freely express whatever thoughts and feelings came into their minds. To the untrained eye, the results were disconnected streams of thought, but to Freud, these free associations represented symbolic clues to the contents of the unconscious.

Another of Freud's important therapeutic tools was **dream analysis:** He felt that it provided a "royal road" to the unconscious. As we discussed in Chapter 5, Freud was convinced that dreams are partly a psychological mechanism for wish fulfillment, a way to satisfy hidden desires that are too anxiety provoking to be allowed to be directly experienced in the conscious state. The storyline of dreams, he believed, is largely symbolic—dreams have a hidden meaning, a *latent content,* that reveals the unconscious. Freud therefore encouraged his patients to describe their dreams, so he could acquire further clues in the search for hidden psychological truth. A third tool, projective tests, was covered in some detail in Chapter 12.

psychoanalysis

Freud's method of treatment that attempts to bring hidden impulses and memories, which are locked in the unconscious, to the surface of awareness, thereby freeing the patient from disordered thoughts and behaviours

free association

A technique used in psychoanalysis to explore the contents of the unconscious; patients are asked to relax and freely express whatever thoughts and feelings happen to come into their minds

dream analysis

A technique used in psychoanalysis; Freud believed that dreams are symbolic and contain important information about the unconscious

Some critics argue that Freud based psychoanalysis far too much on the analysis of his own mind.

Resistance and Transference In classic psychoanalysis, the therapist seeks to understand the contents of the unconscious, but ultimately, it is really the patient who needs the insight. The therapist can't simply relay the hidden meanings that are uncovered—explanation is not enough. Instead, the patient needs to face the emotional conflicts directly and relive them, and the therapist can only act as a kind of expert guide. But the journey toward insight is not an easy one, and the therapist must usually navigate around several roadblocks. For example, patients typically go through periods in which they are uncooperative; they show **resistance,** that is, an unconsciously motivated attempt to subvert the therapy (Adler & Bachant, 1998).

Why would people try to block their own therapy? Because the hidden unconscious conflicts are anxiety provoking. As a result, the patient will do almost anything to reduce the anxiety. As Freud (1912/1964) put it, "Resistance accompanies the treatment at every step; every single association, every act of the patient's ... represents a compromise between the forces aiming at cure and those opposing it" (p. 140). The resistance can express itself in a variety of ways; the patient might become inattentive, claim to forget dreams, skip therapy sessions, or argue with the directions suggested by the therapist.

As resistance begins to wane, a new problem develops. **Transference** is the tendency of patients to express thoughts or feelings toward the therapist that are actually representative of the way the patient feels about other significant people in his or her life. The patient "transfers" feelings of love, hate, or dependence onto a substitute figure, the therapist. Depending on the repressed feelings being tapped, the patient might turn the therapist into an object of passionate love or into a hated and despised individual (see ▶ Figure 15.4). Recent research supports many of these aspects of transference (Andersen & Berk, 1998).

Transference is a significant event in analysis because it means that the patient's hidden memories and conflicts are bubbling up close to the surface of consciousness. The patient is made aware of the strong feelings he or she is experiencing—although the object of those feelings is inappropriate—and the therapist can help the patient work through what those feelings might mean. The patient is no longer in denial of powerful emotional urges—they are now ready to be dealt with. At the same time, it's important for the therapist to recognize that the patient's feelings at this point are symbolic. It's not uncommon for the patient to express feelings of strong sexual desire for the therapist, for example, and it would be inappropriate and unethical for the therapist to respond sexually (Tyler & Tyler, 1997).

Current Applications Classical psychoanalysis, as practised by Freud and his contemporaries, is a very time-consuming process. It can take years for the analyst to excavate the secrets of the unconscious, and the patient needs to be properly prepared to accept the insights when they are delivered. It is assumed that the

resistance

In psychoanalysis, a patient's unconsciously motivated attempts to subvert the process of therapy

transference

In psychoanalysis, the patient's expression of thoughts or feelings toward the therapist that are actually representative of the way the patient feels about other significant people in his or her life

© Bettmann/Corbis/Magma

▶ **Figure 15.4**

Resistance and Transference

People in therapy typically go through resistance periods in which they are uncooperative—skipping a session, arriving late, or arguing with the therapist. Subsequently, the patient's feelings toward significant others begin to be transferred onto the therapist.

Resistance

"I know I'm late. I ... uh ... couldn't find my dream notes."

Transference

"You really understand me. I cherish our time together."

patient will set up roadblocks throughout the process. So this kind of therapy is never presented as a quick fix. It's acknowledged to be not only time consuming but also expensive.

For these reasons, modern practitioners of psychoanalysis often streamline the therapeutic process (Coren, 2001). So-called brief forms of psychoanalysis encourage the therapist to take a more active role in the analytic process (Horvath & Luborsky, 1993). Rather than waiting for patients to find insight themselves in response to subtle nudging, the analyst is much more willing to offer interpretations in the early stages of therapy. Rather than waiting for transference to occur on its own, the analyst might actually encourage role-playing in an attempt to get the patient to deal with deep-seated feelings. So, rather than requiring years of analysis, progress can occur in weeks or months (see Charman, 2004).

Besides increasing the speed of treatment, modern versions of psychoanalysis are often tailored to meet the needs of the particular patient (Westen, 1998). No attempt is made to excavate and reconstruct the patient's entire personality; instead, the analyst focuses on selective defence mechanisms or conflicts that are more pertinent to the individual's particular symptoms (Luborsky, Barber, & Crits-Cristoph, 1990). A greater emphasis is often placed on improving the patient's interpersonal and social skills and less of an emphasis is placed on sexual and aggressive drives. Because these forms of treatment differ from classical psychoanalysis, they sometimes go by the more general name: *psychodynamic therapy.*

Cognitive Therapies: Changing Maladaptive Beliefs

According to Freud's theory, a person's conscious thoughts, beliefs, and feelings are of primary importance only because they provide clues to the inner workings of the unconscious mind. **Cognitive therapies,** in contrast, emphasize the conscious beliefs themselves, rather than what those beliefs may mean symbolically. Cognitive therapists assume that irrational beliefs and inappropriate thoughts are primarily responsible for psychological disorders. If the inappropriate thoughts can be altered, the psychological disorder can be alleviated.

Let's take depression as an example. People who are depressed usually do not think constructively. They view themselves as worthless and unlovable, and they see little chance that things will get better in the future. Such negative thinking clouds the interpretation of normal events; everyday experiences are viewed through a negative filter, which means that depressed people often jump to irrational conclusions. For instance, a depressed woman whose husband arrives home slightly late from work might be immediately convinced that her husband is having an affair. The depressed student who fails the test might see the F as confirmation of a fundamental lack of intelligence.

cognitive therapies

Treatments designed to remove irrational beliefs and negative thoughts that are presumed to be responsible for psychological disorders

CRITICAL   THINKING

What do you think Freud would have thought about the value of biomedical therapies? Would he have supported or rejected the idea of treating psychological disorders through medications or ECT?

▶ **Figure 15.5**

The Cognitive View of Depression

Cognitive therapists believe that it is not direct experience, such as failing a test, that leads to depression. Instead, the depression is caused by internal thoughts and beliefs about the event.

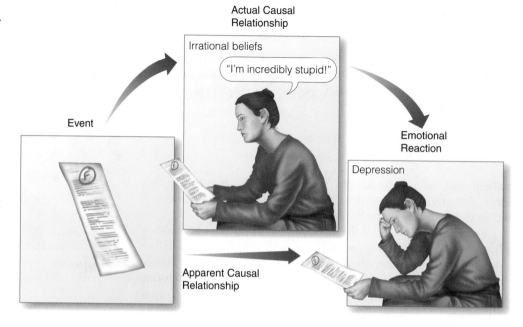

Cognitive therapists argue that it is not direct experience, such as failure on a test, that actually produces depression. Straight thinking tells us that failing a test doesn't tell us much about a student. A student can fail a test for many reasons—most of them having nothing to do with his or her intrinsic worth as a human being. But in the mind of a depressed person, the event (failing the test) is accompanied by an irrational belief ("I'm incredibly stupid"), and it is this belief that leads to negative emotional consequences (feeling sad and depressed). Thus, it is the *interpretation* of the event, not the event itself, that leads to problems (Beck, 1991; Ellis, 1962, 1993) (see ▶ Figure 15.5).

Rational-Emotive Therapy   The goal of cognitive therapy is to remove these irrational beliefs. But how can irrational beliefs be changed? One technique is to challenge the beliefs directly, through active and aggressive confrontation. In **rational-emotive therapy**, developed by Albert Ellis, the therapist acts as a kind of cross-examiner, verbally disputing the client's irrational thought processes. Here's an excerpt from an exchange between a therapist practising rational-emotive therapy and a client showing signs of depressed thinking (from Walen, DiGuiseppe, & Dryden, 1992, pp. 204–205):

rational-emotive therapy

A form of cognitive therapy, developed by Albert Ellis, in which the therapist acts as a kind of cross-examiner, verbally disputing the client's irrational thought processes

> Therapist: You really believe that you're an utterly worthless person. By definition, that means that you always do things poorly. Can you prove to me that that's correct?
>
> Client: But I've failed at so many things.
>
> Therapist: Just how many?
>
> Client: I've lost my job, my wife is threatening to leave me, I don't get along with my kids—my whole life's a mess!
>
> Therapist: Well, let me make two points. First of all, that's not every aspect of your life. Second, you seem to take total responsibility for all of those events, rather than only partial responsibility.
>
> Client: But even if I'm not totally responsible, I'm still a failure.
>
> Therapist: No. You've failed at those things. There are other things you haven't failed at.
>
> Client: Like what?
>
> Therapist: You still manage to get up every morning, you keep up appearances, you manage your finances well considering your economic plight—there are lots of things you do well.
>
> Client: But they don't count!

Therapist: They don't count to you right now because you're overly concerned with negative issues, but they certainly do count. There are lots of people who don't do those things well. Are they failures?

Client: No, but …

Therapist: You know, Jack, you're one of the most conceited people I've ever met!

Client: What do you mean? I've just been telling you how lousy I am!

Therapist: The fact that you hold two different standards tells me how conceited you are. You hold much higher standards for yourself than for anyone else, which implies that you think you're much better than others. It's okay for those lowly slobs to have problems, but not a terrific person like you. Isn't that contradictory to your notion that you're worthless?

Client: Hmmmmm.

Therapist: How about instead of rating yourself as worthless, you just accept the failings that you do have and try your best to improve them?

Client: That sounds sensible.

Therapist: Let's take one of those problem areas now and see how we can improve things.

(From *A Practitioner's Guide to Rational-Emotive Therapy*, Second Edition, by Susan Walen, Raymond DiGiuseppe, and Windy Dryden. Copyright © 1992 by Oxford University Press, Inc. Used by permission of Oxford University Press.)

CRITICAL **THINKING**

Where do you think these irrational beliefs come from? Is it possible that people are taught to think in these absolute and inflexible ways by their parents, by role models, or by the general culture at large?

The important part of rational-emotive therapy is the therapist's attack on the reasonableness of the client's beliefs. The therapist's challenge, often confrontational in manner, assumes that such maladaptive beliefs will ultimately be rejected, thereby alleviating their emotional consequences. The creator of rational-emotive therapy, Albert Ellis (1962), identified the major irrational beliefs he has observed in people seeking treatment for psychological disorders. The therapist tries initially to pinpoint which of these beliefs characterize a particular client's thought processes, so they can be changed accordingly. Here are a few examples from Ellis's list of common irrational beliefs:

1. I must be loved and approved of by every significant person in my life, and if I'm not, it's awful.
2. It's awful when things are not the way I'd like them to be.
3. I should be very anxious about events that are uncertain or potentially dangerous.
4. I am not worthwhile unless I am thoroughly competent, adequate, and achieving at all times or at least most of the time in at least one major area.
5. I need someone stronger than I am on whom to depend or rely.

What makes these beliefs irrational is their inflexibility and absoluteness. I *must* be loved and approved; I *must* be thoroughly competent; I *need* someone stronger than myself. The client firmly believes that things must be a particular way or something awful or catastrophic will happen.

Beck's Cognitive Therapy   Although all forms of cognitive therapy focus on changing irrational thought processes, not all treatments are as direct and harsh as rational-emotive therapy. The rational-emotive therapist will essentially lecture—and in some instances even belittle—the client in an effort to attack faulty beliefs. Other cognitive therapies, such as the treatment procedures pioneered by Aaron Beck, take a more subtle tack. Rather than directly confronting clients with their irrational beliefs, Beck suggests it is more therapeutic to get clients to identify negative forms of thinking themselves. The therapist acts as an adviser, or co-investigator, helping clients discover their own unique kinds of faulty beliefs (Young, Weinberger, & Beck, 2001).

Albert Ellis developed rational-emotive therapy to help people eliminate their irrational thoughts and beliefs.

▶ **Figure 15.6**

Homework from a Cognitive Therapist

During cognitive therapy, people are often asked to record their automatic thoughts and emotions in a notebook. Notice that the daily log requires the person to construct a rational response to the situation and then rate the emotional reaction again. (From Beck, Rush, Shaw, and Emery, "Daily Record of Dysfunctional Thoughts" from *Cognitive Therapy of Depression*, p. 403. Copyright © 1979.)

In a sense, clients who undergo Beck's cognitive therapy are asked to become psychological detectives. Part of the therapy involves extensive record keeping, or "homework." Between therapeutic sessions, Beck asks his clients to record their automatic thoughts and emotions in a notebook as they experience various situations during the day. Clients are then asked to write rational responses to those thoughts and emotions, as if they were scientists evaluating data. Is the thought justified by the actual event? What's the evidence for and against the conclusions that I reached? The therapist hopes clients will eventually discover the contradictions and irrationality in their thinking and realign their beliefs accordingly (see ▶ Figure 15.6).

Situation	Emotion(s)	Automatic Thought(s)	Rational Response	Outcome
1. Actual event leading to unpleasant emotion or 2. Stream of thoughts, daydreams, or recollections, leading to unpleasant emotion	1. Specify sad/ anxious/ angry, etc. 2. Rate degree of emotion, 1–100	1. Record automatic thought(s) that preceded emotion(s) 2. Rate belief in automatic thought(s), 0–100%	1. Write rational response to automatic thought(s) 2. Rate belief in rational response, 0–100%	1. Rerate belief in automatic thought(s), 0–100% 2. Specify and rate subsequent emotions, 0–100
7/15 Audre didn't return my phone call.	Anxious – 75 Sad – 55 Angry – 40	People don't like talking to me. 75% I'm incompetent. 65%	She's out walking the dog so she hasn't had the time to call back. 70%	1. 35% 15% 2. Relieved – 35

Explanation: When you experience an unpleasant emotion, note the situation that seemed to stimulate the emotion. (If the emotion occurred while you were thinking, daydreaming, etc., please note this.) Then note the automatic thought associated with the emotion. Record the degree to which you believe this thought: 0% = not at all, 100% = completely. In rating degree of emotion: 1 = a trace, 100 = the most intense possible.

Humanistic Therapies: Treating the Human Spirit

In cognitive therapy, the goal is for clients to gain understanding or insight into their faulty and irrational ways of thinking. In classical psychoanalysis, the focus of the insight is on the patient's hidden conflicts and desires. In the final type of insight-based treatment that we'll consider—**humanistic therapy**—the purpose of therapy is to help the client gain insight into his or her own fundamental *self-worth* and *value* as a human. Therapy is a process of discovering your own unique potential, your innate capacity to grow and better yourself as a human being.

Humanistic therapists argue that all people are capable of controlling their behaviour—we can fix our own problems—because each of us ultimately has free will. We sometimes lose sight of our potential because we're concerned about what others think of us and our actions. We let others control how we think and feel. It is the therapist's job to help clients rediscover their natural self-worth—to help them get back in touch with their own true feelings, desires, and needs—by acting as a confidant and friend.

Client-Centred Therapy   Humanistic therapies resemble cognitive therapies in their emphasis on conscious thought processes. But the intention of humanistic therapy is not to criticize or correct irrational thinking; quite the contrary, it's to be totally supportive in all respects. The therapist's proper role is to be nonjudgmental, which means the client should be accepted unconditionally. According to humanistic therapists, such as Carl Rogers, the most effective form of therapy is **client-centred**—it is the client, not the therapist, who ultimately holds the key to psychological health and happiness.

We discussed the theoretical ideas of humanistic psychologists, especially Carl Rogers, in some detail in Chapter 12. Rogers was convinced that most psychological problems originate from *incongruence*, which he defined as the discrepancy between people's self-concept and the reality of their everyday experiences. People often hold an inaccurate view of themselves and their abilities, Rogers argued, because of an ingrained need for *positive regard*—they seek the approval, love, and companionship of significant others (such as their parents). But these significant others sometimes attach *conditions of worth* to their approval: They demand that we think and act in ways that may not be consistent with our true inner feelings. The humanistic therapist provides a warm and supportive environment—without conditions of worth—that will encourage clients to accept themselves as they truly are. Attaining this goal may require accepting some disapproval from significant others.

In client-centred therapy, the therapist seeks to provide three essential core qualities to the client: *genuineness, unconditional positive regard,* and *empathy.* As the client's confidant, the therapist must be completely genuine—he or she must act without

> **humanistic therapy**
>
> Treatments designed to help clients gain insight into their fundamental self-worth and value as human beings; therapy is a process of discovering our own unique potential

> **client-centred therapy**
>
> A form of humanistic therapy, developed by Carl Rogers, proposing that it is the client, not the therapist, who holds the key to psychological health and happiness; therapist's role is to provide genuineness, unconditional positive regard, and empathy

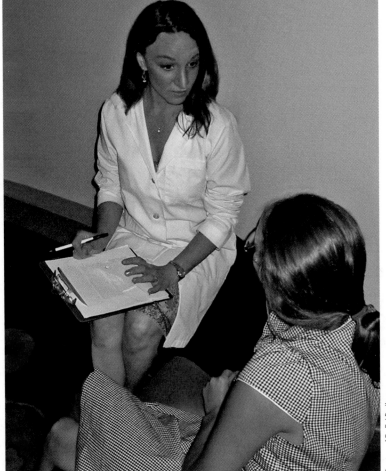

In humanistic therapies, the therapist tries to provide a completely supportive environment that allows clients to rediscover their natural self-worth.

CRITICAL   THINKING

Think about the interactions you've had with a really close friend. Do you see any similarities to the client-centred approach advocated by Carl Rogers?

phoniness and express true feelings in an open and honest way. The second quality, unconditional positive regard, means that the therapist cannot place conditions of worth on the client. The therapist must be totally accepting and respectful of the client at all times, even if the client thinks and acts in a way that seems irrational or inappropriate. Remember, humanists believe that people are essentially good—they simply need to be placed in an environment that will nurture their innate tendencies toward positive growth.

The third quality, empathy, is achieved when the therapist is able to truly understand and accept what the client is feeling—to see things from the client's perspective. Through empathy, the therapist acquires the capacity to reflect those feelings back in a way that helps the client gain insight into himself or herself. Consider the following interaction between Carl Rogers and one of his clients, a woman coming to grips with deep feelings of betrayal and hurt that she's tried to cover up (from Rogers, 1961, p. 94):

Client: I never did really know. But it's—you know, it's almost a physical thing. It's—it's sort of as though I were looking within myself at all kinds of— nerve endings and bits of things that have been sort of mashed.

Rogers: As though some of the most delicate aspects of you physically almost have been crushed or hurt.

Client: Yes. And you know, I do get the feeling, "Oh, you poor thing." (Pause)

Rogers: Just can't help but feel very deeply sorry for the person that is you.

Client: I don't think I feel sorry for the whole person; it's a certain aspect of the thing.

Rogers: Sorry to see the hurt.

Client: Yeah.

Notice that Rogers reflects back the feelings of the client in a completely nonjudgmental fashion. He is seeking to understand and empathize with her feelings, thereby validating their existence and helping her to work through them. Notice also that it is the client, not the therapist, who is doing the analyzing. Client-centred therapy is founded on the idea that it is the clients who understand what truly hurts them psychologically, and it is the clients who have the best sense of how to proceed with therapy. All the therapist can do is provide the right kind of supportive environment and help clients to recognize their own self-worth and trust their own instincts.

CONCEPT SUMMARY

INSIGHT APPROACHES TO PSYCHOTHERAPY

Approach	Source of Psychological Problem	Approach to Treatment (Depression)
Psychoanalysis	Problem arises from unconscious conflict, often rooted in childhood trauma.	Debbie is depressed because of repressed fears that her parents don't really love her. They were not very affectionate while she was growing up. Her therapist tries to get Debbie to talk about her childhood relationship with her parents.
Cognitive	Problem arises from conscious processes, including irrational beliefs and negative thoughts.	Troy is having a tough time with his parents. They want him to major in business, which he hates. He feels like a terrible person for not following his parents' wishes. After all, they're paying his tuition. His therapist attempts to show him that disagreeing with his parents over his university major does not reflect badly on him as a person.
Humanistic	Problem arises from incongruence between self-concept and reality.	Azra feels guilty. She plans on having only one child, but her parents would like lots of grandchildren, and Azra is an only child. Azra feels bad about herself and about her failure to get acceptance from her parents. Her therapist listens as Azra describes her feelings, and tries to be warm, supportive, and open to what she is saying.

Other Humanistic Approaches   Client-centred therapy is the most popular form of humanistic therapy, but it is not the only one. *Gestalt therapy*, developed by Fritz Perls (1969; Perls, Hefferline, & Goodman, 1951), also places the burden of treatment in the hands of a "naturally good" client, but the approach is far less gentle and nondirective than client-centred therapy. In Gestalt therapy, clients are actively encouraged—even forced—to express their feelings openly. The emphasis is on the here and now, and the therapist uses a variety of techniques to get the client to open up. For example, in the "empty chair" technique, clients are asked to project their feelings onto an empty chair in the room and then, literally, "talk" to the feelings. The idea is that only through fully understanding and overtly expressing themselves as a whole person (the word *Gestalt* roughly translates from the German as "whole") can people hope to take responsibility for those feelings and change them for the better.

Another group of humanistic treatments is known collectively as *existential therapies* (Yalom, 1980). Existential therapists believe that psychological problems originate from the anxieties created by personal choices, such as whether to stay in school, get married, or quit a job. These fundamental choices—choices that relate to daily existence as a human being—are often difficult to face, and individuals may choose not to deal with them directly. Existential therapists encourage their clients to accept responsibility for these decisions, but in a supportive environment that encourages positive growth (Trull, 2005).

Group Therapy

Therapy is most commonly perceived as a one-on-one experience—you and the therapist sit alone in a room discussing your problems. In **group therapy,** you join other people who are undergoing treatment for a similar problem. Typically, group sessions include the therapist and somewhere between 4 and 15 clients, although there are few strict rules for conducting group sessions; for example, in some cases there may be more than one therapist involved in the session (Yalom, 1995).

At first glance, the idea of group therapy seems troubling to most people. After all, who wants to talk about their personal problems in front of others? It's hard enough to open up to one person—the therapist—but at least he or she is a trained professional. Yet groups offer a number of advantages over individual sessions (MacKenzie, 2000). First, group therapy can be much more cost effective because the therapist can meet with multiple clients at the same time (Wolff, Helminiak, & Tebes, 1997). Second, hearing other people talk about problems that match your own can be educational (Matano, Yalom, & Schwartz, 1997). You can learn about their strategies for coping with problems, and you can see firsthand how their symptoms compare with your own. Third, and perhaps most important, when you hear testimonies from other people it's easier to realize that you're not alone—you're not the only person who has psychological problems. As you'll discover later in this chapter, empathy is a very important predictor of success in therapy; group settings can improve the trusting relationship you have with your therapist as well as with other people who share your problem (Donigian & Malnati, 1997).

Family Therapy   One place in which group therapy can be particularly appropriate is with the family. Rather than just treating an individual, in **family therapy** the therapist treats the family as a whole, as a kind of *social system* (Cox & Paley, 1997; Lebow & Gurman, 1995). Clearly, if one member of a family suffers from a psychological problem, such as depression, all family members tend to be affected and all can benefit from treatment. Moreover, the family environment can play either a positive or a negative role in helping a particular family member recover from a psychological problem. If the family understands the disorder, and what's

group therapy

A form of therapy in which several people are treated simultaneously in the same setting

family therapy

A form of group therapy in which the therapist treats the family as a whole, as a kind of social system; the goals of the treatment are often to improve interpersonal communication and collaboration

necessary for treatment, the odds of successful treatment go up considerably. Family therapists work on ways to improve interpersonal communication and collaboration among family members (Rivett, 1998).

The critical role that emotions play in family and couples therapy has been emphasized by Canadian researchers Les Greenberg at York University and Susan Johnson at the University of Ottawa. They have shown how the emotions experienced by patient and therapist alike can be used to understand and improve therapy. Their recommendations to therapists include encouraging patients to fully express their emotions, access previously unacknowledged feelings, and restructure their emotions in a more adaptive way (Greenberg & Paivio, 1997; Johnson, 1996).

Test Yourself 15.2

Check your knowledge about insight therapies by matching each of the following statements to a type of therapy. Choose from among the following: psychoanalysis, Gestalt therapy, rational-emotive therapy, Beck's cognitive therapy, client-centred therapy, family therapy. (The answers are in Appendix B.)

1. "You think you're worthless? Well, I'm sitting here spending time with you so how can you be completely worthless? It's a ridiculous idea." _____

2. "I want you to keep a record of your thoughts, and the situations that produce them, so that you can judge whether those thoughts are really appropriate given the situation."
_____

3. "Don't leave. Sit down and tell me again about the dream you had last night." _____

4. "You feel pain, deep pain, and you just can't get beyond the hurt that you feel inside." _____

5. "Talk to the chair ... be the chair. Open up and let your true feelings come out." _____

6. "It's not just your problem. Each of you needs to communicate better and learn to work together to solve problems and avoid conflicts." _____

▶ Changing the Environment: Behavioural Therapies

LEARNING GOALS
1. Understand how conditioning techniques can be used in therapy.
2. Understand how rewards and punishments can be used to improve behaviour.

behavioural therapies

Treatments designed to change behaviour through the use of established learning techniques

Instead of searching the minds of their clients for hidden conflicts, faulty beliefs, or damaged self-worth, some approaches to therapy essentially leave the mind alone. Behavioural therapies treat behaviour rather than thoughts or memories. **Behavioural therapies** are designed to change unwanted or maladaptive behaviour through the application of basic learning principles (Spiegler & Guevremont, 1998).

As we discussed in Chapter 14, many psychologists argue that psychological problems are *learned*, that is, acquired as a result of experience. Afraid of snakes? Perhaps you were bitten by one at some point in your life, or you saw someone else get bitten. That experience caused you to associate snakes with a negative emotional consequence. It's not that the snake is symbolic of some hidden sexual conflict—you feel anxious because you have a chance of being bitten again.

If you believe that a psychological problem has been learned, it doesn't make a lot of sense to spend months or years searching for a hidden reason for the problem. It's better to treat the surface symptoms by learning something new. More productive actions need to be rewarded, and the negative associations you've formed need to be extinguished or counteracted. We'll consider several behavioural approaches in this section of the chapter, beginning with an effective technique for treating phobias that is based on the principles of *classical conditioning*.

Conditioning Techniques

In Chapter 6, we discussed how dogs and people learn about the signalling properties of events. In Pavlov's classic experiments, dogs learned that one event, called the *conditioned stimulus*, signalled the occurrence of a second event, called the *unconditioned stimulus*. After pairing the conditioned stimulus and the unconditioned stimulus together in time, Pavlov found that his dogs responded to the conditioned stimulus in a way that anticipated the arrival of the unconditioned stimulus. For example, if a bell (the conditioned stimulus) was repeatedly presented just before food (the unconditioned stimulus), the dogs would begin to salivate (the conditioned response) to the bell in anticipation of the food. Pavlov also showed that this conditioned response, the drooling, was sensitive to a termination of the association between the conditioned stimulus and the unconditioned stimulus: If the bell was rung repeatedly after conditioning but the food was no longer presented, the dog eventually stopped salivating to the bell (a procedure Pavlov called *extinction*).

Now let's consider the case of a specific phobia, such as fear of snakes. Specific phobias are highly focused fears of objects or situations. When the feared object is present, it produces an intense anxiety reaction. In the 1920s, psychologist Mary Cover Jones proposed that intense fear reactions like these can be treated as if they are classically conditioned responses. A snake produces fear because some kind of earlier experience has taught you to associate snakes with something fearful. Perhaps while standing near one as a child, your brother or sister screamed in terror, thereby scaring you. Jones's analysis suggested a treatment: It might be possible to eliminate phobias by conditioning a new association between the feared object and something pleasurable. As she reported in 1924, she was able to use this logic to treat a little boy's fear of rabbits. She fed the boy some tasty food in the presence of the rabbit, which extinguished the association between the rabbit and an earlier negative experience and replaced it with a more pleasurable association (Jones, 1924).

CRITICAL THINKING

Can you think of a role that reinforcement might play in maintaining a phobia? Isn't it true that every time you stay away from a snake you avoid being bitten?

This child's fear of the water might have been acquired as a result of an earlier frightening experience.

Psychologist Mary Cover Jones proposed that intense fear reactions, such as those seen in phobias, could be treated as if they were classically conditioned responses.

Henning von Holleben/Getty Images

Archives of the History of American Psychology, University of Akron, OH

A technique that uses counterconditioning and extinction to reduce the fear and anxiety that have become associated with a specific object or event; a multistep process that attempts to replace the negative learned association with something relaxing

CRITICAL   THINKING

In what ways is shaping, which we discussed in Chapter 6, similar to and different from the procedures of systematic desensitization?

Systematic Desensitization   The treatment pioneered by Mary Cover Jones was later refined by psychiatrist Joseph Wolpe into a technique known as **systematic desensitization** (Wolpe, 1958, 1982). As with Jones's approach, systematic desensitization uses counterconditioning as a way of reducing the fear and anxiety that have become associated with a specific object or event. The therapist attempts to replace the negative association with something relaxing and pleasurable. It's a gradual process that involves three major steps:

1. The therapist helps the client construct an anxiety hierarchy, which is an ordered list of situations that lead to fearful reactions. The client is asked to imagine a series of anxiety-provoking situations, beginning with the least fear-arousing situation and ending with the feared situation itself.
2. The therapist spends time teaching the client ways to induce deep muscle relaxation. A state of deep relaxation is inconsistent with the experience of anxiety—you can't be afraid and relaxed at the same time.
3. With the help of the therapist the client then attempts to work through the anxiety hierarchy, forming an image of each of the scenes, while maintaining the state of relaxation. The idea is to pair the images of fearful situations with the pleasurable state of relaxation to extinguish the old negative association and replace it with something relaxing.

Let's imagine you have a deep, irrational fear of flying in an airplane. Treatment starts by having you create a list of flying-related situations that are increasingly frightful. Next, you would receive lessons in how to relax yourself fully. Finally, you would begin working through your hierarchy. Perhaps you might start by simply imagining a picture of an airplane. If you can consistently remain relaxed under these conditions, the therapist will direct you to move up the hierarchy to the next most stressful situation—perhaps imagining the airplane actually taking off. Gradually, over time, you will learn to relax in increasingly more stressful situations, even to the point where you can imagine yourself strapped in the seat as the plane rolls down the runway. The key to the technique is to maintain the relaxation. If you can stay relaxed—which is incompatible with fear and anxiety—the fearful association with planes should extinguish and be replaced by an association that is neutral or positive. Eventually, when you move to a real situation, the learning will generalize and you will no longer be afraid to fly in a plane. This type of therapy is summarized in ▶ Figure 15.7, using another specific phobia—the fear of snakes.

▶ **Figure 15.7**

Systematic Desensitization

After learning relaxation techniques, the client works slowly through an anxiety hierarchy. At first she simply imagines the feared object while relaxed. Eventually, the relaxation response can be maintained while she experiences the actual feared situation.

Aversion Therapy   Systematic desensitization attempts to eliminate unpleasant associations by replacing them with pleasant ones. In **aversion therapy,** the therapist tries to replace a pleasant reaction to a harmful stimulus with an unpleasant one: for example, making the client feel bad rather than good after smoking a cigarette or having a drink of alcohol. Once again, the idea is to use a kind of counterconditioning, but the goal is to make the target situation something to be avoided rather than approached.

In the case of alcohol dependency, it's possible to give people a drug (Antabuse) that causes the patient to become nauseated and vomit on taking a drink of alcohol. The drug interacts with alcohol, causing extreme discomfort. Under these conditions, the person who is drinking learns a new association that helps combat the alcohol dependency, namely, that drinking leads to an unpleasant feeling. A similar technique can be used for smoking. There are drugs containing chemicals that leave an extremely bad taste in the mouth after smoking. The old association connecting pleasure with smoking is replaced by a new association: connecting smoking with a terrible taste.

Aversion therapy can be quite effective, as long as the client takes the aversive drug for a sufficient time. The problem is that people who undergo this therapy are often reluctant to continue the treatment unless they're closely supervised. If the client stops the treatment and returns to normal drinking or smoking, the newly learned negative association will extinguish and be replaced by the old, positive association. Ethical concerns have also been raised about this form of treatment. Although those who participate do so voluntarily, they are often people who are desperately seeking a solution to their problems. Because the treatment directly induces extremely unpleasant experiences, many therapists are convinced that it should be used only as a treatment of last resort.

Using Rewards and Punishments to Change Behaviour

As we discussed in Chapter 6, it is possible to change behaviour by teaching people about the direct consequences of their behaviour. You can be shaped, through the application of rewards and punishments, away from abnormal actions and toward more normal behaviours. Although aversion therapy involves elements of punishment (e.g., the act of drinking is followed by an extremely unpleasant consequence), its goal is mainly to replace prior pleasant emotional associations with unpleasant ones. Behavioural therapies that use reward and punishment systems, that is, instrumental conditioning, are designed to modify specific unwanted behaviours by teaching people about the consequences of their actions.

Token Economies   Shaping behaviour through the delivery of reward has proven to be particularly effective in institutional settings. When people are confined to mental hospitals or other kinds of institutions, it is usually because they cannot cope successfully without constant supervision. If people cannot care for themselves—if they don't wash properly, eat proper foods, or protect themselves from harm—they need a structured environment around them. In institutional settings, therapists have found that setting up an economic system in which patients are rewarded for behaving appropriately can be quite effective in teaching patients how to cope with the realities of everyday life (e.g., Seegert, 2003).

In a **token economy,** institutionalized patients are rewarded with small tokens (such as poker chips) whenever they engage in an appropriate activity. Certain rules are established and explained to the patient, which determine when tokens are handed out (or taken away). For example, if Bob, who is suffering from schizophrenia, takes his medication without complaint, he is given a plastic token. Sally might receive tokens for getting out of bed in the morning, washing her hair, and brushing her teeth. The tokens can later be exchanged for certain privileges, such as being able to watch a video or buy soft drinks. Similarly, if a patient acts in

aversion therapy

A treatment for replacing a positive reaction to a harmful stimulus, such as alcohol, with something negative, such as feeling nauseated

token economy

A type of behavioural therapy in which institutionalized patients are rewarded with small tokens when they act in an appropriate way; tokens can then be exchanged for certain privileges

an inappropriate manner, the therapist might choose to take tokens away as a form of punishment. This technique is called a token *economy* because it represents a voluntary exchange of goods and services—the patient exchanges appropriate behaviour for the privileges that tokens provide.

Token economies are highly successful in helping patients develop the skills they'll need to function well inside and outside the institution. Not only do the everyday "maintenance" activities of the patients improve, but token rewards can also be used to shape social behaviour and even vocational skill. Token economies have also been used in classroom settings to reward children for showing appropriate individual and group behaviour and even to increase participation in large college courses (Boniecki & Moore, 2003).

Punishment   Although token economies focus on rewards, we've already seen (in Chapters 6 and 12), that punishment can be an effective way to teach people about the consequences of their behaviour. The method of associating an unwanted behaviour with an aversive stimulus (sometimes even a shock) often seems justified. Consider a patient who is extremely self-destructive—perhaps a disturbed boy who continually bangs his head against the wall. Under these conditions, the safe administration of an aversive event has been shown to reduce these self-destructive behaviours, thereby preventing serious injury (Lovaas, 1987; Lovaas, Koegel, Simmons, & Long, 1973).

But, for several reasons, punishment is rarely used as the sole kind of behavioural intervention. First, punishment has side effects—for example, it can damage the working relationship between the therapist and the client. Second, punishment by itself only teaches someone what not to do; it doesn't deal with the appropriate way to act. Third, punishing someone who is in the grips of a psychological disorder raises ethical concerns. We cannot be sure the person on the receiving end of the aversive event approves of the treatment, even though the therapist and the patient's family may be convinced it's in the patient's best interest.

Social Skills Training

Serious psychological disorders can have a devastating impact on a person's ability to function successfully in any environment—especially in social ones. In schizophrenia, for example, social or occupational dysfunction is one of the defining characteristics of the disorder. Patients with schizophrenia tend to isolate themselves from others, and, when they do interact socially, they typically act in odd or peculiar ways.

Consider the conversational speech of David, a 25-year-old with schizophrenia, during an interaction with his therapist (Barlow & Durand, 1999):

Therapist: I was sorry to hear that your Uncle Bill died a few years ago. How are you feeling about him these days?
David: Yes, he died. He was sick and now he's gone. He likes to fish with me, down at the river. He's going to take me hunting. I have guns. I can shoot you and you'd be dead in a minute.

In the words of his therapist, David's conversational speech "resembled a ball rolling down a rocky hill. Like an accelerating object, his speech gained momentum the longer he went on, and as if bouncing off obstacles, the topics almost always went in unpredictable directions" (Barlow & Durand, 1999, p. 407).

In such cases, therapists face a practical problem: How can they improve the social skills of the person with the disorder? This is a particularly important concern in schizophrenia, which is often difficult to treat. Even with effective medications, many patients suffer relapses of symptoms (Liberman, Kopelowicz, & Young, 1994), and some symptoms of the disorder, including social withdrawal and flat affect, are not helped by conventional psychoactive drugs. For these reasons, therapists sometimes turn to social skills training, which is a form of behavioural therapy that uses modelling and reinforcement to shape appropriate adjustment skills (McFall, 1976; Wong et al., 1993).

Social skills training usually consists of a series of steps. To teach conversational skills, for example, the therapist might begin with a discussion of appropriate verbal responses in a conversation, followed by a videotaped demonstration. The patient is then asked to role-play an actual conversation, and the therapist provides either corrective feedback or positive reinforcement. "Homework" might then be assigned, in which the patient is encouraged to practise his or her skills outside the training session, preferably in new situations. If the training is conducted in an institutional setting, such as a mental hospital, the therapist must monitor the patient's subsequent interactions carefully so that appropriate reinforcement can be delivered (Wallace, 1998).

As with other behavioural techniques, social skills training does not try to cure the underlying schizophrenia. But reviews of the research literature indicate that the application of these simple learning principles—positive reinforcement and modelling—can lead to significant improvements in social functioning and in the quality of life for individuals affected with psychological disorders (Benton & Schroeder, 1990; Bustillo, Lauriello, Horan, & Keith, 2001). Although a major goal of any therapy is to improve global functioning, improvements in specific symptoms—even something as simple as knowing how to answer a casual question in an appropriate way—can make an enormous difference in the life of an individual.

CONCEPT SUMMARY

BEHAVIOURAL THERAPIES

Conditioning Approaches

Approach	Based on the Idea That	Therapeutic Approach
Systematic desensitization	Intense anxiety reactions can be reconditioned.	Uses counterconditioning to reduce the fear and anxiety that have become associated with a particular object or event. The therapist attempts to replace a negative association with something relaxing and pleasurable.
Aversion therapy	Unhealthy attractions can be reconditioned.	The therapist tries to replace a pleasant reaction to a harmful stimulus with an unpleasant reaction. For example, the pleasurable reaction associated with smoking is replaced by a new association between smoking and a terrible taste.

Rewards and Punishments

Approach	Based on the Idea That	Therapeutic Approach
Token economies	Behaviour can be changed by teaching people about the positive consequences of their behaviour.	Therapist and patient have a voluntary exchange of goods and services—the patient exchanges appropriate behaviour for privileges provided by tokens.
Punishment	Behaviour can be changed by teaching people about the negative consequences of their behaviour.	An inappropriate (e.g., self-injurious) behaviour is followed with an aversive stimulus or with the removal of a pleasant stimulus.
Social skills training	Improvements in global functioning help re-engage the otherwise isolated patient.	Specific social skills are trained via repetitive practising in graduated steps of increasing contact with the normal social world.

Test Yourself 15.3

Check your knowledge about behavioural therapies by answering the following questions. (The answers are in Appendix B.)

1. According to the classical conditioning account of phobias, the feared stimulus, such as a snake, acts as
   a. an unconditioned stimulus.
   b. a conditioned stimulus.
   c. a conditioned response.
   d. a conditioned reinforcer.
2. In systematic desensitization, the fear that has become associated with a specific object or event is reduced through
   a. counterconditioning and extinction.
   b. second-order conditioning.
   c. delivery of an aversive consequence.
   d. token rewards.

3. Which of the following is not a major concern in aversion therapy?
   a. Clients cannot truly give informed and voluntary consent.
   b. Effective punishments can't be delivered because pain thresholds are high.
   c. Clients are often reluctant to continue treatment.
   d. Newly learned negative associations can extinguish.
4. In a token economy, the token acts as which of the following?
   a. conditioned stimulus
   b. punishment
   c. conditioned inhibitor
   d. reinforcement

▶ Evaluating and Choosing Psychotherapy

LEARNING GOALS

1. Understand the major findings of clinical evaluation research.
2. Understand the factors that are common across psychotherapies.
3. Appreciate the important personal and cultural factors that should be considered when choosing a therapist.

When people make the decision to enter therapy, they do so because they're in need of help. But how do they know what kind of therapy they need? We've now examined the major types of therapy, but we've said little about their relative effectiveness. How well does psychotherapy actually work? Are all forms of therapy equally effective, or do some forms work better than others?

To assess the effectiveness of any therapy requires carefully controlled research. As we discussed in Chapter 2, just because a change occurs after a manipulation does not guarantee that it was the manipulation that caused the change. Someone might enter therapy and leave improved, but the change could have occurred for reasons unrelated to the actual treatment. As Eysenck (1952) pointed out, many patients simply improve spontaneously with the passage of time. Most people who get the flu improve over time—even if they never see a doctor—and it could be that the same kind of thing happens with psychological disorders. A control group—in which no treatment is given—is needed to confirm that the therapy was indeed responsible for the improvement. Fortunately, a number of such controlled research studies have been conducted (Chambless & Ollendick, 2001).

Clinical Evaluation Research

Let's begin by considering a well-known example of a clinical evaluation study (Sloane, Staples, Cristol, Yorkston, & Whipple, 1975). In this study, conducted at a Philadelphia psychiatric clinic in the mid-1970s, men and women who were seeking treatment primarily for anxiety disorders were assigned at random to one of three treatment conditions. One group of patients was assigned to therapists experienced in the practice of psychodynamic techniques (the analysis of unconscious conflicts and memories); a second group was assigned to experienced behavioural therapists (using systematic desensitization and other learning-based techniques); and a third group—the *control* group—was placed on a "waiting list" and received no immediate

CRITICAL THINKING

Is it ethical to assign patients who are seeking help for their psychological problems to a no-treatment control group?

treatment. After four months, an independent team of therapists, who were unaware of the treatment assignments, was called in to evaluate the progress of the patients.

The results were somewhat surprising. The good news is that the therapies clearly worked. As shown by the green bars in ▶ Figure 15.8, all three groups began with the same symptom severity. The purple bars show that the people given either the psychodynamic or the behavioural therapy showed lower symptom severity after four months than the control group did. Interestingly, the control group also improved slightly. There were no significant differences between the two treatment conditions: The behavioural approach worked just as well as the psychodynamic approach.

The bad news (not shown in the graph) is that, in an eight-month follow-up assessment, the patients in the control group had essentially caught up with the treatment patients. They had improved enough to be comparable with the patients in the other two groups. In short, the treatments worked, but it appears that their primary effect was simply to speed up natural improvement. Problems with this interpretation are discussed below.

Meta-Analysis   The Philadelphia study is important because it's an example of how evaluation research should be conducted—random assignment to groups, the use of a no-treatment control, and an independent assessment procedure (Wolpe, 1975). Since that study was first reported, hundreds of other studies have been conducted (although not all have included the same rigorous control procedures). Rather than picking and choosing from among these studies, mental health professionals often rely on a summary technique called meta-analysis to help them draw overall conclusions. In a **meta-analysis,** all available studies are combined statistically by using some common evaluation measure. The comparison standard is usually something called an *effect size*, which is a standardized measure of the difference in the success rate of the treatment and control conditions (see Robey & Dalebout, 1998). If the average effect size across all available studies is large and positive, then that type of therapy is proved to be effective.

In one of the first extensive meta-analytic studies, Smith and colleagues analyzed the results of 475 research studies designed to evaluate one or more forms of psychotherapy (Smith & Glass, 1977; Smith, Glass, & Miller, 1980). Although the individual studies covered a wide range of psychological problems and therapeutic techniques, in each case it was possible to compare a treatment condition with some kind of control condition (usually an untreated group). Smith and colleagues reached two major conclusions from their meta-analysis of the data. First, a consistent and large treatment advantage existed (see ▶ Figure 15.9 on page 626). People who experienced some kind of active psychotherapy were better off, on average, than roughly 80% of the people who were left untreated. Second, when the various kinds of psychotherapy were compared, few, if any, differences were found. It really didn't matter whether the patient was receiving an insight therapy or a behavioural therapy—all produced the same amount of improvement (see also Wampold et al., 1997).

Hundreds of other attempts to meta-analyze evaluation studies have been made. Some have sought to exercise more control over the research quality of the studies included (Lipsey & Wilson, 1993); others have attempted to extend the areas of examination to such things as client characteristics, experience of the therapist, or length of the treatment (Lambert & Bergin, 1994). In general, the findings support two main conclusions: Therapy works and the effects of therapy are long lasting. For example, one recent review of meta-analysis studies, which examined some 302 published meta-analyses, found that the vast majority were overwhelmingly positive (Lipsey & Wilson, 1993).

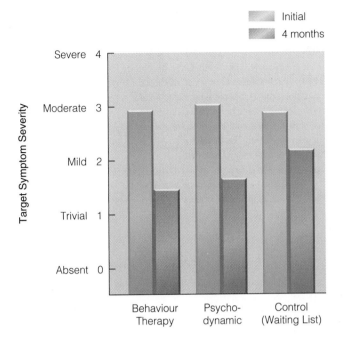

▶ **Figure 15.8**

Evaluating Forms of Treatment

In the study by Sloane and colleagues (1975), men and women seeking treatment for anxiety disorders were randomly assigned to behaviour therapy, psychodynamic therapy, or a control waiting list. After four months, the people receiving therapy showed significantly less severe symptoms than people in the control group, but there were no significant differences between types of therapy (behaviour and psychodynamic). (Data from Sloane et al., 1975.)

meta-analysis

A statistical technique used to summarize findings across all available studies; comparisons are based on some common evaluation index, such as the numerical difference between the success rate of the treatment and control conditions

▶ **Figure 15.9**

The Effectiveness of Psychotherapy

In the meta-analysis by Smith, Glass, and Miller (1980), which assessed hundreds of clinical evaluation studies, people who experienced psychotherapy were better off, on average, than roughly 80% of the people who were not treated. (From *The Benefits of Psychotherapy*, by Mary Lee Smith, Gene V. Glass, and Thomas I. Miller. Copyright © 1980. Reprinted with permission of The Johns Hopkins University Press.)

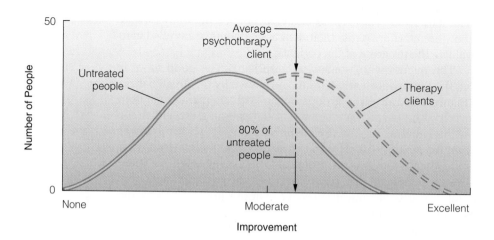

spontaneous remission

Improvement in a psychological disorder without treatment—that is, simply as a function of the passage of time

Controversies   Psychologists generally agree that psychotherapy works, but how to evaluate the evidence remains the subject of debate. For example, what should constitute the proper evaluation "control"? Let's return to the Philadelphia experiment in which two treatment groups (psychodynamic and behavioural) were compared with a group containing people who were left on a waiting list. Remember, the control patients actually got considerably better over time, to a point in which, after a year, they had improved to the same levels as the treatment groups. Psychologists call this kind of improvement in the absence of treatment **spontaneous remission**, and it's been estimated that psychological disorders may improve on their own as much as 30% or more of the time (Eysenck, 1952; Lambert & Bergin, 1994).

But did the people who were left on the waiting list in the Philadelphia experiment really receive no treatment? This is a difficult question to answer—it depends on how you define "treatment." Although those people received no formal psychotherapy, they were given initial psychological tests and were called frequently and given support. Their participation in the study, along with the expectation that they would be receiving some help, may itself have acted as a kind of therapy. Similar effects are commonly found with many placebo controls, in which clients are given attention and support but no formal therapy. Many critics have argued that these no-treatment conditions actually involve factors—such as social support—that are common to most forms of therapy (Horvath, 1988). Even more serious is the high likelihood that some patients secretly sought out—but didn't report—other treatments from other therapists. After all, their overriding goal was to get better, not to aid science. We'll return to this issue in the next section.

The reported finding that all types of psychotherapy are equally effective has also proven to be controversial (Crits-Christoph, 1997). We know that certain treatments work best for certain kinds of problems. For example, psychotherapy researcher Keith Dobson of the University of Calgary conducted a meta-analysis of 28 studies that looked at the effectiveness of different therapies for the treatment of depression (Dobson, 1989). Dobson concluded that cognitive therapy was more effective for treating depression than were other therapies, including drug therapy and behavioural therapy. A similar finding was recently reported for treating anxiety disorders (Compton et al., 2004). However, behavioural therapies may be ideal for combating such anxiety disorders as specific phobias (Bowers & Clum, 1988).

But even if the treatment is matched to the problem, "client variables" can also influence the effectiveness of a therapy. Not all people have the desire or capacity to respond to rational, verbal arguments of the type used by some cognitive therapists or to the probing questions of the psychoanalyst. As a result, it is very difficult to conduct an evaluation study that properly takes all of these factors into account (Chambless & Ollendick, 2001).

Recently, many psychologists have come to support a move toward promoting **empirically supported treatments** as recognized foundations of psychological practice and training. This suggestion involves psychologists coming to an agreement about what we can conclude from the research literature regarding which treatments work best with which disorders (Hunsley, Lee, & Aubry, 1999). This movement also suggests that clinical psychology graduate programs be required to train students in at least two of the "empirically supported treatments." Although some controversy surrounds these suggestions, it is likely that this kind of approach will be a major component guiding the development and application of psychotherapy in the future (McLean & Woody, 2001).

> **empirically supported treatments**
>
> Treatments or therapies that have been shown, based on extensive and well-validated research, to be effective in treating specific psychological disorders and problems

Common Factors across Psychotherapies

Clinical researchers have also considered the possibility that common factors may be shared by all successful therapies, regardless of surface differences. Although the various therapies we've considered are clearly driven by very different assumptions about human psychology, they do share features in common (Grencavage & Norcross, 1990; Rosenzweig, 1936). Michael Lambert and Allen Bergin (1994) have suggested that these common factors can be grouped into three main categories: *support factors*, *learning factors*, and *action factors*.

Support Factors   As Carl Rogers pointed out many years ago, therapeutic success is unlikely without a supportive atmosphere for the client. Of course, the therapist and the patient share the common goal of helping the patient get better. But patients must sense that the therapist is willing to accept and understand their problems. Regardless of their theoretical orientation—psychodynamic, cognitive, behavioural, or humanistic—effective therapists show an interest in listening to and reassuring their clients and in developing a positive, trusting relationship. This notion is backed up by a strong correlation found between the amount of empathy shown by the therapist and the effectiveness of the treatment (Lafferty, Beutler, & Crago, 1991; Miller, Taylor, & West, 1980). One aspect of the relationship between therapist and client that appears to be quite important in the success of therapy is referred to as the **therapeutic alliance,** which refers to the extent to which the therapist and client work together constructively to address the client's problems. Psychotherapy researcher David Zuroff of McGill University and his colleagues have found that the more the client perceives the therapeutic alliance to be strong, and the more that the client actively contributes toward making the therapeutic alliance work, the more successful the therapy (Zuroff et al., 2000). Interestingly, one factor that seemed to be detrimental to successful therapy was a perfectionistic personality style on the part of the client. Particularly in the latter stages of therapy, perfectionist clients tended to have little success in improving their conditions, evidently partly because their perfectionism somehow blocked them from forming a strong therapeutic alliance with the therapist (Flett & Hewitt, 2003).

> **therapeutic alliance**
>
> The bond formed between the client and therapist in successful psychotherapy that is focused on working together constructively to solve the client's problem

Learning Factors   When people go through therapy, they *learn* things about themselves. They learn about their thought processes, about their behaviour, or about important factors in their past that might be contributing to current discomforts. Effective therapists often act as mirrors, reflecting back a client's beliefs and actions in ways that provide critical insight. Regardless of the method of treatment, effective therapists also give feedback about how various experiences relate to one another. They point out connections between experiences—how people might behave and think similarly across different situations. Even if their understanding of the problem is somewhat off the mark, people are often helped because they now have a reason or a rationale for their problems.

PRACTICAL SOLUTIONS

CHOOSING A THERAPIST

At some point in your life, you might find yourself in need of a psychotherapist. Perhaps you'll experience a simple problem in living or maybe something more serious. What should you do? Given our discussion about the relative effectiveness of the various treatment options, it might seem that it doesn't make much difference whom you choose. But those overall results mask the fact that for any specific problem, specific therapists are using specific techniques that work best (Dobson, 1989). Given the complexities involved, the task of making the right choice would seem impossible for the average person. Fortunately, some consumer-oriented books can be of assistance (Engler & Gordon, 1992). Part of the judgment is subjective: The level of trust that you feel with the therapist is critical. So don't be afraid to shop around a bit to find the right person.

It used to be the case that therapists would stick with a particular approach or "school" (such as psychoanalysis or behavioural therapy), but in a recent survey of 800 therapists, 68% of respondents described their orientation as *eclectic* (Jensen, Bergin, & Greaves, 1990). You can expect most therapists to be flexible in their approach, and if one form of treatment is not yielding results—or if you feel uncomfortable with the approach—you can expect the therapist to be open to trying something different. Effective therapy requires open communication, and the therapist is dependent on your feedback as a client throughout the treatment process.

Mental health professionals also now recognize that cultural factors are important in both the diagnosis and the treatment of psychological disorders (Gaw, 2001; Sue & Zane, 1987; Tseng & McDermott, 1975). For many years, cultural barriers have made it difficult for members of ethnic minorities to use and benefit from mental health resources. Language differences between the client and the therapist clearly undermine effective communication, as do differences between the therapist's and the client's worldview. For example, many Asians feel uncomfortable with open self-disclosure and the expression of

Andrea Morini/Getty Images

Cultural barriers sometimes prevent members of ethnic minorities from benefiting from mental health resources. It's essential for a therapist to be sensitive to a client's cultural background and general worldview.

emotions. Indeed, the uniquely Japanese disorder called *taijin kyofusho* is the fear of inappropriately disclosing information to others (Kirmayer, 1991). As a result, it's unlikely that many Japanese patients will benefit from Western therapists who encourage clients to "let it all hang out" (Sue, Zane, & Young, 1994). Instead, there is an increasing use in Canada of traditional Asian methods, such as Morita therapy (Alden, 1988).

Similarly, Aboriginal people have their own traditions of healing, including treating mental and emotional problems, that share some similarities with psychotherapy (Krippner, 1993) and that are in some ways quite different (McCormick, 1996, 2000). For instance, some researchers have found that the most successful substance abuse programs for Aboriginal people were "self-generated, led by a healer or shaman, and organized as healing communities" (Weibel-Orlando, 1989; Wyrostok & Paulson, 2000, p. 15). Most Aboriginal

approaches to healing psychological or emotional problems also emphasize a strong spiritual component and focus on the healing powers of nature (McCormick, 1996). Therapists working with Aboriginal clients are increasingly trying to coordinate their efforts with Aboriginal community-based interventions and to respect these traditions as useful aspects of the healing process.

Does this mean you should always seek a therapist with a cultural background identical to your own? Not necessarily. For one thing, there is still a shortage of therapists from ethnic minorities in Canada. This means that finding a cultural match may be difficult. Moreover, with the increased exposure to cultural influences, many therapists are now making concerted efforts to become culturally sensitive, and almost all clinical psychology graduate programs in Canada have aspects of their curricula devoted to cultural diversity issues (Hertzsprung & Dobson, 2000).

Action Factors   Successful forms of therapy ultimately provide people with a set of specific suggestions for *action*. Troubled clients might be asked to face their fears, take risks, or directly test irrational beliefs. They might be given specific strategies for coping with anxiety or training in how to relax. Irrespective of the specific suggestions, just providing clients with a tangible course of action may be sufficient to give them hope and allow them to feel in control of their problem.

CRITICAL   THINKING
What kind of therapeutic approach would you choose if you needed help? Justify your answer based on what you've learned in this chapter.

Who Uses Psychotherapy and When?   It is interesting to ask, Who are the people most likely to go to a psychotherapist? Clinical researchers John Hunsley, Catherine Lee, and Tim Aubry (1999) of the University of Ottawa addressed this question. They found that approximately 2.15% of Canadians had consulted a psychologist in the 12 months preceding the survey. These people were more likely to be middle-aged, female, and separated, divorced, or widowed. They also tended to have higher incomes than average. One interesting aspect of the study was that the majority of Canadians who were diagnosed as depressed (and who could have presumably benefited from psychotherapy) were not being treated by a psychologist. This suggests that psychological services are probably underutilized in Canada, as is the case in many countries, and steps should be taken to increase people's awareness of how such services could help them and their families. This difference between the number of people who could benefit from psychological services and those who actually receive them has sometimes been referred to as the **service gap** (Cramer, 1999).

What are some of the nondemographic factors (i.e., factors unrelated to ethnicity, age, and gender) that increase the likelihood of people seeking psychological help? Kenneth Cramer of the University of Windsor has examined this question by reanalyzing data from two recent studies of psychology undergraduates (Cramer, 1999). As expected, he found that university students tend to seek psychological help when their level of personal distress is quite high; they also have positive attitudes toward counselling. More interesting, however, was the influence of self-concealment on the decision to seek psychological help. Cramer's analysis suggests that university students who tend to keep their problems to themselves and not share their problems with others (i.e., who self-conceal) tend to have more psychological problems than students who more freely disclose their problems to other people. Another finding was that psychological distress tends to be high when students do not have access to a solid social support network (i.e., understanding and attentive friends and family). Cramer suggests that steps to enhance students' social support systems may both decrease their psychological distress and increase their likelihood of seeking appropriate psychological services when needed. He also points out that it may be useful to conduct public education programs aimed at changing students' attitudes about counselling, so that the students who would benefit from such treatment are more likely to seek it.

service gap

The difference between the number of people who could benefit from receiving psychological services and those who receive them

---

Test Yourself 15.4   *Check your knowledge about behavioural therapies by answering the following questions. (The answers are in Appendix B.)*

1. Psychological disorders may improve on their own as much as 30% of the time. *True or False?*
2. According to most meta-analytic studies, people who experience active psychotherapy are better off, on average, than roughly 80% of the people who are left untreated. *True or False?*
3. Most evaluation studies show that specific disorders, such as depression, require specific forms of therapy, such as psychoanalysis. *True or False?*
4. One factor that is common to all forms of psychotherapy is the need to investigate the traumatic events of childhood. *True or False?*
5. In choosing a therapist, perhaps the most important factor is empathy—finding someone you trust and with whom you feel comfortable. *True or False?*

Therapy

In this chapter, we've discussed the various techniques used to address the practical problem of psychological disorders. The issues have been organized in terms of the three possible origins of disorders: biological, cognitive, and environmental factors. Depending on the particular disorder, psychologists have varied in their success at developing effective therapies.

First, what are the most effective biologically based treatments? Of these three categories, the most dramatic advances continue to be made in *biomedical therapies*. It is not an overstatement to say that, in the past 40 years, drug therapies have revolutionized psychotherapy. Altering the actions of neurotransmitters in the brain has been the primary technique. Great success has been achieved with antidepressants and antipsychotic and antianxiety drugs. Each one has side effects that must be closely monitored to avoid symptoms that may be worse than the original problem.

In the event that other approaches fail, therapists treating depression sometimes turn to other forms of biomedical intervention, particularly electroconvulsive therapy (ECT). Despite the handicap of being used only on extreme cases, there is widespread agreement that ECT works for many patients.

A notable issue common to drug therapies and ECT is that even experts are not sure how they work. Presumably, they will eventually be understood; but until then, their ever-increasing use should be accompanied by some caution and further research.

Second, how can maladaptive thinking be changed? The stereotype of the therapist with the notepad talking to the patient on the couch still holds most closely with insight therapy. Usually, this insight is obtained through prolonged verbal, one-on-one interactions between the therapist and the client (i.e., the "talking cure"). By now, you are quite familiar with the most popular variations—psychoanalysis, cognitive therapy, and humanistic therapy.

Whether used by psychologists or psychiatrists or counsellors, these therapies retain the notion of the mind-body separation. Specifically, psychological disorders are problems of the mind and, therefore, can be cured strictly with techniques applied to the mind.

Third, how can the environment be altered to reduce maladaptive behaviour? If a disorder results from maladaptive conditioning, it makes sense to use behavioural techniques to counteract the disorder. In line with strict behaviourism, pure behavioural therapies aim to treat overt behaviour without considering thought processes. Although not as popular as it once was, this approach has important applications, such as systematic desensitization, token economies, and social skills training, that are effective in specific situations.

Behavioural methods are now flourishing in combination with more cognitive approaches that use cognitive behavioural therapy (CBT). Although agreeing that many kinds of psychological problems have been learned, cognitive-behavioural therapists consider cognitive aspects to be critical to success. An effective treatment of panic disorder, for example, uses a CBT approach that combines reframing and desensitization.

Fourth, how can we evaluate the effectiveness of psychotherapy? We have seen how psychotherapy evaluation research should be done properly: Treatment groups must be compared with appropriate control conditions in rigorous experiments. Many such studies have now been conducted, and meta-analyses of their results typically reach two main conclusions. First, people who receive psychotherapy do significantly better than those left untreated. Second, one type of psychotherapy has few overall advantages over another. Nonetheless, such research may have some hidden problems.

One reason that different forms of treatment appear equally effective may be that success actually depends more on basic process factors of support, learning, and action. If these are carried out adeptly, then patients will get better. If not, any therapeutic approach will fail. Another complication that may hide any differences among approaches is that therapists tend to choose approaches that they are most comfortable with and best trained in. Moreover, patients are apt to select approaches and therapists that they are most comfortable with. Imagine the difficulty of doing a study where therapists and patients could be randomly assigned to a therapy that they despise. A further complication is the growing issue of cultural differences.

Ultimately, we may not be able to answer questions about the effectiveness of psychotherapy without specifying the type of therapist, the type of client, and what sort of improvement the pair are seeking. Those same factors should be considered if you are seeking psychotherapy. You should select a therapist with whom you are comfortable, who is sensitive to your cultural perspective, and who specializes in your particular problem area.

CHAPTER SUMMARY

▶ Treating the Body: Biomedical Therapies

Abnormal functioning in the brain is thought to contribute to a number of psychological disorders. To address these problems, psychologists sometimes consider the use of *biomedical therapies.*

Drug Therapies

Medications (such as chlorpromazine) that treat positive symptoms of schizophrenia are termed *antipsychotic drugs* and quite often act on the neurotransmitter dopamine. However, these drugs are limited in their effect and can produce side effects, such as *tardive dyskinesia,* which produces disabling involuntary movements. *Clozapine* and *risperidone* are newer medications that serve as an effective alternative. *Antidepressant drugs* also modulate the effectiveness of neurotransmitters, particularly norepinephrine and serotonin. Bipolar disorders are often treated with the common salt *lithium carbonate.* *Antianxiety drugs,* or *tranquillizers* (e.g., Valium), come from a class of drugs called *benzodiazepines* and work primarily on the neurotransmitter GABA.

Electroconvulsive Therapy

Most professionals believe that *electroconvulsive therapy (ECT)* is now a reasonably safe and effective treatment for severe depression. Nonetheless, it is typically used as a treatment of last resort. The treatment remains controversial for a number of reasons. The reasons for its effectiveness are not well understood, and it can produce side effects, such as confusion and minor memory loss.

▶ Treating the Mind: Insight Therapies

Psychological disorders are often associated with abnormal thoughts and beliefs. Many psychologists believe that the key to improvement lies in insight. *Insight therapies* encourage clients to gain a clearer understanding of their psychological problems, usually through a one-on-one interaction with a therapist.

Psychoanalysis: Resolving Unconscious Conflicts

Freud believed that through *psychoanalysis,* hidden impulses and memories can be brought to awareness, freeing us from disordered thoughts and behaviours. The tools used to uncover unconscious conflicts include *free association* and *dream analysis. Resistance* (unconsciously motivated attempts to hinder therapy) and *transference* (expression of thoughts or feelings toward the therapist that are representative of how patients feel about others in their lives) also provide clues about unconscious

conflict. Modern versions of psychoanalysis streamline the therapeutic process and are often tailored to meet the specific needs of individuals.

Cognitive Therapies: Changing Maladaptive Beliefs

Unlike the psychoanalytic approach, *cognitive therapies* place emphasis on *conscious* beliefs. Psychological problems arise from maladaptive and negative interpretations of daily events. In *rational-emotive therapy,* the therapist "cross-examines" the client, disputing irrational thought processes. Beck's cognitive therapy takes a more subtle approach, helping clients discover their own unique kinds of faulty beliefs through record-keeping or other types of "homework."

Humanistic Therapies: Treating the Human Spirit

Humanistic therapies help the client gain insight into his or her own fundamental self-worth and value as a person. In *client-centred therapy,* the therapist is warm, empathic, and supportive in all respects, accepting the client unconditionally. This unconditional positive regard helps the client overcome *incongruence.* One variation, *Gestalt therapy,* forces clients to express their feelings openly.

Group Therapy

In *group therapy,* you join others who are undergoing treatment for a similar problem. This can be particularly appropriate in the case of families. In *family therapy,* the therapist treats the family as a kind of social system, attempting to improve interpersonal communication and collaboration among family members.

▶ Changing the Environment: Behavioural Therapies

People may *learn* to feel, think, and act in abnormal ways through the mechanisms of classical and instrumental conditioning and observational learning. *Behavioural therapies* employ basic learning principles to recondition maladaptive behaviour patterns into adaptive behaviour patterns.

Conditioning Techniques

Phobias can be eliminated by teaching a new association between the feared object and something pleasurable. *Conditioning techniques* may be used to change the association to something pleasurable. In *systematic desensitization,* the therapist uses counterconditioning, systematically associating relaxation with feared objects as expressed in an *anxiety hierarchy.* In *aversion therapy,* the therapist attempts to replace a pleasant reaction to a harmful stimulus (e.g., alcohol) with something unpleasant.

Using Rewards and Punishments to Change Behaviour

People can be shaped, through rewards and punishments, away from abnormal actions and toward more normal behaviours. In a *token economy*, institutionalized patients are rewarded with tokens whenever they engage in an appropriate activity. The tokens are later exchanged for certain privileges. *Punishment* may also be effective in teaching people to understand the consequences of their actions and is sometimes used to discourage self-injurious behaviour.

Social Skills Training

Even with serious disorders, such as schizophrenia, the patient's quality of life can be improved dramatically by improving their ability to interact with others. A multistep training process is required, including modelling, role-playing, and homework to reinforce the new skills.

▶ Evaluating and Choosing Psychotherapy

Therapy is a costly and time-consuming process, so it's important to determine the advantages and disadvantages of an intervention. A person must also take a number of factors into account when choosing a therapist.

Clinical Evaluation Research

One well-known study that compared psychoanalytic and behavioural approaches to therapy with a control condition demonstrated that therapy clearly worked, but no reliable differences existed in the effectiveness of the two approaches. *Meta-analyses* of evaluation studies have shown that therapy works, although some problems may improve on their own through *spontaneous remission*. Overall, no one therapeutic approach seems more effective than others, although particular kinds of therapy may work best for certain problems. Psychologists have recently begun to agree on which treatments are *empirically supported* by research as being effective.

Common Factors across Psychotherapies

Common factors are seen in each therapeutic approach: All therapies provide *support* for the client; all people in therapy *learn* something about themselves; and all forms of therapy provide people with some suggestions for *action*. These common factors may account for the finding that approaches are comparable in their overall effectiveness. Also important is the *therapeutic alliance*: the agreement between therapist and client to work together to solve the client's problem.

Terms to Remember

psychotherapy, 601

Treating the Body: Biomedical Therapies
biomedical therapies, 603
antipsychotic drugs, 604
antidepressant drugs, 605
antianxiety drugs, 606
electroconvulsive therapy (ECT), 607

Treating the Mind: Insight Therapies
insight therapies, 608
psychoanalysis, 609
free association, 609
dream analysis, 609
resistance, 610
transference, 610
cognitive therapies, 611
rational-emotive therapy, 612

humanistic therapy, 615
client-centred therapy, 615
group therapy, 617
family therapy, 617

Changing the Environment: Behavioural Therapies
behavioural therapies, 618
systematic desensitization, 620
aversion therapy, 621
token economy, 621

Evaluating and Choosing Psychotherapy
meta-analysis, 625
spontaneous remission, 626
empirically supported treatments, 627
therapeutic alliance, 627
service gap, 629

Recommended Readings

Endler, N. S. (1990). *Holiday of darkness: A psychologist's personal journey out of his depression.* New York: Wall & Emerson. York University psychologist Norman Endler's personal account of struggling with his own depressive episodes. Endler defended the usefulness of ECT for helping people with his kind of depression.

Engler, J., & Goleman, D. (1992). *The consumer's guide to psychotherapy.* New York: Simon & Schuster. This book is a good source for discovering the range of available psychotherapies and for help in picking the kind of therapy that might work best for you.

Mahrer, A. R. (1995). *A complete guide to experiential psychotherapy.* New York: John Wiley. Alvin Mahrer of the University of Ottawa is a distinguished psychotherapy researcher and practitioner. In this volume, he outlines how to conduct experiential psychotherapy (which shares many features with humanistic approaches).

Rosenthal, H. G. (2006). *Therapy's best: Practical advice and gems of wisdom from twenty accomplished counselors and therapists.* St. Louis, MO: Haworth Press. This new book gives an insider's perspective on psychotherapy with interviews of well-known psychotherapists.

 For additional readings, explore InfoTrac® College Edition, your online library. Go to http://www.adaptivemind3e.nelson.com.

Hint: Enter these search terms: Prozac, psychotherapy, psychoanalysis, cognitive therapy, behaviour modification, effectiveness of psychotherapy.

Media Resources

What's on the Web?

Please note that Web addresses are subject to change. Check out the accompanying website for updates: http://www.adaptivemind3e.nelson.com.

This site presents practice quiz questions, hypercontent, information on degrees and careers in psychology, study tips, and more.

Canadian Psychological Association: Clinical Psychology Section Webpage

http://www.cpa.ca/clinical/

This site includes information on psychotherapy's effectiveness and reports and conferences on psychotherapy and other aspects of clinical psychology.

Canadian Traumatic Stress Network

http://www.ctsn-rcst.ca

This site offer resources, support, and advice for people who have suffered traumatic stress and for practitioners working with such people.

Canadian *Journal of Psychiatry and Neuroscience*

http://www.cma.ca/jpn/index.htm

The website for Canada's leading psychiatric journal contains abstracts and some full-text research articles, many of them examining biomedical approaches to the treatment of mental disorders.

Psychotherapy Links

http://www.psychiatry.med.uwo.ca/ecp/

From the University of Western Ontario Department of Psychiatry comes an extensive collection of well-organized links to psychotherapy sites and contacts in rural Ontario.

Society for Interpersonal Theory and Research

http://www.vcu.edu/sitar

The interpersonal approach to therapy emphasizes the emergence of personality in social interaction. It has a long history with strong influences from Canadian researchers, such as Wiggins, Alden, Moskowitz, Trobst, and Trapnell.

ThomsonNOW™ ThomsonNOW™

http://hed.nelson.com

Go to this site for the link to ThomsonNOW™, your one-stop study shop. Take a Pretest for this chapter and ThomsonNOW™ will generate a personalized Study Plan based on your test results. The Study Plan will identify the topics you need to review and direct you to online resources to help you master those topics. You can then take a Posttest to determine what concepts you have mastered and what you still need work on.

Psyk.trek 3.0

Check out Psyk.trek 3.0 for further study of the concepts in this chapter. Psyk.trek's 65 interactive learning modules, simulations, and quizzes offer additional opportunities for you to interact with, reflect on, and retain the material:

Abnormal Behavior and Therapy: Behavioral and Biomedical Therapies
Abnormal Behavior and Therapy: Insight Therapies

Photos.com

. . . most commentators believe that ours is the "age of stress," forgetting that the caveman's fear of attack by wild animals or of death from hunger, cold, or exhaustion must have been just as stressful as our fear of a world war, the crash of the stock exchange, or overpopulation.

—Hans Selye

Stress and Health

Like every generation, we tend to claim exclusive rights to the
"age of stress." It hits us from all sides—school, work, relationships,
family. Everyone expects something from us, and everyone seems to want
it now. Your teachers expect you to read too much material and to write papers
by the deadline; your boss expects overtime in addition to your regular hours;
your parents expect you to show up for family events—and to act as if you enjoy
them. Is it any wonder that you feel tired all the time, can't seem to shake that
cough, and feel the need to keep the antacid tablets by your bedside at night?
Although we can adapt to stress reasonably well in the short run, there are consequences for our physical health in the long run.

The idea that a close relationship exists between your psychological state
and the physical reactions of your body has been around since Freud. The mind
and the body interact, and the forces work in both directions. As we've discussed,
disruptions in the delicate balance of neurotransmitters in the brain can contribute significantly to psychological problems, such as schizophrenia and depression. At the same time, beliefs, expectations, and reactions to the environment
affect how those neurotransmitters are manufactured and used in the brain. In
this chapter, you'll see that the mind-to-body connection affects the way you
think, feel, and react, but it can affect your overall state of health as well.

Our focus in this chapter is the general topic of **health psychology.** Also known as *behavioural medicine,* this field seeks to understand how biological, psychological, environmental, and cultural factors are involved in the promotion of physical health and the prevention of illness. Not surprisingly, health psychologists are particularly interested in the psychological and environmental contributions (Krantz & McCeney, 2002; Nezu, Nezu, & Geller, 2003). They tend to ask such questions as these: Are there particular personality characteristics that determine who becomes sick or who will recover from an illness once it is acquired? Can the same theories that have been used successfully to diagnose and treat psychological disorders be applied to the promotion of physical health? Is it possible to identify the kinds of working environments that lead to illness or promote recovery? Are there specific strategies, or lifestyle choices, that reduce the likelihood of getting sick?

Stress and Health

P R E V I E W

Much of our discussion in this chapter will deal with the topic of psychological stress and its effects on health. Our reactions to stress tend to be adaptive, but prolonged exposure to stressful environments can have a negative long-term impact on health. Our discussion in this chapter will focus on four adaptive problems that are related to stress and to health psychology in general.

First, what is stress, and how is it experienced? Everyone has an intuitive sense of what *stress* is, but the term can actually be defined in a variety of ways. We'll discuss some of the meanings of the term, as well as the various components of the stress response. It's best to conceive of stress not as a single reaction, such as a sudden release of activating hormones, but rather as an extended response that occurs over time.

Second, how does the body react when the exposure to stressful situations is prolonged? The human body is usually well equipped to deal with unexpected trauma by activating those systems that are needed to respond to the emergency. But if the threat continues for an extended period, the body's defences can begin to break down. We'll consider some of the physical consequences of prolonged exposure to stress, including the role that stress plays in the immune system.

Third, what strategies enable us to reduce and cope with stress? Given that prolonged exposure to stress can have negative long-term consequences, psychologists have developed specific methods of treatment for reducing and controlling stress. A number of techniques are available for managing stress, and we'll consider some of them later in the chapter.

Fourth, what general factors and lifestyle choices promote physical and psychological health? Whether you will remain healthy throughout your life depends importantly on the lifestyle habits you choose. Obviously, if you choose to engage in risky behaviours—such as smoking, failing to get adequate nutrition, or practising unsafe sex— then you increase your likelihood of illness or death. Health psychologists have joined with other professionals, including physicians, to offer prescriptions for a healthy lifestyle. We'll discuss some of these recommendations along with their foundations in psychological theory.

▶ Experiencing Stress: Stressors and the Stress Response

LEARNING GOALS

1. Understand the stress response.
2. Be able to explain the role of cognitive appraisal in the stress response.
3. Learn about external sources of stress.
4. Learn about internal sources of stress.

Stress is a concept that is easy to identify but difficult to define precisely. Part of the problem is that the term can be used to refer to two different aspects of the psychological process. Stress can be an actual *stimulus* (such as an event or a person) that places a demand on us or threatens our well-being ("Four final exams in one week is too much stress"). However, we're just as likely to describe stress as a physical *response* or reaction that we feel ("I'm really stressed out"). To complicate matters even further, as you'll see later, whether we experience stress depends on how we interpret the situation we're in (Lazarus, 1966, 1991).

For our purposes, we'll define **stress** as the physical and psychological reaction that people have to threatening or demanding situations, and we'll refer to the demanding or threatening situations that produce stress as **stressors.** For example, the traffic jam that blocks your usual route home from school is a stressor, whereas your fuming physical and emotional reaction to such a situation is stress. In this section of the chapter, we'll first consider some of the physical and psychological characteristics of stress; then we'll examine the external and internal factors that create stress.

stress

People's physical and psychological reactions to demanding or threatening situations

stressors

The demanding or threatening situations that produce stress

The Stress Response

If you're like most people, you probably think of stress as a bad thing. Certainly when you're "stressed out," you tend to feel lousy, and there's no question that extended exposure to stressful situations can have long-term negative

Prolonged exposure to stress can lead to physical and psychological problems.

Jack Hollingsworth/PhotoDisc/Getty Images

The early stages of the stress response are clearly adaptive because they help organisms initiate a fight-or-flight response.

© Tom Brakefield/Corbis

general adaptation syndrome (GAS)

Hans Selye's model of stress as a general, nonspecific reaction that occurs in three phases: alarm reaction, resistance, and exhaustion

consequences. But it's important to understand that stress is in many ways an adaptive reaction. When you're in a threatening situation, or when someone is placing demands on you, it's important that your body become activated so you can respond to the threat with energy. The experience of stress does exactly that— it activates you for responses that are quick and intense.

Physiological Reactions   In Montreal during the 1930s, a physician named Hans Selye introduced an influential model of stress reaction that he called the **general adaptation syndrome (GAS)** (Selye, 1936, 1952, 1974). Selye suggested that our reaction to stressful situations is general and nonspecific, by which he meant that people are biologically programmed to respond to most threats in the same way. He was initially led to this idea as a medical student, when he was struck by the similarities he saw among his patients. Across wildly different illnesses and injuries, his patients seemed to share a "syndrome of just being sick": That syndrome suggested to Selye that the body was reacting to each threatening situation in a very general way (no matter what the illness or the injury). Later, working in the laboratory with rats, he was able to confirm his hypothesis under controlled experimental conditions. Rats subjected to a variety of different kinds of threats— cold, heat, shock, restraint—produced a similar pattern of deteriorating health.

Selye's concept of the GAS proposed that the body reacts to threat or demand in three stages or phases (see ▶ Figure 16.1). The first phase, the *alarm reaction*, corresponds to the adaptive fight-or-flight response we've discussed in previous chapters (Cannon, 1932). The body becomes energized, through activation of the sympathetic division of the autonomic nervous system, and hormones are released by the glands of the endocrine system. Heart rate and respiration rate increase, as does blood flow to the muscles; each of these actions helps prepare the body for immediate defensive or evasive action. The alarm reaction enables people to get out of life-threatening jams, but it is extremely intense and cannot be sustained for long periods without serious negative consequences (even death).

If the threat continues but is not serious enough to demand a continued alarm reaction, the body enters a *resistance phase*. During this phase, the body adjusts its physiological reaction in an effort to reduce, or cope with, the still-present threat. Arousal levels remain higher than normal, but the body is capable of replenishing at least some of its resources. During the resistance phase, people are able to function reasonably well, but they are particularly susceptible to other stressors in the environment and may begin to develop health problems, or what Selye called "diseases of adaptation."

General Adaptation Syndrome

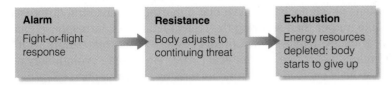

Alarm	Resistance	Exhaustion
Fight-or-flight response	Body adjusts to continuing threat	Energy resources depleted: body starts to give up

▶ **Figure 16.1**

The General Adaptation Syndrome

Hans Selye proposed that the body reacts to threat or demand in three stages or phases: (1) an *alarm reaction*, which corresponds to the fight-or-flight response; (2) a *resistance phase*, during which the body adjusts its reaction in an effort to cope with a threat that is still present; and (3) *exhaustion*, which occurs when the body's energy reserves become so depleted that it starts to give up.

Finally, if the person is unable to find a way to neutralize the threat, the body eventually enters the *exhaustion phase* of the GAS. The body simply cannot continue to maintain a high state of readiness for extended periods. Eventually, energy reserves become so taxed and depleted that the body starts to give up. During this period, resistance declines to the point at which the stress reaction becomes more and more maladaptive. Irreversible damage and even death become real possibilities.

Selye's notion of the GAS has remained influential over the years (Csermely, 1998). But today, many researchers believe that the body's reaction to threat may not be as general and nonspecific as Selye suggested. Different stressors may well produce somewhat different patterns of response in the body (Kemeny, 2003). Moreover, as you'll see momentarily, the stress reaction depends on the cognitive interpretation, or appraisal, of the threatening situation. But the idea that stress is best conceived as a complex process of adaptation is still widely accepted, as is Selye's discovery of the link between stress and health.

Psychological Reactions   Stress is not just a physiological reaction to threat; the reaction has emotional and behavioural components as well. We will consider the psychological consequences of prolonged exposure to stressful situations later in the chapter, but emotional reactions are an important component of the stress response regardless of when or how long it occurs. *Fear* is a common reaction to threat, as is *anger*. Stressful situations can also lead to feelings of *sadness, dejection,* or even *grief* (Lazarus, 1991). Notice that this diverse set of emotional reactions is another piece of evidence suggesting that the stress reaction is not completely general and nonspecific—people are capable of responding emotionally to different stressors in quite different ways.

The psychological consequences of stress are not always negative. Stress can have significant short-term and long-term psychological benefits (Suedfeld, 1997). For example, one study of people who had frequent illnesses found them to be more empathic toward others and more tolerant of uncertainty (Haan, 1977). Stressful situations require people to use their skills and to interact with the environment. Those who can successfully resolve a stressful situation can learn from it and gain confidence in their abilities. Even some survivors of the Holocaust in World War II appeared to gain some long-term benefits, including a more complex worldview (Suedfeld, Krell, Wiebe, & Steel, 1997). Experimental laboratory work showed that rats who were allowed to escape from shock, thereby reducing stress, had better-functioning immune systems than rats who received no shock (Laudenslager, Ryan, Drugen, Hyson, & Maier, 1983). A similar reaction may happen to people: Stress may, at times, lead to the release of hormones that are health enhancing, at least in the short term (Epel, McEwen, & Ickovics, 1998).

CRITICAL   THINKING

Just because two things occur together, such as illness and empathy, doesn't mean that one causes the other. How would you determine whether physical illness truly causes increased empathy?

Gender Differences   Although the basic physiological stress reaction (e.g., activation of the sympathetic nervous system) doesn't differ much between males and females, some psychologists believe that important behavioural differences exist. For example, rather than showing the typical fight-or-flight response that is characteristic of males, females seem predisposed to react to stressors with "tending and befriending" behaviour (Taylor et al., 2000). Because of evolutionary pressures, females may have evolved to respond by tending and protecting offspring (in addition to themselves) rather than fighting or fleeing the scene.

According to Taylor and her colleagues (2000), it's more adaptive for males to react to potential harm by being aggressive or fleeing; females are faced with different pressures, especially the care of the young, and often lack the necessary physical power to ward off threats through aggression. Although women can certainly become physically aggressive in some settings, aggression and flight are secondary reactions to threats. Instead, the first line of defence is to protect and calm offspring, which increases the chances of offspring survival. These reactions are also reflected in longer-term strategies: Females appear more likely to create and maintain social networks that potentially can aid in protecting themselves and their offspring (Haselton & Buss, 2000).

The proposal that males and females differ fundamentally in their behavioural reactions to stressors is new and likely to be controversial—especially the idea that gender-specific stress reactions may be adaptations arising from evolutionary pressures. However, the evidence supporting gender differences appears across the animal kingdom and may have some basis in the biology of male and female brains (Kimura, 1999). As Taylor and her colleagues (2000) note, the majority of research on the behavioural components of the stress response has been conducted on one sex at a time, so much remains to be learned about gender differences in the basic stress response.

Cognitive Appraisal

The experience of stress is critically influenced by the way that people perceive or *appraise* their situation (Lazarus, 1993). To feel stress, it's necessary to (1) perceive that some kind of demand or threat is present and (2) conclude that you may not have adequate resources available to deal with that threat. If you have a black belt in the martial arts, then the sudden appearance of a school bully is not likely to cause much stress—the threat is there, but you have adequate defensive resources should you need to use them.

This idea—that the experience of stress depends on the **cognitive appraisal** of the situation—is reminiscent of what we know about the experience of emotions. As you may remember from Schachter's work in Chapter 11, the same general physiological reaction can lead to different subjective emotional experiences, depending on how people interpret the arousal experienced. The same is true for stress. Identical environmental events can lead to two very different stress reactions, depending on how the event is interpreted. Consider an upcoming exam: Everyone in the class receives the same test, but not everyone will feel the same amount of stress. Those people who are prepared for the exam—the people (like you) who read the chapter—are likely to feel less stress. You, the diligent student, still perceive the threat, but you have adequate resources to deal with it (see ❱ Figure 16.2). The converse is also true—dangerous situations must be perceived as dangerous for a stress response to be produced. A small child does not necessarily understand that a loaded gun is dangerous and so may feel no stress while handling it.

A great deal of evidence confirms the role of cognitive appraisal in the experience of stress (Folkman & Moskowitz, 2004). In one study of elementary schoolchildren, urine samples were taken from the children on both normal school days and on days when they were about to take standardized achievement tests. The urine sample measured the amount of cortisol, an important stress hormone, that

cognitive appraisal

The idea that to feel stress you need to perceive a threat and come to the conclusion that you may not have adequate resources to deal with the threat

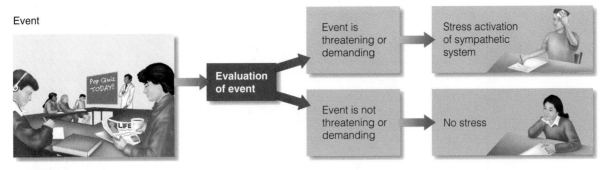

Event

▶ **Figure 16.2**

Cognitive Appraisal

Like emotion, whether an event will create stress depends on how the event is interpreted. A stress reaction is more likely to occur if you feel you have inadequate resources to deal with the potential threat.

each child produced. In formal terms, the authors operationalized stress as the current amount of the hormone in the urine. Not surprisingly, more cortisol was found on test days, suggesting a higher level of stress, but the increase in stress depended on the child's previously recorded overall intelligence score. The children with higher intelligence scores showed less of a stress reaction on test days, presumably because they considered the test to be less of a threat (Tennes & Kreye, 1985).

External Sources of Stress

The fact that the stress reaction depends on appraisal of the situation means that it will never be possible to compile an exhaustive list of life's stressors. We can never predict how everyone will react to an environmental event, even though it may seem clearly stressful to the majority. But it is possible to catalogue external situations, or life events, that induce stress reactions in *most* individuals. We'll consider four major classes of external stressors in this section: significant life events, physical pain, daily hassles, and other factors in the environment.

Significant Life Events   Certain events in our lives are virtually guaranteed to produce stress. We can all agree that the death of a loved one or getting fired from a job is likely to lead to an extended stress reaction in most people. On a larger scale, catastrophes and natural disasters—such as the terrorist attacks that occurred in the United States on September 11, 2001—unquestionably produce stress that is prolonged and widespread. In the case of the terrorist attacks in 2001, a national phone survey conducted three to five days after the attack found that more than 44% of people reported one or more substantial symptoms of stress, and more than 90% reported feeling at least some symptoms (Schuster et al., 2001).

Many studies have found clear relationships between such events and subsequent physical and psychological problems (Dohrenwend, 1998; Heim, Bierl, Nisenbaum, Wagner, & Reeves, 2004). Although it's too early to tell what the long-term health consequences of the terrorist attacks will be, other cases suggest the long-term effects will be widespread. For instance, in the seven months following the 1980 volcanic eruption of Mount St. Helens in Washington State, one nearby town reported a more than 30% increase in the number of hospital emergency room visits, compared with a similar period in the year before the eruption (Adams & Adams, 1984) (see ▶ Figure 16.3 on page 642). These visits were *not* for injuries directly caused by the eruption but rather for general health problems that may have been created or enhanced by the experience of stress.

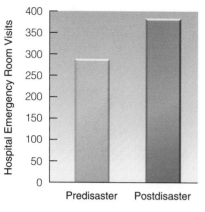
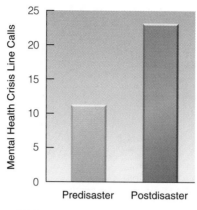
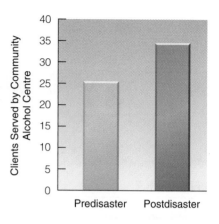

▶ **Figure 16.3**

Reacting to a Natural Disaster

In the seven months following the volcanic eruption of Mount St. Helens in 1980, the residents of nearby Othello, Washington, showed dramatic increases in a variety of stress-related behaviours. The data shown here present the mean monthly hospital emergency room visits, mental health crisis line calls, and number of clients served by a community alcohol centre for comparable time periods before and after the disaster. (Data from Adams & Adams, 1984.)

Over the years researchers have tried to compile lists of external life stressors. The best-known example is the Social Readjustment Rating Scale, which was put together by researchers Thomas Holmes and Richard Rahe (1967). Holmes and Rahe interviewed thousands of people who had health problems and then tried to determine whether certain kinds of events preceded the onset of the health problems. The results are shown in ▶ Table 16.1. This table lists the various significant life events mentioned by the people who were interviewed, ranked in terms of "life change units" (roughly representing the amount of readjustment that the event caused in the person's life).

There are two interesting things to notice about the results shown in the table. First, most of these life events are associated with some kind of change in a person's day-to-day activities. Thus, it may be that the disruption caused by the event is just as important as the event itself in causing the stress reaction. People get stressed, in part, because something happens that requires them to alter their ways or lifestyle. Second, notice that many of the events listed in the table are actually quite positive. For example, marriage and retirement both make the top 10. Even vacations and Christmas make the list. This is not really too surprising if you think about it, because each is associated with some kind of temporary or long-lasting change or disruption of normal routines.

The results listed in Table 16.1 are about 40 years old, but they continue to be used by researchers as an index for predicting the likelihood of stress. Dozens of studies have shown significant correlations among the rankings shown in the table and various measures of stress, including physical and psychological problems (Derogatis & Coons, 1993; Miller, 1993). However, not all experts are satisfied with the methods that have been used to compile such lists (Brett, Brief, Burke, George, & Webster, 1990; Cleary, 1980; Schroeder & Costa, 1984), and recent revisions of the scale have been introduced to take into account such factors as gender, age, and amount of education (Hobson & Delunas, 2001; Miller & Rahe, 1997). Moreover, change by itself will not necessarily lead to stress reactions in all individuals. Remember, it's how you appraise the event that is really important, along with your assessment of whether you have adequate resources to deal with the life change when it occurs.

▶ **Table 16.1** Social Readjustment Rating Scale

Rank	Life Event	Point Value	Rank	Life Event	Point Value
1	Death of spouse	100	23	Son or daughter leaving home	29
2	Divorce	73	24	Trouble with in-laws	29
3	Marital separation	65	25	Outstanding personal achievement	28
4	Jail term	63	26	Wife begins or stops work	26
5	Death of close family member	63	27	Begin or end school	26
6	Personal injury or illness	53	28	Change in living conditions	25
7	Marriage	50	29	Revision of personal habits	24
8	Fired at work	47	30	Trouble with boss	23
9	Marital reconciliation	45	31	Change in work hours or conditions	20
10	Retirement	45	32	Change in residence	20
11	Change in health of family member	44	33	Change in schools	20
12	Pregnancy	40	34	Change in recreation	19
13	Sex difficulties	39	35	Change in church activities	19
14	Gain of new family member	39	36	Change in social activities	18
15	Business readjustment	39	37	Mortgage or loan less than $20 000	17
16	Change in financial state	38	38	Change in sleeping habits	16
17	Death of close friend	37	39	Change in number of family get-togethers	15
18	Change to different line of work	36	40	Change in eating habits	15
19	Change in number of arguments with spouse	35	41	Vacation	13
20	Mortgage over $20 000	31	42	Christmas	12
21	Foreclosure of mortgage or loan	30	43	Minor violations of the law	11
22	Change in responsibilities at work	29			

Source: Reprinted from T. H. Holmes & R. H. Rahe, "The Social Readjustment Rating Scale" from *Journal of Psychosomatic Research, 11,* pp. 218–231. Copyright © 1967 Elsevier Inc. Reprinted with permission from Elsevier Science.

Physical Pain For the last 50 years, scientific research on pain has been led by Canadian researchers, such as Ronald Melzak at McGill University, Ken Craig at the University of British Columbia, and Patrick McGrath at Dalhousie University. Craig and McGrath have developed methods for detecting pain in babies to avoid the possibility that we are inflicting pain on individuals who cannot report it (e.g., Craig, 1978; McGrath, Humphreys, Keene, & Goodman, 1992). These efforts have been extended by a second wave of Canadian researchers, including Thomas and Heather Hadjistavropoulos and Gordon Asmundson at the University of Regina. The ability to evelute pain is important not just in babies but also in seniors (Hadjistavropoulos, 2001). Psychologists are sometimes asked to give objective assessments of pain in individuals requesting compensation for injuries on the job (Asmundson, Frombach, & Hadjistavropoulos, 1998). But judging pain in others is contaminated with a whole set of biases (Hadjistavropolous, Craig, Hadjistavropoulos, & Poole, 1996). For example, observers tend to underestimate pain intensity when judging men and anyone who is physically attractive (Hadjistavropoulos, McMurtry, & Craig, 1999).

Daily Hassles Psychologists also recognize that it is not just the big events that cause problems. The little things, the daily irritations and hassles of life, also contribute significantly to the experience of stress (Cassidy, 2000). Think about how you feel when you're stuck in a long checkout line at the store, when someone's tailgating you on the highway, or when you're hungry and you've waited a half-hour or more for your order at a restaurant. Some psychologists believe the cumulative

CRITICAL   THINKING

Try listing and ranking the life events that cause, or have caused, you the most stress. How do your rank orderings differ from those listed in Table 16.1?

Crowded urban environments can be a source of stress for many people.

effect of these "daily hassles" may actually be more important in creating stress than the kinds of life events that we just considered (Lazarus & Folkman, 1984; Miller, 1993). University of British Columbia psychologist Anita DeLongis and her colleagues (DeLongis, Folkman, & Lazarus, 1988) have developed what they call a Daily Hassles Scale, and it seems to predict, on average, the likelihood of physical and mental health problems. The more hassles you experience in your daily life, the more likely you are to experience health problems. Included on the scale are such things as concern about weight and physical appearance, home maintenance, and worries about misplacing or losing something.

Environmental Factors   People are also subjected to stress by their environment. *Noise* is a good example. Think about how difficult it is to study when someone is talking loudly nearby, or how irritated you get when you're roused from sleep by the whirring, clanging sounds of the morning garbage truck. Chronic exposure to noise interferes with everyday activities and it's been linked with the appearance of such stress-related disorders as ulcers and high blood pressure (Evans, 1997; Nagar & Panady, 1987) and with a general decline in the perceived quality of life (Evans, Hygge, & Bullinger, 1995). Schoolchildren experience more stress when they're exposed to chronic noise, and cognitive measures (such as reading comprehension) appear to suffer (Haines, Stansfeld, Job, Berglund, & Head, 2001). Apparently, it's not the loudness of the noise that really matters; people are bothered most by noises that are new, intermittent, or unpredictable (Graig, 1993).

Another environmental factor that has been linked to stress is *crowding* (Freeman & Stansfeld, 1998). The larger the number of people who live or work around you, the more likely you are to experience a stress reaction (Weiss & Baum, 1987). Living in a crowded environment, on average, makes people more susceptible to health problems and increases the likelihood of aggression. People who live in high-rise apartment buildings, filled with tenants, are more likely to behave aggressively than those who live in apartment buildings with fewer floors (Bell, Fisher, Baum, & Greene, 1990). The effects of crowding on health and aggression have also been studied extensively in prison settings: Again, inmates who live in crowded environments have more health problems and are more likely to act aggressively than inmates housed in less crowded environments (Paulus, 1988). Others have argued that total segregation from others is even more damaging (Bonta & Gendreau, 1990).

Crowding and noise are two examples of environmental stressors, but there are many others. For example, stress and health have been closely linked to the family social environment, to peer interactions, to conditions in the workplace, and to socioeconomic class (Chen & Mathews, 2001; Taylor, Repetti, & Seeman, 1997). In fact, an entire specialty in psychology—called **environmental psychology**—is devoted to the study of such environmental effects as these on behaviour and health (Gifford, 1997). Environmental psychologists have shown a particular interest in the psychology of urban living because living in a large city is likely to expose people to a large variety of environmental stressors—especially noise and crowding. Cities, such as Tokyo and New York, with a fast-paced life, tend to have higher rates of heart disease and smoking (Levine & Norenzayan, 1999). In general, people succumb to stress when they're forced to live in situations with excessive stimulation, constrained movement, or limitations in some important resource (Graig, 1993).

environmental psychology

A specialty area in psychology devoted to the study of environmental effects, such as crowding or noise, on behaviour and health

Internal Sources of Stress

As you are now aware, no single event or set of living conditions will automatically lead to stress in everyone. Stress is a very subjective experience, which means we need to know something about the internal characteristics of the individual before we can predict whether he or she will experience stress. Stress arises out of an interaction between individuals and events in the world—neither alone is sufficient to predict the reaction. The notion of the **hardy personality** was hypothesized to explain why some individuals resist chronic stressors with minimal effects (Kobasa, 1979). Rather than a single personality variable, the hardy personality is currently seen as a collection of adaptive personality traits, attitudes, and skills (Maddi, 2002). We'll consider three in this section: perceived control, explanatory style, and personality characteristics.

Perceived Control   To experience stress, you need to perceive a threat or some kind of demand, and you need to feel you lack the resources to deal effectively with that threat. This second part of the appraisal process, the assessment of resources, is influenced by a psychological construct called **perceived control,** which is the amount of influence you feel you have over the situation and your reaction to it. It turns out that perceived control significantly affects the amount of stress you will experience. If you perceive a demand or threat and you think you have no control over the situation, your body is likely to react with arousal and the release of stress hormones, and there will be changes in the activities of your immune system (Brosschot et al., 1998). If the situation continues for a prolonged period, negative physical and psychological consequences are likely to result.

Many examples, both scientific and anecdotal, support the link between perceived control and stress. Early in the manned space program, for instance, the Mercury astronauts insisted that manual controls and windows be placed in the orbiting space capsule. Although not necessary from an engineering standpoint, doing so gave the astronauts a "sense of control" over their environment, which reduced their stress. In laboratory studies, animals that are exposed to shocks that they can turn off by turning a wheel are less likely to develop ulcers than animals that receive the same amount of shock but cannot control it (Weiss, 1977).

Explanatory Style   The results of the cognitive appraisal process, and therefore susceptibility to stress, are also influenced by people's general style of thinking. At several points in the text, we've discussed the importance of the process of *attribution,* which refers to how we arrive at conclusions about cause and effect. Different kinds of explanations are available for the positive and negative events that occur in the world. For example, use of an *internal*, *stable*, and *global* attribution for a negative event can lead to a sense of personal inadequacy.

We've seen elsewhere that a maladaptive explanatory style can be altered via cognitive therapy (see Chapter 15). Continued use of this explanatory style can undermine physical health and lead to susceptibility to stress. People who consistently make internal, stable, and global attributions for negative events have been found to have increased stress-related health problems in midlife as well as later in life (Kamen-Siegel, Rodin, Seligman, & Dwyer, 1991; Peterson, Seligman, & Vaillant, 1988). In one particularly intriguing study, Peterson and Seligman (1987) analyzed the explanatory styles of 94 members of the Baseball Hall of Fame who had played at some point between 1900 and 1950. Many of these players were dead at the time of the study, so the researchers had to glean the players' explanatory styles from stories and quotations in old newspapers. The players with the negative explanatory styles were found, on average, to have lived shorter lives.

Personality Characteristics   Perceptions of control and explanatory styles are more easily modified than long-term personality traits. Consider the personality characteristic *optimism*—the belief that good things will happen—a relatively

hardy personality

The set of traits, attitudes, and skills that make an individual less vulnerable to stress

perceived control

The amount of influence you feel you have over a situation and your reaction to it

CRITICAL   THINKING

Suppose you discover a group of people living in a crowded and noisy environment who show little or no stress reaction. What kind of explanation would you look for?

Type A personalities expose themselves to stressful situations and then react in a hostile fashion; consequently, they are more likely to develop heart problems than are Type B personalities.

Keith Brofsky/PhotoDisc/Getty Images

enduring trait that changes little over a lifetime (Scheier & Carver, 1993). "Optimism scales" have been developed and used to look for a connection between personality and health. In one study, optimism was assessed on the day before a group of men underwent coronary bypass surgery. The optimists reacted physiologically to the surgery in ways that lowered the risk of heart attack, and they also recovered more quickly after the surgery (Scheier et al., 1989). More recent studies have demonstrated links between optimism and improved functioning of the immune system (Segerstrom, Taylor, Kemeny, & Fahey, 1998). An optimistic view of life, therefore, appears to reduce stress and its associated health risks (Davidson & Prkachin, 1997).

The best-known personality characteristic linked to *higher* levels of stress is the **Type A** pattern. Traditionally, the syndrome included such tendencies as being hard driving, ambitious, easily annoyed, and impatient. Those with a Type A personality seem to be immersed in a sea of perpetual self-imposed stress; they react badly to frustration because they're engaged in a relentless pursuit of success. **Type B** personality types are essentially people who lack the Type A attributes—they put themselves under less pressure and react more calmly when stress does occur.

The connection between behaviour patterns and heart disease was first noted by cardiologists Meyer Friedman and Ray Rosenman (1974). They sought to explain why some people with known risk factors for heart disease (e.g., smoking, obesity, inactivity) do develop heart problems and some don't. Two people can appear to have identical risk profiles but end up healthy in one instance and disease-prone in another. Friedman and Rosenman proposed that the explanation lies in the connection between personality and stress. People who willingly choose a high-stress lifestyle—Type A personalities—will be more susceptible to diseases of the heart.

Over the past several decades, many extensive studies have explored the health consequences of Type A behaviour patterns. The results have generally supported the proposals of Friedman and Rosenman: People who are classified as Type A personality types are at least twice as likely to develop coronary heart problems as Type B personality types (Lyness, 1993).

Recent work has refined the original interpretation of the Type A behaviour pattern or personality. Original diagnoses required that you score high on a number of dimensions—competitiveness, ambition, time urgency, and so on. Some of these

Type A

An enduring pattern of behaviour linked to coronary heart disease; the tendency to be hard driving, ambitious, easily annoyed, and impatient all seem to derive from the trait of hostility

Type B

People who lack the Type A traits—they experience less stress and, therefore, better health outcomes

turn out to be incidental. It now appears that your overall level of hostility is most responsible for producing subsequent coronary artery disease (Krantz & McCeney, 2002). Chronically high levels of hostility naturally lead to a character that, under stress, will show irritability, impatience, and competitiveness. In terms of the Big Five, these are disagreeable individuals. This proclivity is subject to cultural factors—some occupations, subcultures, and even societies encourage competition and others do not (Thoresen & Powell, 1992). In short, those with the Type A personality have a combination of tendencies making them highly vulnerable to both stress and disease: They immerse themselves in stressful situations and then react badly to them (Friedman, Hawley, & Tucker, 1994).

CONCEPT SUMMARY

SOURCES OF STRESS

External Source	Description
Significant life events	Major life events associated with a change in a person's day-to-day activities; can be positive (e.g., getting married) or negative (e.g., death of a loved one)
Physical pain	Chronic or frequent repetitive pain that cannot be entirely alleviated (e.g., migraine headaches, arthritis, back pain)
Daily hassles	Daily irritations and hassles of life, such as getting stuck in traffic
Environmental factors	Stressors present in a person's environment, such as noise and crowding

Internal Source	Description
Perceived control	The amount of influence you feel you have over a situation; a sense of control often lessens the stress
Explanatory style	The general style of thinking about and explaining events; people who make internal, stable, and global attributions for negative events are more likely to have stress-related health problems
Personality characteristics	*Optimism* (the belief that good things will happen) generally reduces stress; *Type A* behaviour pattern (hard driving, ambitious, easily annoyed, impatient) associated with elevated stress and heart problems

Test Yourself 16.1

Check your knowledge about the stress response by answering each of the following questions. (The answers are in Appendix B.)

1. Hans Selye's concept of the general adaptation syndrome (GAS) proposes that the body reacts to stress in three phases. Which of the following shows the correct sequence of these phases?
   a. resistance, alarm, exhaustion
   b. exhaustion, resistance, alarm
   c. alarm, resistance, exhaustion
   d. exhaustion, alarm, resistance

2. The experience of stress is related to the experience of emotion in which of the following ways?
   a. The experience of stress, like emotion, is an inevitable reaction to threat.
   b. The experience of stress, like emotion, is accompanied by very distinctive facial expressions.
   c. The experience of stress, like emotion, depends on the appraisal of the event rather than on the event itself.
   d. The experience of different kinds of stress, like emotion, leads to highly specific kinds of body reactions.

3. According to the Social Readjustment Rating Scale, which of the following events is most likely to cause stress-related health problems?
   a. marriage
   b. death of a close friend
   c. sex difficulties
   d. trouble with your boss

4. Which of the following internal characteristics is least likely to be associated with stress-related health problems?
   a. low levels of perceived control
   b. Type A behaviour pattern
   c. an optimistic outlook
   d. internal, stable, and global attributions

▶ Reacting to Prolonged Stress: Physical and Psychological Effects

LEARNING GOALS

1. Understand the physical consequences of prolonged stress, including the link between stress and the immune system.
2. Understand the psychological consequences of prolonged stress, including posttraumatic stress disorder and burnout.

A definite connection exists between prolonged exposure to stress and subsequent physical and psychological health. Stress is an adaptive reaction to threat—it helps us to fight or flee. But when it is prolonged, we're not able to reduce or eliminate the perceived threat and the mind and body start to break down. If the stress reaction is extreme enough, the breakdown can be sudden and may even result in death; in most cases, however, the effects are gradual and reveal themselves slowly through a growing list of physical and psychological problems. In this section of the chapter, we'll consider the nature of these breakdowns and how and why they occur.

Physical Consequences of Stress

Stress has been implicated in a wide variety of health problems. Besides ulcers and heart disease, it has been linked to everything from the common cold to chronic back pain, multiple sclerosis, and even cancer (Schneiderman, Antoni, Saab, & Ironson, 2001). Most of the scientific evidence is correlational, which means a statistical relationship has been found between the incidence of a health problem, such as heart disease, and some measurement of stress. Large numbers of people are interviewed, and health histories as well as stress levels are measured. The net result is that we can predict whether someone, on average, will have an increased chance of developing a particular kind of health problem by knowing the amount of stress that person experiences on a regular basis. But this does not tell us whether a causal relationship exists between stress and illness. To determine such a relationship, we must turn to experimental research.

Ideally, we would randomly divide people into groups, subject some of them to high levels of stress, and then monitor the later consequences of that manipulation on health. Ethically, however, we cannot knowingly subject people to harmful conditions. Instead, studies have been conducted on groups of people who have been previously identified as having either a high or a low level of stress in their lives. In one study (Cohen, Tyrrell, & Smith, 1993), high- and low-stress people were given nasal drops that either contained or did not contain a common cold virus. It was a double-blind study, so neither the participants nor the researchers were aware during the course of the study who was getting the actual virus and who was not. Afterward, when the subject assignments were "decoded," it was found that the high-stress people who received the virus were the ones most likely to show cold symptoms. Living a stressful life apparently lowers the ability to fight disease.

The Immune Response   To understand why stress increases susceptibility to illness, you need to understand something about the human immune system. The human body has a complex defence system, called the *immune system*, that is constantly on the lookout for foreign substances, such as viruses or bacteria. The primary weapons of the immune system are **lymphocytes,** which are specialized white blood cells that have the job of attacking and destroying most of these foreign invaders. Stress can increase a person's risk for disease by interfering with white blood cells' ability to eliminate foreign substances that have invaded the body (see Cohen & Herbert, 1996; Gonzalez-Quijano, Martin, Millan, &

lymphocytes

Specialized white blood cells that have the job of attacking foreign substances, such as viruses and bacteria

People who are subjected to chronic stress, because of environmental conditions, can show weakened immune system functioning.

Lopez-Calderon, 1998). The underlying mechanisms that produce these changes have not been completely determined, although the prolonged release of stress hormones into the bloodstream probably plays a significant role (Chen, Fisher, Bacharier, & Strunk, 2003; Kiecolt-Glaser, McGuire, Robles, & Glaser, 2002).

Several investigations have shown that stressful life events directly affect the immune response. Medical students, on average, have fewer lymphocytes in their blood during final exams, compared with levels found before exams (Kiecolt-Glaser et al., 1984); they are also more likely to get sick during exams. Depressed individuals who have recently had a spouse or loved one die also show suppressed immune responses (Miller, Cohen, & Herbert, 1999). One investigative team tracked the immune response in men married to women with advanced breast cancer. Samples of the men's blood were taken during the months preceding and following their wife's death. On average, the existing lymphocytes in blood samples drawn *after* the wives had died showed a weaker response to foreign substances (Schleifer et al., 1983).

The fact that stress weakens the immune system has led researchers to wonder about the effects of stress on more chronic illnesses, such as cancer. In the laboratory it's been shown that stress can increase the growth rate of cancerous tumours in rats, although the particular type of tumour apparently matters (Justice, 1985). There have also been reports that cancer patients who are optimistic or who are given therapy to help reduce anxiety and depression survive longer than patients who are hopeless or depressed (Andersen, 1992; Spiegel, Bloom, Kramer, & Gotheil, 1989). Stress may affect not only the body's ability to fight cancer but also the likelihood that cancer cells will form in the first place (Schneiderman, Antoni, Ironson, Laperriere, & Fletcher, 1992).

At present, however, most researchers remain cautious about the link between psychology, the immune system, and cancer (Cohen & Herbert, 1996). Not all studies have found associations between psychological factors and cancer (Schneiderman et al., 2001), and the fact that data linking cancer to stress have come primarily from correlational studies means that it is difficult to draw conclusions about cause and effect. For example, it's possible that "stressful" people, on average, have a greater risk of acquiring cancer because they tend to engage in unhealthy behaviours—such as smoking—as a way of dealing with the stress. It may also be the case that people who are optimistic about their survival from cancer tend to comply more with the recommendations of their doctors. So, although a statistical association may exist between stress and cancer, that does not necessarily mean that stress is causing cancer by compromising the functioning of the immune system.

How might the onset of a psychological disorder, such as depression, be an adaptive reaction to prolonged stress?

Cardiovascular Disease   Health psychologists have also intensively studied the well-documented relationship between stress and cardiovascular disease (problems connected with the heart and blood vessels). We discussed the connection between Type A behaviour and heart problems earlier, but we left the mechanisms through which stress undermines cardiovascular health unspecified. The two most important risk factors in heart disease are high cholesterol levels in the blood and high blood pressure. Prolonged exposure to stress increases exposure to both of these risk factors.

Increased blood pressure, a natural byproduct of the stress response, is generally helpful over the short term (as part of the fight-or-flight response). But if the elevated pressure continues, it causes wear and tear on the blood vessels in the body, which can lead to both cardiovascular disease and kidney problems. Stress can also directly affect the level of cholesterol in the blood. For example, when college students are anticipating an upcoming exam, samples of their blood show higher levels of cholesterol (Van Doornen & Van Blokland, 1987). People who display Type A behaviour patterns have also been found, on average, to have higher levels of blood cholesterol. One possibility is that when people sense threat, the body directs the blood flow to the muscles and away from the internal organs that remove fat and cholesterol from the blood.

Interestingly, it is not just Type A individuals who show this pattern of health problems. Depressed individuals are also at higher risk for cardiovascular disease. One study looked at patients in Montreal who had survived a heart attack. It showed that patients who were depressed in the period shortly after their heart attack were four times more likely to die within the next six months, compared with nondepressed patients (Musselman, Evans, & Nemeroff, 1998). The fact that depressed individuals seem to show the same pattern of health risks as Type A individuals has led researchers to look for common biological mechanisms, such as high blood pressure and altered immune function (Miller, Stetler, Carney, Freeland, & Banks, 2002).

Psychological Consequences of Stress

The mental and emotional consequences of stress can also be profound. You feel anxious, out of control, emotionally drained, and, after a while, possibly even sad and depressed. Stress is not a pleasant experience, and if the stress reaction is intense enough, or if it continues long enough, serious psychological problems can result.

Most psychologists are convinced that stressful life events play a significant role in the onset of many psychological disorders. If you interview people who have major depression or a bipolar disorder, you will find that most have experienced some kind of major stressor just before or early into the depressive episode—they got fired from their job, they moved to a new town, they're mired in a nasty divorce, and so on (Barlow & Durand, 2002). Stress tends to deplete the willpower to resist such unhealthy behaviours as overeating (Vohs & Hetherton, 2000). Stress has also been implicated in the onset of schizophrenia. Several studies have shown that stressful life events tend to immediately precede schizophrenic episodes (Brown & Birley, 1968; Harvey, 2001).

As noted earlier, some hardy individuals are quite resistant to stress. Even some who have endured prolonged imprisonment or torture or survived the horrors of the Holocaust do not show long-term consequences (Bonta & Gendreau, 1990; Suedfeld, 1997, 2001). In fact, the majority of people who experience a traumatic life stressor do not subsequently develop psychological disorders (Bonanno, 2004). But others seem to have some kind of vulnerability, perhaps rooted in the genetic code, and stress can trigger an extreme disorder, such as major depression or schizophrenia. Similar arguments apply to anxiety disorders, such as posttraumatic stress disorder, which we discuss briefly below.

Posttraumatic Stress Disorder   You're familiar with the story: A soldier returns home from war, shell shocked, enduring sleepless nights and flashbacks of traumatic episodes in battle. Hollywood has exploited this image to the point where the "unstable war vet" has become a recurring character in popular books and films. In reality, the vast majority of soldiers who return from war experience no long-term psychological problems. At the same time, even though the percentages are small, psychologists do recognize that exposure to extreme stress can produce a serious psychological condition known as **posttraumatic stress disorder.** This disorder is not limited to battle veterans; it can occur in any individual who has undergone a traumatic episode, such as a physical attack, rape, or a natural disaster (Foa & Riggs, 1995). Canadian researchers have discovered that for some unknown reason women are found to be five times more likely than men to develop posttraumatic stress disorder following exposure to serious trauma (Stein, Walker, & Forde, 2000).

In the *DSM-IV*, posttraumatic stress disorder is classified as an anxiety disorder, and the diagnosis is made if the following three types of symptoms occur for a period lasting longer than one month:

1. *Flashbacks.* When a flashback occurs, the person relives the traumatic event in some way. These flashbacks can take the form of persistent thoughts or images of the traumatic scene, and they can even involve vivid hallucinations; the affected person seems at times to be re-experiencing the event—fighting the battle anew or fending off the attacker.
2. *Avoidance of stimuli associated with the trauma.* People with posttraumatic stress disorder actively try to avoid anything that reminds them of the event. This avoidance behaviour can lead to significant disruptions in normal social functioning, as the affected person turns away from friends and loved ones who in some way remind him or her of the trauma.
3. *Chronic arousal symptoms.* These symptoms can include sleep problems, irritability or outbursts of anger, and difficulties in concentrating.

Obviously, posttraumatic stress disorder is a disabling condition, not only for the individuals who are directly affected but also for family and friends (Sims & Sims, 1998). The cause of the disorder is clear—traumatic stress—but the reason that only some people who experience trauma develop posttraumatic stress disorder remains a mystery. Evidence does suggest that the intensity of the trauma

posttraumatic stress disorder

A trauma-based anxiety disorder characterized by flashbacks, avoidance of stimuli associated with the traumatic event, and chronic arousal symptoms

Witnessing or experiencing traumatic events, such as the bombing of the World Trade Center on September 11, 2001, can lead to disabling psychological conditions.

may be important. For example, soldiers who were in heavy combat were significantly more likely to develop posttraumatic stress disorder than those serving in noncombat roles (Goldberg, True, Eisen, & Henderson, 1990). But, once again, this does not explain why the disorder remains relatively rare even among people who have experienced extreme trauma. If we look to the experience of firefighters, we note that it is certainly not the case that every firefighter develops the disorder, despite their exposure to duty-related trauma (Corneil, Beaton, Murphy, Johnson, & Pike, 1999). As is the case for most psychological disorders, the likelihood that posttraumatic stress disorder will develop undoubtedly depends on a complex mix of biological and environmental factors (Craske, 1999; O'Shea, 2001).

Burnout   Stress does not need to be extreme to produce unpleasant psychological consequences. In the 1970s, the term "burnout" was introduced by psychologists to describe a syndrome that develops in certain people who are exposed to stressful situations that are demanding but not necessarily traumatic (Freudenberger, 1974; Maslach, 1976). Although the term **burnout** has become a household word, to psychologists it refers to "a state of physical, emotional, and mental exhaustion caused by long-term involvement in emotionally demanding situations" (Pines & Aronson, 1988). When burnout occurs, affected individuals essentially lose their spirit—they become emotionally drained, they feel used up, and they lose their sense of personal accomplishment (Maslach & Jackson, 1981).

As in the case of posttraumatic stress disorder, stress is a necessary component but is not a sufficient condition for producing burnout. Not everyone who has a demanding and stressful job becomes burned out. Burnout seems to occur only in idealistic individuals—people who have entered their careers with a high sense of motivation and commitment. In the words of psychologist Ayala Pines (1993), "You cannot burn out unless you were 'on fire' initially." Because burnout tends to occur only in highly motivated individuals, it can have a high cost for organizations as well as for the individual. People who experience burnout lose their edge on the job—they become disillusioned with their work, are frequently absent from the job, and usually are at increased risk for a host of physical problems (Maslach, Schaufeli, & Leiter, 2001). Health care workers seem to be especially vulnerable.

burnout

A state of physical, emotional, and mental exhaustion created by long-term involvement in an emotionally demanding situation

CONCEPT SUMMARY

CONSEQUENCES OF STRESS

Physical

Stress Effects	Nature of the Effect
Immune response	Stressful events directly affect the immune response, lowering the number of disease-fighting *lymphocytes*. Some believe that stress also has an effect on more chronic illnesses, such as cancer.
Cardiovascular disease	Increased blood pressure from prolonged stress causes wear and tear on blood vessels, which can lead to cardiovascular disease.

Psychological

Stress Leads To	Nature of the Effect
Posttraumatic stress disorder	A serious psychological condition that can result from exposure to extreme stress. Classified as an anxiety disorder, it's characterized by flashbacks, avoidance of trauma-associated stimuli, and chronic arousal symptoms.
Burnout	A state of physical, emotional, and mental exhaustion caused by long-term involvement in emotionally demanding situations. It seems to occur in idealistic individuals who are highly motivated, perhaps because of a loss of control or a loss of meaning in life.

Why does burnout occur? The underlying cause may well be related to a loss of meaning in life (Pines, 1993) or to a loss of control in the workplace (McKnight & Glass, 1995). People who are subject to burnout are usually those who think of their work as a kind of "calling." They use success on the job as a way of validating their existence. They identify so closely with their work that when failure happens, their entire lives lose meaning. This failure could be artistic, financial, or, in the case of health care workers, a learned helplessness in their attempts to aid needy patients. If the overall stress levels can be reduced, perhaps by providing a better support system within the work environment, burnout is less likely to occur (Maslach et al., 2001; Pines & Aronson, 1988).

Test Yourself 16.2

Check your knowledge about reacting to stress by deciding whether each of the following statements is true or false. (The answers are in Appendix B.)

1. Lymphocytes are the primary weapons of the human immune system. *True or False?*
2. Much of the data linking cancer and stress have come from correlational studies; researchers are unable, therefore, to draw firm conclusions about cause and effect. *True or False?*
3. Stress is known to affect blood pressure, but no links have been established between stress and cholesterol levels. *True or False?*
4. Posttraumatic stress disorder is a common reaction to experiencing a traumatic event. *True or False?*
5. Burnout is more likely to occur in people who use success on the job as a way of giving life meaning. *True or False?*

▶ Reducing and Coping with Stress: Techniques of Stress Management

LEARNING GOALS

1. Learn how relaxation techniques can be used to reduce stress.
2. Understand the positive and negative effects of social support.
3. Be able to explain how stress can be managed through cognitive reappraisal of the stressful situation.

Because stress is associated with so many physical and psychological problems, it is obviously in our best interest to develop techniques for reducing stress. Unfortunately, stressors are often outside our direct control—you can't prevent the tornado that demolishes the neighbourhood trailer park or the death of a valued friend from accident or illness. But techniques are available for psychological management of stressors when they're present. **Coping** is a term that psychologists use to describe efforts to manage conditions of threat or demand that tax our resources (Lazarus, 1993).

The variety of coping techniques reported by ordinary people is incredibly diverse. They can be organized into techniques that resolve the stress-inducing situation, deal with the negative emotions, or connect with other people (DeLongis & O'Brien, 1990). Specific examples include distracting yourself from the problem, confronting (or actively avoiding) the person responsible for the stress, improving relevant abilities, and turning to religion. Below, we consider three others in detail: (1) using relaxation techniques, (2) exploiting social support networks, and (3) reappraising the environment in a less threatening way.

coping

Efforts to manage or master conditions of threat or demand that tax resources

Relaxation Techniques

By definition, the stress response is incompatible with relaxation. You cannot be prepared to fight or flee if your body is calm, relaxed, and free from arousal-inducing stress hormones. Studies have shown that high-stress individuals can reduce the physically threatening components of the stress reaction—such as high blood pressure—by simply practising a regimen of relaxation techniques. You may remember that in Chapter 15 we discussed how relaxation can be used effectively in the treatment of anxiety disorders; similar relaxation techniques have proven effective in reducing long-term stress reactions (Stoyva & Carlson, 1993).

Several types of relaxation procedures are available to help manage stress. In *progressive muscle relaxation*, you're taught to concentrate on specific muscle groups in the body, to note whether there is any tension, and then to try to relax those specific groups (Jacobson, 1938). Often in progressive relaxation, you learn to address muscle groups in sequence. For example, you might begin with the muscle groups in the neck, move to the shoulders, and so on, first tensing and then relaxing each group. In this way, you learn to pay attention to how muscles in your body feel when tense or relaxed. Progressive relaxation has been used successfully to treat a variety of stress-related health problems, everything from tension headaches (Myers, Wittrock, & Foreman, 1998) to posttraumatic stress disorder (Frueh, de Arellano, & Turner, 1997). In a somewhat different technique, called *autogenic relaxation*, you're taught to focus on directing blood flow toward tense

There are a variety of ways to reduce and cope with stress, including exercise, meditation, social support, and biofeedback.

muscle groups, "warming" and relaxing each group (Linden, 1990); once again, autogenic relaxation has proven beneficial in treating stress-related conditions (Friedlander, Lumley, Farchione, & Doyal, 1997).

Such relaxation techniques as these are sometimes accompanied by *meditation* training. We discussed some of the benefits of meditation in Chapter 5. Meditation essentially involves learning how to relax by using techniques similar to progressive muscle relaxation. But you're also taught some time-tested mental exercises, such as repeating a string of words or sounds over and over again in your head. The mental repetition focuses awareness and helps prevent potentially distracting or stress-producing thoughts from interfering with the relaxation response. (For instance, if you're concentrating on repeating the phrase "I'm at one with the universe," you cannot simultaneously be worrying about whether the relaxation technique is working.) Daily meditation sessions clearly help people deal with stress-related arousal (MacLean, Walton, Wenneberg, & Levitsky, 1997) and are likely to prevent the later development of health problems, such as high blood pressure (Barnes, Treiber, & Davis, 2001).

Biofeedback   The goal of relaxation training is to counteract components of the stress response, such as blood pressure, heart rate, and muscle tension. For example, if stress-related headaches are caused by tension in the muscles of the head and scalp, then people should be able to reduce or eliminate the pain by relaxing these specific muscle groups. Such a feat is made possible by giving people feedback—**biofeedback**—about the effectiveness of their relaxation efforts. With biofeedback, monitoring equipment provides a continuous reading of your physiological state: In the case of tension headaches, the feedback would indicate the tension levels in the muscles of the head; for blood pressure or heart rate, you would be able to read your blood pressure and heart rate directly from appropriate monitoring equipment.

> **biofeedback**
> Specific physiological feedback that people are given about the effectiveness of their relaxation efforts

To say the least, biofeedback works. When people are given information about how well their relaxation efforts are succeeding, compared with control subjects who are given no feedback, it's clearly easier to control the relevant physiological response (Blanchard, 1992). But researchers are still debating exactly why biofeedback produces its beneficial effects. Yes, it may well be that the benefits help the affected person gain control over countermeasures to reduce the physiological problem. Another possibility is that it may simply be the *feeling* of control that leads to reductions in the stress response.

For instance, in one study on tension headaches, three groups of subjects were given a feedback signal that they were led to believe indicated a successful lowering of muscle tension in their foreheads. Actually, unknown to the subjects, the signal had three different meanings: In one group, it appeared only when subjects successfully *increased* the amount of tension in their foreheads; in a second group, the signal appeared whenever the amount of tension decreased; in a third group, it appeared when tension levels remained the same. Remarkably, despite the misleading feedback in two of the groups, everyone reported headache improvement (see ❯ Figure 16.4 on page 656). Apparently, feeling that you have some control over your body can be sufficient to lower stress-induced pain (Andrasik & Holroyd, 1980). This finding does not mean that biofeedback is an ineffective way to treat stress. Whether you will experience a stress response depends on a cognitive appraisal of your resources. If you feel you have the ability to control the threat or demand, even if that control is illusory, you're less likely to experience stress.

Social Support

> **social support**
> The resources that individuals receive from other people or groups, often in the form of comfort, caring, or help

Although it may seem like a cliché, having a good friend or loved one to lean on during a time of stress really does matter. Psychologists use the term **social support** to refer to the resources we receive from other people or groups, often in the

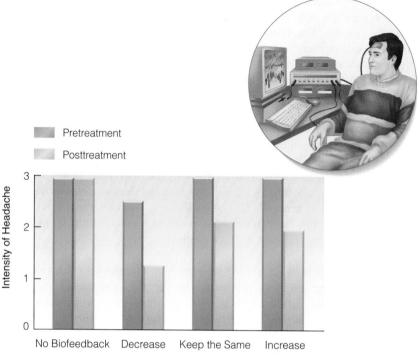

▶ **Figure 16.4**

Biofeedback, Perceived Control, and Stress

In the study by Andrasik and Holroyd (1980), subjects in three groups were led to believe that they could lower the amount of muscle tension in their foreheads through biofeedback. Actually, the subjects learned to increase, decrease, or keep the tension levels the same. Yet all three groups showed significant improvement in headache symptoms, compared with subjects who received no biofeedback. (Data from Andrasik & Holroyd, 1980.)

CRITICAL THINKING
Do you think it's possible that simply believing that you have social support is more important than actually receiving it?

form of comfort, caring, or help. A great deal of research has backed up the claim that people blessed with good social support have better psychological and physical health (Cohen & Wills, 1985). For example, Wolfgang Linden, a health psychologist at the University of British Columbia, has investigated the effect of social support on cardiovascular patients. He showed that patients with well-established social support systems have lower rates of morbidity and mortality than those who have less social support (Linden, Stossel, & Maurice, 1996). Quick recovery from such real world stressors as surgery is also linked to good social support (Schroeder, Schwarzer, & Endler, 1997). Several studies on depression have established that individuals with better social support are less likely to get depressed and to recover more quickly (McLeod, Kessler, & Landis, 1992).

The association between social support and lower stress has several possible explanations (Sarason, Sarason, & Pierce, 1994). Social contacts should help people maintain a healthy lifestyle. Friends and family push you out the door for your morning jog, force you to take your medications, and encourage you to visit the doctor regularly. Family and friends also bolster your confidence in times of stress, so you're more likely to feel that you have the necessary resources to cope with the demand. In a time of loss, such as immediately after the death of a spouse, social support lowers the likelihood that a grieving person will engage in unhealthy behaviours, such as drinking (Jennison, 1992). (For a discussion of how pets can act as a form of positive social support see the Practical Solutions box.)

PRACTICAL SOLUTIONS

PET SUPPORT

Having a loved one or a good friend to talk to about your problems makes a difference, and that friend doesn't even need to be human. The companionship of pets—dogs, cats, even birds—has repeatedly been found to be an effective form of social support. Heart attack victims who own pets, for example, are more likely to survive the first year after the attack than are those who do not own pets. Correlational studies among the elderly have found that pet ownership is inversely related to the severity of psychological problems; people who are attached to their pets are less likely to show the symptoms of depression (Garrity, Stallones, Marx, & Johnson, 1989). Ownership of a dog, in particular, is an excellent predictor of whether or not an elderly person will feel the need to visit a doctor (Siegel, 1990).

Some evidence suggests that having a pet may even be a more effective buffer against stress than is having a human companion. In an experiment conducted by Karen Allen and her colleagues (Allen, Blascovich, Tomaka, & Kelsey, 1991), women dog owners agreed to have several physiological reactions monitored while they tried to solve relatively difficult math problems. Before starting the task, the women were randomly divided into three groups. In one group, the women were allowed to have their dogs with them in the room while completing the math task. In a second group, no dogs were allowed but each woman was allowed the presence of a close human friend. In the third group, no social support was present during the testing.

A variety of physiological reactions were measured, including heart rate and blood pressure. Not surprisingly, solving difficult math problems led directly to stress-related arousal—heart rate increased, as did blood pressure. But the amount of reactivity depended on the group: The women who were allowed to have their dog with them showed the lowest arousal effects compared with the women in the other two groups (see ▶ Figure 16.5). The presence of the pet apparently acted as an effective buffer

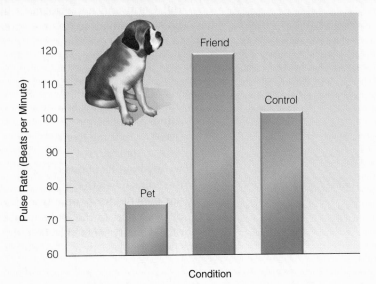

▶ **Figure 16.5**

Pets as Stress Moderators

In one study, a pet's presence during a stressful task significantly lowered the stress reaction (measured here in terms of pulse rate) compared with when a friend was present or with a control condition in which neither a friend nor a pet was present. (Data from Allen et al., 1991.)

against stress. The surprise finding of the study was that having a close human friend sit nearby while solving the math problems actually led to the highest relative stress reaction.

Does this mean that pets are more therapeutic than friends or loved ones? For some people in some situations, the answer may well be yes. Allen and her colleagues argued that pets are often effective buffers against stress because they are essentially nonevaluative. Pets don't make value judgments about their caretakers. Your dog or cat doesn't care one bit about how well you're doing on some math task, but your close human friend might. A friend's expectations can place added pressure on you as you perform an already stressful task. A woman who participated in the study by Allen and colleagues put it this way: "Pets never withhold their love, they never get angry and leave, and they never go out looking for new owners." Another woman offered the following: "Whereas husbands may come and go, and children may grow up and leave home, a 'dog is

forever.'" The opinions of these women may not be shared by everyone, nor do you need to hold these strong views to appreciate the value of pet companionship. The data simply indicate that pets can be an important part of your social network and as such can help you cope with stress.

Pets are effective buffers against stress for many people.

But the reverse causal argument is just as convincing. People who are healthier and experience less stress may have more social support. Who wants to hang out with someone who is always sick and stressed out? Fortunately, some experimental evidence now supports the claim that social support helps reduce stress. Bill Gerin and his associates have conducted laboratory studies by using blood pressure monitors to measure level of stress. They set up a stressful debate between two experimental participants. Debaters were randomly assigned to have a supporter in the room or not to have one. Results showed that debaters with supporters—even if they didn't participate in the debate—showed lower stress levels (Gerin, Pieper, Levy, & Pickering, 1992). Other experimental work has shown that simply having someone to talk things over with can help you cope with stress. James Pennebaker (1990) had college students talk about upsetting events in their lives (everything from a divorce in the family to fears about the future). Compared with a control group, those students given the opportunity to talk it over (or just write about it) showed improved immune functioning and were less likely to visit the college health centre over the next several months. Pennebaker has found similar benefits for people who lived through natural disasters (such as earthquakes) or were part of the Holocaust. Opening up, talking about things, and confiding in others really seemed to help these people cope (Pennebaker, Zech, & Rime, 2001). Given that research, it seems no surprise that a positive relationship with your parents can improve the chances of surviving a stressful episode without depression (Mongrain, 1998).

However, psychologists recognize that social support can have a negative side as well. For example, if you've come to depend on another for support and that support is no longer delivered, your ability to cope can be compromised. Social support can also reduce self-reliance in some people, which may produce psychological distress and impair their ability to cope. It's been found that whether people respond favourably to social support and the receipt of aid, or consider it to be a meddling nuisance, depends to some extent on how much control they feel they have over their own actions and the outcomes of their actions (Hobfoll, Shoham, & Ritter, 1991).

Finally, research at York University has shown how the nature of support provided is linked to the personality of the supporter. By using the interpersonal circle (see Chapter 12), Krista Trobst examined how each of the eight personalities provided a different form of support. She showed, for example, that dominant people tended to be highly directive in their support attempts, whereas nurturant individuals tended to give warm and accepting support (e.g., Trobst, 2000). As with Hobfall's conclusions, which type of support is more beneficial will depend on both the nature of the help and how it is received.

Reappraisal of the Situation

When thinking about how to cope with stress, it's important to remember that the stress reaction is essentially psychological. In most instances, it is not the sudden life event or the daily hassle that leads us to experience stress—it's our *interpretation* of the event that really matters (Lazarus, 1991). Even the death of a spouse or the occurrence of a natural disaster, cruel as it may seem, will create significant stress only if the event is appraised in a negative way (Davis & Nolen-Hoeksema, 2001). Imagine that your spouse had an incurable disease, one that produced extreme and persistent pain. Under these conditions, death could be seen as a kind of blessing.

Remember, too, that many instances of stress are caused by the little things, the daily hassles of life (DeLongis et al., 1988). Getting stuck in traffic or in the wrong line at the store makes us feel stressed only because we have a tendency to "catastrophize" the situation: "This is absolutely awful.... I can't stand waiting here any longer.... I'm going to get home late and my family will be mad." It's not the delay that creates the stress; it's the things we tell ourselves about the delay that cause the problems. As a result, many psychologists feel that stress can be managed effectively through logical reanalysis and positive reappraisal. If you can interpret the hassle in a more rational or empathic manner, you can reduce or eliminate the stress reaction (Preece & DeLongis, 2005).

Stress management techniques that rely on cognitive reappraisal take a variety of forms. For instance, you can be taught to focus on certain aspects of the situation that distract you from catastrophizing. If you're stuck in the slow checkout line at the supermarket, rather than concentrating on why you "must" get home on time, instead, pick up one of the supermarket tabloids and catch up on the latest celebrity gossip. It may be the only time when you have a good excuse to do so. Alternatively, try using your past experiences to reappraise the consequences: "Let's see, this certainly is not the first time I've been stuck in a checkout line, and it's never led to any tragedies." Another approach would be to analyze the situation logically and derive alternatives for the future: "Every time I come to the store at 5:30, right after work, I get stuck in a line—maybe if I wait and go after dinner, there will be less of a wait."

Some stress management programs recommend that clients keep daily records of the specific situations that have led to stress, as well as the specific symptoms and thoughts that arose (an example is shown in ▶ Figure 16.6). The value of a stress record is that it allows the client to recognize any unrealistic thoughts or conclusions on the spot because they need to be written in the record. With time, clients get a pretty good idea of the situations that lead to the highest stress, and they gain insight into the thought processes that underlie their reaction. As each unrealistic thought is recognized, the client can work at reappraising the situation and confronting any negative attitudes or beliefs (Barlow & Rapee, 1991).

CRITICAL THINKING

What's the link between these stress management programs and the techniques used in cognitive therapies, such as rational-emotive therapy?

▶ **Figure 16.6**

A Daily Stress Record

Stress management programs often recommend that clients keep daily records of situations that lead to stress, along with the specific symptoms and thoughts that arise. (From D. H. Barlow & R. M. Rapee, "Daily Stress Record," *Mastering Stress 2001: A Lifestyle Approach*, p. 12. Copyright © 2001. Reproduced with permission of American Health Publishing Company, Dallas, Texas. All rights reserved. For ordering information call 1-800-736-7323.)

Sample Daily Stress Record

Week of _____

	8	Extreme stress
	7	
	6	Great stress
	5	
	4	Moderate stress
	3	
	2	Mild stress
	1	
	0	No stress

	(1)	(2)	(3)	(4)	(5)	(6)
Date	Starting time	Ending time	Highest stress (0-8)	Triggers	Symptoms	Thoughts
1–5	10:00 am	11:00 am	7	Sales meeting	Sweating, headache	My figures are bad.
1–7	5:15 pm	5:35 pm	6	Traffic jam	Tension, impatience	I'll never get home.
1–8	12:30 pm	12:32 pm	3	Lost keys	Tension	I can't find my keys.
1–9	3:30 pm	4:30 pm	4	Waiting for guests	Sweating, nausea	Are they lost?

Check your knowledge about stress management techniques by answering the following questions. (The answers are in Appendix B.)

1. Relaxation techniques, such as meditation or progressive muscle relaxation, appear to work because
   a. They promote a sense of "connectedness" with the therapist.
   b. They lead to positive cognitive reappraisals.
   c. The stress response is incompatible with relaxation.
   d. They cause you to open up and express feelings.
2. Biofeedback may be effective for managing stress because
   a. It gives you a feeling of control.
   b. It leads to muscle relaxation.
   c. It trains neurons to fire in sequence.
   d. It works well with meditation.
3. Which of the following statements about the influence of social support on stress is false?
   a. Social contacts help you maintain a healthy lifestyle.
   b. Social support increases the chances that you'll open up and express feelings.

   c. Social support can reduce the chances of a second heart attack.
   d. Social support makes it easier to cope if the support is no longer delivered.
4. Bernie no longer fumes when he gets stuck in traffic because he's stopped catastrophizing about the consequences. Which of the following stress management techniques is Bernie probably using?
   a. cognitive reappraisal
   b. autogenic relaxation
   c. progressive muscle relaxation
   d. cathartic exploration

▶ Living a Healthy Lifestyle

LEARNING GOALS

1. Be able to explain the physical and psychological benefits of aerobic exercise.
2. Understand the value of proper nutrition.
3. Learn the consequences of tobacco use, and explain why it's difficult to quit smoking.
4. Learn the consequences of drinking alcohol, and explain how intoxication leads us to engage in other risky health-related behaviours.
5. Distinguish among the different types of prevention programs, and learn how to avoid unsafe sexual practices.

One challenge of the health psychology movement is to devise a comprehensive and workable framework for health promotion (Winett, 1995). In a review of the literature, researchers Nancy Adler and Karen Matthews (1994) summed up the goals of the health psychologist by asking three essential questions: "First, who becomes sick and why? Second, among the sick, who recovers and why? Third, how can illness be prevented or recovery be facilitated?" Such questions are appropriately addressed to a psychologist because, as we've seen, a close and intimate connection exists among mind, behaviour, and health.

In offering prescriptions for healthy lifestyles, psychologists recognize that not all risk factors can be controlled. Men, for example, have a much greater risk of developing heart disease than women do, and the elderly are at a greater risk of developing a whole host of health-related problems. Obviously, people have no control over heredity and they can't help the fact that they grow old. Even a sex change won't help. But as you are no doubt aware, lifestyle choices can make a difference.

aerobic exercise

High-intensity activities, such as running and swimming, that increase both heart rate and oxygen consumption

Get Fit: The Value of Aerobic Exercise

Exercise is an excellent example of an activity that can have a substantial positive impact on physical and psychological health, especially if the exercise is sustained and aerobic. **Aerobic exercise** consists of high-intensity activities that increase both heart rate and oxygen consumption, such as fast walking, running, dancing, rowing, swimming, and so on. As you probably know, regular aerobic exercise improves cardiovascular fitness over the long term and, on average, increases the chances that you will live longer (Blair, Kohl, Paffenbarger, Clark, & Gibbons, 1989; Villeneuve, Morrison, Craig, & Schaubel, 1998).

Psychologically, regular exercise improves mood and makes people more resistant to the effects of stressors (Stoyva & Carlson, 1993). For example, in one study (McCann & Holmes, 1984), volunteer female college students who had mild depression were asked to (1) engage in a regular program of aerobic exercise, (2) learn relaxation techniques, or (3) do nothing. After 10 weeks, the aerobic exercise group showed the largest improvement in mood. More recent work indicates that 30 minutes of moderate exercise daily may be sufficient to increase mood (Hansen, Stevens, & Coast, 2001). In another experimental study looking at stress resistance, men were randomly assigned to exercise conditions that involved either aerobic activity or nonaerobic strength-and-flexibility training.

Regular exercise is an important ingredient in living a healthy lifestyle.

After 12 weeks of training, the men in the aerobic group showed lower blood pressure and heart rate when they were exposed to situations involving mental stress (Blumenthal et al., 1988).

But researchers have yet to understand fully how or why exercise improves psychological health and functioning. Over the short term, vigorous exercise increases the amount of oxygen that reaches the brain, which undoubtedly improves cognitive functioning, and sustained exercise may alter mood-inducing neurotransmitters in the brain (Sheridan & Radmacher, 1992). It is also clearly the case that aerobic exercise, since it improves cardiovascular health, will lessen the physiological effects of the stress reaction. But placebo-like effects may also be involved: People who choose to exercise regularly are convinced that they're going to get better, and they subsequently rate themselves as healthier psychologically than they may in fact be (Pierce, Madden, Siegel, & Blumenthal, 1993).

Despite the benefits of exercise, only 56% of men and 58% of women report that they exercise regularly (Statistics Canada, 1999). Obviously, the more people who exercise, the healthier our population will be. Researchers are investigating why people do or do not exercise. Lise Gauvin of Concordia University discovered that regular exercisers differed from individuals with less active lifestyles in a number of ways (Gauvin, 1990). For example, regular exercisers stated that the aspect they enjoyed most about participation was the task itself (e.g., running or weight lifting). In addition, the regular exercisers did not

Photos.com

CRITICAL   THINKING

Do you think there's a connection between age and the chances of living a healthy lifestyle? If so, why do you think this is the case?

need to do any planning to ensure that they regularly attended their workouts. That is, exercise was part of their routine. In fact, the regular exercisers felt that something was missing in their life when they did not exercise.

In an effort to increase exercise participation, James Olson of the University of Western Ontario and Mark Zanna of the University of Waterloo developed a number of recommendations for motivating people to begin exercising (Olson & Zanna, 1987). Olson and Zanna suggest the following:

- Specific exercises should be promoted (e.g., jogging, swimming, or walking) and specific personal gains from exercise should be identified (e.g., you'll feel and look better).
- Negative personal consequences of not exercising should be identified as well as how those consequences can be avoided (e.g., to reduce your risk of cardiovascular disease, you should walk for 15 minutes a day).
- Perceived social pressure for exercising can be created (communicate that respected others value and engage in regular exercise).
- Increase perceived control over exercising (demonstrate how exercising regularly is compatible with lifestyle).
- Provide basic, detailed information about exercising (e.g., how to stretch properly or how much it costs to join exercise facilities).

Eat Right: The Value of Proper Nutrition

In Chapter 11 we dealt with the adaptive problem of how to motivate eating behaviour. Obviously, to maintain proper functioning of body and mind, people need to consume the necessary amounts of food. In our earlier discussion of eating, we didn't pay too much attention to the quality of the food that people consume; instead, our concern was mainly with the internal and external factors that underlie the motivation to eat. But proper nutrition is vitally important to maintaining a healthy body and mind, and health psychologists are engaged in a vigorous campaign to improve people's dietary habits.

The dietary habits of most North Americans leave much to be desired. Our diet tends to be too high in calories, fat, cholesterol, sugar, protein, and salt (Nolan, Gray-Donald, Shatenstein, & O'Loughlin, 1995; Sheridan & Radmacher, 1992). High-fat diets have been linked to heart disease, stroke, and several kinds of cancer, as well as to obesity. Diets that are high in cholesterol contribute to heart disease because the cholesterol can lodge in the walls of arteries, which can lead to hardening and narrowing, which restricts blood flow. Of course, not everyone who maintains a diet high in fat or cholesterol will develop these problems (because genetic predispositions are also a factor), but there's no question that many people eat themselves into an early grave.

Given the overwhelming amount of evidence linking diet to health, why don't people eat better? For many people, it's not the amount of food they eat but their choice of food that creates the problems. Consider the following: A baked potato has 0.5% of its calories as fat; when that same potato is French-fried, it has 42% of its calories as fat (Winikoff, 1983). Everyone has a handy list of reasons for why they give in to fast food, including the fact that it tastes good. Few people admit that their choices are influenced by television commercials that emphasize foods low in nutrition (e.g., beer and candy), yet the media undoubtedly influence our choices (Ostbye, Pomerleau, White, Coolich, & McWhinney, 1993). From a nutritional standpoint, fast foods tend to come up short because they're packed with fat and sodium. The best advice is to eat a variety of foods and to avoid foods with too much fat, cholesterol, sugar, and sodium. This is not a new message for you, we are sure, but remember: You're now much more sophisticated about the psychological factors that influence your choice of foods (see Chapter 11). So think before you eat—it might make a difference.

Don't Smoke: Tobacco and Health

Virtually everyone knows that smoking or the oral ingestion (chewing) of tobacco is bad for your health. There is no shortage of correlational and experimental studies available to document this fact. Few researchers question, for example, that smoking contributes annually to tens of thousands of deaths in Canada alone from associated heart disease, cancer, stroke, and emphysema (Ellison, Morrison, de Groh, & Villeneuve, 1999). And it's not just the smokers who are affected—the babies of women who smoke during pregnancy tend to have lower birth weights and are at increased risk for birth defects; even people who are simply exposed to second-hand smoke may experience subsequent health problems (Byrd, 1992). So why, given that it is so damaging to their health, do people smoke?

First, despite what you might have heard on television (especially from tobacco company executives), smoking is recognized to be *addictive* by the vast majority of mainstream researchers in the health-related sciences (Marlatt & VandenBos, 1997). Many people who smoke regularly become dependent on their daily dosage, and when they try to quit, they have physical and psychological withdrawal symptoms. The *DSM-IV* lists criteria for a diagnosis of "nicotine withdrawal" that include insomnia, irritability, difficulty concentrating, and increased appetite or weight gain. The symptoms of withdrawal can be severe enough to cause a significant disruption in normal everyday functioning (Piasecki, Fiore, & Baker, 1998). This conclusion, of course, comes as no surprise to anyone who has ever tried to quit smoking after prolonged use.

The reinforcing effects of cigarette smoking can be explained by appealing to chemical reactions in the brain and to factors in the culture at large. Within the brain, it takes only seconds for nicotine—the active agent in cigarette smoke—to stimulate the central nervous system, elevating heart rate, blood pressure, and mood. Many smokers report that cigarettes not only improve mood but help alleviate anxiety and stress. At the same time, tobacco companies in the United States launch advertising campaigns designed to make smoking appear desirable. Tobacco use is identified with role models—often thin, vigorous, and healthy people on horseback or frolicking on the beach—or is associated with independence and nonconformity. Unfortunately, these types of advertising campaigns are often particularly effective for those in adolescence, which is the time when most smokers begin. Girls are told that smoking will keep their weight down.

Advertising of tobacco products in Canada has been prohibited by the Hazardous Products Act since May 1988, and by 2003, sponsorships were stopped too. Canada has some of the world's toughest anti-smoking laws; however, the laws don't affect American magazines and periodicals sold in Canada, which still carry cigarette advertising.

You've probably heard the saying that the best way to stop smoking is never to start. It's undoubtedly true, because once started, tobacco use is a difficult habit to break. The psychological and physical withdrawal symptoms associated with tobacco use make quitting extraordinarily difficult.

In an effort to understand what strategies are most effective in helping people quit smoking, Canadian researchers, including Martin Taylor of McMaster University and Mark Zanna of the University of

University of British Columbia researcher Rick Pollay has studied the effects of tobacco advertising. He is shown here with examples of cigarette advertising, including some that attempt to associate smoking with healthy, vigorous lifestyles.

Nick Procaylo/CP Picture Archive

Waterloo, were involved in the most extensive smoking cessation study ever undertaken in North America (e.g., COMMIT Research Group, 1995a, 1995b; Taylor et al., 1998). This study, the Community Intervention Trial for Smoking Cessation (COMMIT), took place in 11 pairs of matched communities (10 in the United States and 1 in Canada) and incorporated a variety of smoking cessation techniques that were developed based on psychological principles. For example, smokers were recruited and became part of the "Smokers' Network"; thus social support was provided. In addition, participants took part in a "Quit and Win" contest whereby contest participants who remained smoke-free for 30 days were eligible to win a substantial prize. The smoking cessation interventions took place for four years, from 1989 to 1993, but the results of these interventions were somewhat disappointing. The results revealed that light to moderate smokers in the intervention communities were more likely to quit than those in the comparison communities. The number of heavy smokers in the intervention communities who quit smoking was not significantly different from the number who quit in the comparison communities. On a more positive note, smokers in all groups came to have stronger beliefs about smoking as a serious public health problem.

Changes in attitudes toward smoking and behaviour are occurring throughout North America. There has been a significant drop in the percentage of people who smoke in Canada and the United States, especially over the past two or three decades. Currently, approximately 25% of Canadians over the age of 12 smoke. Government advertising bans on television, radio, and other media may be at least partly responsible. Large numbers of people are choosing never to start smoking and more and more people are quitting—although often only after many relapses. In the words of Mark Twain: "To cease smoking is the easiest thing I ever did; I ought to know because I've done it a thousand times."

Stop Binge Drinking: One Risky Behaviour Leads to Another

Drinking is commonplace in North America. More than half of Canadians drink alcohol at least once per month (Health Canada, 1999). Although rates of drinking for adults have been decreasing over the last couple of decades, there are disturbing indications that the proportion of adolescents who drink to excess is increasing (Canadian Centre on Substance Abuse, 1999). The act of "binge" drinking (i.e., consuming five or more drinks on one occasion) is also more frequent in adolescents than in adults. Psychologists Roger Tonkin at the McCreary Centre Society and David Cox of Simon Fraser University surveyed more than 25 000 adolescents and found that more than 40% of the 12- to 18-year-olds who reported ever having a drink had engaged in a binge at least once during the past month (McCreary Centre Society, 1999). Canadian Aboriginal adolescents are reported as having a risk that is as much as six times greater than other Canadians for developing alcohol problems (Canadian Centre on Substance Abuse, 1999).

Canadian researchers have also been at the forefront of clarifying the link between personality and drinking behaviour. These researchers include Robert Pihl at McGill, Sherry Stewart at Dalhousie, Patricia Conrod at the University of British Columbia, and Jordan Peterson at the University of Toronto. Together, they have clarified links between personality traits and vulnerability to, as well as choice of, substance abuse (e.g., Conrod, Pihl, Stewart, & Dongier, 2000). Even for the same substance abuse (e.g., alcohol), different motives for use can be traced to underlying biological vulnerabilities (Stewart, Peterson, & Pihl, 1995).

Excessive use of alcohol can have adverse effects on almost every system of the body. For example, chronic alcohol abuse causes liver disease and damage to the stomach, pancreas, and intestines. Moreover, chronic drinking causes high blood pressure, leads to depression of the immune system, and is associated with coronary artery disease and cancer of the throat, larynx, mouth, esophagus, and liver (Alberta Alcohol and Drug Abuse Commission, 1999).

Excessive use of alcohol can have adverse effects on almost every system of the body. The act of binge drinking—that is, consuming five or more drinks on one occasion—is more frequent in adolescents than in adults.

Emma Lee/Life File/PhotoDisc/Getty Images

Alcohol is a depressant drug and, like other depressant drugs (e.g., tranquillizers and painkillers), it slows down the nervous system, which may cause drowsiness, induce sleep, or relieve pain. Even the initial apparent stimulant effect actually results from depression of various centres in the brain. At higher doses—even below a blood-alcohol concentration of 0.08%, the legal limit for driving a car in Canada—thinking and judgment are impaired. Thus, engaging in the health-compromising behaviour of drinking may lead people to engage in other risky health-related behaviours.

Psychologists Tara MacDonald of Queen's University and Mark Zanna and Geoffrey Fong of the University of Waterloo have been studying the effects of alcohol on our attitudes and intentions to engage in risky health-related behaviours, such as drinking and driving and having unprotected sexual intercourse (MacDonald, Zanna, & Fong, 1995, 1996, 1998). For example, in a series of experimental laboratory and field studies, MacDonald, Zanna, and Fong discovered that, compared with sober participants, intoxicated participants report a decrease in their intentions to use condoms, even among those participants who claimed to practise safe sex on a regular basis. These researchers believe that the phenomenon of **alcohol myopia,** developed by Steele and Josephs (1990), explains their findings. According to this theory, "alcohol causes social behaviours to become more extreme, and the direction of the behaviour will be determined by whatever cues are most salient in the environment" (MacDonald et al., 1998, p. 410). In the case of engaging in unprotected sex, intoxicated individuals likely do not have the requisite cognitive capacity to attend to both the costs and the benefits of their actions. Because the salient cue available to people in a situation described as "a possible sexual encounter" is likely sexual satisfaction and not the threat of pregnancy or sexually transmitted diseases, intoxicated individuals are more apt than sober individuals to participate in unprotected sexual intercourse.

alcohol myopia

A state induced by alcohol intoxication that results in more extreme social behaviours

Avoid Risky Behaviour: Protect Yourself from Disease

Choosing a healthy lifestyle requires having the right kind of information about how to prevent health-impairing habits. Health psychologists often distinguish among three main types of prevention programs (Winett, 1995):

1. *Primary prevention* is designed to educate the public as a whole in ways to reduce or eliminate a problem before it starts. Teaching children about the potential hazards of smoking or drug use is an example of primary prevention.
2. *Secondary prevention* involves the early identification of risk factors in specific population groups, such as checking for HIV infection in intravenous drug users or looking for early signs of disease through screening.
3. *Tertiary prevention* seeks to handle and contain an illness or habit once it has been acquired.

All three types of prevention programs are needed, but stopping an illness or habit before it starts—primary prevention—obviously has greater long-term significance.

Unsafe Sexual Behaviours Engaging in unsafe sexual behaviours can lead to serious health consequences, including the contraction of sexually transmitted diseases (STDs), such as human immunodeficiency virus (HIV), the virus that causes acquired immune deficiency syndrome (AIDS). HIV does its damage by attacking cells in the immune system, which leaves the body unable to fight off opportunistic infections that would otherwise be controlled. The disease **AIDS** is diagnosed in the latter stages of HIV infection, when the immune system has been sufficiently compromised. Living in the age of AIDS dramatically underscores the need for primary prevention programs.

Although AIDS and HIV infection are medical conditions, psychologists have two important roles to play. First, the only effective way to control widespread HIV transmission is to prevent risk-taking behaviour—in this case, preventing sexual intercourse without the use of latex condoms. Second, psychologists also play a therapeutic role with those who have contracted STDs.

To control transmission of STDs, psychologists are attempting to understand why people engage in unsafe sexual behaviours and how best to persuade people not to engage in these behaviours. Certainly a large number of our youth are practising unsafe sex. Results from the 1994/1995 National Public Health Survey indicate that more than 50% of female and approximately 35% of male sexually active 15- to 24-year-olds (excluding those with only one sexual partner and those who were married, in a common-law relationship, divorced, or widowed) have had sex without a condom in the past year. These figures are estimated to be even higher for Aboriginal people (Jolly, Orr, Hammond, & Young, 1995).

Why do people not use condoms when engaging in sexual intercourse? Researchers attempted to gain insight into this question by conducting a national survey of 5500 first-year Canadian college and university students between the ages of 16 and 24 years (MacDonald et al., 1990). The students reported not using condoms for a number of reasons: They were embarrassed about purchasing them; they had difficulty discussing condom use with their partner; they believed that condoms interfered with sexual pleasure; they already used oral contraceptives. The students also were found not to use condoms because they lacked knowledge about HIV and STDs. The reasons for participating in unsafe sexual behaviours provided by the students in this study are similar to those provided by surveys of the general population (Boroditsky, Fisher, & Sand, 1996).

In an effort to understand the best method of curtailing the unsafe sexual practices of youth, health psychologist Geoffrey Fong of the University of Waterloo and his colleagues examined which interventions are most effective (Jemmott, Jemmott, & Fong, 1998; Jemmott, Jemmott, Fong, & McCaffree, 1999). In one study, grade 6 and grade 7 students took part in an eight-hour intervention as part of a Saturday program. The adolescents were randomly assigned to one of three different interventions: an abstinence HIV intervention, which acknowledged that condoms can reduce risks but emphasized abstinence to eliminate the

AIDS

Acquired immune deficiency syndrome, a disease that gradually weakens and disables the immune system

Primary prevention is crucial in battling the AIDS epidemic.

GANNETT OUTDOOR

THE SECOND BEST WAY TO PREVENT AIDS.

The Elizabeth Taylor Aids Foundation

2836

© David Young-Wolff/PhotoEdit

risk of pregnancy and STDs, including HIV; a safer-sex HIV intervention, which indicated that abstinence is the best choice but that condom use is important to reduce the risk of pregnancy and STDs, including HIV, if participants were to have sex; or a health promotion intervention, which focused on behaviours associated with risk of cardiovascular disease, stroke, and certain cancers rather than on AIDS or sexual behaviour. Those adolescents assigned to the health promotion intervention served as the control group. The results of this study suggest that both abstinence and safer-sex interventions can reduce unsafe sexual behaviours, but safer-sex interventions may have longer-lasting effects. Not surprisingly, safer-sex interventions may be especially effective with sexually experienced adolescents.

Taking a somewhat different approach, psychologist William Fisher of the University of Western Ontario researched the psychological determinants of human sexual and reproductive health behaviour. With Jeffrey Fisher of the University of Connecticut he proposed the Information-Motivation-Behavioral Skills (IMB) model (Fisher & Fisher, 1992, 1993, 1998). According to this model, successfully achieving safe-sex practices has three fundamental determinants. First, those who are sexually active must be *knowledgeable* about sexual and reproductive health information. If you do not know that STDs exist, or if you do not know what constitutes safe sex, practising safe sex is unlikely. Second, in addition to being knowledgeable about safe-sex practices, you must be *motivated* to act on this information. Finally, you must possess the *behavioural skills* for acting on this information effectively. For example, you must be able to negotiate with your partner to ensure cooperation in safe-sex practices.

The other key role being played by psychologists in the AIDS epidemic is a therapeutic one. Once infected, people with HIV are subjected to an overwhelming amount of stress. Not only are these individuals faced with the prospect of an early death, but they must face the stigma that often accompanies the disease. Psychologists are actively involved in the establishment of treatment programs that can help AIDS patients cope with their disease (Chesney, 1993; Feldman & Christensen, 1997).

Test Yourself 16.4

Check your knowledge about living a healthy lifestyle by deciding whether each of the following statements is true or false. (The answers are in Appendix B.)

1. Aerobic exercise improves cardiovascular health and general mood, but produces few changes in the physiological effects of the stress reaction. *True or False?*

2. For many people, it's not the amount of food they eat but their choice of food that creates health problems. *True or False?*

3. Smoking is recognized to be addictive by the vast majority of mainstream researchers in the health-related sciences. *True or False?*

4. Teaching children about the hazards of smoking or drugs would be classified as an example of secondary prevention. *True or False?*

Stress and Health

The close relationship that exists between thoughts and emotions and the physical reactions of the body means that understanding and promoting physical health requires some attention to psychological factors. Health psychology (also called *behavioural medicine*) seeks to understand the medical consequences of the interaction between body and mind. Health psychologists are interested in the psychological and environmental factors—everything from personality characteristics to the work environment—that both produce illness and affect the likelihood of recovery.

First, what is stress, and how is it experienced? Stress has historically been a somewhat tough concept to define. It can be conceived of as a stimulus, as a response, or as a process through which external events are interpreted as threatening or demanding. We chose to define stress as the physical and psychological reaction that is shown in response to demanding situations. The stress response involves an extended reaction that occurs in phases. According to the general adaptation syndrome proposed by Hans Selye, the body initially reacts to threat with a highly adaptive fight-or-flight response (although there may be gender differences in the behavioural response); if the threat continues, the body goes through resistance and exhaustion phases that make it vulnerable to disease.

Our reactions are critically influenced by the way we perceive or appraise a situation. To experience stress, it's necessary to both perceive a threat and feel that you lack the necessary resources to deal with it effectively. This means that identical environmental events can lead to very different stress reactions, depending on how the situation is interpreted. Overall, however, it is possible to identify some common sources of stress. External sources of stress include significant life events, physical pain, daily hassles, and environmental factors, such as noise and crowding. Internal sources of stress include insufficient perceived control over the situation and a maladaptive explanatory style.

Certain personality characteristics have been linked to stress. Type A individuals—those who are hard driving, ambitious, and impatient—appear to be at increased risk for subsequent heart disease. It has become clear that the decisive element in the Type A behaviour pattern is the tendency toward angry, hostile reactions to stressful situations.

Second, how does the body react when the exposure to stressful situations is prolonged? Stress is an adaptive reaction to threat, but if the threat is extended over time, both body and mind can start to break down. Stress has been implicated in a wide variety of health problems, ranging from heart disease to the common cold. A number of studies have shown that prolonged stress can affect immune functioning, which is the body's method of fighting disease. Stress can compromise the immune response by either lowering the number of specialized white blood cells (lymphocytes) or by somehow suppressing the response of those lymphocytes to foreign substances that have invaded the body.

Two chronic psychological consequences of prolonged stress are posttraumatic stress disorder and burnout. Posttraumatic stress disorder results from exposure to extreme trauma, such as that experienced during battle or as a result of a physical assault, such as rape. The symptoms of the disorder include flashbacks in which the traumatic event is re-experienced, avoidance of stimuli associated with the trauma, and chronic arousal problems. Burnout is a term that psychologists use to describe a state of physical, emotional, and mental exhaustion that sometimes develops after prolonged stress.

Third, what strategies enable us to reduce and cope with stress? The term *coping* describes efforts to manage conditions of threat that tax resources. Effective coping techniques include relaxation training, the use of social support, and reappraisal. The stress response is incompatible with relaxation; therefore, relaxation training can help lower components of the stress response (such as blood pressure and heart rate). In progressive relaxation training, the client is taught to concentrate on specific muscle groups in the body, note whether they seem tense, and then relax those specific groups. Sometimes it's useful to provide biofeedback as well.

Additional evidence indicates that social support—the resources received from other people—can also help you cope effectively with stress. Friends and family help us maintain a healthy lifestyle, boost confidence, or simply provide an avenue for us to open up and express our feelings. Talking about things and confiding in others really seem to help people deal with stress. Finally, because stress depends on how you interpret the threatening or demanding situation, it can often be managed effectively through cognitive reappraisal. You can be taught to reinterpret significant life events or daily hassles in a less stressful way. Some stress management programs encourage clients to keep daily stress records. By identifying the kinds of situations that create stress, as well as the negative thoughts those situations induce, you become better prepared to reinterpret those situations and thoughts in a more adaptive manner.

Fourth, what general factors and lifestyle choices promote physical and psychological health? Aerobic exercise is one example of an activity that can have a substantial effect on physical and psychological health. Regular exercise improves mood and makes people more resistant to the effects of stressors. Proper nutrition is another important ingredient in maintaining a healthy body and mind. The North American diet tends to be too high in calories, fat, cholesterol, sugar, protein, and salt. Poor dietary habits can lead to significant long-term health problems. Another lifestyle choice that directly affects physical health is the decision not to smoke. Smoking and other tobacco use contribute to tens of thousands of deaths annually in Canada alone, from associated heart disease, cancer, stroke, and emphysema.

Tobacco use stimulates activity in the central nervous system, which is immediately reinforcing, but prolonged use leads to addiction or dependence that can be difficult to overcome. Choosing to drink is a lifestyle choice that affects health both immediately and over time. Alcohol is a depressant drug that slows down the nervous system, altering judgment and decision-making skills. With excessive use alcohol can have adverse effects on several organs and almost every system of the body, including the liver, stomach, pancreas, intestines, and cardiovascular and immune systems. Finally, maintaining a healthy lifestyle includes avoiding risky behaviours and preventing disease. For example, psychologists are playing an important role in the AIDS epidemic by educating the public about risky behaviour, and through the establishment of treatment programs they are helping AIDS patients cope with the psychological effects of the disease.

CHAPTER SUMMARY

▶ Experiencing Stress: Stressors and the Stress Response

How does the body produce stress? How is it experienced? *Stress* is best conceived of as an extended response that occurs over time rather than as a single reaction.

The Stress Response

One influential model of the stress reaction is known as the *general adaptation syndrome (GAS)*, which proposes that we respond to threat or demand in three phases. The *alarm reaction* corresponds to a fight-or-flight response; during the *resistance stage*, the threat continues and the body adjusts its reaction to cope; if the person is unable to neutralize the threat, *exhaustion* occurs. Fear, anger, sadness, dejection, and grief are common psychological responses to stress. Despite the negative health consequences, this sequence of reactions to stress seems to have adaptive value. Because of different evolutionary strategies, sex differences in coping behaviour may have evolved.

Cognitive Appraisal

The experience of stress is critically affected by how people appraise the situation they're in. People must feel that a threat is present and that they may not have adequate resources to deal with the threat. The role of *cognitive appraisal* in the stress response is consistent with what we know about the role of cognition in the experience of emotion.

External Sources of Stress

Significant life events can introduce a good deal of stress into a person's life. Holmes and Rahe (1967) developed a life-change stress scale that indicates that stressful events are often associated with some type of change in day-to-day activities, which can be either positive or negative. Pain is an obvious warning signal that the body is being stressed and can contribute to stress as well. Less obviously stressful, daily hassles and environmental factors, such as noise, may nonetheless contribute to daily stress. The specialty area of *environmental psychology* is devoted to the study of environmental effects on behaviour and health.

Internal Sources of Stress

The *hardy personality*—that is, the one resistant to stress—includes a number of adaptive perceptions, styles, and traits. One such factor is *perceived control*, or the amount of influence you feel you have over a situation and your reaction to it. Generally, less perceived control is associated with higher stress. A second factor is *explanatory style*, which is also related to psychological disorders, such as depression. In contrast, the higher level of stress and heart disease in *Type A* personalities is linked to their preference for high-stress occupations and activities and a hostile reaction to people and events that interfere with their goals.

Reacting to Prolonged Stress: Physical and Psychological Effects

The human body is usually able to deal with unexpected trauma, but if the threat continues for an extended period, the body's defences can begin to break down.

Physical Consequences of Stress

Stress has been implicated in a wide variety of health problems. Living a stressful life seems to lower the ability to fight disease. The immune system and its primary weapons, *lymphocytes*, are affected by stress. The immune response is lowered, decreasing the number of lymphocytes, or the response of lymphocytes to foreign substances is suppressed. The link between stress and the immune system has led some to speculate about the possible relationship between stress and more chronic illnesses, such as cancer, although researchers remain cautious in their conclusions. Prolonged exposure to stress is also associated with two major risk factors in cardiovascular disease: high blood pressure and high cholesterol.

Psychological Consequences of Stress

Most psychologists believe that stressful life events play a significant role in the onset of many psychological disorders. Psychologists assume that a (perhaps genetic) vulnerability interacts with stress to produce a psychological disorder. One psychological disorder resulting from extreme stress is *posttraumatic stress disorder* (*PTSD*), which is characterized by flashbacks, avoidance of trauma-associated stimuli, and chronic arousal symptoms. *Burnout*, another effect of prolonged stress, is "a state of emotional and mental exhaustion caused by long-term involvement in emotionally demanding situations" (Pines & Aronson, 1988). Burnout may be caused by loss of control in the workplace or of meaning in life.

Reducing and Coping with Stress: Techniques of Stress Management

Given the negative consequences that long-term exposure to stress can have, psychologists have developed specific methods for reducing and controlling stress. *Coping* is the term psychologists use to describe efforts to manage conditions of threat or demand that tax resources.

Relaxation Techniques

Relaxation is an effective stress reducer because of its incompatibility with the stress response. *Progressive muscle relaxation* involves concentrating on specific muscle groups of the body, noting tension, and trying to relax those specific groups. In *autogenic relaxation*, a person is taught to focus on directing blood flow toward specific muscle groups, warming and relaxing them. Relaxation techniques are sometimes accompanied by *meditation* training. Giving people feedback (*biofeedback*) about the effectiveness of their relaxation efforts has proven successful.

Social Support

Social support refers to the resources that we receive from other people or groups, often in the form of comfort, caring, or help. Studies indicate that social support can improve one's psychological and physical health. Social support can also have a negative side if one has come to depend on such support and it is no longer available.

Reappraisal of the Situation

Interpretation of events plays a large role in how stressful the situation is; many stress management techniques involve *cognitive reappraisal*. This might involve focusing on aspects of the situation that distract one from catastrophizing, or analyzing a situation logically and deriving alternatives.

Living a Healthy Lifestyle

Whether you will remain healthy throughout your life depends significantly on your lifestyle habits. Health psychologists and other professionals have offered prescriptions for a healthy lifestyle.

Get Fit: The Value of Aerobic Exercise

Aerobic exercise, which consists of high-intensity activities that increase both heart rate and oxygen consumption, can have a substantial positive impact on psychological and physical health. It can improve mood and increase resistance to the effects of stressors. Researchers have not yet discovered exactly how or why exercise improves functioning; placebo-like effects may be involved.

Eat Right: The Value of Proper Nutrition

Proper nutrition is vital to maintaining a healthy body and mind; yet the foods most North Americans eat tend to be high in calories, cholesterol, fat, and other substances that are damaging in excess. Problems usually involve the type of food that is eaten, not the amount.

Don't Smoke: Tobacco and Health

A wealth of correlational and experimental evidence has demonstrated the link between tobacco and serious health problems. People continue to smoke because smoking is addictive and associated with withdrawal effects. In addition, smoking seems to produce chemical reactions in the brain that lead to reinforcing effects. Although smoking is a difficult habit to break, rates of smoking do seem to be on the decline.

Stop Binge Drinking: One Risky Behaviour Leads to Another

Drinking alcohol to the point of intoxication affects brain functioning. *Alcohol myopia* means that judgment and decision-making processes are altered, and this may lead to people engaging in other risky health-related behaviours that they wouldn't partake in if sober (e.g., drinking and driving, engaging in unsafe sex). Excessive and chronic use of alcohol may lead to serious health problems.

Avoid Risky Behaviour: Protect Yourself from Disease

Health psychologists distinguish among three types of prevention. *Primary prevention* attempts to reduce or eliminate a problem before it starts. *Secondary prevention* involves early identification of risk factors in specific population groups. *Tertiary prevention* seeks to handle and contain an illness or habit once it has been acquired. The prevalence of STDs, such as *AIDS*, underscores the importance of primary prevention programs.

Terms to Remember

health psychology, 636

Experiencing Stress: Stressors and the Stress Response
stress, 637
stressors, 637
general adaptation syndrome (GAS), 638
cognitive appraisal, 640
environmental psychology, 644
hardy personality, 645
perceived control, 645
Type A, 646
Type B, 646

Reacting to Prolonged Stress: Physical and Psychological Effects
lymphocytes, 648
posttraumatic stress disorder, 651
burnout, 652

Reducing and Coping with Stress: Techniques of Stress Management
coping, 653
biofeedback, 655
social support, 655

Living a Healthy Lifestyle
aerobic exercise, 660
alcohol myopia, 665
AIDS, 666

Recommended Readings

Friedman, H. S. (1991). *The self-healing personality: Why some people achieve health and others succumb to illness.* New York: Holt. An excellent introduction to the link between psychological factors and health.

Gifford, R. (1997). *Environmental psychology: Principles and practice* (2nd ed.). Needham Heights, MA: Allyn & Bacon. Robert Gifford of the University of Victoria is a leading researcher in the field of environmental psychology. This textbook is a comprehensive overview of contemporary research, model research, and practical applications in this area.

Pennebaker, J. W. (1990). *Opening up.* New York: William Morrow & Company. An in-depth discussion of the role that oral or written expression of painful experiences might play in reducing stress and improving health.

Poole, G. D., Matheson, D. H., & Cox, D. (2001). *The psychology of health and health care: A Canadian perspective.* Toronto: Prentice Hall. The first Canadian health psychology undergraduate textbook. This textbook, written by health psychologists from the University of British Columbia, the University of Victoria, and Simon Fraser University, covers many aspects of stress, health, and behaviour.

 For additional readings, explore InfoTrac® College Edition, your online library. Go to http://www.adaptivemind3e.nelson.com.

Hint: Enter these search terms: reactions to stress, causes of stress, stress and illness, coping with stress, posttraumatic stress disorder, health psychology.

Media Resources

🌐 What's on the Web?

Please note that Web addresses are subject to change. Check out the accompanying website for updates: http://www.adaptivemind3e.nelson.com.

This site presents practice quiz questions, hypercontent, information on degrees and careers in psychology, study tips, and more.

Canadian Institute for Health Information

http://www.cihi.ca

This is a convenient website to use as a starting point when conducting a general search for Canadian health-related information. The main function of the Canadian Institute for Health Information is to bring together health-related information from Statistics Canada, Health Canada, the Hospital Medical Records Institute, and other organizations.

Health Canada

http://www.hc-sc.gc.ca

This site provides a wealth of information on the health of Canadians. The information is available in the form of statistics, articles, and other documents, all of which are organized alphabetically, from "Aboriginal Health" all the way to "Youth."

American Institute of Stress

http://www.stress.org

This site provides some very useful information about stress, how to avoid it, how to cope with it, and how it can affect your life. It presents some surprising statistics. For example, 75% to 90% of visits to primary care physicians are for stress-related problems, and 78% of Americans describe their jobs as stressful (the majority claim that this has worsened in the last 10 years). Clearly, we are living in stressful times.

U.S. Center for PTSD

http://www.ncptsd.va.gov/

This site is devoted to education and research on posttraumatic stress disorder; it provides a wealth of information related to the topic, including information for trauma survivors and veterans and fact sheets on a variety of topics, including PTSD and children, PTSD and community violence, and PTSD and the family.

ThomsonNOW™ ThomsonNOW™

http://hed.nelson.com

Go to this site for the link to ThomsonNOW™, your one-stop study shop. Take a Pretest for this chapter and ThomsonNOW™ will generate a personalized Study Plan based on your test results. The Study Plan will identify the topics you need to review and direct you to online resources to help you master those topics. You can then take a Posttest to determine what concepts you have mastered and what you still need work on.

Statistics. The word causes many students to shudder with fear and loathing. One reason for this negative reaction is that many students expect the topic to be incredibly difficult. But, in truth, the basics of statistics are fairly easy to understand, and most students are surprised at how quickly they pick them up. The core concepts can be understood intuitively as well as mathematically, and most of the math is pretty easy. (Adding, subtracting, multiplying, and dividing will get you a long way in statistics.)

Another reason that statistics has a bad reputation is that many people are wary of it—they know that it is easy to lie (or at least mislead) with statistics, and some are uncomfortable with the whole idea of quantifying human experience. These concerns have legitimate grounds: Statistics can be presented in ways that are misleading, and quantifying psychological phenomena can be done poorly. But far from being good reasons for staying ignorant of statistics, these are excellent reasons for learning about them: Knowledge of statistics can protect you from being bamboozled by misleading uses of statistics, and engaging the problem of quantifying aspects of human experience can enhance your appreciation of the subtlety and complexity of human beings.

This appendix offers only a simplified and limited introduction to statistics, intended to supplement the information presented in Chapter 2. There are many textbooks that provide a more complete and sophisticated introduction to the use of statistics in psychology (e.g., Pagano, 2007).

DESCRIPTIVE STATISTICS

Statistics are used to summarize and make inferences about measurements of variables. A variable is a dimension or characteristic that can vary across or within individuals (e.g., height, gender, hours of sleep, creativity). Some psychological variables are inherently qualitative (e.g., gender), but many variables can be usefully quantified (i.e., we can use numbers to describe many psychological variables in terms of strength, amount, frequency, speed, etc.). Before we quantify a psychological variable, we must think carefully about the nature of whatever it is we want to measure (e.g., what *is* creativity, and how can we quantify it?). The development of theoretically sound, methodologically rigorous, and practically useful ways of quantifying psychological variables is a central task for psychology, and one on which considerable

progress has been made. Briefly, a good measure is *reliable* (the same result is obtained when the same thing is measured on different occasions or by different investigators), *valid* (it measures what it is intended to measure), and *sensitive* (it detects subtle but real differences).

Nominal Data versus Score Data

Suppose that you wanted to describe the students in your introductory psychology course in terms of their favourite hobbies and their performance on a psychology exam. If they all completed a questionnaire with this information, you would want some way of summarizing the responses. That is, you would want to use *descriptive statistics* to characterize the hobbies and test performance of the class.

Different sorts of variables lend themselves to different sorts of statistical analyses. Statisticians differentiate between several different sorts of variables, but here we focus on the two most common kinds: *nominal data* and *score data*.

"Hobbies" is an example of a "nominal" (namelike) variable: You could put the hobbies that students reported into various categories (e.g., sports, collecting, music), and you could quantify the data by reporting the number or percentage of students reporting the various kinds of hobbies. "Hobbies" in this example is a nominal variable because there is no underlying quantitative scale along which the different categories range (i.e., there isn't a quantitative scale running from "sports" to "collecting" to "music"). Gender and cultural heritage are other examples of nominal variables.

You can quantify nominal data in terms of the number (or percentage or proportion of the total) in the various nominal categories. You can also examine relationships between two different nominal variables; for example, you could compare men's and women's reports of their favourite hobbies. One useful way of depicting the relationship between two nominal variables is by creating a *cross-tabulation table*. ▶ Table A.1 on page 674 presents such a table, with data from the 2001 Canada census on the percentage of Canadians who classified themselves as cigarette smokers as a function of age and gender. Notice how the prevalence of smoking increases over the teens and early 20s, then levels off, then drops in late life (with that drop being partly due to people quitting smoking by dying). Also notice that in the two youngest age groups smoking is more common among females than males.

▶ **Table A.1**   Cross-Tabulation of the Percentage
of Canadians by Gender and Age Group
Classified as Cigarette Smokers

	Age (years)					
	12–14	15–19	20–34	35–44	45–64	65+
Female	3.8	18.9	22.7	24.9	22.6	11.7
Male	2.2	17.7	29.5	29.2	27.3	9.5

Source: Data from Canada census, 2001, http://www40.statcan.ca/l01/cst01/
health07a.htm.

Nominal categories—such as different hobbies or genders—are not quantitative scales. You couldn't, for example, assign numbers to the different categories of hobbies (e.g., sports = 1, collecting = 2, music = 3), add up all of the respondents' responses, divide by the total number of respondents, and come out with a meaningful "average hobby." This wouldn't make sense because "hobbies" is not a quantitative scale but rather a set of qualitatively different categories.

In contrast, performance on an exam (expressed as number, percentage, or proportion correct) is an example of a "score" variable. Score variables are inherently quantitative in a variety of senses. Most obviously, scores have an underlying quantitative dimension, ranging from 0% to 100% correct. Also, the intervals between scores are equal at different parts of the scale; for example, scores of 6 and 8 differ by the same amount as scores of 7 and 9. Because score data have these quantitative properties, we can meaningfully perform mathematical operations on them (e.g., calculate the mean to describe the average score on an exam). Psychologists often use measures that produce score data (e.g., IQ tests, measures of creativity, reaction time).

Normal Distributions of Score Data

Frequency Distribution Tables and Frequency Histograms

Chapter 2 introduced you to frequency histograms (graphs that depict the frequency of cases getting various scores on some measurement). We will review them here in greater depth. Suppose that you randomly selected 20 students from your introductory psychology class and gave each of them a test on the material in this textbook. ▶ Table A.2 shows the raw data you might obtain, scored in terms of percentage correct and sorted into rank order from the lowest to the highest.

A frequency histogram summarizes data graphically in a way that depicts the distribution of the scores. In this case, we want to show how many students got particular scores on the psychology test. To do so, we must first select ranges of scores; once we've done that, we'll simply count up the number of cases with scores falling within each of those ranges. Score ranges are selected such that the total range is sufficient to include all the data and that there are enough different intervals along that total range to depict the distribution of scores in a clear and informative manner.

▶ **Table A.2**   Percentage Correct on a Psychology Test by 20 Students in an Introductory Psychology Course

Rank	Name	Score (x)
1	Mary	59
2	Betty	68
3	Colleen	69
4	Amy	72
5	Tanya	74
6	René	74
7	Inez	75
8	Pierre	75
9	Petra	76
10	Frances	76
11	Cheryl	76
12	Steve	76
13	Martin	77
14	James	77
15	Belinda	79
16	Helene	80
17	Daphne	80
18	Jean	81
19	Deborah	85
20	Theresa	91

Let's say we decide to use six ranges of test scores: 41–50, 51–60, 61–70, 71–80, 81–90, and 91–100. Now we can construct a *frequency distribution table* that shows the number of students whose scores fell in each of those ranges. ▶ Table A.3 is a frequency distribution table of the data shown in Table A.2. Compare Tables A.2 and A.3, and make sure you understand the relationship between them. Notice, for example, that Table A.2 includes two students (Betty and Colleen) with scores between 61 and 70 and that Table A.3 indicates that the frequency of scores from 61 to 70 is 2 (i.e., Betty and Colleen).

A *frequency histogram* is simply a graphic depiction of the numeric information in a frequency distribution table. Frequency histograms come in a variety of styles, but one of the most common has the ranges of scores along the horizontal axis (called the *abscissa*). The vertical axis (called the *ordinate*) is used to represent the frequency (number) of cases.[1] Vertical bars are used to represent the frequency of cases within each of the ranges of scores, with the height of each bar corresponding to the number of cases within that range, as indexed by the values marked on the ordinate. ▶ Figure A.1 is a frequency histogram of the data in Tables A.2 and A.3. Take a look now, and make sure you understand how the data in Tables A.2 and A.3 have been depicted in Figure A.1. A good way to test your grasp of this material is to make up a small set of data (e.g., 10 single-digit numbers) and then construct a frequency histogram for that data set.

▶ **Table A.3** Frequency Distribution Table of the Raw Data Presented in Table A.2 (Percentage Correct on a Psychology Test by 20 Students in an Introductory Psychology Course)

Test Score Range	Frequency (Number of Cases)
41–50	0
51–60	1
61–70	2
71–80	14
81–90	2
91–100	1

Normal Distributions

The distribution of scores depicted in Figure A.1 is an approximately "normal" or "bell curve" distribution: The most frequent or common cases are at or near the mean (arithmetic average), and as score values move below or above the mean, the frequency of cases declines. Note that in a normal distribution the rate of the decline in frequency is approximately symmetrical around the mean; in other words, rarity increases at about the same rate as score values move above or below the mean. Notice also that in a normal distribution the mean, median, and mode are all quite close to one another (indeed, in a perfectly symmetrical normal distribution these three measures of central tendency are identical). Think about this for a moment, and make sure you understand why it makes sense that the mean, median, and mode are similar in a normal distribution (and identical in a perfectly symmetrical normal distribution).

Many physical and psychological variables have approximately normal distributions. For example, if you measured the IQ of the members of your introductory psychology course and calculated the mean IQ, you'd find that most of the class would be at or near that mean, with fewer and fewer students having IQ scores farther and farther from the mean. The same would hold for height, weight, creativity, performance on an exam, and numerous other score variables.[2]

Measuring Variability in Distributions: The Standard Deviation

Suppose that we once again recruited the same 20 students from your introductory psychology course, this time quizzing them about current events. Introductory psychology students vary a great deal from one another in their knowledge of current events: Some are total media hounds, up on all sorts of news items, others avoid such information like the plague, and yet others are somewhere between these extremes. We might therefore expect that there would be a lot of variability from one student to another on scores on the current-events test. ▶ Table A.4 presents the raw data

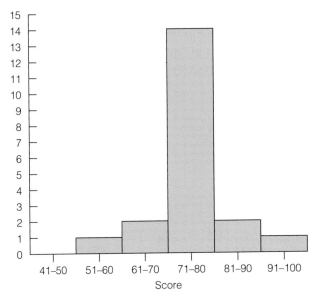

▶ **Figure A.1**

Frequency Histogram of the Data in Tables A.2 and A.3 (Percentage Correct on a Psychology Test by 20 Students in an Introductory Psychology Course)

▶ **Table A.4** Percentage Correct on a Test of Current Events by 20 Students in an Introductory Psychology Course

Rank	Name	Score (x)
1	Tanya	48
2	René	55
3	Colleen	57
4	Amy	61
5	Mary	70
6	Betty	73
7	Frances	74
8	Pierre	75
9	Petra	75
10	Deborah	76
11	Cheryl	77
12	Belinda	79
13	Martin	80
14	James	82
15	Steve	84
16	Jean	84
17	Daphne	88
18	Helene	89
19	Inez	95
20	Theresa	98

▶ **Table A.5**   Frequency Distribution Table of the Raw Data Presented in Table A.4 (Percentage Correct on a Test of Current Events by 20 Students in an Introductory Psychology Course)

Test Score Range	Frequency (Number of Cases)
41–50	1
51–60	2
61–70	2
71–80	8
81–90	5
91–100	2

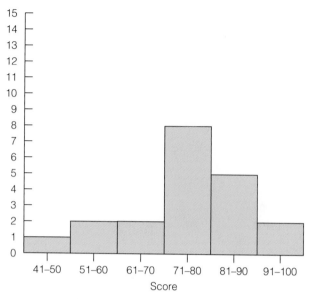

▶ **Figure A.2**

Frequency Histogram of the Data in Tables A.4 and A.5 (Percentage Correct on a Test of Current Events by 20 Students in an Introductory Psychology Course)

from the current-events test, and ▶ Table A.5 is a frequency distribution table of those same data, using the same score ranges as were used with the psychology test (Table A.3).

▶ Figure A.2 is a frequency histogram of the current-events test scores. Note first that this distribution is approximately normal; that is, the most common cases are at or near the mean, and rarity increases approximately symmetrically as score values move above and below the mean. In this regard, Figure A.2 is similar to Figure A.1. The two figures are also similar in that the mean of each set of scores is 76. The two figures differ, however, in how "flat" versus "narrow" the normal distributions are. The distribution in Figure A.1 is quite narrow because a very large percentage of the students had scores at or quite close to the mean; that is, there is relatively little variability in this data set. The distribution in Figure A.2 is wider because quite a few students had scores that were above or below the mean; that is, there is a fair amount of variability in the current-events data set.

Frequency histograms are very useful because they clearly depict both the mean and the amount of variability around that mean in a set of score data. It is often handy, though, to describe the amount of variability in a set of data quantitatively, that is, with a number that indicates the average extent to which scores in the data set differ from the mean. The most common quantitative index of variability in score data is the *standard deviation (SD)*. The SD is a standardized measure of the average extent to which scores in a data set deviate or differ from the mean of that data set. To use a somewhat silly but illustrative example, suppose you measured the number of bellybuttons on each of your classmates. What do you think the mean would be? How about the SD? Of course, the mean would be 1 and the SD would be 0; that is, every student would be exactly at the mean value, so the average amount of deviation from the mean would be 0. The SD would be larger than 0 for the scores on the psychology test shown in Figure A.1 and even larger for the scores on the current-events test shown in Figure A.2, because there is more variability around the mean for those measures.

To calculate the SD, you first determine the mean for the data set (i.e., add up the scores and divide by the number of scores). Then, for each individual score, you subtract the mean from that score. (See ▶ Table A.6, which depicts the steps involved in calculating the SD for the current-events test scores graphed in Figure A.2.) Obviously, if a score is the same as the mean, this difference will be 0 (e.g., Deborah scored 76 on the test, so her difference from the mean is 0); if a score deviates from the mean by a large amount, then this difference will be a lot different from 0. For example, as shown in the first line of Table A.6, Tanya's score of 48 is 28 points below the mean of 76, so Tanya's difference from the mean is −28. Given that we're trying to measure the average extent to which the scores in the data set differ from the mean, you might think that all you have to do now is add up those difference scores and divide by the number of scores (*N*), but that wouldn't work. Can you think why? By definition, some scores are above the mean and others below the mean, so some differences from the mean will be negative (as in Tanya's case) and others positive (such as Theresa), and if you simply added up the difference scores you'd get a grand total of 0. Think this through while looking at the difference scores in the third column of Table A.6 and make sure you understand why the difference scores would sum to 0.

To get around this problem, each difference score is squared (multiplied by itself): By the rules of mathematics, a negative number times a negative number equals a positive number, so this eliminates the problem of the differences from the mean adding to 0. Notice that the farther a particular score is from the mean, the larger the squared difference

▶ **Table A.6**   Calculating the Standard Deviation of the Data in Table A.4 (Percentage Correct on a Test of Current Events by 20 Students in an Introductory Psychology Course)

Rank	Name	Score (x)	x − x̄	(x − x̄)²
1	Tanya	48	48 − 76 = −28	784
2	René	55	55 − 76 = −21	441
3	Colleen	57	57 − 76 = −19	361
4	Amy	61	61 − 76 = −15	225
5	Mary	70	70 − 76 = −6	36
6	Betty	73	73 − 76 = −3	9
7	Frances	74	74 − 76 = −2	4
8	Pierre	75	75 − 76 = −1	1
9	Petra	75	75 − 76 = −1	1
10	Deborah	76	76 − 76 = 0	0
11	Cheryl	77	77 − 76 = 1	1
12	Belinda	79	79 − 76 = 3	9
13	Martin	80	80 − 76 = 4	16
14	James	82	82 − 76 = 6	36
15	Steve	84	84 − 76 = 8	64
16	Jean	84	84 − 76 = 8	64
17	Daphne	88	88 − 76 = 12	144
18	Helene	89	89 − 76 = 13	169
19	Inez	95	95 − 76 = 19	361
20	Theresa	98	98 − 76 = 22	484
N = 20		Sum = 1520	Sum = 0	Sum = 3210
		Mean = x = 1520/20 = 76		SD = √3210/(20 − 1) = 13.00

from the mean. For example, in Tanya's case, the mean of 76 is subtracted from her score of 48; that equals −28, and −28 squared equals 784. The squared differences from the mean are then summed, yielding a measure called *the sum of squared differences from the mean* (or *sum of squares*, for short). The sum of squares is then divided by the number of scores minus 1 ($N − 1$) to yield an estimate of the average extent to which scores in the data set deviate from the mean; this measure is called the *variance*.[3]

As shown in Table A.6, the sum of squares for the current-events test data is 3210, so the variance of that data set is 3210/(20 − 1) = 168.95. For reasons that will become clear in a moment, statisticians don't usually use the variance to index variability, but rather go one step further and get the square root of the variance (i.e., the number that, when multiplied by itself, equals the variance). The square root of the variance is the standard deviation, or SD. For the current-events test data, the SD is 13.0 (rounded from 12.997). (You can assess your understanding of the steps involved in calculating SD by calculating it for the psychology test data in Table A.4; the correct answer is 6.50.)

Whew! That seems like a lot of work! But it's worth it, because the SD has some very important properties (which is why statisticians usually prefer it to the variance). The marvellous thing about the SD is that for *any* normal distribution

(no matter how "narrow" or "wide"), approximately 34.1% of the scores are between the mean and 1 SD above the mean, and 34.1% of the scores are between the mean and 1 SD below the mean (see ▶ Figure A.3 on page 678).[4] Thus, in any normal distribution, approximately 68.2% of the scores are within ±1 SD of the mean. In the current-events test scores, for example, the mean is 76 and the SD is 13.0, so about 68.2% of the scores should be between 63 (1 SD below the mean) and 89 (1 SD above the mean); in fact, 14 of the 20 scores (70%) fall in this range, which is as close to 68.2% as possible given there are only 20 scores. Further, for any normal distribution, approximately 13.6% of the scores are between 1 SD and 2 SD above the mean, and approximately 13.6% are between 1 SD and 2 SD below the mean. So what proportion of the scores in a normal distribution is within ±2 SD of the mean? About 34.1 + 34.1 + 13.6 + 13.6 = 95.4%. Only about 2.1% of the scores in a normal distribution are between 2 SD and 3 SD above the mean (and 2.1% are between 2 SD and 3 SD below the mean), so about 99.6% of the scores are within ±3 SD of the mean.

Figure A.3 shows a particular normal distribution, with a particular mean and a particular SD. There are an infinite number of possible normal distributions, differing from each other in terms of their means or SD or both. ▶ Figure A.4 on page 678 shows four different normal distributions, each

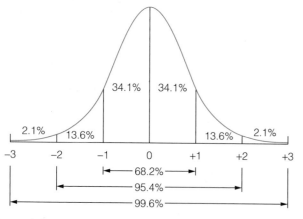

▶ **Figure A.3**

Areas under the Normal Curve as a Function of Standard Deviation from the Mean[5]

From http://qreview.cera.net/Chapters-HTML/Chap4_html/chapter4.htm. Reprinted by permission of Carl D. Nocera.

with a different mean and a different SD. Note that in a fairly wide distribution, such as that shown in panel (a) of Figure A.4, each SD is fairly wide and short; in contrast, in a relatively narrow distribution, such as that shown in panel

(b), each SD is fairly narrow and tall. Thus, the proportion of each curve that falls between the mean and a given number of SDs is the same in all four of the distributions.

INFERENTIAL STATISTICS

Typically, psychologists want to do more than simply describe the data obtained from a sample. Usually we measure a sample because we are interested in some larger population that the sample is supposed to represent. Therefore, we need to estimate the likelihood that the sample represents the population in terms of the dependent variable(s) of interest in a study. For example, opinion researchers might ask a sample of 100 Canadian teenagers about their views on peer-to-peer file sharing of copyrighted materials on the Web. The point of such a study would not merely be to measure the opinions of those 100 Canadian teenagers but rather to use them to represent the larger population of some 3 million Canadian teenagers. That is, measures of the sample are used to make inferences about a larger population.

Sampling Error

Suppose you selected two random samples of Canadian teenagers and measured their opinions of peer-to-peer file

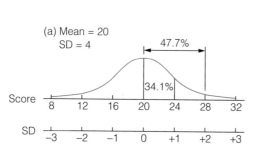

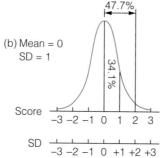

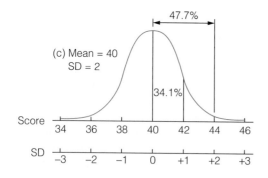

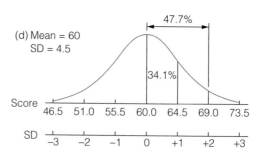

▶ **Figure A.4**

Four Normal Distributions, with Different Means and SDs, Illustrating that the Percentage of the Scores in a Normal Distribution between the Mean and a Given SD Is Always Approximately the Same

From *Statistics: Tool of the Social Sciences*, ed. 1, by M. K. Johnson and R. M. Leibert. Copyright © 1997. Reprinted and electronically reproduced by permission of Pearson Education, Inc., Upper Saddle River, NJ.

sharing. The two samples would probably not be identical in their opinions on this issue; for example, flukes of chance might lead to an overrepresentation, in one sample, of people who disapprove of file sharing, whereas by chance alone the other sample might be more representative of the population. This variation from sample to sample—or, more fundamentally, the discrepancy between any particular sample and the population from which it was drawn—is called "sampling error." That is, sampling error—random flukes of who gets selected by chance to be in the sample versus who doesn't—can lead a sample to differ from the population it is supposed to represent.

Given that proper procedures were used to select a sample (see Chapter 2, pp. 43–44), two factors determine the amount of sampling error: (1) the size of the sample (the larger the sample the smaller the sampling error) and (2) the amount of variability in the population on the dependent variable measured in the sample (the greater the variability the larger the sampling error). The size of the sample and the amount of variability on the dependent variable within the population interact with each other to determine the amount of sampling error: Sampling error is greatest when samples are small and variability is large. To return to our earlier, rather silly example, suppose you wanted to use a sample of students in your introductory psychology class to estimate the number of bellybuttons per student in the whole class. In this case, a sample of 1 would be perfectly representative because there is no variability in the population (the class) in the number of bellybuttons: Every person in the class has 1 bellybutton, so any sample will be perfectly representative of the class on this variable. More generally, if a population has only a little bit of variability on a particular measure, then even a fairly small sample is likely to be representative of that sample because all or most of the people selected to be in the sample are likely to have scores very close to the mean (because most of the population has scores very close to the mean). The greater the amount of variability in the population, the more opportunities for individuals who differ greatly from the mean to be selected as part of the sample. In other words, as the amount of variability in the population goes up, so too does sampling error. If there is a lot of variability and the sample is small, then by chance it would be easy to get a sample whose mean is very different from the true population mean.

How can we figure out how much variability there is in the population on the dependent variable we want to measure? In theory, we might find out by measuring everyone in the population, but if we did so we'd no longer be concerned about sampling error. (Who needs a sample if you've measured the whole population?)

Here's a key idea: The variability in a population on a particular dependent variable can be estimated by measuring the variability in the sample on that variable. How much variability in bellybuttons would there be in a sample of your classmates? None, and based on that we would estimate the population variability to be low. How much variability would there be in a sample of your classmates on current-events knowledge? Lots, and based on that we would estimate the population variability on that measure to be high.

Measurement Error

Measurement tools are imperfect. Even measuring something as crude and simple as weight is subject to error; scales may be affected by factors such as barometric pressure, and their accuracy tends to deteriorate with age and use. Psychological measures likewise are imperfect. For example, your instructor may give you a test of your knowledge of the material in this appendix. Your performance on the test would almost certainly correlate with your understanding of the material, but it wouldn't be a perfect index of it. Some of the questions on the test might be vague or ambiguous, or maybe the questions focused on particular parts of the appendix that you didn't understand very well, or maybe you slept so poorly the night before that you weren't able to demonstrate on the test how much you'd learned. Thus, the "reading" we get when we apply a psychological measurement is unlikely to perfectly reflect whatever it is we are seeking to measure. This difference between what we are attempting to measure and the measurement obtained is called measurement error.

Experts in research methods and statistics have developed means of assessing measurement error, and means of minimizing it. But measurement error cannot be entirely eliminated. The crucial thing is to ensure that the amount and direction of measurement error does not systematically vary with the conditions being compared in a research study. If the measurement tool is systematically (i.e., consistently, nonrandomly) biased in favour of one condition (e.g., if a math test somehow overestimates boys' math skills or underestimates girls'), then interpretation of the findings is fundamentally compromised.

Even measurement error that is essentially random (i.e., not systematically related to the conditions being compared) can distort the results of psychological research. The problem here is similar to that with random sampling error; even if there is no systematic measurement error or bias in favour of one condition, flukes of chance might lead random measurement error to favour one condition. Fortunately, statisticians have developed techniques to estimate the probability that a particular set of results would occur as a fluke of random chance. We turn next to a review of those techniques.

Inferential Statistics for Comparing Conditions

Psychologists often compare behaviour under different conditions. Sometimes this is exploratory, simply to discover whether or not different conditions lead to differences in behaviours. More often, conditions are compared with test hypotheses derived from theories. In any case, psychologists use statistics to make inferences about the results of such studies. We divide our treatment of statistics for comparing conditions into three subparts: (1) experiments comparing scores in independent groups of participants, (2) experiments comparing scores when the same subjects are tested under different conditions, and (3) nonexperimental comparisons.

Experiments Comparing Scores in Independent Conditions

Many psychological experiments compare independent groups of research participants, each in a different experimental condition, to see if they differ on a dependent variable. The conditions are "independent" in that different people are *randomly* assigned to each; thus, whether or not a particular person gets assigned to a particular condition is independent of what that condition is, what the person is like, and of who else gets assigned to that condition.

Suppose, for example, that at the beginning of the term the students in your introductory psychology class were randomly divided into two groups: Half of the students were required to sit in the front half of the lecture hall throughout the term, whereas the remaining students were required to sit in the back half. This is an experiment in which the independent variable is seating location. Suppose further that we find that the average percentage correct on the midterm exam (the dependent variable) was 86 for front-sitters and 81 for back-sitters. If all we cared about was this particular sample, measured on this particular midterm, then we could simply report the average scores (and perhaps the SDs) for each group and note that the average score was 5 points higher for front-sitters than for back-sitters.

How could the 5-point difference in average midterm scores between front- and back-sitters be explained? (For research on this subject, see Burda & Brooks, 1996.) There are many potential explanations, but for present purposes we put them into two major categories. One category of explanations has to do with causal effects of the independent variable (seat location) on test performance. It could be, for example, that sitting in the front makes it easier to hear the lecture and see the visuals the lecturer uses, or that sitting in the front makes it more difficult to chat with neighbours; hence, students who sit in the front learn more from lectures. Whatever the specific mechanism(s), the important point is that something about sitting in the front versus the back of the classroom appears to *cause* a difference in average marks on the midterm.

Another category of explanations has nothing to do with the independent variable of where people sit. It could be that the difference in midterm scores between front- and back-sitters was a mere fluke of chance. After all, if you had just randomly divided the class into two groups, called *X* and *Y*, without regard to where they sit or anything else, the two groups probably wouldn't have come out with exactly identical scores on the midterm. Just as in sampling error, flukes of chance in which people got assigned to which condition could easily lead the average score in the two groups to be nonidentical (and the smaller the samples the more likely they would be to differ by flukes of random chance alone). Similarly, flukes of measurement error could favour one condition over another, contributing to the difference between groups. In sum, maybe the difference between front- and back-sitters is just a fluke.

How could we estimate the likelihood that the 5-point difference in average midterm scores between front- and back-sitters was a fluke? One approach would be to repeat the experiment many times, with a different class each time. The more times we find a difference favouring front-sitters, the less likely that the difference is a fluke of random assignment. By their nature, flukes of chance don't happen consistently over and over. But this approach would be very time consuming and expensive. The alternative is to use inferential statistics to estimate the likelihood that a difference would occur by chance alone.

To estimate the likelihood that a difference in scores between two conditions would occur by chance alone, inferential statistic tests simultaneously take three considerations into account: how big the difference is, how large the samples are, and how much variability there is in the scores within each condition.

It is easy to see that, all else being equal, a large difference between conditions is less likely to occur by chance alone than is a small difference. For example, a small difference in mean midterm scores is quite likely to occur by chance alone when two random groups are compared, but a large difference is less likely to occur by chance alone.

The importance of sample size is also fairly easy to appreciate intuitively. As we've already mentioned, the larger the sample, the more likely that it will accurately represent the population from which it is drawn: If you randomly selected just one student to represent the population of front-sitters and another student to represent the back-sitters, it would be very likely that the two students would differ on the midterm (not because of where they sit, but just because they are two different individuals). The more people you randomly assign to the two conditions, the less likely that a mean difference between the conditions is a fluke of chance; again, by their nature flukes don't tend to happen over and over again in a consistent manner, which is what would have to happen to get a difference between large groups by chance alone.

Finally, the importance of the extent to which scores within each condition vary from one another is also intuitive: All else being equal, the greater the variability in exam scores, the greater the likelihood that flukes of random assignment could lead to average differences between the groups. As per our discussion of sampling error and bellybuttons, the less variability there is from one participant to another in whatever is being measured, the fewer opportunities there are for atypical participants to be assigned, by flukes of random chance, to one condition rather than another.

We're not going to get into the details of inferential statistical tests for comparing scores in independent conditions. For present purposes the important point is that these tests simultaneously combine measures of (1) how much the conditions differ in terms of the dependent variable (e.g., their scores on the midterm), (2) how many participants were tested, and (3) how much variability there is from one person to another within each condition. By combining these three considerations, inferential statistical tests yield an estimate of the likelihood of the difference between the two groups occurring by chance alone. If the likelihood of the difference occurring as a random fluke is estimated to be quite small (by convention, fewer than 5 times out of 100), then the difference is said to be *statistically significant* (meaning it probably didn't occur by chance alone).

It is important to grasp that the statistical significance of a difference between conditions depends on all three of these considerations—the size of the difference, the amount of variability within conditions, and sample size—not just on the size of the difference. A difference between conditions that appears to be quite large might be nonsignificant if there is a lot of variability within conditions or if sample sizes are very small. That is, with small samples or large amounts of variability from one participant to another, fairly large differences between conditions are expected to occur quite often by chance alone. Conversely, a very small difference between conditions might turn out to be statistically significant, if there is little variability within conditions or the samples are very large. Keep in mind that in the context of statistics *significant* means "unlikely to occur by chance alone"; *significant* does not necessarily mean "large" or "important."

Experiments Comparing Scores in Dependent Conditions

If an independent variable has only a small effect, and if the variability across participants on the dependent variable of interest is large, then the effect of the independent variable may not be detected when two independent groups of participants are compared (unless the sample sizes are very large). Suppose, for example, that we want to see if people with myopia gain greater visual acuity from a new kind of contact lens compared with regular contact lenses. We could take a group of people with myopia, randomly assign half of them to wear regular contacts and half to wear the new contacts, and test their visual acuity. But we might well end up with a "null" result (i.e., no statistically significant difference) even if the new lenses do lead to slightly better acuity, because there would probably be large differences in visual acuity from one participant to another within each condition. It's hard to detect a small effect of an independent variable when there's lots of within-condition variability in the dependent variable.

One way to deal with this situation would be to test large numbers of people; even if there is a lot of within-condition variability in the dependent variable and the effect of the independent variable is small, it will become statistically significant if a large enough number of people is tested. But that gets expensive and time consuming.

An alternative is to conduct a dependent-conditions experiment to test the hypothesis that the new lenses give people better visual acuity. The most popular type of dependent-conditions experiment is aptly referred to as a *repeated-measures experiment*. In a repeated-measures experiment, we would test each participant in both conditions (with regular contacts and with the new contacts). In such an experiment, it is important to *counterbalance* the order of the two conditions (i.e., half of the participants are tested first with regular and then with new contacts, whereas the others are tested first with the new contacts and then with regular ones). Counterbalancing the order of conditions eliminates the possibility that differences between the conditions are caused by improvements because of practice on the acuity test or decrements because of fatigue.

In a repeated-measures experiment, individual differences between people cannot lead to a fluke difference between the two conditions (because the same people are in both conditions). The score that is analyzed in a repeated-measures inferential test is a difference score: In this example, the difference (for each participant) between visual acuity with the new contacts and visual acuity with regular contacts. Even if the participants differ wildly from one another in acuity, and even if the size of the advantage of the new contacts is small, if there *is* a small but fairly consistent advantage then there will be a small but fairly consistent tendency for the new minus regular difference score to be greater than 0.

Repeated-measures experiments are quite powerful (i.e., they are able to detect small effects even when variability across individuals is large and samples are fairly small). Unfortunately, they cannot always be used because it is not always possible to test the same individual in different conditions. Imagine, for example, that we were interested in comparing visual acuity in myopic people treated with two different forms of laser surgery. We couldn't test each person in both conditions because once they've had one kind of surgery we cannot undo that surgery and then give them the other.

Nonexperimental Comparisons of Scores between Conditions

The two preceding sections discussed inferential statistics as they apply to experiments, in which the researcher manipulates an independent variable and measures a dependent variable while ensuring that all other factors are either held constant or allowed to vary randomly. The beauty of experiments, done properly, is that differences between conditions can only plausibly be attributed to two sources: an effect of the independent variable or flukes of random chance.

But psychologists are often interested in variables that they cannot manipulate. We may, for example, be interested in differences between men and women, or between teens and people in their twenties, or between adults who were versus those who were not abused in childhood. In these and many other cases, researchers may have hypotheses about different conditions affecting a dependent variable (e.g., a researcher might predict that women will do better than men on a test of memory for the locations of objects), but the researcher cannot test that hypothesis by randomly assigning some participants to be women and others to be men. In some cases it is impossible to manipulate the variable (e.g., age or genetic sex), in others it is impractical (e.g., wealth), in others it is unethical (e.g., torture). So psychologists go ahead and study such variables nonexperimentally, taking care to interpret their results cautiously as explained below.

For example, Tottenham, Saucier, Elias, and Gutwin (2003) compared men and women on a test of memory for the spatial location of objects. Performance was measured with an efficiency score, with more efficient task performance yielding lower scores. As predicted, on average women's performance (mean = 0.61, SD = 0.12) was more efficient than men's (mean = 0.69, SD = 0.10). The inferential statistical tests used to assess the results of nonexperimental comparisons of scores between conditions are exactly the same as those used for experimental comparisons. Such tests yield estimates of the likelihood that an observed difference would occur by chance alone. In this case the test indicated that, based on the fairly large number of people tested (62) and the relatively small amount of variability from one person to another within each group, the likelihood of a difference this large occurring by chance alone was less than 5 in 100. Thus, the result was statistically significant, meaning that it was unlikely to have occurred by chance alone.

The problem with nonexperimental comparisons like this is that it's difficult to know what it is about the groups being compared that leads to the difference. In this case, we might wonder whether there's something essential and inherent about being female that tends to lead to superior memory for object location, or rather whether something about our culture creates this gender difference. Similarly, if we compare, say, self-esteem in children whose parents split up versus stayed together, we can use inferential statistics to estimate the likelihood that such a difference would occur by chance alone, but if we find that the difference is significant, we are left with many questions about what causes the difference (e.g., maybe parents with low self-esteem are more likely to split up and maybe self-esteem is heritable). Of course, chasing down such questions is part of the fun of research.

Estimating the Strength and Statistical Significance of Relationships between Pairs of Scores or Measures

We've just finished talking about nonexperimental comparisons between groups. Now we're going to talk about assessments of the relationship between pairs of scores or measures. The two topics are virtually identical, the only difference between them being that in the former we're interested in whether qualitatively different groups (e.g., men vs. women, children vs. adults, Caucasian vs. Asian) differ in their scores on some dependent variable, whereas in the latter we're interested in whether two different scores (e.g., a measure of wealth and a measure of happiness) are related to one another. Accordingly, we need to use slightly different statistical tests when comparing groups versus when assessing pairs of scores.

As discussed in Chapter 2 (pp. 46–50), the relationship between pairs of scores or measurements can be expressed in terms of correlation, or the tendency of scores on one measure to covary with scores on another measure. For example, ▶ Figure 2.4 (p. 48) depicts data from 40 individuals, each measured in terms of their body-mass index and how much time they spend exercising. It's a negative correlation, because people who exercise a lot tend to have low BMIs, whereas those who exercise little tend to have higher BMIs. ▶ Figure A.5 presents scatter plots depicting various directions and strengths of correlation.

Chapter 2 also introduced the correlation coefficient, a value that can range from −1.0 (a perfect negative correlation) to 0 (no relationship) to +1.0 (a perfect positive correlation). We're not going to go through the details of the equation here. Briefly, the correlation coefficient measures how closely the points on a scatter plot conform to a straight line that slopes up (positive) or down (negative) from left to right. For example, if you measured the height of a group of people in inches, then measured their height in centimetres, and then made a scatter plot of those data, all the data points would fall on a straight, upward-sloping line, and the correlation would be +1.0 (assuming accurate measurements). If you also measured each person's weight and made a scatter plot of weight and height, there would still be a positive correlation (because on average, taller people tend to weigh more than shorter people), but the data points would not all perfectly conform to a straight line: The correlation coefficient would be different from 0 and it would be positive, but it would be substantially less than +1. Note that the degree of steepness of the line does not affect the size of the correlation coefficient; as long as the line is not flat (i.e., slopes either up or down) what determines the strength of the correlation is how closely points conform to that line.

We remind you that the fact that two variables are correlated does not compel the conclusion that one variable has a causal effect on the other (for review, see Chapter 2, pp. 49–50). It is also worth noting here that correlation is only good for measuring the strength of linear relationships, not curvilinear relationships. An example of a curvilinear relationship is the relationship between arousal and memory. At very low levels of arousal (e.g., when people are half asleep), memory tends to be poor (wake up!). As arousal increases from very low levels to moderate levels, memory improves, but as arousal continues to increase (e.g., toward panic), memory may begin to suffer. If you plotted memory performance across a wide range of degrees of arousal, you would therefore expect to see an inverted U-shaped function. Even if the data points conformed to that inverted U-shaped function very well, a correlation coefficient would be low, because correlation coefficients assess how closely the data fit a simple straight line (there are other statistics for measuring the strength of curvilinear relationships, but we will not discuss those here).

Another point to be made about correlation is that the sample that is measured must have a fair amount of variability

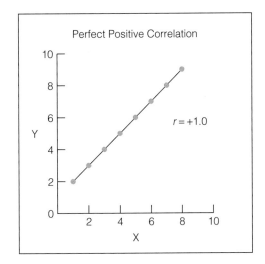

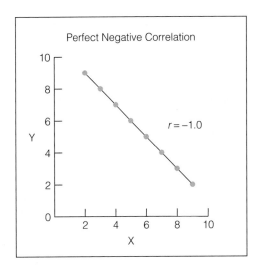

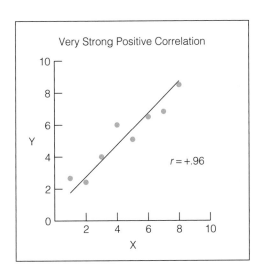

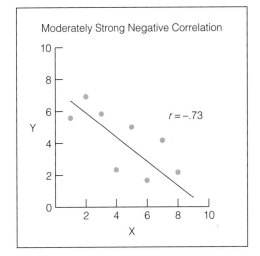

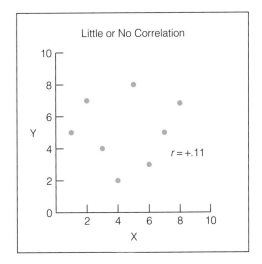

▶ **Figure A.5**

Various Directions and Degrees of Correlation

on both of the dependent variables for a correlation to be detected. For example, the correlation between performance on the Graduate Records Examination (which many graduate schools in Canada consider when deciding whether or not to admit applicants for higher degrees) and grades in graduate school is quite weak (in psychology, about $r = .15$; Chernyshenko & Ones, 1999). This isn't because ability to perform well on the GRE is very weakly related to ability to perform well in graduate school, but rather because only people with fairly good GRE scores get admitted to graduate school. For example, about 80% of applicants to graduate school in psychology are turned down; the top 20% who are admitted all have pretty high GREs (Norcross, Kohout, & Wicherski, 2005). If applicants with very low GREs were admitted, they would likely often perform poorly in graduate school and hence the correlation would be stronger. Of course, GRE scores are imperfect predictors of performance, so the correlation would never be perfect. Indeed, Chernyshenko and Ones (1999) used statistical techniques to estimate that the correlation between GRE scores and graduate school grades if everyone who took the test went to graduate school would be $r = .36$, which might be described as a moderately sized relationship. (For research on the GRE as a predictor of success in graduate school, see Kuncel et al., 2001; for a study of a small Canadian sample, see Symons, 1999.)

The final point to be made here about correlations is that the correlation coefficient measures the *strength* or consistency of the relationship between two variables, not its statistical significance. The statistical significance of a correlation between two variables is estimated by simultaneously assessing (1) the strength of the relationship as indexed by the correlation coefficient and (2) the sample size. The size of the correlation coefficient is inversely related to the amount of random variability in the relationship (e.g., if the correlation coefficient is -1.0 or $+1.0$, then there is no variability at all across participants in the relationship; as the correlation coefficient approaches 0, the amount of variability across participants in the relationship increases). Thus, the logic here is the same as in the other inferential statistical tests: Large correlations are less likely to occur as flukes of chance than are small ones, and correlations of a given size are less likely to occur as flukes of chance in larger samples than in smaller ones.

CONCLUSION

This appendix introduced many ideas, yet we have barely scratched the surface of statistics. Also, with the exception of the most elementary and foundational statistical procedures (e.g., those used to calculate SD), we have not covered the nitty-gritty of the mathematical formulas involved in performing particular statistical tests. For a more complete and comprehensive introduction to this important topic, we recommend a good text such as Pagano (2007) (or ask your instructor what text he or she recommends). Despite its brevity and rather abstract nature, we hope that this appendix has sharpened your intuitive grasp of how statistical analyses work and that it has allayed any fears you may have had about the subject.

Notes

1. To remember which of these terms is which, say "abscissa" aloud, and notice that your lips stretch horizontally; then say "ordinate" aloud, noting that your lips purse together somewhat vertically.

2. Not all score variables have normal distributions. For example, the distribution of annual income by Canadian residents is "positively skewed": Most adults in Canada have incomes between $10 000 and $100 000 per year; by definition, none have incomes less than 0, but a few make millions of dollars per year. Other distributions are non-normal in other ways (e.g., negatively skewed, bimodal). This appendix focuses on normal distributions because they are by far the most common in psychology.

3. The rationale for dividing by $N - 1$ rather than by N is beyond the scope of this appendix; very briefly, with small samples variability tends to be underestimated if the sum of squares is divided by N; dividing by $N - 1$ corrects for this problem.

4. The values given here for the percentage of scores falling in various parts of a normal distribution (e.g., 34.1% between the mean and $+1$ SD) refer to perfectly normal distributions (i.e., those in which frequency declines symmetrically as score values move above and below the mean) of a very large number of scores. They don't work out perfectly for small samples or for distributions that are not perfectly normal, but even in such cases they will be quite close.

5. Unlike the vertical bars used to represent the frequency of particular score ranges in Figures A.1 and A.2, a smooth line is used in Figure A.3 to represent the frequency of cases across the distribution; think of that smooth line as comprising a large number of points, each of which indicates the frequency of a particular score value.

Appendix B

Answers to the "Test Yourself" Boxes

CHAPTER 1

Test Yourself 1.1

1. *False.* Psychologists cannot directly observe the thoughts or feelings of other individuals, but they can and do make inferences about them based on other measures (verbal reports of what people think or feel, physiological measures that are indicative of emotions, etc.).
2. *True*
3. *False*
4. *False.* Psychiatrists are medical doctors who receive specialized training in psychology, but the psychological problems of their clients are not fundamentally different from those of psychologists. Both clinical psychologists and psychiatrists work on severe psychological problems such as schizophrenia.
5. *False.* The master's degree is a lower-level qualification than the doctoral degree; the latter is the highest level of formal training in psychology.

Test Yourself 1.2

1. *b.* Most psychologists believe that mental events arise entirely from activity in the brain.
2. Functionalists and structuralists used the technique of *introspection* to understand immediate conscious experience. The *structuralists* believed that it was best to break the mind down into basic parts, much as a chemist would seek to understand a chemical compound. The *functionalists* were influenced by Darwin's views on natural selection and focused primarily on the purpose and adaptive value of mental events. *Behaviourism,* founded by John Watson, steered psychology away from the study of immediate conscious experience toward an emphasis on *behaviour.*
3. *d.* Psychoanalysis often places a strong emphasis on hidden urges and memories related to sex and aggression.
4. Mary Salter Ainsworth was a pioneering Canadian psychologist, best known for her work (with Bowlby) on how infants develop attachments to their parents.

Test Yourself 1.3

1. *c.* Clinical psychologists who adopt an eclectic approach often consider the preferences of the client, as well as

the type of problem presented, in deciding on the most appropriate therapy.
2. Over the past several decades, psychologists have returned to the study of internal mental phenomena such as consciousness. This shift away from strict behaviourism has been labelled the *cognitive* revolution. An important factor that helped fuel this revolution was the development of the *computer,* which became a model of sorts for the human mind. Developments in *biology* are also playing an important role in shaping modern psychology and in creating effective treatments for psychological problems.
3. *b.* Our cultural background can influence how we think, reason, and remember.

CHAPTER 2

Test Yourself 2.1

1. To define a psychological variable operationally is to define it in terms of the steps or procedures that are used to *measure* that variable.
2. The *case study* technique, in which one or a few individuals are studied in depth, is open to criticism because its results may lack *external validity*; that is, the results may not generalize to or be representative of the population as a whole.
3. When behaviour changes as a result of the observation process, the study may suffer from the problem of *reactivity.*
4. The descriptive research technique used to gather information from many people is called a *survey.*

Test Yourself 2.2

1. *negative*
2. *positive*
3. *positive*
4. *zero correlation*

Test Yourself 2.3

1. In experimental research, the researcher actively manipulates the environment in order to observe its effect on behaviour. The aspect of the environment that is manipulated is called the *independent* variable; the

behaviour of interest is measured by the *dependent* variable. To draw conclusions about cause and effect, the experimenter must make certain that the *independent* variable is the only thing changing systematically in the environment.
2. *b.* The independent variable—Brad versus Barney—is not the only factor changing across the groups.
3. *c.* Random assignment increases the likelihood that subject differences will be equally represented in each group.

Test Yourself 2.4

1. The middle score in a rank-ordered set of scores is the *median.*
2. The most common value in a set of scores is the *mode.*
3. The mean is calculated by dividing the *total sum* of all of the scores by the *number* of scores.
4. It's likely that in my intro psych class, the mean number of bellybuttons per student is +1.00 and that the standard deviation is *very small* (almost certainly zero).
5. *b.* How big the difference is between the groups, how much subjects within each group differed from one another, and how many subjects were tested (see Appendix A)

Test Yourself 2.5

1. All psychologists have a responsibility to respect the rights and dignity of other people. To ensure that research participants are treated ethically, psychologists use (a) *informed consent*, which means that all potential participants are fully informed about the potential risks of the project, (b) *confidentiality*, which ensures that the subject's right to privacy will be maintained, and (c) *debriefing*, which is designed to provide participants with more information about the purpose and procedures of the research once their participation is complete.
2. *c.* Is justified but only under some circumstances
3. *c.* Animals cannot give informed consent.

CHAPTER 3

Test Yourself 3.1

1. The *soma* is the main body of the cell, where excitatory and inhibitory messages combine.
2. The *axon* is the long tail-like part of a neuron that serves as the cell's main transmitter device.
3. The *action potential* is the all-or-none electrical signal that leads to the release of chemical messengers.
4. The *dendrites* are the branch-like fibres that receive information from other neurons.
5. *Neurotransmitters.*
6. In a reflex response, *sensory* neurons carry information about a stimulus (such as intense heat) to the *spinal cord*, where they synapse on to *interneurons*, which in turn synapse with *motor* neurons that stimulate muscles to contract.

Test Yourself 3.2

1. The *hindbrain* is the primitive part of the brain that controls basic life support functions such as heart rate and respiration.
2. The *hypothalamus* is a structure thought to be involved in a variety of motivational activities, including eating, drinking, and sexual behaviour.
3. The *frontal lobes* are believed to be involved in higher-order thought processes (such as planning) as well as the initiation of motor movements.
4. The *cerebellum* is a structure near the base of the brain that is involved in coordination of complex activities such as walking.
5. An *EEG* is a device used to monitor gross electrical activity in the brain.

Test Yourself 3.3

1. *nervous system*
2. *endocrine system*
3. *endocrine system*
4. *endocrine system*
5. *nervous system*

Test Yourself 3.4

1. *natural selection*
2. *trait*
3. *recessive*
4. *mutation*
5. To the extent that a trait is inherited, *identical* twins would be expected to be more similar to one another on that trait than *fraternal* twins.
6. To qualify as an evolutionary adaptation, a trait must be *adaptive, heritable*, and *universal.*
7. *environment of evolutionary adaptedness (EEA)*

CHAPTER 4

Test Yourself 4.1

1. a. *Fovea.* The "central pit" area where most of the cone receptors are located.
   b. *Cones.* Receptors that are responsible for visual acuity, or our ability to see fine detail.
   c. *Accommodation.* Process through which the lens changes its shape temporarily in order to help focus light on the retina.
   d. *Retina.* The "film" at the back of the eye that contains the light-sensitive receptor cells.
   e. *Cornea.* The protective outer layer of the eye.
2. a. *False.* The majority of visual messages are analyzed in the lateral geniculate and primary visual cortex, although some messages are relayed to the superior colliculus.
   b. *True*
   c. *True*
   d. *True*

3. a. *Top-down processing.* The part of perception that is controlled by our beliefs and expectations about how the world is organized.
   b. *Perceptual constancy.* Perceiving an object, or its properties, to remain the same even though the physical input received by the eyes is changing.
   c. *Convergence.* The depth cue that is based on calculating the degree to which the two eyes have turned inward to focus on an object.
   d. *Recognition by components.* The view, developed by Biederman, that object perception is based on the analysis of simple building blocks, called geons.
   e. *Lower region.*

Test Yourself 4.2

1. *True*
2. *False.* Place, not frequency, theory proposes that the location of activity on the basilar membrane is a critical cue for determining pitch.
3. *False.* Hair cells are located in the cochlea, not the pinna, and they are "bent" by movement of the basilar membrane.
4. *False.* Figure-ground organization occurs in hearing as well as in vision.
5. *True*

Test Yourself 4.3

1. *b.* Our perception of temperature is based on the changes that occur from one stimulus (or environment) to another.
2. *c.* Psychological factors are thought to block pain messages from reaching higher neural centres.
3. *d.* The vestibular sacs are part of the structures of the inner ear.

Test Yourself 4.4

1. *Chemoreceptors.* The general term for receptor cells that are activated by molecules scattered about in the air or dissolved in liquids.
2. *Olfactory bulb.* One of the main brain destinations for odour stimuli.
3. *Flavour.* A psychological term used to describe the entire gustatory experience.
4. *Olfaction.* The technical name for the sense of smell.
5. *Gustation.* The technical name for the sense of taste.

Test Yourself 4.5

1. *False.* The point on the intensity curve at which an individual reliably detects a stimulus varies over time.
2. *True*
3. *False.* Detection of a JND in magnitude depends on the intensity of the standard.
4. *True*
5. *True*

CHAPTER 5

Test Yourself 5.1

1. *False.* The cocktail party effect suggests that we do at least some monitoring of unattended messages. We hear our name when it's spoken from across the room.
2. *True*
3. *True*
4. *False.* Damage to the right side of the brain, in visual neglect, means that people will fail to recognize things on the left side of the body.
5. *False.* Although some aspects of attention deficit/hyperactivity disorder may be learned, most researchers believe that some kind of neurological problem also contributes to the disorder.
6. *False*

Test Yourself 5.2

1. a. *Theta waves.* The characteristic pattern found in stage 1 sleep.
   b. *K complex.* Often triggered by loud noises during stage 2 sleep.
   c. *Delta activity.* Another name for the slow-wave patterns that are found during stage 3 and stage 4 sleep.
   d. *REM.* The characteristic pattern of paradoxical sleep.
2. *c.* Cats sleep more than cows.
3. a. *Insomnia.* Difficulty initiating and maintaining sleep.
   b. *Night terror.* Sleeper awakens suddenly, screaming, but the EEG pattern indicates a period of non-REM sleep.
   c. *Sleep apnea.* Sleeper repeatedly stops breathing during the night, usually for short periods lasting less than one minute.
   d. *Nightmare.* A frightening dream that usually occurs during the REM stage of sleep.

Test Yourself 5.3

1. *Stimulant.* Increases central nervous system activity.
2. *Opiate.* Reduces pain by mimicking the brain's own natural pain-reducing chemicals.
3. *Depressant.* Tends to produce inhibitory effects by increasing the effectiveness of the neurotransmitter GABA.
4. *Hallucinogen.* Distorts perception and may lead to flashbacks.
5. *Caffeine.* The active ingredient found in your morning cup of coffee.

Test Yourself 5.4

1. *False.* The EEG patterns of a hypnotized person more closely resemble the patterns typical of people who are awake and relaxed, not asleep.
2. *False.* Hypnosis increases the chances of fabrication and does not generally lead to better memory.
3. *True*

4. *False.* Hilgard's experiments support the idea of hypnotic dissociations.
5. *True*

CHAPTER 6

Test Yourself 6.1

1. *sensitization*
2. *orienting response*
3. *habituation*
4. *habituation*
5. *habituation*

Test Yourself 6.2

1. a. The unconditioned stimulus is the *screaming.*
   b. The unconditioned response is *wincing and covering your ears.*
   c. The conditioned stimulus is the *sound of running water.*
   d. The conditioned response is *wincing.*
2. a. The unconditioned stimulus is the *puff of air.*
   b. The unconditioned response is *blinking.*
   c. The conditioned stimulus is the *word "ready."*
   d. The conditioned response is the *urge to blink.*
3. *d. Extinction.* It's likely that the boy looked at the neighbour's yard many times after the neighbours moved, without being frightened by the now-departed dogs. So, the association was extinguished.
4. *e. Inhibitory conditioning.* Your grandmother has become a conditioned stimulus that signals to Rascal that scraps will not be forthcoming and hence inhibits his begging.

Test Yourself 6.3

1. a. *Negative punishment.* Arriving home late is punished by the removal of freedom.
   b. *Positive reinforcement.* The bonus is presented to increase the chances of similar sales behaviour again.
   c. *Positive punishment.* The ticket is delivered to lower the likelihood of speeding in a school zone.
   d. *Positive reinforcement.* Crying increases because Mom delivers a kiss and a story.
   e. *Positive punishment.* Dad delivers a stern lecture for crying, which lowers the likelihood of crying in his presence.
2. a. *Variable-ratio.* Reinforcement depends on the number of calls, but the number of calls is not constant or predictable.
   b. *Fixed-ratio.* Reinforcement always occurs when she goes to a rally.
   c. *Variable-interval.* Reinforcement cannot be predicted and depends on the passage of time rather than the number of responses.
   d. *Fixed-ratio.* Reinforcement is delivered after a fixed number of purchases.

e. *Variable-interval.* Reinforcement is not predictable and depends on the passage of time.

Test Yourself 6.4

1. *False.* Observational learning often applies to our own behaviour—we learn to act in a certain way by observing a role model.
2. *True*
3. *False.* Our beliefs about how well we can perform a task (self-efficacy) play an important role in observational learning.
4. *True*
5. *True*

CHAPTER 7

Test Yourself 7.1

1. *sensory memory*
2. *short-term memory*
3. *sensory memory*
4. *short-term memory*
5. *sensory memory*
6. *short-term memory*
7. *short-term memory*

Test Yourself 7.2

1. a. semantic
   b. episodic
   c. semantic
   d. procedural
   e. procedural
2. *c.* Form a visual image of each word.
3. a. *Method of loci.* A mnemonic device in which you visualize items sitting in locations along a well-learned path.
   b. *Distinctiveness.* The extent to which your mental representation of an event differs from your mental representations of other events.
   c. *Elaboration.* The formation of connections between an item and other things in memory.
   d. *Link-word system.* The French word for "dog," *chien,* sounds like the English word "chin," so to learn the French word you might imagine a person's face with a tiny dog sitting on the chin.
   e. *Distributed practice.* Spacing practice episodes across time, with other activities between them.
   f. *Massed practice.* Opposite of distributed practice.

Test Yourself 7.3

1. *Schema.* An organized structure of knowledge stored in long-term memory.
2. *Implicit memory.* Using memory automatically and without awareness of doing so.
3. *Transfer-appropriate processing.* Studying for a multiple-choice test by writing and answering your own multiple-choice questions.

4. *Encoding specificity principle.* The idea that retrieval cues must match the information stored in the original memory record.
5. *Flashbulb memory.* Very detailed and vivid recollection of an emotionally significant and surprising event, such as hearing the news of the September 11, 2001, attacks.
6. *Free recall.* Remembering material without the aid of any specific external retrieval cues.

Test Yourself 7.4

1. *False.* Most forgetting occurs early and is followed by more gradual loss.
2. *True*
3. *False.* Proactive interference occurs when prior learning interferes with later remembering.
4. *True.* People with anterograde amnesia can learn new things, but lose the ability to access those memories consciously (although they can still form memories, as shown by preserved performance on tests of implicit memory).
5. *True*
6. *True*

CHAPTER 8

Test Yourself 8.1

1. a. *Phonemes.* The smallest significant sound units in speech.
   b. *Pragmatics.* The term used for the practical knowledge that helps us understand the intentions of a speaker and pick an effective response.
   c. *Linguistic relativity.* The hypothesis that proposes that language determines the characteristics and content of thought.
   d. *Syntax.* The rules that govern how words are combined into sentences.
   e. *Morphemes.* The smallest units in a language that carry meaning.
2. a. *True*
   b. *False.* Babies appear to learn language rules implicitly and often produce phrases, and commit errors, that they never hear from their parents.
   c. *True*
   d. *True*
   e. *False.* Kanzi appears able to understand and follow spoken requests from this trainers.
   f. *True*

Test Yourself 8.2

1. a. *defining features*
   b. *category exemplars*
   c. *family resemblance*
   d. *prototype*
2. *b.* Basic level ("look, it's a cat").

Test Yourself 8.3

1. a. Finding your way to a restaurant is a well-defined problem, because the starting and goal states can be clearly specified, and a well-specified series of steps will take you from one state to the other.
   b. Getting an A in psychology is an ill-defined problem; you can specify what your current mark would be, and the criteria for an A are (or at least should be!) clearly defined in the syllabus, but the precise steps that would take you from the former to the latter cannot be formally specified.
   c. Making your lab partner fall madly in love with you is an ill-defined problem, because it would be difficult to precisely define how he or she currently feels and difficult to define "madly in love." It would be even more difficult to specify how to get from the former to the latter state.
   d. Baking a delicious cheesecake is an ill-defined problem, because it is unclear what constitutes "deliciousness" and room to debate how to achieve it in the cheesecake domain.
2. a. *searching for analogies*
   b. *algorithm*
   c. *means-ends analysis*
   d. *algorithm*

Test Yourself 8.4

1. *availability heuristic*
2. *confirmation bias*
3. *framing*
4. *illusory correlation*
5. *representativeness heuristic*

CHAPTER 9

Test Yourself 9.1

1. *Sternberg's intelligences.* "Street smarts" is an example of practical intelligence.
2. *Cognitive.* Intelligence is defined by the speed of mental processes.
3. *Gardner's intelligences.* Musical ability is considered to be a type of intelligence in Gardner's theory.
4. *Psychometric.* Intelligence is measured by analyzing performance on mental tests.
5. *Psychometric.* Factor analysis is a statistical technique used to analyze test performance.
6. *Gardner's intelligences.* Insight into the feelings of others is a type of intelligence in Gardner's theory.
7. *Sternberg's intelligences.* Applying what's been learned to new situations is a kind of creative intelligence.

Test Yourself 9.2

1. a. *Reliability.* Donna's performance is consistent across testing.
   b. *Validity.* Larry's new test doesn't measure what it's supposed to measure.
   c. *Reliability.* Chei-Wui is checking on the consistency of test scores.
   d. *Standardization.* Robert makes certain that the testing and scoring procedures are the same for everybody who takes the test.
2. a. *True*
   b. *False.* Average IQ, based on the deviation IQ method, is always 100 regardless of age.
   c. *False.* The diagnosis of mental retardation depends on many factors, such as one's ability to adapt.
   d. *True.* But the correlation is not very high.

Test Yourself 9.3

1. *False.* Fluid intelligence shows declines over the life span.
2. *False.* Identical twins reared apart tend to have more similar IQs than fraternal twins raised together.
3. *True*
4. *False.* Heritability tells us only that for a given group, a certain percentage of the differences in intelligence can be explained by genetic factors.
5. *True*

Test Yourself 9.4

1. *False.* No such bias exists.
2. *False.* Our perceptions show a significant degree of accuracy.
3. *False.* Entity theorists believe that intelligence is fixed.
4. *True.* Although the effects are small, there is evidence that such labels affect our expectations about people and, consequently, our behaviour toward them.
5. *True.* There are a number of such examples in the history of testing in the 20th century.

CHAPTER 10

Test Yourself 10.1

1. *False.* The period from implantation to the end of the eighth week is called the embryonic period.
2. *True*
3. *False.* The cells increase in size and complexity, not in number. The number of glial cells in the brain, however, may increase with age.
4. *False.* The timing of motor development is determined primarily by nature—the genetic code—although the environment may play some role.
5. *False.* We all lose brain cells with age, but the vast majority of people over 70 will not develop dementia.

Test Yourself 10.2

1. a. *Reward.* In the reward technique, the baby is given reinforcement when he or she performs a movement, such as kicking a leg, in response to a presented event.
   b. *Habituation.* The decline in responsiveness to repeated presentations, called habituation, can be used to infer that the baby recognizes that elements of the event have been repeated.
   c. *Cross-sectional.* In a cross-sectional design, different age groups are studied at the same time.
   d. *Longitudinal.* In a longitudinal design, the same individual is tested repeatedly across the life span.
2. *Conservation.* Conservation refers to the ability to recognize that certain physical properties of an object, such as mass, remain the same despite changes in the object's appearance.
3. a. *Conventional.* According to Kohlberg, individuals at the conventional level of moral reasoning decide the correctness of actions on the basis of whether or not the action disrupts the social order.
   b. *Postconventional.* At the postconventional level, moral reasoning is based on abstract principles that may or may not conflict with accepted standards.
   c. *Preconventional.* At the preconventional level, moral decisions are made on the basis of the action's immediate consequences.

Test Yourself 10.3

1. a. *secure*
   b. *avoidant*
   c. *resistant*
   d. *resistant*
2. *d.* Not all teenagers suffer anxiety during this period.
3. *False.* Gender identity is already being formed by age two or three.
4. a. *False.* Most elderly people are not sick and do not have disabilities, although physical problems certainly do increase with age.
   b. *False.* Some stereotypes about the elderly are positive, such as the belief that all elderly people are wise and kind.
   c. *False.* Research suggests the opposite.
   d. *False.* Research suggests that most elderly people prefer to strive to keep on living in such circumstances.

CHAPTER 11

Test Yourself 11.1

1. *c.* Instincts lead to fixed response patterns; drives do not.
2. a. *Incentive motivation.* Whitney jogs because of the reward.
   b. *Intrinsic motivation.* Celine's playing is self-motivated.

c. *Achievement motivation.* Candice studies to satisfy a need for achievement.

d. *Intrinsic motivation.* Jerome has become less motivated because of the reward.

3. *b.* Satisfying basic survival and social needs.

Test Yourself 11.2

1. *False.* A high level of glucose, or blood sugar, is associated with a decreased desire for food.
2. *False.* Binging and purging are the principal symptoms of bulimia nervosa.
3. *False.* Stimulation of the lateral hypothalamus causes an animal to start eating, not stop eating.
4. *False.* Obesity is caused by many factors, not necessarily poor dietary habits.
5. *False.* Destruction of the ventromedial hypothalamus increases hunger and leads to large weight gains.

Test Yourself 11.3

1. *True*
2. *False.* Women tend to not include condom use in their sexual scripts.
3. *True*
4. *True*

Test Yourself 11.4

1. a. Dancing is an *expressive reaction.*
   b. Grimacing and wrinkling her nose is an *expressive reaction.*
   c. A racing heart is a *body reaction.*
   d. Robert is telling us about his *subjective experience.*
2. *c.* Receiving a C when you expected to flunk is the largest change in expectation (i.e., adaptation level).
3. a. *James-Lange*
   b. *Schachter*
   c. *Cannon-Bard*
   d. *Schachter*

CHAPTER 12

Test Yourself 12.1

1. a. *openness*
   b. *extraversion*
   c. *agreeableness*
   d. *neuroticism*
   e. *conscientiousness*
2. a. *TAT*
   b. *MMPI*
   c. *NEO-PI-R*
   d. *Rorschach*
   e. *16 Personality Factor*

Test Yourself 12.2

1. *psychodynamic*
2. *cognitive-behavioural*

3. *humanistic*
4. *psychodynamic*
5. *humanistic*
6. *cognitive-behavioural*
7. *psychodynamic*

Test Yourself 12.3

1. *True*
2. *True*
3. *False.* High self-monitors tend to adapt their behaviour to the situation.
4. *False.* Genetics appear to play a significant role in personality as measured by the MMPI.
5. *False.* Personality traits may only reveal themselves if they are relevant, or needed, in the situation.

CHAPTER 13

Test Yourself 13.1

1. a. *True*
   b. *False.* Exemplar, not prototype, theories assume that we represent stereotypes with particular individuals, or exemplars.
   c. *False.* It is the belief that out-groups are opposed to traditional values that appears to be more of a concern for authoritarian individuals.
   d. *False.* The "personal/group" discrepancy refers to the fact that people tend to report discrimination against their group is high when they themselves report personally experiencing little discrimination.
2. a. *internal*
   b. *internal*
   c. *external*
   d. *internal*
3. a. *True*
   b. *False.* The central, not peripheral, route to persuasion operates when our level of involvement in or commitment to a message is high.
   c. *True*
   d. *False.* Mere exposure is most likely to lead to attitude change when we're processing a message peripherally.

Test Yourself 13.2

1. a. *conformity*
   b. *bystander effect*
   c. *social facilitation*
   d. *deindividuation*
   e. *group polarization*
   f. *Social loafing,* although conformity is also a possibility.
2. *d.* The experiment is conducted in the teacher's home.

Test Yourself 13.3

1. *True*
2. *False.* Averaged faces tend to be rated as most attractive.
3. *False.* Your ratings would go down.
4. *True*
5. *True*
6. *False.* Companionate love typically leads to more feelings of warmth and trust.
7. *True*

CHAPTER 14

Test Yourself 14.1

1. *False.* When a behaviour occurs infrequently among members of a population it meets the criterion of statistical deviance.
2. *False.* Not all people with psychological disorders are emotionally distressed.
3. *True*
4. *True*

Test Yourself 14.2

1. *somatoform disorder* (hypochondriasis or conversion disorder)
2. *anxiety disorder* (obsessive-compulsive disorder)
3. *anxiety disorder* (panic disorder, agoraphobia)
4. *mood disorder* (depressive disorder)
5. *dissociative disorder* (dissociative fugue)
6. *personality disorder* (antisocial personality disorder)
7. *schizophrenia* (paranoia)
8. *schizophrenia* (catatonia)

Test Yourself 14.3

1. *b.* excessive amounts of the neurotransmitter dopamine
2. *d.* If your identical twin has schizophrenia, you have about a 50% chance of developing the disorder yourself.
3. *d.* internal, stable, and global
4. *b.* observational learning

CHAPTER 15

Test Yourself 15.1

1. a. *schizophrenia* (clozapine)
   b. *depression* (Prozac)
   c. *depression* (ECT)
   d. *generalized anxiety disorder* (benzodiazepine)
2. *d.* ECT is used regularly to treat schizophrenia.

Test Yourself 15.2

1. *rational-emotive therapy*
2. *Beck's cognitive therapy*
3. *psychoanalysis*

4. *client-centred therapy*
5. *Gestalt therapy*
6. *family therapy*

Test Yourself 15.3

1. *b.* conditioned stimulus
2. *a.* counterconditioning and extinction
3. *b.* Effective punishments can't be delivered because pain thresholds are high.
4. *d.* reinforcement

Test Yourself 15.4

1. *True*
2. *True*
3. *False.* Many evaluation studies show that the particular form of treatment doesn't matter.
4. *False.* Some types of treatment, such as most behavioural therapies, show concern only for the present symptoms.
5. *True*

CHAPTER 16

Test Yourself 16.1

1. *c.* alarm, resistance, exhaustion
2. *c.* The experience of stress, like emotion, depends on the appraisal of the event rather than on the event itself.
3. *a.* marriage
4. *c.* an optimistic outlook

Test Yourself 16.2

1. *True*
2. *True*
3. *False.* Stress has been shown to affect cholesterol levels.
4. *False.* Most people who suffer trauma do not develop posttraumatic stress disorder.
5. *True*

Test Yourself 16.3

1. *c.* The stress response is incompatible with relaxation.
2. *a.* It gives you a feeling of control.
3. *d.* Social support makes it easier to cope if the support is no longer delivered.
4. *a.* Cognitive reappraisal.

Test Yourself 16.4

1. *False.* Aerobic exercise can lessen the physiological effects of the stress reaction.
2. *True*
3. *True*
4. *False.* Teaching children about the hazards of smoking or drugs would be classified as an example of *primary* prevention.

Glossary

abnormal behaviour An observed behaviour that is unusual, maladaptive, socially deviant, or accompanied by continuing distress

absolute threshold The level of intensity that lifts a stimulus over the threshold of conscious awareness; it's defined as the intensity level at which a person detects the presence of the stimulus 50% of the time

accommodation In vision, the process by which the lens changes shape temporarily to help focus light on the retina; also, in human development, the modification of existing schemas to accommodate new experiences when they occur

acetylcholine A neurotransmitter that plays several roles in the central and peripheral nervous systems, including the excitation of muscle contractions

achievement motivation tests Psychological tests that measure your desire to perform challenging tasks and reach difficult goals

achievement motive A need that varies in strength across individuals; its strength on any given task depends on (1) expectations about success and (2) how much value a person places on succeeding at the task

achievement tests Psychological tests that measure your current level of knowledge or competence in a particular subject

action potential The all-or-none electrical signal that travels down a neuron's axon

activation-synthesis hypothesis The idea that dreams represent the brain's attempt to make sense out of random patterns of neural activity generated during sleep

actor-observer effect The tendency to attribute others' behaviour to internal forces and our own behaviour to external forces

adoption studies The traits of children adopted at an early age are compared with those of their biological parents and siblings, with whom they share genetic material but not rearing environment

adrenal glands Glands that secrete norepinephrine and epinephrine into the bloodstream

aerobic exercise High-intensity activities, such as running and swimming, that increase both heart rate and oxygen consumption

afterimage A sensation experienced after removal of a stimulus. For example, after staring at a red maple leaf for several seconds, when you shift your focus to a blank part of the page you will see a green afterimage

aggression Behaviour meant to harm someone

agoraphobia An anxiety disorder that causes an individual to restrict his or her normal activities; someone who has agoraphobia tends to avoid public places out of fear that a panic attack will occur

AIDS Acquired immune deficiency syndrome, a disease that gradually weakens and disables the immune system

alcohol myopia A state induced by alcohol intoxication that results in more extreme social behaviours

algorithms Step-by-step rules or procedures that, if applied correctly, guarantee a problem solution eventually

alpha waves The pattern of brain activity observed in someone who is in a relaxed state, with his or her eyes closed

anal stage Freud's second stage of psychosexual development, occurring in the second year of life; pleasure is derived from the process of defecation

anorexia nervosa An eating disorder diagnosed when an otherwise healthy person refuses to maintain a normal weight level because of an intense fear of being overweight

anterograde amnesia Memory loss for events that happen after the physical injury

antianxiety drugs Medications that reduce tension and anxiety; many work on the inhibitory neurotransmitter GABA

antidepressant drugs Medications that modulate the availability or effectiveness of the neurotransmitters implicated in mood disorders; Prozac, for example, increases the action of the neurotransmitter serotonin

antipsychotic drugs Medications that reduce the positive symptoms of schizophrenia; the majority act on the neurotransmitter dopamine

antisocial personality disorder A personality disorder characterized by repeated criminal behaviour and a failure to learn from punishment

anxiety disorders A class of disorders marked by excessive apprehension and worry that in turn impairs normal functioning

applied psychologists Psychologists who apply the principles of scientific psychology to practical, everyday problems in the world

aptitude tests Psychological tests that measure your ability to learn and solve problems in a particular subject area

artificial intelligence The attempt to understand the meaning of intelligence by building intelligent machines; such machines—usually computer programs—can simulate or surpass many human capabilities

assimilation The process through which people fit—or assimilate—new experiences into existing schemas

attachments Strong emotional ties formed to one or more intimate companions

attention The internal processes people use to set and follow priorities for mental functioning

attention deficit/hyperactivity disorder A psychological condition marked by difficulties in concentrating and sustaining attention and by high levels of fidgety physical activity; occurs most often in children

attitude A positive or negative evaluation or belief held about something, which in turn may affect behaviour; are typically broken down into cognitive, affective, and behavioural components

attributions The inference processes people use to assign cause and effect to behaviour

automaticity Fast and almost effortless processing that requires little or no focused attention

autonomic system Nerves that control the more automatic needs of the body, such as heart rate, digestion, blood pressure, and so on; part of the peripheral nervous system

auto-stereotyping A belief system about discrimination that is widely shared by group members

availability heuristic The tendency to base estimates of frequency or probability on the ease with which examples come to mind; for example, if you've just heard about a plane crash, your estimate of the likelihood of plane crashes may increase because the recent plane crash easily comes to mind

aversion therapy A treatment for replacing a positive reaction to a harmful stimulus, such as alcohol, with something negative, such as feeling nauseated

axon The long tail-like part of a neuron that serves as the cell's transmitter device

basic-level categories The level in a category hierarchy that most efficiently provides a lot of useful and predictive information; the basic level is usually an intermediate level in a category hierarchy

basilar membrane A flexible membrane running through the cochlea that, through its movement, displaces the auditory receptor cells (hair cells)

behaviour Observable actions, such as moving, talking, gesturing, and so on; can also refer to the activities of cells, as measured through physiological recording devices, and to thoughts and feelings, as measured through oral and written expression

behavioural therapies Treatments designed to change behaviour through the use of established learning techniques

behaviourism A school of psychology proposing that the proper subject matter of psychology is directly observable behaviour and the situations that lead to changes in behaviour, rather than immediate conscious experience

bell curve The plot of frequencies obtained for many psychological tests; most people's scores are in the middle range, and the decline in frequencies is similar whether scores get higher or lower than the mean

Big Five The five dimensions of personality—extroversion, agreeableness, conscientiousness, neuroticism, and openness—that have been isolated through the application of factor analysis; it is widely believed that virtually all personality terms in language can be accounted for by appealing to one or more of these basic dimensions

binocular depth cues Cues for depth that depend on comparisons between the two eyes

biofeedback Specific physiological feedback that people are given about the effectiveness of their relaxation efforts

biological clocks Brain structures that schedule rhythmic variations in bodily functions by triggering them at the appropriate times

biomedical therapies Biologically based treatments, including drug therapies, shock treatments, and, very rarely, psychosurgery

bio-psycho-social perspective The idea that psychological disorders are influenced, or caused, by a combination of biological, psychological (cognitive), and social (environmental) factors

bipolar disorder A type of mood disorder in which the person experiences disordered mood shifts in two directions—from depression to a manic state

blind spot The point where the optic nerve leaves the back of the eye; the blind spot has no rods or cones

bottom-up processing Processing that is driven by the physical input contacting the sensory receptors

brightness The aspect of the visual experience that changes with light intensity; in general, as the intensity of light increases, so does its perceived brightness

bulimia nervosa An eating disorder in which the principal symptom is binge eating (consuming large quantities of food), followed by purging in which the person voluntarily vomits or uses laxatives to prevent weight gain

burnout A state of physical, emotional, and mental exhaustion created by long-term involvement in an emotionally demanding situation

bystander effect The reluctance to come to the aid of a person in need when other people are present

Cannon-Bard theory A theory of emotion that argues that body reactions and subjective experiences occur together but independently

cardinal traits Allport's term to describe personality traits that dominate an individual's life, such as a passion to serve others or to accumulate wealth

case study A descriptive research technique in which the research effort is focused on one or a few individuals who are studied in great depth

catalepsy A hypnotically induced behaviour characterized by an ability to hold one or more limbs of the body in a rigid position for long periods without tiring

category A collection of objects (people, places, or things) or events that most people in a given culture agree belong together

category exemplars Specific examples of category members that are stored in long-term memory

central nervous system The brain and the spinal cord

central traits Allport's term to describe the 5 to 10 descriptive traits that you would use to describe someone you know—friendly, trustworthy, and so on

cerebellum A hindbrain structure at the base of the brain that is involved in the coordination of complex motor skills (e.g., walking, throwing) and may contribute to the performance of other tasks as well

cerebral cortex The outer layer of the brain, considered to be the seat of higher mental processes

chemoreceptors Receptor cells that react to molecules in the air or dissolved in liquids, leading to the senses of smell and taste

chunking A short-term memory strategy that involves mentally rearranging many pieces of information into a familiar and meaningful pattern; a single chunk can represent a wealth of information

circadian rhythms Biological activities that rise and fall in a 24-hour cycle

classical conditioning A set of procedures, initially developed by Pavlov, used to investigate how organisms learn about the signalling properties of events; leads to the learning of relations between events—conditioned and unconditioned stimuli—that occur outside of our control

client-centred therapy A form of humanistic therapy, developed by Carl Rogers, proposing that it is the client, not the therapist, who holds the key to psychological health and happiness; therapist's role is to provide genuineness, unconditional positive regard, and empathy

clinical psychologists Professional psychologists who specialize in the diagnosis and treatment of psychological problems

cochlea The snail shell–shaped sound processor in the inner ear, where sounds are transduced into nerve impulses

cocktail party effect The ability to focus on one auditory message, such as a friend's voice at a noisy party, and largely ignore others, yet notice when your own name is spoken among the auditory stimuli that you have been ignoring

cognitive appraisal The idea that to feel stress you need to perceive a threat and come to the conclusion that you may not have adequate resources to deal with the threat

cognitive dissonance The tension produced when people act in a way that is inconsistent with their attitudes; attitude change may occur as a result of attempting to reduce cognitive dissonance

cognitive revolution The shift away from strict behaviourism, begun in the 1950s, characterized by renewed interest in the study of consciousness and internal mental processes

cognitive therapies Treatments designed to remove irrational beliefs and negative thoughts that are presumed to be responsible for psychological disorders

cognitive-behavioural theories An approach to personality that suggests it is reward-punishment experiences, and interpretations of those experiences, that determine personality growth and development

cold fibres Neurons that respond to a cooling of the skin by increasing the production of neural impulses

collective unconscious The notion proposed by Carl Jung that certain kinds of universal symbols and ideas are present in the unconscious of all people

companionate love A kind of emotional attachment characterized by feelings of trust and companionship; marked by a combination of intimacy and commitment, but passion may be lacking

computerized tomography scan (CT scan) The use of highly focused beams of X-rays to construct detailed anatomical maps of the living brain

concrete operational period Piaget's third stage of cognitive development, lasting from age 7 to age 11; children acquire the capacity to perform a number of mental operations but still lack the ability for abstract reasoning

conditioned inhibition Learning to associate a previously neutral stimulus with the absence of an unconditioned stimulus

conditioned reinforcer A stimulus that has acquired reinforcing properties through prior learning

conditioned response (CR) The acquired response that is produced to the conditioned stimulus in anticipation of the arrival of the unconditioned stimulus; often resembles the unconditioned response, although not always

conditioned stimulus (CS) A neutral stimulus (one that does not produce the unconditioned response before training) that is paired with the unconditioned stimulus during classical conditioning and thereby comes to give rise to conditioned response

conditions of worth The expectations or standards that we believe others place on us

cones Receptor cells in the central portion of the retina that transduce light energy into neural activity; they operate best when light levels are fairly high, and they are primarily responsible for the ability to sense fine detail and colour

confidentiality The principle that all personal information obtained from a participant in research or therapy should not be revealed without the individual's permission

confirmation bias The tendency to emphasize hypothesis-confirming evidence when making decisions

conformity The tendency to go along with the wishes of the group; when people conform, their opinions, feelings, and behaviours generally start to move toward the group norm

confounding variable An uncontrolled variable that changes along with the independent variable

conscious mind The contents of awareness—those things that occupy the focus of your current attention

consciousness The subjective awareness of internal and external events

conservation The ability to recognize that the physical properties of an object remain the same despite superficial changes in the object's appearance

conventional level In Kohlberg's theory of moral development, the stage in which actions are judged to be right or wrong based on whether they maintain or disrupt the social order

convergence A binocular cue for depth that is based on the extent to which the two eyes move inward, or converge, when looking at an object

conversion disorder The presence of real physical problems, such as blindness or paralysis, that seem to have no identifiable physical cause

coping Efforts to manage or master conditions of threat or demand that tax resources

cornea The transparent and protective outer covering of the eye

corpus callosum The collection of nerve fibres that connect the two cerebral hemispheres and allow information to pass from one side to the other

correlation coefficient A statistic that indicates whether two variables are related or vary together in a systematic way; correlation coefficients vary from $+1.00$ (perfect positive relationship) to 0.00 (no relationship) to -1.00 (perfect negative relationship)

counselling psychologists Professional psychologists who deal with milder problems, such as family and personal adjustment issues

counsellor An individual who provides some sort of therapy or support to clients but who (typically) does not have advanced training in providing psychological treatment; some counsellors (or therapists) are skilled and effective, but others are not

creativity The ability to generate ideas that are original, novel, and useful

cross-sectional design A research design in which people of different ages are compared at the same time

crystallized intelligence The knowledge and abilities acquired as a result of experience (as from schooling and cultural influences)

cued recall A testing condition in which subjects are given specific retrieval cues to help them remember: subjects might be given hints or cues, such as "some of the words were fruits; others were vegetables"

cue-dependent forgetting The idea that forgetting is caused by a failure to retrieve memories because of a lack of appropriate retrieval cues

cultural deviance criterion Behaviour is abnormal if it violates the rules or accepted standards of society

culture The shared values, customs, and beliefs that are characteristic of a group or community

culture-fair test Tests that avoid the use of language (e.g., by using only pictures or symbols) so that the test is fair to all cultures

dark adaptation The process through which the eyes adjust to dim light

debriefing At the conclusion of an experimental session, informing the participants about the purpose of the experiment, including any deception that was involved

decay The proposal that memories are forgotten or lost spontaneously with the passage of time (or with some passive chemical processes that occur over time, akin to rusting)

decision making The thought processes involved in evaluating and choosing from among a set of alternatives; it usually involves some degree of risk

deep structure The underlying representation of meaning in a sentence

defence mechanisms According to Freud, unconscious processes used by the ego to ward off the anxiety that comes from conflicts between the superego and the id

defining features A set of features that define membership in a category, such that all members of that category (and no non-members of that category) have all those features; for example, the defining features of the category *triangle* might be (1) a two-dimensional figure that is (2) composed of three straight lines with (3) each end of each line joined to an end of one of the other lines

deindividuation The loss of individuality, or depersonalization, that comes from being in a group

delta activity The pattern of brain activity observed in stage 3 and stage 4 sleep; it's characterized by synchronized slow waves (also called *slow-wave* patterns)

dementia Physically based losses in mental functioning

dendrites The branchlike fibres that extend outward from a neuron and receive information from other neurons

denial A defence mechanism involving the refusal to accept an external reality that creates anxiety

dependent personality disorder A personality disorder characterized by an excessive and persistent need to be taken care of by others

dependent variable The behaviour that is measured in an experiment

depressants A class of drugs that slow or depress the ongoing activity of the central nervous system

descriptive research The methods used to measure and describe aspects of behaviour and experience

descriptive statistics Mathematical techniques that help researchers describe and summarize their data

development The age-related physical, intellectual, social, and personal changes that occur throughout an individual's lifetime

deviation IQ An intelligence score that is derived from determining where your performance sits in an age-based distribution of test scores

dichotic listening A technique in which two different auditory messages are presented simultaneously, one to each ear; usually the subject's task is to shadow, or repeat aloud, one message while ignoring the other

difference threshold The smallest difference in the magnitude of two stimuli that an observer can reliably detect

diffusion of responsibility The idea that when people know, or think, that others are present in a situation, they allow their sense of responsibility for action to diffuse, or spread out widely, among those who are present

discrimination Behaving in an unfair way toward members of another group

discriminative stimulus The stimulus situation that sets the occasion for a response to be followed by reinforcement or punishment

dissociative amnesia A psychological disorder characterized by an inability to remember important personal information

dissociative disorders A class of disorders characterized by the separation, or dissociation, of conscious awareness from previous thoughts or memories

dissociative fugue A loss of personal identity that is often accompanied by a flight from home

dissociative identity disorder A condition in which an individual alternates between what appear to be two or more distinct identities or personalities (also known as *multiple personality disorder*)

distinctiveness A term used to refer to how unique or different a memory record is, compared with other information in memory; distinctive memory records tend to be recalled well

distributed practice Spacing the repetitions of to-be-remembered information over time

dominant versus recessive genes Many traits have two genes: one dominant and the other recessive; if the two such genes for a given trait differ, the dominant gene controls the observable characteristic

dopamine A neurotransmitter that often leads to inhibitory effects; decreased levels have been linked to Parkinson's disease, and increased levels have been linked to schizophrenia; dopamine also plays an important role in the neurological mechanisms of reward

double-blind study An experimental design in which neither the participants nor the research observers are aware of who has been assigned to the experimental and control groups; it's used to control for both subject and experimenter expectancies

dream analysis A technique used in psychoanalysis; Freud believed that dreams are symbolic and contain important information about the unconscious

drug dependency A condition in which an individual experiences a physical or psychological need for continued use of a drug

DSM-IV The *Diagnostic and Statistical Manual of Mental Disorders* (4th ed.), which is used for the diagnosis and classification of psychological disorders; comprises five major rating dimensions, called *axes*

dysfunction criterion Behaviour is abnormal if it interferes with the ability to pursue daily activities, such as work and relationships

eclectic approach The position adopted by many psychologists that it's useful to integrate information from several sources; we need not rely exclusively on any single theoretical perspective

ego In Freud's theory, the portion of personality that induces people to act with reason and deliberation and helps them conform to the requirements of the external world

egocentrism The tendency to see the world from your own unique perspective only; a characteristic of thinking in the preoperational period of development

elaboration An encoding process that involves the formation of connections between to-be-remembered input and other information in memory

electroconvulsive therapy (ECT) A treatment used primarily for depression in which a brief electric current is delivered to the brain

electroencephalograph (EEG) A device used to monitor the electrical activity of the brain by measuring tiny changes in the electrical fields on the scalp

embryonic period The period of prenatal development lasting from implantation to the end of the eighth week; during this period, the human develops from an unrecognizable mass of cells to a somewhat familiar creature

emotion A psychological event involving (1) a physiological reaction, usually arousal, (2) some kind of expressive reaction, such as a distinctive facial expression, and (3) some kind of subjective experience, such as the conscious feeling of being happy or sad

emotional distress criterion Behaviour is abnormal if it regularly leads to personal distress or emotional upset

emotional intelligence The ability to perceive, understand, and express emotion in ways that are useful and adaptive

empirically supported treatments Treatments or therapies that have been shown, based on extensive and well-validated research, to be effective in treating specific psychological disorders and problems

empiricism The idea that knowledge comes directly from experience

encoding The processes that control the acquisition of information into memory

encoding specificity principle The idea that the effectiveness of retrieval cues depends on the extent to which they match the specifics of the to-be-remembered material; the more similar the cue and the testing situation to the to-be-remembered material and the studying situation, the more likely the memories will be accessed

endocrine system A network of glands that uses the bloodstream to send chemical messages that regulate growth and other internal functions

endorphins Morphine-like chemicals that act as the brain's natural painkillers

entity theorists People who see intelligence as fixed, a permanent quality that people are born with

environment of evolutionary adaptedness (EEA) The environment, or environments, in which a species' evolutionary adaptations were selected

environmental psychology A specialty area in psychology devoted to the study of environmental effects, such as crowding or noise, on behaviour and health

episodic memory Remembering a particular past event or episode that happened to you personally, such as recalling having breakfast this morning or recollecting your high-school graduation ceremony

event-related potentials (ERP) EEG patterns observed shortly after presentation of a stimulus

evolutionary adaptation A heritable trait that provided an organism with an advantage in surviving or reproducing during its evolutionary history

evolutionary psychology The study of the human mind and behavioural processes as products of natural selection

experimental method A technique in which the investigator actively manipulates or alters some aspect of the environment independently of other variables and observes the effect of the manipulation on behaviour

explicit memory Deliberate uses of memory with conscious awareness of remembering

external attribution Attributing the cause of a person's behaviour to an external event or situation in the environment

external validity The extent to which the results of an observation generalize to other situations or are representative of real life

extinction Presenting a conditioned stimulus repeatedly, after conditioning, without the unconditioned stimulus, resulting in a gradual loss of the conditioned response

facial-feedback hypothesis The proposal that muscles in the face deliver signals to the brain that are then interpreted, depending on the pattern, as a subjective emotional state

factor analysis A statistical procedure developed by Charles Spearman that determines how many subsets of highly correlated items are in a larger test; each subset is called a common factor, useful for summarizing the subset under a single name

family resemblance The idea that categories are defined by a set of characteristic features, which category members share in varying degrees; each member of the category will have some but not necessarily all of these features

family studies The study of similarities and differences between biological (blood) relatives to help discover the role heredity plays in physical or psychological traits; rarely provide conclusive evidence because genes and the environment are usually entangled

family therapy A form of group therapy in which the therapist treats the family as a whole, as a kind of social system; the goals of the treatment are often to improve interpersonal communication and collaboration

feature detectors Cells in the visual cortex that respond to very specific visual events, such as bars of light at particular orientations

fetal period The period of prenatal development lasting from the ninth week until birth, during which the fetus develops functioning organ systems, and increases are seen in body size and in the size and complexity of brain tissue

fixed-interval schedule A schedule in which the reinforcement is delivered for the first response that occurs following a fixed interval of time

fixed-ratio schedule A schedule in which the number of responses required for reinforcement is fixed and does not change from trial to trial

flashbulb memory Highly detailed and vivid recollections of the circumstances under which one first learned of an emotionally significant and surprising event

flavour A psychological term used to describe the overall gustatory (eating) experience; flavour is influenced by taste, smell, the visual appearance of food, and expectations about the food's quality

fluid intelligence The natural ability to solve problems, reason, and remember; fluid intelligence is thought to be relatively uninfluenced by experience

forebrain The outer portion of the brain, including the cerebral cortex and the structures of the limbic system

forgetting The loss in accessibility of previously accessible memory information

formal operational period Piaget's last stage of cognitive development; thought processes become adult-like, and people gain mastery over abstract thinking

fovea The "central pit" area in the centre portion of the retina where most of the cone receptors are located

framing The way the alternatives in a decision-making situation are structured and described

free association A technique used in psychoanalysis to explore the contents of the unconscious; patients are asked to relax and freely express whatever thoughts and feelings happen to come into their minds

free recall A testing condition in which a person is asked to remember information without specific retrieval cues: subjects might simply be asked to "recall the words you studied a few minutes ago"

frequency theory The idea that pitch perception is determined partly by the *frequency* of neural impulses travelling up the auditory pathway

frontal lobes One of four anatomical regions of each hemisphere of the cerebral cortex, located on the top front of the brain; contain the motor cortex and are involved in initiating higher-level thought processes

functional fixedness The tendency to see objects, and their functions, in certain fixed and typical ways, and thereby to fail to see alternative uses of objects that would enable us to solve a problem

functionalism An early school of psychology; functionalists believe that the proper way to understand mind and behaviour is to analyze their function and purpose; you can only truly understand a mental process, functionalists argue, by first knowing the purpose of that process

fundamental attribution error The fact that causal attributions tend to overestimate the influence of internal personal factors and underestimate the role of situational factors

g (general intelligence) factor The large underlying factor that contributes to performance on a variety of ability tests

gamma-amino-butyric acid (GABA) A neurotransmitter that may play a role in the regulation of anxiety; it generally produces inhibitory effects

gate-control theory The idea that neural impulses generated by pain receptors can be blocked, or gated, in the spinal cord by signals produced in the brain

gender roles Specific patterns of behaviour that are consistent with how society dictates males and females should act

gender schemas The organized sets of beliefs and perceptions held about men and women

general adaptation syndrome (GAS) Hans Selye's model of stress as a general, nonspecific reaction that occurs in three phases: alarm reaction, resistance, and exhaustion

generalized anxiety disorder Excessive worrying, or freefloating anxiety, that lasts for at least six months and cannot be attributed to any single identifiable source

genes Segments of chromosomes that contain chemically coded instructions for creating particular hereditary characteristics

genital stage Freud's final stage of psychosexual development, during which a person develops mature sexual relationships with members of the opposite sex

genotype The genetic information inherited from parents

germinal period The period in prenatal development from conception to implantation of the fertilized egg in the wall of the uterus

Gestalt principles of organization The organizing principles of perception proposed by the Gestalt psychologists, which are the laws of proximity, similarity, closure, continuation, and common fate

gifted A label commonly assigned to someone who scores above 130 on a standard IQ test

glial cells Cells in the nervous system that are not neurons and hence do not transmit or receive information but perform a variety of functions, such as removing waste, filling empty space, and helping neurons to communicate efficiently

glucose A kind of sugar that cells require for energy production

grammar The rules or procedures of language that allow the communicator to combine arbitrary symbols in an infinite number of ways to convey meaning; includes the rules of phonology, syntax, and semantics

group polarization The tendency for a group's dominant point of view to become stronger and more extreme with time

group therapy A form of therapy in which several people are treated simultaneously in the same setting

groupthink The tendency for members of a group to become so interested in seeking a consensus of opinion that they start to ignore and even suppress dissenting views

gustation The sense of taste

habituation The decline in responsiveness to repeated stimulation; habituation has been used to investigate the perceptual capabilities of infants

hallucinogens A class of drugs that tend to disrupt normal mental and emotional functioning and produce distorted perceptions

hardy personality The set of traits, attitudes, and skills that make an individual less vulnerable to stress

health psychology The study of how biological, psychological, environmental, and cultural factors are involved in physical health and the prevention of illness

heritability A mathematical index that represents the extent to which IQ differences in a particular population can be accounted for by genetic factors

heuristics The rules of thumb we often use to solve problems; are quick and easy but do not guarantee a correct solution

hindbrain A primitive part of the brain that sits at the juncture where the brain and spinal cord merge; structures in the hindbrain, including the medulla, pons, and reticular formation, control the basic life-support systems of the body

homeostasis The process through which the body maintains a steady state, such as a constant internal temperature or an adequate amount of fluids

hormones Chemicals released into the blood by the various endocrine glands to help control a variety of internal regulatory functions

hue The dimension of light that produces colour; hue is typically determined by the wavelength of light reflecting from an object

humanistic psychology An approach to personality that focuses on people's unique capacity for choice, responsibility, and growth

humanistic therapy Treatments designed to help clients gain insight into their fundamental self-worth and value as human beings; therapy is a process of discovering our own unique potential

hypersomnia A chronic condition marked by excessive sleepiness

hypnosis A social interaction between a person perceived to be a hypnotist and a person who perceives himself or herself to be a hypnotic subject; the interaction produces a heightened state of suggestibility in the subject

hypnotic dissociation A hypothesized, hypnotically induced splitting of consciousness during which two streams of awareness are said to coexist: one that is fully under the sway of the hypnotist's suggestions and one that remains more aloof and objective

hypnotic hypermnesia The supposed enhancement of memory that is said to occur under hypnosis; little evidence supports the existence of this effect

hypochondriasis A long-lasting preoccupation with the idea that one has developed a serious disease, based on what turns out to be a misinterpretation of normal body reactions

hypothalamus A forebrain structure thought to play a role in the regulation of various motivational activities, including eating, drinking, and sexual behaviour

iconic memory The system that produces and stores visual sensory memories

id In Freud's theory, the portion of personality that is governed by inborn instinctual drives, particularly those related to sex and aggression

ill-defined problem A problem, such as "becoming a better person," for which the starting point and goal cannot be clearly specified

illusory correlation Perception of a relationship between variables (e.g., handwriting and personality) that does not really exist

implicit memory Use of memory that occurs automatically and without conscious awareness of remembering

incentive motivation External factors in the environment—such as money, an attractive person, or tasty food—that exert pulling effects on people's actions

incongruence A discrepancy between the image we hold of ourselves—our self-concept—and the sum of all our experiences

incremental theorists People who see intelligence as malleable and something that people gradually acquire through hard work

independent variable The aspect of the environment that is manipulated by the researcher in an experiment; the manipulation must consist of at least two conditions

inferential statistics Mathematical techniques that help researchers estimate the likelihood that recorded behaviours are representative of a population or the likelihood that differences or relationships between observations are due to chance

informed consent The principle that before consenting to participate in research, people must be fully informed of any significant factors that might affect their willingness to participate

ingratiation The attempt to get someone to like you for some ulterior motive

in-group A group that you belong to or identify with

insanity A legal term used in the United States usually defined as the inability to understand that certain actions are wrong, in a legal or moral sense, at the time of a crime

insight therapies Treatments designed to give clients self-knowledge, or insight, into their psychological problems, usually through one-on-one interactions with a therapist

insomnia A chronic condition marked by difficulties in initiating or maintaining sleep, lasting for a period of at least one month

instincts Unlearned characteristic patterns of responding that are controlled by specific triggering stimuli in the world; not thought to be an important factor in explaining goal-directed behaviour in humans

instrumental or operant conditioning A procedure for studying how organisms learn about the consequences of their own voluntary actions: their behaviours are instrumental in producing rewards and punishments

insulin A hormone released by the pancreas that helps pump nutrients in the blood into the cells, where they can be stored as fat or metabolized into needed energy

intelligence An internal capacity hypothesized to explain people's ability to solve problems, learn new material, and adapt to new situations; the strength of this capacity appears to differ across individuals

intelligence prototype The list of characteristics that each person believes are present in the perfectly intelligent person

intelligence tests Tests that evaluate your overall cognitive ability to learn and solve problems

internal attribution Attributing the cause of a person's behaviour to an internal personality characteristic

internal validity The extent to which an experimenter has effectively controlled for confounding variables; internally valid experiments allow for the determination of causality

interneurons Neurons that make no direct contact with the external world but rather convey information from one neuron to another

intrinsic motivation Goal-directed behaviour that seems to be entirely self-motivated

IQ (intelligence quotient) A single number calculated to represent a person's intelligence; originally, mental age divided by chronological age and then multiplied by 100; more recently, defined in terms of deviation from the average score on an IQ test

iris The ring of coloured tissue surrounding the pupil; if you have brown eyes, your irises are (mostly) brown

James-Lange theory A theory of emotion that argues that body reactions precede and drive the subjective experience of emotions

kinesthesia In perception, the ability to sense the position and movement of one's body parts

latency period Freud's period of psychosexual development, from age five to puberty, during which the child's sexual feelings are largely suppressed

latent content According to Freud, the true psychological meaning of objects and events in dreams, which are said to represent hidden wishes and desires that are too disturbing to be confronted directly

lateral hypothalamus A portion of the hypothalamus that, when lesioned, causes an animal to be reluctant to eat; probably plays some role in eating behaviour, but the precise role is unknown

lateralization Asymmetry in the functions of the right and left hemispheres of the cerebral cortex (e.g., in most individuals, most language skills are lateralized to the left hemisphere)

law of effect If a response in a particular situation is followed by a satisfying or pleasant consequence, the response will be strengthened; if a response in a particular situation is followed by an unsatisfying or unpleasant consequence, the response will be weakened

learned helplessness A general sense of helplessness that is acquired when people repeatedly fail in their attempts to control their environment; learned helplessness may play a role in depression

learning A relatively permanent change in behaviour, or potential to respond, that results from experience

lens The flexible, transparent disk of tissue that helps focus light toward the back of the eye

leptin A hormone that may regulate the amount of energy stored in fat cells

light The small portion of the electromagnetic spectrum that is processed by the visual system; light is typically classified in terms of *wavelength* (the physical distance from one energy cycle to the next) and *intensity* (the amount of light falling on an object)

limbic system A system of structures thought to be involved in motivational and emotional behaviours (the amygdala) and memory (the hippocampus)

linguistic relativity hypothesis The proposal that language determines the characteristics and content of thought

link-word system A mnemonic device for remembering foreign language vocabulary in which you (1) think of an English word that sounds similar to the to-be-learned foreign word and (2) form a visual image connecting the meaning of the to-be-remembered word with the similar-sounding English word

locus of control The amount of control that a person feels he or she has over the environment

longitudinal design A research design in which the same people are studied or tested repeatedly over time

long-term memory The system used to maintain information for extended periods, from several seconds to a lifetime

loudness The psychological experience that results from the auditory processing of a particular *amplitude* of sound

lower region Bias to perceive the lower part of a visual scene as the "figure" (meaningful object of perception) rather than "ground" (background)

lymphocytes Specialized white blood cells that have the job of attacking foreign substances, such as viruses and bacteria

magnetic resonance imaging (MRI) A device that uses magnetic fields and radio-wave pulses to construct detailed, three-dimensional images of the brain

major depressive episode A type of mood disorder characterized by depressed mood and other symptoms

manic state A disordered state in which the person becomes hyperactive, talkative, and has a decreased need for sleep; a person in a manic state may engage in activities that are self-destructive or dangerous

manifest content According to Freud, the objects and events experienced in a dream

massed practice Clustering repetitions of to-be-remembered information close together in time

mean The arithmetic average of a set of scores, obtained by dividing the sum of all scores by the number of scores

means-ends analysis A problem-solving heuristic that involves devising actions, or means, that reduce the distance between the current starting point and the desired end (the goal)

median The middle point in an ordered set of scores; half the scores fall below the median score and half fall above the median score

medical model The view that abnormal behaviour is symptomatic of an underlying "disease" that can be "cured" with the appropriate therapy

meditation A technique for self-induced manipulation of awareness, often used for relaxation and self-reflection

memory The capacity to preserve and recover information

memory span The largest number of items that can reliably be recalled from short-term memory in their proper presentation order

menopause The time during which a woman's menstrual cycle slows down and finally stops

mental age The chronological age that best fits a child's level of performance on a test of mental ability; typically calculated by comparing a child's test score with the average scores for different age groups

mental retardation A label commonly assigned to someone who scores below 70 on a standard IQ test; other factors, such as the ability to adapt to the environment, are also considered before putting someone in this category

mental sets Well-established habits of perception and thought used to solve problems; typically efficient and effective, but sometimes make problem solving more difficult

meta-analysis A statistical technique used to summarize findings across all available studies; comparisons are based on some common evaluation index, such as the numerical difference between the success rate of the treatment and control conditions

meta-stereotyping A person's beliefs regarding the stereotype that out-group members hold about his or her own group

method of loci A mnemonic device in which you first memorize a series of locations along a familiar real-world pathway, such as the route from your residence to the university, and then form visual images of the to-be-remembered items sitting in the various locations along that pathway; to recall the items, you mentally traverse the pathway, checking each location as a retrieval cue

midbrain The middle portion of the brain, containing such structures as the tectum, superior colliculus, and inferior colliculus; midbrain structures serve as neural relay stations and may help coordinate reactions to sensory events

middle ear The portion of the ear between the eardrum and the cochlea containing three small bones (the malleus, incus, and stapes) that intensify and prepare the sound vibrations for passage into the inner ear

mind The contents and processes of subjective experience: sensations, thoughts, and emotions

Minnesota Multiphasic Personality Inventory (MMPI) A widely used self-report inventory for assessing personality traits and for diagnosing psychological problems

mnemonic devices Special mental tricks that help people think about material in ways that improve later memory; most use visual imagery and elaboration during encoding and a systematic strategy for searching memory during retrieval

mode The most frequently occurring score in a set of scores

monocular depth cues Cues for depth for which input from one eye is sufficient

mood disorders Prolonged and disabling disruptions in emotional state

morality The ability to distinguish between appropriate and inappropriate actions; a child's sense of morality may be tied to his or her level of cognitive development

morphemes The smallest units in a language that carry meaning (words, prefixes, suffixes)

motivation The set of factors that initiate and direct behaviour, usually toward some goal

motor neurons Neurons that carry information away from the central nervous system to the muscles and glands that directly produce behavioural responses

multiple intelligences The notion proposed by Howard Gardner that people possess a set of separate and independent "intelligences" ranging from musical to linguistic to interpersonal abilities

mutation Error in the process by which chromosomes are copied that changes the genotype specified by those chromosomes

myelin sheath An insulating material that protects the axons of some neurons and helps to speed up neural transmission

nativism The idea that certain kinds of knowledge and ideas are innate, or present at birth; innate ideas do not need to be learned

natural selection The differential production and survival of offspring by species members with advantageous traits

naturalistic observation A research technique that involves recording only naturally occurring behaviour, as opposed to behaviour produced in the laboratory

need hierarchy The idea popularized by Maslow that human needs are prioritized in a hierarchy; some needs, especially physiological ones, must be satisfied before others, such as the need for achievement or self-actualization, can be pursued

negative punishment An event that, when *removed* after a response, lowers the likelihood of that response occurring again

negative reinforcement An event that, when *removed* after a response in a situation, increases the likelihood of that response occurring in that situation again

NEO-PI-R A self-report inventory developed to measure the Big Five personality dimensions

nerves Bundles of axons that make up neural "transmission cables"

neural plasticity Ability of neurons to alter synaptic connections during learning and during recovery from brain injury

neurons The cells in the nervous system that receive, integrate, and transmit information by generating an electrochemical signal; neurons are the basic building blocks of the nervous system

neuroscience An interdisciplinary field of study directed at understanding the brain and its relation to experience and behaviour

neurotransmitters Chemical messengers that relay information from one neuron to the next; they are released from the terminal buttons into the synapse, where they interact chemically with the cell membrane of the next neuron; the result is either an excitatory or an inhibitory influence on the recipient neuron

night terrors A condition in which the sleeper, usually a child, awakens suddenly in an extreme state of panic

nightmares Frightening dreams that occur primarily during the REM stage of sleep

nodes of Ranvier Spaces separating the segments of the myelin covering of the neuron; they help speed the nerve impulse along the axon

norepinephrine and epinephrine Hormones that cause a surge of energy that increases the heart rate, directing blood to areas that require it (and away from the stomach and intestine) and making glucose available to the muscles

obedience The form of compliance that occurs when people respond to the orders of an authority figure

obesity A weight problem characterized by excessive body fat

object permanence The ability to recognize that objects still exist when they're no longer in sight

objective test A test that is scored in a standardized fashion so that anyone calculating the result gets the same answer

observational learning, social learning, or modelling Learning that occurs as a result of observing the experiences of others

obsessive-compulsive disorder An anxiety disorder that manifests itself through persistent and uncontrollable thoughts, called *obsessions*, or by the compelling need to perform repetitive acts, called *compulsions*

occipital lobes One of four anatomical regions of each hemisphere of the cerebral cortex, located at the back of the brain; visual processing is controlled here

olfaction The sense of smell

operational definition A definition that defines a concept in terms of the steps and procedures used to measure that concept

opiates A class of drugs that reduce anxiety, lower sensitivity to pain, and elevate mood; opiates often act to depress nervous system activity

opponent process theory A theory of colour vision proposing that certain cells in the visual pathway increase their activation levels to one colour and decrease their activation levels to another colour (e.g., increasing to red and decreasing to green)

oral stage The first stage in Freud's conception of psychosexual development, occurring in the first year of life; in this stage, pleasure is derived primarily from sucking and placing things in the mouth

organic amnesia Forgetting that is caused by physical problems in the brain, such as those induced by injury or disease

orienting response An inborn tendency to shift our focus of attention toward a novel or surprising event

out-group A group of individuals that you do not belong to or identify with

pain An adaptive response by the body to any stimulus that is intense enough to cause tissue damage

panic disorder A condition marked by recurrent discrete episodes or attacks of extremely intense fear or dread

parallel processing Processing that occurs in many different brain regions at the same time, in parallel

paranoid personality disorder A personality disorder characterized by pervasive distrust of others

parasympathetic system The division of the autonomic nervous system that helps the body calm down

parietal lobes One of four anatomical regions of each hemisphere of the cerebral cortex, located roughly on the top middle portion of the brain; contain the somatosensory cortex, which controls the sense of touch

partial reinforcement schedule A schedule in which reinforcement is delivered only some of the time after the response has occurred

passionate love An intense emotional state characterized by a powerful longing to be with a specific person; marked by a combination of intimacy and passion, but commitment may be lacking

perceived control The amount of influence you feel you have over a situation and your reaction to it

perception The processes used to arrive at a meaningful interpretation of sensations; through perception, the simple component sensations are organized and interpreted into meaningful, recognizable forms, such as the appearance of a boulder or the taste of lime

perceptual constancy Perceiving the properties of an object as remaining the same even though the physical properties of the sensory input from that object are changing

perceptual illusions Inappropriate interpretations of physical reality; perceptual illusions often occur as a result of the brain's use of otherwise adaptive organizing principles

perfectionistic personality disorder A personality disorder characterized by an excessive and rigid need to achieve the highest level of quality in achievements

peripheral nervous system The network of nerves that link the central nervous system with the rest of the body

personal/group discrimination discrepancy The tendency for members of groups experiencing discrimination to minimize discrimination directed toward themselves as individuals, but to agree with other group members that discrimination against the group as a whole is significant

personal identity A sense of who we are as individuals and how well we stack up against peers; Erik Erikson's theory postulates that personal identity is shaped by a series of personal crises that each person confronts at characteristic stages of development

personality disorders Chronic or enduring patterns of behaviour that lead to significant impairments in social functioning

personality profiling Estimating the personality makeup of an individual based on indirect evidence, such as his or her eating habits, room arrangement, and so on

person-situation debate A controversial debate centring on whether people really do behave consistently across situations

phallic stage Freud's third stage of psychosexual development, lasting from about age three to age five; pleasure is gained from self-stimulation of the sexual organs

phenotype A person's observable characteristics, such as hair colour; controlled partly by the genotype and partly by the environment

phonemes The smallest significant, difference-making sound units in speech

phonology The rules and procedures for combining sounds to make words in a language

pinna The external flap of tissue commonly referred to as the "ear"; it helps direct sounds toward the tympanic membrane

pitch The psychological experience that results from the auditory processing of a particular *frequency* of sound

pituitary gland A kind of master gland that controls the release of hormones from other glands in response to signals from the hypothalamus

place theory The idea that the *location* of auditory receptor cells activated by movement of the basilar membrane plays a role in the perception of pitch

placebo An inactive, or inert, substance or treatment that resembles an experimental substance or treatment

polygraph A device that measures various indexes of physiological arousal in an effort to determine whether someone is telling a lie; the logic behind the test is that lying leads to greater emotionality, which can be picked up through such measures of arousal as heart rate, blood pressure, breathing rate, and perspiration

positive punishment An event that, when *presented* after a response, lowers the likelihood of that response occurring again

positive regard The idea that we value what others think of us and constantly seek others' approval, love, and companionship

positive reinforcement An event that, when *presented* after a response in a certain situation, increases the likelihood of that response occurring again in that situation

positron emission tomography (PET) A method for measuring how radioactive substances are absorbed in the brain; it can be used to detect how different tasks activate different areas of the living brain

postconventional level Kohlberg's highest level of moral development, in which moral actions are judged on the basis of personal codes of ethics that are general and abstract and that may not agree with societal norms

posttraumatic stress disorder A trauma-based anxiety disorder characterized by flashbacks, avoidance of stimuli associated with the traumatic event, and chronic arousal symptoms

pragmatics The practical knowledge used to comprehend the intentions of a speaker and to produce an appropriate response

preconscious mind The part of the mind that contains all the inactive but potentially accessible thoughts and memories

preconventional level In Kohlberg's theory, the lowest level of moral development, in which decisions about right and wrong are made primarily in terms of external consequences

prejudice An unrealistic negative evaluation of a group and its members

preoperational period Piaget's second stage of cognitive development, lasting from age two to about age seven; children begin to think symbolically but often lack the ability to perform mental operations, like conservation

primacy effect The better memory for items near the beginning of a studied list compared with mid-list items

primary drive A psychological state that arises in response to an internal physiological need, such as hunger or thirst

primary mental abilities The seven distinct forms of intelligence that Thurstone uncovered with modern forms of factor analysis

proactive interference A process in which old memories interfere with the establishment and retrieval of new memories

procedural memory Memory for how to do things, such as ride a bike or swing a golf club

projection A defence mechanism in which unacceptable feelings or desires are dealt with by attributing them to others

projective test A type of personality test in which individuals are asked to interpret ambiguous stimuli; the idea is that subjects will project their true thoughts and feelings into the interpretation, thereby revealing elements of their personality

prototype The best or most representative member of a category (such as robin for the category "bird")

proximate factors Causes of behaviour that derive from an organism's immediate internal or external environment

psychiatrists Medical doctors who specialize in the diagnosis and treatment of psychological problems; unlike psychologists, psychiatrists are licensed to prescribe drugs

psychoactive drugs Drugs that affect behaviour and mental processes, and produce alterations of conscious awareness

psychoanalysis A term used by Freud to describe his theory of mind and system of therapy, which involves analyzing the conscious mind to discover underlying unconscious influences; also, Freud's method of treatment that attempts to bring hidden impulses and memories, which are locked in the unconscious, to the surface of awareness, thereby freeing the patient from disordered thoughts and behaviours

psychodynamic theory An approach to personality development, based largely on the ideas of Sigmund Freud, which holds that much of behaviour is governed by unconscious forces

psychological disorder A specific psychological problem that causes abnormal behaviour to occur

psychology The scientific study of behaviour and mind

psychometrics The use of psychological tests to measure the mind, especially individual differences

psychopathy An alternative construct to the antisocial personality disorder; as well as criminal tendencies, it focuses on the underlying personality traits of manipulation, callousness, and impulsive thrill-seeking

psychophysics A field of psychology in which researchers search for ways to describe the transition from the physical stimulus to the psychological experience of that stimulus

psychotherapy Treatment designed to help people deal with mental, emotional, or behavioural problems

puberty The period during which a person reaches sexual maturity and is potentially capable of producing offspring

punishment Consequences that decrease the likelihood of responding in a similar way again

pupil The hole in the centre of the iris through which light enters the eye; the size of the pupil changes with light intensity

radical behaviourism A perspective on the analysis of human and animal behaviour that emphasizes explaining behaviour in terms of environmental events and that minimizes the use of internal explanations, like thoughts, beliefs, and intentions

random assignment A technique that ensures that each participant in an experiment has an equal chance of being assigned to any of the conditions in the experiment

random sampling A procedure for selecting a representative subset of a target population; the procedure guarantees that everyone in the population has an equal likelihood of being selected for the sample

range The difference between the largest and smallest scores in a distribution

rational-emotive therapy A form of cognitive therapy, developed by Albert Ellis, in which the therapist acts as a kind of cross-examiner, verbally disputing the client's irrational thought processes

reaction formation A defence mechanism used to transform an anxiety-producing desire into a kind of opposite—people behave in a way counter to the way they truly feel

reactivity The extent to which an individual's behaviour changes as a result of being observed; the behaviour is altered in reaction to being observed

recency effect The better memory for items near the end of a studied list compared with mid-list items

receptive field In vision, the portion of the retina that, when stimulated, causes the activity of a higher-level neuron (such as a ganglion cell or an even higher-level neuron in the visual cortex) to change

reciprocal determinism The idea that beliefs, behaviour, and the environment interact to shape what is learned from experience

reciprocity The tendency for people to return in kind the feelings that are shown toward them

recognition by components The idea proposed by Biederman that people recognize objects perceptually through smaller components called *geons*

reflex A largely automatic body movement, such as the knee jerk, that is controlled by a simple network of sensory neurons, interneurons in the spinal cord, and motor neurons

refractory period The period of time following an action potential during which more action potentials cannot be generated

rehearsal A strategic process that helps maintain short-term memories through the use of internal repetition

reinforcement Response consequences that increase the likelihood of responding in a similar way again

reliability A measure of the consistency of test results; reliable tests give people similar scores across time and across parts of the test

REM A stage of sleep characterized by rapid eye movements and low-amplitude, irregular EEG patterns similar to those found in the waking brain; REM is typically associated with dreaming

REM rebound The tendency to increase the proportion of sleeping time spent in REM sleep after a period of REM deprivation

representativeness heuristic The tendency to base judgments on similarity to an abstract ideal, expectation, or stereotype; for example, when deciding whether a sequence of coin-toss outcomes is random, people who use the representativeness heuristic focus on how irregular the sequence looks, because they think short random sequences should look irregular

repression A defence mechanism used to bury anxiety-producing thoughts and feelings in the unconscious

research psychologists Psychologists who conduct experiments or collect observations designed to discover the basic principles of behaviour and mind

resistance In psychoanalysis, a patient's unconsciously motivated attempts to subvert the process of therapy

resting potential The tiny electrical charge in place between the inside and outside of the resting neuron

retina The thin layer of tissue that covers the back of the inside of the eye and contains the light-sensitive receptor cells for vision

retinal disparity A binocular cue for depth that is based on differences between the images in each eye

retrieval The processes that control how information is recovered from memory and translated into performance

retroactive interference A process in which the formation of new memories hurts the retrieval of old memories

retrograde amnesia Memory loss for events that happened before the brain injury

rods Receptor cells in the retina, located mainly on the periphery of the retina, that transduce light energy into neural inputs; these visual receptors are highly sensitive and are active in dim light

Rorschach test A projective test that requires people to interpret ambiguous inkblots

s (specific) residual The remainder part of a specific ability test that is unique and not explained by *g*

savant An individual with a special talent despite generally low intelligence

Schachter theory A theory of emotion that argues that the cognitive interpretation, or appraisal, of a body reaction creates the subjective experience of emotion

schedule of reinforcement A rule that an experimenter uses to determine when particular responses will be reinforced: in a continuous reinforcement schedule, a reward is delivered every time the target behaviour is performed; partial reinforcement schedules, in contrast, can be fixed or variable, and ratio or interval

schema An organized knowledge structure in long-term memory

schemas Mental models of the world that people use to guide and interpret their experiences

schizophrenia A class of disorders characterized by fundamental disturbances in thought processes, emotion, or behaviour

scientific method A method for acquiring knowledge by combining (1) the principles of rational thought (that is, logic) with (2) information derived from systematic measurements of the object of study (that is, empirical research)

searching for analogies A problem-solving heuristic that involves trying to find a connection between the current problem and some previous problem you have solved successfully

secondary drive A drive learned by association with a primary drive (e.g., the need for money)

secondary traits The less obvious characteristics of an individual's personality that do not always appear in his or her behaviour, such as grouchiness at morning meetings

second-order conditioning A procedure in which an established conditioned stimulus is used to condition a second neutral stimulus

self-actualization The ingrained desire to reach our true potential as human beings

self-concept An organized set of perceptions that we hold about our abilities and characteristics

self-efficacy The beliefs that we hold about our own ability to perform a task or accomplish a goal

self-fulfilling prophecy effect When our expectations about the actions of another person actually lead that person to behave in the expected way

self-monitoring The degree to which a person monitors a situation closely and changes his or her behaviour accordingly; people who are high self-monitors may not behave consistently across situations

self-perception theory The idea that people use observations of their own behaviour as a basis for inferring their internal beliefs

self-report questionnaires Personality tests that ask the person of interest a set of questions about how he or she thinks, acts, or feels

self-serving bias The tendency to make internal attributions about our own behaviour when the outcome is positive and to blame the situation when our behaviour leads to something negative

semantic memory Knowledge about language and the world, retrieved as abstract facts or beliefs that make little or no reference to any particular episode in personal experience

semantics The rules and procedures for communicating meaning through words and combinations of words

semicircular canals A receptor system attached to the inner ear that responds to movement, acceleration, and deceleration and to changes in upright posture

sensations The elementary components, or building blocks, of perception, such as a pattern of light and dark contrast detected by the eye or a bitter taste on the tongue

sensitization An increase in the tendency to respond to an event that has been repeated; sensitization is more likely when a repeated stimulus is intense

sensorimotor period Piaget's first stage of cognitive development, lasting from birth to about two years of age; schemas revolve around sensory and motor abilities

sensory adaptation The tendency of sensory systems to reduce sensitivity to a stimulus that remains constant

sensory memory The capacity to preserve sensory information in a relatively pure, unanalyzed form for a very brief period

sensory neurons Neurons that make initial contact with the environment and carry the message inward toward the spinal cord and brain

serotonin A neurotransmitter that has been linked to sleep, dreaming, and general arousal and may also be involved in some psychological disorders, such as depression and schizophrenia

service gap The difference between the number of people who could benefit from receiving psychological services and those who receive them

set point A natural body weight, perhaps produced by genetic factors, that the body seeks to maintain; when body weight falls below the set point, people are motivated to eat; when weight exceeds the set point, people feel less motivated to eat

sexual orientation The direction of a person's sexual and emotional attraction: homosexuality, heterosexuality, and bisexuality are all sexual orientations

sexual scripts Learned cognitive programs that instruct us on how, why, and what to do in our interactions with sexual partners; their nature differs across gender and may vary across cultures

shaping A procedure in which reinforcement is delivered for successive approximations of the desired response

short-term memory A limited-capacity "working memory" system that people use to hold information, after it has been perceptually analyzed, usually for less than a minute; the system used to temporarily store, think about, and reason with new information and with information retrieved from long-term memory

signal detection A technique that can be used to determine an individual's ability to detect the presence of a stimulus and to measure the individual's response bias

single-blind study An experimental design in which the participants do not know to which of the conditions they have been assigned (e.g., experimental versus control); it's used to control for subject expectancies

16 Personality Factor (16PF) A self-report inventory developed by Cattell and colleagues to measure 16 primary personality factors

sleepwalking A condition in which the sleeper rises during sleep and wanders about; not thought to be associated with dreaming

social cognition The study of how people use cognitive processes—such as perception, memory, thought, and emotion—to make sense of other people as well as themselves

social facilitation The enhancement in performance that is sometimes found when an individual performs in the presence of others

social influence The study of how the behaviours and thoughts of individuals are affected by the presence of others

social interference The impairment in performance that is sometimes found when an individual performs in the presence of others

social learning theory The idea that most important personality traits come from modelling, or copying, the behaviour of others

social loafing The tendency to put out less effort when several people are supposed to be working on a task than when only one is working

social phobia An incapacitating fear of social interactions

social psychology The study of how people think about, influence, and relate to other people

social schema A general knowledge structure, stored in long-term memory, that relates to social experiences or people

social support The resources that individuals receive from other people or groups, often in the form of comfort, caring, or help

socially desirable responding The tendency to describe ourselves as having positive, or at least normal, traits

sociological model The view that abnormality is a label that each society assigns to behaviours that it finds unacceptable, even if the behaviours are not criminal in nature

soma The cell body of a neuron

somatic system Nerves that transmit information from sensory organs to the brain, and from the brain to the skeletal muscles; part of the peripheral nervous system

somatization disorder A long-lasting preoccupation with body symptoms that have no identifiable physical cause

somatoform disorders Psychological disorders that focus on the physical body

sound The physical input to the auditory system, a mechanical energy travelling in waves that requires a medium, such as air or water, through which to move

specific phobic disorder A highly focused fear of a specific object or situation

split-half reliability The ability of a test to give the same scores in the first and second halves of the test

spontaneous recovery The recovery of an extinguished conditioned response after a period without exposure to the conditioned stimulus

spontaneous remission Improvement in a psychological disorder without treatment—that is, simply as a function of the passage of time

standard deviation An indication of how much individual scores differ or vary from the mean in a set of scores

standardization Keeping the testing, scoring, and interpretation procedures similar across all administrations of a test

statistical deviance criterion A criterion for abnormality based on a low frequency of occurrence among the members of a population

stereotypes The collection of beliefs and impressions held about a group and its members; common stereotypes include those based on gender, race, and age

Sternberg's three facets of intelligence Robert Sternberg's theory of intelligence that includes three types of intelligence: analytic, creative, and practical

stimulants A class of drugs that increase central nervous system activity, enhancing neural transmission

stimulus discrimination Responding to a new stimulus in a way that is different from the response to an established conditioned stimulus

stimulus generalization Responding to a new stimulus in a way similar to the response produced by an established conditioned stimulus

storage The processes that determine how information is maintained over time

strange situation test Gradually subjecting a child to a stressful situation and observing his or her behaviour toward the parent or caregiver; this test is used to classify children according to type of attachment: secure, resistant, or avoidant

stress People's physical and psychological reactions to demanding or threatening situations

stressors The demanding or threatening situations that produce stress

structuralism An early school of psychology; structuralists attempted to understand the mind by breaking it down into its basic constituent parts, much as a molecular biologist might try to understand an organic compound

subjective definition A definition based on personal opinion; each person's definition seems designed to suit his or her personal needs and worldviews

sublimation A defence mechanism used to channel unacceptable impulses into socially acceptable activities

superego In Freud's theory, the portion of personality that motivates people to act in a proper fashion, that is, in accordance with the moral customs defined by parents and culture

surface structure The literal ordering of words in a sentence

survey A descriptive research technique designed to gather limited amounts of information from many people, usually by administering a questionnaire

sympathetic system The division of the autonomic nervous system that helps the body respond to emergencies

synapse The junction, or small gap, between a terminal button of one neuron and a dendrite of another neuron

syntax The rules and procedures for combining words to form sentences

systematic desensitization A technique that uses counterconditioning and extinction to reduce the fear and anxiety that have become associated with a specific object or event; a multistep process that attempts to replace the negative learned association with something relaxing

tacit knowledge The special knowledge in a particular area that allows one to think quickly and efficiently

taste buds The receptor cells on the tongue involved in taste

temperament Behavioural tendencies that have biological origins

temporal lobes One of four anatomical regions of each hemisphere of the cerebral cortex, located roughly on the sides of the brain; involved in certain aspects of speech and language perception

teratogens Environmental agents—such as disease, organisms, or drugs—that can potentially damage the developing embryo or fetus

terminal buttons The tiny swellings at the end of a neuron's axon that contain chemicals that, when released into the synapse, are taken up by the dendrites of other neurons, thereby stimulating them

test-retest reliability The ability of a test to give consistent scores across time

texture gradient Gradual reduction, with increasing distance, of the apparent coarseness of a surface (such as the ground or floor); provides a powerful cue to the distances of objects located on that surface

thalamus A relay station in the forebrain thought to be an important gathering point for input from the senses

Thematic Apperception Test (TAT) A projective personality test that requires people to make up stories about the characters in ambiguous pictures

therapeutic alliance The bond formed between the client and therapist in successful psychotherapy that is focused on working together constructively to solve the client's problem

theta waves The pattern of brain activity observed in stage 1 sleep

thinking The processes that underlie the mental manipulation of knowledge, images, and ideas, often in an attempt to reach a goal, such as solving a problem

token economy A type of behavioural therapy in which institutionalized patients are rewarded with small tokens when they act in an appropriate way; tokens can then be exchanged for certain privileges

tolerance An adaptation that the body makes to compensate for the continued use of a drug such that increasing amounts of the drug are needed to produce the same physical, psychological, and behavioural effects

top-down processing Processing that is driven by beliefs and expectations about how the world is organized

trait A distinguishable characteristic of an organism

trait taxonomies Systems for distinguishing the most important individual differences in personality; these traits taxonomies are usually associated with an inventory of psychometric tests designed to measure these traits

transcranial magnetic stimulation (TMS) Powerful pulses of magnetic energy applied to the scalp stimulate action potentials in regions of the cortex; behavioural responses cast light on the function of the stimulated brain region

transduction The process by which external inputs are translated into the internal language of the brain

transfer-appropriate processing The idea that the likelihood of correct retrieval increases as a function of the similarity between mental processes during encoding and those during test

transference In psychoanalysis, the patient's expression of thoughts or feelings toward the therapist that are actually representative of the way the patient feels about other significant people in his or her life

trichromatic theory A theory of colour vision proposing that colour information is extracted by comparing the relative activations of three different types of cone receptors

twin studies Identical twins, who share genetic material, are compared with fraternal twins in an effort to disentangle the roles of heredity and environment in giving rise to psychological traits

tympanic membrane The eardrum, which responds to incoming sound waves by vibrating

Type A An enduring pattern of behaviour linked to coronary heart disease; the tendency to be hard driving, ambitious, easily annoyed, and impatient all seem to derive from the trait of hostility

Type B People who lack the Type A traits—they experience less stress and, therefore, better health outcomes

ultimate factors Causes of behaviour that refer to the evolutionarily adaptive significance and reproductive consequences for the organism

unconditioned response (UR) The observable response that is produced automatically, before training, on presentation of an unconditioned stimulus

unconditioned stimulus (US) A stimulus that automatically produces—or elicits—an observable response prior to any training

unconscious mind The part of the mind that Freud believed housed all the memories, urges, and conflicts that are truly beyond awareness

validity An evaluation of how well a test measures what the label of the test says it is measuring: *Content validity* assesses the degree to which the content of a test samples broadly across the domain of interest; *predictive validity* assesses how well the test predicts an important criterion; *construct validity* assesses how well the test captures all the details of the theoretical construct

variability A measure of how much the scores in a data set differ from one another

variable-interval schedule A schedule in which the allotted time before a response will yield reinforcement changes from trial to trial

variable-ratio schedule A schedule in which a certain number of responses is required for reinforcement, but the number of required responses typically changes from trial to trial

ventromedial hypothalamus A portion of the hypothalamus that, when lesioned, causes an animal to typically overeat and gain a large amount of weight; once thought to be a kind of "stop eating," or satiety, centre in the brain; its role in eating behaviour is currently unknown

vestibular sacs Small organs in the inner ear that contain receptors responsible for the sense of balance

visual acuity The ability to see fine detail

visual imagery The processes used to construct an internal visual image through the use of some of the same brain mechanisms as in perception

visual neglect A complex attention disorder characterized by a tendency to ignore things that appear on one side of the body, usually the left side

warm fibres Neurons that respond vigorously when the temperature of the skin increases

Weber's law States that the ability to notice a difference in the magnitude of two stimuli is a constant proportion of the intensity of the standard stimulus; psychologically, the more intense a stimulus is to begin with, the more intense it will need to become for a person to notice a difference

well-defined problem A problem with a clear starting point and a fully specified goal

withdrawal Clear and measurable physical reactions, such as sweating, vomiting, tremors, or changes in heart rate, that occur when a person stops taking certain drugs after continued use

working backward A problem-solving heuristic that involves mentally starting at the goal and mentally moving backward toward the starting point to see how the goal can be reached

zygote The fertilized human egg, containing 23 chromosomes from the father and 23 chromosomes from the mother, which pair up to form the master genetic blueprint

References

Abdullaev, Y. G., & Posner, M. I. (1998). Time course of activating brain areas in generating verbal associations. *Psychological Science, 8,* 56–59.

Aboud, F. E. (1988). *Children and prejudice.* New York: Blackwell.

Aboud, F. E. (1993). A fifth grade program to reduce prejudice. In K. McLeod (Ed.), *Multicultural education: The state of the art* (pp. 20–27). Toronto: University of Toronto Press.

Aboud, F. E., & Doyle, A. B. (1996). Does talk of race foster prejudice or tolerance in children? *Canadian Journal of Behavioural Science, 28,* 161–170.

Abramson, L. Y., Metalsky, G. I., & Alloy, L. B. (1989). Hopelessness depression: A theory-based subtype of depression. *Psychological Review, 96,* 358–372.

Achenbach, T. M. (1992). Developmental psychopathology. In M. H. Bornstein & M. E. Lamb (Eds.), *Developmental psychology: An advanced textbook* (pp. 405–450). Hillsdale, NJ: Erlbaum.

Adair, J. G. (2001). Ethics of psychological research: New policies; continuing issues; new concerns. *Canadian Psychology, 42,* 25–37.

Adair, J. G., Paivio, A., & Ritchie, P. (1996). Psychology in Canada. *Annual Review of Psychology, 47,* 341–370.

Adair, R., Bauchner, H., Phillip, B., Levenson, S., & Zuckerman, B. (1991). Night waking during infancy: Role of parent presence at bedtime. *Pediatrics, 87,* 500–504.

Adamec, R. E. (2000). Evidence that long-lasting potentiation of amygdala efferents in the right hemisphere underlies pharmacological stressor (FG-7142) induced lasting increases in anxiety-like behaviour: Role of GABA tone in initiation of brain and behavioural changes. *Journal of Psychopharmacology, 14,* 323–339.

Adams, P. R., & Adams, G. R. (1984). Mount Saint Helens's ash-fall: Evidence for a disaster stress reaction. *American Psychologist, 39,* 252–260.

Adler, A. (1927). *Understanding human nature.* New York: Greenberg.

Adler, E., & Bachant, J. (1998). Intrapsychic and interactive dimensions of resistance: A contemporary perspective. *Psychoanalytic Psychology, 15,* 451–479.

Adler, N., & Matthews, K. (1994). Health psychology: Why do some people get sick and some stay healthy? *Annual Review of Psychology, 45,* 229–259.

Adorno, T. W., Frenkel-Brunswik, E., Levinson, D. J., & Sanford, R. N. (1950). *The authoritarian personality.* New York: Harpur & Brothers.

Aggleton, J. P. (1993). The contribution of the amygdala to normal and abnormal emotional states. *Trends in Neuroscience, 16,* 328–333.

Agras, W. S., Sylvester, D., & Oliveau, D. (1969). The epidemiology of common fears and phobia. *Comprehensive Psychiatry, 10,* 151–156.

Aiello, J. R., & Douthitt, E. A. (2001). Social facilitation from Triplett to electronic performance monitoring. *Group Dynamics, 5,* 163–180.

Ainsworth, M. D. S. (1979). Attachment as related to mother-infant interaction. In J. S. Rosenblatt, R. A. Hinde, C. Beer, & M. Busnel (Eds.), *Advances in the study of behavior* (Vol. 9, pp. 1–51). New York: Academic Press.

Ainsworth, M. D. S., Blehar, M., Waters, E., & Wall, S. (1978). *Patterns of attachment.* Hillsdale, NJ: Erlbaum.

Ainsworth, M. D. S., & Bowlby, J. (1954). Research strategy in the study of mother-child separation. *Courrier, 4,* 105–131.

Ainsworth, M. D. S., & Wittig, B. A. (1969). Attachment and exploratory behavior of one-year-olds in a strange situation. In B. M. Foss (Ed.), *Determinants of infant behaviour* (Vol. 4, pp. 111–136). London: Methuen.

Ajzen, I. (2001). Nature and operation of attitudes. *Annual Review of Psychology, 52,* 27–58.

Ajzen, I., & Fishbein, M. (1977). Attitude-behavior relations: A theoretical analysis and review of empirical research. *Psychological Bulletin, 84,* 888–918.

Akiskal, H. S., & Cassano, G. B. (Eds.). (1997). *Dysthymia and the spectrum of chronic depression.* New York: Guilford Press.

Albert, M. S., & Moss, M. B. (1992). The assessment of memory disorders in patients with Alzheimer's disease. In L. R. Squire & N. Butters (Eds.), *Neuropsychology of memory* (2nd ed., pp. 211–219). New York: Guilford Press.

Alberta Alcohol and Drug Abuse Commission. (1999). *Beyond the ABCs: Information for professionals.* Retrieved August 8, 2000, from http://www.gov.ab.ca/aadac/addictions/beyond/

Alda, M. (2001). Genetic factors and treatment of mood disorders. *Bipolar Disorders, 3,* 318–324.

Alden, L. E. (1988). Morita therapy with socially avoidant clients. *International Bulletin of Morita Therapy, 1,* 43–51.

Alden, L. E. (2001). Interpersonal perspectives on social phobia. In W. R. Crozier & L. E. Alden (Eds.), *International handbook of social anxiety: Concepts, research and interventions relating to the self and shyness* (pp. 381–404). New York: John Wiley & Sons.

Alden, L. E., Ryder, A. G., & Mellings, T. M. B. (2002). Perfectionism in the context of social fears: Toward a two-component model. In G. L. Flett & P. L. Hewitt (Eds.), *Perfectionism: Theory, research, and treatment* (pp. 373–391). Washington, DC: American Psychological Association.

Allan, L. G., & Siegel, S. (1997). Contingent color aftereffects: Reassessing old conclusions. *Perception and Psychophysics, 59,* 129–141.

Allen, K. M., Blascovich, J., Tomaka, J., & Kelsey, R. M. (1991). Presence of human friends and pet dogs as moderators of autonomic responses to stress in women. *Journal of Personality and Social Psychology, 61*, 582–589.

Allen, S. W., & Vokey, J. R. (1998). Directed forgetting and rehearsal on direct and indirect memory tests. In J. M. Golding & C. M. MacLeod (Eds.), *Intentional forgetting: Interdisciplinary approaches* (pp. 173–195). Mahwah, NJ: Erlbaum.

Alley, T. R., & Cunningham, M. R. (1991). Average faces are attractive, but very attractive faces are not average. *Psychological Science, 2*, 123–125.

Allison, D. B., & Faith, M. S. (1997). Issues in mapping genes for eating disorders. *Psychopharmacology Bulletin, 33*, 359–368.

Allison, T., & Cicchetti, D. V. (1976). Sleep in mammals: Ecological and constitutional correlates. *Science, 194*, 732–734.

Alloy, L. B., Abramson, L. Y., Tashman, N. A., Berrebbi, D. S., Hogan, M. E., Whitehouse, W. G., et al. (2001). Developmental origins of cognitive vulnerability to depression: Parenting, cognitive, and inferential feedback styles of the parents of individuals at high and low cognitive risk for depression. *Cognitive Therapy and Research, 25*, 397–423.

Alloy, L. B., & Clements, C. M. (1998). Hopelessness theory of depression: Tests of the symptom component. *Cognitive Therapy and Research, 22*, 303–335.

Allport, A. (1989). Visual attention. In M. I. Posner (Ed.), *Foundation of cognitive science* (pp. 631–682). Cambridge, MA: MIT Press.

Allport, G. W. (1937). *Personality: A psychological interpretation.* New York: Holt.

Allport, G. W. (1954). *The nature of prejudice.* Cambridge, MA: Addison-Wesley.

Allport, G. W., & Odbert, H. H. (1936). Trait-names: A psycho-lexical study. *Psychological Monographs, 47*(1, Whole No. 211).

Altemeyer, B. (1988). *Enemies of freedom: Understanding right-wing authoritarianism.* San Francisco: Jossey-Bass.

Altemeyer, B. (1994). Reducing prejudice in right-wing authoritarians. In M. P. Zanna & J. M. Olson (Eds.), *The psychology of prejudice: The Ontario symposium* (pp. 131–148). Hillsdale, NJ: Erlbaum.

Altemeyer, B. (1996). *The authoritarian specter.* Cambridge, MA: Harvard University Press.

Amabile, T. M. (1983). *The social psychology of creativity.* New York: Springer-Verlag.

American Psychiatric Association. (1994). *Diagnostic and statistical manual of mental disorders* (4th ed.). Washington, DC: Author.

Amzica, F., & Steriade, M. (1996). Progressive cortical synchronization of ponto-geniculo-occipital potentials during rapid eye movement sleep. *Neuroscience, 72*, 309–314.

Anastasi, A. (1985). Psychological testing: Basic concepts and common misconceptions. *G. Stanley Hall Lecture Series, 5*, 87–120.

Andersen, B. L. (1992). Psychological interventions for cancer patients to enhance quality of life. *Journal of Consulting and Clinical Psychology, 60*, 552–568.

Andersen, S. M., & Berk, M. S. (1998). Transference in everyday experience: Implications of experimental research for relevant clinical phenomena. *Review of General Psychology, 2*, 81–120.

Anderson, C. A., Berkowitz, L., Donnerstein, E., Huesmann, L. R., Johnson, J. D., Linz, D., Malamuth, N. M., et al. (2003). The influence of media violence on youth. *Psychological Science in the Public Interest, 4*(3), 81–110.

Anderson, J. L., & Crawford, C. B. (1992). Modelling the costs and benefits of reproductive suppression. *Human Nature, 3*, 299–334.

Anderson, J. R. (1990). *The adaptive character of thought.* Hillsdale, NJ: Erlbaum.

Anderson, L. E., & Walsh, J. A. (1998). Prediction of adult criminal status from juvenile psychological assessment. *Criminal Justice and Behavior, 25*, 226–239.

Anderson, M. C., Ochsner, K. N., Kuhl, B., Cooper, J., Robertson, E., & Gabrieli, S. W., et al. (2004). Neural systems underlying the suppression of unwanted memories. *Science, 303*, 232–235.

Andrasik, F., & Holroyd, K. A. (1980). A test of specific and nonspecific effects in the biofeedback treatment of tension headache. *Journal of Consulting and Clinical Psychology, 48*, 575–586.

Andreasen, N. C. (1987). Creativity and mental illness: Prevalence rates in writers and their first-degree relatives. *American Journal of Psychiatry, 144*, 1288–1292.

Anisman, H., Hayley, S., Staines, W., & Merali, Z. (2001). Cytokines, stress, and neurochemical change: Immediate and proactive effects. In C. A. Shaw & J. C. McEachern (Eds.), *Toward a theory of neuroplasticity* (pp. 301–320). Philadelphia: Taylor & Francis.

Antle, M. C., & Silver, R. (2005). Orchestrating time: Arrangements of the brain circadian clock. *Trends in Neurosciences, 28*(3), 145–151.

Antrobus, J. (1991). Dreaming: Cognitive processes during cortical activation and high afferent thresholds. *Psychological Review, 98*, 96–121.

Apgar, V., & Beck, J. (1974). *Is my baby all right?* New York: Pocket Books.

Araoz, D. L. (1982). *Hypnosis and sex therapy.* New York: Brunner/Mazel.

Arguin, M., & Bub, D. (1993). Modulation of the directional attention deficit in visual neglect by hemispatial factors. *Brain and Cognition, 22*, 148–160.

Arguin, M., Bub, D., & Dudek, G. (1996). Shape integration for visual object recognition and its implication in category-specific visual agnosia. *Visual Cognition, 3*, 221–275.

Aronoff, J., Lynn, S. J., & Malinoski, P. (2000). Are cultic environments psychologically harmful? *Clinical Psychology Review, 20*, 91–111.

Aronson, E. (1992). The return of the repressed: Dissonance theory makes a comeback. *Psychological Inquiry, 3*, 303–311.

Aronson, E. (1997). The theory of cognitive dissonance: The evolution and vicissitudes of an idea. In C. McGarty & S. Haslam (Eds.), *The message of social psychology: Perspectives on mind in society* (pp. 20–35). Oxford, England: Blackwell.

Arvanitogiannis, A., Riscaldino, L., & Shizgal, P. (1999). Effects of NMDA lesions of the medial basal forebrain on LH and VTA self-stimulation. *Physiology and Behavior, 65*, 805–810.

Asch, S. E. (1951). Effects of group pressure on the modification and distortion of judgments. In H. Guetzkow

(Ed.), *Groups, leadership, and men* (pp. 177–190). Pittsburgh, PA: Carnegie Press.

Asch, S. E. (1955, May). Opinions and social pressures. *Scientific American, 193,* 31–35.

Aserinsky, E., & Kleitman, N. (1955). Two types of ocular motility occurring in sleep. *Journal of Applied Physiology, 8,* 1–10.

Ashton, C. H. (2001). Pharmacology and effects of cannabis: A brief review. *British Journal of Psychiatry, 178,* 101–106.

Ashton, M. C., Lee, K., & Son, C. (2000). Honesty as the sixth factor of personality: Correlations with Machiavellianism, primary psychopathy, and social adroitness. *European Journal of Personality, 14,* 359–369.

Asmundson, G. J. G., Carleton, R. N., & Wright, K. D. (2004). Psychological sequelae of remote exposure to the September 11th terrorist attacks in Canadians with and without panic. *Cognitive Behaviour Therapy, 33*(2), 51–59.

Asmundson, G. J. G., Frombach, I. K., & Hadjistavropoulos, H. D. (1998). Anxiety sensitivity: Assessing factor structure and relationship to multidimensional aspects of pain in injured workers. *Journal of Occupational Rehabilitation 8*(3), 223–234.

Assanand, S., Pinel, J. P. J., & Lehman, D. R. (1998). Personal theories of hunger and eating. *Journal of Applied Social Psychology, 28*(11), 998–1015.

Atkinson, J. W. (1957). Motivational determinants of risk-taking behavior. *Psychological Review, 64,* 359–372.

Atkinson, J. W., & Raynor, J. O. (Eds.). (1974). *Motivation and achievement.* Washington, DC: Winston.

Atkinson, R. C., & Shiffrin, R. M. (1968). Human memory: A proposed system and its control processes. In K. W. Spence (Ed.), *The psychology of learning and motivation: Advances in research and theory* (pp. 89–195). New York: Academic Press.

Aubé, J., & Whiffen, V. E. (1996). Depressive styles and social acuity. *Communication Research, 23,* 407–425.

Ayton, P., & Fischer, I. (2004). The hot hand fallacy and the gambler's fallacy: Two faces of subjective randomness? *Memory & Cognition, 32*(8), 1369–1378.

Baddeley, A. D. (1992). Working memory. *Science, 255,* 556–559.

Baddeley, A. D. (2000). The episodic buffer: A new component of working memory? *Trends in Cognitive Sciences, 4,* 417–423.

Baddeley, A. D., Gathercole, S. E., & Papagno, C. (1998). The phonological loop as a language device. *Psychological Review, 105,* 158–173.

Baddeley, A. D., & Hitch, G. (1974). *Working memory.* In G. H. Bower (Ed.), *The psychology of learning and motivation* (Vol. 8, pp. 47–90). New York: Academic Press.

Baddeley, A. D., & Lieberman, K. (1980). Spatial working memory. In R. Nickerson (Ed.), *Attention and performance VIII* (pp. 521–617). Hillsdale, NJ: Erlbaum.

Baddeley, A. D., & Longman, D. J. A. (1978). The influence of length and frequency of training sessions on the rate of learning to type. *Ergonomics, 21,* 627–635.

Baddeley, A. D., Thomson, N., & Buchanan, M. (1975). Word length and the structure of short-term memory. *Journal of Verbal Learning and Verbal Behavior, 14,* 575–589.

Bahrick, H. P. (1984). Semantic memory content in permastore: 50 years of memory for Spanish learned in school. *Journal of Experimental Psychology: General, 113,* 1–29.

Bahrick, H. P., & Hall, L. K. (1991). Lifetime maintenance of high school mathematics content. *Journal of Experimental Psychology: General, 120,* 20–33.

Bailey, J. M., & Pillard, R. C. (1991). A genetic study of male sexual orientation. *Archives of General Psychiatry, 48,* 1089–1096.

Bailey, J. M., & Pillard, R. C. (1995). Genetics of human sexual orientation. *Annual Review of Sex Research, 6,* 126–150.

Bailey, J. M., Pillard, R. C., Neale, M. C. I., & Agyei, Y. (1993). Heritable factors influence sexual orientation in women. *Archives of General Psychiatry, 50,* 217–223.

Bailey, J. M., & Zucker, K. J. (1995). Childhood sex-typed behavior and sexual orientation: A conceptual analysis and quantitative review. *Developmental Psychology, 31*(1), 43–55.

Baillargeon, R. (2004). Infants' physical world. *Current Directions in Psychological Science, 13,* 89–94.

Bakan, D. (1966). *The duality of human existence.* Boston: Beacon Press.

Baker, T. B., & Tiffany, S. T. (1985). Morphine tolerance as habituation. *Psychological Review, 92,* 78–108.

Baldo, J. V., & Shimamura, A. P. (1998). Letter and category fluency in patients with frontal lobe lesions. *Neuropsychology, 12,* 259–267.

Baldwin, M. W., Carrell, S. E., & Lopez, D. F. (1990). Priming relationship schemas: My advisor and the Pope are watching me from the back of my mind. *Journal of Experimental Social Psychology, 26,* 435–454.

Baldwin, M. W., Granzberg, A., Pippus, L., & Pritchard, E. T. (2003). Cued activation of relational schemas: Self-evaluation and gender effects. *Canadian Journal of Behavioural Science, 35,* 153–163.

Balota, D. A., Dolan, P. O., & Duchek, J. M. (2000). Memory changes in healthy older adults. In E. Tulving & F. I. M. Craik (Eds.), *The Oxford handbook of memory* (pp. 395–410). Oxford: Oxford University Press.

Banaji, M. R., & Crowder, R. G. (1989). The bankruptcy of everyday memory. *American Psychologist, 44,* 1185–1193.

Bandura, A. (1986). *Social foundations of thought and action.* Englewood Cliffs, NJ: Prentice-Hall.

Bandura, A. (1993). Perceived self-efficacy in cognitive development and functioning. *Educational Psychologist, 28,* 117–148.

Bandura, A., Ross, D., & Ross, S. A. (1963). Imitation of film-mediated aggressive models. *Journal of Abnormal and Social Psychology, 66,* 3–11.

Banks, M. S., & Salapatek, P. (1983). Infant visual perception. In M. M. Haith & J. J. Campos (Eds.), *Infancy and developmental psychobiology: Vol. 2, Handbook of child psychology* (pp. 435–571). New York: Wiley.

Banks, M. S., & Shannon, E. (1993). Spatial and chromatic visual efficiency in human neonates. In C. E. Granrud (Ed.), *Visual perception and cognition in infancy* (pp. 1–46). Hillsdale, NJ: Erlbaum.

Barber, T. X. (1976). *Pitfalls in human research: Ten pivotal points.* New York: Pergamon Press.

Barcelo, F., & Gale, A. (1997). Electrophysiological measures of cognition in biological psychiatry: Some cautionary notes. *International Journal of Neuroscience, 92,* 219–240.

Barenbaum, N. B. (1997). The case(s) of Gordon Allport. *Journal of Personality, 65,* 743–755.

Bargones, J. Y., & Werner, L. A. (1994). Adults listen selectively; infants do not. *Psychological Science, 5,* 170–174.

Barkley, R. A. (1997). Behavioral inhibition, sustained attention, and executive functions: Constructing a unified theory of ADHD. *Psychological Bulletin, 121,* 65–94.

Barkley, R. A. (2003). Issues in the diagnosis of attention-deficit/hyperactivity disorder in children. *Brain & Development, 25*(2), 77–83.

Barkow, J. H., Cosmides, L., & Tooby, J. (1992). *The adapted mind: Evolutionary psychology and the generation of culture.* New York: Oxford.

Barlow, D. H. (1988). *Anxiety and its disorders: The nature and treatment of anxiety and panic.* New York: Guilford Press.

Barlow, D. H., & Durand, V. M. (1999). *Abnormal psychology: An integrative approach* (2nd ed.). Pacific Grove, CA: Brooks/Cole.

Barlow, D. H., & Durand, V. M. (2002). *Abnormal psychology: An integrative approach* (3rd ed.). Pacific Grove, CA: Brooks/Cole.

Barlow, D. H., & Rapee, R. M. (1991). *Mastering stress: A lifestyle approach.* Dallas, TX: American Health.

Barnes, S. J., Floresco, S. B., Kornecook, T. J., & Pinel, J. P. J. (2000). Reversible lesions of the rhinal cortex produce delayed non-matching-to-sample deficits in rats. *Neuroreport: For Rapid Communication of Neuroscience Research, 11,* 351–354.

Barnes, V. A., Treiber, F., & Davis, H. (2001). Impact of Transcendental Meditation (R) on cardiovascular function at rest and during acute stress in adolescents with high normal blood pressure. *Journal of Psychosomatic Research, 51,* 597–605.

Barnier, A. J., Conway, M. A., Mayoh, L., Speyer, J., & Avizmil, O. (in press). Controlling memories of the past: Directed forgetting of recently recalled autobiographical memories. *Journal of Experimental Psychology: General.*

Bar-On, R., & Parker, J. D. A. (Eds.). (2000). *The handbook of emotional intelligence.* New York: John Wiley/Jossey-Bass.

Baron-Cohen, S. (1994). Cognitive mechanisms in mind-reading. *Current Psychology of Cognition, 13,* 513–552.

Barsalou, L. W. (1983). Ad hoc categories. *Memory and Cognition, 11,* 211–227.

Bartholomew, K., Henderson, A. J. Z., & Dutton, D. G. (2000). Insecure attachment and abusive intimate relationships. In C. Clulow (Ed.), *Attachment and couple work: Applying the "secure base" concept in research and practise* (pp. 43–61). London: Routledge.

Bartlett, F. C. (1932). *Remembering.* Cambridge: Cambridge University Press.

Bassok, M., Wu, L. L., & Olseth, K. L. (1995). Judging a book by its cover: Interpretative effects of content on problem-solving transfer. *Memory and Cognition, 23,* 354–367.

Bastien, C., & Campbell, K. (1992). The evoked K-complex: All or none phenomenon? *Sleep, 15,* 236–245.

Baumeister, R. F. (1997). Identity, self-concept, and self-esteem: The self lost and regained. In R. Hogan, J. Johnson, & S. R. Briggs (Eds.), *Handbook of personality psychology* (pp. 681–711). San Diego, CA: Academic Press.

Baumeister, R. F. (2004). Gender and erotic plasticity: Sociocultural influences on the sex drive. *Sexual and Relationship Therapy, 19,* 133–139.

Baumeister, R. F., Catanese, K. R., & Vohs, K. D. (2001). Is there a gender difference in strength of sex drive? Theoretical views, conceptual distinctions, and a review of relevant evidence. *Personality and Social Psychology Review, 5,* 242–273.

Baumeister, R. F., & Leary, M. R. (1995). The need to belong: Desire for interpersonal attachment as a fundamental human motivation. *Psychological Bulletin, 117,* 497–529.

Baumeister, R. F., & Vohs, K. D. (2004). *Handbook of self-regulation: Research, theory, and applications.* New York: Guilford Press.

Baumrind, D. (1964). Some thoughts on the ethics of research: After reading Milgram's "Behavioral study of obedience." *American Psychologist, 19,* 421–423.

Baumrind, D. (1985). Research using intentional deception: Ethical issues revisited. *American Psychologist, 40,* 165–174.

Beal, A. L., Dumont, R. P., Cruse, C. L., & Branche, A. H. (1996). Practical implications of differences between the American and Canadian norms for WISC-III and a short form for children with learning disabilities. *Canadian Journal of School Psychology, 12,* 7–14.

Beaubrun, G., & Gray, G. E. (2000). A review of herbal medicines for psychiatric disorders. *Psychiatric Services, 51,* 1130–1134.

Beaumont, S. (1995). Adolescent girls' conversations with mothers and friends: A matter of style. *Discourse Processes, 11,* 325–356.

Beaumont, S. (1996). Adolescent girls' perceptions of conversations with mothers and friends. *Journal of Adolescent Research, 11,* 325–346.

Beaumont, S., & Cheyne, J. A. (1998). Interruptions in adolescent girls' conversations: Comparing mothers and friends. *Journal of Adolescent Research, 13,* 272–292.

Beauregard, K. S., & Dunning, D. (1998). Turning up the contrast: Self-enhancement motives prompt egocentric contrast effects in social judgments. *Journal of Personality and Social Psychology, 74,* 606–621.

Beck, A. T. (1991). Cognitive therapy: A 30-year retrospective. *American Psychologist, 46,* 368–375.

Beck, A. T., Rush, A. J., Shaw, B. F., & Emery, G. (1979). Cognitive therapy for depression. New York: Guilford Press.

Beech, J. R., & Whittaker, J. (2001). What is the female image projected by smoking? *Psychologia: An International Journal of Psychology in the Orient, 44,* 230–236.

Beer, J. M., Arnold, R. D., & Loehlin, J. C. (1998). Genetic and environmental influences on MMPI factor scales: Joint model fitting to twin and adoption data. *Journal of Personality and Social Psychology, 74,* 818–827.

Beers, M. J., Lassiter, G. D., & Flannery, B. C. (1997). Individual differences in person memory: Self-monitoring and the recall of consistent and inconsistent behavior. *Journal of Social*

Behavior and Personality, 12, 811–820.

Begg, I. M., Needham, D. R., & Bookbinder, M. (1993). Do backward messages unconsciously affect listeners? No. *Canadian Journal of Experimental Psychology, 47,* 1–14.

Behrmann, M., Winocur, G., & Moscovitch, M. (1992). Dissociation between mental imagery and object recognition in a brain-damaged patient. *Nature, 359,* 636–637.

Békésy, G. von (1960). *Experiments in hearing.* New York: McGraw-Hill.

Bell, A. P., Weinberg, M. S., & Hammersmith, S. K. (1981). *Sexual preference: Its development in men and women.* Bloomington: Indiana University Press.

Bell, P. A., Fisher, J. D., Baum, A., & Greene, T. E. (1990). *Environmental psychology* (3rd ed.). Fort Worth, TX: Holt, Rinehart & Winston.

Bem, D. J. (1967). Self-perception: An alternative interpretation of cognitive dissonance phenomena. *Psychological Review, 74,* 183–200.

Bem, D. J. (1972). Self-perception theory. In L. Berkowitz (Ed.), *Advances in experimental social psychology* (Vol. 6, pp. 1–62). New York: Academic Press.

Bem, S. L. (1981). Gender schema theory: A cognitive account of sex-typing. *Psychological Review, 88,* 354–364.

Benbow, C. P., Lubinski, D., Shea, D. L., & Eftekhari-Sanjani, H. (2000). Sex differences in mathematical reasoning ability at age 13: Their status 20 years later. *Psychological Science, 11,* 474–480.

Benes, F. M., Turtle, M., Khan, Y., & Farol, P. (1994). Myelination of a key relay zone in the hippocampul formation occurs in the human brain during childhood, adolescence, and adulthood. *Archives of General Psychiatry, 51,* 477–484.

Benjafield, J. G. (2004). *A history of psychology* (2nd ed.). New York: Oxford University Press.

Benson, P. L., Dehority, J., Garman, L., Hanson, E., Hochschwender, M., Lebod, C., et al. (1980). Intrapersonal correlates of nonspontaneous helping behavior. *Journal of Social Psychology, 110,* 87–95.

Bentall, R. P. (1990). The illusion of reality: A review and integration of psychological research on hallucina-tions. *Psychological Bulletin, 107,* 82–95.

Benton, M. K., & Schroeder, H. E. (1990). Social skills training with schizo-phrenics: A meta-analytic evaluation. *Journal of Consulting and Clinical Psychology, 58,* 741–747.

Bergvall, A., Fahlke, C., & Hansen, S. (1996). An animal model for Type 2 alcoholism? Alcohol consumption and aggressive behavior following lesions in the raphe nuclei, medial hypothalamus, or ventral striatum-septal area. *Physiology and Behavior, 60,* 1125–1135.

Berkowitz, L., & Harmon-Jones, E. (2004). Toward an understanding of the determinants of anger. *Emotion, 4,* 107–130.

Berman, K. F., & Weinberger, D. R. (1990). Lateralization of cortical func-tion during cognitive tasks: Regional cerebral blood flow studies of normal individuals and patients with schizo-phrenia. *Journal of Neurology, Neurosurgery, and Psychiatry, 53,* 150–160.

Bernal, E. M. (1984). Bias in mental testing: Evidence for an alternative to the heredity-environment controversy. In C. R. Reynolds & R. T. Brown (Eds.), *Perspectives on bias in mental testing.* New York: Plenum Press.

Berndt, T. J. (1988). The nature and sig-nificance of children's friendships. In R. Vasta (Ed.), *Annals of child devel-opment* (Vol. 5, pp. 155–186). Greenwich, CT: JAI Press.

Berndt, T. J., & Keefe, K. (1995). Friends' influence on adolescents' adjustments to school. *Child Development, 66,* 1312–1329.

Bernstein, I. H., Lin, T., & McClelland, P. (1982). Cross- vs. within-racial judg-ments of attractiveness. *Perception and Psychophysics, 32,* 495–503.

Bernstein, I. L. (1978). Learned taste aversions in children receiving chemotherapy. *Science, 200,* 1302–1303.

Berridge, K. C. (2004). Motivation con-cepts in behavioral neuroscience. *Physiology & Behavior, 81,* 179–209.

Berry, J. W. (1999). Intercultural relations in plural societies. *Canadian Psychology, 40,* 12–21.

Berry, J. W., & Kalin, R. (1995). Multicultural and ethnic attitudes in Canada: An overview of the 1991 national survey. *Canadian Journal of Behavioural Science, 27,* 301–320.

Berry, J. W., Poortinga, Y. H., & Pandey, J. (Eds.). (1997). *Handbook of cross-cultural psychology: Theory and method.* Boston: Allyn & Bacon.

Berscheid, E. (1985). Interpersonal attraction. In G. Lindzey & E. Aronson (Eds.), *Handbook of social psychology* (3rd ed., pp. 413–484). New York: Random House.

Bertenthal, B. I., Campos, J. J., & Kermoian, R. (1994). An epigenetic perspective on the development of self-produced locomotion and its con-sequences. *Current Directions in Psychological Science, 3,* 140–145.

Berthoud, H. (2004). Mind versus metab-olism in the control of food intake and energy balance. *Physiology & Behavior, 81,* 781–793.

Best, J. B. (1989). *Cognitive psychology* (2nd ed.). St. Paul, MN: West Publishing.

Beutler, L. E., & Berren, M. R. (Eds.). (1995). *Integrative assessment of adult personality.* New York: Guilford Press.

Biederman, I. (1987). Recognition-by-components: A theory of human image understanding. *Psychological Review, 94,* 115–147.

Biederman, I. (1990). Higher-level vision. In D. H. Osherson, S. M. Kosslyn, & J. M. Hollerbach (Eds.), *An invitation to cognitive science: Visual cognition and action* (Vol. 2, pp. 41–72). Cambridge, MA: MIT Press.

Bigelow, H. J. (1850). Dr. Harlow's case of recovery from the passage of an iron bar through the head. *American Journal of Medical Science, 20,* 13–22.

Binet, A., & Simon, T. (1973). *The devel-opment of intelligence in children.* New York: Arno Press. (Original work published 1916)

Bischof, W. R., & Boulanger, P. (2003). Spatial navigation in virtual reality environments: An EEG analysis. *CyberPsychology & Behavior, 6,* 487–495.

Bisiach, E. (1992). Understanding con-sciousness: Clues from unilateral neglect and related disorders. In A. D. Milner & M. D. Rugg (Eds.), *The neu-ropsychology of consciousness* (pp. 113–137). London: Academic Press.

Bisiach, E., & Rusconi, M. L. (1990). Break-down of perceptual awareness in unilateral neglect. *Cortex, 26,* 643–649.

Bjork, R. A. (1989). Retrieval inhibition as an adaptive mechanism in human memory. In H. L. Roediger & F. I. M. Craik (Eds.), *Varieties of memory and consciousness: Essays in honor of Endel Tulving* (pp. 309–330). Hillsdale, NJ: Erlbaum.

Bjorklund, D. F. (1997). The role of immaturity in human development. *Psychological Bulletin, 122*, 153–169.

Blagrove, M. (1996). Problems with the cognitive psychological modeling of dreaming. *Journal of Mind and Behavior, 17*, 99–134.

Blair, H. A., & Sanford, K. (1999). TV and zines: Media and the construction of gender for early adolescents. *Alberta Journal of Educational Research, 45*, 103–105.

Blair, S. N., Kohl, H. W., Paffenbarger, R. S., Clark, K. H., & Gibbons, L. W. (1989). Physical fitness and all-cause mortality: A prospective study of healthy men and women. *Journal of the American Medical Association, 262*, 2395–2401.

Blake, J., Austin, W., Cannon, M., & Lisus, A. (1994). The relationship between memory span and measures of imitative and spontaneous language complexity in preschool children. *International Journal of Behavioral Development, 17*, 91–107.

Blanchard, E. B. (1992). Psychological treatment of benign headache disorders. *Journal of Consulting and Clinical Psychology, 60*, 537–551.

Blanchard, R. (1997). Birth order and sibling sex ratio in homosexual versus heterosexual males and females. *Annual Review of Sex Research, 8*, 27–67.

Blanton, H., Cooper, J., Skurnik, I., & Aronson, J. (1997). When bad things happen to good feedback: Exacerbating the need for self-justification with self-affirmations. *Personality and Social Psychology Bulletin, 23*, 684–692.

Blass, T. (Ed.). (2000). *Obedience to authority: Current perspectives on the Milgram paradigm.* Mahwah, NJ: Erlbaum.

Blatt, S. J., & Zuroff, D. C. (1992). Interpersonal relatedness and self-definition: Two prototypes for depression. *Clinical Psychology Review, 12*, 527–562.

Bleuler, E. (1908). Die prognose der Dementia praecox (Schizophreniegruppe). *Allgemeine Zeitschrift für Psychiatrie, 65*, 436–464.

Block, J. (2002). *Ego-resiliency and ego-control through time.* New York: Guilford Press.

Bloomfield, L. (1933). *Language.* New York: Holt.

Blumenthal, J. A., Emery, C. F., Walsh, M. A., Cox, D. R., Kuhn, C. M., Williams, R. B., et al. (1988). Exercise training in healthy Type A middle-aged men: Effects on behavioral and cardiovascular responses. *Psychosomatic Medicine, 50*, 418–433.

Blundell, J. E., & Rogers, P. J. (1991). Hunger, hedonics, and the control of satiation and satiety. In M. I. Friedman, M. G. Tordoff, & M. R. Kare (Eds.), *Chemical senses: Vol. 4. Appetite and nutrition* (pp. 127–148). New York: Marcel Dekker.

Bock, G. R., & Cardew, G. (Eds.). (1997). *Characterizing human psychological adaptations.* New York: Wiley.

Bodner, G. E., & Masson, M. E. J. (2003). Beyond spreading activation: An influence of relatedness proportion on masked semantic priming. *Psychonomic Bulletin & Review, 10*, 645–652.

Bogaert, A. F. (2005). Sibling sex ratio and sexual orientation in men and women: New tests in two national probability samples. *Archives of Sexual Behavior, 34*, 111–116.

Boivin, D. B. (2000). Influence of sleep-wake and circadian rhythm disturbances in psychiatric disorders. *Journal of Psychiatry and Neuroscience, 25*, 446–458.

Bolanowski, S. J., Gescheider, G. A., & Verrillo, R. T. (1994). Hairy skin: Psychophysical channels and their physiological substrates. *Somatosensory and Motor Research, 11*, 279–290.

Bolanowski, S. J., Jr. (1989). Four channels mediate vibrotaction: Facts, models, and implications. *Journal of the Acoustical Society of America, 85*, S62.

Bolles, R. C. (1972). Reinforcement, expectancy, and learning. *Psychological Review, 79*, 394–409.

Bolles, R. C. (1993). *The story of psychology: A thematic history.* Pacific Grove, CA: Brooks/Cole.

Bonanno, G. A. (2004). Loss, trauma, and human resilience: Have we underestimated the human capacity to thrive after extremely aversive events? *American Psychologist, 59*(1), 20–28.

Bonanno, G. A., Field, N. P., Kovacevic, A., & Kaltman, S. (2002). Self-enhancement as a buffer against extreme adversity: Civil war in Bosnia and traumatic loss in the United States. *Personality and Social Psychology Bulletin, 28*, 184–196.

Boniecki, K. A., & Moore, S. (2003). Breaking the silence: Using a token economy to reinforce classroom participation. *Teaching of Psychology, 30*, 224–227.

Bonta, J., & Gendreau, P. (1990). Reexamining the cruel and unusual punishment of prison life. *Law and Human Behavior, 14*, 347–372.

Book, A. S., & Quinsey, V. L. (2003). Psychopaths: Cheaters or warrior-hawks? *Personality and Individual Differences, 36*, 33–45.

Boone, K. B., & Lu, P. (2000). Gender effects in neuropsychological assessment. In E. Fletcher-Janzen, T. L. Strickland, & C. R. Reynolds (Eds.), *Handbook of cross-cultural neuropsychology* (pp. 73–85). Dordrecht, Netherlands: Kluwer Academic Publishers.

Bootzin, R. R., Manber, R., Perlis, M. L., Salvio, M., & Wyatt, J. K. (1993). Sleep disorders and the elderly. In P. B. Sutker & H. F. Adams (Eds.), *Comprehensive handbook of psychopathology* (2nd ed.). New York: Plenum Press.

Boring, E. G. (1950). *A history of experimental psychology* (2nd ed.). New York: Appleton-Century-Crofts.

Borkenau, P., & Liebler, A. (1995). Observable attributes as manifestations and cues of personality and intelligence. *Journal of Personality, 63*, 1–25.

Borkowski, J. G., Ramey, S. L., & Bristol-Power, M. (Eds.). (2001). *Parenting and the child's world: Influences on academic, intellectual, and social-emotional development.* Mahwah, NJ: Erlbaum.

Bornstein, M. H. (1989). Stability in early mental development: From attention and information processing in infancy to language and cognition in childhood. In M. H. Bornstein & N. A. Krasnegor (Eds.), *Stability and continuity in mental development: Behavioral and biological perspectives* (pp. 147–170). Hillsdale, NJ: Erlbaum.

Bornstein, M. H. (1992). Perception across the life span. In M. H. Bornstein & M. E. Lamb (Eds.), *Developmental psychology: An advanced textbook* (3rd ed., pp. 731–789). Hillsdale, NJ: Erlbaum.

Bornstein, M. H., Kessen, W., & Weiskopf, S. (1976). Color vision and hue categorization in young human infants. *Journal of Experimental Psychology: Human Perception and Performance, 2*, 115–129.

Boroditsky, R., Fisher, W., & Sand, M. (1996). The 1995 Canadian contraception study. *Journal SOGC, 18*(Suppl.), 1–31.

Bortz, W. M. (1990). The trajectory of dying: Functional status in the last year of life. *Journal of the American Geriatrics Society, 38*, 146–150.

Bosco, A., Longoni, A. M., & Vecchi, T. (2004). Gender effects in spatial orientation: Cognitive profiles and mental strategies. *Applied Cognitive Psychology, 18*(5), 519–532.

Bouchard, C., Tremblay, A., Despres, J., Nadeau, A., Lupien, P. J., Theriault, G., et al. (1990). The response to long-term overfeeding in identical twins. *New England Journal of Medicine, 322*, 1477–1487.

Bouchard, T. J., Jr. (1997). IQ similarity in twins reared apart: Findings and responses to critics. In R. J. Sternberg & E. L. Grigorenko (Eds.), *Intelligence, heredity, and environment* (pp. 126–160). New York: Cambridge University Press.

Bouchard, T. J., Jr., Lykken, D. T., McGue, M., Segal, N. L., & Tellegean, A. (1990). Sources of human psychological differences: The Minnesota study of twins reared apart. *Science, 250*, 223–228.

Bouchard, T. J., Jr., & McGue, M. (1981). Familial studies of intelligence: A review. *Science, 212*, 1055–1059.

Boucher, J. D., & Carlson, G. E. (1980). Recognition of facial expression in three cultures. *Journal of Cross-Cultural Psychology, 11*, 263–280.

Boudreau, R. A. (1983). An evaluation of graduate record examinations as predictors of graduate success in a Canadian context. *Canadian Psychology, 24*, 191–199.

Bouton, M. E. (1991). Context and retrieval in extinction and other examples of interference in simple associative learning. In L. Dachowski & C. F. Flaherty (Eds.), *Current topics in animal learning* (pp. 25–53). Hillsdale, NJ: Erlbaum.

Bouton, M. E., Mineka, S., & Barlow, D. H. (2001). A modern learning theory perspective on the etiology of panic disorder. *Psychological Review, 108*, 4–32.

Bower, G. H. (1973). How to . . . uh . . . remember. *Psychology Today, 7*, 63–70.

Bower, T. G. R. (1982). *Development in infancy* (2nd ed.). San Francisco: Freeman.

Bowers, T., & Clum, G. (1988). Relative contributions of specific and nonspecific treatment effects: Meta-analysis of placebo-controlled behavior therapy research. *Psychological Bulletin, 103*, 315–323.

Bowlby, J. (1969). *Attachment and loss: Vol. 1. Attachment*. New York: Basic Books.

Bowlby, J. (1988). *A secure base: Parent-child attachment and healthy human development*. New York: Basic Books.

Bowman, E. S. (1998). Pseudoseizures. *Psychiatric Clinics of North America, 21*, 649–657.

Boynton, R. M. (1979). *Human color vision*. New York: Holt, Rinehart, & Winston.

Braff, D. L., & Huey, L. (1988). Methylphenidate-induced information processing dysfunction in non-schizophrenic patients. *Archives of General Psychiatry, 45*, 827–832.

Bransford, J. D., & Stein, B. S. (1993). *The IDEAL problem solver* (2nd ed.). New York: Freeman.

Braungart, J. M., Plomin, R., DeFries, J. C., & Fulker, D. W. (1992). Genetic influence on tester-rated infant temperament as assessed by Bayley's Infant Behavior Record: Nonadoptive and adoptive siblings and twins. *Developmental Psychology, 28*, 40–47.

Breggin, P. R. (1991). *Toxic psychiatry*. New York: St. Martin's.

Bregman, A. S. (1990). *Auditory scene analysis*. Cambridge, MA: Bradford/MIT Press.

Breland, K., & Breland, M. (1961). The misbehavior of organisms. *American Psychologist, 16*, 681–684.

Brenneis, C. B. (1994). Can early childhood trauma be reconstructed from dreams? On the relation of dreams to trauma. *Psychoanalytic Psychology, 11*, 429–447.

Brett, J. F., Brief, A. P., Burke, M. J., George, J. M., & Webster, J. (1990). Negative affectivity and the reporting of stressful life events. *Health Psychology, 9*, 57–68.

Brewer, K. R., & Wann, D. L. (1998). Observational learning effectiveness as a function of model characteristics: Investigating the importance of social power. *Social Behavior and Personality, 26*, 1–10.

Briere, J., & Conte, J. (1993). Self-reported amnesia for abuse in adults molested as children. *Journal of Traumatic Stress, 6*, 21–31.

Brigham, J. C., & Pfeifer, J. E. (1996). Euthanasia: An introduction. *Journal of Social Issues, 52*, 1–11.

Brimacombe, C. A. E., Jung, S., Garrioch, L., & Allison, M. (2003). Perceptions of older adult eyewitnesses: Will you believe me when I'm 64? *Law and Human Behavior, 27*, 507–522.

Broad, W., & Wade, N. (1982). *Betrayers of the truth*. New York: Simon & Schuster.

Broadbent, D. E. (1952). Failures of attention in selective listening. *Journal of Experimental Psychology, 44*, 428–433.

Broadbent, D. E. (1958). *Perception and communication*. London: Pergamon Press.

Broberg, D. J., & Bernstein, I. L. (1987). Candy as a scapegoat in the prevention of food aversions in children receiving chemotherapy. *Cancer, 60*, 2344–2347.

Broca, P. (1861). Remarques sur le siege de la faculté du langage article, suivies d'une observation d'aphemie (perte de la parole). *Bulletin de la Societé Anatomique (Paris), 36*, 330–357.

Brody, J. L., Gluck, J. P., & Aragon, A. S. (2000). Participants' understanding of the process of psychological research: Debriefing. *Ethics & Behavior, 10*(1), 13–25.

Brody, N. (1992). *Intelligence* (2nd ed.). San Diego, CA: Academic Press.

Brooks, D. C. (2000). Recent and remote extinction cues reduce spontaneous recovery. *Quarterly Journal of Experimental Psychology, 53B*, 25–58.

Brooks, L. R. (1968). Spatial and verbal components of the act of recall. *Canadian Journal of Psychology, 22*, 349–368.

Brosschot, J. F., Godaert, G. L. R., Benschop, R. J., Olff, M., Ballieux, R. E., & Heijnen, C. J. (1998).

Experimental stress and immunological reactivity: A closer look at perceived uncontrollability. *Psychosomatic Medicine, 60,* 359–361.

Broughton, R., Trapnell, P. D., & Boyes, M. C. (1991). Classifying personality types with occupational prototypes. *Journal of Research in Personality, 25,* 302–321.

Brown, A. D., & Murphy, D. R. (1989). Cryptomnesia: Delineating inadvertent plagiarism. *Journal of Experimental Psychology: Learning, Memory, and Cognition, 15,* 432–442.

Brown, D., Scheflin, A. W., & Hammond, D. C. (1998). *Memory, trauma treatment, and the law.* New York: W. W. Norton.

Brown, G. W., & Birley, J. L. T. (1968). Crisis and life change and the onset of schizophrenia. *Journal of Health and Social Behavior, 9,* 203–214.

Brown, J. (1958). Some tests of the decay theory of immediate memory. *Quarterly Journal of Experimental Psychology, 10,* 12–21.

Brown, R., & Kulick, J. (1977). Flashbulb memories. *Cognition, 5,* 73–99.

Brown, R. E. (1992). Responses of dominant and subordinate male rats to the odors of male and female conspecifics. *Aggressive Behavior, 18*(2), 129–138.

Brown, T. A., Barlow, D. H., & Liebowitz, M. R. (1994). The empirical basis of generalized anxiety disorder. *American Journal of Psychiatry, 151,* 1272–1280.

Brown, T. A., O'Leary, T. A., & Barlow, D. H. (2001). Generalized anxiety disorder. In D. H. Barlow (Ed.), *Clinical handbook of psychological disorders: A step-by-step treatment manual* (3rd ed., pp. 154–205). New York: Guilford Press.

Bruce, D. (1985). The how and why of ecological memory. *Journal of Experimental Psychology: General, 114,* 78–90.

Bub, D. N. (2000). Methodological issues confronting PET and MRI studies of cognitive function. *Cognitive Neuropsychology, 17,* 467–484.

Buck, L. (1996). Information coding in the vertebrate olfactory system. *Annual Review of Neuroscience, 19,* 517–544.

Buck, L., & Axel, A. (1991). A novel multigene family may encode odorant receptors: A molecular basis for odor recognition. *Cell, 65,* 175–187.

Buehler, R., Griffin, D., & Ross, M. (1994). Exploring the "planning fallacy": Why people underestimate their task completion times. *Journal of Personality and Social Psychology, 67,* 366–381.

Buell, S. J., & Coleman, P. D. (1979). Dendritic growth in the aged human brain and failure of growth in senile dementia. *Science, 206,* 854–856.

Burda, J. M., & Brooks, C. I. (1996). College classroom seating position and changes in achievement motivation over a semester. *Psychological Reports, 78,* 331–336.

Burger, J. M., & Caldwell, D. F. (2003). The effects of monetary incentives and labeling on the foot-in-the-door effect: Evidence for a self-perception process. *Basic & Applied Social Psychology, 25,* 235–241.

Buscemi, N., Vandermeer, B., Hooton, N., Pandya, R., Tjosvold, L., Hartling, L., Baker, G., et al. (2006). Efficacy and safety of exogenous melatonin for secondary sleep disorders and sleep disorders accompanying sleep restriction: Meta-analysis. *BMJ: British Medical Journal, 332*(7538), 1–9.

Bushman, B. J., & Anderson, C. A. (2001). Media violence and the American public: Scientific facts versus media misinformation. *American Psychologist, 56,* 477–489.

Buss, A. H. (1988). *Personality: Evolutionary heritage and human distinctiveness.* Hillsdale, NJ: Erlbaum.

Buss, D. M. (1991). Evolutionary personality psychology. *Annual Review of Psychology, 42,* 459–491.

Buss, D. M. (1994). *The evolution of desire: Strategies of human mating.* New York: Basic Books.

Buss, D. M. (1999). *Evolutionary psychology: The new science of the mind.* Needham Heights, MA: Allyn & Bacon.

Buss, D. M. (2000). *The dangerous passion: Why jealousy is as dangerous as love and sex.* New York: Free Press.

Buss, D. M. (2004). *Evolutionary psychology: The ultimate origins of human behavior* (2nd ed.). Boston: Allyn & Bacon.

Buss, D. M. (2005). *The murderer next door: Why the mind is designed to kill.* New York: Penguin Press.

Buss, D. M., & Schmitt, D. P. (1993). Sexual strategies theory: An evolutionary perspective on human mating. *Psychological Review, 100,* 204–232.

Buss, D. M., & Shackelford, T. K. (1997). Human aggression in evolutionary psychological perspective. *Clinical Psychology Review, 17,* 605–619.

Bustillo, J. R., Lauriello, J., Horan, W. P., & Keith, S. J. (2001). The psychosocial treatment of schizophrenia: An update. *American Journal of Psychiatry, 158,* 163–175.

Butcher, J. N. (1995). Interpretation of the MMPI-2. In L. E. Beutler & M. R. Berren (Eds.), *Integrative assessment of adult personality* (pp. 206–239). New York: Guilford Press.

Butcher, J. N., & Rouse, S. V. (1996). Personality: Individual differences and clinical assessment. *Annual Review of Psychology, 47,* 87–111.

Butterworth, G. (1992). Origins of self-perception in infancy. *Psychological Inquiry, 3,* 103–111.

Byers, S. E., Purdon, C., & Clark, D. A. (1998). Sexual intrusive thoughts of college students. *Journal of Sex Research, 35,* 359–369.

Byrd, J. C. (1992). Environmental tobacco smoke: Medical and legal issues. *Medical Clinics of North America, 76,* 377–398.

Byrne, D. (1971). *The attraction paradigm.* New York: Academic Press.

Cabeza, R., Locantore, J. K., & Anderson, N. D. (2003). Lateralization of prefrontal activity during episodic memory retrieval: Evidence for the production-monitoring hypothesis. *Journal of Cognitive Neuroscience, 15,* 249–259.

Cacioppo, J. T., Berntson, G. G., Sheridan, J. F., & McClintock, M. K. (2000). Multilevel integrative analyses of human behavior: Social neuroscience and the complementing nature of social and biological approaches. *Psychological Bulletin, 126*(6), 829–843.

Cahn, B. R., & Polich, J. (2006). Meditation states and traits: EEG, ERP, and neuroimaging studies. *Psychological Bulletin, 132*(2), 180–211.

Cameron, J., & Pierce, W. D. (1994). Reinforcement, reward, and intrinsic motivation: A meta-analysis. *Review of Educational Research, 64,* 363–423.

Camic, P. M., Rhodes, J. E., & Yardley, L. (2003). *Qualitative research in psychology: Expanding perspectives in methodology and design.* Washington, DC: American Psychological Association.

Campbell, D. T., & Stanley, J. C. (1966). *Experimental and quasi-experimental designs for research.* Chicago: Rand McNally.

Campbell, D. W., & Eaton, W. O. (1999). Sex differences in the activity level of infants. *Infant and Child Development, 8,* 1–17.

Campfield, L. A., Smith, F. J., Rosenbaum, M., & Hirsch, J. (1996). Human eating: Evidence for a physiological basis using a modified paradigm. *Neuroscience & Biobehavioral Reviews, 20,* 1133–1137.

Campos, J. J., Langer, A., & Krowitz, A. (1970). Cardiac responses on the visual cliff in prelocomotor human infants. *Science, 170,* 196–197.

Canadian Centre on Substance Abuse. (1999). *Canadian Profile, 1999.* Retrieved August 20, 2000, from http://www.ccsa.ca/CCSA/EN/Statistics/CanadianProfile1999.htm

Canadian Institutes of Health Research, Natural Sciences and Engineering Research Council of Canada, Social Sciences and Humanities Research Council of Canada. (2005). Tri-council policy statement: Ethical conduct for research involving humans. Ottawa, ON: Interagency Advisory Panel on Research Ethics.

Canadian Psychological Association. (1991). *Canadian code of ethics for psychologists.* Ottawa, ON: Author. Also available at www.cpa.ca/ethics.html

Cannon, W. B. (1927). The James-Lange theory of emotions: A critical examination and an alternative theory. *American Journal of Psychology, 39,* 106–124.

Cannon, W. B. (1929). *Bodily changes in pain, hunger, fear, and rage.* New York: Appleton.

Cannon, W. B. (1932). *The wisdom of the body.* New York: Norton.

Cantor, N. (1990). From thought to behavior: "Having" and "doing" in the study of personality and cognition. *American Psychologist, 45,* 735–750.

Cantor, N., & Harlow, R. E. (1994). Personality, strategic behavior, and daily-life problem solving. *Current Directions in Psychological Science, 3,* 169–172.

Cantor, N., & Malley, J. (1991). Life tasks, personal needs, and close relationships. In G. Fletcher & F. Fincham (Eds.), *Cognition in close relationships* (pp. 101–125). Hillsdale, NJ: Erlbaum.

Cantor, N., & Mischel, W. (1978). Prototypes in person perception. *Advances in Experimental Social Psychology, 12,* 3–52.

Cantwell, D. P. (1996). Attention deficit disorder: A review of the past 10 years. *Journal of the American Academy of Child and Adolescent Psychiatry, 35,* 978–987.

Capaldi, E. D. (Ed.). (1996). *Why we eat what we eat: The psychology of eating.* Washington, DC: American Psychological Association.

Carlsmith, J. M., & Gross, A. E. (1969). Some effects of guilt on compliance. *Journal of Personality and Social Psychology, 11,* 240–244.

Carlsson, A., Waters, N., Holm-Waters, S., Tedroff, J., Nilsson, M., & Carlsson, M. L. (2001). Interactions between monoamines, glutamate, and GABA in schizophrenia: New evidence. *Annual Review of Pharmacology and Toxicology, 41,* 237–260.

Carpendale, J. (1997). An explication of Piaget's constructivism: Implications for social cognitive development. In S. Hala (Ed.), *The development of social cognition* (pp. 35–64). Hove, England: Erlbaum.

Carrasco, M., & Ridout, J. B. (1993). Olfactory perception and olfactory imagery: A multidimensional analysis. *Journal of Experimental Psychology: Human Perception and Performance, 19,* 287–301.

Carrazana, E. J., Rivas-Vazquez, R. A., & Rey, G. J. (2001). SSRI discontinuation and buspirone. *American Journal of Psychiatry, 158,* 966–967.

Carstensen, L. L. (1995). Evidence for a life-span theory of socioemotional selectivity. *Current Directions in Psychological Science, 4,* 151–156.

Cartwright, J. (2000). *Evolution and human behavior.* Cambridge, MA: MIT Press.

Cartwright, R. (1991). Dreams that work: The relation of dream incorporation to adaptation to stressful events. *Dreaming, 1,* 2–9.

Caspi, A., & Silva, P. A. (1995). Temperamental qualities at age three predict personality traits in young adulthood: Longitudinal evidence from a birth cohort. *Child Development, 66,* 486–498.

Caspi, A., Sugden, K., Moffitt, T. E., Taylor, A., Craig, I. W., Harrington, H., et al. (2003). Influence of life stress on depression: Moderation by a polymor-phism in the 5-HTT gene. *Science, 301,* 386–389.

Cassidy, T. (2000). Stress, healthiness and health behaviours: An exploration of the role of life events, daily hassles, cognitive appraisal and the coping process. *Counselling Psychology Quarterly, 13,* 293–311.

Castillo, R. J. (1997). *Culture and mental illness: A client-centered approach.* Pacific Grove, CA: Brooks/Cole.

Cattell, R. B. (1963). Theory of fluid and crystallized intelligence: A critical experiment. *Journal of Educational Psychology, 54,* 1–22.

Cattell, R. B. (1998). Where is intelligence? Some answers from the triadic theory. In J. J. McArdle & R. W. Woodcock (Eds.), *Human cognitive abilities in theory and practice* (pp. 29–38). Mahwah, NJ: Erlbaum.

Cattell, R. B., Eber, H. W., & Tatsuoka, M. M. (1970). *Handbook of the 16 personality factor questionnaire (16PF).* Champaign, IL: Institute for Personality and Ability Testing.

Cavanaugh, J. C. (1993). *Adult development and aging* (2nd ed.). Pacific Grove, CA: Brooks/Cole.

Cavanaugh, J. C., & Blanchard Fields, F. (2002). *Adult development and aging* (4th ed.). Belmont, CA: Wadsworth.

Ceci, S. J. (1991). How much does schooling influence intellectual development and its cognitive components? A reassessment of the evidence. *Developmental Psychology, 27,* 703–722.

Ceci, S. J., & Liker, J. K. (1986). A day at the races: A study of IQ, expertise, and cognitive complexity. *Journal of Experimental Psychology: General, 115,* 255–266.

Cermak, L. S. (1982). The long and the short of it in amnesia. In L. S. Cermak (Ed.), *Human memory and amnesia* (pp. 43–56). Hillsdale, NJ: Erlbaum.

Cermakian, N., & Sassone-Corsi, P. (2002). Environmental stimulus perception and control of circadian clocks. *Current Opinion in Neurobiology, 12*(4), 359–365.

Chakos, M., Lieberman, J., Hoffman, E., Bradford, D., & Sheitman, B. (2001). Effectiveness of second-generation antipsychotics in patients with treatment-resistant schizophrenia: A review and meta-analysis of randomized trials. *American Journal of Psychiatry, 158,* 518–526.

Challis, B. H. (1993). Spacing effects on cued-memory tests depend on level of processing. *Journal of Experimental Psychology: Learning, Memory, and Cognition, 19,* 389–396.

Chambless, D. L., & Ollendick, T. H. (2001). Empirically supported psychological interventions: Controversies and evidence. *Annual Review of Psychology, 52,* 685–716.

Chan, J. C. K., McDermott, K. B., & Roediger, H. L., III. (in press). Retrieval-induced facilitation: Initially nontested material can benefit from prior testing of related material. *Journal of Experimental Psychology: General.*

Chandler, M. J., & Lalonde, C. E. (1996). Shifting toward an interpretive theory of the mind: Five- to seven-year-olds' changing conceptions of mental life. In A. Sameroff & M. Haith (Eds.), *Reason and responsibility: The passage through childhood* (pp. 111–139). Chicago: University of Chicago Press.

Chandler, M. J., Lalonde, C. E., & Sokol, B. W. (2000). Continuities of selfhood in the face of radical developmental and cultural change. In L. P. Nucci, G. Saze, & E. Turiel (Eds.), *Culture, thought, and development: The Jean Piaget symposium series* (pp. 68–84). Mahwah, NJ: Erlbaum.

Chapman, L. J., & Chapman, J. P. (1967). Genesis of popular but erroneous psychodiagnostic observations. *Journal of Abnormal Psychology, 72,* 193–204.

Chapman, M. (1988). *Constructive evolution: Origins and development of Piaget's thought.* New York: Cambridge University Press.

Charman, D. P. (Ed.). (2004). Core processes in brief psychodynamic psychotherapy: Advancing effective practice (pp. 231–250). Hillsdale, NJ: Erlbaum.

Charney, D. S. (2000). The use of placebos in randomized clinical trials of mood disorders: Well justified, but improvements in design are indicated. *Biological Psychiatry, 47,* 687–688.

Chase, W. G., & Simon, H. A. (1973). The mind's eye in chess. In W. G. Chase (Ed.), *Visual information processing* (pp. 215–281). New York: Academic Press.

Chaudhari, N., Landin, A. M., & Roper, S. D. (2000). A metabotropic glutamate receptor variant functions as a taste receptor. *Nature Neuroscience, 3,* 113–119.

Cheesman, J., & Merikle, P. M. (1986). Distinguishing conscious from unconscious perceptual processes. *Canadian Journal of Psychology, 40*(4), 343–367.

Chen, E., Fisher, E. B., Jr., Bacharier, L. B., & Strunk, R. C. (2003). Socioeconomic status, stress, and immune markers in adolescents with asthma. *Psychosomatic Medicine, 65,* 984–992.

Chen, E., & Mathews, K. A. (2001). Cognitive appraisal biases: An approach to understanding the relation between socioeconomic status and cardiovascular reactivity in children. *Annals of Behavioral Medicine, 23,* 101–111.

Chen, S. C. (1937). Social modification of the activity of ants in nest-building. *Physiological Zoology, 10,* 420–436.

Chen, X., Rubin, K. H., & Sun, Y. (1992). Social reputation and peer relationships in Chinese and Canadian children: A cross-cultural study. *Child Development, 63,* 1336–1343.

Chernyshenko, O. S., & Ones, D. S. (1999). How selective are psychology graduate programs? The effect of the selection ratio on GRE score validity. *Educational and Psychological Measurement, 59,* 951–961.

Cherry, E. C. (1953). Some experiments on the recognition of speech with one and with two ears. *Journal of the Acoustical Society of America, 25,* 975–979.

Chesney, M. A. (1993). Health psychology in the 21st century: Acquired immunodeficiency syndrome as a harbinger of things to come. *Health Psychology, 12,* 259–268.

Chia, R. C., Allred, L. J., Grossnickle, W. F., & Lee, G. W. (1998). Effects of attractiveness and gender on the perception of achievement-related variables. *Journal of Social Psychology, 138,* 471–477.

Chomsky, N. (1957). *Syntactic structures.* The Hague: Mouton.

Chomsky, N. (1986). *Knowledge of language: Its nature, origins, and use.* New York: Praeger.

Chumlea, W. C. (1982). Physical growth in adolescence. In B. J. Wolman (Ed.), *Handbook of developmental psychology.* Englewood Cliffs, NJ: Prentice-Hall.

Cialdini, R. B., & Goldstein, N. J. (2004). Social influence: Compliance and conformity. *Annual Review of Psychology, 55,* 591–621.

Cicirelli, V. G. (1997). Relationship of psychosocial and background variables to older adults' end-of-life decisions. *Psychology and Aging, 12,* 72–83.

Clark, H. H. (1992). *Arenas of language use.* Chicago: University of Chicago Press.

Clarke, L. A., & Livesley, W. J. (1994). Two approaches to identifying the dimensions of personality disorder: Convergence on the five-factor model. In P. T. Costa, Jr., & T. A. Widiger (Eds.), *Personality disorders and the five-factor model of personality* (pp. 261–278). Washington, DC: American Psychological Association.

Cleary, L. J., Lee, W. L., & Byrne, J. H. (1998). Cellular correlates of long-term sensitization in Aplysia. *Journal of Neuroscience, 18,* 5988–5998.

Cleary, P. J. (1980). A checklist for life event research. *Journal of Psychosomatic Research, 24,* 199–207.

Cleghorn, J. M., Franco, S., Szechtman, B., Kaplan, R., Szechtman, H., Brown, G. M., et al. (1992). Toward a brain map of auditory hallucinations. *American Journal of Psychiatry, 149,* 1062–1069.

Clendenen, V. I., Herman, C. P., & Polivy, J. (1994). Social facilitation of eating among friends and strangers. *Appetite, 23,* 1–13.

Cohen, J. D., & Schooler, J. W. (Eds.). (1997). *Scientific approaches to consciousness.* Mahwah, NJ: Erlbaum.

Cohen, J. S., Simpson, A., Westlake, K., & Hamelin, P. (2002). Integration and representation in rats' serial pattern learning in the T-maze. *Animal Learning and Behavior, 30*(3), 261–274.

Cohen, S., & Herbert, T. B. (1996). Health psychology: Psychological factors and physical disease from the perspective of human psychoneuroimmunology. *Annual Review of Psychology, 47,* 113–142.

Cohen, S., Tyrrell, D. A., & Smith, D. A. (1993). Negative life events, perceived stress, negative affect, and susceptibility to the common cold. *Journal of Personality and Social Psychology, 64,* 131–140.

Cohen, S., & Wills, T. A. (1985). Stress, social support, and the buffering hypothesis. *Psychological Bulletin, 98,* 310–357.

Coile, D. C., & Miller, N. E. (1984). How radical animal activists try to mislead humane people. *American Psychologist, 39*, 700–701.

Cole, M. (1992). Culture in development. In M. H. Bornstein & M. E. Lamb (Eds.), *Developmental psychology: An advanced textbook* (3rd ed., pp. 731–789). Hillsdale, NJ: Erlbaum.

Cole, N. S. (1981). Bias in testing. *American Psychologist, 36,* 1067–1077.

Coles, R., & Stokes, G. (1985). *Sex and the American teenager.* New York: Harper & Row.

Colombo, J., Frick, J. E., & Gorman, S. A. (1997). Sensitization during visual habituation sequences: Procedural effects and individual differences. *Journal of Experimental Child Psychology, 67,* 223–235.

Colwill, R. M. (1994). Associative representations of instrumental contingencies. In D. L. Medin (Ed.), *The psychology of learning and motivation* (Vol. 31, pp. 1–72). San Diego, CA: Academic Press.

Colwill, R. M., & Rescorla, R. A. (1986). Associative structures in instrumental learning. In G. H. Bower (Ed.), *The psychology of learning and motivation* (pp. 55–104). Orlando, FL: Academic Press.

COMMIT Research Group. (1995a). Community intervention trial for smoking cessation (COMMIT): I. Cohort results from a four-year community intervention. *American Journal of Public Health, 85,* 183–192.

COMMIT Research Group. (1995b). Community intervention trial for smoking cessation (COMMIT): II. Changes in adult cigarette smoking prevalence. *American Journal of Public Health, 85,* 193–200.

Compas, B. E., Hinden, B. R., & Gerhardt, C. A. (1995). Adolescent development: Pathways and processes of risk and resilience. *Annual Review of Psychology, 46,* 265–293.

Compton, S. N., March, J. S., Brent, D., Albano, A. M., Weersing, V. R., & Curry, J. (2004). Cognitive-behavioral psychotherapy for anxiety and depressive disorders in children and adolescents: An evidence-based medicine review. *Journal of the American Academy of Child & Adolescent Psychiatry, 43,* 930–959.

Connolly, J., Pepler, D., Craig, W., & Taradash, A. (2000). Dating experiences of bullies in early adolescence. *Journal of the American Professional Society on the Abuse of Children, 5,* 299–310.

Connolly, J. F., & D'Arcy, R. C. N. (2000). Innovations in neuropsychological assessment using event-related brain potentials. *International Journal of Psychophysiology, 37,* 31–47.

Conrad, R. (1964). Acoustic confusion in immediate memory. *British Journal of Psychology, 55,* 75–84.

Conrod, P. J., Pihl, R. O., Stewart, S. H., & Dongier, M. (2000). Validation of a system of classifying female substance abusers on the basis of personality and motivational risk factors for substance abuse. *Psychology of Addictive Behaviors, 14,* 243–256.

Conway, A. R. A., Kane, M. J., & Engle, R. W. (2003). Working memory capacity and its relation to general intelligence. *Trends in Cognitive Science, 7,* 547–552.

Conway, M. A. (1995). *Flashbulb memories.* London: Taylor and Francis.

Cook, M., & Mineka, S. (1989). Observational conditioning of fear to fear-relevant versus fear-irrelevant stimuli in rhesus monkeys. *Journal of Abnormal Psychology, 98,* 448–459.

Cook, T. D., & Campbell, D. T. (1979). *Quasi-experimentation: Design and analysis for field settings.* Chicago: Rand McNally.

Cooper, A., Scherer, C. R., Boies, C., & Gordon, B. L. (1999). Sexuality on the Internet: From sexual exploration to pathological expression. *Professional Psychology: Research and Practice, 30,* 154–164.

Cooper, E. (1991). A critique of six measures for assessing creativity. *Journal of Creative Behavior, 25,* 194–204.

Cooper, J. (1992). Dissonance and the return of the self-concept. *Psychological Inquiry, 3,* 320–323.

Cooper, P. E. (1991). Neuroendocrinology. In W. G. Bradley, R. B. Daroff, D. G. Fenichel, & C. D. Marsden (Eds.), *Neurology in clinical practice: Principles of diagnosis and management* (pp. 611–625). Boston: Butterworth Heinemann.

Cooper, W. H. (1983). An achievement motivation nomological network. *Journal of Personality and Social Psychology, 44,* 841–861.

Coplan, R. J., Rubin, K. H., Fox, N. A., Calkins, S. D., & Stewart, S. (1994). Being alone, playing alone, and acting alone: Distinguishing among reticence and passive and active solitude in young children. *Child Development, 65,* 129–137.

Corballis, M. C. (1991). *The lopsided ape: Evolution of the generative mind.* New York: Oxford University Press.

Coren, A. (2001). *Short-term psychotherapy: A psychodynamic approach.* New York: Palgrave.

Coren, S. (1992). The moon illusion: A different view through the legs. *Perceptual and Motor Skills* (3, Pt. 1), 827–831.

Coren, S. (1995). *The intelligence of dogs.* New York: Bantam Books.

Coren, S. (1996). *Sleep thieves.* New York: Free Press.

Coren, S. (1999). Psychology applied to animal learning. In D. A. Bernstein & A. Stec (Eds.), *Psychology: Fields of application* (pp. 199–217). Boston: Houghton Mifflin.

Coren, S. (2000). *Why we love the dogs we do: How to find the dog that matches your personality.* New York: Fireside.

Coren, S., Ward, L. M., & Enns, J. T. (1999). *Sensation and perception* (5th ed.). Fort Worth, TX: Harcourt Brace.

Coren, S., Ward, L. M., & Enns, J. T. (2004). *Sensation and perception* (6th ed.). New York: Wiley.

Corneil, W., Beaton, R., Murphy, S., Johnson, C., & Pike, K. (1999). Exposure to traumatic incidents and prevalence of posttraumatic stress symptomatology in urban firefighters in two countries. *Journal of Occupational Health Psychology, 4,* 131–141.

Corsica, J. A., & Perri, M. G. (2003). Obesity. In A. M. Nezu, C. M. Nezu, & P. A. Geller (Eds.), *Handbook of psychology: Vol. 9. Health psychology* (pp. 121–146). New York: Wiley.

Cosmides, L., & Tooby, J. (1997). Dissecting the computational architecture of social inference mechanisms. In G. R. Bock & G. Cardew (Eds.), *Characterizing human psychological adaptations* (pp. 132–161). New York: Wiley.

Costa, P. T., & McCrae, R. R. (1989). *NEO/PI/FFI manual supplement.* Odessa, FL: Psychological Assessment Resources.

Cote, K. A., Etienne, L., & Campbell, K. B. (2001). Neurophysiological evidence for the detection of external stimuli during sleep. *Sleep: Journal of Sleep and Sleep Disorders Research, 24,* 791–803.

Courage, M. L., & Howe, M. L. (2004). Advances in early memory development research: Insights about the dark side of the moon. *Developmental Review, 24,* 6–32.

Couturier, J. L. (2005). Efficacy of rapid-rate repetitive transcranial magnetic stimulation in the treatment of depression: A systematic review and meta-analysis. *Journal of Psychiatry & Neuroscience, 30,* 83–90.

Covington, M. V., & Mueller, K. J. (2001). Intrinsic versus extrinsic motivation: An approach/avoidance reformulation. *Educational Psychology Review, 13,* 157–176.

Cowan, N. (1984). On short and long auditory stores. *Psychological Bulletin, 96,* 341–370.

Cowan, N. (1995). *Attention and memory: An integrated framework.* New York: Oxford University Press.

Cowan, N., Saults, J. S., & Nugent, L. D. (1997). The role of absolute and relative amounts of time in forgetting within immediate memory: The case of tone-pitch comparisons. *Psychonomic Bulletin and Review, 4,* 393–397.

Cox, B. J., Yu, N., Afifi, T. O., & Ladouceur, R. (2005). A national survey of gambling problems in Canada. *Canadian Journal of Psychiatry, 50*(4), 213–217.

Cox, C. (1926). *Eminent men and women.* London: Bantam Books.

Cox, M. J., Owen, M. T., Henderson, V. K., & Margand, N. A. (1992). Prediction of infant-father and infant-mother attachment. *Developmental Psychology, 28,* 474–483.

Cox, M. J., & Paley, B. (1997). Families as systems. *Annual Review of Psychology, 48,* 243–267.

Craig, J. C. (1985). Attending to two fingers: Two hands are better than one. *Perception and Psychophysics, 38,* 496–511.

Craig, K. D. (1978). Social disclosure, coactive peer companions, and social modeling determinants of pain communications. *Canadian Journal of Behavioural Science, 10,* 91–104.

Craig, W., Pepler, D., & Atlas, R. (2000). Observations of bullying in the playground and in the classroom. *School Psychology International, 21,* 22–36.

Craik, F. I. M. (1994). Memory changes in normal aging. *Current Directions in Psychological Science, 5,* 155–158.

Craik, F. I. M., & Jacoby, L. L. (1979). Elaboration and distinctiveness in episodic memory. In L. Nilsson (Ed.), *Perspectives on memory research: Essays in honor of Upsala University's 500th anniversary* (pp.145–166). Hillsdale, NJ: Erlbaum.

Craik, F. I. M., & Lockhart, R. S. (1972). Levels of processing: A framework for memory research. *Journal of Verbal Learning and Verbal Behavior, 11,* 671–684.

Craik, F. I. M., & McDowd, J. M. (1987). Age differences in recall and recognition. *Journal of Experimental Psychology: Learning, Memory, and Cognition, 13,* 474–479.

Craik, F. I. M., & Tulving, E. (1975). Depth of processing and the retention of words in episodic memory. *Journal of Experimental Psychology: General, 104,* 268–294.

Cramer, K. M. (1999). Psychological antecedents to help-seeking behavior: A reanalysis using path modeling structures. *Journal of Counseling Psychology, 46,* 381–387.

Cramer, K. M., & Barry, J. E. (1999a). Conceptualizations and measures of loneliness: A comparison of subscales. *Personality and Individual Differences, 27,* 491–502.

Cramer, K. M., & Barry, J. E. (1999b). Psychometric properties and confirmatory factor analysis of the Self-Concealment Scale. *Personality and Individual Differences, 27,* 629–637.

Cramer, K. M., & Neyedley, K. A. (1998). Sex differences in loneliness: The role of masculinity and femininity. *Sex Roles, 38,* 645–653.

Cramer, K. M., Nickels, J. B., & Gural, D. M. (1997). Uncertainty of outcomes, prediction of failure, and lack of control as factors explaining perceived helplessness. *Journal of Social Behavior and Personality, 12*(3), 611–630.

Craske, M. G. (1999). *Anxiety disorders: Psychological approaches to theory and treatment.* Boulder, CO: Westview Press.

Craske, M. G., & Barlow, D. H. (1993). Panic disorder and agoraphobia. In D. H. Barlow (Ed.), *Clinical handbook of psychological disorders* (2nd ed., pp. 1–47). New York: Guilford Press.

Craske, M. G., & Rowe, M. K. (1997). Nocturnal panic. *Clinical Psychology: Science and Practice, 4,* 153–174.

Crawford, C. B. (1989). The theory of evolution: Of what value to psychology? *Journal of Comparative Psychology, 103,* 4–22.

Crawford, C. B. (1998a). The theory of evolution in the study of human behavior: An introduction and overview. In C. B. Crawford & D. L. Krebs (Eds.), *Handbook of evolutionary psychology: Ideas, issues and applications* (pp. 3–42). Mahwah, NJ: Erlbaum.

Crawford, C. B. (1998b). Environments and adaptations: Then and now. In C. B. Crawford & D. L. Krebs (Eds.), *Handbook of evolutionary psychology: Ideas, issues and applications* (pp. 275–302). Mahwah, NJ: Erlbaum.

Crawford, C. B., & Krebs, D. L. (1998). *Handbook of evolutionary psychology: Ideas, issues, and applications.* Mahwah, NJ: Erlbaum.

Crits-Christoph, P. (1997). Limitations of the dodo bird verdict and the role of clinical trials in psychotherapy research: Comment on Wampold et al. *Psychological Bulletin, 122,* 216–220.

Croft, R. J., Mackay, A. J., Mills, A. T. D., & Gruzelier, J. G. H. (2001). The relative contributions of ecstasy and cannabis to cognitive impairment. *Psychopharmacology, 153,* 373–379.

Cronbach, L. J. (1957). The two disciplines of scientific psychology. *American Psychologist, 12,* 671–684.

Crooks, R., & Baur, K. (2002). *Our sexuality* (8th ed.). Belmont, CA: Wadsworth.

Cropley, A. J. (1996). Recognizing creative potential: An evaluation of the usefulness of creativity tests. *High Ability Studies, 7,* 203–219.

Crowder, R. G., & Neath, I. (1991). The microscope metaphor in human memory. In W. E. Hockley & S. Lewandowsky (Eds.), *Relating theory and data: Essays on human memory in honor of Bennet B. Murdock* (pp. 111–125). Hillsdale, NJ: Erlbaum.

Crowder, R. G., & Surprenant, A. M. (2000). Sensory memory. In A. E. Kazdin (Ed.), *Encyclopedia of psychology* (pp. 227–229). New York: Oxford University Press and American Psychological Association.

Crowne, D. P., & Marlowe, D. (1964). *The approval motive.* New York: Wiley.

Csermely, P. (Ed.). (1998). *Stress of life: From molecules to man.* New York: New York Academy of Sciences.

Csernansky, J. G., & Bardgett, M. E. (1998). Limbic-cortical neuronal damage and the pathophysiology of schizophrenia. *Schizophrenia Bulletin, 24,* 231–248.

Cunningham, M. D., & Reidy, T. J. (1998). Antisocial personality disorder and psychopathy: Diagnostic dilemmas in classifying patterns of antisocial behavior in sentencing evaluations. *Behavioral Sciences and the Law, 16,* 333–351.

Cunningham, W. A., Raye, C. L., & Johnson, M. K. (2004). Implicit and explicit evaluation: FMRI correlates of valence, emotional intensity, and control in the processing of attitudes. *Journal of Cognitive Neuroscience, 16*(10), 1717–1729.

Currie, P. J., & Wilson, L. M. (1993). Central injection of 5-hydroxtryptamine reduces food intake in obese and lean mice. *Neuroreport, 3,* 59–61.

Curtis, R. C., & Miller, K. (1986). Believing another likes or dislikes you: Behaviors making the beliefs come true. *Journal of Personality and Social Psychology, 51,* 284–290.

Cutler, W. B., Friedmann, E., & McCoy, N. L. (1998). Pheromonal influences on sociosexual behavior in men. *Archives of Sexual Behavior, 27,* 1–13.

Dabbs, J. M. (2000). *Heroes, rogues, and lovers: Outcroppings of testosterone.* New York: McGraw-Hill.

Daly, M., Salmon, C., & Wilson, M. (1997). Kinship: The conceptual hole in psychological studies of social cognition and close relationships. In J. A. Simpson & D. T. Kenrick (Eds.), *Evolutionary social psychology* (pp. 265–296). Mahwah, NJ: Erlbaum.

Daly, M., & Wilson, M. (1983). *Sex, evolution and behavior* (2nd ed.). Boston: PWS.

Daly, M., & Wilson, M. (1987). The Darwinian psychology of discriminative parental solicitude. In D. W. Leger (Ed.), *Comparative perspectives in modern psychology: Nebraska symposium on motivation, 1987* (Vol. 35, pp. 163–189). New York: John Wiley & Sons.

Daly, M., & Wilson, M. (1990). Is parent–offspring conflict sex-linked?

Freudian and Darwinian models. *Journal of Personality, 58,* 163–189.

Daly, M., & Wilson, M. (1995). Discriminative parental solicitude and the relevance of evolutionary models to the analysis of motivational systems. In M. S. Gazzaniga (Ed.), *The cognitive neurosciences* (pp. 1269–1286). Cambridge, MA: MIT Press.

Daly, M., & Wilson, M. (1998). The evolutionary social psychology of family violence. In C. Crawford & D. L. Krebs (Eds.), *Handbook of evolutionary psychology: Ideas, issues and applications* (pp. 431–456). Mahwah, NJ: Erlbaum.

Daly, M., & Wilson, M. (1999a). *The truth about Cinderella: A Darwinian view of parental love.* New Haven, CT: Yale University Press.

Daly, M., & Wilson, M. I. (1999b). Human evolutionary psychology and animal behaviour. *Animal Behaviour, 57*(3), 509–519.

Damasio, A. R. (1994). *Descartes' error: Emotion, reason, and the human brain.* New York: Grosset/Putnam.

Damhorst, M. L. (1990). In search of a common thread: Classification of information communicated through dress. *Clothing and Textiles Research Journal, 8,* 1–12.

Damon, W., & Hart, D. (1992). Self-understanding and its role in social and moral development. In M. H. Bornstein & M. E. Lamb (Eds.), *Developmental psychology: An advanced textbook* (pp. 421–464). Hillsdale, NJ: Erlbaum.

Darley, J. M., & Berscheid, E. (1967). Increased liking as a result of the anticipation of personal contact. *Human Relations, 20,* 29–39.

Darley, J. M., & Latané, B. (1968). Bystander intervention in emergencies: Diffusion of responsibilities. *Journal of Personality and Social Psychology, 8,* 377–383.

Darou, W. G. (1992). Native Canadians and intelligence testing. *Canadian Journal of Counselling, 26,* 96–99.

Darwin, C. (1859). *On the origin of species.* London: Murray.

Darwin, C. (1871). *Descent of Man.* London: Murray.

Das, J. P. (2002). A better look at intelligence. *Current Directions in Psychological Science, 11,* 28–33.

Davidson, K., & Prkachin, K. (1997). Optimism and unrealistic optimism

have an interacting impact on health-promoting behavior and knowledge changes. *Personality and Social Psychology Bulletin, 23,* 617–625.

Davidson, M., Keefe, R. S. E., Mohs, R. C., Siever, L. J., Losonczy, M. F., Horvath, T. B., et al. (1987). L-dopa challenge and relapse in schizophrenia. *American Journal of Psychiatry, 144,* 934–938.

Davidson, T. L. (1993). The nature and function of interoceptive signals to feed: Toward integration of physiological and learning perspectives. *Psychological Review, 100,* 640–657.

Davidson, T. L. (1998). Hunger cues as modulatory stimuli. In N. A. Schmajuk & P. C. Holland (Eds.), *Occasion setting: Associative learning and cognition in animals* (pp. 223–249). Washington, DC: American Psychological Association.

Davidson, T. L., & Jarrard, L. E. (1993). A role for hippocampus in the utilization of hunger signals. *Behavioral and Neural Biology, 59,* 167–171.

Davies, I. (1998). A study of colour grouping in three languages: A test of the linguistic relativity hypothesis. *British Journal of Psychology, 89,* 433–452.

Davies, I., & Corbett, G. G. (1997). A cross-cultural study of colour grouping: Evidence for a weak linguistic relativity. *British Journal of Psychology, 88,* 493–517.

Davies, S. N., Pertwee, R. G., & Riedel, G. (2002). Functions of cannabinoid receptors in the hippocampus. *Neuropharmacology, 42,* 993–1007.

Davis, C. G., & Nolen-Hoeksema, S. (2001). Loss and meaning: How do people make sense of loss? *American Behavioral Scientist, 44,* 726–741.

Davis, K. L., Kahn, R. S., Ko, G., & Davidson, M. (1991). Dopamine in schizophrenia: A review and reconceptualization. *American Journal of Psychiatry, 148,* 1474–1486.

Davis, M., & Lee, Y. (1998). Fear and anxiety: Possible roles of the amygdala and bed nucleus of the stria teminalis. *Cognition and Emotion, 12,* 277–305.

Dawkins, R. (1989). *The selfish gene* (2nd ed.). New York: Oxford University Press.

Dawson, G., Ashman, S., & Carver, L. J. (2000). The role of early experience in shaping behavioral and brain development and its implications for social policy. *Development and Psychopathology, 12,* 695–712.

Dawson, G., & Fischer, K. W. (Eds.). (1994). *Human behavior and the developing brain.* New York: Guilford Press.

Deary, I. J. (2001). *Intelligence: A very short introduction.* Oxford, England: Oxford University Press.

Deaux, K., & Lewis, L. L. (1984). The structure of gender stereotypes: Interrelationships among components and gender label. *Journal of Personality and Social Psychology, 46,* 991–1004.

Debner, J. A., & Jacoby, L. L. (1994). Unconscious perception: Attention, awareness, and control. *Journal of Experimental Psychology: Learning, Memory, and Cognition, 20,* 304–317.

de Boysson-Bardies, B., Sagat, L., & Durand, C. (1984). Discernable differences in the babbling of infants according to target language. *Journal of Child Language, 11,* 1–16.

DeCasper, A. J., & Fifer, W. P. (1980). Of human bonding: Newborns prefer their mothers' voices. *Science, 208,* 1174–1176.

DeCasper, A. J., & Spence, M. J. (1986). Prenatal maternal speech influences newborns' perception of speech sounds. *Infant Behavior and Development, 9,* 133–150.

Deci, E. L., & Ryan, R. M. (1985). *Intrinsic motivation and self-determination in human behavior.* New York: Plenum Press.

DeCola, J. P., & Fanselow, M. S. (1995). Differential inflation with short and long CS-US intervals: Evidence of a nonassociative process in long-delay taste avoidance. *Animal Learning and Behavior, 23,* 154–163.

Deese, J. (1959). On the prediction of occurrence of particular verbal intrusions in immediate recall. *Journal of Experimental Psychology, 58,* 17–22.

DeGrandpre, R. J. (2000). A science of meaning: Can behaviorism bring meaning to psychological science? *American Psychologist, 55,* 721–773.

Degroot, A., & Parent, M. B. (2001). Infusions of physostigmine into the hippocampus or the entorhinal cortex attenuate avoidance retention deficits produced by intra-septal infusions of the GABA agonist muscimol. *Brain Research, 920,* 10–18.

De Jesus-Zayas, S., Baker, M., Banes, D., & Lozano-Blanco, C. (2001). Opinions

on insanity according to federal law, rule 17 and the M'Naghten standard. *American Journal of Forensic Psychology, 19,* 23–36.

de Lacoste-Utamsing, C., & Holloway, R. L. (1982). Sexual dimorphism in the human corpus callosum. *Science, 216,* 1431–1432.

de la Fuente-Fernandez, R., & Stoessl, A. J. (2002). The placebo effect in Parkinson's disease. *Trends in Neurosciences, 25,* 302–306.

DeLisi, L. E., Sakuma, M., Tew, W., Kushner, M., Hoff, A. L., & Grimson, R. (1997). Schizophrenia as a chronic active brain process: A study of progressive brain structural change subsequent to the onset of schizophrenia. *Psychiatry Research: Neuroimaging, 74,* 129–140.

DeLongis, A., & O'Brien, T. (1990). An interpersonal framework for stress and coping: An application to the families of Alzheimer's patients. In M. A. P. Stephens, J. H. Crowther, S. E. Hobfall, & D. L. Tennenbaum (Eds.), *Stress and coping in later-life families* (pp. 221–239). New York: Hemisphere Publishing.

DeLongis, A., Folkman, S., & Lazarus, R. S. (1988). The impact of daily stress on health and mood: Psychological and social resources as mediators. *Journal of Personality and Social Psychology, 54,* 486–498.

Dement, W. C. (1978). *Some must watch while some must sleep.* New York: Norton.

Dement, W. C., & Kleitman, N. (1957). The relation of eye movements during sleep to dream activity: An objective method for the study of dreaming. *Journal of Experimental Psychology, 53,* 339–346.

Dement, W. C., & Vaughan, C. (1999). *The promise of sleep: A pioneer in sleep medicine explores the vital connection between health, happiness, and a good night's sleep.* New York: Delacorte.

Dennett, D. C. (1995). *Darwin's dangerous idea: Evolution and the meanings of life.* New York: Simon & Schuster.

Dennis, W., & Dennis, M. G. (1940). The effect of cradling practices upon the onset of walking in Hopi children. *Journal of Genetic Psychology, 56,* 77–86.

Derogatis, L. R., & Coons, H. L. (1993). Self-report measures of stress. In

L. Goldberger & S. Breznitz (Eds.), *Handbook of stress: Theoretical and clinical aspects* (2nd ed., pp. 200–233). New York: Free Press.

Déry, M., Toupin, J., Pauzé, R., & Verlaan, P. (2004). Frequency of mental health disorders in a sample of elementary school students receiving special educational services for behavioural difficulties. *Canadian Journal of Psychiatry, 49*(11), 769–775.

DeSaint, V., Smith, C., Hull, P., & Loboschefski, T. (1997). Ten-month-old infants' retrieval of familiar information from short-term memory. *Infant Behavior and Development, 20,* 111–122.

DeValois, R. L., & DeValois, K. K. (1980). Spatial vision. *Annual Review of Psychology, 31,* 309–341.

Dewey, J. (1896). The reflex arc concept in psychology. *Psychological Review, 3,* 357–370.

DiBattista, D., & Shepherd, M.-L. (1993). Primary school teachers' beliefs and advice to parents concerning sugar consumption and activity in children. *Psychological Reports, 72,* 47–55.

Dickinson, A. (1989). The detrimental effects of extrinsic reinforcement on "intrinsic motivation." *The Behavior Analyst, 12,* 1–15.

Dickinson, A., & Charnock, D. J. (1985). Contingency effects with a constant probability of instrumental reinforcement. *Quarterly Journal of Experimental Psychology, 37B,* 397–416.

Diener, E., & Seligman, M. E. P. (2004). Beyond money: Toward an economy of well-being. *Psychological Science in the Public Interest, 5,* 1–31.

Digman, J. M. (1990). Personality structure: Emergence of the five-factor model. *Annual Review of Psychology, 41,* 417–440.

DiLollo, V., & Bischof, W. F. (1995). Inverse-intensity effect in duration of visible persistence. *Psychological Bulletin, 118,* 223–237.

DiMaggio, P. (1997). Culture and cognition. *Annual Review of Sociology, 23,* 263–287.

Dinges, D. F., Whitehouse, W. G., Orne, E. C., & Powell, J. W. (1992). Evaluating hypnotic memory enhancement (hypermnesia and reminiscence) using multitrial forced recall. *Journal of Experimental Psychology: Learning, Memory, and Cognition, 18,* 1139–1147.

Dion, K., & Kawakami, K. (1996). Ethnicity and perceived discrimination in Toronto: Another look at the personal/group discrimination discrepancy. *Canadian Journal of Behavioural Science, 28*, 203–213.

Dixon, J. A., & Moore, C. F. (1997). Characterizing the intuitive representation in problem solving: Evidence from evaluating mathematical strategies. *Memory and Cognition, 25*, 395–412.

Dixon, M., Bub, D. N., & Arguin, M. (1997). The interaction of object form and object meaning in the identification performance of a patient with category-specific visual agnosia. *Cognitive Neuropsychology, 14*, 1085–1130.

Dixon, M. J., Cudahy, C., Merikle, P. M., & Smilek, D. (2000). Five plus two equals yellow: Mental arithmetic in people with synaesthesia is not coloured by visual experience. *Nature, 406*(6794), 365.

Djordjevic, J., Zatorre, R. J., Petrides, M., & Jones-Gotman, M. (2004). The mind's nose: Effects of odor and visual imagery on odor detection. *Psychological Science, 15*, 143–148.

Dobson, K. S. (1989). A meta-analysis of the efficacy of cognitive therapy for depression. *Journal of Consulting and Clinical Psychology, 37*, 414–419.

Dohrenwend, B. P. (Ed.). (1998). *Adversity, stress, and psychopathology.* New York: Oxford University Press.

Domhoff, G. (1996). *Finding meaning in dreams: A quantitative analysis.* New York: Plenum Press.

Domjan, M. (1998). *The principles of learning and behavior* (4th ed.). Pacific Grove, CA: Brooks/Cole.

Domjan, M., & Purdy, J. E. (1995). Animal research in psychology: More than meets the eye of the general psychology student. *American Psychologist, 50*, 496–503.

Dong, W. K., Chudler, E. H., Sugiyama, K., Roberts, V. J., & Hayashi, T. (1994). Somatosensory, multisensory, and task-related neurons in cortical area 7b (PF) of unanesthetized monkeys. *Journal of Neurophysiology, 72*, 542–564.

Donigian, J., & Malnati, R. (1997). *Systemic group therapy: A triadic model.* Pacific Grove, CA: Brooks/Cole.

Dorward, F. M. C., & Day, R. H. (1997). Loss of 3-D shape constancy in interior spaces: The basis of the Ames-room illusion. *Perception, 26*, 707–718.

Doucet, C., & Stelmack, R. M. (1999). The effect of response execution on P3 latency, reaction time, and movement time. *Psychophysiology, 36*, 351–363.

Douvan, E. (1997). Erik Erikson: Critical times, critical theory. *Child Psychiatry and Human Development, 28*, 15–21.

Doyle, A. B., & Aboud, F. E. (1995). A longitudinal study of White children's racial prejudice as a social cognitive development. *Merrill-Palmer Quarterly, 41*, 210–229.

Drachman, D. A. (2005). Do we have brain to spare? *Neurology, 64*, 2004–2005.

Draguns, J. G. (1997). Abnormal behavior patterns across cultures: Implications for counseling and psychotherapy. *International Journal of Intercultural Relations, 21*, 213–248.

Drevets, W. C., Burton, H., Videen, T. O., & Snyder, A. Z. (1995). Blood flow changes in human somatosensory cortex during anticipated stimulation. *Nature, 373*, 249–252.

Druckman, D., & Bjork, R. A. (1991). *In the mind's eye: Enhancing human performance.* Washington, DC: National Academy Press.

Druckman, D., & Swets, J. A. (Eds.). (1988). *Enhancing human performance: Issues, theories, and techniques.* Washington, DC: National Academy Press.

Duckworth, A. L., & Seligman, M. E. P. (2005). Self-discipline outdoes IQ in predicting academic performance of adolescents. *Psychological Science, 16*, 939–944.

Dugas, M. J., Freeston, M. H., Ladouceur, R., Rheaume, J., Provencher, M., & Boisvert, J. (1998). Worry themes in primary GAD, secondary GAD, and other anxiety disorders. *Journal of Anxiety Disorders, 12*, 253–261.

Duncan, R. (1995). Piaget and Vygotsky revisited: Dialogue or assimilation? *Developmental Review, 15*, 458–472.

Duncan, R., & Pratt, M. (1997). Microgenetic change in preschoolers' private speech. *International Journal of Behavioral Development, 20*, 367–383.

Duncan, R. M., & Cheyne, J. A. (1999). Incidence and functions of self-reported private speech in young adults: A self-verbalization questionnaire. *Canadian Journal of Behavioural Science, 31*, 133–136.

Duncker, K. (1945). On problem solving. *Psychological Monographs, 58*(5, Whole No. 270).

Dunning, D. (2005). *Self-insight: Roadblocks and detours on the path to knowing thyself.* New York: Psychology Press.

Dupont, P., Orban, G. A., De-Bruyn, B., & Verbruggen, A. (1994). Many areas in the human brain respond to visual motion. *Journal of Neurophysiology, 72*, 1420–1424.

Durgin, F. H., Tripathy, S. P., & Levi, D. M. (1995). On the filling in of the visual blind spot: Some rules of thumb. *Perception, 24*, 827–840.

Durie, D. J. (1981). Sleep in animals. In D. Wheatley (Ed.), *Psychopharmacology of sleep.* New York: Raven Press.

Dutton, D. G. (1998). *The abusive personality: Violence and control in close relationships.* New York: Guilford.

Dutton, D. G., & Aron, A. P. (1974). Some evidence for heightened sexual attraction under conditions of high anxiety. *Journal of Personality and Social Psychology, 30*, 510–517.

Dweck, C. S. (1999). *Self-theories: Their role in motivation, personality, and development.* Philadelphia: Psychology Press.

Dweck, C. S., Chiu, C. Y., & Hong, Y. Y. (1995). Implicit theories: Elaboration and extension of the model. *Psychological Inquiry, 6*, 322–333.

Dywan, J., & Bowers, K. (1983). The use of hypnosis to enhance recall. *Science, 222*, 184–185.

Eagly, A. H., Ashmore, R. D., Makhijani, M. G., & Longo, L. C. (1991). What is beautiful is good, but . . .: A meta-analytic review of research on the physical attractiveness stereotype. *Psychological Bulletin, 110*, 109–128.

Eagly, A. H., & Steffen, F. J. (1986). Gender and aggressive behavior: A meta-analytic review of the social psychological literature. *Psychological Bulletin, 100*, 309–330.

Easterbrook, M. A., Kisilevsky, B. S., Muir, D. W., & Laplante, D. P. (1999). Newborns discriminate schematic faces from scrambled faces. *Canadian Journal of Experimental Psychology, 53*, 231–241.

Eaton, W. O., & Saudino, K. J. (1992). Prenatal activity level as a temperament dimension? Individual differences and developmental functions in fetal movement. *Infant Behavior and Development, 15,* 57–70.

Ebbinghaus, H. (1885/1964). *Memory: A contribution to experimental psychology.* New York: Dover.

Eccles, J., Adler, T. F., Futterman, R., Goff, S. B., Kaczala, C. M., Meece, J., et al. (1983). Expectancies, values, and academic behaviors. In J. T. Spence (Ed.), *Achievement and achievement motives* (pp. 77–146). San Francisco: Freeman.

Edelman, G. M. (1987). *Neural Darwinism.* New York: Basic Books.

Edwards, J. (1999). Refining our understanding of language attitudes. *Journal of Language and Social Psychology, 18,* 101–110.

Egan, D., & Schwartz, B. (1979). Chunking in recall of symbolic drawings. *Memory and Cognition, 7,* 149–158.

Ehrlich, S. (1999). Communities of practice, gender, and the representation of sexual assault. *Language and Society, 28,* 239–256.

Eibl-Eibesfeldt, I. (1973). The expressive behavior of the deaf-and-blind born. In M. von Cranach & I. Vine (Eds.), *Social communication and movement* (pp. 163–194). San Diego, CA: Academic Press.

Eich, E., Macaulay, D., Loewenstein, R. J., & Dihle, P. H. (1997). Memory, amnesia, and dissociative identity disorder. *Psychological Science, 8,* 417–422.

Eich, E., & Schooler, J. W. (2000). Cognition/emotion interactions. In E. Eich, J. F. Kihlstrom, G. H. Bower, J. P. Forgas, & P. M. Niedenthal (Eds.), *Cognition and emotion* (pp. 3–29). New York: Oxford University Press.

Eisenberger, R. (1992). Learned industriousness. *Psychological Review, 99,* 248–267.

Ekman, P. (1992). Are there basic emotions? *Psychological Review, 99,* 350–353.

Ekman, P. (1994). Strong evidence for universals in facial expressions: A reply to Russell's mistaken critique. *Psychological Bulletin, 115,* 268–287.

Ekman, P., & Friesen, W. V. (1975). *Unmasking the face.* Englewood Cliffs, NJ: Prentice-Hall.

Ekman, P., & Friesen, W. V. (1986). A new pan-cultural facial expression of emotion. *Motivation and Emotion, 10,* 159–168.

Ekman, P., & Keltner, D. (1997). Universal facial expressions of emotion: An old controversy and new findings. In U. C. Segerstrale & P. Molnar (Eds.), *Nonverbal communication: Where nature meets culture* (pp. 27–46). Mahwah, NJ: Erlbaum.

Elicker, J., Englund, M., & Sroufe, L. A. (1992). Predicting peer competence and peer relationships in childhood from early parent-child relationships. In R. D. Parke & G. W. Ladd (Eds.), *Family-peer relationships: Modes of linkage* (pp. 77–106). Hillsdale, NJ: Erlbaum.

Ellard, C. G. (2000). Landmark navigation in gerbils. The role of the posterior parietal cortex. *Psychobiology, 28,* 325–338.

Ellard, J. H., & Rogers, T. B. (1993). Teaching questionnaire construction effectively: The ten commandments of question writing. *Contemporary Social Psychology, 17*(1), 17–20.

Elliot, A. J., & Thrash, T. M. (2001). Achievement goals and the hierarchical model of achievement motivation. *Educational Psychology Review, 13,* 139–156.

Ellis, A. (1962). *Reason and emotion in psychotherapy.* Secaucus, NJ: Prentice-Hall.

Ellis, A. (1993). Fundamentals of rational-emotive therapy for the 1990s. In W. Dryden & L. K. Hill (Eds.), *Innovations in rational-emotive therapy* (pp.1–32). Newbury Park, CA: Sage.

Ellis, R. R., & Lederman, S. J. (1998). The "golf-ball" illusion: Evidence for top-down processing in weight perception. *Perception, 27,* 193–202.

Ellis, R. R., & Lederman, S. J. (1999). The material-weight illusion revisited. *Perception and Psychophysics, 61,* 1564–1576.

Ellison, L. F., Morrison, H. I., de Groh, M., & Villeneuve, P. J. (1999). Health consequences of smoking among Canadian smokers: An update. *Chronic Diseases in Canada, 20,* 36–39.

Ellman, S. J., Spielman, A. J., Luck, D., Steiner, S. S., & Halperin, R. (1991). REM deprivation: A review. In S. J. Ellman & J. S. Antrobus (Eds.), *The mind in sleep* (2nd ed., pp. 327–376). New York: Wiley.

Ellsworth, P. C. (1994). William James and emotion: Is a century of fame worth a century of misunderstanding? *Psychological Review, 101,* 222–229.

Elmes, D. G., Kantowitz, B. H., & Roediger, H. L., III. (1995). *Research methods in psychology* (5th ed.). St. Paul, MN: West Publishing.

Elsabagh, S., Hartley, D. E., Ali, O., Williamson, E. M., & File, S. E. (2005). Differential cognitive effects of Ginkgo biloba after acute and chronic treatment in healthy young volunteers. *Psychopharmacology, 179,* 437–446.

Endler, N. S. (1990). *Holiday of darkness: A psychologist's personal journey out of his depression.* New York: Wall & Emerson.

Engler, J., & Goleman, D. (1992). *The consumer's guide to psychotherapy.* New York: Simon & Schuster.

Epel, E., Lapidus, R., McEwen, B., & Brownell, K. (2001). Stress may add bite to appetite in women: A laboratory study of stress-induced cortisol and eating behavior. *Psychoneuroendocrinology, 26,* 37–49.

Epel, E. S., McEwen, B. S., & Ickovics, J. R. (1998). Embodying psychological thriving: Physical thriving in response to stress. *Journal of Social Issues, 54,* 301–322.

Epstein, S. (1979). The stability of behavior: On predicting most of the people much of the time. *Journal of Personality and Social Psychology, 37,* 1097–1126.

Erdberg, P. (1990). Rorschach assessment. In A. Goldstein & M. Hersen (Eds.), *Handbook of personality assessment.* (pp. 387–399) New York: Pergamon Press.

Erickson, M. A., & Kruschke, J. K. (1998). Rules and exemplars in category learning. *Journal of Experimental Psychology: General, 127,* 107–140.

Erickson, M. H. (1964). A hypnotic technique for resistant patients. *American Journal of Clinical Hypnosis, 7,* 8–32.

Ericsson, K. A., & Chase, W. G. (1982). Exceptional memory. *American Scientist, 70*(6), 607–615.

Ericsson, K. A., & Simon, H. A. (1993). *Verbal reports as data* (Rev. ed.). Cambridge, MA: MIT Press.

Erikson, E. (1963). *Childhood and society.* New York: Norton.

Erikson, E. (1968). *Identity: Youth and crisis.* New York: Norton.

Erikson, E. (1982). *The life cycle completed: Review.* New York: Norton.

Ernst, C. E., & Angst, J. (1983). *Birth order: Its influence on personality.* Berlin and New York: Springer-Verlang.

Esser, J. K. (1998). Alive and well after 25 years: A review of groupthink research. *Organizational Behavior and Human Decision Processes, 73,* 116–141.

Esses, V. M., Haddock, G., & Zanna, M. P. (1993). Values, stereotypes, and emotions as determinants of intergroup attitudes. In D. M. Mackie & D. L. Hamilton (Eds.), *Affect, cognition, and stereotyping: Interactive processes in group perception* (pp. 137–166). San Diego, CA: Academic Press.

Evans, C. L., McGuire, P. K., & David, A. S. (2000). Is auditory imagery defective in patients with auditory hallucinations? *Psychological Medicine, 30,* 137–148.

Evans, E. F. (1982). Functional anatomy of the auditory system. In H. B. Barlow & J. D. Mollon (Eds.), *The senses* (pp. 251–305). Cambridge: Cambridge University Press.

Evans, G. W. (1997). Environmental stress and health. In A. Baum, T. Revenson, & J. E. Singer (Eds.), *Handbook of health psychology* (pp. 365–385). Hillsdale, NJ: Erlbaum.

Evans, G. W., Hygge, S., & Bullinger, M. (1995). Chronic noise and psychological stress. *Psychological Science, 6,* 333–338.

Eysenck, H. J. (1952). The effects of psychotherapy: An evaluation. *Journal of Consulting Psychology, 16,* 319–324.

Eysenck, H. J. (1970). *The structure of human personality* (3rd ed.). London: Methuen.

Eysenck, H. J. (1991). Dimensions of personality: 16, 5, or 3? Criteria for a taxonomic paradigm. *Personality and Individual Differences, 12,* 773–790.

Eysenck, H. J., & Eysenck, S. B. G. (1975). *Manual of the Eysenck Personality Questionnaire.* San Diego, CA: EdITS.

Eysenck, H. J., & Kamin, L. (1981). *The intelligence controversy: H. J. Eysenck vs. Leon Kamin.* New York: Wiley.

Fackelmann, K. A. (1993). Marijuana and the brain. *Science News, 143,* 88–94.

Fahy, T. A. (1988). The diagnosis of multiple personality: A critical review. *British Journal of Psychiatry, 153,* 597–606.

Fallon, A. E., & Rozin, P. (1985). Sex differences in perceptions of desirable body shape. *Journal of Abnormal Psychology, 94,* 102–105.

Fallon, A. E., Rozin, P., & Pliner, P. (1984). The child's conception of food: The development of food rejections with special reference to disgust and contamination sensitivity. *Child Development, 55,* 566–575.

Fantz, R. L. (1961, May). The origin of form perception. *Scientific American, 204,* 66–72.

Farah, M. J. (1994). Specialization within visual object recognition: Clues from prosopagnosia and alexia. In M. J. Farah & G. Ratcliff (Eds.), *The neuropsychology of high-level vision: Collected tutorial essays* (pp. 133–146). Hillsdale, NJ: Erlbaum.

Faust, I. M. (1984). Role of the fat cell in energy balance physiology. In A. J. Stunkard & E. Stellar (Eds.), *Eating and its disorders* (pp. 97–107). New York: Raven.

Fazio, R. H. (1986). How do attitudes guide behavior? In R. M. Sorrentino & E. T. Higgins (Eds.), *Handbook of motivation and cognition: Foundations of social behavior.* New York: Guilford Press.

Fechner, G. T. (1887/1987). My own viewpoint on mental measurement. *Psychological Research/ Psychologische Forschung, 49*(4), 213–219. (Original work published 1887)

Fehr, B., & Russell, J. A. (1991). The concept of love: Viewed from a prototype perspective. *Journal of Personality and Social Psychology, 60,* 425–438.

Feingold, A. (1988). Matching for attractiveness in romantic partners and same-sex friends: A meta-analysis and theoretical critique. *Psychological Bulletin, 104,* 226–235.

Feingold, A. (1990). Gender differences in effects of physical attractiveness on romantic attraction: A comparison across five research paradigms. *Journal of Personality and Social Psychology, 59,* 981–993.

Feingold, A. (1992). Good-looking people are not what we think. *Psychological Bulletin, 111,* 304–341.

Feist, J. (1994). *Theories of personality* (3rd ed.). Fort Worth, TX: Harcourt Brace.

Feldman, D. H. (2003). Cognitive development in childhood. In R. M. Lerner, M. A. Easterbrook, & J. Mistry (Eds.), *Handbook of psychology* (Vol. 6, pp. 195–210). New York: Wiley.

Feldman, M. D., & Christensen, J. F. (Eds.). (1997). *Behavioral medicine in primary care: A practical guide.* Stamford, CT: Appleton & Lange.

Fentress, J. C. (1999). Organization of behaviour revisited. *Canadian Journal of Experimental Psychology, 53,* 8–20.

Fenwick, K. D., & Morrongiello, B. A. (1998). Spatial co-location and infants' learning of auditory-visual associations. *Infant Behavior and Development, 21,* 745–759.

Ferguson, N. B. L., & Keesey, R. E. (1975). Effect of a quinine-adulterated diet upon body weight maintenance in male rats with ventromedial lesions. *Journal of Comparative and Physiological Psychology, 89,* 478–488.

Ferster, C. B., & Skinner, B. F. (1957). *Schedules of reinforcement.* New York: Appleton-Century-Crofts.

Festinger, L. (1957). *A theory of cognitive dissonance.* Stanford, CA: Stanford University Press.

Festinger, L., & Carlsmith, J. M. (1959). Cognitive consequences of forced compliance. *Journal of Abnormal and Social Psychology, 58,* 203–210.

Festinger, L., Riecken, H. W., & Schachter, S. (1956). *When prophecy fails.* Minneapolis: University of Minnesota Press.

Festinger, L., Schachter, S., & Back, K. (1950). *Social pressures in informal groups: A study of human factors in housing.* New York: Harper.

Fiedler, K. (1988). The dependence of the conjunction fallacy on subtle linguistic factors. *Psychological Research, 50,* 123–129.

Fink, M. (2001). Convulsive therapy: A review of the first 55 years. *Journal of Affective Disorders, 63,* 1–15.

Fishbain, D. A., & Goldberg, M. (1991). The misdiagnosis of conversion disorder in a psychiatric emergency service. *General Hospital Psychiatry, 13,* 177–181.

Fisher, J. D., & Fisher, W. A. (1992). Changing AIDS risk behavior. *Psychological Bulletin, 111,* 455–474.

Fisher, W. A., & Fisher, J. D. (1993). A general social psychological model for changing AIDS risk behavior. In J. Pryor & G. Reeder (Eds.), *The social psychology of HIV infection* (pp. 127–154). Hillsdale, NJ: Erlbaum.

Fisher, W. A., & Fisher, J. D. (1998). Understanding and promoting sexual and reproductive health behavior: Theory and method. *Annual Review of Sex Research, 9,* 39–77.

Fiske, S. T. (1993). Social cognition and social perception. *Annual Review of Psychology, 44,* 155–194.

Fiss, H. (1991). Experimental strategies for the study of the function of dreaming. In S. J. Ellman & J. S. Antrobus (Eds.), *The mind in sleep* (2nd ed., pp. 308–326). New York: Wiley.

Flanagan, J. R., & Beltzner, M. A. (2000). Independence of perceptual and sensorimotor predictions in the size-weight illusion. *Nature Neuroscience, 3,* 737–741.

Flanagan, O. (2000). *Dreaming souls: Sleep, dreams, and the evolution of the conscious mind.* New York: Oxford University Press.

Flavell, J. H. (1971). Stage-related properties of cognitive development. *Cognitive Psychology, 2,* 421–453.

Flavell, J. H., Miller, P. A., & Miller, S. A. (1993). *Cognitive development* (3rd ed.). Englewood Cliffs, NJ: Prentice-Hall.

Flaxman, S. M., & Sherman, P. W. (2000). Morning sickness: A mechanism for protecting mother and embryo. *Quarterly Review of Biology, 75,* 113–148.

Flett, G. L., & Hewitt, P. L. (2003). *Perfectionism: Theory, research and treatment.* Washington, DC: American Psychological Association.

Flett, G. L., Hewitt, P. L., Blankstein, K. R., & Gray, L. (1998). Psychological distress and the frequency of perfectionistic thinking. *Journal of Personality and Social Psychology, 75,* 1363–1381.

Flett, G. L., Hewitt, P. L., Blankstein, K. R., & Pickering, D. (1998). Perfectionism in relation to attributions for success or failure. *Current Psychology: Developmental, Learning, Personality, Social, 17,* 249–262.

Flett, G. L., Hewitt, P. L., & Hallett, C. J. (1995). Perfectionism and job stress in teachers. *Canadian Journal of School Psychology, 11,* 32–42.

Foa, E. B., & Franklin, M. E. (2001). Obsessive-compulsive disorder. In D. H. Barlow (Ed.), *Clinical handbook of psychological disorders: A step-by-step treatment manual* (3rd ed., pp. 209–263). New York: Guilford Press.

Foa, E. B., & Riggs, D. S. (1995). Posttraumatic stress disorder following assault: Theoretical considerations and empirical findings. *Current Directions in Psychological Science, 4,* 61–65.

Foersterling, F., Buehner, M., & Gall, S. (1998). Attributions of depressed persons: How consistent are they with the covariation principle? *Journal of Personality and Social Psychology, 75,* 1047–1061.

Folkman, S., & Moskowitz, J. T. (2004). Coping: Pitfalls and promise. *Annual Review of Psychology, 55,* 745–774.

Fong, G. T., Krantz, D. H., & Nisbett, R. E. (1986). The effects of statistical training on thinking about everyday problems. *Cognitive Psychology, 18,* 253–292.

Fong, G. T., & Nisbett, R. E. (1991). Immediate and delayed transfer of training effects in statistical reasoning. *Journal of Experimental Psychology: General, 120,* 34–45.

Forest, B., & Gross, P. R. (2004). *Creationism's Trojan horse: The wedge of intelligent design.* New York: Oxford University Press.

Forgas, J. P., Williams, K. D., & Laham, S. M. (2005). *Social motivation: Conscious and unconscious processes.* Cambridge, UK: Cambridge University Press.

Foulkes, D. (1985). *Dreaming: A cognitive-psychological analysis.* Hillsdale, NJ: Erlbaum.

Frankham, C., & Cabanac, M. (2003). Nicotine lowers the body-weight setpoint in male rats. *Appetite, 41,* 1–5.

Frazer, J. G. (1890/1959). *The new golden bough: A study in magic and religion* (T. H. Gaster, Ed., Abridged ed.). New York: Macmillan.

Fredericks, D. W., & Williams, L. W. (1998). New definition of mental retardation for the American Association of Mental Retardation. *Image—the Journal of Nursing Scholarship, 30,* 53–56.

Freedman, J. L. (1988). Television violence and aggression: What the evidence shows. In S. Oskamp (Ed.), *Television as a social issue: Applied psychology annual* (Vol. 8, pp. 144–162). Beverly Hills, CA: Sage.

Freedman, J. L., & Fraser, S. C. (1966). Compliance without pressure: The foot-in-the-door technique. *Journal of Personality and Social Psychology, 4,* 195–202.

Freeman, H. L., & Stansfeld, S. A. (1998). Psychosocial effects of urban environments, noise, and crowding. In A. Lundberg (Ed.), *The environment and mental health: A guide for clinicians* (pp. 147–174). Mahwah, NJ: Erlbaum.

Freud, S. (1900/1990). *The interpretation of dreams.* New York: Basic Books.

Freud, S. (1905/1962). *Three contributions to the theory of sexuality.* New York: Dutton.

Freud, S. (1910). The origin and development of psychoanalysis. *American Journal of Psychology, 21,* 181–218.

Freud, S. (1912/1964). The dynamics of transference. In J. Strachey (Trans. & Ed.), *The standard edition of the complete works of Sigmund Freud* (Vol. 12, pp. 97–108). London: Hogarth Press.

Freud, S. (1940). *An outline of psychoanalysis.* New York: Norton.

Freudenberger, H. J. (1974). Staff burnout. *Journal of Social Issues, 30,* 159–165.

Friedlander, L., Lumley, M. A., Farchione, T., & Doyal, G. (1997). Testing the alexithymia hypothesis: Physiological and subjective responses during relaxation and stress. *Journal of Nervous and Mental Disease, 185,* 233–239.

Friedman, H. S., Hawley, P. H., & Tucker, J. S. (1994). Personality, health, and longevity. *Current Directions in Psychological Science, 3,* 37–41.

Friedman, M., & Rosenman, R. F. (1974). *Type A behavior and your heart.* New York: Knopf.

Friedrich-Cofer, L., & Huston, A. C. (1986). Television violence and aggression: The debate continues. *Psychological Bulletin, 100,* 364–371.

Frueh, B. C., de Arellano, M. A., & Turner, S. M. (1997). Systematic desensitization as an alternative exposure strategy for PTSD. *American Journal of Psychiatry, 154,* 287–288.

Fukuda, T., Kanada, K., & Saito, S. (1990). An ergonomic evaluation of lens accommodation related to visual circumstances. *Ergonomics, 33,* 811–831.

Funder, D. C. (2001). Personality. *Annual Review of Psychology, 52,* 197–221.

Fyer, A. J., Mannuzza, S., Gallops, M. S., Martin, L. Y., Aaronson, C., Gorman, J. M., et al. (1990). Familial transmission of simple phobias and fears: A preliminary report. *Archives of General Psychiatry, 47,* 252–256.

Gabrieli, J. D. E. (1998). Cognitive neuroscience of human memory. *Annual Review of Psychology, 49,* 87–115.

Gaetz, M., Weinberg, H., Rzempoluck, E., & Jantzen, K. J. (1998). Neural network classifications and correlational analysis of EEG and MEG activity accompanying spontaneous reversals of the Necker Cube. *Cognitive Brain Research, 6,* 335–346.

Gagnon, J., & Simon, W. (1973). *Sexual conduct: The social sources of human sexuality.* Chicago: Aldine.

Galambos, N. L., & Tilton-Weaver, L. C. (1998). Multiple-risk behavior in adolescents and young adults. *Health Reports, 10,* 9–20.

Galef, B. G., Jr. (1985). Social learning in wild Norway rats. In T. D. Johnston & A. T. Pietrewicz (Eds.), *Issues in the ecological study of learning* (pp. 143–165). Hillsdale, NJ: Erlbaum.

Galinsky, A. D., & Moskowitz, G. B. (2000). Perspective-taking: Decreasing stereotype expression, stereotype accessibility, and in-group favoritism. *Journal of Personality and Social Psychology, 78,* 708–724.

Gallistel, C. R., & Gibbon, J. (2000). Time, rate, and conditioning. *Psychological Review, 107,* 289–344.

Galton, F. (1869). *Hereditary genius: An inquiry into its laws and consequences.* New York: Appleton.

Galton, F. (1883). *Inquiries into human faculty and development.* London: Macmillan.

Gandelman, R. (1992). *Psychobiology of behavior development.* New York: Oxford University Press.

Gandevia, S. C., McCloskey, D. I., & Burke, D. (1992). Kinaesthetic signals and muscle contraction. *Trends in Neurosciences, 15,* 62–65.

Gangestad, S. W., & Snyder, M. (1985). On the nature of self-monitoring: An examination of latent causal structure. In P. Shaver (Ed.), *Review of personality and social psychology* (pp. 65–85). Beverly Hills, CA: Sage.

Ganis, G., Thompson, W. L., & Kosslyn, S. M. (2004). Brain areas underlying visual mental imagery and visual perception: An fMRI study. *Cognitive Brain Research, 20,* 226–241.

Ganis, G., Thompson, W. L., Mast, F. W., & Kosslyn, S. M. (2003). Visual imagery in cerebral visual dysfunction. *Neurologic Clinics, 21,* 631–646.

Gardner, E. B., & Costanzo, R. H. (1981). Properties of kinesthetic neurons in somatosensory cortex of awake monkeys. *Brain Research, 214,* 301–319.

Gardner, E. L. (1997). Brain reward mechanisms. In J. H. Lowinson, P. Ruiz, R. B. Millman, & J. G. Langrod (Eds.), *Substance abuse: A comprehensive textbook* (3rd ed., pp. 51–85). Baltimore: Williams & Wilkins.

Gardner, H. (1983). *Frames of mind: The theory of multiple intelligences.* New York: Basic Books.

Gardner, H. (1993). *Multiple intelligences: The theory in practice.* New York: Basic Books.

Gardner, R. A., & Gardner, B. T. (1969). Teaching sign language to a chimpanzee. *Science, 165,* 664–672.

Gardner, R. A., Gardner, B. T., & Van Cantfort, T. E. (Eds.). (1989). *Teaching sign language to chimpanzees.* Albany, NY: SUNY Press.

Garland, A. F., & Zigler, E. (1993). Adolescent suicide prevention: Current research and social policy implications. *American Psychologist, 48,* 169–182.

Garrity, T. F., Stallones, L., Marx, M. B., & Johnson, T. P. (1989). Pet ownership and attachment as supportive factors in the health of the elderly. *Anthrozoos, 3,* 35–44.

Gauvin, L. (1990). An experiential perspective on the motivational features of exercise and lifestyle. *Canadian Journal of Sport Science, 15,* 51–58.

Gaw, A. C. (2001). *Concise guide to cross-cultural psychiatry.* Washington, DC: American Psychiatric Association.

Gazzaniga, M. S. (1970). *The bisected brain.* New York: Appleton-Century-Crofts.

Gazzaniga, M. S. (2005). Forty-five years of split-brain research and still going strong. *Nature Reviews Neuroscience, 6,* 653–659.

Gazzaniga, M. S., Bogen, J. E., & Sperry, R. W. (1965). Observations on visual perception after disconnection of the cerebral hemispheres in man. *Brain, 88,* 221–236.

Gazzaniga, M. S., Eliassen, J. C., Nisenson, L., Wessinger, C. M., Fendrich, R., & Baynes, K. (1996). Collaboration between the hemispheres of a callosotomy patient: Emerging right hemisphere speech and the left hemisphere interpreter. *Brain, 119,* 1255–1263.

Gazzaniga, M. S., & LeDoux, J. E. (1978). *The integrated mind.* New York: Plenum Press.

Gebotys, R. J., & Claxton, O. S. P. (1989). Errors in the quantification of uncertainty: A product of heuristics or minimal probability knowledge base? *Applied Cognitive Psychology, 3,* 157–170.

Gegenfurtner, K. R., Xing, D., Scott, B. H., & Hawken, M. J. (2003). A comparison of pursuit eye movement and perceptual performance in speed discrimination. *Journal of Vision, 3,* 865–876.

Geiselman, R. E., Fisher, R. P., MacKinnon, D. P., & Holland, H. L. (1985). Eyewitness memory enhancement in the police interview: Cognitive retrieval mnemonics versus hypnosis. *Journal of Applied Psychology, 70,* 401–412.

Gerbner, G., & Gross, L. (1976). Living with television: The violence profile. *Journal of Communications, 26,* 172–199.

Gerin, W., Pieper, C., Levy, R., & Pickering, T. G. (1992). Social support in social interaction: A moderator of cardiovascular reactivity. *Psychosomatic Medicine, 54,* 324–336.

Gernsbacher, M. A., & Kaschak, M. P. (2003). Neuroimaging studies of language production and comprehension. *Annual Review of Psychology, 54,* 91–114.

Gershon, E. S. (1990). Genetics. In F. K. Goodwin & K. R. Jamison (Eds.), *Manic-depressive illness* (pp. 369–401). New York: Oxford University Press.

Gershon, E. S., & Reider, R. O. (1992, April). Major disorders of mind and brain. *Scientific American, 267,* 126–133.

Gianoulakis, C. (2001). Influence of the endogenous opioid system on high alcohol consumption and genetic predisposition to alcoholism. *Journal of Psychiatry and Neuroscience, 26,* 304–318.

Gibson, E. J., & Walk, R. D. (1960, April). The "visual cliff." *Scientific American, 202,* 64–71.

Gibson, J. J. (1966). *The senses considered as perceptual systems.* Boston: Houghton Mifflin.

Gick, M. L., & McGarry, S. J. (1992). Learning from mistakes: Inducing analogous solution failures to a source problem produces later successes in analogical transfer. *Journal of Experimental Psychology: Learning, Memory, and Cognition, 18,* 623–639.

Gifford, R. (1997). *Environmental psychology: Principles and practice* (2nd ed.). Needham Heights, MA: Allyn & Bacon.

Gigerenzer, G. (1996). On narrow norms and vague heuristics: A reply to Kahneman & Tversky. *Psychological Review, 103,* 592–596.

Gigerenzer, G. (1997). Ecological intelligence: An adaptation for frequencies. In D. Cummins & C. Allen (Eds.), *The evolution of mind* (pp. 9–29). New York: Oxford University Press.

Giguere, C., & Abel, S. M. (1993). Sound localization: Effects of reverberation time, speaker array, stimulus frequency, and stimulus rise/decay. *Journal of Acoustical Society of America, 94,* 769–776.

Gilbert, D. T. (1989). Thinking lightly about others: Automatic components of the social inference process. In J. S. Uleman & J. A. Bargh (Eds.), *Unintended thought* (pp. 189–210). New York: Guilford Press.

Gilligan, C. (1982). *In a different voice: Psychological theory and women's development.* Cambridge, MA: Harvard University Press.

Gladue, B. A. (1994). The biopsychology of sexual orientation. *Current Directions in Psychological Research, 3,* 150–154.

Glaser, B. G., & Strauss, A. L. (1968). *Time for dying.* Chicago: Aldine.

Gleaves, D. H., May, M. C., & Cardena, E. (2001). An examination of the diagnostic validity of dissociative identity disorder. *Clinical Psychology Review, 21,* 577–608.

Glucksberg, S. (1998). Understanding metaphors. *Current Directions in Psychological Science, 7*(2), 39–43.

Godey, B., Atencio, C. A., Bonham, B. H., Schreiner, C. E., & Cheung, S. W. (2005). Functional organization of squirrel monkey primary auditory cortex: Responses to frequency-modulation sweeps. *Journal of Neurophysiology, 94,* 1299–1311.

Goldberg, J., True, W. R., Eisen, S. A., & Henderson, W. G. (1990). A twin study of the effects of the Vietnam War on posttraumatic stress disorder. *Journal of the American Medical Association, 263,* 1227–1232.

Goldberg, L. R. (1993). The structure of phenotypic personality traits. *American Psychologist, 48,* 26–34.

Goldberg, L. R., & Stycker, L. A. (2002). Personality traits and eating habits: The assessment of food preferences in a large community sample. *Personality and Individual Differences, 32,* 49–65.

Goldstein, B. (1994). *Psychology.* Pacific Grove, CA: Brooks/Cole.

Goldstone, R. L., & Kersten, A. (2003). Concepts and categorization. In A. Healy & R. Proctor (Eds.), *Handbook of psychology: Vol. 4. Experimental psychology* (pp. 599–621). New York: Wiley.

Goleman, D. (1995). *Emotional intelligence.* New York: Bantam.

Golub, S. (1992). *Periods: From menarche to menopause.* Newbury Park, CA: Sage.

Gonzalez-Quijano, M. I., Martin, M., Millan, S., & Lopez-Calderon, A. (1998). Lymphocyte response to mitogens: Influence of life events and personality. *Neuropsychobiology, 38,* 90–96.

Goodale, M. A., & Humphrey, G. K. (2000). Separate visual systems for action and perception. In E. B. Goldstein (Ed.), *Blackwell handbook of perception* (pp. 311–343). Malden, MA: Blackwell.

Goodale, M. A., & Westwood, D. A. (2004). An evolving view of duplex vision: Separate but interacting cortical pathways for perception and action. *Current Opinion in Neurobiology, 14*(2), 203–211.

Goodall, J. (1990). *Through a window: My thirty years with the chimpanzees of Gombe.* Boston: Houghton Mifflin.

Goodenough, D. R. (1991). Dream recall: History and current status of the field. In S. J. Ellman & J. S. Antrobus (Eds.), *The mind in sleep* (2nd ed., pp. 143–171). New York: Wiley.

Goodwin, K. F., & Jamison, K. R. (1990). *Manic depressive illness.* New York: Oxford University Press.

Gopnik, M. (1999). Some evidence for impaired grammars. In R. Jackendoff, P. Bloom, & K. Wynn (Eds.), *Language, logic, and concepts: Essays in memory of John Macnamara* (pp. 263–283). Cambridge, MA: MIT Press.

Gore-Felton, C., Koopman, C., Thoresen, C., Arnow, B., Bridges, E., & Spiegel,

D. (2000). Psychologists' beliefs and clinical characteristics: Judging the veracity of childhood sexual abuse memories. *Professional Psychology: Research and Practice, 31*(4), 372–377.

Gorwood, P., Bouvard, M., Mouren-Simeoni, M. C., Kipman, A., & Ades, J. (1998). Genetics and anorexia nervosa: A review of candidate genes. *Psychiatric Genetics, 8,* 1–12.

Gosling, S. D., Ko, S. J., Mannareli, T., & Morris, M. E. (2002). Room with a cue: Personality judgments based on offices and bedrooms. *Journal of Personality and Social Psychology, 82,* 379–398.

Gottesman, I. I. (1991). *Schizophrenia genesis: The origins of madness.* New York: Freeman.

Gottesman, I. I., & Moldin, S. O. (1998). Genotypes, genes, genesis, and pathogenesis in schizophrenia. In M. F. Lenzenweger & R. H. Dworkin (Eds.), *Origins and development of schizophrenia: Advances in experimental psychopathology* (pp. 5–26). Washington, DC: American Psychological Association.

Gougoux, F., Lepore, F., Lassonde, M., Voss, P., Zatorre, R. J., & Belin, P. (2004). Pitch discrimination in the early blind: People blinded in infancy have sharper listening skills than those who lost their sight later. *Nature, 430,* 309–309.

Gould, M. S. (1990). Suicide clusters and media exposure. In S. J. Blumenthal & D. J. Kupfer (Eds.), *Suicide over the life cycle: Risk factors, assessments and treatment of suicidal patients* (pp. 517–532). Washington, DC: American Psychiatric Press.

Gould, M. S., & Kramer, R. A. (2001). Youth suicide prevention. *Suicide and Life-Threatening Behavior, 31*(Suppl.), 6–31.

Gould, R. L. (1978). *Transformations: Growth and change in adult life.* New York: Simon & Schuster.

Gould, S. J. (2000). More things in heaven and earth. In H. Rose & S. Rose (Eds.), *Alas, poor Darwin: Arguments against evolutionary psychology* (pp. 85–128). New York: Harmony Books.

Graber, J. A., Brooks-Gunn, J., & Warren, M. P. (1995). The antecedents of menarcheal age: Heredity, family environment, and stressful life events. *Child Development, 66,* 346–359.

Graf, P., Mandler, G., & Haden, P. E. (1982). Simulating amnesic symptoms in normal subjects. *Science, 218,* 1243–1244.

Graf, P., & Schacter, D. L. (1985). Implicit and explicit memory for new associations in normal and amnesic subjects. *Journal of Experimental Psychology: Learning, Memory, and Cognition, 11,* 501–518.

Graf, P., & Uttl, B. (1995). Component processes of memory: Changes across the adult lifespan. *Swiss Journal of Cognitive Psychology, 6,* 113–129.

Graf, P., & Uttl, B. (2001). Prospective memory: A new focus for research. *Consciousness and Cognition, 10,* 437–450.

Graffen, N. F., Ray, W. J., & Lundy, R. (1995). EEG concomitants of hypnosis and hypnotic susceptibility. *Journal of Abnormal Psychology, 104,* 123–131.

Graig, E. (1993). Stress as a consequence of the urban physical environment. In L. Goldberger & S. Breznitz (Eds.), *Handbook of stress: Theoretical and clinical aspects* (2nd ed., pp. 316–322). New York: Free Press.

Granrud, C. E. (Ed.). (1993). *Visual perception and cognition in infancy.* Hillsdale, NJ: Erlbaum.

Granvold, D. K. (Ed.). (1994). *Cognitive and behavioral treatment: Methods and applications.* Pacific Grove, CA: Brooks/Cole.

Gray, J. R., & Thompson, P. M. (2004). Neurobiology of intelligence: Science and ethics. *Nature Reviews Neuroscience, 5,* 471–482.

Graziano, W. G., & Bryant, W. H. M. (1998). Self-monitoring and the self-attribution of positive emotions. *Journal of Personality and Social Psychology, 74,* 250–261.

Graziano, W. G., & Tobin, R. M. (2002). Agreeableness: Dimension of personality or social desirability artifact? *Journal of Personality, 70,* 695–727.

Greenberg, D. L. (2004). President Bush's false "flashbulb" memory of 9/11/01. *Applied Cognitive Psychology, 18,* 363–370.

Greenberg, L. S., & Paivio, S. C. (1997). *Working with emotions in psychotherapy.* New York: Guilford Press.

Greenblatt, D. J., & Shader, R. I. (1978). Pharmacotherapy of anxiety with benzodiazepines and beta-adrenergic blockers. In M. Lipton, A. DiMascio, & F. Killiam (Eds.),

Psychopharmacology: A generation of progress. New York: Raven.

Greene, R. L. (1992). *Human memory: Paradigms and paradoxes.* Hillsdale, NJ: Erlbaum.

Greenspoon, P. J., & Saklofske, D. H. (1998). Confirmatory factor analysis of the multidimensional Students' Life Satisfaction Scale. *Personality and Individual Differences, 25,* 965–971.

Greenwald, A. G. (1980). The totalitarian ego: Fabrication and revision of personal history. *American Psychologist, 35,* 603–618.

Greenwald, A. G., Schuh, E. S., & Klinger, M. R. (1995). Activation of marginally perceptible ("subliminal") stimuli: Dissociation of unconscious from conscious cognition. *Journal of Experimental Psychology: General, 124,* 22–42.

Greenwald, A. G., Spangenberg, E. R., Pratkanis, A. R., & Eskenazi, J. (1991). Double-blind tests of subliminal self-help audiotapes. *Psychological Science, 2,* 119–122.

Grencavage, L. M., & Norcross, J. C. (1990). Where are the common factors? *Professional Psychology: Research and Practice, 21,* 372–378.

Grice, D. E., Halmi, K. A., & Fitcher, M. M. (2002). Evidence for a susceptibility gene for anorexia nervosa on Chromosome 1. *American Journal of Human Genetics, 70,* 787–792.

Grice, H. P. (1975). Logic and conversation. In P. Cole & J. L. Morgan (Eds.), *Syntax and semantics: Speech acts* (pp. 44–58). New York: Seminar Press.

Grill, H. J., & Kaplan, J. M. (1990). Caudal brainstem participates in the distributed neural control of feeding. In E. M. Stricker (Ed.), *Handbook of behavioral neurobiology* (pp. 125–149). New York: Plenum Press.

Grove, P. M., Gillam, B., & Ono, H. (2002). Content and context of monocular regions determine perceived depth in random dot, unpaired background and phantom stereograms. *Vision Research, 42,* 1859–1870.

Groves, P. M., & Thompson, R. F. (1970). Habituation: A dual-process theory. *Psychological Review, 77,* 419–450.

Gruneberg, M. M., Sykes, R. N., & Gillett, E. (1994). The facilitating effects of mnemonic strategies on two learning tasks in learning disabled adults. *Neuropsychological Rehabilitation, 4,* 241–254.

Grusec, J. E., & Kuczynski, L. (Eds.). (1997). *Parenting and children's internalization of values: A handbook of contemporary theory.* New York: John Wiley & Sons.

Gulick, W. L., Gescheider, G. A., & Frisina, R. D. (1989). *Hearing: Physiological acoustics, neural coding, and psychoacoustics.* New York: Oxford University Press.

Gunderson, J. G. (1992). Diagnostic controversies. In A. Tasman & M. B. Riba (Eds.), *Review of psychiatry* (Vol. 11, pp. 9–24). Washington, DC: American Psychiatric Press.

Gurman, E. B. (1994). Debriefing for all concerned: Ethical treatment of human subjects. *Psychological Science, 5,* 139.

Haan, N. (Ed.). (1977). *Coping and defending: Processes of self-environment organization.* New York: Academic Press.

Haber, R. N. (1985). An icon can have no worth in the real world: Comments on Loftus, Johnson, and Shimamura's "How much is an icon worth?" *Journal of Experimental Psychology: Human Perception and Performance, 11,* 374–378.

Hadjistavropoulos, T. (2001). Pain and aging. *Pain Research & Management 6*(3), 116–117.

Hadjistavropoulos, T., & Craig, K. D. (Eds.). (2004). *Pain: Psychological perspectives.* New York: Erlbaum.

Hadjistavropoulos, H. D., Craig, K. D., Hadjistavropoulos, T., & Poole, G. D. (1996). Subjective judgments of deception in pain expression: Accuracy and errors. *Pain, 65*(2–3), 251–258.

Hadjistavropoulos, T., McMurtry, B., & Craig, K. D. (1999). Beautiful faces in pain: Biases and accuracy in the perception of pain. *Psychology and Health, 11,* 411–420.

Haerich, P. (1997). Long-term habituation and sensitization of the human acoustic startle response. *Journal of Psychophysiology, 11,* 103–114.

Haidt, J. (2001). The emotional dog and its rational tail: A social intuitionist approach to moral judgment. *Psychological Review, 108,* 814–834.

Haines, M. M., Stansfeld, S. A., Job, R. F. S., Berglund, B., & Head, J. (2001). Chronic aircraft noise exposure, stress responses, mental health and cognitive performance in school children. *Psychological Medicine, 31,* 265–277.

Hall, J. A. Y., & Kimura, D. (1994). Dermatoglyphic asymmetry and sexual orientation in men. *Behavioral Neuroscience, 108,* 1203–1206.

Halpern, B. P. (2002). Taste. In H. Pashler & S. Yantis (Eds.), *Steven's handbook of experimental psychology: Vol. 1. Sensation and perception* (3rd ed., pp. 653–690). New York: John Wiley & Sons.

Halpern, D. F. (1989). The disappearance of cognitive gender differences: What you see depends on where you look. *American Psychologist, 44,* 1156–1158.

Halpern, D. F. (2000). *Sex differences in cognitive abilities* (3rd ed.). Mahwah, NJ: Erlbaum.

Hamer, D. H., Hu, S., Magnuson, V. L., Hu, N., & Pattatucci, A. M. L. (1993). A linkage between DNA markers on the X chromosome and male sexual orientation. *Science, 261,* 321–327.

Hammen, C. (2003). Mood disorders. In G. Stricker & T. A. Widiger (Eds.), *Handbook of psychology: Clinical psychology* (Vol. 8, pp. 93–118). New York: Wiley.

Hansen, C. J., Stevens, L. C., & Coast, J. R. (2001). Exercise duration and mood state: How much is enough to feel better? *Health Psychology, 20,* 267–275.

Hanson, G. R., Rau, K. S., & Fleckenstein, A. E. (2004). The methamphetamine experience: A NIDA partnership. *Neuropharmacology, 47*(Suppl. 1), 92–100.

Hanson, V. L. (1990). Recall of order information by deaf signers: Phonetic coding in temporal order recall. *Memory and Cognition, 18,* 604–610.

Harbluk, J. L., Noy, Y. I., & Eizenman, M. (2002). *The impact of cognitive distraction on driver visual behaviour and vehicle control.* Retrieved September 10, 2006, from the Transport Canada website: http://www.tc.gc.ca/roadsafety/tp/tp13889/pdf/tp13889es.pdf

Hare, R. D. (1996). Psychopathy. *Criminal Justice & Behavior, 23,* 25–54.

Hare, R. D. (2003). *Manual for the Psychopathy Checklist – Revised* (2nd version). Toronto: Multi-Health Systems.

Harlow, H. F., Harlow, M. K., & Meyer, D. R. (1971). From thought to therapy: Lessons from a primate laboratory. *American Scientist, 59,* 538–549.

Harlow, H. F., & Zimmerman, R. R. (1959). Affectional responses in the infant monkey. *Science, 130,* 421–432.

Harmon, T. M., Hynan, M. T., & Tyre, T. E. (1990). Improved obstetric outcomes using hypnotic analgesia and skill mastery combined with childbirth education. *Journal of Consulting and Clinical Psychology, 58,* 525–530.

Harnad, S. (2003). Can a machine be conscious? How? In O. Holland (Ed.), *Machine consciousness* (pp. 66–75). Exeter, UK: Imprint Academic.

Harper, G. (2001). Cultural influences on diagnosis. *Child & Adolescent Psychiatric Clinics of North America, 10,* 711–728.

Harris, G. T., Rice, M. E., & Cormier, C. A. (1994). Psychopaths: Is a therapeutic community therapeutic? *Therapeutic Communities: International Journal for Therapeutic and Supportive Organizations, 15,* 283–299.

Harris, G. T., Rice, M. E., & Quinsey, V. L. (1993). Violent recidivism of mentally disordered offenders: The development of a statistical prediction instrument. *Criminal Justice and Behavior, 20,* 315–335.

Harris, J. R. (1995). Where is the child's environment? A group socialization theory of development. *Psychological Review, 102,* 458–489.

Harris, J. R. (1998). *The nurture assumption.* New York: Free Press.

Hartshorne, H., & May, A. (1928). *Studies in the nature of character: Studies in deceit.* New York: Macmillan.

Hartup, W. W., & Stevens, N. (1997). Friendships and adaptation in the life course. *Psychological Bulletin, 121,* 355–370.

Harvey, P. D. (2001). Vulnerability to schizophrenia in adulthood. In R. E. Ingram & J. M. Price (Eds.), *Vulnerability to psychopathology: Risk across the lifespan* (pp. 355–381). New York: Guilford Press.

Haselton, M. G., & Buss, D. M. (2000). Error management theory: A new perspective on biases in cross-sex mind reading. *Journal of Personality and Social Psychology, 78,* 81–91.

Hasher, L., Stolzfus, E. R., Zacks, R. T., & Rypma, B. (1991). Age and inhibition. *Journal of Experimental Psychology:*

Learning, Memory, and Cognition, 17, 163–169.

Hasher, L., & Zacks, R. R. (1979). Automatic and effortful processes in memory. *Journal of Experimental Psychology: General, 108,* 356–388.

Hasselmo, M. E., Rolls, E. T., & Baylis, G. C. (1989). The role of expression and identity in the face-selective responses of neurons in the temporal visual cortex of the monkey. *Behavioral Brain Research, 32,* 203–218.

Hastings, M. H., Reddy, A. B., & Maywood, E. S. (2003). A clockwork web: Circadian timing in brain and periphery, in health and disease. *Nature Reviews Neuroscience, 4*(8), 649–661.

Hatala, R., Norman, G. R., & Brooks, L. R. (1999). Influence of a single example on subsequent electrocardiogram interpretation. *Teaching and Learning in Medicine, 11*(2), 110–117.

Hatfield, E. (1988). Passionate and companionate love. In R. J. Sternberg & M. L. Barnes (Eds.), *The psychology of love* (pp. 191–217). New Haven, CT: Yale University Press.

Hatfield, E., & Rapson, R. L. (1993). *Love, sex, and intimacy.* New York: HarperCollins.

Hauri, P. (1982). *The sleep disorders.* Kalamazoo, MI: Upjohn.

Hayes, C. (1952). *The ape in our house.* London: Gollacz.

Hayes, K. J., & Hayes, C. (1951). The intellectual development of a home-raised chimpanzee. *Proceedings of the American Philosophical Society, 95,* 105–109.

Hayward, W. G. (2003). After the viewpoint debate: Where next in object recognition? *Trends in Cognitive Sciences, 7,* 425–427.

Health Canada. (1999). *Toward a healthy future: Second report on the health of Canadians.* Ottawa, ON: Health Canada Publications.

Health Canada. (2005). *Baseline natural health products survey among consumers: Final report.* Ottawa, ON: Health Canada Publications. Retrieved July 4, 2006, from http://www.hc-sc.gc.ca/dhp-mps/alt_formats/hpfb-dgpsa/pdf/pubs/eng_cons_survey_e.pdf

Hearold, S. (1986). A synthesis of 1043 effects of television on social behavior. In G. Comstock (Ed.),

Public communication and behavior (pp. 66–135). New York: Academic Press.

Hearst, E., & Franklin, S. R. (1977). Positive and negative relations between a signal and food: Approach-withdrawal behavior to the signal. *Journal of Experimental Psychology: Animal Behavior Processes, 3*, 37–52.

Hebb, D. O. (1949/2002). *The organization of behavior: A neuropsychological theory*. Mahwah, NJ: Erlbaum.

Hector, R. I. (1998). The use of clozapine in the treatment of aggressive schizophrenia. *Canadian Journal of Psychiatry, 43*, 466–472.

Heider, E. (1972). Universals of color naming and memory. *Journal of Experimental Psychology, 93*, 10–20.

Heider, F. (1944). Social perception and phenomenal causality. *Psychological Review, 51*, 358–374.

Heim, C., Bierl, C., Nisenbaum, R., Wagner, D., & Reeves, W. C. (2004). Regional and prevalence of fatiguing illnesses in the United States before and after the terrorist attacks of September 11, 2001. *Psychosomatic Medicine, 66*, 672–678.

Heiman, G. A. (1995). *Research methods in psychology*. Boston: Houghton Mifflin.

Heine, S. J., & Lehman, D. R. (1999). Culture, self-discrepancies, and self-satisfaction. *Personality and Social Psychology Bulletin, 25*, 915–925.

Heine, S. J., Takata, T., & Lehman, D. R. (2000). Beyond self-presentation: Evidence for self-criticism among Japanese. *Personality and Social Psychology Bulletin, 26*(1), 71–78.

Hellerstein, D. J., & Little, S. (2000). Current perspectives on the diagnosis and treatment of double depression. In K. J. Palmer (Ed.), *Managing depressive disorders* (pp. 59–73). Auckland, New Zealand: Adis International.

Hellige, J. B. (1990). Hemispheric asymmetry. *Annual Review of Psychology, 41*, 55–80.

Helmes, E., & Reddon, J. R. (1993). A perspective on developments in assessing psychopathology: A critical review of the MMPI and MMPI-2. *Psychological Bulletin, 113*, 453–471.

Henderson-King, E. I., & Nisbett, R. E. (1996). Anti-Black prejudice as a function of exposure to the negative behavior of a single Black person.

Journal of Personality and Social Psychology, 71, 654–664.

Henley, N. M. (1989). Molehill or mountain? What we know and don't know about sex bias in language. In M. Crawford & M. Gentry (Eds.), *Gender and thought: Psychological perspectives* (pp. 59–78). New York: Springer-Verlag.

Herman, C. P., & Polivy, J. (1988). Studies of eating in normal dieters. In B. T. Walsh (Ed.), *Eating behavior in eating disorders* (pp. 95–111). Washington, DC: American Psychiatric Press.

Herrmann, D., Raybeck, D., & Gruneberg, M. (2002). *Improving memory and study skills: Advances in theory and practice*. Ashland, OH: Hogrefe & Huber.

Hertzsprung, E. A. M., & Dobson, K. S. (2000). Diversity training: Conceptual issues and practices for Canadian clinical psychology programs. *Canadian Psychology, 41*, 184–191.

Herz, R. S., & Cahill, E. D. (1997). Differential use of sensory information in sexual behavior as a function of gender. *Human Nature, 8*, 275–286.

Herz, R. S., Eliassen, J., Beland, S., & Souza, T. (2004). Neuroimaging evidence for the emotional potency of odor-evoked memory. *Neuropsychologia, 42*, 371–378.

Herzog, D. B., Greenwood, D. N., Dorer, D. J., Flores, A. T., & Ekeblad, E. R. (2000). Mortality in eating disorders: A descriptive study. *Journal of Eating Disorders, 28*, 20–26.

Hetherington, A. W., & Ranson, S. W. (1942). The relation of various hypothalamic lesions to adiposity in the rat. *Journal of Comparative Neurology, 76*, 475–499.

Hewitt, P. L., Caelian, C. F., & Flett, G. L. (2002). Perfectionism in children: Associations with depression, anxiety, and anger. *Personality and Individual Differences, 32*(6), 1049–1061.

Hewstone, M., & Brown, R. (1986). *Contact and conflict in intergroup encounters*. Oxford, England: Basil Blackwell.

Hilgard, E. R. (1965). *Hypnotic susceptibility*. New York: Harcourt, Brace, & World.

Hilgard, E. R. (1987). *Psychology in America: An historical survey*. New York: Harcourt Brace Jovanovich.

Hilgard, E. R. (1992). Dissociation and theories of hypnosis. In E. Fromm & M. Nash (Eds.), *Contemporary hypnosis research* (pp. 60–101). New York: Guilford Press.

Hill, J. O., & Peters, J. C. (1998). Environmental contributions to the obesity epidemic. *Science, 280*, 1371–1374.

Hilton, J. L., & von Hippel, W. (1996). Stereotypes. *Annual Review of Psychology, 47*, 237–271.

Hines, M. (1982). Prenatal gonadal hormones and sex differences in human behavior. *Psychological Bulletin, 92*, 56–80.

Hintzman, D. L. (1986). "Schema abstraction" in a multiple-trace memory model. *Psychological Review, 93*, 411–428.

Hirsh, I. J., & Watson, C. S. (1996). Auditory psychophysics and perception. *Annual Review of Psychology, 47*, 461–484.

Hirst, W. (1995). Cognitive aspects of consciousness. In M. S. Gazzaniga (Ed.), *The cognitive neurosciences* (pp. 1307–1319). Cambridge, MA: MIT Press.

Hitch, G. J., & Halliday, M. S. (1983). Working memory in children. *Philosophical Transactions of the Royal Society London B, 302*, 325–340.

Hobfoll, S. E., Shoham, S. B., & Ritter, C. (1991). Women's satisfaction with social support and their receipt of aid. *Journal of Personality and Social Psychology, 61*, 332–341.

Hobson, C. J., & Delunas, L. (2001). National norms and life-event frequencies for the revised Social Readjustment Rating Scale. *International Journal of Stress Management, 8*, 299–314.

Hobson, J. A., & McCarley, R. W. (1977). The brain as a dream state generator: An activation-synthesis hypothesis of the dream process. *American Journal of Psychiatry, 134*, 1335–1348.

Hobson, J. A., Pace-Schott, E. F., & Stickgold, R. (2000). Dreaming and the brain: Toward a cognitive neuroscience of conscious states. *Behavioral and Brain Sciences, 23*(6), 793–842; 904–1018; 1083–1121.

Hodges, J., & Tizard, B. (1989). IQ and behavioral adjustment of ex-institutional adolescents. *Journal of Child Psychology and Psychiatry, 30*, 53–75.

Hoff, T. (1992). Psychology in Canada one hundred years ago: James Mark Baldwin at the University of Toronto. *Canadian Psychology, 33*, 683–694.

Hoffman, M. L. (1986). Affect, cognition, and motivation. In R. M. Sorrentino & E. T. Higgins (Eds.), *Handbook of motivation and cognition: Foundations of social behavior* (pp. 244–280). New York: Guilford Press.

Hoffmann, P. (1997). The endorphin hypothesis. In W. P. Morgan (Ed.), *Physical activity and mental health* (pp. 163–177). Washington, DC: Taylor & Francis.

Hofmann, S. G., Lehman, C. L., & Barlow, D. H. (1997). How specific are specific phobias? *Journal of Behavior Therapy and Experimental Psychiatry, 28*, 233–240.

Hofstadter, M. C., & Reznick, J. S. (1996). Response modality affects human infant delayed-response performance. *Child Development, 67*, 646–658.

Hogan, R., Hogan, J., & Roberts, B. W. (1996). Personality measurement and employment decisions: Questions and answers. *American Psychologist, 51*, 469–477.

Hohmann, G. W. (1966). Some effects of spinal cord lesions on experienced emotional feelings. *Psychophysiology, 3*, 143–156.

Holden, R. R., Kerr, P. S., Mendonca, J. D., & Velamoor, V. R. (1998). Are some motives more linked to suicide proneness than others? *Journal of Clinical Psychology, 54*, 569–576.

Holland, P. C. (1977). Conditioned stimulus as a determinant of the form of the Pavlovian conditioned response. *Journal of Experimental Psychology: Animal Behavior Processes, 3*, 77–104.

Holmes, D. S. (1976). Debriefing after psychological experiments: I. Effectiveness of postdeception dehoaxing. *American Psychologist, 31*, 858–867.

Holmes, T. H., & Rahe, R. H. (1967). The Social Readjustment Rating Scale. *Journal of Psychosomatic Research, 11*, 213–218.

Holroyd, C. B., & Coles, M. G. H. (2002). The neural basis of human error processing: Reinforcement learning, dopamine, and the error-related negativity. *Psychological Review, 109*, 679–709.

Holt, E. B. (1931). *Animal drive and the learning process: An essay toward radical empiricism.* New York: Holt.

Holtzheimer, P. E., & Neumaier, J. F. (2003). Treatment of acute mania. *CNS Spectrums, 8*, 917–928.

Honzik, M. P., Macfarlane, J. W., & Allen, L. (1948). The stability of mental test performance between two and eighteen years. *Journal of Experimental Education, 17*, 309–324.

Horn, J. L. (1976). Human abilities: A review of research and theory in the early 1970s. *Annual Review of Psychology, 27*, 437–485.

Horn, J. L. (1982). The aging of human abilities. In J. Wolman (Ed.), *Handbook of developmental psychology* (pp. 847–870). Englewood Cliffs, NJ: Prentice-Hall.

Horn, J. L., & Cattell, R. B. (1966). Refinement and test of the theory of fluid and crystallized ability intelligences. *Journal of Educational Psychology, 57*, 253–270.

Horn, J. L., & Noll, J. (1997). Human cognitive capabilities: Gf-Gc theory. In D. P. Flanagan & J. L. Genshaft (Eds.), *Contemporary intellectual assessment: Theories, tests, and issues* (pp. 53–91). New York: Guilford Press.

Horne, J. (2001). State of the art: Sleep. *Psychologist, 14*, 302–306.

Horne, J. A., & Minard, A. (1985). Sleep and sleepiness following a behaviourally "active" day. *Ergonomics, 28*, 567–575.

Horney, K. (1945). *Our inner conflicts: A constructive theory of neurosis.* New York: Norton.

Horney, K. (1967). *Feminine psychology.* New York: Norton.

Horvath, A. O., & Luborsky, L. (1993). The role of the therapeutic alliance in psychotherapy. *Journal of Consulting and Clinical Psychology, 61*, 561–573.

Horvath, P. (1988). Placebos and common factors in two decades of psychotherapy research. *Psychological Bulletin, 104*, 214–225.

Houle, M., McGrath, P. A., Moran, G., & Garrett, O. J. (1988). The efficacy of hypnosis- and relaxation-induced analgesia on two dimensions of pain for cold pressor and electrical tooth pulp stimulation. *Pain, 33*, 241–251.

Hoyle, R. H., Kernis, M. H., Leary, M. R., & Baldwin, M. W. (Eds.) (1999). *Selfhood: Identity, esteem, regulation.* New York: Westview.

Hser, Y., Anglin, M. D., & Powers, K. (1993). A 24-year follow-up of California narcotics addicts. *Archives of General Psychiatry, 50*, 577–584.

Hubbel, J. C. (1990, January). Animal rights war on medicine. *Reader's Digest,* 70–76.

Hubel, D. H., & Wiesel, T. N. (1962). Receptive fields, binocular interaction, and functional architecture in the cat's visual cortex. *Journal of Physiology, 160*, 106–154.

Hubel, D. H., & Wiesel, T. N. (1979, September). Brain mechanisms and vision. *Scientific American, 241*, 150–162.

Huesmann, L., Moise-Titus, J., Podolski, C. P., & Eron, L. D. (2003). Longitudinal relations between childhood exposure to media violence and adult aggression and violence: 1977–1992. *Developmental Psychology, 39*, 201–221.

Hull, C. L. (1943). *Principles of behavior.* New York: Appleton-Century.

Hull, J. G., & Bond, C. F., Jr. (1986). Social and behavioral consequences of alcohol consumption and expectancy: A meta-analysis. *Psychological Bulletin, 99*, 347–360.

Hultsch, D. F., Hertzog, C., Small, B. J., & Dixon, R. A. (1999). Use it or lose it: Engaged lifestyle as a buffer of cognitive decline in aging? *Psychology and Aging, 14*, 245–263.

Humphrey, G. K., James, T. W., Gati, J. S., Menon, R. S., & Goodale, M. A. (1999). Perception of the McCollough effect correlates with activity in extrastriate cortex: A functional magnetic resonance imaging study. *Psychological Science, 10*, 444–448.

Hunnicutt, C. P., & Newman, I. A. (1993). Adolescent dieting practices and nutrition knowledge. *Health Values, 17*, 35–40.

Hunsley, J., Lee, C. M., & Aubry, T. (1999). Who uses psychological services in Canada? *Canadian Psychology, 40*(3), 232–240.

Hunt, E. (1985). The correlates of intelligence. In D. K. Detterman (Ed.), *Current topics in human intelligence: Vol. 1, Research Methodology* (pp. 157–178). Norwood, NJ: Ablex.

Hunt, M. (1993). *The story of psychology.* New York: Anchor Books.

Hunt, R. R., & Einstein, G. O. (1981). Relational and item-specific information in memory. *Journal of Verbal*

Learning and Verbal Behavior, 20, 497–514.

Hunt, R. R., & McDaniel, M. A. (1993). The enigma of organization and distinctiveness. *Journal of Memory and Language, 32,* 421–445.

Hurt, S. W., Reznikoff, M., & Clarkin, J. F. (1995). The Rorschach. In L. E. Beutler & M. R. Berren (Eds.), *Integrative assessment of adult personality* (pp. 187–205). New York: Guilford Press.

Hyde, J. S., & Lin, M. C. (1988). Gender differences in verbal ability: A developmental meta-analysis. *Psychological Bulletin, 104,* 53–69.

Hynie, M., Lydon, J. E., Cote, S., & Weiner, S. (1998). Relational sexual scripts and women's condom use: The importance of internalized norms. *Journal of Sex Research, 35,* 370–380.

Iezzi, T., Duckworth, M. P., & Adams, H. E. (2001). Somatoform and factitious disorders. In P. B. Sutker & H. E. Adams (Eds.), *Comprehensive handbook of psychopathology* (3rd ed., pp. 211–242). New York: Kluwer Academic/Plenum.

Inoue-Nakamura, N., & Matsuzawa, T. (1997). Development of stone tool use by wild chimpanzees (Pan troglodytes). *Journal of Comparative Psychology, 111,* 159–713.

Iverson, G. L., King, R. J., Scott, J. G., & Adams, R. L. (2001). Cognitive complaints in litigating patients with head injuries or chronic pain. *Journal of Forensic Neuropsychology, 2,* 19–30.

Izard, C. E. (1994). Innate and universal facial expressions: Evidence from developmental and cross-cultural research. *Psychological Bulletin, 115,* 288–299.

Jackson, D. N., & Messick, S. (1961). Acquiescence and desirability as response determinants on the MMPI. *Educational and Psychological Measurement, 21,* 771–790.

Jackson, D. N., Paunonen, S. V., Fraboni, M., & Goffin, R. D. (1996). A five-factor versus six-factor model of personality structure. *Personality and Individual Differences, 20,* 33–45.

Jacobson, E. (1938). *Progressive relaxation.* Chicago: University of Chicago Press.

Jacoby, L. L., & Brooks, L. R. (1984). Nonanalytic cognition: Memory, per-

ception, and concept learning. In G. H. Bower (Ed.), *The psychology of learning and motivation: Advances in research and theory* (pp. 1–47). New York: Academic Press.

Jacoby, L. L., & Dallas, M. (1981). On the relationship between autobiographical memory and perceptual learning. *Journal of Experimental Psychology: General, 110,* 306–340.

Jacoby, L. L., & Witherspoon, D. (1982). Remembering without awareness. *Canadian Journal of Psychology, 36,* 300–324.

Jacoby, L. L., Woloshyn, V., & Kelley, C. M. (1989). Becoming famous without being recognized: Unconscious influences of memory produced by dividing attention. *Journal of Experimental Psychology: General, 118,* 115–125.

James, W. (1884). Some omissions of introspective psychology. *Mind, 9,* 1–26.

James, W. (1890). *The principles of psychology.* New York: Holt.

James, W. (1894). The physical basis of emotion. *Psychological Review, 1,* 516–529.

Jamison, K. R. (1986). Suicide and bipolar disorders. *Annals of the New York Academy of Science, 487,* 301–315.

Jamison, K. R. (1989). Mood disorders and patterns of creativity in British writers and artists. *Psychiatry, 52,* 125–134.

Jang, K. L., Livesley, W. J., & Vernon, P. A. (1996a). Heritability of the big five personality dimensions and their facets: A twin study. *Journal of Personality, 64,* 577–591.

Jang, K. L., Livesley, W. J., & Vernon, P. A. (1996b). The genetic basis of personality at different ages: A cross-sectional twin study. *Personality and Individual Differences, 21,* 299–301.

Jang, K. L., McCrae, R. R., Angleitner, A., Riemann, R., & Livesley, W. J. (1998). Heritability of facet-level traits in a cross-cultural twin sample: Support for a hierarchical model of personality. *Journal of Personality and Social Psychology, 74,* 1556–1565.

Jang, K. L., Vernon, P. A., Livesley, W. J., Stein, M. B., & Wolf, H. (2001). Intra- and extra-familial influences on alcohol and drug misuse: A twin study of gene-environment correlation. *Addiction, 96*(9), 1307–1318.

Janicki, M. G., & Krebs, D. L. (1998). Evolutionary approaches to culture. In C. Crawford & D. L. Krebs (Eds.),

Handbook of evolutionary psychology: Ideas, issues and applications (pp. 163–209). Mahwah, NJ: Erlbaum.

Janis, I. L. (1982). *Victims of groupthink* (2nd ed.). Boston: Houghton Mifflin.

Janis, I. L. (1989). *Crucial decisions: Leadership in policymaking and crisis management.* New York: Free Press.

Jarrad, L. E. (1993). On the role of the hippocampus in learning and memory in the rat. *Behavioral and Neural Biology, 60,* 9–26.

Jausovec, N. (1997). Differences in EEG activity during the solution of closed and open problems. *Creativity Research Journal, 10,* 317–324.

Jaynes, J. (1976). *The origin of consciousness in the breakdown of the bicameral mind.* Boston: Houghton Mifflin.

Jemmott, J. B., III, Jemmott, L. S., & Fong, G. T. (1998). Abstinence and safer sex HIV risk-reduction interventions for African American adolescents. *Journal of the American Medical Association, 279,* 1529–1536.

Jemmott, J. B., III., Jemmott, L. S., Fong, G. T., & McCaffree, K. (1999). Reducing HIV risk-associated sexual behavior among African American adolescents: Testing the generality of intervention effects. *American Journal of Community Psychology, 27,* 161–187.

Jenike, M. A., Baer, L., & Minichiello, W. E. (Eds.). (1986). *Obsessive-compulsive disorders: Theory and management.* Littleton, MA: PSG Publishing.

Jenkins, H. M., Barrera, F. J., Ireland, C., & Woodside, B. (1978). Signal-centered action patterns of dogs in appetitive classical conditioning. *Learning and Motivation, 9,* 272–296.

Jenkins, J. G., & Dallenbach, K. M. (1924). Obliviscence during sleep and waking. *American Journal of Psychology, 35,* 605–612.

Jenner, P. (1990). Parkinson's disease: Clues to the cause of cell death in the substantia nigra. *Seminars in the Neurosciences, 2,* 117–126.

Jennison, K. M. (1992). The impact of stressful life events and social support on drinking among older adults: A general population survey. *International Journal of Aging and Human Development, 35,* 99–123.

Jensen, A. R. (1992). Commentary: Vehicles of g. *Psychological Science, 3,* 275–278.

Jensen, A. R. (1993). Why is reaction time correlated with psychometric *g*? *Current Directions in Psychological Science, 2,* 53–56.

Jensen, A. R., & Weng, L. (1994). What is a good *g*? *Intelligence, 18,* 231–258.

Jensen, J. P., Bergin, A. E., & Greaves, D. W. (1990). The meaning of eclecticism: New survey and analysis of components. *Professional Psychology: Research and Practice, 21,* 124–130.

John, O. P., & Robins, R. W. (1994). Accuracy and bias in self-perception: Individual differences in self-enhancement and the role of narcissism. *Journal of Personality and Social Psychology, 66,* 206–219.

Johnson, E. A. (1995). Self-deceptive coping: Adaptive only in ambiguous contexts. *Journal of Personality, 63,* 759–191.

Johnson, E. A., Vincent, N., & Ross, L. (1997). Self-deception versus self-esteem in buffering the negative effects of failure. *Journal of Research in Personality, 31,* 385–405.

Johnson, L. M., & Morris, E. K. (1987). Public information on research with nonhumans. *American Psychologist, 42,* 103–104.

Johnson, M. H., Dziurawiec, S., Ellis, H., & Morton, J. (1991). Newborns' preferential tracking of face-like stimuli and its subsequent decline. *Cognition, 40,* 1–19.

Johnson, M. K., Hashtroudi, S., & Lindsay, D. S. (1993). Source monitoring. *Psychological Bulletin, 114,* 3–28.

Johnson, R. C., McClearn, C. G., Yuen, S., Nagoshi, C. T., Ahern, F. M., & Cole, R. E. (1985). Galton's data a century later. *American Psychologist, 40,* 875–892.

Johnson, S. M. (1996). *The practice of emotionally focused marital therapy: Creating connection.* New York: Guilford Press.

Johnson, S. P. (1997). Young infants' perception of object unity: Implications for the development of attentional and cognitive skills. *Current Directions in Psychological Science, 6,* 5–11.

Johnston, C. (1988). A behavioral-family systems approach to assessment: Maternal characteristics associated with externalizing behavior in children. In R. Prinz (Ed.), *Advances in behavioral assessment of children and families* (Vol. 4, pp. 163–189). Greenwich, CT: JAI Press.

Johnston, C., & Freeman, W. S. (1997). Attributions for child behavior in parents of nonproblem children and children with attention deficit hyperactivity disorder. *Journal of Consulting and Clinical Psychology, 65,* 636–645.

Johnston, V. S. (2000). Female facial beauty: The fertility hypothesis. *Pragmatics and Cognition, 8,* 107–122.

Joiner, T. E., Jr., Steer, R. A., Abramson, L. Y., Alloy, L. B., Metalsky, G. I., & Schmidt, N. B. (2001). Hopelessness depression as a distinct dimension of depressive symptoms among clinical and non-clinical samples. *Behaviour Research and Therapy, 39,* 523–536.

Jolly, A. M., Orr, P. H., Hammond, G., & Young, T. K. (1995). Risk factors for infection in women undergoing testing for *Chlamydia trachomatis* and *Neisseria gonorrhoeae* in Manitoba, Canada. *Sexually Transmitted Diseases, 22,* 289–295.

Jones, E. E. (1964). *Ingratiation.* New York: Appleton-Century-Crofts.

Jones, E. E. (1990). *Interpersonal perception.* New York: Freeman.

Jones, E. E., & Davis, K. E. (1965). A theory of correspondent inferences: From acts to dispositions. In L. Berkowitz (Ed.), *Advances in experimental social psychology* (Vol. 2, pp. 219–266). New York: Academic Press.

Jones, E. E., & Harris, V. A. (1967). The attribution of attitudes. *Journal of Experimental Social Psychology, 3,* 1–24.

Jones, E. R., & Childers, R. L. (1993). *Contemporary college physics* (2nd ed.). Reading, MA: Addison-Wesley.

Jones, G. V., & Martin, M. (1992). Misremembering a familiar object: Mnemonic illusions, not drawing bias. *Memory and Cognition, 20,* 211–213.

Jones, L. A. (1988). Motor illusions: What do they reveal about proprioception? *Psychological Bulletin, 103,* 72–86.

Jones, M. C. (1924). A laboratory study of fear: The case of Peter. *Pedagogical Seminary, 31,* 308–315.

Jones, R. T. (1971). Tetrahydrocannabinol and the marijuana-induced social "high" or the effects on the mind of marijuana. In A. J. Singer (Ed.), Marijuana: Chemistry, pharmacology, and patterns of social use. *Annals of the New York Academy of Sciences, 191,* 155–165.

Jonides, J. (2000). Mechanisms of verbal working memory revealed by neuroimaging studies. In B. Landau & J. Sabini (Eds.), *Perception, cognition, and language: Essays in honor of Henry and Lila Gleitman* (pp. 87–104). Cambridge, MA: MIT Press.

Josephson, W. L. (1995). *Television violence: A review of the effects on children of different ages.* Ottawa, ON: Canadian Heritage.

Joule, R. V. (1986). Twenty-five on: Yet another version of cognitive dissonance theory? *European Journal of Social Psychology, 16,* 65–78.

Jung, C. G. (1923). *Psychological types.* New York: Pantheon Books.

Jussim, L. (1989). Teacher expectations: Self-fulfilling prophecies, perceptual biases, and accuracy. *Journal of Personality and Social Psychology, 57,* 469–480.

Justice, A. (1985). Review of the effects of stress on cancer in laboratory animals: Importance of time stress application and type of tumor. *Psychological Bulletin, 98,* 108–138.

Kagan, J. (1997). Temperament and the reactions to unfamiliarity. *Child Development, 68,* 139–143.

Kagan, J., & Snidman, N. (1991). Temperamental factors in human development. *American Psychologist, 46,* 856–862.

Kahneman, D. (1973). *Attention and effort.* Englewood Cliffs, NJ: Prentice-Hall.

Kahneman, D., Slovic, P., & Tversky, A. (Eds.). (1982). *Judgment under uncertainty: Heuristics and biases.* Cambridge: Cambridge University Press.

Kail, R., & Salthouse, T. A. (1994). Processing speed as a mental capacity. *Acta Psychologica, 86,* 199–225.

Kalakoski, V., & Saariluoma, P. (2001). Taxi drivers' exceptional memory of street names. *Memory & Cognition, 29,* 634–638.

Kalat, J. W. (1992). *Biological psychology* (4th ed.). Belmont, CA: Wadsworth.

Kalat, J. W. (1996). *Introduction to psychology* (4th ed.). Pacific Grove, CA: Brooks/Cole.

Kaler, S. R., & Freeman, B. J. (1994). Analysis of environmental deprivation: Cognitive and social development in Romanian orphans. *Journal of Child Psychology and Psychiatry, 35,* 769–781.

Kalick, S. M., Zebrowitz, L. A., Langlois, J. H., & Johnson, R. M. (1998). Does human facial attractiveness honestly advertise health? Longitudinal data on an evolutionary question. *Psychological Science, 9,* 8–13.

Kalin, R. (1996). Ethnic attitudes as a function of ethnic presence. *Canadian Journal of Behavioural Science, 28,* 171–179.

Kalin, R., & Berry, J. W. (1996). Interethnic attitudes in Canada: Ethnocentrism, consensual hierarchy and reciprocity. *Canadian Journal of Behavioural Science, 28,* 253–261.

Kamen-Siegel, L., Rodin, J., Seligman, M. E. P., & Dwyer, J. (1991). Explanatory style and cell-mediated immunity in elderly men and women. *Health Psychology, 10,* 229–235.

Kamil, A. C., & Balda, R. P. (1990). Differential memory for different cache sites by Clark's nutcrackers (Nucifraga columbiana). *Journal of Experimental Psychology: Animal Behavior Processes, 16,* 162–168.

Kamin, L. J. (1968). "Attention-like" processes in classical conditioning. In M. R. Jones (Ed.), *Miami symposium on the prediction of behavior: Aversive stimulation* (pp. 9–33). Miami, FL: University of Miami Press.

Kamin, L. J. (1974). *The science and politics of IQ.* Oxford, England: Erlbaum.

Kandel, E. R. (1991). Cellular mechanisms of learning and the biological basis of individuality. In E. R. Kandel, J. H. Schwartz, & T. M. Jessel (Eds.), *Principles of neural science* (3rd ed., pp. 1009–1032). New York: Elsevier.

Kane, J. M., Woerner, M., Weinhold, P., Wegner, J., Kinon, B., & Bernstein, M. (1986). Incidence of tardive dyskinesia: Five-year data from a prospective study. *Psychopharmacology Bulletin, 20,* 387–389.

Kanwisher, N., McDermott, J., & Chun, M. M. (1997). The fusiform face area: A module in human extrastriate cortex specialized for face perception. *Journal of Neuroscience, 17*(11), 4302–4311.

Kaplan, R. M. (1985). The controversy related to the use of psychological tests. In B. B. Wolman (Ed.), *Handbook of intelligence: Theories, measurements, and applications* (pp. 465–504). New York: Wiley.

Kapur, S., & Mann, J. J. (1993). Antidepressant action and the neurobiologic effects of ECT: Human studies. In C. E. Coffey (Ed.), *The clinical science of electroconvulsive therapy* (pp. 183–210). Washington, DC: American Psychiatric Press.

Karau, S. J., & Hart, J. W. (1998). Group cohesiveness and social loafing: Effects of a social interaction manipulation on individual motivation with groups. *Group Dynamics, 2,* 185–191.

Karau, S. J., & Williams, K. D. (1993). Social loafing: A meta-analytic review and theoretical integration. *Journal of Personality and Social Psychology, 65,* 681–706.

Karmiloff-Smith, A., Plunket, K., Johnson, M. H., Elman, J. L., & Bates, E. A. (1998). What does it mean to claim that something is "innate"? Response to Clark, Harris, Lightfoot and Samuels. *Mind and Language, 13*(4), 588–604.

Karni, A., Tanne, D., Rubenstein, B. S., Askenasy, J., & Sagi, D. (1994). Dependence on REM sleep of overnight improvement of a perceptual skill. *Science, 265,* 679–682.

Kass, S. J., Ahlers, R. H., & Dugger, M. (1998). Eliminating gender differences through practice in an applied visual spatial task. *Human Performance, 11,* 337–349.

Katz, A. N., Blasko, D. G., & Kazmerski, V. A. (2004). Saying what you don't mean: Social influences on sarcastic language processing. *Current Directions in Psychological Science, 13,* 186–189.

Kaufman, A. S., & Horn, J. L. (1996). Age changes on tests of fluid and crystallized ability for women and men on the Kaufman Adolescent and Adult Intelligence Test (KAIT) at ages 17–94 years. *Archives of Clinical Neuropsychology, 11,* 97–121.

Kawakami, K., Dovidio, J. F., & van Kamp, S. (2005). Kicking the habit: Effects of nonstereotypic association training and correction processes on hiring decisions. *Journal of Experimental Social Psychology, 41,* 68–75.

Kawakami, K., Young, H., & Dovidio, J. F. (2002). Automatic stereotyping: Category, trait, and behavioral activations. *Personality and Social Psychology Bulletin, 28,* 3–15.

Keel, P. K., & Klump, K. L. (2003). Are eating disorders culture-bound syndromes? Implications for conceptualizing their etiology. *Psychological Bulletin, 129,* 747–769.

Keesey, R. E., & Powley, T. L. (1975). Hypothalamic regulation of body weight. *American Scientist, 63,* 558–565.

Keller, M. B., & Shapiro, R. W. (1982). Double depression: Superimposition of acute depressive episodes on chronic depressive disorders. *American Journal of Psychiatry, 139,* 438–442.

Keller, W. C., & Rueda, M. G. (1998). Mechanisms of action in dopaminergic agents in Parkinson's disease. *Neurology, 50,* 511–514.

Kellerman, J. M., & Laird, J. D. (1982). The effect of appearance on self-perception. *Journal of Personality, 50,* 296–315.

Kelley, C. M. (1999). Subjective experience as basis of "objective" judgments: Effects of past experience on judgments of difficulty. In D. Gopher & A. Koriat (Eds.), *Attention and performance XVII: Cognitive regulation of performance: Interaction of theory and application* (pp. 515–536). Cambridge, MA: MIT Press.

Kelley, H. H. (1967). Attribution theory in social psychology. In D. Levine (Ed.), *Nebraska Symposium on Motivation 1967* (Vol. 15, pp. 192–238). Lincoln: University of Nebraska Press.

Kelley, H. H. (1983). Love and commitment. In H. H. Kelley, E. Berscheid, A. Christensen, J. H. Harvey, T. L. Huston, G. Levinger, et al. (Eds.), *Close relationships* (pp. 265–314). New York: Freeman.

Kelley, K. (1985). Sex, sex guilt, and authoritarianism: Differences in responses to explicit heterosexual and masturbatory slides. *Journal of Sex Research, 21,* 68–85.

Kellogg, W. N., & Kellogg, L. A. (1933). *The ape and the child.* New York: McGraw-Hill.

Kelly, T. M., Lynch, K. G., Donovan, J. E., & Clark, D. B. (2001). Alcohol use disorders and risk factor interactions for adolescent suicidal ideation and attempts. *Suicide and Life-Threatening Behavior, 31,* 181–193.

Kemeny, M. E. (2003). The psychobiology of stress. *Current Directions in Psychological Science, 12,* 124–129.

Kemper, T. L. (1994). Neuroanatomical and neuropathological changes in normal aging and in dementia. In M. L. Albert & J. E. Knoefel (Eds.), *Clinical neurology of aging* (2nd ed., pp.

3–78). New York: Oxford University Press.

Kenrick, D. T. (1994). Evolutionary social psychology: From sexual selection to social cognition. In M. Zanna (Ed.), *Advances in experimental social psychology* (Vol. 26, pp. 75–122). San Diego, CA: Academic Press.

Kenrick, D. T., & Funder, D. C. (1988). Profiting from controversy: Lessons of the person-situation debate. *American Psychologist, 43,* 23–34.

Kenrick, D. T., Gutierres, S. E., & Goldberg, L. (1989). Influence of erotica on judgments of strangers and mates. *Journal of Experimental Social Psychology, 25,* 159–167.

Kenrick, D. T., McCreath, H. E., Govern, J., King, R., & Bordin, J. (1990). Person-environment intersections: Everyday settings and common trait dimensions. *Journal of Personality and Social Psychology, 58,* 685–698.

Keppel, G., & Underwood, B. J. (1962). Proactive inhibition in short-term retention of single items. *Journal of Verbal Learning and Verbal Behavior, 1,* 153–161.

Kerkhoff, G., Munssinger, U., & Meier, E. K. (1994). Neurovisual rehabilitation in cerebral blindness. *Archives of Neurology, 51,* 474–481.

Kerns, K. A., & Price, K. J. (2001). An investigation of prospective memory in children with ADHD. *Child Neuropsychology, 7,* 162–171.

Kessler, R. C., McGonagle, K. A., Shanyang, Z., Nelson, C. B., Hughes, M., Eshleman, S., Wittchen, H., et al. (1994). Lifetime and 12-month prevalence of DSM-III-R psychiatric disorders in the United States. *Archives of General Psychiatry, 51,* 8–19.

Keysar, B., Barr, D. J., Balin, A., & Paekm, T. S. (1998). Definite reference and mutual knowledge: Process models of common ground in comprehension. *Journal of Memory and Language, 39,* 1–20.

Khan, A., Khan, S., Kolts, R., & Brown, W. A. (2003). Suicide rates in clinical trials of SSRIs, or other antidepressants, and placebo: Analysis of FDA reports. *American Journal of Psychiatry, 160,* 790–792.

Kiecolt-Glaser, J. K., Garner, W., Speicher, C., Penn, G. M., Holliday, J., & Glaser, R. (1984). Psychosocial modifiers of immunocompetence in medical students. *Psychosomatic Medicine, 46,* 7–17.

Kiecolt-Glaser, J. K., McGuire, L., Robles, T. F., & Glaser, R. (2002). Emotions, morbidity, and mortality: New perspectives from psychoneuroimmunology. *Annual Review of Psychology, 53,* 83–107.

Kihlstrom, J. (1985). Hypnosis. *Annual Review of Psychology, 36,* 385–418.

Kihlstrom, J., & Cantor, N. (1984). Mental representations of the self. In L. Berkowitz (Ed.), *Advances in experimental social psychology* (Vol. 15, pp. 1–47). New York: Academic Press.

Kihlstrom, J., & McConkey, K. M. (1990). William James and hypnosis: A centennial reflection. *Psychological Science, 1,* 174–178.

Kilgour, A. R., Kitada, R., Servos, P., James, T. W., & Lederman, S. J. (2005). Haptic face identification activates ventral occipital and temporal areas: An fMRI study. *Brain and Cognition, 59*(3), 246–257.

Kilgour, A. R., & Lederman, S. J. (2002). Face recognition by hand. *Perception & Psychophysics, 64*(3), 339–352.

Kim, B. J., Williams, L., & Gill, D. L. (2003). A cross-cultural study of achievement orientation and intrinsic motivation in young USA and Korean athletes. *International Journal of Sport Psychology, 34,* 168–184.

Kimble, G. A. (1993). A modest proposal for a minor revolution in the language of psychology. *Psychological Science, 4,* 253–255.

Kimelberg, H. K., & Norenberg, M. D. (1989, April). Astrocytes. *Scientific American, 260,* 66–76.

Kimura, D. (1999). *Sex and cognition.* Cambridge, MA: Bradford/MIT Press.

Kimura, D. (2004). Human sex differences in cognition, fact, not predicament. *Sexualities, Evolution & Gender, 6,* 45–53.

Kimura, D., & Hampson, E. (1994). Cognitive pattern in men and women is influenced by fluctuations in sex hormones. *Current Directions in Psychological Science, 3,* 57–61.

King, R. N., & Koehler, D. J. (2000). Illusory correlations in graphological inference. *Journal of Experimental Psychology: Applied, 6,* 336–348.

Kirchgessner, A. L., & Sclafani, A. (1988). PVN-hindbrain pathway involved in the hypothalamic hyperphagia-obesity syndrome. *Physiology and Behavior, 42,* 517–528.

Kirmayer, L. J. (1991). The place of culture in psychiatric nosology: Taijin kyofusho and DSM-III-R. *The Journal of Nervous and Mental Disease, 179,* 19–28.

Kirsch, I. (1999). Automaticity in clinical psychology. *American Psychologist, 54,* 504–515.

Kirsch, I., Montgomery, G., & Sapirstein, G. (1995). Hypnosis as an adjunct to cognitive behavioral psychotherapy: A meta-analysis. *Journal of Consulting and Clinical Psychology, 63,* 214–220.

Kirsch, I., & Sapirstein, G. (1999). Listening to Prozac but hearing placebo: A meta-analysis of antidepressant medication. In I. Kirsch (Ed.), *How expectancies shape experience* (pp. 303–320). Washington, DC: American Psychological Association.

Klatzky, R. L. (1984). *Memory and awareness: An information-processing perspective.* New York: Freeman.

Klein, R. M. (1999). Hebb legacy. *Canadian Journal of Experimental Psychology, 53,* 1–3.

Kleinfeld, J., & Nelson, P. (1991). Adapting instruction to Native Americans' learning style. *Journal of Cross-Cultural Psychology, 22,* 273–282.

Kline, P. (1991). *Intelligence: The psychometric view.* New York: Routledge, Chapman, & Hall.

Klinger, E. (1977). *Meaning and void: Inner experience and the incentive in people's lives.* Minneapolis: University of Minnesota Press.

Kluft, R. P. (1991). Multiple personality disorder. In A. Tasman & S. M. Goldfinger (Eds.), *Review of psychiatry* (pp. 161–188). Washington, DC: American Psychiatric Press.

Kobasa, S. C. (1979). Stressful life events, personality and health: An inquiry into hardiness. *Journal of Personality and Social Psychology, 42,* 168–177.

Kocsis, R. N., Irwin, H. J., Hayes, A. F., & Nunn, R. (2002). Expertise in psychological profiling: A comparative assessment. *Journal of Interpersonal Violence, 15,* 311–331.

Kohlberg, L. (1963). The development of children's orientations toward a moral order: I. Sequence in the development of moral thought. *Vita Humana, 6,* 11–33.

Kohlberg, L. (1969). Stage and sequence: The cognitive-developmental approach to socialization. In D. A. Goslin (Ed.), *Handbook of socializa-*

tion theory and research (pp. 347–480). Chicago: Rand McNally.

Kohlberg, L. (1984). *Essays on moral development: The psychology of moral development.* San Francisco: Harper & Row.

Kohlberg, L. (1986). *The psychology of moral development.* New York: Harper & Row.

Kolb, B. (1999). Synaptic plasticity and the organization of behaviour after early and late brain injury. *Canadian Journal of Experimental Psychology, 53,* 62–75.

Kolb, B. (2004). Mechanisms of cortical plasticity after neuronal injury. In J. Ponsford (Ed.), *Cognitive and behavioral rehabilitation: From neurobiology to clinical practice* (pp. 30–58). New York: Guilford Press.

Kolb, B., & Whishaw, I. Q. (2002). *Fundamentals of human neuropsychology* (5th ed.). New York: Freeman.

Kosky, R. J., Eshkevari, H. S., Goldney, R. D., & Hassan, R. (1998). *Suicide prevention: The global context.* New York: Plenum Press.

Kosonen, P., & Winne, P. H. (1995). Effects of teaching statistical laws on reasoning about everyday problems. *Journal of Educational Psychology, 87,* 33–46.

Kosslyn, S. M., Alpert, N. M., Thompson, W. L., & Maljkovic, V. (1993). Visual mental imagery activates topographically organized visual cortex: PET investigations. *Journal of Cognitive Neuroscience, 5,* 263–287.

Kosslyn, S. M., Ball, T. M., & Reiser, B. J. (1978). Visual images preserve metric spatial information: Evidence from studies of image scanning. *Journal of Experimental Psychology: Human Perception and Performance, 4,* 47–60.

Kouider, S., & Dupoux, E. (2005). Subliminal speech priming. *Psychological Science, 16*(8), 617–625.

Kowalski, T. J. (2004). The future of genetic research on appetitive behavior. *Appetite, 42,* 11–14.

Kraemer, P. J., & Golding, J. M. (1997). Adaptive forgetting in animals. *Psychonomic Bulletin and Review, 4,* 480–549.

Kramer, P. D. (1993). *Listening to Prozac.* New York: Viking.

Kramer, R. M. (1998). Revisiting the Bay of Pigs and Vietnam decisions 25 years later: How well has the group-think hypothesis stood the test of time? *Organizational Behavior and Human Decision Processes, 73,* 236–271.

Krank, M. D., & O'Neill, S. (2002). Environmental context conditioning with ethanol reduces the aversive effects of ethanol in the acquisition of self-administration in rats. *Psychopharmacology, 159,* 258–265.

Krantz, D. S., & McCeney, M. K. (2002). Effects of psychological and social factors on organic disease: A critical assessment of research on coronary heart disease. *Annual Review of Psychology, 53,* 341–369.

Kraus, S. J. (1995). Attitudes and the prediction of behavior. *Personality and Social Psychology Bulletin, 21,* 58–75.

Krebs, D. L. (1998). The evolution of moral behaviors. In C. Crawford & D. L. Krebs (Eds.), *Handbook of evolutionary psychology: Ideas, issues and applications* (pp. 337–368). Mahwah, NJ: Erlbaum.

Krebs, D. L., & Denton, K. (1997). Social illusions and self-deceptions: The evolution of biases in person perception. In J. A. Simpson & D. T. Kenrick (Eds.), *Evolutionary social psychology* (pp. 21–47). Mahwah, NJ: Erlbaum.

Krebs, D. L., & Denton, K. (2005). Toward a more pragmatic approach to morality: A critical evaluation of Kohlberg's model. *Psychological Review, 112,* 629–649.

Krechevsky, M., & Seidel, S. (1998). Minds at work: Applying multiple intelligences in the classroom. In R. J. Sternberg & W. M. Williams (Eds.), *Intelligence, instruction, and assessment: Theory into practice* (pp.17–42). Mahwah, NJ: Erlbaum.

Kreuz, R. J. (2000). The production and processing of verbal irony. *Metaphor and Symbol, 15*(1–2), 99–107.

Krippner, S. (1993). Some contributions of native healers to knowledge about the healing process. *International Journal of Psychosomatics, 40,* 96–99.

Krug, E. G., Kresnow, M., Peddicord, J., Dahlberg, L., Powell, K., Crosby, A., et al. (1998). Suicide after natural disasters. *New England Journal of Medicine, 338,* 373–378.

Krystal, A. D., & Coffey, C. E. (1997). Neuropsychiatric considerations in the use of electroconvulsive therapy. *Journal of Neuropsychiatry and Clinical Neurosciences, 9,* 283–292.

Kübler-Ross, E. (1969). *On death and dying.* New York: Macmillan.

Kübler-Ross, E. (1974). *Questions and answers on death and dying.* New York: Macmillan.

Kuhn, D. (1992). Cognitive development. In M. H. Bornstein & M. E. Lamb (Eds.), *Developmental psychology: An advanced textbook* (3rd ed., pp. 211–272). Hillsdale, NJ: Erlbaum.

Kuhn, W., Winkel, R., Woitalla, D., Meves, S., Przuntek, H., & Mueller, T. (1998). High prevalence of Parkinsonism after exposure to lead-sulfate batteries. *Neurology, 50,* 1885–1886.

Kuncel, N. R., Hezlett, S. A., & Ones, D. S. (2001). A comprehensive meta-analysis of the predictive validity of the graduate record examinations: Implications for graduate student selection and performance. *Psychological Bulletin, 127,* 162–181.

Kunda, Z. (1999). *Social cognition: Making sense of people.* Cambridge, MA: MIT Press.

Kunda, Z., & Sanitioso, R. (1989). Motivated changes in the self-concept. *Journal of Experimental Social Psychology, 25,* 272–328.

Kunda, Z., & Thagard, P. (1996). Forming impressions from stereotypes, traits, and behaviors: A parallel-constraint-satisfaction theory. *Psychological Review, 103,* 284–308.

Labouvie-Vief, G., Hakim-Larson, J., & Hobart, C. J. (1987). Age, ego level, and the life-span development of coping and defense processes. *Psychology and Aging, 2,* 286–293.

Labov, W. (1973). The boundaries of words and their meanings. In C. J. N. Bailey & R. W. Shuy (Eds.), *New ways of analyzing variation in English* (pp. 340–373). Washington, DC: Georgetown University Press.

Lackner, J. R., & DiZio, P. (1991). Decreased susceptibility to motion sickness during exposure to visual inversion in microgravity. *Aviation, Space, and Environmental Medicine, 62,* 206–211.

Ladd, G. T. (1896). *Psychology: Descriptive and explanatory.* New York: Charles Scribner's Sons.

Lafferty, P., Beutler, L. E., & Crago, M. (1991). Differences between more or less effective psychotherapists: A study of select therapist variables. *Journal of Consulting and Clinical Psychology, 57,* 76–80.

Lakoff, G. (1987). *Women, fire, and dangerous things: What categories reveal about the human mind.* Chicago: University of Chicago Press.

Lalonde, C. E., & Chandler, M. J. (1995). False belief understanding goes to school: On the social-emotional consequences of coming early or late to a first theory of mind. *Cognition and Emotion, 9,* 167–185.

Lalumière, M. L., Blanchard, R., & Zucker, K. J. (2000). Sexual orientation and handedness in men and women: A meta-analysis. *Psychological Bulletin, 126*(4), 575–592.

Lalumière, M. L., & Quinsey, V. L. (1999). A Darwinian interpretation of individual differences in male propensity for sexual aggression. *Jurimetrics, 39,* 201–216.

Lamb, M. E., Ketterlinus, R. D., & Fracasso, M. P. (1992). Parent-child relationships. In M. H. Bornstein & M. E. Lamb (Eds.), *Developmental psychology: An advanced textbook* (3rd ed., pp.465–518). Hillsdale, NJ: Erlbaum.

Lambert, M. J., & Bergin, A. E. (1994). The effectiveness of psychotherapy. In A. E. Bergin & S. L. Garfield (Eds.), *Handbook of psychotherapy and behavior change* (4th ed., pp. 143–189). New York: Wiley.

Lancet, D., Gross-Isseroff, R., Margalit, T., & Seidemann, E. (1993). Olfaction: From signal transduction and termination to human genome mapping. *Chemical Senses, 18,* 217–225.

Landauer, T. K. (1962). Rate of implicit speech. *Perceptual and Motor Skills, 15,* 646.

Landrum, R. E., & Chastain, G. (1995). Experiment spot-checks: A method for assessing the educational value of undergraduate participation in research. *IRB: A Review of Human Subjects Research, 17,* 4–6.

Lang, P. J. (1994). The varieties of emotional experience: A meditation on James-Lange theory. *Psychological Review, 101,* 211–221.

Langer, E. J. (1989). *Mindfulness.* Cambridge, MA: Addison-Wesley.

Langlois, J. H., & Roggman, L. A. (1990). Attractive faces are only average. *Psychological Science, 1,* 115–121.

Langlois, J. H., Roggman, L. A., Casey, R. J., Ritter, J. M., Rieser-Danner, L. A., & Jenkins, V. Y. (1987). Infant preferences for attractive faces: Rudiments of a stereotype? *Developmental Psychology, 23,* 363–369.

Langlois, J. H., Roggman, L. A., & Musselman, L. (1994). What is average and what is not average about attractive faces? *Psychological Science, 5,* 214–220.

Laprelle, J., Hoyle, R. H., Insko, C. A., & Bernthal, P. (1990). Interpersonal attraction and descriptions of the traits of others: Ideal similarity, self similarity, and liking. *Journal of Research in Personality, 24,* 216–240.

Larose, H., & Standing, L. (1998). Does the halo effect occur in the elderly? *Social Behavior and Personality, 26,* 147–150.

Lassonde, M., & Jeeves, M. A. (Eds.). (1994). *Callosal agenesis: A natural split brain?* New York: Plenum Press.

Latané, B. (1981). The psychology of social impact. *American Psychologist, 36,* 343–356.

Latané, B., & Nida, S. A. (1981). Ten years of research on group size and helping. *Psychological Bulletin, 89,* 308–324.

Latané, B., Williams, K., & Harkins, S. (1979). Many hands make light the work: The causes and consequences of social loafing. *Journal of Personality and Social Psychology, 37,* 822–832.

Laudenslager, M. L., Ryan, S. M., Drugen, R. L., Hyson, R. L., & Maier, S. F. (1983). Coping and immunosuppression: Inescapable but not escapable shock suppresses lymphocyte proliferation. *Science, 221,* 568–570.

Lavoie, K. L., & Fleet, R. P. (2002). Should psychologists be granted prescription privileges? A review of the prescription privilege debate for psychiatrists. *Canadian Journal of Psychiatry, 47,* 443–449.

Lay, C., & Verkuyten, M. (1999). Ethnic identity and its relation to personal self-esteem: A comparison of Canadian-born and foreign-born Chinese adolescents. *Journal of Social Psychology, 139,* 288–299.

Lazarus, A. A., & Messer, S. B. (1991). Does chaos prevail? An exchange on technical eclecticism and assimilative integration. *Journal of Psychotherapy Integration, 1,* 143–158.

Lazarus, R. S. (1966). *Psychological stress and the coping process.* New York: McGraw-Hill.

Lazarus, R. S. (1991). *Emotion and adaptation.* New York: Oxford University Press.

Lazarus, R. S. (1993). Why we should think of stress as a subset of emotion. In L. Goldberger & S. Breznitz (Eds.), *Handbook of stress: Theoretical and clinical aspects* (2nd ed., pp. 21–39). New York: Free Press.

Lazarus, R. S., & Folkman, S. (1984). *Stress, appraisal and coping.* New York: Springer.

Leach, M. M., & Harbin, J. J. (1997). Psychological ethics codes: A comparison of 24 countries. *International Journal of Psychology, 32,* 181–192.

Leadbeater, B. J., Blatt, S., & Quinlan, D. M. (1995). Gender-linked vulnerabilities to depressive symptoms, stress, and problem behaviours in adolescents. *Journal of Research on Adolescence, 5,* 1–29.

Leadbeater, B. J., Kuperminc, G. P., Blatt, S. J., & Hertzog, C. (1999). A multivariate model of gender differences in adolescents' internalizing and externalizing problems. *Developmental Psychology, 35,* 1268–1282.

Leadbeater, B. J., & Way, N. (Eds.). (1996). *Urban adolescent girls: Resisting stereotypes, creating identities.* New York: New York University Press.

Lebow, J. L., & Gurman, A. S. (1995). Research assessing couple and family therapy. *Annual Review of Psychology, 46,* 27–57.

Leclerc, G., Lefrancois, R., Dube, M., Hebert, R., & Gaulin, P. (1998). The self-actualization concept: A content validation. *Journal of Social Behavior and Personality, 11,* 69–84.

Lederman, S. J., & Klatzky, R. L. (2004). Haptic identification of common objects: Effects of constraining the manual exploration process. *Perception & Psychophysics, 66*(4), 618–628.

Lee, E. K. (1998). Periodic left temporal sharp waves during acute psychosis. *Journal of Epilepsy, 11,* 79–83.

Lee, K., & Homer, B. (1999). Children as folk psychologists: The developing understanding of the mind. In A. Slater & D. Muir (Eds.), *The Blackwell reader in development psychology* (pp. 228–252). Malden, MA: Blackwell.

Lefcourt, H. M. (1982). *Locus of control: Current trends in theory and research.* Waterloo, ON: University of Waterloo.

Leger Marketing. (2001). *Canadians and the use of cellular phones.* Retrieved September 10, 2006, from http://www.legermarketing.com/documents/spclm/011008eng.pdf

Lehman, D. R., Chiu, C., & Schaller, M. (2004). Psychology and culture. *Annual Review of Psychology, 55,* 689–714.

Leith, K. P., & Baumeister, R. F. (1996). Why do bad moods increase self-defeating behavior? Emotion, risk taking, and self-regulation. *Journal of Personality and Social Psychology, 71,* 1250–1267.

Lenneberg, E. H. (1967). *Biological foundations of language.* New York: Wiley.

Lepper, M. R., Greene, D., & Nisbett, R. E. (1973). Undermining children's intrinsic interest with external reward: A test of the "overjustification" hypothesis. *Journal of Personality and Social Psychology, 28,* 129–137.

Lerman, H. G. (1986). From Freud to feminist personality theory: Getting here from there. *Psychology of Women Quarterly, 10,* 1–18.

LeVay, S. (1991). A difference in hypothalamic structure between heterosexual and homosexual men. *Science, 253,* 1034–1037.

Levenson, R. W. (1992). Autonomic nervous system differences among emotions. *Psychological Science, 3,* 23–27.

Levin, I. P., & Gaeth, G. J. (1988). How consumers are affected by the framing of attribute information before and after consuming the product. *Journal of Consumer Research, 15,* 374–378.

Levine, D. N., Warach, J., & Farah, M. J. (1985). Two visual systems in mental imagery: Dissociation of "what" and "where" in imagery disorders due to bilateral posterior cerebral lesions. *Neurology, 35,* 1010–1018.

Levine, G., & Parkinson, S. (1994). *Experimental methods in psychology.* Hillsdale, NJ: Erlbaum.

Levine, R. V., & Norenzayan, A. (1999). The pace of life in 31 countries. *Journal of Cross-Cultural Psychology, 30,* 178–205.

Levinson, D. J., Darow, C. N., Klein, E. B., Levinson, M. H., & McKee, B. (1978). *The seasons of a man's life.* New York: Knopf.

Lewis, M., & Brooks-Gunn, J. (1979). *Social cognition and the acquisition of self.* New York: Plenum Press.

Lewontin, R. (1976). Race and intelligence. In N. J. Block & G. Dworkin (Eds.), *The IQ controversy: Critical readings* (pp. 107–112). New York: Pantheon.

Li, X., Sano, H., & Merwin, J. C. (1996). Perception and reasoning abilities among American, Japanese, and Chinese adolescents. *Journal of Adolescent Research, 11,* 173–193.

Liberman, R. P., Kopelowicz, A., & Young, A. S. (1994). Biobehavioral treatment and rehabilitation of schizophrenia. *Behavior Therapy, 25,* 89–107.

Lickey, M. E., & Gordon, B. (1991). *Medicine and mental illness: The use of drugs in psychiatry.* New York: Freeman.

Liebert, R. M., & Liebert, L. L. (1995). *Science and behavior: An introduction to methods of psychological research* (4th ed.). Englewood Cliffs, NJ: Prentice-Hall.

Lilienfeld, S. O. (1994). Conceptual problems in the assessment of psychopathy. *Clinical Psychology Review, 14,* 17–38.

Lilienfeld, S. O., Wood, J. M., & Garb, H. N. (2000). The scientific status of projective tests. *Psychological Science in the Public Interest, 1,* 27–66.

Linden, W. (1990). *Autogenic training: A clinical guide.* New York: Guilford Press.

Linden, W., Stossel, C., & Maurice, J. (1996). Psychosocial interventions for patients with coronary artery disease. *Archives of Internal Medicine, 156,* 745–752.

Lindsay, D. S. (2002). Children's source monitoring. In H. L. Westcott, G. Davies, & R. H. C. Bull (Eds.), *Children's testimony: Psychological research and forensic practice* (pp. 83–98). Sussex, England: John Wiley & Sons.

Lindsay, D. S., Hagen, L., Read, J. D., Wade, K. A., & Garry, M. (2004). True photographs and false memories. *Psychological Science, 15,* 149–154.

Lindsay, D. S., & Kelley, C. M. (1996). Creating illusions of familiarity in a cued recall remember/know paradigm. *Journal of Memory and Language, 35,* 197–211.

Lindsay, D. S., & Poole, D. A. (1998, Fall). The Poole et al. (1995) surveys of therapists: Misinterpretations by both sides of the recovered memories controversy. *Journal of Psychiatry and Law, 26,* 383–399.

Lindsay, D. S., & Read, J. D. (1994). Psychotherapy and memories of childhood sexual abuse: A cognitive perspective. *Applied Cognitive Psychology, 8,* 281–338.

Lindsay, D. S., & Read, J. D. (2001). The recovered memories controversy: Where do we go from here? In G. Davies & T. Dalgleish (Eds.), Recovered memories: Seeking the middle ground (pp. 71–94). London: Wiley.

Lindsay, D. S., & Read, J. D. (2006). Adults' memories of long-past events. In L. Nilsson & N. Ohta (Eds.), *Memory and society: Psychological perspectives* (pp. 51–72). New York: Psychology Press.

Lindsay, D. S., Wade, K. A., Hunter, M. A., & Read, J. D. (2004). Adults' memories of childhood: Affect, knowing, and remembering. *Memory, 12,* 27–43.

Lindsay, R. C. L., Brigham, J. C., & Brimacombe, C. A. E. (2002). Eyewitness research. In J. R. P. Ogloff (Ed.), *Taking psychology and law into the twenty-first century* (pp. 199–223). New York: Kluwer Academic/Plenum.

Linton, M. (1975). Memory for real-world events. In D. A. Norman & D. E. Rumelhart (Eds.), *Explorations in cognition* (pp. 376–404). San Francisco: Freeman.

Linville, P. W., Fischer, G. W., & Fischhoff, B. (1993). AIDS risk perceptions and decision biases. In J. B. Pryor & G. D. Reeder (Eds.), *The social psychology of HIV infection* (pp. 5–38). Hillsdale, NJ: Erlbaum.

Lippa, R. A. (2006). Is high sex drive associated with increased sexual attraction to both sexes? *Psychological Science, 17,* 46–52.

Lipsey, M. W., & Wilson, D. B. (1993). The efficacy of psychological, educational, and behavioral treatment: Confirmation from meta-analysis. *American Psychologist, 48,* 1181–1209.

Little, B. R. (1996). Free traits, personal projects and idio-tapes: Three tiers for personality psychology. *Psychological Inquiry, 7,* 340–344.

Little, B. R. (2000). Persons, contexts, and personal projects: Assumptive themes of a methodological transactionalism. In S. Wapner, J. Demick, T. Yamamoto, & H. Minami (Eds.), *Theoretical perspectives in environment-behavior research: Underlying assumptions, research problems, and methodologies* (pp. 79–88). Dordrecht, Netherlands: Kluwer.

Liu, Z. (1996). Viewpoint dependency in object representation and recognition. *Spatial Vision, 9,* 491–521.

Livesley, W. J. (2001). *Handbook of personality disorders: Theory, research, and treatment.* New York: Guilford Press.

Livingstone, M., & Hubel, D. H. (1988). Segregation of form, color, movement, and depth: Anatomy, physiology, and perception. *Science, 240,* 740–749.

Lockard, J. S., & Mateer, C. A. (1988). Neural bases of self-deception. In J. S. Lockard & D. L. Paulhus (Eds.), *Self-deception: An adaptive mechanism?* (pp. 23–39). Englewood Cliffs, NJ: Prentice-Hall.

Lockard, J. S., & Paulhus, D. L. (Eds.). (1988). *Self-deception: An adaptive mechanism?* Englewood Cliffs, NJ: Prentice-Hall.

Locke, J. L. (1994). Phases in the child's development of language. *American Scientist, 82,* 436–445.

Loehlin, J. C. (1992). *Genes and environment in personality development.* Newbury Park, CA: Sage.

Loewenstein, R. J. (1996). Dissociative amnesia and dissociative fugue. In L. K. Michelson & W. J. Ray (Eds.), *Handbook of dissociation: Theoretical, empirical, and clinical perspectives* (pp. 307–336). New York: Plenum Press.

Loftus, E. L. (1979). *Eyewitness testimony.* Cambridge, MA: Harvard University Press.

Loftus, E. L. (1991). *Witness for the defense.* New York: St. Martin's.

Loftus, E. L. (1993). The reality of repressed memories. *American Psychologist, 48,* 518–537.

Loftus, E. L., & Palmer, J. C. (1974). Reconstruction of automobile destruction: An example of the interaction between language and memory. *Journal of Verbal Learning and Verbal Behavior, 13,* 585–589.

Loftus, G. R., & Harley, E. M. (2005). Why is it easier to identify someone close than far away? *Psychonomic Bulletin & Review, 12*(1), 43–65.

Logan, G. D. (1988). Toward an instance theory of automatization. *Psychological Review, 95,* 492–527.

Logan, G. D. (1991). Automaticity and memory. In W. E. Hockley & S. Lewandowsky (Eds.), *Relating theory and data: Essays on human memory in honor of Bennet B. Murdock* (pp. 347–366). Hillsdale, NJ: Erlbaum.

Looy, H., & Weingarten, H. P. (1992). Facial expressions and genetic sensitivity to 6-n-propylthiouracil predict hedonic response to sweet. *Physiology and Behavior, 52*(1), 75–82.

Lorenz, K. (1966). *On aggression.* New York: Harcourt, Brace & World.

Lorenz, K. (1970). *Studies in animal and human behaviour.* London: Methuen.

Lorenz, K. Z. (1958, December). The evolution of behavior. *Scientific American, 199,* 67–78.

Lovaas, O. I. (1987). Behavioral treatment and normal educational and intellectual functioning in young autistic children. *Journal of Consulting and Clinical Psychology, 55,* 3–9.

Lovaas, O. I., Koegel, R., Simmons, J. Q., & Long, J. S. (1973). Some generalization and follow-up measures on autistic children in behavior therapy. *Journal of Applied Behavior Analysis, 6,* 131–166.

Loverock, D. S., & Modigliani, V. (1995). Visual imagery and the brain: A review. *Journal of Mental Imagery, 19,* 91–132.

Lowe, J., & Carroll, D. (1985). The effects of spinal cord injury on the intensity of emotional experience. *British Journal of Clinical Psychology, 24,* 135–136.

Luborsky, L., Barber, J. P., & Crits-Cristoph, P. (1990). Theory-based research for understanding the process of dynamic psychotherapy. *Journal of Consulting and Clinical Psychology, 58,* 281–287.

Lucy, J. A. (1997). Linguistic relativity. *Annual Review of Anthropology, 26,* 291–312.

Lutz, C. (1982). The domain of emotion words in Ifaluk. *American Ethnologist, 9,* 113–128.

Lykken, D. T. (1998). *A tremor in the blood: Uses and abuses of the lie detector.* New York: Plenum Press.

Lyness, S. A. (1993). Predictors of differences between type A and type B individuals in heart rate and blood pressure reactivity. *Psychological Bulletin, 114,* 266–295.

Lynn, S. J., Myers, B., & Malinoski, P. (1997). Hypnosis, pseudomemories, and clinical guidelines: A sociocognitive perspective. In J. D. Read & D. S. Lindsay (Eds.), *Recollections of trauma: Scientific evidence and clinical practice* (pp. 305–336). New York: Plenum Press.

Lynn, S. J., Rhue, J. W., & Weekes, J. R. (1990). Hypnotic involuntariness: A social cognitive analysis. *Psychological Review, 97,* 169–184.

Lyubomirsky, S., King, L., & Diener, E. (2005). The benefits of frequent positive affect: Does happiness lead to success? *Psychological Bulletin, 131,* 803–855.

Maccoby, E. (2000). Parenting and its effects on children: On reading and misreading behavioral genetics. *Annual Review of Psychology, 51,* 1–27.

MacDonald, N. E., Wells, G. A., Fisher, W. A., Warren, W. K., Ding, M. A., Doherty, J. A., et al. (1990). High-risk STD/HIV behavior among college students. *Journal of the American Medical Association, 263,* 3155–3159.

MacDonald, S., Uesiliana, K., & Hayne, H. (2000). Cross-cultural and gender differences in childhood amnesia. *Memory, 8,* 365–376.

MacDonald, T. K., & Ross, M. (1999). Assessing the accuracy of predictions about dating relationships: How and why do lovers' predictions differ from those made by observers? *Personality and Social Psychology Bulletin, 25,* 1417–1429.

MacDonald, T. K., Zanna, M. P., & Fong, G. T. (1995). Decision-making in altered states: The effects of alcohol on attitudes toward drinking and driving. *Journal of Personality and Social Psychology, 68,* 973–985.

MacDonald, T. K., Zanna, M. P., & Fong, G. T. (1996). Why common sense goes out the window: The effects of alcohol on intentions to use condoms. *Personality and Social Psychology Bulletin, 22,* 763–775.

MacDonald, T. K., Zanna, M. P., & Fong, G. T. (1998). Alcohol and intentions to engage in risky health-related behaviors: Experimental evidence for a causal relationship. In J. G. Adair, D. Bélanger, & K. L. Dion (Eds.), *Advances in psychological science, Vol. 1: Social, personal, and cultural aspects* (pp. 407–428). Hove, England: Psychology Press/Erlbaum.

Mackay, D. G. (1983). Prescriptive grammar and the pronoun problem. In B. Thorne, C. Kramarae, & N. Henley (Eds.), *Language, gender, and society* (pp. 38–53). Rowley, MA: Newbury House.

MacKenzie, K. R. (2000). Current approaches to time-limited group psychotherapy services. In F. Flach (Ed.), *The Hatherleigh guide to psychiatric* disorders, Part II. *The Hatherleigh guides series* (pp. 112–127). Long Island City, NY: Hatherleigh.

MacKinnon, D. W. (1962). The nature and nurture of creative talent. *American Psychologist, 17,* 484–495.

MacLean, C. R. K., Walton, K. G., Wenneberg, S. R., & Levitsky, D. K. (1997). Effects of the transcendental meditation program on adaptive mechanisms: Changes in hormone levels and responses to stress after 4 months of practice. *Psychoneuroendocrinology, 22,* 277–295.

MacLennan, R. N., & Peebles, J. W. E. (1996). Survey of health problems and personality in air traffic controllers. *International Journal of Aviation Psychology, 6,* 43–55.

MacLeod, C. M. (1999). The item and list methods of directed forgetting: Test differences and the role of demand characteristics. *Psychonomic Bulletin and Review, 6,* 123–129.

Macmillan, N. A., & Creelman, C. D. (1991). *Detection theory: A user's guide.* New York: Cambridge University Press.

MacNeill, P., & Webster, I. (1995). *Canada's alcohol and other drugs survey of 1994: A discussion of the findings.* Ottawa, ON: Health Canada.

Macrae, C. N., & Bodenhausen, G. V. (2000). Social cognition: Thinking categorically about others. *Annual Review of Psychology, 51,* 93–120.

Maddi, S. R. (2002). The story of hardiness: Twenty years of theorizing, research, and practice. *Consulting Psychology Journal: Practice and Research, 54,* 175–185.

Madon, S., Guyll, M., Spoth, R., & Willard, J. (2004). Self-fulfilling prophecies: The synergistic accumulative effect of parents' beliefs on children's drinking behavior. *Psychological Science, 15,* 837–845.

Maestripieri, D. (2001). Biological basis of maternal attachment. *Current Directions in Psychological Science, 10,* 79–83.

Mahrer, P., & Miles, C. (2002). Recognition memory for tactile sequences. *Memory, 10,* 7–20.

Maier, N. R. F. (1931). Reasoning in humans II: The solution to a problem and its appearance in consciousness. *Journal of Comparative Psychology, 12,* 181–194.

Maier, N. R. F., & Burke, R. J. (1967). Response availability as a factor in the problem-solving performance of males and females. *Journal of Personality and Social Psychology, 5,* 304–310.

Malt, B. C., & Smith, E. E. (1984). Correlated properties in natural categories. *Journal of Verbal Learning and Verbal Behavior, 23,* 250–269.

Mandal, M. K., Bryden, M. P., & Bulman-Fleming, M. B. (1996). Similarities and variations in facial expressions of emotions: Cross-cultural evidence. *International Journal of Psychology, 31*(1), 49–58.

Mandler, J. M. (1992). How to build a baby: II. Conceptual primitives. *Psychological Review, 99,* 587–604.

Manly, T., Cornish, K., Grant, C., Dobler, V., & Hollis, C. (2005). Examining the relationship between rightward visuo-spatial bias and poor attention within the normal child population using a brief screening task. *Journal of Child Psychology and Psychiatry, 46*(12), 1337–1344.

Mann, J. J. (1998). Neurobiological correlates of the antidepressant action of electroconvulsive therapy. *Journal of ECT, 14,* 172–180.

Mann, T. (1994). Informed consent for psychological research: Do subjects comprehend consent forms and understand their legal rights? *Psychological Science, 5,* 140–143.

Manson, S. M. (1995). Culture and major depression: Current challenges in the diagnosis of mood disorders. *Psychiatric Clinics of North America, 18,* 487–501.

Maratos, O. (1998). Neonatal, early and later imitation: Same order phenomena? In F. Simion & G. Butterworth (Eds.), *The development of sensory, motor and cognitive capacities in early infancy: From perception to cognition* (pp. 145–160). Hove, England: Psychology Press.

Marche, T. A. (1999). Memory strength affects reporting of misinformation. *Journal of Experimental Child Psychology, 73*(1), 45–71.

Marcia, J. E. (1966). Development and validation of ego identity status. *Journal of Personality and Social Psychology, 3,* 551–558.

Markman, A. B., & Wisniewski, E. J. (1997). Similar and different: The differentiation of basic-level categories. *Journal of Experimental Psychology: Learning, Memory, and Cognition, 23,* 54–70.

Markus, H. (1977). Self-schemata and processing information about the self. *Journal of Personality and Social Psychology, 35,* 63–78.

Marlatt, G. A., & VandenBos, G. R. (Eds.). (1997). *Addictive behaviors: Readings on etiology, prevention, and treatment.* Washington, DC: American Psychological Association.

Marquardt, C. J. G., Bonato, R. A., & Hoffmann, R. F. (1996). An empirical investigation into the day-residue and dream-lag effects. *Dreaming: Journal of the Association for the Study of Dreams, 6,* 57–65.

Marsella, A. J., & Yamada, A. M. (2000). Culture and mental health: An introduction and overview of foundations, concepts, and issues. In I. Cuellar & F. A. Paniagua (Eds.), *Handbook of multicultural mental health* (pp. 3–24). San Diego, CA: Academic Press.

Marsh, R. L., Landau, J. D., & Hicks, J. L. (1997). Contributions of inadequate source monitoring to unconscious plagiarism during idea generation. *Journal of Experimental Psychology: Learning, Memory, and Cognition, 23,* 886–897.

Marshall, J. C., & Halligan, P. W. (1988). Blindsight and insight in visuo-spatial neglect. *Nature, 336,* 766–767.

Marson, L., & McKenna, K. E. (1994). Stimulation of the hypothalamus initiates the urethrogenital reflex in male rats. *Brain Research, 638,* 103–108.

Martin, G., & Pear, J. (1999). *Behavior modification: What it is and how to do it* (6th ed.). Upper Saddle River, NJ: Prentice Hall.

Martin, K. M., & Aggleton, J. P. (1993). Contextual effects on the ability of divers to use decompression tables. *Applied Cognitive Psychology, 7,* 311–316.

Martin, P., & Bateson, P. (1993). *Measuring behavior: An introductory guide* (2nd ed.). Cambridge: Cambridge University Press.

Martin, R. J., White, B. D., & Hulsey, M. G. (1991). The regulation of body weight. *American Scientist, 79,* 528–541.

Martinson, B. C., Anderson, M. S., & de Vries, R. (2005). Scientists behaving badly. *Nature, 435*(7043), 737–738.

Marx, M. H., & Cronan-Hillix, W. A. (1987). *Systems and theories in psychology.* New York: McGraw-Hill.

Maser, J. D., Kaelber, C., & Weise, R. E. (1991). International use and attitudes toward DSM-III and DSM-III-R: Growing consensus in psychiatric classification. *Journal of Abnormal Psychology, 100,* 271–279.

Maslach, C. (1976). Burned out. *Human Behavior, 5,* 16–22.

Maslach, C., & Jackson, S. E. (1981). The measurement of experienced burnout. *Journal of Occupational Behavior, 2,* 99–113.

Maslach, C., Schaufeli, W. B., & Leiter, M. P. (2001). Job burnout. *Annual Review of Psychology, 52,* 397–422.

Maslow, A. H. (1954). *Motivation and personality.* New York: Harper.

Mason, J. R., & Reidinger, R. F. (1982). Observational learning of aversions in red-winged blackbirds (*Agelaius phoeniceus*). *Auk, 99,* 548–554.

Masson, J. (1984). *The assault on truth: Freud's suppression of the seduction theory.* New York: Farrar, Straus, & Giroux.

Masson, M. E. J., & MacLeod, C. M. (1997). Episodic enhancement of processing fluency. In D. L. Medin (Ed.), *Psychology of learning and motivation: Advances in research and theory* (Vol. 37, pp. 155–210). San Diego, CA: Academic Press.

Masuda, T., & Kitayama, S. (2004). Perceiver-induced constraint and attitude attribution in Japan and the US: A case for the cultural dependence of the correspondence bias. *Journal of Experimental Social Psychology, 40,* 409–416.

Matano, R. A., Yalom, I. D., & Schwartz, K. (1997). Interactive group therapy for substance abusers. In J. L. Spira (Ed.), *Group therapy for medically ill patients* (pp. 296–325). New York: Guilford Press.

Mateer, C. A. (2005). Fundamentals of cognitive rehabilitation. In P. W. Halligan & D. T. Wade (Eds.), *Effectiveness of rehabilitation for cognitive deficits* (pp. 21–29). Oxford, England: Oxford University Press.

Matlin, M. W. (2003). From menarche to menopause: Misconceptions about women's reproductive lives. *Psychology Science, 45,* 106–122.

Matsumoto, D. (1987). The role of facial response in the experience of emotion: More methodological problems and a meta-analysis. *Journal of Personality and Social Psychology, 52,* 769–774.

Matsumoto, D. (1994). *People: Psychology from a cultural perspective.* Pacific Grove, CA: Brooks/Cole.

Matthews, G. (1997). Intelligence, personality and information-processing: An adaptive perspective. In J. Kingma & W. Tomic (Eds.), *Advances in cognition and educational practice: Reflections on the concept of intelligence* (pp. 175–200). Greenwich, CT: JAI Press.

Matthews, K. A. (1992). Myths and realities of the menopause. *Psychosomatic Medicine, 54,* 1–9.

Matzel, L. D., Held, F. P., & Miller, R. R. (1988). Information and expression of simultaneous and backward associations: Implications for contiguity theory. *Learning and Motivation, 9,* 317–344.

Mauss, I. B., Evers, C., Wilhelm, F. H., & Gross, J. J. (2006). How to bite your tongue without blowing your top: Implicit evaluation of emotion regulation predicts affective responding to anger provocation. *Personality and Social Psychology Bulletin, 32,* 589–602.

Mauss, M. (1902/1972). *A general theory of magic* (R. Brain, Trans.). New York: Norton.

Mayberg, H. S., Silva, J. A., Brannan, S. K., Tekell, J. L., Mahurin, R. K., McGinnis, S., et al. (2002). The functional neuroanatomy of the placebo effect. *American Journal of Psychiatry, 159,* 728–737.

Mayer, D. J. (1953). Glucostatic mechanism of regulation of food intake. *New England Journal of Medicine, 249,* 13–16.

Mazur, A., & Booth, A. (1998). Testosterone and dominance in men. *Brain and Behavioral Sciences, 21,* 353–397.

McAdams, D. P. (2000). *The person: An integrated introduction to personality psychology.* New York: Harcourt.

McAdams, D. P. (2001). The psychology of life stories. *Review of General Psychology, 5*(2), 100–122.

McAllister-Williams, R. H., Ferrier, I. N., & Young, A. (1998). Mood and neuropsychological function in depression: The role of corticosteriods and serotonin. *Psychological Medicine, 28,* 573–584.

McArthur, L. Z., & Berry, D. S. (1987). Cross-cultural agreement in perceptions of babyfaced adults. *Journal of Cross-Cultural Psychology, 18,* 165–192.

McBride, C., Zuroff, D. C., Bacchiochi, J., & Bagby, R. M. (2006). Depressive experiences questionnaire: Does it measure maladaptive and adaptive forms of dependency? *Social Behavior and Personality, 34,* 1–16.

McCall, M. (1994). Decision theory and the sale of alcohol. *Journal of Applied Social Psychology, 24,* 1593–1611.

McCall, M. (1997). The effects of physical attractiveness on gaining access to alcohol: When social policy meets social decision making. *Addiction, 92,* 597–600.

McCall, R. B., & Carriger, M. S. (1993). A meta-analysis of infant habituation and recognition memory performance as predictors of later IQ. *Child Development, 64,* 57–79.

McCann, I. L., & Holmes, D. S. (1984). Influence of aerobic exercise on depression. *Journal of Personality and Social Psychology, 46,* 1142–1147.

McClelland, D. C. (1961). *The achieving society.* Princeton, NJ: Von Nostrand.

McClelland, D. C., Atkinson, J. W., Clark, R. A., & Lowell, E. W. (1953). *The achievement motive.* New York: Appleton-Century-Crofts.

McClelland, J. L., & Elman, J. L. (1986). The TRACE model of speech perception. *Cognitive Psychology, 18,* 1–86.

McCormick, R. (2000). Aboriginal traditions in the treatment of substance abuse: Let only the good spirits guide you. *Canadian Journal of Counselling, 34,* 25–32.

McCormick, R. M. (1996). Culturally appropriate means and ends of counselling as described by the First Nations people of British Columbia. *International Journal for the Advancement of Counselling, 34,* 25–32.

McCrae, R. R., & Costa, P. T., Jr. (1985). Updating Norman's "adequate taxonomy": Intelligence and personality dimensions in natural language and in questionnaires. *Journal of Personality and Social Psychology, 49,* 710–721.

McCrae, R. R., & Costa, P. T., Jr. (1990). *Personality in adulthood.* New York: Guilford Press.

McCrae, R. R., & Costa, P. T., Jr. (1997). Personality trait structure as a human universal. *American Psychologist, 52,* 509–516.

McCrae, R. R., Costa, P. T., Jr., & Yik, M. S. M. (1996). Universal aspects of Chinese personality structure. In M. H.

Bond (Ed.), *The handbook of Chinese psychology* (pp. 189–207). Hong Kong: Oxford University Press.

McCreary Centre Society. (1999). *Healthy connections: Listening to BC Youth.* Burnaby, BC: Author.

McDaniel, E., & Anderson, P. A. (1998). International patterns of interpersonal tactile communication: A field study. *Journal of Nonverbal Behavior, 22,* 59–75.

McDermott, K. B., & Roediger, H. L., III. (1994). Effects of imagery on perceptual implicit memory tests. *Journal of Experimental Psychology: Learning, Memory, and Cognition, 20,* 1379–1390.

McDermott, K. B., & Roediger, H. L., III. (1998). Attempting to avoid illusory memories: Robust false recognition of associates persists under conditions of explicit warnings and immediate testing. *Journal of Memory and Language, 39,* 508–520.

McDonald, J. J., & Ward, L. M. (2000). Involuntary listening aids seeing: Evidence from human electrophysiology. *Psychological Science, 11,* 167–171.

McDonald, M. P., & Crawley, J. N. (1997). Galanin-acetylcholine interactions in rodent memory tasks and Alzheimer's disease. *Journal of Psychiatry and Neuroscience, 22,* 303–317.

McDougall, W. (1908). *An introduction to social psychology.* London: Methuen.

McFall, R. M. (1976). Behavioral training: A skill-acquisition approach to clinical problems. In J. T. Spence, R. C. Carson, & J. W. Thibaut (Eds.), *Behavioral approaches to therapy.* Morristown, NJ: General Learning Press.

McFarland, C., & Miller, D. T. (1994). The framing of relative performance feedback: Seeing the glass as half empty or half full. *Journal of Personality and Social Psychology, 66,* 1061–1073.

McGrath, P. J., Humphreys, P., Keene, D., & Goodman, J. T. (1992). The efficacy and efficiency of a self-administered treatment for adolescent migraine. *Pain, 49,* 321–324.

McGuire, P. K., Shah, G. M. S., & Murray, R. M. (1993). Increased blood flow in Broca's area during auditory hallucinations. *Lancet, 342,* 703–706.

McGuire, W. J. (1985). Attitudes and attitude change. In G. Lindzey & E. Aronson (Eds.), *Handbook of social psychology* (3rd ed., Vol. 2, pp. 233–346). New York: Random House.

McGuire, W. J., & McGuire, C. V. (1988). Content and process in the experience of the self. In L. Berkowitz (Ed.), *Advances in experimental social psychology* (pp. 97–144). San Diego, CA: Academic Press.

McIntosh, A. R., Grady, C. L., Ungerleider, L. G., & Haxby, J. V. (1994). Network analysis of cortical visual pathways mapped with PET. *Journal of Neuroscience, 14,* 655–666.

McIntosh, D. N., Zajonc, R. B., Vig, P. S., & Emerick, S. W. (1997). Facial movement, breathing, temperature, and affect: Implications of the vascular theory of emotional efference. *Cognition and Emotion, 11,* 171–195.

McIntyre, J. S., & Craik, F. I. (1987). Age differences in memory for item and source information. *Canadian Journal of Psychology, 41*(2), 175–192.

McKenna, S. P., & Glendon, A. I. (1985). Occupational first aid training: Decay in cardiopulmonary resuscitation (CPR) skills. *Journal of Occupational Psychology, 58,* 109–117.

McKinlay, S. M., Brambilla, D. J., & Posner, J. G. (1992). The normal menopause transition. *Maturitas, 14,* 103–115.

McKnight, J. D., & Glass, D. C. (1995). Perceptions of control, burnout, and depressive symptomatology: A replication and extension. *Journal of Consulting and Clinical Psychology, 63,* 490–494.

McLean, K. C. (2005). Late adolescent identity development: Narrative meaning making and memory telling. *Developmental Psychology, 41*(4), 683–691.

McLean, P. D., & Woody, S. R. (2001). *Anxiety disorders in adults: An evidence-based approach to psychological treatment.* London: Oxford University Press.

McLeod, J. D., Kessler, R. C., & Landis, K. R. (1992). Speed of recovery from major depressive episodes in a community sample of married men and women. *Journal of Abnormal Psychology, 101,* 277–286.

McNeil, B. J., Pauker, S. G., Cox, H. C., Jr., & Tversky, A. (1982). On the elicitation of preferences for alternative therapies. *New England Journal of Medicine, 306,* 1259–1262.

Mealey, L. (1995). The sociobiology of sociopathy: An integrated evolutionary model. *Behavioral and Brain Sciences, 18,* 523–599.

Medin, D. L. (1989). Concepts and conceptual structure. *American Psychologist, 44,* 1469–1481.

Medin, D. L., & Shaffer, M. M. (1978). A context theory of classification learning. *Psychological Review, 85,* 207–238.

Mednick, S. A. (1962). The associative basis of the creative process. *Psychological Review, 69,* 220–232.

Mednick, S. C., Nakayama, K., Cantero, J. L., Atienza, M., Levin, A. A., Pathak, N., et al. (2002). The restorative effect of naps on perceptual deterioration. *Nature Neuroscience, 5,* 677–681.

Meeus, W. H. J., & Raaijmakers, Q. A. W. (1987). Administrative obedience as a social phenomenon. In W. Doise & S. Moscovici (Eds.), *Current issues in European social psychology* (Vol. 2, pp. 183–230). Cambridge, England: Cambridge University Press.

Meisel, A., & Roth, L. H. (1983). Toward an informed discussion of informed consent: A review and critique of the empirical studies. *Arizona Law Review, 25,* 265–346.

Melamed, B. G., & Siegel, L. J. (1975). Reduction of anxiety in children facing hospitalization and surgery by use of filmed modeling. *Journal of Consulting and Clinical Psychology, 43,* 511–521.

Melton, A. W. (1963). Implications of short-term memory for a general theory of memory. *Journal of Verbal Learning and Verbal Behavior, 2,* 1–21.

Melzack, R. (1973). *The puzzle of pain.* New York: Basic Books.

Melzack, R., & Katz, J. (2004). The gate control theory: Reaching for the brain. In T. Hadjistavropoulos & K. D. Craig (Eds.), *Pain: Psychological perspectives* (pp. 13–34). New York: Erlbaum.

Melzack, R., & Wall, P. D. (1965). Pain mechanisms: A new theory. *Science, 150,* 971–979.

Mendez, I., Baker, K. A., & Hong, M. (2000). Simultaneous intrastriatal and intranigral grafting (double grafts) in the rat model of Parkinson's disease. *Brain Research Reviews, 32*(1), 328–339.

Mennin, D. S., Heimberg, R. G., & Holt, C. S. (2000). Panic, agoraphobia, phobias, and generalized anxiety disorder. In M. Hersen & A. S. Bellack (Eds.), *Psychopathology in adulthood* (2nd ed., pp. 169–207). Needham Heights, MA: Allyn & Bacon.

Meredith, C. W., Jaffe, C., Ang-Lee, K., & Saxon, A. J. (2005). Implications of chronic methamphetamine use: A literature review. *Harvard Review of Psychiatry, 13*(3), 141–154.

Merikle, P. M., & Skanes, H. E. (1992). Subliminal self-help audiotapes: A search for placebo effects. *Journal of Applied Psychology, 77*, 772–776.

Merikle, P. M., Smilek, D., & Eastwood, J. D. (2001). Perception without awareness: Perspectives from cognitive psychology. *Cognition, 79*, 115–134.

Merlin, D. (1999). Preconditions for the evolution of protolanguages. In M. Corballis & S. E. G. Lea (Eds.), *The descent of mind. Psychological perspectives on hominid evolution* (pp. 138–154). New York: Oxford University Press.

Merton, R. (1948). The self-fulfilling prophecy. *Antioch Review, 8*, 193–210.

Meston, C. M. (2000). The psychophysiological assessment of female sexual function. *Journal of Sex Education & Therapy, 25*, 6–16.

Meston, C. M., & Frohlich, P. F. (2003). Love at first fright: Partner salience moderates roller-coaster-induced excitation transfer. *Archives of Sexual Behavior, 32*, 537–544.

Metcalfe, J. (2002). Is study time allocated selectively to a region of proximal learning? *Journal of Experimental Psychology: General, 131*, 349–363.

Metcalfe, J., & Jacobs, W. J. (2000). "Hot" emotions in human recollection: Toward a model of traumatic memory. In E. Tulving (Ed.), *Memory, consciousness, and the brain: The Tallinn conference* (pp. 228–242). Philadelphia: Psychology Press.

Miklowitz, D. J. (2001). Bipolar disorder. In D. H. Barlow (Ed.), *Clinical handbook of psychological disorders: A step-by-step treatment manual* (3rd ed., pp. 523–561). New York: Guilford Press.

Mikulincer, M., & Shaver, P. R. (2005). Mental representations of attachment security: Theoretical foundation for a positive social psychology. In M. W. Baldwin (Ed.), *Interpersonal cognition* (pp. 233–266). New York: Guilford Press.

Milgram, S. (1963). Behavioral study of obedience. *Journal of Abnormal and Social Psychology, 67*, 371–378.

Milgram, S. (1974). *Obedience to authority.* New York: Harper & Row.

Miller, D. B. (1977). Roles of naturalistic observation in comparative psychology. *American Psychologist, 32*, 211–219.

Miller, D. T., & Ross, M. (1975). Self-serving biases in the attribution of causality: Fact or fiction? *Psychological Bulletin, 82*, 213–225.

Miller, G. (2005). What is the biological basis of consciousness? *Science, 309*(5731), 79.

Miller, G. A. (1956). The magical number seven plus or minus two: Some limits on our capacity for processing information. *Psychological Review, 63*, 81–97.

Miller, G. A., Galanter, E., & Pribram, K. H. (1960). *Plans and the structure of behavior.* New York: Holt.

Miller, G. E., Cohen S., & Herbert, T. B. (1999). Pathways linking major depression and immunity in ambulatory female patients. *Psychosomatic Medicine, 61*, 850–860.

Miller, G. E., Stetler, C. A., Carney, R. M., Freeland, K. E., & Banks, W. A. (2002). Clinical depression and inflammatory risk markers for coronary heart disease. *American Journal of Cardiology, 90*, 1279–1283.

Miller, G. F. (1998). How mate choice shaped human nature: A review of sexual selection and human evolution. In C. Crawford & D. Krebs (Eds.), *Handbook of evolutionary psychology* (pp. 87–129). Mahwah, NJ: Erlbaum.

Miller, J. G. (1994). Cultural diversity in the morality of caring: Individually oriented versus duty-based interpersonal moral codes. *Cross-Cultural Research: The Journal of Comparative Social Science, 28*, 3–39.

Miller, L. T., & Vernon, P. A. (1996). Intelligence, reaction time, and working memory in 4- to 6-year-old children. *Intelligence, 22*, 155–190.

Miller, L. T., & Vernon, P. A. (1997). Developmental changes in speed of information processing in young children. *Developmental Psychology, 22*, 549–554.

Miller, M. A., & Rahe, R. H. (1997). Life changes scaling for the 1990s. *Journal of Psychosomatic Research, 43*, 279–292.

Miller, N. E. (1985). The value of behavioral research on animals. *American Psychologist, 40*, 423–440.

Miller, N. E. (1991). Commentary on Ulrich: Need to check truthfulness of statements by opponents of animal research. *Psychological Science, 2*, 422–424.

Miller, S. D. (1989). Optical differences in cases of multiple personality disorder. *Journal of Nervous and Mental Disease, 177*, 480–486.

Miller, T. W. (1993). The assessment of stressful life events. In L. Goldberger & S. Breznitz (Eds.), *Handbook of stress: Theoretical and clinical aspects* (2nd ed, pp. 161–173). New York: Free Press.

Miller, W. R., Taylor, C. A., & West, J. C. (1980). Focused versus broad-spectrum behavior therapy for problem drinkers. *Journal of Consulting and Clinical Psychology, 48*, 590–601.

Milner, A. D., & Rugg, M. D. (Eds.). (1992). *The neuropsychology of consciousness.* London: Academic Press.

Milner, B. (1966). Amnesia following operation on the temporal lobes. In C. W. M. Whitty & O. L. Zangwill (Eds.), *Amnesia* (pp. 109–133). London: Butterworths.

Milner, B. (2005). The medial temporal-lobe amnesic syndrome. *Psychiatric Clinics of North America, 28*, 599–611.

Milner, B., Corkin, S., & Teuber, H. L. (1968). Further analysis of the hippocampal amnesic syndrome: 14-year follow-up study of H. M. *Neuropsychologia, 6*, 215–234.

Mineka, S. (1987). A primate model of phobic fears. In H. Eysenck & I. Martin (Eds.), *Theoretical foundations of behavior therapy* (pp. 81–111). New York: Plenum Press.

Mirmiran, M., van Soneren, E. J. W., & Swaab, D. F. (1996). Is brain plasticity preserved during aging and in Alzheimer's disease? *Behavioral Brain Research, 78*, 43–48.

Mischel, W. (1968). *Personality and assessment.* New York: Wiley.

Mischel, W., & Peake, P. K. (1982). Beyond déjà vu in the search for cross-situational consistency. *Psychological Review, 89*, 730–755.

Mischel, W., & Shoda, Y. (1995). A cognitive-affective system theory of personality: Reconceptualizing situations, dispositions, dynamics, and invariance in personality structure. *Psychological Review, 102*, 246–268.

Mischel, W., & Shoda, Y. (1998). Reconciling processing dynamics and personality dispositions. *Annual Review of Psychology, 49*, 229–258.

Mistlberger, R. E. (2005). Circadian regulation of sleep in mammals: Role of the suprachiasmatic nucleus. *Brain Research Reviews, 49*(3), 429–454.

Mix, J. A., & Crews, W. D. J. R. (2002). A double-blind, placebo-controlled, randomized trial of Ginkgo biloba extract EGb 761(R) in a sample of cognitively intact older adults: Neuropsychological findings. *Human Psychopharmacology Clinical and Experimental, 3*, 267–277.

Molden, D. C., & Dweck, C. S. (2000). Meaning and motivation. In C. Sansone & J. M. Harackiewicz (Eds.), *Intrinsic and extrinsic motivation: The search for optimal motivation and performance* (pp. 131–153). San Diego, CA: Academic Press.

Mondor, T. A., Zatorre, R. J., & Terrio, N. A. (1998). Constraints on the selection of auditory information. *Journal of Experimental Psychology: Human Perception and Performance, 24*, 66–79.

Mongrain, M. (1998). Parental representations and support-seeking behaviors related to dependency and self-criticism. *Journal of Personality, 66*, 151–173.

Mook, D. G. (1995). *Motivation: The organization of action* (2nd ed.). New York: Norton.

Moore, T. E. (1995). Subliminal self-help auditory tapes: An empirical test of perceptual consequences. *Canadian Journal of Behavioural Science, 27*, 9–20.

Moray, N. (1959). Attention in dichotic listening: Affective cues and the influence of instructions. *Quarterly Journal of Experimental Psychology, 11*, 56–60.

Moret, V., Forster, A., Laverriere, M. C., & Lambert, H. (1991). Mechanism of analgesia induced by hypnosis and acupuncture: Is there a difference? *Pain, 45*, 135–140.

Moretti, M. M., Rein, A. S., & Wiebe, V. J. (1998). Relational self-regulation: Gender differences in risk for dysphoria. *Canadian Journal of Behavioural Science, 30*(4), 243–252.

Moretti, M. M., Segal, Z. V., McCann, C. D., & Shaw, B. F. (1996). Self-referent versus other-referent information processing in dysphoric, clinically depressed, and remitted depressed

subjects. *Personality and Social Psychology Bulletin, 22*, 68–80.

Morf, C. C., & Rhodewalt, F. (2001). Unraveling the paradoxes of narcissism: A dynamic self-regulatory processing model. *Psychological Inquiry, 12*, 177–196.

Morris, C. D., Bransford, J. D., & Franks, J. J. (1977). Levels of processing versus transfer appropriate processing. *Journal of Verbal Learning and Verbal Behavior, 16*, 519–533.

Morris, P. E., Fritz, C. O., Jackson, L., Nichol, E., & Roberts, E. (2005). Strategies for learning proper names: Expanding retrieval practice, meaning and imagery. *Applied Cognitive Psychology, 19*, 779–798.

Morrongiello, B. A., Fenwick, K. D., Hillier, L., & Chance, G. (1994). Sound localization in newborn human infants. *Developmental Psychobiology, 27*, 519–538.

Morton, J. (2005). Ecstasy: Pharmacology and neurotoxicity. *Current Opinion in Pharmacology, 5*(1), 79–86.

Moskowitz, D. S. (1994). Cross-situational generality and the interpersonal circumplex. *Journal of Personality and Social Psychology, 66*, 921–933.

Moskowitz, H. (1985). Marihuana and driving. *Accident Analysis and Prevention, 17*, 323–345.

Moulton, P. L., Boyko, L. N., Fitzpatrick, J. L., & Petros, T. V. (2001). The effect of Ginkgo biloba on memory in healthy male volunteers. *Physiology and Behavior, 73*(4), 659–665.

Mueller, C. M., & Dweck, C. S. (1998). Praise for intelligence can undermine children's motivation and performance. *Journal of Personality and Social Psychology, 75*, 33–52.

Muir, D., Hains, S. M. J., & Symons, L. A. (1994). Baby and me: Infants need minds to read. *Current Psychology of Cognition, 13*, 669–682.

Mullen, M. (1994). Earliest recollection of childhood: A demographic analysis. *Cognition, 52*, 55–79.

Müller, J. P. (1838–1842). *Elements of physiology* (2 vols.) (W. Baly, Trans.). London: Taylor & Walton. (Original work published in 1833)

Multimodal Treatment Study of Children with ADHD Cooperative Group. (1999). Moderators and mediators of treatment response for children with attention-deficit/hyperactivity disorder: The multimodal treatment study of children with attention-

deficit/hyperactivity disorder. *Archives of General Psychiatry, 56*(12), 1088–1096.

Mumby, D. G., Glenn, M. J., Nesbitt, C., & Kyriazis, D. A. (2002). Dissociation in retrograde memory for object discriminations and object recognition in rats with perirhinal cortex damage. *Behavioural Brain Research, 132*, 215–226.

Munakata, Y., McClelland, J. L., Johnson, M. H., & Siegler, R. S. (1997). Rethinking infant knowledge: Toward an adaptive process account of successes and failures in object permanence tasks. *Psychological Review, 104*, 686–713.

Munhall, K. G., Jones, J. A., Callan, D. E., Kuratate, T., & Vatikiotis-Bateson, E. (2004). Visual prosody and speech intelligibility: Head movement improves auditory speech perception. *Psychological Science, 15*, 133–136.

Murdock, B. B. (1995). Primacy and recency in the chunking model. In C. A. Weaver, III, & S. Mannes (Eds.), *Discourse comprehension: Essays in honor of Walter Kintsch* (pp. 49–63). Hillsdale, NJ: Erlbaum.

Murdock, B. B., Jr. (1960). The distinctiveness of stimuli. *Psychological Review, 67*, 16–31.

Murnen, S. K., & Stockton, M. (1997). Gender and self-reported sexual arousal in response to sexual stimuli: A meta-analytic review. *Sex Roles, 37*, 135–153.

Murphy, G. L., & Lassaline, M. E. (1997). Hierarchical structure in concepts and the basic level of categorization. In K. Lamberts & D. R. Shanks (Eds.), *Knowledge, concepts and categories: Studies in cognition* (pp. 93–132). Cambridge, MA: MIT Press.

Murray, H. A. (1938). *Explorations in personality.* New York: Oxford University Press.

Murray, H. A. (1943). *Thematic Apperception Test.* Cambridge, MA: Harvard University Press.

Musselman, D. L., Evans, D. L., & Nemeroff, C. B. (1998). The relationship of depression to cardiovascular disease: Epidemiology, biology, and treatment. *Archives of General Psychiatry, 55*(7), 580–592.

Muter, P. (1980). Very rapid forgetting. *Memory and Cognition, 8*, 174–179.

Myers, D. G. (1982). Polarizing effects of social interaction. In H. Brandstatter, J. H. Davis, & G. Stocker-Kreichgauer

(Eds.), *Group decision making* (pp. 125–161). New York: Academic Press.

Myers, D. G., & Diener, E. (1995). Who is happy? *Psychological Science, 6,* 10–19.

Myers, T. C., Wittrock, D. A., & Foreman, G. W. (1998). Appraisal of subjective stress in individuals with tension-type headache: The influence of baseline measures. *Journal of Behavioral Medicine, 21,* 469–484.

Nader, K., Bechara, A., & van der Kooy, D. (1997). Neurobiological constraints on behavioral models of motivation. *Annual Review of Psychology, 48,* 85–114.

Nadon, R., Hoyt, I. P., Register, P. A., & Kihlstrom, J. F. (1991). Absorption and hypnotizability: Context effects reexamined. *Journal of Personality and Social Psychology, 60,* 144–153.

Nagar, D., & Panady, J. (1987). Affect and performance on cognitive tasks as a function of crowding and noise. *Journal of Applied Social Psychology, 17,* 147–157.

Nairne, J. S. (1990). A feature model of immediate memory. *Memory and Cognition, 18,* 251–269.

Nairne, J. S. (2002). Remembering over the short term: The case against the standard model. *Annual Review of Psychology, 53,* 53–81.

Nairne, J. S., & Rescorla, R. A. (1981). Second-order conditioning with diffuse auditory reinforcers in the pigeon. *Learning and Motivation, 12,* 65–91.

Nathan, P. E., & Langenbucher, J. (2003). Diagnosis and classification. In G. Stricker & T. A. Widiger (Eds.), *Handbook of psychology: Clinical psychology* (Vol. 8, pp. 3–26). New York: Wiley.

Nathan, P. J., Tanner, S., Lloyd, J., Harrison, B., Curran, L., Oliver, C., et al. (2004). Effects of a combined extract of Ginkgo biloba and bacopa monniera on cognitive function in healthy humans. *Human Psychopharmacology: Clinical and Experimental, 19,* 91–96.

Nathan, R. (2006). *My freshman year: What a professor learned by becoming a student.* New York: Penguin.

Nathanson, C., Paulhus, D. L., & Williams, K. M. (2006). Personality and misconduct correlates of body modification and other cultural deviance markers. *Journal of Research in Personality, 40,* pp. 779–802.

Naveh-Benjamin, M., & Ayres, T. J. (1986). Digit span, reading rate, and linguistic relativity. *Quarterly Journal of Experimental Psychology, 38A,* 739–751.

Neath, I. (1993). Distinctiveness and serial position effects in recognition. *Memory and Cognition, 21,* 689–698.

Neath, I. (1998). *Human memory: An introduction to research, data, and theory.* Pacific Grove, CA: Brooks/Cole.

Neath, I., & Surprenant, A. (2003). *Human memory: An introduction to research, data, and theory* (2nd ed.). Belmont, CA: Wadsworth.

Neisser, U. (1967). *Cognitive psychology.* New York: Appleton-Century-Crofts.

Neisser, U. (2000). Memorists. In U. Neisser & I. E. Hyman, Jr. (Eds.), *Memory observed: Remembering in natural contexts* (pp. 475–478). New York: Worth.

Neisser, U., & Harsch, N. (1992). Phantom flashbulbs: False recollections of hearing the news about Challenger. In E. Winograd & U. Neisser (Eds.), *Affect and accuracy in recall: Studies of "flashbulb memories"* (pp. 9–31). Cambridge: Cambridge University Press.

Neisser, U., & Hyman, I. E., Jr. (Eds.). (1999). *Memory observed: Remembering in natural contexts* (2nd ed.). New York: Worth.

Nelson, K. (1973). Structure and strategy in learning to talk. *Monographs of the Society for Research in Child Development, 38*(Serial No. 149).

Nelson, K., & Shaw, L. K. (2002). Developing a socially shared symbolic system. In E. Amsel & J. P. Byrnes (Eds.), *Language, literacy, and cognitive development: The development and consequences of symbolic communication* (pp. 27–57). Mahwah, NJ: Erlbaum.

Newcomb, A. F., & Bagwell, C. L. (1995). Children's friendship relations: A meta-analytic review. *Psychological Bulletin, 117,* 306–347.

Newcombe, N. E., Drummey, A. B., Fox, N. A., Lie, E., & Ottinger-Alberts, W. (2000). Remembering early childhood: How much, how, and why (or why not)? *Current Directions in Psychological Science, 9,* 55–58.

Newell, A., & Simon, H. A. (1972). *Human problem solving.* Englewood Cliffs, NJ: Prentice-Hall.

Nezu, A. M., Nezu, C. M., & Geller, P. A. (Eds.). (2003). *Handbook of psychology: Health psychology* (Vol. 9). New York: Wiley.

Nichols, D. S., & Greene, R. L. (1997). Dimensions of deception in personality assessment: The example of the MMPI-2. *Journal of Personality Assessment, 68,* 251–266.

Nickerson, R. S. (1999). How we know—and sometimes misjudge—what others know: Imputing one's own knowledge to others. *Psychological Bulletin, 125,* 737–759.

Nickerson, R. S., & Adams, M. J. (1979). Long-term memory for a common object. *Cognitive Psychology, 11,* 287–307.

Nicolaus, L. K., & Nellis, D. W. (1987). The first evaluation of the use of conditioned taste aversion to control predation by mongooses upon eggs. *Applied Animal Behaviour Science, 17,* 329–346.

Nielsen, T. A., & Powell, R. A. (1992). The day-residue and dream-lag effects: A literature review and limited replication of two temporal effects in dream formation. *Dreaming: Journal of the Association for the Study of Dreams, 2,* 67–77.

Nisbett, R. E. (Ed.). (1993). *Rules for reasoning.* Hillsdale, NJ: Erlbaum.

Nisbett, R. E., & Wilson, T. D. (1977). Telling more than we can know: Verbal reports on mental processes. *Psychological Review, 84,* 231–259.

Nobel, K. D., Robinson, N. M., & Gunderson, S. A. (1993). All rivers lead to the sea: A follow-up study of gifted young adults. *Roeper Review, 15,* 124–130.

Nolan, C. C., Gray-Donald, K., Shatenstein, B., & O'Loughlin, J. (1995). Dietary patterns leading to high fat intake. *Canadian Journal of Public Health, 86,* 389–391.

Norcross, J. C., Kohout, J. L., & Wicherski, M. (2005). Graduate study in psychology: 1971–2004. *American Psychologist, 60,* 959–975.

Norenzayan, A., Choi, I., & Nisbett, R. E. (2002). Cultural similarities and differences in social inference: Evidence from behavioral predictions and lay theories of behavior. *Personality and Social Psychology Bulletin, 28,* 109–120.

Norenzayan, A., & Nisbett, R. E. (2000). Culture and causal cognition. *Current Directions in Psychological Science, 9,* 132–135.

Norton, G. R., Cox, B. J., Hewitt, P. L., & McLeod, L. (1997). Personality factors associated with generalized and non-generalized social anxiety. *Personality and Individual Differences, 22,* 655–660.

Nosofsky, R. M. (1992). Exemplar-based approach to relating categorization, identification, and recognition. In G. F. Ashby (Ed.), *Scientific psychology series: Multidimensional models of perception and cognition* (pp. 363–393). Hillsdale, NJ: Erlbaum.

Nowak, A., Vallacher, R. R., & Miller, M. E. (2003). Social influence and group dynamics. In T. Millon & M. J. Lerner (Eds.), *Handbook of psychology: Personality and social psychology* (Vol. 5, pp. 383–417). New York: Wiley.

Nowakowski, R. S. (1987). Basic concepts of CNS development. *Child Development, 58,* 568–595.

Oakes, J. (1985). *Keeping track: How schools structure inequality.* New Haven, CT: Yale University Press.

O'Donnell, P., & Grace, A. (1998). Dysfunctions in multiple interrelated systems as the neurobiological bases of schizophrenic symptom clusters. *Schizophrenia Bulletin, 24,* 267–283.

Offer, D., & Schonert-Reichl, K. A. (1992). Debunking the myths of adolescence. *Journal of the American Academy of Child and Adolescent Psychiatry, 31,* 1003–1013.

Offord, D. R., Boyle, M. H., Campbell, D., Goering, P., Lin, E., Wong, M., et al. (1996). One-year prevalence of psychiatric disorder in Ontarians 15 to 64 years of age. *Canadian Journal of Psychiatry, 41*(9), 559–563.

Ogden, J. A., & Corkin, S. (1991). Memories of HM. In W. C. Abraham, M. C. Corballis, & K. G. White (Eds.), *Memory mechanisms: A tribute to G. V. Goddard* (pp. 195–215). Hillsdale, NJ: Erlbaum.

Ogloff, J. R. P., & Pfeifer, J. E. (1992). Cults and the law: A discussion of the legality of alleged cult activities. *Behavioral Sciences and the Law, 10,* 117–140.

Ogloff, J. R. P., Roberts, C. F., & Roesch, R. (1993). The insanity defense: Legal standards and clinical assessment. *Applied and Preventive Psychology, 2,* 163–178.

Okada, Y., & Stark, C. (2003). Neural processing associated with true and false memory retrieval. *Cognitive, Affective, & Behavioral Neuroscience, 3,* 323–334.

Oldani, R. (1997). Causes of increases in achievement motivation: Is the personality affected by parental environment? *Personality and Individual Differences, 22,* 403–410.

Olds, J., & Milner, P. (1954). Positive reinforcement produced by electrical stimulation of the septal area and other regions of the rat brain. *Journal of Comparative and Physiological Psychology, 47,* 419–427.

Olson, J. M., & Maio, G. R. (2003). Attitudes in social behavior. In T. Millon & M. J. Lerner (Eds.), *Handbook of psychology: Personality and social psychology* (Vol. 5, pp. 299–325). New York: Wiley.

Olson, J. M., & Zanna, M. P. (1987). Understanding and promoting exercise: A social psychological perspective. *Canadian Journal of Public Health, 78,* S1–S7.

Olson, J. M., & Zanna, M. P. (1993). Attitudes and attitude change. *Annual Review of Psychology, 44,* 117–154.

O'Mahony, M. (1978). Smell illusions and suggestion: Reports of smells contingent on tones played on television and radio. *Chemical Senses and Flavor, 3,* 183–187.

Orne, M. T. (1959). The nature of hypnosis: Artifact and essence. *Journal of Abnormal and Social Psychology, 58,* 277–299.

Orne, M. T. (1969). Demand characteristics and the concept of quasi-controls. In R. Rosenthal & R. L. Rosnow (Eds.), *Artifact in behavioral research* (pp. 143–179). New York: Academic Press.

Ortmann, A., & Hertwig, R. (1997). Is deception acceptable? *American Psychologist, 52,* 746–747.

Ortony, A., & Turner, T. J. (1990). What's basic about basic emotions? *Psychological Review, 97,* 315–331.

Oscar-Berman, M., Shagrin, B., Evert, D. L., & Epstein, C. (1997). Impairments of brain and behavior: The neurological effects of alcohol. *Alcohol Health and Research World, 21,* 65–75.

O'Shea, B. (2001). Post-traumatic stress disorder: A review for the general psychiatrist. *International Journal of Psychiatry in Clinical Practice, 5,* 11–18.

Ostbye, T., Pomerleau, J., White, M., Coolich, M., & McWhinney, J. (1993). Food and nutrition in Canadian "prime time" television commercials. *Canadian Journal of Public Health, 84,* 370–374.

Otto, M. W., Demopulos, C. M., McLean, N. E., Pollack, M. H., & Fava, M. (1998). Additional findings on the association between anxiety sensitivity and hypochondriacal concerns: Examination of patients with major depression. *Journal of Anxiety Disorders, 12,* 225–232.

Ozgen, E. (2004). Language, learning, and color perception. *Current Directions in Psychological Science, 13,* 95–98.

Ozgen, E., & Davies, I. R. L. (2002). Acquisition of categorical color perception: A perceptual learning approach to the linguistic relativity hypothesis. *Journal of Experimental Psychology: General, 131,* 477–493.

Pagano, R. R. (2007). *Understanding statistics in the behavioral sciences* (8th ed.). St. Paul, MN: Brooks/Cole.

Pahl, J. J., Swayze, V. W., & Andreasen, N. C. (1990). Diagnostic advances in anatomical and functional brain imaging in schizophrenia. In A. Kales, C. N. Stefanis, & J. A. Talbott (Eds.), *Recent advances in schizophrenia* (pp.163–189). New York: Springer-Verlag.

Paivio, A. (1995). Imagery and memory. In M. S. Gazzaniga (Ed.), *The cognitive neurosciences* (pp. 977–986). Cambridge, MA: MIT Press.

Pappas, B. A., Bayley, P. J., Bui, B. K., Hansen, L. A., & Thal, L. J. (2000). Choline acetyltransferase activity and cognitive domain scores of Alzheimer's patients. *Neurobiology of Aging, 21,* 11–17.

Park, N. W., Moscovitch, M., & Robertson, I. H. (1999). Divided attention impairments after traumatic brain injury. *Neuropsychologia, 37,* 1119–1133.

Parker, E. S., Cahill, L., & McGaugh, J. L. (2006). A case of unusual autobiographical remembering. *Neurocase, 12,* 35–49.

Parker, J. D. A. (Ed.). (2000). *Emotional intelligence: Clinical and therapeutic implications. The handbook of emotional intelligence.* New York: John Wiley/Jossey-Bass.

Parkes, J. D., & Block, C. (1989). Genetic factors in sleep disorders. *Journal of Neurology, Neurosurgery, and Psychiatry, 52*, 101–108.

Parkin, A. J., & Java, R. (2001). Determinants of age-related memory loss. In T. J. Perfect & E. I. Maylor (Eds.), *Models of cognitive aging* (pp. 188–203). New York: Oxford University Press.

Parmelee, A. H., & Sigman, M. D. (1983). Perinatal brain development and behavior. In M. M. Haith & J. J. Campos (Eds.), *Handbook of child psychology: Infancy and developmental psychobiology* (pp. 95–155). New York: Wiley.

Parrott, A. C. (2005). Chronic tolerance to recreational MDMA (3,4-methylenedioxymethamphetamine) or Ecstasy. *Journal of Psychopharmacology,19*, 71–83.

Pashler, H. (1992). Attentional limitations in doing two tasks at the same time. *Current Directions in Psychological Science, 1*, 44–48.

Pashler, H. (1998). *The psychology of attention.* Cambridge, MA: MIT Press.

Pasveer, K. A., & Ellard, J. H. (1998). The making of a personality inventory: Help from the WWW. *Behavior Research Methods, Instruments, and Computers, 30*, 309–313.

Patterson, D. R. (2004). Treating pain with hypnosis. *Current Directions in Psychological Science, 13*(6), 252–255.

Patterson, F. G. (1978). The gesture of a gorilla: Language acquisition in another pongid. *Brain and Language, 5*, 72–97.

Paulhus, D. L. (1998). Interpersonal and intrapsychic adaptiveness of trait self-enhancement: A mixed blessing? *Journal of Personality and Social Psychology, 74*, 1197–1208.

Paulhus, D. L., & John, O. P. (1998). Egoistic and moralistic bias in self-perceptions: The interplay of self-deceptive styles with basic traits and motives. *Journal of Personality, 66*, 1024–1060.

Paulhus, D. L., Lysy, D., & Yik, M. S. M. (1998). Self-report measures of intelligence: Are they useful as proxy measures of IQ? *Journal of Personality, 66*, 525–554.

Paulhus, D. L., & Reid, D. B. (1991). Enhancement and denial in socially desirable responding. *Journal of Personality and Social Psychology, 60*, 307–317.

Paulhus, D. L., & Reynolds, S. R. (1995). Enhancing target variance in personality impressions: Highlighting the person in person perception. *Journal of Personality and Social Psychology, 69*, 344–354.

Paulhus, D. L., & Trapnell, P. D. (1998). Typological measures of shyness: Additive, interactive, and categorical. *Journal of Research in Personality, 32*, 183–201.

Paulhus, D. L., Trapnell, P. D., & Chen, D. (1999). Effects of birth order on achievement and personality within families. *Psychological Science, 10*, 482–488.

Paulhus, D. L., Wehr, P., Harms, P. D., & Strasser, D. I. (2002). Use of exemplar surveys to reveal implicit theories of intelligence. *Personality and Social Psychology Bulletin, 28*, 1051–1062.

Paulhus, D. L., & Williams, K. M. (2002). The dark triad of personality: Narcissism, machiavellianism, and psychopathy. *Journal of Research in Personality, 36*, 556–563.

Paulus, P. B. (1988). *Prison crowding: A psychological perspective.* New York: Springer.

Paunonen, S. V. (1998). Hierarchical organization of personality and prediction of behavior. *Journal of Personality and Social Psychology, 74*, 538–556.

Paunonen, S. V., Jackson, D. N., & Keinonen, M. (1990). The structured nonverbal assessment of personality. *Journal of Personality, 58*, 481–501.

Paunonen, S. V., Zeidner, M., Engvik, H. A., Oosterveld, P., & Maliphant, R. (2000). The nonverbal assessment of personality in five cultures. *Journal of Cross-Cultural Psychology, 31*, 220–239.

Paus, T., & Barrett, J. (2004). Transcranial magnetic stimulation (TMS) of the human frontal cortex: Implications for repetitive TMS treatment of depression. *Journal of Psychiatry and Neuroscience, 29*, 268–279.

Penfield, W., & Boldrey, E. (1958). Somatic motor and sensory representation in the cerebral cortex as studied by electrical stimulation. *Brain, 60*, 389–443.

Penfield, W., & Perot, P. (1963). The brain's record of auditory and visual experience. *Brain, 86*, 595–696.

Pennebaker, J. W. (1990). *Opening up: The healing power of confiding in others.* New York: Morrow.

Pennebaker, J. W., Zech, E., & Rime, B. (2001). Disclosing and sharing emotion: Psychological, social, and health consequences. In M. S. Stoebe & R. O. Hansson (Eds.), *Handbook of bereavement research: Consequences, coping, and care* (pp. 517–544). Washington, DC: American Psychological Association.

Pepler, D., Craig, W. M., & O'Connell, P. (1999). Understanding bullying from a dynamic systems perspective. In A. Slater & D. Muir (Eds.), *The Blackwell reader in development psychology* (pp. 440–451). Malden, MA: Blackwell.

Peretz, I., & Zatorre, R. J. (2005). Brain organization for music processing. *Annual Review of Psychology, 56*, 89–114.

Perls, F. S. (1969). *Gestalt therapy verbatim.* Moab, UT: Real People Press.

Perls, F. S., Hefferline, R. F., & Goodman, P. (1951). *Gestalt therapy.* New York: Julian.

Perrett, D. I., & Mistlin, A. M. (1987). Visual neurones responsive to faces. *Trends in Neuroscience, 10*, 358–364.

Perry, W. (1970). *Forms of intellectual and ethical development in the college years.* New York: Holt, Rinehart, & Winston.

Pert, C. B., & Snyder, S. H. (1973). The opiate receptor: Demonstration in nervous tissue. *Science, 179*, 1011–1014.

Peterson, A. C. (1988). Adolescent development. *Annual Review of Psychology, 39*, 583–607.

Peterson, C., & Seligman, M. E. P. (1987). Explanatory style and illness. *Journal of Personality, 55*, 237–265.

Peterson, C., Seligman, M. E. P., & Vaillant, G. E. (1988). Pessimistic explanatory style is a risk factor for physical illness: A thirty-five-year longitudinal study. *Journal of Personality and Social Psychology, 55*, 23–27.

Peterson, L. R., & Peterson, M. J. (1959). Short-term retention of individual items. *Journal of Experimental Psychology, 58*, 193–198.

Petitto, L. A. (2000). The acquisition of natural signed languages: Lessons in the nature of human language and its biological foundations. In C. Chamberlain, J. P. Morford, & R. Mayberry (Eds.), *Language acquisition by eye* (pp. 41–50). Mahwah, NJ: Erlbaum.

Petty, R. E., & Cacioppo, J. T. (1986). *Communication and persuasion: Central and peripheral routes to attitude change.* New York: Springer-Verlag.

Petty, R. E., DeSteno, D., & Rucker, D. D. (2001). The role of affect in attitude change. In J. P. Forgas (Ed.), *Handbook of affect and social cognition* (pp. 212–233). Mahwah, NJ: Erlbaum.

Petty, R. E., Wegener, D. T., & Fabrigar, L. R. (1997). Attitudes and attitude change. *Annual Review of Psychology, 48,* 609–647.

Petty, R. E., Wheeler, C., & Tormala, Z. L. (2003). Persuasion and attitude change. In T. Millon & M. J. Lerner (Eds.), *Handbook of psychology: Personality and social psychology* (Vol. 5, pp. 353–382). New York: Wiley.

Pexman, P. M., & Olineck, K. M. (2002). Understanding irony: How do stereotypes cue speaker intent? *Journal of Language and Social Psychology, 21,* 245–274.

Pezdek, K., Finger, K., & Hodge, D. (1997). Planting false childhood memories: The role of event plausibility. *Psychological Science, 8,* 437–441.

Pfaus, J. G., Kippin, T. E., & Coria-Avila, G. (2003). What can animal models tell us about human sexual response? *Annual Review of Sex Research, 14,* 1–63.

Pfeiffer, S. I. (2001). Emotional intelligence: Popular but evasive construct. *Roeper Review, 23,* 138–142.

Phelps, E. A. (2006). Emotion and cognition: Insights from studies of the human amygdala. *Annual Review of Psychology, 57,* 27–53.

Phelps, E. A., O'Connor, K. J., Cunningham, W. A., Funayama, E. S., Gatenby, J. C., Gore, J., et al. (2000). Performance on indirect measures of race evaluation predicts amygdala activation. *Journal of Cognitive Neuroscience, 12,* 729–738.

Piaget, J. (1929). *The child's conception of the world.* New York: Harcourt Brace.

Piaget, J. (1952). *The origins of intelligence in children.* New York: International Universities Press.

Piaget, J. (1970). Piaget's theory. In P. H. Mussen (Ed.), *Carmichael's manual of child psychology* (pp. 703–732). New York: Wiley.

Piasecki, T. M., Fiore, M. C., & Baker, T. B. (1998). Profiles in discourage-ment: Two studies of variability in the time course of smoking withdrawal symptoms. *Journal of Abnormal Psychology, 107,* 238–251.

Pickles, J. O. (1988). *An introduction to the physiology of hearing* (2nd ed.). London: Academic Press.

Pierce, T. W., Madden, D. J., Siegel, W. C., & Blumenthal, J. A. (1993). Effects of aerobic exercise on cognitive and psychosocial functioning in patients with mild hypertension. *Health Psychology, 12,* 286–291.

Pillsworth, E. G., Haselton, M. G., & Buss, D. M. (2004). Ovulatory shifts in female sexual desire. *Journal of Sex Research, 41,* 55–65.

Pinel, J. P. J. (1997). *Biopsychology* (3rd ed.). Boston: Allyn & Bacon.

Pines, A. (1993). Burnout. In L. Goldberger & S. Breznitz (Eds.), *Handbook of stress: Theoretical and clinical aspects* (2nd ed., pp. 386–402). New York: Free Press.

Pines, A., & Aronson, E. (1988). *Career burnout: Causes and cures* (2nd ed.). New York: Free Press.

Pinker, S. (1994). *The language instinct.* New York: HarperCollins.

Pinker, S. (1997a). *How the mind works.* New York: Norton.

Pinker, S. (1997b). Language as a psychological adaptation. In G. R. Bock & G. Cardew (Eds.), *Characterizing human psychological adaptations* (pp. 162–180). New York: John Wiley.

Pinker, S. (2002). *The blank slate.* New York: Viking-Penguin.

Pinker, S., & Bloom, P. (1992). Natural language and natural selection. In J. H. Barkow & L. Cosmides (Eds.), *The adapted mind: Evolutionary psychology and the generation of culture* (pp. 451–493). New York: Oxford University Press.

Piper, A., Jr. (1997). *Hoax and reality: The bizarre world of multiple personality disorder.* Northvale, NJ: Jason Aronson.

Pittenger, D. J. (1996). Reconsidering the overjustification effect: A guide to critical resources. *Teaching of Psychology, 23,* 234–236.

Plomin, R., Corley, R., Caspi, A., Fulker, D. W., & DeFries, J. (1998). Adoption results for self-reported personality: Evidence for nonadditive genetic effects? *Journal of Personality and Social Psychology, 75,* 211–218.

Plomin, R., Fulker, D. W., Corley, R., & DeFries, J. C. (1997). Nature, nurture, and cognitive development from 1 to 16 years: A parent-offspring adoption study. *Psychological Science, 8,* 442–447.

Plous, S. (1991). An attitude survey of animal rights activists. *Psychological Science, 2,* 194–196.

Plous, S. (1996). Attitudes toward the use of animals in psychological research and education: Results from a national survey of psychologists. *American Psychologist, 51*(11), 1167–1180.

Polivy, J., & Herman, C. P. (2002). Causes of eating disorders. *Annual Review of Psychology, 53,* 187–213.

Poole, D. A., & Lindsay, D. S. (2002). Reducing child witnesses' false reports of misinformation from parents. *Journal of Experimental Child Psychology, 81,* 117–140.

Poole, D. A., Lindsay, D. S., Memon, A., & Bull, R. (1995). Psychotherapy and the recovery of memories of childhood sexual abuse: U.S. and British practitioners' opinions, practices, and experiences. *Journal of Consulting and Clinical Psychology, 63,* 426–437.

Poore, A. G., Gagne, F., Barlow, K. M., Lydon, J. E., Taylor, D. M., & Wright, S. C. (2002). Contact and the personal/group discrimination discrepancy in an Inuit community. *Journal of Psychology: Interdisciplinary and Applied, 136,* 371–382.

Pope, H. G., Gruber, A. J., Hudson, J. I., Huestis, M. A., & Yurgelun-Todd, D. (2001). Neuropsychological performance in long-term cannabis users. *Archives of General Psychiatry, 58,* 909–915.

Pope, K. S. (1996). Memory, abuse, and science: Questioning claims about the False Memory Syndrome epidemic. *American Psychologist, 51,* 957–974.

Porter, R. H., Makin, J. W., Davis, L. B., & Christensen, K. M. (1992). Breast-fed infants respond to olfactory cues from their own mother and unfamiliar lactating females. *Infant Behavior and Development, 15,* 85–93.

Posner, M. I., & Rothbart, M. K. (1992). Attentional mechanisms and conscious experience. In A. D. Milner & M. D. Rugg (Eds.), *The neuropsychology of consciousness* (pp. 91–112). London: Academic Press.

Postmes, T., & Spears, R. (1998). Deindividuation and antinormative behavior: A meta-analysis. *Psychological Bulletin, 123,* 238–259.

Potter, W. Z., & Manji, H. K. (1993). Are monamine metabolites in cerebral spinal fluid worth measuring? *Archives of General Psychiatry, 50,* 653–656.

Pratkanis, A. R., & Greenwald, A. G. (1989). A sociocognitive model of attitude structure and function. *Advances in Experimental Social Psychology, 22,* 245–285.

Pratt, G. J., Wood, D., & Alman, B. M. (1988). *A clinical hypnosis primer.* New York: Wiley.

Preece, M., & DeLongis, A. (2005). A contextual examination of stress and coping processes in stepfamilies. In T. A. Revenson, K. Kayser, & G. Bodenmann (Eds.) Couples coping with stress: Emerging perspectives on dyadic coping (pp. 51–69). Washington, DC: American Psychological Association.

Preilowski, B. (1975). Bilateral motor interaction: Perceptual-motor performance of partial and complete split-brain patients. In K. J. Zulch, O. Creutzfeldt, & G. C. Galbraith (Eds.), *Cerebral localization* (pp. 115–132). New York: Springer-Verlag.

Premack, D. (1976). *Intelligence in ape and man.* Hillsdale, NJ: Erlbaum.

Proctor, R. W., & Van Zandt, T. (1994). *Human factors in simple and complex designs.* Boston: Allyn & Bacon.

Profet, M. (1992). Pregnancy sickness as adaptation. In J. H. Barkow, L. Cosmides, & J. Tooby (Eds.), *The adapted mind: Evolutionary psychology and the generation of culture* (pp. 327–365). New York: Oxford University Press.

Prud'homme, M. J. L., Cohen, D., & Kalaska, J. F. (1994). Tactile activity in primate somatosensory cortex during active arm movements: Cytoarchitectonic distribution. *Journal of Neurophysiology, 71,* 173–181.

Prudic, J., Sackeim, H. A., & Devanand, D. P. (1990). Medication resistance and clinical response to electroconvulsive therapy. *Psychiatry Research, 31,* 287–296.

Putnam, F. W., Guroff, J. J., Silberman, E. K., Barban, L., & Post, R. M. (1986). The clinical phenomenology of multiple personality disorder: Review of 100 recent cases. *Journal of Clinical Psychiatry, 47,* 285–293.

Quinsey, V. L., Harris, G. T., Rice, M. E., & Cormier, C. (1998). *Violent offenders: Appraising and managing risk.*

Washington, DC: American Psychological Association.

Quirion, R. (1993). Cholinergic markers in Alzheimer's disease and the autoregulation of acetylcholine release. *Journal of Psychiatry and Neuroscience, 18,* 226–234.

Rachman, S. J. (1990). *Fear and courage.* New York: Freeman.

Raichle, M. E. (1994). Visualizing the mind. *Scientific American, 270,* 58–64.

Raij, T. (1999). Patterns of brain activity during visual imagery of letters. *Journal of Cognitive Neuroscience, 11,* 282–299.

Rakic, P. (1991). Plasticity of cortical development. In S. E. Brauth, W. S. Hall, & R. J. Dooling (Eds.), *Plasticity of development* (pp. 127–161). Cambridge, MA: Bradford/MIT Press.

Ramachandran, V. S. (1992). Filling in gaps in perception: I. *Current Directions in Psychological Science, 1,* 199–205.

Ramachandran, V. S., & Hirstein, W. (1998). The perception of phantom limbs: The D. O. Hebb lecture. *Brain: A Journal of Neurology, 121,* 1603–1630.

Ramsay, D. S., & Woods, S. C. (1997). Biological consequences of drug administration: Implications for acute and chronic tolerance. *Psychological Review, 104,* 170–193.

Ranganath, C., Yonelinas, A. P., Cohen, M. X., Dy, C. J., Tom, S. M., & D'Esposito, M. (2004). Dissociable correlates of recollection and familiarity within the medial temporal lobes. *Neuropsychologia, 42,* 2–13.

Rankin, C. H. (2002). A bite to remember. *Science, 296,* 1624–1625.

Raugh, M. R., & Atkinson, R. C. (1975). A mnemonic method for learning a second-language vocabulary. *Journal of Educational Psychology, 67,* 1–16.

Raven, J. C., Court, J. H., & Raven, J. (1985). *A manual for Raven's progressive matrices and vocabulary scales.* London: H. K. Lewis.

Rea, C. P., & Modigliani, V. (1988). Educational implications of the spacing effect. In M. M. Gruneberg & P. E. Morris (Eds.), *Practical aspects of memory: Current research and issues: Memory in everyday life* (pp. 402–406). New York: John Wiley & Sons.

Read, J. D. (1996). From a passing thought to a false memory in 2 minutes:

Confusing real and illusory events. *Psychonomic Bulletin and Review, 3,* 105–111.

Read, J. D., Connolly, D., & Turtle, J. W. (2001). Memory in legal contexts: Remembering events, circumstances, and people. In R. A. Schuller & J. R. P. Ogloff (Eds.), *Introduction to psychology and law: Canadian perspectives* (pp. 95–125). Toronto: University of Toronto Press.

Read, J. D., & Lindsay, D. S. (2000). "Amnesia" for summer camps and high school graduation: Memory work increases reports of prior periods of remembering less. *Journal of Traumatic Stress, 13,* 129–147.

Rechtschaffen, A., Bergmann, B. M., Everson, C. A., Kushida, C. A., & Gilliland, M. A. (2002). Sleep deprivation in the rat: X integration and discussion of the findings. *Sleep: Journal of Sleep and Sleep Disorders Research, 25,* 68–87.

Redelmeier, D. A., & Tibshirani, R. J. (1997). Association between cellular-telephone calls and motor vehicle collisions. *New England Journal of Medicine, 336,* 543–548.

Ree, M. J., & Earles, J. A. (1992). Intelligence is the best predictor of job performance. *Current Directions in Psychological Science, 1,* 86–89.

Reed, T. E., & Jensen, A. R. (1992). Conduction velocity in a brain nerve pathway correlates with intelligence. *Intelligence, 16,* 259–272.

Regan, D. (1981). Evoked potential studies of visual perception. *Canadian Journal of Psychology, 35*(2), 77–112.

Reingold, E. M. (2004). Unconscious perception: Assumptions and interpretive difficulties. *Consciousness and Cognition: An International Journal, 13*(1), 117–122.

Reisberg, D. (2001). *Cognition: The science of the mind* (2nd ed.). New York: W. W. Norton.

Reisberg, D., & Chambers, D. (1991). Neither pictures nor propositions: What can we learn from a mental image? *Canadian Journal of Psychology, 45,* 336–352.

Reker, G. T. (1995). Quantitative and qualitative methods. In M. Kimble, S. McFadden, J. W. Ellor, & J. Seeber (Eds.), *Aging, spirituality, and religion: A handbook* (pp. 568–588). Minneapolis, MN: Fortress Press.

Reker, G. T. (1997). Personal meaning, optimism and choice: Existential problems of depression in community and institutional elderly. *The Gerontologist, 37*, 709–716.

Rennie, D. L. (2002). Making a clearing: Qualitative research in anglophone Canadian psychology [Special issue–Qualitative research: History, theory and practice]. *Canadian Psychology, 43*(3), 139–140.

Rentfrow, P. J., & Gosling, S. D. (2003). The do-re-mi's of everyday life: Examining the structure and personality correlates of music preferences. *Journal of Personality and Social Psychology, 84*, 1236–1256.

Rescorla, R. A. (1980). Simultaneous and successive associations in sensory preconditioning. *Journal of Experimental Psychology: Animal Behavior Processes, 6*, 207–216.

Rescorla, R. A. (1988). Pavlovian conditioning: It's not what you think it is. *American Psychologist, 43*, 151–160.

Resnick, S. M., Berenbaum, S. A., Gottesman, I. I., & Bouchard, T. J. (1986). Early hormonal influences on cognitive functioning in congenital adrenal hyperplasia. *Developmental Psychology, 22*, 191–198.

Revelle, W. (1995). Personality processes. *Annual Review of Psychology, 46*, 295–328.

Revonsuo, A. (2000). Did ancestral humans dream for their lives? *Behavioral and Brain Sciences, 23*, 1063–1082; 1083–1121.

Revonsuo, A. (2001). Can functional brain imaging discover consciousness in the brain? *Journal of Consciousness Studies, 8*(3), 3–23.

Reynolds, D. J., & Gifford, R. (2001). The sounds and sights of intelligence: A lens model channel analysis. *Personality and Social Psychology Bulletin, 27*, 187–200.

Rhodes, G., & Tremewan, T. (1996). Averageness, exaggeration, and facial attractiveness. *Psychological Science, 7*, 105–110.

Ribaupierre, F. (1997). Acoustical information processing in the auditory thalamus and cerebral cortex. In G. Ehret & R. Romand (Eds.), *The central auditory system* (pp. 317–397). New York: Oxford University Press.

Riccio, D. C., Millin, P. M., & Gisquet-Verrier, P. (2003). Retrograde amnesia: Forgetting back. *Current Directions in Psychological Science, 12*, 41–44.

Rice, M. E. (1997). Violent offender research and implications for the criminal justice system. *American Psychologist, 52*(4), 414–423.

Richards, F. A., & Commons, M. L. (1990). Postformal cognitive-developmental theory and research: A review of its current status. In C. N. Alexander & E. J. Langer (Eds.), *Higher stages of human development: Perspectives on adult growth* (pp. 139–161). New York: Oxford University Press.

Rickels, K., Schweizer, E., Case, W. G., & Greenblatt, D. J. (1990). Long-term therapeutic use of benzodiazepines. I. Effects of abrupt discontinuation. *Archives of General Psychiatry, 47*, 899–907.

Rieber, R. W. (1999). Hypnosis, false memory and multiple personality: A trinity of affinity. *History of Psychiatry, 10*(37, Pt. 1), 3–11.

Riegel, K. F. (1976). The dialectics of human development. *American Psychologist, 31*, 689–700.

Riggs, D. A., & Foa, E. B. (1993). Obsessive-compulsive disorder. In D. H. Barlow (Ed.), *Clinical handbook of psychological disorders* (2nd ed., pp. 180–239). New York: Guilford Press.

Rijsdijk, F. V., Vernon, P. A., & Boomsma, D. I. (1998). The genetic basis of the relation between speed-of-information processing and IQ. *Behavioural Brain Research, 95*, 77–84.

Rivett, M. (1998). The family therapy journals in 1997: A thematic review. *Journal of Family Therapy, 20*, 423–430.

Robbins, T. W. (1997). Arousal systems and attentional processes. *Biological Psychology, 45*, 57–71.

Robey, R. R., & Dalebout, S. D. (1998). A tutorial on conducting meta-analyses of clinical outcome research. *Journal of Speech Language and Hearing Research, 41*, 1227–1241.

Robins, R. W., Gosling, S. D., & Craik, K. H. (1999). An empirical analysis of trends in psychology. *American Psychologist, 54*, 117–128.

Robinson, J. O., Rosen, M., Revill, S. I., David, H., & Rus, G. A. D. (1980). Self-administered intravenous and intramuscular pethidine. *Anaesthesia, 35*, 763–770.

Robinson, T. E., & Kolb, B. (2004). Structural plasticity associated with exposure to drugs of abuse. *Neuropharmacology, 47*, 33–46.

Rodin, J. (1981). Current status of the internal-external hypothesis for obesity: What went wrong? *American Psychologist, 36*, 361–372.

Rodin, J., Schank, D., & Striegal-Moore, R. H. (1989). Psychological features of obesity. *Medical Clinics of North America, 73*, 47–66.

Roediger, H. L., III, & Karpicke, J. D. (2006). Test-enhanced learning: Taking memory tests improves long-term retention. *Psychological Science, 17*, 249–255.

Roediger, H. L., III, & McDermott, K. B. (1993). Implicit memory in normal human subjects. In F. Boller & J. Grafman (Eds.), *Handbook of neuropsychology* (Vol. 8, pp. 63–131). Amsterdam: Elsevier.

Roediger, H. L., III, & McDermott, K. B. (1995). Creating false memories: Remembering words not presented in lists. *Journal of Experimental Psychology: Learning, Memory, and Cognition, 21*, 803–814.

Roediger, H. L., III, Weldon, M. S., & Challis, B. H. (1989). Explaining dissociations between implicit and explicit measures of retention: A processing account. In H. L. Roediger & F. I. M. Craik (Eds.), *Varieties of memory and consciousness: Essays in honour of Endel Tulving* (pp. 355–389). Hillsdale, NJ: Erlbaum.

Roediger, H. L., III, Weldon, M. S., Stadler, M. L., & Riegler, G. L. (1992). Direct comparison of two implicit memory tests: Word fragment and word stem completion. *Journal of Experimental Psychology: Learning, Memory, and Cognition, 18*, 1251–1269.

Roesler, A., & Witztum, E. (1998). Treatment of men with paraphilia with a long-acting analogue of gonadotropin-releasing hormone. *New England Journal of Medicine, 338*, 416–422.

Rogers, C. R. (1951). *Client-centered therapy*. Boston: Houghton Mifflin.

Rogers, C. R. (1961). *On becoming a person: A therapist's view of psychotherapy*. Boston: Houghton Mifflin.

Rogers, C. R. (1963). The actualizing tendency in relation to "motives" and to consciousness. In M. R. Jones (Ed.), *Nebraska symposium on motivation* (Vol. 11, pp. 1–24). Lincoln: University of Nebraska.

Rogers, S. M., & Turner, C. F. (1991). Male-male sexual contact in the U.S.A.: Findings from five sample surveys, 1970–1990. *Journal of Sex Research, 28,* 491–519.

Roitblat, H. L., & von Ferson, L. (1992). Comparative cognition: Representations and processes in learning and memory. *Annual Review of Psychology, 43,* 671–710.

Rolls, E. T. (1995). Central taste anatomy and neurophysiology. In R. L. Doty (Ed.), *Handbook of olfaction and gustation* (pp. 549–573). New York: Dekker.

Roney, C. J. R., & Trick, L. M. (2003). Grouping and gambling: A gestalt approach to understanding the gambler's fallacy. *Canadian Journal of Experimental Psychology, 57*(2), 69–75.

Rosch, E., & Mervis, C. B. (1975). Family resemblances: Studies in the internal structure of categories. *Cognitive Psychology, 7,* 573–605.

Rosch, E., Mervis, C. B., Gray, W. D., Johnson, D. M., & Bayes-Braem, P. (1976). Basic objects in natural categories. *Cognitive Psychology, 8,* 382–439.

Rosen, D. L., & Singh, S. (1992). An investigation of subliminal embed effect on multiple measures of advertising effectiveness. *Psychology and Marketing, 9,* 157–173.

Rosenbaum, M. E. (1986). The repulsion hypothesis: On the nondevelopment of relationships. *Journal of Personality and Social Psychology, 51,* 1156–1166.

Rosenhan, D. L. (1973). On being sane in insane places. *Science, 179,* 250–258.

Rosenthal, R. (1966). *Experimenter effects in behavioral research.* New York: Appleton-Century-Crofts.

Rosenthal, R. (1994). Science and ethics in conducting, analyzing, and reporting psychological research. *Psychological Science, 5,* 127–134.

Rosenthal, R. (2002). Covert communication in classrooms, clinics, courtrooms, and cubicles. *American Psychologist, 57*(11), 839–849.

Rosenthal, R., & Jacobson, L. (1968). *Pygmalion in the classroom: Teachers' expectations and pupils' intellectual development.* New York: Holt, Rinehart & Winston.

Rosenthal, R., & Rosnow, R. L. (Eds.). (1969). *Artifact in behavioral research.* New York: Academic Press.

Rosenthal, R., & Rosnow, R. L. (1975). *The volunteer subject.* New York: Wiley.

Rosenthal, R., & Rosnow, R. L. (1991). *Essentials of behavioral research:*

Methods and data analysis (2nd ed.). New York: McGraw-Hill.

Rosenzweig, S. (1936). Some implicit common factors in diverse methods of psychotherapy. *American Journal of Orthopsychiatry, 6,* 422–425.

Ross, C. A., Miller, S. D., Reagor, P., Bjornson, L., Fraser, G. A., & Anderson, G. (1990). Structured interview data on 102 cases of multiple personality disorder from four centers. *American Journal of Psychiatry, 147,* 596–601.

Ross, L. (1977). The intuitive psychologist and his shortcomings: Distortions in the attribution process. In L. Berkowitz (Ed.), *Advances in experimental social psychology* (Vol. 10, pp. 174–214). New York: Academic Press.

Ross, M., & Wilson, A. E. (2000). Constructing and appraising past selves. In D. L. Schacter & E. Scarry (Eds.), *Memory, brain, and belief* (pp. 231–258). Cambridge, MA: Harvard University Press.

Rothbart, M. K., Ahadi, S. A., Hershey, K., & Fisher, P. (2001). Investigations of temperament at three to seven years: The children's behavior questionnaire. *Child Development, 72*(5), 1394–1408.

Rotter, J. B. (1966). Generalized expectancies for internal versus external locus of control of reinforcement. *Psychological Monographs, 80*(Whole No. 609).

Rotter, J. B., Liverant, S., & Crowne, D. P. (1961). The growth and extinction of expectancies in change controlled and skilled tasks. *Journal of Psychology, 52,* 161–177.

Rovee-Collier, C. (1993). The capacity for long-term memory in infancy. *Current Directions in Psychological Science, 2,* 130–135.

Roy, M. M., & Christenfeld, N. J. S. (2004). Do dogs resemble their owners? *Psychological Science, 15,* 361–363.

Rozin, P. (1990). Development in the food domain. *Developmental Psychology, 26,* 555–562.

Rozin, P., & Fallon, A. E. (1987). A perspective on disgust. *Psychological Review, 94,* 23–41.

Rozin, P., Hammer, L., Oster, H., Horowitz, T., & Marmara, V. (1986). The child's conception of food: Development of categories of accepted and rejected substances.

Journal of Nutrition Education, 18, 75–81.

Rubinsky, H., Eckerman, D., Rubinsky, E., & Hoover, C. (1987). Early-phase physiological response patterns to psychosexual stimuli: Comparisons of male and female patterns. *Archives of Sexual Behavior, 16,* 45–55.

Ruble, D. N., Balaban, T., & Cooper, J. (1981). Gender constancy and the effects of sex-typed televised toy commercials. *Child Development, 52,* 667–673.

Ruble, D. N., & Martin, C. L. (1998). Gender development. In W. Damon & N. Eisenberg (Eds.), *Handbook of child psychology: Social, emotional, and personality development* (pp. 933–1016). New York: Wiley.

Rudman, L. A., & Borgida, E. (1995). The afterglow of construct accessibility: The behavioral consequences of priming men to view women as sexual objects. *Journal of Experimental Social Psychology, 31,* 493–517.

Rumbaugh, D. M. (Ed.). (1977). *Language learning by a chimpanzee: The Lana project.* New York: Academic Press.

Rummel, A., & Feinberg, R. (1988). Cognitive evaluation theory: A meta-analytic review of the literature. *Social Behavior and Personality, 16,* 147–164.

Rushton, J. P. (2000). *Race, evolution, and behavior: A life-history perspective* (3rd ed.). Port Huron, MI: Charles Darwin Research Institute.

Russek, M. (1971). Hepatic receptors and the neurophysiological mechanisms controlling feeding behavior. *Neuroscience Research, 4,* 213–282.

Russell, J. A. (1994). Is there universal recognition of emotion from facial expression? A review of the cross-cultural studies. *Psychological Bulletin, 115,* 102–141.

Russell, J. A. (2003). Core affect and the psychological construction of emotion. *Psychological Review, 110,* 145–172.

Russell, J. A., Bachorowski, J., & Fernandez-Dols, J. (2003). Facial and vocal expressions of emotion. *Annual Review of Psychology, 54,* 329–349.

Russell, J. A., & Yik, M. S. M. (1996). Emotion among the Chinese. In M. H. Bond (Ed.), *The handbook of Chinese psychology* (pp. 166–188). Hong Kong: Oxford University Press.

Ryan, K. M. (2004). Further evidence for a cognitive component of rape. *Aggression & Violent Behavior, 9,* 579–604.

Ryckman, R. M. (2004). *Theories of personality* (8th ed.). Belmont, CA: Wadsworth.

Ryder, A. G., Alden, L., & Paulhus, D. L. (2000). Is acculturation unidimensional or bidimensional? A head-to-head comparison in the prediction of demographics, personality, self-identity, and adjustment. *Journal of Personality and Social Psychology, 79,* 49–65.

Sackeim, H. (1999). The anticonvulsant hypothesis of the mechanisms of action of ECT. Current status. *Journal of ECT, 15,* 5–26.

Sackeim, H. A. (1983). Self-deception, self-esteem, and depression: The adaptive value of lying to oneself. In J. Masling (Ed.), *Empirical studies of psychoanalytic theories* (pp. 101–157). Hillsdale, NJ: Erlbaum.

Sackeim, H. A., Prudic, J., Devanand, D. P., Nobler, M. S., Lisanby, S. H., Peyser, S., et al. (2000). A prospective, randomized, double-blind comparison of bilateral and right unilateral electroconvulsive therapy at different stimulus intensities. *Archives of General Psychiatry, 57,* 425–434.

Sagie, A., Elizur, D., & Yamauchi, H. (1996). The structure and strength of achievement motivation: A cross-cultural comparison. *Journal of Organizational Behavior, 17,* 431–444.

Saitoh, T., Kang, D., Mallory, M., DeTeresa, R., & Masliah, E. (1997). Glial cells in Alzheimer's disease. Preferential effect of APOE risk on scattered microglia. *Gerontology, 43,* 109–118.

Sakai, F., Stirling Meyer, J., Karacan, I., Yamaguchi, F., & Yamamoto, M. (1979). Narcolepsy: Regional cerebral blood flow during sleep and wakefulness. *Neurology, 29,* 61–67.

Saklofske, D. H., & Greenspoon, P. J. (2000). Confirmatory factor analysis of the MSLSS: A reply to Shevlin et al. *Personality and Individual Differences, 28,* 187–190.

Salkovskis, P. M. (1985). Obsessional compulsive problems: A cognitive behavioral analysis. *Behaviour Research and Therapy, 23,* 571–577.

Salman, M. S. (2002). The cerebellum: It's about time! But timing is not everything—New insights into the role of the cerebellum in timing motor and cognitive tasks. *Journal of Child Neurology, 17,* 1–9.

Salmon, C. A., & Daly, M. (1998). Birth order and familial sentiment: Middleborns are different. *Evolution and Human Behavior, 19,* 299–312.

Salovey, P., & Mayer, J. D. (1990). Emotional intelligence. *Imagination, Cognition, and Personality, 9,* 185–211.

Salthouse, T. A. (1994). The nature of the influence of speed on adult age differences in cognition. *Developmental Psychology, 30,* 240–259.

Sameroff, A. J., Seifer, R., Baldwin, A., & Baldwin, C. (1993). Stability of intelligence from preschool to adolescence: The influence of social and family risk factors. *Child Development, 64,* 80–97.

Sanders, R. J. (1989). Sentence comprehension following agenesis of the corpus callosum. *Brain and Language, 37,* 59–72.

Sanderson, W. C., & Barlow, D. H. (1990). A description of patients diagnosed with a DSM-II-R anxiety disorder. *Journal of Nervous and Mental Disease, 178,* 588–591.

Sanson, A., & di-Muccio, C. (1993). The influence of aggressive and neutral cartoons and toys on the behaviour of preschool children. *Australian Psychologist, 28,* 93–99.

Sansone, C., & Harackiewicz, J. M. (Ed.). (2000). *Intrinsic and extrinsic motivation: The search for optimal motivation and performance.* San Diego, CA: Academic Press.

Santi, A., Weise, L., & Kuiper, D. (1995). Memory for event duration in rats. *Learning and Motivation, 26,* 83–100.

Sarason, I. G., Sarason, B. R., & Pierce, G. R. (1994). Social support: Global and relationship-based levels of analysis. *Journal of Social and Personal Relationships, 11,* 295–312.

Sarbin, T. R., & Coe, W. C. (1972). *Hypnosis: A social psychological analysis of influence communication.* New York: Holt, Rinehart & Winston.

Saron, C. D., & Davidson, R. J. (1989). Visual evoked potential measures of interhemispheric transfer times in humans. *Behavioral Neuroscience, 103,* 1115–1138.

Sato, W., Kochiyama, T., Yoshikawa, S., Naito, E., & Matsumura, M. (2004). Enhanced neural activity in response to dynamic facial expressions of emotion: An fMRI study. *Cognitive Brain Research, 20,* 81–91.

Saunders, B. A. C., & van Brakel, J. (1997). Are there nontrivial constraints on colour categorization? *Behavioral and Brain Sciences, 20*(2), 167–228.

Savage-Rumbaugh, S., McDonald, D., Sevcik, R., Hopkins, W., & Rupert, E. (1986). Spontaneous symbol acquisition and communicative use by pygmie chimpanzees. *Journal of Experimental Psychology: General, 115,* 211–235.

Savage-Rumbaugh, S., Murphy, J., Sevcik, R., Brakke, K., Williams, S., & Rumbaugh, D. M. (1993). Language comprehension in ape and child. *Monographs of the Society for Research in Child Development, 58*(3–4, Serial No. 233).

Scarr, S., & Weinberg, R. A. (1976). IQ test performance of black children adopted by white families. *American Psychologist, 31,* 726–739.

Schachter, S. (1971). *Emotion, obesity, and crime.* New York: Academic Press.

Schachter, S., & Gross, L. (1968). Manipulated time and eating behavior. *Journal of Personality and Social Psychology, 10,* 98–106.

Schachter, S., & Singer, J. E. (1962). Cognitive, social, and physiological determinants of emotional state. *Psychological Review, 69,* 379–399.

Schacter, D. L. (2001). *The seven sins of memory: How the mind forgets and remembers.* Boston: Houghton Mifflin.

Schacter, D. L., Norman, K. A., & Koutstaal, W. (1998). The cognitive neuroscience of constructive memory. *Annual Review of Psychology, 49,* 289–318.

Schaie, K. W. (1983). The Seattle Longitudinal Study: A twenty-one-year exploration of psychometric intelligence in adulthood. In K. W. Schaie (Ed.), *Longitudinal studies of adult psychological development* (pp. 64–135). New York: Guilford Press.

Schaie, K. W. (1989). The hazards of cognitive aging. *Gerontologist, 29,* 484–493.

Schaie, K. W. (1993). The Seattle Longitudinal Studies of Adult Intelligence. *Current Directions in Psychological Science, 2,* 171–175.

Schaie, K. W. (1998). The Seattle Longitudinal Studies of Adult Intelligence. In M. P. Lawton & T. A. Salthouse (Eds.), *Essential papers on the psychology of aging. Essential papers in psychoanalysis* (pp. 263–271). New York: New York University Press.

Schall, J. D. (2004). On building a bridge between brain and behavior. *Annual Review of Psychology, 55,* 23–50.

Schaller, M. (1997). The psychological consequences of fame: Three tests of the self-consciousness hypothesis. *Journal of Personality, 65,* 291–309.

Schaller, M., Conway, L. G., & Tanchuk, T. L. (2002). Selective pressures on the once and future contents of ethnic stereotypes: Effects of the communicability of traits. *Journal of Personality and Social Psychology, 82,* 861–877.

Schedlowski, M., Fluge, T., Richter, S., & Tewes, U. (1995). b-Endorphin, but not substance-P, is increased by acute stress in humans. *Psychoneuroendocrinology, 20,* 103–110.

Scheich, H., & Zuschratter, W. (1995). Mapping of stimulus features and meaning in gerbil auditory cortex with 2–deoxyglucose and c-fos antibodies. *Behavioural Brain Research, 66,* 195–205.

Scheier, M. F., & Carver, C. S. (1993). On the power of positive thinking: The benefits of being optimistic. *Current Directions in Psychological Science, 2,* 26–30.

Scheier, M. F., Matthews, K. A., Owens, J. F., Magovern, G. J., Sr., Lefebvre, R. C., Abbott, R. A., et al. (1989). Dispositional optimism and recovery from coronary artery bypass surgery: The beneficial effects on physical and psychological well-being. *Journal of Personality and Social Psychology, 57,* 1024–1040.

Schifano, F. (2004). A bitter pill. Overview of ecstasy (MDMA, MDA) related fatalities. *Psychopharmacology, 173*(3–4), 242–248.

Schiller, P. H., Logothetis, N. K., & Charles, E. R. (1990). Functions of the colour-opponent and broad-channels of the visual system. *Nature, 343,* 68–70.

Schleifer, S. J., Keller, S. E., Meyerson, A. T., Raskin, M. J., Davis, K. L., & Stein, M. (1983). Suppression of lymphocyte stimulation following bereavement.

Journal of the American Medical Association, 250, 374.

Schlenker, B. R., & Forsyth, D. R. (1977). On the ethics of psychological research. *Journal of Experimental Social Psychology, 13,* 369–396.

Schmahmann, J. D., & Sherman, J. C. (1998). The cerebellar cognitive affective syndrome. *Brain, 121,* 561–579.

Schmidt, F. L., & Hunter, J. E. (1993). Tacit knowledge, practical intelligence, general mental ability, and job knowledge. *Current Directions in Psychological Science, 2,* 8–9.

Schmidt, F. L., & Hunter, J. E. (1998). The validity and utility of selection methods in personnel psychology: Practical and theoretical implications of 85 years of research findings. *Psychological Bulletin, 124,* 262–274.

Schmitt, D. P. (2003). Universal sex differences in the desire for sexual variety: Tests from 52 nations, 6 continents, and 13 islands. *Journal of Personality and Social Psychology, 85,* 85–104.

Schmuckler, M. A., & Proffitt, D. R. (1994). Infants' perception of kinetic depth and stereokinetic displays. *Journal of Experimental Psychology: Human Perception and Performance, 20,* 122–130.

Schnapf, J. L., & Baylor, D. A. (1987, April). How photoreceptor cells respond to light. *Scientific American, 256,* 40–47.

Schneider, J. S., Sun, Z. Q., & Roeltgen, D. P. (1994). Effects of dopamine agonists on delayed response performance in chronic low-dose MPTP-treated monkeys. *Pharmacology, Biochemistry, and Behavior, 48,* 235–240.

Schneiderman, N., Antoni, M. H., Ironson, G., Laperriere, A., & Fletcher, M. A. (1992). Applied psychological science and HIV-1 spectrum disease. *Applied and Preventive Psychology, 1,* 67–82.

Schneiderman, N., Antoni, M. H., Saab, P. G., & Ironson, G. (2001). Health psychology: Psychosocial and biobehavioral aspects of chronic disease management. *Annual Review of Psychology, 52,* 555–580.

Schooler, J. W. (2002). Verbalization produces a transfer inappropriate processing shift. *Applied Cognitive Psychology, 16*(8), 989–997.

Schooler, J. W., Reichle, E. D., & Halpern, D. V. (2004). Zoning out while reading: Evidence for dissociations between

experience and metaconsciousness. In D. T. Levin (Ed.), *Thinking and seeing: Visual metacognition in adults and children* (pp. 203–226). Cambridge, MA: MIT Press.

Schooler, J. W., & Schreiber, C. A. (2004). Experience, meta-consciousness, and the paradox of introspection. *Journal of Consciousness Studies, 11*(7), 17–39.

Schreiber, F. (1973). *Sybil.* New York: Warner Books.

Schretlen, D., Pearlson, G. D., Anthony, J. C., Ayward, E. H., Augustine, A., Davis, A., et al. (2000). Elucidating the contributions of processing speed, executive ability, and frontal lobe volume to normal age-related differences in fluid intelligence. *Journal of the International Neuropsychological Society, 6,* 52–61.

Schroeder, D. H., & Costa, P. T. (1984). Influence of life event stress on physical illness: Substantive effects or methodological flaws? *Journal of Personality and Social Psychology, 46,* 853–863.

Schroeder, K. E., Schwarzer, R., & Endler, N. S. (1997). Predicting cardiac patients' quality of life from the characteristics of their spouses. *Journal of Health Psychology, 2,* 231–244.

Schuller, R. A., & Ogloff, J. R. P. (Eds.). (2001). *Introduction to psychology and law: Canadian perspectives.* Toronto: University of Toronto Press.

Schuster, M. A., Stein, B. D., Jaycox, L. H., Collins, R. L., Marshall, G. N., Elliott, M. N., et al. (2001). A national survey of stress reactions after the September 11, 2001, terrorist attacks. *New England Journal of Medicine, 345,* 1507–1512.

Schwartz, B. (1990). The creation and destruction of value. *American Psychologist, 45,* 7–15.

Schwartz, C. E., Snidman, N., & Kagan, J. (1996). Early childhood temperament as a determinant of externalizing behavior in adolescence. *Development and Psychopathology, 8,* 527–537.

Schweickert, R., Guentert, L., & Hersberger, L. (1990). Phonological similarity, pronunciation rate, and memory span. *Psychological Science, 1,* 74–77.

Schweinberger, S. R., & Stief, V. (2001). Implicit perception in patients with visual neglect: Lexical specificity in repetition priming. *Neuropsychologia, 39,* 420–429.

Sclafani, A. (1994). Eating rates in normal and hypothalamic hyperphagic rats. *Physiology and Behavior, 55,* 489–494.

Sebrechts, M. M., Marsh, R. L., & Seamon, J. G. (1989). Secondary memory and very rapid forgetting. *Memory and Cognition, 17,* 693–700.

Seegert, C. R. (2003). Token economies and incentive programs: Behavioral improvement in mental health inmates housed in state prisons. *Behavior Therapist, 208,* 210–211.

Seeman, P., Lee, T., Chau Wong, M., & Wong, K. (1976). Antipsychotic drug doses and neuroleptic/dopamine receptors. *Nature, 261,* 717–719.

Segall, M. H., Dasen, P. R., Berry, J. W., & Poortinga, Y. (1990). *Human behavior in global perspective.* New York: Pergamon Press.

Segerstrom, S. C., Taylor, S. E., Kemeny, M. E., & Fahey, J. L. (1998). Optimism is associated with mood, coping, and immune change in response to stress. *Journal of Personality and Social Psychology, 74,* 1646–1655.

Seidenberg, M. S., & Petitto, L. A. (1987). Communication, symbolic communication, and language: Comment on Savage-Rumbaugh, McDonald, Sevcik, Hopkins, and Rupert (1986). *Journal of Experimental Psychology: General, 116*(3), 279–287.

Sekular, R., & Blake, R. (1990). *Perception* (2nd ed.). New York: McGraw-Hill.

Sekuler, A. B. (1994). Local and global minima in visual completion: Effects of symmetry and orientation. *Perception, 23,* 529–545.

Seligman, M. E. P. (1975). *Helplessness: On depression, development, and death.* San Francisco: Freeman.

Seligman, M. E. P. (2002). *Authentic happiness: Using the new positive psychology to realize your potential for lasting fulfilment.* New York: Free Press.

Selkoe, D. J. (1992, September). Aging brain, aging mind. *Scientific American, 267,* 135–142.

Sellers, J. G., Mehl, M. R., & Josephs, R. A. (in press). Hormones and personality: Testosterone as a marker of individual differences. *Journal of Research in Personality.*

Selye, H. (1936). A syndrome produced by diverse nocuous agents. *Nature, 138,* 32.

Selye, H. (1952). *The story of the adaptation syndrome.* Montreal: Acta.

Selye, H. (1974). *Stress without distress.* Philadelphia: Lippincott.

Sepple, C. P., & Read, N. W. (1989). Gastrointestinal correlates of the development of hunger in man. *Appetite, 13,* 183–191.

Servos, P., & Goodale, M. A. (1995). Preserved visual imagery in visual form agnosia. *Neuropsychologia, 33*(11), 1383–1394.

Servos, P., Wilson, D., Gati, J., & Lederman, S. (2001). fMRI-derived cortical maps for haptic shape, texture, and hardness. *Cognitive Brain Research, 12*(2), 307–313.

Shaffer, D. R. (1993). *Developmental psychology: Childhood and adolescence* (3rd ed.). Pacific Grove, CA: Brooks/Cole.

Shaffer, D. R. (2002). *Developmental psychology: Childhood and adolescence* (6th ed.). Pacific Grove, CA: Brooks/Cole.

Shane, M. S., & Peterson, J. B. (2004). Defensive copers show a deficit in passive avoidance learning on Newman's go/no-go task: Implications for self-deception and socialization. *Journal of Personality, 72,* 939–965.

Shapiro, A. K. (1960). A contribution to a history of the placebo effect. *Behavioral Science, 5,* 109–135.

Shapiro, K. L., & Raymond, J. E. (1994). Temporal allocation of visual attention: Inhibition or interference? In D. Dagenbach & T. H. Carr (Eds.), *Inhibitory processes in attention, memory, and language* (pp. 151–188). San Diego, CA: Academic Press.

Shapley, R. (1990). Visual sensitivity and parallel retinocortical channels. *Annual Review of Psychology, 41,* 635–658.

Sharma, K. N., Anand, B. K., Due, S., & Singh, B. (1961). Role of stomach in regulation of activities of hypothalamic feeding centers. *American Journal of Physiology, 201,* 593–598.

Sharpe, D., & Adair, J. G. (1993). Reversibility of the hindsight bias: Manipulation of experimental demands. *Organizational Behavior and Human Decision Processes, 56,* 233–245.

Shaw, C. A., & McEachern, J. C. (Eds.). (2001). *Toward a theory of neuroplasticity.* Philadelphia: Psychology Press.

Shepard, R. N. (1990). *Mind sights.* New York: W. H. Freeman.

Shepard, R. N., & Cooper, L. A. (1986). *Mental images and their transformations.* Cambridge, MA: MIT Press.

Sher, L. (2004). Hypothalamic-pituitary-adrenal function and preventing major depressive episodes. *Canadian Journal of Psychiatry, 49,* 574–575.

Sheridan, C. L., & Radmacher, S. A. (1992). *Health psychology: Challenging the biomedical model.* New York: Wiley.

Shields, S. A. (1975). Functionalism, Darwinism, and the psychology of women: A study in social myth. *American Psychologist, 30,* 739–754.

Shiffrin, R. M., & Schneider, W. (1977). Controlled and automatic human information processing II: Perceptual learning, automatic attending, and a general theory. *Psychological Review, 84,* 127–190.

Shirley, S. G., & Persaud, K. C. (1990). The biochemistry of vertebrate olfaction and taste. *Seminars in the Neurosciences, 2,* 59–68.

Shweder, R. A., Mahapatra, M., & Miller, J. G. (1990). Culture and moral development. In J. W. Stigler, R. A. Shweder, & G. Herdt (Eds.), *Cultural psychology* (pp. 1–83). New York: Cambridge University Press.

Siegel, J. M. (1990). Stressful life events and use of physician services among the elderly: The moderating role of pet ownership. *Journal of Personality and Social Psychology, 58,* 1081–1086.

Siegel, S. (2005). Drug tolerance, drug addiction, and drug anticipation. *Current Directions in Psychological Science, 14,* 296–300.

Siegel, S., Baptista, M. A. S., Kim, J. A., McDonald, R. V., & Weise-Kelly, L. (2000). Pavlovian psychopharmacology: The associative basis of tolerance. *Experimental and Clinical Psychopharmacology, 27,* 125–136.

Siegler, R. S. (1996). *Children's thinking: Beyond the immaculate transition.* New York: Oxford University Press.

Sigelman, C. K., & Shaffer, D. R. (1995). *Life-span human development* (2nd ed.). Pacific Grove, CA: Brooks/Cole.

Sigmundson, H. K. (1994). Pharmacotherapy of schizophrenia: A review. *Canadian Journal of Psychiatry, 39,* 570–575.

Silber, M. H. (2001). Sleep disorders. *Neurologic Clinics, 19,* 173–186.

Silverman, I., & Choi, J. (2005). Locating places. In D. M. Buss (Ed.), *The handbook of evolutionary psychology* (pp. 177–199). New York: John Wiley & Sons.

Silverstein, B., Perdue, L., Peterson, B., & Kelly, E. (1986). The role of the mass media in promoting a thin standard of bodily attractiveness for women. *Sex Roles, 14*, 519–532.

Simon, H. A. (1969). *The sciences of the artificial.* Cambridge, MA: MIT Press.

Simon, H. A. (1992). What is an "explanation" of behavior? *Psychological Science, 3*, 150–161.

Sims, A. C. P., & Sims, D. (1998). The phenomenology of post-traumatic stress disorder: A symptomatic study of 70 victims of psychological trauma. *Psychopathology, 31*, 96–112.

Single, E., Robson, L., Xie, X., Rehm, J., in collaboration with Moore, R., Cho, B., Desjardins, S., & Anderson, J. (1996). *The cost of substance abuse in Canada.* Ottawa, ON: Canadian Centre of Substance Abuse.

Single, E. W., Brewster, J. M., MacNeil, P., Hatcher, J., & Trainor, C. (1995). The 1993 General Social Survey II: Alcohol problems in Canada. *Canadian Journal of Public Health, 86*(6), 402–407.

Siqueland, E. R., & DeLucia, C. A. (1969). Visual reinforcement of nonnutritive sucking in human infants. *Science, 165*, 1144–1146.

Skinner, B. F. (1938). *The behavior of organisms: An experimental analysis.* New York: Appleton-Century.

Skinner, B. F. (1948). "Superstition" in the pigeon. *Journal of Experimental Psychology, 38*, 168–172.

Skinner, B. F. (1956). A case history in scientific method. *American Psychologist, 11*, 221–233.

Skinner, B. F. (1969). *Contingencies of reinforcement: A theoretical analysis.* New York: Appleton-Century-Crofts.

Skinner, B. F. (1974). *About behaviorism.* New York: Knopf.

Slater, A., Von der Schulenburg, C., Brown, E., Badenoch, M., Butterworth, G., Parsons, S., et al. (1998). Newborn infants prefer attractive faces. *Infant Behavior and Development, 21*, 345–354.

Slater, E., & Glithero, E. (1965). A follow-up of patients diagnosed as suffering from hysteria. *Journal of Psychosomatic Research, 9*, 9–13.

Sloane, R. B., Staples, F. R., Cristol, A. H., Yorkston, N. J., & Whipple, K. (1975). *Psychotherapy versus behavior therapy.* Cambridge, MA: Harvard University Press.

Slovic, P., Fischoff, B., & Lichtenstein, S. (1982). Facts versus fears: Understanding perceived risk. In D. Kahneman, P. Slovic, & A. Tversky (Eds.), *Judgment under uncertainty: Heuristics and biases* (pp. 463–492). Cambridge: Cambridge University Press.

Slugoski, B. R., & Wilson, A. E. (1998). Contribution of conversation skills to the production of judgmental errors. *European Journal of Social Psychology, 28*(4), 575–601.

Small, D. M., Zald, D. H., Jones-Gotman, M., Zatorre, R. J., Pardo, J. V., Frey, S., et al. (1999). Human cortical gustatory areas: A review of functional neuroimaging data. *Neuroreport: For Rapid Communication of Neuroscience Research, 10*, 7–14.

Smiley, P. A., & Dweck, C. S. (1994). Individual differences in achievement goals among young children. *Child Development, 65*, 1723–1743.

Smith, B. N., Kerr, N. A., Markus, M. J., & Stasson, M. F. (2001). Individual differences in social loafing: Need for cognition as a motivator in collective performance. *Group Dynamics: Theory, Research, and Practice, 5*, 150–158.

Smith, D. V., & Margolskee, R. F. (2001). Making sense of taste. *Scientific American, 284*, 32–39.

Smith, E. E. (1989). Concepts and induction. In M. Posner (Ed.), *Foundations of cognitive science* (pp. 501–526). Cambridge, MA: MIT Press.

Smith, E. E., Patalano, A. L., & Jonides, J. (1998). Alternative strategies of categorization. *Cognition, 65*, 167–196.

Smith, E. R., Stewart, T. L., & Buttram, R. T. (1992). Inferring a trait from a behavior has long-term, highly-specific effects. *Journal of Personality and Social Psychology, 62*, 753–759.

Smith, E. R., & Zárate, M. A. (1992). Exemplar-based model of social judgment. *Psychological Review, 99*, 3–21.

Smith, F. J., & Campfield, L. A. (1993). Meal initiation occurs after experimental induction of transient declines in blood glucose. *American Journal of Physiology, 265*, R1423–R1429.

Smith, J. D., Redford, J. S., & Washburn, D. A. (2005). Specific-token effects in screening tasks: Possible implications for aviation security. *Journal of Experimental Psychology: Learning, Memory, and Cognition, 31*(6), 1171–1185.

Smith, M. L., & Glass, G. V. (1977). Meta-analysis of psychotherapy outcome studies. *American Psychologist, 32*, 752–760.

Smith, M. L., Glass, G. V., & Miller, T. I. (1980). *The benefits of psychotherapy.* Baltimore: Johns Hopkins University Press.

Smuts, B. B., Cheney, D. L., Seyfarth, R. M., Wrangham, R. W., & Struhsaker, T. T. (Eds.). (1987). *Primate societies.* Chicago: University of Chicago Press.

Snyder, M. (1974). The self-monitoring of expressive behavior. *Journal of Personality and Social Psychology, 30*, 526–537.

Snyder, M. (1987). *Public appearances/ private realities: The psychology of self-monitoring.* New York: Freeman.

Snyder, M., Tanke, E. D., & Berscheid, E. (1977). Social perception and interpersonal behavior: On the self-fulfilling nature of social stereotypes. *Journal of Personality and Social Psychology, 35*, 656–666.

Snyder, S. H. (1976). The dopamine hypothesis of schizophrenia: Focus on the dopamine receptor. *American Journal of Psychiatry, 133*, 197–202.

Sohlberg, M. M., & Mateer, C. A. (2001). *Cognitive rehabilitation: An integrative neuropsychological approach.* New York: Guilford Press.

Solomon, P. R., Adams, F., Silver, A., Zimmer, J., & DeVeaux, R. (2002). Ginkgo for memory enhancement: A randomized control trial. *JAMA: Journal of the American Medical Association, 288*, 835–840.

Solowij, N., Stephens, R. S., Roffman, R. A., Babor, T., Kadden, R., Miller, M., et al. (2002). Cognitive functioning of long-term heavy cannabis users seeking treatment. *JAMA: Journal of the American Medical Association, 287*, 1123–1131.

Sorrentino, R. M., & Higgins, E. T. (Eds.). (1996). *Handbook of motivation and cognition: The interpersonal context* (pp. 570–590). New York: Guilford Press.

Sorrentino, R. M., & Roney, C. J. R. (2000). *The uncertain mind: Individual differences in facing the unknown*. Philadelphia: Psychology Press.

Soudino, K. J., Plomin, R., & DeFries, J. C. (1996). Tester-rated temperament at 14, 20, and 24 months: Environmental change and genetic continuity. *British Journal of Developmental Psychology*, *14*, 129–144.

Spanos, N. P. (1982). Hypnotic behavior: A cognitive, social psychological perspective. *Research Communications in Psychology, Psychiatry, and Behavior*, *7*, 199–213.

Spanos, N. P. (1994). Multiple identity enactments and multiple personality disorder: A sociocognitive perspective. *Psychological Bulletin*, *116*, 143–165.

Spanos, N. P. (1996). *Multiple identities and false memories: A sociocognitive perspective*. Washington, DC: American Psychological Association.

Spanos, N. P., Weeks, J. R., & Bertrand, L. D. (1985). Multiple personality: A social psychological perspective. *Journal of Abnormal Psychology*, *92*, 362–376.

Sparks, D. L. (1988). Neural cartography: Sensory and motor maps in the mammalian superior colliculus. *Brain, Behavior, and Evolution*, *31*, 49–56.

Spearman, C. (1904). "General intelligence," objectively determined and measured. *American Journal of Psychology*, *15*, 201–293.

Spelke, E., Hirst, W., & Neisser, U. (1976). Skills of divided attention. *Cognition*, *4*, 215–230.

Spelke, E. S. (2005). Sex differences in intrinsic aptitude for math and science? A critical review. *American Psychologist*, *60*, 950–958.

Spelke, E. S., Breinlinger, K., Macomber, J., & Jacobson, K. (1992). Origins of knowledge. *Psychological Review*, *99*, 605–632.

Spence, S., Shapiro, D., & Zaidel, E. (1996). The role of the right hemisphere in the physiological and cognitive components of emotional processing. *Psychophysiology*, *33*, 112–122.

Sperling, G. (1960). The information available in brief visual presentations. *Psychological Monographs*, *74*(Whole No. 48).

Spetch, M. L., & Friedman, A. (2003). Recognizing rotated views of objects: Interpolation versus generalization by humans and pigeons. *Psychonomic Bulletin & Review*, *10*(1), 135–140.

Spiegel, D. (1995). Hypnosis and suggestion. In D. L. Schacter (Ed.), *Memory distortion: How minds, brains, and societies reconstruct the past* (pp. 129–149). Cambridge, MA: Harvard University Press.

Spiegel, D. (1998). Social psychological theories cannot fully account for hypnosis: The record was never crooked. *American Journal of Clinical Hypnosis*, *41*, 158–161.

Spiegel, D., Bloom, J. R., Kramer, H. C., & Gotheil, E. (1989). Effect of psychosocial treatment on survival of patients with metastatic breast cancer. *Lancet*, *14*, 888–891.

Spiegler, M. D., & Guevremont, D. C. (1998). *Contemporary behavior therapy* (3rd ed.). Pacific Grove, CA: Brooks/Cole.

Spitzer, R. L., Gibbon, M., Skodol, A. E., Williams, J. B., & First, M. B. (Eds.). (1994). *DSM-IV casebook*. Washington, DC: American Psychiatric Press.

Sponheim, S. R., Clementz, B. A., Iacono, W. G., & Beiser, M. (1994). Resting EEG in first episode and chronic schizophrenia. *Psychophysiology*, *31*, 37–43.

Springer, S. P., & Deutsch, G. (1989). *Left brain, right brain* (3rd ed.). New York: Freeman.

Squire, L. R. (1992). Memory and the hippocampus: A synthesis of findings with rats, monkeys, and humans. *Psychological Review*, *99*, 195–231.

Srivastava, S., John, O. P., Gosling, S. D., & Potter, J. (2003). Development of personality in early and middle adulthood: Set like plaster or persistent change? *Journal of Personality and Social Psychology*, *84*, 1041–1053.

Staddon, J. E. R. (1998). The dynamics of memory in animal learning. In M. Sabourin, F. Craik, & M. Robert (Eds.), *Advances in psychological science: Biological and cognitive aspects* (pp. 259–274). Hove, England: Psychology Press/Erlbaum.

Stajduhar, K. I., & Davies, B. (2005). Variations in and factors influencing family members' decisions for palliative home care. *Palliative Medicine*, *19*(1), 21–32.

Standing, L., & Curtis, L. (1989). Subvocalization rate versus other predictors of the memory span. *Psychological Reports*, *65*, 487–495.

Stanovich, K. E. (1999). *Who is rational? Studies of individual differences in reasoning*. Mahwah, NJ: Erlbaum.

Statistics Canada. (1997a, November 17). Impaired driving, 1996. *The Daily*. Ottawa, ON: Author.

Statistics Canada. (1997b). *Suicides, and suicide rates, by sex, by age group*. Ottawa, ON: Author. Retrieved July 9, 2006, from http://www.statcan.ca/english/Pgdb/People/Health/health01.htm

Statistics Canada. (1999). *Toward a healthy future: Second report on the health of Canadians*. Ottawa, ON: Author.

Statistics Canada. (2000, March 31). Health reports: How healthy are Canadians? *The Daily*. Ottawa, ON: Author.

Statistics Canada. (2004a). Average earnings of the population 15 years and over, by highest level of schooling, by province and territory. *Census of population*. Ottawa, ON: Author. Retrieved July 9, 2006, from http://www40.statcan.ca/l01/cst01/labor50a.htm

Statistics Canada. (2004b). *Canadian community health survey: Mental health and well-being*. Ottawa, ON: Author. Catalogue No. 82-617-XIE. Retrieved August 3, 2006, from http://www.statcan.ca/english/freepub/82-617-XIE/index.htm

Statistics Canada. (2004c, July 21). Health reports: Use of cannabis and other illicit drugs, 2002. *The Daily*. Ottawa, ON: Author. Retrieved August 10, 2006, from http://www.statcan.ca/Daily/English/040721/d040721a.htm

Steblay, N. M., & Bothwell, R. K. (1994). Evidence for hypnotically refreshed testimony: The view from the laboratory. *Law and Human Behavior*, *18*, 635–651.

Steele, C. M., & Josephs, R. A. (1990). Alcohol myopia: Its prized and dangerous effects. *American Psychologist*, *45*, 921–933.

Stein, M., Ottenberg, P., & Roulet, N. (1958). A study of the development of olfactory preferences. *American Medical Association Archives of Neurology and Psychiatry*, *80*, 264–266.

Stein, M. B., Walker, J. R., & Forde, D. R. (2000). Gender differences in susceptibility to posttraumatic stress disorder. *Behaviour Research and Therapy*, *38*, 619–628.

Stein, R. M., & Ellinwood, E. H. (1993). Stimulant use: Cocaine and amphetamine. In D. L. Dunner (Ed.), *Current psychiatric therapy* (pp. 98–105). Philadelphia: W. B. Saunders.

Steinberg, L., & Morris, A. S. (2001). Adolescent development. *Annual Review of Psychology, 52,* 83–100.

Steiner, J. E. (1977). Facial expressions of the neonate infant indicating the hedonics of food-related chemical stimuli. In J. M. Weiffenbach (Ed.), *Taste and development* (pp. 173–190). Bethesda, MD: Department of Health, Education, and Welfare.

Stern, R. S., & Cobb, J. P. (1978). Phenomenology of obsessive-compulsive neurosis. *British Journal of Psychiatry, 132,* 233–234.

Sternberg, R. J. (1985). *Beyond IQ: A triarchic theory of human intelligence.* New York: Cambridge University Press.

Sternberg, R. J. (1986). A triangular theory of love. *Psychological Review, 93,* 119–135.

Sternberg, R. J. (1988a). Triangulating love. In R. J. Sternberg & M. L. Barnes (Eds.), *The psychology of love* (pp. 119–138). New Haven, CT: Yale University Press.

Sternberg, R. J. (1988b). *The triarchic theory of mind: A new theory of human intelligence.* New York: Viking Press.

Sternberg, R. J. (1997). The concept of intelligence and its role in lifelong learning and success. *American Psychologist, 52,* 1030–1037.

Sternberg, R. J. (1998). Principles of teaching for successful intelligence. *Educational Psychologist, 33,* 65–72.

Sternberg, R. J., Castejon, J. L., Prieto, M. D., Hautamaeki, J., & Grigorenko, E. L. (2001). Confirmatory factor analysis of the Sternberg Triarchic Abilities Test in three international samples: An empirical test of the triarchic theory of intelligence. *European Journal of Psychological Assessment, 17,* 1–16.

Sternberg, R. J., & Grajek, S. (1984). The nature of love. *Journal of Personality and Social Psychology, 47,* 312–329.

Sternberg, R. J., & Kaufman, J. C. (1998). Human abilities. *Annual Review of Psychology, 49,* 479–502.

Sternberg, R. J., Torff, B., & Grigorenko, E. L. (1998). Teaching triarchically improves school achievement. *Journal of Educational Psychology, 90,* 374–384.

Sternberg, R. J., & Wagner, R. K. (1993). The g-ocentric view of intelligence and job performance is wrong. *Current Directions in Psychological Science, 2,* 1–5.

Stevens, S. S. (1939). Psychology and the science of science. *Psychological Bulletin, 36,* 221–263.

Stewart, D. D., & Stasser, G. (1995). Expert role assignment and information sampling during collective recall and decision making. *Journal of Personality and Social Psychology, 69,* 619–628.

Stewart, S. H., Peterson, J. B., & Pihl, R. O. (1995). Anxiety sensitivity and self-reported alcohol consumption rates in university women. *Journal of Anxiety Disorders, 9,* 283–292.

Stewart, T. L., Doan, K. A., Gingrich, B. E., & Smith, E. R. (1998). The actor as context for social judgments: Effects of prior impressions and stereotypes. *Journal of Personality and Social Psychology, 75,* 1132–1154.

Stickgold, R., Hobson, J. A., Fosse, R., & Fosse, M. (2001). Sleep, learning, and dreams: Off-line memory reprocessing. *Science, 294,* 1052–1057.

Stock, S. L., Werry, J. S., & McClellan, J. M. (2001). Pharmacological treatment of pediatric anxiety. In W. K. Silverman & P. D. Treffers (Eds.), *Anxiety disorders in children and adolescents: Research, assessment, and intervention* (pp. 335–367). New York: Cambridge University Press.

Stolarz-Fantino, S., Fantino, E., & Kulik, J. (1996). The conjunction fallacy: Differential incidence as a function of descriptive frames and educational context. *Contemporary Educational Psychology, 21*(2), 208–218.

Stopfer, M., & Laurent, G. (1999). Short-term memory in olfactory network dynamics. *Nature, 402,* 664–668.

Stoyva, J. M., & Carlson, J. G. (1993). A coping/rest model of relaxation and stress management. In L. Goldberger & S. Breznitz (Eds.), *Handbook of stress: Theoretical and clinical aspects* (2nd ed., pp. 745–763). New York: Free Press.

Strassman, R. J. (1992). Human hallucinogen interactions with drugs affecting serotonergic neurotransmission. *Neuropsychopharmacology, 7,* 241–243.

Strauss, E., Sherman, E. M. S., & Spreen, O. (2006). *A compendium of neuropsychological tests: Administration, norms, and commentary* (3rd ed.). New York: Oxford University Press.

Strauss, E., Slick, D. J., Levy-Bencheton, J., Hunter, M., MacDonald, S. W. S., & Hultsch, D. F. (2002). Intraindividual variability as an indicator of malingering in head injury. *Archives of Clinical Neuropsychology, 17,* 423–444.

Strayer, D. L., & Johnston, W. A. (2001). Driven to distraction: Dual task studies of simulated driving and conversing on a cellular telephone. *Psychological Science, 6,* 462–466.

Strough, C., Clarke, J., Lloyd, J., & Nathan, P. J. (2001). Neuropsychological changes after 30-day Ginkgo biloba administration in healthy participants. *International Journal of Neuropsychopharmacology, 4*(2), 131–134.

Stuss, D. T., Rosenbaum, R. S., Malcolm, S., Christiana, W., & Keenan, J. P. (2005). The frontal lobes and self-awareness. In T. E. Feinberg & J. P. Keenan (Eds.), *The lost self: Pathologies of the brain and identity* (pp. 50–64). Oxford, England: Oxford University Press.

Stuss, D. T., Winocur, G., & Robertson, I. H. (Eds.). (1999). *Cognitive neurorehabilitation.* New York: Cambridge University Press.

Sue, S., & Zane, N. (1987). The role of culture and cultural techniques in psychotherapy: A critique and reformulation. *American Psychologist, 42,* 37–45.

Sue, S., Zane, N., & Young, K. (1994). Research on psychotherapy with culturally diverse populations. In A. E. Bergin & S. L. Garfield (Eds.), *Handbook of psychotherapy and behavior change* (4th ed., pp. 783–817). New York: Wiley.

Suedfeld, P. (1997). Reactions to societal trauma: Distress and/or eustress. *Political Psychology, 18,* 849–861.

Suedfeld, P. (2001). Theories of the Holocaust: Trying to explain the unimaginable. In D. Chirot & M. E. Seligman (Eds.), *Ethnopolitical warfare: Causes, consequences, and possible solutions* (pp. 51–70). Washington, DC: American Psychological Association.

Suedfeld, P., Krell, R., Wiebe, R. E., & Steel, G. D. (1997). Coping strategies in the narratives of Holocaust survivors. *Anxiety, Stress and Coping: An International Journal, 10,* 153–179.

Sullivan, J. M. (2000). Cellular and molecular mechanisms underlying learning and memory impairments produced by cannabinoids. *Learning and Memory, 7,* 132–139.

Sulloway, F. J. (1997). *Born to rebel: Birth order, family dynamics, and creative lives.* New York: Vintage.

Surbey, M. K. (1987). Anorexia nervosa, amenorrhea, and adaptation. *Ethology and Sociobiology, 8,* 47S–61S.

Surbey, M. K. (1990). Family composition, stress and human menarche. In T. E. Ziegler & F. B. Bercovitch (Eds.), *The socioendocrinology of primate reproduction* (pp. 11–32). New York: Wiley.

Surbey, M. K. (1998). Developmental psychology and modern Darwinism. In C. Crawford & D. L. Krebs (Eds.), *Handbook of evolutionary psychology: Ideas, issues and applications* (pp. 369–404). Mahwah, NJ: Erlbaum.

Sutton, D. A., Moldofsky, H., & Badley, E. M. (2001). Insomnia and health problems in Canadians. *Sleep: Journal of Sleep & Sleep Disorders Research, 24,* 665–670.

Suzdak, P. D., Glowa, J. R., Crawley, J. N., Schwartz, R. D., Skolnick, P., & Paul, S. M. (1986). A selective imidazobenzodiazepine antagonist of ethanol in the rat. *Science, 234,* 1243–1247.

Swinson, R. P., Antony, M. M., Rachman, S., & Richter, M. A. (Eds.). (1998). *Obsessive-compulsive disorder: Theory, research, and treatment.* New York: Guilford Press.

Symons, D. K. (1999). GRE predictive validity in a master's program. *Canadian Psychology, 40,* 71–73.

Symons, D. K., & Clark, S. E. (2000). A longitudinal study of mother-child relationships and theory of mind in the preschool period. *Social Development, 9,* 3–23.

Symons, L. A., Hains, S. M. J., & Muir, D. (1998). Look at me: Five-month-old infants' sensitivity to very small deviations in eye-gaze during social interactions. *Infant Behavior and Development, 21,* 531–536.

Szaflarski, J. P., Binder, J. R., & Possing, E. T. (2002). Language lateralization in left-handed and ambidextrous people: fMRI data. *Neurology, 59*(2), 238–244.

Szasz, T. (1961). *The myth of mental illness: Foundations of a theory of personal conduct.* New York: Hoeber-Harper.

Szasz, T. (1990). Law and psychiatry: The problems that will not go away. *The Journal of Mind and Behavior, 11,* 557–564.

Tanaka, J. W., & Curran, T. (2001). A neural basis for expert object recognition. *Psychological Science, 12,* 43–47.

Tanaka, J. W., Curran, T., & Sheinberg, D. L. (2005). The training and transfer of real-world perceptual expertise. *Psychological Science, 16,* 145–151.

Tanford, S., & Penrod, S. (1984). Social influence model: A formal integration of research on majority and minority influence processes. *Psychological Bulletin, 95,* 189–225.

Tateyama, M., Asai, M., Hashimoto, M., Bartels, M., & Kasper, S. (1998). Transcultural study of schizophrenic delusions: Tokyo versus Vienna versus Tuebingen (Germany). *Psychopathology, 31,* 59–68.

Taylor, D. M., Ruggiero, K. M., & Louis, W. R. (1996). Personal/group discrimination discrepancy: Towards a two-factor explanation. *Canadian Journal of Behavioural Science, 28,* 193–202.

Taylor, D. M., Wright, S. C., Moghaddam, F. M., & Lalonde, R. N. (1990). The personal/group discrimination discrepancy: Perceiving my group but not myself to be a target for discrimination. *Personality and Social Psychology Bulletin, 16,* 256–262.

Taylor, F. K. (1965). Cryptomnesia and plagiarism. *British Journal of Psychiatry, 111,* 1111–1118.

Taylor, F. W. (1911). *Principles of scientific management.* New York: Harper.

Taylor, G. J., Bagby, R. M., & Parker, J. D. A. (1997). *Disorders of affect regulation: Alexithymia in medical and psychiatric illness.* Cambridge: Cambridge University Press.

Taylor, H. (1997). The very different methods used to conduct telephone surveys of the public. *Journal of the Marketing Research Society, 39,* 421–432.

Taylor, S. E., & Brown, J. D. (1988). Illusion and well-being: A social psychological perspective on mental health. *Psychological Bulletin, 103,* 193–210.

Taylor, S. E., Klein, L. C., Lewis, B. P., Gruenewald, T. L., Gurung, R. A. R., & Updegraff, J. A. (2000). Biobehavioral responses to stress in humans: Tend-and-befriend, not fight-or-flight. *Psychological Review, 107,* 411–429.

Taylor, S. E., Repetti, R., & Seeman, T. (1997). Health psychology: What is an unhealthy environment and how does it get under the skin? *Annual Review of Psychology, 48,* 411–447.

Taylor, S. M., Ross, N. A., Cummings, K. M., Glasgow, R. E., Goldsmith, C. H., Zanna, M. P., et al. (1998). Community intervention trial for smoking cessation (COMMIT): Changes in community attitudes toward cigarette smoking. *Health Education Research, 13,* 109–122.

Telford, L., & Frost, B. J. (1993). Factors affecting the onset and magnitude of linear vection. *Perception and Psychophysics, 53,* 682–692.

Tellegen, A., Lykken, D. T., Bouchard, T. J., Jr., Wilcox, K. J., Segal, N. L., & Rich, S. (1988). Personality similarity in twins reared apart and together. *Journal of Personality and Social Psychology, 54,* 1031–1039.

Templeton, J. J. (1998). Learning from others' mistakes: A paradox revisited. *Animal Behaviour, 55,* 79–85.

Tennes, K., & Kreye, M. (1985). Children's adrenocortical responses to classroom activities and tests in elementary school. *Psychosomatic Medicine, 47,* 451–460.

Terman, L. M. (1925). *Mental and physical traits of a thousand gifted children.* Stanford, CA: Stanford University Press.

Terman, L. M. (1954). The discovery and encouragement of exceptional talent. *American Psychologist, 9,* 221–238.

Terman, L. M., & Ogden, M. (1947). *Genetic studies of genius: The gifted child grows up.* Stanford, CA: Stanford University Press.

Terrace, H. S. (1986). *Nim: A chimpanzee who learned sign language.* New York: Columbia University Press.

Tesser, A. (1993). The importance of heritability in psychological research: The case of attitudes. *Psychological Review, 100,* 129–142.

Thagard, P. (2005). *Mind: Introduction to cognitive science* (2nd ed.). Cambridge, MA: MIT Press.

Thigpen, C. H., & Cleckley, H. A. (1957). *Three faces of Eve.* New York: McGraw-Hill.

Thomas, A., & Chess, S. (1977). *Temperament and development.* New York: Bruner/Mazel.

Thomsen, P. H. (1998). Obsessive-compulsive disorder in children and adolescents: Clinical guidelines. *European Child and Adolescent Psychiatry, 7,* 1–11.

Thoresen, C. E., & Powell, L. H. (1992). Type A behavior pattern: New perspectives on theory, assessment and intervention. *Journal of Consulting and Clinical Psychology, 60,* 595–604.

Thorndike, E. L. (1898). Animal intelligence: An experimental study of the associative processes in animals. *Psychological Review, Monograph Supplements, 2*(Serial No. 8).

Thurstone, L. L. (1938). *Primary mental abilities.* Chicago: University of Chicago Press.

Tiffany, S. T. (1990). A cognitive model of drug urges and drug-use behavior: Role of automatic and nonautomatic processes. *Psychological Review, 97,* 147–168.

Timberlake, W., & Silva, F. J. (1994). Observation of behavior, inference of function, and the study of learning. *Psychonomic Bulletin and Review, 1,* 73–88.

Tinbergen, N. (1951). *The study of instinct.* London: Oxford University Press.

Titchener, E. B. (1899). Structural and functional psychology. *Philosophical Review, 8,* 290–299.

Tjepkema, M. (2002). Alcohol and illicit drug dependence. Ottawa: ON: Statistics Canada. Retrieved August 10, 2006, from http://www.statcan.ca/english/freepub/82-003-SIE/2004000/pdf/82-003-SIE20040007447.pdf

Tolman, C. W. (1968). The role of the companion in social facilitation of animal behavior. In E. C. Simmel, R. A. Hoppe, & G. A. Milton (Eds.), *Social facilitation and imitative behavior* (pp. 33–54). Boston: Allyn & Bacon.

Tombaugh, T. N. (1997). The Test of Memory Malingering (TOMM): Normative data from cognitively intact and cognitively impaired individuals. *Psychological Assessment, 9,* 260–268.

Tombs, S., & Silverman, I. (2004). Pupillometry: A sexual selection approach. *Evolution and Human Behavior, 25,* 221–228.

Tombu, M., & Jolicœur, P. (2005). Testing the predictions of the central capacity sharing model. *Journal of Experimental Psychology: Human Perception and Performance, 31*(4), 790–802.

Tomkins, S. S. (1962). *Affect, imagery, and consciousness.* New York: Springer.

Tooby, J., & Cosmides, L. (1995). Mapping the evolved functional organization of mind and brain. In M. S. Gazzaniga (Ed.), *The cognitive neurosciences* (pp. 1185–1197). Cambridge, MA: MIT Press.

Torrance, E. P. (1981). Empirical validation of criterion-referenced indicators of creative ability through a longitudinal study. *Creative Child and Adult Quarterly, 6,* 136–140.

Tottenham, L., Saucier, D., Elias, L., & Gutwin, C. (2003). Female advantage for spatial location memory in both static and dynamic environments. *Brain and Cognition, 53*(2), 381–383.

Towler, G. (1986). From zero to one hundred: Coaction in a natural setting. *Perceptual and Motor Skills, 62,* 377–378.

Tracy, J. L., & Robins, R. W. (2004). Show your pride: Evidence for a discrete emotion expression. *Psychological Science, 15,* 194–197.

Trapnell, P. D., & Wiggins, J. S. (1990). Extension of the Interpersonal Adjective Scales to include the Big Five dimensions of personality. *Journal of Personality and Social Psychology, 59,* 781–790.

Travis, C. B., Phillippi, R. H., & Tonn, B. E. (1989). Judgment heuristics and medical decisions. *Patient Education and Counseling, 13,* 211–220.

Trehub, S. E., Hill, D. S., & Lamenetsky, S. B. (1997). Parents' sung performances for infants. *Canadian Journal of Experimental Psychology, 51,* 385–396.

Treiman, R. A., Clifton, C., Meyer, A. S., & Wurm, L. H. (2003). Language comprehension and production. In A. Healy & R. Proctor (Eds.), *Handbook of psychology Vol. 4: Experimental psychology* (pp. 527–547). New York: Wiley.

Treisman, A. (1960). Contextual cues in selective listening. *Quarterly Journal of Experimental Psychology, 12,* 242–248.

Treit, D., & Menard, J. (2000). The septum and anxiety. In R. Numan (Ed.), *The behavioral neuroscience of the septal region* (pp. 210–233). New York: Springer-Verlag.

Triplett, N. (1898). The dynamogenic factors in pacemaking and competition. *American Journal of Psychology, 9,* 507–533.

Trobst, K. K. (2000). An interpersonal conceptualization and quantification of social support transactions. *Personality and Social Psychology Bulletin, 26,* 971–986.

Trull, T. J. (2005). *Clinical psychology* (7th ed.). Belmont, CA: Wadsworth.

Trull, T. J., & McCrae, R. R. (1994). A five-factor perspective on personality disorder research. In P. T. Costa, Jr., & T. A. Widiger (Eds.), *Personality disorders and the five-factor model of personality* (pp. 45–67). Washington, DC: American Psychological Association.

Trull, T. J., & Widiger, T. A. (2003). Personality disorders. In G. Stricker & T. A. Widiger (Eds.), *Handbook of psychology: Clinical psychology* (Vol. 8, pp. 149–172). New York: Wiley.

Tseng, W., & McDermott, J. F. (1975). Psychotherapy: Historical roots, universal elements, and cultural variations. *American Journal of Psychiatry, 132,* 378–384.

Tuckey, M. R., & Brewer, N. (2003). The influence of schemas, stimulus ambiguity, and interview schedule on eyewitness memory over time. *Journal of Experimental Psychology: Applied, 9,* 101–118.

Tuckman, B. W. (1998). Using tests as an incentive to motivate procrastinators to study. *Journal of Experimental Education, 66,* 141–147.

Tugrul, K. (1998). Newer antipsychotic agents: Impact on quality of life and alternative applications. *Journal of the American Psychiatric Nurses Association, 4,* S35–S41.

Tulving, E. (1983). *Elements of episodic memory.* New York: Oxford University Press.

Tulving, E. (2002). Episodic memory: From mind to brain. *Annual Review of Psychology, 53*(1), 1–25.

Tulving, E., & Pearlstone, Z. (1966). Availability versus accessibility of information in memory for words. *Journal of Verbal Learning and Verbal Behavior, 5,* 381–391.

Tulving, E., & Thomson, D. M. (1973). Encoding specificity and retrieval processes in episodic memory. *Psychological Review, 80,* 352–373.

Turner, T. J., & Ortony, A. (1992). Basic emotions: Can conflicting criteria converge? *Psychological Review, 99,* 566–571.

Tversky, A., & Kahneman, D. (1973). On the psychology of prediction. *Psychological Review, 80,* 237–251.

Tversky, A., & Kahneman, D. (1974). Decision making under uncertainty: Heuristics and biases. *Science, 185,* 1124–1131.

Tyversky, A., & Kahneman, D. (1983). Extensional versus intuitive reasoning: The conjunction fallacy in probability judgment. *Psychological Review, 90,* 293–315.

Tyversky, A., & Kahneman, D. (1987). Rational choice and the framing of decisions. In R. M. Hogarth & M. W. Reder (Eds.), *Rational choice: The contrast between economics and psychology* (pp. 67–94). Chicago: University of Chicago Press.

Tweed, R. G., & Lehman, D. R. (2003). Confucian and Socratic learning. *American Psychologist, 58,* 148–149.

Tychsen, L. (2001). Critical periods for the development of visual acuity, depth perception, and eye tracking. In D. Bailey & J. Bruer (Eds.), *Critical thinking about critical periods* (pp. 67–80). Baltimore: Paul H. Brookes.

Tyler, J. M., & Tyler, C. L. (1997). Ethics in supervision: Managing supervisee rights and supervisor responsibilities. *Hatherleigh Guide to Ethics in Therapy, 10,* 75–95.

Uddin, L. Q., Rayman, J., & Zaidel, E. (2005). Split-brain reveals separate but equal self-recognition in the two cerebral hemispheres. *Consciousness and Cognition: An International Journal, 14,* 633–640.

UK ECT Review Group. (2003). Efficacy and safety of electroconvulsive therapy in depressive disorders: A review and meta-analysis. *Lancet, 36,* 799–808.

Ulrich, R. E. (1991). Commentary: Animal rights, animal wrongs and the question of balance. *Psychological Science, 2,* 197–201.

Uttl, B., Graf, P., Miller, J., McIsaac, H., & Tuokko, H. (2001). Age-related changes in pro- and retrospective memory. *Consciousness and Cognition, 10,* 451–472.

Valenstein, E. S. (1986). *Great and desperate cures: The rise and decline of psychosurgery and other radical treatments for mental illness.* New York: Basic Books.

Vallortigara, G., & Rogers, L. J. (2005). Survival with an asymmetrical brain: Advantages and disadvantages of cerebral lateralization. *Behavioral and Brain Sciences, 28*(4), 575–633.

van Anders, S. M., & Watson, N. V. (2006). Relationship status and testosterone in North American heterosexual and non-heterosexual men and women: Cross-sectional and longitudinal data. *Psychoneuroendocrinology, 31,* 715–723.

van Dongen, M. C. J. M., van Rossum, E., Kessels, A. G. H., Sielhorst, H. J. G., & Knipschild, P. G. (2000). The efficacy of ginkgo for elderly people with dementia and age-associated memory impairment: New results of a randomized clinical trial. *Journal of the American Geriatrics Society, 48*(10), 1183–1194.

Van Doornen, L. J., & Van Blokland, R. (1987). Serum-cholesterol: Sex-specific psychological correlates during rest and stress. *Journal of Psychosomatic Research, 31,* 239–249.

van Rijzingen, I. M. S., Gispen, W. H., & Spruijt, B. M. (1997). Postoperative environmental enrichment attenuates fimbria-fornix lesion-induced impairments in Morris maze performance. *Neurobiology of Learning and Memory, 67,* 21–28.

Vazire, S., & Gosling, S. D. (2003). *www.knowingmeknowingyou.com: Judging personality from web sites.* Paper presented at the meeting of the Western Psychological Association, Vancouver, BC.

Vazire, S., & Gosling, S. D. (2004). e-Perceptions: Personality impressions based on personal websites. *Journal of Personality and Social Psychology, 87,* 123–132.

Vecera, S. P., Vogel, E. K., & Woodman, G. F. (2002). Lower region: A new cue for figure-ground assignment. *Journal of Experimental Psychology: General, 131*(2), 194–205.

Vernon, P. E. (1983). Speed of information processing and general intelligence. *Intelligence, 7,* 53–70.

Verschueven, S., Cordo, P. J., & Swinnen, S. P. (1998). Representation of wrist joint kinematics by the ensemble of muscle spindles from synergistic muscles. *Journal of Neurophysiology, 79,* 2265–2276.

Vertes, R. P., & Eastman, K. E. (2000). The case against memory consolidation in REM sleep. *Behavioral & Brain Sciences, 23,* 867–876; 904–1018; 1083–1121.

Victor, M. (1996). Conflicting communicative behavior in a split-brain patient: Support for dual consciousness. In S. Hameroff & A. W. Kaszniak (Eds.), *Toward a science of consciousness: The first Tucson discussions and debates* (pp. 189–196). Cambridge, MA: MIT Press.

Villeneuve, P. J., Morrison, H. I., Craig, C. L., & Schaubel, D. E. (1998). Physical activity, physical fitness, and risk of dying. *Epidemiology, 9,* 626–631.

Vitz, P. C. (1988). *Sigmund Freud's Christian unconscious.* New York: Guilford Press.

Vogel, G. W., Buffenstein, A., Minter, K., & Hennessey, A. (1990). Drug effects on REM sleep and on endogenous depression. *Neuroscience and Biobehavioral Reviews, 14,* 49–63.

Vohs, K. D., & Heatherton, T. F. (2000). Self-regulatory failure: A resource-depletion approach. *Psychological Science, 11,* 249–254.

Vokey, J. R., & Brooks, L. R. (1992). Salience of item knowledge in learning artificial grammars. *Journal of Experimental Psychology: Learning, Memory, and Cognition, 18,* 328–344.

Vokey, J. R., & Read, J. D. (1985). Subliminal messages: Between the media and the devil. *American Psychologist, 40,* 1231–1239.

von Frisch, K. (1967). *The dance language and orientation of bees.* Cambridge, MA: Belknap Press.

Vorauer, J. D., Hunter, A. J., Main, K. J., & Roy, S. A. (2000). Meta-stereotype activation: Evidence from indirect measure for specific evaluative concerns experienced by members of dominant groups in intergroup interaction. *Journal of Personality and Social Psychology, 78,* 690–707.

Vorauer, J. D., Main, K. J., & O'Connell, G. B. (1998). How do individuals expect to be viewed by members of lower status groups? Content and implications of meta-stereotypes. *Journal of Personality and Social Psychology, 75,* 917–937.

Vygotsky, L. S. (1978). *Mind in society: The development of higher psychological processes.* Cambridge, MA: Harvard University Press.

Wada, J. A. (Ed.). (1991). *Kindling, 4.* New York: Plenum Press.

Waddill, P. J., & McDaniel, M. A. (1998). Distinctiveness effects in free recall: Differential processing or privileged retrieval? *Memory and Cognition, 26,* 108–120.

Wagenaar, W. A. (1986). My memory: A study of autobiographical memory over six years. *Cognitive Psychology, 18,* 225–252.

Wager, T. D., & Nitschke, J. B. (2005). Placebo effects in the brain: Linking mental and physiological processes. *Brain, Behavior, and Immunity, 19,* 281–282.

Wager, T. D., & Smith, E. E. (2003). Neuroimaging studies of working memory: A meta-analysis. *Cognitive, Affective, & Behavioral Neuroscience, 3,* 255–274.

Wagner, A. R. (1981). SOP: A model of automatic memory processing in animal behavior. In N. E. Spear & R. R. Miller (Eds.), *Information processing in animals: Memory mechanisms* (pp. 5–47). Hillsdale, NJ: Erlbaum.

Wagner, R. K., & Sternberg, R. J. (1985). Practical intelligence in real-world pursuits: The role of tacit knowledge. *Journal of Personality and Social Psychology, 49,* 436–458.

Waldman, I. D., Weinberg, R. A., & Scarr, S. (1994). Racial-group differences in IQ in the Minnesota Transracial Adoption Study: A reply to Levin and Lynn. *Intelligence, 19,* 29–44.

Walen, S. T., DiGuiseppe, R., & Dryden, W. (1992). *A practitioner's guide to rational-emotive therapy.* New York: Oxford University Press.

Walker, E., Kestler, L., Bollini, A., & Hochman, K. M. (2004). Schizophrenia: Etiology and course. *Annual Review of Psychology, 55,* 401–430.

Walker, L. J. (1989). A longitudinal study of moral reasoning. *Child Development, 60,* 157–166.

Wallace, C. J. (1998). Social skills training in psychiatric rehabilitation: Recent findings. *International Review of Psychiatry, 10,* 9–10.

Wallhagen, M. I., Strawbridge, W., & Shema, S. (1997). *Perceived control:*

Mental health correlates in a population-based aging cohort. Paper presented at the 50th Annual Scientific Meeting of the Gerontological Society of America.

Walters, J. M., & Gardner, H. (1986). The theory of multiple intelligences: Some issues and answers. In R. J. Sternberg & R. K. Wagner (Eds.), *Practical intelligence: Nature and origins of competence in the everyday world* (pp. 163–182). New York: Cambridge University Press.

Walton, D. (2002, October). Police in Calgary make big ecstasy bust. *The Globe and Mail,* p. A10. Retrieved August 10, 2006, from http://www.mapinc.org/drugnews/v02/ n2012/ a02.html

Walton, G. E., & Bower, T. G. R. (1993). Newborns form "prototypes" in less than 1 minute. *Psychological Science, 4,* 203–205.

Wampold, B. E., Mondin, G. W., Moody, M., Stich, F., Benson, K., & Ahn, H. (1997). A meta-analysis of outcome studies comparing bona fide psychotherapies: Empiricially, "all must have prizes." *Psychological Bulletin, 122,* 203–215.

Wasow, T. (1989). Grammatical theory. In M. I. Posner (Ed.), *Foundations of cognitive science* (pp. 161–202). Cambridge, MA: MIT Press.

Wasserman, E. A., & Miller, R. R. (1997). What's elementary about associative learning? *Annual Review of Psychology, 48,* 573–607.

Waters, E., Wippman, J., & Sroufe, L. A. (1979). Attachment, positive affect, and competence in the peer group: Two studies in construct validation. *Child Development, 50,* 821–829.

Watson, J. B. (1913). Psychology as a behaviorist views it. *Psychological Review, 20,* 158–177.

Watson, J. B. (1919). *Psychology from the standpoint of a behaviorist.* Philadelphia: Lippincott.

Watson, S. J., Benson, J. A., Jr., & Joy, J. E. (2000). Marijuana and medicine: Assessing the science base. A summary of the 1999 Institute of Medicine Report. *Archives of General Psychiatry, 57,* 547–552.

Webb, E. J., Campbell, D. T., Schwartz, R. D., Sechrist, L., & Grove, J. B. (1981). *Nonreactive research in the social sciences.* Boston: Houghton Mifflin.

Webb, W. B. (1981). The return of consciousness. *G. Stanley Hall Lecture Series, 1,* 129–152.

Webb, W. B. (1992). *Sleep: The gentle tyrant.* Bolton, MA: Anker Publishing.

Wechsler, D. (1996). *WISC-III Manual Canadian Supplement.* Toronto: Psychological Corporation.

Wegner, D. M. (1994). *White bears and other unwanted thoughts: Suppression, obsession, and the psychology of mental control.* New York: Guilford Press.

Weibel-Orlando, J. (1989). Treatment and prevention of Native American alcoholism. In T. D. Watts & R. Wright (Eds.), *Alcoholism in minority populations* (pp. 121–139). Springfield, IL: Charles C. Thomas.

Weinberg, R. A., Scarr, S., & Waldman, I. D. (1992). The Minnesota Transracial Adoption Study: A follow-up of IQ test performance at adolescence. *Intelligence, 16,* 117–135.

Weingarten, H. P. (1983). Conditioned cues elicit feeding in sated rats: A role for learning in meal initiation. *Science, 220,* 431–433.

Weingarten, H. P. (1985). Stimulus control of eating: Implications for a two-factor theory of hunger. *Appetite, 6,* 387–401.

Weingarten, H. P., Chang, P. K., & McDonald, T. J. (1985). Comparison of the metabolic and behavioral disturbances following paraventricular and ventro-medial-hypothalamic lesions. *Brain Research Bulletin, 14,* 551–559.

Weinstein, L. N., Schwartz, D. G., & Arkin, A. M. (1991). Qualitative aspects of sleep mentation. In S. J. Ellman & J. S. Antrobus (Eds.), *The mind in sleep* (2nd ed., pp. 172–213). New York: Wiley.

Weinstein, S., & Graves, R. E. (2002). Are creativity and schizotypy products of a right hemisphere bias? *Brain and Cognition, 49*(1), 138–151.

Weisberg, H. F., Krosnick, J. A., & Bowen, B. D. (1989). *An introduction to survey research and data analysis* (2nd ed.). Glenview, IL: Scott, Foresman.

Weisberg, R. W. (1994). Genius and madness? A quasi-experimental test of the hypothesis that manic-depression increases creativity. *Psychological Science, 5,* 361–367.

Weiskrantz, L. (1992). Introduction: Dissociated issues. In A. D. Milner & M. D. Rugg (Eds.), *The neuropsy-*

chology of consciousness (pp. 1–10). London: Academic Press.

Weiss, J. M. (1977). Psychological and behavioral influences on gastrointestinal lesions in animal models. In J. D. Maser & M. E. P. Seligman (Eds.), *Psychopathology: Experimental models*. San Francisco: Freeman.

Weiss, L., & Baum, A. (1987). Physiological aspects of environment-behavior relationships. In E. Zube & G. Morre (Eds.), *Advances in environment, behavior, and design* (Vol. 1, pp. 221–247). New York: Plenum Press.

Weiten, W. (1995). *Psychology: Themes and variations* (3rd ed.). Pacific Grove, CA: Brooks/Cole.

Welder, A. N., & Graham, S. A. (2001). The influences of shape similarity and shared labels on infants' inductive inferences about nonobvious object properties. *Child Development, 72,* 1653–1673.

Weldon, M. S., & Roediger, H. M., III. (1987). Altering retrieval demands reverses the picture superiority effect. *Memory and Cognition, 15,* 269–280.

Wells, G. L., Malpass, R. S., Lindsay, R. C. L., Fisher, R. P., Turtle, J. W., & Fulero, S. M. (2000). From the lab to the police station: A successful application of eyewitness research. *American Psychologist, 55,* 581–598.

Welsh, R. S. (2003). Prescription privileges: Pro or con? *Clinical Psychology: Science & Practice, 10,* 371–372.

Wender, P. H., Kety, S. S., Rosenthal, D., Schlusinger, F., Ortmann, J., & Lunde, I. (1986). Psychiatric disorders in the biological and adoptive families of adopted individuals with affective disorders. *Archives of General Psychiatry, 43,* 923–929.

Wenner, A. (1998). Honey bee "dance language" controversy. In G. Greenberg & M. M. Haraway (Eds.), *Comparative psychology: A handbook* (pp. 823–836). New York: Garland.

Werker, J. F., & Desjardins, R. N. (2001). Listening to speech in the 1st year of life. In M. Tomasello & E. Bates (Eds.), *Language development: The essential readings* (pp. 26–33). Malden, MA: Blackwell.

Werker, J. F., & Tees, R. C. (1999). Influences on infant speech processing: Toward a new synthesis. *Annual Review of Psychology, 50,* 509–535.

Wernicke, C. (1874). *Der Aphasische Symptomenkomplex*. Breslau, Poland: Cohn & Weigert.

Wertheimer, M. (1987). *A brief history of psychology* (3rd ed.). New York: Holt, Rinehart & Winston.

Wertsch, J. V., & Tulviste, P. (1992). L. S. Vygotsky and contemporary developmental psychology. *Developmental Psychology, 28,* 548–557.

Wesnes, K. A., Ward, T., McGinty, A., & Petrini, O. (2000). The memory enhancing effects of a Ginkgo biloba/Panax ginseng combination in healthy middle-aged volunteers. *Psychopharmacology, 152,* 353–361.

Westen, D. (1998). The scientific legacy of Sigmund Freud: Toward a psychodynamically informed psychological science. *Psychological Bulletin, 124,* 333–371.

Wheeler, L., & Kim, Y. (1997). What is beautiful is culturally good: The physical attractiveness stereotype has different content in collectivistic cultures. *Personality and Social Psychology Bulletin, 23,* 795–800.

Wheeler, M. A., Stuss, D. T., & Tulving, E. (1997). Toward a theory of episodic memory: The frontal lobes and autonoetic consciousness. *Psychological Bulletin, 121,* 331–354.

Whishaw, I. Q., Hines, D. J., & Wallace, D. G. (2001). Dead reckoning (path integration) requires the hippocampal formation: Evidence from spontaneous exploration and spatial learning tasks in light (allothetic) and dark (idothetic) tests. *Behavioural Brain Research, 127,* 49–69.

Whitbourne, S. K. (1985). *The aging body*. New York: Springer.

Whitbourne, S. K., Zuschlag, M. K., Elliot, L. B., & Waterman, A. S. (1992). Psychosocial development in adulthood: A 22-year sequential study. *Journal of Personality and Social Psychology, 63,* 260–271.

White, L., Tursky, B., & Schwartz, G. E. (1985). *Placebo: Theory, research, and mechanisms*. New York: Guilford Press.

Whittlesea, B. W. A., Brooks, L. R., & Westcott, C. (1994). After the learning is over: Factors controlling the selective application of general and particular knowledge. *Journal of Experimental Psychology: Learning, Memory, and Cognition, 20*(2), 259–274.

Whittlesea, B. W. A., & Leboe, J. P. (2000). The heuristic basis of remembering and classification: Fluency, generation, and resemblance. *Journal of Experimental Psychology: General, 129,* 84–106.

Whittlesea, B. W. A., & Williams, L. D. (2000). The source of feelings of familiarity: The discrepancy-attribution hypothesis. *Journal of Experimental Psychology: Learning, Memory, and Cognition, 26,* 547–565.

Whorf, B. L. (1956). *Language, thought, and reality: Selected writings of Benjamin Lee Whorf*. New York: Wiley.

Wickelgren, W. A. (1999). Webs, cell assemblies, and chunking in neural nets: Introduction. *Canadian Journal of Experimental Psychology, 53,* 118–131.

Widiger, T. A. (1998). Personality disorders. In D. F. Barone & M. Hersen (Eds.), *Advanced personality. The Plenum series in social/clinical psychology* (pp.335–352). New York: Plenum Press.

Widiger, T. A., & Sankis, L. M. (2000). Adult psychopathology: Issues and controversies. *Annual Review of Psychology, 51,* 377–404.

Wigfield, A. (1994). Expectancy-value theory of achievement motivation: A developmental perspective. *Educational Psychology Review, 6,* 49–78.

Wiggins, J. S. (1979). A psychological taxonomy of trait descriptive terms: The interpersonal domain. *Journal of Personality and Social Psychology, 37,* 395–412.

Wiggins, J. S., & Broughton, R. (1991). A geometric taxonomy of personality scales. *European Journal of Personality, 5,* 343–365.

Wiggins, J. S., & Pincus, A. L. (1992). Personality: Structure and assessment. *Annual Review of Psychology, 43,* 473–504.

Wiggins, J. S., & Trapnell, P. D. (1997). Personality structure: The return of the Big Five. In R. Hogan, J. A. Johnson, & S. R. Briggs (Eds.), *Handbook of personality psychology* (pp. 737–764). San Diego, CA: Academic Press.

Wilde, G. J. S. (1994). *Target risk: Dealing with the danger of death, disease and damage in everyday decisions*. Toronto: PDE.

Williams, D. A., Frame, K. A., & LoLordo, V. M. (1991). Reexamination of contextual conditioning with massed versus distributed unconditioned stimuli. *Journal of Experimental Psychology: Animal Behavior Processes, 17,* 202–209.

Williams, K. M., Paulhus, D. L., & Hare, R. D. (in press). Capturing the four-factor structure of psychopathy in college students via self-report. *Journal of Personality Assessment.*

Williams, L. M. (1994). Recall of childhood trauma: A prospective study of women's memories of child sexual abuse. *Journal of Consulting and Clinical Psychology, 62,* 1167–1176.

Willoughby, T., Wood, E., McDermott, C., & McLaren, J. (2000). Enhancing learning through strategy instruction and group interaction: Is active generation of elaborations critical? *Applied Cognitive Psychology, 14*(1), 19–30.

Wilson, E. O. (1963, May). Pheromones. *Scientific American, 208,* 100–114.

Wilson, L. M., Stewart, M. L., & McAnanama, E. P. (1989). Milk intakes of genetically obese (ob/ob) and lean mouse pups differ with enhanced milk supply. *Physiology and Behavior, 46,* 823–827.

Wilson, M., & Daly, M. (1997). Relationship-specific social psychological adaptations. In G. R. Bock & G. Cardew (Eds.), *Characterizing human psychological adaptations* (pp. 253–268). New York: John Wiley.

Windgassen, K. (1992). Treatment with neuroleptics: The patient's perspective. *Acta Psychiatrica Scandinavica, 86,* 405–410.

Winett, R. A. (1995). A framework for health promotion and disease prevention programs. *American Psychologist, 50,* 341–350.

Winikoff, B. (1983). Nutritional patterns, social choices, and health. In D. Mechanic (Ed.), *Handbook of health, health care, and the health professions.* New York: Free Press.

Winkielman, P., & Berridge, K. C. (2004). Unconscious emotion. *Current Directions in Psychological Science, 13,* 120–123.

Winkielman, P., Berridge, K. C., & Wilbarger, J. L. (2005). Unconscious affective reactions to masked happy versus angry faces influence consumption behavior and judgments of value.

Personality and Social Psychology Bulletin, 1, 121–135.

Winman, A. (2004). Do perfume additives termed human pheromones warrant being termed pheromones? *Physiology & Behavior, 82*(4), 697–701.

Winner, E. (1997). Exceptionally high intelligence and schooling. *American Psychologist, 52,* 1070–1081.

Winter, D. G., John, O. P., Stewart, A. J., Klohnen, E. C., & Duncan, L. E. (1998). Traits and motives: Toward an integration of two traditions in personality research. *Psychological Review, 105,* 230–250.

Wintre, M. G., Polivy, J., & Murray, M. A. (1990). Self-predictions of emotional response patterns: Age, sex, and situational determinants. *Child Development, 61*(4), 1124–1133.

Wise, R. A., & Bozarth, M. A. (1987). A psychomotor theory of addiction. *Psychological Review, 94,* 469–492.

Wise, R. A., & Rompre, P. P. (1989). Brain dopamine and reward. *Annual Review of Psychology, 40,* 191–225.

Wissler, C. (1901). The correlation of mental and physical tests. *Psychological Review, Monograph Supplement 3*(No. 6).

Witelson, S. F. (1992). Cognitive neuroanatomy: A new era. *Neurology, 42,* 709–713.

Wixted, J. T., & Ebbesen, E. B. (1991). On the form of forgetting. *Psychological Science, 2,* 409–415.

Wolff, N., Helminiak, T. W., & Tebes, J. K. (1997). Getting the cost right in cost-effectiveness analyses. *American Journal of Psychiatry, 154,* 736–743.

Wolford, G., Miller, M. B., & Gazzaniga, M. S. (2004). Split decisions. In M. S. Gazzaniga (Ed.), *The cognitive neurosciences* (3rd ed., pp. 1189–1199). Cambridge, MA: MIT Press.

Wolpe, J. (1958). *Psychotherapy by reciprocal inhibition.* Stanford, CA: Stanford University Press.

Wolpe, J. (1975). Foreword. In B. Sloane, F. Staples, A. Cristol, N. Yorkston, & K. Whipple (Eds.), *Psychotherapy versus behavior therapy.* Cambridge, MA: Harvard University Press.

Wolpe, J. (1982). *The practice of behavior therapy.* New York: Pergamon Press.

Wong, S. E., Martinez-Diaz, J. A., Massel, H. K., Edelstein, B. A., Wiegand, W., Bowen, L., et al. (1993). Conversational skills training with schizophrenic inpa-

tients: A study of generalization across settings and conversants. *Behavior Therapy, 24,* 285–304.

Wood, J. M., Bootzin, R. R., Kihlstrom, J. F., & Schacter, D. L. (1992). Implicit and explicit memory for verbal information presented during sleep. *Psychological Science, 3,* 236–239.

Wood, W. (2000). Attitude change: Persuasion and social influence. *Annual Review of Psychology, 51,* 539–570.

Woods, D. L., Alain, C., & Ogawa, K. H. (1998). Auditory and visual feature conjunction during high-rate serial presentation: Processing two features can be faster than processing one. *Perception and Psychophysics, 60,* 239–249.

Woods, E. R., Lin, Y. G., Middleman, A., Beckford, P., Chase, L., & DuRant, R. (1997). The associations of suicide attempts in adolescents. *Pediatrics, 99,* 791–796.

Woods, S. C., Schwartz, M. W., Baskin, D. G., & Seeley, R. J. (2000). Food intake and the regulation of body weight. *Annual Review of Psychology, 51,* 255–277.

Woods, S. C., Seeley, R. J., Porte, D., & Schwartz, M. W. (1998). Signals that regulate food intake and energy homeostasis. *Science, 280,* 1378–1383.

Woodward, T. S., Dixon, M. J., Mullen, K. T., Christensen, K. M., & Bub, D. N. (1999). Analysis of errors in color agnosia: A single-case study. *Neurocase, 5*(2), 95–108.

Woody, E. Z., & McConkey, K. M. (2003). What we don't know about the brain and hypnosis, but need to: A view from the Buckhorn Inn. *International Journal of Clinical and Experimental Hypnosis, 51*(3), 309–338.

Woody, G. E., & Cacciola, J. (1997). Diagnosis and classification: DSM-IV and ICD-10. In J. H. Lowinson, P. Ruiz, R. B. Millman, & J. G. Langrod (Eds.), *Substance abuse: A comprehensive textbook.* Baltimore: Williams & Wilkins.

Woody, S., & McLean, P. D. (2001). *Anxiety disorders in adults: An evidence based approach to psychological treatment.* New York: Oxford University Press.

Worringham, C. J., & Messick, D. M. (1983). Social facilitation of running: An unobtrusive study. *Journal of Social Psychology, 121,* 23–29.

Wright, E. F., Voyer, D., Wright, R. D., & Roney, C. (1995). Supporting audiences and performance under pressure: The home-ice disadvantage in hockey championships. *Journal of Sport Behavior, 18*, 21–28.

Wright, M. J. (2002). Flashbacks in the history of psychology in Canada: Some early "headline" makers. *Canadian Psychology, 43*(1), 21–34.

Wundt, W. (1896). *Outlines of psychology* (C. M. Judd, Trans.). New York: Stechart.

Wyrostok, N., & Paulson, B. (2000). Traditional healing practices among First Nations students. *Canadian Journal of Counselling, 34*(1), 14–24.

Yalom, I. D. (1980). *Existential psychotherapy*. New York: Basic Books.

Yalom, I. D. (1995). *The theory and practice of group psychotherapy* (4th ed.). New York: Basic Books.

Yamaguchi, S., Tsuchiya, H., & Koboyashi, S. (1998). Visuospatial attention shift and motor responses in cerebellar disorders. *Journal of Cognitive Neuroscience, 10*, 95–107.

Yapko, M. D. (1994). Suggestibility and repressed memories of abuse: A survey of psychotherapists' beliefs. *American Journal of Clinical Hypnosis, 36*, 163–179.

Yates, F. A. (1966). *The art of memory.* Chicago: University of Chicago Press.

Yik, M. S. M., & Russell, J. A. (1999). Interpretation of faces: A cross-cultural study of a prediction from Fridlund's theory. *Cognition and Emotion, 13*, 93–104.

Yin, R. K. (1998). The abridged version of case study research: Design and method. In L. Bickman & D. J. Rog (Eds.), *Handbook of applied social research methods* (pp. 229–259). Thousand Oaks, CA: Sage.

Yonelinas, A. P., & Jacoby, L. L. (1995). The relation between remembering and knowing as bases for recognition: Effects of size congruency. *Journal of Memory and Language, 34*, 622–643.

Young, J. E., Beck, A. T., & Weinberger, A. (1993). Depression. In D. H. Barlow (Ed.), *Clinical handbook of psychological disorders* (2nd ed., pp. 240–277). New York: Guilford Press.

Young, J. E., Weinberger, A. D., & Beck, A. T. (2001). Cognitive therapy for depression. In D. H. Barlow (Ed.), *Clinical handbook of psychological disorders* (3rd ed., pp. 264–308). New York: Guilford Press.

Young, K. S. (1998). *Caught in the net.* New York: John Wiley & Sons.

Young, K. S. (1999). Internet addiction: Symptoms, evaluation and treatment. In L. VandeCreek & T. Jackson (Eds.), *Innovations in clinical practice: A source book* (pp. 19–31). Sarasota, FL: Professional Resource Press.

Young, L. R., & Shelhamer, M. (1990). Microgravity enhances the relative contribution of visually-induced motion sensation. *Aviation and Space Environmental Medicine, 61*, 525–530.

Yuille, J. C. (1993). We must study forensic eyewitnesses to know about them. *American Psychologist, 48*, 572–573.

Zacks, R. T., & Hasher, L. (1994). Directed ignoring: Inhibitory regulation of working memory. In D. Dagenbach & T. H. Carr (Eds.), *Inhibitory processes in attention, memory, and language* (pp. 241–264). San Diego, CA: Academic Press.

Zahorik, D. M., Houpt, K. A., & Swartzman-Andert, J. (1990). Taste-aversion learning in three species of ruminants. *Applied Animal Behaviour Science, 26*, 27–39.

Zajonc, R. B. (1965). Social facilitation. *Science, 149*, 269–274.

Zajonc, R. B. (1968). Attitudinal effects of mere exposure. *Journal of Personality and Social Psychology, 9*(Monograph Suppl. 2, Pt. 2).

Zajonc, R. B. (1983). Validating the confluence model. *Psychological Bulletin, 93*(3), 457–480.

Zajonc, R. B. (2001). Mere exposure: A gateway to the subliminal. *Current Directions in Psychology Science, 10*, 224–228.

Zajonc, R. B., Heingartner, A., & Herman, E. M. (1969). Social enhancement and impairment of performance in the cockroach. *Journal of Personality and Social Psychology, 13*, 83–92.

Zajonc, R. B., Murphy, S. T., & McIntosh, D. N. (1993). Brain temperature and subjective emotional experience. In M. Lewis & J. M. Haviland (Eds.), *Handbook of emotions* (pp. 209–220). New York: Guilford Press.

Zametkin, A. J., Nordahl, T., Gross, M., King, A. C., Semple, W. E., Rumsey, J., et al. (1990). Cerebral glucose metabolism in adults with hyperactivity of childhood onset. *New England Journal of Medicine, 323*, 1361–1366.

Zanna, M. P. (1994). On the nature of prejudice. *Canadian Psychology, 35*, 11–23.

Zatorre, R. J. (2003). Sound analysis in auditory cortex. *Trends in Neurosciences, 26*, 229–230.

Zeki, S. (1992, September). The visual image in mind and brain. *Scientific American, 267*, 68–76.

Ziegert, D. I., Kistner, J. A., Castro, R., & Robertson, B. (2001). Longitudinal study of young children's responses to challenging achievement situations. *Child Development, 72*, 609–624.

Zotterman, Y. (1959). Thermal sensations. In J. Fields, H. W. Magoun, & V. E. Hall (Eds.), *Handbook of physiology: Section I. Neurophysiology, 1*(pp. 431–458). Washington, DC: Physiological Society.

Zucker, K. J. (1987). Commentary on Kohlberg, Ricks, and Snarey's (1984) "Childhood development as a predictor of adaptation in adulthood." *Genetic, Social, and General Psychology Monographs, 113*(1), 127–130.

Zuroff, D. C., Sotsky, S. M., Martin, D. J., Sanislow, C. A., Blat, S. J., Krupnick, J. L., et al. (2000). Relation of therapeutic alliance and perfectionism to outcome in brief outpatient treatment of depression. *Journal of Consulting and Clinical Psychology, 68*, 114–124.

Name Index